# THE GOOD
# FOOD GUIDE
## 2010

D1494419

Distributed by Littlehampton Book Services Ltd
Faraday Close, Durrington, Worthing, West Sussex BN13 3RB

Copyright © Which? Ltd 2009

Base mapping by Cosmographics
Data management and export by AMA DataSet Limited, Preston
Printed and bound by Charterhouse, Hatfield

A catalogue record for this book is available from the British Library

ISBN: 978 1 84490 0664

Consultant Editor: Elizabeth Carter
Senior Editor: Lisa Grey

The Good Food Guide makes every effort to be as accurate and up-to-date as possible.
All Good Food Guide inspections are anonymous but every main entry has been
contacted separately for details.

As we are an annual Guide, we have strict guidelines for fact-checking
information ahead of going to press, so some restaurants were dropped if they failed
to provide the information we required. Readers should still check details at the
time of booking, particularly if they have any special requirements.

For a full list of Which? books, please call 01903 828557, access our website at
www.which.co.uk, or write to Littlehampton Book Services. For other enquiries
call 0800 252100.

Please send updates to: goodfoodguide@which.co.uk or 2 Marylebone Road,
London NW1 4DF.

To submit feedback on any restaurant, please visit www.which.co.uk/gfgfeedback

**FSC**
**Mixed Sources**
Product group from well-managed
forests and other controlled sources

Cert no. SGS-COC-003131
www.fsc.org
© 1996 Forest Stewardship Council

*"You can corrupt one man.*
*You can't bribe an army."*

Raymond Postgate, founder of
The Good Food Guide, 1951

Inverness 510
513
Aberdeen

**SCOTLAND**

500
Dundee

503

500
Edinburgh
Glasgow 480
491 477

348

NORTHERN 479 Newcastle
IRELAND Upon Tyne
569 Belfast Carlisle 414
212 248 Middlesbrough

440 York
Blackpool 315 Leeds

REPUBLIC OF 269
IRELAND Liverpool Manchester
330
195 224 351 326
544 542
384
WALES Leicester Norwich
366 322 336
421 189
Birmingham Cambridge
537 435 418 346 386
292 173
552 ENGLAND
183
255 Oxford 296 251
532 356 London
Swansea 525 175 19
Cardiff Bristol 394
427 302
278
370 Southampton 407 398
230 242 Bournemouth
Exeter 283
199
Plymouth

Please turn to the page
number listed on the
map to find restaurant
reviews corresponding
to the region.

561                                    **FRAN**

# CONTENTS

# About The Good Food Guide

*The Good Food Guide* is Britain's longest-running restaurant guide. Since 1951, it has cast a critical eye over cafés, pubs, bistros and restaurants throughout the UK.

Each year the Guide is completely rewritten and compiled from scratch. Our research list is based on the huge volume of feedback that we receive from readers (the list of contributors at the back of the book is testimony to this). This feedback, together with anonymous inspections, ensures that every entry is assessed afresh. We believe that the restaurants included in this Guide are the very best in the UK.

Although much has changed since Raymond Postgate founded *The Good Food Guide*, the ethos of the original book remains: we do not accept any sponsorship, advertising or free meals. It is because of this, and because the Guide will always be the voice of the consumer, not the catering industry, that *The Good Food Guide* remains the UK's most trusted, best-selling and best-loved restaurant bible.

# Introduction

The year 2009 was one of recession, and restaurants have suffered as much as any kind of business. The more enlightened adjusted their menus and prices, offering more of what people wanted at a price they could afford. Some even started to break away from the conventions of set mealtimes.

As the trend for all-day eating gains momentum, we are beginning to see a welcome spread of good-quality restaurants in the middle and lower price bands. At their best, these are part of the community in their area, acting as the hub of the local food economy and establishing a reputation for local produce. Two of the new entries in the Guide this year, Entropy in Leicester and The Allotment in Dover, are such places, open non-stop from breakfast to dinner and charging realistic prices. They provide an example of how small, owner-run dining rooms can, and do, work in direct opposition to the high-street chains.

Pubs, too, are going back to their roots. In the last year or so, British pubs have enjoyed a boom in traditional pub food. What was once regarded as cheap grub, and therefore abandoned in the first wave of the gastropub food revolution, has received a luxury makeover. It is no longer enough for a sausage or pork pie to be stuffed with any old pork, they are now made of choice cuts from a rare-breed pig; even pork scratchings are homemade. Some pubs, like The Nut Tree Inn at Murcott, Oxfordshire, are even rearing their own pigs in the garden.

The ability of the discerning consumer to insist on standards by contacting *The Good Food Guide* may well play an important role. To everyone who has used our feedback system (www.which.co.uk/gfgfeedback) over the last year, many thanks, and please keep the reports coming in. In buying and using this Guide you are supporting its aim to improve standards of food and restaurateuring.

# How to use the Guide

The Guide is organised by county/region. Maps in each section work alongside the full-page atlas maps at the back of the book. London is divided into six: Central, North, East, South, West and Greater London. See page 18 for more details.

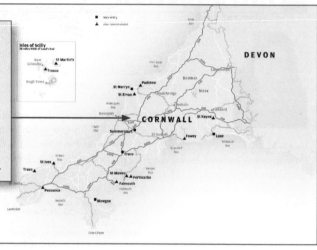

**CORNWALL** | England

## ▌St Ives

### Little Harbour Restaurant

Modern cuisine by the harbour
1 The High Street, New Town, NT1 1AB
Tel no: 01234 567890
www.littleharbourrestaurant.co.uk
**Modern European | £43**
**Cooking score: 3**
**V**

If you want to secure the much-desired view over the harbour from this former lifeboat house, ask for a table by the window on the upper floor. The décor throughout is light, bright and minimalist, with white-painted walls and white napery. Dinner starts with an amuse-bouche – maybe creamed cauliflower and Stilton soup served in a tiny tureen – and 'excellent' home-made granary and tomato bread. Fish is a strong suit, as in a creamy nage of black bream or mackerel tempura with a sesame and soy dipping sauce which 'was an absolute *tour de force*' at inspection. Or you could start with terrine of duck with fig chutney. Finish

with a taster selection of chocolate, including a mould of dark chocolate and orange mousse, and banana and white chocolate ice cream. Plenty of wines are served by the glass from an international list. House Australian is £12.95
**Chef:** Frederick Igor **Open:** all week 11.30 to 2, 5 to 10 (6 to 9.30 low season) **Closed:** 25 and 26 Dec
**Meals:** alc (£5 to £25) **Service:** not inc.
**Extra details:** Car parking. Children allowed.

ALSO RECOMMENDED

### Jasper Jones

2 The Cresent, Old Town, OT1 1AB
Tel no: 01234 567890
Seaside café with a great position overlooking the beach and St Ives Bay. The lively menu offers simple stuff using the freshest seafood: crisp calamari or moules marinière (both £5.95) to start, followed by fish, chips and mushy peas in herb batter (£9.95) or whole local grilled lemon sole (£10.95). Breakfast and light lunches are also served (baguettes from £5.50). Wines from £10.95. Open all week, Apr to Oct.

'Also Recommended' establishments are not scored but we think they are worth a visit.

48                    the content on these pages is sample text only

## CORNWALL

### The White Bar and Grill
**Spectacular alfresco beach dining**
10 The High Street, New Town, NT2 2BC
Tel no: 01234 567890
www.thewhitebarandgrill.co.uk
Global/Seafood | £46
Cooking score: 4

The position of this restaurant is rather special, with unbeatable views over the sea. It is closed over winter, so there's no opportunity to enjoy the view over the bay on the stormiest of days, but there's a large terrace for a truly Mediterranean experience in summer. Lunch can be a satisfying Cornish crab sandwich or crispy fried chilli squid with black spice, Thai salad and citrus white miso. In the evening, Jones pushes the boat out with scallop risotto with piquillo peppers, mascarpone and lemon vodka, followed by twice-cooked Barbary duck on braised salsify with seared foie gras and a gooseberry and Cointreau sauce. Finish with blood orange and Campari posset with a ginger glass biscuit.
**Chef:** Chris White **Open:** all week 12 to 3.45, 6 to 10 **Closed:** Nov to Mar **Meals:** alc (main courses £15-£30) **Service:** not inc.
**Extra details:** 70 seats outside.

### READERS RECOMMEND

#### Bistro Eleven
**Modern British**
Harbour Road, Old Town, OT2 2AB
Tel no: 01234 567890
'Fantastic fish in a harbourside setting'

#### Café Cod
**Modern British**
20 The High Street, New Town, NT1 1AB
Tel: 01234 567890
'Excellent food in a quirky, hippy-style setting'

#### Barry the Fish
**Fish**
Harbour Road, Old Town, OT1 1AB
Tel no: 01234 567890
'Fast, slick and stylish dining'

Send your reviews to: www.which.co

**Chris Bradley** Mr Underhill's

**Who or what inspired you to become a chef?**
When we opened in 1981 we could not afford to employ a chef.

**What do you like cooking when you are 'off duty'?**
Anything Italian. When growing up in Glasgow in the sixties I lived with an Italian family for a short while who ran an outstanding deli.

**What is your favourite restaurant and why?**
I love going to restaurants; at my age it's impossible to single out just one.

**What do you do to relax when out of the kitchen?**
I'm allowed out of the kitchen?

**What is your top culinary tip?**
Use the very best ingredients and don't make it complicated just for the sake of it.

**What is the best part of your job?**
That moment when a member of staff clicks and realises that cooking will never be just a job for them.

9

# Scoring

We should begin by saying that a score of 1 is actually a significant achievement. We reject many restaurants during the compilation of the Guide. Obviously, there are always subjective aspects to rating systems, but our inspectors are equipped with extensive scoring guidelines, so that restaurant bench-marking around the UK is accurate. We also take into account the reader feedback that we receive for each restaurant, so that any given review is based on several meals.

1/10    Capable cooking, with simple food combinations and clear flavours, but some inconsistencies.

2/10    Decent cooking, displaying good basic technical skills and interesting combinations and flavours. Occasional inconsistencies.

3/10    Good cooking, showing sound technical skills and using quality ingredients.

4/10    Dedicated, focused approach to cooking; good classical skills and high-quality ingredients.

5/10    Exact cooking techniques and a degree of ambition; showing balance and depth of flavour in dishes, while using quality ingredients.

6/10    Exemplary cooking skills, innovative ideas, impeccable ingredients and an element of excitement.

7/10    High level of ambition and individuality, attention to the smallest detail, accurate and vibrant dishes.

8/10    A kitchen cooking close to or at the top of its game – highly individual, showing faultless technique and impressive artistry in dishes that are perfectly balanced for flavour, combination and texture. There is little room for disappointment here.

9/10    This mark is for cooking that has reached a pinnacle of achievement, making it a hugely memorable experience for the diner.

10/10    It is extremely rare that a restaurant can achieve perfect dishes on a consistent basis. We have awarded this mark for the second time in two years.

# Symbols

Restaurants that may be given main entry status are contacted ahead of publication and asked to provide key information about their opening hours and facilities. They are also invited to participate in the £5 voucher scheme. The symbols on these entries are therefore based on this feedback from restaurants, and are intended for quick, at-a-glance identification.

This year we have changed the criteria for the vegetarian symbol so that the symbol now indicates where more than three vegetarian main courses are available. The wine bottle symbol is an accolade assigned by the Guide's team, based on their judgement of the wine list available.

Accommodation is available.

**£30** It is possible to have three courses at the restaurant for less than £30.

**V** There are more than three vegetarian main courses on the menu.

**£5 OFF** The restaurant is participating in our £5 voucher scheme. (Please see the vouchers at the end of the book for terms and conditions.)

The restaurant has a wine list that our inspector and wine expert have deemed to be exceptional.

**£XX** The price indicated on each review represents the average price of a three-course dinner, excluding wine.

4

3

2

10

5

9

7

8

6

# Reader Awards

The Good Food Guide has always recognised excellence and good service at restaurants throughout the UK. The Good Food Guide Restaurant of the Year award is run annually between March and May, and presents readers with the opportunity to nominate their favourite local establishment. For this year's award, members of the public were invited to nominate establishments for ten different regions, with the criteria that restaurants should be independently owned and offer regional or local produce. Nominations were submitted via our online feedback form (www.which.co.uk/gfgfeedback), and by postal vote. We received thousands of nominations and The Good Food Guide team picked the overall winner from the list of regional winners.

## The Readers' Restaurant of the Year (2010 edition)
RONNIES, THORNBURY

**1.** WALES - Tyddyn Llan, Llandrillo

**2.** EAST ENGLAND - Maison Bleue, Bury St Edmunds

**3.** LONDON - L'Etranger, South Kensington

**4.** MIDLANDS - Entropy, Leicester

**5.** NORTHERN IRELAND - Mourne Seafood, Belfast

**6.** NORTH EAST - The Yorke Arms, Ramsgill

**7.** NORTH WEST - Nutters, Norden

**8.** SCOTLAND - Ubiquitous Chip, Glasgow

**9.** SOUTH EAST - The Mulberry Tree, Boughton Monchelsea

**10.** SOUTH WEST - Ronnies, Thornbury

# Editors' Awards

Other awards in this Guide have been allocated by *The Good Food Guide* team and are as follows:

## Best new entry 2010
Da Piero, Merseyside

## Pub newcomer of the year
The Harwood Arms, London

## Wine list of the year
Fraiche, Merseyside

## Best chef
Stephen Harris, The Sportsman, Kent

## Up-and-coming chef
Ryan Simpson, The Goose, Oxfordshire

## Best pub chef
Guy Manning, Red Lion, Wiltshire

## Best fish restaurant
The Café at Brovey Lair, Norfolk

## Best value for money
The Dogs, Edinburgh

## Best set menu
Michael Caines at ABode Manchester for the set lunch

## Best use of local produce
The Nut Tree Inn, Oxfordshire

# Top 50 2010

In 2008, *The Good Food Guide* started listing the top 40 restaurants in the UK in order of merit. Now, with more chefs than ever scoring 7 out of 10 and some strong contenders scoring 6 out of 10, that list has expanded to become the Top 50.

1. The Fat Duck, Bray, Berkshire (10)
2. Gordon Ramsay, Royal Hospital Road, London (9)
3. Marcus Wareing at the Berkeley, London (8)
4. Le Manoir aux Quat' Saisons, Great Milton, Oxfordshire (8)
5. The Square, London (8)
6. Le Champignon Sauvage, Cheltenham, Gloucestershire (8)
7. Le Gavroche, London (8)
8. The Vineyard at Stockcross, Newbury, Berkshire (8)
9. Pied-à-Terre, London (8)
10. Restaurant Nathan Outlaw, Fowey, Cornwall (8)
11. Maze, London (8)
12. Tom Aikens, London (8)
13. L'Enclume, Cartmel, Cumbria (8)
14. Restaurant Martin Wishart, Edinburgh, Scotland (8)
15. The Capital, London (7)
16. The Waterside Inn, Bray, Berkshire (7)
17. Bohemia, St Helier, Jersey (7)
18. Hibiscus, London (7)
19. Danesfield House, Marlow, Buckinghamshire (7)
20. L'Atelier de Joël Robuchon, London (7)
21. Restaurant Sat Bains, Nottingham (7)
22. Gidleigh Park, Chagford, Devon (7)
23. Holbeck Ghyll, Windermere, Cumbria (7)
24. Fischer's Baslow Hall, Baslow, Derbyshire (7)
25. Anthony's, Leeds, Yorkshire (7)
26. Simon Radley at the Chester Grosvenor, Cheshire (7)
27. Andrew Fairlie at Gleneagles, Auchterarder, Scotland (7)
28. Michael Wignall at the Latymer, Pennyhill Park Hotel, Surrey (7)
29. Whatley Manor, Easton Grey, Wiltshire (7)
30. Fraiche, Oxton, Merseyside (7)
31. Tyddyn Llan, Llandrillo, Wales (7)
32. Mr Underhill's, Ludlow, Shropshire (7)
33. Murano, London (7)
34. Midsummer House, Cambridge (7)
35. Hambleton Hall, Hambleton, Leicestershire & Rutland (7)
36. The Crown at Whitebrook, Whitebrook, Wales (7)
37. Robert Thompson at the Hambrough, Ventnor, Isle of Wight (7)
38. The Creel, St Margaret's Hope, Scotland (7)
39. Harry's Place, Great Gonerby, Lincolnshire (7)
40. The Old Vicarage, Ridgeway, Derbyshire (7)
41. The Ledbury, London (7)
42. The Greenhouse, London (6)
43. Club Gascon, London (6)
44. The Kitchin, Edinburgh, Scotland (6)
45. Galvin at Windows, London (6)
46. The Sportsman, Whitstable, Kent (6)
47. Purnell's, Birmingham, West Midlands (6)
48. The Yorke Arms, Ramsgill, Yorkshire (6)
49. ramsons, Ramsbottom, Greater Manchester (6)
50. La Bécasse, Ludlow, Shropshire (6)

# Longest-serving restaurants

*The Good Food Guide* was founded in 1951. Here is a list of restaurants which have appeared consistently since their first entry into the Guide.

The Connaught, London, 57 years
Gay Hussar, London, 53 years
Gravetye Manor, East Grinstead, 53 years
Porth Tocyn Hotel, Abersoch, 53 years
Sharrow Bay, Ullswater, 49 years
Rothay Manor, Ambleside, 41 years
Le Gavroche, London, 40 years
Summer Isles Hotel, Achiltibuie, 40 years
The Capital, London, 39 years
Ubiquitous Chip, Glasgow, 38 years
The Druidstone, Broad Haven, 37 years
Plumber Manor, Sturminster Newton, 37 years
The Waterside Inn, Bray, 37 years
White Moss House, Grasmere, 37 years
Isle of Eriska, Eriska, 36 years
Airds Hotel, Port Appin, 34 years
Farlam Hall, Brampton, 33 years
Corse Lawn House, Corse Lawn, 32 years
Hambleton Hall, Hambleton, 31 years

The Pier Hotel, Harbourside Restaurant, Harwich, 31 years
Grafton Manor, Bromsgrove, 30 years
Magpie Café, Whitby, 30 years
RSJ, London, 29 years
The Seafood Restaurant, Padstow, 29 years
Sir Charles Napier, Chinnor, 29 years
The Dower House, The Royal Crescent, Bath, 29 years
Kalpna, Edinburgh, 28 years
Le Caprice, London, 28 years
Little Barwick House, Barwick, 28 years
Moss Nook, Manchester, 28 years
Ostlers Close, Cupar, 27 years
The Cellar, Anstruther, 26 years
Clarke's, London, 25 years
Read's, Faversham, 24 years
ramsons, Ramsbottom, 23 years
Le Champignon Sauvage, Cheltenham, 21 years

# Notable wine lists

The qualities we are looking for in a good wine list are a conscientious eye to the best growers, clearly comprehensible presentation (with or without tasting notes), and – most elusively of all – fair value.

We have presented this year's Editors' Award for best wine list to Fraiche, in Oxton, Merseyside. Below are listed other restaurants from around the country that we commend for their approach to wine.

### London
Chez Bruce, Wandsworth
La Trompette, Chiswick
Odette's, Primrose Hill
Pied-à-Terre, Fitzrovia
Ransome's Dock, Battersea
Rex Whistler Restaurant at Tate Britain, Westminster

### England
Crown Hotel, Southwold, Suffolk
Holbeck Ghyll, Windermere, Cumbria
The Horn of Plenty, Gulworthy, Devon
The Old Vicarage, Ridgeway, Derbyshire
ramsons, Ramsbottom, Greater Manchester
Sir Charles Napier, Chinnor, Oxfordshire

### Scotland
Kinloch House Hotel, Blairgowrie, Tayside
Ubiquitous Chip, Glasgow
Valvona & Crolla Caffè Bar, Edinburgh

### Wales
The Crown at Whitebrook, Whitebrook, Gwent
Fairyhill, Reynoldston, Glamorgan
Tyddyn Llan, Llandrillo, North-East Wales

### Northern Ireland
Cayenne, Belfast

 Other notable wine lists are marked with a bottle symbol and can be found throughout the Guide.

# London explained

This year we have changed the way London is ordered. London is split into six regions: Central, North, East, South, West and Greater. Restaurants within each region are listed alphabetically. Each main entry and 'also recommended' entry has a map reference.

The lists below are a guide to the areas covered in each region.

## London – Central
Belgravia, Bloomsbury, Chinatown, Covent Garden, Fitzrovia, Green Park, Holborn, Hyde Park, Knightsbridge, Lancaster Gate, Marble Arch, Marylebone, Mayfair, Oxford Circus, Piccadilly, Soho, St James's Park, Trafalgar Square, Westminster

## London – North
Belsize Park, Camden, Crouch End, Dalston, Euston, Golders Green, Hampstead, Highbury, Highgate, Islington, King's Cross, Primrose Hill, Stoke Newington, Swiss Cottage, Willesden

## London – East
Barbican, Bethnal Green, Canary Wharf, City, Clerkenwell, Hackney, Limehouse, Shoreditch, Spitalfields, Tower Hill, Wapping, Whitechapel

## London – South
Balham, Battersea, Bermondsey, Blackheath, Clapham, East Dulwich, Elephant and Castle, Forest Hill, Greenwich, Putney, South Bank, Southwark, Tooting, Wimbledon

## London – West
Chelsea, Chiswick, Earls Court, Fulham, Hammersmith, Kensal Rise, Kensington, Knightsbridge, Maida Vale, Notting Hill, Paddington, Shepherd's Bush, South Kensington, Westbourne Park

## London – Greater
Barnes, Croydon, Harrow-on-the-Hill, Kew, Richmond, Southall, Tottenham Hale, Twickenham, Wood Green

# LONDON

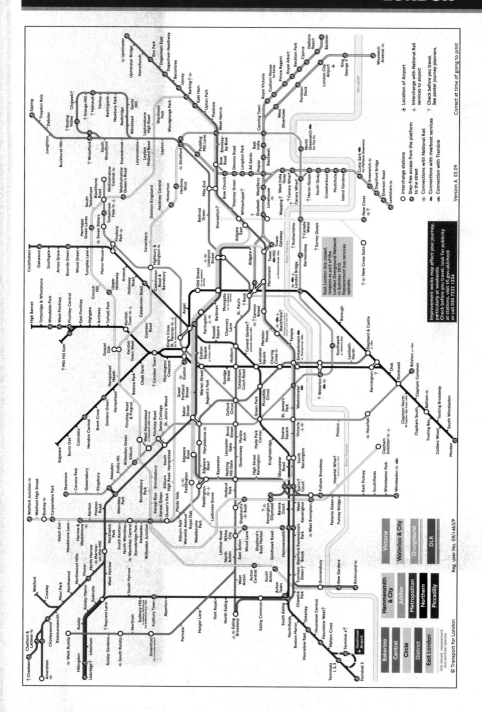

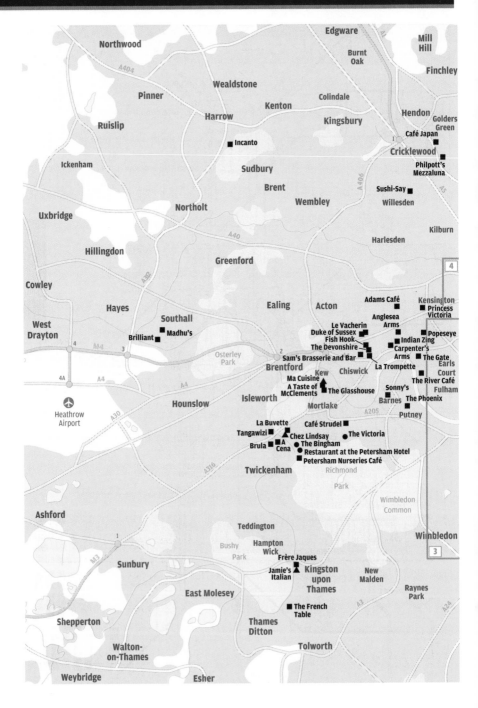

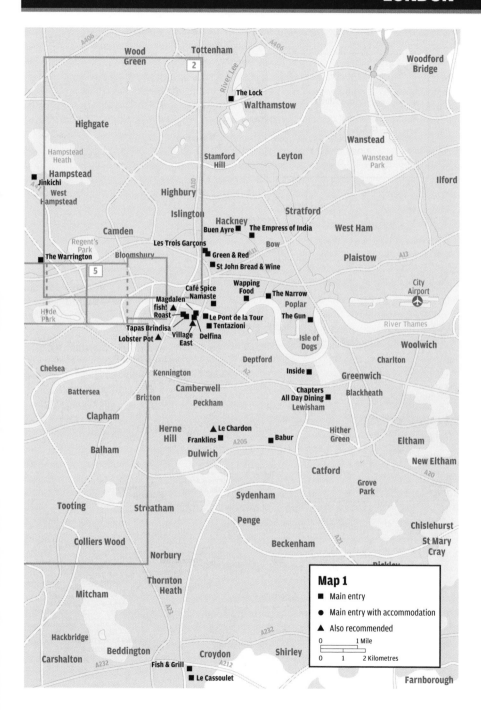

**Map 1**

■ Main entry

● Main entry with accommodation

▲ Also recommended

0      1 Mile

0   1     2 Kilometres

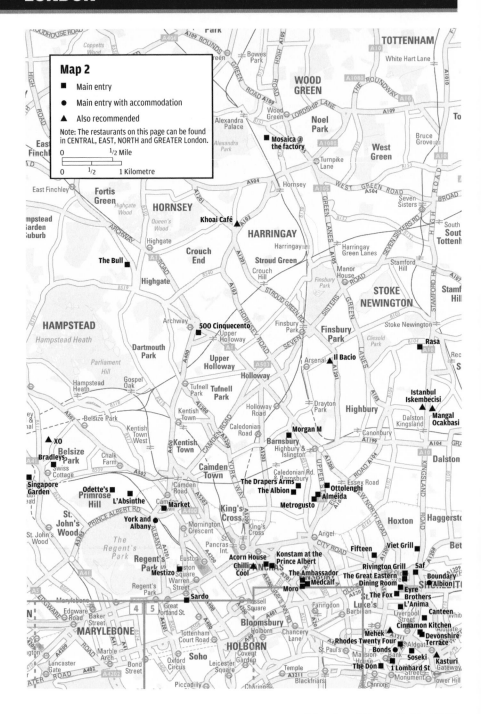

**Map 2**

- ■ Main entry
- ● Main entry with accommodation
- ▲ Also recommended

Note: The restaurants on this page can be found in CENTRAL, EAST, NORTH and GREATER London.

0 ___ ½ Mile

0 ___ ½ ___ 1 Kilometre

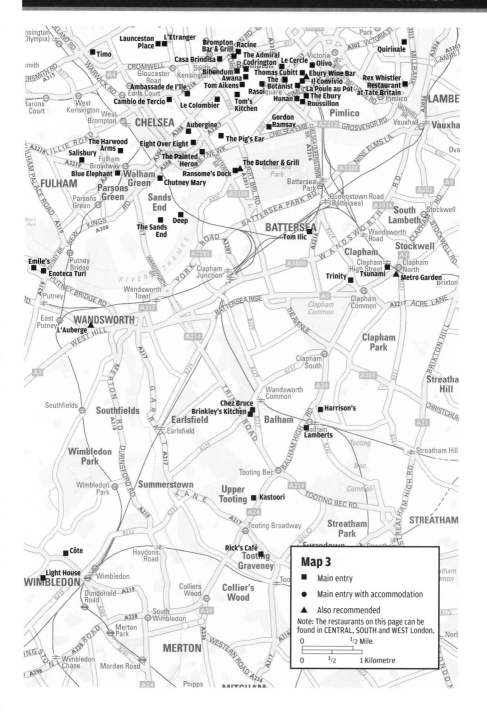

**Map 3**

■ Main entry

● Main entry with accommodation

▲ Also recommended

Note: The restaurants on this page can be found in CENTRAL, SOUTH and WEST London.

0 ————— ½ Mile

0 ——— ½ ——— 1 Kilometre

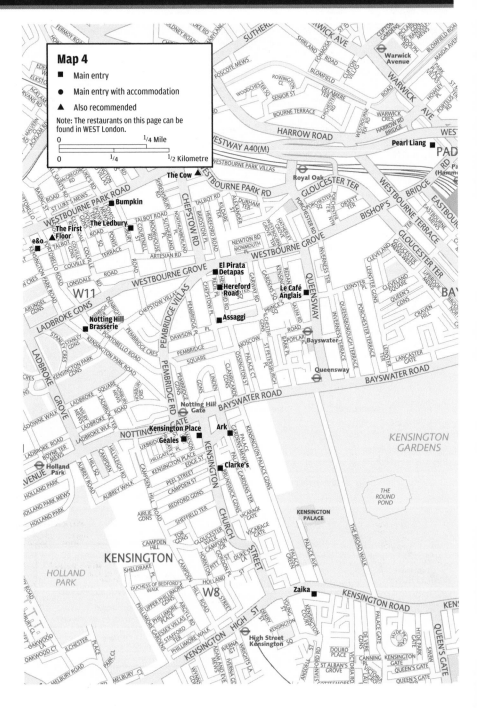

**Map 4**

- ■ Main entry
- ● Main entry with accommodation
- ▲ Also recommended

Note: The restaurants on this page can be found in WEST London.

0                    ¼ Mile

0          ¼              ½ Kilometre

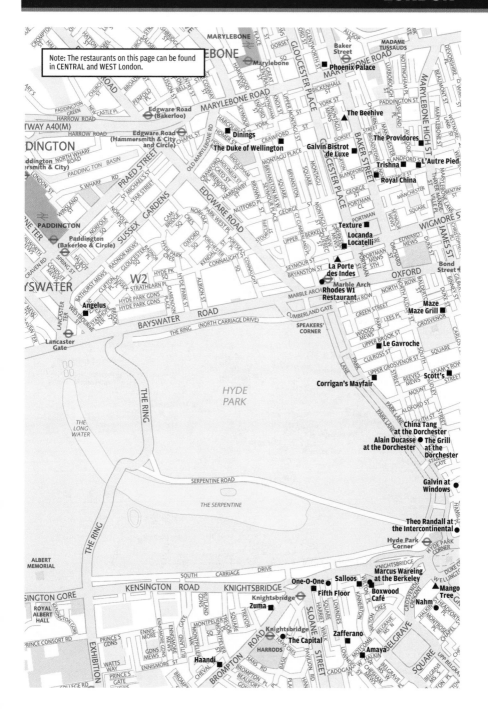

Note: The restaurants on this page can be found in CENTRAL and WEST London.

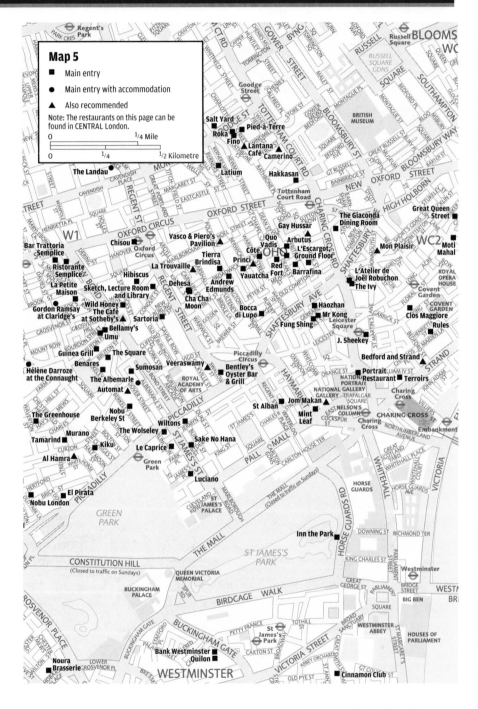

**Map 5**

■ Main entry

● Main entry with accommodation

▲ Also recommended

Note: The restaurants on this page can be found in CENTRAL London.

0                    ¹/₄ Mile

0          ¹/₄          ¹/₂ Kilometre

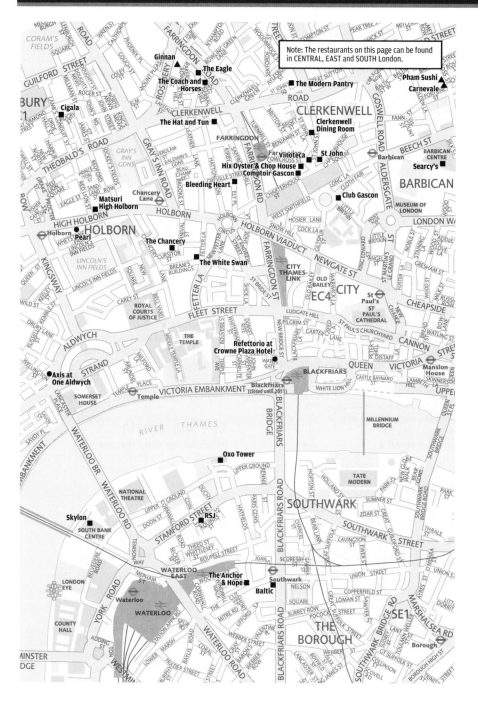

Note: The restaurants on this page can be found in CENTRAL, EAST and SOUTH London.

## ALSO RECOMMENDED

### ▲ Al Hamra

31-33 Shepherd Market, Green Park, W1J 7PT
Tel no: (020) 7493 1954
www.alhamrarestaurant.co.uk
⊖ Green Park, Hyde Park Corner, map 5
Lebanese

Set in the narrow alleyways of Shepherd Market, Al Hamra is counted among the capital's most venerable Middle Eastern restaurants. An epic selection of meze ranges from the usual suspects – hummus with tahina (£5), falafel and tabbouleh (£6.50) – to signature dishes, such as manakeish Al Hamra (£7.50), Lebanese-style pizza topped with tomato, onion, chilli and wild oregano. For those who favour Beirut over Bordeaux, a French-dominated wine list sees Lebanese bottles starting at £22. Open all week.

## Alain Ducasse at the Dorchester

**Luxury-laden French aristocrat**
The Dorchester Hotel, 53 Park Lane, Hyde Park, W1K 1QA
Tel no: (020) 7629 8866
www.alainducasse-dorchester.com
⊖ Hyde Park Corner, map 4
French | £75
Cooking score: 6

🛏

Jet-setting über-restaurateur Alain Ducasse rules over a gastronomic empire that stretches across some nine countries, so for the Dorchester to get his name above the door was quite a coup. His London venue creates a muted, cocooned world of upper-crust affluence, and its fine-dining comes with an eye-watering price tag – although the all-inclusive set lunch is relatively gentle on the wallet. Luxury ingredients are scattered across the menu, which reads like twenty-first century Escoffier lacquered with fashionable quirks from the Far East (simmered duck foie gras with mango and 'dolce forte' sauce or braised halibut with citrus, Swiss chard and 'eggplant condiment', say). This is overtly rich,

aristocratic and flawlessly presented food, although flavours can seem a tad safe and rather 'subdued'. Highlights from recent meals have included a starter of roasted lobster with chicken 'sticks', pasta and black truffles followed by a well-conceived dish of seared meagre (a relative of sea bass) with cauliflower purée, capers, parsley and chicken jus. The kitchen saves the best till last, with a cavalcade of supremely crafted desserts including a glorious orange cream tart ('a very fine creation') matched with a pitch-perfect ginger sorbet. Service runs like silk, and all the incidentals are just so – a generous pile of dainty gougères to start, spot-on breads baked in-house, ripe cheeses and excellent ad lib coffee. The imposing wine list is dominated by some of the most auspicious French names in the business, but mark-ups are 'sky high'. House selections start at £25.

**Chef/s:** Jocelyn Herland. **Open:** Tue to Fri L 12 to 2, Tue to Sat D 6.30 to 10. **Closed:** Sun, Mon, Easter, 3 weeks Aug, 26 Dec to 5 Jan (exc 31 Dec). **Meals:** Set L £39.50 (2 courses) to £45. Set D £55 (2 courses) to £75. Tasting menu £115 (8 courses). **Service:** 12.5% (optional). **Details:** Cards accepted. 82 seats. Air-con. No mobile phones. Wheelchair access. Music. Car parking.

## The Albemarle

**Delightful old-world charmer**
Brown's Hotel, 30 Albemarle Street, Mayfair, W1S 4BP
Tel no: (020) 7518 4060
www.roccofortehotels.com
⊖ Green Park, map 5
British | £45
Cooking score: 4

🛏 V

The other-worldly atmosphere of Browns Hotel continues to delight. It exerts a strong pull – both for its ambience and for Lee Streeton's cooking. The handsome dining room (formerly The Grill) is done out in oak panelling and pillars, and the old-fashioned club-room effect is softened by neutral colours. A bevy of staff helps to maintain a high degree of efficiency. Not all experiences

are equally happy – service lapses in particular have concerned readers this year – but the consensus is that the food is 'superb'. The menu features great British classics such as potted Morecambe Bay shrimps, beer-battered haddock with chips and mushy peas, and Lancashire hotpot, alongside monkfish cheeks with veal sweetbreads and hedgerow garlic, and wild rabbit braised in cider with capers. It is simple, ingredients-led cooking of a high order. Good old British puddings take in steamed treacle sponge and scrumpy-battered apple fritters with Somerset cider brandy ice cream. House wines from £26.
**Chef/s:** Lee Streeton and Mark Hicks. **Open:** all week L 12 to 3 (Sun 12.30 to 4) D 5.30 to 10.30. **Meals:** alc (main courses £15 to £33). Set L and pre-theatre (5.30 to 7.30) £25 (2 courses) to £30. **Service:** 12.5%. **Details:** Cards accepted. 80 seats. Air-con. Separate bar. No music. Wheelchair access. Children allowed.

## Amaya
**Sleek, high-gloss Indian**
15 Halkin Arcade, Motcomb Street, Knightsbridge, SW1X 8JT
Tel no: (020) 7823 1166
www.amaya.biz
⊖ Knightsbridge, map 4
**Indian | £35**
**Cooking score: 3**
V

Smartly located in Knightsbridge's fashion nirvana – near Sloane Street – Amaya is as well turned-out as its clientele. Vibrant murals and Indian statues contribute to the interior's sleek look, and there's the added theatre of chefs going about their work in a spectacular open kitchen. The modern Indian food is designed for sharing – the recommended six to eight portions between four is equivalent to a two-course meal. Mixing and matching flavours and textures is what the kitchen aims to do, and to this end the menu may deliver rock oysters flash-grilled with coconut and ginger moilee sauce, tandoori monkfish tikka, and slow-cooked lamb osso buco with

fenugreek and fresh coriander. Rose and rhubarb brûlée is an interesting twist on a Western classic. House wine is £23.50.
**Chef/s:** Karunesh Khanna. **Open:** all week L 12.30 to 2.15 (12.45 to 2.45 Sun), D 6.30 to 11.30 (6 to 10.30 Sun). **Closed:** 25 Dec. **Meals:** alc (main courses £11 to £26). Set L £17. Tasting menu £38.50. Gourmet menu £65. **Service:** 12.5% (optional). **Details:** Cards accepted. 100 seats. Air-con. Separate bar. Music.

## Andrew Edmunds
**Romantic Soho treasure**
46 Lexington Street, Soho, W1F 0LP
Tel no: (020) 7437 5708
⊖ Oxford Street, Piccadilly Circus, map 5
**Modern European | £25**
**Cooking score: 2**

With a reputation as one of London's most romantic restaurants, this independent Soho bistro takes up two candlelit rooms, a pleasant flower-filled ground floor and a rather duller basement. 'Cramped and with little ambience', sniffs one reader of its 'Dickensian' charm. Detractors call the modern European menu 'dinner party food'. Fans rave about generous prices and generous portions – for example pork cheek and pea salad, seared tuna with ratte potatoes and fennel, and damson and sloe gin ice cream. Let's hope the 'first-daters' who pile in are taking advantage of the low wine mark-ups – the owner is an expert and the list offers bargains galore – Pol Roger NV at £35 and house fizz at £5.50 a glass. Reservations are taken one week in advance to the day.
**Chef/s:** Rebecca St John-Cooper. **Open:** all week L 12.30 to 3 (1 to 3 Sat, 1 to 3.30 Sun), D 6 to 10.45 (10.30 Sun). **Closed:** 23 Dec to 2 Jan, Easter, August bank hol. **Meals:** alc (main courses £10 to £18). **Service:** 12.5% (optional). **Details:** Cards accepted. 40 seats. 4 seats outside. Air-con. No music. No mobile phones. Children allowed.

## Angelus

**Gallic charm and romance**
4 Bathurst Street, Lancaster Gate, W2 2SD
Tel no: (020) 7402 0083
www.angelusrestaurant.co.uk
⊖ Lancaster Gate, map 4
Modern French | £38
Cooking score: 4

**V**

Thierry Tomasin's establishment has a certain Gallic charm. It's rather romantic, and beautifully lit – spotlights bounce off white linen and sparkling silverware in the Art Nouveau-inspired dark wood and red banquette bistro interior. Judging by a recent test meal, new chef Martin Nisbet can produce skilled, careful cooking, including an earthy, perfectly balanced lentil and truffle soup, a smoked eel salad with Jersey royals, and a flying-saucer chicken raviolo with a rich tarragon, pea and bacon broth that begged to be mopped up with the accompanying golden, crusty bread. Only poached pollack with fennel purée and lemon verbena sauce was frustratingly short of sublime, sunk by a tasteless piece of fish – possibly more the fish's fault than the chef's. Desserts included a notable white chocolate bavarois, flecked with hazelnuts and passion fruit sauce. There's a discreet cocktail bar and, as you might expect from a former sommelier, an excellent wine list with bottles from £22.
**Chef/s:** Martin Nisbet. **Open:** all week 12 to 11. **Closed:** 23 Dec to 2 Jan. **Meals:** alc (main courses £19 to £29). Set L £36. Set D £38. **Service:** 12.5% (optional). **Details:** Cards accepted. 60 seats. 12 seats outside. Air-con. Separate bar. Wheelchair access. Music. Children allowed.

## Arbutus

**Buzzy bistro borders on fine-dining**
63-64 Frith Street, Soho, W1D 3JW
Tel no: (020) 7734 4545
www.arbutusrestaurant.co.uk
⊖ Tottenham Court Road, map 5
Modern European | £33
Cooking score: 6

Anthony Demetre and Will Smith's smart Soho address offers bistro cooking that 'borders on fine-dining'. The hybrid 'smart-casual' concept extends to the plain dining room which, with its linen-free tables, suits low-key suppers and business lunches, yet is buzzy and impressive enough for a special occasion. Luxury food lovers should probably move on, as Demetre keeps prices low (notably the 'fabulous value' prix fixe) by majoring in provincial French classics such as bouillabaisse and pieds et paquets (trotters and tripe) and by making 'extraordinary use of regular ingredients', for example Elwy Valley lamb breast with sweetbreads or braised pig's head with potato purée. Always 'inventive and well-presented', even simple-sounding assemblies of broccoli and goats' curd or crab, peas and broad beans are greater than the sum of their parts. Only desserts such as hazelnut ice cream with Pedro Ximinez can feel slightly apologetic after all the assertive flavours. Feedback remains largely positive, with just the occasional gripe about 'tough bavette' and 'fatty pork'. The wine list, all served by either 250ml carafe (from £5) or bottle (from £14.50), is a pleasure to work through, sampling unusual picks such as Argentinian Torrontes and German Pinot Noir. Readers appreciate 'not being ripped off' for 'extras' such as coffee and water.
**Chef/s:** Anthony Demetre. **Open:** all week L 12 to 2.30 (3 Sun), D 5 to 11 (11.30 Fri and Sat, 6 to 10.30 Sun). **Closed:** 25 and 26 Dec, 1 Jan. **Meals:** alc (main courses £15 to £20). Set L £15.50. Set D (pre theatre) £17.50. Sun L £15.50. **Service:** 12.5% (optional). **Details:** Cards accepted. 65 seats. Air-con. Separate bar. No music. Wheelchair access. Children allowed.

## L'Atelier de Joël Robuchon

**Astonishing, original and beautiful food**
13-15 West Street, Covent Garden, WC2H 9NE
Tel no: (020) 7010 8600
www.joel-robuchon.com
⊖ Leicester Square, map 5
French | £80
Cooking score: 7

£5
OFF

Culinary global superstar Joël Robuchon has
created what must be the world's most
glamorous chain with this Atelier brand. The
London outpost is split into two spaces, the
black-and-white chequered La Table on the
first floor (where only the carte is served) and
the penumbral, street-level Atelier in
Robuchon's signature black and red with its
central eating 'bar'. A meal begins with an
explanation of 'The Concept of Monsieur Joël
Robuchon' – a tedious spiel the waiter must
rattle through. However it leaves the diner
little wiser about how much to order from the
poorly designed menu, with its mix of small
and conventionally proportioned dishes. The
awkward start is a prelude to some of London's
most astonishing, original and beautiful food,
'full of flavours and textures' and 'with
ingredients treated with the utmost respect'.
At inspection, foie gras ravioli in clear chicken
broth – a very jazzy liver dumpling soup! –
was the winner, Asian-style with fresh
coriander and ginger and a swirl of fresh
cream. A more conventional main of sole
meunière didn't quite hit the same heights,
although a complex Chartreuse and raspberry
dessert came close. The pre-theatre menu
(with two choices at each course) is a good
deal: a sweet onion soup, hanger steak with
pommes dauphinoise and a selection of tarts
have all impressed. Cooking in this league
doesn't come cheap and bills soon mount.
However the international wine list does a
game job of offering something for everyone,
starting with Chilean house at £18, a dozen
by the glass (from £5), and a dozen in 375cl
format (from £21). Staff are efficient and
thorough, a little brusque at times, but
generally kindly.

**Chef/s:** Olivier Limousin. **Open:** all week L 12 to
2.30, D 5.30 to 10.30. **Meals:** alc (main courses £14
to £29). Set L and D (pre-theatre) £19 (2 courses) to
£25. Tasting menu £105. **Service:** 12.5% (optional).
**Details:** Cards accepted. 97 seats. Air-con. Separate
bar. Wheelchair access. Music. Children allowed. Car
parking.

## ALSO RECOMMENDED

### ▲ Automat

33 Dover Street, Mayfair, W1S 4NF
Tel no: (020) 7499 3033
www.automat-london.com
⊖ Green Park, map 5
North American

Breakfast and weekend brunches have won
ringing endorsements from readers this year,
with eggs Benedict (£10) and buttermilk
pancakes singled out for praise. Like any all-
day diner this is not the place for a long,
leisurely meal or expectations of fine dining –
simpler choices are the best: onion soup,
macaroni cheese and the house burger (£12)
have all been endorsed. Wherever you're
seated, in the booth-lined diner or split-level
eatery looking on to the kitchen, service is
spot-on. House wine £16. Open all week.

### L'Autre Pied

**Class act with an easy price tag**
5-7 Blandford Street, Marylebone, W1U 3DB
Tel no: (020) 7486 9696
www.lautrepied.co.uk
⊖ Bond Street, map 4
Modern European | £40
Cooking score: 6

Just off Marylebone High Street, this bijou
other 'Pied' is a relaxed and accessible version
of its renowned big brother Pied-à-Terre (see
entry). Not surprisingly, it too is a class act,
serving food of ambition and style. The
fashionable décor fits the bill, too, pleasant
without being edgy or pretentious, and
featuring backlit flower-pattern glass panels,
silk wallpaper and chic seating. Forgoing the
formality of tablecloths and stiff service, it's a

kind of entry-level haute cuisine with reasonable prices: 'one goes for the food rather than the surroundings'. Choose the lunch/ early-evening menu for a limited choice, three-course 'bargain', perhaps showcasing loin of Gloucestershire Old Spot, served with tarragon pomme purée, crushed carrot and swede, and a thyme jus. Young Marcus Eaves appears to take it all in his stride, delivering ambitious, complex food noted for its seasonality, light touch, balance, texture and emphatic flavour. From a winter carte, pan-fried pollack partnered with potato gnocchi, chanterelles and Vacherin Mont d'Or has been praised, as has the citrus fruit bavarois with black cherry sorbet that caught one reporter's eye at dessert stage. One niggle is portion size – just right for some, but 'tiny' to others. Wines are keenly priced, well chosen and Eurocentric with a strong by-the-glass selection. Bottles start at £19.20.

**Chef/s:** Marcus Eaves. **Open:** all week L 12 to 2.45 (2.30 Sat, 3.30 Sun), D 6 to 10.45 (6.30 to 9.30 Sun). **Closed:** 23 to 27 Dec. **Meals:** alc (main courses £18 to £27). Set L £17.95 (2 courses) to £20.95. Sun L £26.95. Tasting menu £55 (7 courses). **Service:** 12.5% (optional). **Details:** Cards accepted. 53 seats. Air-con. No mobile phones. Music. Children allowed.

## Axis at One Aldwych

**Unfussy hotel dining**
1 Aldwych, Covent Garden, WC2B 4RH
Tel no: (020) 7300 0300
www.onealdwych.com/axis
⊖ Covent Garden, map 5
Modern British | £33
Cooking score: 3

🛏 V

A contemporary take on a metropolitan hotel dining room, Axis occupies a radically designed, subterranean space below the swanky One Aldwych. Green Thai silk panels, comfy black and purple leather armchairs, a double-height ceiling and a row of slender tree trunks gilded with satin nickel create quite an impact, but the food aims to keep things straightforward. The short, unfussy

menu avoids fancy descriptions in favour of telling it like it is: Welsh rarebit with beef tomato salad, smoked salmon fishcakes with gribiche sauce, roast chicken 'properly garnished', and duck confit with colcannon, lentils, plum and port jus. A few lighter main courses are also welcome (monkfish niçoise, say), while desserts could involve poached rhubarb with custard or apple and hazelnut crumble. Wines start at £19 (£4.75 a glass).

**Chef/s:** Tony Fleming. **Open:** Mon to Fri L 12 to 2.30, Mon to Sat D 5.30 to 10.45 (5 to 11.30 Sat). **Closed:** Sun, bank hols. **Meals:** alc (main courses £13 to £24). Set L and D £16.75 (2 courses) to £19.75. **Service:** not inc. **Details:** Cards accepted. 110 seats. Air-con. Separate bar. Wheelchair access. Music. Children allowed.

## Bank Westminster

**Globe-trotting brasserie**
45 Buckingham Gate, Westminster, SW1E 6BS
Tel no: (020) 7630 6644
www.bankrestaurants.com
⊖ St James's Park, map 5
Modern European | £35
Cooking score: 2

🛏 V

The restaurant is set inside a Victorian pile – now the Crowne Plaza Hotel – and dining takes place in a light-washed space overlooking a delightful courtyard. The room is big, the modern design a bit brash. The menu traverses the globe, but the kitchen takes the diversity in its stride, producing well-cooked wild mushroom risotto with a Parmesan wafer, and seared yellowfin tuna, capers, tomato and olives. However the impact of the flavours can occasionally be 'too clement'. Passion fruit crème brûleé is a nice way to end. Wines, equally well-travelled, start from £14.95. There is a provincial outpost in Birmingham (see entry).

**Chef/s:** Alan Larch. **Open:** Mon to Fri 12 to 11, Sat 5.30 to 11. **Closed:** Sun, 25 and 26 Dec, bank hols. **Meals:** alc (main courses £11 to £23). **Service:** 12.5% (optional). **Details:** Cards accepted. 150 seats. 12 seats outside. Air-con. Separate bar. Wheelchair access. Music. Children allowed.

**NEW ENTRY**
# Bar Trattoria Semplice
Simply lives up to its name
22-23 Woodstock Street, Mayfair, W1C 2AP
Tel no: (020) 7491 8638
www.bartrattoriasemplice.com
⊖ Bond Street, map 5
Italian | £24
Cooking score: 3
 V

Hidden in the corner of Woodstock Street, a few yards from Oxford Street, this offshoot of nearby Ristorante Semplice (see entry) lives up to its name. The simple décor is light and bright, with blond wood and an almost café-like feel, and the food, built around the best bought-in ingredients, is presented with unfussy aplomb. Wooden boards of fabulous meaty antipasti and the wonderful Italian cheeses are a highlight, but speciality menus focusing on the various regions of Italy are a feature – Lazio's sweetbread, artichoke and black olive salad, as well as grilled lamb rump with a semolina gnocco and a sauce of red and yellow peppers. Trolley-borne desserts include the endearingly frumpy-looking torta della nonna. The Italian wine list starts at £13.50.
**Chef/s:** Marco Torri and Marco Squillace. **Open:** all week L 12 to 2.30 (12.30 Sat, 1 Sun), D 6.30 to 10.30 (11 Sat, 9.30 Sun). **Closed:** 24 to 26 Dec, bank hols. **Meals:** alc (main courses £12 to £15). Set L £14.50 (3 courses). **Service:** not inc. **Details:** Cards accepted. 70 seats. 30 seats outside. Air-con. Separate bar. Wheelchair access. Music. Children allowed.

# Barrafina
Real-deal tapas
54 Frith Street, Soho, W1D 4SL
Tel no: (020) 7813 8016
www.barrafina.co.uk
⊖ Tottenham Court Road, map 5
Spanish | £28
Cooking score: 4
V

'The kitchen just keeps rolling on here', notes a regular at Sam and Eddie Hart's homage to Catalonia. It comes in the shape of an authentic tapas bar that would stand up well to those in Barcelona. It's nothing more than a long bar with an open kitchen behind and high bar stools (to discourage lingering too long) in front. The food is strictly traditional Spanish, built around impeccably sourced ingredients. The menu features plenty of charcuterie (excellent jamón de Jabugo), seafood such as sardines a la plancha and gambas al ajillo, individual tortillas – jamón and spinach, for example – and the likes of ham croquetas, grilled chicken with romesco sauce and lamb cutlets. Chips with brava sauce is a fine take on a tapas staple, and grilled quail with aïoli has been a highlight. Crema catalana and Santiago tart are good ways to finish. Wines from £15.50.
**Chef/s:** Nieves Barragan. **Open:** all week L 12 to 3 (1 to 3.30 Sun), D 5 to 11 (5.30 to 10 Sun). **Closed:** 24 to 26 Dec, bank hols. **Meals:** alc (main courses £7 to £13). **Service:** 12.5% (optional). **Details:** Cards accepted. 23 seats. 10 seats outside. Air-con. No music. Children allowed.

## Symbols

 Accommodation is available

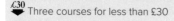 Three courses for less than £30

V More than three vegetarian main courses

£5 OFF £5-off voucher scheme

🍾 Notable wine list

## ALSO RECOMMENDED
## ▲ Bedford and Strand
1a Bedford Street, Covent Garden, WC2E 9HH
Tel no: (020) 7836 3033
www.bedford-strand.com
⊖ Covent Garden, map 5
European

Attractive Parisian-style décor features tiled floors, dark wood furniture and marble-topped tables at this welcoming wine bar and bistro on the Covent Garden fringes. The owners are passionate about wine, and it shows in a great, accessibly laid-out list (from £13.25) with enthusiastic staff happy to make recommendations. Charcuterie and cheese plates satisfy lighter appetites at the bar, while potted crab and toast (£7.50) and crisp-crumbed fishcakes with spinach and poached egg (£13.50) stand out on a menu of bistro classics. Closed Sun.

## ▲ The Beehive

**126 Crawford Street, Marylebone, W1U 6BF**
**Tel no: (020) 7486 8037**
**www.thebeehive-pub.co.uk**
**⊖ Baker Street, map 4**
**Gastropub**

It may have been taken over by restaurateur Claudio Pulze, but this traditional boozer in a residential Marylebone street is still very much a pub. Wooden floors and uncomplicated décor strike the right note and the one large bar doubles as a dining room for food that is served all day. Classic pub dishes include steak sandwich or sausage and mash with onion gravy (£8.90). Other options might range from Caesar salad to crackling roasted pork belly with mash (£13.90). House wine £16. Open all week.

## Bellamy's

**Classy French cooking**
**18-18a Bruton Place, Mayfair, W1J 6LY**
**Tel no: (020) 7491 2727**
**www.bellamysrestaurant.co.uk**
**⊖ Green Park, map 5**
**French | £40**
**Cooking score: 4**

Simplicity is surely the key to success here – dishing up the finest, most luxurious ingredients available, from smoked salmon to Périgord truffles or even Beluga caviar, with a minimum of fuss. Such quality invariably doesn't come cheap, but this popular Bruton Place establishment finds plenty willing to pay, and you get some classy French cooking for your money, including uncomplicated main courses such as roast turbot with hollandaise and veal sweetbreads meunière.

For those feeling slightly less extravagant, the set-lunch menu doesn't skimp on quality, and the Oyster Bar alongside the deli provides open sandwiches, simple dishes and a glass of wine in a more informal setting. The all-French wine list by John Armit garners high praise, even with scant choice under £30, and the only grumble comes in response to a suggested donation on the bill. Readers are, apparently, 'quite capable of working out their own charitable giving'.

**Chef/s:** Stéphane Pacoud. **Open:** Mon to Fri L 12 to 3, Mon to Sat D 6 to 11. **Closed:** Sun, bank hols, Christmas. **Meals:** alc (main courses £19 to £29). Set L and D £24 (2 courses) to £28.50. **Service:** 12.5% (optional). **Details:** Cards accepted. 76 seats. Air-con. No music. Wheelchair access. Children allowed.

## Benares

**Innovative new-wave Indian**
**12a Berkeley Square, Mayfair, W1J 6BS**
**Tel no: (020) 7629 8886**
**www.benaresrestaurant.com**
**⊖ Green Park, map 5**
**Indian | £50**
**Cooking score: 3**

Designed as a snazzy Lilliputian snapshot of the holy city of Benares, this high-flying Mayfair thoroughbred is a world away from curry house expectations. Atul Kochhar's enlightened approach to Indian cuisine breaks rules and challenges expectations with its innovative blend of old and new, classic and crossover. Bhindi bhaji and chicken korma now share the billing with the likes of fennel-infused Kentish lamb chops with goats' cheese and wild rocket. Elsewhere, wild rabbit is given the tandoori treatment and fillet of roe deer is accompanied by yellow pumpkin risotto and pear chutney, while the creative impetus also extends to, say, Savoy cabbage 'dolmas' with fenugreek-infused concassé and soured cream. Wines have been chosen with care and sensitivity to the food; prices start at £18. Atul Kochhar also runs Vatika at the Wickham Vineyard, Hampshire (see entry).

**Chef/s:** Atul Kochhar. **Open:** all week L 12 to 2.30, D 5.30 to 11 (6 to 10.30 Sun). **Closed:** 25 and 26 Dec. **Meals:** alc (main courses £18 to £43). Set L and D £24.95 (2 courses) to £29.95. **Service:** 12.5% (optional). **Details:** Cards accepted. 130 seats. Air-con. Separate bar. Wheelchair access. Music.

## Bentley's Oyster Bar & Grill
**Classic seafood and seriously good desserts**
11-15 Swallow Street, Piccadilly, W1B 4DG
Tel no: (020) 7734 4756
www.bentleys.org
⊖ Piccadilly Circus, map 5
Seafood | £40
Cooking score: 4

🍾 V

'I had the fortune to lunch at Bentley's today', noted a reader in March, 'and I have to say the shellfish bisque starter was a delight and a meal in itself'. Indeed, Richard Corrigan's menu is a classic run through potted salmon and brown shrimps, cold dressed crab mayonnaise, beef tartare, steamed mutton pudding and a fish pie stuffed with lobster, scallop, haddock and tiger prawn. Reports have praised 'excellent condition' oysters and a massive Dover sole for two ('a superb fish, beautifully grilled and prepared') served in the clubby upstairs dining room. But though the cooking has pleased, sometimes the advertised flavours have been more muted than might be expected from the description, and service occasionally lets the side down. Desserts are seriously enjoyed, the trifle, especially, is well-loved. Inviting fish-friendly whites and a good slate of sherries offer serious drinking opportunities, but the wine list is full of diverting treasures – with an excellent choice by the glass if you fancy exploring. Bottle prices start at £16.95.
**Chef/s:** Richard Corrigan and Brendan Fyldes.
**Open:** all week 12 to 11.30. **Closed:** 25 Dec, 1 Jan.
**Meals:** alc (main courses £14 to £38). Set L and D (including wine) £18.50 (2 courses) to £22.50.
**Service:** 12.5% (optional). **Details:** Cards accepted. 120 seats. 40 seats outside. Air-con. Separate bar. No music. Wheelchair access. Music. Children allowed.

### Best value in London

**The Beehive** The one large bar doubles as a dining room for good-value food that is served all day.

**El Pirata Detapas** This offshoot of El Pirata in Mayfair (see entry) is a convivial place for reasonably priced tapas.

**Jom Makan** Cheerful, fast-paced, keenly priced Malaysian restaurant close to the National Gallery.

**Lantana Café** Great value, generous portions, and high-quality ingredients.

**Albion, Boundary Street** The food is heroically British and most dishes are under £10.

**Tangawizi** Décor is basic, service friendly, and the kitchen delivers good food at reasonable prices.

**Chilli Cool** Modestly appointed Bloomsbury address that delivers better-than-usual Szechuan food.

**Jinkichi** People drop in for the good sushi and yakitori.

**Market** Unpretentious, wholesome approach, warm service and pared-back British menu.

**Kastoori** Affable restaurant offers Gujarati vegetarian food with a very personal stamp.

NEW ENTRY

## Bocca di Lupo

**Simple, modern Italian food**
12 Archer Street, Piccadilly, W1D 7BB
Tel no: (020) 7734 2223
www.boccadilupo.com
⊖ Piccadilly Circus, map 5
Italian | £30
Cooking score: 4

V

Since opening in November 2008, Jacob Kenedy's restaurant has built up a loyal following who keep returning for simple, modern Italian food. It's a long, narrow room split into a bar which is lined with stools, tapas-style, and a dining area with close-set tables. Neither area is particularly large, so the staff can set a steady pace at busy times. The menu turns its back on conventional courses, offering instead a choice of large and small plates. Simplicity and careful sourcing are seen in rabbit tonnato with broad beans and capers, and wild garlic and ricotta tortelloni with morels, both highlights of an inspection meal that also included sheep's milk ricotta gnudi with lamb ragù, and cream of red prawn risotto with basil. Desserts offer sanguinaccio from Abruzzo – a sweet pâté of pig's blood and chocolate – for the very adventurous, an exemplary rum baba for the rest of us. Service, too, is exemplary. House wine is £10 for a 500ml carafe.
**Chef/s:** Jacob Kenedy. **Open:** all week L 12.30 to 3, Mon to Sat D 5.30 to 12. **Meals:** alc (main courses £10 to £24). **Service:** 12.5% (optional).
**Details:** Cards accepted. 100 seats. Air-con. Wheelchair access. Music. Children allowed.

## Boxwood Café

**New York comes to Knightsbridge**
Berkeley Hotel, Wilton Place, Knightsbridge, SW1X 7RL
Tel no: (020) 7235 1010
www.gordonramsay.com
⊖ Knightsbridge, map 4
Modern British | £40
Cooking score: 3

V

The buzz, the praiseworthy service, and the chic-yet-comfortable interior of Gordon Ramsay's Boxwood Café are imported straight from New York. So are some updated brasserie dishes, such as veal and foie gras burger or pancakes with bacon and maple syrup (the latter on the new Sunday brunch menu). 'Fine-dining' touches sneak on to a trendily global menu which features crab tagliolini, whole Label Anglais chicken for two with artichoke salad, and marinated pineapple with star anise. Quality ingredients and sexy pairings give dishes that 'eat me' quality, although prices are a shade 'Knightsbridge', as are the portions. The wine list (from £22), with a dozen by the glass, tacks from Old World to New, with strengths in France and Italy.
**Chef/s:** Stuart Gillies. **Open:** all week L 12 to 3 (4 Sat and Sun), all week D 6 to 11 (12 Thur to Sat). **Meals:** alc (main courses £12 to £33). Set L £21 (2 courses) to £25. Sun L £21. **Service:** 12.5% (optional). **Details:** Cards accepted. 120 seats. Air-con. Separate bar. Wheelchair access. Music. Children allowed.

## ALSO RECOMMENDED

### ▲ The Café at Sotheby's

34–35 New Bond Street, Mayfair, W1A 2AA
Tel no: (020) 7293 5077
www.sothebys.com
⊖ Bond Street, Oxford Circus, map 5
Modern European

However tumultuous the art market, you can always be assured of a good meal here. Chef Laura Greenfield consistently impresses with dishes like twice-baked goats' cheese soufflé

(£14), salt beef with latkes or a simple lobster club sandwich (£18). Located in the bustling foyer, it's open for breakfast, lunch and tea. Wines are selected by Sotheby's own MW Serena Sutcliffe (house is £18). Afterwards go for a spin around the galleries, where you can check out highlights of forthcoming sales. Open Mon to Fri.

##  Camerino

16 Percy Street, Fitzrovia, W1T 1DT
Tel no: (020) 7637 9900
www.camerinorestaurant.com
⊖ Tottenham Court Road, Goodge Street, map 5
Italian

'Good value, slightly smarter than average' Italian noted for bold design – blocks of fuchsia softened by pink tones – and well-crafted, if conventional, cooking that explores the food of regional Italy. Starters of borlotti bean and spelt soup or gnocchi with swordfish sauce (£9) and mains of calf's liver with spinach (£16.50) or roasted halibut with sautéed lentils show the style. The kitchen makes its own bread, pasta and ice creams. House wine is £16.50. Closed Sat L and all Sun.

## Le Caprice

**Classy modern brasserie fare**
Arlington House, Arlington Street, Mayfair, SW1A 1RJ
Tel no: (020) 7629 2239
www.le-caprice.co.uk
⊖ Green Park, map 5
Modern European | £45
Cooking score: 4

**V**

One doesn't hear too much about 1980s darling Le Caprice these days. While her sister restaurants The Ivy (now with private members' club) and J Sheekey (with new oyster bar) get all the attention, dear dependable Le Caprice just gets on with it, turning out the kind of classy modern brasserie fare it always did. This seems to bother its many regulars not a bit. It's comforting to pop into the bright, modern

dining room for a great burger (or 'chopped steak Americaine' in Caprice-speak), or salmon fishcake with sorrel sauce. Rather more interesting are the weekly specials boasting wonderful seasonal ingredients – maybe oxtail cappelletti with barba di frate (monk's beard) or roasted guinea fowl with morel macaroni. Prices are surprisingly good for the quality and locale. Likewise the French-focused wine list, from £19.50. Reservations remain hard to come by.
**Chef/s:** Lee Bull. **Open:** all week L 12 to 3 (4 Fri and Sat), D 5.30 to 12 (12 to 11 Sun). **Closed:** 25 and 26 Dec, 1 Jan. **Meals:** alc (main courses £13 to £28). Pre/post theatre set D £15.75 (2 courses) to £19.75. **Service:** 12.5%. **Details:** Cards accepted. 90 seats. Air-con. No mobile phones. Music. Children allowed.

## Cha Cha Moon

**Super-stylish noodle bar**
15-21 Ganton Street, Soho, W1F 9BN
Tel no: (020) 7297 9800
www.chachamoon.com
⊖ Oxford Circus, map 5
Chinese | £10
Cooking score: 1

Peak-time queues prove that Alan Yau (the brains behind Wagamama and a succession of high-profile eateries) has come up trumps again with Cha Cha Moon. Hong Kong street food is served at breakneck speed in a stylish canteen clad with bamboo and indigo glass. Top-dollar dishes reach just £7.80, but execution is hit-and-miss. Stick to hits, such as ribeye beef lao mian, XO vermicelli noodles with prawns and chilli-spiked Szechuan dumplings, and it's 'very, very good value'. Wash down with wines (by the 250ml glass at £4.90). A second branch is at Whiteleys, 151 Queensway, W2 4YN, tel no: (020) 7792 0088.
**Chef/s:** Weng Kong Wong. **Open:** all week, 12 to 11 (11.30 Fri and Sat, 10.30 Sun). **Closed:** 25 Dec. **Meals:** alc (main courses £5 to £8). **Service:** not inc. **Details:** Cards accepted. 90 seats. 40 seats outside. Air-con. No music. Wheelchair access. Children allowed.

## The Chancery

Chic bolt-hole in lawyerland
9 Cursitor Street, Holborn, EC4A 1LL
Tel no: (020) 7831 4000
www.thechancery.co.uk
⊖ Chancery Lane, map 5
Modern European | £34
Cooking score: 4

£5
OFF

A smart space for the moneyed denizens of lawyerland, the lofty, stone-faced Chancery offers its wares in a setting of mahogany parquet floors, brown leather chairs and walls hung with abstract art. The food here is assured, with plenty of sharp ideas, exciting combinations and eye-catching possibilities on the regularly updated menus. 'Truly exceptional', was one correspondent's verdict. Mediterranean flavours give the cooking a suntanned look – roast fillet of mackerel is partnered by a crisp tomato and onion tart, while steamed hake comes with a potage of squid and mussels with red peppers and pesto. Away from the sea, expect exotically tinged combos (spiced rump of lamb with aubergines, couscous and merguez sausage) alongside tweaked favourites (calf's liver and onions served with smoked potato cream). Finish with something intricate – perhaps sablé of blackberries and poached pears with crème chiboust, or go for the tart of the day. The wine list is a tidy package of carefully sourced global bottles from £16 (£6 a glass). **Chef/s:** Andrew Thompson. **Open:** Mon to Fri L 12 to 2.30, D 6 to 10. **Closed:** Sat, Sun, bank hols, 23 Dec to first week Jan. **Meals:** Set L and D £27.50 (2 courses) to £34. **Service:** 12.5% (optional). **Details:** Cards accepted. 55 seats. Air-con. Separate bar. Wheelchair access. Music.

### Average price

The average price listed in main-entry reviews denotes the price of a three-course meal, without wine.

## China Tang at the Dorchester

Scintillating Shanghai glitz
The Dorchester Hotel, 53 Park Lane, Hyde Park, W1K 1QA
Tel no: (020) 7629 9988
www.thedorchester.com
⊖ Hyde Park Corner, map 4
Chinese | £65
Cooking score: 2

 V

Conceived by lifestyle guru and entrepreneur Sir David Tang, this glamorous subterranean dining room evokes colonial Hong Kong and Shanghai with its grand sweeping staircase, fabulous chinoiserie, swathes of silk and staff parading around in white uniforms. It's a scintillating prospect that comes with an eye-watering price tag – although there's nothing unsettling about the menu itself. Peking duck, steamed scallops with black-bean sauce and Singapore noodles inhabit a reassuringly familiar world, with rare abalone and suckling pig included for the really big spenders. At lunchtime you can ease the financial strain with dependable dim sum, but expect to pay upwards of £30 if you fancy something from the elite wine list. **Chef/s:** Lin Low. **Open:** all week, L 11 to 3.30 (4.30 Sun), D 5.30 to 12 (11.30 Sun). **Closed:** 25 Dec. **Meals:** alc (main courses from £10 to £60). Set L £15 (2 courses). **Service:** 12.5%. **Details:** Cards accepted. 180 seats. Air-con. Separate bar. Wheelchair access. Music. Children allowed.

## Chisou

A taste of Tokyo
4 Princes Street, Mayfair, W1B 2LE
Tel no: (020) 7629 3931
www.chisou.co.uk
⊖ Oxford Circus, map 5
Japanese | £45
Cooking score: 4

V

A slice of Japan in a quiet enclave near Oxford Circus, Chisou evokes fond echoes of Tokyo's sociable eating houses – which is probably why it is a treasured bolt-hole for homesick

salarymen. Its sleekily groomed, glass-and-slate interior creates a mood of uncluttered Zen-like affluence, and the food lives up to the restaurant's name ('spirit of the feast'). All-comers descend on the place for sushi lunch boxes and bowls of noodles, while evening brings a more creative edge to proceedings: check out the chef's specialities, which might include monkfish liver with ponzu, spring onions and grated mooli served in a saké cup, or deep-fried and marinated baby octopus. The regular menu explores all the benchmark techniques, from visually stunning sashimi and fascinating appetisers (raw tuna 'yukke' mixed with sesame seeds and miso, topped with a raw quail's egg and dried seaweed) to clear-flavoured salads, teriyaki and tempura. Chisou is a saké lover's wonderland, with a glorious selection of vintage and blended tipples on offer. Wines start at £14.80.
**Chef/s:** Kodi Aung. **Open:** Mon to Sat L 12 to 2.30 (3 Sat), D 6 to 10.15. **Closed:** Sun, bank hols, 2 weeks Aug, 2 weeks Christmas. **Meals:** alc (main courses £10 to £25). Set L £17 (2 courses). Set D £25 (2 courses) to £35. **Service:** 13% (optional). **Details:** Cards accepted. 52 seats. 8 seats outside. Air-con. Music. Children allowed.

# Cigala

**Unbuttoned Spanish hangout**
54 Lamb's Conduit Street, Bloomsbury, WC1N 3LW
Tel no: (020) 7405 1717
www.cigala.co.uk
⊖ Holborn, Russell Square, map 5
Spanish | £26
Cooking score: 1

Chef/proprietor Jake Hodges helped to set up Moro (see entry), so he knows his way around the byways of Hispanic cuisine – no wonder this defiantly cliché-free venue is often 'full almost to bursting'. Feed on tapas in the animated downstairs bar or explore the more vigorous offerings in the dining room: expect a daily repertoire that runs from cecina (oak-smoked beef) with caperberries and grilled sardines with churrasco to Asturian fabada stew and a brace of paellas. Wines from £7.75.

**Chef/s:** Jake Hodges. **Open:** Mon to Fri 12 to 10.45, Sat 12.30 to 10.45, Sun 12.30 to 9.45. **Meals:** alc (main courses £12 to £19). Set L £15 (2 courses) to £18. Tapas menu available. **Service:** 12.5% (optional). **Details:** Cards accepted. 60 seats. 16 seats outside. Air-con. Separate bar. No music. Wheelchair access. Children allowed.

# Cinnamon Club

**Grand Indian high-roller**
30-32 Great Smith Street, Westminster, SW1P 3BU
Tel no: (020) 7222 2555
www.cinnamonclub.com
⊖ Westminster, map 5
Indian | £50
Cooking score: 3
£5 OFF **V**

A favourite with political movers and shakers from the nearby Houses of Parliament, this patrician Indian occupies the hallowed halls of the Old Westminster Library. Antique bookcases, mahogany panels and parquet flooring provide a cultured backdrop to sophisticated modern food that makes the most of top-notch ingredients: tandoori squab pigeon is served with confit leg and black lentils, roast saddle of Oisin deer has been cooked medium-rare with pickling spices, and grilled Label Anglais chicken might appear with a citrus crust and tomato quinoa. Side dishes could include a stir-fry of lamb's heart with sweetbread, as well as lightly spiced mushrooms with spinach. The eclectic wine list is a telling match for the good, although prices (from £25) are pitched at high-rollers. A City offshoot, the Cinnamon Kitchen, is now open on Devonshire Square (see entry).
**Chef/s:** Vivek Singh. **Open:** Mon to Sat L 12 to 2.45, D 6 to 10.45. **Closed:** Sun, 26 Dec, bank hols (exc 25 Dec L and Good Fri D). **Meals:** alc (main courses £14 to £37). Set L and early eve D £19 (2 courses) to £22. **Service:** 12.5% (optional). **Details:** Cards accepted. 130 seats. Air-con. Separate bar. No music. Children allowed.

## Clos Maggiore

**Comfortable, with skilful service and food**
33 King Street, Covent Garden, WC2E 8JD
Tel no: (020) 7379 9696
www.closmaggiore.com
⊖ Covent Garden, map 5
Modern European | £35
Cooking score: 2

**V**

This Covent Garden stalwart feels 'small but comfortable', especially in the open-roofed conservatory 'with trees and plants round the walls so it feels like you're sitting outside'. Service comes with a 'sense of humour' and the brisk efficiency of a well-oiled machine, and there's skill in the kitchen too, with the Mediterranean-style food well-timed and attractively presented. The set menu appears to offer the best value – escabèche of red mullet with a fruit salsa, and gnocchi with pear, Gorgonzola and asparagus, as well as slow-cooked rabbit with a casserole of yellow peas have all been recommended. There's an excellent selection of wines by the glass (from £4.50). Bottles start at £18.

**Chef/s:** Marcellin Marc. **Open:** all week L 12 to 3, D 5 to 10.45 (11 Fri, 10 Sun). **Meals:** alc (main courses £15 to £21). Set L and D £19.50. **Service:** 12.5% (optional). **Details:** Cards accepted. 45 seats. Air-con. Wheelchair access. Music. Children allowed.

**NEW ENTRY**

## Corrigan's Mayfair

**Irish chef in fine fettle**
28 Upper Grosvenor Street, Mayfair, W1K 7EH
Tel no: (020) 7499 9943
www.corrigansmayfair.com
⊖ Marble Arch, map 4
Modern British | £45
Cooking score: 6

🍶 **V**

Following the closure of Lindsay House in Soho, Richard Corrigan now channels his energies into this swanky new dining room tacked onto the Grosvenor House Hotel. The move has 'revitalised' him, although not everyone is sold on the feathered lampshades and hunting-themed interior – or indeed the precise but 'simpering' French service. The kitchen certainly started off with a shotgun bang, and its winter game specialities received universally ecstatic plaudits. Saddle of hare with roast pumpkin and sprout tops, butter-poached pheasant with chestnuts, bacon and game toast, and roe deer in 'excellent pastry' with pickled cabbage have all been eaten and endorsed with gusto. Since then, this big-boned metropolitan dazzler has eased off a tad, with recent reports mentioning 'very tame' food and inconsistencies. That said, meals begin with 'instantly addictive' soda bread, and diners continue to be wowed by all manner of Anglo-Irish delights from an earthy combo of crubeens, beetroot and horseradish to 'ruby-red' spring lamb chops with peas and mint or John Dory with Jerusalem artichokes and langoustine sauce. To finish, carrot cake with pickled walnuts and clementines has been as warmly inviting as a Christmas stocking, and the kitchen also deserves applause for its 'stand-out' rhubarb soufflé. The wine list is a delicious read, and it nails its 'terroir' colours to the mast when it comes to supporting organic and biodynamic producers. France, Italy and Spain share most of the glory, and every page is stuffed with real corkers. Prices rise rapidly from £15, but there is the bonus of fine drinking from £5.60 a glass.

**Chef/s:** Richard Corrigan. **Open:** Mon to Fri L 12 to 3 (4 Sun), all week D 6 to 11 (10 Sun). **Closed:** 24 to 27 Dec. **Meals:** alc (main courses £16 to £24). Set L Mon to Fri £19.50 (2 courses) to £23.50. Sun L £27. **Service:** 12.5% (optional). **Details:** Cards accepted. 100 seats. Air-con. Separate bar. Wheelchair access. Music. Children allowed.

### Please send us your feedback

To register your opinion about any restaurant listed in the Guide, or a new restaurant that you wish to bring to our attention, please visit the web address at the bottom of the page. Your feedback informs the content of the book and will be used to compile next year's reviews.

# Côte

**Bustling brasserie**
124-126 Wardour Street, Soho, W1F 0TY
Tel no: (020) 7287 9280
www.cote-restaurants.co.uk
⊖ **Tottenham Court Road, map 5**
**French | £25**
**Cooking score: 2**

Success breeds success, and this second link in
the Côte chain – also at Wimbledon (see
entry), Covent Garden, Kensington and
Richmond – got off to a cracking start when
it opened in 2008. The preferred spot is the
ground-floor dining room, which buzzes
with noise and chatter – there's a further
dining room downstairs. The kitchen turns
out classic French regional dishes along the
lines of chicken liver parfait, steak tartare,
cassoulet de Toulouse and chargrilled Landes
chicken with frites, alongside good value plats
rapides (steak frites), afternoon and weekend
set deals, and a good-value all-French wine list
with bottles from £13.95.
**Chef/s:** Albert Ndrew. **Open:** Mon to Fri 8am to
11pm (midnight Thur to Sat), Sat 9am to 11pm, Sun
9am to 10.30pm. **Closed:** 25 Dec. **Meals:** alc (main
courses £9 to £18). Set L £9.70 (2 courses) to £11.70.
**Service:** 12.5% (optional). **Details:** Cards accepted.
140 seats. Air-con. Wheelchair access. Music.
Children allowed.

# Dehesa

**Chilled-out chic and charcuterie**
25 Ganton Street, Oxford Circus, W1F 9BP
Tel no: (020) 7494 4170
www.dehesa.co.uk
⊖ **Oxford Circus, map 5**
**Spanish/Italian | £22**
**Cooking score: 3**
£5 OFF  **V**  £30

Named after the woodland area and home to
Ibérico pigs in Spain, Dehesa puts a strong
emphasis on charcuterie, with whole hams on
display. This younger sibling to Salt Yard (see
entry) occupies a chic corner site and gives out
a casual feel – with no reservations and bar

stools at high narrow tables this is for quick
pit-stops. The cooking relies on exceptional
ingredients, with the kitchen displaying the
confidence to juggle contrasting flavours, so
expect unusual Italo-Spanish tapas such as
crispy salmon with sautéed aubergines, honey
and Padron peppers, or confit Old Spot belly
pork with rosemary-scented cannellini beans,
as well as classics of patatas fritas and chorizo.
Finish with turron parfait and figs. The Italian/
Spanish wine list opens at £15.
**Chef/s:** Brent Loam. **Open:** all week 12 to 11 (5 Sun).
**Closed:** 25 Dec to 1 Jan. **Meals:** alc (tapas £3 to £7).
**Service:** 12.5% (optional). **Details:** Cards accepted.
38 seats. 22 seats outside. Air-con. Music. Children
allowed.

# Dinings

**Harmonious Japanese flavours**
22 Harcourt Street, Marylebone, W1H 4HH
Tel no: (020) 7723 0666
www.dinings.co.uk
⊖ **Marylebone, map 4**
**Japanese | £36**
**Cooking score: 3**

There's barely enough room to swing a
chopstick in the ground-floor sushi bar, and
the basement's utilitarian furnishings are the
antithesis of luxury, but the regular custom
and necessary bookings suggest, rightly, that
the food is Dining's real draw. Chef/owner
Tomonari Chiba honed his trade at Nobu
London (see entry) and has a sublime knack
for uniting harmonious flavours and textures.
Tackle the lengthy menu by sharing several
small dishes: thin slivers of sea bass sashimi
with fragrant yuzu and jalapeño salsa, buttery
scallops in a creamy wasabi-spiked sauce, and
silky black cod grilled with chilli and garlic.
It's all a pleasure to eat, with the added extras
of fair pricing and obliging staff. Wines start at
£16 and there is plenty of beer and saké.
**Chef/s:** Tomonari Chiba and Masaki Sugisaki. **Open:**
Mon to Fri L 12 to 2.30, all week D 6 to 10.30 (10
Sun). **Closed:** 25 and 26 Dec. **Meals:** alc (main
courses £4 to £16). **Service:** 10% (optional).
**Details:** Cards accepted. 28 seats. Music. Children
allowed.

## The Duke of Wellington
Groovy gastropub
94a Crawford Street, Marylebone, W1H 2HQ
Tel no: (020) 7723 2790
www.thedukew1.co.uk
⊖ Marylebone, Baker Street, map 4
Gastropub | £25
Cooking score: 1

Once a Dickensian-style nook stuffed with Wellingtonian memorabilia, this Marylebone boozer has joined the ranks of the gastropub brigade – and sports the abstract artwork, leather banquettes and groovy lighting to prove it. Eat in the shabby-chic bar or the cosy upstairs dining room from menus that work their way through dressed Cornish crab on toast, chargrilled monkfish with a curried mussel and spinach ragoût or slow-roast Tamworth pork belly with parsnip purée and red cabbage. End with rhubarb crumble or rice pudding. House wine is £15.
**Chef/s:** Fred Smith. **Open:** all week L 12 to 3 (11.30 to 4 Sat, 12.30 to 4.30 Sun), D 6.30 to 10 (7 to 10 Sat, 7 to 9 Sun). **Closed:** 26 Dec. **Meals:** alc (main courses £10 to £18). **Service:** 12.5% (optional). **Details:** Cards accepted. 60 seats. 48 seats outside. Separate bar. Wheelchair access. Music. Children allowed.

## L'Escargot, Ground Floor
Soho's French ambassador
48 Greek Street, Soho, W1D 4EF
Tel no: (020) 7439 7474
www.lescargotrestaurant.co.uk
⊖ Tottenham Court Road, Leicester Square, map 5
French | £31
Cooking score: 3

Soho's legendary 'snail' slithered onto the London restaurant scene in 1927 and has been an exclusive fixture ever since. These days it's a repository for owner Jimmy Lahoud's art collection, displayed in the aptly named Picasso Room or the ever-buzzing Ground Floor brasserie. Designer of the moment David Collins has re-shaped the interiors, and the kitchen feeds the downstairs crowd with fashionably dressed-up French food. Snails are given the bordelaise treatment with red wine, or you could start with 'subtly flavoured' guinea fowl and Savoy cabbage terrine. Mains draw on carefully sourced raw materials, as in organic salmon with Puy lentils and samphire or confit of Barbary duck with braised red cabbage and 'raisin sec'. To finish, consider cinnamon crème brûlée with roasted fig and sugared almonds. Wines start at £17.
**Chef/s:** Joseph Croan. **Open:** Mon to Fri L 12 to 2.30, Mon to Sat D 6 to 11.30 (5.30 Sat). **Closed:** Sun, 25 and 26 Dec, 1 Jan. **Meals:** alc (main courses £13 to £16). Set L and pre-theatre D £15 (2 courses) to £18. **Service:** 12.5% (optional). **Details:** Cards accepted. 90 seats. Air-con. Music. Children allowed.

## Fifth Floor
Foodie heaven
Harvey Nichols, 109-125 Knightsbridge, Knightsbridge, SW1X 7RJ
Tel no: (020) 7235 5250
www.harveynichols.com
⊖ Knightsbridge, map 4
Modern British | £40
Cooking score: 3

The top floor of Harvey Nicks' Knightsbridge flagship is foodie heaven with its displays of trendy comestibles; it also provides indulgent opportunities aplenty, whether you choose the suave leather-clad bar, groovy café or futuristic, all-white restaurant lit by state-of-the-art fibre optics. Swedish chef Jonas Karlsson feeds the glammed-up ladies who shop – and the men who don't – with a swanky menu of posh modern food. Among the voguish possibilities might be seared wood pigeon with pickled apples, pancetta and hazelnut polenta, followed by pan-fried stone bass with chickpea ragoût, pak choi and smoked eel tortellini. For afters, chocolate fondue is made for sharing; otherwise try light-toned blood orange parfait with orange salad and citrus foam. In addition, 'market menus' take their cue from seasonal ingredients sold in the store's Foodmarket. The stellar wine list is a mammoth tome with hardly a dud in sight; own-label house selections (from £18) are on the money, and there's an irresistible choice by the glass. Otherwise, go for broke with one of the definitive, three-figure Super Tuscans or pedigree Bordeaux.

**Chef/s:** Jonas Karlsson. **Open:** all week L 12 to 3 (4 Fri and Sat, 5 Sun), Mon to Sat D 6 to 10.45. **Closed:** 25 and 26 Dec, Easter Sun. **Meals:** alc (main courses £17 to £26). Set L and D £19.50. Sun L £19.50 (2 courses) to £24.50. **Service:** 12.5%. **Details:** Cards accepted. 120 seats. Air-con. Separate bar. Wheelchair access. Music. Children allowed. Car parking.

# Fino

**Top-notch tapas**
33 Charlotte Street (entrance in Rathbone Street), Fitzrovia, W1T 1RR
Tel no: (020) 7813 8010
www.finorestaurant.com
⊖ **Goodge Street, map 5**
**Spanish | £40**
**Cooking score: 3**

After closing for a subtle refurbishment in early 2009, Fino is back on track as one of London's best for modern classic tapas. The new softer interior, flower-filled and candle-lit, suits the spacious basement dining room and better reflects the oft-praised hospitality of its owners, Sam and Eddie Hart. A clubby corner bar is good fun for a glass of sherry (from a choice of 20) before hitting the excellent, though compact, Iberian wine list. The menu remains structured to include specials, seafood, 'plancha' dishes and so on, but prices are lower (and dishes smaller), allowing guests to sample more. Crisp crab croquetas, hand-cut pata negra ham, Basque fish stew 'marmitako' and chorizo tortilla are fine choices. Please note: Fino's entrance is off Charlotte Street, on Rathbone Street.

**Chef/s:** Nevis Barragan. **Open:** Mon to Fri L 12 to 2.30, Mon to Sat D 6 to 10.30. **Closed:** Sun, 25 and 26 Dec, 1 Jan, bank hols. **Meals:** alc (main courses

£7 to £28). **Service:** 12.5% (optional). **Details:** Cards accepted. 75 seats. Air-con. Separate bar. No music. Wheelchair access. Children allowed.

# Fung Shing

**Utterly reliable Cantonese food**
15 Lisle Street, Soho, WC2H 7BE
Tel no: (020) 7437 1539
www.fungshing.co.uk
⊖ **Leicester Square, map 5**
**Chinese | £25**
**Cooking score: 2**
£5 OFF ♦ **V** £30

For long one of the premier eating houses in Chinatown, Fung Shing maintains good standards from year to year. Smart table settings and charming staff elevate the place above many nearby competitors, and the cooking is utterly reliable, with dishes that range from the expected Cantonese standards to some highly unusual house specials. Venison marinated in oolong tea and stir-fried crispy pigeon extend the repertoire productively, and there are supremely tasty seafood offerings, such as baby squid stuffed with chilli and garlic. The wine list, too, is an object-lesson in quality control and fair pricing. You may not see the Chinese customers ordering Argentinian Torrontes, but there is a world of experimentation to be undertaken. Southern French house wines are £16.

**Chef/s:** Frank Cheung. **Open:** all week 12 to 11.30. **Closed:** 24 to 26 Dec. **Meals:** alc (main courses £9 to £75). Set L and D £17 (2 courses). **Service:** 10% (optional). **Details:** Cards accepted. 100 seats. Air-con. Separate bar. No mobile phones. Music. Children allowed.

## Galvin at Windows

**Food that's as good as the views**
Hilton Hotel, 22 Park Lane, Mayfair, W1K 1BE
Tel no: (020) 7208 4021
www.galvinatwindows.com
⊖ **Hyde Park Corner, Green Park, map 4**
French | £58
**Cooking score: 6**

≒ V

It goes without saying that the panoramic view over Buck House from the 28th floor is commanding. What isn't remarked upon enough is the equally commanding modern French cuisine from the kitchen. This modern Art Deco-style restaurant at the smart – if corporate – Park Lane Hilton exhibits the same Francophile streak as the Galvin Brothers' Bistrot de Luxe (see entry), only with haute cuisine flair, delivering rich, seasonal tastes and ingredients that make happy bedfellows. One might find foie gras with pomme d'épices and hazelnuts, halibut with lemon oil and crab pommes ecrasées or tarte Tatin with Calvados crème fraîche. 'It's not cheap, but you get what you pay for' notes a fan. The all-inclusive lunch is a doozy. The dramatic setting works best for business by day, dates by night: the 'professional and friendly' service team tailor their spiel to suit, and largely get it right. Wine is a big part of it. The very French list (from £18.50) and service get better year on year. Strong on the big-hitting regions, if weak at the cheaper end, there is plenty by the glass and half-bottle.
**Chef/s:** Chris Galvin and André Garrett. **Open:** Sun to Fri L 12 to 3 (11.45 Sun), Mon to Sat D 6 to 11 (5 Sat). **Closed:** 26 Dec, bank hols, Easter Mon. **Meals:** Set L £29. Set D £58. **Service:** 12.5% (optional). **Details:** Cards accepted. 108 seats. Air-con. Separate bar. No music. Wheelchair access. Children allowed. Car parking.

## Galvin Bistrot de Luxe

**Sophisticated food and a bistro vibe**
66 Baker Street, Marylebone, W1V 7DH
Tel no: (020) 7935 4007
www.galvinrestaurants.com
⊖ **Baker Street, map 4**
French | £30
**Cooking score: 5**

The well-composed menu at the Galvin brothers' 'bistrot de luxe' pleases diners old and new, with a roster of house classics and enticing new dishes 'at affordable prices'. There's effusive praise for the steak tartare, oeufs à la neige and crab 'lasagne' in the former category; for 'meltingly tender lamb tagine' and 'impeccable' red mullet with carrots in the latter. We'll add our tuppence in favour of the perfect veal brains with beurre noisette enjoyed at inspection. The lunchtime business crowd certainly appreciates the generous portions and the set lunch – 'the best value in London'. The Galvins have nailed the bistro vibe as well as the food – although for some the 'buzz' of the wood-panelled room is more din than 'fantastic atmosphere'. The acoustics seem to magnify noise: 'it's difficult to hold a conversation', beefs one reader. On another note, it's delightful to see a restaurant commanding as much comment for service as for cuisine. The 'professional, charming and efficient' team greets one 'like an old friend'. The Francophile wine list draws criticism for 'over-pricing', but with house at £16.50 and some small appellations and young producers represented at the cheaper end, there's a lot to like.
**Chef/s:** Chris and Jeff Galvin and Sian Rees. **Open:** all week L 12 to 2.30 (3.30 Sun), D 6 to 11 (9.30 Sun). **Closed:** 24 to 26 Dec, 1 Jan. **Meals:** alc (main courses £12 to £19). Set L £15.50. Set D £17.50. **Details:** Cards accepted. 105 seats. 12 seats outside. Air-con. Separate bar. Wheelchair access. Car parking.

## Le Gavroche

**Peerless gastronomy from a French legend**
43 Upper Brook Street, Mayfair, W1K 7QR
Tel no: (020) 7408 0881
www.le-gavroche.co.uk
⊖ Marble Arch, map 4
French | £85
Cooking score: 8

🍾

Now into its fifth decade as a 'grand bastion' of top-end French haute cuisine, Le Gavroche still manages to epitomise cosseted 'special event' dining in the capital, while many of its neighbours experiment with foams, dusts and powders. The basement dining room hasn't changed in years, but despite its subterranean setting it never feels claustrophobic: all is polished, mellow, luxurious and somehow comfortingly familiar – even for first-timers. Protocol from a bygone era is still strictly observed, but it's handled with good grace. The retirement of indefatigable maître d' Silvano Giraldin must have unnerved a few of the restaurant's faithful devotees, but they needn't have worried. His replacement is a 'more than worthy successor' – astute, well-informed, ever-courteous and a smooth orchestrator of proceedings in this supremely professional set-up. Some things never change on the menu, from the mousseline de homard to the petite tarte Tatin, but Michel Roux Jnr's cooking isn't about to get preserved in aspic. Lighter contemporary ideas increasingly float to the surface, witness grilled scallops with spicy aubergine, fennel pollen and parsley coulis or poached John Dory with winkles and clams in a clear lobster broth pointed up with ginger and seaweed. Prices on the carte might make you flinch, but there's also the inviting prospect of a nigh-on irresistible set lunch, which everyone agrees is the best deal of its kind in the West End. Those who have indulged talk ecstatically about mousseline of chicken with Roquefort sauce, a glorious tourte au gibier with 'magnificent game flavours and a wonderfully sticky meat reduction' and 'suitably warming' preserved 'collier' of lamb with braised turnips. Desserts are impeccably wrought designs defined by masterly pastrywork and high-end technique, whether it's the kitchen's peerless take on crème brûlée, the wondrous homemade ice creams or that crowning creation, the bitter chocolate and praline 'indulgence' overlaid with pure gold leaf. Michel Roux's bespoke beer menu is a sign of the times, but nothing can match the sheer aristocracy of the wine list, with page upon page of the finest vintages from the finest growers in all the major French regions – and more besides. Much is eye-wateringly expensive, although there are a few bottles under £30 for those feeling the crunch.

**Chef/s:** Michel Roux. **Open:** Mon to Fri L 12 to 2, Mon to Sat D 6.30 to 11. **Closed:** Sun, bank hols, 25 Dec to 2 Jan. **Meals:** alc (main courses £26 to £49). Set L £48 (including wine). Tasting menu £95 (£150 with wine). **Service:** 12.5% (optional). **Details:** Cards accepted. 65 seats. Air-con. Separate bar. No music. Children allowed.

## ALSO RECOMMENDED

### ▲ Gay Hussar

2 Greek Street, Soho, W1D 4NB
Tel no: (020) 7437 0973
www.gayhussar.co.uk
⊖ Tottenham Court Road, map 5
Hungarian

A bastion of old Hungary for more than 50 years, this redoubtable warhouse still stands its ground – even if its status as a Soho icon often overshadows what goes on in the kitchen. Curious tourists now mingle with the hard-core journos and Old Labour diehards who congregate in the low-lit ground-floor room, sure in the knowledge that there will be wild cherry soup (£4.25), duck liver cooked in Tokaji, and veal goulash with galouksa dumplings (£15.25) on the menu, followed by caramel-topped dobos torta (£4.50). Bull's Blood (£16.50) is also guaranteed. Open Mon to Sat.

## NEW ENTRY
# The Giaconda Dining Room
**Real cooking at fair prices**
9 Denmark Street, Soho, WC2 H8LS
Tel no: (020) 7240 3334
www.giacondadining.com
⊖ Tottenham Court Road, map 5
Modern European | £29
Cooking score: 3

'Not flashy, not grand, just tasty food', writes
Paul Merrony, summing up his 'pint-sized'
restaurant in London's famous music street –
the place takes its name from the Giaconda
Café, a haunt of many rock legends. Tables are
close-set, service is friendly and the menu is
principally focused on dishes from France and
Italy – vitello tonnato alongside duck confit
with lyonnaise potatoes. Start with baked eggs
with spinach, cream and cheese and go on to
cod, 'roasted to perfection' and simply served
with roasted tomatoes and portabello
mushrooms, or grilled calf's liver with onion
and currant gravy, and finish with chocolate
mousse cake with caramel sauce. As with the
cooking, the wine list is well-considered,
affordable and European, with prices
from £19.
**Chef/s:** Paul Merrony. **Open:** Mon to Fri L 12 to 2.15,
D 6 to 9.15. **Closed:** Sat, Sun, 25 Dec to 2 Jan, last 2
weeks Aug, bank hols. **Meals:** alc (main courses £11
to £15). **Service:** not inc. **Details:** Cards accepted.
32 seats. Air-con. No music.

# Gordon Ramsay at Claridge's
**Aristocrat à la mode**
Brook Street, Mayfair, W1A 2JQ
Tel no: (020) 7499 0099
www.gordonramsay.com
⊖ Bond Street, map 5
Modern European | £70
Cooking score: 5

Ever since Gordon Ramsay stormed the
hallowed portals of Claridge's in 2001, this has
been one of the more unlikely alliances on the
London restaurant scene – but it works. The
palatial foyer still captures the spirit of those
Art Deco glory days when London's
aristocratic hotels ruled the world, but the re-
branded restaurant can come as a bit of a
culture shock with its extraordinary
centrepiece light fittings, orange-pink walls
and purple chairs. Thankfully, it is all steadied
with the kind of polished modern food that is
synonymous with the Ramsay stable. Mark
Sargeant is no longer in charge, but readers
continue to praise the classical grounding and
technical knowhow that is applied to British
ingredients of irreproachable quality: Isle of
Skye scallops are roasted and served with sage
gnocchi, butternut squash and Parmesan
velouté, while Suffolk pork belly might
appear crisped-up with roast langoustines,
crushed white beans, fennel purée, lemon and
sage jus. Other partnerships are equally vivid,
if less Med-inspired – say braised brill with
smoked duck and glazed parsnips. As for
desserts, expect trademark finesse and artistry
all the way, from marinated pineapple with
coconut ice cream, coriander and pink
peppercorns to Valrhona chocolate fondant,
served cold with banana and passion fruit
sorbet. The wine list is an outstanding slate
that can live with the best in the land, whether
you are looking for noble Champagnes or
fabulous stickies. Vintages and growers are
peerless – although prices sky-rocket rapidly
from £20.
**Chef/s:** Steve Allen. **Open:** all week L 12 to 3, D 5.45
to 11. **Meals:** Set L £30, Set D £70 to £80 (6
courses). **Service:** 12.5%. **Details:** Cards accepted.
100 seats. Air-con. No music. No mobile phones.
Wheelchair access. Children allowed.

## Great Queen Street
**No-frills, flavour-packed Brit food**
32 Great Queen Street, Covent Garden, WC2B 5AA
Tel no: (020) 7242 0622
⊖ Covent Garden, map 5
**British | £27**
**Cooking score: 4**

 £30

Bustling and cheery, with bare boards and closely packed tables helping to crank up the volume, what is offered is very much in tune with modern times. Tom Norrington-Davies has made a success of providing sensible, unfussy dishes in that no-frills modern British style pioneered by older sibling the Anchor & Hope in Waterloo (see entry). The food deserves credit for its lack of ostentation, with the kitchen often using modest ingredients and simple treatments in heroically seasonal dishes: from a winter menu comes cockles and mussels on toast, baked mackerel with fennel and breadcrumbs, and game such as partridge and lentils or braised leg of hare and pickled walnuts. Needless to say, robust flavours are hallmarks. Equally well-handled desserts have included buttermilk pudding with rhubarb, and service has been well reported this year. The modern wine list offers 14 by the glass or carafe, with house French £12 a bottle.
**Chef/s:** Tom Norrington-Davies. **Open:** Tue to Sun 12 to 2.30 (3 Sun), Mon to Sat D 6 to 10.30. **Closed:** Christmas, bank hols. **Meals:** alc (main courses £11 to £25). Sun L £25. **Service:** not inc. **Details:** Cards accepted. 60 seats. 8 seats outside. Separate bar. No music. Wheelchair access. Children allowed.

## Jason Atherton  Maze

**Who or what inspired you to become a chef?**
Being naturally creative.

**If you hadn't become a chef, what would you have been?**
A businessman.

**What do you like cooking when you are off duty?**
Mostly Asian food.

**If you were to have one abiding principle in the kitchen, what would it be?**
To do everything at 100 per cent or don't do anything at all.

**What is your favourite restaurant and why?**
Barfina, Spain, as it reminds me of when I was training back in Spain, and had excellent traditional food.

**What do you do to relax when out of the kitchen?**
Run.

**What's coming up next for you?**
Working hard keeping Maze one of the top restaurants in the country. Doing TV and working towards expanding Maze all over the world.

## The Greenhouse

**A world away from busy Mayfair**
27a Hays Mews, Green Park, W1J 5NX
Tel no: (020) 7499 3331
www.greenhouserestaurant.co.uk
⊖ Green Park, map 5
**Modern European | £65**
Cooking score: 6

🍶 V

A stroll down the quiet garden walkway puts customers in the right frame of mind for the Greenhouse. Like its mews location it is discreet and high-end, buzzing with the satisfaction of solid budgets put to tasteful good use. The fripperies surrounding Antonin Bonnet's carefully seasonal menu – surprisingly successful date-and-coffee bread, say, or an amuse of bright green jelly bursting with a liquid celery, basil and apple centre – are bolder than the central dishes, especially for business lunchers using the set menu to sweeten their deals. Nevertheless, things are rarely dull in a dining room that evokes nature through pale green detailing and the odd twiggy design feature. Start, perhaps, with smoked lambs' sweetbreads, which give off a delicate woodsy scent against cool wedges of beetroot, or 'superbly fresh' Scottish langoustines with cocoa and white beans. At this level, missteps stick out like a badly trimmed box hedge – a curl of tough squid and under-powered mushroom velouté distracted from the quality of a piece of skate, slow-cooked so that the flesh formed soft ropes and served with St George's mushrooms and sweet winkles. Desserts, such as a soft, pretty marzipan and strawberry cake, offer no such disappointments. For wine, a user-friendly by-the-glass list (from £5.50, £22 a bottle) gives way to many crisp, closely typed pages that promise excitement and adventure to guests with deep pockets.

**Chef/s:** Antonin Bonnet. **Open:** Mon to Fri L 12 to 2.30, Mon to Sat D 6.45 to 11. **Closed:** Sun, bank hols, 24 Dec to early Jan. **Meals:** Set L £25 (2 courses) to £29. Set D £65. Tasting menu £65. **Service:** 12.5% (optional). **Details:** Cards accepted.

70 seats. Air-con. Separate bar. No music. No mobile phones. Wheelchair access. Children allowed.

## The Grill at the Dorchester

**Confident cooking and baronial splendour**
The Dorchester Hotel, 53 Park Lane, Hyde Park, W1K 1QA
Tel no: (020) 7629 8888
www.thedorchester.com
⊖ Hyde Park Corner, map 4
**Modern British | £60**
Cooking score: 4

🛏 V

It's impossible to ignore the Scottish-ness of this big gilt-edged dining room with tartan in every corner and murals of Highlanders. Brian Hughson has taken over from Aiden Byrne, and has devised a modern menu where grills are offered alongside fair-value lunch and tasting menus. The cooking has a welcome uncomplicated appeal: seared scallops with a sardine pie and cauliflower purée was a success, the cauliflower providing just the right inflection. Dishes also have a balanced richness and use clean flavours to good effect: roasted pigeon comes with the breast braised with Swiss chard and onion confit, the leg stuffed with a little offal for extra depth. Brandy soufflé with a grassy sage sorbet is of equally high standard. Staff ensure it all goes well – a bonus for the numerous people celebrating special milestones. Wines, from £23.50, are global and serious.

**Chef/s:** Brian Hughson. **Open:** all week L 12 to 2.30 (12.30 to 3.30 Sat and Sun), D 6.30 to 11 (6 to 11 Sat, 7 to 10.30 Sun). **Meals:** alc (main courses £20 to £42). Set L and D £25 (2 courses) to £27.50. Sun L £35. Tasting menu £70. **Service:** 12.5% (optional). **Details:** Cards accepted. 80 seats. Air-con. Separate bar. No music. No mobile phones. Wheelchair access. Children allowed.

## The Guinea Grill
**Beefy true Brit**
30 Bruton Place, Mayfair, W1J 6NL
Tel no: (020) 7409 1728
www.theguinea.co.uk
⊖ Bond Street, map 5
British | £35
Cooking score: 2

A traditional experience that has remained largely unchanged over the years is why the loyal (and distinguished) clientele are still drawn to this Bruton Place stalwart. A cordial greeting from the doorman, then through the pub, past a glass cabinet stacked with steaks from the Scotch Beef Club and seafood ready to be slapped on to the giant smoking grill. The interior is looking a bit tired, and the menu won't win any awards for innovation – typical dishes include pies, asparagus with Parmesan and grilled Dover sole – but regulars say standards remain high. Prices seem uncompetitive, though, especially given local alternatives. House wine is £18.
**Chef/s:** Mark Newbury. **Open:** Mon to Fri L 12.30 to 3, Mon to Sat D 6 to 10.30. **Closed:** Sun, bank hols. **Meals:** alc (main courses £13 to £36). Bar menu available. **Service:** 12.5% (optional). **Details:** Cards accepted. 47 seats. Air-con. Separate bar. No music. No mobile phones. Children allowed.

## Hakkasan
**Chinese dining on a grand scale**
8 Hanway Place, Fitzrovia, W1T 1HD
Tel no: (020) 7927 7000
www.hakkasan.com
⊖ Tottenham Court Road, map 5
Chinese | £50
Cooking score: 5

🍸 V

Alan Yau's pace-setting east Asian restaurants continue to draw the crowds. Such is the likelihood of finding famous faces at a nearby table that there's a ban on taking pictures. Almost as head-turning as the clientele is the décor, with its low-lit, sleek, dark ambience enhanced by candlelight and incense. The oft-repeated description of the place as a kind of designer opium den reflects this sultry feel, rather than anything that might crop up on the menu. Dim sum is of a very high standard, with exquisitely light har gau prawn dumplings, delicate gai lan greens steamed with garlic, properly fluffy, sweetly spicy char siu bao, and a crab and pork item that gushes forth rice vinegar for an interesting sweet-sour contrast. Eating more substantially, you might opt for soft-shell crab or chilli quail to start, followed by miraculously tender steamed lobster with glass vermicelli in yellow-bean sauce. Tofu, for one seasoned traveller, 'is the most tender and moist I have tasted outside China'. Drinking is taken seriously, from the East-meets-West cocktail list to the well-chosen wines (from £7.90 a glass), and a lengthy listing of speciality tequilas.
**Chef/s:** Tong Chee Hwee. **Open:** all week L 12 to 3 (3.30 Thur and Fri, 4 Sat and Sun) D 6 to 12 (12.30 Fri to Sun). **Closed:** 24 and 25 Dec. **Meals:** alc (main courses £13 to £52). Set menus £40 to £100. **Service:** 13% (optional). **Details:** Cards accepted. 220 seats. Air-con. Separate bar. Wheelchair access. Music. Children allowed.

## Haozhan
**Chinatown thriller**
8 Gerrard Street, Soho, W1D 5PJ
Tel no: (020) 7434 3838
www.haozhan.co.uk
⊖ Leicester Square, map 5
Chinese | £25
Cooking score: 3

V

Soho Chinatown's new stars have a habit of fading fast, but Haozhan is waxing strongly and remains a hot ticket for fans of thrilling new-wave food. Inside, it puts on a modish, contemporary face and the kitchen fuses the regional traditions of Chinese cuisine with 'modern Oriental' influences pulled from Thailand, Malaysia and Japan. You can play safe with lemon chicken or pork chops in batter with sweet-and-sour sauce, but exploration pays dividends. Crispy quail blasted with chilli, spring onion and salt continues to wow, lobster is 'to die for' and it's worth shelling out for the baked black cod with Champagne and buttered honey sauce. The homemade silken tofu also takes some beating (try it topped with chopped spinach and scallops), likewise earthy Malaysian ho fun noodles with 'sharply defined' tastes and textures. Wines start at £13.50; heady fragrant teas are available too.

**Chef/s:** Min Wei Lai. **Open:** all week 12 to 11.30 (midnight Fri and Sat, 11 Sun). **Closed:** 24 and 25 Dec. **Meals:** alc (main courses from £9 to £39). **Service:** 12.5% (optional). **Details:** Cards accepted. 80 seats. Air-con. Music. Children allowed.

## Hélène Darroze at the Connaught

**A French star in Mayfair**
16 Carlos Place, Mayfair, W1K 2AL
Tel no: (020) 3147 7200
www.the-connaught.co.uk
⊖ Bond Street, Green Park, map 5
French | £75
Cooking score: 6

 V

After a five-year Italian interlude, the Connaught dining room has reverted to French form, with Hélène Darroze dividing her time between London and Paris. The no-expense-spared makeover makes an appropriate backdrop to her fairly classical French cooking, which is built on sound technique, impeccable produce and the return of unfashionable butter and stocks. Foie gras from Darroze's native Les Landes figures strongly, often delivered with an urbane swagger (foie gras crème brûlée with apple sorbet and peanut), and she excels at hearty rustic dishes such as her take on the Catalan dish, arroz negro (baby squid with chorizo, confit tomatoes and Carnaroli Acquarello rice). For some, however, it is 'a great disappointment'. Pink, flavourful spit-roasted pigeon with grilled foie gras begged a better accompaniment than pea mousseline and its vague hint of peppermint. There are readers who wonder at the cost of it all. The entry-level 'business lunch' does the kitchen few favours: a faultless but stingy cauliflower

velouté, a no more generous Savoy cabbage roll stuffed with shellfish farce, nor a rustic chicken fricassee with its delicious sauce and quartered sprout on the side. Thank goodness for superb Manjari chocolate with coconut sorbet, terrific bread and huge wedges of excellent Bernard Antony cheese. The weighty wine list focuses on France, but includes a wide selection of growers and less obvious choices from Slovenia and Greece. Mark-ups are lower than comparable establishments, but prices start high at £29.

**Chef/s:** Hélène Darroze. **Open:** Tue to Sat L 12 to 2.30 (11 to 3 Sat), D 6.30 to 10.30. **Closed:** Sun, Mon, bank hols. **Meals:** Set L £29 (2 courses) to £32. Set D £60 (2 courses) to £75. Tasting menu £85 (8 courses). **Service:** 12.5% (optional). **Details:** Cards accepted. 62 seats. Air-con. Separate bar. No music. No mobile phones. Wheelchair access. Children allowed.

## Hibiscus

**Offbeat French lessons**
29 Maddox Street, Mayfair, W1S 2PA
Tel no: (020) 7629 2999
www.hibiscusrestaurant.co.uk
⊖ Oxford Circus, map 5
Modern French | £65
Cooking score: 7

V

Even without the tripe à la lyonnaise, it would be clear that Hibiscus's menu is 100% Claude Bosi. Behind the voile that separates this small restaurant from bland Mayfair, the strapping Frenchman does as he pleases, overdosing on seasonal ingredients (spring menus are gorged with asparagus, fricasseed soya beans and gariguette strawberries) and making sweet tarts of ceps, peas or sweet potatoes. Guests are by now accustomed to the sideways thinking and esoteric ingredients that can, though only if they wish, make a fine French meal into a learning experience. The lessons are easy to take in a panelled wood-and-slate dining room where all-comers are put at their ease. Crusty gougères and excellent petits fours bookend an experience that emphasises texture as well as taste, playing around with each mouthful. To start, a fat quenelle of iced foie gras in a warm, buttery brioche 'emulsion' is blowsy and soft until the spoon finds little bombs of confit rhubarb, and pale, glistening tartare of mackerel gets a highly effective wake-up call from spots of wasabi and honey dressing. To follow, a star ingredient often arrives in two related services. Label Anglais chicken breast might be lined with a razor clam stuffing and served with crisp soya beans and blood orange purée, followed by a piece of thigh with impressively crunchy skin, airy liver parfait, and – slightly misplaced but hardly tear-jerking – rillettes of confit wing and more clams. An offbeat (some say 'weird') dessert might be creamy white asparagus tart with goats' cheese ice cream and crumbs of black olive, made with exemplary pastry. Staff honour the fun of a banana cake soufflé, gleefully slicing and dicing to admit a ball of excellent coffee ice cream and the contents of an ampoule of banana syrup, though at inspection there was a distinct post-coffee retreat. Wine selections start at £19.75 (£5.25 a glass), with plenty of halves. Though a low budget is no barrier to courteous discussion and some flexibility, the French highlights are best approached with a treat mentality.

**Chef/s:** Claude Bosi. **Open:** Mon to Fri L 12 to 2.30, Mon to Sat D 6.30 to 10. **Closed:** Sun, bank hols, 10 days Christmas and New Year. **Meals:** Set L £25. Set D £65. Tasting menu £80 (7 courses). **Service:** 12.5% (optional). **Details:** Cards accepted. 48 seats. Air-con. No music. No mobile phones. Wheelchair access. Children allowed.

## READERS RECOMMEND

## Ibérica

**Spanish**
195 Great Portland Street, Fitzrovia, W1W 5PS
Tel no: (020) 7636 8650
www.ibericalondon.com
**'Try the tapas bar for the best Spanish food in town'**

## Il Baretto

**Italian**
43 Blandford Street, Marylebone, W1U 7HF
Tel no: (020) 7486 7340
www.ilbaretto.co.uk
**'Just a pleasure eating there, the food is always brilliant'**

## Inn the Park

**A tribute to all things British**
St James's Park, SW1A 2BJ
Tel no: (020) 7451 9999
www.innthepark.com
⊖ **St James's Park, map 5**
**British | £32**
**Cooking score: 2**

A 'great location' in St James's Park, with a fair-weather terrace and a striking, light-filled space inside, Oliver Peyton's homage to all things British gives both takeaway and sit-down diners a chance to eat simply prepared, fresh food from breakfast to dinner. During the day, the lively, happy atmosphere puts families at their ease, though an early evening visit in April found the place 'cold and uninviting'. Seasonal offerings include grilled Herefordshire asparagus with hollandaise sauce and gurnard with spring greens, brown shrimp and tarragon butter. Bakewell tart and an all-British cheeseboard to finish. The short, no-nonsense wine list opens at £15.50.

**Chef/s:** Amanda Fuller. **Open:** all week L 12 to 3, Mon to Sat D 5 to 11. **Closed:** 25 Dec. **Meals:** alc (main courses £13 to £20). Set L and D £25.50 (2 courses) to £29.50. **Service:** 12.5% (optional). **Details:** Cards accepted. 90 seats. 80 seats outside. No music. Wheelchair access. Children allowed.

## The Ivy

**Hot ticket for people-watchers**
5 West Street, Covent Garden, WC2H 9NQ
Tel no: (020) 7836 4751
www.the-ivy.co.uk
⊖ Leicester Square, map 5
**Modern British | £49**
**Cooking score: 3**
**V**

At peak times, the tiny bar can be a squeeze while waiting for that over-running table booked weeks in advance. And some may wonder what all the fuss is about, what with steak and kidney pudding, Lancashire hotpot, treacle tart and baked Alaska on the menu. Otherwise, a fillet of brill teamed with pied de mouton mushrooms, bacon and curly kale might feature among more challenging, well-executed options. Some may criticise a £2 cover charge, or the feeling of being 'rushed' by the 'rapid turnover of tables', yet the Ivy's trump card is its bustling atmosphere and low-key, clubby décor of wood panelling, green leather seating and stained glass; it's one of the 'best people-watching tickets around'. Wines lean towards Europe, starting at £18.50, with plenty by the glass and half-bottle.
**Chef/s:** Gary Lee. **Open:** all week L 12 to 3 (3.30 Sat and Sun), D 5.30 to 12 (11 Sun). **Meals:** alc (main courses £11 to £39). **Service:** 12.5% (optional). **Details:** Cards accepted. 100 seats. Air-con. Separate bar. No music. No mobile phones. Wheelchair access. Children allowed.

**NEW ENTRY**
## J. Sheekey Oyster Bar

**Good-looking Sheekey sibling**
33-34 St Martin's Court, Covent Garden, WC2N 4AL
Tel no: (020) 7240 2565
www.j-sheekey.co.uk
⊖ Leicester Square, map 5
**Seafood | £42**
**Cooking score: 4**

J. Sheekey has spread its wings with the purchase of an adjoining bookshop to create this good-looking oyster bar extension. It was originally intended as a no-booking venue, but that policy was reversed because of overwhelming popularity – it's perfectly pitched in both pricing and atmosphere. Whether you are perched on stools at the bar or ensconced in one of the handful of window tables, the place runs like a well-oiled machine, thanks to excellent staff and nifty chefs preparing food in full view behind the bar. The simple, uncluttered presentation of small plates highlights the quality raw materials. Ingredients are everything – potted shrimps, razor clams perfectly partnered by chorizo and broad beans, baked spiced crab, Sheekey's famous fish pie – all fairly priced and served alongside oysters, caviar and plateaux de fruits de mer. The wine list is a whistlestop tour of old and new, with everything available by the glass (from £4). Bottles from £15.
**Chef/s:** Martin Dickinson. **Open:** all week L 12 to 3 (3.30 Sun), D 5.30 to 12 (6 to 11 Sun). **Closed:** 25 and 26 Dec. **Meals:** alc (main courses £10 to £29). Set L £25.50 (Sat and Sun only). **Service:** 12.5% (optional). **Details:** Cards accepted. 32 seats. Air-con. Separate bar. No music. Wheelchair access. Children allowed.

## J. Sheekey

**Old-school seafood stalwart**
28-32 St Martin's Court, Covent Garden, WC2N 4AL
Tel no: (020) 7240 2565
www.j-sheekey.co.uk
⊖ Leicester Square, map 5
**Seafood | £48**
**Cooking score: 4**

However fashionable this theatreland stalwart gets, it still delivers the classic true-Brit seafood on which its reputation was founded in 1896. Tucked down an alley, J.Sheekey's frosted windows and top-hatted doorman can intimidate, but that's apparently 'self-mocking pomposity'. Inside it's charm personified, with 'helpful advice' about the global wine list (starting at £18) and a crowd-pleasing menu featuring Cornish fish stew, jellied eels and, according to one reader, 'the best fish and chips

I know'. Specials of pan-fried slip soles with buttered alexanders or goats' curd cheesecake with ruby plums are enticing too. The team knows the drill pre- and post-theatre: 'amazingly consistent food' is 'produced, served and cleared most efficiently'. Less well-thought of is the £2 cover charge.

**Chef/s:** Martin Dickinson and Richard Kirkwood. **Open:** all week L 12 to 3, D 5.30 to 12 (6 to 11 Sun). **Closed:** 25 and 26 Dec, 1 Jan. **Meals:** alc (main courses £14 to £40). **Service:** 12.5% (optional). **Details:** Cards accepted. 100 seats. Air-con. Separate bar. No music. No mobile phones. Children allowed.

## ALSO RECOMMENDED

### ▲ Jom Makan

5-6 Pall Mall East, Trafalgar Square, SW1Y 5BA
Tel no: (020) 7925 2402
www.jommakan.co.uk
⊖ **Charing Cross, Piccadilly Circus, map 5**
**Malaysian**

Spacious, modern and clean sums up the décor at this cheerful, fast-paced Malaysian restaurant close to the National Gallery. Chicken satay, rendang daging (beef braised in coconut milk and spicy herbs, £8.50), kari kambing (lamb curry with tomato and potato) and kway teow goring (fried rice noodles with chicken, seafood, egg and vegetables, £7.60) have all found favour. Extraordinary desserts include a delicious concoction of tapioca topped with palm sugar and coconut cream (£2.85). The minimal wine list opens at £12.95. Open all week.

Eating with chefs

The idea behind the chef's table is that you eat in, or adjacent to, the kitchen and that the chef cooks a special meal for you.

Gordon Ramsay is credited with introducing the first chef's table in his kitchen at Claridge's in 2001; he then extended the idea to some of his top London restaurants – one of the best is at **Maze**, with its ringside kitchen seating and plenty of hot cooks. Nearly a decade on and watching chefs at work remains popular: **Ambassade de l'Ile** in South Kensington, **Angelus** in Lancaster Gate and two new entries this year – **Murano** and **Corrigan's Mayfair** – all incorporated chef's tables into their design.

But these tables require a significant outlay of cash, so some restaurants have come up with a more affordable way into the trend. **Barrafina** is a tapas bar where you eat at a bar counter in full view of the open kitchen; **J. Sheekey Oyster Bar** chose the same concept when it opened at the end of 2008. But, if you go to **Terroirs** near Charing Cross station, ask for a bar seat rather than a table in order to watch Ed Wilson and team hard at work.

Otherwise look to the American brasserie **Automat**, which has a 12-seater table overlooking the kitchen at the rear of the restaurant, but offers the normal à la carte as well as set menu options.

## Kiku

**Dependable Japanese achiever**
17 Half Moon Street, Mayfair, W1J 7BE
Tel no: (020) 7499 4208
www.kikurestaurant.co.uk
⊖ **Green Park, map 5**
**Japanese | £40**
**Cooking score: 4**
£5 OFF **V**

Since arriving on the Mayfair scene in 1978, Kiku – the name means 'chrysanthemum' – has forged a reputation as an ever-dependable bastion of traditional Japanese cuisine in the capital. The exterior's classically luxurious tone gives way to minimalist contemporary features – stone floors, black tables, bamboo blinds, and one of London's largest sushi bars for fans of exquisite, top-dollar nigiri, maki rolls and the like. In the serene dining room you can choose between formal kaiseki banquets and the rigorously organised carte, which homes in on specific cooking techniques – grilled (mackerel marinated in citrus, yuzu and miso paste), casseroled (chicken and white radish) and fried (prawn tempura). Hot and cold appetisers are suitably zingy palate-sharpeners (try grated yam with quail's egg yolk), while sunomono and salads involve octopus, jellyfish, seaweed and vegetables. Various beancurd specialities, soups and sharing hotpots (shabu-shabu and sukiyaki) make up the remainder of the inventory. Drink beer or saké; otherwise, Corney & Barrow house wines are £14.50.
**Chef/s:** Hirofumi Shiraishi and Yoichi Hattori. **Open:** Mon to Sat L 12 to 2.30, all week D 6 to 10.15 (Sun 5.30 to 9.45). **Closed:** 25 and 26 Dec, 1 Jan.
**Meals:** alc (main courses £10 to £35). Set L £20 to £23.50. Set D £46 (8 courses) to £65.
**Service:** 12.5%. **Details:** Cards accepted. 100 seats. Air-con. Wheelchair access. Music. Children allowed.

## The Landau

**Trademark tasting menus and stunning wine**
Langham Hotel, 1c Portland Place, Oxford Circus, W1B 1JA
Tel no: (020) 7636 1000
www.thelandau.com
⊖ **Oxford Circus, map 5**
**Modern European | £50**
**Cooking score: 4**
🍷 ⇋ **V**

Part of the ongoing regeneration of the grandly imposing Langham, this flagship restaurant occupies the hotel's one-time ballroom – now transformed into a glittering, no-expense-spared dining room courtesy of design wonder boy David Collins. Chef Andrew Turner garners impeccable supplies from Britain's 'food hero' elite for a range of trademark tasting menus. These multi-course, pan-European extravaganzas might encompass anything from Cornish crab and avocado with Parmesan crumble, fennel pollen and pickled apple purée to slow-cooked (at 59°C) fillet of Castle Mey beef with salsify, ox tongue and wild mushrooms or fillet and breast pudding of Merton Farm lamb with charcutière sauce. Similar dishes also appear on the carte, along with more classic lunchtime options (think organic salmon with Savoy cabbage or calf's liver with bacon and spinach). Desserts tend to be intricate, as in orange parfait with banana, fromage frais and allspice sorbet. Sommelier Zack Saghir and John Atkinson MW have put together a stunning wine list that mixes tradition with the fruits of cutting-edge production. Contributions from the likes of Telmo Rodriguez, California's Paul Draper and Jean-Louis Chave in Hermitage add to the thrill of it all. The bidding starts at £28.
**Chef/s:** Andrew Turner. **Open:** Sun to Fri L 12.30 to 2.30, Mon to Sat D 5.30 to 10.30. **Meals:** alc (main courses £18 to £30). Set L £19.95 (2 courses) to £26.50. Pre-theatre D £20 (2 courses) to £27.50. Tasting menus £57.50 (5 courses) to £72.50 (8 courses). **Service:** 12.5% (optional). **Details:** Cards accepted. 89 seats. Air-con. Separate bar. Wheelchair access. Music. Children allowed.

## ALSO RECOMMENDED

### ▲ Lantana Café

13 Charlotte Place, Fitzrovia, W1T 1SN
Tel no: (020) 7637 3347
www.lantanacafe.co.uk
⊖ Goodge Street, Tottenham Court Road, map 5
Café

Tucked behind Charlotte Street, this laid-back little Antipodean outfit is run by Shelagh Ryan, and the big breakfasts and surfer's soundtrack are pure Bondi. It's all great value: generous portions, high-quality ingredients. Brunch might be fritters with crispy bacon, roasted tomato and garlicky aïoli or a sandwich of bacon, egg, rocket and tomato (£4.50). Lunchtime salads (£7.80) are upper-class (fennel with blood orange, radicchio and pearl barley) and your authentically Australian flat white coffee has a decent pedigree. Bottles of wine from £13.50. Open for breakfast and lunch only, Mon to Sat.

### Latium

**Unsung Italian hero with ravishing ravioli**
21 Berners Street, Fitzrovia, W1T 3LP
Tel no: (020) 7323 9123
www.latiumrestaurant.com
⊖ Goodge Street, Tottenham Court Road,
Oxford Circus, map 5
Italian | £30
Cooking score: 2

£5 OFF **V**

Latium boasts neither the celebrity diners nor glamorous surroundings of higher-profile West End Italians, but it still has plenty going for it. Comfortable interiors, colourful cooking and fair prices tick all the right boxes. Prime ingredients are left to their own devices in starters of beef tartare with rocket and Parmesan and main courses such as roast Gressingham duck with spinach and blood orange. But it's the ravioli menu that steals the show: rich oxtail ravioli cut through with celery sauce, or pert chicken tortellini floating in comforting hen broth. The wine list tours Italy's finest regions, working up from £15.50 house bottles to revered Antinoris.

Chef/s: Maurizio Morelli. Open: Mon to Fri L 12 to 3, Mon to Sat D 6.30 to 10.30 (11 Sat). Closed: Sun, 24 to 26 Dec, 1 Jan, bank hols. Meals: alc (main courses £14 to £18). Set L £15.50 (2 courses) to £19.50. Set D £26.50 (2 courses) to £29.50. Service: 12.5% (optional). Details: Cards accepted. 56 seats. Air-con. Wheelchair access. Music. Children allowed.

### Locanda Locatelli

**Celeb chef's swanky flagship**
8 Seymour Street, Marble Arch, W1H 7JZ
Tel no: (020) 7935 9088
www.locandalocatelli.com
⊖ Marble Arch, map 4
Italian | £45
Cooking score: 5

Still a dream ticket for West End A-listers, celeb chef Giorgio Locatelli's self-named restaurant is as much about style as cooking, with truckloads of hype surrounding the place and relentless ogling of the stunning David Collins interior – think leather surrounds, etched-glass screens, discreet booths and sexy spotlights. The kitchen aims for ingredients-led regional Italian 'cucina' without frills or frivolity, which translates as ox tongue with green sauce, potato and caper salad or stewed cuttlefish with white polenta and black ink among the antipasti, and orecchiette with turnip tops, chilli, garlic and anchovies for fans of homemade pasta. Chargrilled mackerel in a herb crust is a typically straight main course, while desserts embrace a tasting of Amedei chocolate, a daily tart and Montebianco (Muscavado sponge, whipped cream and chestnut ice cream). Recent reports suggest a noticeable dip in performance of late, with complaints alluding to extortionate prices, 'dull' food and snail-paced, 'condescending service'. Thankfully, the 'excellent' wine list makes amends: this is a 'Serie A', all-Italian selection organised by region, with peerless growers in abundance, plus a broad choice from £3.50 a glass. Bottle prices start around £15, but shoot skyward for three-figure Super Tuscans and more.

Chef/s: Giorgio Locatelli. **Open:** all week L 12 to 3 (3.30 Sat and Sun), D 6.45 to 11 (11.30 Fri and Sat, 10.15 Sun). **Closed:** bank hols, 24 to 26 Dec. **Meals:** alc (main courses £15 to £30). **Service:** not inc. **Details:** Cards accepted. 80 seats. Air-con. No music. No mobile phones. Wheelchair access. Children allowed.

## Luciano
**Glamorous rather than glorious**
72-73 St James's Street, Mayfair, SW1A 1PH
Tel no: (020) 7408 1440
www.lucianorestaurant.co.uk
⊖ Green Park, map 5
Italian | £35
Cooking score: 3

**V**

With Marco Pierre White's increasing profile, television appearances and expanding global empire drawing inevitable comparisons to a certain other jetsetting TV chef, some readers are left with the distinct impression that his original Mayfair venture is being neglected. While no one disputes the glamour of the place – the masculine dining room is rockstar cool, with Pirelli-style nudes adorning the dark red walls – an uneven standard of food including 'tasteless' zucchini fritti, and 'unexceptional' main courses like 'dry' halibut with leeks and porcini make the high prices seem unjustifiable. It's not all bad news though, chargrilled calamari and risotto alla milanese come in for high praise, and there's still a definite, if occasionally deafening, buzz in the artfully decorated gunmetal and mosaic front bar. House wine is £16.
**Chef/s:** Marco Corsica. **Open:** Mon to Sat L 12 to 3 (2.30 Sat), D 6 to 11. **Closed:** Sun, 25 and 26 Dec, 1 Jan. **Meals:** alc (main courses £16 to £26). Set L £17.95 (2 courses). Set D £20.95 (2 courses). **Service:** 12.5% (optional). **Details:** Cards accepted. 170 seats. Air-con. Separate bar. No music. Wheelchair access. Music. Children allowed.

## ALSO RECOMMENDED

▲ **Mango Tree**
46 Grosvenor Place, Belgravia, SW1X 7EQ
Tel no: (020) 7823 1888
www.mangotree.org.uk
⊖ Victoria, Hyde Park Corner, map 4
Thai

Bringing a fragrant waft of Thailand to the Belgravia/Victoria borders, Mango Tree's spacious and sleek dining room attracts a lively crowd. Spices are tempered to suit Western tastes, but dishes still pack a punch – from hot-and-sour tom yum soup (£5.95) via green chicken curry (£13.20) and various stir-fries to banana and coconut pudding (£5.50). Also try the more interesting likes of slow-cooked lamb shank in Penang curry sauce. Wines, from £19, have been selected to stand up to the spice. Open all week.

## Marcus Wareing at the Berkeley
**Among London's finest**
The Berkeley, Wilton Place, Belgravia, SW1X 7RL
Tel no: (020) 7235 1200
www.marcus-wareing.com
⊖ Hyde Park Corner, Knightsbridge, map 4
Modern French | £75
Cooking score: 8

🍷 🚗 **V**

The kerfuffle following the much publicised falling-out with Gordon Ramsay has died down, leaving Marcus Wareing in charge of the restaurant formerly known as Pétrus – and his cooking to speak for itself. Otherwise there has been no discernible change. Masculine tones of mahogany and claret give a sober, clubby feel to the large dining room, creating a look in keeping with the prices. However, there is a lack of stuffiness and service at table, though formal and correct, is friendly. Finely crafted appetisers get proceedings off to a good start: hummus with a sweet onion bavarois, and cod and black pudding with lime crème fraîche are particularly impressive. Then comes a pre-starter (of course), maybe a velouté of sweetcorn topped with a tarragon froth with crème fraîche. Intelligent texture and flavour contrasts are to the fore – witness 'various miniature cuts of hare' partnered with spiced pear salad, port jelly and candied walnuts, while white onion fondue, butternut squash and a baked potato foam gives a pleasant earthy counterpoint to roasted and marinated breast of quail. Accurately timed turbot is served garnished with frogs' legs, a garlicky snail beignet and caper raisin purée, the sweet acidity of the last enhancing the overall flavour without dominating. To finish, there is cheese supplied by Jacques Vernier of Paris & Paxton and Whitfield. Sweets continue the theme of exploring particular ingredients and extracting contrasting textures while maximizing flavours – for instance iced lime mousse with sweet-and-sour pineapple, soft-baked meringue and liquorice. There are pre-desserts, petits fours and a vast wine list of serious producers from France and beyond. Prices are high with entry level around £24, but a page of wines by the glass offers good choice.

**Chef/s:** Marcus Wareing. **Open:** Mon to Fri L 12 to 2.30, Mon to Sat D 6 to 11. **Closed:** Sun, 1 Jan. **Meals:** Set L £35. Set D £75. Tasting menu £90 (7 courses). **Service:** 12.5% (optional). **Details:** Cards accepted. 70 seats. Air-con. No music. No mobile phones. Wheelchair access. Children allowed.

# Matsuri High Holborn

**Traditional Japanese dining**
71 High Holborn, Holborn, WC1V 6EA
Tel no: (020) 7430 1970
www.matsuri-restaurant.com
⊖ Holborn, map 5
Japanese | £35
Cooking score: 3

A trio of elegant dining spaces is on offer at the High Holborn outpost of Matsuri. There is a sushi counter, a basement room for the teppanyaki specialities and a spacious main dining room with banquette seating and simple bare-wood tables. Overall, the various menus offer a neat balance of traditional Japanese and fusion styles, depending on

whether you're in the market for maki rolls, tempura and nigiri, or dishes such as Scottish beef fillet with foie gras teriyaki. The all-important freshness is accompanied by precision and artistry. Interest is maintained by featured seasonal dishes such as baked rockfish served in a soup of dashi stock and Japanese herbs, with white asparagus on the side. Wines start at £18, and there is a good showing of saké. Also at 15 Bury Street, SW1Y 6AL, tel no: (020) 7839 1101.

**Chef/s:** Hiroshi Sudo. **Open:** Mon to Sat L 12 to 2.30, D 6 to 10. **Closed:** Sun, Christmas, bank hols. **Meals:** alc (main courses £20 to £30). **Service:** 12.5% (optional). **Details:** Cards accepted. 120 seats. Air-con. Separate bar. No mobile phones. Wheelchair access. Music. Children allowed.

# Maze

**Pace-setting invention and endless pleasure**
10-13 Grosvenor Square, Mayfair, W1K 6JP
Tel no: (020) 7107 0000
www.gordonramsay.com
⊖ Bond Street, map 4
Modern European | £50
Cooking score: 8

The crunch may be hurting, but there are few more enticing gastronomic antidotes to the downturn than Jason Atherton's star-spangled hot spot overlooking Grosvenor Square. Inside, the glamorously understated David Rockwell design shows its class in a modishly comfortable way. Tapas-sized tasting dishes are Maze's USP, and avid supporters devour these high-calibre miniatures with wide-eyed excitement and lip-smacking gusto. No wonder, because the food is a procession of addictive, mouth-filling surprises; you may not want it to end, but – as one fan noted gleefully – you'll leave 'with a big fat smile on your face'. Recent meals suggest the cooking is actually getting better; pace-setting invention and audacious combos come thick and fast, but it's not cleverness for its own sake. The kitchen currently has a penchant for powders: sweetly bland pressed skate is energised by a dusty trio representing the deconstructed components of grenobloise sauce. Elsewhere, 'pinkies' of braised octopus ('very brave') appear with an intensely potent oxtail vinaigrette, dehydrated olive and confit lemon. Tiny details make a huge impact – a dab of blazing-red chorizo and pimento purée with roasted hake, the sweetness of butterscotch with scallops, and stupendously good iron-bark pumpkin 'latte' beside a dinky, fungus-shaped cep brioche fashioned with a mycologist's eye for accuracy. Even the unctuous pomme purée served with confit rare-breed Sussex pork belly is a delight – and who could resist the fun-filled 'assiette of sandwiches'? Desserts also provide endless pleasure, from elaborately re-invented îles flottantes involving cylinders of meringue that look like polystyrene packaging (but taste like heaven) to rice pudding with fig jam and fig roll. If needs must, you can follow the conventional route by ordering from the carte, which features similar dishes in different sizes; the set lunch is also a financial fillip in these lean times. Wine 'flights' offer a tantalising introduction to the platinum-standard list which is a wine fan's dream, from its vintage Champagnes and premium sakés to its luscious dessert tipples – including that sexy sparkling Italian bestseller Moscati d'Asti.

**Chef/s:** Jason Atherton. **Open:** all week L 12 to 2.30, D 5.45 to 11. **Meals:** alc (main courses £22 to £30). Set L £28.50 (4 courses) to £42.50 (6 courses). Set D £60 (7 courses). **Service:** 12.5% (optional). **Details:** Cards accepted. 75 seats. Air-con. Separate bar. Wheelchair access. Music. Children allowed.

## Maze Grill
**Serious beef with pedigree**
10-13 Grosvenor Square, Mayfair, W1K 6JP
Tel no: (020) 7495 2211
www.gordonramsay.com
⊖ Bond Street, map 4
North American | £40
Cooking score: 5

On the other side of the entrance foyer to its elder sibling Maze (see entry), Maze Grill is Jason Atherton's homage to American steakhouses, with all their beefed-up

masculinity. It goes about its meaty business in a fashionable setting of pale oak, sage-green leather and decorative brown flourishes, with a communal table up at one end by the red-hot open kitchen. Five types of beef are on offer, and deceptively strong waitresses carry huge butcher's slabs of the raw red stuff to each table. Take your pick from grass-fed Hereford, Aberdeen Angus, Casterbridge, Creekstone USDA or expense-account ninth-grade Wagyu. The kitchen's trump card is a specially imported broiler which blasts the meat to 650°C after it has been flashed over coals. Steaks arrive as a designer package on wooden boards, with knives in sheaths reading 'rare' and so forth, plus sides, sauces and other classy accompaniments. If steak isn't really your bag, consider something like whole baby sea bass with spicy couscous or Cornish lamb bourguignon. To start the ball rolling, there are small plates and starters (think salt-and-pepper squid or 'pigs on toast'), while cinnamon doughnuts or winter fruit sundae provide a suitably transatlantic finish. The wine list majors in classic Old World reds and zesty New World whites, with prices from £20.

**Chef/s:** Jason Atherton. **Open:** all week L 12 to 2.30, D 5.45 to 11. **Meals:** alc (main courses £14 to £28). Set L £15 (2 courses) to £18. **Service:** 12.5% (optional). **Details:** Cards accepted. 60 seats. Air-con. Separate bar. Wheelchair access. Music. Children allowed.

## Mint Leaf
**Cool subterranean Indian**
Suffolk Place, Haymarket, SW1Y 4HX
Tel no: (020) 7930 9020
www.mintleafrestaurant.com
⊖ Piccadilly Circus, Charing Cross, map 5
Indian | £35
Cooking score: 2

**V**

A sober stone façade gives little clue to the action taking place in this vast subterranean Indian close to theatreland's heartbeat. The funky bar gets fired up as the cocktails flow, while the restaurant puts on a suave, cool face with its fibre-optic lighting and intimate spaces divided by wire-mesh screens. The kitchen adds a healthy, fashionable gloss to deep-rooted traditional ideas, turning out sharing dishes ranging from duck kebabs with mint and coriander to seared scallops with sour mango and peanut salad. Tandooris and biryanis are cleverly sexed up, and curries might run to poached sea bass in tomato and fenugreek sauce or stewed morels with cashews and peas. The wine list provides invigorating drinking from £15. A sister restaurant, the fizzy Mint Leaf Lounge, is at Angel Court, EC2R 7HB, tel no: (020) 7600 0992.

**Chef/s:** Ajay Chopra. **Open:** Mon to Fri L 12 to 3, all week D 5.30 to 11 (6 Sun). **Closed:** 25 and 26 Dec, 1 Jan. **Meals:** alc (main courses £15 to £25). Set L £12.95 (2 courses) to £15. Set menus £40 to £70. **Service:** 12.5%. **Details:** Cards accepted. 270 seats. Air-con. Separate bar. Wheelchair access. Music. Children allowed.

## ALSO RECOMMENDED

### ▲ Mon Plaisir

21 Monmouth Street, Covent Garden, WC2H 9DD
Tel no: (020) 7836 7243
www.monplaisir.co.uk
⊖ Covent Garden, map 5
French

This most French of French restaurants celebrates 66 years in Monmouth Street in 2010. Not much has changed: the tables are still cramped, there's plenty of noise and pâté en croûte (£7.50), cuisse de canard and coq au vin (£16.95) are typical of a menu that is stoically patriotic. Readers have praised the value of the fixed-price menus (lunch and theatre) and there's a handy brasserie menu served in the afternoons. Attentive service. House French is £16. Open all week.

NEW ENTRY
## Moti Mahal
**Ambitious modern Indian**
45 Great Queen Street, Covent Garden, WC2B 5AA
Tel no: (020) 7240 9329
www.motimahal-uk.com
⊖ Covent Garden, map 5
Indian | £40
Cooking score: 3

Born in Delhi and now trading in Covent Garden, Moti Mahal is a singular establishment on two vividly decorated floors – with glimpses of the kitchen from the lower level. Classy contemporary Indian cooking is the order of the day, and chef Anirudh Arora brings a new-wave sensibility to dishes such as rabbit kebab, which is spiked with cinnamon and cracked black pepper then served on an asparagus and chestnut rösti. Elsewhere, spicy Goan-style wild boar and okra curry comes with masala fried egg, and flash-grilled wild bream turns up with garlic, baked crab, bean cakes and quail's egg (a wow at inspection). On more familiar ground, you might also find a South Indian vegetable korma, lamb biryani and murgh makhani. House wines start at £20.

**Chef/s:** Anirudh Arora. **Open:** Mon to Fri L 12 to 3, all week D 5.30 to 11.30 (10.45 Sun). **Closed:** Sat, Sun. **Meals:** alc (main courses £13 to £18). Set L £10 (2 courses) to £13.50. Set D £20. **Service:** 12.5 % (optional). **Details:** Cards accepted. 85 seats. Air-con. Separate bar. Wheelchair access. Music. Children allowed.

## Mr Kong

**A king in Chinatown**
21 Lisle Street, Soho, WC2H 7BA
Tel no: (020) 7437 7341
www.mrkongrestaurant.com
⊖ Leicester Square, map 5
Chinese | £20
Cooking score: 3

V

Over the years, the Kong family dynasty has established this Lisle Street warhorse as one of the emblematic Cantonese survivors in ever-changing Chinatown. Following a fire in 2007, dining now takes place on two floors, with the kitchen occupying what was the basement dining area. Little has changed as regards the menu, which still touts seafood in a big way: soft-shell crabs, scallops, lobster and sea bass are perennial favourites. Barbecued spare ribs and the like are capably handled, but it's worth making a beeline for the chef's specials if you fancy something a tad more adventurous. Among the tempters might be steamed razor clams with glass noodles, 'King Kong burgers' (minced pork with salted fish) and spicy pork knuckle served cold with jellyfish, plus vegetarian curiosities including mock abalone with pea shoots. House wine is £9.50.
**Chef/s:** K Kong Yw Lo. **Open:** all week 12 to 3am (2am Sun). **Closed:** 24 and 25 Dec. **Meals:** alc (main courses £7 to £30). Set L and D £9.80 (2 courses) to £23 (4 courses). **Service:** 10% (optional). **Details:** Cards accepted. 120 seats. Air-con. No music. No mobile phones. Children allowed.

### Please send us your feedback

To register your opinion about any restaurant listed in the Guide, or a new restaurant that you wish to bring to our attention, please visit the web address at the bottom of the page. Your feedback informs the content of the book and will be used to compile next year's reviews.

NEW ENTRY
## Murano

**Elegant showcase for subtle Italian food**
20-22 Queen Street, Mayfair, W1J 5PR
Tel no: (020) 7592 1222
www.gordonramsay.com
⊖ Green Park, map 5
Italian | £55
Cooking score: 7

V

In moving from the Connaught to new premises in Mayfair, Angela Hartnett has upped her game considerably. Murano is a stylish and elegant room, handsomely decorated in neutral tones with carefully judged lighting. Service is professional, effortless and exceptionally polite, while the menu showcases Hartnett's understanding of the subtleties of Italian food. There's much to surprise and delight at prices that seem like kindness itself. Indeed, the lunch menu is considered some of the best-value fine dining in London. Reporters have praised a delicate mackerel tart served with confit lemon and olive vinaigrette, and braised rabbit leg with apricot stuffing and wet polenta, as well as ravioli of king prawn with pickled fennel 'complemented by wonderful raisin purée', and the 'great combination of flavours' found in a loin of pork braised in milk and served with crushed new potatoes and black pudding. Not to be outdone, a tasting menu that took in turbot confit in olive oil with celeriac purée and red wine reduction, a herb salad with apple, sesame seeds and cider vinaigrette, then English lamb with caramelised sweetbreads and artichokes showed no gimmickry – everything was perfectly fresh. Meals open with Parma ham and coppa, great olive oil and a selection of breads. Miniature sorbets ('the basil was stunning') precede desserts such as pistachio soufflé with warm chocolate sauce and passion fruit granité. The 19-page wine list features particularly well-chosen growers and is impressive in its scope, with a strong Italian

section. However prices and mark-ups are high, with £23 the starting point for an Umbrian white.
**Chef/s:** Angela Hartnett. **Open:** Mon to Sat L 12 to 2.30, D 6.30 to 10.30. **Closed:** Sun. **Meals:** Set L £25. Set D £55. Tasting menu £70 (7 courses). **Service:** 12.5% (optional). **Details:** Cards accepted. 50 seats. Air-con. Separate bar. No music. Wheelchair access. Children allowed.

# Nahm

**Flavourburst food for the senses**
Halkin Hotel, 5 Halkin Street, Belgravia, SW1X 7DJ
Tel no: (020) 7333 1234
www.nahm.como.bz
⊖ Hyde Park Corner, map 4
**Thai | £40**
**Cooking score: 3**

🍴 V

David Thompson's contemporary Thai cuisine awakens slumbering palates with vibrant combinations of taste and texture evinced by the likes of salty chicken wafers with sweet longans or sour prawn curry with acacia omelette. One can order piecemeal from curry, salad, stir-fry, relish and soup sections, but the traditional Nahm Arharn menu comprising five dishes served 'family-style' is another option, with dishes nicely balanced both in themselves and in combination. Desserts are intriguing, for example a refreshing combination of coconut and sweetcorn or pandan cake. Prices are steep although the street food lunch offers better value. It's a shame to see the minimalist dining room so sorry-looking and quiet at lunch and on school nights, with only bland muzak and a handful of diners to fill the space. Watch your wine spend: the spice-appropriate list starts at £32, but only hits its stride post-£50.
**Chef/s:** Matthew Albert. **Open:** Mon to Fri L 12 to 2.30, all week D 7 to 10.15 (10 Sun). **Closed:** bank hol Mon, 24 to 27 Dec. **Meals:** alc (main courses £15 to £19). Set L £15 (2 courses) to £20. Set D £40 (2 courses) to £55. **Service:** 12.5% (optional). **Details:** Cards accepted. 70 seats. Air-con. Separate bar. Wheelchair access. Music. Children allowed. Car parking.

# National Portrait Gallery, Portrait Restaurant

**A feast for the eyes**
Orange Street, Trafalgar Square, WC2H 0HE
Tel no: (020) 7312 2490
www.searcys.co.uk
⊖ Leicester Square, Charing Cross, map 5
**Modern British | £26**
**Cooking score: 2**

£5 OFF   £30 ▼

'I thought that the whole experience was more pleasurable than the sum of its parts', wrote one who found this rooftop restaurant a wonderful place to pass a lunchtime: comfortable, good service, lots of people to observe, great rooftop views, and some fabulous paintings on the way up and down – all in all, an event. Yet the prices will deter most people ('you pay for the view here') and the standard of cooking is sometimes variable. Starters might include beef carpaccio with truffle cheese, rocket and pine nuts, while mains take in pollack with marsh samphire, brown shrimps, lemon and 'very muted' horseradish butter. Wines from £14.95.
**Chef/s:** Katarina Todosijevic. **Open:** all week L 11.30 to 3, Thur and Fri D 5.30 to 8.30. **Closed:** 24 to 26 Dec. **Meals:** alc (main courses £11 to £18). Set L £20 (2 courses) to £25. Set D £17 (2 courses) to £22. Sun L £20.75. **Service:** 12.5% (optional). **Details:** Cards accepted. 100 seats. Air-con. Separate bar. No music. Wheelchair access. Children allowed.

# Nobu Berkeley St

**Cool international brand**
15 Berkeley Street, Mayfair, W1J 8DY
Tel no: (020) 7290 9222
www.noburestaurants.com
⊖ Green Park, map 5
**Japanese | £70**
**Cooking score: 5**

Part of a global enterprise that stretches from Honolulu to Melbourne, the Nobu phenomenon is still among the premier league players on the Japanese restaurant scene. At Berkeley Street, the dramatic décor riffs on arborial themes, with wintry trees dominating the panoramic windows and echoed in the light fittings. Furniture is minimally plain, except for the grill-top hibachi tables. The cooking gives a vigorous spin to classical notions of Japanese fine dining, with Latin American chilli heat applied to salmon, chicken and Wagyu beef dishes, as an alternative, to, say traditional teriyaki. Presentation is reliably exquisite, from appetisers such as octopus carpaccio with bottarga to show-stoppers like the Scottish lobster roasted in a wood-fired oven with spices, lemon and garlic. Fixed-price menus served with miso soup and rice prove abidingly popular, and meals might conclude with the enticing yuzu pie, served with oat cookie crumble and dulce de leche ice cream. Wines are a carefully chosen bunch, arranged stylistically with the food in mind. If the credit crunch hasn't ruined you yet, the Reserve listings are a dream. Prices open at £26.

**Chef/s:** Mark Edwards. **Open:** Mon to Fri L 12 to 2.15, all week D 6 to 11 (12 Thur to Sat, 9.15 Sun). **Closed:** 25 and 26 Dec. **Meals:** alc (main courses £5 to £32). Set L £26. Set D £21 to £32. **Service:** 15%. **Details:** Cards accepted. 200 seats. Separate bar. Music. Children allowed.

## Nobu London
**Innovative Japanese fusion**
19 Old Park Lane, Mayfair, W1K 1LB
Tel no: (020) 7447 4747
www.noburestaurants.com
⊖ Hyde Park Corner, map 5
Japanese | £70
Cooking score: 5

🍶 V

This was the original of Nobu's London operations (see also Nobu Berkeley St), and indeed the group's first outing into Europe. Launched in 1997, it revolutionised at a stroke what Londoners expected of high-end Japanese dining. Nobu offered not just the traditional roll call of tempura, sashimi, bento boxes and the like, but a style of Latino-Japanese fusion that creatively applied the

spicey edge to what was then too often seen as the almost subliminal delicacy of Japanese food. Since then the concept has continued to develop, slowly but productively, under the inspired aegis of Mark Edwards. Specialities here include Wagyu and foie gras gyoza dumplings, soft-shell crab harumaki with creamy wasabi, the exquisite sea urchin tempura, and anti-cucho (Peruvian-style) spicy tea-smoked lamb. Preparations are unimpeachable, and even the smallest bites are loaded with umami, pointedly seasoned and impeccably fresh. Desserts don't let you down either. Not for Nobu the default plates of carved fresh fruit served by other restaurants – here you might be offered, say, tofu cheesecake with mandarin jelly and a sweet Malaga wine ice cream. Wines, as at Berkeley Street, are opulent and chosen with discrimination, but prices will weight the bill all the more heavily.

**Chef/s:** Mark Edwards. **Open:** all week L 12 to 2.15 (12.30 to 2.30 Sat and Sun), D 6 to 10.15 (11 Fri and Sat, 9.30 Sun). **Closed:** 25 and 26 Dec, 1 Jan. **Meals:** alc (main courses £10 to £32). Set L £28 to £60. Set D £70 to £90. **Service:** 15% (optional). **Details:** Cards accepted. 150 seats. Air-con. Separate bar. No music. Wheelchair access. Children allowed.

## Noura Brasserie
**Favourite Lebanese fixture**
16 Hobart Place, Belgravia, SW1W 0HH
Tel no: (020) 7235 9444
www.noura.co.uk
⊖ Victoria, map 5
Lebanese | £32
Cooking score: 3

£5 OFF V

You can't argue with the 10 years in business that this original branch of the Noura chain has notched up in the capital. There's also no doubting the popularity of its Lebanese and mainstream Middle Eastern food, which continues to guarantee steady custom. Such longevity does mean that the décor could do with a revamp, but the kitchen continues to deliver – especially when it comes to highly rated meze such as fatayer (spinach baked in pastry) and kibbeh (cracked wheat with deep-fried lamb). By contrast, chargrilled main courses are reckoned to be more 'ordinary', although vegetarian options and sweets such as baklava all come in for high praise. The extensive wine list includes Chateau Kefraya at £29 a bottle – a real highlight from the Lebanon. Noura has branches in Knightsbridge, Mayfair and Piccadilly.

**Chef/s:** Badih Asmar. **Open:** all week 11.30am to 11.30pm. **Meals:** alc (main courses £12 to £23). Set L £18 (2 courses) to £24. Set D £22 (2 courses) to £30. **Service:** not inc. **Details:** Cards accepted. 130 seats. Air-con. No mobile phones. Wheelchair access. Music. Children allowed.

## One-O-One
**Original, subtle seafood**
Sheraton Park Tower, 101 Knightsbridge, Knightsbridge, SW1X 7RN
Tel no: (020) 7290 7101
www.oneoonerestaurant.com
⊖ Knightsbridge, map 4
Seafood | £45
Cooking score: 5

⊟ V

One-O-One is at the base of the Sheraton Park Tower, its separate entrance allowing it to stand alone from the hotel. Huge glass windows embrace the sleek space within, where Pascal Proyart delivers assured dishes from versatile and flexible menus. He puts the emphasis on seafood, combining truly original touches and the subtlest of flavours with essentially modern French techniques. From the 'Petit Plats' section of the menu come small tasting dishes ranging from native lobster and fennel macedoine salad with red king crab pastilla, apple jelly and sorbet, via red mullet bouillabaisse with shellfish ragoût, rouille and seaweed mouillette, to Scottish beef fillet cooked in a rich red Burgundy sauce and served with creamed salsify, sautéed potatoes and trompette mushrooms. If a succession of small dishes doesn't appeal, there is a carte with larger versions as starters and main courses such as slow-cooked Arctic cod with Joselito chorizo carpaccio and squid à la

plancha, and classics such as Dover sole meunière. Anise-infused pineapple is the accompaniment to rum baba and coconut Chantilly; more mainstream is coupe liégeoise with dark Manjari chocolate. The wine list is pricey (from £22) and appropriately French, but New World and modern styles are well represented.

**Chef/s:** Pascal Proyart. **Open:** all week L 12 to 2.30 (12.30 Sat and Sun), D 6.30 to 10. **Meals:** alc (main courses £23 to £29). Set L £19. Set D £38. **Service:** not inc. **Details:** Cards accepted. 52 seats. Air-con. Separate bar. Wheelchair access. Music. Children allowed. Car parking.

## READERS RECOMMEND

## Osteria Dell'Angolo
**Italian**
47 Marsham Street, Westminster, SW1P 3DP
Tel no: (020) 3268 1077
www.osteriadellangolo.co.uk
**'Enjoyed a wonderful, but not cheap meal'**

## Pearl
**Sound flavours and a stunning setting**
252 High Holborn, Holborn, WC1V 7EN
Tel no: (020) 7829 7000
www.pearl-restaurant.com
⊖ Holborn, map 5
Modern French | £55
Cooking score: 5

Jun Tanaka, something of a minor-league telly chef these days, is (in spite of that) held in high regard by his peers. A visit to Pearl explains why. The warm, attractive high-ceilinged room, in an old Pearl Assurance banking hall, is hung with pearls and finished in soft pinks and creams. It's a fitting setting for Tanaka's modern French cuisine, deemed 'a feast for the eyes as well as the stomach'. The set lunch offers six choices per course. As such, 'it has to be one of the best places to lunch in London', according to one fan. Here, 'neglected' foodstuffs such as mackerel and oxtail get the haute treatment. A dish of mallard (pink slices of breast alongside braised leg) with salsify and cavolo nero is warmly praised. From the dinner menu, dishes could include Orkney beef ribeye with braised cheek, Roscoff onion and bone marrow or brill with oyster tortellini. The wine list has been described as 'superior', but with prices that are 'a bit steep', offering little under £30. There is, however, plenty by the glass or half-bottle (although none of it is exactly a bargain).

**Chef/s:** Jun Tanaka. **Open:** Mon to Fri L 12 to 2.30, Mon to Sat D 6 to 10. **Closed:** Sun, bank hols, last 2 weeks Aug, 25 and 26 Dec. **Meals:** Set L £26 (2 courses) to £29. Set D £47. Tasting menu £56. **Service:** 12.5% (optional). **Details:** Cards accepted. 72 seats. Air-con. Separate bar. Wheelchair access. Music. Children allowed.

## La Petite Maison

**Sharing's the name of the game**
54 Brook Mews, Mayfair, W1K 4EG
Tel no: (020) 7495 4774
www.lpmlondon.co.uk
⊖ **Bond Street, map 5**
**French | £60**
**Cooking score: 3**

V

This smart, wedge-shaped restaurant, with its plate-glass windows offering views of the bonhomie (and kitchen) within is 'French to its fingertips', with a noisy buzz, and a long carte of regional and modern French dishes. 'Each dish will be served when ready', announces the menu. Sharing is the idea, but the consensus is that some starters and mains are not really designed for it – the lemony roast baby chicken is one you might want to keep to yourself. A recent (shared) meal opened with deep-fried baby squid and pissaladière, before going on to the undisputable star of the menu – whole black-leg chicken with foie gras. It finished with pear clafoutis and yoghurt ice cream. There's little under £30 on the mainly French wine list.

**Chef/s:** Raphael Duntoye. **Open:** all week L 12 to 3 (12.30 to 3.30 Sat and Sun), D 6 to 11. **Closed:** 25 and 26 Dec. **Meals:** alc (main courses £14 to £70). **Service:** 12.5% (optional). **Details:** Cards accepted. 85 seats. 16 seats outside. Air-con. Separate bar. Wheelchair access. Music. Children allowed.

## Phoenix Palace

**Temple to Chinese cooking**
3-5 Glentworth Street, Marylebone, NW1 5PG
Tel no: (020) 7486 3515
www.phoenixpalace.uk.com
⊖ **Baker Street, map 4**
**Chinese | £25**
**Cooking score: 2**

V

Palace is an overstatement, but this vast restaurant is a temple to Chinese cooking. Expect weekend lunchtime queues when the lengthy dim sum selection takes centre-stage – neatly folded parcels stuffed with everything from prawn and chive to barbecued pork. In the evening, diners contend with a wide-ranging à la carte that boasts superb renditions of all the classics, plus myriad more interesting options such as wild boar stir-fried with fragrant lemongrass or piquant fried eel with chilli and garlic – all delivered quickly from the creative kitchen. A brief, Old World-centred wine list kicks off with house white at £12 a bottle.

**Chef/s:** Marco Li. **Open:** all week 12 to 11.30 (11 to 10.30 Sun). **Closed:** 25 Dec. **Meals:** alc (main courses £7 to £38). Set D £25. **Service:** 12.5% (optional). **Details:** Cards accepted. 250 seats. Air-con. Separate bar. Wheelchair access. Music. Children allowed.

## Pied-à-Terre

**One of London's best**
34 Charlotte Street, Fitzrovia, W1T 2NH
Tel no: (020) 7636 1178
www.pied-a-terre.co.uk
⊖ **Goodge Street, map 5**
**Modern French | £68**
**Cooking score: 8**

£5 OFF ♦ V

Easy enough to miss amid the wealth of eating options on Charlotte Street, Pied-à-Terre is nonetheless a destination address. The dimensions are on the bijou side, yet the narrow main room with its skylight, as well as the smaller front area where three tables are shielded from pavement view, are

comfortable. Table settings scream quality and the staff are reassuringly civil, without any of the hauteur that can come with a place of this reputation. Shane Osborn has skill to spare, both in the imagination of his dishes and his sheer technique. Menu descriptions are long, but what arrives at the table fully lives up to its billing. How about a starter of seared scallops and poached oysters in Champagne and cucumber nage, with samphire, wood sorrel and trout roe? Or a main course that sees Gressingham duck breast teamed with morteau sausage, kohlrabi, baby turnips and almonds, with a muscular port sauce. The fixed-price lunch deal is exemplary value – a spring outing delivered wood pigeon and foie gras boudin in a slew of Puy lentils and diced ventrèche, followed by roast sea bream with carrot and runner bean threads and a Day-Glo sauce of orange and caraway. With classy canapés, an amuse and a pre-dessert, you might be forgiven for passing up an actual dessert, in which case you'll be missing the likes of chestnut mousse wrapped in a chocolate pancake, with chocolate sabayon, tonka bean and butterscotch ice cream and little pearls of Pedro Ximenez jelly. Too rich? Then consider a straightforward white chocolate mousse with strawberry ice cream and coulis, accompanied by diced nectarine, pear and strawberry. Almost as great as the wine collection itself is the manner of its service. The wines that come with the tasting menu are served 'blind' with the dishes, and then informatively unmasked. Separate volumes for different colours come in a slipcase, which all sounds rather daunting, until you look at the quality. With wines by the glass from £5 and bottles from £22, the sky's the limit thereafter, but there is a true feeling that every bottle has earned its place on the list.
**Chef/s:** Shane Osborn. **Open:** Mon to Fri L 12 to 2.30, Mon to Sat D 6 to 11. **Closed:** Sun, 10 days Christmas and New Year. **Meals:** alc (main courses £19 to £35). Set L £24.50 (2 courses) to £32. Set D £54.50 (2 courses) to £68. Tasting menu £85. **Service:** 12.5% (optional). **Details:** Cards accepted. 38 seats. Air-con. Separate bar. Wheelchair access. Music. Children allowed.

# El Pirata
**Bargain tapas in Mayfair**
5-6 Down Street, Mayfair, W1J 7AQ
Tel no: (020) 7491 3810
www.elpirata.co.uk
⊖ Hyde Park Corner, map 5
Spanish | £19
Cooking score: 1

**V**

Although tucked away, this tapas bar draws the crowds with its tightly packed tables, brightly coloured paintings and rapid delivery of traditional Spanish tapas at bargain prices –'in Mayfair!' Bag a table on the ground floor rather than in the basement and order plates of jamón Ibérico, chorizo in red wine, and stuffed red peppers. For something more substantial, there are generous main courses of roast suckling pig or a classic paella valenciana. The all-Spanish wine list opens at £14.30.
**Chef/s:** Rosendo Gimbana. **Open:** Mon to Fri 12 to 11.30, Sat D 6 to 11.30. **Closed:** Sun. **Meals:** alc (main courses £13 to £18). Set L £9.95 (2 courses). Set L and D tapas £14.95 to £19.50. **Service:** 10% (optional). **Details:** Cards accepted. 95 seats. 16 seats outside. Air-con. Separate bar. Wheelchair access. Music. Children allowed.

## ALSO RECOMMENDED
### ▲ La Porte des Indes
32 Bryanston Street, Marble Arch, W1H 7EG
Tel no: (020) 7224 0055
www.laportedesindes.com
⊖ Marble Arch, map 4
Indian

There are echoes of Bollywood and Disney World in this extravagant Indian with its kitsch OTT surrounds, giant palms, cascading waterfall and luxurious drapes. Mainstream Mughal favourites such as Bombay chaat, tandoori chicken and Hyderabadi lamb biryani (£17) are bolstered by a sizeable contingent of Creole-style dishes from 'Les Indes Françaises' including pepper crabs with green mango sauce (£10.50), revved-up bouillabaisse and duck with tamarind sauce. Round off with pistachio kulfi or gulab jamun. Vegetarians do well, with thalis from £20. Well-chosen, spice-friendly wines from £19.50 (£5.50 a glass). Open all week.

## ▲ Princi

**135 Wardour Street, Soho, W1F 0UT**
**Tel no: (020) 7478 8888**
**www.princi.co.uk**
**⊖ Tottenham Court Road, map 5**
**Italian**

Restaurateur Alan Yau and Milanese baker Rocco Princi's nifty Italian bakery-cum-café bears all the hallmarks of a slick, professional operation. There's a busy buzz to the glossy, good-looking room where cheerful staff dispense food and drink with a can-do charm. Select your choice from counter displays of breads, pastries, quiches, pizza slices, salads (beetroot, walnut and gorgonzola, £4.50) or generous hot dishes (spinach and ricotta cannelloni, £6). It's all well-made and keenly-priced. House wine £16. Open all week.

## The Providores

**Thrilling fusion trailblazer**
**109 Marylebone High Street, Marylebone, W1U 4RX**
**Tel no: (020) 7935 6175**
**www.theprovidores.co.uk**
**⊖ Baker Street, Bond Street, map 4**
**Fusion | £42**
**Cooking score: 4**

🍶 V

'My palate is consistently entertained', wrote one reporter about Peter Gordon's seminal fusion gaff in trend-conscious Marylebone. It's certainly 'fun' to eat here, whether you choose the ground floor Tapa Room or the monochrome Providores Restaurant. Downstairs is a boisterous, brash, no-bookings drop-in with high decibels, elbow-to-elbow seating and global grazing as the foodie business of the day (think smoked Gressingham duck breast with pan-fried Manouri ewe's cheese, kumquat and pomegranate chutney). Breakfast is worth a punt, too. Meanwhile, things take a serious turn on the first floor, as the kitchen sets about

assaulting the senses with even more esoteric ingredients and complex left-field partnerships. How about roast Norwegian cod on ginger and wasabi tobbiko arancini with pickled red cabbage, tomato chilli jam and miso beurre blanc, followed by a dessert of warm chocolate prune cake with hazelnut-crusted palm sugar ice cream and a puffed rice wafer? Like Peter Gordon, the fascinating wine list has Kiwi blood in its veins: expect a breathtaking in-depth tour of New Zealand's vineyards, plus a round-up of seriously good 'other world' selections. Prices start at £14.50 (£4.75 a glass).
**Chef/s:** Peter Gordon. **Open:** all week L 12 to 2.30, D 6 to 10.30. **Closed:** 25 to 27 Dec, 1 to 3 Jan. **Meals:** alc (main courses £18 to £26). Set L £48. Set D £42. **Service:** 12.5% (optional). **Details:** Cards accepted. 38 seats. Air-con. Wheelchair access. Music. Children allowed.

## Quilon

**A fascinating galaxy of flavours**
**41 Buckingham Gate, Westminster, SW1E 6AF**
**Tel no: (020) 7821 1899**
**www.quilon.co.uk**
**⊖ St James's Park, Victoria, map 5**
**Indian | £50**
**Cooking score: 4**

🍽 V

Quilon's street entrance lends a stand-alone feel to this hotel-based Indian restaurant. One reporter thought the interior was a not-too-successful mix of the 'Days of the Raj meets contemporary India', but concluded that while the ambience may suffer, Sriram Aylur's South Indian coastal cuisine 'is an exciting, balanced and light affair'. With its focus on seafood and vegetarian options, and blending ethnic and progressive ideas with prime produce and imported spices, the cooking delivers a 'fascinating galaxy of flavours', though with due refinement and subtlety. The fixed-price lunch is a steal: spinach poriyal (spinach cooked with mustard seeds, whole red chillies and fresh grated coconut), or a 'cracking' koondapoor fish curry, with its chunks of succulent halibut simmered in coconut, chilli,

onions and tamarind gravy. There are wonderful appams (dish-shaped rice pancakes) to accompany, while a spice-friendly wine list offers plenty by glass (from £5), carafe or bottle (from £20).
**Chef/s:** Sriram Aylur. **Open:** Sun to Fri L 12 to 2.30 (12.30 to 3.30 Sun), all week D 6 to 11 (10.30 Sun). **Closed:** 25 and 26 Dec. **Meals:** alc (main courses £15 to £25). Set L £20. Set D £37. Sun L £20. **Service:** 12.5% (optional). **Details:** Cards accepted. 25 seats.

## Quirinale

**Good-looking, rich Italian**
1 Great Peter Street, Westminster, SW1P 3LL
Tel no: (020) 7222 7080
www.quirinale.co.uk
⊖ Westminster, map 3
Italian | £26
Cooking score: 3

**V**

Quirinale continues to enjoy faithful support among the denizens of Westminster for its good looks and simply prepared northern Italian food. Stefano Savio orders a fair amount of the kitchen's supplies direct from Italy, guaranteeing a reassuring degree of authenticity in what is served. A salad of roast beetroot, endive, Robiola cheese and walnut dressing might go before an intermediate dish such as bigoli pasta with porcini mushrooms and duck ragù. Main courses are rich and filling, wrapping fillet of pork in prosciutto and sage and serving with balsamic-glazed onions, or adding chickpea purée and rosemary-scented olive oil to fillet of cod. Look forward to versions of Italian favourites at dessert stage, from tiramisu to homemade ice creams and sorbets. The (almost) all-Italian wine list opens at £17.
**Chef/s:** Stefano Savio. **Open:** Mon to Fri L 12 to 3, D 6 to 10.30. **Closed:** Sat, Sun, 24 Dec to first Mon in Jan, 7 Aug to 7 Sept. **Meals:** alc (main courses £17 to £21). **Service:** 12.5%. **Details:** Cards accepted. 50 seats. Air-con. Music. Children allowed.

## Quo Vadis

**Reviving the classic old-school grill**
26-29 Dean Street, Soho, W1D 3LL
Tel no: (020) 7437 9585
www.quovadissoho.co.uk
⊖ Tottenham Court Road, map 5
Modern British | £45
Cooking score: 2

Brothers Sam and Eddie Hart have breathed new life into this famous, history-etched Soho veteran: Marx once lived upstairs and the old dining room has seen plenty of action over the years. Its stained glass and art-hung walls will strike a chord with fans of the Ivy (see entry), and the revamped menu also has a familiar ring with its mix of comfort food and old-school grills. It looks tempting on paper, but the results on the plate have been mixed, judging by feedback: glowing reports of 'flawless' turbot with salsa verde and sea bream with razor clams have been tempered by niggles about 'rubbery' shellfish and 'recklessly fried' gnocchi. Prices soon add up, although the impressive wine list (from £16.50) is fair, with some unusual pickings such as Austrian Zweigelt and Montlouis-sur-Loire on offer.
**Chef/s:** Jean Philippe Patruno. **Open:** Mon to Sat L 12 to 2.30, Mon to Sat D 5.30 to 10.30. **Closed:** Sun, bank hols, 24 to 29 Dec. **Meals:** alc (main courses £12 to £33). Set L (Sat only) £16.50 (2 courses) to £19.50. Set D (pre-theatre 5.30-6) £16.50 (2 courses) to £19.50. **Service:** 12.5% (optional). **Details:** Cards accepted. 86 seats. Air-con. Separate bar. No music. Wheelchair access. Children allowed.

## Red Fort

**Indian new-wave veteran**
77 Dean Street, Soho, W1D 3SH
Tel no: (020) 7437 2525/2115
www.redfort.co.uk
⊖ Tottenham Court Road, map 5
Indian | £40
Cooking score: 2

£5 OFF **V**

When it opened in 1983, the Red Fort's upmarket take on Indian food was a bold stroke, but the years have passed, chefs have come and gone and the place now feels less of a ground-breaker. Meals begin well with exquisite homemade pickles, and the kitchen aims for creativity – although there have been grumbles about 'overcooking' and a lack of freshness of late. Tandooris and tikkas are given some interesting twists – lamb chops in star anise and pomegranate jus, say – while curries might include chicken breast with fenugreek, cashew nut and creamed tomato sauce. Overall, prices are reckoned to be 'high', with wines starting at £25.
**Chef/s:** Mohammed Rais. **Open:** Mon to Fri L 12 to 2.15, all week D 5.45 to 11.15. **Closed:** 25 Dec. **Meals:** alc (main courses £15 to £33). Set L £12 (2 courses) to £25. Set D £16 (2 courses) to £35. **Service:** not inc. **Details:** Cards accepted. 84 seats. Air-con. Separate bar. Wheelchair access. Music. Children allowed.

## Rex Whistler Restaurant at Tate Britain

**Drink to a national treasure**
Millbank, Westminster, SW1P 4RG
Tel no: (020) 7887 8825
www.tate.org.uk
⊖ Pimlico, map 3
Modern British | £29
Cooking score: 2

£5 OFF

The lunchtime restaurant is well worth booking if you're planning to spend a day at Tate Britain. It's an altogether civilised option – the service is agreeably genteel, and the cooking scores some palpable hits. A tart composed of Lancashire's Blacksticks Blue cheese and red onion is a good savoury start, and might be followed by chargrilled Devon beef with chanterelles and peppercorn jus. Finish with gingerbread mousse. The wine list has always been as much of a national treasure as the art collection, a cornucopia of delights with France, Italy and Australia leading the charge. Many mature vintages are on offer, there is a fine spread of dessert wines and many by the glass, from £4.10. Bottles start at £15.50. All this, and an original Rex Whistler mural to contemplate too.
**Chef/s:** Richard Oxley. **Open:** all week L only 11.30 to 3. **Closed:** 24 to 26 Dec. **Meals:** alc (main courses £16 to £19). Set L £15.95 (2 courses) to £19.95. **Service:** 12.5% (optional). **Details:** Cards accepted. 80 seats. 20 seats outside. Air-con. No music. Wheelchair access. Children allowed.

## Rhodes W1 Restaurant

**Modern British cooking in a luxurious setting**
Great Cumberland Place, Marble Arch, W1A 4RF
Tel no: (020) 7479 3737
www.rhodesw1.com
⊖ Marble Arch, map 4
Anglo-French | £65
Cooking score: 5

£5 OFF

Although part of the Cumberland Hotel, Rhodes W1 has its own entrance. The dining room, designed by the 'queen of taupe' Kelly Hoppen is a real looker, with glittering chandeliers, antique chairs and pearl-effect walls. The cooking is modern, and British, but it comes with a strong French accent. At inspection, a rather 'wee helping' of Scottish langoustines (coated in tempura batter) arrived with three types of melon, an unusual pairing of cucumber ice cream and an orange dressing, and was pronounced 'a qualified victory'. The kitchen delivers some highbrow dishes with tip-top presentation: meticulously prepared wild salmon, again sourced from Scotland, was teamed unusually but successfully with confit snails, parsley gnocchi, samphire and an emulsion of roasted garlic. Desserts are distinctive and intricate –

apple parfait came with green apple sorbet, as well as cinnamon foam and comforting mini apple doughnuts. The urge to add foam to everything could do with some tempering, though. Service is 'well schooled'. France holds most of the cards on the noteworthy wine list, which starts from £24, but high premiums can make it difficult to find much below £40.

**Chef/s:** Paul Welburn. **Open:** Tue to Fri L 12 to 2.30; Tue to Sat D 7 to 10.30. **Closed:** Sun, Mon, 2 weeks Aug, Christmas, New Year, bank hols. **Meals:** alc (main courses £28). Set L £19.95 (2 courses) to £23.95. Set D £55 (2 courses) to £65. **Service:** 12.5% (optional). **Details:** Cards accepted. 46 seats. Air-con. Separate bar. Wheelchair access. Music. Children allowed.

## Ristorante Semplice
**Suave metropolitan Italian**
9-10 Blenheim Street, Mayfair, W1S 1LJ
Tel no: (020) 7495 1509
www.ristorantesemplice.com
⊖ Bond Street, Green Park, map 5
Italian | £35
Cooking score: 5

 V

The name may translate as 'simplicity', but that's about as far it goes in this intimate Italian off Bond Street. Ristorante Semplice exudes suave metropolitan style, with gold-frescoed walls, walnut panels and slinky leather furnishings, while the kitchen has its finger firmly on the regional pulse. Much of the repertoire is defined by top-drawer ingredients imported from the home country: Fassone beef finds its way into a signature Alba-style carpaccio as well as tagliata with French beans, while milk-fed Piedmontese veal is wrapped in Parma ham and served with shiitake mushrooms, courgettes and cherry tomatoes. British produce also has its say, from Cornish sea bass with sautéed spinach and chickpea purée to Herdwick lamb ragù with Gragnano paccheri and Calabrese chilli. On the pasta front, the kitchen has also delivered 'heavenly' crab ravioli and spaghetti 'alla chitarra' with squid. To finish, readers have

been won over by the pineapple and polenta cake ('how can they cook something so simple and make it so exquisite?' mused one fan). Otherwise, try apple fritters with cinnamon custard cream. The stellar Italian wine list is a connoisseur's tour of the country's vineyards, with superstar names, little-known gems and quality drinking all the way from Piedmont to Sicily. Prices start at £19. An informal sibling, Bar Trattoria Semplice, is just around the corner (see entry).

**Chef/s:** Marco Torri. **Open:** Mon to Fri L 12 to 2.30, Mon to Sat D 7 to 10.30. **Closed:** Sun, bank hols, 2 weeks Christmas. **Meals:** alc (main courses £18 to £27). Set L £16 (2 courses) to £22. **Service:** 12.5% (optional). **Details:** Cards accepted. 55 seats. Air-con. Wheelchair access. Music. Children allowed.

## Roka
**Chic Japanese with electric atmosphere**
37 Charlotte Street, Fitzrovia, W1T 1RR
Tel no: (020) 7580 6464
www.rokarestaurant.com
⊖ Goodge Street, map 5
Japanese | £40
Cooking score: 4

V

Five years since opening, Roka hasn't lost one jot of its X-factor: the chic wood interiors are holding up well, service from an army of staff remains nicely up to scratch and the modern Japanese food is a knockout night after night. Start proceedings with oriental cocktails in the seductive subterranean bar, Shochu, before gearing up to the electric atmosphere of the dining room. The focal point is the open-plan robata grill, behind which chefs conjure up sublime mini-plates of scallop skewers with punchy wasabi, the tenderest Korean-spiced lamb cutlets and sweet quail marinated in plum wine and red miso. Presentation is second to none and extends beyond robata dishes to sashimi platters served in bamboo baskets, nori-wrapped rounds of foie gras parfait cut through with tart umeshu plum and melt-in-the-mouth butterfish tataki with white asparagus. Wines start at a stiff £28 a bottle, but there is wide choice under £40.

Chef/s: Nicholas Watt. Open: all week L 12 to 3.30 (12.30 Sat and Sun), D 5.30 to 11.30 (10.30 Sun). Closed: 25 Dec, 1 Jan. Meals: alc (L £25 to £30, D £40 to £50). Service: 13.5% (optional). Details: Cards accepted. 105 seats. 24 seats outside. Air-con. Separate bar. Wheelchair access. Music. Children allowed.

## Royal China
**Dim sum is still a class act**
24–26 Baker Street, Marylebone, W1U 3BZ
Tel no: (020) 7487 4688
www.royalchinagroup.co.uk
⊖ Baker Street, map 4
Chinese | £30
Cooking score: 3

At this glitzily decorated restaurant, with its black lacquer and gold motif, the dim sum seldom disappoints. But Royal China's popularity means it can be noisy, with patchy service. If you like the Chinese predilection for texture, try jellyfish with pork knuckle. The cooking can also deliver elsewhere, as in a hotpot of beef brisket Szechuan-style, laced with fiery bird's-eye chillies, or the equally good pan-fried aubergine stuffed with minced shrimp with black bean sauce. However, complacency has crept in; at inspection the chef's specials had vanished from the menu, and dishes can suffer from oiliness and over-seasoning. Chilled mango pudding is a welcome relief after the strong flavours. Wines start from £18. There are also branches in Queensway, Docklands and Fulham. Our questionnaire was not returned, so some of these details may be incorrect.
Chef/s: Mr Man. Open: all week 12 to 11 (11.30 Sat, 11 to 10 Sun). Closed: Christmas. Meals: alc (main courses L £8 to £15, D £10 to £25). Service: 12.5% (optional). Details: Cards accepted. 160 seats. Air-con. Wheelchair access. Music. Children allowed.

## Marcus Wareing  The Berkeley

**If you hadn't become a chef, what would you have been?**
I would have worked with my dad in his fruit and potato business.

**What is your top culinary tip?**
If you are not a competent cook, don't stray from the recipe.

**Which chefs do you admire?**
Those that know how to run a business and cook.

**If you were to have one abiding principle in the kitchen, what would it be?**
Lead by example.

**What is your favourite restaurant and why?**
Marcus Wareing at the Berkeley because it's all mine!

**What do you do to relax when out of the kitchen?**
I spend time with my kids - it's far from relaxing though!

**What do you like cooking when 'off duty'?**
Full English or roast - cannot choose.

# Rules

**Britannia rules in Covent Garden**
35 Maiden Lane, Covent Garden, WC2E 7LB
Tel no: (020) 7836 5314
www.rules.co.uk
⊖ Covent Garden, Leicester Square, Charing
Cross, map 5
British | £37
Cooking score: 3

London's longest surviving restaurant purrs
along like a vintage Bentley and continues to
champion Bulldog British food in an inspired
setting that makes tourists dewy-eyed with
admiration. Those who cross the threshold can
expect genuine courtesy and good-humoured
hospitality without a whiff of tight-collared,
conservative pomposity. Rare-breed beef
from the owners' Pennine farm is a feature, but
game is the real star: furred and feathered
specials vary with the season, from Rules'
'famous grouse' to loin of roe deer (a 'deeply
flavoured piece of Bambi') with caramelised
chicory and Victoria plums. Readers have also
endorsed the brown Windsor soup topped
with Welsh rarebit (a cheeky Brit take on
French onion), potted Wiltshire rabbit and
textbook steak and kidney pud, while ever-
reliable spotted dick and raspberry trifle are
flag-waving finales. House wine is £22,
London tap water is free.
**Chef/s:** Richard Sawyer. **Open:** all week 12 to 11.45.
**Closed:** 4 days Christmas. **Meals:** alc (main courses
£18 to £28). **Service:** 12.5% (optional).
**Details:** Cards accepted. 98 seats. Air-con. Separate
bar. No music. No mobile phones. Wheelchair
access. Children allowed.

# St Alban

**Modern flair, cosmopolitan accent**
Rex House, 4-12 Lower Regent Street, Piccadilly,
SW1Y 4PE
Tel no: (020) 7499 8558
www.stalban.net
⊖ Piccadilly Circus, map 5
Modern European | £37
Cooking score: 4
**V**

Chris Corbin and Jeremy King's St Alban can
still show a clean pair of heels to most of its
nearby rivals and has blossomed into a mature,
confident restaurant – despite its unpromising
location on the ground floor of an office block.
A slight refurb has seen the installation of two
Damien Hirst artworks and plate glass
windows 'un-etched so that you can look out
into the street, successfully opening the
restaurant up to its location'. Chef Dale
Osborne has settled into his stride: expect
precise cooking of food that is a wonderful
amalgam of flavours, textures and
combinations. Cornish squid with black rice,
clams and aïoli is a harmonious combination,
rare organic salmon comes with crisply
flavoursome skin, lentils and wild
mushrooms, while slow-cooked braised lamb
enjoys an equally forthright partnership with
chilli and chickpeas. Desserts aim for gently
flavoured richness, as in homemade yoghurt
with crushed honeycomb. House wine
from £17.
**Chef/s:** Dale Osborne. **Open:** Mon to Sat L 12 to 3, D
5.30 to 11. **Closed:** Sun, 25 to 26 Dec, 1 Jan, Aug
bank hol. **Meals:** alc (main courses £9 to £30). Set
Sat L £15.50 (2 courses) to £19.75 (also pre and post
theatre). **Service:** 12.5% (optional). **Details:** Cards
accepted. 140 seats. Air-con. Separate bar. No
music. Wheelchair access. Children allowed.

## Sake No Hana

**Alan Yau's homage to Japanese food**
23 St James's Street, Mayfair, SW1A 1HA
Tel no: (020) 7925 8988
www.sakenohana.com
⊖ Green Park, map 5
Japanese | £65
Cooking score: 5

V

The frontage is dark and discreet and unless you are heading for the ground-floor sushi bar an escalator whisks you up to the first-floor restaurant. It's a soothing, soaring space with acres of pale wood, the only blush of colour coming from the tatami mat seating area. The smart move is to go at lunchtime when it is not crowded, eat from one of a selection of kaiseki bento lunch boxes and order a carafe of saké for £10. That way you may be able to afford to plot another visit. The young waiters are less sharp then, but the ingredients are always sensational and the cooking dazzles. Indeed, this young sibling of Alan Yau's Hakkasan and Yauatcha (see entries) sets a radical new tone for Japanese dining in London. Standout dishes this year have included a salad of warm soft-shell crab with wasabi sauce, miso Chilean sea bass (which came wrapped in a houba leaf and had flesh that slipped apart into fine pearly flakes), delicate tempura, and sushi and sashimi that showed the excellent quality of the raw fish. The only misstep was French patisserie-style desserts. Universally pricey French wines move from £24 very quickly.
**Chef/s:** Matsuno San. **Open:** Mon to Sat L 12 to 3, all week D 6 to 11. **Closed:** 24 and 25 Dec. **Meals:** alc (main courses from £8 to £27). Set L £25 to £28. Set D £55. **Service:** 13% (optional). **Details:** Cards accepted. 95 seats. Air-con. Separate bar. No music. Wheelchair access. Children allowed.

## Salloos

**Consistent quality from a long-runner**
62-64 Kinnerton Street, Knightsbridge, SW1X 8ER
Tel no: (020) 7235 4444
⊖ Knightsbridge, map 4
Pakistani | £55
Cooking score: 3

V

Thankfully little has changed at this long-running Pakistani restaurant, which occupies a mews house in a quiet corner of Knightsbridge. Abdul Aziz is still the chef (as he has been for several decades) and consistency of quality and service remain the restaurant's guiding principles. The deceptively simple menu of Mughlai cuisine offers excellent tandoori options, from chicken tikka to a signature dish of tender lamb chops, marinated for 24 hours before being baked. Other specialities include king prawn karahi and the marvellous haleem akbari (shredded lamb cooked for a day with whole wheatgerm, lentils and spices). Kebabs are a popular choice, and a decent selection of classic vegetable dishes includes familiar names such as dahl, bhindi and baingan. Wines start at £19.50 a bottle.
**Chef/s:** Abdul Aziz. **Open:** Mon to Sat L 12 to 2.15, D 7 to 11.30. **Closed:** Sun, 25 and 26 Dec. **Meals:** alc (main courses £17 to £20). **Service:** 12.5% (optional). **Details:** Cards accepted. 60 seats. Air-con. Separate bar. No music. No mobile phones.

## Salt Yard

**Classic tapas with a sophisticated edge**
54 Goodge Street, Fitzrovia, W1T 4NA
Tel no: (020) 7637 0657
www.saltyard.co.uk
⊖ **Goodge Street, map 5**
**Spanish/Italian | £25**
**Cooking score: 2**

V

Salt Yard's resolutely unflashy surroundings of ground-floor bar and basic dining room are matched by unshowy food in which fine ingredients are treated simply. Best described as contemporary tapas – Spanish classics with an Italian twist – the menu might start with spicy chorizo with marinated peppers or squid with chickpeas and chilli jam. Lamb shoulder is slow-roasted and teamed with a wonderful tomato compote, while patatas fritas come with both romesco and aïoli. Spanish and Italian wines complement the food, the list opening with a good selection of sherries. House wine is £15.
**Chef/s:** Ben Tish. **Open:** Mon to Fri L 12 to 3, Mon to Sat D 6 to 11 (5 Sat). **Closed:** Sun, 24 Dec to 2 Jan, bank hols. **Meals:** alc (tapas £4 to £9). **Service:** 12.5% (optional). **Details:** Cards accepted. 70 seats. 6 seats outside. Air-con. Separate bar. Music. Children allowed.

## Sardo

**Faithful family-run Sardinian**
45 Grafton Way, Fitzrovia, W1T 5DQ
Tel no: (020) 7387 2521
www.sardo-restaurant.com
⊖ **Warren Street, map 2**
**Sardinian | £29**
**Cooking score: 4**

Sardinian cooking is becoming gradually more known in the UK, thanks in large measure to restaurants such as Sardo, now embarked on its second decade. Inside, it's light and relaxing, with staff full of Mediterranean warmth. There are subtle inflections on more familiar Italian modes throughout a menu that is structured classically, starting with antipasti of, say, stuffed squid in a sauce of tomatoes, olives and basil, before launching into pasta such as the island speciality, maloreddus, served with Sardinia's spicy sausage, salsiccia sarda. Main course might be grilled Scotch beef topped with Ovinfort (a north Sardinian sheeps' cheese), accompanied by spinach and potatoes. Desserts ply a more traditional trade, with tiramisu, pannacotta and semifreddo all present and deliciously correct. If your knowledge of Sardinia's wines is rusty to non-existent, there can be no further excuse. A great list of the island's reds and whites is on hand, bolstered by selections from the other Italian regions. Prices start at £15.
**Chef/s:** Roberto Sardu. **Open:** Mon to Fri L 12 to 3, Mon to Sat D 6 to 11. **Closed:** Sun, 25 and 26 Dec, Easter, bank hols. **Meals:** alc (main courses £11 to £18). **Service:** 12.5% (optional). **Details:** Cards accepted. 60 seats. 8 seats outside. Air-con. Wheelchair access. Music. Children allowed.

## Sartoria

**Sharply cut Italian**
20 Savile Row, Mayfair, W1S 3PR
Tel no: (020) 7534 7000
www.danddlondon.com
⊖ **Oxford Circus, Piccadilly Circus, map 5**
**Italian | £44**
**Cooking score: 2**

V

Named for its location in the heart of Savile Row, a world of bespoke suiting and handmade shoes, Sartoria is an elegant restaurant with good linen, gentle lighting and a menu of earthy, uncomplicated Italian food. Tagliatelle with rabbit ragù and black olives is one of a range of pasta dishes that may be taken in two sizes, and main courses extend from grey mullet with Sicilian couscous to grilled lamb chops with deep-fried artichokes. Start, perhaps, with a serving of coppa with fennel and apple sauce, and finish classically with tiramisu. A commendable list of Italian wines allows exploration of the regions, from £18.

**Chef/s:** Alan Marchetti. **Open:** Mon to Fri L 12 to 3, Mon to Sat D 5.30 to 11. **Closed:** Sun, 25 and 26 Dec, 1 Jan, bank hols. **Meals:** alc (main courses £9 to £26). Set L and D £17.50 (2 courses) to £19.50. **Service:** 12.5% (optional). **Details:** Cards accepted. 150 seats. Air-con. Separate bar. Wheelchair access. Music. Children allowed.

## Scott's
**Celebs?** Seafood's the real star
20 Mount Street, Mayfair, W1K 2HE
Tel no: (020) 7495 7309
www.scotts-restaurant.com
⊖ Green Park, map 4
Seafood | £60
Cooking score: 4

**V**

Some nights, Scott's really is the celeb circus the gossip rags would have us believe. But, frankly, the appeal of 'star-gazing' soon gives way to a focus on dinner. Seafood is the star here, often raw or unadorned, as befits its high quality. British classics litter the menu, for example potted shrimps, a retro shellfish cocktail, and deep-fried haddock with mushy peas. Slightly trendier 'foodie' options feature too, with rare or seasonal ingredients such as skate knobs, herring milts and 'seashore vegetables'. Meat options are few: exemplary game in season or a ribeye steak, perhaps. Getting in takes planning, although early tables and last-minute seats at the shellfish bar (a ravishing affair fashioned in onyx and stingray skin) are options. The wine list, from £20, offers little under £30. On the plus side, it has plenty by the glass and carafe.
**Chef/s:** Dave McCarthy. **Open:** all week 12 to 10.30 (10pm Sun). **Closed:** 25 and 26 Dec, 1 Jan, Aug bank hol. **Meals:** alc (main courses £17 to £39). **Service:** 12.5% (optional). **Details:** Cards accepted. 120 seats. 20 seats outside. Air-con. Separate bar. No music. No mobile phones. Wheelchair access.

## Serpentine Bar & Kitchen
**Modern British**
Serpentine Road, Hyde Park, W2 2UH
Tel no: (020) 7706 8114
www.serpentinebarandkitchen.com
'Lovely all day café – was in two minds whether to recommend this as it is such a find'

## Sketch, Lecture Room and Library
**A sumptuous pleasure palace**
9 Conduit Street, Mayfair, W1S 2XG
Tel no: (020) 7659 4500
www.sketch.uk.com
⊖ Oxford Circus, map 5
Modern European | £65
Cooking score: 6

Persons who might be bemused rather than delighted by ornate handbag tables, padded walls and, in the loos, toilet paper swinging languorously on a crystal trapeze should look away now. At the top of Mourad Mazouz's extraordinarily gilded Mayfair toybox, the Lecture Room and Library multiplies the trappings of fabulousness, creating a singular experience during which guests will want for nothing except deeper pockets. Pierre Gagnaire's whimsical, nature-inspired ideas are given substance by head chef Jean-Denis Le Bras, and many appear as 'combinations' of dishes, rotated by softly moving staff with a fine line in knowing deference. To start, they could include avocado fluff with pale mozzarella ice cream and redcurrants, salty rabbit rillettes, a carpaccio of bitter turnips scattered with strawberries and a 'minestrone' of orzo pasta, tomatoes and beans; it might seem bitty, but concentrate and the mist clears, leaving fresh, celebratory natural flavours. A main course called 'piglet' (it could be 'perfume of the earth' or 'sea garden No 4') might be a surprisingly rustic braise of bright, sweet peppers and suckling pig shoulder, but at dessert the combi approach is back; a chocolate délice, perhaps, alongside strawberry sorbet and the perfect fruit salad. The wine list, which runs from £19 (£5 by

the glass) to £10,000, dispenses with the fripperies, concentrating on quality and range. The set lunch offers a fine opportunity for dipping a toe into the whole experience.
**Chef/s:** Jean-Denis Le Bras and Pierre Gagnaire. **Open:** Tue to Fri L 12 to 4, Tue to Sat D 6.30 to 12. **Closed:** Sun, Mon, 25 to 30 Dec, 2 weeks Aug, bank hols. **Meals:** alc (main courses £28 to £35). Set L £30 (2 courses) to £35. Tasting menu from £70 (7 courses). **Service:** 12.5% (optional). **Details:** Cards accepted. 50 seats. Air-con. Separate bar. No mobile phones. Wheelchair access. Music. Children allowed.

## The Square
**One of Britain's most talented chefs**
6-10 Bruton Street, Mayfair, W1J 6PU
Tel no: (020) 7495 7100
www.squarerestaurant.com
♦ Green Park, map 5
French | £75
Cooking score: 8

The Square is a handsome room with a muted colour scheme and the odd abstract painting to divert the eye. It's the domain of Philip Howard, one of the most talented chefs in Britain, whose classically orientated cooking is committed to technical excellence without reaching for outré combinations to sustain interest. Quail served several ways, for example, cleverly delivers a lightly truffled consommé; a jelly topped with bacon foam with pearl barley added for texture; a beignet of soft-boiled quail's egg with raisin purée; and a 'club sandwich' with layers of quail breast, foie gras, truffle cream and raw apple. It is all adventurous and visually stimulating enough to be exciting, yet it is balanced by finely honed discipline. Main courses gain lustre through the pedigree of their components, as is the case with a delicate ragoût of Dover sole with lobster ravioli, sea kale and leek hearts, which arrives in a light broth finished with crème fraîche, the whole assemblage pointed up with the addition of a single oyster giving 'a lovely salty note'. Desserts reveal the full extent of the kitchen's

dexterity, as in an unusual warm truffled honey jelly topped with a rich hazelnut cream and served with mead-flavoured financiers and Cannelés de Bordeaux on the side. Prices are at the top end of the national spectrum, but then so is the quality, and you do get a lot for your money. Meals start with a succession of nibbles and a pre-starter of, say, foie gras with apple jelly and Parmesan, and puddings are preceded by a beautifully crafted miniature dessert such as a small glass of yoghurt topped with layers of rhubarb and blood orange. To round off the meal, coffee is served with a panoply of impressive petits fours. The wine list centres on classic French regions, but the focus on the rest of the world is equally impressive. Bottles start at £19.
**Chef/s:** Philip Howard. **Open:** Mon to Fri L 12 to 2.30, all week D 6.30 to 10. **Closed:** 23 to 31 Dec. **Meals:** Set L £30 (2 courses) to £35. Set D £75. Tasting menu £95. **Service:** 12.5% (optional). **Details:** Cards accepted. 90 seats. Air-con. Separate bar. No music. Wheelchair access. Children allowed.

## Sumosan
**Modern Japanese for the in-crowd**
26 Albemarle Street, Mayfair, W1S 4HY
Tel no: (020) 7495 5999
www.sumosan.com
♦ Green Park, map 5
Japanese | £45
Cooking score: 4
**V**

The suave contemporary design – soft purple panels offsetting the light oak floor and macassar wood tables – makes a fittingly modern backdrop for the most up-to-the-minute kind of concept cooking. Japanese-based fusion food gone expat is what the Wolkow family are about, and the place has three branches in Moscow. A stylish cocktail bar is a glamorous adjunct to the dining room, which offers teppan grilling and sushi as well as a range of fixed-price menus served communally for sharing. Creamy, spicy rock shrimp tempura with yuzu is one memorable dish. Tuna might come tartare-style with avocado, a quail's egg, sevruga caviar and truffle oil. Meatier bites include spiced nori-crusted lamb cutlets, and the relatively mainstream chicken yakitori. Finish with two-tone chocolate fondant with green tea ice cream. Wines and sakés are chosen to complement the often highly seasoned food, and prices are not all as plutocratic as may be feared. They start at £24.

**Chef/s:** Bubker Belkhit. **Open:** Mon to Fri L 12 to 2.45, all week D 6 to 11.30 (10.30 Sun). **Closed:** 25 and 26 Dec, Easter, bank hols. **Meals:** alc (main courses £9 to £26). Set menus £22.50 to £70. **Service:** 15% (optional). **Details:** Cards accepted. 120 seats. Air-con. Separate bar. Wheelchair access. Music. Children allowed.

## Tamarind
**First-rate contemporary Indian**
20-22 Queen Street, Mayfair, W1J 5PR
Tel no: (020) 7629 3561
www.tamarindrestaurant.com
⊖ Green Park, map 5
Indian | £32
**Cooking score: 4**

£5 OFF **V**

Tamarind has been a destination address for up-to-date Indian Mughal cooking since the mid-1990s. With smart table settings and an opulent staircase on which to make an entrance, it's as well-designed as subterranean dining rooms get and in Alfred Prasad, who has risen through the kitchen ranks here, it has a skilled interpreter of the north-west Indian culinary palette. The Tamarind house salad, with apple, plum and kumquat in pine nuts and honey, makes a refreshing appetiser, or you might begin with enlivening aloo tikki, sago-crusted spiced potato cakes filled with creamed spinach, with tamarind chutney. Vegetarian dishes throughout impress, while the fish and meat – such as meen kozhambu (kingfish and mango simmered in tomatoes and coconut), or Kashmiri shank (a hunk of lamb slow-cooked in yoghurt, saffron and chillies) – are never less than striking. Traditional desserts include carrot halva, or grilled spiced pineapple with rose-petal ice cream. Wines start at £19, or £5 a glass.

**Chef/s:** Alfred Prasad. **Open:** Sun to Fri L 12 to 2.30, all week D 5.30 to 11 (6 to 10.30 Sun). **Meals:** alc (main courses £16 to £25). Set L £19.95 (2 courses) to £24.95. Set D £28 (2 courses) to £37. **Service:** 12.5% (optional). **Details:** Cards accepted. 90 seats. Air-con. Music. Children allowed.

**NEW ENTRY**
## Terroirs
**Easy-on-the-pocket crowd-pleaser**
5 William IV Street, Covent Garden, WC2N 4DW
Tel no: (020) 7036 0660
www.terroirswinebar.com
⊖ Charing Cross, map 5
French | £25
**Cooking score: 3**

 £30

Good places to eat in the area around Charing Cross are thin on the ground so it's no surprise that this Gallic wine bar has proved popular – 'a real swerve to the cooking', fantastic wines, and prices 'attuned to a depressed economy', have all proved a great lure. The menu is neatly divided into bar snacks (try the duck scratchings), charcuterie, generous small plates of plump, garlicky snails with bacon, potted brown shrimps or piperade basquaise, plus plats du jour along the lines of bavette with shallots and red wine, and French cheeses or crêpes with salted butter caramel to finish. There's a great buzz to the split-level room, so it's a shame that the rather too easy-going service wilts under pressure. Wines are sourced with an eager eye for provenance with plenty of organic and biodynamic names on show. Prices (from £13.95) are eminently fair and attractive.

**Chef/s:** Ed Wilson. **Open:** Mon to Sat L 12 to 3, D 5.45 to 11. **Closed:** Sun, bank hols. **Meals:** alc (main courses £12 to £14). **Service:** 12.5% (optional). **Details:** Cards accepted. 75 seats. Air-con. Separate bar. Wheelchair access. Music. Children allowed.

# Texture

**Dynamic dining from young guns**
34 Portman Street, Marble Arch, W1H 7BY
Tel no: (020) 7224 0028
www.texture-restaurant.co.uk
⊖ Marble Arch, map 4
Modern European | £40
Cooking score: 4

Texture's young owners are smooth operators. They met at Le Manoir aux Quat' Saisons (see entry), and their high-pedigree backgrounds have served them well: sommelier Xavier Rousset oversees front-of-house with panache and Agnar Sverrisson heads up an inspired kitchen where his Icelandic roots shine through. Bold, clean flavours punctuate dishes in which a lack of cream and butter give a light touch, and Sverrisson adds playful flourishes – witness bacon popcorn served with drinks in the Champagne bar. To start, delicate Cornish crab is harmoniously accompanied by cucumber, beetroot and rye bread, and – for main course – buttery Faroe Island cod is teamed with wholesome barley risotto, juicy crayfish tails and Sauternes sauce. Skyr (Icelandic yoghurt) forms the basis of at least one dessert, including a delightful sorbet with poached rhubarb. Vivid Scandinavian art brightens up the grand dining room in which Rousset leads a charming team of staff; he also gives intelligent advice on the French-dominated wine list (bottles from £19.50).
**Chef/s:** Agnar Sverrisson. **Open:** Tue to Sat L 12 to 2.30, D 6.30 to 11. **Closed:** Sun, Mon, 2 weeks Aug, 2 weeks Christmas (excluding New Year's Eve).
**Meals:** alc (main courses £20 to £28). Set L £18.50 (2 courses) to £22. Set D £29.50. Tasting menu £59 (7 courses). **Service:** 12.5% (optional).
**Details:** Cards accepted. 54 seats. Air-con. Separate bar. Wheelchair access. Music. Children allowed. Car parking.

# Theo Randall at the InterContinental

**Gutsy, alluring Italian flavours**
InterContinental London Hotel, 1 Hamilton Place, Mayfair, W1J 7QY
Tel no: (020) 7318 8747
www.theorandall.com
⊖ Hyde Park Corner, map 4
Italian | £45
Cooking score: 6

The über-rich setting of Park Lane's InterContinental Hotel might seem far removed from the rustic byways of Italian regional cooking, but its reinvented restaurant now bridges the gap with marble tiles, a pistachio and brown colour scheme and a wood-fired oven in the open kitchen. For many years chef Theo Randall was the unsung hero of the River Café (see entry) and he's lost none of his instinct for mainline, ingredients-led cooking – those who track down this rather unexpected venue are in for a real treat. His food goes straight to the gutsy heart of things, with bold, alluring flavours and the stamp of earthy authenticity on every plate. Chargrilled Limousin veal chops with seasonal accompaniments (perhaps chanterelles and trompette mushrooms, spinach and salsa verde) are the succulent stars of the show, closely followed by wood-roasted fish – say, turbot on the bone with capers, parsley, Roman artichokes and Swiss chard. Pasta is also a surefire success, whether it's pappardelle with a ragù of slow-cooked beef in Chianti or green ravioli 'de erbette' with rocket, sheep's ricotta and sage. Blood orange sorbet is a cleansing dessert, if the soft chocolate cake with mascarpone cream sounds too calorific. Set lunches and supper menus are great value, and the lengthy global wine list has strong Italian leanings. House selections start at £20.
**Chef/s:** Theo Randall. **Open:** Mon to Fri L 12 to 3, Mon to Sat D 5.45 to 11.15. **Closed:** Sun, 12 days Jan.
**Meals:** alc (main courses £20 to £32). Set L and D £21 (2 courses) to £25. **Service:** 12.5% (optional).

**Details:** Cards accepted. 124 seats. Air-con. Separate bar. Wheelchair access. Music. Children allowed. Car parking.

**NEW ENTRY**
## Tierra Brindisa
**A true taste of Spain**
46 Broadwick Street, Soho, W1F 7AF
Tel no: (020) 7534 1690
www.tierrabrindisa.com
⊖ Oxford Circus, map 5
Spanish | £22
Cooking score: 3

When Spanish produce supplier Brindisa opened Tapas Brindisa (see entry) it earned a reputation for running one of the most authentic Spanish venues in town. This Soho offshoot is no different. There's a stab at interior design with a 'garish' green-and-white tiled dining room (with rather cramped tables) and a lovely light bar area next to the open kitchen. On the food front things kick off simply, with a plate of Joselito ham before going on to other staples of the tapas repertoire such as lamb cutlets served with a good romesco sauce. More unusual is lentil stew with soft Tiétar goats' curd or quails in escabèche. Iberian cheeses make a fine alternative to desserts such as pears in Rioja. House Spanish from £14.50.
**Chef/s:** Jose Pizarro. **Open:** Mon to Sat 12 to 11. **Closed:** Sun, 25 and 26 Dec, 2 weeks Aug, bank hols. **Meals:** alc (main courses £4 to £16). Set menus £25 to £35. **Service:** 12.5% (optional). **Details:** Cards accepted. 50 seats. 4 seats outside. Air-con. Wheelchair access. Music. Children allowed.

**Michel Roux Jnr** Le Gavroche

**Who or what inspired you to become a chef?**
Father and uncle.

**If you hadn't become a chef, what would you have been?**
I would have done anything as long as it was in the catering industry. It's my life and I love it.

**What is the best meal you have ever eaten?**
Salt beef on rye after a freezing cold New York marathon.

**What is your favourite restaurant and why?**
Too many to list, but Zuma London is great for a family get together.

**If you were to have one abiding principle in the kitchen, what would it be?**
Taste before presentation.

**What do you do to relax when out of the kitchen?**
Run marathons and follow Man United home and away and in Europe.

**What is your top culinary tip?**
Foams are pointless.

**NEW ENTRY**

## Trishna

**Indian seafood star**
15-17 Blandford Street, Marylebone, W1U 3DG
Tel no: (020) 7935 5624
www.trishnalondon.com
⊖ Marylebone, Bond Street, map 4
Indian/Seafood | £28
Cooking score: 3

V

The sleek new arrival in Marylebone – all painted brick walls and cool colours – is the London sister of an iconic Mumbai seafood restaurant. They share the same coastal spicing ('a little restrained', according to one inspector), but here it is married with excellent, mainly British, seafood in dishes like hariyali bream with coconut and coriander, mussels in coconut turmeric masala and (less successfully) Cornish crab with butter and garlic. One is encouraged to share from a menu with sections of pakora, chargrills and 'Trishna dishes', plus bread, rice and vegetables. Dessert might be carrot halva or mango rice pudding. Indian house wine is £17.50.
**Chef/s:** Ravi Deulkar. **Open:** all week 12 to 10.30 (10 Sun). **Closed:** 25 to 29 Dec. **Meals:** alc (main courses £12 to £25). Set L £19.50 to £21.50. Set D £19.50 (2 courses) to £25. **Service:** 12.5% (optional). **Details:** Cards accepted. 62 seats. 12 seats outside. Air-con. Music. Children allowed.

## ALSO RECOMMENDED

### ▲ La Trouvaille

12a Newburgh Street, Soho, W1F 7RR
Tel no: (020) 7287 8488
www.latrouvaille.co.uk
⊖ Oxford Circus, map 5
French

A dish of snails, cured ham and preserved tomato quenelles with lettuce coulis is typical of the unorthodox food served in this quirky bistro/wine bar close to Carnaby Street. The kitchen also scours the French byways for the likes of veal cutlet with Swiss chard gratin, cassava chips and morels, and dreams up some snappy desserts including pain perdu with maple syrup and 'milk jam' ice cream. Two-course lunch is £16.50, dinner £29. 'Eclectic' and biodynamic French regional wines from £17. Open Mon to Fri L, Tue to Sat D.

## Umu

**Gilt-edged Kyoto cuisine**
14-16 Bruton Place, Mayfair, W1J 6LX
Tel no: (020) 7499 8881
www.umurestaurant.com
⊖ Green Park, Bond Street, map 5
Japanese | £50
Cooking score: 5

V

When it opened in 2004, Umu brought the 'haute cuisine' multi-course kaiseki dining of Kyoto, the ancient Japanese capital, to the UK. The restaurant's interior is a modern interpretation of a traditional kaiseki house, with dark woods and Venetian mirrors creating a subdued, soothing feel. Ichiro Kubota, the son of a master-chef, learned his craft in Japan and practised in France before arriving here. A plethora of set menus allows you to set your budget, if budget is quite the word (they rise to £135), and the array of tastes, textures and seasonings is fascinating. One dish might combine Savoy cabbage, crab, foie gras, girolles and wasabi, while umami, the Japanese taste element best described as a kind of concentrated savouriness, is abundant in dishes that partner monkfish with shiitake mushrooms, the famous Wagyu beef with blackberries and foie gras, and even the single sushi items, such as red mullet with pesto and dried grey mullet roe. Desserts also bridge the cultural divide, with chocolate fondant and white miso ice cream. Sakés of all descriptions, from sweet to dry to sparkling and including vintage versions going back to 1975, are the main draw on the drinks list. The wines feature torrents of claret and Burgundy to go at. Prices start at £24 and rocket upwards.
**Chef/s:** Ichiro Kubota. **Open:** Mon to Fri L 12 to 2.30, Mon to Sat D 6 to 11. **Closed:** Sun, 24 Dec to early Jan. **Meals:** alc (main courses £10 to £55). Set L from £21. Kaiseki tasting menu from £65.

Service: 12.5% (optional). Details: Cards accepted. 67 seats. Air-con. No mobile phones. Wheelchair access. Music. Children allowed.

## ALSO RECOMMENDED

### ▲ Vasco & Piero's Pavilion

15 Poland Street, Soho, W1F 8QE
Tel no: (020) 7437 8774
www.vascosfood.com
⊖ Oxford Circus, map 5
Italian

Stars of stage, screen and politics have been flocking to this Soho local for years, enjoying the elegant tone of the dining room and the lively cooking of central Italy's Umbria region. Fixed-price menus are £19.50 for two courses for early-evening diners, £31.50 for three courses for those with more time. Start with roast Umbrian ham, rocket, radicchio and Parmesan, and go on to sautéed squid with cannellini beans, garlic and chilli, or roast duck with wild fennel and cabbage. Italian dolci include limoncello mousse. Wines from £17.50. Closed Sat L and Sun.

### ▲ Veeraswamy

Victory House, 99-101 Regent Street, Piccadilly, W1B 4RS
Tel no: (020) 7734 1401
www.veeraswamy.com
⊖ Piccadilly Circus, map 5
Indian

Established in the 1920s, Veeraswamy was the first Indian restaurant in Britain, and it has been beguiling diners in the very heart of London ever since. Amid an ambience fit for a Mughal prince, with a silver ceiling and gold-speckled floor, some out-of-the-ordinary cooking is on show. Mussels in coconut and ginger sauce (£8.25), or skewered flash-grilled oysters are possible starters, with the likes of tandoori-cooked lamb shank (£21.50) following on. Indian dessert delicacies include kheer – rice pudding with a grilled plum (£7.50). Wines from £5.50 a glass. Open all week.

## The White Swan

**Latest star in a gastropub galaxy**
108 Fetter Lane, Holborn, EC4A 1ES
Tel no: (020) 7242 9696
www.thewhiteswanlondon.com
⊖ Chancery Lane, map 5
Gastropub | £30
Cooking score: 3

The Fetter Lane branch of Tom and Ed Martin's expanding gastropub galaxy is a narrow building comprising a lively, pubby ground-floor bar, mezzanine level and a smart upstairs dining room which features a mirrored ceiling, crisp-clothed tables and plenty of wood. There has been another change of chef since the last edition of the *Guide*, but the kitchen continues to take a modern British approach: a straightforward carte offers the likes of smoked monkfish cheeks with a well-flavoured bacon and kale broth, and saddle of Blackface lamb with broad bean and morel fricassee and mille-feuille potato. A lemon curd tart might come with raspberries and elderflower sorbet, and cheese is taken seriously. House wine is £15.

**Chef/s:** Lee Coulson. **Open:** Mon to Fri L 12 to 3, D 6 to 10. **Closed:** Sat, Sun, 25 and 26 Dec, bank hols. **Meals:** alc (main courses £10 to £18). Set L £24 (2 courses) to £29. **Service:** 12.5% (optional). **Details:** Cards accepted. 52 seats. Air-con. Separate bar. Music. Children allowed.

## Wild Honey

**Affordable, unpretentious, intelligent food**
12 St George Street, Mayfair, W1S 2FB
Tel no: (020) 7758 9160
www.wildhoneyrestaurant.co.uk
⊖ Bond Street, Oxford Circus, map 5
Modern European | £33
Cooking score: 6

Like its elder sibling Arbutus (see entry), Wild Honey is in the front line of British gastonomy's new order and is driven by the same guiding principles. 'Fine food at affordable prices' neatly sums up its intentions, and the setting for this disarmingly simple cooking is a high-ceilinged, clubby room with swathes of oak panelling, an ornate mirrored mantelpiece and polished floors offset by contemporary artwork. The menu changes daily and the kitchen mines a rich vein, allowing ingredients (lordly or otherwise) to bask in the limelight. Above all, Wild Honey's food is confident, intelligent and skilfully crafted stuff, where full-blooded flavours matter more than chi-chi assemblages. Warm beetroot tart with smoked eel and horseradish is a pitch-perfect starter, the 'plat du jour' might be pot-au-feu, and main courses bring on authentic Marseilles bouillabaisse as well as roast haunch of venison with Jerusalem artichokes and curly kale or sea bass with leeks and preserved lemon. To finish, it has to be wild honey ice cream with crushed honeycomb, unless you fancy spiced pannacotta with poached pear or the pungently ripe cheeseboard. Just about everything on the carefully assembled wine list is available by the carafe. Bottle prices (from £14.50) are eminently fair.

**Chef/s:** Colin Kelly. **Open:** all week L 12 to 2.30 (3 Sun), D 6 to 11 (11.30 Sat, 10.30 Sun). **Closed:** 25 and 26 Dec, 1 Jan. **Meals:** alc (main courses £15 to £19). Set L £16.95 (3 courses), pre-theatre D (6 to 7) £18.95. **Service:** 12.5% (optional). **Details:** Cards accepted. 64 seats. Air-con. No music. Children allowed.

## Wiltons

**Old-school British aristocrat**
55 Jermyn Street, Mayfair, SW1Y 6LX
Tel no: (020) 7629 9955
www.wiltons.co.uk
⊖ Green Park, map 5
British | £50
Cooking score: 4

Wiltons' heart has belonged to the blue-blooded streets of St James's ever since its early years as a shellfish stall, and it has always attracted famous faces: Winston Churchill once dined here, now it's home to Hugh Grant and his peers. Like an impeccably groomed gentlemen's club, it's swish, archaic and revered as a classic of the old school – right down to the uniformed doorman and 'jacket

and tie' policy. This is the place to come if your fancy turns to dressed crab, baked Dover sole 'Silver Jubilee', poached haddock Monte Carlo or even something like teal with artichoke and truffle sauce. The old-faithful mix of grills, crustacea and nostalgia-inducing dishes is crowned by angels on horseback and other silver-plated English savouries, but – if pudding is required – the kitchen can also oblige with apple and plum crumble or sherry trifle. The patrician wine list is stuffed with pedigree clarets and Burgundies dating back to the golden years; prices from £34.

**Chef/s:** Jerome Ponchelle. **Open:** Mon to Fri L 12 to 2.30, D 6 to 10.30. **Closed:** Sat, Sun, Christmas, New Year, bank hols. **Meals:** alc (main courses £18 to £60). Set L £45 with wine. Tasting D £80 (8 courses) to £150 (8 courses with wine). **Service:** 12.5% (optional). **Details:** Cards accepted. 100 seats. Air-con. No music. No mobile phones. Wheelchair access. Children allowed.

## The Wolseley

**Splendid all-day dining haven**
160 Piccadilly, Mayfair, W1J 9EB
Tel no: (020) 7499 6996
www.thewolseley.com
⊖ Green Park, map 5
Modern European | £40
Cooking score: 2

Conceived in the grand café style, the Wolseley is both useful and beautiful. The converted bank is 'really splendid', lending a sense of occasion to coffee and cake (try the sachertorte). Its 'glamorous atmosphere' is 'even welcoming to the style-deficient'. The all-day menu accommodates all appetites and budgets, running from croque-monsieur or Hungarian goulash to crustacea and caviar. The wine list, from £18, isn't quite so all-encompassing but makes up for it with its ample by the glass selection. 'Superb quality' afternoon teas beat many a nearby hotel on price and portion size. Getting in can be a headache, so plan ahead.

**Chef/s:** Julian O'Neill. **Open:** all week 7am to midnight (8am to midnight Sat, 8am to 11pm Sun). **Closed:** 25 and 26 Dec, 1 Jan, August bank hol.

**Meals:** alc (main courses £10 to £29). **Service:** 12.5% (optional). **Details:** Cards accepted. 150 seats. Air-con. Separate bar. No music. Wheelchair access. Children allowed.

## Yauatcha

**Dazzling dim sum**
15 Broadwick Street, Soho, W1F 0DL
Tel no: (020) 7494 8888
www.yauatcha.com
⊖ Tottenham Court Road, map 5
Chinese | £35
Cooking score: 4

**V**

A sexy, drop-dead cool amalgam of tea house, all-day dim sum joint and slinky night-time restaurant, Yauatcha spreads itself over two floors: a boisterous café-style room behind opaque blue-frosted windows at street level and a formal, softly lit basement that mirrors its elder sibling Hakkasan (see entry). The dazzling dim sum menu moves quickly from re-worked versions of Chinatown staples into the esoteric world of steamed scallop and kumquat dumplings, spinach cubes with prawn and water chestnut, or duck and shiitake rolls. Larger plates also set out to impress: fried sea bass with green mango and sweet chilli dressing, black pepper ostrich or jasmine tea-smoked organic pork ribs, say. To finish, exquisite patisserie and desserts jet from exotic macaroons or strawberry and mint tart to matcha shortbread with yuzu cream, green tea marshmallow and green tea chocolate. Snazzy smoothies and cocktails are the in-vogue tipples of choice, although the heady tea list should keep aficionados enthralled for hours. Trendy, cosmopolitan wines start at £24.

**Chef/s:** Soon Wah Cheong. **Open:** all week 12 to 11.30 ( 10.30 Sun). **Closed:** 24 and 25 Dec. **Meals:** alc (£4 to £38). Set L and D £40 (3 courses). **Service:** 12.5% (optional). **Details:** Cards accepted. 170 seats. Air-con. Wheelchair access. Music. Children allowed.

## Zafferano

**Upscale Italian that consistently delivers**
15 Lowndes Street, Belgravia, SW1X 9EY
Tel no: (020) 7235 5800
www.zafferanorestaurant.com
⊖ Knightsbridge, Hyde Park Corner, map 4
Italian | £45
Cooking score: 6

Few upscale Italian restaurants in the capital deliver as consistently as Zafferano – a loyal Knightsbridge servant for many a year and still highly valued for its all-round excellence. It may strike a rather discreet and serious pose, although the interior now has lighter tones and an easier ambience. Zafferano's real trump card is its dedication to superb ingredients of unimpeachable quality, and it shows particularly in star-turn pasta dishes from its seasonal repertoire: maltagliati with saffron and braised pig's cheeks or pappardelle with broad beans and rocket, for example. Salads are also pitch-perfect – try the cured tuna with orange and fennel. Seafood waxes strongly when it comes to main courses (basil-crusted plaice with potatoes and tomatoes, say); otherwise enjoy the meaty delights of calf's liver with white asparagus and Marsala sauce. Truffles have their say in season, and exemplary tiramisu holds court when it comes to desserts. Of course this is SW1, and Italian food never comes cheap in these parts, which is fine when service is as smooth and charming as can be, but grates a little when there's no greeting on arrival and no drinks offered while waiting (has happened to an inspector). Tuscany is a big player on the regional Italian wine list, although the bidding starts with a Sicilian Inziola at £22; better deals lurk further up the scale.

**Chef/s:** Andrew Needham. **Open:** all week L 12 to 2.30 (3 Sat and Sun), D 7 to 11 (10.30 Sun). **Closed:** 25 and 26 Dec. **Meals:** Set L £29.50 (2 courses) to £34.50. Set D £34.50 (2 courses) to £44.50. **Service:** 13.5%. **Details:** Cards accepted. 100 seats. Air-con. Separate bar. Wheelchair access. Music. Children allowed.

## L'Absinthe

**Gallic neighbourhood bonhomie**
40 Chalcot Road, Primrose Hill, NW1 8LS
Tel no: (020) 7483 4848
www.labsinthe.co.uk
⊖ Chalk Farm, map 2
French | £22
Cooking score: 3

There's a feeling of Gallic neighbourhood bonhomie about Jean-Christophe Slowik's dyed-in-the-wool bourgeois bistro, and it chimes agreeably with the locals in this part of Primrose Hill. The mood is casual, décor is functional (think candles on bare tables), prices are refreshing and the food is unashamedly traditional. Come here for leeks vinaigrette with poached egg, well-rendered ribeye steak frites, confit duck with braised Savoy cabbage, or something from the specials board – say grilled tuna with ratatouille and sauce vierge. To finish, it has to be absinthe crème brûlée – unless you fancy tarte Tatin or a shot from the Colonel (lemon sorbet and vodka). L'Absinthe also operates as a wine business, and everything on the all-French list is generously offered at retail price (from £6.50) – plus corkage (from £6).
**Chef/s:** Christophe Fabre. **Open:** Tue to Sun L 12 to 2.30 (4 Sat and Sun), D 6 to 10.30 (9.30 Sun). **Closed:** Mon. **Meals:** alc (main courses £9 to £16). Set L Tue to Sat £8.50 (2 courses). Sun L £14.95 (2 courses) to £18.50. **Service:** 12.5% (optional). **Details:** Cards accepted. 60 seats. 14 seats outside. Air-con. Wheelchair access. Music. Children allowed.

### Please send us your feedback

To register your opinion about any restaurant listed in the Guide, or a new restaurant that you wish to bring to our attention, please visit the web address at the bottom of the page. Your feedback informs the content of the book and will be used to compile next year's reviews.

## Acorn House

**Green is good**
69 Swinton Street, King's Cross, WC1X 9NT
Tel no: (020) 7812 1842
www.acornhouserestaurant.com
⊖ King's Cross, map 2
Modern British | £28
Cooking score: 2

V

Acorn House trumpets its green message almost within earshot of the St Pancras Eurostar terminal: 'environment, community, training, health' is its upbeat mantra and the whole place is driven by a crusading, eco-friendly ethos and seasonally attuned cooking. The flavours of winter, for example, might extend to pan-fried mackerel with pickled red cabbage and walnuts, twice-cooked pork belly with Madeira, or beetroot tagliatelle with blue cheese and horseradish, followed by 'sweet stuff' such as toffee pannacotta with pear. Boxes of produce surround the crowds seated on apple-green chairs, although the daytime mood of boisterous canteen camaraderie is replaced by salubrious low-lit intimacy come evening. House wine is £16.
**Chef/s:** Arthur Potts Dawson. **Open:** Mon to Fri L 12 to 3, Mon to Sat D 6 to 10. **Closed:** Sun, bank hols, Christmas, New Year. **Meals:** alc (main courses £12 to £18). **Service:** 12.5% (optional). **Details:** Cards accepted. 66 seats. Air-con. Wheelchair access. Music. Children allowed.

**NEW ENTRY**
## The Albion

**Irish flavours in Islington**
10 Thornhill Road, Islington, N1 1HW
Tel no: (020) 7607 7450
www.the-albion.co.uk
⊖ Angel, Highbury and Islington, map 2
Gastropub | £28
Cooking score: 3

Surrounded by upmarket Georgian houses, this recent arrival from Richard Turner has a suitably eighteenth-century feel, with candles and chandeliers casting a dim glow over an uncluttered and tasteful interior of soft blue and stripped wood. Equally smart are dishes like salted mallard with cranberry sauce, pork belly and caper terrine, and Arbroath fishcakes with bacon, duck egg and sweet pea sauce. But dig a little deeper, into Irish stew and roast beef marrow with caper gravy, and you'll find the same rustic Anglo-Irish cooking that helped chef Liam Kirwan put his previous venture, the Sand's End (see entry), on the culinary map. For a party of 10, you can go the whole hog and order a roast suckling pig. House wine is £14.

**Chef/s:** Liam Kirwan. **Open:** all week L 12 to 3 (10 to 4 Sat and Sun), D 6 to 10. **Meals:** alc (main courses £11 to £18). Set L £12.50 (2 courses) to £15. **Service:** 10% (optional). **Details:** Cards accepted. 94 seats. 108 seats outside. Wheelchair access. Music. Children allowed.

## Almeida
**Sleek Islington performer**
30 Almeida Street, Islington, N1 1AD
Tel no: (020) 7354 4777
www.danddlondon.com
⊖ Angel, Highbury & Islington, map 2
Modern French | £30
**Cooking score: 4**
🍷 V

Almeida is a boon for cast and audience alike as it stands directly opposite the renowned Islington theatre of the same name. It's a smart-casual kind of place with a sleek, elegant look, vivid modern art on the walls and a menu that adds some Mediterranean vibrancy to the core French repertoire. Asparagus velouté with a soft poached egg and grilled ribeye with béarnaise sauce represent the old guard, while carpaccio of yellowfin tuna and scallops with marinated cucumber and citrus dressing strikes a contemporary note. To finish, glazed passion fruit tart with yoghurt sorbet is typical of the patisserie on offer. You can also enjoy all-day nibbles and 'petits plats' in the bar, along with many wines by the glass or 'pot lyonnais'. The full list is a weighty, French-centred march-past, with regional bottles from the south-west making

the most telling impression. Top-flight South Africans and Italians are also worth a punt. Prices start at £16 (£4 a glass).

**Chef/s:** Alan Jones. **Open:** Tue to Sun L 12 to 3 (4 Sun), Mon to Sat D 5.30 to 10.30. **Closed:** 26 to 28 Dec, 1 Jan. **Meals:** Set L and theatre menu £14.50 (2 courses) to £17.50. Set D £24.50 (2 courses) to £29.50. Sun L £24.50. **Service:** 12.5% (optional). **Details:** Cards accepted. 88 seats. 10 seats outside. Air-con. Separate bar. No music. Wheelchair access. Children allowed.

## ALSO RECOMMENDED

### ▲ Il Bacio
178-184 Blackstock Road, Highbury, N5 1HA
Tel no: (020) 7226 3339
www.ilbaciohighbury.co.uk
⊖ Arsenal, map 2
Italian

This glass-fronted Sardinian restaurant and pizzeria draws a lively local crowd. Pizzas themselves are several steps up from what's offered in the chains – try a saporita, with Gorgonzola and bresaola (£8) – but it's the speciali della Sardegna that attract the eye, with their useful introduction to the island's cuisine. Malloreddus pasta with Sardinian sausage, garlic, tomato and chilli (£8.95) might be followed by sea bass baked in foil with clams, cherry tomatoes and white wine (£12.95). House wines are £10.95. Open all week D, Sat and Sun L.

## Bradleys
**Bright and breezy**
25 Winchester Road, Swiss Cottage, NW3 3NR
Tel no: (020) 7722 3457
www.bradleysnw3.co.uk
⊖ Swiss Cottage, map 2
French | £30
**Cooking score: 3**
£5 OFF 🍷

The setting is as pastoral as it is possible for a London restaurant to be – the dining room, with soft pastels and fresh flowers, overlooks a courtyard garden. The culinary accent is breezy modern French – starters such as fish

bourride with fennel precede mains that go to town with the likes of haunch of venison in sauce poivrade with celeriac purée and beetroot confit. The precision and careful judgement are what impress, and when you can finish with something like a perfect chocolate fondant with Seville orange ice cream, happiness is complete. A quality-driven wine list (from £14.50) doesn't just linger in France, but pulls in distinguished bottles from all over, grouping them by style. Close to Hampstead Theatre.
**Chef/s:** Simon Bradley. **Open:** all week L 12 to 3, Mon to Sat D 6 to 11. **Meals:** alc (main courses £14 to £18). Set L £12.50 (2 courses) to £16.50. Set D £22.50. Sun L £22.50 (2 courses) to £26.50. **Service:** 12.5% (optional). **Details:** Cards accepted. 60 seats. Air-con. No music. No mobile phones. Wheelchair access. Children allowed.

## READERS RECOMMEND

### The Bull & Last
**Gastropub**
168 Highgate Road, Hampstead, NW5 1QS
Tel no: (020) 7267 3641
www.thebullandlast.co.uk
'Well worth a visit'

### The Bull
**Relaxed, stylish pub dining**
13 North Hill, Highgate, N6 4AB
Tel no: (0845) 456 5033
www.inthebull.biz
⊖ Highgate, map 2
Gastropub | £25
Cooking score: 1

Perched atop Highgate Hill, this boutique gastropub is less leisurely pints and more fine dining, although there's a terrace for summer drinking and it's not overly formal. On inspection, broad bean, pea and pancetta risotto wasn't greater than the sum of its parts, although braised ox cheeks with pearl barley in a rich, dark jus was more successful. The all-budgets, global wine list (from £15) also gets the thumbs-up, and lots of staff ensure attentive service.

**Chef/s:** Paul Rice. **Open:** Tue to Sun L 12 to 2.30 (4 Sat, 4.30 Sun), D 6 to 10.30 (6.30 to 9.30 Sun). **Meals:** alc (main courses £10 to £18). Set L £12.95 (2 courses) to £14.95. **Service:** not inc. **Details:** Cards accepted. 150 seats. 60 seats outside. Air-con. Separate bar. Wheelchair access. Music. Children allowed. Car parking.

## Café Japan
**Super-sushi**
626 Finchley Road, Golders Green, NW11 7RR
Tel no: (020) 8455 6854
www.cafejapan.co.uk
⊖ Golders Green, map 1
Japanese | £25
Cooking score: 3

A chorus of 'irashaimasei' ('welcome' in Japanese) from hospitable staff greets visitors to Café Japan. Spartan blond wood furnishings aren't eye-catching, but the array of top-class sushi certainly is: silky slices of yellowtail, sea bream and scallop sit together on supremely fresh sashimi platters, sushi rolls encase the likes of lightly battered soft-shell crab, asparagus and omelette, while generous hunks of grilled salmon, butterfish or mackerel come lacquered with teriyaki sauce. Enticing daily specials are also offered. With all the food so good you might be tempted to keep on ordering, watch out as prices do add up. Bento boxes (from £12) help keep bills in check, while green tea, saké and wine (from £12 a bottle) provide adequate liquid refreshment. Cash only at lunchtime.
**Chef/s:** Masaki Anayama. **Open:** Wed to Sun L 12 to 2, D 6 to 10 (9.30 Sun). **Closed:** Mon, Tue, 25 and 26 Dec. **Meals:** alc (main courses £12 to £20). Set L £7.50 (2 courses). Set D £12 (2 courses). **Service:** not inc. **Details:** Cards accepted. 37 seats. Air-con. No mobile phones. Music. Children allowed.

## Average price

The average price listed in main-entry reviews denotes the price of a three-course meal, without wine.

## ALSO RECOMMENDED

### ▲ Chilli Cool

15 Leigh Street, King's Cross, WC1H 9EW
Tel no: (020) 7383 3135
www.chillicool.com
⊖ Russell Square, King's Cross, map 2
Chinese

Cheerful, modestly appointed Bloomsbury address that delivers better-than-usual Szechuan food. It is the heat of the spicing that gives the cooking its impact, from ma po tofu (£6.80) and aubergine in yellow bean sauce, to a generous (enough for three) hotpot of fish with fresh chilli (£15.80). As always with Chinese cooking, pork figures enterprisingly: hot-and-spicy pigs' feet, slices of ear in sesame oil, but there's also steamed sliced pork with rice powder. House wine £10. Open all week.

**NEW ENTRY**

## The Drapers Arms

Easy food with flair
44 Barnsbury Street, Islington, N1 1ER
Tel no: (020) 7619 0348
www.thedrapersarms.com
⊖ Highbury & Islington, Angel, map 2
Gastropub | £25
Cooking score: 3

 £30

Expectations have been running unusually high for this new gastropub in affluent, leafy Islington. Why? Because Ben Maschler (his mother Fay is one of London's most revered restaurant critics) is a partner. Inside it's colourful, spacious and uncluttered, but on a balmy summer's evening the garden is the place to be. The short, modern British menu feels easy and shows flair – whether potted pork with spicy pickles or half a native lobster with rough-cut herb and potato salad. Plenty of sharing options for two to four people, like a whole shoulder of lamb with fennel and aïoli are also appreciated, and it's all pleasantly family-friendly. Service could be sharper, but no doubt this will come with time. House wine is £13.50.

Chef/s: Karl Goward. Open: all week L 12.30 to 3 (3.30 Sat, 12 to 4 Sun), D 6.30 to 10.30 (10 Sun). Meals: alc (main courses £9 to £16). Service: 12.5% (optional). Details: Cards accepted. 115 seats. 40 seats outside. Music. Children allowed.

## READERS RECOMMEND

### The Elk in the Woods

British
39 Camden Passage, Islington, N1 8EA
Tel no: (020) 7226 3535
www.the-elk-in-the-woods.co.uk
'Wonderfully warm atmosphere...small but perfectly formed menu'

### Eriki

Indian
4-6 Northways Parade, Finchley Road, Swiss Cottage, NW3 5EN
Tel no: (020) 7722 0606
www.eriki.co.uk
'Most adventurous and creative Indian restaurant I've been to'

**NEW ENTRY**

## 500 Italian Restaurant

Affordable gem of a trattoria
782 Holloway Road, Archway, N19 3JH
Tel no: (020) 7272 3406
www.500restaurant.co.uk
⊖ Archway, map 2
Italian | £30
Cooking score: 2

The name reflects the owners' affection for the iconic car. Apart from this quirky touch, the restaurant seems unassuming – the dining room is understated, with a flourish of pale wood accented by blue-grey walls. But when it comes to the cooking, 500 Cinquecento punches above its weight – even breads are made on the premises. At inspection, gnocchi with ragù of Italian sausage was spot-on, followed by glistening pan-fried fillets of sea bass, paired with a zippy salad of shiitake mushrooms, pea shoots and grapes. For dessert, apple and almond tart was winning in its simplicity. You can also drink affordably from the wine list, starting from £12.50 (glasses from £2.05). Generosity pervades the place, making it an affordable little gem. **Chef/s:** Mario Magli. **Open:** Tue to Sat L 12 to 3, Tue to Sun D 5.30 to 10. **Closed:** Mon, 10 days Christmas. **Meals:** alc (main courses £12 to £13). **Service:** not inc. **Details:** Cards accepted. 35 seats. Wheelchair access. Music. Children allowed.

## READERS RECOMMEND
### The Horseshoe
Gastropub
28 Heath Street, Hampstead, NW3 6TE
Tel no: (020) 7431 7206
**'Delicious, beautifully presented British gastropub grub, with microbrewery onsite'**

## ALSO RECOMMENDED
### ▲ Istanbul Iskembecisi
9 Stoke Newington Road, Stoke Newington, N16 8BH
Tel no: (020) 7254 7291
www.istanbuliskembecisi.co.uk
⊖ Dalston, map 2
Turkish

Worth a try for its 'delicious, reasonably priced Turkish cuisine', this simply decorated restaurant majors in kebabs, grills and traditional dishes such as hummus (£3), falafel (£8) and moussaka (£9). There is a decent selection of meat-free options and a short list of fish dishes such as traditionally prepared grilled sea bass with salad and chips (£11). A selection of flexible set menus start at £11.50 for two courses. The short wine list kicks off at £10. Open all week.

**NEW ENTRY**
## Jinkichi
**Sociable sushi and specials**
73 Heath Street, Hampstead, NW3 6UG
Tel no: (020) 7794 6158
www.jinkichi.com
⊖ Hampstead, map 1
Japanese | £25
Cooking score: 1

 V £30

It's a marvel that this cramped, no-frills space produces such a broad menu. The sociable atmosphere can be a draw and people drop in for the good sushi and yakitori. Look to the specials for creativity, such as sashimi of turbot fin muscle with ponzu. Kaki-age, a tempura of diced prawns and vegetables, is a winning mix. Finish with chestnut ice cream. Wines and sakés start from £16. **Chef/s:** Atsushi Matsumoto. **Open:** Sat and Sun L 12.30 to 2, Tue to Sun D 6 to 11 (10 Sun). **Closed:** Mon, bank hols, Christmas and New Year. **Meals:** alc (main courses £7 to £17). Set menu £8.80 to £15.90. **Service:** 10%. **Details:** Cards accepted. 44 seats. Air-con. Music. Children allowed.

## ALSO RECOMMENDED
### ▲ Khoai Café
6 Topsfield Parade, Middle Lane, Crouch End, N8 8PR
Tel no: (020) 8341 2120
⊖ Finsbury Park, map 2
Vietnamese

A hit with Crouch End families in search of cheap-and-cheerful Vietnamese food without frills. There's not much décor, but the food makes amends with its freshness, punch and fragrance. Pho and other flavour-packed noodle soups (from £5.45) are the stars, although the kitchen also delivers decent appetisers including banh xeo (savoury stuffed pancakes, £6.45) plus big dishes such as caramelised braised basa fish (£7.50). Drink tea, Vietnamese beer or house wine (£9.95). Open all week. A second branch is 362 Ballards Lane, Finchley, N12 0EE, tel no: (020) 8445 2039.

## Konstam at the Prince Albert

Local hero
2 Acton Street, King's Cross, WC1X 9NA
Tel no: (020) 7833 5040
www.konstam.co.uk
⊖ King's Cross, map 2
Modern British | £35
Cooking score: 3

Although serving 'locally sourced' and 'seasonal' produce is something of a mantra for many restaurants, Konstam can claim to test this ethos to its limits. Oliver Rowe tries to build his menu from produce found within the M25, a challenge chronicled three years ago in the BBC2 documentary *Urban Chef*. Media attention may have waned, but Konstam continues to offer precise, unpretentious cooking to the King's Cross clientele. Beetroot, spinach and Russian kale have often featured on the short, ever-changing menu, while starters might include charcoal-grilled Mersea cuttlefish with dill-seed and lemon and garlic dressing. Braised shoulder of Amersham lamb – served with roast Jerusalem artichokes and caper sauce – is a popular main. A short wine list (sourced from well outside the M25) starts at £16 a bottle.
**Chef/s:** Oliver Rowe. **Open:** Sun to Fri L 12.30 to 2 (10.30 to 4 Sun, 3 Mon), Mon to Sat D 6.30 to 10.30. **Closed:** bank hols, 24 Dec to 1 Jan. **Meals:** alc (main courses £13 to £20). **Service:** not inc. **Details:** Cards accepted. 62 seats. Air-con. Wheelchair access. Music. Children allowed.

## ALSO RECOMMENDED
### ▲ Mangal Ocakbasi

4 Stoke Newington Road, Dalston, N16 8BH
Tel no: (020) 7254 7888
www.mangal2.com
⊖ Dalston, map 2
Turkish

There are queues for a reason at this no-frills, BYO Turkish 'ocakbasi' grill by the Arcola Theatre. The menu, such as it is, is basic: the idea is to choose from the chiller filled with the likes of lamb spare ribs, quails and perfectly spiced lamb kofte (£10.45). Accompaniments and starters are limited to little more than warm homemade bread, some superior aubergine and tomato salads, hummus (£3.25) and lahmahcun (£2.95). Quality is excellent across the board, although service is often barely there. Open all week.

## Market

Brit classics in Camden
43 Parkway, Camden, NW1 7PN
Tel no: (020) 7267 9700
www.marketrestaurant.co.uk
⊖ Camden Town, map 2
British | £24
Cooking score: 2

When people sing the praises of Camden's Market, they're talking about this attractive little restaurant rather than the stalls selling wacky clothing and black nail polish. It's valued for its unpretentious, wholesome approach: from cosy surroundings of blasted-brick walls and zinc-topped tables to the warm service and pared-back British menu. Hearty, uncomplicated flavours prevail: herring roes on toast or ham hock, soft egg and crackling salad to start, followed by lemon sole with mussels and chips or a butch chicken and ham pie. Steamed jam sponge with custard wraps meals up nicely, while a brief globetrotting wine list kicks off at £13 and refrains from rising too steeply.
**Chef/s:** Dan Spence. **Open:** all week L 12 to 2.30 (1 to 3.30 Sun), Mon to Sat D 6 to 10.30. **Closed:** bank hols. **Meals:** alc (main courses £10 to £15). Set L £10 (2 courses). **Service:** 12.5% (optional).
**Details:** Cards accepted. 38 seats. 4 seats outside. Air-con. Wheelchair access. Music. Children allowed.

## Mestizo

**A breath of Mexican fire**
103 Hampstead Road, Euston, NW1 3EL
Tel no: (020) 7387 4064
www.mestizomx.com
⊖ Warren Street, Euston Square, map 2
Mexican | £25
Cooking score: 2

Aztec artwork on red walls and shelves lined
with scores of tequilas set the tone at this
livewire Mexican joint in the bleak Euston/
Camden hinterland, and its hot, sexy vibes are
matched by food with genuine fiery intensity.
Forget the timid travesties of Tex-Mex – here
you will find ceviche, salads and soups
(perhaps poblano pepper and sweetcorn)
ahead of enchiladas and richly spiced mains
such as chuleta de cordero (lamb chops topped
with potent, tequila-spiked salsa borracha).
Also don't miss the classic chocolate-sauced
'mole' dishes or the house special molecajete –
an extravagant sharing combo served in a
stone bowl. Head to the funky basement
lounge for cocktails and authentic Latin
sounds, antojitos (Mexican tapas) and trays of
tacos. Chilean house wine is £12.50.
**Chef/s:** Dalce Aguilera. **Open:** all week 12 to 11
(Thur to Sat to 11.30, Sun to 10.30). **Closed:** 24 to 27
Dec, Good Fri, Easter Mon. **Meals:** alc (main courses
£5 to £12). Sun L £19. **Service:** not inc.
**Details:** Cards accepted. 80 seats. Air-con.
Separate bar. Wheelchair access. Music. Children
allowed.

## Metrogusto

**Idiosyncratic Italian eatery**
13 Theberton Street, Islington, N1 0QY
Tel no: (020) 7226 9400
www.metrogusto.co.uk
⊖ Angel, map 2
Italian | £28
Cooking score: 3

A quirky take on the neighbourhood trattoria,
Metrogusto's self-styled 'progressive Italian
cooking' has long beguiled the Islington set.

The décor is wilfully eccentric – bottles, jars
and miscellaneous *objets d'art* are scattered
about the dining room, while bright,
flamboyant paintings hang on the walls. The
menu caters primarily for meat-eaters, and
regional Italian dishes are well represented. A
starter of trenette al pesto Genovese with
French beans and saffron potatoes could be a
fitting prelude to a classic Tuscan main –
fettuccine fresche, served with wild boar and
rosemary ragù – or perhaps pan-fried calf's
liver with butter and sage sauce. Lime
pannacotta with liquorice sauce stars on an
extensive dessert menu, which also includes
Silician sorbets and ice creams. An exclusively
Italian wine lists sees bottles starting at £17.
**Chef/s:** Giuseppe Emanuele Giusini. **Open:** Fri to
Sun L 12 to 2.30, Mon to Sat D 6.30 to 10.30 (11 Fri
and Sat). **Closed:** Christmas, Easter. **Meals:** alc (£13
to £19). Set L and D £14.50 (2 courses) to £18.50.
Sun L £14.50. **Service:** 12.5% (optional).
**Details:** Cards accepted. 65 seats. 10 seats outside.
Air-con. Wheelchair access. Music. Children allowed.

## Morgan M

**Stylish venue for serious dining**
489 Liverpool Road, Islington, N7 8NS
Tel no: (020) 7609 3560
www.morganm.com
⊖ Highbury & Islington, map 2
Modern French | £39
Cooking score: 6

Morgan Meunier's neighbourhood restaurant
inspires loyalty – the draw is flexible,
seasonally inspired menus packed with dishes
of a consistently high standard. The single
room has lots of natural light, and plush
burgundy walls and oak panelling create a
feeling of intimacy. Professional service
matches the ambition of the kitchen. Terrine
of seared foie gras makes a fine opening dish,
served with compote of cherries, griottine
granité and toasted Poilâne bread. It sets the
scene for very refined cooking, with intricate
flavours, creative combinations and superb
presentation. Classic French modes may well
bring on main courses such as new season's

lamb (the shoulder confit, the rack roasted) teamed with artichoke barigoule and courgette and onion soubise. The kitchen hardly ever fails in its accuracy, so that a pavé of turbot is flawlessly timed. Good pastry work distinguishes desserts such as mille-feuille of summer fruits, which comes with a light crème patissière, rhubarb and Jurançon ice cream and blackcurrant jus. A thoroughly commendable and mostly French wine list has been assembled. Expect to pay £15 for a white vin du Gers and £18 for red vin du Pay d'Oc.
**Chef/s:** Morgan Meunier and Sylvain Soulard. **Open:** Wed to Fri and Sun L 12.15 to 2.30, Tue to Sat D 7 to 10.30. **Closed:** Mon, 24 to 30 Dec. **Meals:** Set L £22.50 (2 courses) to £26.50. Set D £39. Sun L £39. **Service:** 12.5% (optional). **Details:** Cards accepted. 50 seats. Air-con. No music. No mobile phones. Wheelchair access. Children allowed.

## Odette's

**Prowess and virtuosity**
130 Regents Park Road, Primrose Hill, NW1 8XL
Tel no: (020) 7586 8569
www.odettesprimrosehill.com
⊖ Chalk Farm, map 2
Modern British | £32
Cooking score: 5

Welsh chef Bryn Williams is now owner as well as kitchen supremo at this re-energised Primrose Hill veteran, having taken over the reins from entrepreneur Vince Power. Little else has changed, and the place maintains its iconic status with locals and the arty crowd. Following its dramatic makeover in 2006, the restaurant now flaunts a swaggering look, although the jury is still out on the garish yellow chairs, billowing drapes, bejewelled lampshades and leaf-motif wallpaper. However, any dissenting voices are silenced when it comes to the food, as Bryn Williams continues to show off his prowess and virtuosity – especially when it comes to cooking fish. Seafood fans might relish the prospect of tuna tartare with beetroot gazpacho and tomato confit, organic salmon with minestrone vegetables and liquorice jus

or pan-fried turbot with braised oxtail, cockles and samphire. Others could consider peppered wood pigeon with sweetcorn pannacotta, Bayonne ham and trompette mushrooms ahead of roast loin of Welsh lamb with braised shoulder, aubergine purée and baby onions. Desserts bring some seasonal fruitiness to the table in the shape of, say, poached apple and blackberry with walnut frangipane and apple sorbet. Aristocratic names from France jostle to the front of the prestigious wine list, although those whose allegiances lie with Marlborough, Stellenbosch or Mendoza won't be disappointed. House selections start at £19 (£5 a glass).
**Chef/s:** Bryn Williams. **Open:** Tue to Sun L 12 to 2.30 (3 Sat, 3.30 Sun), Tue to Sat D 6 to 10.30. **Closed:** Mon, 1 week Christmas. **Meals:** alc (main courses £15 to £22). Set L and early evening D £12 (2 courses) to £16. Sun L £20 (2 courses) to £25. Tasting menu £58 (6 courses). **Service:** 12.5% (optional). **Details:** Cards accepted. 60 seats. 35 seats outside. Air-con. Separate bar. Wheelchair access. Music. Children allowed. Car parking.

## Ottolenghi

**Ultra-hip deli diner**
287 Upper Street, Islington, N1 2TZ
Tel no: (020) 7288 1454
www.ottolenghi.co.uk
⊖ Angel, Highbury & Islington, map 2
Mediterranean | £30
Cooking score: 2

**V**

Passers-by can't help but 'eye up' the collage of meringues, cakes and 'highly imaginative salads' that line Ottolenghi's window – and those lured in don't leave disappointed. Whether it's a morning slice of apple and olive oil cake with coffee, lunch of broccoli and Gorgonzola quiche or evening meals comprised of several small plates, the food tastes as good as it looks. Mediterranean, Maghreb and Middle Eastern influences abound on a daily changing menu that touts cinnamon-roasted butternut squash with mint-lime yoghurt and pan-fried sea bass with baba ganoush and pomegranate sauce. Diners share a central table or sit at smaller tables round the side – it's a little cramped, but staff are efficient. Wines from £15. The Ottolenghi brand has also reached Notting Hill, Kensington and Belgravia (see website for details).

**Chef/s:** Sami Tamimi. **Open:** all week L 11 to 3, Mon to Sat D 6 to 10 (10.30 Thur to Sat). **Closed:** 25 and 26 Dec, 1 Jan, bank hols. **Meals:** alc (main courses £9 to £12). **Service:** not inc. **Details:** Cards accepted. 48 seats. 6 seats outside. Air-con. Wheelchair access. Music. Children allowed.

## Philpott's Mezzaluna

Value-for-money Italian
424 Finchley Road, Golders Green, NW2 2HY
Tel no: (020) 7794 0455
⊖ Golders Green, map 1
Italian | £25
Cooking score: 4

£5 OFF £30

The atmosphere at this bright, friendly neighbourhood restaurant is generally bustling without being overwhelming. The place certainly seems to have established a winning formula with the partnership of David Philpott and Alex Ross continuing to bring a taste of Italy to Child's Hill. A big attraction is the choice of good-value, flexible menus that aim to please all-comers. Alongside standard fare such as spaghetti with meatballs, penne with tomato and basil, and fillet steak with tarragon and mustard butter, there are some interesting options: fritto of cod cheeks with cauliflower, lemon and cumin, followed by partridge with Parma ham and thyme or black bream with pink peppercorns and rhubarb. Finish with hazelnut semifreddo. It's all very good value for money – and that extends to the sound selections on the mainly Italian wine list; bottles from £14.

**Chef/s:** David Philpott. **Open:** Tue to Fri and Sun L 12 to 2.30 (3 Sun), Tue to Sun D 7 to 11. **Closed:** Mon, 25 and 26 Dec, 1 Jan. **Meals:** Set L £12 (1 course) to £25 (4 courses). Set D £20 (2 courses) to £25 (4 courses). **Service:** 10% (optional). **Details:** Cards

accepted. 60 seats. 9 seats outside. Air-con. Separate bar. Wheelchair access. Music. Children allowed.

## Rasa

Indian vegetarian hot-spot
55 Stoke Newington Church Street, Stoke Newington, N16 0AR
Tel no: (020) 7249 0344
www.rasarestaurants.com
⊖ Finsbury Park, map 2
Indian Vegetarian | £17
Cooking score: 2

V

Although a further six branches have opened since its inception in 1997, Rasa purists generally agree that the original Stoke Newington restaurant – and its inimitable approach to Keralan vegetarian cooking – still leads the pack. Staff remain staunchly proud of their culinary heritage, and are eager to explain the historical and cultural background of the dosas and curries on offer. A starter of masala vadai – lentil patties with ginger, chillies and coconut chutney – might be followed by beet cheera pachadi (spinach and beetroot blended into a yoghurt sauce). A comprehensive stock of breads, rices and sides provide ample opportunity to offset some of the more powerful flavours on the menu. House wines start at £11.

**Chef/s:** Rajan Karatill. **Open:** Sat and Sun L 12 to 3, all week D 6 to 11 (12 Sat and Sun). **Closed:** 24 to 26 Dec. **Meals:** alc (main courses £3 to £6). Set L and D £16.50. **Service:** 12.5% (optional). **Details:** Cards accepted. 50 seats. Air-con. Wheelchair access. Music. Children allowed.

### Please send us your feedback

To register your opinion about any restaurant listed in the Guide, or a new restaurant that you wish to bring to our attention, please visit the web address at the bottom of the page. Your feedback informs the content of the book and will be used to compile next year's reviews.

## Singapore Garden

South-Asian spice in suburbia
83 Fairfax Road, Swiss Cottage, NW6 4DY
Tel no: (020) 7328 5314
www.singaporegarden.co.uk
⊖ Swiss Cottage, map 2
Malaysian | £30
Cooking score: 2

**V**

An unusual find in a Swiss Cottage backwater, Singapore Garden delivers Asian-themed interiors, attentive service and above-average food to an appreciative audience. Culinary inspiration comes from China, Singapore and Malaysia, with textbook versions of the Cantonese classics dominating the menu. To sample the kitchen's finest wares, look to the Singaporean and Malaysian specials: kuay pie tee translates as crisp pastry cups filled with stir-fried bamboo shoots, chicken and prawns and, to follow, both slow-cooked beef curry and fragrant laksa noodle soup with prawns and Chinese-style fishcakes score highly. Prices reflect the quality of the cooking, and spice-friendly wines start at £16. **Chef/s:** Kok Sum Toh. **Open:** all week L 12 to 3 (5 Sun), D 6 to 11 (11.30 Fri and Sat). **Closed:** 4 days at Christmas. **Meals:** alc (main courses £8 to £29). Set L £20 (3 courses). Set D £28 (4 courses). **Service:** 12.5% (optional). **Details:** Cards accepted. 85 seats. 12 seats outside. Air-con. Wheelchair access. Music. Children allowed.

## Sushi-Say

Sparklingly-fresh fish favourite
33b Walm Lane, Willesden, NW2 5SH
Tel no: (020) 8459 2971
⊖ Willesden Green, map 1
Japanese | £30
Cooking score: 4

The fish comes sparklingly fresh and the diners come from far and wide to this Willesden Green Japanese joint – so bookings are recommended. Behind the sushi bar, bandana-wearing chefs nip and tuck pearly fillets of fish before piling thick slices on to wooden platters to be served to appreciative

tables in the narrow dining room. Mackerel, turbot and razor clams are among the many types of nigiri and sashimi available. Sushi rolls feature minced fatty tuna and spring onion, or the texturally interesting salmon skin, sticky soya beans and pickled radish. Hot dishes include well-executed renditions of the usual suspects – prawn tempura or chicken katsu – plus more adventurous plates of slow-cooked pork belly in special sauce. Set menus help curb spending, otherwise prepare for your bank balance to take a beating. Cut costs by passing on wine (from £14 a bottle) and drinking green tea instead. **Chef/s:** Katsuharu Shimizu. **Open:** Sat and Sun L 12 to 3.30, Tue to Sun D 6.30 to 10 (10.30 Sat, 9.30 Sun). **Closed:** Mon, 25 and 26 Dec, bank hols, Tue after bank hols, 1 week Jul, 2 weeks Jan. **Meals:** alc (main courses £9 to £23). Set L £10.80 to £16.80. Set D £25 to £37. **Service:** not inc. **Details:** Cards accepted. 42 seats. Air-con. No music. Wheelchair access. Children allowed.

## ALSO RECOMMENDED

### ▲ XO

29 Belsize Lane, Belsize Park, NW3 5AS
Tel no: (020) 7433 0888
www.rickerrestaurants.com
⊖ Belsize Park, map 2
Pan-Asian

XO attracts a more sedate crowd than its fashionable West London siblings from the Will Ricker stable. A small bar dispenses Asian-tinted cocktails while dishes in the glossy, mirror-lined dining room roam Asia with variable results, particularly when high prices are factored in. Guaranteed high notes are hit with chilli-salt squid flecked with roasted garlic and red chilli (£6.50) and grilled black cod in miso (£23.50). There's scant choice under £20 on the wine list, and staff, though perfectly efficient, could flash more smiles. Open all week.

## Shane Osborn Pied-à-Terre

**Who or what inspired you to become a chef?**
My mother was a cook, so I followed her to work from the age of 11.

**What is the best meal you have ever eaten?**
Dinner at Arzak in San Sebastian in 2003. I still haven't stopped talking about it.

**What do you do to relax when out of the kitchen?**
Make cookies with my two young children.

**Which chefs do you admire?**
The list is too long to mention. However, any chef that works hard, to the best of their ability and enjoys the job as much as I do.

**What is your top culinary tip?**
Remove your meat from the fridge at least half an hour before cooking.

**What is the best part of your job?**
Teaching and working with passionate, knowledge-hungry cooks is a great inspiration and also a great way of keeping me motivated.

**NEW ENTRY**

## York and Albany
**Delivering some real treats**
127-129 Parkway, Camden, NW1 7PS
Tel no: (020) 7388 3344
www.gordonramsay.com
⊖ Camden Town, map 2
Modern European | £30
Cooking score: 5

Angela Hartnett can do creative fine dining (see Murano), but she's also got a respect for simpler brasserie dishes. The reincarnation of this majestic John Nash building by Gordon Ramsay Holdings is the perfect showcase for the latter. Behind the large windows of the former Regency coaching inn lies a high-ceilinged room that operates variously as a bar, café, restaurant and meeting place, with a deli next door and a flight of stairs leading down to exotic-looking dining rooms – all red silk walls, slouchy red sofas and high-backed red chairs. The menu works throughout, and the kitchen can deliver some real treats: impeccable Italian touches show in pumpkin risotto with sage butter and aged Gorgonzola, and loin of venison with wet polenta and braised Swiss chard. There's also plenty of flavour and bite in a simple fixed-price Sunday lunch of home-cured salmon with beetroot, horseradish and cucumber, and rump of lamb with Puy lentils and roasted pumpkin. It is undoubtedly the quality of the raw materials that lifts these dishes above their natural simplicity – an impression made again by a delicate vanilla pannacotta with pineapple compote. Service is practised and well-paced. The wide-ranging wine list is startlingly good, with some reasonably priced easy drinking from £16.50.
**Chef/s:** Angela Hartnett. **Open:** Mon to Sat L 12 to 3, D 6 to 11, Sun 12 to 9. **Meals:** alc (main courses £15 to £20). Set L (and D before 7) £18. Sun L £25. **Service:** 12.5% (optional). **Details:** Cards accepted. 80 seats. 12 seats outside. Air-con. Separate bar. Wheelchair access. Music. Children allowed.

## NEW ENTRY
# Albion

**Stylish caff won't bust your budget**
2-4 Boundary Street, Shoreditch, E2 7JE
Tel no: (020) 7729 1051
www.albioncaff.co.uk
 Old Street, Liverpool Street, map 2
British | £20
Cooking score: 2

Sir Terence Conran has transformed this Victorian warehouse into a boutique hotel with various eating options including the basement Boundary (see entry) and this 'caff' and bakery on the ground floor. It has quite a swagger, with big windows giving lots of light and street views, and there's all the theatre of an open-plan kitchen. The food is heroically British, so expect kedgeree or toad-in-the-hole. Eating here will not mess up your budget – most dishes are under £10. Start by nibbling on some crackling before moving on to a heart-warming chicken, leek and crayfish pie, and finish with summer pudding. There's praise for the cheery service, and wines start from £15.
**Chef/s:** Ian Wood. **Open:** all week 8am to midnight. **Meals:** alc (main courses £5 to £10). **Service:** 12.5% (optional). **Details:** Cards accepted. 80 seats. 20 seats outside. Wheelchair access. Music. Children allowed.

# The Ambassador

**Streetwise all-day winner**
55 Exmouth Market, Clerkenwell, EC1R 4QL
Tel no: (020) 7837 0009
www.theambassadorcafe.co.uk
 Farringdon, Angel, map 2
Modern European | £23
Cooking score: 2

Competition is fierce in bustling Exmouth Market, but Clive Greenhalgh's neighbourhood pit-stop more than holds its own. There's a clean, light and attractive interior for evening dining with banquette seating for a good sprawl and tables outside providing a popular spot for brunch – eggs Benedict or Royale perhaps. Crusty homemade bread with salty butter almost merits the visit alone, while the rest of the simple French brasserie food – say pear, walnut and Roquefort salad or bacon and snail tart – is tasty and competently produced. Service is friendly and it's all eminently affordable, with set-lunch and pre-theatre menus providing further incentive. A keenly priced wine list offers much under £20.
**Chef/s:** Chris Dyer and Josh Wortley. **Open:** all week 8.30am to 2.30 (11 to 3.30 Sat, 11 to 4 Sun), D 6 to 10.15 (9.30 Sun). **Closed:** 25 Dec to 2 Jan. **Meals:** alc (main courses £11 to £18). Set L and D £12.50 (2 courses) to £16. **Service:** not inc. **Details:** Cards accepted. 70 seats. 20 seats outside. Separate bar. Wheelchair access. Music. Children allowed.

# L'Anima

**Breathtaking flavours and wicked pasta**
1 Snowden Street, City, EC2A 2DQ
Tel no: (020) 7422 7000
www.lanima.co.uk
 Liverpool Street, map 2
Italian | £45
Cooking score: 5

It may be hidden in a maze of buildings near the Broadgate Centre ('even the taxi driver wasn't sure of the street'), but Francesco Mazzei's modern Italian restaurant hasn't wanted for custom since opening in spring 2008. It achieves an easy balance of sophistication and unpretentious urban chic. The airy, minimalist space is split into a bar and dining room with lots of glass, stone and white leather. The menu may read quite plainly, but the emphasis is on exceptional ingredients and the kitchen displays the skill and confidence to bring out their full, remarkable flavours. These were apparent in a starter of stunningly fresh chargrilled scallops with n'duja (a spicy Calabrian salami) and garlicky salsa verde. Pasta is always well considered, as when pappardelle is served lightly sauced with duck ragù or butternut squash tortellini teamed with nothing more

than brown butter and deep-fried sage leaves. Flavours are clean and clear, and dishes know what they are about: witness the breathtaking sweet-and-sour flavour conjured out of a main-course Sicilian rabbit. Breads and pasta are made in-house, and service never misses a beat. Wines can help bump up the bill; prices on a strong, but not exclusive, Italian list start at £18, although most bottles are over £25.
**Chef/s:** Francesco Mazzei and Lucca Terraneo. **Open:** Mon to Fri L 1.45 to 3, Mon to Sat D 5.30 to 10.30 (11 Sat). **Closed:** Sun, Christmas, bank hols. **Meals:** alc (main courses £6 to £28). Set L £23.50 (2 courses) to £25.50. **Service:** 12.5% (optional). **Details:** Cards accepted. 80 seats. Air-con. Separate bar. No mobile phones. Wheelchair access. Music. Children allowed.

# Bleeding Heart
**Romantic venue for fine French dining**
Bleeding Heart Yard, Greville Street, Clerkenwell, EC1N 8SJ
Tel no: (020) 7242 2056
www.bleedingheart.co.uk
⊖ Farringdon, map 5
Modern French | £30
Cooking score: 2

Bleeding Heart Yard – the site of an infamous murder in 1626 – is home to this 'very French restaurant'. It does a roaring trade in business lunches, though its warm, glowing rooms are equally good for romantic liaisons. Service is generally agreed to be 'impeccable'. Gallic, wine-themed décor and atmospheric lighting set the tone for Peter Reffell's inventive take on classic French cooking: perhaps foie gras crème brûlée with pineapple compote followed by roast suckling pig with confit shoulder of pork, apple boudin blanc and green peppercorn sauce. Finish with wild cherry and almond clafoutis with amaretti ice cream. The wine list is noted for its broad and generous spread, with fine drinking extending way beyond France into the nether regions of the New World – the proprietors own the Trinity Hill Vineyard in Hawkes Bay, New Zealand. Prices start at £16.25.

**Chef/s:** Peter Reffell. **Open:** Mon to Fri L 12 to 2.30, D 6.30 to 10.30. **Closed:** Sat, Sun, bank hols, Christmas to New Year. **Meals:** alc (main courses £13 to £24). **Service:** 12.5% (optional). **Details:** Cards accepted. 140 seats. 15 seats outside. Air-con. No music. No mobile phones. Children allowed.

# Bonds
**Banking on quality**
Threadneedle Hotel, 5 Threadneedle Street, City, EC2R 8AY
Tel no: (020) 7657 8090
www.theetoncollection.com
⊖ Bank, map 2
Modern French | £35
Cooking score: 6

Hard though it may be to recall, but there was a time before the recent unpleasantness when Britain's banks were the pillars of a confident empire, that confidence reflected in their monumental architecture. One glance around as you enter Threadneedles confirms it, as the light shimmers down through a dome of stained glass built in insolent Victorian imitation of St Paul's. Now a boutique City hotel, the place also boasts an opulent mirrored and columned restaurant in the form of Bonds, where Barry Tonks caters to a knowledgeable business crowd. Based on conscientiously sourced ingredients, from Dorset Bay crab to Elwy Valley lamb, Limousin veal to Denham Estate venison, the cooking is both supremely assured and sensitively presented. Start perhaps with that crab, served in tarragon mayonnaise with fennel and apple, and proceed to slow-cooked Pyrenean pork belly with pearl barley and chorizo (cleverly cooked to resemble a risotto) and caramelised onions. French cheeses with figs and almonds are the alternative to a dessert such as floating island with pink praline and custard. It all comes with a formidably comprehensive wine list, glasses (from £5.95) and half-bottles to the fore. Prices reflect the location, but quality is indisputable.

Chef/s: Barry Tonks. **Open:** Mon to Fri L 12 to 2.30,
D 6 to 10. **Closed:** Sat, Sun, bank hols, 25 and 26
Dec, 1 Jan. **Meals:** alc (main courses £15 to £20). Set
L and D £17.50. **Service:** 12.5% (optional).
**Details:** Cards accepted. 80 seats. Air-con.
Separate bar. Wheelchair access. Music. Children
allowed.

**NEW ENTRY**
## Boundary
**Love affair with the Paris brasserie**
2-4 Boundary Street, Shoreditch, E2 7DD
Tel no: (020) 7729 1051
www.theboundary.co.uk
⊖ Old Street, Liverpool Street, map 2
**French | £30**
**Cooking score: 4**

Sir Terence Conran's new project is housed in a
Victorian warehouse and retains something of
an industrial air about it. At ground level there
is a large, airy British caff with adjoining food
shop (see the Albion), on the roof is a fair-
weather open-air grill restaurant and bar, and
in between is a 12-bed hotel. Boundary in the
basement feels like a secret restaurant, reached
down concrete stairs. But it's some spacious
basement – all bare brick and soaring ceilings,
white-clad tables and an open-to-view
kitchen. The food reflects Conran's love affair
with the Paris brasserie – oysters, rotisserie
chicken, steak au poivre, shellfish platters and
tarte Tatin. Reports have applauded French
onion soup and calf's liver as well as potted
shrimps served with Melba toast and a navarin
of lamb fragrant with the perfumes of an early
summer vegetable basket. The modern wine
list offers good drinking from £19.
Chef/s: Ian Wood and Henrik Ritzen. **Open:** all week
L 12 to 2.30 (3.30 Sun), Mon to Sat D 6.30 to 10.30.
**Meals:** alc (main courses £12 to £24). Set L £23.50.
**Service:** 12.5% (optional). **Details:** Cards accepted.
124 seats. Air-con. Separate bar. Music. Children
allowed.

## Buen Ayre
**Friendly grill with top-quality steaks**
50 Broadway Market, Hackney, E8 4QJ
Tel no: (020) 7275 9900
www.buenayre.co.uk
⊖ Bethnal Green, map 1
**Argentinian | £35**
**Cooking score: 1**

£5
OFF

A hit with Hackney locals, this friendly
neighbourhood Argentine grill offers a simple
formula of quality steaks (expertly cooked on
the chargrill) accompanied by similarly beefy
Argentinian wines (from £12.50). Top choices
include ribeye with a side of the house's super-
garlicky chips, and the tabletop 'parillada'
featuring kidney, black pudding and short
ribs. Puddings major on the dulce de leche,
with pancakes, cheesecake and crème caramel
all featuring the stuff. The waiting staff are
almost as sweet.
Chef/s: John Rattagan. **Open:** Sat and Sun L 12 to
3.30, all week D 6 to 10.30. **Closed:** 25 and 26 Dec, 1
Jan. **Meals:** alc (main courses £10 to £28).
**Service:** 12% (optional). **Details:** Cards accepted. 38
seats. 24 seats outside. Air-con. Wheelchair access.
Music. Children allowed.

## Café Spice Namaste
**Rich, exotic high-profile Indian**
16 Prescot Street, Tower Hill, E1 8AZ
Tel no: (020) 7488 9242
www.cafespice.co.uk
⊖ Tower Hill, map 1
**Indian | £30**
**Cooking score: 2**

 **V**

Banners flutter outside and the interior is
ablaze with rich, exotic colours – a fitting
backdrop for the food on offer in Cyrus
Todiwala's high-profile contemporary Indian.
Culinary influences come from the
Subcontinent and beyond, although the
kitchen looks to Britain's regional larder for
many of its ingredients: samosas are stuffed
with Cheltenham beetroot and coconut,
Denham Estate venison is fashioned into

minced kebabs with Hunza apricots, dates and ginger, and organic British Lop pork finds its way into a vindaloo. Arabic and Keralan influences also show up strongly, and Todiwala's Parsee roots guarantee that dhansaks are beyond reproach. Retreat to the Ginger Garden for fine-weather chill-outs. Carefully selected wines start at £16.95. **Chef/s:** Angelo Collaco. **Open:** Mon to Fri L 12 to 3, Mon to Sat D 6.15 to 10.30 (6.30 to 10.30 Sat). **Closed:** Sun, bank hols, 24 Dec to 1 Jan. **Meals:** alc (main courses £14 to £20). Set L £19.95 (2 courses) to £30. Set D £25 (2 courses) to £30. **Service:** 12.5% (optional). **Details:** Cards accepted. 130 seats. 40 seats outside. Air-con. Wheelchair access. Music. Children allowed.

## Canteen
**Big on nostalgia and all-day breakfasts**
Crispin Place, Spitalfields, E1 6DW
Tel no: (0845) 6861 122
www.canteen.co.uk
⊖ **Liverpool Street, map 2**
**Modern British | £22**
**Cooking score: 3**

The epicentre of East End-chic might seem an unlikely location for a restaurant trading in nostalgic British cooking, but Canteen has become something of an institution in Spitalfields Market. The plate-glass exterior, marble surfaces and communal oak tables make for a utilitarian but sharply contemporary setting for Cass Titcombe to reinvent bygone classics. An all-day breakfast menu is a popular port of call: bacon, eggs and bubble and squeak or hot buttered Arbroath smokie tempt the peckish pedestrians of E1. Mains are equally unpretentious: sausages and mash with caramelised onion gravy continues a theme of simple cooking from rigorously scrutinised ingredients. The wine list (starting at £13 a bottle) plays second fiddle to a good range of lagers, ales and stouts. Branches have opened on the South Bank and Baker Street. **Chef/s:** Cass Titcombe. **Open:** all week 8am to 11pm. **Closed:** 25 and 26 Dec. **Meals:** alc (main courses £7 to £15). **Service:** 12.5% (optional).

**Details:** Cards accepted. 80 seats. 50 seats outside. Air-con. Separate bar. Wheelchair access. Music. Children allowed.

## ALSO RECOMMENDED
## ▲ Carnevale
**135 Whitecross Street, Barbican, EC1 8JL**
Tel no: (020) 7250 3452
www.carnevalerestaurant.co.uk
⊖ **Barbican, map 5**
**Vegetarian**

Vegetarian food with a sunny disposition is the prospect at this pint-sized hangout near the Barbican. The place doubles as a deli by day, but punters can look forward to colourful Med-inspired food at any time. Starters (£6.25) could include goats' cheese parcels with fig and almond salad, while mains (£12.50) might range from asparagus and herb risotto to pumpkin gnocchi in roast garlic cream. Chocolate rum pudding (£5.25) is a typically down-the-line dessert. House wine is £13.50. Open Mon to Fri L, Mon to Sat D.

**NEW ENTRY**
## Cinnamon Kitchen
**Strong Indian flavours in the City**
9 Devonshire Square, City, EC2M 4YL
Tel no: (020) 7626 5000
www.cinnamon-kitchen.com
⊖ **Liverpool Street, map 2**
**Indian | £25**
**Cooking score: 4**

The Westminster politico's favourite, Cinnamon Club (see entry), gets a hip reworking for the City boys. This means polo-shirted service, a cool, grey, semi-industrial room, and marginally lower prices. Chef Vivek Singh's modern Indian cuisine comes fully plated, modern European-style: for example, pork chop with masala mash, lamb saddle with mint-onion sauce and banana tarte Tatin. Starters of fat chilli stuffed with lamb or a juicy wild African prawn sizzled on the showpiece grill make a very direct appeal

to the palate. It's still early days for Cinnamon Kitchen, which could explain the clingy service and over-cautious wine suggestions at inspection. A global list opens at £19.
**Chef/s:** Abdul Yaseen. **Open:** Mon to Fri B 7 to 10.30, L 12 to 3.30, Mon to Sat D 6 to 10.30. **Closed:** Sun, bank hols. **Meals:** alc (main courses £12 to £22). Sel L and D £15 (2 courses) to £18.
**Service:** 12.5% (optional). **Details:** Cards accepted. 120 seats. 44 seats outside. Air-con. Separate bar. Wheelchair access. Music. Children allowed.

## Clerkenwell Dining Room
**Confident, civilised favourite**
69-73 St John Street, Clerkenwell, EC1M 4AN
Tel no: (020) 7253 9000
www.theclerkenwell.com
⊖ Farringdon, map 5
**Modern European | £34**
**Cooking score: 3**

Andrew Thompson's popular Clerkenwell restaurant strikes a quietly confident, civilised note, despite its rather unpromising location on the ground floor of an office block. Inside, understated colours and restrained design provide the backdrop to imaginative European-influenced food that maintains a healthy balance between familiarity and innovation. You could take the well-tried route with game terrine and grape chutney followed by calf's liver and onions with smoked potato cream. Otherwise, head off into the world of seared scallops with aubergine pakora and curry spices before sampling roast halibut with corned beef hash and Savoy cabbage. To finish there's always a French tarte of the day, alongside more elaborate creations such as sablé of blackberries and poached pears with crème chiboust. Keenly priced global wines start at £16 (£6 a glass). Sister to the Chancery (see entry).
**Chef/s:** Andrew Thompson. **Open:** Mon to Fri L 12 to 2.30, Mon to Sat D 6 to 11. **Closed:** Sun, bank hols, 23 Dec to first week Jan. **Meals:** alc (main courses from £16 to £22). **Service:** 12.5% (optional).
**Details:** Cards accepted. 130 seats. Air-con. Separate bar. Wheelchair access. Music. Children allowed. Car parking.

## Club Gascon
**Passion, innovation and foie gras**
57 West Smithfield, City, EC1A 9DS
Tel no: (020) 7796 0600
www.clubgascon.com
⊖ Barbican, Farringdon, St Paul's, map 5
**French | £45**
**Cooking score: 6**
£5 OFF 🍾 V

'Unlike anywhere else', observed one reporter about Club Gascon, and it's hard to disagree. Secreted near Smithfield Market, this one-time Lyons tea house has been home to Pascal Aussignac's passionate and diligent endeavours for more than a decade and – judging by feedback – he is 'getting better every year'. The rich, potent flavours of southwest France are his lifeblood and he explores them in miraculous detail. Foie gras is – of course – king of the hill, and this velvet delicacy is served six ways (as carpaccio with ginger pearls, paired with sherry, braised quince and candied chicory, even magicked into 'popcorn'). There are no conventional courses at Club Gascon: instead, guests seated in the faux marble-walled dining room are offered clusters of dishes with headings such as 'la route de sel' or 'l'oceane'. Aussignac's cooking has no truck with convention either – it's radical and audacious by turns, but also knows exactly where it's going. Confit organic salmon with violet tea and citrus chutney is one of the more accessible creations, and the menu also promises snails caviar fricassee with salsify sorbet and almonds, sturgeon bordelaise with braised rhubarb, and milk-fed lamb cooked on vine-shoot embers with dates. To finish, Champagne granité with mango and pineapple cannelloni might provide the final thrill, unless you are tempted by the earthy possibilities of Bleu des Causses with chicory and clementine chutney. The mighty wine list gives Champagne and Bordeaux plenty of attention before heading south into the treasured realms of Tursan, Gaillac and Irouléguy. 'Vins de verre' start at £5.50 a glass.

Chef/s: Pascal Aussignac. **Open:** Mon to Fri L 12 to 2, Mon to Sat D 7 to 10 (10.30 Fri and Sat). **Closed:** Sun, bank hols, 2 weeks Christmas and New Year. **Meals:** alc (main courses £13 to £23). Set L £28. Set D £35 (2 courses) to £55. **Service:** 12.5% (optional). **Details:** Cards accepted. 45 seats. Air-con. Separate bar. Wheelchair access. Music. Children allowed.

## The Coach and Horses
**More pubby grub than gastro**
26-28 Ray Street, Clerkenwell, EC1R 3DJ
Tel no: (020) 7278 8990
www.thecoachandhorses.com
⊖ Farringdon, map 5
**Gastropub | £25**
**Cooking score: 2**

New chef Henry Herbert takes this wood-panelled boozer into more 'pubby', less 'gastro' terrain, at least at lunch, when local office workers pile in for a pint of Landlord or Stella with a burger, Scotch egg or – for the more daring – devilled kidneys on toast. The kitchen ups its game by night with rabbit pie, confit lamb breast and green sauce, and elderflower Turkish delight. The wine list is overly safe, but all 16 choices are under £21.95 and are available by glass and carafe. Service is too casual in our experience to justify a (discretionary) 12.5% service charge.
**Chef/s:** Henry Herbert. **Open:** Mon to Fri and Sun L 12 to 3, Mon to Sat D 6 to 10. **Closed:** bank hols, 24 to 31 Dec. **Meals:** alc (main courses £11 to £14). Bar menu available. **Service:** 12.5% (optional). **Details:** Cards accepted. 78 seats. 38 seats outside. Separate bar. Wheelchair access. Music. Children allowed.

### Best for brunch in London

London may be second to none for the variety and quality of its restaurants, but it still doesn't do good middle-range eateries with the panache of our European or transatlantic cousins. A few places are beginning to fill the gap as the trend for quality all-day eating gains momentum. Even conventional restaurants have started to break away from set meal times, making breakfast/brunch a popular option.

**The Wolseley** pulls in the crowds with French viennoiserie, full English and American pancakes.

The American brasserie **Automat** is the place to go for pancakes, French toast and steak and eggs.

**The Modern Pantry** is ideal if you are looking for something funkier, say poached tamarillo, Greek yoghurt and Manuka honey.

There's a French spin to **Côte** in Soho and Wimbledon, with crêpes complet, croque-monsieur and bacon baguettes.

Expat Aussies get homesick devouring corn fritters with crispy bacon and great banana bread at **Lantana Café**.

Every weekend there are eggs rancheros, posh porridge and buttermilk pancakes at **Harrison's** in Balham.

## Comptoir Gascon

**Hearty cooking and Gallic charm**
61-63 Charterhouse Street, Clerkenwell, EC1M 6HJ
Tel no: (020) 7608 0851
www.comptoirgascon.com
⊖ **Farringdon, Barbican, map 5**
French | £21
**Cooking score: 4**

Club Gascon's deli/café, located on the opposite side of Smithfield to its illustrious sibling (see entry), is a picture of rustic French charm. Rough painted walls and simple wooden tables set the scene for hearty cooking of such southwestern treats as duck confit with garbure béarnaise or a fantastic cassoulet Toulousian, although the kitchen is not above turning out brasserie staples along the lines of beef onglet with bordelaise sauce. Portions are generous, so share a plate of potted duck rillettes or fresh oysters with grilled chipolatas to start, and if you can't manage dessert, buy some well-sourced artisan cheese or choose from the selection of classic French patisserie in the deli to take home. Open all day from 9am, it's a good spot for breakfast and afternoon tea, too. All wines are sourced from the south of France, with a good choice by the glass from £6. Bottles start at £19.
**Chef/s:** Romuald Sanfourche. **Open:** Tue to Sat L 12 to 2 (10.30 to 2.30 Sat), D 7 to 10. **Closed:** Sun, Mon, 24 Dec to 1st Tue after New Year. **Meals:** alc (main courses £8 to £14). **Service:** 12.5% (optional). **Details:** Cards accepted. 35 seats. 8 seats outside. Air-con. Wheelchair access. Music. Children allowed.

### Please send us your feedback

To register your opinion about any restaurant listed in the Guide, or a new restaurant that you wish to bring to our attention, please visit the web address at the bottom of the page. Your feedback informs the content of the book and will be used to compile next year's reviews.

NEW ENTRY
## Devonshire Terrace

**Laid-back dining**
9 Devonshire Square, Liverpool Street, EC2M 4WY
Tel no: (020) 7256 3233
www.devonshireterrace.co.uk
⊖ **Liverpool Street, map 2**
Modern European | £30
**Cooking score: 1**

This laid-back restaurant and bar comprises a smart central dining room and various private dining spaces and alfresco terraces. Eggs Benedict satisfies early birds, and grilled meat and fish with mix-and-match sauces and sides take over later on. Pan-fried red mullet might be paired with zesty lime and chilli dressing and seasonal veg, or you could fancy the prospect of tender Black Angus sirloin bolstered by a pungent Muscat and Stinking Bishop sauce. Sticky toffee pudding provides a sweet finish. Global wines from £14.
**Chef/s:** Justin Abbott Charles. **Open:** Mon to Fri B 8 to 11, L 12 to 3, D 6 to 11. **Closed:** Sat, Sun, 25 and 26 Dec, bank hols. **Meals:** alc (main courses £10 to £24). **Service:** 12.5% (optional). **Details:** Cards accepted. 62 seats. 100 seats outside. Air-con. Separate bar. Wheelchair access. Music. Children allowed.

## The Don

**Blue-chip wines and modish menus**
The Courtyard, 20 St Swithin's Lane, City, EC4N 8AD
Tel no: (020) 7626 2606
www.thedonrestaurant.co.uk
⊖ **Bank, map 2**
Modern European | £30
**Cooking score: 2**

A vintage City treasure, and formerly HQ for Sandeman's (of port and sherry fame), the Don is now a favoured destination for power lunches and evening get-togethers, thanks to its discreet courtyard location, blue-chip wine list and dependable modern food. Pride of place goes to the chic ground-floor restaurant, with its abstract canvases, sculptures and modish cosmopolitan menu – think salt cod brandade on salmon tartare, and roast venison with fig and walnut Tatin, followed by iced jasmine tea and lime parfait. The brick-walled cellar bistro majors in simpler dishes. France claims much of the high ground on the stupendous wine list, but the New World also makes a thrilling impact – and don't forget the matchless collection of ports, Madeiras and sherries, a tribute to Sandeman's emblematic caped 'Don'. 'Vins du patron' start at £16.95 (£4.50 a glass). Sister to the Bleeding Heart (see entry).

**Chef/s:** Matthew Burns. **Open:** Mon to Fri L 12 to 2.30, D 6 to 10. **Closed:** Sat, Sun, bank hols, Christmas and New Year. **Meals:** alc (main courses £13 to £27). **Service:** 12.5% (optional). **Details:** Cards accepted. 80 seats. Air-con. Separate bar. No music. No mobile phones. Wheelchair access.

## The Eagle

**Gastropub grandaddy**
159 Farringdon Road, Clerkenwell, EC1R 3AL
Tel no: (020) 7837 1353
⊖ Farringdon, map 5
Gastropub | £20
Cooking score: 2

Still flying high after all these years, Michael Belben's gastropub pioneer has clung to the deliberately deconstructed formula that made it such a mould-breaker when it opened back in 1991. Food is advertised on blackboards hung over the bar: expect around a dozen dishes, with influences from the Med shining out. Spring might bring Romney Marsh lamb chops with grilled artichokes and olives, asparagus salad with pecorino, mint and broad beans or pan-fried plaice with greens and tartare sauce. Bifeana (the Eagle's legendary marinated steak sandwich) is a fixture that no one would dare remove, while tapas goes well as a filler with real ales or gluggable wines (from £12.50).

**Chef/s:** Ed Mottershaw. **Open:** all week L 12.30 to 3 (3.30 Sat and Sun), Mon to Sat D 6.30 to 10.30. **Closed:** 1 week Christmas, bank hols (except Good Fri D). **Meals:** alc (main courses £5 to £16). **Service:** not inc. **Details:** Cards accepted. 60 seats. 24 seats outside. Music. Children allowed.

## READERS RECOMMEND

### Eastside Inn

**Modern European**
40 St John Street, Clerkenwell, EC1M 4AY
Tel no: (020) 7490 9240
www.esilondon.com
'Only eaten in the bistro but love the food'

## The Empress of India

**Confident all-day operation**
130 Lauriston Road, Hackney, E9 7LH
Tel no: (020) 8533 5123
www.theempressofindia.com
⊖ Mile End, Bethnal Green, map 1
Gastropub | £22
Cooking score: 3

The Empress of India's boozer history, brasserie interior, pints on tap and all-day gastropub/café menu suggest something of a muddle. But E9's Empress is a confident operator, not one in the throes of an identity crisis. The menu segues smoothly from breakfast (Fri to Sun) of kippers or porridge and syrup to Sunday roasts – for example Angus sirloin or whole roast chicken for two – then to afternoon tea and tiffin. The kitchen also sends out reliable rotisserie specials and classics like London Particular, pint o' prawns, and oxtail with celeriac mash. Plum and almond tart makes a good finale. The wine list, which is fittingly commitment-phobic, zig-zags across the globe from England to Chile. Prices from £16.

**Chef/s:** Daniel Doherty. **Open:** Mon to Fri L 12 to 2.30 (12 to 10 Sat), D 7 to 10. **Closed:** Sun, 25 and 26 Dec. **Meals:** alc (main courses £9 to £14). Sun L £14.95. **Service:** 12.5% (optional). **Details:** Cards accepted. 60 seats. 16 seats outside. Separate bar. Wheelchair access. Music. Children allowed.

## Eyre Brothers

**Full-on Iberian flavours**
70 Leonard Street, Shoreditch, EC2A 4QX
Tel no: (020) 7613 5346
www.eyrebrothers.co.uk
⊖ Old Street, map 2
Modern European | £30
Cooking score: 2
£5 OFF

The Eyre brothers, David and Robert, opened in these extravagantly spacious warehouse premises in 2000, with a mission to bring the lively flavours of southwest European cooking to a trendy part of the capital. Roast morcilla (blood sausage) with black-eyed beans and turnip greens, dressed in garlic and sherry vinegar, is a starter that gives a good indication of the style. Materials are carefully sourced, with Ibérico pork, 35-day aged beef and Mozambique tiger prawns with rice pilaf among the main course options. Finish with tarta de Santiago (Spanish almond cake) with orange and lime confit. A thoroughly commendable array of international wines is especially strong in Iberian listings, with plenty by the glass, including a useful slate of Valdespino and Gonzalez Byass sherries.
**Chef/s:** David Eyre and João Cleto. **Open:** Mon to Fri L 12 to 3, Mon to Sat D 6.30 to 10.45. **Closed:** Sun, Christmas to New Year. **Meals:** alc (main courses £12 to £25). Bar menu available. **Service:** 12.5% (optional). **Details:** Cards accepted. 70 seats. Air-con. Separate bar. Wheelchair access. Music. Children allowed.

## Fifteen London

**Jamie's trendy Italian hangout**
15 Westland Place, Shoreditch, N1 7LP
Tel no: (0871) 330 1515
www.fifteen.net
⊖ Old Street, map 2
Italian | £36
Cooking score: 3

Jamie Oliver's Fifteen Foundation is a training programme for underprivileged youngsters and has been running for eight years. Yet the former warehouse in Hoxton which houses

the ground-floor trattoria and basement restaurant has lost none of its appeal, continuing to draw praise for its 'buzzy atmosphere', welcoming, friendly and professional staff, and for just being 'simply marvellous'. In the restaurant, dishes are based on 'wonderful, lovely fresh ingredients' with lots of twists on traditional Italian ideas – say tagliatelle with Welsh lamb ragù and gremolata, or perfectly timed cod with Italian peppers 'agro dolce', spianata piccante sausage, cuttlefish and wild rocket. The informal trattoria has slightly cheaper prices, with penne alla Siciliana or roasted spatchcock poussin with wild garlic pesto typical choices. House wine in both is £20.
**Chef/s:** Andrew Parkinson. **Open:** all week L 12 to 3, D 6 to 10. **Closed:** 25 and 26 Dec. **Meals:** Set L £22.50 (2 courses) to £25. Set D £60 (5 courses). **Service:** 12.5% (optional). **Details:** Cards accepted. 68 seats. Air-con. Wheelchair access. Music. Children allowed.

## The Fox

**Streetwise City gastropub**
28 Paul Street, City, EC2A 4LB
Tel no: (020) 7729 5708
www.thefoxpublichouse.com
⊖ Old Street, Liverpool Street, map 2
Gastropub | £25
Cooking score: 3
£30

Like many of its cousins in the capital, this natural-born City gastropub takes a dressed-down, casual, streetwise approach to things, with rough-and-ready furnishings, animated local vibes and no standing on ceremony. At ground level is a rumbustious bar for drinks and socialising, while the main foodie action takes place in a quirky first-floor dining room lit by chandeliers and Gothic candelabra. The short, regularly changing menu trumpets no-frills, seasonal dishes with strong Mediterranean leanings, from chicken liver and chorizo salad with capers and red onion to vanilla pannacotta with mango, or chocolate mousse cake with clementine sorbet. In between, generous satisfaction comes in the shape of, say, grilled tuna with new potatoes, fennel and tapenade, mixed seafood linguine with parsley and garlic or ribeye steak with rosemary, chips, watercress and aïoli. Around 30 affordable wines start at £13.50 (£3.50 a glass).

**Chef/s:** Amanda Pritchett. **Open:** Sun to Fri L 12 to 3 (4 Sun), Mon to Sat D 6 to 10. **Closed:** bank hols, 1 week Christmas. **Meals:** alc (main courses £9 to £17). Set L and D £18.50 (2 courses) to £22.50. Sun L £14 (2 courses). **Service:** not inc. **Details:** Cards accepted. 40 seats. 30 seats outside. Music. Children allowed.

## ALSO RECOMMENDED

### ▲ Ginnan

1-2 Rosebery Court, Rosebery Avenue, Clerkenwell, EC1R 5HP
Tel no: (020) 7278 0008
⊖ Angel, Farringdon, map 5
Japanese

Try to ignore the strong smell of cooking oil in this dimly lit room furnished with simple dark wood. The extensive menu features katsu curry as well as Korean bulgogi. Come here for the 'surprisingly good' sushi – eel and yellowtail (£3) deserves attention. Miso soup, agedashi tofu and chicken teriyaki (£9) are workmanlike, and green tea ice cream is a better bet than red bean custard cake. Set menus are good value. Wines from £16.

### The Great Eastern Dining Room

**Impeccably hip all-rounder**
54-56 Great Eastern Street, Shoreditch, EC2A 3QR
Tel no: (020) 7613 4545
www.rickerrestaurants.com
⊖ Old Street, map 2
Pan-Asian | £30
Cooking score: 3

£5 OFF **V**

The Hoxton outpost of Will Ricker's pan-Asian empire provides an impeccably hip setting for anything from a quick lunch to a long evening, ending in the DJ bar downstairs. The straight-talking menu 'is diverse enough for a knowledgeable palate and familiar enough for the novice', and divides into crowd-pleasing categories including dim sum, curry and sashimi. You could kick off with prawn dumplings or baby spare ribs, and move on to Korean barbecue chicken, vegetable pad thai or roasted aromatic duck with plum sauce. Typical sides might be sugar snaps with garlic and soy, and black pepper noodles. Service is 'beyond excellent'. Fusion desserts run to stem ginger cheesecake, and sticky toffee pudding with chai ice cream. Wines start at £15.20.

**Chef/s:** Cameron MacLean. **Open:** Mon to Fri L 12 to 3, Mon to Sat D 6 to 11. **Closed:** Sun, 23 Dec to 1 Jan. **Meals:** alc (main courses £10 to £22). **Service:** 12.5% (optional). **Details:** Cards accepted. 60 seats. Air-con. Separate bar. No music. Children allowed. Car parking.

### Green & Red

**Tequila thriller with good tapas**
51 Bethnal Green Road, Bethnal Green, E1 6LA
Tel no: (020) 7749 9670
www.greenred.co.uk
⊖ Liverpool Street, map 1
Mexican | £25
Cooking score: 2

£5 OFF  £30 ▼

Tequila is the name of the game – this Mexican bar/cantina claims the biggest collection of 100% agave tequila in Europe ('more than 200 kinds'). The décor is basic, the decibels high and the food from the Mexican state of Jalisco can seem rough-hewn, but tapas such as chorizo with potatoes, onion and coriander, and beef and pork meatballs in a chipotle chilli and tomato salsa are generally well-reported. Substantial mains such as slow-roast pork belly and ribs with chicharron (crackling) and an avocado salsa arrive with fresh tortillas, cabbage salad and refried beans. House wine is £14.90.

**Chef/s:** Otis Quigley. **Open:** Mon to Fri L 12 to 3, all week D 6 to 11 (10.30 Sun). **Closed:** Christmas, banks hols. **Meals:** alc (main courses £11 to £15). **Service:** 12.5% (optional). **Details:** Cards accepted. 60 seats. Air-con. Separate bar. Wheelchair access. Music. Children allowed.

## The Gun

**Popular Docklands gastropub**
27 Coldharbour, Canary Wharf, E14 9NS
Tel no: (020) 7515 5222
www.thegundocklands.com
⊖ Canary Wharf, map 1
Gastropub | £28
Cooking score: 3

 £30

Great urban views over The Thames to the 02
Arena are part of the pull of Tom and Ed
Martin's docklands pub: 'We were there at full
moon. The Gun was really romantic', affirms
one reader. It combines atmosphere and
history with earthy British food – potted salt
beef or pig's head terrine with sauce gribiche
and watercress made a good lunch opener one
Sunday, while roast rack, shoulder and leg of
Herdwick mutton with puréed celeriac, roast
red onion and lamb gravy offered substantial
satisfaction. In the bar, 'excellent pub food'
such as crispy pork belly with apple sauce, shin
burger with hand-cut chips and ox cheeks
with mashed potato adds to the appeal of the
place. However poor service is a point that
concerns reporters. House wine is £15.
**Chef/s:** David George. **Open:** all week L 12 to 3
(11.30 to 4 Sat and Sun), D 6 to 10.30 (9.30 Sun).
**Closed:** 25 Dec. **Meals:** alc (main courses £11 to
£18). **Service:** 12.5% (optional). **Details:** Cards
accepted. 70 seats. 120 seats outside. Air-con.
Separate bar. Wheelchair access. Music. Children
allowed.

## READERS RECOMMEND

## Hawksmoor

**North American**
157 Commercial Street, City, E1 6BJ
Tel no: (020) 7247 7392
www.thehawksmoor.co.uk
'Amazing blend of local and top end restaurant;
great food, charming service'

## Hix Oyster & Chop House

**Making a virtue of plain food**
35-37 Greenhill Rents, Cowcross Street,
Clerkenwell, EC1M 6BN
Tel no: (020) 7017 1930
www.hixoysterandchophouse.co.uk
⊖ Farringdon, map 5
British | £40
Cooking score: 4

Bare floorboards and brown paper menus
suggest that this high-decibel Clerkenwell
bolt-hole is intended as a bistro, Brit-style. It's
too expensive and mannered for that, but still
makes a virtue of plain food, done almost
plainly. Aside from the oysters, a warm salad
of purple sprouting broccoli with sheep's
cheese and a punchy mustard dressing is a
feelgood way to start. Follow it, perhaps, with
an ugly but tasty encounter with a whole roast
gurnard and brown shrimps. The meat board
(porterhouse, fillet on the bone, salt marsh
lamb) is paraded with pride; for a rewardingly
chewy experience choose gamey, fibrous
hanger steak. Desserts like buttermilk
pudding and treacle sponge have a nursery
feel, but the Bakewell pudding, topped with
crisp flaked almonds and served to share with a
bowl of clotted cream, is the stuff of dreams.
Last year's problems with service seem to have
been charmingly resolved, but the chips still
need work. House wine, from £15.50 (£3.75
a glass), is bolstered by a thorough beer and
cider list.
**Chef/s:** Stuart Tattersall. **Open:** Sun to Fri L 12 to 3,
all week D 6 to 11 (10.30 Sun). **Closed:** 25 and 26
Dec, 1 Jan. **Meals:** alc (main courses £15 to £39).
**Service:** 12.5% (optional). **Details:** Cards accepted.
65 seats. 8 seats outside. Air-con. No music.
Wheelchair access. Children allowed.

## ALSO RECOMMENDED

### Kasturi

57 Aldgate High Street, Whitechapel, EC3N 1AL
Tel no: (020) 7480 7402
www.kasturi-restaurant.co.uk
⊖ Aldgate, map 2
**Indian**

Flashy design touches and a striking Art Deco interior signal that this smart City Indian is a notch or two above the local curry house average. The food also makes a statement, with a strong showing of regional dishes – especially from the North West Frontier. Tandooris have been praised, but the kitchen also tackles traditional biryanis (from £9.95), 'popular' staples (think sag gosht and chicken tikka masala) and more ambitious specialities including jumbo prawns malabar cooked with coconut milk (£14.95). Good-value vegetarian thalis, too. House wine is £15.95. Closed Sun.

## Medcalf

**Lively bistro with nakedly simple food**
40 Exmouth Market, Clerkenwell, EC1R 4QE
Tel no: (020) 7833 3533
www.medcalfbar.co.uk
⊖ Farringdon, map 2
**Modern British | £25**
**Cooking score: 2**

£30

The starkly functional look of this long, narrow dining room matches the naked simplicity of the food. With a lively, relaxed atmosphere, and short, modestly priced menu it's a winning format. Straightforward dishes include smoked bacon and duck terrine or pork pie and piccalilli, while mains run to slow-cooked belly of pork with apple and cider sauce, and skate wing with curly kale, beurre noisette and capers. Not all reports have been positive this year, but on the whole this is 'pleasant enough cooking'. The wine list comprises two pages of French, Spanish and Italian bottles from £15.25.

**Chef/s:** Andrew Fila. **Open:** all week L 12 to 3 (4 Sat and Sun), Mon to Sat D 6 to 10 (5.30 Thur, 5.30 to 10.30 Fri and Sat). **Meals:** alc (main courses £9 to £15). Set L £12.50 (2 courses) to £16. **Service:** 12.5% (optional). **Details:** Cards accepted. 65 seats. 28 seats outside. Air-con. Wheelchair access. Music.

## ALSO RECOMMENDED
### Mehek

45 London Wall, City, EC2M 5TE
Tel no: (020) 7588 5043
www.mehek.co.uk
⊖ Moorgate, Liverpool Street, map 2
**Indian**

The name means 'fragrance', when applied in the gastronomic context, and that's certainly apt for the pan-regional Indian cooking on offer in this beautifully decorated, wood-panelled restaurant on the London Wall. Begin, perhaps, wth crisply fried spicy whitebait in garlic and chilli (£4.50), before going on to main course selections such as Goan king prawns served in a coconut shell (£15.90) and Hyderabadi duck marinated in peanuts, mustard and sesame seeds (£10.50). Wines from £14.50 (£3.75 a glass). Open Mon to Fri.

**NEW ENTRY**
## The Modern Pantry

**Fusion makes a comeback**
47-48 St John's Square, Clerkenwell, EC1V 4JJ
Tel no: (020) 7553 9210
www.themodernpantry.co.uk
⊖ Farringdon, map 5
**Fusion | £31**
**Cooking score: 3**

£5 OFF

That brand of cuisine formerly known as fusion or Pacific Rim makes a comeback at ex-Providores chef Anna Hansen's hard-working EC1 venture of café, 'traiteur' and dining room. At street level, the sunlit café's communal tables and dressed-down staff create a refreshing Antipodean ambience. This is reflected in the menu, too, from breakfast of Vegemite toast or sugar-cured prawn omelette with sambal, to lunch or dinner (also served in the first-floor restaurant) of miso-marinated onglet steak with cassava chips, or date, feta and mint fritters. Such sprightly combinations make a change, but they aren't all successful (for example peanut pannacotta with wasabi and lime jelly) and can be let down by imprecise cooking. Wines, spanning the globe from Kent to New Zealand, start at £13, with a dozen by glass/carafe.

**Chef/s:** Anna Hansen. **Open:** Café all week 8am to 11pm (from 9 Sat, 10 to 10 Sun), Restaurant Tue to Fri and Sun L 12 to 3 (4 Sun), Tue to Sat D 6 to 10.30. **Closed:** 25 Dec, bank hols. **Meals:** alc (main courses £12 to £22). Set L £17.50 (2 courses) to £22. **Service:** 12.5% (optional). **Details:** Cards accepted. 60 seats. 36 seats outside. Air-con. Wheelchair access. Music. Children allowed.

## Moro

**Vibrant big-on-flavour favourite**
34-36 Exmouth Market, Clerkenwell, EC1R 4QE
Tel no: (020) 7833 8336
www.moro.co.uk
⊖ Farringdon, map 2
Spanish/North African | £32
Cooking score: 4

The Clarks are into their second decade in charge at this laid-back, no frills restaurant at the heart of Exmouth Market... and they're going from strength to strength. Regulars return repeatedly for the big-on-flavour blend of Spanish and Moorish influences presented in the form of a short-choice, weekly changing menu. Driven by well-sourced ingredients and unfussy execution, the open-to-view kitchen's wood-fired oven and charcoal grill inspire many dishes. Early autumn might see the simplicity of crab brik with harissa or the engaging straightforwardness of roasted bream ('among the better restaurant dishes I have had'), with green tahini, pan-fried potatoes and cauliflower. Elsewhere, there's wood-roasted pork chop with slow-cooked red cabbage and chorizo, or superb chargrilled lamb and fava bean purée with artichoke hearts cooked in preserved lemon. For dessert there's chocolate

and apricot tart. Tapas are served at the bar, and Spanish wines from £13 are complemented by a good sherry selection.

**Chef/s:** Samuel and Samantha Clark. **Open:** Mon to Sat L 12.30 to 2.30, D 7 to 10.30. Tapas 12.30 to 10.30. **Closed:** Sun, 2 weeks Christmas, Easter, bank hols. **Meals:** alc (main courses £15 to £19). **Service:** not inc. **Details:** Cards accepted. 85 seats. 12 seats outside. Air-con. Separate bar. Wheelchair access. Music. Children allowed.

## The Narrow

**Dapper riverside gastropub**
44 Narrow Street, Limehouse, E14 8DP
Tel no: (020) 7592 7950
www.gordonramsay.com
⊖ Limehouse, map 1
Gastropub | £22
Cooking score: 3

This was Gordon Ramsay's first toe in pubby waters and its success has made him dip in two more (the Devonshire and the Warrington, see entries). A dapper riverside pub serving real ales, ciders and unpretentious food, the Narrow occupies a listed building which was originally a customs/dockmaster's house. Classic bar snacks including ploughman's lunches should plug a gap, but for a full meal try smoked ham and veal pie, hake and chips with marrowfat peas, and then a nostalgic pudding like lemon meringue pie. There has been a murmur of discontent about the service ('we came for lunch, not tea'), but otherwise diners seem happy. The mostly European wine list starts at £13.50.

**Chef/s:** John Collin. **Open:** all week L 11.30 to 3 (12 to 4 Sat and Sun), D 6 to 11 (5 to 11 Sat, 5 to 10.30 Sun). **Meals:** alc (main courses £11 to £17). **Service:** 12.5% (optional). **Details:** Cards accepted. 70 seats. 40 seats outside. Air-con. Separate bar. No music. Wheelchair access. Children allowed. Car parking.

### Also recommended

Also recommended entries are not scored but we think they are worth a visit.

## 1 Lombard Street

**Cultured City high-roller**
1 Lombard Street, City, EC3V 9AA
Tel no: (020) 7929 6611
www.1lombardstreet.com
⊖ Bank, map 2
Modern European | £55
Cooking score: 6

£5 OFF ▮ V

A converted, neo-classical banking hall in the fibrillating heart of the recession-ravaged Square Mile, 1 Lombard Street makes the most of its spectacular Georgian interior. The brasserie is a frenetic rendezvous for local suits with bonuses still to spend, while the capacious restaurant strikes a more exclusive, cultured pose, with Titian's *The Rape of Europa* looking down on the scene. Assertive flavours and high levels of technical skill define Herbert Berger's cooking, which overlays modern themes with classic French gloss and exotica. Raw materials are top-drawer and the kitchen is happy to drift into the eclectic flavour zone for the likes of tuna carpaccio with toasted sesame seeds, black radish, ginger and lime vinaigrette or steamed scallops with shellfish tortellini, Thai velouté, green papaya pickle and sweet basil oil. Meat dishes tap into the Gallic mainstream for rack and confit of lamb with sarladaise potatoes or tournedos of Angus beef with wild mushrooms and oxtail sauce – although squab pigeon with chorizo and chickpea rissoles strikes a sunny Iberian note. To finish, bitter chocolate fondant with iced pistachio parfait and sea-salted caramel is balanced by the oriental caprice of roast pineapple with Szechuan pepper, coriander syrup and coconut sorbet. Great names from France hold centre-stage on the distinguished wine list, but there are also gems from the world cellar. High-rollers can delve into the treasured 'Lombard Vault' while the money lasts; lesser mortals will find plenty of pleasures from around £20.

**Chef/s:** Herbert Berger. **Open:** Mon to Fri L 12 to 2.30, D 6 to 10. **Closed:** Sat, Sun. **Meals:** alc (main courses £27 to £32). Tasting menu £45 (9 courses).

**Service:** 12.5%. **Details:** Cards accepted. 40 seats. Air-con. Separate bar. Wheelchair access. Music. Children allowed.

## ALSO RECOMMENDED

### ▲ Pham Sushi

159 Whitecross Street, Barbican, EC1Y 8JL
Tel no: (020) 7251 6336
www.phamsushi.co.uk
⊖ Old Street, Barbican, map 5
Japanese

A simple canteen feel points up the lack of pretension about this straightforward Japanese restaurant, with no-nonsense close-packed tables and brisk staff. The menus major on sushi but also offer a variety of cooked dishes such as vegetable tempura (£6), beef teriyaki (£8), and crispy fried salmon. Ordering is made easier with various set menus and combination platters of sushi (from £7.50) and sashimi. Booking is advisable. House wine is £11.90.

## Refettorio at the Crowne Plaza Hotel

**Traditional Italian in elegant surroundings**
19 New Bridge Street, City, EC4V 6DB
Tel no: (020) 7438 8052
www.refettorio.com
⊖ Blackfriars, map 5
Italian | £40
Cooking score: 2

The palace that stood here until the Great Fire of 1666 was bequeathed by Henry VIII to his son, Edward VI, who turned it into an incoherent mixture of school and prison, but that's teenagers for you. The site now houses an elegant Blackfriars hotel, incorporating a refectory-style dining room. The Italian menus are structured traditionally, with antipasti, pastas and risottos preceding mains such as chargrilled swordfish with cherry tomatoes and rocket, or beef fillet with spinach in Marsala. Ricotta tart with candied fruits and raspberry sauce is a good way to finish. An all-Italian wine list (bar Champagnes) starts from £16.

**Chef/s:** Giorgio Locatelli. **Open:** Mon to Fri L 12 to 2.30, Mon to Sat D 6 to 10.30 (10 Fri and Sat). **Closed:** Sun, Christmas. **Meals:** alc (main courses £17 to £24). **Service:** 12.5% (optional). **Details:** Cards accepted. 110 seats. Air-con. Separate bar. Wheelchair access. Music. Children allowed.

## Rhodes Twenty Four

**Jaw-dropping views and flag-waving food**
Tower 42, 25 Old Broad Street, City, EC2N 1HQ
Tel no: (020) 7877 7703
www.rhodes24.co.uk
⊖ Liverpool Street, map 2
British | £50
Cooking score: 5

You'll need a head for heights once you've negotiated the 'pre-flight' check-in procedures and security scanners, and taken the lift to 24th floor of the old NatWest building. Needless to say, the views are some of the most jaw-dropping in the capital – so try to bag one of the sought-after window seats if possible. Thankfully the décor doesn't try to compete with the cityscape vistas: muted colours and well-spaced tables are the order of the day, while the food panders to the current longing for unbuttoned British heritage. Chef Adam Gray delivers trademark interpretations of Gary Rhodes' home-grown vernacular morphed into cheeky haute cuisine. It's a style that allows foie gras and Lincolnshire smoked eel terrine with piccalilli dressing or glazed lobster omelette thermidor to share the billing with potted rabbit, steamed mutton suet pudding, and Dover sole with Jerusalem artichoke and cockle casserole. Everything depends on diligently sourced ingredients – pork is free-range meat from Blythburgh, salmon is organic and crab arrives from Cornwall. To conclude, desserts glance backwards into the wistful world of steamed rhubarb and ginger sponge and the like, while practising the art of re-invention (iced caramelised pear mousse with soft dark chocolate ice cream, say). The wine list has an imaginative spread, although prices (from £20) reflect the City location.

**Chef/s:** Adam Gray. **Open:** Mon to Fri L 12 to 2.30, D 6 to 9. **Closed:** Sat, Sun, bank hols, 1 week Christmas. **Meals:** alc (main courses £16 to £32). **Service:** 12.5% (optional). **Details:** Cards accepted. 75 seats. Air-con. Separate bar. Wheelchair access. Music. Children allowed.

## Rivington Grill

**No-frills, nostalgic Brit food**
28-30 Rivington Street, Shoreditch, EC2A 3DZ
Tel no: (020) 7729 7053
www.rivingtongrill.co.uk
⊖ Old Street, map 2
British | £30
Cooking score: 2

£5 OFF **V**

Camped in the arty 'Shoreditch Triangle', this swanky warehouse conversion looks the part, with its whitewashed walls, leather sofas and long eating counters – plus clothed tables for a little more luxury. Brit food from days gone by is Rivington's stock-in-trade, and the menu tugs at the nostalgic heartstrings with soft herring roes on toast, Barnsley chop with bubble and squeak, and bread-and-butter pud. The kitchen also serves up a few surprises – breaded rose veal with wilted nettles, lobster with chips, and sweet cicely added to gooseberry pie. Spanish house wine is £15. A second branch sits cheek-by-jowl with the Greenwich Picturehouse, tel no: (020) 8293 9270.

**Chef/s:** Simon Wadham. **Open:** all week L 12 to 3 (11 to 4 Sat and Sun), D 6 to 11 (10 Sun). **Closed:** 25 and 26 Dec, 1 Jan. **Meals:** alc (main courses £10 to £26). Sun L £18.50. **Service:** 12.5% (optional). **Details:** Cards accepted. 75 seats. Air-con. Separate bar. Wheelchair access. Music. Children allowed.

### Average price

The average price listed in main-entry reviews denotes the price of a three-course meal, without wine.

## Rosemary Lane

**Modern European**
61 Royal Mint Street, Tower Hill, E1 8LG
Tel no: (020) 7481 2602
www.rosemarylane.btinternet.co.uk
'The food is a very high standard; lovingly prepared and good value'

## Saf

**Eat raw, eat vegan**
152 Curtain Road, Shoreditch, EC2A 3AT
Tel no: (020) 7613 0007
www.safrestaurant.co.uk
⊖ Old Street, map 2
Vegetarian | £23
**New chef**

**V** £30 ⊗

Saf gives some street cred and urban chic to raw food and dedicated vegan cuisine, and it pleads its case in a groovy minimalist setting tailor-made for Shoreditch's eco-crowd. A new chef was due to be appointed as the *Guide* was going to press, but the format looks set to continue with snappy global flavours and cute touches at every turn: 'caviar' is actually 'chive pearls', maki rolls are fashioned around parsnip rice, and pesto au poivre involves cashew cheese, sage and a pink peppercorn crust. Rawness is king, and the temperature of any 'cooked' dishes is not allowed to exceed 48°C to preserve nutrients. The bar deals in zany 'botanical' cocktails, and the wine list is a specialist line-up of organic/biodynamic bottles (from £19).
**Open:** all week L 12 to 3.30 (4 Sun), Mon to Sat D 6 to 10.15. **Closed:** 24 to 27 Dec, most bank hols.
**Meals:** alc (main courses £10 to £13).
**Service:** 12.5% (optional). **Details:** Cards accepted. 68 seats. 38 seats outside. Air-con. Wheelchair access. Music. Children allowed.

## St John

**Nose-to-tail standard bearer**
26 St John Street, Clerkenwell, EC1M 4AY
Tel no: (020) 7251 0848
www.stjohnrestaurant.com
⊖ Farringdon, map 5
British | £35
**Cooking score: 6**

It all seemed rather revolutionary back in the '90s: buy up a defunct smokehouse round the corner from Smithfield Market, fill it with a ramshackle selection of old furniture and devise a stripped-bare menu stuffed with thrifty offcuts from the larder, the farm and the countryside. There was even a clever hook and slogan for the whole thing: it was dubbed 'nose-to-tail eating'. Since then, the concept has spread faster than a patch of nettles, and no one bats an eyelid if St John's menu lists kohlrabi as a starter or Eccles cake with Lancashire cheese for afters. It's all in the detail – or the uncompromising lack of it. Fergus Henderson's serious obsession with offal and butchery's less glamorous bits is legendary (lamb's tongue, ox heart, bone marrow and pig's trotters are his stock in trade) and he understands that flavour, freshness and provenance come first. Just about everything on his bold, twice-daily selection has a simple, unadulterated earthiness, whether it's resplendently unadorned cured beef and horseradish, mallard with beetroot or – if fish is your thing – braised squid with fennel and aïoli or brill with salsify. Sides of sprout tops are in keeping, and if the Eccles cakes don't tempt, how about pigging out on spotted dick with custard or blood orange trifle? The decent-value, all-French wine list opens with vins de pays at £18.
**Chef/s:** Christopher Gillard. **Open:** Mon to Fri L 12 to 3, Sun L 1 to 3, Mon to Sat D 6 to 11. **Closed:** Christmas to New Year, Easter. **Meals:** alc (main courses £14 to £20). **Service:** 12.5% (optional). **Details:** Cards accepted. 110 seats. Air-con. Separate bar. No music. No mobile phones. Children allowed.

## St John Bread & Wine

**The upper crust of City brasseries**
94-96 Commercial Street, Spitalfields, E1 6LZ
Tel no: (020) 7251 0848
www.stjohnbreadandwine.com
⊖ Liverpool Street, map 1
British | £25
Cooking score: 3

As with elder sibling St John (see entry above), Fergus Henderson's Spitalfields off-shoot is noted for spartan surrounds and an easy-going atmosphere. The gutsy, no-frills British cooking puts the emphasis firmly on quality ingredients and it's the sort of place where you can drop in for breakfast (doorstop-sized Old Spot bacon sandwich or porridge and prunes) and expect to see ox heart with pickled walnut and watercress or pig's head with white beans and black cabbage on the short carte. While these may not be for the faint-hearted, you might also find smoked mackerel and sorrel and whole crab with a dollop of mayonnaise. The key to it all is simplicity. Cheese are English and wines French, starting at £18.
**Chef/s:** James Lowe. **Open:** all week 9 to 11 (10.30 Sun). **Closed:** 25 Dec to 2 Jan. **Meals:** alc (main courses £11.50 to £13). **Service:** not inc.
**Details:** Cards accepted. 54 seats. Air-con. Children allowed.

## Searcy's

**Stylish dining for culture vultures**
Level 2, Barbican Centre, Silk Street, Barbican, EC2Y 8DS
Tel no: (020) 7588 3008
www.barbican.org.uk
⊖ Barbican, Moorgate, map 5
Modern British | £29
Cooking score: 3

The L-shaped room, looking out over an artificial lake to St Giles Cripplegate Church, wears its new livery well. Stylish and inviting, it makes a fitting backdrop for Quentin Fitch's modern British cooking. Searcy's purpose is obviously to feed concert and theatre-goers,

but it does more much than that. The set-price menus take in a deeply flavoured carrot and sweet potato soup, gurnard fillet with mussels and ratte potatoes, and a typically earthy dish of roast hogget (year-old lamb) with mash and baby onions. Puddings might offer praline burnt cream or a fine Seville orange and chocolate tart. Front-of-house displays plenty of care and attention and the international wine list is organised by style. Bottles from £17.50.
**Chef/s:** Quentin Fitch. **Open:** Mon to Fri L 12 to 2.30, Mon to Sat D 5 to 10.30. **Closed:** Sun, 24 and 25 Dec. **Meals:** Set L and D £24.50 (2 courses) to £28.50. **Service:** 12.5%. **Details:** Cards accepted. 120 seats. Air-con. Separate bar. Wheelchair access. Music. Children allowed. Car parking.

**NEW ENTRY**
## Soseki

**City stunner with sustainable fish**
20 Bury Street, City, EC3A 5AX
Tel no: (020) 7621 9211
www.soseki.co.uk
⊖ Liverpool Street, Bank, map 2
Japanese | £35
Cooking score: 3

Right by the Gherkin, this first-floor dining room looks beautiful, with swathes of embroidered silks, cedar and exquisite screens. It is more than just a pretty face too, with awards for its sustainability policy towards fish. The format is kaiseki-kappo: an informal style of fine dining where chefs and customers face each other across a counter. Fish forms the base of the multi-course banquets. From the Haiku menu, inspection started with supple monkfish liver with wasabi and finished with black sesame blamange as well as green tea tiramisu. In between were raw, simmered and fried dishes, exemplary sashimi and inventive sushi. Savoury chawan mushi, clear soups and tempura were good, but not in the same class. Sakés and wines start from £18.
**Chef/s:** Takanori Kurokowa. **Open:** Mon to Fri L 12 to 2.30, D 6 to 10. **Closed:** bank hols, 1 week Christmas. **Meals:** Set menus £25 to £65.

**Service:** 12.5% (optional) for tables of 6 plus.
**Details:** Cards accepted. 70 seats. Air-con. Separate bar. Wheelchair access. Music.

## Les Trois Garçons
**Bejewelled burlesque dining**
1 Club Row, Shoreditch, E1 6JX
Tel no: (020) 7613 1924
www.lestroisgarcons.com
⊖ Liverpool Street, map 1
French | £50
Cooking score: 3
£5 OFF

Flamboyantly high-camp décor hits you between the eyes in this ravishing burlesque dining room. 'Les trois garçons' of the title have filled this one-time East End boozer with gigantic wine glasses filled with bejewelled fruit and a menagerie of stuffed animals adorned with bling; weird chandeliers hang from the ceiling and lights flash from a working carousel. Once you have caught your breath, focus on the French-inspired menu, which is overlaid with vivid Mediterranean influences. Foie gras is ever-present, and the kitchen also tackles a salad of Jersey tomatoes and Lyme Bay crab with parsley vinaigrette, an assiette of Landroc pork, and braised beef with Scottish langoustines, white asparagus, cauliflower and wild garlic. Artisan Swiss cheeses reflect the chef's homeland, and desserts play it straight with the likes of Tahitian vanilla crème brûlée. Mainly French wines start at £20.
**Chef/s:** Jérôme Henry. **Open:** Mon to Sat D 7 to 12. **Closed:** Sun, Christmas, New Year, bank hols, 2 weeks Aug. **Meals:** Set D £42.50 (2 courses) to £49.50. Tasting menu £72 (8 courses). **Service:** 12.5% (optional). **Details:** Cards accepted. 80 seats. Air-con. Wheelchair access. Music. Children allowed.

### £5 OFF voucher scheme
Also recommended entries can also take part in the £5-off voucher scheme. For a full list of participating restaurants, please visit: www.which.co.uk/gfgvoucherscheme

## Viet Grill
**Glossy vibes and fun wines**
58 Kingsland Road, Shoreditch, E2 8DP
Tel no: (020) 7739 6686
www.vietgrill.co.uk
⊖ Old Street, map 2
Vietnamese | £15
Cooking score: 2
 £5 OFF **V** £30

A shining star on Kingsland Road's 'Little Saigon', Viet Grill has raised the bar, leaving the competition looking rather drab. The glossy interior, Malcolm Gluck-authored wine list and modern menu (inspired by contemporary Vietnamese cooking) make for slightly higher bills, but the extra expenditure is worth it. The commendably brief menu covers interesting territory, for example, 'Saigon ceviche' or beef brisket simmered with star anise, as well as 'one-dish meals' like classic pho (noodle soup). Similarly commendable is the wine offer defined by low mark-ups, fun choices (white Crozes or Austrian Zweigelt) and – oh joy – decent glasses. House wine starts at £17.
**Chef/s:** Vinh Bu. **Open:** all week L 12 to 3, D 5.30 to 11. **Meals:** alc (main courses £6 to £8). Set L £17.50 (2 courses) to £19.50. Set D £21.50 (2 courses) to £25.50. **Service:** 12.5% (optional). **Details:** Cards accepted. 150 seats. Air-con. Separate bar. Wheelchair access. Music. Children allowed.

NEW ENTRY
## Vinoteca
**Wines and food to savour**
7 St John Street, Farringdon, EC1M 4AA
Tel no: (020) 7253 8786
www.vinoteca.co.uk
⊖ Farringdon, Barbican, map 5
Modern British | £25
Cooking score: 3
 £30

This unpretentious, fairly priced wine bar, run by staff passionate about wine and food, boasts an open kitchen that prepares simple, lovingly sourced food. Be prepared to wait for a table – 'it's always heaving' – but with a display of some 275 wines, time can be spent choosing the right bottle to drink now (from £14.25) or to take home later. The menu changes daily (as does the selection of 25 wines by the glass), perhaps a selection of cheese accompanied by peach and fennel chutney and homemade oatcakes followed by mains of char-grilled bavette steak with shallot, chervil and bottarga butter, chips and salad or pan-fried grey mullet with broad beans, peas, Jersey Royals and green olive dressing. Baked white chocolate and caramel cheesecake with fresh blueberries makes a great finish. **Chef/s:** Ross Goodall. **Open:** all week L 12 to 2.45 (11 to 4 Sun), Mon to Sat D 6 to 10. **Closed:** 25 Dec to 2 Jan. **Meals:** alc (main courses £10 to £16). **Service:** 12.5% (optional). **Details:** Cards accepted. 38 seats. 8 seats outside. Air-con. Music. Children allowed.

## Wapping Food
**Industrial-chic food arena**
Wapping Hydraulic Power Station, Wapping, E1W 3ST
Tel no: (020) 7680 2080
www.thewappingproject.com
⊖ Wapping/Shadwell, map 1
**Modern European | £30**
**Cooking score: 3**

£5
OFF

The ever-popular Wapping Project is a London phenomenon, combining an informal restaurant with innovative and experimental art installations, all within a stark, cavernous former hydraulic power station. An Anglo-Mediterranean menu delivers energetic flavour combinations in dishes such as chargrilled squid with chickpeas and morcilla or fried goats' cheese with baby beetroot, chestnut honey, chicory and pecans. Big-hearted main courses include vine leaf-wrapped sea bream with new potatoes, olive and romesco or confit duck with Jerusalem artichoke, red cabbage and pancetta. Blood orange, polenta and pistachio cake with mascarpone has made an impressive finish. An

appealing contemporary wine list opens at £16.25, and there's a great range of cocktails. Brunch is available at weekends (10 to 12.30). **Chef/s:** Camron Emirali. **Open:** all week L 12 to 3 (1 to 3.30 Sat, 1 to 4 Sun), Mon to Sat D 6.30 to 11 (7 Sat). **Closed:** 23 Dec to 2 Jan, bank hols. **Meals:** alc (main courses £12 to £20). Set L and D £25 and £47.50. **Service:** 12.5% (optional). **Details:** Cards accepted. 150 seats. 60 seats outside. Separate bar. Wheelchair access. Music. Children allowed. Car parking.

## READERS RECOMMEND

## Whitechapel Gallery Dining Room
**Modern British**
77-82 Whitechapel High Street, Whitechapel, E1 7QX
Tel no: (020) 7522 7896
www.whitechapelgallery.org
'Whole experience perfectly enhancing a visit to this interesting art gallery'

## The Anchor & Hope
**No-frills food with rustic flavours**
36 The Cut, South Bank, SE1 8LP
Tel no: (020) 7928 9898
⊖ Waterloo, Southwark, map 5
**Gastropub | £25**
**Cooking score: 3**

Pared-back décor proclaims strong pub credentials at this corner building not far from the Young Vic. Drinkers congregate in one half of the large open-plan space, those looking for solid sustenance bag a table in the other half (no bookings). The open kitchen knows what it's doing with seasonal dishes that may seem relatively plain, but have a feel for rustic flavours. Start with a heap of smoked cod's roe on toast or excellent potted shrimps, while for a main course breast of kid with pearl barley stuffing and Puy lentils is 'as good as it gets in this style'. Pace yourself if you are going to order dessert, especially sticky date pudding with butterscotch sauce. House French is £12. **Chef/s:** Trish Hilferty and Warren Fleet. **Open:** Tue to Sat L 12 to 2.30, Sun L at 2 (1 sitting), Mon to Sat D 6 to 10.30. **Closed:** Christmas, New Year, bank hols. **Meals:** alc (main courses £11 to £27). Sun L £30. **Service:** not inc. **Details:** Cards accepted. 40 seats. 28 seats outside. Separate bar. No music. Wheelchair access. Children allowed.

## Babur
**Adventurous Indian**
119 Brockley Rise, Forest Hill, SE23 1JP
Tel no: (020) 8291 2400
www.babur.info
map 1
**Indian | £25**
**Cooking score: 2**

Stylishly simple décor – exposed brickwork and ducting, bare wood tables and abstract artworks – is the hallmark of this contemporary Indian eatery. Seared hake with roast aubergine and red onion salsa is an unusual starter, and so is red sandalwood ostrich, marinated in ground fennel seeds with beetroot. Mains continue that out-of-the-ordinary theme with buffalo vindaloo. For those feeling less adventurous, there is proper biryani made with black-leg chicken, or jumbo tandoori prawns on a masala uttapam griddle cake. Finish with ginger and honey kulfi, or in western style with banana and date pudding and butterscotch sauce. Sunday lunch buffets are abidingly popular. The wine list opens at £13.95. **Chef/s:** Jiwan Lal. **Open:** all week L 12 to 2.30 (4 Sun), D 6 to 11.30. **Closed:** 26 Dec. **Meals:** alc (main courses £10 to £15). **Service:** not inc. **Details:** Cards accepted. 72 seats. Air-con. No mobile phones. Music. Children allowed. Car parking.

## Baltic
**East European chic**
74 Blackfriars Road, Southwark, SE1 8HA
Tel no: (020) 7928 1111
www.balticrestaurant.co.uk
⊖ Southwark, map 5
**Eastern European | £28**
**Cooking score: 3**

Baltic brings some urbane chic to the winter-warming world of East European cooking, and it pleads its case in a stunningly converted, eighteenth-century coachbuilder's workshop with white walls, wooden trussed ceilings, skylights and galleries. To start, try your luck with chlodnik (chilled beetroot, radish and yoghurt soup) or Siberian pelmeni (little veal and pork dumplings) before tackling schabowy (pork escalopes with mizeria and mushrooms) or golonka (ham hock with braised sauerkraut and caraway). Blinis and pierogi are on hand for the diehards, while adventurous souls might branch out into the realms of roast hake with clams, broad beans and wild mushroom broth. Sour cherry crème brûlée is a good way to finish. Baltic is also dedicated to the sinful pleasures of high-proof vodka, although wine fans will find plenty of gluggable stuff from £15.50 (£4 a glass). **Chef/s:** Piotr Repinski. **Open:** Mon to Sat L 12 to 3, D 5.30 to 11, Sun 12 to 10.30. **Meals:** alc (main courses £10 to £17). Set L and D £14.50 (2 courses) to £17.50.

**Service:** 12.5% (optional). **Details:** Cards accepted. 120 seats. 20 seats outside. Air-con. Separate bar. No music. Wheelchair access. Children allowed.

## Brinkley's Kitchen
**Vibrant crowd-pleaser**
35 Bellevue Road, Wandsworth, SW17 7EF
Tel no: (020) 8672 5888
www.brinkleys.com
⊖ Balham, map 3
**Modern European | £28**
**Cooking score: 1**

**V**

The latest addition to the Brinkley's stable occupies a leafy spot overlooking Wandsworth Common, and is already scoring a hit with yummy mummies, famished workers and socialising types. An open kitchen holds centre stage, and the brigade aims to please with a vibrant menu that runs from asparagus and pea risotto to rack of lamb with roasted sweet potato or seared scallops with Puy lentils, chilli and mint dressing. Brinkley's burgers, meze plates and chicken Caesar salad fill the gaps in between. Wines from £12.50.
**Chef/s:** Paolo Zanca. **Open:** all week L 12 to 4 (11 Sat and Sun), Mon to Sat D 6 to 11. **Closed:** 24 to 27 Dec. **Meals:** alc (main courses £10 to £23). Set L £12 (2 courses) to £15. Set D £23 (2 courses) to £27.50. **Service:** 12.5% (optional). **Details:** Cards accepted. 95 seats. 20 seats outside. Air-con. Separate bar. Wheelchair access. Music. Children allowed.

## ALSO RECOMMENDED
### ▲ The Butcher and Grill
39-41 Parkgate Road, Battersea, SW11 4NP
Tel no: (020) 7924 3999
www.thebutcherandgrill.com
map 3
**Modern European**

A bespoke butcher's shop, restaurant and bar rolled into one, this family-friendly venue is cutting the mustard down by Battersea's riverside. Its selling point is ethically reared meat, and everything is handled with aplomb – there are no frills, just slabs of animal protein (from £15.50), burgers and seafood flashed on the grill. Caesar salad (£7.50) is a decent starter, and you could finish with hot Valrhona chocolate brownie (£5.50). Beefy wines from £14.50. Closed Sun D. Also at 33 High Street, Wimbledon SW19 5BY, tel no: (020) 8944 8269.

## Chapters All Day Dining
**From morning coffee to brasserie classics**
43-45 Montpelier Vale, Blackheath, SE3 0TJ
Tel no: (020) 8333 2666
www.chaptersrestaurants.co.uk
map 1
**Modern British | £25**
**Cooking score: 4**

Chapter Two has marched on, changing its format, look and name. It now does exactly what it says on the tin. A flexible menu delivers everything from morning coffee to brasserie classics amid the modernist, unfussy décor which is de rigueur for this kind of open-all-day operation. There is likely to be risotto of wild mushrooms, and maybe confit duck leg or lamb tagine with couscous, while chargrilled steaks are something of a speciality and come with a choice of sauces. Light bites (served from 3 to 6) deliver comfort food in the shape of beef and Guinness pie or battered hake and chips, while desserts feature a good coffee, walnut and pear trifle. Trevor Tobin remains in charge of the kitchen and early feedback is positive – more reports please. A global clutch of wines offers good value from £14.50, with a decent selection by the glass or pichet.
**Chef/s:** Trevor Tobin. **Open:** all week 8am to 11pm. **Closed:** 9 days in Jan. **Meals:** alc (main courses £9 to £22). **Service:** 12.5% (optional). **Details:** Cards accepted. 95 seats. Air-con. Separate bar. Wheelchair access. Music. Children allowed.

## ALSO RECOMMENDED
### ▲ Le Chardon
65 Lordship Lane, East Dulwich, SE22 8EP
Tel no: (020) 8299 1921
www.lechardon.co.uk
**map 1**
**French**

A former Scottish grocer's emblazoned with thistle-motif tiles, Le Chardon offers all-day French bistro food. Following breakfast, it delivers a tried-and-trusted repertoire that runs from moules marinière and fish soup with rouille (£5.75) via whole roast sea bass with olive oil, coq au vin and Barbary duck breast with blackcurrant sauce (£12.95) to crêpes and tarte Tatin (£4.95). House wine is £11.95. Open all week. A sister restaurant is at 32 Abbeville Road, Clapham SW4 9NG, tel no: (020) 8673 9300.

## Chez Bruce
**Superb food, gutsy flavours, big hits**
2 Bellevue Road, Wandsworth, SW17 7EG
Tel no: (020) 8672 0114
www.chezbruce.co.uk
⊖ **Balham, map 3**
**Modern British | £40**
**Cooking score: 6**
🍷

One reader got it spot-on when he described Chez Bruce as a 'great small "local" restaurant that consistently produces superb food'. Bruce Poole has been impressing the denizens of Wandsworth and beyond since 1995 and shows no sign of taking his foot off the pedal in these penny-pinching times. The animated, elbow-to-elbow interior has seen some tweaking and tinkering over the years, but it still conveys a mood of unadorned simplicity – perfect for the kitchen's unfussy, highly personal take on modern cuisine. Poole revels in the gutsy flavours of southern France and the Med, serving up oxtail and chestnut ragoût with herb ravioli and 'lardo di colonnata' as well as roast cod with olive oil mash, Provençal tomato and gremolata. He also delivers some unexpected big hits, adding

a Middle Eastern mélange of spiced kofta, chickpeas, hummus and pomegranate to a dish of lamb rump, and matching Orkney salmon with oysters, crêpes Parmentier, beetroot, horseradish and dill. Desserts also spring a few surprises – perhaps peanut, caramel and milk chocolate mille-feuille. The cheeseboard is a joy to behold ('the best in London', according to one reporter), and it's as much a part of the restaurant's lifeblood as the stupendous global wine list. Intriguing representatives from Canada, Switzerland and Slovenia add an extra dimension to the pages of top-flight French and Australian names, while 16 house selections start at £16.95 (£4.50 a glass) for Sicilian white and Sardinian red.
**Chef/s:** Bruce Poole. **Open:** all week L 12 to 2 (2.30 Sat, 3 Sun), D 6.30 to 10 (10.30 Fri and Sat, 7 to 9.30 Sun). **Closed:** 24 to 26 Dec, 1 Jan. **Meals:** Set L Mon to Fri £19.50 (2 courses) to £25.50. Set L Sat and Sun £32.50. Set D £31.50 (2 courses) to £40. **Service:** 12.5% (optional). **Details:** Cards accepted. 75 seats. Air-con. No music. No mobile phones. Wheelchair access.

## Côte
**Tempting food that's 'stonking good value'**
8 High Street, Wimbledon Village, Wimbledon, SW19 5DX
Tel no: (020) 8947 7100
www.cote-restaurants.co.uk
⊖ **Wimbledon, map 3**
**French | £25**
**Cooking score: 2**

With the look and buzzy feel of a Parisian brasserie, Côte is fast becoming a local institution. The kitchen continues to keep customers satisfied, with flexible menus featuring robust French regional dishes at keen prices. Lunch and early evening deals are 'stonking good value', while duck and pork rillettes, mushrooms feuilleté, tuna niçoise, lamb shank (with wholegrain mustard mash) and steaks with various sauces are equally tempting choices from the carte. Weekend breakfasts (9am to 1pm) bring eggs Benedict and croque-monsieur. The all-French wine

list continues the value-for-money theme with bottles from £13.95. Branches in Soho (see entry), Covent Garden, Richmond and Kensington.
**Open:** Mon to Fri 12 to 11, Sat 9am to 11pm, Sun 9am to 10.30pm. **Closed:** 25 Dec. **Meals:** alc (main courses £9 to £18). Set menu £9.70 (two courses) to £11.70. **Service:** 12.5% (optional). **Details:** Cards accepted. 90 seats. 4 seats outside. Air-con. Wheelchair access. Music. Children allowed.

## Delfina
**Food that packs a flavour punch**
50 Bermondsey Street, Southwark, SE1 3UD
Tel no: (020) 7357 0244
www.thedelfina.co.uk
⊖ **London Bridge, map 1**
**Fusion | £35**
**Cooking score: 4**

More or less round the corner from London Bridge station, Delfina is a converted chocolate factory, a big, open, daylight-filled venue with an expansive exhibition space at the back. Mainly a lunch venue (plus Friday nights), it has always offered up-to-the-minute fusion cooking that is built of quality ingredients and influences drawn from all round the Mediterranean and beyond. Chilli-crusted coley with a sweet potato blini, pak choi and confit tomatoes may be hard to place culturally, but it packs a punch of flavour whatever, while a lentil curry full of cumin and coriander might be garnished with halloumi. Prior to that, you might have started with a chargrilled quail with courgette and a fig and chestnut pannacotta. Meals end aromatically with pistachio macaroons, served with lavender cream and rosewater syrup. A short international wine list starts at £18.60.
**Chef/s:** Richard Simpson. **Open:** Mon to Fri L 12 to 3, Fri D 7 to 10. **Closed:** Sat, Sun, bank hols, 10 days Christmas. **Meals:** alc (main courses £13 to £16). Set L £10 (2 courses). **Service:** 12.5% (optional). **Details:** Cards accepted. 90 seats. 20 seats outside. Wheelchair access. Music. Children allowed.

## Emile's
**An enduring favourite**
96-98 Felsham Road, Putney, SW15 1DQ
Tel no: (020) 8789 3323
www.emilesrestaurant.co.uk
⊖ **Putney Bridge, map 3**
**Anglo-French | £27**
**Cooking score: 1**

A long-established neighbourhood restaurant near the starting-point of the University Boat Race, Emile's is comprised of three dining areas, one in the tiled basement. A mix of traditional French and modern British cuisine is what the monthly changing menus are about, with, say, seared squid and chorizo combining in a pasta-based starter, followed perhaps by grilled veal chop with sweet potato fondant. Cheeses tack to the Anglo side of the Anglo-French compass, and so does sticky ginger and date pudding with toffee sauce. Wine prices open at £12.95.
**Chef/s:** Andrew Sherlock. **Open:** Mon to Sat D only 7.30 to 11. **Closed:** Sun, banks hols, 24 to 30 Dec, 2 Jan, Easter Sat. **Meals:** Set D £23.50 (2 courses) to £26.50. **Service:** not inc. **Details:** Cards accepted. 100 seats. No mobile phones. Wheelchair access. Music. Children allowed.

## Enoteca Turi
**Corkingly good crowd-pleaser**
28 Putney High Street, Putney, SW15 1SQ
Tel no: (020) 8785 4449
www.enotecaturi.com
⊖ **Putney Bridge, map 3**
**Italian | £32**
**Cooking score: 3**

 **V**

Quiet lunches and early evenings can give this long-standing Putney Italian a misleading air of forlornness, but come 8.30 on almost any night of the week, the restaurant is packed to the gunnels with well-heeled locals looking for a decent supper and a glass or two of wine. The red walls and wine racks give the place a country feel, and indeed there's a rustic quality to the menu. The food is good: slivers of marinated pork belly have the fattiness of the meat offset with fresh apple and carrot, and a fillet of black bream served on a herby broth with fresh borlotti beans is nicely timed. But what is really impressive is the wine – proprietor Giuseppe Turi is passionate about the stuff and his carefully annotated all-Italian list (starting around £5 a glass) is over 300 bins long. Follow his recommendations for food and wine matches to add a new dimension to your meal.

**Chef/s:** Giuseppe Turi and Massimo Tagliaferri. **Open:** Mon to Sat L 12 to 2.30, D 7 to 11. **Closed:** Sun, 25 and 26 Dec, 1 Jan. **Meals:** alc (main courses £18 to £22). Set L £15.50 (3 courses). Set D £25.50 (3 courses). **Service:** 12.5% (optional). **Details:** Cards accepted. 85 seats. Air-con. No mobile phones. Wheelchair access. Music. Children allowed.

## ALSO RECOMMENDED

### ▲ fish!

Cathedral Street, Southwark, SE1 9AL
Tel no: (020) 7407 3803
www.fishkitchen.com
⊖ London Bridge, map 1
Seafood

In the heart of Borough Market, close to Southwark Cathedral and London Bridge station, fish! does exactly what it says on the tin. A menu of sustainable seafood is served amid an atmosphere of cheerful bustle, and there's a terrace with outdoor seating. Calamari with rocket and lemon mayonnaise (£7.95), classic fish pie (£10.95) and a whole range of steamed or grilled items (from £9.95 for sardines), served with your choice of sauce, are all impeccably fresh and accurately cooked. Wines from £15.95. Open all week.

## READERS RECOMMEND

### Franco Manca

**Italian**
4 Market Row, Electric Lane, Brixton, SW9 8LD
Tel no: (020) 7738 3021
www.francomanca.co.uk
'Traditional Neapolitan-style pizzas – unlike anything you've tasted before'

## Franklins

**British food with a beating heart**
157 Lordship Lane, East Dulwich, SE22 8HX
Tel no: (020) 8299 9598
www.franklinsrestaurant.com
map 1
British | £24
Cooking score: 2

With raw brick, paper tablecloths and a tiny open kitchen, Rodney Franklin has got his restaurant down to bare bones. The 'interesting' menu is equally basic, proffering chitterlings, ox heart and rabbit which taste of themselves. Nevertheless, Franklins is far from stark, with the buzz of the wine bar and the promise of elemental but enjoyable food to take the edge off. There's more impeccable sourcing at the Kennington branch, and the new 'farm shop' deli across the road. Wine starts at £13.50, although feisty Australian Stump Jump (£18.50) is the popular choice.

**Chef/s:** Ralf Wittig. **Open:** all week L 12 to 4 (5 Sat and Sun), D 6 to 10.30. **Meals:** alc (main courses £12 to £19). Set L £13 (2 courses) to £16. **Service:** not inc. **Details:** Cards accepted. 50 seats. Air-con. Separate bar. No music. Wheelchair access. Children allowed. Car parking.

## Harrison's

**A happy local eatery**
15-19 Bedford Hill, Balham, SW12 9EX
Tel no: (020) 8675 6900
www.harrisonsbalham.co.uk
⊖ Balham, map 3
Modern British | £28
Cooking score: 1

**V**

Having donated his first name to Sam's Brasserie in Chiswick (see entry), Sam Harrison has finished the job with this congenial Balham eatery – a happy place that is ideal for 'singles', yummy mummies, hot dates and the local brunch crowd. The kitchen delivers sound, robust cooking – think goats' curd on toast with shallot jam, grilled lamb chops with bubble and squeak or roast cod

with saffron mash and green sauce, followed by warm rice pudding and blueberry compote. Jazz on Sunday nights. House wine is £13.50.
**Chef/s:** Dan Edwards. **Open:** all week L 12 to 3 (9 to 4 Sat and Sun), D 6 to 10.30 (6.30 to 10.30 Sat, 10 Sun). **Closed:** 24 to 27 Dec. **Meals:** alc (main courses £11 to £18). Set L £12 (2 courses) to £15. Set D £14 (2 courses) to £17. Sun L £17.50.
**Service:** 12.5% (optional). **Details:** Cards accepted. 90 seats. 12 seats outside. Air-con. Separate bar. Wheelchair access. Music. Children allowed.

READERS RECOMMEND

## Hudson's

**British**
113 Lower Richmond Road, Putney, SW15 1EX
Tel no: (020) 8785 4522
'Unpretentious, friendly and a fantastically varied menu'

## Indian Moment

**Indian**
47 Northcote Road, Clapham, SW11 1NJ
Tel no: (020) 7223 6575
www.indianmoment.com
'Perfect for when you don't want to cook, but want interesting, tasty, good-value food'

## Inside

**Good-natured Greenwich bistro**
19 Greenwich South Street, Greenwich, SE10 8NW
Tel no: (020) 8265 5060
www.insiderestaurant.co.uk
map 1
**Modern European | £28**
**Cooking score: 1**

Simple, modern décor and a friendly atmosphere are the hallmarks of this 'excellent' little neighbourhood restaurant, arguably 'the best in Greenwich'. Expect fresh, modern European cooking: perhaps pan-fried halibut with herb risotto and parsley velouté followed by roast Barbary duck breast with Puy lentils, spiced red cabbage, fondant potatoes and balsamic jus, with treacle tart and ginger ice

cream for dessert. Alongside the carte, there's a good-value set lunch or dinner. Wines start at £12.95.
**Chef/s:** Guy Awford and Brian Sargeant. **Open:** Tue to Sun L 12 to 2.30 (3 Sat and Sun), Tue to Sat D 6.30 to 11. **Closed:** Mon, 24 Dec to 2 Jan. **Meals:** alc (main courses £13 to £18). Set L £11.95 (2 courses) to £15.95. Set D £16.95 (2 courses) to £20.95. Sun L £17.95 (2 courses) to £21.95. **Service:** not inc.
**Details:** Cards accepted. 38 seats. Air-con. Wheelchair access. Music. Children allowed.

READERS RECOMMEND

## Jaffna House

**Indian**
90 Tooting High Street, Tooting, SW17 0RN
Tel no: (020) 8672 7786
www.jaffnahouse.co.uk
'Basic, but great for Sri Lankan dishes'

## Kastoori

**Tooting's Gujarati treasure**
188 Upper Tooting Road, Tooting, SW17 7EJ
Tel no: (020) 8767 7027
www.kastoorirestaurant.com
⊖ Tooting Broadway, map 3
**Indian Vegetarian | £21**
**Cooking score: 3**

**V**

A Tooting treasure since opening in 1987, Manoj and Dinesh Thanki's affable restaurant continues to offer Gujarati vegetarian food with a very personal stamp. Vivid colours and Hindu statuettes add some exotic lustre to the dining room, while the kitchen focuses on the regional cuisine of the owners' native Katia Wahd (a temperate region noted for its tomato-based recipes). Classic street snacks such as bhel puri and dahi vada set things up for a range of zingy, fresh-tasting curries ranging from paneer pasanda in cashew and melon seed sauce to channa bateta (chickpeas with potatoes). Their great-value menu also includes a few West African-inspired 'family specials' such as stuffed banana and chillies in tomato sauce or kasodi (sweetcorn in coconut milk with peanut sauce). House wine is £10.95.

**Chef/s:** Manoj Thanki. **Open:** Wed to Sun L 12.30 to 2.30, all week D 6 to 10.30. **Closed:** 25 and 26 Dec. **Meals:** alc (main courses £5 to £7). **Service:** not inc. **Details:** Cards accepted. 82 seats. Air-con. Separate bar. Wheelchair access. Music. Children allowed. Car parking.

## ALSO RECOMMENDED

### ▲ L'Auberge
22 Upper Richmond Road, Putney, SW15 2RX
Tel no: (020) 8874 3593
www.ardillys.com
⊖ East Putney, map 3
French

As patriotically Gallic as *La Marseillaise*, Pascal Ardilly's bistro is a real asset to the neighbourhood, and Putney locals pack the place for bourgeois French food without frippery. A classic starter of roasted pear filled with walnuts and Roquefort (£5.95) could set the scene for authentic cassoulet de Castelnaudary (£15.90) or baked monkfish on beluga lentils with horseradish foam. Close with, say, nougat glacé (£6.75) or moelleux au chocolat. House wine is £14.50. Open Tue to Sat D only.

## Lamberts
**Bijou eatery with excellent food**
2 Station Parade, Balham, SW12 9AZ
Tel no: (020) 8675 2233
www.lambertsrestaurant.com
⊖ Balham, map 3
British | £30
Cooking score: 3

£5
OFF

Though there are local bars and eateries aplenty in the area, there's precious little to draw outsiders to this corner of London. One of the exceptions is this bijou eatery where the chef has gone out of his way to source his ingredients carefully and prepare them thoughtfully. The menu is a tribute to good British produce, and the cooking, on the whole, is excellent in a straightforward way – a simple fish and mussel stew bursts with flavour and braised ham hock with grain

mustard mash and parsley broth is full of soft salty meatiness. The wine list sticks to its English principles – there's plenty of Chapel Down etc. on offer – but it deigns to travel abroad as well. A huge proportion come by the glass (starting at £5) and 300ml decanter. **Chef/s:** David Johnson. **Open:** Sat and Sun L 12 to 3 (5 Sun), Tue to Sat D 7 to 10.30. **Closed:** Mon, 25 and 26 Dec, 1 Jan. **Meals:** alc (main courses £14 to £19). Set L and D £17 (2 courses) to £20. Sun L £20 (2 courses) to £24. **Service:** 12.5% (optional). **Details:** Cards accepted. 50 seats. Air-con. Wheelchair access. Music. Children allowed.

## Light House
**Local favourite with vibrant global food**
75-77 Ridgway, Wimbledon, SW19 4ST
Tel no: (020) 8944 6338
www.lighthousewimbledon.com
⊖ Wimbledon, map 3
Modern European | £30
Cooking score: 3

£5
OFF **V**

A well-liked Wimbledon stalwart that lives up to its name, the 10-year-old Light House continues to beam brightly as a congenial neighbourhood destination with a taste for the exotic when it comes to food. The kitchen dips into the world larder for a menu of palate-teasing dishes gleaned from all over. Here you might encounter beef koftas with sumac onions, hummus and flatbread beside salmon nori rolls with carrot, coriander and chilli sambal, or slow-roast pork belly with molasses, rosemary and tomato baked beans up against confit duck with red lentil and sweet potato dhal. Desserts stay closer to home for the likes of prune frangipane tart or chocolate brownie parfait with cardamom ice cream. House wines start at £14.25 (£3.75 a glass). **Chef/s:** Chris Casey. **Open:** all week L 12 to 2.45 (3.30 Sun), Mon to Sat D 6 to 10.30. **Closed:** 25 and 26 Dec. **Meals:** alc (main courses £13 to £17). Early evening set D £14.50 (2 courses) to £18.50. Sun L £18 (2 courses) to £23. **Service:** 12.5% (optional). **Details:** Cards accepted. 75 seats. 15 seats outside. Air-con. Wheelchair access. Music. Children allowed.

## Family affair

They work together, they stay together: great hospitality from happy families and solid partnerships.

Herefordshire's **Three Crowns** may be fiendishly difficult to find, but the Castle family are great hosts. In game season, one of them may well have shot your lunch.

In a Cotswolds village, Erica Graham (pictured) runs **Allium**'s dining room in assured style, while husband James cooks with the seasons.

Stephen and Tracy Jackson share a vision of self-sufficiency and style at the **Weavers Shed** at Golcar, near Huddersfield.

Andrew and Jacquie Pern are an award-winning partnership, making **The Star Inn** at Harome one of Yorkshire's cosiest bolt-holes.

While Anthony Flinn's partner Olga Garcia sets service standards high at **Anthony's**, his dad crunches the numbers and sister Holly runs the Flannels offshoot.

Matt Tebbutt and wife Lisa turned their ex-pub, **The Foxhunter**, into something smarter while living upstairs with their two young children.

Ex-Dorchester chef Aiden Byrne and partner Sarah Broadley are making **The Church Green**, Lymm, their own.

## ALSO RECOMMENDED
### ▲ Lobster Pot
3 Kennington Lane, Elephant and Castle, SE11 4RG
Tel no: (020) 7582 5556
www.lobsterpotrestaurant.co.uk
⊖ Kennington, map 1
Seafood

The landlocked Elephant and Castle has never been any bar to the maritime yearnings of Hervé Régent. His eatery summons up the Brittany coast with a backdrop of seascapes and lifebelts. Enter into the spirit with avruga-topped crab and mango salad (£12.50), soupe de poissons with the trimmings (£8.50), and mains such as monkfish and wild mushrooms, sauced with Pernod (£19.50) – not to mention the all-important lobsters. Finish with profiteroles and ice cream (£5.30). Wines from £14.50. Closed Sun and Mon.

## Magdalen
**Earthy classics with vim and vigour**
152 Tooley Street, Southwark, SE1 2TU
Tel no: (020) 7403 1342
www.magdalenrestaurant.co.uk
⊖ London Bridge, map 1
**Modern British | £30**
**Cooking score: 3**

A godsend for this part of town, James Faulks' two-tier restaurant does the area proud. The ingredients-led daily menu reads well. The execution tends towards the simple, with roasting, grilling and slow-cooking making the most of ingredients that are more seasonal than luxurious. Potted crab on toast might be a homely way to start, or you could venture forth into the more speculative waters of fried calf's brain and gribiche sauce. Main course choices include pheasant and bacon pie (for two), as well as slow-roast Bresse chicken with mash, and sea bream with baby artichokes, Spanish ham and olive oil. Comforting desserts include French toast with strawberry jam and vanilla ice cream. Prices on the French-centred wine list start at £17.

Chef/s: James Faulks. **Open:** Mon to Fri L 12 to 2.30, Mon to Sat D 6.30 to 10.30. **Closed:** Sun, 2 weeks Aug, bank hols. **Meals:** alc (main courses £14 to £23). Set menu £15.50 (2 courses) to £18.50. **Service:** not inc. **Details:** Cards accepted. 90 seats. Air-con. Wheelchair access. Music. Children allowed.

## ALSO RECOMMENDED
## ▲ Metro Garden Restaurant & Bar

9 Clapham Common Southside, Clapham, SW4 7AA
Tel no: (020) 7627 0632
⊖ Clapham Common, map 3
**Modern European**

'Excellent post-cinema stalwart for locals', confirms a supporter of this popular restaurant opposite Clapham Common tube. A big pull is the 'very atmospheric' gazebo-style extension in the rear garden with patio heaters and twinkling white fairy lights – 'cosy, even in winter'. The menu shows concessions to global modernity with, say, chicken liver parfait (£6.50) ahead of black cod with pak choi and teriyaki dressing (£14.25). Staff are lovely, but 'over-zealous with topping up your wine' (from £14.50). Open all week, D only.

## READERS RECOMMEND
## Numero Uno

**Italian**
139 Northcote Road, Clapham, SW11 6PX
Tel no: (020) 7978 5837
'The food is fabulous, the atmosphere and staff are wonderfully Italian'

---

£5 OFF voucher scheme

Also recommended entries can also take part in the £5-off voucher scheme. For a full list of participating restaurants, please visit: www.which.co.uk/gfgvoucherscheme

## Oxo Tower
**Fashionable food and awesome views**
Oxo Tower Wharf, Barge House Street, South Bank, SE1 9PH
Tel no: (020) 7803 3888
www.harveynichols.com
⊖ Waterloo, Southwark, map 5
**Modern European | £50**
Cooking score: 2
♦ V

Depending on your bank balance, turn left for the relatively affordable brasserie or right for the giddily priced restaurant. Either way, the eighth-floor views over the river and cityscapes are spectacular – especially from the 250-foot terrace. The kitchen's approach is fashionably eclectic, flirting with the Med and the Orient as well as tipping its hat to British produce. In the restaurant, you will find crab salad with sweetcorn ice cream and seaweed bread, and grilled Herdwick mutton with asparagus, land cress and wild garlic salad. The full wine wist list is awesome in its breadth and content – legions of pedigree vintages rub shoulders with cult-status contenders. Prices start at £20, and there's a dazzling choice by the glass.
Chef/s: Jeremy Bloor. **Open:** all week L 12 to 2.30 (3 Sun), D 6 to 11 (6.30 to 10.30 Sun). **Closed:** 25 and 26 Dec. **Meals:** alc (main courses £20 to £32). **Service:** 12.5% optional. **Details:** Cards accepted. 130 seats. 70 seats outside. Air-con. Separate bar. No music. Wheelchair access. Children allowed.

## The Phoenix
**Friendly Italian worth seeking out**
162-164 Lower Richmond Road, Putney, SW15 1LY
Tel no: (020) 8780 3131
www.sonnys.co.uk
⊖ Putney Bridge, map 1
**Italian | £27**
Cooking score: 4
£5 OFF V £30

Though rather off the beaten restaurant track, this Putney local is worth seeking out for good quality, modern Italian cooking in comfortable, grown-up surroundings.

Clement weather has customers clamouring to sit on the sheltered, heated patio, but the art-filled dining room makes a pleasant backdrop to a civilised meal. The house speciality is vincigrassi maceratesi, an eighteenth-century concoction of cream, pasta, cheese and ham, but there's also fettuccine with rosemary sausage and wild mushrooms, and strozzapreti tricolore with clams and artichokes. Wild boar ham with soft caprino cheese and a Sicilian-style sea bass with mussels and clams in a tomato and basil broth with bruschetta reveal a chef who obviously likes food and tastes it – seasoning is balanced and flavours are designed to meld. Set menus are particularly good value. Wine from the Italian heavy list opens at £13.
**Chef/s:** Paola Sibilla. **Open:** all week L 12 to 2.30 (3 Sun), Mon to Sat D 7 to 10.30 (11 Fri and Sat). **Closed:** 25 and 26 Dec, bank hols. **Meals:** alc (main courses £10 to £19). Set L £13.50 (2 courses) to £15.50. Set D £15.50 (2 courses) to £17.50. Sun L £16.50 to £19.50. **Service:** 12.5% (optional). **Details:** Cards accepted. 80 seats. 50 seats outside. Air-con. Separate bar. Wheelchair access. Music. Children allowed.

## Le Pont de la Tour
**Seafood in the spotlight**
36d Shad Thames, Bermondsey, SE1 2YE
Tel no: (020) 7403 8403
www.lepontdelatour.com
⊖ Tower Hill, London Bridge, map 1
**Modern French | £55**
**Cooking score: 3**
£5 OFF 🍾

Le Pont de la Tour has occupied this enviable position on the river overlooking Tower Bridge for 19 years. Inside, it is designed to comfort and reassure, helped along by a kitchen that reads from a largely European script and recognises the benefits of simplicity and the appeal of familiar ideas. Seafood remains in the spotlight – mousseline of scallop and crab with ginger velouté, say, or John Dory with winter vegetable and squid broth – supported by dishes such as roasted foie gras with sweet onion marmalade and

toasted almond sauce, and beef fillet with oxtail risotto. The restaurant is well-known for wine, and the impressive list has some rare treats. France is the first love, but the rest of the world maintains high standards. Bottles open at £22.
**Chef/s:** Lee Bennett. **Open:** all week L 12 to 3 (4 Sun), Mon to Sat D 6 to 11. **Meals:** alc (main courses £15 to £26). Set L and D £20 (2 courses) to £25. Sun L £26. **Service:** 12.5% (optional). **Details:** Cards accepted. 110 seats. 70 seats outside. Air-con. Separate bar. No mobile phones. Wheelchair access. Music. Children allowed.

## Ransome's Dock
**Wines with wow and classic food**
35-37 Parkgate Road, Battersea, SW11 4NP
Tel no: (020) 7223 1611
www.ransomesdock.co.uk
⊖ Sloane Square, map 3
**Modern British | £33**
**Cooking score: 3**
£5 OFF 🍾

This longstanding Battersea restaurant is a site to which all wine merchants in the capital pay homage – its wine list, put together by owner and expert Martin Lam is well-priced, brilliantly annotated and rejects many big names for better-value, more interesting alternatives. What's more, when Lam himself is not present, the manager is more than able to guide diners through its many pages. But don't make the mistake of overlooking the cooking. Both Lam and his wife Vanessa run the kitchen. The menu is littered with classic British produce – Morecambe Bay potted shrimps, lamb from the Elwy Valley – carefully prepared and served in generous portions. Greatly innovative it may not be, but quail salad with dates and oranges, and calf's liver with chorizo and spinach, carefully prepared and cooked, are a pleasure to eat. House wine is £13.50 a bottle.
**Chef/s:** Martin and Vanessa Lam. **Open:** all week L 12 to 5.30 (3.30 Sun), Mon to Sat D 6 to 11. **Closed:** 25 and 26 Dec, Aug bank hol. **Meals:** alc (main courses £11 to £23). Set L and D £15.50 (2 courses). Sun L £20. **Service:** 12.5% (optional). **Details:** Cards

accepted. 55 seats. 24 seats outside. Separate bar. No mobile phones. Wheelchair access. Music. Children allowed.

**NEW ENTRY**

## Rick's Café

**Local favourite with sumptuous treats**
122 Mitcham Road, Tooting, SW17 9NH
Tel no: (020) 8767 5219
⊖ Tooting Broadway, map 3
European | £20
Cooking score: 1

£5 OFF £30

There was a brief hiatus while Rick Gibbs took a sabatical in Spain, but he's back at the helm of this Tooting favourite with a daily changing menu which might include fresh oysters served on a bed of seaweed followed by melt-in-the-mouth pan-fried sea bass for main. Sumptuous desserts include seasonal fruit crumbles and sticky toffee pudding. Regular events such as 'Steak Tuesday' and 'Lobster Friday' provide treats for those on a budget. House wine from £14.
**Chef/s:** Ricardo Gibbs. **Open:** Tue to Sun L 12 to 3 (10 to 4 Sat and Sun), Mon to Sat D 6 to 11. **Meals:** alc (main courses £8 to £16). Set L and D £18.20 (3 courses). Sun L £10. **Service:** 12.5% (optional). **Details:** Cards accepted. 38 seats. Wheelchair access. Music. Children allowed.

## Roast

**Boldy showcasing the best of British**
Floral Hall, Borough Market, Stoney Street, Southwark, SE1 1TL
Tel no: (0845) 034 7300
www.roast-restaurant.com
⊖ London Bridge, map 1
Modern British | £38
Cooking score: 3

£5 OFF

The glass portico of a former flower market sets the scene for this heroically British restaurant. The room is bright even on the dullest day and, with little in the way of soft furnishings, noisy at peak times. The kitchen boldly showcases ingredients found in

Borough Market below and sourced from a network of producers around the country – all listed on the menu. You may find Welsh Black beef hash with coddled egg and English mustard to start, and there could be cod with samphire, peas and sea spinach alongside lamb's kidneys with wild mushrooms and garlic for mains. However, not everyone has been impressed this year – reports have described food that was just 'adequate', while a Sunday lunch was 'disappointing'. House wines from £18. More reports please.
**Chef/s:** Lawrence Keogh. **Open:** all week 7am to 11pm (8am Sat, 11.30am to 4pm Sun). **Meals:** alc (main courses £14 to £25). Sun L £26 (2 courses) to £30. **Service:** 12.5%. **Details:** Cards accepted. 110 seats. Air-con. Separate bar. No music. Wheelchair access. Children allowed.

## RSJ

**Well-supported South Bank veteran**
33 Coin Street, Southwark, SE1 9NR
Tel no: (020) 7928 4554
www.rsj.uk.com
⊖ Waterloo, Southwark, map 5
Modern European | £30
Cooking score: 3

£5 OFF 🍾

The unprepossessing frontage may not stop you in your tracks, but persevere. For many, a meal here is a 'real treat', with one regular singling out first courses for special mention, especially risottos, which 'can be, and often are, outstanding'. Contemporary crossover dishes such as seared tuna with guacamole, gazpacho and crostini, and tandoori poussin teamed with okra provençale and mango relish reveal plenty of original ideas and novel presentations, but the focus is on sound culinary principles and traditional techniques. The cooking may not always be consistent, sometimes getting the timing or balance wrong, but on the whole reporters are happy. When it comes to wine, RSJ's heart is in France. The list, concentrating almost entirely on the Loire, has been put together with something like evangelical glee, with realistic notes and prices from £16.50.

**Chef/s:** Ian Stabler and Alex Lovett. **Open:** Mon to Fri L 12 to 2.30, Mon to Sat D 5.30 to 11. **Closed:** Sun, 24 to 27 Dec, bank hols. **Meals:** alc (main courses £11 to £19). Set L and D £15.95 (2 courses) to £18.95. **Service:** 12.5% (optional). **Details:** Cards accepted. 95 seats. 12 seats outside. Air-con. No music. Children allowed.

## Skylon
**The setting's the star**
Southbank Centre, Belvedere Road, South Bank, SE1 8XX
Tel no: (020) 7654 7800
www.skylonrestaurant.co.uk
⊖ Waterloo, map 5
Modern British | £42
Cooking score: 2

With plenty of sky, less of London (trees obscure some of the view across the Thames), the sheer scale and size make Skylon very impressive. The space is split by a cocktail bar into the livelier (and cheaper) grill or more formal restaurant, although there's not a wealth of difference between the two – both enjoy similar space, stylish waiters and a grey-green colour scheme. Reports of improved cooking this year were found mainly correct at inspection. A silky smooth chilled asparagus soup fell slightly flat on flavour, but a generous and careful crab, haddock and samphire risotto was rich and deeply satisfying. Ultimately, however, the setting is the main draw here. House wine is £19.
**Chef/s:** Helena Puolakka. **Open:** Restaurant all week L 12 to 2.30 (4 Sun), Mon to Sat D 5.30 to 10.30. Grill all week L 12 to 5, D 5.30 to 11. **Closed:** 25 Dec. **Meals:** alc (main courses £7 to £23). Grill Set L £17.50 (2 courses). Restaurant Set L £21.50 (2 courses). **Service:** 12.5% (optional). **Details:** Cards accepted. 92 seats. Air-con. Separate bar. Wheelchair access. Music. Children allowed. Car parking.

## Tandoori Nights
73 Lordship Lane, East Dulwich, SE22 8EP
Tel no: (020) 8299 4077
'Small, popular and delicious; traditional dishes but lots of interesting modern touches too'

## Tapas Brindisa
**Palate-teasing taste of Spain**
18-20 Southwark Street, Southwark, SE1 1TJ
Tel no: (020) 7357 8880
www.brindisatapaskitchens.com
⊖ Borough, London Bridge, map 1
Tapas | £20
Cooking score: 3

V

A few steps from the foodie distractions of Borough Market, cheery Tapas Brindisa peddles the true Spanish experience in an evocative setting of concrete floors and mirrored walls. Placemats double as menus and everything hinges on the sheer quality of the ingredients, whether it's Gran Reserva Joselito ham or luscious Nunez del Prado olive oil. Stand at the bar or squeeze into one of the tight-packed tables and graze on an irresistible selection of palate-teasers – perhaps beetroot with Picos blue cheese, cured Leon beef with pomegranate and frisée or sea bream with morcilla de Burgos and roasted pepper purée – not forgetting standbys such as patatas bravas. To finish, take a chance on creamed white chocolate on toast with Arbequina olive oil and black pepper. Gorgeous sherries and gluggable Spanish wines (from £14.95) round off the package. Newcomers Casa Brindisa and Tierra Brindisa are out of the same stable (see entries).
**Chef/s:** José Pizarro. **Open:** Mon to Sat L 11 to 3 (9 to 4 Fri and Sat), D 5.30 to 11. Sun 10 to 10. **Meals:** alc (tapas from £4 to £13). **Service:** 12.5% (optional). **Details:** Cards accepted. 42 seats. 10 seats outside. Air-con. Separate bar. Wheelchair access. Music. Children allowed.

## Tentazioni
**Modern Italian with passion**
Lloyds Wharf, 2 Mill Street, Bermondsey, SE1 2BD
Tel no: (020) 7237 1100
www.tentazioni.co.uk
⊖ Bermondsey, London Bridge, map 1
Italian | £30
Cooking score: 3

£5 OFF **V**

With slick red and white décor and modern
artwork, this narrow warehouse restaurant
near Tower Bridge is dressed to impress. Chef/
owner Riccardo Giacomini 'makes customers
feel as if they are visiting his home', and 'is
passionate about the food he serves'. Expect a
monthly changing selection of modern Italian
dishes, with options ranging from a
reasonably priced set menu with traditional
undertones to a more sophisticated tasting
menu. Typical dishes from the carte are
marinated fresh tuna salad with oregano,
caperberries and spring onions followed by
roasted rabbit leg wrapped in Black Forest
ham with wild mushrooms and Parmesan
fondue. Classic tiramisu is among the desserts,
but the excellent selection of Italian cheeses is
equally tempting. The 'magnificent' Italian
wine list starts at £12.50 a bottle.
**Chef/s:** Riccardo Giacomini. **Open:** Tue to Fri L 12 to
2.45, Mon to Sat D 6.30 to 10.45. **Closed:** Sun, 24 to
28 Dec. **Meals:** alc (main courses £12 to £19). Set L
£11.95 (2 courses) to £15. Set D £19.95 (2 courses) to
£24.95. Tasting menu £41.50 (7 courses).
**Service:** 12.5% (optional). **Details:** Cards accepted.
60 seats. Wheelchair access. Music. Children
allowed.

## Tom Ilic

**Who or what inspired you to become
a chef?**
It's one way to 'travel' the world
through ingredients without going
anywhere.

**If you hadn't become a chef, what
would you have been?**
Truck driver.

**Which chefs do you admire?**
Those that still work in their kitchen.

**If you were to have one abiding
principle in the kitchen, what
would it be?**
Follow your instinct.

**What is your favourite restaurant
and why?**
My local 'Little Dragon'. The kids and
my wife love Chinese and they look
after us well.

**What do you like cooking when you
are 'off duty'?**
Anything that doesn't involve too
much time.

**What is the best part of your job?**
Seeing happy faces on my customers.

## Tom Ilic

**Cracking rendezvous with barnstorming food**
123 Queenstown Road, Battersea, SW8 3RH
Tel no: (020) 7622 0555
www.tomilic.com
map 3
European | £25
Cooking score: 4

Tom Ilic used to cook at this address when it was the Stepping Stone, and he's back with a vengeance, dishing up big-hearted food in a dressed-down setting of bare tables and pot plants. His self-named restaurant looks, feels and acts like everyone's idea of a cracking neighbourhood rendezvous, with short menus, competitive prices and bags of flavour emanating from the kitchen. Ilic's logo is a cartoon pig and he obviously relishes the delights of earthy porcine cookery – sautéed fillet and roast belly pork with pickled white cabbage, chorizo and caramelised apple is a suitably barnstorming main course. Those with a taste for red meat might also fancy a trio of lamb with potato gratin and spiced aubergine, while fish fans could go for baked brill with roast langoustine, braised fennel, clam and mussel velouté. Desserts keep it simple with, say, tarte Tatin and cardamom ice cream. Wines are a nifty bunch, arranged by style; prices start at £14.75.
**Chef/s:** Tom Ilic. **Open:** Wed to Fri and Sun L 12 to 2.30 (3.30 Sun), Tue to Sat D 6 to 10.30. **Closed:** Mon, 25 to 31 Dec, last week Aug. **Meals:** alc (main courses £11 to £16). Set L £14.50 (2 courses) to £16.95. Sun L £16.95 (2 courses) to £21.50.
**Service:** 12.5% (optional). **Details:** Cards accepted. 58 seats. Air-con. No mobile phones. Wheelchair access. Music. Children allowed.

## Trinity

**Quality cooking that's easy on the wallet**
4 The Polygon, Clapham, SW4 0JG
Tel no: (020) 7622 1199
www.trinityrestaurant.co.uk
⊖ Clapham Common, map 3
Modern European | £32
Cooking score: 4

Locals and those from further afield seek out this smart Clapham restaurant, beguiled by great cooking, the buzzy atmosphere and – compared to the West End – cheap prices for the quality. Adam Byatt works interesting ingredients into clever, complicated dishes. A tarragon broth with a won ton-like raviolo of crab is brought together with the addition of a crisp deep-fried oyster, while a gently cooked rump of veal served with tuna and wild garlic mayonnaise is an inspirational take on the classic vitello tonnato. Elsewhere, there's carefully prepared red mullet escabèche with saffron aïoli and slow-cooked short rib of beef, bourguignonne style. Chocolate 'hot pot' and poached pear with chocolate sorbet are as evolved as the rest of the menu. The wine list has plenty by the glass (from £4) and a policy of charging less mark-up the higher up the list one ventures.
**Chef/s:** Adam Byatt. **Open:** Tue to Sun L 12.30 to 2.30 (4 Sun), Mon to Sat D 6.30 to 10 (11 Fri and Sat). **Closed:** 25 and 26 Dec, 1 and 2 Jan. **Meals:** alc (main courses £16 to £19). Set L £15 (2 courses) to £20. Set D £20 (3 courses). Sun L £25.
**Service:** 12.5% (optional). **Details:** Cards accepted. 62 seats. Air-con. Separate bar. No music. Wheelchair access. Children allowed.

## Tsunami
**Fusion-tinged Japanese food**
5-7 Voltaire Road, Clapham, SW4 6DQ
Tel no: (020) 7978 1610
www.tsunamirestaurant.co.uk
⊖ Clapham North, map 3
Japanese | £35
Cooking score: 2
**V**

One of two Tsunami restaurants (the other is in Charlotte Street in the West End), this is a popular venue for modern Japanese food with European influences. Starters range from snow crab shu mai to lamb cutlets with Korean kimchee chilli. After that, maybe sizzling teryaki chicken or Aberdeen Angus beef fillet with sea urchin and foie gras butter. There's a good sushi menu, plus a list of specials that further explore the Japanese/European fusion theme (chargrilled chicken with creamed leeks, oriental mushrooms and wasabi pepper sauce, for instance). Drinks include saké, cocktails and plenty of wines by the glass. Bottles start at £16.
**Chef/s:** Tommy Cheung. **Open:** Sat and Sun L 12.30 to 4, all week D 6 to 10.30 (11 Fri, 5.30 to 11 Sat, 9.30 Sun). **Closed:** 24 to 26 Dec, 1 Jan. **Meals:** alc (main courses £8 to £18). Set L £10.50 (3 courses). Set D £35 to £45. **Service:** 12.5% (optional). **Details:** Cards accepted. 85 seats. 8 seats outside. Air-con. Separate bar. Wheelchair access. Music. Children allowed.

## ALSO RECOMMENDED
### ▲ Village East
171-173 Bermondsey Street, Southwark, SE1 3UW
Tel no: (020) 7357 6082
www.villageeast.co.uk
⊖ London Bridge, map 1
Modern European

The restaurant unfolds through a converted glass-fronted warehouse development, with polished concrete and rough wooden pillars and a kitchen that's fashionably open to view. Modern European cooking is in tune with the surroundings, offering ash-coated St Maure goats' cheese with roasted beetroot, truffle

honey and balsamic (£7.20), and seared venison with red cabbage and Jerusalem artichokes (£17.60). Side dishes are charged separately, mostly at £3.50, and there are tempting desserts such as chocolate fondant with pistachio ice cream (£6). Wines start at £14.50. Open all week.

## READERS RECOMMEND
### Wright Brothers of Borough Market
Seafood
11 Stoney Street, Southwark, SE1 9AD
Tel no: (020) 7403 9554
www.wrightbros.eu.com
'Buzzing atmosphere of Borough Market and best oysters I've ever had'

## Adams Café

**Zingy flavours and rock-bottom prices**
77 Askew Road, Shepherd's Bush, W12 9AH
Tel no: (020) 8743 0572
⊖ Ravenscourt Park, Stamford Brook, map 1
North African | £17
Cooking score: 3

Totally unpretentious surrounds and totally authentic North African food at 'incredible' prices guarantee regular full houses at this Shepherd's Bush favourite. It's a busy, bubbly, elbow-to-elbow place serving up heady aromatic dishes redolent of the street markets of Morocco and Tunisia – seven stomach-filling versions of couscous, assorted grills accompanied by rice and salad, plus a handful of slow-cooked stews and zingy, flavour-packed tagines (try the monkfish version with saffron potatoes, peppers and coriander or chicken with pickled lemons and green olives). Kick off with grilled merguez sausages, filo pastry 'cigars' filled with cheese and herbs or ojja tunisien (ratatouille topped with an egg), and conclude with sticky baklava pastries or fragrant orange salad with dates, orange blossom water and cinnamon. Quaffable house French is £10 – otherwise BYO (£3 corkage).
**Chef/s:** Sofiene Chahed. **Open:** Mon to Sat D only 7 to 11. **Closed:** Sun, bank hols, 25 Dec to 1 Jan. **Meals:** Set D £14.50 (2 courses) to £16.95. **Service:** 12.5%. **Details:** Cards accepted. 60 seats. Wheelchair access. Music. Children allowed.

## The Admiral Codrington

**Nautical but nice**
17 Mossop Street, Chelsea, SW3 2LY
Tel no: (020) 7581 0005
www.theadmiralcodrington.com
⊖ South Kensington, map 3
Gastropub | £27
Cooking score: 3

V

'The Cod' can get fairly raucous on an evening, but elbow your way through (mind the rutting Sloanes) into the more civilised

surrounds of the conservatory-style restaurant, where skylights, fishy prints and a galley kitchen ensure a suitably nautical feel. Enticing starters like ash-rolled baked goats' cheese, and scallops with wild garlic give way to less exciting, almost ubiquitous main courses like pot-roast chicken with bacon and broad beans. On inspection fish and chips was near perfect, accompanied by chunky, delicately minted mushy peas. Friendly service and exquisite truffles also impressed. A global wine list offers fair choice under £20.
**Chef/s:** Simon Levy. **Open:** all week L 12 to 2.30 (3.30 Sat, 4 Sun), D 6.30 to 11 (7 to 10.30 Sun). **Closed:** 24 to 26 Dec. **Meals:** alc (main courses £11 to £15). Set L £13.75 (2 courses) to £17.75. Bar menu available. **Service:** 12.5% (optional). **Details:** Cards accepted. 50 seats. 25 seats outside. Separate bar. Wheelchair access. Music. Children allowed.

## Ambassade de l'Ile

**French cuisine at its glitziest**
117-119 Old Brompton Road, South Kensington, SW7 3RN
Tel no: (020) 7373 7774
www.ambassadedelile.com
⊖ Gloucester Road, map 3
French | £45
Cooking score: 6

 V

Ambassade de l'Ile is a contemporary design experience, a bold monochrome scheme with sepulchral black areas offset by walls in bright white leather, giving the effect of a supremely civilised padded cell. Jean-Christophe Ansanay-Alex arrived here from a base in Lyon, where accolades have tumbled over him like April showers. Importing formidable Gallic technique (together with some butter and cheeses), his mission is to apply it to the best of British produce. The monthly changing tasting menu is the bedrock for a seasonal approach that also informs a short carte and prix-fixe lunch and dinner menus. Prepare to be spellbound by the concentrated intensity of dishes such as crab served in a curried creamy broth in the shell, the richness offset with shards of cucumber, tart apple and

croûtons of pain d'épice. Properly hung beef fillet turns up in a sauce of wondrous depth, based on a painstaking reduction incorporating Guinness and the lingering tang of fresh oyster. Dessert at a spring inspection offered rhubarb cooked lightly in a mille-feuille of dark brown, buttery pastry layers, with vanilla ice cream, puréed wild strawberries and sugared pistachios. Incidentals are mostly superb and staff have the tone just right, all tender French solicitude and flawless professionalism. Wines are catalogued in an almost unliftable volume big enough to contain wallpaper samples. French classics at astronomic prices are supplemented by good New World selections. The few wines by the glass aren't cheap either, but are interesting choices, not least for their impressive maturity. Bottles start at £25.
**Chef/s:** Jean-Christophe Ansanay-Alex. **Open:** Tue to Sat L 12 to 2, D 7 to 10. **Closed:** Sun, Mon, 9 to 31 Aug, 20 to 28 Dec. **Meals:** Set L £20 (2 courses) to £25. Set D £45 (3 courses). Tasting menu £70. **Service:** 12.5% (optional). **Details:** Cards accepted. 50 seats. Air-con. Wheelchair access. Music. Children allowed.

## Anglesea Arms
**Top-notch gastropub**
35 Wingate Road, Shepherd's Bush, W6 0UR
Tel no: (020) 8749 1291
⊖ Ravenscourt Park, map 1
Gastropub | £24
Cooking score: 2

The Victorian pub in Ravenscourt Park enjoys some notoriety as the place where plans for the Great Train Robbery were hatched in the early 60s. These days, it is a fine neighbourhood hostelry that operates a no-booking policy. The menu is chalked up on a blackboard, the cooking is enjoyably robust with smoked eel in potato broth with a poached egg, stuffed pig's trotter with choucroute, and game birds such as roast woodcock with braised endive typical choices. Unusual desserts have included mulberry and mascarpone tart with mulberry ice cream, and there are great British

cheeses too. A wine list arranged by price is weighted towards France, with bottles starting at £14.
**Chef/s:** Matthew Cranston. **Open:** all week L 12.30 to 2.45 (3 Sat, 3.30 Sun), D 7 to 10.30 (10 Sun and Mon). **Closed:** 25 to 27 Dec. **Meals:** alc (mains £10 to £17). **Service:** not inc (12.5% groups, optional). **Details:** Cards accepted. 80 seats. 25 seats outside. Air-con. Separate bar. No music. Wheelchair access. Children allowed.

## Ark
**Inviting neighbourhood Italian**
122 Palace Gardens Terrace, Notting Hill, W8 4RT
Tel no: (020) 7229 4024
www.ark-restaurant.com
⊖ Notting Hill Gate, map 4
Italian | £37
Cooking score: 2

Chic and stylish, this Notting Hill Italian is a popular spot for yummy mummies to enjoy lunch, or for couples on a date. Fresh flowers, soft lighting and a long conservatory-style room all contribute to the romantic ambience, and there's a diminutive cocktail bar and small terrace amidst climbing foliage for an aperitif. On inspection, pastas such as veal and mortadella tortellini with sage and butter sauce and taglioni with monkfish, cherry tomatoes and olives were watery, although other dishes fared better. A notable truffle menu, with matching wines, is available from October to November. Italian wines are a strong point, with house selections at £14.50.
**Chef/s:** Daniele Cefero. **Open:** Tue to Sat L 12 to 3, Mon to Sat D 6.30 to 11. **Closed:** Sun, bank hols. **Meals:** alc (main courses £12 to £19). **Service:** 12.5% (optional). **Details:** Cards accepted. 60 seats. 15 seats outside. Air-con. Separate bar. Music. Children allowed.

### Average price

The average price listed in main-entry reviews denotes the price of a three-course meal, without wine.

## Assaggi

**Fine-tuned rustic Italian food**
The Chepstow, 39 Chepstow Place, Notting Hill,
W2 4TS
Tel no: (020) 7792 5501
⊖ Notting Hill Gate, map 4
Italian | £40
Cooking score: 4

Don't be fooled by the location, above a gastropub in a row of terraced houses. Assaggi may look prosaic, but its cheerful mix of vibrant minimalism and Notting Hill cool is just perfect for the local punters, and chef Nino Sassu punches well above his weight when it comes to fine-tuned rustic Italian food. Impeccably sourced native ingredients are at the centre of things, and much of the food has a pumping regional heartbeat. Rustic Sardinian breads set the scene, before the kitchen moves into gear for antipasti – say, king prawns with artichokes, polenta with cuttlefish and leeks or pecorino with San Daniele ham. Pasta might feature tagliolini with crab, while mains hit the target with grilled sea bass, veal chops and fritto misto. To conclude, artisan cheeses share the limelight with desserts such as Amaretto semifreddo and flourless torta di ciocollato. The sharp Italian regional wine list has house selections from £21.95.
**Chef/s:** Nino Sassu. **Open:** Mon to Sat L 12.30 to 2.30 (1 to 2.30 Sat), D 7.30 to 11. **Closed:** Sun, 2 weeks from 25 Dec. **Meals:** alc (main courses £14 to £27). **Service:** not inc. **Details:** Cards accepted. 35 seats. Air-con. No music. Children allowed.

## Aubergine

**Well-heeled Gallic grandee**
11 Park Walk, Chelsea, SW10 0AJ
Tel no: (020) 7352 3449
www.auberginerestaurant.co.uk
⊖ South Kensington, map 3
Modern French | £68
New chef

🍾

A fixture of the Chelsea scene and a famous gastronomic address, Aubergine has cruised along effortlessly in recent years, delivering fine food in a well-heeled, soft-focus setting. However, change may be in the air. Long-serving head chef William Drabble left suddenly as the *Guide* was going to press, and Christophe Renou was promoted from the current brigade. The kitchen has always been known for its serious take on modern French cuisine, and its telling amalgam of top-end luxuries (foie gras, truffles, lobster) with humbler ingredients (snails, neck of lamb, collar of bacon). Typical dishes from the recent past have included carpaccio of monkfish with apple and fennel salad ahead of duck breast with figs and port wine jus. As for desserts, the line-up has featured coffee soufflé with chocolate sauce and soaked Savarin with fresh raspberries. The wine list is a mighty Francophilic beast, with pure class in the classics, affordable drinking from lesser-known regions and some very decent new-wave competition from Italy and California. Prices start at £27. Meanwhile, it's business as usual at Aubergine's out-of-town sibling in the Compleat Angler, Marlow (see entry).
**Chef/s:** Christophe Renou. **Open:** Tue to Sat L 12 to 2.15, D 7 to 10.30. **Closed:** Sun, Mon, bank hols. **Meals:** Set L £29 (3 courses). Set D Tue to Fri £34 (3 courses). Gourmand menu £78. **Service:** 12.5%. **Details:** Cards accepted. 50 seats. Air-con. No music.

## Awana

**Suave Malaysian high-flyer**
85 Sloane Avenue, Chelsea, SW3 3DX
Tel no: (020) 7584 8880
www.awana.co.uk
⊖ South Kensington, map 3
Malaysian | £40
Cooking score: 1

£5 OFF **V**

A sleekly designed Malaysian restaurant in well-heeled Chelsea, Awana is a vision of Malaysian hardwood, silk panelling and glass screens. It encompasses a satay bar and fine-dining restaurant, where the menu offers a mix of Malaysian favourites, an adventurous carte, and the chance of a five-course 'journey' for the uninitiated. Eye-catching dishes from the extensive range might include otak-otak (minced seafood with lime and lemongrass in a banana leaf), and sambal kangkung (stir-fried prawns and morning glory with chilli). An aficionado's wine list starts at £19.
**Chef/s:** Mark Read. **Open:** all week L 12 to 3, D 6 to 11 (11.30 Thur to Sat, 10.30 Sun). **Closed:** 25 and 26 Dec, 1 Jan. **Meals:** alc (main courses £11 to £25). Set L £12.50 (2 courses) to £15. Set D £35 (3 courses). **Service:** 12.5% (optional). **Details:** Cards accepted. 100 seats. Air-con. Separate bar. Music. Children allowed.

## Bibendum

**Icon with a magical dining room**
Michelin House, 81 Fulham Road, South Kensington, SW3 6RD
Tel no: (020) 7581 5817
www.bibendum.co.uk
⊖ South Kensington, map 3
French | £45
Cooking score: 4

🍾

The Michelin building is a late Edwardian architectural masterpiece and when it was acquired by the Conran group in 1987 the renovations left its idiosyncratic features to shine forth. Let's say again that the best time to see it is on a sunny lunchtime or early evening, when the bright first-floor room with its stained glass windows becomes one of the most magical dining rooms in London. Matthew Harris maintains the style of traditional French cooking in which the place has always traded. Dishes such as sauté veal brains in beurre noisette and capers, grilled onglet steak with sweet potato purée and pine nuts, and anise parfait with caramelised orange represent the best cuisine de terroir tradition. Service is friendly, even endearingly bumbling at times. A busy, less formal oyster bar is on the ground floor. The French-led wine list is spilling over with opulent, gorgeous listings for those with the means. Other countries provide a little price relief from £17.95.
**Chef/s:** Matthew Harris. **Open:** all week L 12 to 2.30 (3 Sat and Sun), D 7 to 11 (10.30 Sun). **Closed:** 25 and 26 Dec, 1 Jan. **Meals:** alc (main courses £18 to £27). Set L and D £25 (2 courses) to £29.50. Sun L £29.50. **Service:** 12.5% (optional). **Details:** Cards accepted. 90 seats. Air-con. Separate bar. Wheelchair access. Children allowed.

## Blue Elephant

**Extravagant Thai fantasies**
3-6 Fulham Broadway, Fulham, SW6 1AA
Tel no: (020) 7385 6595
www.blueelephant.com
⊖ Fulham Broadway, map 3
Thai | £35
Cooking score: 1

£5 OFF **V**

A dazzling setting bursting with luxuriant foliage and water features, this restaurant – one link in a successful international chain – is a reliable source of authentic Thai food, but also offers some intriguing inventions, including foie gras in a Thai tamarind sauce. For a more traditional experience, start with mieng kham (betel leaves filled with roasted peanuts, lime, shallots, ginger and dried shrimp) then a fresh and fiery green curry of free-range chicken. Wines start at £19.
**Chef/s:** Sompong Sae-Jew. **Open:** all week L 12 to 2.30 (3 Sun), D 7 to 11.30 (6.30 Fri, 6 Sat, 6.30 to 10.30 Sun). **Closed:** 25 Dec, 31 Dec, 1 Jan. **Meals:** alc (main courses £6 to £28). Set L £12 (2 courses) to

£15. Set D £35 to £39. Sun L £25. **Service:** 12.5%
(optional). **Details:** Cards accepted. 350 seats. Air-
con. Separate bar. No mobile phones. Wheelchair
access. Music. Children allowed.

## READERS RECOMMEND

## Books for Cooks

**International**
4 Blenheim Crescent, Notting Hill, W11 1NN
Tel no: (020) 7221 1992
www.booksforcooks.com
**'You never know what is going to be on the menu'**

## The Botanist

**Hot spot with impressive brasserie food**
7 Sloane Square, Chelsea, SW1W 8EE
Tel no: (020) 7730 0077
www.thebotanistsloanesquare.com
⊖ Sloane Square, map 3
**Modern British | £30**
**Cooking score: 3**

Brothers Tom and Ed Martin launched this
Sloane Square hot spot in 2008, and it
continues to thunder away – a busy, noisy
interior and crowds spilling on to the
pavement are testament to its popularity.
Inside it's smart and stylish, with low lighting
and botanical prints making the top-drawer
clientele feel at home. Upmarket brasserie
food in a dining room overlooking Sloane
Square includes impressive dishes such as
lobster and salmon ravioli with pea purée, and
roast pheasant with boudin noir and Calvados
jus. However, grumbling from reporters
focuses on lapses in execution, some inept
service and the fact that it isn't cheap, perhaps
due to the location. Still, house wine is
£14.50, and the impressive list includes
Chapel Down sparkling wine from Kent.
**Chef/s:** Andrew Beddoes. **Open:** all week L 12 to
3.30 (4 Sat and Sun) D 6 to 10.30. **Closed:** 25 and
26 Dec. **Meals:** alc (main courses £12 to £19).
**Service:** 12.5% (optional). **Details:** Cards accepted.
100 seats. 8 seats outside. Air-con. Separate bar.
Wheelchair access. Music. Children allowed.

**NEW ENTRY**
## Brompton Bar & Grill

**Boisterous reborn brasserie**
243 Brompton Road, South Kensington, SW3 2EP
Tel no: (020) 7589 8005
www.bromptonbarandgrill.com
⊖ South Kensington, map 3
**Modern British | £35**
**Cooking score: 2**

In late 2008, longstanding Brasserie St
Quentin was rebooted and reverted to the
name that put it on the culinary map in the
1960s. Now awash with modish grey and fab
artwork, the rejuvenated room is more
boisterous as a result of the blurring between
bar and dining. The low-key menu keeps to
familiar ground, but cheeseburger or
vegetable curry do seem a tad school-dinner.
More grown-up is fresh, rich Dorset crab on
toast, and ingredients shine in an up-to-the-
minute flat-iron steak that's served with
textbook chips and béarnaise sauce. Biscuity
apple crumble is a fair ending. Admirably
priced wines start low from £10.
**Chef/s:** Gary Durrant. **Open:** all week L 12 to 3 (4
Sat and Sun) D 6 to 11. **Closed:** 25 and 26 Dec.
**Meals:** alc (main courses £12 to £24). Set L £12 (2
courses). **Service:** 12.5% (optional). **Details:** Cards
accepted. 50 seats. 4 seats outside. Air-con.
Separate bar. Wheelchair access. Music. Children
allowed.

## Cooking score

A score of 1 is a significant achievement.
The score in any review is based on
several meals, incorporating feedback
from both our readers and inspectors.
As a rough guide, 1 denotes capable
cooking with some inconsistencies,
rising steadily through different levels
of technical expertise, until the scores
between 6 and 10 indicate exemplary skills,
along with innovation, artistry and ambition.
If there is a new chef, we don't score the
restaurant for the first year of entry. For
further details, please see the scoring
section in the introduction to the Guide.

## Bumpkin

**Fun-loving Notting Hillbilly**
209 Westbourne Park Road, Notting Hill, W11 1EA
Tel no: (020) 7243 9818
www.bumpkinuk.com
⊖ Westbourne Park, Ladbroke Grove, map 4
British | £22
Cooking score: 2

V

Notting Hill's prized Bumpkin is a good-natured soul famed for its happy-go-lucky attitude and liking for funky British food – especially if it's from sustainable local sources. For daytime bonhomie or a quick-fix lunch, choose the cacophonous ground-floor brasserie; otherwise graduate to the less raucous restaurant on the next level. The menu ploughs its way through 'pots, pies and stews', plus 'pans, roasts and grills' (say organic Scottish salmon with slow-braised fennel and roasted tomatoes or chump of Elwy Valley lamb with minted Heritage potatoes and wild rocket). Start with Plantation pork terrine and piccalilli; finish with a nursery pud. A cracking drinks list includes snappy wines from £15. Bumpkin can also be found at 102 Old Brompton Road SW7 3RD, tel no: (020) 7341 0802.

**Chef/s:** Steven Rangiwahia. **Open:** all week L 12 to 3 (11 to 3.30 Sat and Sun), D 6 to 10.30. **Closed:** 25 and 26 Dec, 1 Jan, Aug bank hol. **Meals:** alc (main courses £8 to £24). Sun L £22. **Service:** 12.5%. **Details:** Cards accepted. 88 seats. 4 seats outside. Air-con. Wheelchair access. Music. Children allowed.

## Le Café Anglais

**Brasserie dishes to set you salivating**
8 Porchester Gardens, Notting Hill, W2 4DB
Tel no: (020) 7221 1415
www.lecafeanglais.co.uk
⊖ Bayswater, map 4
French | £40
Cooking score: 5

Rowley Leigh was king of the hill at Kensington Place (see entry) for some 20 years and has brought the same vitality and gusto to his new venture on the second floor of the Whiteley's Centre. It's a bold, high-decibel brasserie on a grand scale, part Art Deco salon, with floor-to-ceiling windows, satin curtains and leather banquettes. At the centre of things is an open kitchen dominated by a blazing rotisserie with joints and chickens on the go. Named after the seminal Café Anglais in Paris (forever remembered in the film *Babette's Feast*), it peddles populist food with a strong Anglo-French drift. A glance at the huge card of attractive dishes is enough to set you salivating, and just about every dish begs to be ordered. Enticing plates of mixed hors d'oeuvres are one of the star turns (pickled herrings, oyster fritters, rabbit rillettes); elsewhere, warm smoked eel and bacon salad has pleased reporters. Roasts head the main courses (pungent grouse served whole with ultra-thin game chips, say), while fish fans might fancy mackerel fillets with pine nuts, rosemary and apple sauce. By comparison, desserts can waver – pear Belle Hélène with chocolate sauce has outshone a rather unbalanced sherry trifle. The 80-bin wine list is Eurocentric, with plenty by the glass and carafe; bottle prices start at £16.50.

**Chef/s:** Colin Westal. **Open:** all week L 12 to 3.30, D 6.30 to 11 (10.30 Sun). **Closed:** 25 and 26 Dec, 1 Jan. **Meals:** alc (main courses £9 to £23). Set L (Mon to Fri) £16.50 (2 courses) to £19.50. Set D £20 (2 courses) to £25. **Service:** 12.5% (optional). **Details:** Cards accepted. 160 seats. Air-con. Separate bar. No music. Wheelchair access. Children allowed.

## Cambio de Tercio

**Striking Spanish innovator**
163 Old Brompton Road, Earls Court, SW5 0LJ
Tel no: (020) 7244 8970
www.cambiodetercio.co.uk
⊖ Gloucester Road, map 3
Spanish | £40
Cooking score: 3
£5 OFF 🍷

The name is a bullfighting reference, and the décor hits you between the eyes like a matador's espada, with its black slate floors and striking paintings on blood-red and yellow walls. The food ranges from plates of challenging tapas to more refined tasting dishes a world away from most Iberian clichés served up in the capital. 'It's hard to resist a haunch of top-quality pata negra ham', mused one aficionado, 'but that's just the beginning. Other star turns have included vivid red tuna tartare with tomato seeds and avocado aïoli, and skate wing with pig's ear 'a la plancha', Alegrias chilli and citrus vinaigrette. And don't miss 'clever' desserts such as white chocolate and yoghurt ganache with pistachio powder, passion fruit coulis and ginger ice cream. The all-Spanish, region-by-region wine list features encyclopaedic coverage of native grape varieties and vineyards. Glorious vintages and rareties abound, with prices from £17.50. Tendido Cero (directly opposite) and Tendido Cuatro on New King's Road are sister restaurants.

**Chef/s:** Alberto Criado. **Open:** all week L 12 to 2.30, D 7 to 11.30 (11 Sun). **Closed:** 23 Dec to 3 Jan. **Meals:** alc (main courses £17 to £23). Set menus for parties over 6 £35, £40 or £50. Tasting menu £35 (6 courses). **Service:** 12.5% (optional). **Details:** Cards accepted. 50 seats. 12 seats outside. Air-con. Separate bar. Music. Children allowed.

## The Capital

**Finely tuned French gem**
22 Basil Street, Knightsbridge, SW3 1AT
Tel no: (020) 7589 5171
www.capitalhotel.co.uk
⊖ Knightsbridge, map 4
French | £70
Cooking score: 7
🍷 🛏

Reporters love the 'small size, intimacy and charming French ambience' of this hotel dining room, still a 'little-known gem'. The timeless interior combines classic elegance with retro charm via pale wood panelling and 1970s-style chandeliers. The result is intimate, relaxed and highly personal. Eric Chavot's cooking is solidly French, gently modern and at times surprisingly simple. Rump of venison might come with sweet pickled cabbage, velvety blackcurrant jus and an artful sprinkling of nuts and berries – a forest theme where each ingredient is given ample space to shine. The same passion for quality runs through every aspect of the meal – olive oil adds a fragrant, peppery warmth to a salt-crusted focaccia that is second-to-none, while an amuse of sea bass tartare comes with a 'perfect chorizo cromesqui'. Similarly, a crab lasagne arrives with a seared scallop and a 'gloriously intense, silky' langoustine cappuccino that calls for 'more crusty, oven-fresh bread to mop up every trace'. Further delights are to be had in a burgeoning cheese trolley and exemplary petits fours. This is cooking that rarely misses a beat. At inspection a dessert that combined creamy vanilla tapioca pearls, roasted banana, crunchy popcorn, tart mango sorbet and boozy rum pannacotta was the only instance of flavour overload. The wine list may have you digging deep. French regions are covered in detail (look out for bottles from the hotel's own vineyard, the Levin winery in the Loire Valley), but the rest of the world gets more than a passing glance. There are some excellent wines by the glass – just as well, since bottles start from £31.

Chef/s: Eric Chavot. **Open:** all week L 12 to 2.30, D 7 to 11 (10.30 Sun). **Meals:** Set L £27.50 (2 courses) to £33. Set D £55 (2 courses) to £63. **Service:** 12.5% (optional). **Details:** Cards accepted. 32 seats. Air-con. Separate bar. No music. Wheelchair access. Children allowed. Car parking.

## The Carpenter's Arms
**Great gastropubby grub**
89-91 Black Lion Lane, Hammersmith, W6 9BG
Tel no: (020) 8741 8386
www.carpentersarmsw6.co.uk
⊖ Stamford Brook, Ravenscourt Park, map 1
Gastropub | £30
Cooking score: 2

The Carpenter's Arms has been teleported into the gastropub age without losing any of its original pubby bonhomie. The cooking is a nice mix of English and Mediterranean ways, with 'stunningly fresh crab salad' cropping up among the likes of smoked eel with bacon and choucroute or roast bone marrow and parsley salad. The place's identity as a pub is expressed in simply prepared main courses like a 'thick, centre-cut of plaice with crisp chips' and braised oxtail, but there are usually one of two more obvious restaurant dishes, including the whole grilled sea bass with curly kale, Jerusalem artichokes, hazelnuts and red wine that appeared on a winter menu. The wine list starts at £14.50. The large walled garden is a summer bonus.
Chef/s: Paul Adams. **Open:** all week L 12 to 2.30 (12.30 to 3 Sat, 4 Sun), D 7 to 10 (7.30 to 9.30 Sun). **Meals:** alc (main courses from £10 to £18). Set L £12.50 (2 courses) to £15.50. **Service:** 12.5% (optional). **Details:** Cards accepted. 40 seats. 34 seats outside. Music. Children allowed.

**NEW ENTRY**
## Casa Brindisa
**The perfect Spanish retreat**
7-9 Exhibition Road, South Kensington, SW7 2HQ
Tel no: (020) 7590 0008
www.casabrindisa.com
⊖ South Kensington, map 3
Spanish | £25
Cooking score: 3

Just a moment's walk from the museums of Kensington, this most recent addition to the Brindisa family (Tierra Brindisa and Tapas Brindisa – see entries) is the perfect Spanish retreat. Sit at the bar with a sherry and enjoy Gordal olives with orange and marjoram and a regional charcuterie selection or linger in the main restaurant, entertained by the open kitchen creating authentic delights such as Galician octopus and roasted pork belly with pea purée. For tapas, the portions are generous, the service is relaxed, and if you can't get enough of the speciality cheeses and Ibérico charcuterie, you can pop downstairs to the deli. Desserts do not disappoint; the highlight at inspection was creamed white chocolate on toast with Arbequina olive oil and pink pepper. The Spanish wine list kicks off at £14.95.
Chef/s: José Pizarro. **Open:** all week 12 to 11 (10 Sat and Sun). **Closed:** 25 and 26 Dec. **Meals:** alc (tapas £6 to £20). **Service:** 12.5% (optional). **Details:** Cards accepted. 62 seats. 6 seats outside. Air-con. Separate bar. No music. Wheelchair access. Children allowed.

## Le Cercle

**Exquisite harmony and precision**
1 Wilbraham Place, Belgravia, SW1X 9AE
Tel no: (020) 7901 9999
www.lecercle.co.uk
⊖ Sloane Square, map 3
Modern French | £22
Cooking score: 5

£5 OFF  V £30

The Sloane Street sister to Smithfield's Club Gascon (see entry), Le Cercle is a hidden basement destination for some very fine cooking. The modern French dishes are served in 'petit plat' format as a pick-and-mix tasting menu of sorts, with choices grouped under headings of 'végétal', 'marin', 'terroirs', 'fermier', 'plaisirs', plus cheese and dessert. The system draws praise for 'providing variety in small but exquisite proportions'. This is certainly the case for the likes of monkfish with tarbais beans and bacon, rump of lamb with creamy, cheesy aligot potato, or chocolate fondant with pistachio. Combinations can be quite wacky, and flavours unapologetic, but ingredients are as good as you'll get. The carte is not expensive; lunch and pre/post-theatre deals also offer great value. The 'lively atmosphere' attracts locals on Champagne-guzzling missions, but there are curtained-off booths for greater privacy. Like the cuisine, the wine list does the 'tour de France', with choices (many by the glass) from the Savoie, Jura and Provence, as well as big-hitters from Burgundy and Bordeaux. Service can be 'patchy', though it is praised for friendliness, good wine recommendations and for replacing faulty wine 'without fuss'.
**Chef/s:** Pierre Sang Boyer. **Open:** Tue to Sat L 12 to 3, D 6 to 11. **Closed:** Sun, Mon and bank hols. **Meals:** alc (main courses £6 to £35). Set L £15. Set D £17.50. **Service:** 12.5% (optional). **Details:** Cards accepted. 80 seats. Air-con. Separate bar. Wheelchair access. Music. Children allowed.

## Chutney Mary

**Glamorous modern Indian**
535 King's Road, Fulham, SW10 0SZ
Tel no: (020) 7351 3113
www.realindianfood.com
⊖ Fulham Broadway, map 3
Indian | £33
Cooking score: 3

V

The words 'seductive, slick and silky' catch the prevailing mood in this glamorous Chelsea Indian. Following a stunningly romantic makeover, the dramatically lit subterranean dining room and luxuriant conservatory now sparkle with rich colours, mirrors, etchings and crystal-studded silk wall hangings. Chef Siddharth Krishna has also upped the game, and his cooking shines with a renewed creative intensity fuelled by vibrant, unexpected flavours – witness a stand-out starter of Gressingham duck kebabs with blueberry chutney. Elsewhere, slow-roast masala lamb shank is invigorated with an amalgam of 21 spices and grilled tuna comes with a zingy mustard and coconut sauce. Tantalising vegetables run to crispy pickled potatoes, 'purple cloud' aubergine, lotus root and white pumpkin (served as a raita). The wine list has been intelligently tailored to match the food, with serious drinking from £20.50 (£5.50 a glass).
**Chef/s:** Siddharth Krishna. **Open:** Sat and Sun L 12.30 to 2.30 (3 Sun), all week D 6.30 to 11 (10.30 Sun). **Meals:** alc (main courses £14 to £23). Set L £22. **Service:** 12.5% (optional). **Details:** Cards accepted. 110 seats. Air-con. Music. Children allowed.

## Clarke's

**Enticing flavours at a local favourite**
124 Kensington Church Street, Notting Hill,
W8 4BH
Tel no: (020) 7221 9225
www.sallyclarke.com
⊖ **Notting Hill Gate, High Street Kensington,**
**map 4**
**Modern British | £35**
**Cooking score: 4**

🍷 **V**

'A good neighbourhood regular', is how one reader describes this long-standing stalwart – the restaurant turns 26 in 2010 – with Sally Clarke MBE ensuring that high standards are maintained. Choice in the daily menus has increased, and the idea of taking fresh, seasonal produce and cooking it simply has always been a winning formula. Flavour combinations are enticing – witness beetroot, Bramley apple and fennel soup served with chive cream and onion-seed bread stick, followed by roasted fillet of Cornish mackerel with black olive, celery and red onion relish with marinated organic spelt, or chargrilled lamb chop with red wine and sage glaze and soft Parmesan polenta. To finish, soft ginger meringue 'bombe' with spring rhubarb sauce has proved well balanced. Service is efficient and attentive. Wines are a well-chosen selection, starting with vin de pays d'Oc at £17 and offering a good selection by the glass and half-bottle. Check out the sexy numbers from Sally's beloved California as well as top-name labels from elsewhere.
**Chef/s:** Sally Clarke and Raffaele Colturi. **Open:** all week L 12.30 to 2, Mon to Sat D 7 to 10. **Closed:** 10 day Christmas and New Year, bank hols. **Meals:** alc (main courses £16 to £23). Set D £35.
**Service:** 12.5% (optional). **Details:** Cards accepted. 80 seats. Air-con. No music. No mobile phones. Wheelchair access. Children allowed.

**Vineet Bhatia** Rasoi Restaurant

### Who or what inspired you to become a chef?
I always wanted to be a pilot and, since I didn't qualify, I started looking for other options. As a summer trainee I worked in the service side of a hotel. Shortage of manpower meant I was put in the kitchen and that opened my eyes.

### What is the best meal you have ever eaten?
Nothing beats home-cooked Sunday brunches eaten with the family!

### What do you like cooking when you are 'off duty'?
I love cooking food for my sons and my wife - be it a burger, pizza or masala scrambled eggs with toast.

### If you were to have one abiding principle in the kitchen, what would it be?
Nothing is impossible - give it your best shot, before saying it is!

### What is your culinary tip?
Start with the best ingredients, don't overpower with too many flavours, finally a clean simple presentation - and you can't go wrong.

## Le Colombier

**French through and through**
145 Dovehouse Street, Chelsea, SW3 6LB
Tel no: (020) 7351 1155
www.lecolombier-sw3.co.uk
⊖ South Kensington, map 3
French | £32
Cooking score: 2

The 'entente' couldn't be more 'cordiale' in Didier Garnier's buzzy Gallic bistro. A tiled terrace out front is ideal for fine-weather chilling, while the interior looks the part with its wide floorboards, Art Deco lights and etched windows. The kitchen pilfers a few ideas from the Med (seared tuna with oregano dressing), but the rest is staunchly patriotic stuff – oeufs en meurette, steak tartare, confit duck with curly endive salad, pan-fried veal kidneys with mustard sauce and the like. There are high-protein grills, too, plus a raft of old-school desserts headed by crêpes Suzette and tarte Tatin. The all-French wine list has house selections from £15.90.

**Chef/s:** Philippe Tamet. **Open:** all week L 12 to 3 (3.30 Sun), D 6.30 to 10.30 (10 Sun). **Meals:** alc (main courses £16 to £26). Set L £17.50 (2 courses). Sun L £22. **Service:** 12.5%. **Details:** Cards accepted. 42 seats. 30 seats outside. No music. No mobile phones. Wheelchair access.

## ALSO RECOMMENDED

### ▲ The Cow

89 Westbourne Park Road, Westbourne Park, W2 5QH
Tel no: (020) 7221 0021
www.thecowlondon.co.uk
⊖ Royal Oak, map 4
Gastropub

Tom Conran has injected some urban pizzazz into this re-born Bayswater boozer, which now wears two fashionable hats. Join the rumbustious hordes for pints of 'black stuff' and plates of oysters in the ground-floor bar or graduate upstairs for something with a touch more substance. Evening menus follow the seasons, with crowd-pleasers running from cod chitterlings, garlic and capers (£6.50) via braised mallard with black beans and redcurrant jelly (£17.50) to rhubarb crumble (£6.50). Affordable wines from £15.75. Open all week.

## Deep

**Fish by the river**
The Boulevard, Imperial Wharf, Fulham, SW6 2UB
Tel no: (020) 7736 3337
www.deeplondon.co.uk
⊖ Fulham Broadway, map 3
Seafood | £28
Cooking score: 3

 £30

In a sparkling new development with an interior to match – white walls, pastel-coloured booths and soft neon lighting lending a cool, modern look – it's more Miami Beach than Thameside Fulham. The Scandinavian-influenced seafood menu, which features oyster soup with cucumber tagliatelle, prawn toast with dill and lemon, and Dover sole meunière, alongside more decadent crab and lobster options, ought to have young professionals flocking here. But however good the cooking, there's a dearth of customers, either due to Imperial Wharf being underpopulated or a failure to capture the imagination of local residents, in an otherwise isolated spot. As we went to press a good-value café-style menu was running during the day. House wine is £17.

**Chef/s:** Fredrik Bolin. **Open:** Tue to Fri and Sun L 12 to 3, Tue to Sat D 7 to 11. **Closed:** Mon, 2 weeks Christmas. **Meals:** alc (main courses £15 to £24). Set L and D £20.50 (2 courses) to £27.50. **Service:** 12.5% (optional). **Details:** Cards accepted. 120 seats. 200 seats outside. Air-con. Separate bar. Wheelchair access. Music. Children allowed. Car parking.

## The Devonshire

**The Ramsay treatment**
126 Devonshire Road, Chiswick, W4 2JJ
Tel no: (020) 7592 7962
www.gordonramsay.com
 Turnham Green, map 1
Gastropub | £21
Cooking score: 2

£30

This high-ceilinged, wood-panelled Chiswick boozer got the full-on Gordon Ramsay treatment in 2007 and has slotted into his ever-expanding portfolio with relative ease. Fans of Ramsay's other gastropubs will instantly recognise the tell-tale design trademarks and the carefully considered culinary style – a mix of canny patriotic dishes that tick all the boxes from 'nostaglia' to 'retro reinvention' and 'Med influences'. This is the world of rabbit terrine with prunes, braised lamb neck with turnip, swede and horseradish, and sea bass with clams and white bean broth. Puds include apple Charlotte and treacle tart. A typically stylish Ramsay wine list starts at £13.50 (£3.50 a glass).
**Chef/s:** Chris Arkadieff and Mark Sergeant. **Open:** Fri to Sun L 12 to 3, Wed to Sun D 6 to 10 (10.30 Sat, 9 Sun). **Closed:** Mon, Tue. **Meals:** alc (main courses £10 to £17). **Service:** 12.5% (optional). **Details:** Cards accepted. 70 seats. 15 seats outside. No music. Children allowed. Car parking.

**NEW ENTRY**
## Duke of Sussex

**A local worth cheering**
75 South Parade, Chiswick, W4 5LF
Tel no: (020) 8742 8801
 Chiswick Park, map 1
Gastropub | £23
Cooking score: 2

£5 OFF  £30

It may be building a reputation for food, but readers are pleased to see that this late nineteenth-century building continues to maintain its pubbiness with a range of real ales and a large beer garden. The dining room blends skylights, chandeliers and cherubs,

service is friendly (but slow on occasions), and the kitchen offers a mix of British and Spanish classics. Choose between pressed ox tongue and piccalilli or salt cod croquette, then go on to mutton stew and dumplings or a hearty Asturian fabada made from slow-cooked pork, chorizo and tender butter beans. Bread 'is a treat'. The wine list opens at £13.50.
**Chef/s:** Chris Payne. **Open:** Tue to Sun 12 to 10.30 (9.30 Sun). Mon D only 6 to 10.30. **Meals:** alc (main courses £8 to £16). **Details:** Cards accepted. 112 seats. 130 seats outside. Separate bar. Wheelchair access. Music. Children allowed.

## e&o

**Style-dining for the Notting Hill set**
14 Blenheim Crescent, Notting Hill, W11 1NN
Tel no: (020) 7229 5454
www.rickerrestaurants.com
 Ladbroke Grove, map 4
Pan-Asian | £40
Cooking score: 3

**V**

Stylish to the hilt, e&o is one of a group of pace-setting restaurants owned by Will Ricker. Set amid the buzz of Notting Hill, not far from Portobello Market, it is composed of a darkly inviting, womb-like interior with a cool bar area and small restaurant tables. The food is pan-Asian fusion, with a spread that ranges from dim sum such as XO cod shuymai and chilli salt squid, through sushi and sashimi variations (don't miss the sea bass with yuzu and truffle oil), to tempura, south-east Asian curries, eastern BBQ dishes, and specials like Korean-style lamb with kimchee. Desserts maintain the dizzying, multi-oriented standard with cookies-and-cream mochi, or frozen berries and white chocolate ganache. A varietally arranged wine list is mostly good stuff, with prices from £16.
**Chef/s:** Simon Tredway. **Open:** all week L 12 to 3 (12 to 11 Sat, 12.30 to 10.30 Sun), D 6 to 11. **Closed:** 25 and 26 Dec, 1 Jan, Aug bank hol. **Meals:** alc (main courses £10 to £24). **Service:** 12.5% (optional). **Details:** Cards accepted. 85 seats. 16 seats outside. Air-con. Separate bar. Wheelchair access. Music. Children allowed.

## ALSO RECOMMENDED

### ▲ Ebury Wine Bar

139 Ebury Street, Belgravia, SW1W 9QU
Tel no: (020) 7730 5447
www.eburywinebar.co.uk
⊖ Victoria, map 3
**Modern British**

This long-running Pimlico rendezvous occupies an attractive Georgian building with bow-fronted windows. There's a clubby feel throughout, from the front bar to the back restaurant, courtesy of a dark green colour scheme and trompe l'oeil paintings. The menu embraces everything from Thai fishcakes with wasabi coleslaw (£7.50) and plaice and crab roulade to pork mignons with prunes, brandy sauce and dauphinoise potato (£15.95) and various steaks. Finish with white and dark chocolate parfait. The superior wine list starts at £13.50. Open all week except Sun L.

### The Ebury

**Fashionable Pimlico bar/brasserie**
11 Pimlico Road, Chelsea, SW1W 8NA
Tel no: (020) 7730 6784
www.theebury.co.uk
⊖ Sloane Square, Victoria, map 3
**Modern European | £30**
**Cooking score: 2**

**V**

With both the ground-floor seafood bar and the upstairs fine-dining restaurant gone, this corner-sited, large-windowed bar/brasserie is less sophisticated these days. It now combines fashionable good looks with a more relaxed, accessible approach to dining and service. The printed menu offers simple, clean-cut brasserie-style assemblies, blending no-nonsense home-grown classics like calf's liver with bacon, onion marmalade and mash with sunnier, Med-influenced options such as grilled tuna steak with ratatouille and pesto. Desserts hit the sticky toffee pudding/chocolate fondant comfort zone, while most wines come by glass, carafe and bottle (from £15). A separate bar menu bolsters output.

**Chef/s:** Christophe Clerget. **Open:** all week L 12 to 3.30 (11 to 4 Sat and Sun), D 6 to 10.30 (10 Sun). Bar menu available. **Closed:** 25 Dec. **Meals:** alc (main courses £13 to £17). Set L £13.50 (2 courses) to £16.50. Set D £22.50 (2 courses) to £25. **Service:** 12.5% (optional). **Details:** Cards accepted. 56 seats. Air-con. Separate bar. Wheelchair access. Music. Children allowed.

### Eight Over Eight

**Glitz, glamour and grazing**
392 King's Road, Chelsea, SW3 5UZ
Tel no: (020) 7349 9934
www.rickerrestaurants.com
⊖ Sloane Square, map 3
**Pan-Asian | £30**
**Cooking score: 2**

**V**

The orientation of the food should come as no surprise, since this outpost of the Will Ricker empire is named after the Chinese lucky number eight. Starters and main courses are bypassed in favour of a flexible assortment of well-conceived pan-Asian fusion ideas, which are divided up into categories like dim sum (black cod and king prawn gyoza), sushi and sashimi, salads, a couple of curries, tempura (soft shell crab), BBQ roasts including rack of ribs with black pepper sauce, and specials (black cod with sweet yuzo miso). The idea is for each table to share. Wine from £16.
**Chef/s:** Clifton Muil. **Open:** Mon to Sat L 12 to 3, all week D 6 to 11 (10.30 Sun). **Closed:** 24 to 26 Dec, Easter Sun. **Meals:** alc (main courses £11 to £23). Set L £15. Set D £35 to £55. **Service:** 12.5% (optional). **Details:** Cards accepted. 95 seats. Air-con. Separate bar. Wheelchair access. Music. Children allowed.

> ## Average price
>
> The average price listed in main-entry reviews denotes the price of a three-course meal, without wine.

**NEW ENTRY**

## El Pirata Detapas
**A cheerful buzz and superb food**
115 Westbourne Grove, London, W2 4UP
Tel no: (020) 7727 5000
www.elpiratadetapas.co.uk
⊖ Notting Hill Gate, Bayswater, map 4
Spanish | £20
Cooking score: 3

V

Cheery vibes and energetic staff give this offshoot of Mayfair's El Pirata (see entry) an infectiously convivial buzz. There's also plenty of action in the kitchen, which delivers some cracking tapas and genuine Spanish flavours. Most dishes are 'superb', according to reporters who have singled out plates of pata negra ham and seared scallops with artichoke hearts and wafer-thin pancetta. An inspector was also impressed by the contrasts and balance in roasted pork belly with sweet pear and parsnip purée. Desserts deliver some unusual pairings, as in a deliciously light confit of strawberries with fresh cheese foam, and rich chocolate truffles with a smooth chocolate mousse and crisp saffron toffee. A keenly priced Native Selection heads up the wine list, with a decent range from £13.50 (£3.75 a glass).
**Chef/s:** Omar Allyboy. **Open:** Mon to Fri L 12 to 3, D 6 to 11. Sat and Sun 12 to 11. **Closed:** 24 Dec to 2 Jan. **Meals:** alc (tapas £3 to £17). Set L £9. Set D £18. **Service:** 10% (optional). **Details:** Cards accepted. 90 seats. Air-con. Separate bar. Wheelchair access. Music. Children allowed.

## READERS RECOMMEND

## Esarn Kheaw
**Thai**
314 Uxbridge Road, Shepherd's Bush, W12 7LJ
Tel no: (020) 8743 8930
www.esarnkheaw.com
'A top local restaurant and the food is great'

## L'Etranger
**France with a difference**
36 Gloucester Road, South Kensington, SW7 4QT
Tel no: (020) 7584 1118
www.circagroupltd.co.uk
⊖ Gloucester Road, map 3
Modern French | £45
Cooking score: 4

🍷 V

L'Etranger represents some kind of departure among London's French establishments, nailing its colours neither to the mainstream brasserie nor the modern French masts. Indeed, its 'blend of Japanese and European food is amazing', with Kingshuk Dey's unusual pairing of ingredients and constructions appealing to many readers. Scallop and butterfish in a shiso broth with edamame and smoked shiitake mushrooms or wild rabbit with honey mustard sauce and char sui pineapple are two successful east-meets-west combinations, but there are also good renditions of French classics such as Charolais beef tartare and confit shoulder of Pyrenean mountain lamb with grilled aubergine and onion chutney. Among starters, expect to find oysters with yuzu jelly, cucumber and wasabi granita. Mango and Thai basil soufflé with mango margarita is a good way to finish. The subtle lilac and grey dining room is a sophisticated backdrop for the cooking and the innovative, gently priced wine list (from £20) with its lunch deals, good-by-the-glass selection and extraordinary collection of Champagnes.
**Chef/s:** Kingshuk Dey. **Open:** Mon to Fri and Sun L 12 to 3, all week D 6 to 11 (6 to 10 Sun). **Closed:** 24 to 26 Dec, 1 Jan. **Meals:** alc (main courses £16 to £49). Set L and early D £16.50 (2 courses) to £19.50. Brunch £18.50 (2 courses) to £22.50. **Service:** 12.5% (optional). **Details:** Cards accepted. 80 seats. Air-con. Wheelchair access. Music. Children allowed.

## ALSO RECOMMENDED

### ▲ The First Floor

186 Portobello Road, Notting Hill, W11 1LA
Tel no: (020) 7243 0072
www.firstfloorportobello.co.uk
⊖ Notting Hill Gate, map 4
Modern British

This free-thinking conversion of a grand
Victorian pub, which was at the epicentre of
Notting Hill's 'big bang' during the 90s, is now
a local landmark. Portobello Road's faded
boho charms define the lofty first-floor
restaurant, with its centrepiece chandelier, tall
windows and on-trend contemporary food.
Expect a mix of modern British and Med-
influenced culinary ideas running from
swordfish carpaccio with quail's egg (£6.50)
through Welsh lamb rump with Charlotte
potatoes and juniper jus (£14.50) to tarte Tatin
with cardamom ice cream (£5.50). House
wine is £14.50. Closed Sun D.

### Fish Hook

A fine catch in Chiswick
6-8 Elliott Road, Chiswick, W4 1PE
Tel no: (020) 8742 0766
www.fishhook.co.uk
⊖ Turnham Green, map 1
Seafood | £30
Cooking score: 2

W4 isn't exactly bereft of eateries, but locals
agree that chef/patron Michael Nadra's fish
restaurant is a stand-out success. Inside, it is
simple, clean and contemporary, with cool
marble floors, banquette seating and black-
and-white fishy prints. With each day comes a
new catch and a new menu. The skilful
cooking treats raw ingredients with respect,
but doesn't shy away from the opportunity to
inject some creativity and flair into the
accoutrements – grilled sea bass comes with
crab ravioli, basil and bisque sauce, and roast
salmon with caviar and deep-fried truffled
egg. Elsewhere, a particularly fine classic fish
soup with crostini and aïoli is usually on the
carte. House wine is £15.

**Chef/s:** Michael Nadra. **Open:** all week L 12 to 2.30
(3.30 Sat and Sun), D 6 to 10.30 (10 Sun). **Closed:**
25 and 26 Dec. **Meals:** alc (main courses £17 to £27).
Set L £12.50 (2 courses) to £15. Set D £16 (2 courses)
to £18.50. Sun L £15. **Service:** 12.5% (optional).
**Details:** Cards accepted. 54 seats. Air-con.
Wheelchair access. Music. Children allowed.

### The Gate

No vegetarian clichés here
51 Queen Caroline Street, Hammersmith, W6 9QL
Tel no: (020) 8748 6932
www.thegate.tv
⊖ Hammersmith, map 1
Vegetarian | £23
Cooking score: 2

£5 OFF  V  £30

The vaulted ceiling, large window and
minimalist décor of this 'calm, serene' space
make it easy to picture the artist's studio it once
was (Sir Frank Brangwyn lived and worked
here at the turn of the last century). The
imaginative menu 'tries hard to spurn the
vegetarian clichés', with dishes such as
aubergine schnitzel or truffled risotto cake. A
wild mushroom Eccles cake with well-made
pastry impressed one reporter, as did goats'
cheese ravioli, although flavours and
seasoning were generally felt to be
understated. Wholesome desserts include
apple and fig crumble and maple syrup crème
brûlée. The two-page wine list opens
at £15.60.
**Chef/s:** Mariusz Wegrodzki. **Open:** Mon to Fri L 12 to
3, Mon to Sat D 6 to 11. **Closed:** Sun, 24 Dec to 2
Jan, bank hols. **Meals:** alc (main courses £9 to £14).
**Service:** 12.5% (optional). **Details:** Cards accepted.
59 seats. 38 seats outside. Air-con. Music. Children
allowed.

## Geales

**Posh fish and chips**
2 Farmer Street, Notting Hill, W8 7SN
Tel no: (020) 7727 7528
www.geales.com
⊖ Notting Hill Gate, map 4
Seafood | £25
Cooking score: 1

Famous for putting on the style ('fish and chips with a bottle of Bolly, please'), Geales became a Notting Hill legend in its glory years. Following an extreme makeover by Messrs Fuller and Hollihead, it's now enjoying a comeback – even if some think the food is 'hugely overpriced'. The new owners have applied some gentle improvements (pale grey walls, leather chairs) and cranked up the menu: the main event (battered cod, haddock, hake and pollack) now competes with Thai soft-shell crab, lobster tagliatelle, macaroni cheese and lemon posset. House wine is £14.50.
**Chef/s:** Garry Hollihead. **Open:** Tue to Sun L 12 to 2.30, all week D 6 to 11. **Meals:** alc (main courses £10 to £19). Set L £8.95 (2 courses). **Service:** 12.5% (optional). **Details:** Cards accepted. 80 seats. 20 seats outside. Air-con. No music. Wheelchair access. Children allowed.

## Gordon Ramsay

**As haute as cuisine comes**
68-69 Royal Hospital Road, Chelsea, SW3 4HP
Tel no: (020) 7352 4441
www.gordonramsay.com
⊖ Sloane Square, map 3
French | £90
Cooking score: 9

Gordon Ramsay must regard 2009 as his *annus horribilis*, though he would probably use something more Anglo-Saxon to describe the year when his international business empire took a battering during the economic downturn (among other things). But standards remain impressive and Ramsay's flagship restaurant has the presence of a grand establishment. This has become one of London's institutions and is therefore in an enviable position. Everyone wants to come here at some stage. Ramsay's head chef Clare Smyth has not deviated from the task of modern haute cuisine and you do see labour and effort, as well as taste and flavour, for your money. The menu has an edge to it that gives life to many dishes: sautéed foie gras with roasted veal sweetbreads, Cabernet Sauvignon vinegar and almond velouté, for example, and slow-braised pig's trotter pressed then pan-fried, served with ham knuckle, poached quail's egg and hollandaise sauce. And people have spoken well of fish cookery that includes sea bass served with steamed Charlotte potatoes, cucumber, oyster beignet and a caviar velouté. There is an easy assurance to much of the cooking. A summer lunch that included a paella-style saffron risotto with clams, mussels, langoustines, chorizo and tomatoes, also took in a perfect salad of artichokes and heritage apples served on a chicken liver and foie gras croûton with Périgord truffle vinaigrette. Other stand-outs were a braised shin of Angus beef with horseradish pommes purée, stuffed mushrooms and red wine sauce that allied simplicity with the voluptuous; and confit milk-fed Suffolk pork belly with caramelised endive, apples, grelot onions and Madeira jus. The success continued through superb cheeses to desserts of lemon meringue and almond tart – a welcome variation – and a banana parfait with passion fruit and salted caramel ice cream. Petits fours (balls of strawberry ice cream in white chocolate served Fat Duck-style in a cloud of dry ice) and the seasonally correct amuse bouche of intense tomato essence with langoustine were tip-top. What needs to be stressed here is that the whole experience is enjoyable. The wine waiter is tremendously knowledgeable and the lengthy list does not quite ignore people who want to drink inexpensively. For those with a less relaxed schedule, there are well-kept wines by the glass. A bottle of 2007 Bordeaux Blanc Sec is £20, a Fayard Côtes de Ventoux 2007 is £28.

Chef/s: Clare Smyth. **Open:** Mon to Fri L 12 to 2.30, D 6.30 to 11. **Closed:** Sat, Sun, 1 week Christmas. **Meals:** Set L £45. Set D £90. Tasting menu £120 (8 courses). **Service:** 12.5%. **Details:** Cards accepted. 45 seats. Air-con. Separate bar. No music. No mobile phones. Wheelchair access. Children allowed.

## Haandi

**Classy Indian food near Harrods**
136 Brompton Road, Knightsbridge, SW3 1HY
Tel no: (020) 7823 7373
www.haandi-restaurants.com
⊖ Knightsbridge, map 4
Indian | £25
Cooking score: 4

This popular and upmarket Knightsbridge restaurant gets its name from a type of Indian cooking vessel with a concave bottom. These vessels are much in evidence here – used in the kitchen (which you can view through a curved window) and as miniature serving dishes. The North Indian cooking stays mainly with familiar favourites like lamb rogan josh, chicken makhani, tandooris and tikkas, but with branches in Nairobi and Kampala, it's no surprise to find specialities like the Kenyan dish of jeera chicken served in a 'rich, complex, spicy masala'. The food is generally executed with flair, and dishes that have impressed this year have included chicken burra tikka , Bombay aloo chat, 'consistently good' gobi tak-a-tak, and spicy Goan chilli prawns. Breads include 'nice naan, better paratha, excellent bhatura'. Finish with mango kulfi. House wine £14.95. A second London outlet is at 301-303 Hale Lane, Edgware, tel no (020) 8905 4433.
**Chef/s:** Ratan Singh. **Open:** all week L 12 to 3, D 5.30 to 11. **Closed:** 25 Dec. **Meals:** alc (main courses £7 to £14). Set L £8.90. **Service:** 12.5% (optional). **Details:** Cards accepted. 65 seats. Air-con. Separate bar. Music. Children allowed.

★ PUB NEWCOMER OF THE YEAR ★

**NEW ENTRY**
## The Harwood Arms

**Patriotic newcomer raises the gastropub bar**
Walham Grove, Fulham, SW6 1QP
Tel no: (020) 7386 1847
www.harwoodarms.com
⊖ Fulham Broadway, map 3
Gastropub | £22
Cooking score: 5

In a quiet backstreet location, two of the big players behind the Ledbury in Notting Hill and the Pot Kiln, Berkshire (see entries) have teamed up to create a venue that raises the bar for the whole gastropub experience. It's little wonder that this newcomer is proving such a hit with the local crowd. Inside, the Harwood Arms is comfortable and pleasant (if a tad unspectacular), and the place is almost entirely given over to proper dining – although casual bar snacks such as real savoury mince pies and hot Scotch eggs give a taste of what's on offer. The menu is peppered with inventive seasonal ideas: chopped pig's trotters and crisp ears on toast with tarragon mustard, roe deer stewed with sloe gin, and wood pigeon with chicory braised in mead have an English rustic edge, with deft use of wild herbs, foraged leaves and scarcely an ingredient from beyond Britain's shores. Patriotism also extends to the dessert menu, where you might find warm Bramley apple doughnuts with spiced sugar or Colston Bassett Stilton marinated in British cassis with celery biscuits. Aside from the occasional hiccup, the cooking and execution are skilful, dishes are reasonably priced and fair mark-ups distinguish the well-annotated wine list (from £14).
**Chef/s:** Stephen Williams. **Open:** all week L 12 to 3 (4 Sat), D 6.30 to 9.30 (7 to 9 Sun). **Closed:** 25 Dec. **Meals:** alc (main courses £13 to £16). **Service:** 10% (optional). **Details:** Cards accepted. 60 seats. Air-con. Separate bar. Wheelchair access. Music. Children allowed.

## Hereford Road
**Barnstorming British cooking**
3 Hereford Road, Notting Hill, W2 4AB
Tel no: (020) 7727 1144
www.herefordroad.org
⊖ Bayswater, map 4
British | £30
Cooking score: 4

**V**

One of the new champions of untarnished British food, Hereford Road is an easy-paced, sociable beast – a cracking neighbourhood venue that delivers 'consistently exciting' dishes in a converted Notting Hill butcher's shop. Dining takes place in a functional split-level space where the preferred seating option is to snuggle into cosy red leather booths. Start with grilled razor clams with piquant red onions and thyme, soft roes on toast or crispy pork with dandelion and mustard. Moving on, whole red-leg partridge with red cabbage and lentils is a warming dish in winter, while summer brings lemon sole with cucumber and kohlrabi salad. This is good food without the gratuitous trimmings: pristine ingredients are brought together with dexterity and flavours are 'on point'. Buttermilk pudding or apple crumble and custard guarantee a satisfying end. Service is welcoming, portions are generous and the daily menu ensures that even local regulars remain thrilled. The carefully researched, quaffable wine list is priced from £18.80 (£3.60 a glass).
**Chef/s:** Tom Pemberton. **Open:** all week L 12 to 3 (4 Sun), D 6 to 10.30 (10 Sun). **Closed:** 1 week Christmas. **Meals:** alc (main courses from £10 to £14). Set L £13 (2 courses) to £15.50. **Service:** not inc. **Details:** Cards accepted. 60 seats. 8 seats outside. Air-con. No music. Wheelchair access. Children allowed.

### Readers recommend

A 'readers recommend' review is a genuine quote from a report sent in by one of our readers. We intend to follow up these suggestions throughout the year to come.

## Hunan
**Home-style Hunanese favourites**
51 Pimlico Road, Chelsea, SW1W 8NE
Tel no: (020) 7730 5712
www.hunanlondon.com
⊖ Sloane Square, map 3
Chinese | £39
Cooking score: 3

A breath of fresh air on the plutocrats' paradise that is Pimlico Road, Hunan offers a thorough taste of home-style Hunanese cooking at reasonable prices. Chef Michael Peng cooks 'light food with minimal rice and noodles'. His simple but varied set-price menu includes favourites such as crispy aromatic duck with pancakes as part of a balanced selection of meat (stir-fried beef fillet in spicy Szechuan peppercorn sauce, sautéed spicy shredded chicken) and fish dishes (steamed monkfish and salmon rolls, prawn and bitter melon dumplings). Finish with a sweet red bean pancake with almond jelly. The wine list far surpasses those usually offered with Chinese food; expertly annotated and divided by style, it starts at just at £14.
**Chef/s:** Michael Peng. **Open:** Mon to Sat L 12.30 to 2, D 6.30 to 11. **Closed:** Sun, Christmas, bank hols. **Meals:** Set menus from £38.80. **Service:** 12.5%. **Details:** Cards accepted. 44 seats. Air-con. Music. Children allowed.

## Il Convivio
**Sleek eatery with vivid modern menus**
143 Ebury Street, Chelsea, SW1W 9QN
Tel no: (020) 7730 4099
www.etruscarestaurants.com
⊖ Victoria, Sloane Square, map 3
Italian | £38
Cooking score: 2

£5
OFF

Dante coined the word 'convivio' for a meeting of minds over food and drink, and lines from his poetry are emblazoned on the deep-red walls of this sleek Belgravia Italian. The bilingual menu strikes a vivid contemporary note, and the kitchen steps up to the mark with plenty of vigorous ideas. A terrine of

octopus is accompanied by tomato essence and radishes, black cod is caramelised with aged balsamic (not über-trendy miso), and pasta fans could treat themselves to duck and pea ravioli with foie gras sauce. 'Chocolate trilogy' is an enticing dessert, organic artisan cheeses are a must, and the wine list is firmly camped on Italian soil. House vino is £15.
**Chef/s:** Lukas Pfaff. **Open:** Mon to Sat L 12 to 3, D 7 to 10.30. **Closed:** Sun, bank hols, 2 weeks Christmas. **Meals:** alc (main courses £13 to £26). Set L £14.50 (2 courses). Set D £17.50 (2 courses). **Service:** 12.5% (optional). **Details:** Cards accepted. 65 seats. Air-con. Separate bar. Music. Children allowed.

**NEW ENTRY**
## Indian Zing
**Hot venue with cool cooking**
236 King Street, Hammersmith, W6 0RF
Tel no: (020) 8748 5959
www.indianzing.co.uk
⊖ Ravenscourt Park, map 1
Indian | £22
Cooking score: 4

Manoj Vasaikar's cool, modern restaurant has established itself as one of the top places to eat Indian food in west London. The décor is light – the hidden patio at the back is a draw in fine weather – and the cooking interesting with a few dishes you would have difficulty finding anywhere else in Britain: vegetable bhanavia, for example, is an improvement on the ubiquitous onion bhaji, while prawn and aubergine kharphatla is a delicious combo served with caramelised onions and tomato and pickle masala. Chicken makhani (free-range chicken tikka simmered in a good tomato and fenugreek sauce) has been praised, as has nilgiri lamb (a tender hill station curry made using stone-ground spices, coconut and fresh green herbs). The bread selection is very good, and desserts such as tandoori figs and apple muesli crumble are more than a cut above the average. Wines (from £14.95) are carefully selected to match the food.

**Chef/s:** Manoj Vasaikar. **Open:** all week L 12 to 3 (1 to 4 Sun) D 6 to 11 (10 Sun). **Meals:** alc (main courses £9 to £17) Set L £12 (2 courses) to £15. **Service:** 12.5% (optional). **Details:** Cards accepted. 51 seats. 23 seats outside. Air-con. Wheelchair access. Music. Children allowed. Car parking.

## Kensington Place
**Fast-paced brasserie icon**
201-209 Kensington Church Street, Notting Hill, W8 7LX
Tel no: (020) 7727 3184
www.danddlondon.com
⊖ Notting Hill Gate, Kensington High Street, map 4
Modern European | £20
Cooking score: 4

Hard-edged, big-city vibes and clamorous babbling come with the territory in this capacious, glass-fronted brasserie icon, which has lost none of its appetite for fast-paced eating or affordability. Since founder Rowley Leigh departed to Le Café Anglais (see entry), the kitchen has regrouped and launched some new dishes – although metropolitan flavours still cut a swathe through the menu. Comforting familiar standards (pork rillettes with pear chutney, fish pie, chocolate fondant with crunchy honeycomb) now co-exist with a gang of flashy new kids (anything from octopus sopressata with smoked paprika and shallot tempura to passion fruit curd with lime leaf foam, mango, coconut sorbet and chilli oil). In between, dishes such as glazed lamb's sweetbreads with pea purée and wild garlic or confit pork belly with lentils, apple compote and beetroot salad are totally in tune with the popular mood. The wine list remains a model of its kind, dealing in thrilling names, excitement and serious-minded international drinking at prices few would argue with (the bidding starts at £16.50). A host of top-drawer selections from £4.75 a glass encourage exploration.
**Chef/s:** Henry Vigar. **Open:** all week L 12 to 3 (3.30 Sat and Sun) D 6.30 to 10.30 (11 Fri and Sat, 10 Sun). **Meals:** alc (main courses £13 to £17). Set L

and D £16.50 (2 courses) to £19.50. **Service:** 12.5% (optional). **Details:** Cards accepted. 90 seats. Air-con. Separate bar. Wheelchair access. Music. Children allowed.

## READERS RECOMMEND
## Kiasu
**Malaysian**
48 Queensway, Notting Hill, W2 3RY
Tel no: (020) 7727 8810
**'Good-value cooking'**

## Launceston Place
**Cross-town-for-it cooking**
1a Launceston Place, South Kensington, W8 5RL
Tel no: (020) 7937 6912
www.egami.co.uk
⊖ **Gloucester Road, map 3**
**Modern European | £38**
**Cooking score: 4**

That Launceston Place so successfully combines 'cross-town-for-it' cooking with the charm of a friendly (though moodily chic) neighbourhood restaurant is testament to the skill of ex-Pétrus boy Tristan Welch. He knows when to play it trad (a top-value Sunday lunch of roast beef with all the trimmings) and when to play it cool (the edgier modern British dinner menu). Welch does quirky re-workings of ham, egg and chips and Death by Chocolate alongside more serious dishes of venison, chestnuts and red cabbage or suckling pig with apple, always ravishingly presented. Prices are very fair, even at dinner. If only the same could be said for the wine list – which begins at £18.50 and stings with its high mark-ups. At inspection service was competent, never engaging. A reader draws attention to the 'overbearing bureaucracy' of the group booking policy.
**Chef/s:** Tristan Welch. **Open:** Tue to Sun L 12 to 2.30 (3 Sun), D 6.30 to 10.30. **Closed:** Mon. **Meals:** Set L £18 (3 courses). Set D £42. Tasting menu £55. **Service:** 12.5% (optional). **Details:** Cards accepted. 60 seats. Air-con. Separate bar. Wheelchair access. Children allowed.

## The Ledbury
**Intense food, indelible memories**
127 Ledbury Road, Westbourne Park, W11 2AQ
Tel no: (020) 7792 9090
www.theledbury.com
⊖ **Notting Hill Gate, Westbourne Park, map 4**
**Modern European | £60**
**Cooking score: 7**

🍷 **V**

On a fine day with the terrace doors open to the light, airy dining room and the place packed with a well-heeled cosmopolitan crowd, you could almost imagine yourself to be in Paris or New York (well, you know what we mean). At a meal in May an appetiser of the most intensely flavoured beetroot meringue, sandwiching a smear of rich foie gras, proved an indelible memory, so too the ceviche of scallops, which was brilliantly partnered with seaweed and herb oil, kohlrabi and frozen horseradish snow. A superbly balanced dish of celeriac baked in ash with hazelnuts and wood sorrel and paired unusually with a kromeski of wild boar was a clever marriage of contrasting flavours and textures. Not to be outdone, a calf's sweetbread roasted on liquorice found empathy with grilled white asparagus, date and almonds. Timing is good, textures carefully considered and there is an appealing simplicity to much of the cooking, even among desserts, such as an exceptional brown sugar tart with Muscat grapes, white raisin ice cream and vin cotto. While the cooking puts the Ledbury in the premier league of London restaurants, sadly the service lags a few steps behind – a consistent niggle in reports this year. The wine cellar is magnificent, but with few bargains for those on a budget. House wines start at £23.
**Chef/s:** Brett Graham. **Open:** all week L 12 to 2.30 (3 Sun), D 6.30 to 10.30 (7 to 10 Sun). **Closed:** 24 to 26 Dec, Aug bank hol. **Meals:** Set L £19.50 (2 courses) to £24.50. Set D £60. Tasting menu £70 (8 courses). Sun L £40. **Service:** 12.5% optional. **Details:** Cards accepted. 60 seats. 25 seats outside. Air-con. No music. No mobile phones. Wheelchair access. Children allowed.

## Madsen

Scandinavian
20 Old Brompton Road, South Kensington,
SW7 3DL
Tel no: (020) 7225 2772
www.madsenrestaurant.com
'Good value...clean, Scandinavian, IKEA feel to
the restaurant'

## Notting Hill Brasserie

Romantic atmosphere and appealing food
92 Kensington Park Road, Notting Hill, W11 2PN
Tel no: (020) 7229 4481
www.nottinghillbrasserie.com
⊖ Notting Hill Gate, map 4
Modern European | £45
Cooking score: 4

With its subdued lighting and live jazz piano
music, you could say the Notting Hill
Brasserie has a romantic atmosphere. The
British menu offers some confidently
produced and appealing cooking. Karl
Burdock seems at home with dishes such as the
pair of carefully cooked, sweet scallops served
with creamy peas, beans, pieces of morel and
good herb gnocchi, and the well-seasoned
chicken breast with seasonal white asparagus
and wild mushroom lasagne tried at
inspection. Desserts, however, were 'not at the
same level' and service seems too often left in
the hands of the unskilled, especially when the
food comes at elevated prices. There is relief at
lunch, however, with a good-value fixed price
deal. The manageable, predominantly French
wine list starts with a glass at £4.50.
**Chef/s:** Karl Burdock. **Open:** Tue to Sun L 12 to 3, all
week D 7 to 11 (10 Sun). **Closed:** bank hols.
**Meals:** alc (main courses £25 to £29). Set L £17.50 (2
courses) to £21.50. Sun L £25 (2 courses) to £30.
**Service:** 12.5%. **Details:** Cards accepted. 90 seats.
Air-con. Separate bar. Wheelchair access. Music.
Children allowed.

## Olivo

A showcase for Sardinian cooking
21 Eccleston Street, Belgravia, SW1W 9LX
Tel no: (020) 7730 2505
www.olivorestaurants.com
⊖ Victoria, map 3
Sardinian | £29
Cooking score: 1

Inside this showcase for Sardinian cooking
you may find yourself sitting too close to
strangers. Popularity certainly keeps the staff
busy – which may explain their mood swings,
but doesn't excuse their lack of charm.
Spaghetti is made special thanks to the delicate
flavour of sea urchins, garlic and chilli, an
understated steamed fillet of hake comes with
potatoes and parsley, and it's easy to see why
frozen yoghurt with blueberries is a perennial
favourite. Wines from £17.50 kick off with a
Sardinian aperitif, Vernaccia Di Oristano.
**Chef/s:** Sandro Medda. **Open:** Mon to Fri L 12 to
2.30, all week D 7 to 11. **Closed:** bank hols.
**Meals:** alc (main courses £16 to £20). Set L £19.50
(2 courses) to £22.50. **Service:** not inc.
**Details:** Cards accepted. 45 seats. Air-con. No
music. Wheelchair access. Children allowed.

## The Painted Heron

Mould-breaking Indian tickles the fancy
112 Cheyne Walk, Chelsea, SW10 0DJ
Tel no: (020) 7351 5232
www.thepaintedheron.com
⊖ Sloane Square, map 3
Indian | £35
Cooking score: 3
£5 OFF 🍷 V

This flagship of contemporary Indian cuisine
arrived with all guns blazing in 2002 and is
still cutting a considerable culinary dash.
Starters alone tickle the fancy, with the likes of
soft-shell crab in Cobra beer batter spiked
with sesame and chilli. The voyage of
discovery continues in mains such as tiger
prawn and scallop Goan curry. Rack of lamb
and guinea fowl breast are among other
possibilities not normally seen on Indian

menus, the latter stir-fried with spring onions, masala and cottage cheese. Finish with a spin on kulfi, served with a citrus compote of clementine, lemon and lime. Wines by the glass from £5 head up a creative international mix, with lashings of quality and imagination all the way through.
**Chef/s:** Yogesh Datta. **Open:** all week L 12 to 2.30, D 6 to 11. **Closed:** 25 and 26 Dec, 1 Jan. **Meals:** alc (main courses £12 to £17). **Service:** 12.5% (optional). **Details:** Cards accepted. 70 seats. 16 seats outside. Air-con. Wheelchair access. Music. Children allowed.

## READERS RECOMMEND

## Patio
**Polish**
5 Goldhawk Road, Shepherd's Bush, W12 8QQ
Tel no: (020) 8743 5194
www.patio-restaurant.com
**'I love it – it's like sitting in someone's living room drinking vodka and eating smoked herring'**

## Pearl Liang
**Finely prepared dim sum**
8 Sheldon Square, Paddington, W2 6EZ
Tel no: (020) 7289 7000
www.pearlliang.co.uk
⊖ Paddington, map 4
Chinese | £40
Cooking score: 2

**V**

Pearl Liang is tucked away in the well-hidden, pedestrianised Paddington Basin complex of offices in a location that is a culinary dead spot. But the lavishly decorated restaurant draws crowds with its finely prepared dim sum (especially the attractive lunch deal with 10 items for under a tenner) and mainly Cantonese carte – though it can stray a little into south-east Asia for, perhaps Thai green curry or fried Malaysian kweitio (noodles) with prawn. Recent highlights have included a delicate steamed sea bass with ginger and spring onion, gutsy stewed belly pork with preserved vegetables and silky ma po bean curd. House wine is £14.50.

**Chef/s:** Paul Ngo. **Open:** all week 12 to 11. **Closed:** 24 and 25 Dec. **Meals:** alc (main courses £7 to £33). Set D £23 to £68. **Service:** 12.5% (optional). **Details:** Cards accepted. 120 seats. Air-con. Separate bar. Wheelchair access. Music. Children allowed.

## The Pig's Ear
**Altogether very charming gastropub**
35 Old Church Street, Chelsea, SW3 5BS
Tel no: (020) 7352 2908
www.turningearth.co.uk
⊖ South Kensington, map 3
Gastropub | £30
Cooking score: 2

Friendly staff play cards over the bar with regulars in this laid-back, Bohemian, almost messy pub – fairy lights sparkle, film prints adorn the dark red walls, and it's altogether very charming. Foodwise it's also a bit of a jumble, featuring everything from Spanish charcuterie to an Asian rare beef salad or baked Camembert for two. Dishes can be hit-and-miss, although a naked version of fish and chips – chunks of un-battered cod stacked with architectural precision – scored highly. Wines, which start at £15, are chalked up on the wall, or try a glass of cold Breton cider.
**Chef/s:** Taavi Adamson. **Open:** all week L 12.30 to 3 (3.30 Sat, 4 Sun), D 7 to 10 (9.30 Sun). **Closed:** 24 to 27 Dec, 31 Dec to 2 Jan. **Meals:** alc (main courses £11 to £15). Sun L £14. **Service:** 12.5% (optional). **Details:** Cards accepted. 53 seats. Air-con. Separate bar. Music. Children allowed.

## Popeseye
**Sticking with steak and chips**
108 Blythe Road, Kensington, W14 0HD
Tel no: (020) 7610 4578
www.popeseye.com
⊖ Olympia, map 1
Steaks | £25
Cooking score: 1

Ian Hutchinson has been in business here for 15 years and the formula has not changed. His menu consists only of steaks – sirloin, fillet or rump (popeseye) – served with chips and optional salad. That's it – except that the steaks are Aberdeen Angus, delivered daily from the Scottish Highlands, and hung for a minimum of two weeks, with weights ranging from a dainty six ounces to a whopping 30 ounces. A few puddings, ices and cheese to finish, while a good list of mostly red wines (with some fine clarets) opens at £12.50.

**Chef/s:** Ian Hutchinson. **Open:** Mon to Sat D only 6.30 to 10.30. **Closed:** Sun, 10 days Christmas. **Meals:** alc (steaks £10 to £46). **Service:** 12.5%. **Details:** Cash only. 34 seats. Air-con. Wheelchair access. Music. Children allowed.

## La Poule au Pot
**Classic French bistro cooking**
231 Ebury Street, Belgravia, SW1W 8UT
Tel no: (020) 7730 7763
⊖ Sloane Square, map 3
French | £38
Cooking score: 2

'Farmhouse style (rustic), very few changes in 40 years', is how the proprietor (of 14 years) describes this unequivocally French restaurant. Interconnecting rooms, closely spaced tables, wooden floorboards and large windows draped in lace add to the Gallic feel, while the menu disdains the presentational fripperies of modern French fashion. Choose from the full repertoire of classics: fish soup or onion tart, beef bourguignon, steak béarnaise or bouillabaisse. Even desserts such as tarte Tatin and crème brûlée are high on tradition. The equally patriotic wine list starts at a reasonable £14.

**Chef/s:** Chris Groboski. **Open:** all week L 12.30 to 3 (4 Sat and Sun), D 6.45 to 11.15 (10 Sun). **Closed:** 25 and 26 Dec. **Meals:** alc (main courses £15 to £25). Set L £18.75 (2 courses) to £22.75. **Service:** 12.5% (optional). **Details:** Cards accepted. 70 seats. 36 seats outside. Air-con. No music. No mobile phones. Wheelchair access. Children allowed.

## Marcus Eaves  L'Autre Pied

**Who or what inspired you to become a chef?**
After washing pots and pans in a small hotel at the age of 15, I felt a great sense of achievement and eventually found myself working alongside the chef. This is when I thought maybe I could become a chef one day.

**What is the best meal you have ever eaten?**
Has to be the tasting menu at Lettonie in Bath many years ago. It was the first time I had eaten in a restaurant of that standard before. An interesting, unique and faultless experience.

**Which chefs do you admire?**
The chefs I admire are: Heston Blumenthal, Brett Graham, Claude Bosi – all for different reasons, but each giving something unique to the Great British restaurant scene.

**What did it mean to you to be awarded 'Up-and-coming Chef' in The Good Food Guide 2009?**
The award was totally out of the blue; for me to get some recognition in such early stages at L'Autre Pied was fantastic.

**NEW ENTRY**
## Princess Victoria
**Smart pub with thoughtful, thrifty food**
217 Uxbridge Road, Shepherd's Bush, W12 9DT
Tel no: (020) 8749 5886
www.princessvictoria.co.uk
⊖ Goldhawk Road, Shepherd's Bush, map 1
Gastropub | £28
Cooking score: 3

Even if you're planning to give Westfield shopping a wide berth, it's worth making the trek to this reinvigorated Victorian boozer. An unassuming location and exterior hides a decent pub and a stately dining room, where the fire roars amidst dark marble, gilt mirrors and high ceilings. More down-to-earth are the working-class origins of the food, with dishes like crispy, buttery cakes of pig's head with mash and Madeira jus or pot-au-feu of beef, sausage, bone-marrow dumplings and salted tongue. This isn't thrifty because it's trendy, however – carefully thought-out dishes are greater than the sum of their parts, and are backed up by an immense wine list, starting at £16.90.
**Chef/s:** James McLean. **Open:** all week L 12 to 3 (4.30 Sun), D 6.30 to 10.30 (9.30 Sun). **Closed:** 25 and 26 Dec. **Meals:** alc (main courses £12 to £18). Set L £12.50 (2 courses) to £15. Sun L £12.50. **Service:** not inc. **Details:** Cards accepted. 150 seats. 45 seats outside. Air-con. Separate bar. Music. Children allowed. Car parking.

## Racine
**Sophisticated and comforting French bistro**
239 Brompton Road, Knightsbridge, SW3 2EP
Tel no: (020) 7584 4477
⊖ Knightsbridge, South Kensington, map 3
French | £33
Cooking score: 4

The dining room, dressed in dark brown with mirror-lined walls, exudes a comforting lived-in feel. This past year has seen the return of Henry Harris, but most of the front-of-house staff have departed; while service is still courteous, it lacks the polish of old. But

Racine's formula of timeless dining can be a rewarding strategy. Hot duck foie gras served with bitter bigarade orange sauce makes a wonderful starter. And with a poached Scottish wild salmon paired with pickled cucumber and a classic hollandaise sauce, flavours are on point. Desserts do not vary much: crème caramel is as good as it gets and clafoutis with griottine cherries will guarantee a happy ending. The quaffable wine list, bolstered by a good selection of glasses and half-bottles, starts from £18, has now stretched a little beyond the shores of France.
**Chef/s:** Henry Harris and Mark Blanchford. **Open:** all week L 12 to 3 (3.30 Sat and Sun), D 6 to 10.30 (10 Sun). **Closed:** 25 Dec. **Meals:** alc (main courses £13 to £26). Set L £17.50. Set D £19.50. **Service:** 14.5% (optional). **Details:** Cards accepted. 75 seats. 4 seats outside. Air-con. Wheelchair access. Children allowed.

## Rasoi
**A spicy treat for the taste buds**
10 Lincoln Street, Chelsea, SW3 2TS
Tel no: (020) 7225 1881
www.rasoirestaurant.co.uk
⊖ Sloane Square, map 3
Indian | £55
Cooking score: 5

 V

The interior styling of Vineet Bhatia's upscale Indian restaurant is an improbably effective blend of Chelsea town house and south Asian exotic. There is plenty to look at, from murals and masks to temple bells and statues of the elephant god Ganesha, in an L-shaped ground-floor room that extends into a conservatory section. To access it all, however, you must first ring the doorbell. The cooking that awaits is a vivacious treat for the taste buds, with precisely spiced dishes based on quality ingredients. The new-wave style takes in masala-dusted foie gras with raisins and cashews and wild mushroom naan, followed, perhaps, by tandoori sea bass with crispy okra, or peppered duck korma with truffled potato and apricot chutney. Vegetarian dishes, such as wild mushroom kofta with fennel and tomato sauce and saffron pulao, are equally well-focused. Spices find their way into desserts too, so expect pineapple and fennel-seed tart with yoghurt and cardamom sorbet, or a 'drum' of apricot, white chocolate and chilli, served with carrot fudge and gulab jamun in spiced orange reduction. A page of wines by the glass from £5.50 leads off a list that offers extravagantly wide choice at largely extravagant prices, and doesn't just concentrate on the usual spicy suspects.

**Chef/s:** Vineet Bhatia. **Open:** Mon to Fri L 12 to 3, all week D 6 to 11 (10.30 Sun). **Closed:** bank hols. **Meals:** Set L £19 (2 courses) to £25. Set D £45 (2 courses) to £55. **Service:** 12.5% (optional). **Details:** Cards accepted. 55 seats. Air-con. No music. No mobile phones. Children allowed.

## The River Café
**Flawlessly of-the-moment food**
Thames Wharf, Rainville Road, Hammersmith, W6 9HA
Tel no: (020) 7386 4200
www.rivercafe.co.uk
⊖ Hammersmith, map 1
Italian | £65
Cooking score: 6

Given the damage wrought by a fire in 2008, it's striking that a huge white wood-burning oven is the most distinctive feature of a refurbished River Café. Still airy, the long dining room stretches away from the business end of the open kitchen, with industrial detailing and a stubbly blue carpet adding a distinct but not unpleasant whiff of the 1980s. Food is, of course, flawlessly of-the-moment; seasonality prevails in all things, leading to dalliances with, for example, blood oranges, agretti and new peas. Readers rightly note that an Italophile's procession through four courses can come to 'an awful lot of money', although half-portions are often arranged, with good grace, by a gentle, professional waiting team. After house-made bread and good olive oil, they'll bring chilli squid, complete with squat pyramids of sea salt and the bitter tang of the chargrill, and then perhaps super-light taglierini with tomato, marjoram and

shavings of firm, salted ricotta. Fish, such as wild sea bass served with silky treviso hearts, rosemary and capers, is a highlight, and a generous wedge of chocolate nemesis a delicious cliché. Guidance through the famously comprehensive Italian wine list, which starts at £12.50, is friendly and considered, and carafes of sparkling filtered water at £1.50 a kindly touch. The river is a minor player unless there's a sunny outside table up for grabs.

**Chef/s:** Rose Gray and Ruth Rogers. **Open:** all week L 12.30 to 5 (12 Sun), Mon to Sat D 7 to 11. **Closed:** 22 Dec to 2 Jan, bank hols. **Meals:** alc (main courses £25 to £30). **Service:** 12.5% (optional). **Details:** Cards accepted. 130 seats. 75 seats outside. Air-con. Separate bar. No music. Wheelchair access. Children allowed. Car parking.

## Roussillon
**Polished Gallic gem with real class**
16 St Barnabas Street, Chelsea, SW1W 8PE
Tel no: (020) 7730 5550
www.roussillon.co.uk
⊖ Sloane Square, map 3
Modern French | £55
Cooking score: 6

🍷 V

Quiet, understated elegance combined with French polish, soothing colours and a dash of suave Gallic charm lends real class to Alexis Gauthier's two-roomed gem of a restaurant. He offers a personal take on modern cuisine that is refined, artlessly creative and faithful to the seasons – witness an autumn dish of roast Highland venison with poached pear, celeriac, caramelised pumpkin and truffles. Elsewhere, Anjou squab pigeon comes in a pot, and wild sea bass is dutifully prepared in three contrasting ways (confit, smoked and steamed) with larded salisify, Swiss chard and a lemon thyme-infused broth. To conclude, the *pièce de resistance* is Le Louis XV, a classical masterpiece of praline and chocolate – although contemporary ideas such as pineapple and lime ravioli with lime sorbet are almost as alluring. This is one of the few French big-hitters in London to lay on a creative vegetarian tasting menu and Alexis Gauthier also ventures into the arcane world of 'umami' (the mysterious 'fifth' taste). Prices are par for the course in posh Pimlico, but those looking for a bargain should take advantage of the set lunch (which includes a half-bottle of wine). Given the restaurant's geographical name, it's no surprise that the wine list heads south for some truly fascinating stuff. Elsewhere, the rest of France plays a starring role and the stunning 400-bin slate also has a mini love affair with Italy. Around 20 top-flight house selections start at £18 (£6 a glass). **Chef/s:** Alexis Gauthier. **Open:** Mon to Fri L 12 to 2.30, Mon to Sat D 6.30 to 11. **Closed:** Sun, most bank hols. **Meals:** Set L £35 (includes half bottle of wine). Set D £48 (2 courses) to £55. Tasting menu £65 (vegetarian), £75 (non-vegetarian). **Service:** 12.5% (optional). **Details:** Cards accepted. 70 seats. Air-con. No music. Wheelchair access. Children allowed.

## READERS RECOMMEND

### Saigon Saigon
**Vietnamese**
313-317 King Street, Hammersmith, W6 9NH
Tel no: (0870) 220 1398
www.saigon-saigon.co.uk
'Excellent overall, outstanding food'

**NEW ENTRY**
### Salisbury
**Revamped pub with gutsy cooking**
21 Sherbrooke Road, Fulham, SW6 7HX
Tel no: (020) 7381 4005
www.thesalisbury.co.uk
Θ Fulham Broadway, map 3
Gastropub | £17
Cooking score: 1
 **V**

Light streams in through big windows on to large comfortable sofas in the bar, while the modern dining room blends wooden floors, mirrored walls and bright blue banquette seating. This revamped corner pub in a residential area close to Fulham Broadway makes a fitting contemporary backdrop for Adrian Jones's classic British cooking. From an open kitchen he sends out gutsy dishes, drawing on quality ingredients to show off his cooking skills: sharing plates (rabbit kidneys with mustard, say, or goats' cheese with radish and mint), rump of beef with gnocchi, greens and foie gras, then cinder toffee and rhubarb Eton mess. House wine is £14. **Chef/s:** Adrian Jones. **Open:** all week L 12 to 3, D 6.30 to 9.30. **Closed:** 25 Dec, 1 Jan. **Meals:** alc (main courses £8 to £14). **Service:** 12.5% (optional). **Details:** Cards accepted. 110 seats. Air-con. Separate bar. Wheelchair access. Music. Children allowed.

### Sam's Brasserie and Bar
**All-singing, all-dancing venue**
11 Barley Mow Passage, Chiswick, W4 4PH
Tel no: (020) 8987 0555
www.samsbrasserie.co.uk
Θ Chiswick Park, Turnham Green, map 1
Modern European | £26
Cooking score: 3
£30

This bustling venue housed in premises that were once a paper factory also comes with a big, trendy bar attached. It's a proper brasserie, the kind of place where you can drop in any time throughout the day, and order anything from a bar snack (Scotch quail's eggs with mustard mayonnaise) to full-dress dinner. Evening dishes on a great-value fixed-price deal that might take in potato and wild garlic soup, followed by crisp-skinned sea bass with roast tomato and fennel risotto, while the main carte offers grilled calf's liver with champ, cabbage and pancetta, or lamb steak with rosemary roast potatoes, spinach and salsa verde. Lemon posset with bramble jelly is a lighter finale. A kindly priced wine list accompanies (from £14, or £3.75 a glass). **Chef/s:** Ian Leckie. **Open:** all week L 12 to 3 (4 Sat and Sun), D 6.30 to 10.30. **Closed:** 24 Dec to 27 Dec. **Meals:** alc (main courses £10 to £18). Set L £12 (2 courses) to £15. Set D £14 (2 courses) to £17. Sun L £21. **Service:** 12.5% (optional). **Details:** Cards accepted. 100 seats. Air-con. Separate bar. Wheelchair access. Music. Children allowed.

## NEW ENTRY
## The Sands End

**Low-key local with a country vibe**
135-137 Stephendale Road, Fulham, SW6 2PR
Tel no: (020) 7731 7823
www.thesandsend.co.uk
⊖ Fulham Broadway, map 3
Gastropub | £27
Cooking score: 2

Mismatched wooden kitchen tables and dogs sleeping by the fire give this accomplished low-key local a warm, laid-back, country feel that clearly resonates with the clientele – which includes Princes William and Harry and similarly schooled local chums. Expect rustic Anglo-Irish food on daily menus that include celeriac soup with walnut oil, corn-fed chicken risotto with peas, tarragon and bacon, and seasonal highlights like razor clams and game. Also noteworthy are outstanding bar snacks including Welsh rarebit and Scotch eggs the size of cricket balls. Occasional grumbles focus on inconsistency from the kitchen and the relaxed vibe extending to service. House wine is £14.50.
**Chef/s:** Tom Coleman. **Open:** all week L 12 to 3 (4 Sat and Sun), D 6 to 10 (9.30 Sun). **Closed:** 25 and 26 Dec. **Meals:** alc (main courses £11 to £17). Set L £12.50 (2 courses). **Service:** 12.5%. **Details:** Cards accepted. 60 seats. 16 seats outside. Air-con. Separate bar. Wheelchair access. Music. Children allowed.

## The Thomas Cubitt

**Dapper Belgravia gastropub**
44 Elizabeth Street, Belgravia, SW1W 9PA
Tel no: (020) 7730 6060
www.thethomascubitt.co.uk
⊖ Victoria, map 3
Gastropub | £33
Cooking score: 3

'More ambitious than most gastropubs', notes a reporter of this upmarket Belgravia watering hole that takes its name from the nineteenth-century builder responsible for much of the surrounding area. Very busy, even during the week, it comprises a lively oak-floored bar downstairs and a more staid dining room upstairs decked out with pale walls and white napery. On a recent visit, the clear flavours of a cauliflower and wild mushroom soup with pea shoots and truffle oil impressed, as did carefully cooked venison with soothing creamed sprouts, wild mushrooms and a cherry sauce. Sticky toffee pudding with a satisfying butterscotch milk ice cream and tarte Tatin are typical desserts. The 20-page wine list opens at £16 and includes plenty of Champagne.
**Chef/s:** Phillip Wilson. **Open:** all week L 12 to 3, D 6 to 10. **Closed:** 24 Dec to 1 Jan. **Meals:** alc (main courses £15 to £22). Set D £19.50 (2 courses) to £24.50. Sun L £14.95. **Service:** 12.5% (optional). **Details:** Cards accepted. 125 seats. 20 seats outside. Air-con. Separate bar. Music. Children allowed.

## Timo

**Smart neighbourhood Italian**
343 Kensington High Street, Kensington, W8 6NW
Tel no: (020) 7603 3888
www.timorestaurant.net
⊖ High Street Kensington, map 3
Italian | £29
Cooking score: 2

At the Olympia end of Kensington High Street, this upmarket neighbourhood Italian continues to delight local residents. Service is attentive and helpful without being intrusive, and everything seems to happen at a relaxed pace. Well-rendered rusticity and good timing are notable traits of Franco Gatto's cooking – broad beans, pea and rocket salad with soft goats' cheese and sweet-and-sour dressing opened one early summer meal. Linguine with fresh clams, chilli, olive oil, garlic and parsley followed, then plaice in a lemon sauce with Sicilian capers and grilled asparagus. Desserts could include chocolate and hazelnut fondant with vanilla ice cream or almond and pine nut tart with vanilla sauce. House wine is £17. Lunch and weekly pre-cinema deals (7 to 8) are very good value.

**Chef/s:** Franco Gatto. **Open:** Mon to Sat L 12 to 2.30, D 7 to 11. **Closed:** Sun, 25 and 26 Dec, bank hols. **Meals:** alc (main courses £7 to £24). Set L £13.90 (2 courses) to £17.90. **Service:** not inc. **Details:** Cards accepted. 58 seats. 2 seats outside. Air-con. Separate bar. Wheelchair access. Music. Children allowed.

## Tom Aikens

**Exudes confidence without making a fuss**
43 Elystan Street, Chelsea, SW3 3NT
Tel no: (020) 7584 2003
www.tomaikens.co.uk
⊖ South Kensington, map 3
Modern French | £65
Cooking score: 8

🍷 V

Tom Aikens' status as one of the most talked-about players at the epicentre of modern French cooking is all the more impressive because he has achieved stardom without parading himself around the celeb-chef TV circus. His ever-so-discreet Chelsea flagship exudes confidence without making a fuss, and it's the perfect backdrop for his immaculate culinary conceptions. The décor takes a back seat – just some mirrors and flowers, black leather chairs and a few pieces of modern art on the white walls. Nothing distracts from the food on the plate. Aikens is his own man, and his cooking is even more distinctive than his haircuts, although there's less firebrand bravado than before. These days, ideas are meticulously thought through and executed without needless over-dressing. Everything fits. Meals proceed at a leisurely pace – a good thing, given the seemingly inexhaustible cavalcade of extras and mid-course diversions that arrive at table. Canapés are brilliantly conceived, from an intense red pepper tuile with carrot foam and spiced bread to unctuous deep-fried foie gras mousse – a 'pop-in-the-mouth' dazzler. As a finale, expect an array of petits fours involving shot glasses, lollipops, jelly, doughnuts and more. Aiken's repertoire is spread over three menus (carte, classic and tasting) with plenty of overlap, but triumphs abound. Seasonality is a big theme, and there's

nothing more evocatively autumnal than steamed Anjou pigeon married with chestnut cannelloni, turnip fondant, chestnut and truffle sauce. The kitchen also gives full exposure to impeccably sourced ingredients – perhaps venison in two contrasting forms (cured and carpaccio) aligned on a slate with pickled beetroot, poached pear and toasted hazelnuts. Fish shines brightly, with a little help from some unexpected bedfellows: scallops poached in red wine with Daylesford organic beef shin, confit cabbage and ox tongue or line-caught cod with paprika, chickpeas, pork belly and Jabugo oil, for example. Artful complexity is the hallmark of faultlessly fashioned desserts, which are often an elaborate exploration of just one ingredient – perhaps mangoes, coffee or pistachios (meringue, mousse, cassonade and jelly). The stellar wine list delves into all manner of fascinating French byways, while giving the rest of the world its due. Sommelier Gearoid Devaney is a consummately knowledgeable guide and his recommendations are impeccable. Gilt-edged prices (from £22) are well worth the investment.

**Chef/s:** Tom Aikens. **Open:** Mon to Fri L 12 to 2.30, D 6.45 to 11. **Closed:** Sat, Sun, bank hols, last 2 weeks Aug, 24 Dec to 5 Jan. **Meals:** Set L £29 (3 courses). Set D £45 (2 courses) to £65. Tasting menu £80. Classic menu £100. **Service:** 12.5% (optional). **Details:** Cards accepted. 55 seats. Air-con. No music. Wheelchair access. Children allowed.

## Tom's Kitchen

**Brasserie food for strapping appetites**
27 Cale Street, Chelsea, SW3 3QP
Tel no: (020) 7349 0202
www.tomskitchen.co.uk
⊖ Sloane Square, South Kensington, map 3
Modern British | £35
Cooking score: 4

V

The brash brasserie offshoot of Tom Aikens' high-ranking restaurant in nearby Elystan Street (see entry) occupies the shell of the old Blenheim pub, and is just about as far from haute cuisine as you can get. Spread over two

floors, it pulsates as crowds sit elbow-to elbow around massive refectory tables. Brunch and daytime fill-ups suit the locals, while others might call in for something a bit more substantial from a busy menu of retro and on-trend dishes designed for strapping appetites. Chicken Caesar salad, moules marinière spiked with Calvados and steaks with 'big chips' share the billing with scallops, red endive, roasted peppers and salsa verde or roast chicken breast with Cabernet Sauvignon vinegar, mustard and tarragon jus. Otherwise, order a plate of macaroni cheese with braised ham hock or share a seven-hour braised shoulder of Daylesford organic lamb, before rounding off with passion fruit and white chocolate crème brûlée. House wine is £10.50.
**Chef/s:** Rob Aikens and Julien Maisonneuve. **Open:** all week L 12 to 3 (10 Sat and Sun), D 6 to 11. **Meals:** alc (main courses £12 to £32). **Service:** 12.5% (optional). **Details:** Cards accepted. 76 seats. Air-con. Separate bar. Wheelchair access. Music. Children allowed.

## La Trompette
**Hitting new heights**
5-7 Devonshire Road, Chiswick, W4 2EU
Tel no: (020) 8747 1836
www.latrompette.co.uk
⊖ Turnham Green, map 1
Modern European | £38
Cooking score: 6
🍾

Since 2001, La Trompette has been the jewel in the crown for lovers of fine food in this part of west London. Behind the blue-fronted façade, the interior is a cool, relaxed place with bare wood floors, cloth-covered tables, discreet lighting and infectiously enthusiastic service. James Bennington has taken the place to new heights in recent years, with cooking that focuses on the best-loved modern European styles and a distinctly French grounding underpinning it. The balance is remarkable, even in something as complex as a starter comprised of seared tuna with a king prawn beignet, oyster vinaigrette and radish, seasoned with coriander, soy and sesame oil.

Fish main courses are equally daring, bringing off carefully timed sea bass with cauliflower purée, roast beetroot, raisins, capers and pine nuts. Meat dishes might offer duck magret with a pastilla made from the confit leg meat, foie gras, glazed endive and a spicy jus. Attention to detail is sound all the way through to desserts such as Valrhona chocolate marquise with vanilla ice cream and macadamia praline. It all comes with a fabulous wine list too, with an extensive selection of glasses and many out-of-the-way regions covered. Slovenia? Uruguay? No problem. The bidding opens at £18.
**Chef/s:** James Bennington. **Open:** all week L 12 to 2.30 (3 Sun), D 6.30 to 10.30 (7 to 10 Sun). **Closed:** 25 and 26 Dec, 1 Jan. **Meals:** Set L £19.50 (2 courses) to £23.50. Set D £32.50 (2 courses) to £37.50. Sun L £29.50. **Service:** 12.5% (optional). **Details:** Cards accepted. 72 seats. 16 seats outside. Air-con. No music. Wheelchair access. Children allowed.

## Urban Turban
**Mumbai street food, tapas-style**
98 Westbourne Grove, Westbourne Park, W2 5RU
Tel no: (020) 7243 4200
www.urbanturban.uk.com
⊖ Royal Oak, Bayswater, Queensway, map 4
Indian | £25
Cooking score: 2
£5 OFF  V  £30

Vineet Bhatia's second London restaurant (see also Rasoi) is an attempt to bring the traditions of Indian street food to a western urban clientele. Timber wall-panels, textured wallpaper and throbbing colours echo the vibrancy of the cooking, which is best enjoyed in the form of small tapas-sized dishes meant for sharing, family-style. Spicy scallops in garlic and coriander, crab and sweetcorn cakes with ketchup, and chilli chicken tossed with spring onions, soy and coriander are among the options. 'Classic Helpings' are more conventional dishes where you might order masala lime lamb in coconut and chilli. Finish with cardamom pannacotta with berries, rose infusion and basil. Wines from £20.

**Chef/s:** Vineet Bhatia. **Open:** all week L 12 to 3 (1 to 4 Sat and Sun), D 6 to 11 (10.30 Sun). **Closed:** 25 and 26 Dec. **Meals:** alc (main courses £5 to £12). **Service:** 12.5% (optional). **Details:** Cards accepted. 140 seats. Air-con. Wheelchair access. Music. Children allowed.

## Le Vacherin
**Gay Paree and bags of bonhomie**
76-77 South Parade, Chiswick, W4 5LF
Tel no: (020) 8742 2121
www.levacherin.co.uk
⊖ Chiswick Park, map 1
French | £33
Cooking score: 4

Malcom John manages to summon up the spirit of Gay Paree in this Chiswick neighbourhood favourite – thanks to authentic brasserie trappings, staff with bags of bonhomie and food that brings bourgeois flavours to the table. Le Vacherin's seasonal signature dish is the French mountain cheese it's named after, gilded with a truffle and almond crust and served with Bayonne ham and other fitting accompaniments – a feast for two to share. The remainder of the menu moves quickly from the entrenched bistro world of escargots, cassoulet and côte de boeuf into the realms of seared yellowfin tuna with green beans and walnut salad, salt marsh lamb with pumpkin purée and beetroot, and halibut with sautéed Jerusalem artichokes and cockles. After that, you can look forward to a true Gallic finale – perhaps apple fritters with vanilla ice cream and a shot of Calvados. The wine list is French to the core and offers sound value from £15.50.
**Chef/s:** Malcolm John. **Open:** Tue to Sun L 12 to 3 (4 Sun), all week D 6 to 10.30 (11 Fri and Sat, 10 Sun). **Closed:** 25 and 26 Dec, 1 Jan, bank hols. **Meals:** alc (main courses £12 to £21). Set L £20 (2 courses) to £28. Set D £28 (2 courses) to £38. Sun L £23.50. **Service:** 12.5% (optional). **Details:** Cards accepted. 72 seats. Air-con. Wheelchair access. Music. Children allowed.

## The Warrington
**Gordon's gastropubs roll on**
93 Warrington Crescent, Maida Vale, W9 1EH
Tel no: (020) 7592 7960
www.gordonramsay.com
⊖ Maida Vale, Warwick Avenue, map 1
Gastropub | £25
Cooking score: 2

Gordon Ramsay's gastropub bandwagon rolls on. The latest London boozer to receive the treatment is the old Warrington Hotel – a slab of grandiose Victoriana complete with a pillared portico, mosaic floors and Art Nouveau friezes. Treat yourself to a pork pie and a pint in the sympathetically preserved bar, or go for something bolder in the upstairs dining room. The seasonal menu mixes regional British heritage with a dash of French bistro largesse: Gloucester Old Spot pork belly is matched with quinces, pollack is paired with pickled girolles, and Cornish Blue appears in a salad with endive and pears. Start with potted duck and finish with steamed treacle pud. The trademark Ramsay wine list opens at £13.75.
**Chef/s:** Daniel Kent. **Open:** all week L 12 to 3 (12 to 9 Sun), Tue to Sat D 6 to 10.30. **Meals:** alc (main courses £12 to £19). **Service:** 12.5% (optional). **Details:** Cards accepted. 64 seats. Air-con. Separate bar. No music. Wheelchair access. Children allowed.

## Zaika
**Dependable contemporary Indian**
1 Kensington High Street, Kensington, W8 5NP
Tel no: (020) 7795 6533
www.zaika-restaurant.co.uk
⊖ High Street Kensington, map 4
Indian | £30
Cooking score: 3

 V

Sophisticated East-meets-West décor and a menu to match make Zaika a long-running favourite for contemporary Indian food. One reporter was impressed by an unusual starter of fried soft-shell crab, followed by a generous fillet of tandoor-grilled kingfish in Goan spices served with a sauce of coconut milk infused with fresh coriander, shallots, green chillies and ginger. If you order chicken biryani, expect a top-flight version – Goosnargh chicken and basmati rice in a clay pot, sealed with a flaky pastry crust. For the indecisive there are several attractively priced tasting menus, including a seafood version comprising innovative dishes such as spiced crab risotto with crab chutney. To finish, maybe try the 'excellent' mango kulfi. A wine list well-matched to spices starts at £18.50. **Chef/s:** Sanjay Dwivedi. **Open:** all week L 12 to 2.45, D 6 to 10.30 (9.30 Sun). **Closed:** 25 Dec. **Meals:** alc (main courses £17 to £21). Set L £16 (2 courses) to £19.50. **Service:** 12.5% (optional). **Details:** Cards accepted. 80 seats. Air-con. Separate bar. Music. Children allowed.

chops with pickled onions and myoga ginger. The long list of small dishes and salads presents opportunities for grazing, east Asian style, or you might fancy blowing it all on the daikoku menu, a chef's tasting tour. Finish with green tea and banana cake with coconut ice cream and peanut toffee sauce. A saké bar extends to cocktail-mixing as well as the reverential serving of the best grades, and there is also an inevitably fine wine list, starting at £22. **Chef/s:** Ross Shonhan. **Open:** all week L 12 to 2.15 (2.45 Fri, 12.30 to 3.15 Sat and Sun), D 6 to 10.45 (10.15 Sun). **Closed:** 25 and 25 Dec, 1 Jan. **Meals:** alc (main courses £14 to £75). Tasting menu £96. **Service:** 13.5% (optional). **Details:** Cards accepted. 150 seats. Air-con. Separate bar. Wheelchair access. Music. Children allowed.

## Zuma
**Super-cool and dynamic**
5 Raphael Street, Knightsbridge, SW7 1DL
Tel no: (020) 7584 1010
www.zumarestaurant.com
⊖ Knightsbridge, map 4
**Japanese | £60**
**Cooking score: 5**

**V**

With branches in Dubai, Hong Kong and Istanbul as well as Knightsbridge, Zuma is an ambitious global enterprise. Its mission is to bring more informal Japanese dining (known as izakaya) to sophisticated urban diners, in a setting of awe-inspiring contemporary design. Noriyoshi Muramatsu has created an environment of blond wood, marble and stone, complete with a sushi counter, robata grill and open-plan kitchen. The cooking has all the precision, pin-sharp seasonings, exquisite presentation and freshness we look to Japan to provide. Maki and other rolls (try dynamite spider roll, which involves soft-shell crab, chilli mayo and cucumber in wasabi) and a comprehensive range of sushi and sashimi are followed up by specialities such as roasted lobster in green chilli and garlic hojiso-leaf butter or miso-marinated lamb

## A Cena

**Well-regarded neighbourhood Italian**
418 Richmond Road, Twickenham, TW1 2EB
Tel no: (020) 8288 0108
www.acena.co.uk
⊖ Richmond, map 1
Italian | £35
Cooking score: 2

V

The model of a thriving neighbourhood Italian, A Cena really kicks into life come evening, when Twickenham's smart set descend on the stylish white-walled dining room. Menus change daily and the kitchen's dedication to seasonal produce is seldom in doubt – whether it's an appetiser of asparagus with Italian fried egg and Parmesan or whole roast sea bass with wild garlic leaves, lemon and 'patate agrodolce'. Pasta might feature linguine with mussels and broad beans, while desserts could embrace red wine zabaglione with strawberries or chocolate tartufo with homemade honeycomb. Gluggable Italian wines at 'not unreasonable prices' include several by the 'quartino' (250ml carafe) from £12.

**Chef/s:** Nicola Parsons. **Open:** Tue to Sun L 12 to 2.30, Mon to Sat D 7 to 10.30. **Closed:** 24 to 27 Dec, bank hols. **Meals:** alc (main courses £13 to £22). Sun L £25. **Service:** not inc. **Details:** Cards accepted. 55 seats. Air-con. Wheelchair access. Music. Children allowed.

## READERS RECOMMEND

## Angelo's

Italian
144 Heath Road, Twickenham, TW1 4BN
Tel no: (020) 8891 3750
www.angelosoftwickenham.com
'A great local, good-value Italian... love the pizzas'

## The Bingham

**A stylish setting and stylish food**
61-63 Petersham Road, Richmond, TW10 6UT
Tel no: (020) 8940 0902
www.thebingham.co.uk
⊖ Richmond, map 1
Modern British | £38
Cooking score: 5

 £5 OFF

This chic boutique hotel overlooking the River Thames and its towpath houses an equally stylish restaurant. Tables are scattered around the adjoining dining rooms, making the most of the space and the view without ever feeling crowded. On sunny days and balmy evenings the riverside balcony comes into its own. Shay Cooper, an ambitious chef, cooks a menu to match the setting, using great ingredients in complicated and intricate dishes. His repertoire is full of intriguing combinations, which in lesser hands could be disastrous but here are a triumph. Artichoke salad, presented with a beautiful collection of baby leaves and a truffle hollandaise, is given a necessary acidic kick from the accompanying cep marmalade; cured duck served with foie gras parfait is set off with a blood orange salad and carefully diced mandarin jelly. Follow with an equally wrought dish of suckling pig, accompanied by braised pineapple, meltingly soft pig cheek and turnip and cardamom purée. To finish, a superb chocolate mousse arrives with a smooth-as-butter rice pudding – an accompanying grapefruit sorbet makes it more digestible. The wine list is not wildly long for a hotel, but it's got the bases covered for all eventualities, whether dropping in for lunch or staying for a full-blown celebration. House wine from £16.

**Chef/s:** Shay Cooper. **Open:** all week L 12 to 2.30 (4 Sun), Mon to Sat D 7 to 10. **Meals:** alc (main courses £14 to £28). Set L £19 (2 courses) to £25. Set D £39. Sun L £33. **Service:** 12.5%. **Details:** Cards accepted. 38 seats. 20 seats outside. Air-con. Separate bar. Wheelchair access. Music. Children allowed. Car parking.

## Brilliant

**Shining Punjabi flagship**
72-76 Western Road, Southall, UB2 5DZ
Tel no: (020) 8574 1928
www.brilliantrestaurant.com
map 1
North Indian | £25
Cooking score: 3

£5 OFF **V** £30

The Anand brothers are now venerated as the restaurant kings of Southall, and their world-famous flagship restaurant has become a well-oiled hospitality machine sporting everything from function rooms and karaoke to a wedding licence. At its heart is invigorating Punjabi cooking out of the top drawer, with bags of flavour, subtlety and razor-sharp spicing. Above all, Brilliant shines because its dishes are made 'perfectly fresh'. Regulars could probably recite the menu by heart – butter chicken, fish pakoras, aloo chollay, mighty bowls of palak lamb and keema peas for sharing – although there are some nutritionally aware 'healthy options' too (tandoori quail and methi chicken, for example). Exemplary extras include romali roti – reckoned to be among the best Indian breads in London. Lassi, beer and house wine (£10) are the drinks of choice.
**Chef/s:** Jasvinderjit Singh and Gulu Anand. **Open:** Tue to Fri L 12 to 2.30, Tue to Sun D 6 to 11.30. **Closed:** Mon. **Meals:** alc (main courses £5 to £14). Set £20 (4 courses, parties over 10). **Service:** 10% (optional). **Details:** Cards accepted. 225 seats. Air-con. Wheelchair access. Music. Children allowed. Car parking.

READERS RECOMMEND

## The Brown Dog

**Gastropub**
28 Cross Street, Barnes, SW13 0AP
Tel no: (020) 8392 2200
www.thebrowndog.co.uk
'Properly and freshly cooked British food... a local favourite'

## Brula

**Informality and bourgeois cooking**
43 Crown Road, St Margarets, Twickenham, TW1 3EJ
Tel no: (020) 8892 0602
www.brula.co.uk
⊖ Richmond, map 1
French | £30
Cooking score: 3

This wooden-floored, delightfully informal St Margarets' bistro offers a pleasing menu that's a mix of European styles, although its beating heart is French cuisine bourgeoise. Roast wood pigeon on celeriac rémoulade makes a robust starter, served with sweetcorn and walnuts, or there might be escabèche of Cornish mackerel with pink grapefruit, olives and pine nuts. A main course of sea bass was accurately cooked and came with a good tarte fine of anchovies and red onion, while onglet steak was given the full treatment with chanterelles, pomme purée and red wine sauce. Desserts include the likes of buttermilk pudding and whisky-soaked prunes. The French wine list covers the main regions, with house wines from £14.50.
**Chef/s:** Toby Williams. **Open:** all week L 12 to 3 (4.30 Sun), Mon to Sat D 6 to 10. **Closed:** 25 to 30 Dec, Mon in Aug, all L in Aug except Sun L. **Meals:** alc (main courses £10 to £16). Set L £10 (2 courses) to £14. Set D £22.50 (2 courses) to £29. **Service:** 12.5% (optional). **Details:** Cards accepted. 44 seats. 8 seats outside. No music. Wheelchair access. Children allowed.

## La Buvette

**Idiosyncratic bistro charmer**
6 Church Walk, Richmond, TW9 1SN
Tel no: (020) 8940 6264
www.labuvette.co.uk
⊖ Richmond, map 1
French | £27
Cooking score: 3

£5 OFF £30

La Buvette has its own idiosyncratic charm. A 'buvette' is a refreshment stall or bar and, while the place offers somewhat more comfort

than that, its location in what was once the refectory of the parish church of St Mary Magdalene (complete with walled courtyard) has eccentricity on its side. The repertoire is Francocentric, with occasional brushstrokes of Italian and even English domestic. One reporter returns repeatedly for the meltingly tender Sunday roast beef with enormous Yorkshire pudding. Otherwise, expect moules marinière, duck confit and chicken terrine, rainbow trout amandine, or pork chop with choucroute and apple compote. A chocolate and praline mousse with Kirsch cream is the no-holds-barred way to finish. The French wine list is appealingly old-school, with house Languedoc blends at £13.75 a bottle.
**Chef/s:** Buck Carter. **Open:** all week L 12 to 3, D 6 to 10. **Closed:** 25 and 26 Dec, Good Fri, Easter Sun. **Meals:** Set L £12.75 (2 courses) to £14.50. Set D £17 (2 courses) to £19.50. Sun L £15 (2 courses) to £17. **Service:** 12.5% (optional). **Details:** Cards accepted. 50 seats. 35 seats outside. No music. No mobile phones. Wheelchair access. Children allowed.

## Café Strudel
**Viennese cuisine in East Sheen**
429 Upper Richmond Road, East Sheen, SW14 7PJ
Tel no: (020) 8487 9800
www.cafestrudel.co.uk
⊖ Richmond, **map 1**
Austrian | £27
**Cooking score: 2**

Café Strudel does its best to conjure up the notion of a Viennese café on the busy Upper Richmond Road. Wood floors, old mirrors and traditional globe lights are mixed with daily newspapers, doilies for tablecloths and a hint of cinnamon in the air. Cakes are good, as is the coffee, but the lunch and dinner menu is worth exploring for a creditable rendition of wiener schnitzel or confit duck leg with sweet potato and red wine sauce, followed by palatschinken (pancakes stuffed with cream cheese and raisins) and apple strudel. The wine list, mostly Austrian with a few French offerings, has detailed tasting notes and opens at £9.99.

**Chef/s:** Yacine Bengazahl. **Open:** Tue to Sun L 12 to 3, Tue to Sat D 6.30 to 9.30. Café open all day. **Closed:** Mon, 25 and 26 Dec. **Meals:** alc (main courses £13 to £18). **Service:** 12.5%. **Details:** Cards accepted. 42 seats. 10 seats outside. Wheelchair access. Music. Children allowed.

## Le Cassoulet
**Gascony in the suburbs**
18 Selsdon Road, Croydon, CR2 6PA
Tel no: (020) 8633 1818
www.lecassoulet.co.uk
**map 1**
French | £17
**Cooking score: 3**

Having wowed Chiswick's Francophiles with his earthy food at Le Vacherin (see entry), Malcolm John decided to branch out and bring his big-hearted take on regional cuisine to the suburban environs of South Croydon. Varnished woodwork, lamps and upholstered seats create just the right mood and the food is being lapped up by well-heeled locals. The kitchen's heart is in Gascony and the menu celebrates the rich delights of smoked duck with rémoulade and foie gras toast, baked St Marcellin with thyme, endive and walnuts, cassoulet, and sweetbreads with caper butter. To finish, ripe cheeses might be more tempting than classic crème brûlée or petit pot au chocolat. Patriotic French regional wines start at £14 (£3.60 a glass). Malcolm John recently firmed up his Croydon presence with the Fish and Grill on South End (see entry).
**Chef/s:** Philip Amponsa. **Open:** all week L 12 to 3, D 6 to 10 (Fri and Sat 11). **Meals:** alc (main courses £5 to £17). Set L £12.50 (2 courses) to £16.50. Sun L £19.50. **Service:** 12.5% (optional). **Details:** Cards accepted. 60 seats. Air-con. Wheelchair access. Music. Children allowed.

**£5 OFF voucher scheme**
Also recommended entries can also take part in the £5-off voucher scheme. For a full list of participating restaurants, please visit: www.which.co.uk/gfgvoucherscheme

## ALSO RECOMMENDED

### ▲ Chez Lindsay

11 Hill Rise, Richmond, TW10 6UQ
Tel no: (020) 8948 7473
www.chezlindsay.co.uk
⊖ Richmond, map 1
French

This Richmond rendezvous is into its third decade, and the enduring attraction is Lindsay Wooton's devotion to the twin peaks of Breton cuisine – galettes and seafood. Her savoury buckwheat pancakes (from £3.85) and sweet crêpes are legendary, but the kitchen also turns out everything from fish soup (£6.50) to grilled sea bass with mixed pepper butter (£18.75) and steak frites. Wash it down with bière, cider or wine from the Loire Valley (prices from £14.95). Open all week.

## READERS RECOMMEND

### The Exhibition Rooms

Modern British
69-71 Westow Hill, Crystal Palace, SE19 1TX
Tel no: (020) 8761 1175
www.theexhibitionrooms.com
'Unpretentious yet sophisticated British dishes in a cosy, relaxed setting'

---

**NEW ENTRY**
### Fish & Grill

Just as the name says
48-50 South End, Croydon, CR0 1DP
Tel no: (020) 8774 4060
www.fishandgrill.co.uk
map 1
Modern British | £25
Cooking score: 3

**V**

Malcom John, who also owns nearby Le Cassoulet and Le Vacherin in Chiswick (see entries), has spread his wings further still with this new high-street restaurant, which seems perfectly pitched for the area in both pricing and atmosphere. Floorboards, exposed brick walls, plain tables and a menu and wine list printed on either side of paper placemats create the right casual impression. The emphasis is on fresh fish and grilled meats. Plump scallops on a bed of spinach gratin, and Montgomery cheddar and leek tart are among first course options, while halibut with crayfish butter and parsley mash, Aberdeen Angus steaks or an Old Spot pork chop with BBQ seasoning could be mains. Finish with Valrhona chocolate pots. House wine is £14.95.

**Chef/s:** Jason Nott. **Open:** all week 12 to 11.
**Meals:** alc (main courses £12 to £32). Set L £11.95 (2 courses) to £14.95. **Service:** 12.5% (optional).
**Details:** Cards accepted. 72 seats. 6 seats outside. Air-con. Wheelchair access. Music. Children allowed.

### The French Table

Ambition and good value
85 Maple Road, Surbiton, KT6 4AW
Tel no: (020) 8399 2365
www.thefrenchtable.co.uk
map 1
French | £30
Cooking score: 3

The cooking at Eric and Sarah Guignard's 'light, airy' restaurant may not be at the cutting edge of culinary fashion, but the menu is littered with impressive, high-end ingredients, wrought into clever and ambitious dishes. A main course of classic roast chicken with vin jaune and morels is terrific. The duo of foie gras starter, which delivers perfectly pan-fried liver alongside a slightly odd foie gras crème brûlée concoction, is rather less than the sum of its parts. But generally the kitchen succeeds in its efforts, with homemade bread singled out for praise in a number of reports and 'delectable desserts' including homemade ice creams, ginger bread-and-butter pudding and profiteroles. There's 'a superb cheeseboard' too, and service is always spot-on. House wines start a £14.95.

**Chef/s:** Eric Guignard. **Open:** Tue to Sun L 12 to 2.30, Tue to Sat D 7 to 10.30. **Closed:** Mon, 25 to 27 Dec, 2 weeks end of Aug, bank hols except Good Friday. **Meals:** alc (main courses £12 to £19). Set weekday L £15.50 (2 courses) to £18.50. Set L Sat and Sun £22.50. **Service:** 12.5% (optional).

**Details:** Cards accepted. 50 seats. Air-con. No mobile phones. Wheelchair access. Music. Children allowed.

## Frère Jacques

**Upbeat waterfront brasserie**
10–12 Riverside Walk, Kingston-upon-Thames, KT1 1QN
Tel no: (020) 8546 1332
www.frerejacques.co.uk
**map 1**
**French | £27**
**Cooking score: 2**
£5 OFF £30

On warm summer days there's a touch of the Med at this well-established French-themed brasserie beside the Thames and Kingston Bridge. With red-clothed tables and front terrace it's a perfect spot to watch the world go by. All the seasons are covered though, with further tables beneath a permanent awning and an unstuffy, cheerful dining area inside. The kitchen delivers accomplished Gallic classics (from moules marinière to tarte Tatin) alongside more challenging choices (oven-roasted monkfish wrapped in bacon and teamed with dill-infused potatoes, wilted spinach and a shellfish and mussel bisque). An optional fixed-price menu and accessible wines (from £14.25) continue the upbeat form.
**Chef/s:** Gerhard Peleschka. **Open:** all week L 12 to 5, D 5 to 11. **Closed:** 25 and 26 Dec, 1 Jan. **Meals:** alc (main courses £12 to £18). Set L £12 (2 courses) to £16. **Service:** 12.5% (optional). **Details:** Cards accepted. 52 seats. 48 seats outside. Air-con. Wheelchair access. Music. Children allowed.

### Average price

The average price listed in main-entry reviews denotes the price of a three-course meal, without wine.

## The Glasshouse

**A great all-rounder**
14 Station Parade, Kew, TW9 3PZ
Tel no: (020) 8940 6777
www.glasshouserestaurant.co.uk
⊖ Kew Gardens, map 1
**Modern European | £38**
**Cooking score: 5**
🍸 V

Restaurateurs struggling to fill tables must look enviously through the enormous plate-glass windows of the Glasshouse and wonder what magic formula keeps this restaurant where it is. The recipe for success is deceptively simple: a set-price menu of carefully prepared, robust food that people want to eat, served politely and professionally by people who care. The menu is tweaked every day but the bases are the same – foie gras and chicken liver parfait with dressed lentils is a clever revamp of an old classic, beautifully prepared rare tuna with soy and lime dressing a palate-cleansing, zingy starter. Look to the main courses for the star dish, an assiette of pork with apple tarte fine and choucroute, an astonishingly accomplished layering of textures, flavours, sweet, sour and salt. Those looking for less gutsy pleasure should be satisfied with a Moroccan-inspired lamb rump or crisp sea bass with braised celery. Vegetarian dishes are inspired, and if the puds are not particularly unusual, they are perfectly executed without the silliness that comes of trying too hard. The Glasshouse sports a serious wine list and a sommelier to guide customers through it, but if the occasion doesn't warrant it, there's no need to go overboard – house wine by the glass starts at £5.
**Chef/s:** Anthony Boyd. **Open:** all week L 12 to 2.30 (2.45 Sun), D 6.30 to 10.30 (7 Sun). **Closed:** 24 to 26 Dec, 1 Jan. **Meals:** Set L £18.50 (2 courses) to £23.50. Set D £32 (2 courses) to £37.50. Sun L £29.50. Tasting menu £50. **Service:** 12.5% (optional). **Details:** Cards accepted. 65 seats. Air-con. No music. No mobile phones. Children allowed.

## Incanto

**Friendly, charming local favourite**
41 High Street, Harrow-on-the-Hill, HA1 3HT
Tel no: (020) 8426 6767
www.incanto.co.uk
⊖ Harrow-on-the-Hill, map 1
Italian | £27
Cooking score: 2
£5 OFF **V** £30

Housed in a listed building which was once a post office, this charming neighbourhood restaurant specialises in the cooking of southern Italy. Reporters consistently praise the sympathetic friendliness with which the place is run – regulars are greeted like the old friends they are. Freshness and care distinguish the cooking, with a nice balance of simple and labour-intensive dishes. Smoked salmon roulade with artichoke butter is one way to start, before attention turns to slow-cooked pork leg on braised red cabbage with agrodolce sauce. Leave room for a dessert like blood orange panettone pudding with vanilla cream. The international wine list is arranged by style, with prices from £14.95.
**Chef/s:** Franco Montone. **Open:** Tue to Sun L 12 to 2.30 (4 Sun), Tue to Sat D 6.30 to 11. **Closed:** Mon, 25 and 26 Dec, Easter Sun. **Meals:** alc (main courses £14 to £19). Set L £15.95 (2 courses) to £19.95. Set D £18.95 (2 courses) to £22.50. **Service:** 10% (optional). **Details:** Cards accepted. 64 seats. Air-con. Separate bar. No mobile phones. Wheelchair access. Music. Children allowed.

## ALSO RECOMMENDED

### ▲ Jamie's Italian

19-23 High Street, Kingston-upon-Thames, KT1 1LL
Tel no: (020) 8912 0110
www.jamiesitalian.com
map 1
Italian

Surrey outpost of Jamie Oliver's 'popular, fun, accessible-to-all' Italian chain, a roll-out of the unfussy, affordable, colourful, Latin-lifestyle food he's inspired TV viewers with over the years. Be prepared to queue for a table and enjoy the likes of 'pukka' Italian breads

(£2.95), meat antipasti (£6.50) presented on a plank balanced on tomato cans at the table, decent pasta (sausage pappardelle, £9.95), or an Italian Bakewell tart (£4.95). Wines from £14.95. Open all week.

## The Lock

**Enticing eatery by the canal**
Heron House, Hale Wharf, Ferry Lane, Tottenham Hale, N17 9NF
Tel no: (020) 8885 2829
www.thelockrestaurant.com
⊖ Tottenham Hale, map 1
Modern European | £25
Cooking score: 5
£5 OFF **V** £30

A haven in a 'chaotic area' that is being transformed prior to the 2012 Olympics, the Lock delivers 'West End nosh without the hefty price tag', according to one reader. The location is hardly auspicious – next to a canal lock near the Lea Valley reservoirs and Tottenham marshes, with industrial estates all around – but the owners clearly sniffed a good-time opportunity when they shifted the emphasis from 'Dining Bar' to fully fledged 'Restaurant'. The kitchen is right at home when it comes to on-trend contemporary flavours, although it's also determined to go its own way – witness a *Jeux Sans Frontières* combo of pan-fried Scottish salmon with ackee, salt fish, steamed courgette and crab mousse, or roast goose with a cassoulet of mixed beans and soya chunks. Elsewhere, the menu moves into well-trodden territory for a salad of smoked pigeon and caramelised pears with honey dressing or body-bulking platefuls of sirloin steak, pork sausage and mash with Yorkshire pudding, artichokes and roast carrots. Desserts are straightforward but equally enticing, whether it's blueberry clafoutis or hot chocolate fondant with caramel and cinnamon ice cream. Crunch-busting lunches make the whole prospect even more attractive, and the savvy modern wine list also does its bit with wallet-friendly price tags from £14 (£3.95 a glass).

**Chef/s:** Adebola Adeshina. **Open:** Tue to Fri and Sun L 12 to 2 (5 Sun), Tue to Sat D 6 to 10. **Closed:** Mon. **Meals:** alc (main courses £8 to £15). Set L £11 (2 courses) to £15. Tasting menu £40 (7 courses, pre-booked). **Service:** 10%. **Details:** Cards accepted. 60 seats. 25 seats outside. Separate bar. Wheelchair access. Music. Children allowed. Car parking.

## ALSO RECOMMENDED
### ▲ Ma Cuisine
9 Station Approach, Kew, TW9 3QB
Tel no: (020) 8332 1923
www.macuisinekew.co.uk
⊖ Kew Gardens, map 1
**French**

A branch of John McClements' mini-chain of emphatically patriotic 'French bistrots', delivering creditable food in a setting of posters, gingham-clothed tables and rustic wooden chairs. The kitchen deals in bourgeois classics along the lines of black pudding en croûte with Dijon mustard sauce (£6), coq au vin (£12.50) and roast sea bream with fennel, clams and Pernod, followed by crème brûlée (£4.50). Wines from £12.95. Open all week. There are branches at 6 Whitton Road, Twickenham, tel: (020) 8607 9849, and 7 White Hart Lane, Barnes, tel: (020) 8878 4092.

## Madhu's
**High-gloss Indian favourite**
39 South Road, Southall, UB1 1SW
Tel no: (020) 8574 1897
www.madhusonline.com
map 1
**Indian | £20**
**Cooking score: 3**
£5 OFF **V** £30

The Anand family has been running this Southall favourite through three generations, serving authentic Punjabi cooking to a wide audience of faithful followers. It's the sibling of the equally successful Brilliant (see entry), not far away. The cooking is generous, sharply seasoned and characterised by appreciable freshness. Zafrani chicken malai tikka is

marinated overnight in saffron before being cooked in a tandoor and served in a garlic cream sauce. Classics along the lines of prawn biryani are well rendered, and the wide range of vegetarian main courses turns up many hits, including a nicely textured cauliflower in fenugreek and garlic. Kenyan specialities from the Masai Mara, such as chargrilled lamb ribs marinated in lemon and chilli, add lustrous depth to the menu. Desserts include kulfi and gulab jamun. Wines start at £9.

**Chef/s:** Rakesh Verma. **Open:** Mon and Wed to Fri L 12.30 to 3, Wed to Mon D 6 to 11.30. **Closed:** Tue. **Meals:** alc (main courses £5 to £10). Set L £15. Set D £20. **Service:** not inc. **Details:** Cards accepted. 104 seats. Air-con. Separate bar. Wheelchair access. Music. Children allowed. Car parking.

## Mosaica @ the factory
**Funky flavour-fest for local foodies**
Chocolate Factory, Clarendon Road, Wood Green, N22 6XJ
Tel no: (020) 8889 2400
www.mosaicarestaurants.com
⊖ Wood Green, map 2
**Modern European | £29**
**Cooking score: 3**
£5 OFF £30

The factory in question once made chocolate, but these days the old building on a north London trading estate deals in all kinds of eclectic flavours for foodie locals. Inside it's a funky space with art on the walls, lots of noise and plenty to watch in the open kitchen. The no-nonsense menu is stripped bare to reveal seared scallops with lime and leaves, 'spot-on' rare ribeye with garlic mash and spinach, caramelised goats' cheese with Mediterranean veg and Charlotte potatoes, and 'loch' salmon provençal with samphire. There's no wordy exuberance when it comes to the tidy assortment of hand-crafted desserts, either: vanilla pannacotta with espresso topping should provide a decent flavour hit. Around 50 affordable wines start at £13.50.

**Chef/s:** Johnnie Mountain. **Open:** Tue to Fri and Sun L 12 to 2.30 (1 to 4 Sun), Tue to Sat D 6.30 to 9.30 (7 to 10 Sat). **Closed:** Mon, 25 and 26 Dec. **Meals:** alc (main courses £11 to £17). Set L £15 (2 courses) to £20. Set D £20 (2 courses) to £25. **Service:** 10% (optional). **Details:** Cards accepted. 80 seats. 40 seats outside. Air-con. Wheelchair access. Music. Children allowed. Car parking.

## Petersham Nurseries Café

**Secret oasis with attitude**
Church Lane, off Petersham Road, Richmond, TW10 7AG
Tel no: (020) 8605 3627
www.petershamnurseries.com
⊖ Richmond, map 1
**Modern British | £40**
**Cooking score: 4**

Getting to Skye Gyngell's quirky, upwardly mobile café in the Petersham Nurseries is 'something of an adventure', but there's no doubting the allure of this secret, horticulturally minded oasis with attitude. Tucked away at the end of a narrow lane, PNC has been under threat from Richmond Council with regards to permanent planning consent – although that battle now seems to be won. Despite noticeably steep prices, fans reckon this place is a stunner – and it's become a coveted bolt-hole for the local lunch set. Who could resist eating at antique tables amid the foliage in the ramshackle greenhouse or – even better – outside under fragrant Indian 'tatti' shades? Seasonal pickings define the menu, and the kitchen is generous with sunny, health-giving flavours: a simple dish of girolles with young spinach has pleased, although the day's choice could range from salt cod brandade with white polenta to grilled rabbit with lentils, speck and Gorgonzola dressing. To finish, freshen up with, say, lemon sherbet and candied peel. House wine is £16. **Chef/s:** Skye Gyngell. **Open:** Wed to Sun L only 12 to 2.45. **Closed:** Mon, Tue. **Meals:** alc (main courses £14 to £27). **Service:** 12.5% (optional). **Details:** Cards accepted. 80 seats. No music. Wheelchair access. Children allowed.

## Restaurant at the Petersham Hotel

**Compelling cooking and a fabulous view**
Nightingale Lane, Richmond, TW10 6UZ
Tel no: (020) 8939 1084
www.petershamhotel.co.uk
⊖ Richmond, map 1
**Modern British | £39**
**Cooking score: 4**

🛏 V

The slightly old-fashioned hotel lobby gives way to a dining room on the dowdy side, but all negatives melt away with the astounding view – a panoramic sweep of the River Thames. Alex Bentley's cooking is an equally compelling reason to visit. He has developed a menu and style that keeps the conservative customers happy, but with plenty to tempt the younger, more inquisitive palate too. Fillet steak will be cooked as ordered, Dover sole served grilled or meunière and boned, old style, at the table. Smoked salmon and country terrines are on offer to start. The more adventurous might prefer a velvet ballottine of foie gras with green peppercorns and pistachio or sea bass with piquillo peppers, couscous and mussels. The wine list (starting at £5 a glass) carries everything one would expect of a restaurant of this style, from an impressive parade of Bordeaux and Burgundies to some much more esoteric numbers. **Chef/s:** Alex Bentley. **Open:** all week L 12 to 2.15 (12.30 to 3.30 Sun), D 7 to 9.45 (8.45 Sun). **Closed:** 24 to 27 Dec. **Meals:** alc (main courses £13 to £27). Set L £18.50 (2 courses) to £25.50. Sun L £31.50. **Service:** 10% (optional). **Details:** Cards accepted. 80 seats. Air-con. Separate bar. No music. No mobile phones. Wheelchair access. Children allowed. Car parking.

## READERS RECOMMEND

## Skipjacks

**Seafood**
268-270 Streatfield Road, Harrow, HA3 9BY
Tel no: (020) 8204 7554
**'Old fashioned, with the best quality fish... amazing value for money'**

## Sonny's

**Spruced-up eatery with reliable cooking**
94 Church Road, Barnes, SW13 0DQ
Tel no: (020) 8748 0393
www.sonnys.co.uk
map 1
Modern European | £28
Cooking score: 3

A major spruce-up at this Barnes stalwart has left Sonny's looking neat and tidy. A bar offering enticing snacks now dominates the front overlooking the street, and the dining room at the rear is refreshed without losing its cosiness. The refurb didn't extend to the kitchen, however, and the cooking is much the same as ever – dependable and reliable. White crab tortellini with caper and chive beurre blanc is a combination of classic flavours, fillet of sea bass with Spanish white beans is perfectly cooked. A flabby mock cassoulet with pork belly is less successful but chocolate fondant and the like are generously indulgent. The short wine list starts at an affordable £3.50 per glass; when taken with the very reasonably priced set menus, lunch and dinner here can be a steal.

**Chef/s:** Owen Kenworthy. **Open:** all week L 12.30 to 2.30 (4 Sat, 12 to 4 Sun), Mon to Sat D 7 to 10.30 (11 Fri and Sat). **Closed:** bank hols. **Meals:** alc (main courses £11 to £27). Set L £13.50 (2 courses) to £15.50. Set D £15.50 (2 courses) to £18.50. Sun L £21.50. **Service:** 12.5% (optional). **Details:** Cards accepted. 100 seats. Air-con. Separate bar. No music. Wheelchair access. Children allowed.

### Please send us your feedback

To register your opinion about any restaurant listed in the Guide, or a new restaurant that you wish to bring to our attention, please visit the web address at the bottom of the page. Your feedback informs the content of the book and will be used to compile next year's reviews.

NEW ENTRY
## Tangawizi

**Godsend for Richmond locals**
406 Richmond Road, Richmond Bridge, Richmond, TW1 2EB
Tel no: (020) 8891 3737
www.tangawizi.co.uk
⊖ Richmond, map 1
Indian | £20
Cooking score: 2

At the foot of Richmond Bridge on the St Margaret's side, Tangawizi has been building up a loyal following since it opened in 2005. It's just the kind of Indian you might wish for at the end of your road. Décor is basic, but service is friendly and competent and the kitchen delivers good naan, homemade chutneys, superb tandoori prawns, tender duck tikka with tamarind sauce, rich, buttery methi chicken, and makhani dhal 'as superb here as at Bhukara in Delhi' (where the chef worked). Prawn gulnar – the prawns marinated in garlic, honey and dill – has also been praised. House wine is £11.95.

**Chef/s:** SS Rana. **Open:** all week D 6.30 to 11 (10.30 Sun). **Closed:** 25 and 26 Dec, 1 Jan. **Meals:** alc (main courses £7 to £13). **Service:** not inc. **Details:** Cards accepted. 50 seats. Air-con. Wheelchair access. Music. Children allowed.

NEW ENTRY
## A Taste of McClements

**Complex combinations**
8 Station Approach, Kew, TW9 3QB
Tel no: (020) 8940 6617
www.tasteofmcclements.com
⊖ Kew Gardens, map 1
Modern European | £35
Cooking score: 3

This addition to the Kew landscape offers a no-choice menu of up to 17 dishes in 12 separate courses. John McClements deserves his reputation as a very able chef, whether his customers share that vision of a perfect dinner is a different matter. Many combinations are worth a try: barely cooked sweet scallops with the salt of crisp pancetta; perfectly rendered turbot with a herb crust, but a cold, deep-purple borscht with cubes of vodka jelly and a floating langoustine proved to be 'clashing in colour and taste'. There's a lot to eat and it can be hard to feel anticipation for chocolate praline Louis XV and Calvados soufflé after 10 or so courses. But at £35 per head for dinner, to complain about a couple of less-than-great courses in the mix seems churlish. Wine from £15.

**Chef/s:** John McClements and Reality Champ. **Open:** Tue to Sat L 12 to 2.30, D 6.30 to 9.30. **Closed:** Sun, Mon, bank hols, 2 weeks Aug. **Meals:** Tasting menu L £18 to £25. Tasting menu D £35. **Service:** 10% (optional). **Details:** Cards accepted. 20 seats. 10 seats outside. Air-con. No mobile phones. Music. Children allowed.

**NEW ENTRY**

## The Victoria

**Upmarket gastropub with appealing menus**
10 West Temple, East Sheen, SW14 7RT
Tel no: (020) 8876 4238
www.thevictoria.net
⊖ Richmond, map 1
**Gastropub | £28**
**Cooking score: 3**

Bought by TV chef Paul Merrett in the summer of 2008, this upmarket gastropub-with-rooms is set in a quiet, leafy residential road near Sheen Common. It draws appreciative families for well-priced Saturday brunch and Sunday lunch offerings, but there's a more grown-up ambience in the evening. The appealing modern menus combine classics (crispy chicken Caesar salad with poached egg, boiled collar of bacon with spinach dumplings and parsley sauce) with more avant-garde offerings (salmon sashimi with a shallot and chilli crunch and cucumber pickle to start, or a main course of butternut squash and chickpea tagine with medjool dates, coriander yoghurt and flatbread). There

are good chocolate brownies for dessert. The fashionable wine list fits the bill, with house wine at £14.

**Chef/s:** Paul Merrett. **Open:** all week L 12 to 2.30 (8.30 to 3 Sat, 12 to 8 Sun), D 6 to 10 (6 to 10.30 Sat, 6 to 8 Sun). **Meals:** alc (main courses £11 to £18). **Service:** 12.5% (optional). **Details:** Cards accepted. 45 seats. 60 seats outside. Air-con. Separate bar. Wheelchair access. Music. Children allowed. Car parking.

# ENGLAND

Bedfordshire, Berkshire,
Buckinghamshire, Cambridgeshire,
Cheshire, Cornwall, Cumbria, Derbyshire,
Devon, Dorset, Durham, Essex,
Gloucestershire & Bristol,
Greater Manchester,
Hampshire (inc. Isle of Wight),
Herefordshire, Hertfordshire, Kent,
Lancashire, Leicestershire and Rutland,
Lincolnshire, Merseyside, Norfolk,
Northamptonshire, Northumberland,
Nottinghamshire, Oxfordshire, Shropshire,
Somerset, Staffordshire, Suffolk, Surrey,
Sussex – East, Sussex – West,
Tyne & Wear, Warwickshire,
West Midlands, Wiltshire, Worcestershire,
Yorkshire

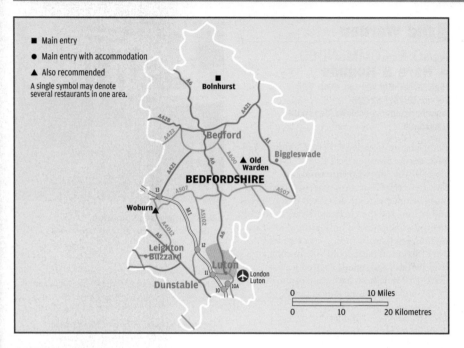

■ Main entry
● Main entry with accommodation
▲ Also recommended

A single symbol may denote
several restaurants in one area.

## Bolnhurst

### The Plough
**Big-flavour food shines out**
Kimbolton Road, Bolnhurst, MK44 2EX
Tel no: (01234) 376274
www.bolnhurst.com
**Modern British | £30**
**Cooking score: 5**

In a county not richly endowed with good
eating, the Plough shines out like a beacon. It's
a whitewashed Tudor inn with tiny windows
(and not many of them) contributing to a
most singular feel. Low beamed ceilings frame
the candlelit scene and the kitchen is open to
view from both bar and restaurant, which
proves a powerful lure. Satisfied customers
write that 'this is top-quality local produce
cooked to produce big, wonderful flavours,
with no daft eclectic combinations'. In
particular, they have enjoyed the house black
pudding as a starter (which may come with
Montgomery Cheddar hash, pancetta and red

wine sauce), braised beef and a side of red
cabbage followed by apple tart –
unimpeachable winter comfort food. Other
good ideas have included a raviolo of Portland
crab in crab and coriander bisque, roast turbot
with confit garlic and cavolo nero, and an
Indian-influenced veggie main course of lentil
dhal with cauliflower, spinach, raita and an
onion bhaji. Bread-and-butter pudding and a
range of homemade ice creams are among the
sweet options. It all takes place in an
atmosphere of great conviviality. An
exemplary wine list, arranged by style, is
crammed with pedigree bottles,
enthusiastically annotated and offered at fair
prices. Choice by the glass (from £3.25) is
handsome enough in itself.
**Chef/s:** Martin Lee. **Open:** Tue to Sun L 12 to 2, Tue
to Sat D 6.30 to 9.30. **Closed:** Mon, 26 Dec to 14
Jan. **Meals:** alc (main courses £12 to £25). Set L £13
(2 courses) to £17. **Service:** not inc. **Details:** Cards
accepted. 80 seats. 30 seats outside. No music.
Wheelchair access. Children allowed. Car parking.

## ▌Old Warden

### ALSO RECOMMENDED
### ▲ Hare & Hounds

High Street, Old Warden, SG18 9HQ
Tel no: (01767) 627225
www.hareandhoundsoldwarden.co.uk
**Gastropub**

Bedfordshire's top dog for pub food is tucked
away on the Shuttleworth Estate – you can
occasionally spot a Spitfire from the
Shuttleworth Collection wheeling overhead.
Cosy beamed bars are decorated in warm reds
and creams and the kitchen delivers a monthly
changing menu that is built around local and
organic produce, including estate-reared
pork. A typical meal could take in chicken
liver parfait (£6), whole roasted sea bass
marinated in lemon, garlic and rosemary
(£15), and caramelised lemon tart (£6).
House wine is £12.50. Closed Sun and
Mon D.

## ▌Woburn

### ALSO RECOMMENDED
### ▲ Paris House

Woburn Park, Woburn, MK17 9QP
Tel no: (01525) 290692
www.parishouse.co.uk
**French**

Brought piece by piece from the Paris
Exhibition of 1878 to rise again in Woburn
Park, this timbered house makes a suitably
opulent setting for the French-influenced
modern cooking of Peter Chandler. The
principal menu is the £55 carte, available at
lunch and dinner, which might go from foie
gras and prune terrine with red onion
marmalade, through pollack with bacon,
chorizo and saffron or belly pork with
redcurrants and port, to light strawberry sablé
at the end. Wines from £20. Closed Sun and
Mon D.

### Best value in England

**Blas Burgerworks, Cornwall**
Cheerful, feel-good atmosphere in this
burger bar.

**Lucca Enoteca, Essex**
Sherri Singleton's kid-friendly pizzeria with
wood-fired, upper-crust toppings.

**Gabriel's Kitchen, Greater Manchester**
Good food at Peter Booth's eminently
affordable university-district café.

**Caracoli, Hampshire**
Bridges a gap in the food market – between
a tea shop and a bistro.

**Delilah, Nottinghamshire**
Primarily a deli, but also serves tapas-style
dishes, good sandwiches, salads and fondues.

**At the Chapel, Somerset**
A sensitively converted chapel, with a menu
of keenly priced crowd-pleasers.

**East Beach Café, West Sussex**
Eyecatching design, good-value all-week
lunch menu and weekend breakfasts.

**The Almanack, Warwickshire**
More bar-restaurant than full-blown
gastropub, the place buzzes from 8am.

**Jyoti's Vegetarian, West Midlands**
Vegetarian eateries are thin on the ground,
but this one is going great guns. BYO wine.

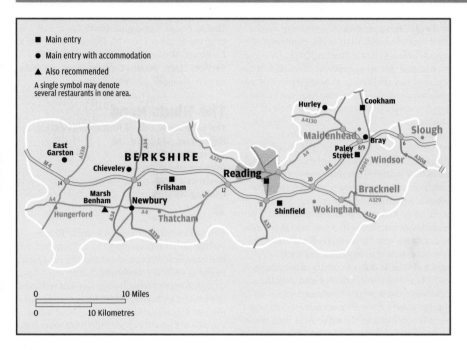

## ▮ Bray

### The Fat Duck
**In a word, genius**
1 High Street, Bray, SL6 2AQ
Tel no: (01628) 580333
www.fatduck.co.uk
**Modern European | £140**
**Cooking score: 10**

If Leonardo da Vinci was spirited back to us as a chef, he would probably be a bit like Heston Blumenthal – a virtuoso, twenty-first century renaissance man. Since floating the Fat Duck in the early 90s, Bray's media-wise polymath has dazzled everyone with his talents as a showman and scientist, educator and experimentalist, food historian and grand master of the gastronomic arts. If that sounds a bit intimidating, fear not. The 'most extraordinary restaurant in Britain' is an egalitarian, non-reverential kind of place, invested with all the fun, fantasy and wide-eyed wonderment of a child's imagination.

Kids are positively encouraged, jeans are no problem, and even the stuffed shirts may summon up a smile at an electrifying cavalcade of thrills without spills that may last up to four hours. At first glance, the food can seem like weird science (just look at that 'amazing palate cleanser' – nitrogen-poached green tea and lime mousse), but it's actually an astute amalgam of meticulous research, culinary know-how, daredevil wizardry and whizz-bang surprises. To make things even more interesting, lots of new ideas are coming on stream: the *Heston's Feasts* TV series is yielding some real crackers, including the zany Mad Hatter's mock turtle soup and a barnstorming dessert that summons up the sensory ghosts of Christmas past. Like Alice's adventures, things are seldom what they seem in Duckland. Elsewhere, Blumenthal is happy to plunder his back-catalogue, re-visiting and re-inventing favourite themes and motifs. Snail porridge with Jabugo ham and shaved fennel is a fixture, his scrambled egg and bacon ice cream has entered popular mythology, and the evocatively named 'Sound of the Sea' remains a *tour de force*: strap on the iPod provided and listen as the memories of seaside holidays come flooding back. Devotees may notice that an assortment of cured fish has replaced raw shellfish as the centrepiece of this emblematic dish – a positive response to the much-publicised scare that closed the Fat Duck early in 2009. For the record, this was due to the norovirus rather than food poisoning, but it says a great deal about Blumenthal's professionalism that he handled the whole matter with impeccable honesty – and is conducting his own research into the subject. Significantly, this episode has done nothing to dampen customers' ecstatic enthusiasm for the food: some rave about the 'spectacular' oak moss and truffle toast or the salmon poached in liquorice gel with asparagus, little dots of vanilla mayonnaise and Manni olive oil; others drool over the fabulous roast foie gras 'benzaldehyde' – its intense cherry flavours miraculously cutting the silky richness of the offal. And then there are the outrageously cheeky, breakfast-themed desserts. 'Good morning' says the waiter, as you are presented with sweet, crisp parsnip flakes in a bowl of parsnip milk – a giggle-inducing prelude to the nitro-fuelled tableside finale (complete with a mini magic show as your attendant transforms a rose petal into an egg). The wine list is as starry as any in the UK, with impeccable sourcing, gilt-edged vintages and mouthwatering possibilities for discerning drinkers. However, there's hardly a bottle below £30 and even a glass of Sancerre will set you back £12. In truth, the Fat Duck requires serious financial outlay: the carte was dropped in July 2009 and meals now revolve around the tasting menu at £140 a head (and rising) with the additional option of suggested wines (from £90). But, to put things in perspective, the bill for this consummate, once-in-a-lifetime experience could be on a par with 'a long weekend in a good hotel abroad'. It sounds like a no-brainer – just remember to book two months in advance.

**Chef/s:** Heston Blumenthal. **Open:** Tue to Sun L 12 to 2, Tue to Sat D 7 to 9.30. **Closed:** Mon, 2 weeks Christmas. **Meals:** Tasting menu L and D £140. **Service:** 12.5%. **Details:** Cards accepted. 40 seats. Air-con. No music. Children allowed.

## The Hinds Head
**The traditional side of Heston Blumenthal**
**High Street, Bray, SL6 2AB**
**Tel no: (01628) 626151**
**www.hindsheadhotel.co.uk**
**Gastropub | £28**
**Cooking score: 4**

When Heston Blumenthal bought Bray's village pub it represented a branching out, for the intention was not to extend the Fat Duck's brand of culinary fireworks, but to offer straightforward British cooking that reflected the building's heritage. Little has changed in the late seventeenth-century inn, and while the place is now food-focused it has stayed in touch with its roots and retains local drinkers. Try and bag a table in the pub rather than the restaurant extension, as tables are less crowded and there is more atmosphere. Expect a menu that changes rarely but delivers sound renditions of pea and ham soup or oxtail and kidney pudding, with sides of the famed triple-cooked chips. Seasonal specials ring the changes (free-range ham with asparagus, pheasant eggs and hollandaise sauce). There are snacks of devils on horseback, and treacle tart for pudding. Wines from £15.75.
**Chef/s:** Heston Blumenthal and Clive Dixon. **Open:** all week L 12 to 2.30, Mon to Sat D 6.30 to 9.30. **Meals:** alc (main courses £14 to £20). **Service:** 12.5%. **Details:** Cards accepted. 90 seats. Air-con. Separate bar. Children allowed.

# The Waterside Inn

**A perfectly pleasing place**
Ferry Road, Bray, SL6 2AT
Tel no: (01628) 620691
www.waterside-inn.co.uk
French | £120
Cooking score: 7

☕ V

**Chef/s:** Alain Roux. **Open:** Wed to Sun L 12 to 2 (2.30 Sun), D 7 to 10, also Tue D 1 Jun to 31 Aug. **Closed:** Mon, 26 Dec to 29 Jan, bank hols. **Meals:** alc (main courses £48 to £68). Set L £39.50 (2 courses) to £54. Sun L £68.50. Menu exceptionnel £109.50. **Service:** 12.5%. **Details:** Cards accepted. 70 seats. Air-con. Separate bar. No music. No mobile phones. Car parking.

It's not hard to define its particular quality, and this riverside inn with a large riverbank extension to house the dining room, two small pavilions for sheltered drinks and coffee on the terrace, and an electric launch for messing about (£54 for half an hour) exerts a strong pull for those with something to celebrate. The set-price lunch, which keeps costs understandable – if not in check – is a boon to many people planning an outing. Most leave happy, though the infinite layers of waiting staff and silver domes, plus prehistoric habits such as priced menus given only to the host, have caused the odd niggle. Alain Roux's repertoire holds firm to the dual strands of haute cuisine and adaptations of cuisine bourgeoise. As cooking calculated never to offend, it is extremely accurate. People have praised the langoustine soufflé served with a cassolette of langoustines scented with truffles, and the roasted Challandais duck (carved at table) with lightly spiced prunes, Puy lentils and Grande Chartreuse jus. As such it pleases perfectly, but would leave those used to comparatively expressive cookery wondering why they need pay so much. A summer set lunch saw the kitchen dispatch rich foie gras parfait with accompanying pan-fried slices, alongside leeks in a truffle dressing and a fragrant navarin of lamb, though red mullet fillets served with crushed potatoes, Provençal vegetable terrine and a warm barigoule-style coulis could have been bolder. Manjari chocolate with a raspberry filling and lychee and raspberry sorbet is textbook, but then there's no questioning the brilliance of the pastry work. It is when the wine list (from £28) is reached that most people wince; the range is of course impressive, but so are the profit margins.

# ▮ Chieveley

## The Crab at Chieveley

**Seafood for landlubbers**
Wantage Road, Chieveley, RG20 8UE
Tel no: (01635) 247550
www.crabatchieveley.com
Seafood | £38
Cooking score: 3

£5 OFF ☕

A prosperous pub/restaurant in the depths of verdant Berkshire countryside might not conjure up thoughts of 'amazing, freshly cooked seafood', but that's the main event at this aptly named venue packed with an eccentric clutter of seafaring artefacts and curios. Supplies of fish arrive daily from Cornwall, and the kitchen sets about its business with gusto. Scallops appear with a riot of garlic butter, sweet chilli, white chocolate, caviar and basil pesto, and other eclectic flavours are also added to the mix (caramelised mango, red pepper and lime syrup with crab ravioli, say). Meat eaters are not forgotten, while desserts such as roasted pear with pain perdu and cinnamon ice cream please the sweet-toothed brigade. The well-spread wine list kicks off with house selections at £13.85 a carafe.
**Chef/s:** Jamie Hodson. **Open:** all week L 12 to 2.30, D 6 to 10 (9 Sun). **Meals:** alc (main courses £19 to £40). Set menu £16 (2 courses) to £20. Sun L £23. **Service:** 10% (optional). **Details:** Cards accepted. 90 seats. 40 seats outside. Separate bar. Wheelchair access. Music. Children allowed. Car parking.

## Cookham

NEW ENTRY
### Maliks

Proper, honest Indian cooking
High Street, Cookham, SL6 9SF
Tel no: (01628) 520085
www.maliks.co.uk
Indian | £40
Cooking score: 2

 **V**

Forget the heavy conventional décor and concentrate on the better-than-average food and excellent service in Malik Ahmed's popular, well-established Indian restaurant. Unusually good are the spiced tandoori king prawns, nazakat (chicken breast grilled in the tandoor) and fragrant lamb pasanda. Chicken jalfrezi and seafood bhuna are also delicately spiced, while naan and rice are impeccable. The restaurant caters well for vegetarians, with aloo gobi jhalpiazi (potato and cauliflower fried with shallots, peppers, spring onion and fresh chilli) and sabzi biryani (stir-fried spiced vegetables with basmati rice, chopped herbs and fresh coriander) singled out for praise. Drink lassi, beer or wines from £14. Reporters also recommend a second branch in Gerrards Cross, Buckinghamshire, tel no: (01753) 880888.
**Chef/s:** Malik Ahmed and Shapon Mia. **Open:** all week L 12 to 2.30 (3 Sun), D 6 to 11 (10.30 Sun). **Closed:** 25 and 26 Dec. **Meals:** alc (main courses £8 to £16). Set D £21 (2 courses) to £30. Sun buffet £10. **Service:** 10% (optional). **Details:** Cards accepted. 70 seats. Wheelchair access. Music. Children allowed. Car parking.

### Please send us your feedback

To register your opinion about any restaurant listed in the Guide, or a new restaurant that you wish to bring to our attention, please visit the web address at the bottom of the page. Your feedback informs the content of the book and will be used to compile next year's reviews.

## East Garston

NEW ENTRY
### Queen's Arms Hotel

Simple, light and local menus
Newbury Road, East Garston, RG17 7ET
Tel no: (01488) 648757
www.queensarmshotel.co.uk
British | £26
Cooking score: 2

Like its sister properties in Hampshire (Peat Spade, Longstock and Anchor Inn, Lower Froyle – see entries), the Queen's Arms follows the same delightful country-style modus operandi. It's been remodelled with period furnishings, a soothing colour scheme and an array of old prints and *objets d'art*. The seasonal English menu comes with modish twists (think eggs Benedict with black pudding or perhaps a chocolate version of Eton mess) and keeps things simple, light and local. Bastable Brothers' crisp pork belly and loin might be teamed with pearl barley and apple purée, while a chicken, leek and bacon pie suits traditionalists. Well-chosen wines start out at £14.50.
**Chef/s:** Matt Green-Armytage. **Open:** all week L 12 to 3 (4 Sun), D 7 to 9.30. **Closed:** 25 Dec. **Meals:** alc (main courses £11 to £18). Set L £17.50 (2 courses). Sun L £24.50. **Service:** not inc. **Details:** Cards accepted. 50 seats. 30 seats outside. Wheelchair access. Music. Children allowed. Car parking.

## Frilsham
### The Pot Kiln

Rooted in the countryside
Frilsham, RG18 0XX
Tel no: (01635) 201366
www.potkiln.co.uk
Gastropub | £26
Cooking score: 1

Surrounded by woods and meadows, the 300-year-old Pot Kiln is Berkshire rusticity personified. Fittingly, TV chef/landlord Mike Robinson is keen on local, country flavours

and his menus have a gutsy edge. Some new dishes have impressed of late – including onion tarte Tatin with goats' cheese and pesto, and devilled chicken livers on toast. Elsewhere, expect anything from confit pork belly with braised red cabbage to Braeburn apple crumble. Real ales are taken seriously, and wines start at £12.95. Mike Robinson is also involved in the Harwood Arms, London SW6 (see entry).
**Chef/s:** Mike Robinson. **Open:** all week L 12 to 2 (2.30 Sun), Mon to Sat D 7 to 9. **Closed:** Sun D and Tue in winter, 25 Dec. **Meals:** alc (main courses £13 to £17). Set L £14.50 (2 courses) to £19.50. **Service:** 10% (optional). **Details:** Cards accepted. 48 seats. 80 seats outside. Separate bar. No music. No mobile phones. Wheelchair access. Children allowed. Car parking.

## Hurley
### Black Boys Inn
**Cuisine bourgeoise with flair**
Henley Road, Hurley, SL6 5NQ
Tel no: (01628) 824212
www.blackboysinn.co.uk
**Modern French | £28**
**New chef**

This former roadside pub dates from the sixteenth century and looks out onto open countryside. Its relaxed and comfortable dining room with pale walls, highly polished oak floors and tables with fine starched napkins may strike a rather conservative note, but the food has integrity and workmanship is meticulous. But, as the *Guide* went to press, we learnt that Simon Bonwick had left after cooking here for five distinguished years and his number two Marc Paley (also here five years) had taken over as head chef. It is unlikely that the classically entrenched style spiked with touches of modern invention will change, and among the dishes that have found favour this year have been pheasant and goose liver terrine with peach chutney, which showed 'great depth of flavour', a rich gratin of river trout and crayfish, a well-timed sea bass served with 'intense, sublime' rocket purée,

and a 'wonderful take on chocolate fondue brownie'. Service, however, remains an issue: 'consistently aloof and superior' being just one of many comments received in recent months. The international wine list starts at £17.50 and has an exceptional choice by the glass.
**Chef/s:** Marc Paley. **Open:** all week L 12 to 2, Mon to Sat D 7 to 9. **Closed:** 1 week Christmas. **Meals:** alc (main courses £14 to £19). Set L and D £9.95 (1 course with glass of wine). **Service:** not inc. **Details:** Cards accepted. 45 seats. 30 seats outside. Separate bar. Wheelchair access. Music. Car parking.

## Marsh Benham
### ALSO RECOMMENDED
### ▲ The Red House
Marsh Benham, RG20 8LY
Tel no: (01635) 582017
**Gastropub**

A new chef is continuing to make food the main business at this prettily thatched pub which overlooks water meadows and is just a 10-minute walk from the Kennet and Avon Canal. Comfort food appears in the guise of slow-braised lamb shank (£15.95) or sausage and mash, with modern European and Asian influences featuring in tiger prawns and mussel tagliatelle (£11.95) and Asian stir-fry on Chinese noodles. House wine is £15.50. Closed Mon and Tue D. Reports please.

## Newbury
### The Vineyard at Stockcross
**Striking cooking in stunning surroundings**
Newbury, RG20 8JU
Tel no: (01635) 528770
www.the-vineyard.co.uk
**Modern European | £68**
**Cooking score: 8**

The Vineyard is a country house hotel cast in a contemporary mode, its older core carefully wrapped around with extensions. A fire and water feature dominates the entrance, but there's no vineyard – the opulent building is named in honour of owner Sir Peter Michael's winery in California. Smartly dressed but refreshingly unstuffy staff ensure everything runs smoothly in the split-level dining room, which has been cleverly divided up to feel both intimate and spacious. Lighting that subtly changes colour throughout the evening and widely spaced tables add to the feeling of luxury. John Campbell dissects modern cooking, reshuffling the components in an intelligent way, and visitors are struck by the brilliant marriage of flavours and textures from the word go. One of the highlights has to be salmon mi cuit served on a bed of lentils with a breathtaking combination of foie gras, apple purée and beetroot. There is both artistry and complexity in Campbell's approach, with dishes being built up in deceptively simple layers. Venison is given an extra dimension by the addition of smoked bacon, celeriac, trompette de mort, choucroute and sloe gin jelly ('such a range of flavours'), while scallop ceviche is perfectly matched by cod brandade and a hint of confit lemon, and an inspirational pre-desert of cucumber, lime, mango and yoghurt is 'the ultimate palate cleanser'. There are some 2,000 bottles listed on the superb wine list, which opens with a good international selection from £15 to £25, but then moves with swift ease past the £30 mark. A renowned collection from California is backed by an impressive Old World selection.

**Chef/s:** John Campbell. **Open:** all week L 12 to 2.30, D 7 to 9.30. **Meals:** Set L £19 (2 courses) to £24. Set D £58 (2 courses) to £68. Sun L £35. **Service:** not inc. **Details:** Cards accepted. 100 seats. 20 seats outside. Air-con. Separate bar. No mobile phones. Wheelchair access. Music. Children allowed. Car parking.

**Dominic Chapman** The Royal Oak

**Who or what inspired you to become a chef?**
My dad.

**What is the best meal you have ever eaten?**
A big fresh sea bream sitting by the sea in Greece – amazing.

**Which chefs do you admire?**
Heston and Phil Howard.

**If you were to have one abiding principle in the kitchen, what would it be?**
A good attitude to work.

**What is your favourite restaurant and why?**
The Waterside – it's pure class.

**What do you do to relax when out of the kitchen?**
Walk the dog or go horse racing.

**What did it mean to you to be awarded 'Best Pub Chef' in The Good Food Guide 2009?**
It was a real honour. The Good Food Guide is something I have followed for years, so to be recognised in it was very special.

## ◼ Paley Street
### The Royal Oak
Upper-tier pub food
Paley Street, SL6 3JN
Tel no: (01628) 620541
www.theroyaloakpaleystreet.com
Gastropub | £35
Cooking score: 5

£5 OFF | ▌ V

'The welcome was warm and genuine, the menu interesting and well-balanced, and overall this was just a fab evening out', was the verdict of one reporter who had clearly enjoyed a dinner at this beamed village pub a little off the M4. Owned by Sir Michael Parkinson and his son Nick, the place is a haven of old-school comfort, with sofas to sink into and artwork on the walls. It also boasts a hugely accomplished chef in Dominic Chapman, whose menus reflect a fondness for traditional British food, conscientiously sourced and prepared with obvious care and skill. Smoked haddock soup comes with a poached egg to create vivid impact, while main courses are full of nostalgic appeal, running from oxtail and kidney pudding to grilled lemon sole with chips. They also find room for the odd idea from beyond these shores – perhaps roast halibut with spiced aubergine, cucumber and mint. Desserts bring it all back home with Cambridge burnt cream or lemon posset, and there are fine British cheeses too. A great choice of 13 wines by the glass leads off a diverse and fascinating list of quality drinking, with a wealth of options at the affordable end of the spectrum. Prices start at £17.
**Chef/s:** Dominic Chapman. **Open:** all week L 12 to 3 (4 Sun), Mon to Sat D 6.30 to 9.30 (10 Fri and Sat). **Closed:** 25 Dec. **Meals:** alc (main courses £12 to £25). Set L £15 (2 courses) to £19.95. Set D £25 (3 courses). **Service:** 12.5% (optional). **Details:** Cards accepted. 46 seats. 20 seats outside. Air-con. Separate bar. Music. Children allowed. Car parking.

## ◼ Reading
### London Street Brasserie
Thoughtful menus by the river
2-4 London Street, Reading, RG1 4SE
Tel no: (01189) 505036
www.londonstbrasserie.co.uk
Modern European | £35
Cooking score: 3

V

A characterful brasserie in a building that was once the tollhouse for traffic coming into Reading over the Duke Street bridge, London Street has built up a loyal local following. The outdoor terrace on the River Kennet is one reason, and Paul Clerehugh's thoughtfully conceived menus are another. Choice is extravagantly wide, from starters that take in salt-and-pepper squid with chilli dressing, or crab and sweetcorn chowder, to substantial mains like fallow deer fillet with haggis mash, fig compote and redcurrant jus. The special lunch deal should prove a boon in these straitened times, and the desserts – sticky toffee pudding, blackberry and apple crumble with custard – could hardly be more comforting. Argentinian house wines are £17 (£4.65 a glass).
**Chef/s:** Paul Clerehugh. **Open:** all week L 12 to 6, D 6 to 11. **Meals:** alc (main courses £13 to £20). Set L and D £14.95 (2 courses) to £18.80. **Service:** not inc. **Details:** Cards accepted. 80 seats. 20 seats outside. Separate bar. No mobile phones. Wheelchair access. Music. Children allowed. Car parking.

## ◼ Shinfield
### L'Ortolan
A fine-dining institution
Church Lane, Shinfield, RG2 9BY
Tel no: (01189) 888500
www.lortolan.com
French | £65
Cooking score: 6

V

As you swing through the gates on a summer's day, with the scrunch of gravel on the drive, trees handsomely mature and the dapper old vicarage draped in wisteria, 'you could be deep in the countryside – apart from the drone of the close-by M4'. Once inside, the attention to detail – contemporary design, professional service and white linen – affirms a serious fine-dining outfit. There are a couple of conservatory areas – one a lounge – plus a boldly decorated bar and an alfresco terrace. In the soft pastel dining room, the cooking doesn't disappoint. Peripherals, from appetisers to petits fours, add 'cracking little flavour awakenings'. Smartly engineered dishes offer a light touch, like a 'beguiling' starter of foie gras and pain d'épices sandwich with rhubarb chutney, its flavours, colours and textures a perfect marriage delivered with trademark head-turning presentation. A 'perfectly timed and seasoned' fillet of halibut (teamed with crushed minted peas and cucumber beurre blanc) 'oozes deceptive simplicity and summer flavour', and 'ethereal desserts' – perhaps a sticky carrot and ginger cake served with carrot sorbet and ginger cream – continue the theme. Wines range from £18 to starry names and prices, with France a major player. There's also a decent by the glass selection. Sister restaurant is La Bécasse in Ludlow (see entry).

**Chef/s:** Alan Murchison and Robin Gosse. **Open:** Tue to Sat L 12 to 2, D 7 to 9. **Closed:** Sun, Mon, 25 Dec to 6 Jan. **Meals:** Set L £22 (2 courses) to £26. Set D £56 (2 courses) to £65. **Service:** 12.5% (optional). **Details:** Cards accepted. 64 seats. Separate bar. Wheelchair access. Children allowed. Car parking.

## ▌Sunningdale

### READERS RECOMMEND
### Bluebells Restaurant and Bar

**Modern European**
Shrubbs Hill, London Road, Sunningdale, SL5 0LE
Tel no: (01344) 622722
www.bluebells-restaurant.co.uk
'This is the best restaurant for miles around . . . always faultless'

## Restaurants with fabulous rooms

**The Café at Brovey Lair, Norfolk**
Elegant in a *Vogue* shoot kind of way, with the terrace and brightly painted swimming pool giving a Mediterranean touch outside.

**Devonshire Arms, Derbyshire**
The Duchess of Devonshire's trademark modern touches give this pretty, estate-owned inn a chic, rustic tone.

**The Great House, Suffolk**
This ancient timber-framed restaurant-with-rooms has an air of civilized charm.

**Hand & Flowers, Buckinghamshire**
Expect hot tubs and individual touches in rooms in a pair of cottages a few steps from this inn of high local repute.

**Lord Poulett Arms, Somerset**
Lap up the gentrified, rural chic interior, as well as the fragrant herb garden, wildflower meadow and lavender-edged boules 'piste'.

**Mr Underhill's, Shropshire**
Visitors are still seduced by the Bradley's special 'cocktail of intimacy, wonderful hospitality and superb food'.

**Russell's, Worcestershire**
Honey-coloured Georgian building that has been painstakingly restored and transformed into a boutique-style restaurant-with-rooms.

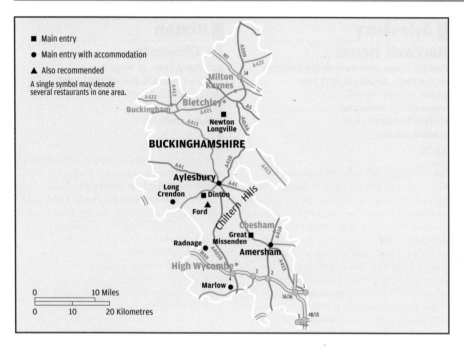

## Amersham

**NEW ENTRY**
### The Crown Inn
**Rustic chic and unfussy food**
16 High Street, Amersham, HP7 0DH
Tel no: (01494) 721541
www.thecrownamersham.co.uk
Gastropub | £25
Cooking score: 2

The Crown's brushed-up brick frontage
dominates Old Amersham's main drag, and it
chimes perfectly with the town's affluent
demeanour. Its cheery feel, rustic chic interior
(courtesy of Ilse Crawford) and unfussy food
also provide a refreshing antidote to prissy
Home Counties' posturing. Rosie Sykes cut
her teeth with Joyce Molyneux and Shaun
Hill, so it's no surprise that her cooking goes
for natural flavour in a big way – pigeon with
quince and watercress, grilled lemon sole with
purple sprouting broccoli, and duck leg with
carrots (plus a helping of 'healthily

invigorating' spring greens) are typical of her
daily menu. After all that generosity, refresh
with a seasonal rhubarb sorbet – served
intriguingly in a little pewter vessel. 'Slap
Bang' lunches are a snip. Wines start at £15.
**Chef/s:** Rosie Sykes and Mark Briston. **Open:** all
week L 12.30 to 3 (4 Sun), Mon to Sat D 6 to 10.
**Meals:** alc (main courses £10 to £18). Set L Mon to
Sat £9.90 (2 courses) to £12.90. **Service:** 12.5%
(optional). **Details:** Cards accepted. 80 seats. 60
seats outside. Separate bar. Music. Children
allowed. Car parking.

### Symbols

Accommodation is available

Three courses for less than £30

**V** More than three vegetarian main courses

£5 £5-off voucher scheme

Notable wine list

## Aylesbury
### Hartwell House
Country house splendour in the Chilterns
Oxford Road, Aylesbury, HP17 8NR
Tel no: (01296) 747444
www.hartwell-house.com
**Modern European | £40**
**Cooking score: 4**

Set in 90 acres of landscaped parkland, Hartwell is an elegant country house hotel in the contemporary style, right down to the spa treatments, themed evenings and even the odd piano recital. Since September 2008, it has been owned by the National Trust, along with its siblings, Bodysgallen Hall at Llandudno and Middlethorpe Hall, York (see entries). The primrose dining room is the scene for some vibrant modern cooking, along the lines of wood pigeon and leek cannelloni with shallots and figs, and fillet of sea bass with potato confit, Jerusalem artichoke purée and a port and truffle butter sauce. Menu descriptions are on the wordy side, but no less alluring for that, when the temptation might be loin of venison with Lapsang Souchong, braised kale, honey-roast parsnip purée and a blackberry jus. Desserts might be as traditional as treacle tart with clotted-cream ice cream, and there are some fabulous cheeses. If you haven't had this year's bonus stopped, a luxurious wine list awaits you, with roll calls of the great and good in profusion. House blends, a Spanish white and a French red, are £17.95.
**Chef/s:** Daniel Richardson. **Open:** all week L 12.30 to 1.45, D 7.30 to 9.45. **Meals:** alc (main courses £23 to £28). Set L £22.95 (2 courses) to £29.95. Set D £39 (3 courses). Sun L £32.95. **Service:** not inc.
**Details:** Cards accepted. 60 seats. Separate bar. No music. No mobile phones. Wheelchair access. Children allowed. Car parking.

---

### Average price

The average price listed in main-entry reviews denotes the price of a three-course meal, without wine.

## Dinton
### La Chouette
Inn with a taste of Belgium
Westlington Green, Dinton, HP17 8UW
Tel no: (01296) 747422
**Belgian | £35**
**Cooking score: 4**

The sixteenth-century, creeper-covered inn opposite the village green is a singular testament to the enterprising Frédéric Desmette. He is coming up to 20 years at the helm, and is as tireless as the day he opened. His menu is influenced by the culinary traditions of his native Belgium, but it goes way beyond the usual mussels and chips; witness main-course game birds – pheasant with chicory, partridge with cabbage – and Scottish salmon served with bacon in the Ardennes fashion. As a curtain-raiser you might consider shrimps or smoked eel in salads, and there is, naturally, Belgian chocolate to finish in some form or other. Not the least delight, and certainly worth the detour, is an unexpectedly stunning wine list, which wouldn't look out of place in the kind of hotel where they make you wear a tie. It's all French, and it's all good. If the spirit of adventure fails you, house wines are £14.
**Chef/s:** Frédéric Desmette. **Open:** Mon to Fri L 12 to 2, Mon to Sat D 7 to 9. **Closed:** Sun. **Meals:** alc (main courses £15 to £17). Set L £14.50. Set D £30 (2 courses) to £40. **Service:** 12.5% (optional).
**Details:** Cards accepted. 35 seats. Separate bar. Music. Children allowed. Car parking.

## Ford
ALSO RECOMMENDED
### ▲ Dinton Hermit
Water Lane, Ford, HP17 8XH
Tel no: (01296) 747473
www.dintonhermit.co.uk
**Gastropub**

Impressively thick walls testify to the age of this carefully extended 400-year-old inn deep in the Aylesbury Vale. The kitchen deals happily with sharing platters and 'old favourites' (fish and chips et al), but the best stuff is on the full menu of satisfying gastropub standards. A starter of chargrilled asparagus salad (£5.95) might be followed by cod cheek and saffron stew or 'melting' braised lamb shoulder on Savoy cabbage and mash (£14.95). Banana bavarois with chocolate ice cream (£4.95) has pleased as a finale. Wines from £14 (£3.50 a glass). Accommodation available. Closed Sun D.

## ▌Great Missenden
## La Petite Auberge

**French cooking with charm and cheer**
107 High Street, Great Missenden, HP16 0BB
Tel no: (01494) 865370
www.lapetiteauberge.co.uk
**French | £34**
**Cooking score: 3**

£5
OFF

Hubert Martel's French bistro does exactly what is required, as confirmed by the couple who report, 'we continue to come back to this restaurant year after year and we are very rarely disappointed'. Crab and tiger prawn gratin sauced with brandy, turbot with anchovies in caper sauce, beef fillet in grain mustard: these are the kinds of dishes, capably executed, that first lured the British across the Channel. They are served with impeccable charm and cheer and, what's more, you can ease gently to a halt with a slice of caramelised lemon tart. The all-French drinking extends from a good Muscadet at £15.50 to Henriot rosé Champagne and Pineau des Charentes for the desserts.
**Chef/s:** Hubert Martel. **Open:** Mon to Sat D only 7 to 10. **Closed:** Sun, 2 weeks Christmas, 2 weeks Easter. **Meals:** alc (main courses £17 to £19). **Service:** not inc. **Details:** Cards accepted. 30 seats. No music. No mobile phones. Wheelchair access. Children allowed.

## ▌Long Crendon
## Angel Restaurant

**Positively appealing home counties' stalwart**
47 Bicester Road, Long Crendon, HP18 9EE
Tel no: (01844) 208268
www.angelrestaurant.co.uk
**Modern British | £25**
**Cooking score: 2**

£5
OFF ♦ 🍷 ▭ V £30

An engaging, recession-proof all-rounder, this Angel 'seems as positively appealing as ever', according to one reporter. Originally a pub, it still has a bar with real ales and leather sofas around the fire, although food and wine is its main business. Fish specials are a big draw (perhaps grilled Cornish lemon sole with lime and basil butter), but vigorous meat dishes also impress: Sandy Lane pork fillet 'with bags of flavour' on grilled black pudding with Savoy cabbage tart and punchy cider gravy, for example. Portions are unashamedly generous, but it's worth finding room for, say, lemon tart with zingy kiwi sorbet. The cracking global wine list offers really interesting drinking at prices that won't offend, with loads available by the 50cl pichet ('a real winner'). Lesser-known grape varieties pop up everywhere, and house selections start at £15.95 (£4.50 a glass).
**Chef/s:** Trevor Bosch. **Open:** all week L 12 to 2.30, Mon to Sat D 7 to 10. **Meals:** alc (main courses £15 to £29). Set L £14 (2 courses) to £19.95. Set D £20 (2 courses) to £24.95. Sun L £15.95 (2 courses) to £22.50. **Service:** not inc. **Details:** Cards accepted. 65 seats. 30 seats outside. Air-con. Separate bar. Wheelchair access. Music. Children allowed. Car parking.

# Marlow

**NEW ENTRY**

## Aubergine at the Compleat Angler

Smooth-flowing food and service
The Compleat Angler Hotel, Marlow, SL7 1RG
Tel no: (01628) 405405
www.auberginemarlow.com
French | £55
Cooking score: 4

💺 V

Marlow is a busy place and the Compleat Angler's prime spot beside the Thames is a magnet for visitors. The hotel is now playing host to a country outpost of Chelsea favourite Aubergine (see entry), and the consensus is that this recent arrival, with its river and weir views, delivers 'great value for the setting and service'. The kitchen deals in straightforward ideas, be it a set lunch of delicate smoked salmon velouté with cucumber and mint, followed by slow-cooked pork cheeks with a rich potato purée and creamy grain mustard sauce, or, from the carte, a warm salad of quail with hazelnut and orange dressing, and saddle of Lune valley lamb with braised peas, onions and lettuce. A set vanilla cream with strawberries marinated in mint and vanilla was as good as it should be. Elsewhere, there's praise for 'great little flavoured bread rolls' and the 'generous' wine waiter. House wine is £19. **Chef/s:** Miles Nixon. **Open:** Tue to Sun L 12 to 2.30, Tue to Sat D 7 to 10.30. **Closed:** Mon. **Meals:** Set L £28.50. Set D £45 (2 courses) to £55. Tasting menu £65. **Service:** 12.5% (optional). **Details:** Cards accepted. 50 seats. Air-con. Separate bar. No mobile phones. Wheelchair access. Music. Children allowed. Car parking.

## Readers recommend

A 'readers recommend' review is a genuine quote from a report sent in by one of our readers. We intend to follow up these suggestions throughout the year to come.

## Danesfield House, Oak Room

Breathlessly modern food and pure theatre
Henley Road, Marlow, SL7 2EY
Tel no: (01628) 891010
www.danesfieldhouse.co.uk
Modern European | £55
Cooking score: 7

£5 OFF 🍷 🛏

The vast white edifice is set in 65 acres and overlooks the Thames. It opened as a hotel in the early 1990s and offers the complete country house package, including the pale-panelled Oak Room, which is the fine-dining arm of the set and a showcase for Adam Simmonds' breathlessly modern cooking. As a chef who cooks at low-temperatures and goes in for jellies and foams, his menus are imaginative without running riot, and style never seems to get in the way of substance. Indeed, the sheer flavour of the food dazzles, as when langoustines are teamed with yoghurt, samphire, a few dots of Oscietra caviar and finished with an intense cucumber essence, or when the soul of spring is evoked in a dish of poached fillet of brill dotted with tiny cubes of wild garlic leaf pannacotta, fresh peas, fèves and morels. The less speculative assemblages work equally well, as when the richness of confit foie gras is pointed by black fig purée, fig compote, hazelnut crunch and Pedro Ximenez jelly, or when slices of meltingly tender slow-cooked loin of lamb come interspersed with braised tongue and juxtaposed with tomato-spiced couscous, aubergine caviar and goats' cheese in a crisp tomato cornet. The incidentals at inspection included a gin and tonic jelly with lime foam, an asparagus soup with a slow-cooked quail's egg, and a stunning pre-dessert that deconstructed the components of a classic trifle using the flavours of orange and cardamon. This is eye-catching food – 'theatre, pure theatre', as one fan enthused – delivered by unfailingly helpful and knowledgeable staff. The polished wine list is arranged by styles, with gentle coaching on how each will partner food. Prices start at £25.

Chef/s: Adam Simmonds. Open: Wed to Sat L 12 to 2.30, Tue to Sat D 7 to 9.30. Closed: Sun, Mon, 20 Dec to 19 Jan, bank hols. Meals: Set L £25 (2 courses) to £29.50. Set D £55. Tasting menu £75. Service: 12.5% (optional). Details: Cards accepted. 30 seats. Separate bar. No mobile phones. Wheelchair access. Car parking.

## Hand & Flowers

**Modern, feet-on-the-ground cooking**
126 West Street, Marlow, SL7 2BP
Tel no: (01628) 482277
www.thehandandflowers.co.uk
**Modern British | £36**
**Cooking score: 6**

Some readers have been critical of the Kerridges' smart roadside pub/restaurant-with rooms, but inspectors and other readers remain firm – this is a restaurant of high local repute. With low, beamed ceilings, evening candles and simple but comfortable décor, it is the setting for modern cooking with its feet on the ground – even the fish and chips served in the bar at lunchtime is a cut above the norm. A couple directed here by word of mouth were glad they took the advice: their red mullet soup came with toasted fennel grissini, crispy squid and 'layers of flavour', while the main course, slow-cooked beef with 'an incredibly light' bone marrow bread pudding, pomme galette and braising juices was a dish of strong appeal. Others might enjoy terrine of Old Spot pork and bacon with hot pickled pineapple or fillet of sea bream with braised Puy lentils, smoked butter, mussels and parsley. Desserts include lavender pannacotta with heather honey, honeycomb and whisky. The wine list opens at £16.
Chef/s: Tom Kerridge. Open: all week L 12 to 2.30 (3 Sun), Mon to Sat D 7 to 9.30. Closed: 24 to 26 Dec. Meals: alc (main courses £16 to £20). Service: not inc. Details: Cards accepted. 50 seats. 20 seats outside. Wheelchair access. Music. Children allowed. Car parking.

## Vanilla Pod

**House of hidden delights**
31 West Street, Marlow, SL7 2LS
Tel no: (01628) 898101
www.thevanillapod.co.uk
**Modern British | £40**
**Cooking score: 5**

£5 OFF V

One of the more discreet players in Marlow's generously endowed foodie scene, Vanilla Pod hides its delights behind the black door of a two-storey townhouse that was once home to poet T.S. Eliot. 'What a smashing little place', observed one reporter, musing on the warm-hearted, domestic intimacy of the narrow dining room with its French doors leading to a little garden out back. Michael Macdonald's cooking is 'clear and concise', sure-footed and gastronomically erudite, with much depending on the details – for example, a supremely light potato gnocchi 'cake' with rump of lamb and vivid red pepper jus, or dollops of smoked aubergine compote alongside a wobbly slab of pressed skate terrine interleaved with spinach. He also extracts the best from top-drawer ingredients, whether it's crunchy new season's asparagus or juicy loin of Appleton pork with earthy, truffle-infused Puy lentils. To finish, eye-catching desserts set out to impress on swanky white crockery: a ball of exquisitely fragrant lychee sorbet atop ginger cream with cubes of poached pear, say. The lunch menu is 'truly outstanding value', but there's no dumbing down – witness a knockout starter of sublime seared scallops served on a zingy cold escabèche of marinated carrot slivers. Congenial Gallic staff go about their business amid the babble of affluent chatter at heavy-clothed round tables, and the French-centred wine list starts at £18 (£4 a glass).
Chef/s: Michael Macdonald. Open: Tue to Sat L 12 to 2, D 7 to 10. Closed: Sun, Mon, 24 Dec to 8 Jan. Meals: Set L £15.50 (2 courses) to £19.50. Set D £35 (2 courses) to £40. Gourmand menu £50 (8 courses). Service: not inc. Details: Cards accepted. 28 seats. 10 seats outside. Air-con. Separate bar. No music. No mobile phones. Children allowed.

## ▌Newton Longville

### The Crooked Billet
**Pub full of surprises**
2 Westbrook End, Newton Longville, MK17 0DF
Tel no: (01908) 373936
www.thebillet.co.uk
**Modern British | £27**
**Cooking score: 2**

Seriously thatched and solidly antiquated, the Crooked Billet looks like everyone's idea of a picture-perfect village boozer. True, it has all the requisite trappings (including real ales on tap), but these days it's a world away from beer and skittles. Emma Gilchrist (chef) and husband John (sommelier) have applied their skills to telling effect here, creating a venue that stakes its reputation on good food and glorious wine. Restaurant diners can look forward to dishes with a sharp modern edge: think scallops matched with warm ham hock terrine and sweet-and-sour apple dressing, or roast lamb rump with sweetbreads, potato and sage bread pudding and creamed Savoy cabbage. Lunches in the bar are a cut above pub grub. The wine list – a 200-bin stunner – opens up a world of irresistible opportunities for top-class drinking, with a truly fabulous selection offered by the glass. Bottle prices start at £14.

**Chef/s:** Emma Gilchrist. **Open:** Tue to Sun L 12 to 2 (3.30 Sun), Mon to Sat D 7 to 9.30 (10 Fri and Sat). **Meals:** alc (main courses £10 to £24). Set L £12 (2 courses) to £19. Set D £16 (2 courses) to £25. **Service:** not inc. **Details:** Cards accepted. 70 seats. 50 seats outside. Separate bar. Wheelchair access. Children allowed. Car parking.

## ▌Radnage

NEW ENTRY
### The Three Horseshoes
**Precise food with oomph**
Horseshoe Road, Bennett End, Radnage,
HP14 4EB
Tel no: (01494) 483273
www.thethreehorseshoes.net
**Modern British | £28**
**Cooking score: 3**

Simon Crawshaw has added his name to the roll call of chefs who have forsaken the cacophony of big London kitchens in favour of their own gaff in the country. His new home is an ever-so-appealing inn hidden deep in the leafy Chilterns. Inside it looks freshly scrubbed-up, with a minuscule drinkers' bar and a roomy slate-floored restaurant. Mementos of Crawshaw's days at the Connaught are reminders of his serious pedigree, and he can be relied on to extract the best from top-notch ingredients – whether it's wild sea bass fired up with green chilli, garlic and ginger dressing or 'fabulously succulent' veal rump with tiny wild mushrooms, fresh-as-a-daisy spring carrots and tarragon cream. These are precise, big-boned dishes with plenty of oomph, and they are followed by textbook renditions of crème brûlée and soft-centred chocolate fondant. Lunches are upmarket pub grub, tapas is served in the garden, and the short, sharp wine list is agreeably priced from £14.

**Chef/s:** Simon Crawshaw and James Norie. **Open:** Tue to Sun L 12 to 2.30 (4 Sun), Mon to Sat D 7 to 9.30 (9 Mon). **Closed:** Tue after bank hols. **Meals:** alc (main courses £15 to £17). Set L Tue to Sat £12.50 (2 courses) to £16.50. **Service:** 10% (optional). **Details:** Cards accepted. 65 seats. 110 seats outside. Separate bar. Wheelchair access. Music. Children allowed. Car parking.

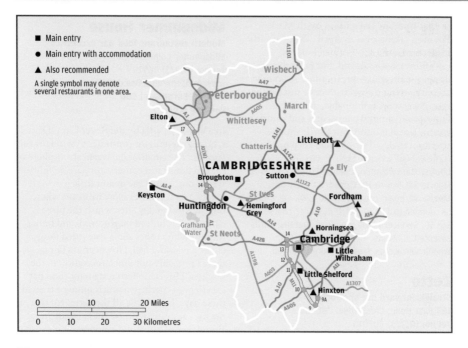

## Broughton

### The Crown Inn

**Heart-warming gastropub**
Bridge Road, Broughton, PE28 3AY
Tel no: (01487) 824428
www.thecrowninnrestaurant.co.uk
**Gastropub | £24**
**Cooking score: 2**

The Crown commands a prime position opposite the church on the road that runs through this hamlet north of Huntingdon. It's a heart-warming country pub with small-paned windows, stone floors, a rustic bar and separate dining room leading onto the garden. The kitchen delivers an eclectic menu that features a number of Mediterranean influences (potato gnocchi with rabbit sauce) to complement modern British dishes of, say, ham hock terrine with piccalilli or roast lamb teamed with mash, thyme and red wine sauce. For dessert, there may be syrup sponge pudding with egg custard. Wines from £13.

**Chef/s:** David Anderson. **Open:** Wed to Sun L 12 to 2.30, Wed to Sat D 7 to 10. **Closed:** Mon, Tue. **Meals:** alc (main courses £10 to £16). Set L £11.50 (2 courses) to £14. **Service:** not inc. **Details:** Cards accepted. 60 seats. 72 seats outside. Separate bar. Wheelchair access. Music. Children allowed. Car parking.

## Cambridge

### Alimentum

**Lively joint with vibrant ideas**
152-154 Hills Road, Cambridge, CB2 8PB
Tel no: (01223) 413000
www.restaurantalimentum.co.uk
**Modern European | £35**
**Cooking score: 4**

This slick, modern restaurant serves contemporary and ethically sourced food in an informal atmosphere with plain wood tables and insistent music. There's also an adjoining bar open to non-diners, plus occasional jazz evenings – no mistaking that Alimentum is a lively venue. There have been several changes of chef since the last edition, with Mark Poynton taking over in April 2009. An early inspection saw a successful velouté of cauliflower with salt cod, but poor timing let down a main course bream fillet – though the accompanying mussel tagliatelle just hit the spot. Sweets are fashionable, delivering frangipane, almond pannacotta and vanilla ice cream. Bread is good, but a little more attention to detail would help keep up the standards of service. House wine is £15.75. **Chef/s:** Mark Poynton. **Open:** all week L 12 to 3, Mon to Sat D 6 to 10. **Closed:** 24 to 31 Dec. **Meals:** alc (main courses £16 to £20). Set L £13.50 (2 courses) to £16.50. Set D £15.50 (2 courses) to £18.50. **Service:** 12.5% (optional). **Details:** Cards accepted. 62 seats. Air-con. Separate bar. Wheelchair access. Music. Children allowed.

## Cotto

**Straightforward but spot-on**
183 East Road, Cambridge, CB1 1BG
Tel no: (01223) 302010
www.cottocambridge.co.uk
**Modern European | £35**
**Cooking score: 1**

**V**

Hans Schweitzer and his team continue to feed a group as diverse as Cambridge can conjure up – academics, students, tourists – in this simple café on two floors. 'Straightforward but spot-on' cooking delivers light lunches of duck and chicken country pâté or risotto with spring vegetables and field mushrooms, while dinner brings velouté of black sea bream, tiger prawns and crayfish, and rack of lamb with herb crust. Home-baked bread and 'exceptional' crème brûlée pleased one reporter. House wine £15.
**Chef/s:** Hans Schweitzer. **Open:** Tue to Sat L 9 to 3, Thur to Sat D 7 to 8.45. **Closed:** Sun, Mon, 25 and 26 Dec, 3 weeks Aug. **Meals:** alc (main courses £6 to £14). Set D £35. **Service:** not inc. **Details:** Cards accepted. 45 seats. 15 seats outside. Wheelchair access. Music. Children allowed.

## Midsummer House

**Modern restaurant food par excellence**
Midsummer Common, Cambridge, CB4 1HA
Tel no: (01223) 369299
www.midsummerhouse.co.uk
**Modern European | £60**
**Cooking score: 7**

In a Victorian villa by the River Cam, Daniel Clifford's restaurant continues to win faithful friends. 'The small-scale, warm atmosphere of the old house and conservatory are delightful,' writes one, 'while the quaint little garden is lovely. You feel miles away from anywhere.' On the kind of day after which the place is named, all is indeed bright, fresh and light. Mainly white tones and a slate-tiled floor create a relaxing feel. However, it's fair to say there's probably not much relaxation in the kitchen. This is modern restaurant food par excellence – perhaps a touch more restrained these days, but maybe all the better for that, as the higher rating reflects. There is still an abundance of novel and convincing ideas, as when sweetbreads caramelised in maple syrup are sharply offset by turnip, pistachio and ox tongue in a first course that sets the tone. Combinations are built up with apposite logic, so tender duck breast as a main course might be accompanied by grapefruit and mouli purée in a modern take on duck à l'orange, and served with spinach, hazelnuts and buerre noisette, plus slivers of the crispest skin. A creative approach to orange cheesecake sees it made with fresh goats' cheese and put together with a 'wonderfully hoppy' Hoegaarden sorbet, caramelised oats and fresh coriander. Extras are no mere fillers; pre-, mid- and post-meal freebies show Clifford is at home with bold flavours and contrasting textures. Most striking is an intensely flavoured gazpacho and a sublime pea velouté with tiger prawns and cubes of onion jelly. There's a generosity, too, that certainly delivers bang per buck. A list of fine wines has been assembled, but with prices starting at around £35, mark-ups aren't about to do anybody any favours.

**Chef/s:** Daniel Clifford. **Open:** Wed to Sat L 12 to 1.30, Tue to Sat D 7 to 9.30. **Closed:** Sun and Mon, 2 weeks Christmas, 1 week Easter, 2 weeks August. **Meals:** Set L £24 (2 courses) to £30. Set D £45 (2 courses) to £60. Tasting menu £80. **Service:** 12.5% (optional). **Details:** Cards accepted. 45 seats. No music. No mobile phones. Children allowed.

## Restaurant 22

**Appealing, fashion-free favourite**
22 Chesterton Road, Cambridge, CB4 3AX
Tel no: (01223) 351880
www.restaurant22.co.uk
**Modern French | £28**
**Cooking score: 2**

This established Cambridge favourite may have fallen behind a little in the fashion stakes, but its professional style and appealing French cooking still add up to a winning formula. Among starters, oriental influences appear in the form of salt-and-pepper squid with onion, orange, chilli and coriander salad, while paupiette and ragoût of rabbit with glazed turnips, shallot confit, salsify and grain mustard sauce represents the cooking's classic strand. An extra fish course is available for a supplement (perhaps seafood panache in a saffron consommé), there's a mid-course sorbet and desserts are things like chocolate délice with salted caramel and brioche ice cream. House wine is £14.95.
**Chef/s:** Martin Cullum. **Open:** Tue to Sat D 7 to 9.45. **Closed:** Sun, Mon, 25 Dec, 2 and 3 Jan. **Meals:** Set D £27.50. **Service:** not inc. **Details:** Cards accepted. 38 seats. Air-con. No mobile phones. Music. Children allowed.

### Readers recommend

A 'readers recommend' review is a genuine quote from a report sent in by one of our readers. We intend to follow up these suggestions throughout the year to come.

## ▌Elton

### ALSO RECOMMENDED
### ▲ The Crown Inn
8 Duck Street, Elton, PE8 6RQ
Tel no: (01832) 280232
www.thecrowninn.org
**Gastropub**

Looking across the green from beneath its towering chestnut tree, the thatched, mellow-stoned Crown is everyone's idea of an English inn. The picture-pretty estate village, set around Elton Hall, draws the crowds and many seek refreshment in the Crown's oak-beamed bar and conservatory restaurant. Reports indicate that few leave disappointed. Pappardelle with venison ragù (£8), baked bream on mussel, chorizo and tomato risotto (£16.50) and chocolate, almond and walnut brownie (£5.95) are some of the dishes that have found favour. House wine is £15.95. Closed Sun D and Mon.

### READERS RECOMMEND
### The Black Horse
**Gastropub**
14 Overend, Elton, PE8 6RU
Tel no: (01832) 280240
**'Relaxed, old-fashioned pub serving really good food'**

## ▌Fordham

### ALSO RECOMMENDED
### ▲ The White Pheasant
21 Market Street, Fordham, CB7 5LQ
Tel no: (01638) 720414
www.whitepheasant.com
**Gastropub**

Handy for Newmarket and the A14, this village pub puts a homely face on its simply decorated interior – there's a log fire, plain wood tables – but the cooking is a cut above the norm. The kitchen sets great store by the provenance of raw materials. Typically, you might find minute steak sandwich or local sausage and mash (£9.95) on the lunch menu, with king scallops teamed with crisp belly pork (£18.95) or fish pie as blackboard specials. House wine is £13.95. Open all week.

## Hemingford Grey

### ALSO RECOMMENDED
### ▲ The Cock

47 High Street, Hemingford Grey, PE28 9BJ
Tel no: (01480) 463609
www.cambscuisine.com
Gastropub

Part local gastro-boozer, part snazzy country restaurant, the revitalised Cock proclaims its wares to a well-heeled, cosmopolitan crowd. Star turns are the homemade sausages with a choice of mash and sauces, although the fish specials board also has its fans. Otherwise, check out the regular menu, which satisfies with the likes of rabbit terrine with grilled polenta (£6), and lamb shank with wilted greens and port sauce (£15). After that, perhaps, sticky toffee pudding (£6). Wines from £13. Open all week.

## Hinxton

### ALSO RECOMMENDED
### ▲ The Red Lion Inn

32 High Street, Hinxton, CB10 1QY
Tel no: (01799) 530601
www.redlionhinxton.co.uk
Gastropub

A valuable local resource and an agreeable stopover, too, for this pink-washed inn is just minutes from the M11/A11. Reporters have endorsed the comfort of the beamed and boarded bar with its chesterfield sofas, log fire and rare roast beef and horseradish sandwiches. Elsewhere there's game terrine with red onion chutney (£6), chicken and leek pie or roast leg of lamb with apricot and rosemary jus (£15), and lemon tart with mango coulis (£5). House wine £12. Accommodation. Open all week.

## Horningsea

### ALSO RECOMMENDED
### ▲ The Crown & Punchbowl

High Street, Horningsea, CB25 9JG
Tel no: (01223) 860643
www.thecrownandpunchbowl.co.uk
Gastropub

A seventeenth-century coaching inn ten minutes' drive from Cambridge, the Crown & Punchbowl offers menus to suit all occasions, amid the English country ambience of exposed beams and wooden floors. Look to the boards for fish, or sausage, sauce and mash variations; otherwise, the carte embraces game terrine with apple and fig compote (£7.95), confit duck leg with potato and orange rösti and Rioja jus (£14.95) and sticky toffee pudding with vanilla ice cream (£5.75). Wines from £13.50. Closed Sun D.

## Huntingdon

### Old Bridge Hotel

Crowd-pleasing modern menu
1 High Street, Huntingdon, PE29 3TQ
Tel no: (01480) 424300
www.huntsbridge.com
Modern British | £28
Cooking score: 3

There has been another change of chef since last year, and indications are that this well-regarded creeper-clad hotel could do with a period of stability. The kitchen fuses great British ingredients with Mediterranean components – potato gnocchi is garnished with Portland crab, lime and chilli, while free-range chicken appears with confit potatoes, leek fondue, Madeira and wild mushroom sauce – but results do not always match ambition. And while the formula of serving modern food in an informal manner is admirable, recent reports suggest that service is lacking. The wine list is the star of the show, priced to encourage adventurous drinking, and you can now buy bottles from the excellent in-house wine shop. House wine is £14.50.

**Chef/s:** Simon Cadge. **Open:** all week L 12 to 2, D 6.30 to 9.30. **Meals:** alc (main courses £13 to £25). Set L £15.50 (2 courses) to £18.95. **Service:** not inc. **Details:** Cards accepted. 80 seats. 30 seats outside. Air-con. Separate bar. No music. No mobile phones. Wheelchair access. Children allowed. Car parking.

## ▮ Keyston
## The Pheasant
**Foodie thatched pub**
Village Loop Road, Keyston, PE28 0RE
Tel no: (01832) 710241
www.thepheasant-keyston.co.uk
**Gastropub | £26**
**Cooking score: 2**

Formerly part of the Huntsbridge group, this ever-so-pretty thatched and beamed village pub now flourishes as an independent set-up, thanks to chef/patron Jay Scrimshaw and his lady, Taffeta. The concise menu changes daily, there's much emphasis on named suppliers and plenty to tempt – perhaps grilled calf's heart salad with pickled walnuts or a slab of roast brill with gnocchi, fennel and smoked salmon sauce. Otherwise, check out the 'favourites' (sausage and mash with mustard sauce, say), before finding room for chocolate marquise with orange jelly and aniseed ice cream. Huntsbridge supremo John Hoskins MW acts as consultant on the wine list – a gold-standard selection of high-class modern names, with a dozen appetising house selections from £15.50 (£4 a glass).

**Chef/s:** Jay Scrimshaw. **Open:** all week L 12 to 2.30 (3 Sun), Mon to Sat D 6.30 to 9.30. **Meals:** alc (main courses £10 to £20). Set L £16.50. Set D £18.50. Sun L £19.50. **Service:** not inc. **Details:** Cards accepted. 96 seats. 40 seats outside. Separate bar. Wheelchair access. Music. Children allowed. Car parking.

## ▮ Little Shelford
## Sycamore House
**Simple yet imaginative**
1 Church Street, Little Shelford, CB22 5HG
Tel no: (01223) 843396
**Modern British | £27**
**Cooking score: 2**

When we talk about restaurants being 'homely', we don't often mean it as literally as here. This place is the ground floor of the Sharpes' house, itself a conversion of a 300-year-old pub in a quiet village not far out of Cambridge. The drill is dinner on four nights a week, with menus of four courses, a simple salad intervening after the first. Good soups include celeriac and Parmesan, or you might start with smoked salmon mousse before going on to the main business, perhaps grilled plaice sauced with vermouth, lime and capers, or slow-cooked Scotch beef with shallots and paprika. Finish with chocolate nemesis or a light apricot sorbet doused in apricot liqueur. Wines zip briskly about the principal producing countries, with house French at £14.

**Chef/s:** Michael Sharpe. **Open:** Wed to Sat D 7.30 to 9. **Closed:** Sun, Mon, Tue, Christmas to New Year. **Meals:** Set D £26.50 (3 courses). **Service:** not inc. **Details:** Cards accepted. 24 seats. No music. No mobile phones. Car parking.

## ▮ Little Wilbraham
## The Hole in the Wall
**Accomplished seasonal cooking**
2 High Street, Little Wilbraham, CB21 5JY
Tel no: (01223) 812282
www.the-holeinthewall.com
**Gastropub | £28**
**Cooking score: 4**

Midway between Cambridge and Newmarket, this heavily timbered sixteenth-century inn makes a highly appealing showcase for Christopher and Jennifer Leeton's friendly approach. Its name comes from the opening where local farm workers once collected their beer after a day's hard graft. In partnership with experienced restaurateur Stephen Bull, a carefully sourced menu has been put together, and the cooking shows real flair. Start, perhaps, with a homemade game sausage, grilled and teamed with pickled red cabbage, apple purée and redcurrant jus, before considering a simple fish dish such as lemon sole served with purple sprouting broccoli, crushed new potatoes and a brown shrimp hollandaise, or the local lamb that is braised for eight hours and accompanied by turnips, lemon thyme mash, creamed carrots and mint jelly. Rhubarb fool with orange and ginger and a passion fruit sorbet is typical of the vibrantly flavoured desserts. Southern French varietals, a Colombard and a Cabernet at £14.50, head up a concise, usefully annotated wine list.

**Chef/s:** Christopher Leeton. **Open:** Tue to Sun L 12 to 2, Tue to Sat D 7 to 9. **Closed:** Mon, 2 weeks Jan, 2 weeks Oct. **Meals:** alc (main courses £11 to £17). Sun L £17.50 (2 courses) to £21. **Service:** not inc. **Details:** Cards accepted. 60 seats. 20 seats outside. Wheelchair access. Children allowed. Car parking.

## ▌Littleport

## ALSO RECOMMENDED
## ▲ Fen House
2 Lynn Road, Littleport, CB6 1QG
Tel no: (01353) 860645
**Anglo-French**

David Warne's beguiling cottage in the Fens is only open two evenings a week – although it's admirably flexible when it comes to hours. The kitchen takes inspiration from across the Channel for dinner menus with a reassuring tone (£36.75 for three courses, plus complimentary cheese). Creamy leek and pine nut risotto topped with grilled goats' cheese could lead on to roast saddle of lamb with celeriac and hazelnut purée, while desserts might promise fennel-scented pannacotta with ruby orange. Eclectic wines from £15. Open Fri and Sat D only.

## ▌Sutton

## The Anchor Inn
**Remote Fenland treasure**
Sutton Gault, Sutton, CB6 2BD
Tel no: (01353) 778537
www.anchorsuttongault.co.uk
**Gastropub | £27**
**Cooking score: 2**

£5 OFF   🛏   £30

In bleak Fen flatlands by the Hundred Foot Drain, the remote Anchor Inn continues to seduce visitors with its infectiously cosy atmosphere, flickering lamps and blazing fires. Menus follow the calendar and the cooking scores with its simplicity and painless prices. Grilled dates wrapped in bacon with mustard sauce has been on the menu since the beginning, but it's now joined by slow-roast Somersham pork belly on juniper-spiced greens and sea bass with almond pesto. As for desserts, consider pear tarte Tatin with cardamom mascarpone. Nothing seems too much trouble here: 'when we couldn't find a taxi, the owner offered us a lift home', observed one couple. House wine is £13.80.

**Chef/s:** Adam Pickup and William Mumford. **Open:** all week L 12 to 2, D 7 to 9, (6.30 to 9.30 Sat, 6.30 to 8.30 Sun). **Meals:** Set L £12 (2 courses) to £16. **Service:** not inc. **Details:** Cards accepted. 60 seats. 36 seats outside. No music. No mobile phones. Wheelchair access. Children allowed. Car parking.

### Symbols

🛏 Accommodation is available

£30 Three courses for less than £30

V More than three vegetarian main courses

£5 OFF £5-off voucher scheme

🍾 Notable wine list

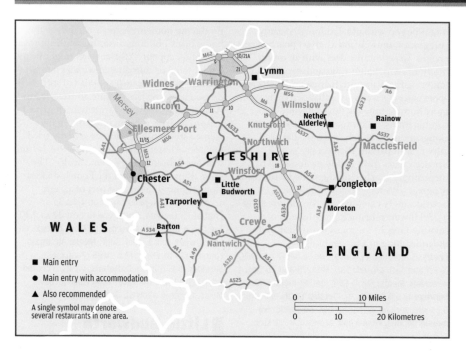

Main entry

Main entry with accommodation

Also recommended

A single symbol may denote several restaurants in one area.

0      10 Miles

0      10      20 Kilometres

## Barton

### ALSO RECOMMENDED
### ▲ Cock O Barton

Barton Road, Barton, SY14 7HU
Tel no: (01829) 782277
www.thecockobarton.co.uk
**Gastropub**

The setting is a sixteenth-century coaching inn, and while many original features have been retained – especially beams and standing timbers – it looks tastefully contemporary inside, with a menu to match. Chef Robert Kisby has moved on to Cabbage Hall (see entry), so expect fish and chips (£13.75), grilled Barnsley chop (£15.95) and steaks with all the trimmings from the new team, alongside grilled baby turbot and Thai-style sea bass. House wine is £13.75. Closed Sun D and Mon. Reports please.

## Chester

### Simon Radley at the Chester Grosvenor

**Formal but fun, with great details**
Eastgate, Chester, CH1 1LT
Tel no: (01244) 324024
www.chestergrosvenor.com
**Modern European | £65**
**Cooking score: 7**

In the newly refurbished dining room that now bears his name, Simon Radley is at his inventive and playful best. The revamped room is still suitably formal, and eating here is still an occasion – but thanks to new, sinkably soft chairs, it's a far more comfortable one. Readers rate the details that bookend a meal: well-loved bread and cheese trolleys, 'fab' canapés such as crispy fried whitebait with fennel mayonnaise, and 'fine' petits fours. What goes between isn't bad, either. Listed with typical brevity as 'spices', one starter might be cod with old-fashioned, creamy curry sauce, mussels and a perfect poached egg raviolo. To follow, roe deer with an onion 'study' of crisp shallot rings and an onion Tatin might share a plate with Ibérico pork belly and apple sauce. Desserts are a chance to play with more humble but well-loved flavour combinations. A 'compression' of banana is alongside an accurately Snickers-like iced salty peanut parfait. Readers say 'wow'. Service ranges from slickly professional to surprisingly gauche, but the skilled wine team is a great advantage to anyone lost in a bewilderingly extensive list. Bottles are from £25. However, being in the presence of (mainly French) greatness is justification for the unleashing of a bigger budget.

**Chef/s:** Simon Radley. **Open:** Tue to Sat D 7 to 9.30 (6 Fri and Sat). **Closed:** Sun, Mon, 25 and 26 Dec, 1 week Jan. **Meals:** Set D £69, Tasting menu £80. **Service:** 12.5% (optional). **Details:** Cards accepted. 45 seats. Air-con. Separate bar. No music. No mobile phones. Wheelchair access. Car parking.

## READERS RECOMMEND
### 1539 Restaurant & Bar
**Modern British**
The Racecourse, Chester, CH1 2LY
Tel no: (01244) 304611
www.restaurant1539.co.uk
'Quality restaurant with a wide appeal at Chester racecourse'

## ▌Congleton
### L'Endroit
**Warm and delicious – a lovely find**
70/72 Lawton Street, Congleton, CW12 1RS
Tel no: (01260) 299548
www.lendroit.co.uk
**French | £25**
**Cooking score: 3**
£5 OFF   V   £30

Behind cheerful yellow awnings, L'Endroit combines French cooking with northern hospitality to happy effect. Jars of honey from the owners' bees are displayed amid a warm colour scheme, and the penchant for

producing homemade treats extends to the house black pudding. Beaming with approval for a good appetite, efficient staff might bring fennel soup, or crab dressed with a grassy herb cream. The details, such as a salad of soft, well-dressed leaves on the side, are all attended to. Readers praise the good treatment of game in season: perhaps venison in a dark, orange-scented stew with no-nonsense herby fried potatoes. Desserts include a tart of the day and shallow, delicately eggy crème brûlée. The wine list is serious, with the French stickies alone running to the best part of a page; accessible house prices start at £12.25.

**Chef/s:** Eli Leconte. **Open:** Tue to Fri L 12 to 2.30, Tue to Sat D 6 to 10. **Closed:** Sun, Mon, 2 weeks end Feb, 1 week Jun, 1 week Sept. **Meals:** alc (main courses £12 to £18). Set L £9.95 (2 courses). **Service:** 10% (optional). **Details:** Cards accepted. 34 seats. 12 seats outside. Wheelchair access. Music. Children allowed. Car parking.

## ▌Little Budworth
**NEW ENTRY**
### Cabbage Hall
**Smart dining pub with French fancies**
Forest Road, Little Budworth, CW6 9ES
Tel no: (01829) 760292
www.cabbagehallrestaurant.com
**Modern British | £30**
**Cooking score: 3**
£5 OFF

A country spot that's decidedly un-rustic, Cabbage Hall could be any smart dining pub in any corner of the country. Chef/patron Robert Kisby's menu is very much Cheshire by way of France, however, offering a combination of regional food platters, Gallic fancies and the odd international influence. Start, perhaps, with gratin Normande, a silky cream of onion soup with Cheshire cider, or the signature lobster, saffron and leek risotto with a potent Cognac sauce. Plain pub dishes such as fish and chips don't fare as well as restauranty mains such as veal suédoise, with more booze and cream in a smooth sherry mushroom sauce. Dessert might be chocolate marquise with a mango and ginger compote, or an excellent crème brûlée studded with raspberries. A reasonably international wine list opens at £14.95 (£3.95 a glass). **Chef/s:** Robert Kisby. **Open:** all week 12 to 10 (8 Sun). **Closed:** first 2 weeks Jan. **Meals:** alc (main courses £16 to £22). Set L and D £14.95. Sun L £17.95 to £26 (2 courses). Platter and dessert Sun L £35 (for 2). **Service:** not inc. **Details:** Cards accepted. 70 seats. 40 seats outside. Separate bar. No mobile phones. Wheelchair access. Music. Children allowed. Car parking.

## ▌Lymm

NEW ENTRY

## The Church Green

**Restaurant food in a country pub**
Higher Lane, Lymm, WA13 0AP
**Tel no: (01925) 752068**
**www.thechurchgreen.co.uk**
**Modern British | £40**
**Cooking score: 4**

Having left The Grill at the Dorchester (see entry, London), Aiden Byrne has moved north to nudge a drinkers' pub in Lymm into culinary life. The transformation starts with the food, a procession of interesting ideas refined into purées and slicked onto slates. Except for Sundays, when the roast beef and fish and chips appear, this is not pub stuff. Start, perhaps, with roast venison loin with sweet beetroot and a fig purée, then maybe a labour-intensive breast of veal, slow-cooked and sealed to resemble a finer cut and served with apples and generous chunks of lobster claw. To finish, a pear and chocolate trifle is less artful brilliance, more something to bury a spoon in. Wine starts at £13.50, and the list is annotated to steer guests towards more offbeat choices. Like the conservatory dining room, it's a work in progress.
**Chef/s:** Aiden Byrne. **Open:** all week L 12 to 3 (6 Sun), Mon to Sat D 6 to 9.30 (10 Fri and Sat). **Meals:** alc (main courses £7 to £24). **Service:** not inc. **Details:** Cards accepted. 80 seats. 50 seats outside. Air-con. No mobile phones. Wheelchair access. Music. Children allowed. Car parking.

## ▌Moreton

## Pecks

**Seriously impressive stuff**
Newcastle Road, Moreton, CW12 4SB
**Tel no: (01260) 275161**
**www.pecksrest.co.uk**
**Modern British | £30**
**Cooking score: 3**
£5 OFF

With its Dinner At Eight concept – where all tables sit down to a seven-course menu in syncronicity and waiters go table-to-table displaying the dishes, Pecks certainly takes a novel approach to dining. Laudably, the concept simply adds to the sterling work done by Les Wassall's kitchen, and it's clear to see why, after 25 years, the restaurant is still popular. From an amuse-bouche shepherd's pie that condenses a field of flavours into a thimble-sized ramekin to the rum and raisin signature dessert, this is impressive stuff. Even the globe trotting menu (cauliflower soup sits next to Singapore laska) is handled deftly. The wine list sticks to safe choices, but customers can BYO with the added bonus of no corkage charge (Tue to Thur only).
**Chef/s:** Les Wassall. **Open:** Tue to Sun L 12 to 2 (3 Sun), Tue to Sat D at 8 (1 sitting). **Closed:** Mon, 25 to 31 Dec. **Meals:** Set L £16.25 (2 courses) to £18.25. Set D Tue and Wed £32.50 (5 courses), Thur and Fri £37.50 (7 courses), Sat £42.50 (7 courses). Sun L £18.25. **Service:** not inc. **Details:** Cards accepted. 110 seats. Air-con. Separate bar. Wheelchair access. Music. Children allowed. Car parking.

## Symbols

| | |
|---|---|
| 🛏 | Accommodation is available |
| £30 | Three courses for less than £30 |
| V | More than three vegetarian main courses |
| £5 OFF | £5-off voucher scheme |
| 🍷 | Notable wine list |

## Nether Alderley

### The Wizard
**A magical place**
Macclesfield Road, Nether Alderley, SK10 4UB
Tel no: (01625) 584000
www.ainscoughs.co.uk
**Modern British | £26**
**Cooking score: 2**

A sixteenth-century, whitewashed inn not far from Alderley Edge is home to one of Martin Ainscough's rapidly growing empire of northern restaurants. The dining room has beamed ceilings and bare wood tables, and the emphasis is on brasserie dishes cooked with style and precision. Beer-battered haddock, gammon with pineapple chutney, and Cumberland sausages with mash and onion gravy will please traditionalists, but there are also more contemporary dishes such as salmon on crushed new potatoes with goats' cheese and basil oil. Chocolate ice cream might bring down the curtain. Wine prices start at £11.50. **Chef/s:** Paul Beattie. **Open:** Tue to Sun L 12 to 2, Tue to Sat D 7 to 9.30. **Closed:** Mon, 6 Dec to 3 Jan. **Meals:** Set L and D £10 (2 courses). **Service:** 10% (optional). **Details:** Cards accepted. 80 seats. 20 seats outside. Wheelchair access. Music. Children allowed. Car parking.

## Rainow

### The Highwayman
**Worth seeking out**
Macclesfield Road, Rainow, SK10 5UU
Tel no: (01625) 573245
www.thehighwaymanrainow.co.uk
**Gastropub | £25**
**Cooking score: 3**

This rambling 350 year-old pub is situated high on the hills above Macclesfield commanding superb views over the Lancashire and Cheshire plains. With many dark, small rooms, 'mind your head' is a good warning. Even allowing for limited parking, this is a gastropub worth seeking out. Try a hearty mushroom soup with Marc Beeley's wonderful bread, while for a main course nothing could be better than homemade pork, chestnut, sage and tarragon sausages with Thwaites Original onion jus and pressed boulangère potato and herb beignet. Finish off with a trio of classic puddings: sticky toffee, red berries rice pudding, and bread-and-butter pudding. Wines from £12.50. **Chef/s:** Tim Finney. **Open:** Tue to Sun L 12 to 2.30 (9.30 Sat, 8 Sun), Tue to Fri D 6 to 9. **Meals:** alc (main courses £10 to £17). **Details:** Cards accepted. 48 seats. 20 seats outside. Separate bar. Music. Children allowed. Car parking.

## Tarporley

**NEW ENTRY**
### The Fox & Barrel
**Reinvigorated country pub**
Foxbank, Cotebrook, Tarporley, CW6 9DZ
Tel no: (01829) 760529
www.foxandbarrel.co.uk
**Gastropub | £25**
**Cooking score: 2**

A new regime and thorough refurbishment has popularised the Fox & Barrel among those who like minimal twee with their open fires and old beams. Space kept for impromptu diners and an order-at-the-bar system contribute to a laid-back atmosphere. The menu, which changes daily, seems designed for customers to eat and be pleased. Along with roasts, chilli and fishcakes, a few fancier dishes deliver bold flavours and pub-sized portions beginning, perhaps, with a twice-baked goats' cheese soufflé with a punchy caper and tomato salsa. Main courses, including sea bass with a mound of chorizo and crab linguine, continue the theme of international generosity. House wine is £13. **Chef/s:** Richard Cotterill and Stephane Tran-Trung. **Open:** all week 12 to 9.30 (9 Sun). **Closed:** D 25 Dec. **Meals:** alc (main courses £8 to £17). **Service:** not inc. **Details:** Cards accepted. 100 seats. 110 seats outside. Separate bar. No music. Wheelchair access. Children allowed. Car parking.

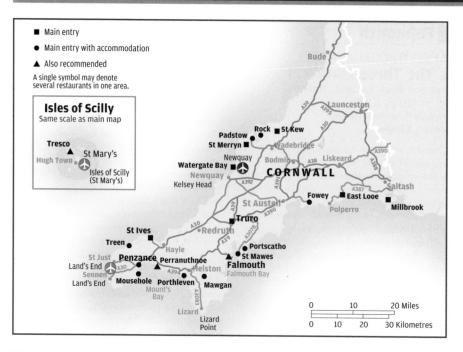

■ Main entry

● Main entry with accommodation

▲ Also recommended

A single symbol may denote
several restaurants in one area.

**Isles of Scilly**
Same scale as main map

# East Looe

## Trawlers on the Quay

**Sea-fresh fish**

The Quay, East Looe, PL13 1AH

Tel no: (01503) 263593

www.trawlersrestaurant.co.uk

**Seafood | £30**

**Cooking score: 3**

 **V**

On a part of the Cornish coast that looks not
unlike the Riviera on a good day, Trawlers
really makes the most of its surroundings.
Gloriously fresh seafood landed metres from
the kitchen door is celebrated on the menus –
and guests can often see the boats bringing in
the day's catch. It's all served with infectious
enthusiasm, in the shape of seafood gumbo,
spicy crab cakes with sweet chilli sauce, and
show-stopping main dishes such as whole
lemon sole with capers and cucumber, or a trio
of the day's haul sauced with beurre blanc. A
couple of meat dishes will cater for those who
aren't fish fans. Meals conclude with chocolate
nut brownie served with the local Treleaven's
vanilla ice cream, or bread-and-butter
pudding made with good Cornish dairy
produce and raisins soaked in rum. The short
wine list, which starts at £15, has a handful of
wines from Cornwall's successful Camel
Valley vineyard, including the renowned
sparkler.

**Chef/s:** Mark Napper. **Open:** Tue to Sat D 6 to 9.
**Closed:** Sun, Mon, 25 and 26 Dec. **Meals:** alc (main
courses £7 to £19). **Service:** not inc. **Details:** Cards
accepted. 40 seats. 12 seats outside. Separate bar.
Wheelchair access. Music. Children allowed.

## Please send us your feedback

To register your opinion about any
restaurant listed in the Guide, or a new
restaurant that you wish to bring to our
attention, please visit the web address at
the bottom of the page. Your feedback
informs the content of the book and will be
used to compile next year's reviews.

## ▌ Falmouth

### ALSO RECOMMENDED
### ▲ The Three Mackerel

Swanpool Beach, Falmouth, TR11 5BG
Tel no: (01326) 311886
www.thethreemackerel.com
**Modern European**

Casual flexibility is the deal at this jauntily decorated hangout, which comes complete with a seductive beachside terrace overlooking Falmouth Bay. The kitchen caters for young and old, changes its menu daily and makes exemplary use of local ingredients for food with a Mediterranean accent. Light lunches and tapas give way to evening menus with plenty of zing – witness fillets of mackerel with couscous and ratatouille (£7.95) and chicken breast wrapped in Parma ham with saffron risotto (£16.95). Also check out the catch of the day. House wine is £12.95. Open all week.

## ▌ Fowey

### Restaurant Nathan Outlaw

**Dazzling, fun food from a wizard**
Marina Villa Hotel, Esplanade, Fowey, PL23 1HY
Tel no: (01726) 833315
www.nathanoutlaw.com
**Modern British | £55**
**Cooking score: 8**

£5 OFF  🍴 ⇌ **V**

Currently king of the hill in the West Country, Nathan Outlaw goes about his business in the highly desirable Marina Villa Hotel – a boutique gem just a pebble's throw from the gorgeous Fowey Estuary. As expected, the views are pretty special (try to bag one of the sought-after window seats in the sleek dining room), although they are comfortably eclipsed by the dazzling food on offer. Cured salmon with marinated beetroot risotto, horseradish and dill ('amazing colour'), is a signature starter that travels with Nathan wherever he chooses to hang up his apron, and it embodies his precise, calendar-friendly style. Clarity, vigorous flavours and a voracious appetite for regional produce are the hallmarks here – although teasingly abrupt menu descriptions generally conceal more than they reveal. 'Squab pigeon – chocolate and spice – potato cake and figs' is an enticing prospect, likewise 'Pork belly – cuttlefish – fennel and clementine'. Every element of each dish impresses, whether it's the hazelnuts with beef rump and mushroom pearl barley or the mussels included in a dish of wreck fish, saffron, peppers and olives. This is scintillating, serious stuff, but it's also invested with a sense of fun – monkfish comes with rosemary dumplings and tomato ketchup, while cauliflower cheese and piccalilli could pop up as renegade gastropub companions for rose veal. Clever desserts such as peanut mousse with banana ice cream and espresso are also guaranteed to raise a cheeky smile, although it's back to the reassuring comfort zone for the likes of apple crumble with doughnut and ice cream. Elsewhere, don't miss the revelatory assortment of artisan British cheeses. This is a labour of love: your choice is brought to the table carefully arranged on a slate with appropriate chutneys, plus a mini menu listing each item according to its strength – 'a really personal touch'. The easy-going mood is reinforced by relaxed staff who strike just the right balance between formality and friendliness, and 'genuinely seem to love the food they are serving'. The wine list is a superior tome, helpfully categorised by style, with cherry-picked selections from across the winemaking world – and easy mark-ups to boot. Prices kick off at £20 (£7 a glass) and half-bottles abound. Nathan Outlaw recently reconnected with his old stamping ground on the north Cornish coast by opening a new restaurant in St Enodoc Hotel, Rock (see entry).
**Chef/s:** Nathan Outlaw. **Open:** Thur to Sat L 12 to 1.30, Tue to Sat D 7 to 8.30 (open Mon in season). **Closed:** Sun, 2 weeks Jan. **Meals:** alc (main courses £24 to £28). Set L £30 (2 courses) to £34.50. Tasting menu £80 (7 courses). **Service:** 10%. **Details:** Cards accepted. 36 seats. 20 seats outside. Separate bar. No mobile phones. Music.

## Sam's

**North American**
20 Fore Street, Fowey, PL23 1AQ
Tel no: (01726) 832273
www.samsfowey.co.uk
'Great burger bar – it's all about the atmosphere'

## ▍Helston

## The Nansloe Restaurant

**Modern British**
Nanslow Manor, Meneage Road, Helston, TR13 0SB
Tel no: (01326) 558400
www.nansloe-manor.co.uk
'Helston would be a poorer place without this restaurant'

## ▍Launceston

## La Bouche Creole

**Modern Creole**
Dockacre Road, Launceston, PL15 8YY
Tel no: (01566) 779294
www.labouchecreole.co.uk
'Creole cooking from Louisiana-born chef'

## ▍Mawgan

## New Yard Restaurant

**A kitchen feeding off its location**
Trelowarren Estate, Mawgan, TR12 6AF
Tel no: (01326) 221595
www.trelowarren.com
**Modern British | £30**
**New chef**
£5 OFF 🛏

Set in one of the county's oldest privately owned estates, the New Yard capitalises brilliantly on its location with the kitchen able to source 90 per cent of what it uses from within a 15-mile radius. A real fire radiates comfort if the weather goes all Cornish on

you, and the menus have much to catch the eye. We learnt of the departure of Greg Laskey too late to send an inspector or receive any feedback. Olly Jackson in now in charge. It seems the lively emphasis on local produce will remain, in the form of pheasant from the estate, Falmouth Bay crab, local asparagus and a Cornish only cheeseboard. Wines start at £15.50.
**Chef/s:** Olly Jackson. **Open:** all week L 12 to 2 (2.30 Sun), Mon to Sat D 7 to 9.30. **Closed:** Mon from mid Sept to Whitsun. **Meals:** alc (main courses £13 to £17). Set L £15.95. Set D £23.50 (3 courses). Sun L £16.95. **Service:** not inc. **Details:** Cards accepted. 50 seats. 20 seats outside. Wheelchair access. Music. Children allowed. Car parking.

## ▍Millbrook

**NEW ENTRY**
## The View

**Local food in a stunning cliff setting**
Treninnow Cliff Road, Millbrook, PL10 1JY
Tel no: (01752) 822345
www.theview-restaurant.co.uk
**British | £28**
**Cooking score: 2**
£5 OFF £30 🛏

Set into the cliff, up high where the paragliders soar, this timber-clad restaurant offers a spectacular view of Whitsand Bay. Hours can be spent on the terrace in summer and it's easy to imagine feeling weather-beaten but cosy inside during the winter months. The daily changing menu focuses on local produce, with nearly all the fresh seafood caught in Looe Harbour. At inspection, dabs and razor clams with lemon and garlic butter shone, as did roast turbot teamed with Cornish crab and roast shallot. Make the most of desserts including hot dark chocolate mousse with crème fraîche or rhubarb and gingerbread crumble before making the trek to the beach below. House wine from £13.95.
**Chef/s:** Matt Corner. **Open:** Wed to Sun L 12 to 2 (and bank hol Mon), D 7 to 9. **Closed:** Mon, Tue, Feb. **Meals:** alc (main courses £10 to £18). **Service:** not inc. **Details:** Cards accepted. 40 seats. 24 seats outside. Music. Children allowed. Car parking.

## █ Mousehole

### 2 Fore Street

**An honest bistro with harbour views**
2 Fore Street, Mousehole, TR19 6PF
Tel no: (01736) 731164
www.2forestreet.co.uk
**Modern British | £26**
**Cooking score: 2**

🛏 🍴£30

The double-fronted restaurant sits close to the harbourside, where the uplifting views stretch across Mounts Bay all the way to the Lizard on clear days. At the back there is a secluded garden area for eating. Joe Wardell's passion for fish together with the warm service make this a powerfully attractive place, and there's a touch of grandeur in dishes such as whole wild sea bass in fennel and ginger, or a plentiful fish stew with tomato, saffron and chilli. Start with local sardines with rosemary and garlic or crab florentine, and round things off with one of the homely puddings such as plum and almond crumble with vanilla ice cream. Wines start at £13.75.
**Chef/s:** Joe Wardell. **Open:** all week L 12 to 2.30, D 6 to 9.30. **Closed:** 4 Jan to 10 Feb. **Meals:** alc (main courses £13 to £17). **Service:** not inc. **Details:** Cards accepted. 36 seats. 20 seats outside. Wheelchair access. Music. Children allowed.

## █ Padstow

### Custard

**Divine diner**
1st Floor, 1a The Strand, Padstow, PL28 8BS
Tel no: (0870) 1700740
www.custarddiner.com
**Modern British | £25**
**Cooking score: 2**

£5 OFF 🍴£30

On the first floor of a historic building in the heart of Padstow, Custard fulfils its function as a contemporary eating house (polished wood floorboards and tables) with a quirky, eclectic feel (chandeliers, a Wurlitzer jukebox). The menu caters for all-comers, opening with breakfast and moving on to lunch of Welsh rarebit, griddled ham and fried eggs or smoked haddock and prawn fish pie. At dinner a grander touch brings on crab rarebit with celery and fennel 'ketchup', and main courses such as spiced pork belly, greens, pickled apple and crackling. There's a great deal of comfort among desserts, which have delivered baked egg custard and lemon posset. Service is particularly welcoming to families, and the fairly priced, global wine list starts at £17.50.
**Chef/s:** Daniel Gedge. **Open:** Wed to Mon L 12 to 2.30, D 7 to 9.30. **Closed:** Tue (except summer), 25 and 26 Dec, 1 May, 2 weeks Nov. **Meals:** alc (main courses £11 to £14). Sun L £15.50. **Service:** not inc. **Details:** Cards accepted. 65 seats. Air-con. Music. Children allowed.

### Paul Ainsworth at No. 6

**Affordable, accomplished food**
6 Middle Street, Padstow, PL28 8AP
Tel no: (01841) 532093
www.number6inpadstow.co.uk
**Modern British | £30**
**Cooking score: 6**

£5 OFF 🍷

Paul Ainsworth now owns the restaurant in which he has cooked for four years. He's changed the style of operation by simplifying the menu, making the carte more affordable and introducing 'bargain lunches'. A 'big improvement' appears to be the consensus. The restaurant (especially service) and the consistency of the cooking needs to settle down a little, but you can eat dishes of a very high standard at prices that won't break the bank. There is superb bread – four different flavoured rolls – and starters of scallops with maple-glazed chicken wings and a 'swipe of celeriac' or mussels with pearl barley in a vegetable broth. Fine main course dishes have included pork belly with a 'beautifully made' black pudding sausage roll, apple compote and crackling, served, at one meal, with a copper pot of purple sprouting broccoli on the side; mackerel atop a broth of cockles, chorizo and chickpeas has also impressed. The sweets – more erratic – are fashionable: slices of Alphonse mango with pistachio ice cream and

madeleines, and chocolate moelleux with peanut butter ice cream. The confident wine list promises plenty of scope for experimentation, whatever your budget. Fine South Africans and Kiwis hold their own alongside the great and good from France. Ten house recommendations begin with vin de pays d'Oc at £14 (£3.75 a glass).
**Chef/s:** Paul Ainsworth and John Walton. **Open:** Tue to Sat L 12 to 2.30, D 6 to 10. **Closed:** Sun (except L in summer), Mon, 19 to 26 Dec, 4 to 25 Jan. **Meals:** alc (main courses £13 to £20). Set L £10 (2 courses) to £13.50. **Service:** not inc. **Details:** Cards accepted. 42 seats. No mobile phones. Wheelchair access. Music. Children allowed.

## Rick Stein's Café

**No-nonsense, cheerful fishy eatery**
10 Middle Street, Padstow, PL28 8AP
Tel no: (01841) 532700
www.rickstein.com
**Seafood**
**Cooking score: 2**

The Café in the centre of Steintown aims to be just that, a no-nonsense, cheerfully bustling venue with tables packed cheek-by-jowl, informal service and a menu that runs from breakfast to dinner. Fish is the abiding theme, with mussels in chilli, tomato and parsley to start, followed by sea bass with Pernod and fennel mayonnaise. A light seasoning of Asian themes brings on Vietnamese pho soup with prawns and rice noodles, or lamb and spinach karahi for main. Finish with lemon tart and clotted cream. The short wine list opens at £15 for a South African rosé.
**Chef/s:** David Sharland and Ross Geach. **Open:** all week L 12 to 3, D 6.30 to 9.30. **Closed:** 25 and 26 Dec, 1 May. **Meals:** alc (main courses £10 to £17). Set D £21.50. **Service:** not inc. **Details:** Cards accepted. 36 seats. 10 seats outside. Music. Children allowed.

## St Petroc's Bistro

**Long-standing fixture of the Rick Stein empire**
New Street, Padstow, PL28 8EL
Tel no: (01841) 532700
www.rickstein.com
**European | £32**
**Cooking score: 2**

Colourful modern art, bare tables and a courtyard and garden for summer days set the tone in another of Rick Stein's Padstow eateries, this one named after the sixth-century Celtic saint. A menu of classic and modern bistro dishes takes in devilled kidneys with wild mushrooms, grilled red mullet with sauce vierge, and mains such as Parisian-style bavette steak with bordelaise sauce and a cheese salad. Padstow's marine bounty is always on hand, perhaps in the form of a whole grilled lemon sole with brown shrimps and mushrooms. Simple desserts include Paris Brest and passion fruit pavlova. The short wine list opens at £16.50 (£4.25 a glass), and includes the celebrated sparkling wines of Cornwall's Camel Valley vineyard.
**Chef/s:** Paul Harwood and David Sharland. **Open:** all week L 12 to 2, D 6.30 to 9.30. **Closed:** 25 and 26 Dec, 1 May. **Meals:** alc (main courses £12 to £20). Set L £17.50. **Service:** not inc. **Details:** Cards accepted. 75 seats. 20 seats outside. Separate bar. Wheelchair access. Music. Children allowed.

## The Seafood Restaurant

**Rick Stein's seafood show**
Riverside, Padstow, PL28 8BY
Tel no: (01841) 532700
www.rickstein.com
**Seafood | £55**
**Cooking score: 4**

Flagship and nerve-centre of the Rick Stein phenomenon ('empire' is too small a word), the Seafood Restaurant is a large, cheerfully bustling, sometimes slightly chaotic space. There's a dramatic seafood bar in the centre, where you can see the brigade assembling the famous platters, and the extensive menu

specialises in what's been landed in the immediate vicinity. However, one or two items have made a longer journey – langoustines from western Scotland, say. Many dishes are the kind of unmuddled preparations people love, as in fish soup with rouille and turbot with hollandaise. More involved offerings often meet with quizzical responses, though they deepen the repertoire (as in Indonesian seafood curry with monkfish, squid and prawns). But reports of offhand, rushed or sloppy service do seem to tarnish the experience uncomfortably often. An expansive, expensive wine list (from £17) of impeccable quality has good names in every corner of the globe to which it ventures; choice by the glass, from £4.25, is wide.
**Chef/s:** Stephane Delourme and David Sharland. **Open:** all week L 12 to 2.30, D 7 to 10 (6.30 Fri to Sun). **Closed:** 25 and 26 Dec, 1 May. **Meals:** alc (main courses £18 to £44). Set L £28.50. Tasting menu £65 (6 courses). **Service:** not inc. **Details:** Cards accepted. 120 seats. Air-con. Separate bar. No music. Wheelchair access.

## ▌ Penzance

## The Bay
**A breath of fresh sea air**
Hotel Penzance, Britons Hill, Penzance, TR18 3AE
Tel no: (01736) 366890
www.bay-penzance.co.uk
**Modern British | £29**
**Cooking score: 3**
£5 OFF ╤ V £30

Not only is The Bay a working gallery which exhibits the work of local artists, it also has a fine dining area, which on clement days opens out on to a decked terrace with seductive views of Mounts Bay, and over the rooftops towards Penzance harbour. Not surprisingly in this setting, fish and seafood feature strongly, with a gamut that ranges from a starter salad of skate and smoked salmon with pickled cucumber and capers, to mains such as baked pollack with fennel purée in an orange and cardamom reduction, or the show-stopping whole grilled lobster served thermidor or with herb and garlic butter.

There's a nice sense of inventiveness running through the menus too, which might result in roast wood pigeon with fine beans, Parma ham, black pudding and a creamy sauce of ceps. Finish with almond pudding and saffron ice cream or Cornish cheeses. Wines start at £14.75 (£4 a glass).
**Chef/s:** Ben Reeve. **Open:** Mon to Fri and Sun L 12 to 2, all week D 6 to 9.30. **Meals:** Set L £11.50 (2 courses) to £15. Set D £23 (2 courses) to £28.50. Sun L £15. **Service:** not inc. **Details:** Cards accepted. 40 seats. 10 seats outside. Air-con. Separate bar. No mobile phones. Wheelchair access. Music. Children allowed. Car parking.

## Harris's
**Risk-free local favourite**
46 New Street, Penzance, TR18 2LZ
Tel no: (01736) 364408
www.harrissrestaurant.co.uk
**Modern European | £33**
**Cooking score: 2**
£5 OFF

Aim for the Humphrey Davy statue in the centre of Penzance if you're trying to find this cosy pink-hued restaurant which is tucked away down a cobbled side street. Roger and Anne Harris have been serving the town for more than 35 years, and are well aware that their loyal customers come here for risk-free, old-wave dishes based on supplies of Cornish produce. Seafood always shows up well on the daily menu, with anything from roast monkfish with wild mushroom risotto to grilled Dover sole with chive butter on offer. Other possibilities might include venison with beetroot and glazed pear. Desserts keep it simple with treacle tart or summer pudding. House wine is £14.95.
**Chef/s:** Roger Harris. **Open:** Tue to Sat L 12 to 2, Mon to Sat D 7 to 9.30. **Closed:** Sun, 25 and 26 Dec, 3 weeks winter. **Meals:** alc (main courses £11 to £26). **Service:** 10% (optional). **Details:** Cards accepted. 40 seats. Separate bar. No mobile phones. Music. Children allowed.

# Perranuthnoe

## ALSO RECOMMENDED
## ▲ Victoria Inn
Perranuthnoe, TR20 9NP
Tel no: (01736) 710309
www.victoriainn-penzance.co.uk
**Gastropub**

Just up from the beach and coast path, Stewart and Anna Eddy's striking pink-washed village inn beckons with Sharp's Doom Bar on tap and some cracking pub food prepared from local seasonal ingredients. The typically Cornish, stone-walled bar is the setting for seafood and shellfish potage (£6.95), ribeye steak with real chips (£14.95), St Buryan pork belly with chorizo and haricot bean stew, black pudding and rosemary sauce, and rhubarb and ginger crumble (£5). House wine £11.50. Closed Sun D.

# Porthleven

## Kota
**Exciting fusion pizzazz**
Harbour Head, Porthleven, TR13 9JA
Tel no: (01326) 562407
www.kotarestaurant.co.uk
**Fusion | £27**
**Cooking score: 2**

Chef/co-owner Jude Kereama has Maori blood in his veins and has brought some exciting fusion pizzazz to this 300-year-old cornmill by Porthleven harbour. Far Eastern influences collide with flavours from elsewhere, and local fish naturally plays a starring role ('kota' is the Maori word for seafood). Falmouth Bay oysters could appear in tempura batter with wasabi tartare sauce, grilled lemon sole comes with soy and ginger dressing, and wild sea bass is partnered by crab raviolo and sauce vierge. Elsewhere, duck is given the full Asian treatment, and pheasant pie is served with braised cavolo nero. Desserts stay in more familiar territory for the likes of poached pear with chocolate pannacotta. House wine is £12.95.

**Chef/s:** Jude Kereama. **Open:** Fri and Sat L 12 to 2, Mon to Sat D 5.30 to 9 (9.30 Fri and Sat). Open Sun on bank hol weekends and Mothering Sun. **Closed:** Sun, Mon and Tue in low season, 1 Jan to first week Feb. **Meals:** alc (main courses £12 to £19). **Service:** not inc. **Details:** Cards accepted. 38 seats. Separate bar. No mobile phones. Wheelchair access. Music. Children allowed.

# Portscatho

## Driftwood
**Seascapes and seasonal food**
Rosevine, Portscatho, TR2 5EW
Tel no: (01872) 580644
www.driftwoodhotel.co.uk
**Modern European | £40**
**Cooking score: 5**

Perched high above the sea with a panoramic view over the water, the setting is beautiful. Inside, a colour scheme of muted neutrals sets a simple tone, and the huge expanse of glass in the dining room makes the most of the light and the view. Chris Eden's ambitions are high, and they are generally met. One summer visitor was pleased by a 'very light, well put together dish' of scallops with black pudding purée and cider apple and sweetcorn and saluted the 'excellent flavours' of chicken with sage, apricot and wild mushroom consommé, but felt an amuse-bouche of a shot glass of pomegranate and grappa jelly with lemon foam would have worked better as a pre-dessert. Others have commented on 'well-designed dishes' that are 'packed with interest in finely judged portions' – perhaps loin of venison with red cabbage, pear mostarda, pumpkin and purple sprouting broccoli or red mullet served with squid bolognese, spaghetti, onion purée and baby artichokes. Summertime desserts include assiette of strawberries – cheesecake, soufflé and sorbet. Service is on the ball and house wine is £16.
**Chef/s:** Chris Eden. **Open:** all week D only 7 to 9. **Closed:** Mid Dec to early Feb. **Meals:** Set D £40. Tasting menu £55. **Service:** not inc. **Details:** Cards accepted. 34 seats. Separate bar. No mobile phones. Music. Car parking.

# Rock

**NEW ENTRY**

## Nathan Outlaw Seafood & Grill

**A new string for the Outlaw's bow**
St Enodoc Hotel, Rock Road, Rock, PL27 6LA
Tel no: (01208) 863394
www.nathan-outlaw.com
British | £28
Cooking score: 4

£5 OFF | £30

Nathan Outlaw has already set a cracking pace at his restaurant in the Marina Villa Hotel in Fowey (see entry), and he's scarcely missed a beat in opening this seafood and grill in the St Enodoc Hotel, if early reports are anything to go by. The hotel is set back from the waterfront in Rock and there are great estuary and countryside views to be had from the uncluttered, two-tiered dining room and terrace. Peter Biggs heads up the kitchen, enthusiastically hauling in local produce and sending it out with the minimum of fuss, the style evident in bowls of mussels, 'really fresh' sardines with romesco sauce and thyme bread and an 'outstanding' fish pie. The sourcing of meat is top-drawer too – ribeye with hand cut chips was pronounced 'just perfect' by one reporter – while desserts maintain the momentum with a dazzling elderflower cream and raspberries. Service is attentive, house wine £15.
**Chef/s:** Peter Biggs. **Open:** all week L 12 to 2, D 6 to 9.30. **Closed:** Dec and Jan. **Meals:** alc (main courses £12 to £16). **Service:** not inc. **Details:** Cards accepted. 40 seats. 30 seats outside. Separate bar. No mobile phones. Wheelchair access. Music. Children allowed. Car parking.

# St Agnes

**READERS RECOMMEND**

## Turk's Head

**Gastropub**
St Agnes, TR22 0PL
Tel no: (01720) 422434
'Excellent, traditional British grub'

### Great-value drinking

Wine can double a restaurant bill, so pick your way economically through the list.

Nobody expects to be done any favours on price in France, but vins de pays can represent fair value – try the Languedoc ('Vin de Pays d'Oc') and regions such as the Loire.

South America remains a source of outstanding value, with Chile and Argentina producing big, complex reds and vibrantly fruity whites at realistic prices.

South Africa's wines have come on in leaps and bounds, with tangy Sauvignons, creamy Chardonnays and richly concentrated Merlots and Cabernet Sauvignons.

Drinking by the glass can be less costly, but watch out – ferocious mark-ups can quickly add up to a bottle of house wine. Carafes have made a comeback so try a 50cl jug of something perfectly drinkable.

Champagne is likely to be pricey. Italy's Prosecco has edged out Spanish Cava as the thriftiest alternative. Both are drier and more grown-up in flavour than they used to be – but Cava is achieving astonishing results now.

If a restaurant has no licence (or even if it does), you may be welcome to BYO, but check the corkage charge isn't extortionate.

# St Ives

## Alba

**Mediterranean zing by the harbour**
Old Lifeboat House, Wharf Road, St Ives, TR26 1LF
Tel no: (01736) 797222
www.thealbarestaurant.com
**Modern European | £27**
Cooking score: 3

 £5 OFF **V** £30

Since 2002, the lifeboat house on St Ives wharf has been doing duty as a contemporary restaurant spread over two floors, with prized window seats looking out onto the harbour. Inside, your eye might also be distracted by the displays of modern art and the chefs at work in the ground-floor kitchen, which is just as well as some have found the tables to be a 'little too small and close together'. Mediterranean influences add some zing to a menu that always features a generous helping of Cornish produce – especially fish. Crab pancakes with deep-fried sea lettuce might precede smoked haddock fishcakes with winter horseradish coleslaw, or pork and fennel meatballs with tagliatelle and fennel sauce. The wide-ranging wine list offers plenty of possibilities from £12.95.
**Chef/s:** Grant Nethercott. **Open:** all week L 12 to 2, D 5 to 10 (6 to 9.30 Oct to May). **Closed:** 25 and 26 Dec. **Meals:** alc (main courses £12 to £19). Set L and D £13.50 (2 courses) to £16.50. **Service:** not inc. **Details:** Cards accepted. 60 seats. Air-con. Wheelchair access. Music. Children allowed.

## Blas Burgerworks

**Feel-good organic burger bar**
The Warren, St Ives, TR26 2EA
Tel no: (01736) 797272
www.blasburgerworks.co.uk
**Burgers | £15**
Cooking score: 1

 £5 OFF **V** £30

There's a cheerful, feel-good atmosphere in this alternative backstreet burger bar, fuelled by the sheer enthusiasm for what the owners do. With just four communal tables (made from reclaimed wood) you may have to wait for a seat, and it's best to check opening times in winter, but readers are full of praise for burgers made from 100% organic Cornish beef and free-range chicken. There's chargrilled fish from sustainable stocks, too, and locally made ice cream to finish. House wine is £13.50.
**Chef/s:** Sally Cuckson, Marie Dixon and Sarah Newark. **Open:** Tue to Sun D 6 to 10 (Mon in summer). **Closed:** Mid Nov to mid Dec and early Feb. **Meals:** alc (main courses £8 to £10). **Service:** not inc. **Details:** Cards accepted. Wheelchair access. Music. Children allowed.

## Porthminster Beach Café

**Racy flavours and awesome views**
Porthminster Beach, St Ives, TR26 2EB
Tel no: (01736) 795352
www.porthminstercafe.co.uk
**Seafood | £30**
Cooking score: 4

 **V**

'Well worth the 700-mile round trip from Cheshire', claimed one fan whose regular sojourns to Cornwall wouldn't be the same without a visit to this stark-white, energetic beachside venue. There's certainly no arguing with the fabulous location beneath the slopes of Porthminster Point or the ozone-fuelled views out across St Ives Bay. Aussie chef Mick Smith and his team deliver 'inventive and enticing' food with shots of fusion and racy flavours that could have been lifted from big-city hot spots Down Under. Local seafood is the main event: grilled oysters are served with chorizo and wasabi mayo, crispy squid appears dramatically with citrus white miso, black spices, coriander and chilli salad, and monkfish turns up in a curry with langoustines and mussels. Meat dishes also tantalise – perhaps sticky pork salad with pickled cucumber – and desserts step up with a tamarillo tasting plate or caramel bananas with cinnamon meringues and pistachio ice cream. 'Expertly selected' global wines from £12.75. The same team also runs the seasonal Porthgwidden Beach Café.

Chef/s: Mick Smith and Zac Anderson. **Open:** all week L 12 to 3.30, D 6 to 9.30. **Closed:** 25 Dec. **Meals:** alc (main courses £13 to £20). **Service:** not inc. **Details:** Cards accepted. 57 seats. 70 seats outside. No mobile phones. Music. Children allowed.

## St Andrews Street Bistro

**Funky, fun bistro**
16 St Andrews Street, St Ives, TR26 1AH
Tel no: (01736) 797074
**Modern European | £18**
**Cooking score: 2**

'What a find', enthused one reporter of this chintzy, eclectically decorated restaurant down a narrow street behind the harbour. It's all very relaxed and casual, with board games available in comfy chairs by the bar and 'funky music' and 'mad art' fitting the seaside surfing mood exactly. The kitchen reads from an international script, with the likes of Jamaican goat curry or 'properly cooked' polenta-crusted plaice fillets served with curry lentils and a refreshing tomato salad both pleasing at inspection. Start with gravlax with horseradish cream, and finish with a light mango mousse with crushed raspberries. Wines from £12.95.
**Chef/s:** Stuart Knight. **Open:** all week D 6 to 11. **Meals:** alc (main courses £8 to £20). **Service:** not inc. **Details:** Cards accepted. 50 seats. Separate bar. Wheelchair access. Music. Children allowed.

## ALSO RECOMMENDED

### ▲ Alfresco

Wharf Road, St Ives, TR26 1LG
Tel no: (01736) 793737
www.stivesharbour.com
**Eclectic**

Fresh seafood and great bay views win the day at this small, open-fronted, harbourside restaurant. You can expect anything from crab cakes with sun-blush tomatoes and red pepper salsa (£6.95) to well-reported scallops set on sweet potato purée with thermidor sauce (£15.95). Otherwise, all tastes are catered for

with shredded duck salad and toasted pine nuts with sweet chilli balsamic and fresh coriander or beef fillet in a rich red wine sauce. House wine is £12.95. Open all week.

## ■ St Kew

**NEW ENTRY**

### St Kew Inn

**Honest pub cooking at reasonable prices**
St Kew, PL30 3HB
Tel no: (01208) 841259
www.stkew-inn.co.uk
**Gastropub | £24**
**Cooking score: 3**

*Guide* readers may remember Paul Ripley from his time in St Merryn. Now he's back, and his new home – much-extended but down-to-earth fifteenth-century pub – really looks the part. It's a 'gorgeous place', with a large garden bordered by a stream. Inside, exposed stone walls and varnished tables are backed up by archetypal beams, winter fires and St Austell ales. Honest pub cooking at reasonable prices is the forte, with the kitchen delivering straightforward classics ranging from Welsh rarebit with fried duck egg and watercress salad to a well-reported chicken and ham pie with homemade piccalilli. St Enodoc asparagus, locally bred steaks and Fowey mussels cooked in cider, cream and chives reveal a dedication to local sourcing. Rhubarb fool with pecan shortbread impressed at inspection. House wine from £12.30. The pub is justifiably popular, so do book ahead.
**Chef/s:** Paul Ripley. **Open:** all week L 12 to 2, Mon to Sat D 6.30 to 9. **Closed:** 25 Dec. **Meals:** alc (main courses £10 to £17). Sun L £10.50 (1 course) to £19.50. **Service:** not inc. **Details:** Cards accepted. 70 seats. 40 seats outside. Separate bar. Music. Children allowed. Car parking.

## St Mawes

### Hotel Tresanton

**Fashionable Cornish retreat**
27 Lower Castle Road, St Mawes, TR2 5DR
Tel no: (01326) 270055
www.tresanton.com
**Modern European | £33**
**Cooking score: 4**

Tresanton drifted into the hospitality arena during the 1940s, when it was a local yachtmen's club serving the nautical brigade. After stepping up to full hotel status, it was given the Olga Polizzi treatment in 1997 and is now one of the darlings of the Cornish weekend set. The hotel cuts a real dash in summer, when the gorgeous terrace comes into its own. Otherwise, there are vicarious whiffs of the Med in the restaurant, with its mosaic floors, seaside colours and sun-drenched menu. A starter of red mullet and scallops with baby fennel, green beans and tomato sets things up for main courses of cod with grilled potatoes, steamed cockles and langoustine or Calenick Farm beef fillet with Swiss chard and wild mushrooms. West Country cheeses with pumpkin pickle are alternatives to sweet offerings such as dark chocolate soufflé with pecan fudge ice cream. Italy and France share most of the glory on the wine list, which kicks off with house selections at £24.
**Chef/s:** Paul Wadham. **Open:** all week L 12 to 2.30, D 7 to 9.30. **Closed:** 2 weeks Jan. **Meals:** Set L £25 (2 courses) to £33. Set D £42. **Service:** not inc. **Details:** Cards accepted. 40 seats. 55 seats outside. Separate bar. Children allowed. Car parking.

## St Merryn

NEW ENTRY
### Rosel & Co

**Satisfying comfort food**
The Dog House, St Merryn, PL28 8NF
Tel no: (01841) 521289
www.roselandco.co.uk
**Modern British | £35**
**Cooking score: 4**

It's 'a hip little place' noted a reporter of this simple, rustic dining room, part of the Dog House Wine Bar. Compact menus limit choice to around four options per course, and dishes aim to comfort rather than challenge. The unfussy modern British-style offerings range from seared salmon with celeriac cream, vanilla and red wine to lamb rack with carrot purée, pea shoots and mustard. Results on the plate may lack a wow factor, but fine ingredients are handled carefully to produce satisfying starters such as scallops in a sweet miso butter with chives, a main course of pork belly with five-spice and apple and ginger sauce, and a 'nice, gooey' hot chocolate pudding with rum caramel and vanilla parfait. Service is 'very relaxed'. A couple of pages of wine offer affordable drinking from £14.
**Chef/s:** Zane Rosel. **Open:** Tue to Sat D 7 to 9. **Closed:** Sun, Mon, 1 Jan to 10 Feb. **Meals:** alc (main courses £15 to £22). Set D £20 (2 courses) to £25. **Service:** not inc. **Details:** Cards accepted. 30 seats. Separate bar. No mobile phones. Music. Children allowed.

## Treen

### The Gurnard's Head

**Fabulous fish in a dramatic setting**
Treen, TR26 3DE
Tel no: (01736) 796928
www.gurnardshead.co.uk
**Gastropub | £25**
**Cooking score: 3**

The curious fishy moniker refers to the brooding rocky promontory of the same name that stretches out below this dramatically situated Cornish inn. 'Eat, drink, sleep' is the GH's motto and the place is eminently cosy – even in the bleakest of weather. Given the name – and the location – it's no surprise that the regularly updated menu generally includes an excellent selection of local fish. The day's haul could yield brill with fennel and tomato stew or mackerel with chorizo, Puy lentils and rocket, while Cornish pastures provide most of the raw materials for lamb's sweetbreads with wild leaves and pancetta or stuffed pork loin with sage gnocchi. British cheeses bring up the rear, alongside no-nonsense puddings including blackberry and almond tart with clotted cream. The global wine list kicks off with 12 selections by the glass or carafe. Bottle prices start at £15.50.

**Chef/s:** Rob Wright. **Open:** all week L 12.30 to 2.30, D 6.30 to 9.30. **Closed:** 24 and 25 Dec. **Meals:** alc (main courses £10 to £16). **Service:** not inc. **Details:** Cards accepted. 50 seats. 30 seats outside. Separate bar. No mobile phones. Music. Children allowed.

# Tresco, Isles of Scilly

## ALSO RECOMMENDED
## ▲ Island Hotel
Tresco, Isles of Scilly, TR24 0PU
Tel no: (01720) 422883
www.tresco.co.uk
**Modern British**

There are panoramic sea views from the terrace and dining room of this hotel on the 'island of flowers'. A colonial-style building with a private beach, it's all the more peaceful thanks to the lack of cars on the island. The set-price dinner menu (£40 for three courses) might offer grilled halloumi with garlic yoghurt, chilli butter and poached egg followed by baked plaice with parsley crust, tomato fondant and lemon butter, and lemon posset for dessert. Wines from £17. Closed Nov to Feb.

# Truro

## Saffron
**Versatile local menus and good value**
5 Quay Street, Truro, TR1 2HB
Tel no: (01872) 263771
www.saffronrestauranttruro.co.uk
**Modern European | £30**
**Cooking score: 2**

The bold and versatile menu at the Tinneys' cheerful, bistro-like restaurant displays a strong commitment to local and regional produce. Falmouth Bay mussels, and Bocaddon cheese with dukkah (a crumbly nut and spice blend) are typical starters, while mains include local veal with lemon thyme and onion polenta, and Newlyn huss with wild garlic, spätzle and parsley sauce. One couple, making a return visit, expressed delight at an excellent-value set lunch of a tapas-style starter plate followed by 'beautifully baked' cod in a spicy vegetable mix. Pannacotta and steamed marmalade pudding get the thumbs-up for dessert. House wine is £12.40.

**Chef/s:** Nik Tinney. **Open:** Mon to Sat L 11.30 to 3.30, D 5 to 10. **Closed:** Sun, Mon Jan to May, 25 and 26 Dec, bank hols. **Meals:** alc (main courses £12 to £17). Set L £12.50 (2 courses) to £15. Early supper £10.50 (2 courses) to £13.50. Set D £19.50. **Service:** not inc. **Details:** Cards accepted. 42 seats. Wheelchair access. Music.

## Tabb's
**Beguiling neighbourhood favourite**
85 Kenwyn Street, Truro, TR1 3BZ
Tel no: (01872) 262110
www.tabbs.co.uk
**Modern British | £30**
**Cooking score: 4**

Occupying what was once a Truro town pub, Tabb's creates a mood of beguiling and stylish intimacy with its slate floors, fresh flowers and soft lilac colours. All the kitchen's familiar trademark touches continue to delight visitors, from the breads baked each morning to the seductive assortment of homemade chocolates and truffles that round off a meal in luxurious style. Nigel Tabb's food is suffused with European flavours, although his cooking also shines the spotlight on seasonal Cornish ingredients. A timbale of chilled duck fillet is married with smoked goats' cheese, lemongrass and spring onion dressing, while baked fillet of mutton comes with sweetbreads, celeriac hash, grain mustard and onion gravy. Fish is also a strong suit – as in grilled fillet of hake with paprika pasta, roasted peppers and harissa dressing. The affordable 40-bin wine list kicks off with a quartet of house selections at £14.95 (£4 a glass). Note that Tabb's is currently open for dinner only.

**Chef/s:** Nigel Tabb. **Open:** Tue to Sat D 7 to 9. **Closed:** Sun, Mon, 25 and 26 Dec, 1 week Jan. **Meals:** alc (main courses £15 to £22). Set D £18.50 (2 courses). **Service:** not inc. **Details:** Cards accepted. 30 seats. Separate bar. No mobile phones. Wheelchair access. Music. Children allowed.

youngsters) is well run and very popular with visitors and locals in equal measure. Enthusiastic dish descriptions, prime ingredients and bold flavours characterise a forthright style that in winter has delivered a well-made celeriac soup with crispy bacon and pollack on a fennel-based ragoût. Early summer brings 'nice and light' frutti di mare of mussels, cockles and clams poached in a broth with Cornish cream, parsley and breadcrumbs, a robust slow-cooked duck leg teamed with smashed Cornish Earlies, spring greens and capers, and a generous sized vanilla pannacotta served with shortbread and apricots poached with elderflower. House wine is £19.

**Chef/s:** Neil Haydock. **Open:** all week B 8.30am to 10, L 12 to 2.30, D 6.15 to 9.15. **Meals:** alc (main courses £14 to £24). Set L £25.45. Set D £55 (5 courses). **Details:** Cards accepted. 100 seats. Wheelchair access. Music. Children allowed. Car parking.

## ■ Wadebridge

READERS RECOMMEND
### The Orchard
**Modern British**
Polmorla Road, Wadebridge, PL27 7ND
Tel no: (01208) 812696
www.theorchardrestaurant.co.uk
**'The food is wonderful, very fresh, local'**

## ■ Watergate Bay
### Fifteen Cornwall
**Pukka Cornish destination**
On the beach, Watergate Bay, TR8 4AA
Tel no: (01637) 861000
www.fifteencornwall.co.uk
**Italian | £55**
**Cooking score: 4**

Picture windows capitalise on the 'spectacular scenery' of Watergate Bay, but the rest is tiled floors, plain tables and subdued colours enlivened by a bit of 1960s *Magic Roundabout*-style psychedelia. This Cornish branch of Jamie Oliver's Fifteen foundation (a chef training programme for underprivileged

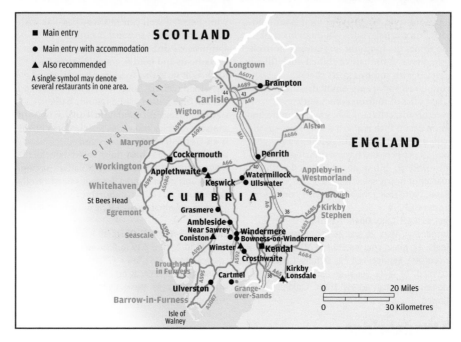

## Ambleside

### The Drunken Duck Inn

**Handsome all-rounder**
Barngates, Ambleside, LA22 0NG
Tel no: (015394) 36347
www.drunkenduckinn.co.uk
**Gastropub | £35**
**Cooking score: 3**

The Duck stands at crossroads high above Ambleside, offering stunning views across distant Lake Windermere to a backdrop of craggy fells. This may be a plush Lakeland pub, but it caters for all-comers, with sandwiches and light lunches of devilled lamb's kidneys or smoked salmon on rye bread served in the smart beamed bar or on the verandah (perhaps enjoyed with Cracker Ale from the on-site Barngates Brewery). Cooking moves up a gear in the evening. The restaurant menu offers the likes of ale-braised pork belly with black pudding and apple, then sea bass and scallops with caviar butter sauce, followed by dark chocolate pannacotta with pistachio ice cream and mint jelly. Smart, antique-furnished dining rooms, swish bedrooms and a fishing tarn complete the picture. The Drunken Duck's impressive wine cellar has something to suit all palates and pockets, with around 20 by the glass and bottle prices from £18.
**Chef/s:** Luke Shaw and Jim Metcalfe. **Open:** all week L 12 to 4, D 6.30 to 9.30 (6 Fri and Sat). **Closed:** 25 Dec. **Meals:** alc (main courses £15 to £25). **Service:** not inc. **Details:** Cards accepted. 70 seats. 40 seats outside. Separate bar. No music. No mobile phones. Wheelchair access. Car parking.

### Please send us your feedback

To register your opinion about any restaurant listed in the Guide, or a new restaurant that you wish to bring to our attention, please visit the web address at the bottom of the page. Your feedback informs the content of the book and will be used to compile next year's reviews.

## Lucy's on a Plate
**A slice of Lakeland enterprise**
Church Street, Ambleside, LA22 0BU
Tel no: (015394) 31191
www.lucysofambleside.co.uk
**Modern British | £25**
**Cooking score: 1**

V

Lucy Nicholson has created a little foodie
empire – a specialist grocer's, wine bar,
cookery school and mail order business – plus
this useful local eatery, which serves as a
family-friendly venue dishing up everything
from all-day breakfasts, through pit-stop
lunches to candlelit dinners. At the heart of
things is a dedication to Cumbrian produce,
although ingredients are often put through the
eclectic mill along the way. Crispy wild duck
with beetroot, almond and red wine glaze
could lead on to Lakeland lamb tagine with
preserved lemons and apricots, with a host of
homemade cakes and desserts to round things
off. House wine £11.95.
**Chef/s:** Mick McMullen. **Open:** all week 10 to 9.
**Closed:** 25 and 26 Dec. **Meals:** alc (main courses £9
to £25). Set D £20 (2 courses) to £25. Sun L £12 (2
courses) to £16. **Service:** not inc. **Details:** Cards
accepted. 100 seats. 12 seats outside. No mobile
phones. Wheelchair access. Music. Children
allowed.

## Rothay Manor
**Classic country house experience**
Rothay Bridge, Ambleside, LA22 0EH
Tel no: (015394) 33605
www.rothaymanor.co.uk
**British | £35**
**Cooking score: 1**

£5 OFF V

A good-looking Regency house a short walk
from the centre of Ambleside is home to this
traditional Lakeland hotel. The dining room
has attractive views over the garden, and the
classic country house mix of chintz curtains,
polished mahogany tables and evening candles
is mirrored in a four-course menu that might
comprise pressed ham terrine, a soup or sorbet

to follow, then mallard braised with damson
gin, with cherries in crème brûlée to finish.
Lunches are lighter, afternoon tea is an event
(booking essential) and the wine list scores
well for both value and variety, with nine by
the glass, half-bottle or bottle (£17).
**Chef/s:** Jane Binns. **Open:** all week L 12.30 to 1.45,
D 7.15 to 9. **Closed:** 3 to 28 Jan. **Meals:** alc L (main
courses £8 to £12). Set L £16.50 (2 courses) to £20.
Set D £36 (2 courses) to £40. Sun L £22.
**Service:** not inc. **Details:** Cards accepted. 65 seats.
Air-con. Separate bar. No music. No mobile phones.
Wheelchair access. Car parking.

# ▌Applethwaite

## Underscar Manor
**Intricate dishes in an Italianate villa**
Applethwaite, CA12 4PH
Tel no: (01768) 775000
www.keswickrestaurant.co.uk
**Modern British | £45**
**Cooking score: 5**

£5 OFF

Set high above Keswick, looking out towards
Derwentwater and Borrowdale, Underscar
Manor is every inch the perfectly positioned
Lakeland retreat. Built as an Italianate villa,
complete with a campanile, it is surrounded
by lush gardens bursting with blooms, while
the interior flaunts its English pedigree. The
whole place is a tribute to serious nurturing.
Meals in the conservatory-style dining room
comprise a succession of exceedingly intricate
dishes drawn from the modern European
repertoire, although Lakeland ingredients
always figure in the mix. The signature cheese
soufflé ('served in different styles') is about as
prosaic as it gets, with other starters moving
quickly into the elaborate world of, say, white
crab and scallop ravioli with a seared scallop,
lemongrass and dry vermouth sauce.
Elsewhere, it's accomplished partnerships all
the way: a dinky steak and mushroom
pudding beside fillet of Cumbrian Fell beef, a
gamey ragoût to accompany loin of local
venison, and an orange puff pastry tart to set
off crispy roast Barbary duck breast and Grand
Marnier sauce. Desserts come full circle with a

hot, sweet soufflé; otherwise, try something relatively simple such as warm apple tart with prune and Armagnac ice cream. France puts down a substantial marker on the reputable wine list; house selections are £24.

**Chef/s:** Robert Thornton. **Open:** all week L 12 to 1, D 7 to 8.30. **Closed:** 2 to 3 days beginning of Jan. **Meals:** Set L £25 (2 courses) to £28. Set D £38 (5 courses). **Service:** not inc. **Details:** Cards accepted. 55 seats. 12 seats outside. No music. No mobile phones. Car parking.

## ▌Bowness-on-Windermere

### Linthwaite House

**Cooking that gets the essentials right**
Crook Road, Bowness-on-Windermere, LA23 3JA
Tel no: (015394) 88600
www.linthwaite.com
**Modern British | £50**
Cooking score: 5

£5
OFF ⓘ ☲ V

After a particularly good meal at Linthwaite House, one reporter was left wondering whether Windermere could be the new Ludlow now that it has 'a few highly rated dining rooms'. Set in 14 acres of woodland overlooking the lake, this nineteenth-century house has a soothing, tranquil yet well-kept feel. Richard Kearsley's cooking doesn't aim for undue sophistication or complexity, but it gets the essentials right: prime materials run from local lamb via Goosnargh duck to Swaledale cheese, and his ideas are carefully considered and skilfully handled. This is evident, for example, in a starter of sesame-crusted tuna loin with dressed crabmeat and oriental dressing, and in a main course of Old Spot pork (fillet teamed with apple, braised belly and cheek) and spiced red cabbage. Fish has impressed, most recently sea bream with vanilla potatoes, salmon and brown shrimp tortellini and a vermouth sauce. 'Very fine' desserts include baked egg custard with poached rhubarb and stem ginger ice cream, and passion fruit soufflé with coconut sorbet. Canapés have also been endorsed, as has an

amuse of butternut squash soup with Parmesan shavings. The *Guide* was not sent the full wine list, though a reporter who drank very well for under £30 was sorry not to 'have done it real justice'. House wine is £19.50.

**Chef/s:** Richard Kearsley. **Open:** all week L 12.30 to 2, D 7 to 9.30. **Closed:** 24 to 27 Dec, 29 Dec to 1 Jan. **Meals:** Set L Mon to Sat £16 (2 courses) to £19. Set D £50 (4 courses). **Service:** not inc. **Details:** Cards accepted. 64 seats. 20 seats outside. Separate bar. No mobile phones. Wheelchair access. Music. Children allowed. Car parking.

## ▌Brampton

### Farlam Hall

**Classic cooking in elegant surroundings**
Brampton, CA8 2NG
Tel no: (016977) 46234
www.farlamhall.co.uk
**Modern British | £43**
Cooking score: 3

☲

Run by the same family since 1975, Farlam Hall is a classic country house hotel on a personal scale. Its lounges are a feast of chintz and antiques – a theme that extends to the dining room, where white napery and polished silverware add to the air of refined elegance. In keeping with English country house tradition, dinner is a one-sitting affair. Barry Quinion's short, daily changing menu draws on excellent regional ingredients, classic techniques and international flavours. Typical of the scope is a starter of guinea fowl terrine with plum chutney, followed by griddled halibut on couscous with herb sauce and a confit of sultanas. For dessert, perhaps lemon tart. A comprehensive wine list starts at £21.50.

**Chef/s:** Barry Quinion. **Open:** all week D only 8 to 8.30. **Closed:** 25 to 30 Dec. **Meals:** Set D £43 (4 courses). **Service:** not inc. **Details:** Cards accepted. 40 seats. No music. No mobile phones. Wheelchair access. Children allowed. Car parking.

# Cartmel

## L'Enclume

**Stand by for thrilling innovation**
Cavendish Street, Cartmel, LA11 6PZ
Tel no: (015395) 36362
www.lenclume.co.uk
**Modern European | £50**
**Cooking score: 8**

£5 OFF 🍷 🍴

Simon Rogan's reputation precedes him. Intellectually, the interplay between charming village location and envelope-shoving food is no longer a surprise. In the chair, it's still a thrill. L'Enclume, once a blacksmith's forge, is now the Lakes' chief culinary attraction, and Rogan teases ingredients from Cumbria's age-old larder with precise modern technique. A spare interior is the setting for a trio of tasting menus, and there's no shame in choosing the shortest. Across eight courses, guests will take in signature dishes, syringes and the squirt of the soda syphon. The latter appears, in the hands of a waiter, to top off a tiny 'martini' of tamarillo juice with pale, boozy foam – an instance of the staff-diner interaction which is carefully measured so as not to poleaxe conversation. Progressing, highlights might include egg drop hot-and-sour soup – a crystal clear, gingery broth with tofu, brown shrimps and spawny tapioca. Noodles are added at the table via a syringe loaded with duck egg, treated to coagulate in the bowl. In such a brave new world, a perfect hit-rate is unlikely. Lamb's tongue, for example, is fabulously crisped up with Japanese breadcrumbs, but its seat of cold white chocolate risotto doesn't appeal to everyone. The kitchen also loves to fool the eye. Almond 'powder', a great match with scallops and white asparagus, is icy and evanescent, and a duo of classic-looking sauces for veal breast harbour, respectively, bewitching star anise and citrus that kicks like a mule. To finish, try the signature 'expearamenthol frappe' topped with excellent eucalyptus ice cream, or a more conventional 'chocolate orange' plate, complete with biscuit crumbs, jellies and slender logs of chocolate mousse, crowned with a ball of fluffy orange sherbet. Readers report 'impersonal' as well as 'friendly' service, and it is possible to encounter both during a single meal. As with the cheese trolley, guidance through a solid, rather French wine list is deft and helpful. House selections start at £21 (£4 a glass), and there are flexible suggestions for possible matches.

**Chef/s:** Simon Rogan. **Open:** Wed to Sun L 12 to 1.30, all week D 6.30 to 9. **Meals:** Set L £25 (3 courses). Set menu £50 (8 courses), £70 (13 courses), £90 (17 courses). **Service:** not inc. **Details:** Cards accepted. 40 seats. Air-con. No music. No mobile phones. Wheelchair access. Car parking.

## Rogan and Company

**Perfect laid-back brasserie**
The Square, Cartmel, LA11 6QD
Tel no: (015395) 35917
www.roganandcompany.co.uk
**Modern European | £26**
**Cooking score: 4**

£5 OFF £30 🍴

The second venture of Simon Rogan – he of L'Enclume, just round the corner (see entry) – is a more down-to-earth brasserie operation for those who don't want cutting-edge experimentation. The surroundings are light and bright, with a characterful, beamed ground-floor bar, and a dining room upstairs with striped chairs, blond wood tables and menus printed on brown paper. Dishes sound appealingly domestic, whether it's starters of smoked ham cannelloni with lentils and runny yoghurt or cod and leek cakes with wilted spinach, or fortifying mains such as braised beef with parsnip purée and bourguignon garnish. Local lamb is always worth a punt in the Lake District, and here it comes with spiced red cabbage, tomato and tarragon. Meals end with alluring dessert combinations like warm cinnamon cake and Granny Smith sorbet. A kindly priced wine list warms the heart with its short but useful selection, starting at £3 a glass, or £12 a bottle, for Languedoc blends.

Chef/s: Simon Rogan and Adam Wesley. **Open:** all week L 12 to 2, D 6.30 to 9.30. **Meals:** alc (main courses £12 to £19). Set L £12.95 (2 courses) to £16.95. Set D £19.95 (2 courses) to £24.95. Sun L £12.95 (2 courses). **Service:** not inc. **Details:** Cards accepted. 80 seats. Air-con. Separate bar. Wheelchair access. Music. Children allowed.

# ▌Cockermouth

## Quince & Medlar
**Vibrantly inventive vegetarian**
13 Castlegate, Cockermouth, CA13 9EU
Tel no: (01900) 823579
www.quinceandmedlar.co.uk
**Vegetarian | £27**
**Cooking score: 4**

**V**

'It is truly a special night out', commented one satisfied pair, after dinner at Colin and Louisa Le Voi's Lakeland vegetarian restaurant next to the castle. In a setting of wood panelling and soft candlelight, the cooking is vibrantly inventive, and founded on some daredevil but successful combinations. Start with chargrilled aubergine and apricot pâté with sesame biscuits, and follow on with leek and butterbean tagine with cheese and herb dumplings, perhaps, or roasted parsnip and cashew ring incorporating bulgur, shallots and thyme, served with sliced butternut squash, topped with crème fraîche and sauced with Madeira. Lime tart makes a zesty spin on traditional tarte au citron, or you might finish with iced fruit and nut meringue with toffee sauce. A short list of vegetarian and vegan wines provides flavours big enough to go with the food. House wines start at £11.90.
**Chef/s:** Colin Le Voi. **Open:** Tue to Sat D 7 to 9.30. **Closed:** Sun, Mon, 24 to 26 Dec, 1 Jan. **Meals:** alc (main courses £14). **Service:** not inc. **Details:** Cards accepted. 26 seats. No mobile phones. Music. Children allowed.

> ### Also recommended
> Also recommended entries are not scored but we think they are worth a visit.

# ▌Coniston

## ALSO RECOMMENDED
## ▲ The Church House Inn
Torver, Coniston, LA21 8AZ
Tel no: (01539) 441282
www.churchhouseinntorver.com
**Gastropub**

This roadside inn has bags of character – the rustic bar boasts flagstones and an open fire, there's a snug for light lunches and a dining room for evening meals – but reports suggest it could do with a facelift. Michael Beaty has cooked for David Bowie, Madonna and other celebrities, but here offers traditional pub fare such as a Sunday lunch of roast rib of aged belted Galloway beef with roast potatoes, Yorkshire pudding and seasonal vegetables (£9.95). There might be rhubarb trifle and a creamy ice cream to finish (£5.25). Wines start at £13.50. Open all week.

# ▌Crosthwaite

## The Punch Bowl
**Stylish country pub with good food**
Lyth Valley, Crosthwaite, LA8 8HR
Tel no: (015395) 68237
www.the-punchbowl.co.uk
**Modern British | £28**
**Cooking score: 3**

Smack next to St Mary's church and overlooking the Lyth Valley, the Punch Bowl has been transformed into a smartly attired pub/restaurant-with-rooms. It still functions as a local, with Cumbrian ales such as Barngates Tag Lag on draught and the day's papers in the bar; you can even buy stamps as the pub functions as the local post office. The food is stylish, too, ranging from simple, light lunches of ham hock terrine with piccalilli, battered hake and chips or salmon niçoise to more ambitious dinner dishes of, say, confit duck and foie gras roulade with spiced plum, ahead of lamb loin with rosemary jus. There could be glazed rice pudding with orange compote to finish. House wine is £16.95.

**Chef/s:** Jonathan Watson. **Open:** all week L 12 to 6, D 6 to 9.30. **Meals:** alc (main courses £14 to £18). **Service:** not inc. **Details:** Cards accepted. 70 seats. 40 seats outside. Separate bar. Wheelchair access. Music. Children allowed. Car parking.

## ▌Grasmere

## The Jumble Room
**Big flavours and hearty bellywarmers**
Langdale Road, Grasmere, LA22 9SU
Tel no: (015394) 35188
www.thejumbleroom.co.uk
Global | £35
Cooking score: 2

Stamped with the individuality of its owners, this arty, eclectic one-off has a loyal band of regulars who praise its 'great food, atmosphere and service'. The cooking is an expansive mix of big flavours and hearty bellywarmers from around the world: try Thai chicken broth with pak choi, shiitake mushrooms and pork dumplings to start, followed by Moroccan lamb tagine or, if you're a home bird, fresh haddock in organic beer batter with mushy peas and hand-cut chips. Finish with raspberry and white chocolate cheesecake. The international wine list kicks off at £11.95.
**Chef/s:** Chrissy Hill and David and Trudy Clay. **Open:** Wed to Sun L 12 to 3.30, Wed to Mon D 6 to 10. **Closed:** Tue, 14 to 27 Dec. **Meals:** alc (main courses £13 to £25). **Service:** not inc. **Details:** Cards accepted. 48 seats. 10 seats outside. Wheelchair access. Music. Children allowed.

## White Moss House
**Captivating Lakeland retreat**
Rydal Water, Grasmere, LA22 9SE
Tel no: (015394) 35295
www.whitemoss.com
British | £40
Cooking score: 5

Famous for its connections with William Wordsworth (the poet bought the house for his son), White Moss is one of those captivating Lakeland retreats with history and heritage on its side. For nigh on 30 years it has been in the devoted hands of Sue and Peter Dixon, who have turned it into one of the most charmingly hospitable country house hotels in the region. Much depends on dinner, and guests are offered a five-course menu that is thoroughly in keeping with the prevailing mood of unaffected Englishness. Ingredients are chosen with due regard for the local larder, and they are proudly deployed in dishes that chime with the seasons. Proceedings open with a soup (perhaps leek and lovage) before a little fish course – a soufflé of Lakeland redfish with Grasmere free-range eggs, Westmorland and Lancashire cheeses, say. Centrepieces such as maize-fed Vale of Lune guinea fowl braised in dry cider and tarragon with Puy lentils are accompanied by a harvest festival of vegetables, while desserts (usually a choice of three) could range from chocolate and Amaretto slice to sticky toffee pudding. Finally, the evening reaches its conclusion with a plate of British cheeses, followed by coffee and sweetmeats. The Dixons should be applauded for squirrelling away a host of fine vintages, with properly matured French regional classics getting most of the plaudits – although the rest of the world chips in with traditional grape varieties from reputable growers. Inviting personal selections start at £13.95 (£4.65 a glass).
**Chef/s:** Peter Dixon. **Open:** Thur to Sat D 7.30 for 8 (1 sitting). **Closed:** Sun to Wed, Dec, Jan, Feb. **Meals:** Set D £39 (5 courses). **Service:** not inc. **Details:** Cards accepted. 18 seats. Separate bar. No music. Wheelchair access. Children allowed. Car parking.

# Kendal

## Bridge Street Restaurant

Local ingredients handled with flair

1 Bridge Street, Kendal, LA9 7DD

Tel no: (01539) 738855

www.one-bridgestreet.co.uk

**Modern British | £25**

**Cooking score: 3**

There is a ground-floor bar, and two small dining rooms upstairs at this Grade II-listed Georgian building. The atmosphere is 'relaxed and enjoyable' and the front-of-house team, led by Elizabeth Ankers, is cheerful and efficient. Julian Ankers is an accomplished chef who shows flair in the way he deals with mainly local produce. Some of his dishes show Asian influences – pak choi and oriental sauce with a crispy duck leg starter, for example. At a test meal, roast chump of Kentmere lamb was pink and tender, and was accompanied by rosemary-infused creamed potatoes with a port and redcurrant sauce. Comforting puddings such as pear and almond flan with a vanilla bean sauce have been well-reported, and ice creams and sorbets are homemade – as is the excellent bread. Note that while a basic three-course dinner is priced at £18, there are supplements on many dishes, and side orders are extra. Wines start at £13.50.

**Chef/s:** Julian Ankers. **Open:** Tue to Sat L 12 to 2, 6.30 to 9. **Closed:** Sun, Mon, 25 Dec to 26 Dec. **Meals:** Set L £9.95 (2 courses) to £12.95. Set D £18. Sun L £16. **Service:** not inc. **Details:** Cards accepted. 36 seats. 8 seats outside. Air-con. Separate bar. Music. Children allowed.

# Keswick

## ALSO RECOMMENDED
### ▲ Swinside Lodge

Grange Road, Newlands, Keswick, CA12 5UE

Tel no: (017687) 72948

www.swinsidelodge.com

**Modern British**

Standing alone in beautiful open countryside, this handsome Georgian residence is just a stroll from lovely Derwentwater. Four-course dinners (£40) are pointed up with local flavours: cream of celeriac and Blengdale Blue cheese soup with white truffle oil might precede fillet of Cumbrian beef in traditional partnership with Savoy cabbage, pickled walnuts and red wine jus. To conclude, choose a slate of Cumbrian cheeses or a dessert such as banana, date and pecan sponge pudding with white chocolate custard. Wines from £16.50. Open all week D only.

# Kirkby Lonsdale

## ALSO RECOMMENDED
### ▲ The Sun Inn

6 Market Street, Kirkby Lonsdale, LA6 2AU

Tel no: (015242) 71965

www.sun-inn.info

**Gastropub**

New owners are keeping things right on track in this quintessential, sympathetically improved, seventeenth-century Cumbrian inn. There's a choice of eating areas – the traditional bar or the contemporary, brasserie-style dining room – and reliable hands in the kitchen conjure up full-flavoured dishes like ham hock and mushroom terrine with parsley jelly (£4.95) and Mediterranean fish stew (£15.95), alongside old-fashioned desserts including rhubarb meringue pie (£4.95). House wine is £12.50. Closed Mon L.

## Near Sawrey

### Ees Wyke

**Beatrix Potter bolt-hole**
Near Sawrey, LA22 0JZ
Tel no: (015394) 36393
www.eeswyke.co.uk
**Anglo-French | £33**
**Cooking score: 2**

The spectacular view over Esthwaite to the fells beyond must be what lured Beatrix Potter to establish a holiday home in this eighteenth-century country house. The Lees now run it as a home-from-home hotel, with a single-sitting, five-course dinner at 7.30 the main attraction. A winter menu indicates the style: leek and potato soup with a Gruyère-topped croûton, followed by grilled salmon and garlic pea mash in lemon butter, then a choice of sea bass, guinea fowl or lamb, the last served with minted wine jus. A dessert such as rhubarb crumble with orange and pine nuts is followed by a platter of regional cheeses. House wines at £16.50 head up a nicely cosmopolitan list.
**Chef/s:** Richard Lee. **Open:** all week D only 7.30 (1 sitting). **Meals:** Set D £33 (5 courses). **Service:** not inc. **Details:** Cards accepted. 16 seats. Separate bar. No music. No mobile phones. Car parking.

## Penrith

**NEW ENTRY**

### George and Dragon

**Gem with genuine country cooking**
Clifton, Penrith, CA10 2ER
Tel no: (01768) 865381
www.georgeanddragonclifton.co.uk
**Gastropub | £21**
**Cooking score: 2**

£5 OFF | £30

One reporter describes this refurbished eighteenth-century coaching inn as 'a real gem'. Food can be eaten in the flagstone-floored bar with open fire, or in the informal dining room with its bare wooden tables and stone walls. Almost all the food is sourced from the farms of the nearby Lowther Estate, where slow-grown animals are reared organically. Chef Paul McKinnon worked with Terry Laybourne in Newcastle and his monthly menu offers the staples of genuine country cooking. Start, perhaps, with a twice-baked cheese soufflé, follow with lamb shank and parsley pie with braised red cabbage and finish off with a classic chocolate tart. Wines start at a very reasonable £11.50.
**Chef/s:** Paul McKinnon. **Open:** all week L 12 to 2.30, D 6 to 9.30. **Meals:** alc (main courses £9 to £14). Sun L £9.95. **Service:** not inc. **Details:** Cards accepted. 100 seats. 60 seats outside. Separate bar. No music. Wheelchair access. Children allowed. Car parking.

## Troutbeck

**READERS RECOMMEND**

### The Queen's Head Hotel

**Gastropub**
Townhead, Troutbeck, LA23 1PW
Tel no: (01539) 432174
www.queensheadhotel.com
'Food is absolutely fabulous, using the best local produce'

## Ullswater

### Sharrow Bay

**Pure class in glorious isolation**
Ullswater, CA10 2LZ
Tel no: (01768) 486301
www.sharrowbay.co.uk
**British | £50**
**Cooking score: 6**

🍾 ⊨ V

The grand old man of Lakeland retreats, Sharrow Bay invented the 'country house hotel' genre and – more than 60 years on – it is still a seductive vision of pure class and enchantment. Much of its special charge comes from the magical setting in lush grounds by the shores of Ullswater: the views are spectacular, whatever the time of year. Dinner is a leisurely extravaganza that lasts the entire evening, and it brings together the kitchen's love of Cumbrian produce with its

classic culinary sensibilities. Sautéed sweetbreads and duck foie gras with Sharrow Bay black pudding, apple and sage sauce is a typically forthright starter, before a little dish of – say – plaice with wild mushroom fricassee is brought to the table. Palates are then refreshed with a sorbet, ahead of the main event: perhaps best end and shoulder of Herdwick lamb with tomato and thyme sauce. To finish, the legendary 'icky sticky' toffee sponge has spawned a galaxy of pale imitations and it remains in pole position, ahead of desserts such as plum and apple strudel with cinnamon ice cream. Factor in the delights of breakfast and incomparable afternoon teas and it's easy to see why Sharrow Bay's 'gentle art' is an experience to be treasured. Finally, there's the wine list – a majestic tome that puts its weight behind pedigree Bordeaux, Burgundies and French regional stars. Other lands – from Portgual to China – are also represented, and prices (from £19) are fair.
**Chef/s:** Colin Akrigg. **Open:** all week L 12.30 for 1, D 7.30 for 8 (1 sitting). **Meals:** Set L £33 (3 courses). Set D £50 (3 courses) to £70 (5 courses). Sun L £43. **Service:** not inc. **Details:** Cards accepted. 50 seats. 20 seats outside. Separate bar. No music. No mobile phones. Wheelchair access. Music. Children allowed. Car parking.

## ▌ Ulverston
### The Bay Horse
**Romantic charmer with breathtaking views**
Canal Foot, Ulverston, LA12 9EL
Tel no: (01229) 583972
www.thebayhorsehotel.co.uk
**Modern British | £38**
**Cooking score: 3**
🛏 V

The views across the Leven Estuary will take your breath away – especially when the sun goes down over the water – and readers continue to be entranced by the 'gentle, romantic atmosphere' of this one-time coaching inn. Guests staying over can also look forward to 'groaning' breakfasts and inviting afternoon teas. Dinner in the Conservatory Restaurant is the main event,

and the kitchen sends out accomplished modern dishes ranging from smoked chicken Caesar salad to roast Waberthwaite pork belly on Calvados and apple sauce, crab and salmon fishcakes or Barbary duck breast on caramelised red onions and grilled pancetta. At lunchtime you can also pick up 'light bites' and hot sandwiches in the bar. Staff are 'trained to perfection' and the wine list is also a source great pleasure (note the South African contingent). Prices start at £16.50.
**Chef/s:** Robert Lyons and Kris Hogan. **Open:** Tue to Sun L 12 to 2, all week D 7.30 for 8 (1 sitting). **Meals:** alc (main courses £15 to £26). Set D £22 (2 courses) to £28. **Service:** not inc. **Details:** Cards accepted. 45 seats. 20 seats outside. Separate bar. No mobile phones. Wheelchair access. Music. Car parking.

## ▌ Watermillock
### Rampsbeck Country House Hotel
**Show-stealing Lakeland views**
Watermillock, CA11 0LP
Tel no: (017684) 86442
www.rampsbeck.co.uk
**Anglo-French | £43**
**Cooking score: 3**
🍷 🛏

If you are turned on by views, take a look across the 18 acres of fantastic grounds that envelope this elegant eighteenth-century country house and marvel at Ullswater in all its photogenic glory. Rampsbeck's dining room is also pretty tasty, if you're fond of knick-knacks, soft lights and luxurious accoutrements. Dinner follows the trusted Lakeland format – four courses at a fixed price, with local ingredients providing the backbone. Game is well represented in season – perhaps roast loin of hare with a confit and purée of beetroot and sautéed chanterelles or venison with spiced blackberries and swede fondant. Fish also makes an impact, as in, say, Dover sole fillets with langoustine risotto, baby fennel and shellfish dressing. Finish invitingly with plum soufflé and cinnamon milkshake with green apple sorbet. Wines are arranged by style, with noteworthy selections from France, Italy and Australia covering everyday quaffers and special-occasion tipples. Prices start at £13.25.

**Chef/s:** Andrew McGeorge. **Open:** all week L 12 to 1.45, D 7 to 8.30 (9 Fri and Sat). **Closed:** 3 to 27 Jan. **Meals:** Set L £23 (2 courses) to £29. Set D £43 (3 courses) to £49.50. Sun L £23 (2 courses) to £29. **Service:** not inc. **Details:** Cards accepted. 40 seats. Separate bar. No music. No mobile phones. Wheelchair access. Children allowed. Car parking.

## ▌ Windermere

### Gilpin Lodge

**Outward-looking Lakeland retreat**
Crook Road, Windermere, LA23 3NE
Tel no: (015394) 88818
www.gilpinlodge.co.uk
**Modern British | £52**
Cooking score: 6

£5 OFF 🍷 ⛓ V

In the same family's hands since 1987, Gilpin Lodge is well-established on tranquil slopes near Windermere. The surrounding greenery is timeless, but Gilpin resists stagnant country house status with quirky touches and utterly modern service standards. The dashing red Champagne bar, where faultless canapés are served, is a new feature, as is chef Russell Plowman. Dinner, served in four candlelit dining rooms, lets guests play it safe – witness a truffled Jerusalem artichoke velouté – but also shows humour and bright thinking, as in a Stichelton soufflé served with dainty cheeseboard garnishes of celery, walnuts and apple. To follow, halibut might be paired with astonishingly light smoked salmon tortellini, braised lettuce and a pale, elegant Champagne sauce, or duck with foie gras and a lime and ginger sauce poured at the table. Accessories are elegant and playful. A pretty glass dessert plate (theme 'lemon') holds a mini bavarois, citrus granita and a swirl of glossy Italian meringue while pistachio crème brûlée is a strangely enticing shade of pond green. Gilpin's wine list is famously extensive and glories in the French side, from which you can

drink happily for under £50. Fans of the New World, half-bottles and entry-level choices (from £17.50, £5.50 a glass) aren't left out in the cold, however, and the list is helpfully annotated.

**Chef/s:** Russell Plowman. **Open:** all week L 12 to 2, D 6 to 9. **Meals:** alc (main courses £8 to £18). Set L £20 (2 courses) to £25. Set D £52 (3 courses). Sun L £30. **Service:** not inc. **Details:** Cards accepted. 65 seats. 35 seats outside. Separate bar. No music. No mobile phones. Wheelchair access. Car parking.

### Holbeck Ghyll

**A taste of life's finer things**
Holbeck Lane, Windermere, LA23 1LU
Tel no: (015394) 32375
www.holbeckghyll.com
**Modern British | £53**
Cooking score: 7

£5 OFF 🍷 ⛓ V

It's no surprise that everyone drools over Holbeck Ghyll's tremendous location and astonishing views: this early Victorian hunting lodge stands majestically overlooking Lake Windermere and the Langdale Fells and is sufficiently far from the madding crowds to offer solace, tranquillity and a taste of the finer things in life. You can make the most of the uninterrupted vistas from the original oak-panelled dining room or the recently refurbished Terrace Restaurant; either way, the food aims to impress with its serious intentions, innovation and technical accomplishments. The kitchen sources ingredients carefully and keeps a sharp eye on the calendar. Cannelloni of crab is tempered with Cartmel Valley smoked salmon, while best end of Cumbrian lamb could be served with Puy lentils, swede purée and haggis beignets. From the West Coast of Scotland there might be hand-dived scallops (enticingly dressed up with spiced cauliflower and apple and raisin purée), while the kitchen's French allegiances show in a salad of warm Périgord quail with white grapes and Sauternes dressing. Other dishes such as breast of Goosnargh duck with pickled beetroot and choucroute bring some earthy rustic tones to the table, and dazzling desserts explore many different avenues, from an extravaganza of cherries involving clafoutis with almond ice cream, a sorbet, sauce and confit, to 'cold' rhubarb crumble. Also leave time (and room) for the impressive cheese menu – a 14-strong line-up of big names from the British Isles and Europe. Service from 'impeccably trained' staff is a big plus, likewise the prudent advice and care lavished on the stupendous, ever-evolving wine list. France is given plenty of attention, but don't ignore other rich pickings – notably the Australian whites and Napa Valley reds. Half-bottles are many and varied, 'Fantastic Finds' throw up some fascinating rarities, and highly praised 'personal house selections' start at £22.50 (£4.25 a glass). **Chef/s:** David McLaughlin. **Open:** all week 12.30 to 2, 7 to 9.30. **Closed:** first 2 weeks Jan. **Meals:** Set L £29.50. Set D £52.50. Gourmet menu £72.50. **Service:** not inc. **Details:** Cards accepted. 60 seats. 30 seats outside. Separate bar. No music. No mobile phones. Wheelchair access. Car parking.

## Jerichos at the Waverley
**Exciting flavours and good value**
College Road, Windermere, LA23 1BX
Tel no: (015394) 42522
www.jerichos.co.uk
**Modern British | £32**
**Cooking score: 5**

Ensconced within the Victorian Waverley Hotel, Chris and Jo Blaydes' white-walled, wood-floored restaurant continues to impress. A party who ate here in winter thought everything about their meal was perfect: 'the sourcing of ingredients, presentation, service, timing – and the value!' They dined on beetroot and black pudding salad with a poached egg, rolled and stuffed plaice with red pepper, spinach and mash, and a triumphant slow-roast of Gloucester Old Spot pork with carrots, swede, roast Bramley apple and Savoy cabbage. Dish descriptions sound complex, but the delivery is mightily convincing, with exciting presentation and deep, clear flavours throughout. Take seared fillet of halibut,

which arrives on a risotto of creamed mushrooms and truffle, along with buttered spinach, a langoustine and tomato fondue sauce, each element of which adds something constructive to the composition. Homemade biscuits with the cheese platter are singled out for praise, while desserts such as apricot and cinnamon sticky toffee sponge with custard and vanilla ice cream could hardly do more to oblige. Wines are usefully classified according to what they might best go with, from smoked fish to beef and game. Prices are extravagantly fair, and a lot is packed in within a relatively modest compass. Six house wines are £14, and even a bottle of Louis Roederer Brut Premier is not much above retail at £39.
**Chef/s:** Chris Blaydes and Tim Dalzell. **Open:** Fri to Wed D only 7 to 9.30. **Closed:** Thur, 24 to 26 Dec, 1 Jan, first 2 weeks Nov, last 3 weeks Jan. **Meals:** alc (main courses £16 to £25). **Service:** not inc. **Details:** Cards accepted. 30 seats. Music. Children allowed. Car parking.

## The Samling
**On-trend cooking in demure surroundings**
Ambleside Road, Windermere, LA23 1LR
Tel no: (015394) 31922
www.thesamling.com
**Modern British | £55**
**Cooking score: 4**

Wordsworth's landlord used to live at the Samling, and the poet would often make the climb up to the house to pay his rent, no doubt admiring the vistas stretching out across Windermere as he walked. These days, it's a demure, pocket-sized country hotel set in a 67-acre estate of woods and landscaped gardens. Refurbishment has added a lighter contemporary tone to the restaurant, where ambitious modern food is the order of the day. The kitchen fashionably brings together scallops, parsley root purée, Serrano ham, sticky chicken and parsley oil, while brill might come with meaty accents in the form of braised oxtail, cauliflower purée and horseradish cream. Desserts often revolve around fruity 'tastings' – including apples from the Samling garden. Otherwise, consider orange caramel flan with sweet ginger parfait and lychee sorbet. The wine list is work in progress, with tantalising choice if money is no barrier; prices start around £40. **Chef/s:** Nigel Mendham. **Open:** all week L 12 to 1.30, D 7 to 9.30. **Meals:** Set L £38 (3 courses). Set D £55 (3 courses). **Service:** not inc. **Details:** Cards accepted. 22 seats. 10 seats outside. No mobile phones. Music. Children allowed. Car parking.

## READERS RECOMMEND

### Miller Howe
**Modern British**
Rayrigg Road, Windermere, LA23 1EY
Tel no: (015394) 42536
www.millerhowe.com
**'The faded look of recent years has gone... food was really good'**

# ▌ Winster

## ALSO RECOMMENDED
### ▲ The Brown Horse Inn
Winster, LA23 3NR
Tel no: (015394) 43443
www.thebrownhorseinn.co.uk
**Gastropub**

The lush Lyth Valley delivers some jaw-dropping views, and the patio at this refurbished inn makes the most of them. Inside, find a traditional flagged bar at one end and a dining room with a hint of Gothic at the other. Food couldn't be more locally sourced – vegetables and herbs come from the back garden, free-range poultry from the smallholding up the road. Follow Blacksticks Blue salad (£5.95) with venison suet pudding, mushy peas and fat chips (£12.95). House wine starts at £12.95. Accommodation. Open all week.

### David McLaughlin Holbeck Ghyll

**Who or what inspired you to become a chef?**
Washing up in the school holidays gave me experience of this trade and I decided I wanted to become part of it.

**What is your top culinary tip?**
Season and continually taste your food. Salt is not good for you, but food without it is horrible.

**Which chefs do you admire?**
All the chefs responsible for turning Britain into a culinary hot spot.

**If you were to have one abiding principle in the kitchen, what would it be?**
No food to leave the kitchen that I wouldn't be happy to sit out there and eat myself.

**What is your favourite restaurant and why?**
At the moment I think it's Pied-à-Terre. Great food, fantastic presentation and not a test tube or syringe in sight!

**What do you do to relax when out of the kitchen?**
Spending time with my wife and trying to stop my two children aged two and five from killing each other!

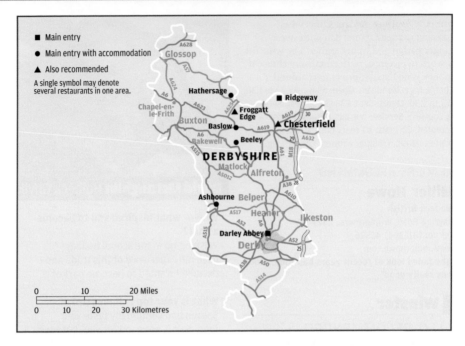

- ■ Main entry
- ● Main entry with accommodation
- ▲ Also recommended

A single symbol may denote several restaurants in one area.

## ■ Ashbourne

### Callow Hall

**Imposing Peak District pile**
Mappleton Road, Ashbourne, DE6 2AA
Tel no: (01335) 300900
www.callowhall.co.uk
**Modern British | £42**
**Cooking score: 3**

🍷 ⇌ V

Following the retirement of long-time owners David and Dorothy Spencer, this imposing Peak District pile overlooking the Dove Valley was acquired by Von Essen Hotels in October 2008 – although son Anthony has been retained as head chef. His home-smoked salmon remains a fixture on the menu – perhaps served with prawn and smoked haddock croquette and horseradish cream. Elsewhere, domestic enterprise shows in the homemade black pudding that accompanies confit of duck. Derbyshire lamb is also a big attraction – a duo of roast loin and rack could appear with slow-roasted courgette, pepper and red onion ratatouille, say. To close the show, expect a line-up of classic desserts such as blackberry and apple tart or meringue pavlova. France is the main contender on the helpfully annotated wine list, but the New World provides ample pleasures at eminently fair prices. House vins de pays d'Oc open the account at £16.95

**Chef/s:** Anthony Spencer. **Open:** all week L 12 to 2, D 7.15 to 9. **Meals:** Set L £20 (2 courses) to £25. Set D £42 (5 courses). Sun L £28. **Service:** not inc. **Details:** Cards accepted. 80 seats. Separate bar. Wheelchair access. Car parking.

## The Dining Room

**Inventive little gem**
33 St John Street, Ashbourne, DE6 1GP
Tel no: (01335) 300666
www.thediningroomashbourne.co.uk
**Modern British | £37**
**Cooking score: 4**

£5
OFF

The mind-your-head ceiling beams and uneven cobbled courtyard indicate the age of the place – it was built at the beginning of the seventeenth century. These days, though, it forms the backdrop for a restaurant that combines stylish intimacy (just six tables, so booking is essential) with an experimental culinary approach. Founded on a network of unrivalled local suppliers, who might appear in chummy first-name terms on the menus (as in, say, an appetiser of Richard's cauliflower), it's food to make you think. And it's had plenty of attention, too. A pair of choices at each stage might furnish two-month aged beef with 16-hour braised ox cheek and a smoked potato fritter, or Cornish pollack with triple-cooked chips, tartare sauce and pea purée. Combinations aren't as outlandish as you might expect – a spaghetti dish comes with mushrooms, three-year-old Parmesan and truffle oil – but that doesn't preclude a dessert such as creamed vanilla rice with passion fruit, cashews, cocoa nibs and chocolate ice cream. Wines, arranged by style, start at £16.
**Chef/s:** Peter Dale. **Open:** Tue to Sat D only 7.15 (1 sitting). **Closed:** Sun, Mon, 1 week over Shrove Tue, 1 week Sept, 2 weeks after 25 Dec. **Meals:** alc (main courses £20). Set L £22 (2 courses) to £29. Set D £30 (2 courses) to £36. Tasting menu £45 (16 courses). **Service:** not inc. **Details:** Cards accepted. 16 seats. No mobile phones. Wheelchair access. Music. Children allowed.

## ▌Baslow

## Cavendish Hotel, Gallery Restaurant

**Grand surroundings and food with style**
Church Lane, Baslow, DE45 1SP
Tel no: (01246) 582311
www.cavendish-hotel.net
**Modern British | £39**
**Cooking score: 4**

Bordering the Duke of Devonshire's Chatsworth House and Estate, the Cavendish lives up to its ducal inheritance with considerable style. The views from the terrace are of the finest Derbyshire countryside; inside all is elegance and serenity, with ancestral portraits lining the walls. The kitchen allies sound technique with thorough use of local produce – Martin Clayton has worked in the county for many years and knows his suppliers. On inspection, a starter of smoked duck breast with cranberry and port dressing was followed by a richly satisfying main of Chatsworth Estate beef, served with caramelised shallot rösti and a butternut squash and spinach purée. Elsewhere, the menu provides the occasional unexpected flourish; a main of Gressingham duck served with honey and vanilla-glazed pak choi, sweet chilli risotto and coriander oil. Toffee apple Bakewell tart is a flagship dessert. A comprehensive wine list opens with house vin de pays at £15.
**Chef/s:** Martin Clayton. **Open:** all week L 12 to 2.30, D 6.30 to 10. **Meals:** Set L and D £29.50 (2 courses) to £38.50. **Service:** 5%. **Details:** Cards accepted. 50 seats. Separate bar. Wheelchair access. Music. Children allowed. Car parking.

## Fischer's Baslow Hall

**Stunning food, unstuffy surroundings**
Calver Road, Baslow, DE45 1RR
Tel no: (01246) 583259
www.fischers-baslowhall.co.uk
**Modern European | £68**
Cooking score: 7

Baslow Hall may look like an archetypal seventeenth-century manor, although it was actually built in 1907 at the behest of a local vicar with a penchant for the past – hence the building's protruding gabled wings, tall chimneys and mullioned windows. Max and Susan Fischer have been in residence here since 1988, and have transformed the place into a much-loved restaurant-with-rooms that cleverly avoids the pomp and circumstance of some self-styled country houses: 'elegance without stuffiness' just about sums up their dedicated efforts. Readers' comments are also full of praise for the quality of the raw materials deployed in the kitchen (excellent rabbit and pigeon, loin of veal, oxtail 'off the bone') and dishes tick all the right boxes when it comes to impeccable local sourcing, stunning technique, invention and deep, intense flavours. There are several fixed-price menus to choose from, culminating in a lavish 'prestige' version for a whole table. Surprises and pleasures come thick and fast – perhaps three 'textures' of foie gras (pan-fried, cured and warm) with mango, pigeon and cappuccino, or slow-poached fillet of wild sea bass with sweet potato tortellini and Thai coconut broth, or even a veggie extravaganza of roasted pumpkin pannacotta with Parmesan ice cream and candied pecans. Cleverly contrived marriages of meat and fish are a favourite culinary device: crispy pork rillettes are paired with John Dory and butternut squash purée, while rolled saddle of rabbit keeps company with king prawns and fennel bavarois. To finish, prune rice pudding with prune and Armagnac ice cream has been a big hit, while pistachio tart with chocolate sorbet turns a classic partnership on its head. Baslow Hall's courteous, well-trained staff

ensure that everything runs like clockwork, and service is reckoned to be 'exemplary'. The top-class wine list breathes class at every turn, with prestigious labels from France, Australia and California shining particularly brightly. Appetising house recommendations start at £22 (£5.50 a glass).
**Chef/s:** Rupert Rowley. **Open:** Tue to Sun L 12 to 1.30, Mon to Sat D 7 to 8.30. **Closed:** 25 and 26 Dec. **Meals:** Set L £23 (2 courses) to £27. Set D £38 (2 courses) to £43. Sun L £38. Tasting menu £63. **Service:** not inc. **Details:** Cards accepted. 38 seats. Separate bar. No music. No mobile phones. Wheelchair access. Car parking.

## Rowley's

**Buzzy brasserie**
Church Lane, Baslow, DE45 1RY
Tel no: (01246) 583880
www.rowleysrestaurant.co.uk
**Modern British | £32**
Cooking score: 3

£5 OFF

'Really buzzy atmosphere whenever you go' was how one reporter summed up the appeal of this cheerful brasserie owned by the Fischers and their chef, Rupert Rowley from nearby Baslow Hall (see entry above). The stone building may look like a former pub from the outside, but inside light wood floors, bold colours and simple table settings give a contemporary look to the all-day bar and casual dining areas. Reports in the main are positive, crispy goats' cheese fritters and tagliatelle of mussels with saffron sauce, for example, but some unevenness has also come through in reports. Nonetheless, plaudits have been given for the likes of lamb hotpot, oxtail suet pudding and desserts such as lime cheesecake with kumquat jelly and mint syrup. House wine £15.95.
**Chef/s:** Richard Barber. **Open:** all week L 12 to 2 (2.30 Sat, 3 Sun). Mon to Sat D 6 to 9 (10 Fri and Sat). **Closed:** 26 Dec and 1 Jan. **Meals:** alc (main courses £14 to £25). **Service:** not inc. **Details:** Cards accepted. 60 seats. 12 seats outside. Separate bar. No mobile phones. Wheelchair access. Music. Car parking.

## Beeley
### Devonshire Arms
Well-to-do country inn
Devonshire Square, Beeley, DE4 2NR
Tel no: (01629) 733259
www.devonshirebeeley.co.uk
Gastropub | £25
Cooking score: 3

 V £30

It might appear to be just a pretty estate-owned village inn close to Chatsworth, but the Duchess of Devonshire's trademark modern touches give this place a chic, rustic tone that just about prepares you for the urban-style, all-glass-and-bold-colours brasserie extension. The flexible menu is generous, with some old-fashioned things on it (honey-glazed Derbyshire ham with fried eggs and chips, local estate Barnsley chop) as well as modern ones (whole roasted wood pigeon with Savoy cabbage, bacon loin and Parmentier potatoes). There's also an all-day menu (served 12 to 6) and lunchtime beef sandwiches. Reports of the food are positive, but there have been mutterings about 'London prices', and one reporter thought some extra staff training might not go amiss. House wine is £14.
Chef/s: Alan Hill. Open: all week 12 to 9.30.
Meals: alc (main courses £9 to £22). Service: not inc. Details: Cards accepted. 70 seats. 20 seats outside. Separate bar. No mobile phones. Wheelchair access. Music. Children allowed. Car parking.

## Chesterfield
### ALSO RECOMMENDED
### ▲ The Old Post
43 Holywell Street, Chesterfield, S41 7SH
Tel no: (01246) 279479
www.theoldpostrestaurant.co.uk
Modern British

Yes, it really was a post office, but since 2002 this venerable Elizabethan building has been home to Hugh and Mary Cocker's diminutive local restaurant. The kitchen is always dreaming up creative ideas – perhaps a 'tasting' of Lincolnshire pork (involving tea-smoked fillet, rillettes and Chinese five-spice belly) or John Dory fillet poached in Cabernet Sauvignon with Jerusalem artichoke étuvée (£22.50). To finish, how about a trio of crème brûlées (£7.55)? Four-course seasonal menus (£28.50) offer value. House wine £13.95. Closed Mon; also Tue and Sat L and Sun D.

## Darley Abbey
### Darleys
Modern food in a terrific setting
Darley Abbey Mills, Haslams Lane, Darley Abbey, DE22 1DZ
Tel no: (01332) 364987
www.darleys.com
Modern British | £35
Cooking score: 4

Darley's was refurbished at the outset of 2009, but it is still brimful of charm, as many regular reporters confirm. It's in the former canteen of an old cotton mill, and has wonderful views (try to bag a table next to the windows). Jonathan Hobson cooks in modern British style, with plaudits coming in this year for wild mushroom and Taleggio ravioli with rosemary and truffle foam, a duo of beef (fillet and shin) with puréed carrot and bay leaf sauce, and venison (cooked to a lovely pink) and served with spinach mousse, parsnip rösti and a sauce of Marsala. If you're in the market for fish, consider spiced monkfish with a smoked haddock beignet and butternut squash purée. Desserts such as warm Black Forest gâteau with cherry jelly and white chocolate ice cream will send you away happy. The single-sheet wine list offers a good international spread from £14.50.
Chef/s: Jonathan Hobson. Open: all week L 12 to 2 (2.30 Sun), Mon to Sat D 7 to 9 (9.30 Sat). Closed: bank hols, 2 weeks after 25 Dec. Meals: alc (main courses £17 to £22). Set L £15.95 (2 courses) to £17.95. Sun L £17.95 (2 courses) to £20. Service: not inc. Details: Cards accepted. 60 seats. 16 seats outside. Air-con. Separate bar. Wheelchair access. Music. Children allowed. Car parking.

## Froggatt Edge

### ALSO RECOMMENDED
### ▲ The Chequers Inn

Froggatt Edge, S32 3ZJ
Tel no: (01433) 630231
www.chequers-froggatt.com
Gastropub

A striking location beneath the steep banks of Froggatt Edge makes this pub-with-rooms a popular refuelling point for outdoor types navigating the Peak District. Restorative food comes in the shape of filling staples (beer-battered haddock, chips and mushy peas) and more upbeat gastro dishes – perhaps grilled sardines on toast with caper oil (£6) or breast of duck with pumpkin mash (£15). Sandwiches and all-day Sunday roasts play their part, while puds (£5.50) might feature sherry and raspberry trifle. House wine is £14.25. Open all week.

## Hathersage
### The George Hotel

Handsome looks and accomplished food
Main Road, Hathersage, S32 1BB
Tel no: (01433) 650436
www.george-hotel.net
Modern British | £35
Cooking score: 4

This rather handsome old coaching inn with its small paned windows, oak beams and open fires once accommodated Charlotte Brontë and provided inspiration for her novel *Jane Eyre*. Today, it is a comfortably appointed hotel with a restaurant at its heart, where Helen Heywood cooks an accomplished modern British menu that attracts a loyal band of regulars. Breast of wood pigeon makes a robust starter with honey-roasted pumpkin salad, while mains run from a thick steak of red pepper-crusted cod (served with warm chorizo and chickpea salad and basil dressing), to sirloin of beef, which comes with a cannelloni of 12-hour braised shin, fondant potato, red wine sauce and roasted garlic foam.

Dessert could offer mandarin jelly with warm chocolate ravioli. Freshly baked breads and petits fours excel too, and tasting notes make choosing wine easier. Bottle prices start at £15.95.
**Chef/s:** Helen Heywood. **Open:** all week L 12 to 2.30, D 6.30 to 10. **Meals:** Set L £28 (2 courses) to £35. Set D £28 (2 courses) to £35. Sun L £19.95 (2 courses) to £39.50 (4 courses). **Service:** not inc. **Details:** Cards accepted. 45 seats. Separate bar. No mobile phones. Wheelchair access. Music. Children allowed. Car parking.

## Ridgeway
### The Old Vicarage

Enchantment and culinary delights
Ridgeway Moor, Ridgeway, S12 3XW
Tel no: (0114) 2475814
www.theoldvicarage.co.uk
Modern British | £60
Cooking score: 7

£5
OFF

It's little wonder that readers endorse this adorable converted vicarage as 'the finest restaurant in the region'. Here is a top-end destination that puts personal comfort and hospitality above grand gestures, thanks to Tessa Bramley's supreme skills as a host and her inspired presence at the culinary heart of things. The enchanting wildflower copses, woodland walks and gardens that surround the house were laid out by a renowned Victorian horticulturist and they still provide the kitchen with valuable pickings. Elsewhere, faultless ingredients from a host of named suppliers are vital to the kitchen's endeavours, and Tessa never shies away from daring ideas, bold flavours or seasonal challenges. Her dishes are often complex and intricately worked, but never outlandish – witness two star turns from recent reports. First a starter of wild halibut fillet with a langoustine raviolo in a lemongrass bisque with tomato fondue followed by a 'quite fantastic' main course of boned Ridgeway partridge breasts layered with local black pudding, rolled, roasted, sliced and served with vanilla-tinged fondant potato, broccoli in lemon oil, prunes and pine nuts. Other ideas, such as fillet of cod with chargrilled leeks, bubble and squeak with cobnuts and passion fruit butter, show off her feel for ingredients and unexpected culinary marriages. Exquisite seasonal desserts often look to the garden for inspiration – notably the sweet woodruff ice cream served in May, and an astonishing confection of apple pie ice cream with almond crumble, apple flapjack, cinnamon milk and apple crisp.

Unpasteurised cheeses are sourced from across the British Isles, and the bespoke selection of coffees, teas and tisanes is also worth investigating. Vicarage Wine Cellars is run as a specialist importer with links to some of the world's most auspicious producers: the result is a wondrous list stuffed full of classics from top estates in France, Italy and Spain, plus exciting stuff from progressive New World vineyards. The list also features a 'cheap and cheerful' selection of 20 wines under £20, all of which can be ordered by the glass.

**Chef/s:** Tessa Bramley and Nathan Smith. **Open:** Tue to Fri L 12.30 to 2, Tue to Sat D 7 to 9.30 (6.30 Fri and Sat). **Closed:** Sun, Mon, bank hol Mon and Tue, 26 Dec to 4 Jan, first 2 weeks Aug. **Meals:** Set L £30 (2 courses) to £40. Set D £60 (4 courses) to £65. **Service:** not inc. **Details:** Cards accepted. 42 seats. 16 seats outside. No music. No mobile phones. Wheelchair access. Children allowed. Car parking.

## ▉ Rowsley

**READERS RECOMMEND**

## The Peacock at Rowsley

Modern British
Rowsley, DE4 2EB
Tel no: (01629) 733518
www.thepeacockatrowsley.com
**'Highly impressed with food, wine and accommodation'**

**Tessa Bramley** The Old Vicarage

**What made you want to become a chef?**
I never thought about being a chef – I just fell into it by accident! I was brought up during the war when food was scarce and basics were on ration. From my grandmother I learnt about country cooking, wild food, free hedgerow ingredients, cooking with spices and the joy of hospitality. Perhaps that's why I love restaurants so much.

**What is the best meal you have ever eaten?**
At Marc Veyrat's restaurant by the lake at Veyrier du Lac. I was impressed by the subtlety and interplay of flavours – it's so similar to how I try to cook myself.

**What is your top culinary tip?**
Take a walk in the countryside and be aware of what's around. Seasonal ingredients always work well together – elderflower with gooseberries, partridge with crab apples and thyme, sweet woodruff with cherries, hare saddle with juniper and pears.

**What's coming up next for you?**
I've no idea. I don't plan too much. That way each day's an adventure.

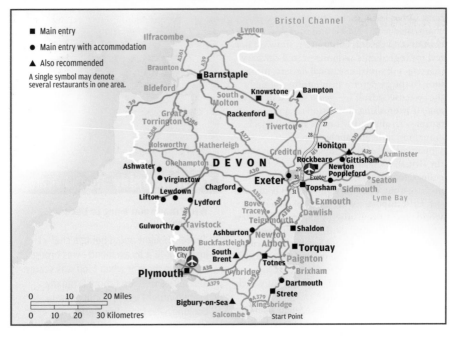

- ■ Main entry
- ● Main entry with accommodation
- ▲ Also recommended

A single symbol may denote several restaurants in one area.

## Ashburton

### Agaric

**'Real food' and pleasing vibes**
30 North Street, Ashburton, TQ13 7QD
Tel no: **(01364) 654478**
www.agaricrestaurant.co.uk
**Modern British | £35**
**Cooking score: 4**

Nick and Sophie Coiley's converted shop in the centre of Ashburton is an unprepossessing little gem, unstuffily informal, good-humoured and dedicated to the principles of 'real food'. There is serious domestic enterprise at work here, and a crusading loyalty to Devon's larder that pays dividends on the plate. Nick's cooking gets straight to the point: starters such as a warm salad of pigeon breast with quince, beetroot, smoked bacon and raspberry vinegar come with home-baked focaccia bread, while mains plunder the region for brill with grilled fennel and Seville orange hollandaise or herb-crusted best end of

lamb with Jerusalem artichoke purée and rosemary gravy. To finish, follow the calendar with forced rhubarb soufflé, rhubarb sauce and Pernod ice cream. This is genuine, unaffected cooking and it's backed by personable vibes and a wine list that offers sound drinking at easy prices (from £15.95). The Coileys also run a seasonal cookery school and offer charming accommodation in a nearby Georgian townhouse.
**Chef/s:** Nick Coiley. **Open:** Wed to Fri L 10 to 2, Wed to Sat D 7 to 9. **Closed:** Mon, Tue, Sun, 2 weeks Aug, 2 weeks Christmas. **Meals:** alc (main courses £15 to £19). Set L £14.95. **Service:** not inc. **Details:** Cards accepted. 28 seats. 14 seats outside. Separate bar. No music. No mobile phones. Wheelchair access. Children allowed.

## Average price

The average price listed in main-entry reviews denotes the price of a three-course meal, without wine.

# Ashwater

## Blagdon Manor

**In a glorious rural setting**
Ashwater, EX21 5DF
Tel no: (01409) 211224
www.blagdon.com
Modern British | £35
Cooking score: 2

The Moreys' seventeenth-century hotel to the north-west of Dartmoor offers a nice balance of country house comfort and a homely approach, right down to the resident pair of chocolate Labradors. With its primrose walls and garden views, the dining room makes a relaxing setting for Steve Morey's cooking, which adds a modern flourish to some traditional pairings. That might translate as skate tempura with mushy peas, onion gravy and tomato relish to open, then braised lamb shoulder with haggis, a steamed kidney pudding, liver and bacon. Passion fruit pannacotta with pineapple, coconut sorbet and chilli syrup is one of the lighter desserts. Wines start at £14 (£4 a glass) for Australian blends.
**Chef/s:** Steve Morey. **Open:** Fri to Sun L 12 to 2, all week D 7 to 9. **Closed:** Jan. **Meals:** Set L £17 (2 courses) to £20. Set D £31 (2 courses) to £35. Sun L £23.50. **Service:** not inc. **Details:** Cards accepted. 28 seats. Separate bar. No music. No mobile phones. Wheelchair access. Car parking.

# Bampton

ALSO RECOMMENDED
## ▲ The Quarryman's Rest

Briton Street, Bampton, EX16 9LN
Tel no: (01398) 331480
www.thequarrymansrest.co.uk
Modern British

Paul and Donna Berry continue to feed Bampton locals and incomers at their unpretentious old coaching inn off the main street. Much of the produce comes from within 25 miles of the pub, with fish delivered from Brixham day boats and all cheeses coming from the South West. Potted salt beef (£4.95), braised lamb shank with rosemary gravy (£11.50), or halibut with bubble and squeak and pea sauce are typical choices, and there could be banana and toffee crumble to finish. House wine £11.95. Closed Sun D.

# Barnstaple

NEW ENTRY
## James Duckett at the Old Custom House

**A godsend for the neighbourhood**
9 The Strand, Barnstaple, EX31 1EU
Tel no: (01271) 370123
www.jamesduckett.co.uk
Modern European | £30
Cooking score: 2

£5
OFF

'This restaurant is the best thing to happen to Barnstaple for years', enthuses one regular. James Duckett's 'smallish restaurant' extends to a courtyard and private dining room and has a light feel, with polished oak floors, beams and simply laid tables. Menus change daily, with a set lunch offered alongside some dozen tapas-style dishes (venison with pickled walnuts and spiced port wine sauce, and risotto of crab with basil and lemon oil have been well-reported) and a short-choice set dinner. Highlights at inspection were an excellent butter-poached cod with samphire, squid ink risotto, carrot and clams, and a well-made lemon tart (though let down by clumsy rhubarb tempura and grainy sorbet). The wine list is a creditable list of affordable bottles from £14.
**Chef/s:** James Duckett. **Open:** Tue to Sat L 12 to 2.30, D 7 to 10.30. **Closed:** Sun, Mon, 26 Dec, first 2 weeks Jan. **Meals:** Tapas-style set L £8 (2 courses) to £12. Set D £24 (2 courses) to £29. Tasting menu £50. **Service:** not inc. **Details:** Cards accepted. 48 seats. 36 seats outside. Wheelchair access. Music. Children allowed.

## ▌Bigbury-on-Sea

### ALSO RECOMMENDED
### ▲ Oyster Shack

Milburn Orchard Farm, Stakes Hill, Bigbury-on-Sea, TQ7 4BE
Tel no: (01548) 810876
www.oystershack.co.uk
**Seafood**

The Shack is a valuable local resource and an agreeable stopover for visitors with absolutely fresh seafood the main attraction, although it may receive plain or elaborately creamy treatment. Expect oysters, lobsters hot and cold, and whole Salcombe crabs (£22), as well as baked haddock with a soft herb crust and home-dried tomato chutney (£15.95) and local trout with creamy curried mussels. House wine from £14.30. Open all week. A second branch is at Hannaford's Landing, 11-13 Island Street, Salcombe; tel no: (01548) 843596.

## ▌Buckfastleigh

### READERS RECOMMEND
### Riverford Field Kitchen

**Modern British**
Wash Barn, Buckfastleigh, TQ11 0LD
Tel no: (01803) 762074
www.riverford.co.uk
'Organic farm where the produce creates the daily menu'

## ▌Chagford

### Gidleigh Park

**Assured cooking in a blissful setting**
Chagford, TQ13 8HH
Tel no: (01647) 432367
www.gidleigh.com
**Modern European | £46**
**Cooking score: 7**
£5 OFF ▪ 🍷 🚆 V

When dinner hour arrives, Gidleigh Park's blissful edge-of-the-moor location, extensive grounds and rumbling river are locked out in the blackness. The smart half-timbered exterior disappears with them, and the focus is on the series of wood-panelled dining rooms, which have an ambience that some guests find 'superb' and others 'dreary'. In truth, a lot depends on whether fellow occupants of these small salons are hushed or exuberant in their enjoyment of Michael Caines' precise modern cooking. Though new dishes do arrive (pastry, particularly, is evolving nicely) menus cleave closely to a repertoire of studiously local protein with tried-and-true garnishes. This matters less than it might, not only because the place screams 'treat' but also because Caines' magpie tendencies make his classic dishes a lively proposition. Thai purée and lemongrass foam, which serve as the baubles on Cornish sea bass, might abut a ballottine of foie gras with melting Madeira jelly and truffle salad, while fennel purée and tapenade jus add mild exotica to a main course of Dartmoor lamb with boulangère potatoes. Cheese, sliced or spooned from the trolley with knowledge and great good humour, is another strength, as are soufflés – perhaps pistachio or prune and Armagnac – so light they're fit to be inhaled. Staff, who must linger in the corridor while their charges butter their bread ('flaky' black olive and tomato is a favourite), are sharp-eyed, proper and mindful of boundaries: over-familiarity is unlikely to be a problem here. A commitment to quality is clear, however, especially when the delights of the 950-bin cellar are being communicated by members of a young but expert wine team. The thinking drinker will find lots to discuss and more to be tempted by, including plenty of French classics, an extensive selection of halves, and a couple of good French ciders. Wine flights may be the relatively easy option, but include both heavenly and interesting matches. Bottle entry level is £28.
**Chef/s:** Michael Caines. **Open:** all week L 12 to 2.30, D 7 to 9.45. **Meals:** Set L £38 (2 courses) to £46. Set D £105 (3 courses). Tasting menu £120 (7 courses). **Service:** not inc. **Details:** Cards accepted. 52 seats. Separate bar. No music. No mobile phones. Wheelchair access. Car parking.

# Dartmouth

## New Angel

Celeb chef's waterfront gaff
2 South Embankment, Dartmouth, TQ6 9BH
Tel no: (01803) 839425
www.thenewangel.co.uk
Modern French | £40
Cooking score: 3

Once home to the iconic Carved Angel, John Burton-Race's high-profile restaurant now has a lighter, brighter tone and a more user-friendly attitude that allows for occasional breakfasts and light lunches as well as full-on French-inspired cooking. Devon produce is at the heart of things, whether it's breast of Creedy Carver duck with foie gras, spring vegetables and Sauternes sauce, Dartmouth crab ('landed by Tony'), grilled day-boat brill accompanied by vegetable tagliatelle, shrimp and sherry vinegar butter, or rib of South Devon beef with bordelaise beans and big fat chips (for two to share). To finish, expertly presented nougat parfait with passion fruit ice cream has hit the target. France is the main contributor to the auspicious wine list, although there are also sharp selections from elite producers worldwide. Bottles start at £22.50 (£6 a glass).
Chef/s: John Burton-Race. Open: Wed to Sun L 12.30 to 2.30, D 6.30 to 9.30. Closed: Mon, Tue, all Jan. Meals: alc (main courses £19 to £28). Set L £19.50 (2 courses) to £24.50. Set D £24.50 (2 courses) to £29.50. Service: 12.5%. Details: Cards accepted. 70 seats. Air-con. Separate bar. Music. Children allowed.

### Please send us your feedback

To register your opinion about any restaurant listed in the Guide, or a new restaurant that you wish to bring to our attention, please visit the web address at the bottom of the page. Your feedback informs the content of the book and will be used to compile next year's reviews.

## The Seahorse

First for fish
5 South Embankment, Dartmouth, TQ6 9BH
Tel no: (01803) 835147
www.seahorserestaurant.co.uk
Seafood | £35
Cooking score: 4

Dartmouth is always worth a visit, and the Seahorse adds sparkle to its growing gastronomic scene. Look for the shell-pink and white frontage on the Dart waterfront. Those with river-legs might take the courtesy boat, *Pearlfisher*, which does the crossing home for restaurant patrons. Fish from Brixham is the name of the game, served in a variety of classic ways (skate with black butter and capers, 'truly excellent' seafood stew scented with saffron and thyme), or else just grilled over charcoal embers. Other local treasures might be Elbury Cove mussels steamed with bay, garlic and parsley. Meat-eaters are not neglected, if Devon lamb seasoned with rosemary, mint and anchovy is anything to go by. Finish with sticky toffee pudding or crème brûlée. The wine list is teeming with good growers and well-chosen vintages, with a particularly strong showing in Italy. Loire house varietals, a Sauvignon and a Gamay, are £14.
Chef/s: Mitch Tonks and Mat Prowse. Open: Wed to Sat L 12 to 3, Tue to Sat D 6 to 10. Closed: Sun, Mon, 3 weeks Jan. Meals: alc (main courses £14 to £25). Set L and D £20 (2 courses) to £25. Service: not inc. Details: Cards accepted. 40 seats. 4 seats outside. Air-con. Wheelchair access. Music. Children allowed.

# Elburton

READERS RECOMMEND
## Lemon Tree Café & Bistro
Modern European
2 Haye Road South, Elburton, PL9 8HJ
Tel no: (01752) 481117
www.lemontreecafe.co.uk
'Good pit-stop outside Plymouth'

## ▌Exeter
### Michael Caines at ABode Exeter

**Clever cooking on an exciting upswing**
Royal Clarence Hotel, Cathedral Yard, Exeter, EX1 1HD
Tel no: (01392) 223638
www.michaelcaines.com
**Modern European | £48**
**Cooking score: 5**

The location, right next to the cathedral, is hard to beat, with the ground-floor of the hotel given over to a luxurious bar for pre-dinner drinks, and the wide, cream room that is the Devon branch of ABode. The cooking is on an exciting upswing, with a carte that features some complex-sounding but clever dishes, based on good local supplies. Start with duck liver terrine and brioche, its conventionally fatty richness offset with the acidic twang of rhubarb served every which way (whole, crisped, puréed and jellied). A main course of John Dory from Brixham at a May lunch was a triumph, the fish timed to a nicety and accompanied by buttery, salty mash, diced tomato and a brace of roasted langoustines. The fixed-price lunch menu is a steal, especially when the main course delivers eloquently flavoured confit lamb shoulder with aubergine caviar and a tapenade jus. Finish with pannacotta, West Countrified with clotted cream, topped with a stingingly intense preserved-lemon sorbet, and served with marinated strawberries. Service, criticised on occasion by readers for lack of attention, has brushed up its act. The varietally arranged wine list opens with a useful glass selection from £4.60, with bottles from £19.25.
**Chef/s:** Tom Williams-Hawkes. **Open:** Mon to Sat L 12 to 2.30, D 6 to 10 (6.30 Sat). **Closed:** Sun. **Meals:** alc (main courses £21 to £24). Set L £14.50 (2 courses) to £19.50. Early D (6 to 7) £14.95. Tasting menu £58. **Service:** 12% (optional). **Details:** Cards accepted. 65 seats. Air-con. Separate bar. No mobile phones. Wheelchair access. Music.

## ▌Gittisham
### Combe House

**Pin-sharp food and splendour**
Gittisham, EX14 3AD
Tel no: (01404) 540400
www.thishotel.com
**Modern British | £45**
**Cooking score: 5**

£5 OFF 🍷 🛏

Set amid acres of rolling Devon, Combe House is a privately owned Elizabethan manor. Pint-sized Arabian horses and pheasants wander the grounds, there is a temple-like summerhouse beside the kitchen garden, and the dining rooms are easy on the eye, one panelled in splendour, the other a smaller, more summery space with wraparound pastoral mural and folding screens. Service is keen as mustard and in Hadleigh Barrett the house has a talented, conscientious chef. Dishes follow the seasons beadily, and draw on the best local supplies. The style is classical country house but with a modern sensibility, offering well-nigh flawless lobster risotto, rich with saffron-scented crustacean sauce. Main course compositions and timings are pin-sharp, as when sea bream appears with a cloud of pomme purée and chargrilled fennel, or guinea fowl breast with finely shredded choucroute and morels. The keen definition of these dishes continues through to desserts such as white chocolate mousse studded with griottine cherries, served with intense pistachio ice cream. West Country cheeses are a selection of the regional stars. A user-friendly list is grouped roughly according to what foods the wines will accompany. The choices are inspired; France is key, but there are good showings from Italy and the New World too. Bottles start at £19.
**Chef/s:** Hadleigh Barrett and Stuart Brown. **Open:** all week L 12 to 2, D 7 to 9.30. **Closed:** last 2 weeks Jan. **Meals:** Set L £25 (2 courses) to £29. Set D £45. Sun L £35. **Service:** not inc. **Details:** Cards accepted. 65 seats. Separate bar. No mobile phones. Wheelchair access. Music. Children allowed. Car parking.

## Gulworthy

### The Horn of Plenty
**Ravishing views and high-flying food**
Gulworthy, PL19 8JD
Tel no: (01822) 832528
www.thehornofplenty.co.uk
**Modern European | £47**
**Cooking score: 6**
£5 OFF

Location is everything, and tranquillity reigns at this soul-soothing country house with ravishing views along the wooded Tamar Valley – a prospect that probably hasn't changed much since the place was built in 1870 for one of the captains of the Devon Mine Consol. These days, visitors make the trek up the hill and through orchards and gardens, in spring ablaze with azaleas and rhododendrons, to enjoy true hospitality and high-flying modern cuisine. The kitchen delivers waves of invention and meticulous technique with no backward glances to sleepy country house cooking. Starters set the tone for what is to follow: fillets of Dover sole are paired with foie gras and salsify, while crispy duck confit is partnered by butternut squash ravioli in a red wine and orange-infused sauce. After that, ideas come thick and fast; witness a main course of saddle of venison atop a tangle of greens with creamy rosemary and garlic polenta or mainstream roasted fillet of sea bass on saffron risotto. Vegetarians are offered a plentiful three-part assiette, while desserts press the comfort button for steamed ginger sponge pudding or caramelised apple crème brûlée with hot apple pancakes and cider sorbet. Astutely chosen house selections (from £18) open the impressively assembled wine list, which explores the classic French regions before looking further afield for gilt-edged global drinking.
**Chef/s:** Peter Gorton. **Open:** all week L 12 to 4, D 7 to 12. **Closed:** 24 to 26 Dec. **Meals:** Set L £26.50. Set D £47. **Service:** not inc. **Details:** Cards accepted. 60 seats. 18 seats outside. Air-con. Separate bar. No mobile phones. Wheelchair access. Music. Children allowed. Car parking.

## Honiton

ALSO RECOMMENDED
### ▲ The Holt
178 High Street, Honiton, EX14 1LA
Tel no: (01404) 47707
www.theholt-honiton.com
**Modern European**

The Holt is noted for a relaxed vibe in its rustic, wood-floored bar and for some great modern pub food in the upstairs dining room. From an open kitchen Angus McCaig cooks imaginative dishes using produce sourced from local farms and estates. Home-cured meats feature in things like smoked duck breast and baby vegetable terrine with apple purée and pickles (£5.50), or there could be confit lamb shoulder with mint jus (£15). Lunch brings sandwiches and tapas dishes. House wine £12.50. Closed Sun and Mon.

## Kingsbridge

READERS RECOMMEND
### Harbour Lights
**Modern British**
Hope Cove, Kingsbridge, TQ7 3HQ
Tel no: (01548) 561376
'Fresh, seasonal and local'

## Knowstone

### The Mason's Arms
**Impeccably crafted modern food**
Knowstone, EX36 4RY
Tel no: (01398) 341231
www.masonsarmsdevon.co.uk
**Modern British | £38**
**Cooking score: 6**

The low-roofed, beamed and thatched inn on the Devon/Somerset border can trace its lineage back eight centuries. That said, the place has been given a bright, modern makeover to create an airy, uplifting dining space alongside a more traditional bar. Mark Dodson was head chef for over a decade at The Waterside Inn (see entry, Bray), and brings a little classic French cuisine refinement to essentially modern British menus. Seared peppered tuna is accompanied by a Thai-style salad dressed in sesame oil and soy, while the leek and potato soup comes bulked with mussels. For mains, there might be monkfish, modishly wrapped in prosciutto and sauced with orange and balsamic, or local beef fillet paired with oxtail and served with potato fondant and parsnip purée. Desserts offer the more traditional likes of pear frangipane tart with butterscotch ice cream, or Amaretto parfait with plums poached in vanilla, as well as impeccable regional cheeses. A shortish wine list opens at £13.60 for a vin de pays Chenin Blanc, with offerings by the glass from £4.75.

**Chef/s:** Mark Dodson. **Open:** Tue to Sun L 12 to 2, Tue to Sat D 7 to 9. **Closed:** Mon, first week Jan. **Meals:** alc (main courses £16 to £21). Sun L £33.50. **Service:** not inc. **Details:** Cards accepted. 28 seats. 24 seats outside. Separate bar. Music. Car parking.

## Lewdown
### Lewtrenchard Manor
**Modern food in country house setting**
Lewdown, EX20 4PN
Tel no: (01566) 783222
www.lewtrenchard.co.uk
**Modern British | £49**
**Cooking score: 6**
£5 OFF  🍷 🚗 V

Nestling in a wooded hollow on the edge of Dartmoor, the Jacobean manor house has been home to some colourful members of the Gould family over the centuries, from the freebooting Oriental trader James Gould to the Reverend Sabine Baring Gould, composer of *Onward Christian Soldiers*. The interiors are of a high order throughout, from the slate-floored hallway onwards, and dining goes on either in an ambience of decorated panelling and stained-glass windows, or outdoors in the courtyard. Jason Hornbuckle continues to maintain a formidable pace, with seasonally based food that draws on local game, fish from the quays at Looe and vegetables from the hotel's own walled garden. An unmistakably modern approach sees sea bass paired with

chorizo cassoulet as a starter, with perhaps a four-way serving of lamb – loin, liver and kidneys with a sweetbread beignet and broccoli purée – to follow. Voguish slow cooking is extended even to fish such as salmon, presented in a nage of scallops and mussels, with spinach and tomato fondue. The purées of recent years are much in evidence, but the cooking retains undeniable depth, all the way to desserts such as advocaat parfait with Malibu syrup and toasted coconut. Wines are a cosmopolitan, well-chosen collection, with prices that are not necessarily as high as you might expect, outside classic France at least. Argentinian house wines are £18.

**Chef/s:** Jason Hornbuckle. **Open:** all week L 12 to 2.30, D 7 to 10. **Meals:** Set L £15 (2 courses) to £19.50. Set D £35 (2 courses) to £55. Sun L £22.50. **Service:** not inc. **Details:** Cards accepted. 45 seats. 20 seats outside. Separate bar. No mobile phones. Wheelchair access. Music. Children allowed. Car parking.

## Lifton
### The Arundell Arms
**Civilised sporting retreat**
Fore Street, Lifton, PL16 0AA
Tel no: (01566) 784666
www.arundellarms.com
**Modern British | £36**
**Cooking score: 5**
🍷 🚗 V

Fishin', shootin' and ridin' types flock to Anne Voss-Bark's civilised country retreat, secreted away in a valley close to the uplands of Dartmoor. This is a sporting hotel *par excellence*, with 20 miles of angling rights on the nearby River Tamar and its tributaries, plus abundant opportunities for other waxed-up Barbour pursuits. After a day out in the open, rest your limbs in the elegantly appointed restaurant, where uncluttered menus make the most of fine, regionally sourced produce. Game and fish are major players, and the choice might extend to grilled fillet of red mullet with a ragoût of clams, lemon and parsley or mignon of venison with oyster mushrooms, rösti and red wine. Elsewhere, Falmouth Bay scallops might be paired with tempura cauliflower, and Devon beef fillet could appear with oxtail pudding, root vegetables and Madeira. For dessert, the kitchen pulls out all the stops for, say, a gratin of strawberries and raspberries with Champagne sabayon. Alternatively, chill out in the bar with a drink and some blue-blooded, pub-style food (think croque-monsieur and spiced venison burgers). The wine list embarks on a thorough-going tour of France, but also gives due attention to high-calibre selections from the rest of the vinous world. Half-bottles and options by the glass abound, with house recommendations from £16.

**Chef/s:** Steven Pidgeon. **Open:** all week L 12 to 3, D 6 to 10 (9.30 Sun). **Closed:** 25 to 27 Dec. **Meals:** Set L £25 (2 courses) to £29. Set D £46 (2 courses) to £49. Sun L £25. **Service:** not inc. **Details:** Cards accepted. 70 seats. 16 seats outside. Separate bar. No mobile phones. Wheelchair access. Music. Children allowed. Car parking.

## ■ Lydford

### The Dartmoor Inn

**Smart high-flier with local leanings**
Moorside, Lydford, EX20 4AY
Tel no: (01822) 820221
www.dartmoorinn.com
Modern British | £26
Cooking score: 3

£5 OFF  🛏  V  £30

Since taking over this gentrified country hostelry in 1998, Philip and Karen Burgess have turned it into a Dartmoor high-flier. The interior has been tricked out in true country-chic style, and the food has local leanings – although ideas are drawn from all over. Fritters are one of the kitchen's trademarks, but the restaurant menu also reaches out into the realms of roast black bream fillet with almonds and coriander, or confit duck with vanilla and apple purée. A few 'easy dining' options are offered in the bar, while desserts stay in the comfort zone for, say, rhubarb and walnut crumble tart. Some reports suggest

that standards are slipping, but supporters continue to applaud the inn's all-round virtues. Real ales and ciders point up the West Country theme, although the wine list (from £14) is global in outlook.

**Chef/s:** Andrew Honey and Philip Burgess. **Open:** Tue to Sun L 12 to 2.15, Mon to Sat D 6.30 to 9. **Meals:** alc (main courses £10 to £22). Set L and D £17 (2 courses) to £22. Sun L £25. **Service:** not inc. **Details:** Cards accepted. 80 seats. 25 seats outside. Children allowed. Car parking.

## ■ Newton Poppleford

### Moores'

**Lovely coastal setting**
6 Greenbank, Newton Poppleford, EX10 0EB
Tel no: (01395) 568100
www.mooresrestaurant.co.uk
Modern British | £28
Cooking score: 1

£5 OFF  🛏  £30

Formerly the village stores, Moores' occupies two cottages dating from the early 1900s. Its interior is smart but homely (think carpets and linen-clad tables) and outside there's a pretty garden for summer dining. Jonathan Moore's cooking is a confident rendition of the modern British theme, offering dishes such as wild mushroom consommé with white truffle oil followed by slowly braised leg and cutlet of prime Devonshire lamb with creamed leek mash and baby vegetables. Finish with poached pear and plum in mulled red wine reduction. Wines start at £12.95.

**Chef/s:** Jonathan Moore. **Open:** Tue to Sun L 12 to 1.30, Tue to Sat D 7 to 9.30. **Closed:** 25 and 26 Dec, first 2 weeks Jan. **Meals:** Set L £14.95 (2 courses) to £19.90. Weekday Set D £17.50 (2 courses) to £22.45. Weekend Set D £22.50 (2 courses) to £27.50. Sun L £14.95. **Service:** not inc. **Details:** Cards accepted. 32 seats. 12 seats outside. No mobile phones. Wheelchair access. Music. Children allowed.

## Plymouth

### Tanners
Lively cooking from brothers in whites
Prysten House, Finewell Street, Plymouth,
PL1 2AE
Tel no: (01752) 252001
www.tannersrestaurant.com
Modern British | £35
Cooking score: 3

V

Prysten House dates from the fifteenth
century and is reputed to be one of the oldest
domestic buildings in Plymouth. But as far as
Chris and James Tanner are concerned, Olde
England stops at the tapestry-covered rough
stone walls in the restaurant. The TV chefs'
modern British food puts the emphasis on
local and regional materials and the repertoire
embraces corn-fed chicken and ham hock
terrine with piccalilli, and steamed black
bream with mussel and saffron risotto.
Reports this year have commented on dishes
lacking sparkle and a lack of attention to
detail, but desserts are pleasing creations like
chocolate torte with peanut brittle and banana
sorbet. A Verre de Vin system allows for a wide
choice of wines by the glass; elsewhere bottles
on the carefully annotated wine list start
at £13.95.
Chef/s: Chris and James Tanner. Open: Tue to Sat L
12 to 2.30, D 7 to 9.30. Closed: Sun, Mon, 25 and 26
Dec, 31 Dec and 1 Jan. Meals: alc (main courses £15
to £25). Set L £14 (2 courses) to £18. Set D £28 (2
courses) to £35. Tasting menu £45. Service: not inc.
Details: Cards accepted. 60 seats. Separate bar. No
mobile phones. Wheelchair access. Music. Children
allowed.

### READERS RECOMMEND

### Perillas
Fish and chips
1A Ford Park Road, Mutley, Plymouth, PL4 6QY
Tel no: (01752) 662220
www.perillasfishandchips.co.uk
'Fish cooked to perfection and to order'

## Rackenford

NEW ENTRY
### The Stag Inn
A strong local accent
Rackenford, EX16 8DT
Tel no: (01884) 881369
www.thestaginn.com
Gastropub | £23
Cooking score: 1

£5 £30
OFF

Reporters think the refurbishment of this
ancient thatched and low-beamed inn has
been over-enthusiastic, but like the way the
Devonian twang of the drinkers in the bar is
picked up on a slate offering North Devon
asparagus with fried duck egg, dressed
Brixham crab, and Red Ruby Devon beef
burger. Intimate, white-clothed areas offer
more formal dinners, say warm salad of wood
pigeon with smoked Yeo bacon and quails'
eggs followed by organic local chicken with
cider sauce. House wine £12.95.
Chef/s: Matthew Robinson. Open: all week L 12 to 3
(4 Sun), Mon to Sat D 6.30 to 11. Meals: alc (main
courses £10 to £19). Sun L £12.50. Service: not inc.
Details: Cards accepted. 50 seats. 40 seats outside.
Separate bar. Wheelchair access. Music. Children
allowed. Car parking.

## Rockbeare

### The Jack in the Green
Devon food champion
London Road, Rockbeare, EX5 2EE
Tel no: (01404) 822240
www.jackinthegreen.uk.com
Modern British | £25
Cooking score: 3

V

Hungry and en route to Cornwall? Then it's
worth the short diversion off the A30 to this
rather unassuming roadside pub. Step inside
and you'll find a traditional bar, a series of cosy,
warmly lit dining rooms and modern,
innovative menus that bristle with seasonal
Devon produce, all sourced from within 25
miles of the pub. Owner Paul Parnell and chefs

Matt Mason and Craig Sampson are an impressive combo, their passion and enthusiasm for local artisan produce deep-rooted. Try a mixed Devon cheese ploughman's in the bar (with a pint of Otter Ale) or settle by by the wood-burning stove next door for own air-dried beef served with rye bread and celeriac rémoulade, then rack of Whimple lamb with honey-roast garlic purée and basil mash, with a chestnut crème brûlée to finish. Wines start at £15.
**Chef/s:** Matt Mason and Craig Sampson. **Open:** all week L 12 to 2 (2.30 Fri and Sat, 12 to 9 Sun), D 6 to 9.30 (10 Fri and Sat). **Closed:** 25 Dec to 4 Jan. **Meals:** alc (main courses £10 to £23). Set L and D £25 (3 courses). Sun L £18.95. **Service:** not inc. **Details:** Cards accepted. 130 seats. 80 seats outside. Air-con. Separate bar. Wheelchair access. Music. Children allowed. Car parking.

## ▍Shaldon

## Ode

**Certified green credentials**
21 Fore Street, Shaldon, TQ14 ODE
**Tel no: (01626) 873977**
www.odetruefood.co.uk
**Modern British | £32**
**Cooking score: 2**

£5 OFF

Tim and Clare Bouget's discreet little restaurant is certified 'organic' by the Soil Association – but its green credentials don't end there. Their three-storey Georgian town house has been re-vamped using recycled and sustainable materials, while the kitchen is committed to Devon produce, ethically reared meat and line-caught fish. The result is a vivid repertoire that is often tweaked with bold global gestures: steamed red mullet might appear with roasted butternut squash, black kale, cumin and orange, while Crediton duck breast is cooked under vacuum with cloves, sweet-and-sour soy and pearl barley. Finish in style with, say, lemon and lime brûlée tart with clementine sorbet. The 100% organic wine list starts at £18.50.

**Chef/s:** Tim Bouget. **Open:** Thur to Fri L 12 to 1.30, Wed to Sat D 7 to 9.30, Sun brunch 11 to 1.30. **Closed:** Mon, Tue, first 2 weeks Oct, bank hols. **Meals:** alc (main courses £16 to £22). Set L £17.50 (2 courses) to £21.50. **Service:** not inc. **Details:** Cards accepted. 24 seats. Wheelchair access. Music. Children allowed. Car parking.

## ▍South Brent

## ALSO RECOMMENDED
## ▲ The Turtley Corn Mill
Avonwick, South Brent, TQ10 9ES
**Tel no: (01364) 646100**
www.avonwick.net
**Gastropub**

Converted to a pub in the 1970s and totally renovated in 2005, this former mill house stands in six acres beside a small lake. Rooms may be rambling, but they have a fresh, contemporary feel, with slate floors, old dining tables, deep sofas and log-burning stoves. Equally modern are the daily printed menus (served all day), which list traditional haddock in Tamar real ale batter (£11.95) alongside game terrine with spiced chutney (£5.75) and seafood cassoulet (£13.95). House wine is £13.75. Open all week.

## ▍Strete

## The Kings Arms
**Pretty pub specialising in seafood**
Dartmouth Road, Strete, TQ6 ORW
**Tel no: (01803) 770377**
www.kingsarms-dartmouth.co.uk
**Seafood | £24**
**Cooking score: 2**

£5 OFF  £30

Hard by the coast road, with glorious views across Start Bay, Rob Dawson's striking eighteenth-century pub draws a loyal crowd with its paean to local seafood. Sit in the traditional carpeted bar or bag one of the window seats in the contemporary dining room, with its fresh, nautical feel. The food is treated in a simple, forthright manner. Fish soup or juicy scallops served with crème fraîche and chilli might be followed by grilled plaice with brown shrimp butter, or hearty, Spanish-style cod with chorizo, pepper and potato stew. There's sirloin steak with Café de Paris butter for die-hard meat-eaters and warm chocolate tart to finish. House wine £15.

**Chef/s:** Rob Dawson. **Open:** all week L 12 to 2 (12 to 9 Sat and Sun), D 6.30 to 9 (5 Fri). **Closed:** Mon in winter, last 3 weeks of Jan. **Meals:** alc (main courses £10 to £17). **Service:** not inc. **Details:** Cards accepted. 36 seats. 48 seats outside. Separate bar. No mobile phones. Wheelchair access. Music. Children allowed. Car parking.

## Topsham
### La Petite Maison
**Well-rendered French style**
35 Fore Street, Topsham, EX3 0HR
Tel no: (01392) 873660
www.lapetitemaison.co.uk
**Anglo-French | £35**
**Cooking score: 4**
£5
OFF

Trendy Topsham, by the River Exe, is the fashionable backdrop for the Pestell family's personable restaurant in a historic curved and bow-windowed building. The name not only sums up the proportions and homely appeal of the place, but also spotlights the Gallic undercurrent that drifts through the cooking. That said, West Country ingredients are the kitchen's building blocks, and they are handled with seasonal sensitivity and aplomb. Lyme Bay crab appears in a risotto with asparagus and crab bisque sauce, while breast of Creedy Carver organic duck comes with confit leg and a plum and star anise sauce. European accents also grace goats' cheese soufflé with pesto dressing, wild mushroom feuilleté and roast chump of local lamb with ratatouille, herb-flecked potato cake and rosemary and mint jus. Desserts are even-handed in their loyalties – sticky toffee pudding alongside poached pear with mulled wine jelly, say. France leads the way on the broadly egalitarian wine list; house selections are £15.95.

**Chef/s:** Douglas Pestell and Sarah Bright. **Open:** Tue to Sat L 12.30 to 2, D 7 to 10. **Closed:** Sun, Mon, 26 Dec. **Meals:** Set L and D £28.95 (2 courses) to £34.95. **Service:** not inc. **Details:** Cards accepted. 30 seats. Music. Children allowed.

## Torquay
### The Elephant
**Foodie fireworks against a bay backdrop**
3-4 Beacon Terrace, Torquay, TQ1 2BH
Tel no: (01803) 200044
www.elephantrestaurant.co.uk
**Modern British | £45**
**Cooking score: 5**
£5
OFF

Torquay's waterfront is a magical sight of an evening and it offers a plethora of eating, from the unmistakable waft of battered fish to the upscale haven that is the Elephant. The establishment is divided into upper and lower rooms; the ground-floor a brasserie with an extensive menu of European favourites, and a more formal space above where culinary fireworks are accompanied by serene bay views. Simon Hulstone has refined his practice and tries some daring turns built upon the sure foundation of pedigree West Country produce. The six-course tasting menu is a route through, taking in a clever 'risotto' of finely chopped squid and cauliflower, pan-roasted halibut with parsnip purée and a verjus butter sauce of delightful acidity, and pure-bred local beef fillet, served with shredded Savoy cabbage and bacon, along with a complex construction of cep and artichoke mousses. An unfashionably assertive approach to salt is perhaps to be praised in the odd dish, but here it accumulates from course to course – beginning with a cup of vividly salty broccoli and blue cheese soup, and ending with salted dark chocolate truffle. This last, however, was offset with candied pistachios, diced raspberry and red pepper jelly and a vibrant passion fruit coulis. A short wine list (from £14.95) finds enough flavours to match the cooking.

Chef/s: Simon Hulstone. **Open:** Brasserie Tue to Sun L 12 to 2.30, Tue to Sat D 6.30 to 9.30. Restaurant Tue to Sat D 7 to 9.30. **Closed:** Mon, first 2 weeks Jan. **Meals:** Brasserie Set L £14.50 (2 courses) to £17.50. Set D £20.50 (2 courses) to £24.50. Restaurant Set D £37.50 (2 courses) to £45. Tasting menu £55. **Service:** not inc. **Details:** Cards accepted. 24 seats. Air-con. Separate bar. No mobile phones. Wheelchair access. Music. Children allowed.

## ▌Totnes

### Effings

**Deli/café with good food and charm**
50 Fore Street, Totnes, TQ9 5RP
Tel no: (01803) 863435
www.effings.co.uk
**Modern European | £20**
**Cooking score: 2**

**V**

Situated on the main street, just below the East Gate arch, is a deli/café that has five tables at the back for daytime eating. Get there early to avoid disappointment at lunchtime (12 to 2.15), and enjoy cooking that's reminiscent of superior gastropub food, with the day's choices chalked up on a board. Salmon terrine with pickled baby cucumbers and toast, black and hog's puddings with potatoes, caramelised apples and cider sauce, and a finale of hot clementine gratin with lemon curd ice cream, might be one hugely satisfying way through the bill of fare. It is served with warmth and charm, and accompanied by a short selection of regularly changing wines, from £13.75 a bottle (£3.75 a glass).
**Chef/s:** Karl Rasmussen. **Open:** Mon to Sat 9 to 4.30. **Closed:** Sun, bank hols. **Meals:** alc (main courses £9 to £14). **Service:** not inc. **Details:** Cards accepted. 14 seats. Air-con. No music. No mobile phones. Wheelchair access. Children allowed.

## ▌Virginstow

## Percy's Country Hotel

**Eco-friendly escape with unfussy menus**
Coombeshead Estate, Virginstow, EX21 5EA
Tel no: (01409) 211236
www.percys.co.uk
**Modern British | £40**
**Cooking score: 4**

£5 OFF 🚗

Looking for a restorative antidote to the big-city rat race? Tony and Tina Bricknell-Webb's enterprising venture might be just the answer. Their converted 400-year-old Devon longhouse (with a zinc bar, stylish guest rooms and other modern additions) is now the hub of a 130-acre, Soil Association-accredited organic estate that supplies much of the produce for the kitchen. Tina puts it all to good use in her admirably unfussy dinner menus, which go straight to the heart of modern country cooking. Roast home-reared meat is always in the limelight – perhaps loin of pork with sage and juniper gravy or lamb with rosemary jus – although the owners also procure fish from Cornwall for dishes such as a duo of John Dory and turbot with béarnaise sauce or monkfish with ginger and saffron. Cheeses are West Country patriots, while desserts include the likes of cardamom and lime crème brûlée. Organic names loom large on the short, thoughtfully chosen wine list, with prices from £20.
**Chef/s:** Tina Bricknell-Webb. **Open:** all week D only 7 to 9. **Meals:** Set D £40. **Service:** not inc.
**Details:** Cards accepted. 16 seats. Separate bar. No mobile phones. Wheelchair access. Car parking.

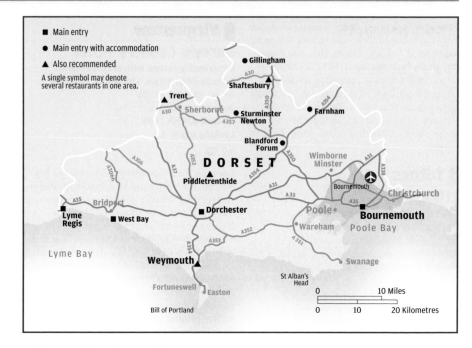

- ■ Main entry
- ● Main entry with accommodation
- ▲ Also recommended

A single symbol may denote several restaurants in one area.

## Blandford Forum

### Castleman Hotel

**A tranquil treasure with convincing food**

Chettle, Blandford Forum, DT11 8DB

Tel no: (01258) 830096

www.castlemanhotel.co.uk

**Modern British | £23**

**Cooking score: 2**

Hailed as a 'tranquil treasure', this handsome hotel was originally the dower house in Chettle – a village that has been owned by the same family for more than 150 years. There is still much to survey in the remodelled Victorian building, from its lovely galleried hall to the fine plasterwork ceilings in the dining room. The food also merits serious attention, and the kitchen delivers convincing renditions of mainstream Eurocentric dishes. Warm pigeon breast and bacon salad with blackerry and balsamic dressing could give way to pine nut-crusted cod with roasted peppers and tapenade or calf's liver with sage

and red wine. After that, lemon syllabub or toffee and banana sponge provide an easy finale. The wine list packs bags of quality and depth into a relatively modest framework: producers are chosen with exemplary care and prices (from £12) are friendly.

**Chef/s:** Barbara Garnsworthy and Richard Morris. **Open:** Sun L 12 to 2, all week D 7 to 10. **Closed:** 25, 26 and 31 Dec, Feb. **Meals:** alc (main courses £10 to £20). Sun L £21. **Service:** not inc. **Details:** Cards accepted. 45 seats. Separate bar. No music. No mobile phones. Wheelchair access. Children allowed. Car parking.

## Please send us your feedback

To register your opinion about any restaurant listed in the Guide, or a new restaurant that you wish to bring to our attention, please visit the web address at the bottom of the page. Your feedback informs the content of the book and will be used to compile next year's reviews.

# Bournemouth

NEW ENTRY
## The Print Room
Bustling all-day Art Deco brasserie
Richmond Hill, Bournemouth, BH2 6HH
Tel no: (01202) 789669
www.theprintroom-bournemouth.co.uk
Modern European | £25
Cooking score: 2

£5 OFF ♦ V ♦£30

The old *Daily Echo* building is the setting for this bustling, light and airy brasserie. The wide-ranging modern European menu is supplemented by 'Express' items such as eggs Benedict, and the cooking shows good technical skills. Locally sourced dishes include a Dorset Smokery meat and fish assiette to start, and pan-fried fillet of Poole Bay sea bream. Well-executed desserts feature a stunning crème brûlée and raspberry mille-feuille. The well-spread wine list, with helpful guidelines, has something to suit all pockets. House wine is £15.95.
**Chef/s:** Nick Baldwin. **Open:** all week 7.45am to 11pm. **Meals:** alc (main courses £9 to £39). **Service:** not inc. **Details:** Cards accepted. 170 seats. Separate bar. Wheelchair access. Music. Children allowed.

## ALSO RECOMMENDED
### ▲ WestBeach
Pier Approach, Bournemouth, BH2 5AA
Tel no: (01202) 587785
www.west-beach.co.uk
Seafood

The food perfectly fits the surroundings at this glass-fronted beachside restaurant close to the pier. Seafood is top of the agenda, say ceviche of scallops with chargrilled red capsicum salsa (£10) or sea bass with roast beetroot glazed with wildflower and vanilla honey (£18.50), but there are lunchtime fish finger sandwiches with chips and Sunday roasts with Yorkshire pudding (£11.50) for those with simpler tastes and tighter budgets. House wine is £14.95. Open all week.

# Dorchester
## Sienna
Engaging intimacy and big aspirations
36 High West Street, Dorchester, DT1 1UP
Tel no: (01305) 250022
www.siennarestaurant.co.uk
Modern British | £39
Cooking score: 4

Russell and Elena Brown's converted shop may be small but it makes a big impact – although it feels more like a tidy 'family bistro' than a restaurant with serious aspirations. Homely touches, colourful flower arrangements and artwork set the scene, and Elena's friendly presence out front adds to the mood of engaging intimacy. In the kitchen, Russell manages to 'wring the maximum flavour' out of carefully sourced seasonal ingredients, and his menus are cleverly contrived showcases for what one reader called 'insightful combinations' – witness pan-fried fillet of brill with a tiger prawn and mushroom tartlet, Jerusalem artichoke velouté and sherry reduction. To start, breast of wood pigeon with roasted beetroot, Puy lentils and horseradish follows the calendar, while in-tune desserts show their class with the likes of pear and maple syrup sponge pudding with a pear and ginger smoothie and crème fraîche ice cream. The carefully chosen, 50-bin wine list has house selections from £15.95 (£10.80 a decanter).
**Chef/s:** Russell Brown. **Open:** Tue to Sat L 12 to 2, D 7 to 9. **Closed:** Sun, Mon, 2 weeks spring and autumn. **Meals:** Set L £21.50 (2 courses) to £24.50. Set D £32.50 (2 courses) to £39. Tasting menu £48.50 (6 courses). **Service:** not inc. **Details:** Cards accepted. 15 seats. Air-con. No mobile phones. Music.

£5 OFF voucher scheme
Also recommended entries can also take part in the £5-off voucher scheme. For a full list of participating restaurants, please visit: www.which.co.uk/gfgvoucherscheme

# Farnham

## The Museum Inn

**Destination restaurant with precision and flair**
Farnham, DT11 8DE
Tel no: (01725) 516261
www.museuminn.co.uk
**Modern British | £29**
**Cooking score: 5**

Set deep in the Dorset countryside, this seventeenth-century inn has become a destination restaurant. Its thatched roof, flagstone floor, inglenook fireplace, old-world prints and wooden furniture belie a very modern approach to cooking. New chef Patrick Davy has maintained the high standards reached in last year's *Guide*. Dishes feature impeccably sourced regional and seasonal produce, such as leg of Dorset spring lamb and bourride of Brixham seafood on the set menu, and cooking shows precision and flair. At inspection, a starter of crispy lamb sweetbreads retained their soft and creamy interior, while layers of white and brown Portland crabmeat and curried mayonnaise were balanced by a Granny Smith sorbet that cut the richness perfectly. A huge rib of Devon Red beef (for two), timed to a tender medium-rare, came with a rich green peppercorn sauce and memorably fragrant truffled chips. Well-made desserts included bitter chocolate tart and rhubarb and ginger crème brûlée. A good alternative was the interesting range of local cheeses, such as Buckland, Dorstone and Sharpham Elmhurst. The wine list was impressive in its diversity, including New and Old World offerings, plus a range of heavyweights. House wines are £17.50, with more than 10 by the glass.
**Chef/s:** Patrick Davy. **Open:** all week L 12 to 2.30 (3 Sun), D 7 to 9.30 (9 Sun). **Closed:** 25 Dec. **Meals:** alc (main courses £14 to £22). **Service:** not inc.
**Details:** Cards accepted. 96 seats. 24 seats outside. Separate bar. Wheelchair access. Children allowed. Car parking.

## Coastal restaurants

Britain has an incomparable shoreline. These restaurants make the most of it.

**Fifteen, Watergate Bay, Cornwall**
The address 'on the beach' says it all.

**Porthminster Beach Café, Cornwall**
Famous for the ozone-fuelled views out across St Ives Bay.

**The Seahorse Restaurant, Devon**
On the Dart waterfront – overlooking the harbour.

**Crab House Café, Dorset**
On Chesil Beach.

**Hix Oyster & Fish House, Dorset**
Overlooking the famous Cobb and fishing harbour.

**Porth Tocyn Hotel, Wales**
Spectacular views across farmland to Cardigan Bay and beyond.

**The Seafood Restaurant, St Monans, Scotland**
The Firth of Forth all but laps up to the doorstep.

**Three Chimneys, Isle of Skye, Scotland**
Total isolation on the shores of Loch Dunvegan.

## Gillingham

### Stock Hill

Austrian flavours in a Dorset domicile
Stock Hill, Gillingham, SP8 5NR
Tel no: (01747) 823626
www.stockhillhouse.co.uk
**Modern European | £40**
**Cooking score: 5**

£5 OFF 🍴 V

Tucked into the border area of Dorset, Somerset and Wiltshire, Stock Hill is many loyal followers' idea of a home-from-home – always assuming you have something like Peter Hauser's hugely accomplished cooking skills to call on at home. A comfortable, elegant dining room with salmon walls and chintzy drapes is served by knowledgeable staff and cooking that is based on impeccable sourcing, a flavour-driven philosophy and constant evolution. The Hausers are Austrian by birth, and that culinary heritage still shows in dishes that are proudly flagged on the menus with the national red-white-and-red. Paprika beef goulash with spätzli, garnished with pickled gherkins and a fried egg, is a long-staying main course, and of course there are desserts to beat the band, such as Esterhazy Torte with berry sauce and cream, or Salzburger Honig Nockerl (baked souffléed dumplings flavoured with honey). Picking a more westerly course through the menu might take you from anchovy niçoise with avocado and tomato, to milk-fed veal with mushrooms in a sherry cream sauce. Wines start at £21.95 for an international selection that confines itself, perhaps surprisingly, to a modest handful of Austrian specimens. Where, you might wonder, are the Grüner Veltliners of yesteryear? (There's one, anyway.)

**Chef/s:** Peter Hauser and Lorna Connor. **Open:** Tue to Sun L 12.15 to 1.45, all week D 7.15 to 8.45 (8 Sun). **Meals:** Set L £17.50 (2 courses) to £21. Set D £40 (3 courses). Sun L £30. **Service:** not inc. **Details:** Cards accepted. 26 seats. 8 seats outside. No music. No mobile phones. Children allowed. Car parking.

## Lyme Regis

NEW ENTRY

### Hix Oyster & Fish House

Menus packed with simple seafood delights
Cobb Road, Lyme Regis, DT7 3JP
Tel no: (01297) 446910
www.hixoysterandfishhouse.co.uk
**Seafood | £40**
**Cooking score: 4**

Mark Hix's expanding group of restaurants are bywords for simple, unpretentious British cooking. The Oyster & Fish House – sister to his Oyster & Chop House in London (see entry) – is set in attractive gardens overlooking Lyme Regis's famous Cobb and fishing harbour, and seats on the small terrace are as highly prized as those by the floor-to-ceiling windows. The daily changing menus are staunchly seasonal, with fish from local day boats and wild food foraged on the beach below. Several types of oyster include Portland Royals from Weymouth, and scallops are hand-dived at Lulworth Cove. The rest of the menu is packed with seafood delights: baked spider crab, cuttlefish and ink stew, Cornish brill with surf clams and buttered alexanders. Meat is treated with equal respect and might include hanger steaks or rump of lamb with mint and cucumber. The exciting wine list starts at £15. Our questionnaire was not returned, so some of the details below may be incorrect.

**Chef/s:** Seldon Curry. **Open:** all week L 12 to 2.30 (3 Fri to Sun), D 6 to 10. **Closed:** Mon (Oct to Jun), 25 and 26 Dec. **Meals:** alc (main courses £11 to £39). Set L (Oct to Jun, Tue to Fri) £17 (2 courses) to £21. **Service:** 12.5% (optional). **Details:** Cards accepted. 45 seats. 10 seats outside. Wheelchair access. Music. Children allowed.

## Piddletrenthide

ALSO RECOMMENDED
### ▲ The European Inn
Piddletrenthide, DT2 7QT
Tel no: (01300) 348308
www.european-inn.co.uk
**Gastropub**

Set the SatNav and book ahead, as this revamped little pub in the Piddle Valley is fast making a name for itself. The old pine tables in the charming bar fill quickly with incomers keen to sample the robust dishes on the short seasonal menu. Meat comes from the Hammicks' family farm up the road, vegetables from local allotments, and the choice may take in Pecker's pigeon breast with black pudding (£6), organic pork loin with cabbage, bacon and apple sauce (£14), and rice pudding with raspberry jam (£5). House wine £13. Closed Mon and Sun D.

## Poole

READERS RECOMMEND
### Guildhall Tavern
**French**
15 Market Street, Poole, BH15 1NB
Tel no: (01202) 671717
'By far the nicest place to eat; seafood is a speciality'

## Shaftesbury

ALSO RECOMMENDED
### ▲ La Fleur de Lys
Bleke Street, Shaftesbury, SP7 8AW
Tel no: (01747) 853717
www.lafleurdelys.co.uk
**Modern British**

A well-liked local rendezvous, this personally run restaurant-with-rooms now resides in a converted girls' boarding house. The kitchen casts its net wide for inspiration, with starters of locally smoked duck, fig, apple and rocket (£7.50) giving way to saddle of Dorset lamb with wild mushrooms, or fillets of sea bass

with sun-blush tomatoes and herb sauce (£23). Desserts include hot raspberry soufflé with raspberry liqueur sorbet (£8). House wine £16. Closed Mon and Tue L and Sun D.

## Sturminster Newton
### Plumber Manor
**Country house dynasty**
Sturminster Newton, DT10 2AF
Tel no: (01258) 472507
www.plumbermanor.com
**Anglo-French | £30**
**Cooking score: 2**

Like a vintage Rolls Royce, Plumber Manor has had just one careful owner – namely the Prideaux-Brune family, who have been its custodians since Jacobean times. Englishness is in its bones, right down to the ancestral portraits and black Labradors padding about. Brian Prideaux-Brune has no truck with culinary fashion, but channels his energies into producing chicken with lemon and tarragon, salmon with pink peppercorns and other Anglo-French staples. Dinner might begin with grilled goats' cheese and blackcurrant vinaigrette or moules marinière, while supplements such as seared scallops with minted pea purée followed by venison with red cabbage keep the regulars interested. The reputable wine list starts from £16.

**Chef/s:** Brian Prideaux-Brune. **Open:** Sun L 12 to 2, all week D 7 to 9. **Closed:** Feb. **Meals:** Set D £26 (2 courses) to £30. Sun L £23. **Service:** not inc. **Details:** Cards accepted. 65 seats. Separate bar. No music. Wheelchair access. Children allowed. Car parking.

### Readers recommend

A 'readers recommend' review is a genuine quote from a report sent in by one of our readers. We intend to follow up these suggestions throughout the year to come.

# Trent

## ALSO RECOMMENDED
## ▲ Rose & Crown
Trent, DT9 4SL
Tel no: (01935) 850776
www.roseandcrowntrent.co.uk
**Gastropub**

Wadworth ales and hearty country cooking set the tone in this unpretentious thatched pub at the end of a lane by the church. Rug-strewn stone floors, crackling log fires and views across open fields to rolling hills are matched by dishes such as mussels in chive and cider sauce (£7.25), game casserole with thyme-roasted root vegetables (£10) or sea bass with rocket and crab risotto (£14.25). House wine is £11.95. Closed Sun and Mon D.

# West Bay
## Riverside Restaurant
**Fresh, flavourful fish with no fuss**
West Bay, DT6 4EZ
Tel no: (01308) 422011
www.thefishrestaurant-westbay.co.uk
**Seafood | £31**
**Cooking score: 3**

Born in 1964 as a seaside café of the old school, the Watsons' unaffected restaurant is still going strong and has never strayed far from its avowed aims – which is why hungry fans continue to traverse the walkway across the water for ample helpings of fresh fish from the Dorset boats. There is no fuss here, just bags of generosity and clean, simple flavours. Lyme Bay dressed crab, mighty seafood platters and Dover sole are joined by specials gleaned from the day's catch – perhaps devilled sprats with lime and coriander mayonnaise or sea bass fillet with celeriac mash and vanilla butter vinaigrette. To finish, consider meringues with marrons glacés, cream and chocolate – a dessert that took one reader back to teatime in Budapest. House wine £13.50. Opening times may vary in winter.

**Chef/s:** George Marsh. **Open:** Tue to Sun L 12 to 2.30, Tue to Sat D 6.30 to 9. **Closed:** Mon, 29 Nov to 12 Feb. **Meals:** alc (main courses £12 to £30). Set L £14.50 (2 courses) to £19.50. **Service:** not inc. **Details:** Cards accepted. 70 seats. 30 seats outside. No music. Wheelchair access. Children allowed.

# Weymouth

## ALSO RECOMMENDED
## ▲ Crab House Café
Ferryman's Way, Portland Road, Weymouth, DT4 9YU
Tel no: (01305) 788867
www.crabhousecafe.co.uk
**Seafood**

Sit outside under frilly pink parasols and gaze across fabulous Chesil Beach if the weather's fine, otherwise cram into this zany wooden beach shack for some cracking fresh seafood. Crabs are the stars (dissecting tools provided), but menus change as supplies come and go. Among the delights might be scallops with wild garlic leaves (£8.50) and roast ling with salt beef and asparagus (£15.50) – not forgetting briny fresh Portland Royal oysters. Desserts (£5.50) could feature poached pear in honey and lavender. House wine £14.50. Closed Sun D, Mon and Tue.

## Cooking score

A score of 1 is a significant achievement. The score in any review is based on several meals, incorporating feedback from both our readers and inspectors. As a rough guide, 1 denotes capable cooking with some inconsistencies, rising steadily through different levels of technical expertise, until the scores between 6 and 10 indicate exemplary skills, along with innovation, artistry and ambition. If there is a new chef, we don't score the restaurant for the first year of entry. For further details, please see the scoring section in the introduction to the Guide.

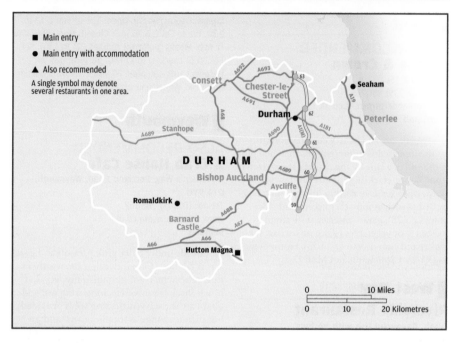

- ■ Main entry
- ● Main entry with accommodation
- ▲ Also recommended

A single symbol may denote several restaurants in one area.

# ▌Durham

## Bistro 21

**Country crowd-pleaser with eclectic food**
Aykley Heads House, Aykley Heads, Durham,
DH1 5TS
Tel no: (0191) 3844354
www.bistrotwentyone.co.uk
**Modern European | £30**
**Cooking score: 2**

**V**

The country cousin of Terry Laybourne's Newcastle-based '21' stable, this cleverly converted seventeenth-century farmhouse is a beacon out in the wilds at Aykley Heads. With its vaulted cellar bar, rustic chic vibes and delightful open courtyard it's a reliable Durham crowd-pleaser that delivers eclectic modern food peppered with home-grown ingredients and Mediterranean influences. Smoked haddock with poached egg and bubble and squeak, devilled beef salad, and Bramley apple crumble with custard sauce share the stage with the likes of grilled aubergines with pesto, roast rump of lamb with tomatoes and olives, and honey pannacotta with mulled wine fruits. Georges Duboeuf house French is £15.40.
**Chef/s:** Tom Jackson. **Open:** all week L 12 to 2.30 (12.30 to 4 Sun), Mon to Sat D 6.30 to 10.30.
**Meals:** alc (main courses £15 to £26). Set L and D £15 (2 courses) to £18. Sun L £16. **Service:** 10% (optional). **Details:** Cards accepted. 55 seats. Separate bar. Music. Children allowed. Car parking.

## Gourmet Spot

**Adventurous menus and capable cooking**
The Avenue, Durham, DH1 4DX
Tel no: (0191) 3846655
www.gourmet-spot.co.uk
**Modern European | £32**
**Cooking score: 2**

£5 OFF  **V**

Ashley Paynton, formerly at the Fisherman's Lodge in Newcastle (see entry Tyne & Wear), is the man tasked with carrying on G-Spot's tradition of adventurous menus in the smart grey, plum and black restaurant attached to the Farnley Tower Hotel. There is a lot of technical playing around, with multiple flavours jostling for attention, despite simple menu descriptions. Yet it can be good, capable cooking, and the traditional elements, like the treatment of pork belly (served with boudin noir beignets, sage foam and Granny Smith apple) and a chocolate fondant with hazelnut ice cream and honeycomb bonbon, are done well. House wine is £14.70.

**Chef/s:** Ashley Paynton. **Open:** Tue to Sat D 6.30 to 10. **Closed:** Sun, Mon, 25 and 26 Dec. **Meals:** alc (main courses £15 to £23). Set D £55. **Service:** not inc. **Details:** Cards accepted. 24 seats. 12 seats outside. Separate bar. Wheelchair access. Music. Children allowed. Car parking.

## ▌Hutton Magna
## The Oak Tree Inn
**Discreet dinners and invention**
Hutton Magna, DL11 7HH
**Tel no: (01833) 627371**
**Modern British | £32**
**Cooking score: 2**

Alastair and Claire Ross run a tight ship at the Oak Tree, meaning that it's essential to book for dinner. Set in a terrace of cottages, the place has all the homely feel you could wish for in a country pub, but the cooking is several cuts above. A warm salad of crisp pork belly and black pudding dressed in apple, honey and mustard is a well-conceived, popular starter, and meals might go on with sea bream fillets with steamed mussels, celery, leeks and cucumber, or roast best end of lamb with boulangère potatoes and niçoise courgettes. Fine selections of malt whiskies and international bottled beers exercise their own attractions. Wines start at £11.95.

**Chef/s:** Alastair Ross. **Open:** Tue to Sun D only 6 to 9 (5.30 to 7.30 Sun). **Closed:** Mon, 25 and 26 Dec, 31 Dec, 1 Jan. **Meals:** alc (main courses £18 to £20). **Service:** not inc. **Details:** Cards accepted. 20 seats. Music. Car parking.

## ▌Romaldkirk
## The Rose and Crown
**Lovingly tended, showpiece village inn**
Romaldkirk, DL12 9EB
**Tel no: (01833) 650213**
www.rose-and-crown.co.uk
**Modern British | £30**
**Cooking score: 3**

£5
OFF

It's 20 years since Christopher and Alison Davy put their names above the door of this showpiece inn overlooking Romaldkirk village green. During their stewardship they have cared lovingly for the place – and it shows in every detail, from the crackling logs in the old stone fireplace to the relentlessly ticking grandfather clock. The bar is just the spot for a lunch or supper of salmon fishcakes or pork sausage and black pudding with mustard mash. By contrast, dinner in the elegant candlelit restaurant is a more sedate affair, with a four-course menu promising precise dishes such as roast Lunesdale duck breast with fruit compote and port jus or chargrilled calf's liver with sweet onion confit and green peppercorn sauce. North Country cheeses, and desserts including sticky toffee pudding close proceedings. House wine is £15.50.

**Chef/s:** Christopher Davy and Andrew Lee. **Open:** Sun L 12 to 1.30, all week D 7.30 to 8.45. **Closed:** 23 to 26 Dec. **Meals:** Set D £30 (4 courses). Sun L £17.75. **Service:** not inc. **Details:** Cards accepted. 24 seats. 24 seats outside. Separate bar. No music. No mobile phones. Wheelchair access. Children allowed. Car parking.

### Please send us your feedback

To register your opinion about any restaurant listed in the Guide, or a new restaurant that you wish to bring to our attention, please visit the web address at the bottom of the page. Your feedback informs the content of the book and will be used to compile next year's reviews.

## Memorable dishes

Culled from all the meals eaten by inspectors for the 2010 Guide, the following are among the most memorable dishes of the year.

Nibbles: Pork scratchings and own-cured ham (**The Sportsman**, Kent)

Amuse-bouche: hummus with a sweet onion bavarois, and cod and black pudding with lime crème fraîche (**Marcus Wareing at the Berkeley**, London)

First course: Celeriac baked in ash with hazelnuts and wood sorrel and paired with a kromeski of wild boar (**The Ledbury**, London)

Main course: Poached fillet of brill with tiny cubes of wild garlic leaf pannacotta, fresh peas, fèves and morels. (**The Oak Room, Danesfield House**, Buckinghamshire)

Cheese course: Incredible Cornish cheeses (**Restaurant Nathan Outlaw**, Cornwall)

Pre-dessert: cucumber, lime, mango and yoghurt – the ultimate palate cleanser, **The Vineyard at Stockcross**, Berkshire)

Dessert: Rhubarb served with wild herb granita and almond granola (**Restaurant Sat Bains**, Nottingham)

Petits fours – violet tarts (**The Fat Duck**, Berkshire)

## ▌Seaham

### Seaham Hall, The White Room
Refined food from a local talent
Lord Byron's Walk, Seaham, SR7 7AG
Tel no: (0191) 5161400
www.seaham-hall.com
**Modern British | £50**
**Cooking score: 5**

🍷 ╤ V

Chef Kenny Atkinson has come home to the North East, and menus packed with local produce, give or take the odd shimeji mushroom, suggest he's glad to be back. His new playground is the White Room, really two pale dining rooms in the hotel where Lord Byron made his ill-advised wedding vows. Neutral apart from pieces of Sunderland glass, the White Room demands that the food be the main feature. Atkinson's response is measured but effective, a series of well-judged dishes whose cumulative effect is very pleasing indeed. The aforementioned shimeji (pickled), are an effective counterpoint to a terrine of confit duck and foie gras, and curry-roasted cod with chestnuts and parsnip velouté plays with various earthy notes. To follow, loin of Northumberland pork with confit belly and braised cheek showcases the animal with finesse, and a Valrhona chocolate pavé is elevated by the presence of fabulous coffee ice cream. Atkinson's arrival isn't the only innovation: though some aesthetic details still beg for attention, the hotel is in the hands of new owners and service is discernibly sharper than it has been. The wine list retains its pleasing scope, with Francophiles well catered for and China-lovers not overlooked. Dr Loosen Riesling (£5.50) does a great job at entry level by the glass; bottles are from £20.
**Chef/s:** Kenny Atkinson. **Open:** Wed to Sun L 12 to 2, all week D 7 to 10. **Meals:** Set L £21.50 (2 courses) to £29.50. Set D £40 or £60 to £80 (7 courses). Sun L £30. **Service:** not inc. **Details:** Cards accepted. 50 seats. Air-con. Separate bar. No mobile phones. Wheelchair access. Music. Children allowed. Car parking.

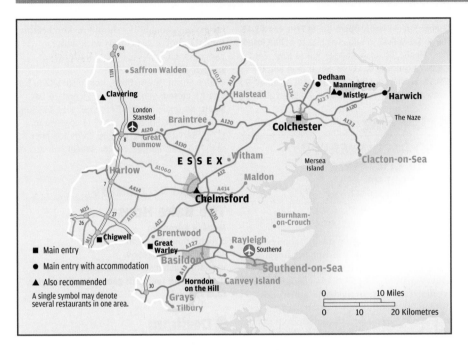

## ■ **Chelmsford**

### ALSO RECOMMENDED
### ▲ **Barda**

30-32 Broomfield Road, Chelmsford, CM1 1SW
Tel no: (01245) 357799
www.barda-restaurant.com
**Modern European**

This light-toned, wood-floored restaurant is
an elegant space that extends on to a decked
patio for aperitifs in sunny weather. East Asian
influences abound in dishes that span a range
from duck tataki with ponzu dip and duck
crackling (£8), to sea bass in tom yum broth
with shiitake mushrooms, tofu and wakame
(£18). Side orders include wasabi mash, and
even desserts catch the mood with coconut
and lemongrass brûlée (£6). Wines from
£13.80. Closed Sat L, Sun D and Mon.

## ■ **Chigwell**

### **The Bluebell**

Mix of old and new
117 High Road, Chigwell, IG7 6QQ
Tel no: (020) 85006282
www.thebluebellrestaurant.co.uk
**Modern European | £35**
**Cooking score: 1**

Greg Molen's surprisingly spacious and
contemporary 500-year-old cottage
restaurant has had yet another change of chef
since last year, and indications are that the
place could do with a period of stability:
service and the modern European dishes have
not always impressed this year. Among menu
choices could be deep-fried calamari with
sweet chilli sauce, a simple chargrilled sirloin
steak with green peppercorn sauce or pollack
with creamed potatoes, wilted spinach and
chive cream sauce, followed by cappuccino
crème brûlée. House wine is £15.50. More
reports please.

**Chef/s:** James Harris. **Open:** Tue to Fri L 12 to 3.45, Tue to Sat D 6.45 to 1am. Sun L 12 to 6.30. **Closed:** Mon. **Meals:** alc (main courses £18 to £26). Set L £15.95 (2 courses) to £19.95. Set D (and Sun L) £24.95. **Service:** not inc. **Details:** Cards accepted. 95 seats. Air-con. No mobile phones. Children allowed.

# Clavering

## ALSO RECOMMENDED
## ▲ The Cricketers
Clavering, CB11 4QT
Tel no: (01799) 550442
www.thecricketers.co.uk
Gastropub

Simple hearty cooking with an Italian twist is as much a draw at this atmospheric English hostelry as the fact that it's run by Jamie Oliver's parents. The regularly changing menu is offered à la carte in the bar at lunch and dinner, but for dinner in the restaurant it is set at £23.50/£29.50 for 2/3 courses. Expect rabbit with gnocchi and wild mushrooms, venison with poached pear and bitter chocolate sauce or free-range chicken with citrus salsa verde. Wines from £12.80. Open all week. Accommodation.

# Colchester
## The Lemon Tree
Easy-going local favourite
48 St Johns Street, Colchester, CO2 7AD
Tel no: (01206) 767337
www.the-lemon-tree.com
Modern European | £20
Cooking score: 1

£5 OFF  V  £30

This comfortable, gently lit, tile-floored restaurant incorporates a bit of the old Roman city wall – and it also offers brasserie-style cooking. Seafood linguine contains crab, king prawns and salmon, as well as pak choi and capers, while tastier cuts of meat form the focal points of dishes such as roasted lamb rump with garlic and herb mash and red wine jus. Parma ham classically dressed with rocket, Parmesan and balsamic might be the curtain-

raiser, and chocoholics should make a beeline for dark chocolate nemesis with white chocolate sauce at the close. House wines are £13.95.

**Chef/s:** Shaan Pallam. **Open:** Mon to Sat L 12 to 5, D 5 to 10. **Closed:** Sun, bank hols, 25 and 26 Dec. **Meals:** alc (main courses £9 to £15). Set L £12.50 (2 courses) to £16.50. Set D £13.95 (2 courses) to £17.95. **Service:** not inc. **Details:** Cards accepted. 80 seats. 40 seats outside. Air-con. Wheelchair access. Music. Children allowed.

## READERS RECOMMEND
## The Bake House
Modern European
5 High Street, Colchester, CO7 9BJ
Tel no: (01206) 824569
www.thebakehouserestaurant.co.uk
'Comfortable feel with good friendly service, food is good'

# Dedham
## The Sun Inn
Ancient inn with Mediterranean soul
High Street, Dedham, CO7 6DF
Tel no: (01206) 323351
www.thesuninndedham.com
Mediterranean | £23
Cooking score: 3

 V £30

It may be deep in Constable country, but this splendidly revitalised fifteenth-century inn is infused with a sunny Mediterranean soul. The interior has a beefy rusticity with its oak floorboards and heavy elm tables – although unfussy pub vibes and real ales contrast with the 'unexpected and understated' contemporary feel of the restaurant. The food is a 'great advert' for home-grown British produce, even though the menu spells out its wares in Italian as well as English. A salad of Dereham duck leg with radicchio and pomegranate might give way to 'piccione ai ceci' (pigeon with chickpeas, spring greens and aged balsamic) or 'stufato' (Gloucester Old Spot stew with Fiano Greco white wine, polenta and rosemary). Walnut tart or semolina budino with rhubarb compote are fitting finales, and the savvy global wine list gives Italy a good run, with carafes from £10. **Chef/s:** Ugo Simonelli. **Open:** all week L 12 to 2.30 (3 Sat and Sun), D 6.30 to 9.30. **Closed:** 25 and 26 Dec. **Meals:** alc (main courses £9 to £17). Set L and D £10.50 (2 courses) to £13.50. Sun L £18. **Service:** not inc. **Details:** Cards accepted. 60 seats. 60 seats outside. Separate bar. Music. Children allowed. Car parking.

## ▮ Great Warley
### The Headley
**Pub and brasserie classics in tandem**
Headley Common, Great Warley, CM13 3HS
Tel no: (01277) 216104
www.theheadley.co.uk
**Gastropub | £20**
**Cooking score: 3**
 £30

Daniel Clifford of Midsummer House, Cambridge (see entry) has pitched a secondary camp at this large, solid and semi-rural pub, reworking both the premises and his own cooking style. What he is offering is very much in tune with modern times, at least for those who don't expect three lots of appetisers and a pre-dessert with their meal. The food makes a virtue out of pub and brasserie classics – pasta, pies, salads and burgers – and successes have been a rich fish soup, fish and chips with decent beer batter and good crushed peas, and a perfectly timed loin of venison with roast chestnuts and a side of creamed Savoy cabbage. The international wine list is packed with good bottles at fair prices from £16. **Chef/s:** Richard Troman. **Open:** Wed to Fri L 12 to 3, D 6 to 9.30. Sat 12 to 10, Sun 12 to 5. **Closed:** Mon, Tue, 27 Dec to 5 Jan (open bank hols). **Meals:** alc (main courses £8 to £15). Sun L £18 (2 courses) to £22. **Service:** not inc. **Details:** Cards accepted. 180 seats. 40 seats outside. Air-con. Separate bar. Wheelchair access. Music. Children allowed. Car parking.

## ▮ Harwich
### The Pier at Harwich, Harbourside Restaurant
**Fresh seafood and harbour views**
The Quay, Harwich, CO12 3HH
Tel no: (01255) 241212
www.milsomhotels.com
**Seafood | £30**
**Cooking score: 2**
 £5 OFF

There are no prizes for guessing the location or the long-lasting appeal of this amenable hotel slap-bang on Harwich quayside. Seafood is the lure, and the kitchen scoops up the pick of the catch for menus that please the old guard and fashion-conscious foodies alike. Diners in the first-floor restaurant can admire the views before partaking of home-smoked salmon, moules marinière or something trendy such as fillet of halibut with passion fruit vinaigrette. Meat-eaters could try venison, wild mushroom and port pie, while crowd-pleasing desserts might include white chocolate and pistachio torte. House wine is £14. Simpler food is also available in the ground-floor Ha'penny Pier bistro. **Chef/s:** Chris Oakley. **Open:** all week L 12 to 2, D 6 to 9.30. **Meals:** alc (main courses £14 to £32). Set L £18.50 (2 courses) to £24. Sun L £25.50. **Service:** 10%. **Details:** Cards accepted. 60 seats. 20 seats outside. Air-con. Separate bar. No mobile phones. Music. Children allowed. Car parking.

## ▮ Horndon on the Hill
### The Bell Inn
**Medieval pub with up-to-date cooking**
High Road, Horndon on the Hill, SS17 8LD
Tel no: (01375) 642463
www.bell-inn.co.uk
**Modern European | £27**
**Cooking score: 2**
 £30

In 1555, a gentleman of Horndon was burned at the stake in the courtyard for professing the wrong denomination of the Christian faith –

a detail that indicates, albeit gruesomely, the age of the inn. Its low-beamed interior is exactly what we like to see in such a venerable place, and so is the confident up-to-date cooking on offer. In the words of one reader, 'it balances a degree of challenge in some of the dishes with impeccable production and interesting and enjoyable flavours'. That might translate as a shellfish terrine with avocado and watercress, roast and confit wild rabbit with fondant potato and spinach, and lemon posset with blueberry compote and pear sorbet. Australian house blends are £12.50.

**Chef/s:** Stuart Fay. **Open:** all week L 12 to 1.45 (2.15 Sun), D 6.30 to 9.45 (7 Sun). **Closed:** 25 and 26 Dec, bank hol Mon. **Meals:** alc (main courses £11 to £22). **Service:** not inc. **Details:** Cards accepted. 80 seats. 36 seats outside. Separate bar. No music. No mobile phones. Wheelchair access. Children allowed. Car parking.

## Manningtree

### ALSO RECOMMENDED
### ▲ Lucca Enoteca

39 High Street, Manningtree, CO11 1AH
Tel no: (01206) 390044
www.luccafoods.co.uk
**Italian**

A spin-off from the Mistley Thorn (see following entry), Sherri Singleton's populist, kid-friendly pizzeria deals in wood-fired pizzas (from £5.95) with creative, upper-crust toppings: try 'picante' (scamorza, Calabrian salami and roasted peppers) or the 'verde' version with spinach, pesto, capers and rocket. Elsewhere, the menu is fleshed out with pastas (linguine with mussels and saffron, £7.95), plus salads and daily specials. To finish, share a sweet pizza Nutella (£4.95) or go for classic raspberry semifreddo. Also good for late breakfasts, bargain lunches and weekend wood-roasts. Italian regional wines from £12.95. Open all week.

## Mistley
### The Mistley Thorn
**Local favourite with speciality seafood**
High Street, Mistley, CO11 1HE
Tel no: (01206) 392821
www.mistleythorn.com
**Seafood | £22**
**Cooking score: 2**

The Mistley Thorn is an eighteenth-century inn with a twenty-first century soul. It overlooks the Stour Estuary. Sherri Singleton is a keen advocate of locally available ingredients, and ventures towards the Mediterranean for culinary ideas, but doesn't seek to impress with outlandish fireworks. Seafood is a speciality, so expect the likes of smoked haddock chowder followed by seared brill with salsa verde and Puy lentils. Vegetarians could try 'wild and tame' mushroom risotto, while meat options include roasted duck breast with a spring onion potato cake and cherry jus. Finish with steamed chocolate cake, and wash it all down with international wines starting at £13.95.
**Chef/s:** Sherri Singleton. **Open:** all week L 12 to 2.30 (5 Sat and Sun), D 6.30 to 9.30 (10 Fri and Sat). **Meals:** alc (main courses £9 to £16). Set L £11.95 (2 courses) to £14.95. Set D Sun and Mon £25 (3 courses for 2 people). Sun L £12.95. **Service:** not inc. **Details:** Cards accepted. 75 seats. 15 seats outside. Wheelchair access. Music. Children allowed. Car parking.

## Tendring
### READERS RECOMMEND
### The Fat Goose
**Gastropub**
Heath Road, Tendring, CO16 0BX
Tel no: (01255) 870060
www.fat-goose.co.uk
**'Imaginative cooking, mostly using locally sourced ingredients'**

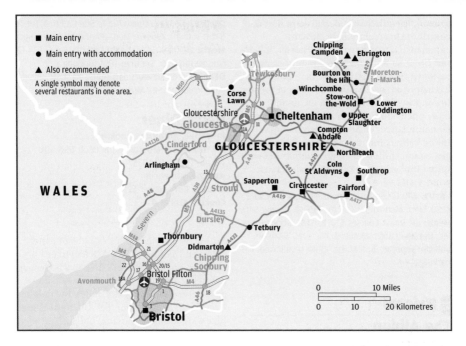

Map legend:
- ■ Main entry
- ● Main entry with accommodation
- ▲ Also recommended

A single symbol may denote several restaurants in one area.

# ▌Arlingham

## The Old Passage Inn

**Idyllic seafood dining by the river**
Passage Road, Arlingham, GL2 7JR
Tel no: (01452) 740547
www.theoldpassage.com
Seafood | £35
Cooking score: 3

The setting is remote and nothing less than beautiful, on the banks of the River Severn with lovely views. A bright colour scheme sets a contemporary tone in the interior. Raoul Moore has now departed, to be replaced by Mark Redwood. He seems content to continue with the mix of familiar and gently inventive cooking of seafood set by his predecessor, much to the delight of readers, who have pronounced him 'well up to standard'. Tea-smoked mackerel and salmon terrine with poached egg sauce makes a good start, followed by roast halibut with braised Little Gem lettuce, baby onions, wild mushrooms and oxtail jus. Desserts run to rhubarb pannacotta with poached rhubarb, hazelnut crisp, stem ginger and rose petal ice cream. House wine is £17.50.
**Chef/s:** Mark Redwood. **Open:** Tue to Sun L 12 to 2, Tue to Sat D 7 to 9. **Closed:** Mon, 25 to 30 Dec. **Meals:** alc (main courses £17 to £40). **Service:** not inc. **Details:** Cards accepted. 40 seats. 30 seats outside. Air-con. No mobile phones. Wheelchair access. Music. Children allowed. Car parking.

# ▌Bourton on the Hill

## Horse and Groom

**Proper pub virtues and lively food**
Bourton on the Hill, GL56 9AQ
Tel no: (01386) 700413
www.horseandgroom.info
Modern British | £25
Cooking score: 2

Panoramic vistas across the Cotswolds are just one of the assets at this honey-coloured stone inn. Locally sourced food (some of it home-grown), friendly staff and well-kept beer also contribute to an 'extremely pleasant experience', according to one reporter. It helps that brothers Will and Tom Greenstock are seasoned innkeepers, because their know-how has helped to preserve the pub's proper virtues. In contrast, daily blackboard menus take a more open-minded view of things – witness fennel and goats' cheese risotto, tandoori-spiced halibut and rack of lamb with mustard greens and chilli jam. Ginger pannacotta with spiced rhubarb makes a zesty finale. House wine is £12.95.

**Chef/s:** Will Greenstock. **Open:** all week L 12 to 2 (2.30 Sun), Mon to Sat D 7 to 9 (9.30 Fri and Sat). **Meals:** alc (main courses £10 to £18). **Service:** not inc. **Details:** Cards accepted. 70 seats. 54 seats outside. Separate bar. Music. Children allowed. Car parking.

# Bristol

## The Albion
**Punchy pub food with a big heart**
Boyces Avenue, Clifton Village, Bristol, BS8 4AA
Tel no: (0117) 9733522
www.thealbionclifton.co.uk
**Gastropub | £28**
**Cooking score: 3**

This listed seventeenth-century inn was transformed from grotty student boozer to foodie-friendly 'public house and dining rooms' in a trademark gastropub reclamation – and it has never looked back. Exposed wood floors, heritage colours and a brick fireplace set just the right tone for punchy food with a big heart. You can eat in the bar or in the more formal upstairs dining room from a menu that avoids purple prose in favour of terse, no-nonsense descriptions: pig's head, white dandelion and capers, then lamb's offal and polenta or lemon sole and brown shrimps, with custard tart and rhubarb or blood orange sorbet and vodka to finish. The results on the plate are suitably emphatic, and the wine list backs things up with a lively global selection from £15 (£3.90 a glass).

**Chef/s:** Jake Platt. **Open:** Tue to Sun L 12 to 3, Tue to Sat D 7 to 10. **Closed:** Mon, 25 and 26 Dec, 1 Jan. **Meals:** alc (main courses £11 to £19). Set D £24 (2 courses) to £30. **Service:** 10% (optional). **Details:** Cards accepted. 60 seats. 40 seats outside. Wheelchair access. Music. Children allowed.

## Bell's Diner
**Inventive, ambitious cooking**
1-3 York Road, Montpelier, Bristol, BS6 5QB
Tel no: (0117) 9240357
www.bellsdiner.com
**Modern European | £29**
**Cooking score: 4**

Sitting on a corner opposite a row of pastel-coloured Georgian houses, Bell's Diner occupies a former grocer's shop in a bohemian quarter of Bristol. The polished wood floor and shelves are a reminder of its past, and the front room has a parlour feel with its duck-egg blue tongue-and-grooving, old jugs, grinders and baskets. The rear dining room is more contemporary, but both areas match the seamless fusion of modern cooking and traditional techniques. Some have found the wannabe Fat Duck-style food amusing rather than enjoyable or value for money, but others are beguiled by the eclectic flavour combinations conjured from top-notch produce, as in a starter of Cornish crab, which arrives with mango, avocado ice cream and hot shellfish bisque. A more conventional chicken breast with summer truffles, peas and morels could follow, while desserts include a traditional crème brûlée served with apple compote and Granny Smith sorbet. An interesting and intelligent wine list starts at £15.

**Chef/s:** Christopher Wicks. **Open:** Tue to Fri L 12 to 2.30, Mon to Sat D 7 to 10. **Closed:** Sun, 24 to 30 Dec. **Meals:** alc (main courses £15 to £19). Tasting menu £45. **Service:** 10% (optional). **Details:** Cards accepted. 50 seats. Music. Children allowed.

## Bordeaux Quay

**Bristol's eco-warrior**
V-Shed, Canons Way, Bristol, BS1 5UH
Tel no: (0117) 9431200
www.bordeaux-quay.co.uk
**Modern European | £28**
Cooking score: 2

This eco-friendly, Bristol harbourside landmark is continually evolving, and the recent launch of a relaxed wine bar next to the upstairs restaurant has been a successful addition. While service in the buzzy downstairs brasserie remains inconsistent, the restaurant appears to have found its feet. Organic and seasonal remain the buzz words throughout and the Mediterranean-influenced dishes are rustic and unpretentious – a salad of broad beans, feta, cherry tomatoes, pea shoots and mint might be followed by wild sea bass, Piedmontese pepper, grilled lemon and rosemary potatoes. Finish with hot chocolate fondant and espresso ice cream. House wine starts at £17 bottle.
**Chef/s:** Barny Haughton. **Open:** Sun to Fri L 12 to 3 (4 Sun), all week D 6 to 10 (5 Sun). **Closed:** 24 to 26 Dec. **Meals:** alc (main courses £9 to £23). Set L £19.50 (2 courses) to £23. Set D £25.50 (2 courses) to £28.50. Sun L £12.50. **Service:** 10% (optional). **Details:** Cards accepted. 120 seats. 60 seats outside. Separate bar. Wheelchair access. Music. Children allowed.

## Café Maitreya

**Vibrant veggie food with edge**
89 St Mark's Road, Easton, Bristol, BS5 6HY
Tel no: (0117) 9510100
www.cafemaitreya.co.uk
**Vegetarian | £23**
Cooking score: 4

There's serious creativity and energy at work in this upbeat veggie hangout, whose name is Sanskrit for 'universal love' – especially when it comes to the cooking. Bright abstract artworks line the walls, staff are 'playful, but at the top of their game', and the open kitchen

delivers mainline flavours that hit the senses full on. Dip into the daily menus and you will find all manner of organic ingredients, wild gleanings and trendy global provisions in wacky combos. A deceptively simple Belgian winter warm salad involves not only caramelised endive but also a crisp pistachio croûte, marinated cauliflower, caper and date dressing, while charred Jerusalem artichokes, parsley root, pickled pear and tarragon sauce keep company with a choux pastry Cheddar gougère. Round things off with a mocca toasted almond pudding with maple-preserved figs and cardamom coconut ice cream. The ever-evolving wine list is a funky Eurocentric assortment with prices from £14.25.
**Chef/s:** Mark Evans. **Open:** Thur to Sun L 11 to 3, Tue to Sat D, 6 to 9.45. **Closed:** Mon, 23 Dec to 2 Jan, 2 weeks Aug. **Meals:** Set L £9.95 (2 courses) to £12.95. Set D £18.95 (2 courses) to £22.50. **Service:** not inc. **Details:** Cards accepted. 50 seats. Separate bar. Wheelchair access. Music. Children allowed.

## Casamia

**Ambitious young chefs aiming high**
38 High Street, Westbury on Trym, Bristol, BS9 3DZ
Tel no: (0117) 9592884
www.casamiarestaurant.co.uk
**Italian | £28**
Cooking score: 5

The unassuming entrance gives nothing away. First impressions are of a low-key neighbourhood restaurant, the neat décor suggesting something a little more traditional than the reality – a glance at the menu should put the uninitiated in the picture. Peter and Jonray Sanchez-Iglesias go about their business with deadly serious intent, their creative and complex ideas mostly executed with considerable intricacy and consummate flair. Their menu descriptions remain in the listing style and the deconstruction of classic dishes is a recurring theme: Caesar salad as a starter and tiramisu at dessert stage have both worked well. However one reporter felt that a proper pesto might have been better than the deconstructed version (basil jelly, piles of parmesan and pine nuts) that accompanied roast organic lamb. But, in general, what appears on the plate has purpose and vigour – as salmon poached in olive oil, with peas, pancetta, rock hyssop and wild mushroom proved for one visitor. Desserts are equally palate-broadening (and 'really good'), with plenty of textural complexity and delicate nuances – as in, say, dark chocolate tart with walnuts and beetroot ice cream. The set lunch has been described as 'extremely good value for the quality involved'. The wine list is mostly Italian, with a good selection by the glass from £4.

**Chef/s:** Jonray and Peter Sanchez-Iglesias. **Open:** Wed to Sat L 12.30 to 2.30, Tue to Sat D 7 to 9.30. **Closed:** Sun, Mon, 25 and 26 Dec, bank hols, 2 weeks Aug. **Meals:** Set L £15 (2 courses) to £20. Set D £23 (2 courses) to £28. Tasting menu £30 (6 courses) to £45 (10 courses). **Service:** not inc. **Details:** Cards accepted. 45 seats. 6 seats outside. Separate bar. No mobile phones. Wheelchair access. Music. Children allowed.

## Culinaria
**Talented chef keeps things simple**
1 Chandos Road, Bristol, BS6 6PG
Tel no: (0117) 9737999
www.culinariabristol.co.uk
**Modern British | £30**
**Cooking score: 4**

With some 30 years in the business, Stephen and Judy Markwick have perfected the personable, unceremonious approach that delights visitors to their informal bistro-style restaurant. There is a short weekly carte and a very short set-price choice at lunchtime (even pre-cooked meals to take away in the small deli area). The range of dishes is comforting: Provençal fish soup; smoked eel, beetroot, horseradish and potato pancake; fillet of brill with crab and prawn risotto; slow-cooked shoulder of mutton; chocolate pot. The lineage from Elizabeth David is plain and Stephen Markwick's verve and honesty is

refreshing, as is his commitment to seasonal and top quality ingredients. The wine list gives prominence to France but also allows fair exposure to other countries, and it is not too expensive. There's a good selection of half-bottles, with house wines from France and Chile £15.50.

**Chef/s:** Stephen Markwick. **Open:** Thur to Sat L 12 to 2, D 6.30 to 9.30. **Closed:** Sun to Wed, Christmas, New Year, 4 other weeks. **Meals:** alc (main courses £16 to £18). Set L £15.50 (2 courses) to £20. **Service:** not inc. **Details:** Cards accepted. 30 seats. No music. Wheelchair access. Children allowed.

## Greens' Dining Room
**Quintessential neighbourhood eatery**
25 Zetland Road, Bristol, BS6 7AH
Tel no: (0117) 9246437
www.greensdiningroom.com
**Modern British | £28**
**Cooking score: 3**

Hidden away in a leafy side street off the main drag, Greens' is the quintessential neighbourhood eatery. Family-run, it has become one of Bristol's most popular restaurants due to its consistency and unpretentiousness. The food pays homage to the likes of Elizabeth David, but there is also a strong Alastair Little influence in some of the unfussy Mediterranean dishes. The cooking is assured, with bold flavours – grilled mackerel with guacamole and sweet chilli to start, followed by fillet of pollack, chickpeas, chorizo and aïoli. Simple and delicious desserts might include quince and almond tart. The global wine list combines value with quality, and cherry-picks some excellent stuff from boutique wineries and reputable old-stagers alike. House selections start at £12.50.

**Chef/s:** Andrew and Simon Green. **Open:** Tue to Sat L 12.30 to 3, Tue to Sat D 6.30 to 10.30. **Closed:** Sun, Mon, 1 week Christmas, 2 weeks late August. **Meals:** Set L £10 (2 courses). Set D £21.50 (2 courses) to £27.50. **Service:** not inc. **Details:** Cards accepted. 36 seats. 14 seats outside. No mobile phones. Music. Children allowed.

**NEW ENTRY**
# Lido

**Smart city oasis with vibrant cooking**
Oakfield Place, Clifton, Bristol, BS8 2BJ
Tel no: (0117) 9339533
www.lidobristol.com
**Eclectic | £25**
**Cooking score: 2**

This Victorian lido was closed for 20 years until it was saved from demolition by locals and ambitious new owners returned it to its former glory. It is now an urban oasis comprising a spa, open-air swimming pool and smart restaurant. Grab a window seat overlooking the blue-tiled pool and candy-striped changing cubicles and enjoy ex-Moro chef Freddy Bird's vibrant seasonal cooking. Bird cooks whatever's good on the day, often with a North African or Middle Eastern slant. Many of the dishes are done in the wood-fired oven, including a starter of mackerel with beetroot, dill and yoghurt salad and a main course of chicken, Pedro Ximenez, butternut squash, pancetta and sage. A dessert menu runs alongside a list of delicious homemade ices. Wine from £12.95.
**Chef/s:** Freddy Bird. **Open:** all week L 12 to 3, D 6.30 to 10. **Closed:** 25 Dec, 1 Jan. **Meals:** alc (main courses £11 to £16.50). **Service:** not inc. **Details:** Cards accepted. 90 seats. 30 seats outside. Separate bar. Wheelchair access. Music. Children allowed.

# riverstation

**Veteran of the harbourside scene**
The Grove, Bristol, BS1 4RB
Tel no: (0117) 9144434
www.riverstation.co.uk
**Modern European | £28**
**Cooking score: 3**

This former 1950s river-police station occupies a prime spot on the city's waterfront. Minimalist décor with lots of glass, wood and steel sets it apart from its neighbours. Downstairs there's a café/bar, while upstairs

the light, spacious restaurant caters to a smarter crowd attracted by the bustling atmosphere and the confident cooking. The menu offers good-quality ingredients, simply prepared and with a strong influence towards the Mediterranean and France. Start with seared Scottish scallops with Jerusalem artichokes and crisp pancetta before moving on to braised breast of lamb with seasonal vegetables, tarragon nage and mint verde. Finish with chocolate St Emilion with morello cherries and cream. Keenly competitive prices are a laudable feature of the vibrant, up-to-the-minute wine list, which is helpfully organised by style. Bottle prices kick off at £14.95, and 13 astute selections are also available by the glass or carafe.
**Chef/s:** Tom Green and Peter Taylor. **Open:** all week L 12 to 2.30 (3 Sun), D 6 to 10.30 (11 Fri and Sat, 9 Sun). **Closed:** 25 and 26 Dec, 1 Jan. **Meals:** alc (main courses £13 to £19). Set L £12.50 (2 courses) to £14.75. **Service:** not inc. **Details:** Cards accepted. 128 seats. 22 seats outside. Separate bar. No music.

# ▋Cheltenham

# Le Champignon Sauvage

**Heartfelt cooking and excellent value**
24-26 Suffolk Road, Cheltenham, GL50 2AQ
Tel no: (01242) 573449
www.lechampignonsauvage.co.uk
**Modern French | £50**
**Cooking score: 8**

After more than two decades David and Helen Everitt-Matthias know a thing or two about sticking power: she heads a composed front-of-house team while his cooking continues to roam between familiar and new ground without ever getting lost. The modest building is set snug to the pavement. The simple interior comprises a small bar bulging with sofas and a spacious, carpeted dining room with an eclectic collection of art. Everything about this place is authentic and heartfelt, and the service is confident enough to be 'unfussy when so many others leave you feeling fussed and tutted over, as if you have never eaten in a grown-up restaurant before'.

An inspection meal began in the bar with a line-up of cheese canapés: cubes of Parmesan mousse with chorizo powder, Gruyère risotto balls in crisp breadcrumb shells, and brittle brioche tuile with a satin-smooth ramsons and goats' cheese dip. An intense and balanced angelica vichysoisse with salt cod mousse was an exemplary amuse. That same clarity of flavour informed a starter of rabbit tortelloni with turnip and vanilla purée, the sweet vanilla notes countered by julienne matchsticks of radish and apple. For the main act, a slightly chewy piece of venison was saved by its glossy, tender bolognese, the flavour pointed by a liquorice root jus and chervil root purée. A firework of rose geranium cream topped with popping candy and a blast of orange and liquorice sorbet preceded crisp teardrops of meringue on lemon pie with sorrel ice cream. Breads are some of the best you'll encounter, from simple oven-fresh rolls to the airy, sweet-savoury delights of a bacon brioche and a classic set of petits fours keep standards high to the last. The 15-page wine list offers good coverage of France and a fair selection from further afield. Like the food it is excellent value, starting at just £12 a bottle.
**Chef/s:** David Everitt-Matthias. **Open:** Tue to Sat L 12.30 to 1.15, D 7.30 to 8.30. **Closed:** Sun, Mon, 10 days Christmas and New Year, 3 weeks June. **Meals:** Set L £25 (2 courses) to £30. Set D £40 (2 courses) to £50. **Service:** not inc. **Details:** Cards accepted. 40 seats. Air-con. Separate bar. No music. No mobile phones. Wheelchair access. Children allowed.

## Lumière
**The light still shines**
Clarence Parade, Cheltenham, GL50 3PA
Tel no: (01242) 222200
www.lumiere.cc
**Modern British | £39**
**Cooking score: 2**

Geoff and Lin Chapman have moved on, but the name endures and the unassuming frontage (sandwiched between an Indian restaurant and a travel shop close to

Cheltenham's central bus station) still hides a relaxed, contemporary restaurant. The white and purple colour scheme and mix of comfortable leather banquettes and distressed cream Georgian chairs adds an understated elegance to the light, airy room. The cooking is modern British with classic French influences and there are some ambitious flavour pairings to be found in dishes such as Cornish hand-dived scallops with crisp pork belly, carrot, anise and orange purée and cumin caramel or Gressingham duck breast with braised red cabbage, vanilla mash and Agen prunes. Wines start at £20.
**Chef/s:** Jon Howe. **Open:** Tue to Sat L 12 to 2, D 7 to 9. **Closed:** Sun, Mon, 1 to 10 Jan. **Meals:** Set L £18 (2 courses) to £22. Set D £34 (2 courses) to £39. **Service:** optional 10% for parties over 6. **Details:** Cards accepted. 34 seats. Air-con. Music. Children allowed.

**NEW ENTRY**
## The Royal Well Tavern
**Tucked-away bistro with gutsy food**
5 Royal Well Place, Cheltenham, GL50 3DN
Tel no: (01242) 221212
www.theroyalwelltavern.com
**French | £20**
**Cooking score: 2**

After working in London restaurants such as the River Café, Kensington Place and the Glasshouse (see entries), chef Humphrey Fletcher has headed west to Cheltenham, where his rustic, gutsy French-inspired cookery has proved a big hit with locals. This tucked-away bistro close to the town's central bus station has a gastropub feel, with its dark wood tables, burgundy banquettes and gilt-framed paintings. There is a small, open kitchen in the corner. The menu is written as one list of dishes – the idea being that people can pop in for a plate of native Cornish oysters and a glass of beer, or stay for the braised lamb shoulder, garlic, shallots, flageolet beans and green sauce accompanied by a well-sourced bottle of wine from the exclusively French list, which kicks off at £15.

**Chef/s:** Humphrey Fletcher. **Open:** all week L 12 to 3 (10 to 4 Sun), Mon to Sat D 5 to 10. **Closed:** 25 and 26 Dec. **Meals:** alc (main courses £7 to £50). Set L and D £10 (2 courses) to £12.50. **Service:** 10% (optional). **Details:** Cards accepted. 48 seats. Air-con. Separate bar. Wheelchair access. Music. Children allowed.

## ALSO RECOMMENDED
### ▲ Brosh
8 Suffolk Parade, Cheltenham, GL50 2AB
Tel no: (01242) 227277
www.broshrestaurant.co.uk
**Eastern Mediterranean**

'Very orginal', 'unstuffy', 'honest' and 'unpretentious' are plaudits tossed in the direction of Raviv and Sharon Hadad's quirky Cheltenham favourite. The food is a heady, hubble-bubble mix of Mediterranean, Israeli and North African influences, with meze (£10.95 for two) and starters such as barley, fig and pistachio salad as standouts. Marinated cod with chermoula, olives and capers (£15.95) typifies the mains, and fragrant haroset ice cream with cardamom, fennel, hazelnuts and sultanas (£5.95) is a must-try dessert. Good-value wines from £12.95 Open Wed to Sat D only.

## ▮ Chipping Campden

## ALSO RECOMMENDED
### ▲ Eight Bells Inn
Church Street, Chipping Campden, GL55 6JG
Tel no: (01386) 840371
www.eightbellsinn.co.uk
**Modern British**

Medieval to the core, this solid Cotswold inn was built in 1380 to house stonemasons working on nearby St James' Church. The building may breathe antiquity, but the food has a modern accent. Home-smoked meat and fish is a strong suit – say, gammon and pea risotto (£6.95) – but the kitchen can also conjure up everything from fish pie to pork fillet stuffed with apricots and thyme (£13.95). Puddings (£5.75) are traditional staples such

as apple and rhubarb cobbler. House wine is £14 (£3.65 a glass). Accommodation available. Open all week.

## ▮ Cirencester

NEW ENTRY
### Made by Bob
**Chic café/deli with big-city vibes**
The Corn Hall, Unit 6, 26 Market Place, Cirencester, GL7 2NY
Tel no: (01285) 641818
**Mediterranean | £22**
**Cooking score: 3**
£5 OFF £30

There is an undeniable London vibe to this chic café/deli. Around the open-plan kitchen are high stools enabling customers to watch ex-Bibendum chef Bob Parkinson and his team at close quarters. At the far end is a well-stocked deli with fruit and veg from Italy, charcuterie, cheese and in-house sauces and dressings with the distinctive Made by Bob packaging. The food is Mediterranean with occasional Asian influences, and the cooking is assured and simple – a starter of bresaola with pecorino, watercress, almonds and sherry vinegar might be followed by roast rump of lamb with crushed potatoes, roast tomato, field mushrooms and salsa verde. Desserts are equally uncomplicated, with, for example, white peach bavarois topped with caramelised almonds. A vibrant wine list starts at £13.10 a bottle.
**Chef/s:** Bob Parkinson and Ben Round. **Open:** Mon to Sat B 7.30 to 10 (10.30 Sat), L 12 to 3. **Closed:** Sun. **Meals:** alc (main courses £9 to £18). **Service:** not inc. **Details:** Cards accepted. 45 seats. Wheelchair access. Music. Children allowed.

### Please send us your feedback

To register your opinion about any restaurant listed in the Guide, or a new restaurant that you wish to bring to our attention, please visit the web address at the bottom of the page. Your feedback informs the content of the book and will be used to compile next year's reviews.

## Coln St Aldwyns

**NEW ENTRY**

### The New Inn

Deliciously English hideaway
Main Street, Coln St Aldwyns, GL7 5AN
Tel no: (01285) 750651
www.new-inn.co.uk
British | £28
Cooking score: 3

£5 OFF 🍽 £30 ♨

This cluster of honey-coloured buildings is a deliciously English hideaway. A small garden overlooks lush fields, and the terrace is dotted with tables and parasols. The inn itself is pure gastropub: exposed brickwork, bare floors, colourful rugs and slick young staff. The menu runs from lunchtime sandwiches to stylish pub meals such as chicken liver parfait with thyme and truffle butter and shallot marmalade, followed by slow-roasted honey-glazed pork belly with dauphinoise potato, black pudding and red wine jus. Flavours and seasoning can err on the shy side – rösti-style salmon and chilli fishcakes with roasted pepper salad lacked any discernable chilli punch – but you can expect good quality ingredients and generous portions. A selection of wines starts at £14.50.
**Chef/s:** Oliver Addis. **Open:** all week L 12.30 to 2.30, D 7 to 9. **Meals:** alc (main courses £10 to £25). **Service:** not inc. **Details:** Cards accepted. 40 seats. 50 seats outside. Separate bar. Wheelchair access. Music. Children allowed. Car parking.

## Compton Abdale

**ALSO RECOMMENDED**

### ▲ The Puesdown Inn

Compton Abdale, GL54 4DN
Tel no: (01451) 860262
www.puesdown.cotswoldinns.com
Modern British

Right beside the A40, this one-time local boozer has been snazzily re-fashioned as a contemporary pub/restaurant-with-rooms. Basic grub is available at lunchtime, but the kitchen shows its real prowess in the evening.

Modern flavours are the order of the day, with starters of roast onion and celeriac ravioli (£7) giving way to skate with caperberries and lemon sauce or lamb rump with a rosemary and roast potato tart (£14.50). To finish, try olive oil and orange cake (£6.25). Wines from £12.50. Open all week L, Tue to Sat D.

## Corse Lawn

### Corse Lawn House Hotel

Classic cuisine in a gracious setting
Corse Lawn, GL19 4LZ
Tel no: (01452) 780771
www.corselawn.com
Anglo-French | £33
Cooking score: 3

🍾 🍽 V

Fronted by a photogenic ornamental pond, this impeccable Queen Anne house has been lovingly nurtured by members of the Hine family since 1978, and it breathes gracious, old-school gentility. The food has evolved over the years, celebrating classic bourgeois cuisine but also making a stand when it comes to eco-friendly sourcing and sustainable fish. Here you might find game terrine with beetroot chutney alongside home-cured salmon, while main courses bring ox tongue with red wine sauce as well as spiced fillet of pollack with lentil and pancetta salsa. The list of puddings covers everything from treacle tart to iced cinnamon parfait with mulled poached pear. A simpler menu is also available in the bistro. The wine list is a well-bred French aristocrat – as you might expect from the Hine family's 'Cognac connections' – although there are prestigious selections from elsewhere and an enviable choice of around 60 half-bottles. House selections are £16.20.
**Chef/s:** Andrew Poole. **Open:** all week L 12 to 2, D 7 to 9.30. **Closed:** 25 and 26 Dec. **Meals:** alc (main courses £14 to £18). Set bistro L £16 (2 courses) to £19. Set bistro D £19 (2 courses) to £22. Set restaurant L £23 (2 courses) to £26. Set restaurant D £33 (3 courses). **Service:** not inc. **Details:** Cards accepted. 60 seats. 30 seats outside. No music. No mobile phones. Wheelchair access. Children allowed. Car parking.

## ▌Didmarton

ALSO RECOMMENDED
### ▲ The Kings Arms

The Street, Didmarton, GL9 1DT
Tel no: (01454) 238245
www.kingsarmsdidmarton.co.uk
**Gastropub**

On the edge of the Badminton Estate, two miles from Westonbirt Arboretum, this seventeenth-century coaching inn is now a smart gastropub with rooms. There is a modern European influence to the cooking, but comforting pub classics are given equal billing, with starters such as seared scallops with chorizo and paprika oil (£7.25) and main dishes including venison casserole with mashed potato (£11.95). A range of local ales are complemented by a concise, affordable wine list starting at £13.75. Open all week.

## ▌Ebrington

ALSO RECOMMENDED
### ▲ The Ebrington Arms

Ebrington, GL55 6NH
Tel no: (01386) 593223
www.theebringtonarms.co.uk
**Modern British**

A singular-looking, seventeenth-century inn in the photogenic hamlet of Ebrington offers a beer garden in fine weather, but also looks a treat in the snow, when log fires will be crackling indoors. James Nixon cooks a modern British menu that might run from clam chowder with chilli and coriander (£5), through noisettes of Cotswold lamb with wild mushroom gratin, celeriac dauphinoise, roasted squash and thyme jus (£14), to passion fruit and orange tart (£5). A well-written, fairly priced wine list goes from £13. Open Tue to Sun L, Tue to Sat D.

## ▌Fairford

### Allium

A country restaurant of some class
1 London Street, Fairford, GL7 4AH
Tel no: (01285) 712200
www.allium.uk.net
**Modern British | £39**
**Cooking score: 6**

In five years the Grahams have established their restaurant as one of the best in the area. A pair of seventeenth-century cottages has been knocked together to create a simple bar and dining room with well-spaced tables – 'first class, yet the restaurant somehow has a homely feel where everyone is very friendly and welcoming'. James Graham oversees a regularly changing seasonal menu that tries out some novel combinations but doesn't overreach itself in ambition. What he is good at is familiar combinations of quality ingredients, mostly sourced from a network of well-chosen local suppliers, and cooked with care. At its best it is cooking that makes a virtue of simplicity and economy and seems to please the great majority on both fronts. A selection of fine homemade breads open proceedings ('Cotswold Crunch is a real favourite'), while the first course might be something as simple as crayfish with wild garlic and almonds. Main courses gain lustre through the pedigree of their components, as is the case with Great Farm chicken served with girolles and white beans. Attractive desserts have included cherry clafoutis with marzipan and basil. The 'always interesting' wine list has a soft spot for France and picks good producers elsewhere. There's a sound house selection from £18.50.

**Chef/s:** James Graham. **Open:** Wed to Sun L 12 to 2, Tue to Sat D 7 to 9. **Closed:** Mon, first 2 weeks Jan, 2 weeks Aug. **Meals:** Set L £18.50 (2 courses) to £22.50. Set D £32.50 (2 courses) to to £38.50. Sun L £13.50. Tasting menu £65 (8 courses). **Service:** not inc. **Details:** Cards accepted. 34 seats. Separate bar. No mobile phones. Wheelchair access. Music. Children allowed.

## Lower Oddington

### The Fox Inn

Rambling hostelry with reliable food
Lower Oddington, GL56 0UR
Tel no: (01451) 870555
www.foxinn.net
Gastropub | £23
Cooking score: 1

Standing proud in an archetypal
Gloucestershire hamlet, this photogenic, ivy-
draped inn is a rambling hostelry with a
reputation for reliable food and classy
drinking opportunities. Hop-garlanded
beams and flagstone floors add to the bucolic
feel in the bar, while the red-walled dining
room feels a touch more sedate. Eat where you
like from a menu that mixes country pub grub
(steak and kidney pie, apple and sultana
sponge) with bistro-style dishes (seared
scallops with ginger dressing, lamb rump with
celeriac and potato purée). House wines
from £13.25.
**Chef/s:** Ray Pearce. **Open:** all week L 12 to 2.30
(3.30 Sun), D 6.30 to 10 (7 to 9.30 Sun). **Closed:** 25
Dec. **Meals:** alc (main courses £11 to £15).
**Service:** not inc. **Details:** Cards accepted. 80 seats.
80 seats outside. Separate bar. No music.
Wheelchair access. Children allowed. Car parking.

## Minchinhampton

READERS RECOMMEND
### The Ragged Cot

Gastropub
Cirencester Road, Minchinhampton, GL6 8PE
Tel no: (01453) 884643
www.theraggedcot.co.uk
'Chef producing modern British cooking of a
high standard'

Average price

The average price listed in main-entry
reviews denotes the price of a three-
course meal, without wine.

## Northleach

ALSO RECOMMENDED
### ▲ The Wheatsheaf Inn

West End, Northleach, GL54 3EZ
Tel no: (01451) 860244
www.cotswoldswheatsheaf.com
Modern British

Under new ownership (the same team behind
the Royal Well Tavern in Cheltenham – see
entry), the Wheatsheaf has been given a
sympathetic makeover and is now a food-
driven pub with comfortable bedrooms.
Located on the edge of the town's lovely
market square, it attracts foodies as well as
local drinkers. Typical dishes might include
treacle-cured salmon, pickled cucumber and
soda bread (£6), Barnsley chop with bubble
and squeak (£14) and seasonal fruit crumble
with crème anglaise (£5). House wine is
£13.50. Open all week.

## Sapperton

### The Bell at Sapperton

Busy local with serious food
Sapperton, GL7 6LE
Tel no: (01285) 760298
www.foodatthebell.co.uk
Gastropub | £30
Cooking score: 4

An agreeable feeling of pastoral prosperity
characterises Paul Davidson and Pat Le Jeune's
pub situated in a pretty Cotswold village. It
still plays its part as a busy local, especially
when the sun shines and the garden comes into
its own, but these days it is better known for
food. When lunch includes faggots of local
game, and seared rare breast of wood pigeon
with soft polenta and braised shallots, it is
clear that cooking is taken seriously. Menus
are daily changing and highlight local and
regionally sourced ingredients. Starters
include crisp-fried Cerney goats' cheese and
aubergine roulade, and hand-pressed terrine
of chicken with house chutney. Mains feature
the likes of slow-braised shank of lamb with
creamed Savoy cabbage or fillet of sea bass on

thyme and Parmesan risotto. Spiced red wine jelly, poached pineapple and sorbet is a fun way to finish. Wines start at £15.

**Chef/s:** Ivan Reid. **Open:** all week L 12 to 2.15, D 7 to 9.30 (9 Sun). **Closed:** 25 Dec. **Meals:** alc (main courses £10 to £20). Set L Mon to Fri £10 (2 courses). **Service:** not inc. **Details:** Cards accepted. 65 seats. 40 seats outside. No music. No mobile phones. Wheelchair access. Car parking.

## ■ Southrop

**NEW ENTRY**
### The Swan at Southrop
**London favourite reborn in the country**
Southrop, GL7 3NU
Tel no: (01367) 850205
www.theswanatsouthrop.co.uk
**Modern British | £25**
**Cooking score: 4**

Sebastian and Lana Snow moved to the country in 2008 after 18 years at their much-loved London eatery – Snows on the Green in Shepherd's Bush. The contrast couldn't be greater. They are now ensconced in a fourteenth-century, creeper-covered Cotswold stone inn, hidden away in a picture-perfect village. It remains a local watering hole, but diners head for the heavy beamed dining room for Sebastian's robust cooking, with its distinct Gallic and Mediterranean slant. Hearty dishes that found favour in London are replicated here: a signature starter of foie gras, fried egg and balsamic vinegar, for example, and comforting plates of crisp belly pork with confit potatoes and artichokes. Elsewhere, you'll find pasta dishes, risottos and puddings like lemon curd tart with raspberry sauce. The set-lunch menu is a steal. Global wines from £13.50.

**Chef/s:** Sebastian Snow. **Open:** all week L 12 to 3, Mon to Sat D 6 to 10. **Meals:** alc (main courses £10 to £18). Set L and D £13 (2 courses) to £16. Sun L £15. **Service:** 12.5% (optional). **Details:** Cards accepted. 60 seats. 20 seats outside. Separate bar. Wheelchair access. Music. Children allowed. Car parking.

## ■ Stow-on-the-Wold
### The Old Butcher's
**Dressed-down, clean-cut flavours**
7 Park Street, Stow-on-the-Wold, GL54 1AQ
Tel no: (01451) 831700
www.theoldbutchers.com
**Modern British | £27**
**Cooking score: 3**

Peter and Louise Robinson's converted butcher's shop has all the creature-comfort niceties of a smart contemporary brasserie, from a bold glass frontage and alfresco tables to a smart bar and high-backed chairs. The mood is dressed-down and relaxed, and the food taps into the current appetite for ingredients-led, straight-down-the-line dishes with clean-cut flavours. Inverurie Angus beef with truffle butter is a carnivorous big-hitter, but the daily menu covers a lot of ground, taking in everything from goose rillettes with sourdough bread to pumpkin and chestnut risotto. The Anglo-Mediterranean alliance also shows up in, say, roast plaice with brown shrimp butter or calf's liver with cavolo nero and balsamic. Desserts pitch buttermilk custard with pomegranate and honey against panettone bread-and-butter pudding. House wine is £15 (£4 a glass).

**Chef/s:** Peter Robinson. **Open:** Tue to Sun L 12 to 2.30, Tue to Sat D 6 to 9.30 (10 Sat). **Closed:** Mon. **Meals:** alc (main courses £11 to £17). Set L £12 (2 courses) to £14. Set D £15 (2 courses) to £17.50. Sun L £12.50. **Service:** not inc. **Details:** Cards accepted. 45 seats. 12 seats outside. Air-con. Separate bar. Wheelchair access. Music. Children allowed.

## Tetbury

### Calcot Manor, The Conservatory

Ambitious, skilful cooking
Tetbury, GL8 8YJ
Tel no: (01666) 890391
www.calcotmanor.co.uk
Modern British | £35
Cooking score: 3

🛏 V

Having outgrown its origins as a Cotswold farmhouse, Calcot Manor is now the full country hotel package, complete with a health spa and luxury accommodation in converted outbuildings. The Conservatory restaurant is also a fairly recent addition, and it provides a suitably bright backdrop for Michael Croft's ambitious food. In a setting of slate floors and candelabra, visitors can sample skilfully wrought dishes such as pressed foie gras and apple terrine followed by poached sea trout with sorrel linguine, chargrilled courgette and lemon butter. Highgrove Estate is close by, and the kitchen also makes admirable use of organically reared Duchy meat for – say – wood-roast rump of beef with smoked garlic purée, ox tongue and artichoke fricassee. Close the show with liquorice crème brûlée or warm rhubarb tartlet and cardamom pannacotta. The French-led wine list starts at £17.50.
Chef/s: Michael Croft. Open: all week L 12 to 2, D 7 to 9.30. Meals: alc (main courses £18 to £21). Set L £19 (2 courses) to £23. Sun L £26.50. Service: not inc. Details: Cards accepted. 100 seats. 12 seats outside. Air-con. Separate bar. Wheelchair access. Music. Children allowed. Car parking.

### The Chef's Table

Classy town centre deli/bistro
49 Long Street, Tetbury, GL8 1AA
Tel no: (01666) 504466
www.thechefstable.co.uk
Modern British | £31
Cooking score: 4

Michael and Sarah Bedford's deli-cum-bistro is now open for lunch and dinner and has upped its game to meet the more demanding needs of evening diners. While the premises 'are less than ideal for an evening operation (ring bell, walk through shop and up the stairs)', reservations are now taken and with the sheer theatre of the open-plan kitchen, menus that make a virtue of simplicity and quality sourcing of raw materials, it all confirms that it's the food that matters. A straightforward dish of robustly flavoured salt cod risotto could precede main courses of 'sublime oxtail' braised in red wine or a modern take on chicken Kiev served with ratatouille and mixed leaves. Finish, perhaps, with warm chocolate brownie. Reports have highlighted the kitchen's perfect timing and 'friendly and obliging' service. House wine is £15.25.
Chef/s: Michael Bedford. Open: Mon to Sat 12 to 2.30, Wed to Sat 7 to 9.30. Closed: Sun, 25 and 26 Dec, 1 Jan. Meals: alc (main courses £14 to £19). Service: not inc. Details: Cards accepted. 30 seats. No music. Children allowed.

## Thornbury

### Ronnies
**Hidden find with food that's a steal**
11 St Mary Street, Thornbury, BS35 2AB
Tel no: (01454) 411137
www.ronnies-restaurant.co.uk
**Modern European | £35**
**Cooking score: 4**

£5
OFF

Hidden away in the town's shopping precinct, Ronnies attracts as many destination diners as it does locals and has built up a fiercely loyal following since opening in 2007. Despite its quirky location, the restaurant is smart and well appointed, its neutral colours blending with stone walls and wooden floors. It's a place to pop in for good coffee in the morning or afternoon, while the two/three-course fixed-price menu is a steal, both at lunch and dinner. The food is modern and chef Ron Faulkner displays solid, precise techniques. A starter of twice-cooked belly pork is accompanied by black pudding and beetroot chutney, while roasted breast of Cotswold chicken comes with baby carrots, asparagus, Jerusalem artichoke purée and chicken jus. Dessert could be chocolate fondant with espresso ice cream. From an interesting and modern list, house wine is £13.75 a bottle, with a dozen by the glass.
**Chef/s:** Ron Faulkner. **Open:** Tue to Sun L 12 to 2.30, D 6.30 to 9.30 (10.30 Sat and Sun). **Closed:** Mon, 25 and 26 Dec, 1 and 2 Jan. **Meals:** alc (main courses £13 to £20). Set L and D £13.75 (2 courses) to £16.75. Sun L £14.50 (2 courses) to £18.50. **Service:** not inc. **Details:** Cards accepted. 62 seats. 32 seats outside. Wheelchair access. Music. Children allowed.

## Upper Slaughter

### Lords of the Manor
**Exciting, attention-grabbing cooking**
Upper Slaughter, GL54 2JD
Tel no: (01451) 820243
www.lordsofthemanor.com
**Modern British | £55**
**Cooking score: 6**

🍷 ☞ V

A picture of rosy-hued Englishness, this honey-coloured Cotswold manor spreads itself comfortably amid eight acres of parkland running down to the River Eye. The idyllic setting doesn't change as the years roll by, although a recent makeover has added some contemporary vibrancy and colour to the one-time rectory's antique-laden, country house interior. Huge canvases now dominate the dining room, where guests can sample the fruits of Matt Weedon's exciting and subtle cooking. Native British ingredients are used to telling effect and the kitchen doesn't need to fall back on luxuries to make diners sit up and take notice. To start, fillet of Cornish red mullet is given some Mediterranean tones with crab cannelloni, warm aubergine gâteau, tapenade and red pepper purée. Mains often have a more emphatic British feel – perhaps fillet and belly of Kelmscott pork with butternut squash, braised shoulder suet pudding, crackling and jus or sirloin of Cotswold Longhorn beef paired with a fricassee of Hereford snails and broad beans. Desserts promise high levels of technical expertise and pinpoint flavours – as in blood orange marshmallow with lemon parfait and blood orange soup. The 16-strong contingent of British artisan cheeses is also worth more than a sniff. A mighty wine list running to more than 600 bins gives plenty of space to the French and Italian regional classics, and the sommelier's food-matching selections by the glass are also worth taking on board. Bottles start at £19.50.
**Chef/s:** Matt Weedon. **Open:** all week L 12 to 2.30, D 7 to 9.45. **Meals:** Set L £29.50. Set D £55. Tasting menu from £65. Sun L £29.50. **Service:** 10% (optional). **Details:** Cards accepted. 60 seats. 28

seats outside. Separate bar. No music. No mobile phones. Wheelchair access. Children allowed. Car parking.

# █ Winchcombe

## 5 North Street

**Stellar cooking and charm**
5 North Street, Winchcombe, GL54 5LH
Tel no: (01242) 604566
**Modern European | £40**
**Cooking score: 6**

**V**

'How lucky I am to have this wonderful local restaurant practically on my doorstep!' is the heartfelt declaration of one reader, summing up the fondness with which regulars view the Ashenfords' rustic Cotswold outfit. Two small, simply decorated rooms in a timber-framed building off the high street make a charming backdrop for what is an extremely professional operation. 'Kate's friendly, attentive service is the perfect complement to her husband's imaginative and nicely judged cooking', another reader rightly notes. The drill is fixed-price menus in ascending order of lavishness, up to the seven-course tasting bonanza, which may be taken in 'surprise' format. This allows Marcus Ashenford's stellar cooking skills to be used to their best effect. A typical evening's dining tour might begin with smoked duck and rillettes, with pea shoot and mooli salad, pumpkin seeds and plum sauce, followed by sea bass with ratatouille, celeriac and horseradish, dressed with tapenade. To conclude, there might be an apple tarte fine, with almond sponge, Calvados and sultana ice cream and a cinnamon biscuit. These are labour-intensive dishes that achieve a deceptive air of effortlessness on the plate. A compact wine list does the job at prices that rarely get silly. Start at £18.50 (or £4.75 a glass) for a pair of Argentinian varietals, Chardonnay and Shiraz. Note that it is essential to book for lunch, so that the owners know it's worth opening.

**Chef/s:** Marcus Ashenford. **Open:** Wed to Sun L 12.30 to 1.30, Tue to Sat D 7 to 9. **Closed:** Mon, first 2 weeks Jan, last week Aug. **Meals:** alc (main courses £15 to £21). Set L £21.50 (2 courses) to £25.50. Set D £34 to £65 (10 courses). **Service:** not inc. **Details:** Cards accepted. 26 seats. Wheelchair access. Music. Children allowed.

## Wesley House

**Big-flavour food with a seasonal accent**
High Street, Winchcombe, GL54 5LJ
Tel no: (01242) 602366
www.wesleyhouse.co.uk
**Modern British | £38**
**Cooking score: 3**

£5 OFF 🛏

John Wesley's former residence has been owned by Matthew Brown since 1992. It's a lovely, half-timbered old building, with mullioned windows and colourful, comfortable interiors, where themed evenings of one sort or another – Thai, Spanish, South African, Seventies – punctuate the year. Martin Dunn cooks a confident version of modern British cuisine with skill and an emphasis on big flavour, and his menus follow the seasons. Start with fennel and juniper-cured salmon with pea shoots in a mustard dressing, and proceed to caramelised pork loin with sweet potato purée and apple sauce. End, perhaps, with a dessert that contrasts the richness of chocolate truffle torte with a sharp passion fruit sorbet. Wines are classified into France, Europe and New World sections, and start with a house selection from £16.50 (£4.50 a glass).

**Chef/s:** Martin Dunn. **Open:** all week L 12 to 2, Mon to Sat D 7 to 9 (9.30 Sat). **Meals:** Set L £19.50 (2 courses) to £24.50. Set D £32.50 (2 courses) to £38. Sun L £19.50. **Service:** not inc. **Details:** Cards accepted. 70 seats. Air-con. Separate bar. No mobile phones. Wheelchair access. Music. Children allowed.

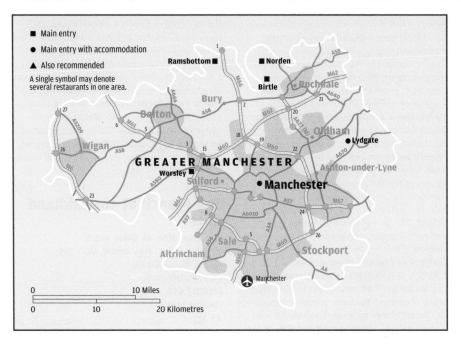

## Birtle

### The Waggon at Birtle

**Vibrant ex-pub with terrific special evenings**
131 Bury and Rochdale Old Road, Birtle, BL9 6UE
Tel no: (01706) 622955
www.thewaggonatbirtle.co.uk
**Modern British | £27**
**Cooking score: 3**

This former pub with its modern, comfortably decorated interior and a vibrant feel has put Birtle on the culinary map. On offer is a carte, a regularly changing market menu, and 'terrific value' special evenings. One such seafood event delivered 'plump and perfect' lobster and tiger prawn ravioli, as well as salmon with sage and lemon butter, and halibut with peas, asparagus and broad beans with oyster butter. Elsewhere, tempura of Chadwick's Bury black pudding has become something of a signature dish, while a meaty main course could be salted ox tongue with creamed potatoes and caramelised onions. A

trio of rhubarb – smoothie, fool and custard ice cream – makes a great finish. House wines at £13.50 a bottle (£3.25 a glass).
**Chef/s:** David Watson. **Open:** Wed to Sat D 6 to 9.30, Sun 12.30 to 7.30. **Closed:** Mon, Tue, 26 Dec for 2 weeks, first 2 weeks Aug. **Meals:** alc (main courses £9 to £19). Set D £13.50 (2 courses) to £15.50. **Service:** not inc. **Details:** Cards accepted. 60 seats. Separate bar. Wheelchair access. Music. Children allowed. Car parking.

## Lydgate

### The White Hart Inn

**Re-invented moorland inn**
51 Stockport Road, Lydgate, OL4 4JJ
Tel no: (01457) 872566
www.thewhitehart.co.uk
**Modern British | £27**
**Cooking score: 4**

You're hardly any distance from the centre of Oldham, but sitting in this handsome old coaching inn perched on the edge of the moors you feel positively remote. Fires roar, good local beer is pulled from gleaming pumps and young, cheerful staff know what they're doing. The bar is a relaxed, easy place; the restaurant, with its white napery and candles, is more formal. The food is good – huge juicy scallops arrive with black pudding hash browns, crispy pancetta and herb butter sauce. Smoked Gressingham duck with asparagus, watercress and a crispy free-range egg is equally rewarding. Follow, perhaps, with seared sea trout, pak choi, carrot and ginger purée and parsley crushed potatoes, the flavours working nicely with the succulent fish. But whatever you do, leave room for dessert. The lemon tart with honey ice cream and red wine jus is 'a big-hitter'. The wine list starts at £16.

**Chef/s:** Paul Cookson. **Open:** Mon to Sat L 12 to 2.30, D 6 to 9.30, Sun 1 to 7.30. **Closed:** 26 Dec, 1 Jan. **Meals:** alc (main courses £11 to £19). Set L £13.50 (2 courses). Bar menu available. **Service:** not inc. **Details:** Cards accepted. 50 seats. 60 seats outside. Air-con. Separate bar. No mobile phones. Wheelchair access. Music. Children allowed. Car parking.

## ▌Manchester

## Chaophraya
**High-quality Thai food**
19 Chapel Walks, Manchester, M2 1HN
Tel no: (0161) 8328342
www.chaophraya.co.uk
Thai | £20
Cooking score: 3
£5 OFF  V  £30

There are as many ways to mangle the pronunciation of Chaophraya as there are options on its extensive Thai menu. With both, the simplest choice is often the best. Since opening in 2006, it has occupied two floors above buzzy Chapel Walks. The large bar might be too cavernous to be truly comfortable, but the top-floor restaurant, cleverly divided into more intimate spaces, is a great setting for the most proficient Thai food in the city. Zingy salads with an unstinting use of fresh herbs, and simple, fresh fish are among

the top choices from a menu that runs and runs. Slow-cooked red curry with duck breast, or a veggie pad thai, rustling with ground peanuts, are also solid options. Service is friendly, if a little rushed. The wine list has several spice-friendly selections from £14.20.

**Chef/s:** Vichai Mumgmai. **Open:** all week 12 to 10.30. **Closed:** 25 Dec, 1 Jan. **Meals:** alc (main courses £8 to £26). Set D £20 to £30 (2 courses). **Service:** 10% (optional). **Details:** Cards accepted. 120 seats. Air-con. Separate bar. Wheelchair access. Music. Children allowed.

## The French at the Midland Hotel
**Still glam after all these years**
16 Peter Street, Manchester, M60 2DS
Tel no: (0161) 2363333
www.qhotels.co.uk
French | £46
Cooking score: 3
£5 OFF 

There is an itch in Manchester that only The French can scratch. Diners who yearn for the expensive, old-fashioned glamour signalled by polished glassware and endless silver will find it in the Midland's discreet *belle époque* dining room. Legendary maître d' Bruno Lucchi has retired, but his assistant of many years, Anibal Cabral, forges on with 'formal and very attentive' service. The customer is still queen, and thanked repeatedly whether she enjoys it or not. A royal feast begins with a laden bread trolley, moving on, perhaps, to a 'well-seasoned' cauliflower velouté with a little rarebit beignet, followed by honey-roasted duck with beetroot tart and orange purée. While you're here, a raspberry soufflé seems more appropriate than custard tart with nutmeg ice cream or an Eccles cake. Bottles from a solid but brief list start at £23 and climb steeply.

**Chef/s:** Paul Beckley. **Open:** Tue to Sat D 7 to 10.30. **Closed:** Sun, Mon, bank hols, 2 weeks Aug. **Meals:** alc (main courses £23 to £33). **Service:** not inc. **Details:** Cards accepted. 40 seats. Air-con. Separate bar. Wheelchair access. Music. Children allowed.

**NEW ENTRY**
# Gabriel's Kitchen
**Affordable, democratic food**
265 Upper Brook Street, Manchester, M13 0HR
Tel no: (0161) 2760911
www.themoderncaterer.co.uk
**Modern European | £10**
**Cooking score: 2**

Good food is rarely more democratic than at Peter Booth's university-district café, where breakfast starts at an eminently affordable £1.45 for hot buttered toast with homemade jam. Booth's daytime enterprises began at the nearby Whitworth Art Gallery (see below), and though Gabriel's occasionally opens for evening events, the emphasis is on decent lunches in relaxed, almost industrial surrounds. Booth knows his suppliers. Excellent local meat makes it into a mutton hotpot, or flank steak with rocket and pecorino, while sandwich fillings like home-cured salt beef or organic Wensleydale are cossetted between great bread. Kids get an inviting £5 meal, finishing with fruit salad or a nutty brownie: cakes also pass muster among the adults.
**Chef/s:** Peter Booth. **Open:** all week 7am to 5 (9 to 5.30 Sat, 10 to 4.30 Sun). **Closed:** 25 and 26 Dec. **Meals:** alc (main courses £7 to £9). **Service:** not inc. **Details:** Cash only. 37 seats. 8 seats outside. Wheelchair access. Music. Children allowed.

# The Gallery Café
**High quality and low prices**
Whitworth Art Gallery, Oxford Road, Manchester, M15 6ER
Tel no: (0161) 2757497
www.themoderncaterer.co.uk
**Modern European | £10**
**Cooking score: 2**

Peter Booth's standalone café (Gabriel's Kitchen, see entry above) has opened not far away, but the quality remains high in his little corner of the Whitworth Art Gallery. Open only at breakfast and lunch, the Gallery Café is all about pleasing combinations of good basics. Bread from Chorlton's much-loved Barbakan deli hunkers down under a bruschetta topping of chilli beetroot, parsley and Kirkham's Lancashire cheese. Ethics play a part, too: the bananas with honey and sultanas in one of the café's home bakes are Fairtrade through and through. Kids are welcome and well looked after with a simple £5 menu, while adults get house wine at £2.50 a glass.
**Chef/s:** Peter Booth. **Open:** Mon to Sat 10 to 4.30, Sun 12 to 3.30. **Closed:** Good Fri, 23 Dec to 4 Jan. **Meals:** alc (main courses £3 to £8). **Service:** not inc. **Details:** Cash only. 52 seats. 48 seats outside. No music. Wheelchair access. Children allowed. Car parking.

# Greens
**Smart veggie restaurant with oomph**
43 Lapwing Lane, West Didsbury, Manchester, M20 2NT
Tel no: (0161) 4344259
www.greensdidsbury.co.uk
**Vegetarian | £21**
**Cooking score: 2**

**V**

Expansion into the shop next door has given Simon Rimmer's vegetarian restaurant a bit of oomph and a lot more space. An outward-looking menu (for example, starters of gado-gado salad or the signature oyster mushrooms with plum sauce and pancakes) is a boon for Didsbury's veggies, but the smart, cheerful space and pleasure of patronising an indie operation lures meat-eaters too. Main courses might be mushroom and Stilton pie with peppercorn gravy, or a slightly less successful nut roast with barbecue sauce and sweet potato mash. Hot puds, such as apple and blueberry crumble with caramel and coconut sauce, are a high point. Wine starts at £13.50.
**Chef/s:** Simon Rimmer. **Open:** Tue to Sun L 12 to 2 (4 Sat and Sun), all week D 5.30 to 10.30. **Meals:** alc (main courses £10 to £11). Set D £13.95 (2 courses). Sun L £13.95. **Service:** not inc. **Details:** Cards accepted. 84 seats. 12 seats outside. Air-con. Separate bar. No mobile phones. Music. Children allowed.

## Lime Tree

'Old favourite' local destination
8 Lapwing Lane, West Didsbury, Manchester,
M20 2WS
Tel no: (0161) 4451217
www.thelimetreerestaurant.co.uk
**Modern British | £27**
**Cooking score: 3**

Lush greenery greets customers at this West Didsbury 'old favourite', which continues to please, courtesy of a sunny conservatory and a menu that strikes a symphony of popular notes. Start, perhaps, with crisp-coated salmon fishcakes with fresh green leaves, or unthreatening seared scallops with sweet chilli and crème fraîche. Main courses could be immaculately fresh sea bass laid over silky greens with a dab of butter sauce, or Mediterranean-inspired roast lamb loin with ratatouille and minted yoghurt. Stay the course for simple, straight-to-the-pleasure-point desserts, such as a faintly boozy chocolate and orange truffle cake with a homely biscuit base. Service can tend towards complacency when the place is packed, but has the relaxed ease which comes with such well-established popularity. A strong wine list favours the Old World with France and Italy holding top slots. Prices are fair, with around 10 house selections from £13 (£3.25 a glass).
**Chef/s:** Jason Parker and Jason Dickinson. **Open:** Tue to Fri and Sun L 12 to 2.30, all week D 5.30 to 10.15. **Closed:** 25 and 26 Dec. **Meals:** alc (main courses £11 to £22). Set L and D (5.30 to 6.30) £15.95. Sun L £17.95. **Service:** not inc. **Details:** Cards accepted. 75 seats. 15 seats outside. Music.

★ BEST SET MENU ★

## Michael Caines at ABode Manchester

Smooth city-centre dining
107 Piccadilly, Manchester, M1 2DB
Tel no: (0161) 2005678
www.michaelcaines.com
**Modern European | £40**
**Cooking score: 4**

There's no getting away from Michael Caines at ABode, the hotel mini-chain at which he leads the gastronomic charge. His name seems etched onto every available surface, but the duty of cooking at the fine-dining restaurant in a low-lit basement goes mainly to executive chef Ian Matfin. His experience as number two at Gidleigh Park (see entry) shows on every plate, which might hold a luxurious salad of wild duck with hollandaise or sea bass with fennel purée and an on-the-nail fish red wine sauce. A grazing menu of tasting-size dishes is hugely popular at lunchtime. Bolstered by the excellent house-baked bread, three courses with matching wines is 'wonderful value' at under £20. The kitchen's ability extends to dessert, which might be a dense chocolate orange mousse with orange confit sorbet. Some readers feel service is less consistent, and charges of gaucheness may stick. Wine, brought from the glassed-in cellar by a capable sommelier, could be one of 65 bins with a decent international reach. The list begins at £22.50.
**Chef/s:** Ian Matfin. **Open:** Mon to Sat L 12 to 2.30, D 6 to 10. **Closed:** Sun. **Meals:** alc (main courses £21 to £24). Set L £12. Set D £14.95 (2 courses) to £19.95. **Service:** 12% (optional). **Details:** Cards accepted. 60 seats. Air-con. Separate bar. No mobile phones. Wheelchair access. Music. Children allowed. Car parking.

**NEW ENTRY**
# The Modern

**Cool cocktails and creative cooking**
Urbis, Cathedral Gardens, Manchester, M4 3GB
Tel no: (0161) 6058282
www.themodernmcr.co.uk
**Modern British | £27**
**Cooking score: 3**

At the top of Urbis – Manchester's museum of urban life – the Modern offers verve, cocktails and cooking with intent. Drinks in the upstairs bar are some of the finest in the city, and a menu dedicated – though not feverishly – to good local produce has serious appeal. Potted this and terrine of that feature heavily. Start, perhaps, with potted smoked mackerel and ribbons of cucumber pickled with dill. Braised Ribble Valley pork hock comes with a hearty but surprisingly effective double-hander of smooth champ and Puy lentils: be assured that lighter alternatives are available. Dessert could be a Valrhona tart with addictive ice cream studded with caramelised hazelnuts. It's all served competently in a long room accented with sage green and muddy brown, streamlined but not unfriendly. House bottles at £15.30 kick off a compact but colourfully described list.
**Chef/s:** Paul Faulkner. **Open:** all week L 12 to 3 (4.45 Sun), Mon to Sat D 5 to 9.45. Bar menu available. **Closed:** 25 and 26 Dec. **Meals:** alc (main courses £10 to £23). Set L and D £15 (2 courses) to £18. **Service:** not inc. **Details:** Cards accepted. 64 seats. Air-con. Separate bar. Wheelchair access. Music. Children allowed.

# Moss Nook

**Silver-service charmer**
2 Trenchard Drive, Ringway Road, Moss Nook, Manchester, M22 5NA
Tel no: (0161) 4374778
www.mossnookrestaurant.co.uk
**Modern British | £42**
**Cooking score: 3**

All traces of the bikers' cafe at 2 Trenchard Drive vanished when it became the Moss Nook in 1973. Since then, major changes have been neither necessary nor desirable; stasis is part of its considerable charm. Long-standing staff put guests at their ease, plying them with outmoded extras such as lamb bolognese tartlets with – drumroll – fresh Parmesan! Yet most components are thoughtfully cooked and presented. Start, perhaps, with a fish special – lobster salad with crab and smoked salmon piles luxury on luxury. Follow with good Cheshire lamb with a lively herb crust. Cloches rattle by on a hefty trolley, and wine (from £19.50, with opportunities to go higher) is poured into cut-glass goblets. The grey pound is undoubtedly a factor in the Moss Nook's continued success, but everyone needs a little silver service from time to time.
**Chef/s:** Kevin Lofthouse. **Open:** Tue to Fri L 12 to 1.30, Tue to Sat D 7 to 9.30. **Closed:** Mon, Sun, 25 and 26 Dec, 2 weeks Jan. **Meals:** alc (main courses £17 to £24). Set L £21 (5 courses). Set D £38.50 (7 courses). **Service:** not inc. **Details:** Cards accepted. 65 seats. 20 seats outside. Air-con. No music. No mobile phones. Wheelchair access. Children allowed. Car parking.

## Second Floor

**Sleek spot with a great view**
Harvey Nichols, 21 New Cathedral Street,
Manchester, M1 1AD
Tel no: (0161) 8288898
www.harveynichols.com
**Modern British | £40**
Cooking score: 3

🍷

A second-floor department store restaurant
doesn't sound a likely prospect for dinner with
a vista, but Harvey Nichols' glass-walled
dining room is elevated just enough to offer
views over busy Exchange Square. Readers
have mainly become inured to the 'clinical'
décor, and the shiny blacks and hard edges are
now the backdrop for food by former sous
Stuart Thomson. A spring inspection found
sound technique and strong ingredients,
undermined occasionally by muddled,
overdone plates. Though executed well, a
starter of red mullet with tuna ballotine,
tapenade, crab cake and spiced aubergine
purée might benefit from ruthless editing, as
would a main course of wild sea bass riddled
with trimmings from earth and sea. An
enjoyable iced peanut parfait, however, stands
alone. Service can waver, but staff rightly have
every confidence in a rather thrilling wine list,
which starts at £18 and shows the same
strength as the in-house wine shop.
**Chef/s:** Stuart Thomson. **Open:** all week L 12 to 3 (4
Sun), Tue to Sat D 6 to 10.30. **Closed:** 25 Dec, 1 Jan,
Easter, bank hols. **Meals:** alc (main courses £20 to
£25). Set L and D £30 (2 courses) to £40. Sun L £25.
Tasting menu £50. **Service:** 10% (optional).
**Details:** Cards accepted. 50 seats. Air-con. Separate
bar. Wheelchair access. Music. Children allowed.

### Please send us your feedback

To register your opinion about any
restaurant listed in the Guide, or a new
restaurant that you wish to bring to our
attention, please visit the web address at
the bottom of the page. Your feedback
informs the content of the book and will be
used to compile next year's reviews.

## Yang Sing

**Dim sum star can still shine**
34 Princess Street, Manchester, M1 4JY
Tel no: (0161) 2362200
www.yang-sing.com
**Chinese | £30**
Cooking score: 2

£5 OFF **V**

Over 30 and looking good on it, thanks to
2006's stylish refurb, Yang Sing retains the
status built on strong Cantonese cooking and
the Yeung family's hospitality. On a good day
in the huge dining room, it still shines. The
trademark flexible banquets contain some of
the dim sum, such as steamed Shanghai-style
pork dumplings, for which Yang Sing is
celebrated, to be followed by excellent roast
duckling or stir-fried scallops with sprightly
greens. Service can be gleeful or lacklustre,
and allegations of inconsistency have also been
levelled at the kitchen. Another venture, the
beautiful Yang Sing Oriental hotel, has sadly
opened and closed; Little Yang Sing, the
smaller, brighter restaurant sibling on George
Street, remains open. House wine is £18.90.
**Chef/s:** Harry Yeung. **Open:** all week 12 to 11.30.
**Closed:** 25 Dec. **Meals:** alc (main courses £9 to £18).
Set menu £22. **Service:** not inc. **Details:** Cards
accepted. 240 seats. Air-con. Wheelchair access.
Music. Children allowed.

## ALSO RECOMMENDED

### ▲ EastzEast

**Princess Street, Manchester, M1 7DL**
Tel no: (0161) 2445353
www.eastzeast.com
**Indian**

The EastzEast mini-chain recently extended
to Preston, but the original, at the base of a
hotel on the outskirts of town, is perhaps still
the best. The restaurant is reliably busy.
Readers are attracted by its relatively
'upmarket' air and Punjabi dishes, which
might include a Lahore lamb chop handi
(£9.95) or karahi chicken masala desi (£8.45),
cooked on the bone with tomatoes galore.
They've also noted the cheek-by-jowl

approach to seating, which can be hair-raising when there's hot food on the move. House wine is £12.50. Open all week D only.

## ▲ The Market Restaurant

104 High Street, Manchester, M4 1HQ
Tel no: (0161) 8343743
www.market-restaurant.com
**Modern European**

This Northern Quarter stalwart changed hands in 2008, and readers praise both its newly reduced quirkiness and solid bistro cooking. In cosy surrounds, start with a creamy croquette of Morecambe Bay shrimps (£5.75) with fried parsley salad, followed, perhaps, by a ribeye steak (£17.95) with a little kidney pudding on the side. Dessert is significant – this is the home of the Sweet Meets pudding club – and might be a blowsy stem ginger pavlova with braised rhubarb (£5.50). Popular elements – like the lovingly annotated beer list, from £2.95 – have survived the subtle changes. Closed Mon.

## ▲ Red Chilli

70-72 Portland Street, Manchester, M1 4GU
Tel no: (0161) 2362888
www.redchillirestaurant.co.uk
**Chinese**

Chilli fiends have trodden a well-worn path to this basement restaurant on the fringes of Chinatown. They glory in Szechuan cooking that balances extreme heat with impressive flavour – not to mention sleek décor and reasonable prices. Aside from chilli-speckled offal and thick, satisfying spring onion bread (£3), house specialities include spicy hot poached lamb (£8) in a powerful savoury broth. Detractors note some variations dish-by-dish and day-by-day, but the Red Chilli factor seems all-powerful; there are now six branches, including a second Manchester site near the university. Wine from £12.95. Open all week.

## ▲ Red N Hot

56 Faulkner Street, Manchester, M1 4FH
Tel no: (0161) 2362650
www.rednhotgroup.com
**Chinese**

Red N Hot is often descibed as Manchester's other Szechuan restaurant, and Red Chilli did get there first. Nonetheless, this interloper has a charm of its own, partly due to its high-tech approach: you send your order to the kitchen via a tiny laptop, and use natty tabletop stoves to keep the signature spicy hotpots bubbling (from £15). Stand-out dishes include the does-what-it-says crushed cucumber in delicious sauce (£3.50) and delicate thinly-sliced lamb fried with cumin (£7.50). House wine £10.90. Open all week.

## ▲ That Café

1031 Stockport Road, Levenshulme, Manchester, M19 2TB
Tel no: (0161) 4324672
www.thatcafe.co.uk
**Modern British**

The owners of this south Manchester institution have recently become smallholders, too. Their own pork, lamb and allotment produce appear regularly on Alison Eason's menu of hearty international dishes. Start, perhaps, with home-cured Burnley ham with figs and pickled beetroot (£6.95), followed by venison with crushed caraway parsnips (£15.95). Service can be muted, but the homely atmosphere – you're eating, essentially, in a converted terraced house – makes up for it. House wine is £10.50. Open Sun L and Tue to Sat D.

## ▲ Vermilion

Lord North Street, Manchester, M40 8AD
Tel no: (0161) 2020055
www.vermilioncinnabar.com
**Pan-Asian**

A hangar-like building in industrial east Manchester looks more likely to offer timber and workbenches than chicken in pandan leaves (£7), but Vermilion really is a pan-Asian restaurant, and an extraordinary one at that. Film-set Zen opulence dominates cocktails in the bar (tired? there are beds) and dinner in the bewilderingly fabulous restaurant. The latter might be a tiptoe through classic Thai cuisine, done adequately, or Indian dishes such as a lamb and spinach curry (£13.50) or tarka dhal. House wine from £15. Closed Sat L.

# Norden

★ READERS' RESTAURANT OF THE YEAR ★
NORTH WEST

## Nutters
**Friendly outfit with loyal fan club**
Edenfield Road, Norden, OL12 7TT
Tel no: (01706) 650167
www.nuttersrestaurant.co.uk
Modern British | £30
Cooking score: 3

V

The Nutter family's restaurant is divertingly sited in a nineteenth-century manor house with some six acres of grounds. Gothic windows and arches give way to a warm, friendly atmosphere in the interconnecting dining rooms, and a seasonally changing menu based on local supplies manages to push most of the right buttons. Vegetarians have their own menu, which might proceed in fine style from twice-baked cauliflower cheese soufflé to leek, potato and Welsh rarebit tart. Others will find a pairing of sea bass with Asian-spiced scallops served with sweet potato and spring onion fritters or soy and sesame-glazed Goosnargh duck teamed with honey roast potatoes and sweet chilli dressing, plus griottine cherry and chocolate brownie torte with Kirsch cream for dessert. House wine is £14.20.

**Chef/s:** Andrew Nutter. **Open:** Tue to Sun L 12 to 2 (4 Sun), D 6.30 to 9.30. **Closed:** Mon. **Meals:** alc (main courses £14 to £20). Set L £13.95 (2 courses) to £16.95. Gourmet D £36 (6 courses). Sun L £22.50. **Service:** not inc. **Details:** Cards accepted. 154 seats. Air-con. Separate bar. No mobile phones. Wheelchair access. Music. Children allowed. Car parking.

# Ramsbottom

## ramsons
**Italian-inspired sophistication**
18 Market Place, Ramsbottom, BL0 9HT
Tel no: (01706) 825070
www.ramsons-restaurant.com
Italian | £45
Cooking score: 6

£5
OFF  🍷 V

'It is on form this year', writes a regular visitor to this intimate, civilised restaurant. With a team of chefs headed by Abdulla Naseem, Chris Johnson brings a high level of sophistication to one of the north-west's pre-eminent kitchens. Fixed-price menus focus strongly on local produce, but the inspiration is Italy, so a breast of Bowland pheasant would be wrapped in pancetta and served with stir-fried radicchio and Castelluccio lentil casserole, its freshness and flavour faultless in an appetiser. Similarly, one reporter's roast white onion with veal ragù, melting Taleggio and rocket pesto opened a memorable winter meal that went on to wholemeal tajarin pasta with veal kidney, pancetta and red wine sauce, while a succeeding intermediate course involved a simple plate of vegetables of 'just the finest, freshest ingredients'. Others have praised 'the chicken liver brûlée, which was then surpassed by the stunning rare-breed pork ravioli', a textbook slow-cooked lamb breast with potato gratin, pea purée and lamb jus, and top-notch desserts such as hot Amadei chocolate fondant with beetroot ice cream. An obvious passion for all things Italian has produced what must be one of the finest selections of Italian wines in the country, and 'Chris Johnson's ability to take a price point and unfailingly pair up a sublime bottle of wine' should be noted. House wines £18.

**Chef/s:** Abdulla Naseem. **Open:** Wed to Sun L 12 to 2.30 (1 to 3.30 Sun), Tue to Sat D 7 to 9.30. **Closed:** Mon. **Meals:** Set L £24 (2 courses) to £30. Set D £36. Tasting menu £50 to £70. Sun L £30. **Service:** not inc. **Details:** Cards accepted. 34 seats. Music. Children allowed.

**NEW ENTRY**
## Sanmini's

**Fabulous flavours from family-run newcomer**
7 Carrbank Lodge, Ramsbottom Lane,
Ramsbottom, BL0 9DJ
Tel no: (01706) 821831
www.sanminis.com
Indian | £26
Cooking score: 3

Dr Mini Sankar and her anaesthetist husband
Dev know how healthy South Indian food can
be and, dosa by dosa, they're showing
Ramsbottom. Set in a handsome stone
gatehouse at the top of the town, Sanmini's is a
simple set-up with kitchen upstairs and small,
pleasant dining room below. Poppadoms with
impressive, vibrant chutneys are a statement of
intent which continues with artfully
presented masala dosa and fluffy rings of deep-
fried medhu vadai, both served with excellent,
toasty coconut chutney. Clear, multi-layered
flavours are evident again in Mini's mutton
Madras and rich nadar kozhi kozhambu –
chicken with fennel and cashew nuts. Service
is handled by the Sankars' grown-up children,
aided by well-drilled local teens, and, while
it's impeccably polite, more guidance would
smooth the ordering process a little. House
wine is £11.95, with lassi at £2.95.
**Chef/s:** Sundara Moorthy and Balraj. **Open:** Sat and
Sun L 11.30 to 3, Tue to Sun D 6.30 to 9.30 (10.30
Fri, Sat and Sun). **Closed:** Mon, 2 weeks Jan.
**Meals:** alc (main courses £8 to £12). Thaali Sat and
Sun £15 to £20. **Service:** not inc. **Details:** Cards
accepted. 40 seats. Separate bar. Wheelchair
access. Music. Children allowed.

## ALSO RECOMMENDED

### ▲ Hideaway
18 Market Place, Ramsbottom, BL0 9HT
Tel no: (01706) 825070
www.ramsons-restaurant.com
Italian

Head downstairs at ramsons (see entry) at 8pm
sharp to discover what happens when a
glamour model turns proficient and passionate

Italian cook. Now happier on the hobs than in
the spotlight, chef Lu Varley cooks a four-
course, single-sitting 'trattoria supper'
(£17.50) in the candlelit basement of
Ramsbottom's exemplary Italian restaurant. It
might feature antipasto, a roast tomato soup,
pasta with a ragù of organic beef and pork and
a light ricotta cheesecake. Half-litre carafes of
house wine are £5, but couples spending
more than £60 on wine from the extensive
cellar eat for free. Open Tue to Sat D.

## ▌Worsley

**NEW ENTRY**
## Grenache

**Warmth and careful home cooking**
15 Bridgewater Road, Walkden, Worsley, M28 3JE
Tel no: (0161) 7998181
www.grenacherestaurant.com
Modern British | £25
Cooking score: 2

Grenache produces everyday luxury, signified
by a slick of well-made sauce or a soft, sticky
brownie. There is genuine warmth in the
welcome to the simple dining room; there's
also generosity in the portion sizes, careful
home cooking and friendly service. Start with
jellied ham hock terrine or pinkish, chilli-
spiked chicken livers, followed by duck with
plum chutney or crisp-skinned sea bass with
buerre blanc and zingy red grapefruit; avoid
the ill-advised dribbles of chilli oil. Brownies
make for a reliably good finish. House wines
are all based on – what else? – Grenache, and
start at £10.95.
**Chef/s:** David Hayden. **Open:** Sun L 2 to 6, Wed to
Sat D 5.30 to 9. **Closed:** Mon, Tue, 25 and 26 Dec, 1
Jan, 2 weeks in Jan. **Meals:** alc (main courses £11 to
£24). Set D and Sun L £13.95 (2 courses) to £16.95.
**Service:** not inc. **Details:** Cards accepted. 34 seats.
Air-con. Separate bar. Wheelchair access. Music.
Children allowed.

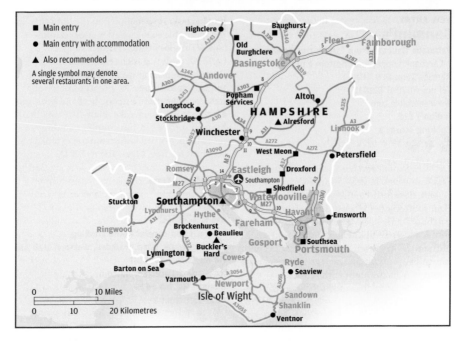

# Alresford

## ALSO RECOMMENDED
### ▲ Caracoli

15 Broad Street, Alresford, SO24 9AR
Tel no: (01962) 738730
www.caracoli.co.uk
**Global**

Caracoli 'bridges a gap in the food market – in between a tea shop and a bistro'. Fresh, local and quality are bywords, with a 'truly excellent range of home-baked cakes and pastries and good coffee' bolstering the short, daily changing lunch menu. Typical dishes might include local watercress and trout rillettes served with house hazelnut brioche (£6), or perhaps smoked duck salad with apple, Manchego and chives (£6.50). Sunday brunch is a draw too. Wines start at £12. Open all week.

# Alton

**NEW ENTRY**
## The Anchor Inn

**Oozing character with classic English menus**
Lower Froyle, Alton, GU34 4NA
Tel no: (01420) 23261
www.anchorinnatlowerfroyle.co.uk
**Modern British | £26**
**Cooking score: 2**

The Anchor (like sister properties the Peat Spade Inn, Longstock and the Queen's Arms Hotel, Garston – see entries) is helping to revitalize our disappearing rural inns. The place oozes character, from main dining area to saloon and snug bars. The remodelling takes in charming country styling, mixing original features with period furnishings, prints and thoughtful *objets d'art*. The seasonal English menu keeps things simple, fresh and local with the likes of skate wing served with capers, brown butter, shrimps and parsley or beer-battered haddock, triple-cooked chips and

mushy peas. Puddings stay in the comfort zone, with the likes of treacle tart or spotted dick. Well-chosen wines start at £15.50.
**Chef/s:** Kevin Chandler. **Open:** all week L 12 to 2 (3.30 Sun), D 7 to 9 (10 Sat). **Meals:** alc (main courses £11 to £19). **Service:** not inc. **Details:** Cards accepted. 74 seats. Separate bar. No music. Wheelchair access. Children allowed. Car parking.

## ▌ Barton on Sea

## Pebble Beach

**Bright and breezy beachside eatery**
Marine Drive, Barton on Sea, BH25 7DZ
Tel no: (01425) 627777
www.pebblebeach-uk.com
**Modern European | £30**
**Cooking score: 3**

🛏 **V**

The breezy, good-time vibes and seaside razzmatazz of Barton on Sea are perfectly in tune with this clifftop eatery-with-rooms, which wows the holiday crowds with its open-air terrace and unrivalled views of the Needles. It's 'a winner every time', noted one fan. The kitchen casts its net wide – although European flavours wax strongly and local fish is the star turn, whether you want something light or the full works. You might kick off with seared scallops, pea purée and crispy speck bacon, or rabbit terrine spiked with Mirabelle plums, before confit of duck, Lancashire hotpot or steamed brill with shrimps and garlicky jus. Chargrills and seafood platters are big sellers, while desserts usher in iced raspberry parfait and the like. Carefully sourced wines (from £13.95) include bottles from the Campillo vineyard in Rioja.
**Chef/s:** Pierre Chevillard. **Open:** all week L 11 to 2.30, D 6 to 11 (10.30 Sun). **Meals:** alc (main courses £13 to £34). **Service:** not inc. **Details:** Cards accepted. 90 seats. 36 seats outside. Air-con. Separate bar. No mobile phones. Wheelchair access. Music. Children allowed. Car parking.

## ▌ Baughurst

## Wellington Arms

**Likeable country dining pub**
Baughurst Road, Baughurst, RG26 5LP
Tel no: (0118) 9820110
www.thewellingtonarms.com
**Gastropub | £27**
**Cooking score: 3**

 £30

Jason King and Simon Page have been hard at work in their likeable country pub, adding Saddleback pigs to the hens and bees (and vegetables) to be found in the garden and paddock behind the building. This has not detracted from the quality of the food served in the small bar-cum-dining room. An excellent cheese soufflé, 'the best rib of pork I have ever tasted' and venison pot pie with delicious gravy constituted one winter meal. Spring could bring local asparagus with poached egg and Rustic White Nancy goats' cheese, or turbot with marsh samphire. Popularity has brought niggles, especially about service, which, according to one reporter, 'with the notable exception of the co-owner is amateurish'. On the plus side, the weekday lunch is good value. House wine is £16.
**Chef/s:** Jason King. **Open:** Wed to Sun L 12 to 2.30 (4 Sun), Tue to Sat D 6.30 to 9. **Closed:** Mon.
**Meals:** alc (main courses £11 to £19). Set L £15 (2 courses) to £18. **Service:** 10% (optional).
**Details:** Cards accepted. 25 seats. 20 seats outside. No mobile phones. Wheelchair access. Music. Children allowed. Car parking.

### Readers recommend

A 'readers recommend' review is a genuine quote from a report sent in by one of our readers. We intend to follow up these suggestions throughout the year to come.

## ◼ Beaulieu

### Montagu Arms Hotel, Terrace Restaurant

Fine-tuned modern food
Palace Lane, Beaulieu, SO42 7ZL
Tel no: (01590) 612324
www.montaguarmshotel.co.uk
Modern British | £45
Cooking score: 5

£5 OFF 🍷 🍴

This well-known New Forest hotel, which dates from 1742, exerts a great pull for lovers of traditional English character. The décor in the Terrace aims to match the classic country house theme, with its white linen, high-back floral patterned chairs, oak panelling and formal service – but Matthew Tomkinson's kitchen takes a clean, modern approach. Prime seasonal produce from the forest and the sea shines in fine-tuned dishes such as wild line-caught sea bass served with crushed Jersey Royal potatoes, Lymington crab, buttered samphire and cucumber. Richer options might deliver roast rump of rose veal alongside a slow-cooked breast croquette, sauté wild garlic, Castelluccio lentils and spring carrots. Invention and flair continue through to dessert (if you have room – 'portions are not shy'), perhaps a warm blackberry sponge cake colourfully teamed with blackberry yoghurt purée, liquorice ice cream and a disc of Valrhona Guanaja chocolate. The wine list is quite a tome, arranged by style and Old World dominant. It includes some blockbusters alongside bottles from £19.50.
Chef/s: Matthew Tomkinson. Open: all week L 12 to 2.30, D 7 to 9.30. Meals: alc (main courses £18 to £26). Set L £17 (2 courses) to £22.50. Sun L £27.50. Service: not inc. Details: Cards accepted. 50 seats. 25 seats outside. Separate bar. No mobile phones. Wheelchair access. Music. Children allowed. Car parking.

## ◼ Brockenhurst

### Le Poussin at Whitley Ridge

Seriously classy cooking
Beaulieu Road, Brockenhurst, SO42 7QL
Tel no: (01590) 622354
www.lepoussin.co.uk
Modern British | £45
Cooking score: 6

🍷 🍴

Closely mown lawns and manicured neatness greet you as you arrive at this dapper Georgian country house hotel squirrelled away in the New Forest. It's just one part of Alex Aitken's burgeoning empire (see Simply Poussin, Brockenhurst). Inside doesn't disappoint – the intimate dining room oozes a sense of occasion. It's the kind of place where you can expect some seriously classy cooking that rarely fails to impress reporters. Aitken's style is classically minded French, but with an innovative streak that might produce an unusual but very successful loin of rabbit filled with its liver, wrapped in prosciutto and served with cutlets and rillette, Puy lentils and wild mushrooms. Another combination that has come in for plenty of praise is fillet of sea bass teamed with a crab risotto, pea shoots, fennel and crab cappuccino. To finish, perhaps a chocolate fondant with baby banana split, chocolate milk and Rice Crispie cake with praline cream or a straightforward but excellent hot passion fruit soufflé. The wine list is a cracker – a notable collection with plenty of big-hitters alongside more wallet-friendly bottles from £16. Note: As we went to press, the total overhaul of Lime Wood – previously called Parkhill – was nearing completion. It was expected to re-open in late summer 2009.
Chef/s: Alex Aitken and Neil Duffet. Open: all week L 12 to 2 , D 6.30 to 9.30. Meals: alc (main courses £21 to £24). Set L £17.50 (2 courses) to £25. Set D £27.50 (2 courses) to £35. Sun L £27.50. Tasting menu £65. Service: 12.5% (optional). Details: Cards accepted. 45 seats. 45 seats outside. Separate bar. No music. No mobile phones. Wheelchair access. Children allowed. Car parking.

## Simply Poussin

**Cutie with brasserie-style cooking**
The Courtyard, Brookley Road, Brockenhurst,
SO42 7RB
Tel no: (01590) 623063
www.simplypoussin.com
**Modern British | £18**
**Cooking score: 3**

 £30

'Cute' is how Alex Aitken describes this, the informal sibling of his headline Le Poussin operation (see entry above), and it's hard to disagree. The mews and courtyard setting, complete with hanging baskets and shrubs in planters, is a particular delight in summer. The cooking here ploughs a more brasserie-style furrow, with the likes of twice-baked cheese soufflé to start, followed perhaps by a seafood medley in butter sauce with saffron potatoes, or herb-crusted lamb rump on a casserole of roots and white beans. Finish with pear Tatin and caramel sauce, or crème brûlée with poached rhubarb. The fixed-price menu offered at lunch and midweek dinners is exemplary value. A short wine list is classified by style, with prices from £15.
**Chef/s:** Alex Aitken and Jamie Stapleton Burns. **Open:** Tue to Sat L 12 to 2, D 6.30 to 9.30 (10 Sat and Sun). **Meals:** alc (main courses £13 to £17). Set L and D £12.50 (2 courses) to £17.50. **Service:** 10% (optional). **Details:** Cards accepted. 28 seats. 12 seats outside. No mobile phones. Wheelchair access. Music. Children allowed. Car parking.

## ■ Buckler's Hard

### ALSO RECOMMENDED
### ▲ The Master Builder's
Buckler's Hard, SO42 7XB
Tel no: (01590) 616253
www.themasterbuilders.co.uk
**Modern British**

Set on the banks of the Beaulieu River, the former house of master shipbuilder Henry Adams has been given more than a dash of urban chic by Hillbrooke Hotels. Output from the cosmopolitan kitchen ranges from rock oysters and dressed Lymington crab to ribeye steak with béarnaise (£18) in the bar or garden (weather permitting), and watercress and wild garlic soup (£6), pork belly with cabbage, bacon and cider sauce (£15), and rhubarb crème brûlée in the restaurant. Wine from £14.50. Open all week. Smart bedrooms, too. One to watch, reports please.

## ■ Droxford

**NEW ENTRY**
## The Bakers Arms
**Friendly inn with generous country cooking**
High Street, Droxford, SO32 3PA
Tel no: (01489) 877533
www.thebakersarmsdroxford.com
**Gastropub | £22**
**Cooking score: 3**

 £30

This small, whitewashed pub on the High Street is quite the hub of the community, for not only does it deliver generous country cooking and Droxford's Bowman ales, but it also serves as the village store and post office. Opened-up and remodelled it may be, but there's a friendly, unpretentious charm that avoids any prosaic gastropub fashioning. Meat-biased menus stay local like the beer, with seasonal produce including grilled Hampshire ribeye steak served with home-cut chips and own-recipe 'Baker's butter'. More modern offerings such as slow-cooked crispy duck leg with pearl barley and chorizo show that the kitchen keeps things simple, accessible, fresh and accurately cooked. Chocolate and fudge brownie with butterscotch ice cream is deemed a 'cracker', while the simple wine list kicks off at £12.95.
**Chef/s:** Adam Cordery and Richard Harrison. **Open:** Tue to Sun L 12 to 2 (2.30 Sun), Tue to Sat D 7 to 9. **Closed:** Mon. **Meals:** alc (main courses £10 to £17). Sun L £12.95. **Service:** not inc. **Details:** Cards accepted. 35 seats. 18 seats outside. No music. Wheelchair access. Children allowed. Car parking.

## Emsworth

### Fat Olives

**Highly polished but homey**
30 South Street, Emsworth, PO10 7EH
Tel no: (01243) 377914
www.fatolives.co.uk
**Modern British | £33**
**Cooking score: 3**

A former fisherman's cottage only a few yards from the quayside provides the setting for the Murphys' friendly, relaxing restaurant. Given the name, you won't be surprised to find yourself nibbling on some plump, ripe specimens with aperitifs. The menu gives a good account of the Anglo-Mediterranean fusion orientation of Lawrence Murphy's culinary thinking, with tiger prawns, gazpacho, pea shoots and chilli oil coming together to make a sharply appetising starter, and mains such as red mullet in bouillabaisse with fennel and tapenade, or more Brit-based South Downs pork with a black pudding fritter, dauphinoise potatoes and cider sauce. Foams of one sort or another add effervescence to desserts like espresso parfait. A single-sheet wine list opens with house Chardonnay and Cabernet from Chile at £13.25 (£3.60 a glass).
**Chef/s:** Lawrence Murphy. **Open:** Tue to Sat L 12 to 1.45, D 7 to 9.15. **Closed:** Sun, Mon, 2 weeks Christmas, 2 weeks Jun/Jul. **Meals:** alc (main courses £15 to £23). Set L £16.95 (2 courses) to £18.75. **Service:** not inc. **Details:** Cards accepted. 28 seats. 10 seats outside. Wheelchair access. Music.

### 36 On The Quay

**A dream ticket for South Coast visitors**
47 South Street, Emsworth, PO10 7EG
Tel no: (01243) 375592
www.36onthequay.co.uk
**Modern European | £47**
**Cooking score: 6**

🍷 🛏

Ramon and Karen Farthing's seventeenth-century cottage down by the cobbled quayside is a dream ticket for visitors to the region – especially when you factor in the stunning location, desirable letting rooms and a self-contained cottage in the village. Ramon's cooking is all about impeccable execution, confidence and intricacy, with lots of little extras and freebies adding to his fixed-price menus. Given the setting, it's no surprise that fish plays a starring role: a starter of brill fillet on caramelised fennel is embellished with confit tomatoes, fennel dust, foam and a roast chicken sauce, while skate wing is flaked and layered with tomato fondue and courgettes, gently steamed and partnered by a baby leek tartlet. By contrast, meat is often given more robust treatment – perhaps pan-fried veal loin with peppered swede, a little veal and mushroom pie and light Jerusalem artichoke cream. Meals end on a triumphant note with a speciality five-part dessert exploring the delights of, say, chocolate and orange. The final trump card is a wine list that is guaranteed to hit the 'wow' button with its idiosyncratic line-up of prestigious bottles from the French regions (notably the south), plus sexy Italians, Iberians and exciting numbers from California. Half-bottles are well represented and appealing house selections start at £17.50.
**Chef/s:** Ramon Farthing. **Open:** Tue to Sat L 12 to 1.45, D 7 to 9.30 (6.45 Sat). **Closed:** Sun, Mon, 3 weeks Jan, 1 week May, 1 week Oct. **Meals:** Set L £20.95 (2 courses) to £25.95. Set D £46.95.
**Service:** not inc. **Details:** Cards accepted. 50 seats. Separate bar. No music. Wheelchair access. Children allowed.

### Symbols

🛏 Accommodation is available

£30 Three courses for less than £30

**V** More than three vegetarian main courses

£5 OFF £5-off voucher scheme

🍷 Notable wine list

## ▌Highclere

### Marco Pierre White's Yew Tree

Smart country inn
Hollington Cross, Andover Road, Highclere, RG20 9SE
Tel no: (01635) 253360
www.theyewtree.net
**Anglo-French | £30**
**Cooking score: 5**

Marco Pierre White, master of all he surveys, owns this rambling roadside inn by the junction of a narrow lane with the busy A343. The day-to-day running of the kitchen is down to Neil Thornley, who does a sound job in interpreting the MPW classics-based style. The appeal of the long and relatively unchanging menu (some of it in gastronomic franglais) is not hard to find. It delivers good renditions of dishes that soothe rather than challenge. The straightforwardness of the cooking is another confidence-booster, as the repertoire runs from Morecambe Bay potted shrimps via omelette Arnold Bennett to Wheeler's of St James's fish pie. Another element at work is the comfort factor, which produces parfait of foie gras en gelée, for example, alongside ribeye steak au poivre (or with béarnaise sauce), and British classics like shepherd's pie, braised oxtail and kidney pud, and rice pudding. Raspberry soufflé is, however, the star turn at dessert. Service is on the ball and the two-page wine list nicely judged, with bottles starting at £15.50 and good choice under £25. France is the focus, although the New World is more than just name-checked.
**Chef/s:** Neil Thornley. **Open:** all week, L 12 to 2.30 (3 Sun), D 6 to 9.30 (9 Sun). **Meals:** alc (main courses £14 to £20). Set L £13.50 (2 courses) to £19.50. **Service:** not inc. **Details:** Cards accepted. 70 seats. 30 seats outside. Separate bar. Wheelchair access. Music. Children allowed. Car parking.

## ▌Isle of Wight

### The George Hotel

Sleek waterfront brasserie
Quay Street, Yarmouth, Isle of Wight, PO41 0PE
Tel no: (01983) 760331
www.thegeorge.co.uk
**Modern European | £37**
**Cooking score: 3**

⇌ V

Nestling comfortably between Yarmouth pier and the town's dinky castle, this dignified Georgian townhouse (once home to the island's governor) makes a delightful sanctuary from the hubbub of the nearby ferry terminal. It also boasts cracking views over the Solent, which you can soak up from the terrace, water garden or sleek modern brasserie. Those who have ventured across the Channel will recognise the tone of the menu, with its French and Italian influences grafted on to spanking fresh island ingredients: hand-picked spider crab comes with spaghettini and chilli, roast fillet of gurnard gets a horseradish and beetroot salsa, and pheasant is braised with red wine and root vegetables. To finish, you might fancy chocolate tart with pistachio ice cream. The concise global wine list opens with house selections from £15.75.
**Chef/s:** Jose Graziosi. **Open:** all week L 12 to 3, D 7 to 10. **Meals:** alc (main courses £15 to £28). Set L £27.75 (2 courses) to £35.95. Set D £41.95.
**Service:** not inc. **Details:** Cards accepted. 65 seats. 120 seats outside. Air-con. Separate bar. Wheelchair access. Music. Children allowed.

**Robert Thompson** The Hambrough

## Who or what inspired you to become a chef?

The amazing feeling of being around and working with food. You can express yourself through your style of cooking and there is nothing like serving 50 covers at dinner - the adrenalin is brilliant.

## If you hadn't become a chef, what would you have been?

Landscape gardener - I love being outside designing and making in the garden. Just being able to picture what you want to achieve and then working towards that goal.

## What is the best meal you have ever eaten?

Restaurant Sant Pau in Sant Pol de Mar in Spain. Amazing.

## If you were to have one abiding principle in the kitchen, what would it be?

Respect your ingredients, your colleagues and also yourself.

## Which chefs do you admire?

The ones who stay in their kitchen and achieve and pass on their skills.

# Robert Thompson at the Hambrough

**Cooking with a touch of genius**
Hambrough Road, Ventnor, Isle of Wight, PO38 1SQ
Tel no: (01983) 856333
www.thehambrough.com
**Modern French | £45**
**Cooking score: 7**

The quirky resort town of Ventnor is enjoying a renaissance, and Robert Thompson's arrival at the Hambrough last summer heralded a sea change in the kitchen at this welcoming boutique hotel, set on an elegant street of Victorian town houses perched above the esplanade. The light, airy and comfortable dining room, now firmly established as the island's premier foodie destination, boasts commanding views over the harbour and out to sea. Thompson turns out beautifully executed, labour-intensive dishes that draw inspiration from their surroundings, showcasing local produce alongside a host of fine ingredients from further afield. The signature starter, a terrine of lightly smoked eel with foie gras, pork belly and Granny Smith apple, is a skilfully concocted study in rich, earthy flavours and mouth-pleasing textures. The stand-out dish at inspection was an exquisite lasagne of local scallops, pungent truffles and silky Jerusalem artichoke purée, sealed and baked in a large scallop shell. Prised open at the table, it filled the room with an attention-grabbing aroma. Main courses maintain the wow factor, with dishes that charm rather than challenge, as in a beautifully composed presentation of succulent black-leg chicken with stuffed morels, crisp tips of asparagus and an intensely flavoured forcemeat boudin. A thick slab of brill was poached to pillowy perfection, topped with a glossy slick of tangy sauce matelote and served on layers of lovage-scented mash, sautéed chanterelle mushrooms and braised salsify. Pre-eminent among the puddings was an inspired combination of unctuous blackberry soufflé and Ventnor Stout ice cream. The

Hambrough's hefty wine list presents a near-comprehensive choice of terroirs and varietals, with some interesting options in the £20-£30 range and ample temptation for big spenders, too. A commendable 16 wines are sold by the glass, from £5 to £9, including a lip-smacking pink Champagne, a crisp Slovenian Pinot Grigio, a supple Pinot Noir and a mouth-filling Margaux.

**Chef/s:** Robert Thompson. **Open:** Tue to Sat L 12 to 1.30, D 7 to 9.30. **Closed:** Sun, Mon, 2 weeks Jan, 2 weeks Nov, 2 weeks Apr. **Meals:** Set L £20 (2 courses) to £24. Set D £38 (2 courses) to £45. Tasting menu £59. **Service:** not inc. **Details:** Cards accepted. 30 seats. 20 seats outside. Air-con. Separate bar. No mobile phones. Music. Children allowed.

## Seaview Hotel

**Cooking with good local produce**
High Street, Seaview, Isle of Wight, PO34 5EX
Tel no: (01983) 612711
www.seaviewhotel.co.uk
**Modern British | £21**
**Cooking score: 2**

£5 OFF 🛏️ £30

The style here is chic, the décor smart, with its vaguely nautical theme. As the name may imply, fish is a strong – though not exclusive – suit. It is not the most ambitious cooking around, but the food is prepared using good local produce. Start with Isle of Wight crab with green chilli, lime and coriander tagliatelle, before pollack with beetroot mash, spinach and lemon balm, or New Close Farm venison haunch with braised red cabbage, creamed potato, sultana and thyme sauce. Desserts range from liquorice pannacotta with vanilla ice cream to dark and white chocolate mousse with lavender ice cream. House wine is £14.95.

**Chef/s:** Graham Walker. **Open:** all week L 12 to 2, D 7 to 9.30. **Closed:** 21 to 26 Dec. **Meals:** alc (main courses £16 to £19). Sun L £14.95. Set D £21. **Service:** not inc. **Details:** Cards accepted. 90 seats. 30 seats outside. Air-con. Separate bar. Wheelchair access. Music. Children allowed. Car parking.

## READERS RECOMMEND

## Mojac's

**Modern European**
10a Shooters Hill, Cowes, Isle of Wight, PO31 7BG
Tel no: (01983) 281118
www.mojacs.co.uk
'Mediterranean-style neighbourhood joint, a very popular, successful one'

## Morgans

**Modern British**
36-38 High Street, Shanklin, Isle of Wight, PO37 6JY
Tel no: (01983) 864900
www.morgansofshanklin.co.uk
'Many fish dishes and other local produce to choose from'

## The Royal Hotel

**Modern European**
Belgrave Road, Ventnor, Isle of Wight, PO38 1JJ
Tel no: (01983) 852186
www.royalhoteliow.co.uk
'Memorable meal; long may it continue'

## ■ Longstock

## The Peat Spade Inn

**Oozing character and charm**
Village Street, Longstock, SO20 6DR
Tel no: (01264) 810612
www.peatspadeinn.co.uk
**Modern British | £21**
**Cooking score: 2**

 🛏️ £30

A thatched estate village in the Test Valley is the setting for Lucy Townsend's dining pub-with-rooms. With scrubbed tables, bare floorboards and red and green walls covered with old photographs and prints, the beautifully remodelled bar and dining room ooze character and charm. The kitchen works with the seasons, using local allotment vegetables and game from the Leckford Estate and is known for classic English cooking delivered on a short, daily changing menu. Expect some great pub classics, perhaps rump steak with garlic butter alongside roast halibut with squid ink risotto and sweet fennel, and sticky toffee pudding to finish. The French-dominated wine list starts at £14.50. Sister to the Anchor Inn, Alton and the Queen's Arms Hotel, Garston — see entries.

**Chef/s:** Chris Mackett. **Open:** all week L 12 to 2 (4 Sun), D 7 to 9.30. **Closed:** 25 Dec. **Meals:** alc (main courses £10 to £19). Set L £21 (2 courses) to £32. **Service:** not inc. **Details:** Cards accepted. 45 seats. 40 seats outside. Separate bar. Wheelchair access. Music. Children allowed. Car parking.

## ▌Lymington

### Egan's
**Easy-going local favourite**
24 Gosport Street, Lymington, SO41 9BE
Tel no: (01590) 676165
**Modern British | £30**
**Cooking score: 2**

**V**

The Egans' welcoming, unpretentious restaurant is housed in a listed late-Victorian building that used to be a police station. John's cooking style overlays a modern British approach with classical French modes and the occasional Asian touch, producing watercress and mushroom risotto cake with a poached egg and Pommery mustard beurre blanc, and monkfish wrapped in Bayonne ham with bouillabaisse jus. Vegetarians get to choose from their own menu, and a reader reports that dishes look 'artistic but generous'. End with rum baba, served with exotic fruits and praline cream. The wine list kicks off with half a dozen house selections at £13.95.

**Chef/s:** John Egan. **Open:** Tue to Sat L 12 to 2, D 6.30 to 10. **Closed:** Sun, Mon, 10 days from 25 Dec. **Meals:** alc (main courses £14 to £19). Set L £12.50 (2 courses) to £14.95. **Service:** not inc. **Details:** Cards accepted. 50 seats. 20 seats outside. Separate bar. No mobile phones. Wheelchair access. Music.

## ▌Micheldever, Popham Services

NEW ENTRY
### Little Chef Popham
**Not just any old Little Chef...**
west-bound on the A303, Micheldever, Popham Services, SO21 3SP
Tel no: (01256) 398490
www.littlechef.co.uk/heston.php
**British | £15**
**Cooking score: 2**

An open kitchen reveals staff squeezing fresh oranges and spit-roasting chickens; blackboards list specials of, say, lamb shank with mustard mash. This is not just any old Little Chef, this is a Heston Blumenthal Little Chef. A prototype for a proposed roll out, it's a splendid reworking by the Fat Duck chef, putting a contemporary spin on the old American-diner-circa-1950s-look. With its range of kidult games — Monopoly, Cluedo — it may not sound like the Little Chef of old, but overall the menu has retained the spirit (and prices) of the original repertoire along with old favourites like the Olympic breakfast and Jubilee pancakes, but tweaked and with much better quality produce. Sweet staff are very family friendly. Wine from £2.75 a glass.

**Open:** all week 7am to 10pm. **Meals:** alc (main courses £6 to £13). **Service:** not inc. **Details:** Cards accepted. Air-con. Wheelchair access. Music. Children allowed. Car parking.

# ■ Old Burghclere

## Dew Pond

**Dreamy views and dependable food**
Old Burghclere, RG20 9LH
Tel no: (01635) 278408
www.dewpond.co.uk
Anglo-French | £32
Cooking score: 3

£5
OFF

Keith and Julie Marshall certainly had an eye for dreamy views when they decided to pitch camp on the Berkshire/Hampshire border: on a clear day you can see for miles across the pond from which the restaurant takes its name towards Watership Down and Highclere Castle. Twenty years on, the Dew Pond still exudes homely domestic warmth, although the dining room has been jazzed up with some contemporary artwork and colourful embellishments. Keith's food rejects flashy fireworks in favour of carefully measured execution – so slow-roast belly pork comes with crackling, black pudding, apple purée and Calvados jus, while peppered saddle of local roe deer gets a classic Armagnac sauce. There's room for fish, too (perhaps served with pesto crushed potato, asparagus and baby fennel), while desserts might include caramel parfait with banana, coconut and rum syrup. Wines start at £15.

**Chef/s:** Keith Marshall. **Open:** Tue to Sat D only 7 to 10. **Closed:** Sun, Mon, 2 weeks Christmas, 2 weeks Aug. **Meals:** Set D £32 (3 courses). **Service:** not inc. **Details:** Cards accepted. 45 seats. Separate bar. Wheelchair access. Music. Children allowed. Car parking.

# ■ Petersfield

## JSW

**Classy, professional set-up**
20 Dragon Street, Petersfield, GU31 4JJ
Tel no: (01730) 262030
www.jswrestaurant.com
Modern British | £50
Cooking score: 6

🍷 ⊑ V

The restaurant behind the white-painted façade on a street of attractive old town houses has an unusually relaxing and welcoming atmosphere. The understated dining room has well-spaced tables and 'discreet and sensitive service'. Menus are fixed-price with a short choice at lunch and dinner, and most reporters reckon that value is good. Fresh materials lay a secure foundation, perhaps in the form of scallops with a well-judged butternut squash purée, and clear flavours and attractive presentation are part of the deal – evident in a trio of rabbit with sweetcorn and tarragon. Timing is impeccable, producing first-class home-smoked duck served with lentils, shallot purée and ceps, but there is also a lightness of touch: for example, in a fricassee of brill and mussels with carrot purée, and a mouthwatering mango mousse with passion fruit and pineapple. Minor details, especially bread, are well-rendered. Jake Watkins is a talented chef – he's also an affable presence, joining in at the end of service, making polite enquiries and putting people at ease. The wide-ranging wine list is both very serious and wholly approachable – due mainly to reasonable prices. House wines start at £15.50 (£4.75 a glass), there's a good half-bottle selection and the choice of dessert wines is huge.

**Chef/s:** Jake Watkins. **Open:** Tue to Sat L 12 to 1.30, D 7 to 9.30. **Closed:** Sun, Mon, 2 weeks Jan and Jun. **Meals:** Set L £15 (2 courses) to £19.50 Set D Tue to Thur £19.50 (2 courses) to £25, Fri and Sat £38.50 (2 courses) to £47. **Service:** not inc. **Details:** Cards accepted. 50 seats. 28 seats outside. No music. No mobile phones. Wheelchair access. Car parking.

## ALSO RECOMMENDED
### ▲ The Harrow Inn
Steep, Petersfield, GU32 2DA
Tel no: (01730) 262685
www.harrow-inn.co.uk
**Gastropub**

In a quiet Hampshire backwater, this seventeenth-century watering hole has been in the same family since 1922. It remains quite unspoilt, the rustic boarded walls, worn tiled floor, open fire in the inglenook, scrubbed wooden tables and hop-adorned beams a perfect match for hearty food cooked on the Rayburn. The limited menu lists thick sandwiches, split-pea and ham soup served with great chunks of bread, generous ham platters and a gooey treacle tart (all £4 to £8). Closed Sun D. House wine from £11.

## ▌Shedfield

**NEW ENTRY**
## Vatika
**Avant-garde Indian food in a vineyard**
Wickham Vineyard, Botley Road, Shedfield,
SO32 2HL
Tel no: (01329) 830405
www.vatikarestaurant.com
**Indian | £30**
**Cooking score: 5**

Vatika is the Hampshire outpost created by Atul Kochhar of Benares (see entry, London), so you can expect some highly innovative Indian cooking. It's billed as 'modern British food with an Indian twist,' and, in this Wickham Vineyard setting overlooking the vines, it seems more than appropriate. The sleek, barn-style interior is all pastel grey-green tones, with big, oblong windows, and, at night, a trio of contemporary chandeliers. White linen and professional service confirm the upmarket aspirations. Vatika takes itself seriously, with different-spiced salts accompanying breads, and plentiful pre- and between-course action delivered with trademark eye-catching presentation.

Kochhar protégé Jitin Joshi heads the kitchen. His refined cooking offers a light touch and the subtlest of spicing. Menus are succinctly scripted, thus 'duck-beans' arrives as succulent honey-glazed magret with broad bean stew and the lightest of korma sauces, accompanied by a jar of warm, spiced polenta. The ambition extends to refreshing western-style desserts such as 'rhubarb-oats': star anise-poached rhubarb with flapjack and ginger beer float – a glass of ginger beer with melting rhubarb sorbet. A serious wine list sees the Old World as a major player, with house from £16.50.
**Chef/s:** Jitin Joshi. **Open:** Wed to Sun L 12 to 2.30, D 6 to 9.30. **Closed:** Mon, Tue. **Meals:** Set L £19.50 (2 courses) to £24.50. Set D £35 (2 courses) to £40. Sun L £35. Tasting menu £65. **Service:** 12.5% (optional). **Details:** Cards accepted. 45 seats. 40 seats outside. Air-con. No music. Wheelchair access. Car parking.

## ▌Southampton

## ALSO RECOMMENDED
### ▲ The White Star Tavern
28 Oxford Street, Southampton, SO14 3DJ
Tel no: (023) 80821990
www.whitestartavern.co.uk
**Modern British**

Named after the White Star Line, which sailed from Southampton, this tavern/restaurant-with-rooms is situated in the heart of Southampton's trendiest street. Some complain that 'the pub noise dominates the dining experience', but others are impressed by the please-all brasserie menu offering dishes such as tempura tiger prawns with smoked chilli jam (£8), pigeon breast with black pudding mash, fish pie with cauliflower cheese mash (£14), and ribeye steak with puttanesca sauce. House wine is £14. Open all week.

## ▌Southsea

### Montparnasse

**Fixture of the Southsea scene**
103 Palmerston Road, Southsea, PO5 3PS
Tel no: (023) 92816754
www.bistromontparnasse.co.uk
**Modern European | £34**
**New chef**

This simple, compact terraced restaurant, the brightest fixture on the Southsea scene for a decade, is facing a period of change as chef Kevin Bingham heads off to pastures new and Nikolas Facey (who has worked at the Fat Olives in Emsworth and the Hambrough Hotel in Ventnor on the Isle of Wight, see entries) takes over the kitchen. This happened just as the *Guide* went to press. Reports are particularly welcome, but the distinctive style is likely to remain, serving up chicken and tarragon boudin with mushroom velouté, perhaps, with a main course of lamb fillet and slow-cooked shoulder of lamb with white onion purée. A short, modern wine list opens at £13.95.
**Chef/s:** Nikolas Facey. **Open:** Tue to Sat L 12 to 1.45, D 7 to 9.30. **Closed:** Sun, Mon, 25 and 26 Dec, 1 Jan. **Meals:** Set D £28.50 (2 courses) to £33.50. **Service:** not inc. **Details:** Cards accepted. 30 seats. Music. Children allowed. Car parking.

## ▌Stockbridge

### The Greyhound Inn

**Good looks and foodie aspirations**
31 High Street, Stockbridge, SO20 6EY
Tel no: (01264) 810833
www.thegreyhound.info/
**Modern British | £35**
**Cooking score: 4**

🍾 ⇌

This fifteenth-century inn is more a relaxed restaurant-with-rooms these days, with its 'glasses of wine' rather than 'pints of ale' atmosphere. Easy-on-the-eye good looks take in a mix of low beams and timbers, scrubbed-wood tables and open fires, complimented by high-back leather chairs, sage walls and

vibrant French posters that embody the kitchen's foodie aspirations. The sensibly compact menu is bolstered by blackboard specials, and offers the likes of pan-fried scallops with linguine, tomato, olives and spring onion, and a super-fresh fillet of sea bass with brown shrimp risotto and a tomato and broad bean velouté. The well-chosen wine list offers house bottles from £15. Other bonuses include a cosy lounge, separate bar menu and a small garden at the back which overlooks the clear-running waters of the Test.
**Chef/s:** Norelle Oberin. **Open:** all week L 12 to 2 (2.30 Fri to Sun), Mon to Sat D 7 to 9 (9.30 Fri and Sat). **Closed:** 24 to 26 Dec, 31 Dec to 2 Jan. **Meals:** alc (main courses £13 to £20). Bar menu available. **Service:** not inc. **Details:** Cards accepted. 50 seats. No music. Wheelchair access. Children allowed. Car parking.

## ▌Stuckton

### The Three Lions

**Quirky, with skilful, intelligent food**
Stuckton, SP6 2HF
Tel no: (01425) 652489
www.thethreelionsrestaurant.co.uk
**Anglo-French | £32**
**Cooking score: 5**

£5 OFF  🍾 ⇌ V

Mike and Jayne Womersley's restaurant-with-rooms is a quirky, homely, 'kind of 60s retro' place, with pine furniture, woodchip-textured walls, patterned carpet and climbing plants. Mike's food has never fallen victim to fads of fashion either, yet his straightforward and accomplished approach matches today's culinary vogue for keeping things simple, fresh and accessible. The tiny adjoining bar oddly comes with modern chocolate-brown seating, but it's just the place to read the blackboard's terse, two-element descriptions. Skate wing and herb crust turns out to be impeccable-quality fish (the skate de-boned) served with a cracking red wine reduction sauce. Like the décor, presentation is a little old-fashioned, with dish-specific vegetable selections delivered on a separate plate, but there's no doubting the skilful, intelligent hand that takes its cue from prime seasonal ingredients and treats them with respect. The friendly service (led by Jayne) explains dishes in detail, thus one knows a Three Lions tart will make an entrance as a citrusy St Clements number with 'lovely light pastry' and vanilla ice cream. The wine list is an enlightened slate, with a bias towards elite independent producers from across the globe. There's an impressive choice – especially in the mid-range – and prices (from £14.75) are drinker-friendly.

**Chef/s:** Mike Womersley. **Open:** Tue to Sun L 12 to 2, Tue to Sat D 7 to 9 (9.30 Fri and Sat). **Closed:** Mon, 2 weeks end Feb. **Meals:** alc (main courses £18 to £25). Set L £19.75. Set D £25. **Service:** not inc. **Details:** Cards accepted. 60 seats. 20 seats outside. Separate bar. No mobile phones. Wheelchair access. Music. Children allowed. Car parking.

## West Meon

NEW ENTRY
### The Thomas Lord
**A local in every sense**
High Street, West Meon, GU32 1LN
Tel no: (01730) 829244
www.thethomaslord.co.uk
**British | £26**
**Cooking score: 3**

Named after Lord's Cricket Ground founder and erstwhile West Meon denizen, this country inn continues to bowl over the Hampshire locals. It's a real pub with traditional character – the pared-back interior provides something of a retirement home for lost country furniture and candlesticks – offering pints of Hampshire ale and a daily changing menu that draws 100% on local produce. This includes seasonal ingredients from its own potager and eggs from the owners' hens and quails. Menus of simple, clean-cut modern British food punch above their weight: say Hyden Farm duck breast teamed with a coriander rösti and mustard sauce, and, to finish, maybe bavarois made with rhubarb picked that morning from the

kitchen garden. The garden – with its own outdoor kitchen – is a big draw in summer. Wines strike out at £14.50 a bottle.

**Chef/s:** Gareth Longhurst. **Open:** all week L 12 to 2 (3 Sat and Sun), D 7 to 9 (9.30 Fri and Sat). **Meals:** alc (main courses £11 to £18). **Service:** not inc. **Details:** Cards accepted. 62 seats. 75 seats outside. Separate bar. No music. Wheelchair access. Children allowed. Car parking.

## Winchester
### The Black Rat
**Unusual menu for relaxed dining**
88 Chesil Street, Winchester, SO23 0HX
Tel no: (01962) 844465
www.theblackrat.co.uk
**Modern British | £32**
**Cooking score: 3**

You wouldn't give this one-time boozer a second glance from the outside, what with its rather unkempt look and less-than-endearing name. But inside it has been remodelled, without losing the charm of old beams and timbers, polished floorboards, exposed brickwork and big inglenook. The accomplished modern British cooking shows plenty of generosity, flavour and 'interesting combinations' – crisp Lincolnshire pork (loin and cheek) with pea purée and braised gem, for example, or fillet of pollack served with sarladaise potatoes, marsh samphire and sauce vierge. Ingredients press all the right seasonal, local and quality buttons. Wines offer balance between Old and New Worlds from £15.50, while upstairs there's a small bar and flock-wallpapered lounge. Out back, a few tropical-style huts offer intimate alfresco dining.

**Chef/s:** Chris Bailey. **Open:** Sat and Sun L 12 to 2.15, all week D 7 to 9.30. **Closed:** 2 weeks Christmas and New Year, 2 weeks end Oct/Nov. **Meals:** alc (main courses £17 to £20). **Service:** not inc. **Details:** Cards accepted. 40 seats. 15 seats outside. Separate bar. Music.

## Chesil Rectory

**Ancient building with relaxed, modern food**
1 Chesil Street, Winchester, SO23 0HU
Tel no: (01962) 851555
www.chesilrectory.co.uk
**Modern British | £30**
**Cooking score: 4**

New owners have taken over Winchester's oldest house (dating from 1450), and have turned their back on the fine dining offered by the previous owner, Robert Quéhan, in favour of a more accessible, relaxed approach to cooking and service. There has also been a makeover – deep-buttoned banquettes, vintage chandeliers, quirky antiques and prints cleverly embrace the ancient timber building and deliver easy-on-the-eye style too. In the kitchen, Damian Brown shows off his pedigree via 'deceptively simple, balanced and clear-flavoured' modern British dishes in a series of regularly changing menus. There's plenty of local produce – from a starter of terrine of local Greenfields pork served with apple and vanilla purée to a main course of pan-fried cod with a casserole of butter beans and curly kale. To finish there could be a 'cracking' lemon posset with orange biscuits or a chocolate and honeycomb parfait with banana sorbet. Well-chosen wines (from £16.95) offer plenty by glass and carafe. The restaurant promises a flat £10-a-bottle mark-up on shop prices.
**Chef/s:** Damian Brown. **Open:** all week L 12 to 2.30 (11 to 2.30 Sat, 12 to 3 Sun), Mon to Sat D 6 to 9.30 (10 Fri and Sat). **Closed:** Mon, 25 and 26 Dec, 1 week Aug, 1 week Christmas. **Meals:** alc (main courses £11 to £18). Set L and D (6 to 7) £14.95 (2 courses) to £19.95. **Service:** not inc. **Details:** Cards accepted. 56 seats. Separate bar. Music. Children allowed.

## Hotel du Vin & Bistro

**Stylish town house hotel with popular bistro**
Southgate Street, Winchester, SO23 9EF
Tel no: (01962) 841414
www.hotelduvin.com
**European | £35**
**Cooking score: 3**

🍷 ⊐ V

'High standards continue at this, the original Hotel du Vin', writes a satisfied reporter, who went on to praise 'friendly, efficient and professional staff, a lively atmosphere (on a packed Saturday night in the bistro anyway) and simple but well-prepared and presented choices'. With old bare wood, small tables and bottles everywhere, it's an amenable setting for good bistro food – from scallops, pancetta and minted pea purée to chargrilled ribeye with peppercorn sauce or sea bass with a sweetcorn purée. Timing and judgement on a recent Sunday lunch has been called into question, but one couple ended on a high note with an excellent selection of cheeses. The wine list shows off plenty of top-quality bottles from classic French appellations before moving to the rest of Europe. Prices are not giveaway, but the quality is outstanding. House wine is £14.75.
**Chef/s:** Adam Fargin. **Open:** all week L 12 to 1.45 (2.15 Sat and Sun), D 7 to 9.45 (10.15 Fri and Sat). **Meals:** alc (main courses £11 to £42). **Service:** 10%. **Details:** Cards accepted. 64 seats. 36 seats outside. Separate bar. No music. Wheelchair access. Children allowed. Car parking.

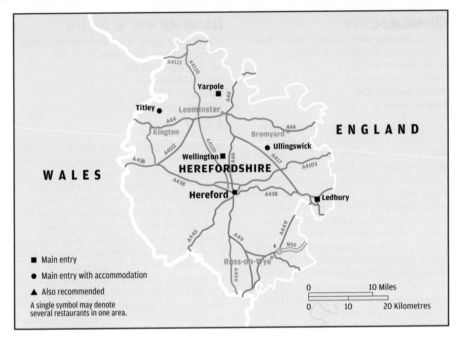

- ■ Main entry
- ● Main entry with accommodation
- ▲ Also recommended

A single symbol may denote several restaurants in one area.

0           10 Miles

0     10     20 Kilometres

## ■ Hereford

## Castle House

**Swish food in a swanky setting**
Castle Street, Hereford, HR1 2NW
Tel no: (01432) 356321
www.castlehse.co.uk
**Modern British | £32**
**Cooking score: 5**

£5 OFF 🍷 🍴

A good-looking Regency townhouse in a prime spot not far from Hereford Cathedral, the Castle House stakes its claim as one of the city's prime hotel destinations. It is also home to a formally appointed restaurant with views over the remains of the castle moat. This provides a swanky setting for Claire Nicholls' open-minded take on contemporary cuisine. To start, a tian of crab and avocado mousse with a pesto wafer might share the bill with an oriental salad of shiitake mushrooms, baby corn and water chestnuts with soy dressing. Mains are equally vigorous assemblages ranging from herb-crusted sea trout with summer-tinged roast fennel, pea and mint casserole to no-frills ribeye with home-cut chips. Apple and blackberry steamed pudding with vanilla custard is one way to finish, otherwise go for something more upbeat such as chocolate and Amaretto parfait with cherry and yoghurt ice and marinated cherries. Lunch is a lighter proposition that moves into the brasserie zone for the likes of Spanish cured meats, open steak sandwiches or pan-fried cod cheeks with Serrano ham and pesto salad. Big-name Bordeaux and Burgundies are the main contenders on the helpfully annotated wine list, although coverage from Italy and the New World should also get the juices flowing. Prices start at £15.50.

**Chef/s:** Claire Nicholls. **Open:** all week L 12 to 2, D 7 to 10. **Meals:** alc (main courses £11 to £19). Sun L £24. Tasting menu £49 (7 courses). **Service:** not inc. **Details:** Cards accepted. 38 seats. 20 seats outside. Air-con. Separate bar. No mobile phones. Wheelchair access. Music. Children allowed. Car parking.

## ■ Ledbury
### The Malthouse
**Inspired and intricate food**
Church Lane, Ledbury, HR8 1DW
Tel no: (01531) 634443
www.malthouse-ledbury.co.uk
**Modern British | £27**
**Cooking score: 3**

Make your way up a cobbled lane just off Ledbury's market square to find this atmospheric restaurant spread over two floors of a converted barn, with a delightful walled courtyard out front. Exposed beams, pictures and mirrors provide the backdrop to Ken Wilson's food, which is 'both inspired and inspiring', according to one reporter. Intricacy is his culinary hallmark, and there's always a great deal happening on the plate, whether it's Japanese crispy pork belly with smoked eel, mushrooms, pea shoots and soy broth or Madgetts Farm duck breast with duck hash, sweet potatoes, turnips and orange pepper sauce. Menus are short, but specials widen the choice – spiced baked cod with couscous, chickpeas and baby tomato stew, say. To finish, consider iced tiramisu parfait with marzipan ice cream and chocolate syrup. House wines are £13.
**Chef/s:** Ken Wilson. **Open:** Sat L 12 to 1.30, Tue to Sat D 7 to 9 (9.30 Fri and Sat). **Closed:** Sun, Mon, 25 Dec, 1 to 5 Jan, 1 week Nov. **Meals:** alc (main courses £15 to £17). **Service:** not inc. **Details:** Cards accepted. 30 seats. 16 seats outside. No mobile phones. Wheelchair access. Music. Children allowed.

## ■ Titley
### The Stagg Inn
**Herefordshire pub star**
Titley, HR5 3RL
Tel no: (01544) 230221
www.thestagg.co.uk
**Modern British | £30**
**Cooking score: 5**

Steve and Nicola Reynolds have done Herefordshire proud during their 10 years in residence at this handsome country inn, which stands at the junction of several ancient drovers' roads. They have retained the feel of the place as a genuine hostelry, while serving top-drawer food. Precise, uncluttered cooking is the deal, and it comes with bright ideas, assured style and honest endeavour in abundance. As you might expect, Steve taps into Herefordshire's rich larder, although he looks to Cornwall for fish specials (perhaps seared scallops on celeriac and cumin purée). Domestic enterprise also shows up across the board, from home-baked breads to home-cured chorizo (perhaps served in a pasta dish with squid, tomato and chilli). Herefordshire beef is given full rein (rump steak with red wine sauce and chips), and other big local names also figure prominently: Madgett's Farm duck breast is pointed up with a complex, sweet and spicy sauce of ginger, mustard and Sauternes. To finish, crème brûlée is subjected to all sorts of twists; otherwise, the kitchen might send out lemon tart with Cassis sorbet. The cracking cheeseboard features a prodigious array from England and Wales, while the 100-bin wine list offers an intelligent choice, with a broad sweep of grape varieties and regions, keen prices and plentiful half-bottles; it even finds room for a local representative from Broadfield Court. House selections start at £13.50 (£2.35 a glass).
**Chef/s:** Steve Reynolds. **Open:** Tue to Sun L 12 to 2, Tue to Sat D 6.30 to 9. **Closed:** Mon, 2 weeks Nov, 2 weeks Jan/Feb. **Meals:** alc (main courses £15 to £18). **Service:** not inc. **Details:** Cards accepted. 70 seats. 16 seats outside. Separate bar. No music. No mobile phones. Children allowed. Car parking.

## Ullingswick

### Three Crowns Inn

**Raggletaggle, easy-going hostelry**
Ullingswick, HR1 3JQ
Tel no: (01432) 820279
www.threecrownsinn.com
**Modern British | £26**
**Cooking score: 4**

An open fire and Wye Valley beers on tap reward the tenacious traveller for finding the Three Crowns, deep in red clay country. Chef/ proprietor Brent Castle makes much of Herefordshire produce, but he isn't immune to the charms of chorizo, black beans or an accurately made French sauce. Visitors are likely to be charmed, too, by the collision of raggletaggle family-run pub and high-reaching, technically able cooking from a chef who enjoys stretching his ladle arm beyond pub cliché. Lunch can easily run into dinner in the beamed bar area or airy modern extension, so comfortable and easy is the atmosphere. Highlights might include a soufflé of spinach and organic Little Hereford cheese or home hot-smoked haddock fishcake, followed by pheasant shot in the surrounding fields and served with Puy lentils, luscious smoked bacon gravy and a chunk of Morteau sausage. Dessert could be winter fruit compote with rice pudding ice cream, and there's always some good cheese about the place. House wine is £14.50. Our questionnaire was not returned so the details below may be incorrect.
**Chef/s:** Brent Castle. **Open:** Tue to Sun L 12 to 3, D 7 to 10. **Closed:** Mon, 25 and 26 Dec. **Meals:** alc (main courses £15). Set L (not Sun) £12.95 (2 courses) to £14.95. **Service:** not inc. **Details:** Cards accepted. 75 seats. 30 seats outside. No music. Wheelchair access. Children allowed. Car parking.

## Set lunch menus

Want to try the big names at accessible prices? Book a table during daylight hours.

At £23.95 for three courses, the lunch deal at **Anthony's Restaurant** (Leeds) is brilliant value.

Many diners believe the best way to enjoy **Le Gavroche** (London) is with the £48 set lunch, which includes half a bottle of wine.

Tasting portions of Michael Caines' dishes from the 'amazing grazing' menu at **ABode Manchester**. At £18 with matching wines, you can afford a lunchtime tipple.

The luxurious setting of **Jesmond Dene House** (Newcastle) makes the £25 Sunday lunch feel like a real bargain.

Midweek, £25.50 will buy three carefully cooked lunch courses and a view of Wandsworth Common at **Chez Bruce**.

With polished full-length windows, **The Vineyard at Stockcross**'s dining room looks great in the sunshine. A three-course John Campbell lunch is £24.

Lunch at Shaun Rankin's **Bohemia** (Jersey) is an accessible £21.50, and you'll avoid the crowds that throng the bar by night.

## ▌ Wellington

### The Wellington
**Cooking that goes down a treat**
Wellington, HR4 8AT
Tel no: (01432) 830367
www.wellingtonpub.co.uk
**Gastropub | £28**
**Cooking score: 2**

Ross Williams opened this appealing rural
pub and restaurant in summer 2002. The
unpretentious approach extends to bare tables
and classic village-local chalkboard menus,
but his cooking is impressively ambitious.
Fried duck hearts on brioche toast is an
enterprising starter, or there might be twice-
baked Hereford Hop soufflé. A reporter eating
in winter was full of praise for a main course of
local venison fillet with beetroot and cheese
gratin, buttered kale and red wine sauce, and
the apple and Calvados crumble with vanilla
custard went down a treat too. A good
selection of real ales and seven wines by the
glass are welcome sights. House wine starts
at £13.
**Chef/s:** Ross Williams. **Open:** Tue to Sun L 12 to 2
(12.30 Sun), Mon to Sat D 7 to 9. **Closed:** 25 and 26
Dec. **Meals:** alc (main courses £11 to £18).
**Service:** not inc. **Details:** Cards accepted. 70 seats.
20 seats outside. Separate bar. Music. Children
allowed. Car parking.

## ▌ Yarpole

### The Bell Inn
**Horse brasses, locals and classic dishes**
Green Lane, Yarpole, HR6 0BD
Tel no: (01568) 780359
www.thebellinnyarpole.co.uk
**Gastropub | £27**
**Cooking score: 2**

**V**

The black-and-white-timbered Bell has the
look and feel of an old-fashioned pub, with
horse brasses hanging from the beams and
locals drinking at the bar. The biggest changes
are seasonal: a welcoming fire in winter, while

in spring and summer the garden comes into
its own. The operation is owned by Claude
Bosi (of Hibiscus, see entry London) and run
by his brother Cedric. Menus are firmly in
keeping with the pub's image – classic dishes
ranging from terrine of ham hock and crayfish
cocktail to haddock and chips or sausages
made from local pork and spring onions.
House wine from £13.95.
**Chef/s:** Neil McCann. **Open:** Tue to Sun L 12 to 2.30,
D 6.30 to 9.30. **Closed:** Mon. **Meals:** alc (main
courses £10 to £16). **Service:** not inc. **Details:** Cards
accepted. 70 seats. 70 seats outside. Separate bar.
No music. Wheelchair access. Children allowed. Car
parking.

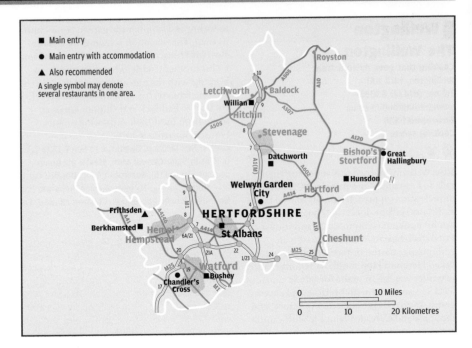

- ■ Main entry
- ● Main entry with accommodation
- ▲ Also recommended

A single symbol may denote
several restaurants in one area.

## ▌Berkhamsted

### Eat Fish

**Local favourite with lively seafood**
163-165 High Street, Berkhamsted, HP4 3HB
Tel no: (01442) 879988
www.eatfish.co.uk
Seafood | £25
Cooking score: 1

'They are a great bunch', enthuses a regular at
this popular neighbourhood restaurant,
referring not just to the service but also to the
unerring freshness of the victuals on offer. The
kitchen's forte is seafood, which gets lively,
contemporary treatments, as in starters of crab
linguine with green chilli, coriander and lime
and mains of whole baked sea bream with
smoked paprika sweet potatoes and spring
onion salsa. Small/large plate options are
offered on many dishes, and meat alternatives
include slow-roast pork belly. House wine
is £13.

**Chef/s:** Paul Sim. **Open:** all week L 12 to 3 (12.30
Sun), D 6 to 10 (9 Sun). **Closed:** 25 to 27 Dec.
**Meals:** alc (main courses £10 to £15). Set L and D
£11 (2 courses) to £15. **Service:** not inc.
**Details:** Cards accepted. 75 seats. 25 seats outside.
Air-con. Wheelchair access. Music. Children allowed.

### READERS RECOMMEND

### The Gatsby

**Modern British**
Rex Cinema, 97 High Street, Berkhamsted,
HP4 2DG
Tel no: (01442) 870403
www.thegatsby.net
**'On-trend brasserie in a fabulously restored Art
Deco cinema'**

## Bushey

### St James

**Contemporary neighbourhood restaurant**
30 High Street, Bushey, WD2 3DN
Tel no: (020) 89502480
www.stjamesrestaurant.co.uk
**Modern British | £40**
**Cooking score: 1**

**V**

This bright, contemporary restaurant stands opposite St James church in the heart of Bushey, and eager reporters testify to its ongoing popularity. The name of the game is to combine good-quality ingredients with uncomplicated cooking to produce a menu with broad appeal. There might be smoked duck with woodland salad and orange vinaigrette, mains of roast saddle of venison with homemade sausage and butternut squash purée or a simple grilled lemon sole. Desserts could take in Toblerone cheesecake. House wine is £13.50.
**Chef/s:** Calvin Hill. **Open:** all week L 12.30 to 2.30, Mon to Sat D 6.30 to 10. **Closed:** bank hols. **Meals:** alc (main courses £13 to £21). Set L £14.95 (2 courses). Set D £16.95 (2 courses). **Service:** 12.5% (optional). **Details:** Cards accepted. 100 seats. 20 seats outside. Air-con. Separate bar. No mobile phones. Wheelchair access. Music. Children allowed. Car parking.

## Chandler's Cross

### The Grove, Colette's

**Out to make an impact**
Chandler's Cross, WD3 4TG
Tel no: (01923) 807807
www.thegrove.co.uk
**Modern European | £58**
**Cooking score: 5**

On a clear night you can see Watford's urban fluorescence glowing in the distance as you stroll around this sprawling hotel complex. Built for the Earls of Clarendon, the Grove's original porticoed mansion now houses its top-end restaurant, and the lofty dining room still feels like an illustrious 'weekend in the country' destination. Everything here is larger than life, from huge canvases and abstract sculptures to a fantastical chandelier of epic proportions. Chef Russell Bateman arrived in 2009 from the Feathers Hotel, Woodstock (see entry) and he is out to make an impact. A starter of creamy lamb's sweetbreads with deep-fried palourdes and crisp parsnip ribbons is given some peppery bite with tiny nasturtium leaves, while the summery sweetness of steamed Scottish lobster tail is offset by astringent lemon thyme, artichokes and baby fennel. Ideas are complex, ingredients top-drawer and flavours neatly judged, although novelties occasionally fall flat – bland chocolate polenta added nothing to a dish of pigeon breasts with baby beetroot, spring cabbage and 'bubble and squawk' (sic). Finally, the kitchen dons its joker's hat for a startling dessert involving violet mousse, blueberries and Laurent Perrier jelly topped with nuggets of excited popping candy that explode like hyperactive fizz bubbles in the mouth. Busy, name-tagged staff in dapper grey outfits are 'a tad too eager to please', and the wine list includes many exceptional bottles. Prices start at £28.
**Chef/s:** Russell Bateman. **Open:** Tue to Sat D 7 to 9.30 (and Sun D on bank hols). **Closed:** Sun (except bank hols), Mon. **Meals:** Set D £57.75. **Service:** 12.5% (optional). **Details:** Cards accepted. 40 seats. Air-con. Separate bar. Wheelchair access. Music. Children allowed. Car parking.

## Datchworth

### The Tilbury

**Fervent local food crusader**
1 Watton Road, Datchworth, SG3 6TB
Tel no: (01438) 815550
www.thetilbury.co.uk
**Modern British | £28**
**Cooking score: 4**

**£5 OFF** **V** **£30**

TV chef Paul Bloxham is a fervent supporter of 'seasonal and regional British foods', and his latest venture – a sympathetically refurbished village pub not far from Knebworth – flies the flag with pride and gusto. In a bid to keep food miles to a minimum, most of the kitchen's culinary building blocks come from named suppliers in Hertfordshire and neighbouring counties – anything from Farmer Sharp's steak tartare with potato biscuits to hefty plates of Great Dunmow free-range pig. Daily market menus and specials also tap into the wider network for the likes of Shetland scallops with smoked black pudding, apple sauce and pea purée, Cornish red mullet with octopus bourride and parsley aïoli, or slow-cooked Herdwick mutton shank with couscous and green sauce. Desserts conjure up a mix of nursery flavours (apple and blackberry crumble) and contemporary hits (honey and ginger pannacotta with poached forced rhubarb). Carafes of house wine (from £9.95) head the intelligently assembled global wine list.

**Chef/s:** Paul Bloxham and Ben Crick. **Open:** all week L 12 to 3 (6 Sun), Mon to Sat D 6 to 11. **Meals:** alc (main courses £10 to £23). Set L £13.95 (2 courses) to £17.95. Set D £17.95 (2 courses) to £21.50. Sun L £16.95. **Service:** not inc. **Details:** Cards accepted. 70 seats. 40 seats outside. Separate bar. No mobile phones. Wheelchair access. Music. Children allowed. Car parking.

# ▌Frithsden

## ALSO RECOMMENDED
## ▲ The Alford Arms
Frithsden, HP1 3DD
Tel no: (01442) 864480
www.alfordarmsfrithsden.co.uk
**Gastropub**

Enveloped in National Trust woodland, this attractive Victorian pub is a riot of rich colours and old furniture inside, with a little light jazz often playing in the background. A refined style of pub cooking brings on small plates either as snacks or starters – perhaps omelette Arnold Bennett (£5.25) – with more substantial offerings to follow. Crisp-cooked pork belly with onion roly-poly and sticky roast parsnips (£13.50) is one option, grilled sea bass on chargrilled spiced aubergine with baby fennel and chorizo oil (£13.75) another.

Vegetables are charged extra. Desserts include vanilla and gingerbread cheesecake (£5.25). Wines from £12.75. Open all week.

# ▌Great Hallingbury

## Anton's Restaurant
**Relaxed, open-minded flexibility**
Great Hallingbury Manor, Tilekiln Green, Great Hallingbury, CM22 7TJ
Tel no: (01279) 506475
www.antonsrestaurant.co.uk
**Modern British | £28**
**Cooking score: 4**

Vast sums have been lavished on this grandiose mock-Tudor manor, which is now a magnet for celebratory bashes and corporate hospitality. It's also home to chef Anton Edelmann, whose self-named restaurant and 'Champagne Barn' occupies a seductive spot overlooking the hotel's lake and swan sanctuary. Great views, jazz prints and glimpses of the chefs at work create a relaxed feel, and the menus encourage open-minded flexibility. There are starters for sharing (try the signature mini toad-in-the-hole with wild mushrooms) and you are welcome to have just one course from a line-up that embraces combos of Mersea shellfish (scallop on black pudding, spice-crusted razor clams, and gratinated oysters), Szechuan-peppered Telmara duck breast with confit leg, and a trio of Wick Manor pork involving braised cheek, crispy belly and fried trotter with pearl barley, chorizo and sweet potato purée. To conclude, try poached rhubarb with vanilla pannacotta. The carefully assembled wine list kicks off with 16 selections by the glass (from £3.75, £16 a bottle).

**Chef/s:** Anton Edelmann. **Open:** Sun to Fri L 12 to 3, Mon to Sat D 6.30 to 9.30. **Meals:** alc (main courses £12 to £26). Set L £12.50 (2 courses) to £17.50. Set D £19.50 (2 courses) to £24.50. Sun L £25.50. Tasting menu £42 (5 courses). **Service:** 10% (optional). **Details:** Cards accepted. 70 seats. 30 seats outside. Air-con. Separate bar. Wheelchair access. Music. Children allowed. Car parking.

Pubs going back to their roots

**Steve Harris** has cooked at the **Sportsman** (Kent) for ten years. In that time he has become increasingly influenced by the raw materials available on his doorstep. He labels his style 'haute barnyard', curing hams in the beer cellar, churning his own butter, making his own salt. His premise is simple, follow locally grown food and 'you end up cooking as they did 1,000 years ago.'

As more pub chefs follow his example, it is clear that this is not a gourmet re-invention, but a return to how traditional British food used to be, before industrialisation and factory farming lowered our standards.

**Wellington Arms** (Hampshire) has added Saddleback pigs to the hens and bees that can be found in their garden and paddock.

**The Mulberry Tree** (Kent) has installed Middle Whites in the back paddock, and **The Nut Tree Inn** (Oxfordshire) are proud owners of Gloucester Old Spot-Tamworth pigs.

London pubs with no space for livestock, and no farms down the road, have responded with stunning, traditional bar food. Go to the **Princess Victoria** for deep-fried pig's cheek with homemade pork scratchings; **The Sands End** for Welsh rarebit and **The Harwood Arms** for real mince pies and hot Scotch eggs made with pork and venison.

## Hemel Hempstead

READERS RECOMMEND
### Cochin Cuisine
Indian
61 High Street (Old Town), Hemel Hempstead, HP1 3AF
Tel no: (01442) 233777
www.thecochincuisine.com
'Sun-kissed Keralan cooking comes to the Home Counties'

## Hunsdon
### Fox & Hounds
**Free-spirited gastropub food**
2 High Street, Hunsdon, SG12 8NH
Tel no: (01279) 843999
www.foxandhounds-hunsdon.co.uk
**Gastropub | £23**
**Cooking score: 2**
£5 OFF   £30

Combining the virtues of born-again local boozer and amenable village eating house, the Fox & Hounds does the business, with real ales on tap, a heated terrace for alfresco meals and lively food with a free-spirited gastropub slant. The daily menu mixes pub favourites with big-city flavours, pitching fishcakes with aïoli and braised oxtail against the likes of line-caught sea bass with a warm salad of lentils and pea shoots. Lunch brings a few more homespun offerings (cod roes on toast, mustard-crusted salt beef), while desserts span everything from whisky and blueberry trifle to bitter chocolate tart with espresso ice cream. Around 40 carefully chosen global wines start at £13.25 (£3.35 a glass).
**Chef/s:** James Rix. **Open:** Tue to Sun L 12 to 3, Tue to Sat D 6.30 to 10. **Closed:** Mon. **Meals:** alc (main courses £10 to £18). Set L £12.50 (2 courses). Set D £13.50 (2 courses). Sun L £19.50 (2 courses) to £23.50. **Service:** 10% (optional). **Details:** Cards accepted. 80 seats. 40 seats outside. Separate bar. Wheelchair access. Music. Children allowed. Car parking.

## ▌St Albans

NEW ENTRY

### Lussmanns

**Relaxed, fuss-free dining**
Waxhouse Gate, Off High Street, St Albans,
AL3 4EW
Tel no: (01727) 851941
www.lussmanns.com
**International | £20**
**Cooking score: 1**

V

This three-tiered link in the Lussmanns chain
(also in Hertford and Bishops Stortford),
offers relaxed, fuss-free dining. The menu is
keen to promote provenance and seasonality,
with starters such as a sourdough bruschetta of
bell peppers, local goats' cheese and anchovies,
or mains of shepherd's pie with cabbage. To
finish you could try sticky toffee pudding.
There's nothing groundbreaking here but
readers love it and it's pleasing to see a kids'
menu offering half portions rather than the
joyless gamut of something with chips. House
wines are £13.50.
**Chef/s:** Andrei Lussmann and Tim Hope. **Open:** all
week 12 to 10 (10.30 Fri and Sat, 9 Sun). **Closed:** 25
and 26 Dec. **Meals:** alc (main courses £7 to £17). Set
L (12 to 5) £11 (2 courses) to £14. **Service:** not inc.
**Details:** Cards accepted. 105 seats. Air-con.
Wheelchair access. Music. Children allowed.

## ALSO RECOMMENDED

### ▲ Darcys

2 Hatfield Road, St Albans, AL1 3RP
Tel no: (01727) 730777
www.darcysrestaurant.co.uk
**Modern European**

Situated in an old smithy, behind original
wrought-iron gates, Darcy's delights for its
welcoming ambience. There are two floors
and a courtyard for fine-weather eating. Ruth
Hurren mixes her influences productively,
offering Moroccan chicken with spiced
pumpkin salad (£7), monkfish and salmon
wrapped in nori with soy and ginger dressing
and jasmine rice, or rack of lamb with fig and

lemon stuffing on parsnip purée with Merlot
jus (£16.50). Desserts, such as a sorbet trio, are
£5.75. Wines from £13.90. Open all week.

## ▌Tring

READERS RECOMMEND

### The Green House

**Vegetarian**
50 High Street, Tring, HP4 5AG
Tel no: (01442) 823993
www.thegreenhousetring.co.uk
**'Green-fingered vegetarian restaurant with
young-at-heart vibes'**

## ▌Welwyn

READERS RECOMMEND

### The Stable Door

**Spanish**
12 High Street, Welwyn, AL6 9EQ
Tel no: (01438) 715200
www.thestabledoor-welwyn.co.uk
**'Tapas that is fast becoming a local favourite'**

### The Wellington

**Gastropub**
1 High Street, Welwyn, AL6 9LZ
Tel no: (01438) 714036
www.wellingtonatwelwyn.co.uk
**'Simple, fresh and lovingly prepared food'**

## ▌Welwyn Garden City

### Auberge du Lac

**Thrilling food and gorgeous surrounds**
Brocket Hall, Welwyn Garden City, AL8 7XG
Tel no: (01707) 368888
www.aubergedulac.co.uk
**Modern French | £55**
**Cooking score: 6**

You need to press the button and identify
yourself before proceeding through the
daunting iron gates that protect the sprawling
acres of Brocket Hall Estate. Once inside, the
Auberge du Lac (a dreamy-looking converted
hunting lodge) beckons. The whole complex

is highly corporate and seriously sporty (golf is king here), but it doesn't feel like that – especially in the relaxed conservatory dining room overlooking the lake. The gorgeous setting positively encourages lingering, and the mood is enhanced by perfectly paced service that never puts a foot wrong. Chef Phil Thompson is on a roll at the moment, delivering precise, 'sharp as a needle' dishes designed to thrill. His food still has a modern French undercurrent but it's not slavishly Gallic, pulling in threads from more exotic climes well as plundering the modern British camp. There are some unusual strokes too: fillets of John Dory are partnered by spinach-stuffed macaroni, chanterelles and split port dressing, while loin of Balmoral venison is invigorated with juniper-infused polenta cake, poached pear and smoked chocolate. Desserts are equally impressive – perhaps vanilla-infused roast fig with sticky toffee pudding and popcorn ice cream. The set lunch (including two glasses of superior wine and extras) has to be one of the best deals in the region, and it has yielded some stellar dishes – notably a 'flavour bomb' of Tamworth pork belly confit on courgette purée with cockles, plumped-up raisins and tendrils of baby watercress woven around it. The regal, 700-bin wine list is a procession of the great and the good from French vineyards, supported by a wealth of eminently drinkable stuff from elsewhere. Prices start at £20.

**Chef/s:** Phil Thompson. **Open:** Tue to Sat L 12 to 2.30, D 7 to 10. **Closed:** Sun, Mon, 27 Dec to 7 Jan. **Meals:** Set L £29.50. Set D £55. Tasting menu £65. **Service:** 10% (optional). **Details:** Cards accepted. 62 seats. 40 seats outside. Air-con. Separate bar. Wheelchair access. Music. Children allowed. Car parking.

## ▌Willian

### The Fox
**Agreeable gastropub with local food**
Willian, SG6 2AE
Tel no: (01462) 480233
www.foxatwillian.co.uk
Gastropub | £25
Cooking score: 2

**V**

This agreeable gastropub seems very happy in its own skin. The menu doesn't punch above its weight, nor does the relaxed friendly service, and dishes are full of seasonal, locally sourced ingredients. Oysters straight from the beds beside The Fox's sister eatery, the White Horse (see entry, Brancaster Staithe, Norfolk) kick things off well. Generously sized mains may feature Willian Manor Farm duo of pork fillet and belly or Hertfordshire lamb with Asian chutney, while passion fruit crème brûlée could be a suitable way to round things off. The wine list offers a decent, global spread and house wine is £13.

**Chef/s:** Harry Kodagoda. **Open:** all week L 12 to 2 (2.45 Sun), Mon to Sat D 6.45 to 9. **Meals:** alc (main courses £9 to £17). **Service:** 10% (optional). **Details:** Cards accepted. 65 seats. 16 seats outside. Air-con. Separate bar. No music. No mobile phones. Wheelchair access. Children allowed. Car parking.

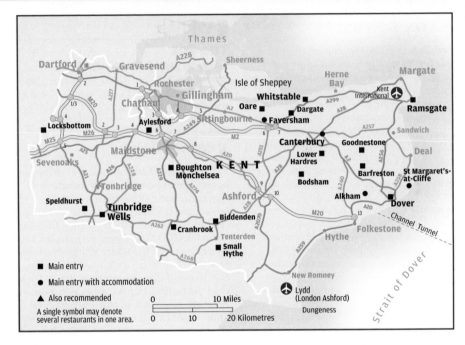

- ■ Main entry
- ● Main entry with accommodation
- ▲ Also recommended

A single symbol may denote several restaurants in one area.

0          10 Miles

0     10     20 Kilometres

## ▌Alkham

**NEW ENTRY**

### The Marquis at Alkham

**Triumphant food in an elegant ex-pub**
Alkham Valley Road, Alkham, CT15 7DF
Tel no: (01304) 873410
www.themarquisatalkham.co.uk
**Gastropub | £23**
**Cooking score: 4**

£5 OFF  🍴  £30

This former village pub in the lovely Alkham Valley between Dover and Folkestone has been extensively converted to give an elegant dining room and a spacious bar lounge; it 'hits all the spots', according to one reader. Charlie Lakin (formerly at the Star at Harome, Yorkshire, see entry) heads the kitchen. His menus make the most of local ingredients and seasonal produce: beetroot-marinated Kentish trout with watercress mousse and confit of lemon, for example, makes a triumphant start. A trio of Chilton Farm chicken (butter-roast breast, chicken liver and spinach pie, ballottine of leg with wild mushroom stuffing) vies for flavour with duck (roast breast, confit of duck hash) served with choucroute, turnips and thyme-scented liquor. The cooking of fish, from scallops to turbot, has also spawned good reports. Pear tarte Tatin is the dessert of choice. The wine list delivers a sound international selection at sensible prices from £15.

**Chef/s:** Charles Lakin. **Open:** Tue to Sun L 12 to 2.30 (6 Sun), Tue to Sat D 6.30 to 9.30. Bar food only Mon 12 to 9, Sun 6 to 9. **Meals:** alc (main courses £11 to £27). Set L £15.50 (2 courses) to £18.50. Set D £17.95 (2 courses) to £22.95. Sun L £19.50. **Details:** Cards accepted. 65 seats. 30 seats outside. Separate bar. Wheelchair access. Music. Children allowed. Car parking.

## Average price

The average price listed in main-entry reviews denotes the price of a three-course meal, without wine.

## Ash, Sevenoaks

### READERS RECOMMEND
## Twig & Spoon
**Modern British**
Woodlands Garden Centre, Ash Lane, Ash, Sevenoaks, TN15 7EG
Tel no: (01474) 852788
www.twigandspoon.co.uk
'Nice, simple selection of seasonal, locally sourced dishes'

## Aylesford

## Hengist
**Modern French cooking in chic surroundings**
7-9 High Street, Aylesford, ME20 7AX
Tel no: (01622) 719273
www.hengistrestaurant.co.uk
**Modern European | £30**
**Cooking score: 4**
£5
OFF

Hengist is named after the first King of Kent (449AD) and is tucked away in one of England's oldest villages. But step inside this sixteenth-century building and you enter a cool, modern restaurant where beams, brick and stone fuse with sophisticated smoked glass and bronze taffeta curtains. The cooking has moved up a notch since chef Daniel Hatton joined Richard Phillips's culinary empire (see entries for Thackeray's and Richard Phillips at Chapel Down). While classic French ideas are bolstered by contemporary touches, it is the careful sourcing of local and seasonal materials, innovative combinations and attention to detail that are key to this shift in gear. Rich chicken liver parfait with mango may kick off proceedings, followed by succulent fat scallops teamed with crab and fennel risotto, then roast duck breast with confit leg, pommes Anna and infused sweet grapes, with an impressive assiette of Yorkshire rhubarb bringing up the rear. A well-composed, French-dominated wine list starts at £15.

**Chef/s:** Daniel Hatton. **Open:** Tue to Sun L 12 to 2.30, Tue to Sat D 6 to 10.30. **Closed:** Mon, 25 Dec, 1 Jan. **Meals:** Set L £10.95 (2 courses) to £12.95. Set D £16.95 (2 courses) to £19.95. Set Sun L £18.50. **Service:** 11% (optional). **Details:** Cards accepted. 74 seats. 25 seats outside. Air-con. Separate bar. No mobile phones. Wheelchair access. Music. Children allowed. Car parking.

## Barfreston

## The Yew Tree
**Secret hideaway with good-value meals**
Barfreston, CT15 7JH
Tel no: (01304) 831000
www.yewtree.info
**Modern British | £25**
**Cooking score: 2**

The winter 2008 departure of chef Ben Williams and front-of-house Lisa Wealleans left this 'secret hideaway' rudderless for a time, but a new team is pulling it back on course with welcoming service, an enlarged terrace that looks onto one of the best preserved Norman churches in England, and a menu that stays faithful to local and regional produce. Fried Sussex halloumi with chickpea and red pepper salsa, cider-braised pork belly with 'perfect crackling', and dark chocolate and hazelnut brownie have all been praised, as have good-value meal deals, local ales and a wine list offering tantalising drinking at ungreedy prices (from £13).

**Chef/s:** Craig Mather. **Open:** all week L 12 to 2 (3 Sun), Mon to Sat D 7 to 9. **Meals:** alc (main courses £13 to £18). Set L £9.95 (2 courses) to £12.95. Set D £16 (2 courses) to £19. Sun L £13. **Service:** 10%. **Details:** Cards accepted. 44 seats. 24 seats outside. Separate bar. No music. Children allowed. Car parking.

## Biddenden

# West House

**Cleverly woven flavours**
28 High Street, Biddenden, TN27 8AH
Tel no: (01580) 291341
www.thewesthouserestaurant.co.uk
**Modern European | £35**
**Cooking score: 5**

Graham Garrett cooks while his wife Jackie serves in their neat, understated restaurant that forms part of a terrace of former weavers' cottages in the centre of this pretty Wealden village. It is one of those places that runs very much to its own rules and booking is essential. On the carte of around five choices per course, the concise dish descriptions hide a great deal of skill, with flavours and textures intelligently considered and juxtaposed. So, West Mersea oysters combine with apple jelly, Avruga caviar and horseradish 'snow', and cold poached pork fillet arrives with warm Scotch egg, dandelion and daisy leaf. Main courses are painstakingly composed: chervil root purée, sautéed chanterelles and sea purslane accompany grilled fillets of John Dory, and a modern riff on duck à l'orange sees roasted breast with confit stuffing, foie gras, red cabbage and bitter orange. Cheeses are always British (from Neal's Yard, perhaps) and sweet treats to finish include creamed rice pudding with apple, vanilla and apple pie ice cream. An international line-up of wines at fair prices (from £14.50) hits just the right note.
**Chef/s:** Graham Garrett. **Open:** Tue to Fri L 12 to 1.45, Sun L 12 to 2.30, Tue to Sat D 7 to 9 (10 Fri and Sat). **Closed:** Mon, 24 Dec through New Year, 2 weeks summer. **Meals:** Set L £22 (2 courses) to £25. Set D £35. Sun L £29.50 (2 courses) to £35. **Service:** 12.5 % (optional). **Details:** Cards accepted. 32 seats. No music. Wheelchair access. Children allowed. Car parking.

## ALSO RECOMMENDED

## ▲ The Three Chimneys

Hareplain Road, Biddenden, TN27 8LW
Tel no: (01580) 291472
www.thethreechimneys.co.uk
**Gastropub**

The pub is pure Kentish picture-postcard – a sixteenth-century country classic that rambles through a series of beamed, low-ceilinged rooms filled with old settles, wood-panelling, wonky brick floors, evening candles and open fires. Cider and ale may be tapped straight from the barrel, but the food is bang-up-to-date – the daily chalkboard lists salmon, cod and smoked haddock fishcakes with tartare sauce (£8.95), ribeye steak with Stilton butter (£18.95) or seared scallops with coconut and coriander velouté (£18.95). House wine is £15.25. Open all week.

## Bodsham

# Froggies at the Timber Batts

**Traditional pub, classic French food**
School Lane, Bodsham, TN25 5JQ
Tel no: (01233) 750237
www.thetimberbatts.co.uk
**French | £35**
**Cooking score: 1**

One for eternal Francophiles. This deeply rural fifteenth-century pub meets authentic French country cooking courtesy of Joel Gross, the well-respected Gallic chef/proprietor. Blackboards in French advertise moules farci, prawns with garlic, and pigeon breast with smoked duck to start, with mains ranging from confit duck leg to carré d'agneau. Bar snacks are served at lunchtime (ham, egg and chips has been endorsed), real ales are on tap and wines grown by a cousin in the Loire open the list at £15.
**Chef/s:** Joel Gross. **Open:** all week L 12 to 2.30, D 7 to 9.30 (9 Sun and Mon). **Closed:** 24 Dec to 3 Jan. **Meals:** alc (main courses £12 to £20). Sun L £23 (2 courses) to £25. **Service:** not inc. **Details:** Cards accepted. 50 seats. 40 seats outside. Separate bar. Music. Children allowed. Car parking.

# Boughton Monchelsea

**NEW ENTRY**

## The Mulberry Tree

Classic food that's worth the effort
Hermitage Lane, Boughton Monchelsea,
ME17 4DA
Tel no: (01622) 749082
www.themulberrytreekent.co.uk
Modern British | £25
Cooking score: 4

It's not the easiest place to find, and the stark modern building can come as a shock given the otherwise serene pastoral setting. Persevere. The dining room is light and contemporary, the patio does brisk alfresco business in summer and Alan Irwin's cooking is heroically seasonal, based on first-class local produce. Poached Finnan haddock with egg and spinach and slow-roast belly of Kentish Middle White pork with boulangère potato are typical of the unpretentious classic style. An impressive selection of Kentish cheeses demands exploration, while marinated blood oranges with cannelloni of white chocolate is a sweet finish. The set menu has been praised, both for value and for the cooking of such dishes as roast lambs' tongues with herb dumplings. House wine is £12.95.
**Chef/s:** Alan Irwin. **Open:** Tue to Sun L 12 to 2 (2.30 Sun), Tue to Sat D 6.30 to 9 (9.30 Fri and Sat). **Closed:** Mon. **Meals:** alc (main courses £13 to £19). Set L and D £12.95 (2 courses) to £15.95. Sun L £14.95 (2 courses) to £17.95. **Service:** not inc. **Details:** Cards accepted. 60 seats. 40 seats outside. Separate bar. Wheelchair access. Music. Children allowed. Car parking.

# Canterbury

## The Goods Shed

Championing local supplies
Station Road West, Canterbury, CT2 8AN
Tel no: (01227) 459153
www.thegoodsshed.net
Modern British | £32
Cooking score: 2

The former Victorian railway shed next to Canterbury West Station is now an acclaimed farmers' market, with a dining area on a raised wooden platform along one wall and the kitchen open to view at one end. It has a laid-back air, though service could be tightened up, but the cooking – much improved this year – is honest and rustic with top-drawer slow-roast belly pork teamed with apple and rhubarb, and chicken with chorizo and wild garlic. Good desserts include a fine lemon posset trifle. Prices are high, but reflect the quality of ingredients, sourced mainly from the market. Wines start at £13. Our questionniare has not been returned so some of the information below may have changed.
**Chef/s:** Rafael Lopez. **Open:** Tue to Sun L 12 to 2.30 (3 Sat and Sun), Tue to Sat D 6 to 9.30. **Closed:** Mon, 25 and 26 Dec, 1 Jan. **Meals:** alc (main courses £10 to £18). **Service:** not inc. **Details:** Cards accepted. 80 seats. Car parking.

## Michael Caines at ABode Canterbury

Modern boutique hotel dining
High Street, Canterbury, CT1 2RX
Tel no: (01227) 766266
www.michaelcaines.com
Modern European | £35
Cooking score: 4

This 'smart, chic abode' part of Michael Caines' mini-hotel group has Mark Rossi in charge of the day-to-day running of the kitchen. He brings great technical skill to fine raw materials, delivering dishes that do not stint on flavour. That was certainly the case for one reporter, who considered the lunchtime

grazing menu of small tasting dishes to be 'the best-value lunch deal in the area'. The meal in question opened with pan-fried marinated mackerel served alongside Provençal vegetables, roast pepper and chorizo purée with fennel cream sauce, went on to pigeon breast with potato salardaise, sweetcorn, pancetta, broad bean ragoût and Madeira sauce vinaigrette, and finished with a superb mint chocolate sundae. At dinner, a grander touch brings on ballottine of chicken and veal sweetbread and local sea bass with saffron velouté and baby leeks. Service, a constant bugbear in the past, has been 'much improved' of late. Wines from £21.50.
**Chef/s:** Mark Rossi. **Open:** all week L 12 to 2.30 (12.30 Sun), Mon to Sat D 6 to 10. **Meals:** alc (main courses £17 to £24). Set L £9.95. Set D £14.95/£19.95 (2 courses) to £20/£25. **Service:** 12% (optional). **Details:** Cards accepted. 74 seats. Air-con. Separate bar. No mobile phones. Wheelchair access. Music. Car parking.

# Cranbrook

## Apicius
**Artistry and big-statement cooking**
23 Stone Street, Cranbrook, TN17 3HF
Tel no: (01580) 714666
www.restaurant-apicius.co.uk
**Modern European | £32**
**Cooking score: 6**

Apicius is a testament to the single-minded persistence of its proprietors, and is warmly appreciated by its faithful followers. A small Kent village might be considered out on a limb but the place has proved a slow-burner, producing cooking that is well worth the drive. What awaits, according to one reporter, is 'sheer artistry, food good enough to weep over'. That report singled out a starter of leek velouté, spooned over a perfectly poached duck egg, as the kind of dish you don't quickly forget; or there might be baked mackerel fillet served with the twin supports of beetroot and mozzarella. Main courses capitalise on quality local (and not so local) supplies for the likes of sea bream with Tarbais beans, 'pied bleu' mushrooms and orange confit, or maybe roast

Barbary duck breast with Puy lentils, pancetta, celeriac purée and garlic cream sauce. Well-constructed desserts include the ingeniously sweet-savoury poached pear with walnut cream, Stilton ice cream and port sauce, as well as tropically themed caramelised pineapple and coconut pannacotta with Malibu sorbet and mango coulis. The short, well-chosen wine list starts at £15 (£3.75 a glass).
**Chef/s:** Timothy Johnson. **Open:** Wed to Fri and Sun L 12 to 2, Tue to Sat D 7 to 9. **Closed:** Mon, 2 weeks Christmas and New Year, 2 weeks summer. **Meals:** Set L £22.50 (2 courses) to £26.50. Set D £25.50 (2 courses) to £29.95. **Service:** 12.5% (optional). **Details:** Cards accepted. 24 seats. No music. No mobile phones. Wheelchair access.

# Dargate

## The Dove Inn
**Good-value food with ambition**
Plum Pudding Lane, Dargate, ME13 9HB
Tel no: (01227) 751360
**Gastropub | £25**
**Cooking score: 1**

Don't let the bare floorboards and wooden furniture fool you – the Dove is predominantly an eating place rather than a straightforward pub nowadays and shows ambition. The lunchtime blackboard offers good value in such dishes as fish pie and Toulouse sausage with red wine shallots. The pricier carte brings a short choice of varied modern European cooking. Ham hock and foie gras terrine is a good start, while main courses might include ribeye steak with a pleasing bordelaise sauce or well-timed Dover sole. House wine is £13.
**Chef/s:** Phillip MacGregor. **Open:** Tue to Sun L 12 to 2.30 (3 Sun), Tue to Sat D 7 to 9. **Closed:** Mon. **Meals:** alc (main courses £10 to £18). **Service:** not inc. **Details:** Cards accepted. 24 seats. 30 seats outside. Wheelchair access. Music. Children allowed. Car parking.

# Dover

NEW ENTRY
## The Allotment

A gem of a find

9 High Street, Dover, CT16 1DP
Tel no: (01304) 214467
www.theallotmentdover.com
Modern British | £24
Cooking score: 3

£5 OFF £30

The best food in Dover is served behind the pretty vine-patterned stained glass window of a former wine shop. It is an idiosyncratic, informal all-day café/restaurant with an open-plan kitchen-cum-dining room, thoroughly good-humoured service from owner David Flynn and a menu that moves with the seasons. There is no standing on ceremony, yet the food can impress. The style is unmistakably modern British brasserie: fresh soups such as a thick, satisfying carrot, prawns with garlic and chilli and 21-day aged sirloin of beef. Vegetables and salads emphasise the theme, although there's a Mediterranean flavour to some dishes, such as an impressive Andalusian lamb with couscous. The breakfast menu is worth exploring, too. With a succinct list of modern wines (from £14), it's 'an absolute gem of a find'.

**Chef/s:** David Flynn. **Open:** Tue to Sat 8.30am to 11pm. **Closed:** Sun, Mon, 2 to 3 weeks after Christmas. **Meals:** alc (main courses £8 to £17). **Service:** not inc. **Details:** Cards accepted. 26 seats. 26 seats outside. Wheelchair access. Music. Children allowed.

## Please send us your feedback

To register your opinion about any restaurant listed in the Guide, or a new restaurant that you wish to bring to our attention, please visit the web address at the bottom of the page. Your feedback informs the content of the book and will be used to compile next year's reviews.

# Faversham

## Read's

Fine-dining grandee

Macknade Manor, Canterbury Road, Faversham, ME13 8XE
Tel no: (01795) 535344
www.reads.com
Modern British | £52
Cooking score: 6

£5 OFF 🍷 � V

This Georgian manor house is home to one of the most renowned and longest-standing fine-dining restaurants in the Home Counties. Five acres of mature gardens, a fifth of which is occupied by a walled produce garden serving the kitchen, enhance the experience, particularly for those who avail themselves of one of the half-dozen guest rooms. In a dining room of understated elegance, the tone is one of grown-up refinement. David Pitchford is well into his fourth decade at the stoves here, and his commitment to quality produce prepared with sensitivity is undimmed. The menu deals in carefully composed dishes that retain a grounding in culinary tradition, so starters might take in butternut squash risotto with shaved Parmesan, sage and rocket, or a terrine of foie gras and confit chicken with pickled mushrooms and toasted brioche. Local supply lines provide the main-course proteins, whether it be pheasant, mallard or lamb, the last served on black cabbage with celeriac purée and a lemon thyme jus. Fish is superbly handled too, as in the halibut that appears with braised fennel and spinach in a prawn sauce. The six-course tasting menu offers a useful way to sample the range, through to desserts such as the sublime deep lemon tart with raspberry sorbet. It all comes with an extremely fine wine list that explores France in depth, and also exerts itself imaginatively in the New World. 'Best Buys' is a digest of the more gently priced options, starting at £18.
**Chef/s:** David Pitchford and Simon McNamara. **Open:** Mon to Sat L 12 to 2.30, D 7 to 10. **Closed:** Sun, 25 and 26 Dec, 1 week beg Jan, 2 weeks beg Sept. **Meals:** Set L £24. Set D £52. Tasting menu £52.

**Service:** not inc. **Details:** Cards accepted. 60 seats. 24 seats outside. Separate bar. No music. No mobile phones. Wheelchair access. Children allowed. Car parking.

## Goodnestone

### The Fitzwalter Arms
The hub of village life
The Street, Goodnestone, CT3 1PJ
Tel no: (01304) 840303
www.thefitzwalterarms.co.uk
Gastropub | £25
Cooking score: 3

£5 OFF  £30

Log fires, real ales, no frills – the Fitzwalter Arms looks and feels like a proper local. But dishes chalked up on a blackboard in the bar and dining room give notice that everyone is here for the food. David Hart's strong relationship with local suppliers and his simple yet unpretentious approach has transformed this village boozer next to the church. Much is made on the premises, from the bread to the madeleines that accompany an exquisite dessert of roasted Champagne rhubarb. Before that, you may have enjoyed starters of Jerusalem artichoke soup with finely diced scallop, or gravlax with pickled cucumber, followed by braised shank of hare with beetroot and red wine sauce, or perfectly timed cod atop a fishcake with fresh egg sauce. House wine is £11.95.
**Chef/s:** David Hart. **Open:** Mon and Wed to Sun L 12 to 2 (2.30 Sun), Mon and Wed to Sat D 7 to 9. **Closed:** Tue, 25 Dec, 1 Jan. **Meals:** alc (main courses £11 to £18). Set L £12.50 (2 courses) to £14.50. **Service:** not inc. **Details:** Cards accepted. 25 seats. 20 seats outside. Separate bar. Music. Children allowed. Car parking.

## Locksbottom

### Chapter One
Refined food at unbeatable prices
Farnborough Common, Locksbottom, BR6 8NF
Tel no: (01689) 854848
www.chaptersrestaurants.co.uk
Modern European | £30
Cooking score: 5

There's a light airy feel to this spacious dining room with smart, linen clad tables where Andrew McLeish offers contemporary European cuisine overlaid with his own tirelessly inventive personal touches. Jugged hare might appear with pancetta and potato espuma and hare satay, as one way to start, while a vegetarian main course might be a pithiviers of wild mushrooms with pommes mousseline, ragoût of artichokes and mushroom sauce. For the rest, it isn't all familiar prime cuts, witness a dish of braised oxtail with pancetta, sautéed spinach, parsnip purée and oxtail jus. The good-value 'menu du jour' impressed one couple with a well-flavoured butternut squash velouté and a 'magnificent dish' of roasted guinea fowl served atop good creamy mashed potato with red wine jus, baby leeks and roasted silverskin onions. Desserts continue to draw praise, including organic lemon tart with crème fraîche sorbet and mille-feuille of passion fruit. The wine list traverses the globe, categorising everything by style and offering a good selection by the glass and half-bottle. House wine is £15.50. There is also a less formal brasserie where you can feast more cheaply on the likes of roast salmon with sautéed potatoes and sauce vierge, and sea salt caramel parfait.
**Chef/s:** Andrew McLeish. **Open:** all week L 12 to 2.30 (2.45 Sun), D 6.30 to 10.30 (11 Fri and Sat, 9.30 Sun). **Closed:** first few days Jan. **Meals:** Set L Mon to Sat £18.50. Set D £29.50. Sun L £19.95. **Service:** 12.5% (optional). **Details:** Cards accepted. 120 seats. 20 seats outside. Air-con. Separate bar. Wheelchair access. Music. Children allowed. Car parking.

# Lower Hardres

## The Granville

Laid-back pub with appealing ideas
Street End, Lower Hardres, CT4 7AL
Tel no: (01227) 700402
Gastropub | £26
Cooking score: 4
£30

You can't miss the Granville, a solid white-painted building a few miles from Canterbury on the road to Hythe. The setting may be a pub, but the large space is plain and uncluttered. An open fire is the central focus of the dining room and there's a distinctly separate bar for drinkers. Menus follow local supply lines, as befits a sibling of the Sportsman, Whitstable (see entry) and they have some appealing ideas: smoked local widgeon with rémoulade or a main course of seared thornback ray with shrimp and parsley butter. Flavours are robust and clear. Reporters continue to enjoy the crispy duck with smoked chilli salsa and sour cream, the excellent homemade foccacia and desserts such as a 'first-class' rhubarb sorbet with burnt cream. While many love the laid-back ambience, some feel the cooking has been undermined by variable service. The wine list is a reasonably priced slate, starting at £12.95. **Chef/s:** Jim Shave. **Open:** Tue to Sun L 12 to 2 (3.30 Sun), Tue to Sat D 7 to 9. **Closed:** Mon, 25 and 26 Dec. **Meals:** alc (main courses £10 to £19). **Service:** not inc. **Details:** Cards accepted. 55 seats. 40 seats outside. Separate bar. Wheelchair access. Music. Children allowed. Car parking.

# Oare

## The Three Mariners

Fuss-free approach to British food
2 Church Road, Oare, ME13 0QA
Tel no: (01795) 533633
www.thethreemarinersoare.co.uk
Gastropub | £22
Cooking score: 3
£30

With a roaring fire, real ales and good food, this seventeenth-century pub close to Oare Creek combines the virtues of thriving boozer with congenial rustic restaurant. Although supplemented by blackboard specials, the daily changing carte is self-sufficient in terms of interest and variety. It literally feeds off its location, one look at the menu tells you that the kitchen is proud of Kentish produce – local skate cheeks, for example, served with lemon, garlic, parsley and tomato. Direct, earthy, heart-on-sleeves dishes include classic duck confit, and fillets of local red mullet with lemon, sage and butternut squash purée. These are good ideas, well executed and backed up by honest desserts such as raisin and walnut tart with cinnamon ice cream. House wines from £12. **Chef/s:** John O'Riordan. **Open:** Tue to Sun L 12 to 3 (4 Sun), Wed to Sat D 6 to 9. **Closed:** Mon. **Meals:** alc (main courses £12 to £18). Set L £11 to £15. **Service:** not inc. **Details:** Cards accepted. 55 seats. 25 seats outside. Separate bar. No mobile phones. Music. Children allowed. Car parking.

# ▌Ramsgate

**NEW ENTRY**

## Age and Sons

Food's the priority here

Charlotte Court, Ramsgate, CT11 8HE
Tel no: (01843) 851515
www.ageandsons.co.uk
Modern British | £29
Cooking score: 3

£5 OFF  £30

In a Victorian wine warehouse in a secluded courtyard off Harbour Street, Toby Leigh gives a much-needed boost to the Ramsgate eating-out scene. The first-floor dining room, over the informal café and open-to-view kitchen, offers plenty of natural light and is unfussily laid out, suggesting that the food itself is the priority here. Dishes display clarity, deliver simple pairings of good raw materials, and offer seasonal focus. Descriptions are robust, but the cumulative impact of the food is surprisingly gentle, even if you opt for something like venison haunch with cabbage and pickled pear. Mussel risotto with gremolata, and salt beef with piccalilli and potato bread both looked as bright as their tastes were harmonious. Ecuadorian chocolate nemesis was the pick of desserts. House wine is £13.60.
**Chef/s:** Toby Leigh. **Open:** Tue to Sun L 12 to 4, Wed to Sat D 6.30 to 9.30. **Closed:** Mon, 25 and 26 Dec, Tue after bank hols. **Meals:** alc (main courses £10 to £17). Set L £17 (2 courses) to £20. Set D £20 (2 courses) to £25. **Service:** not inc. **Details:** Cards accepted. 50 seats. 48 seats outside. Separate bar. Music. Children allowed.

## ALSO RECOMMENDED

## ▲ Surin

30 Harbour Street, Ramsgate, CT11 8HA
Tel no: (01843) 592001
www.surinrestaurant.co.uk
Thai

Close to the harbour, this small, café-like restaurant is owned and run by Damrong Garbutt, who covers the Thai repertoire

extensively with generally sound cooking at reasonable prices. Starters range from chicken satay to mixed seafood soup, while meat, seafood and vegetable main courses (ranging from £6 to £13) include fried salmon with red curry sauce, pork with basil leaves, and vegetable green curry. Good-value set lunch. House wine £9. Closed Sun and Mon L.

# ▌St Margaret's-at-Cliffe

## Wallett's Court

Contemporary food and historic trappings

Westcliffe, St Margaret's-at-Cliffe, CT15 6EW
Tel no: (01304) 852424
www.wallettscourt.com
Modern British | £40
Cooking score: 3

£5 OFF

Just a mile inland from Dover's white cliffs, Wallett's Court is a trove of updated seventeenth-century rusticity – although its origins lie further back in time. The Oakley family have run this one-time farmhouse as a country hotel since 1976. The main house has a uniquely lived-in feel, right down to its weathered timbers and Jacobean staircase. The dining room also has its quota of historic trappings, but the kitchen ensures that the food strikes a more contemporary pose. Starters such as seared sea bream fillet with spiced pear salsa and orange sauce show creative flair, although mains follow the mainstream – witness Gressingham duck breast with sautéed chestnuts and wild mushrooms, port and balsamic jus. Desserts find room for apple crumble, while also exploring the merits of glazed vanilla brûlée with hot blackcurrant compote and liquorice ice cream. The wine list brims with exciting names from prestigious growers across the globe. Bottles start at £15.
**Chef/s:** Stephen Harvey and Paul Birkett. **Open:** Sun L 12 to 2, all week D 7 to 9. **Closed:** 25 and 26 Dec. **Meals:** Set L £19.50 (2 courses) to £25. Set D £32.50 (2 courses) to £40. **Service:** 10% (optional). **Details:** Cards accepted. 70 seats. Separate bar. No mobile phones. Wheelchair access. Music. Children allowed. Car parking.

## READERS RECOMMEND

### The Bay Restaurant

Modern British
The White Cliffs Hotel, High Street, St Margaret's-at-Cliffe, CT15 6AT
Tel no: (01304) 852229
www.thewhitecliffs.com
'Local, free-range, organic, sustainable food very well cooked'

## Small Hythe

NEW ENTRY
### Richard Phillips at Chapel Down

Local wines complementing local produce
Chapel Down, Tenterden Vineyard, Small Hythe, TN30 7NG
Tel no: (01580) 761616
www.richardphillipsatchapeldown.co.uk
Modern British | £28
Cooking score: 3

Richard Phillips, of Thackeray's and Hengist (see entries), has pitched his new venture in the peaceful surrounds of the Chapel Down Vineyard. The combination of warehouse-style winery and interior vision of mellow wood and brilliant splashes of colour is an irresistible one, the more so when the cooking combines excellent use of local produce with value for money. Lunch is the main event (dinner available three evenings) and dishes come beautifully presented with by-the-glass suggestions to match, including home-grown ones. The cooking scores hits with silky sorrel and leek soup with Stilton and spinach tortellini, mains of braised rump of Sussex breed beef with pearl barley risotto, and an excellent, zingy lemon tart, but service seriously lets the kitchen down, being at times 'amateurish without the charm'. House wine is £14.95.
Chef/s: Richard Phillips and Jose Azevedo. Open: all week L 12 to 3 (4 Sun), Thur to Sat D 6.30 to 10.30. Meals: alc (main courses £14 to £20). Set L £12.95 (2 courses) to £14.95. Sun L £16.95 (2 courses) to

£18.95. Chef's table menus £38 to £65. Service: not inc. Details: Cards accepted. 74 seats. 16 seats outside. Air-con. Separate bar. Music. Children allowed. Car parking.

## Speldhurst

### George & Dragon

Good food at a well-heeled pub
Speldhurst, TN3 0NN
Tel no: (01892) 863125
www.speldhurst.com
Gastropub | £25
Cooking score: 4

It is six years since Julian Leffe-Griffiths revitalised this thirteenth-century hostelry, reputedly the second oldest in the country. He has cleverly balanced all the virtues of a well-heeled pub, thanks to genuine hospitality, local ales and good food. The kitchen is proud of the fact that it buys directly from local farmers and producers, and is currently showing off its prowess with confidence. Lunchtime fish and chips keeps things pubby, but there's also squid and clams with nero di sappio tagliolini and chilli, and superb meat – from a huge slab of prime aged rump steak with perfect pommes allumettes and wild garlic butter to a generous piece of slow-roast pork belly topped with the crackliest of crackling and served with rhubarb and apple compote. Someone clearly has a real talent for making bread, too. Meals finish strongly with Valrhona chocolate and nut brownie. Around 50 well-spread wines offer the prospect of interesting drinking at bearable prices, starting at £13.80.
Chef/s: Brett Mather. Open: all week L 12 to 2.30 (3 Sun), Mon to Sat D 7 to 9.30. Closed: 1 Jan. Meals: alc (main courses £9 to £18). Service: 12.5% (optional). Details: Cards accepted. 120 seats. 100 seats outside. Separate bar. Wheelchair access. Music. Children allowed. Car parking.

## ▌ Tunbridge Wells

### Thackeray's

**Elegant French polish**
85 London Road, Tunbridge Wells, TN1 1EA
Tel no: (01892) 511921
www.thackerays-restaurant.co.uk
**Modern French | £43**
**Cooking score: 6**

William Makepeace Thackeray would not recognise the interior of his former home now, but readers love the cool, modern look and locals still regard the white clapboard Georgian house as the best restaurant in the area. But while some demur at Richard Phillips'à la carte prices (there are good value set lunch and dinner options), and what they see as small portions, others report on fine ingredients, accurate timing and spot-on textures. Seafood illustrates what the kitchen can accomplish: for example, a puddle of glossy chive beurre blanc flanked by just-cooked fillet of brill, cod brandade, mussels and fried calamari, the flavours emphatic, the counterpoint well considered. Variations on traditional themes might include terrine of chicken with shiitake mushrooms, Sauternes jelly, wild mushrooms and truffle jus. Likewise a pairing of a ballottine of wild rabbit with a brochette of rabbit offal, served with vegetable ratatouille and a first-class tomato risotto. Desserts have included apple tarte Tatin with cider espuma and cinnamon ice cream. The global wine list abounds with quality producers and there is plenty of drinking at the £25 mark or below (house wine is £14.95) and a good selection of half bottles.
**Chef/s:** Richard Phillips. **Open:** Tue to Sun L 12 to 2.30, Tue to Sat D 6.30 to 10.30. **Closed:** Mon. **Meals:** alc (main courses £23 to £27). Set L £16.50 (2 courses) to £17.50. Set D £24.50 (2 courses) to £26.50. Sun L £24.50 (2 courses) to £28.50. **Service:** 12.5% (optional). **Details:** Cards accepted. 60 seats. 30 seats outside. Air-con. Separate bar. Wheelchair access. Music. Children allowed.

## ▌ Whitstable

### JoJo's

**Appealing, friendly and value for money**
209 Tankerton Road, Tankerton, Whitstable, CT5 2AT
Tel no: (01227) 274591
www.jojosrestaurant.co.uk
**Modern European | £20**
**Cooking score: 4**

Nikki Billington and Paul Watson's intimate blue-painted restaurant is neat and unshowy: functional modern design teams an open-plan kitchen with plain counter stools, simply dressed tables and an uncluttered tapas menu. But this is a very different plate of tapas: top-notch ingredients form the bedrock to an intriguing array of meze from all over the Mediterranean: charcuterie could be Spanish chorizo or Italian lonzino or fioco di spalla, dolmades and hummus served alongside fish from local day boats, garlic mayo served with deep-fried squid, tzatziki with sliced cannon of lamb. As we went to press Paul and Nikki informed us that they plan to move JoJo's to larger premises 'just round the corner' at 2 Herne Bay Road, Tankerton. The move is planned to take place in February 2010. Do check the website or telephone for further information.
**Chef/s:** Nikki Billington and Joe Billington. **Open:** Sat and Sun L 1 to 3, Wed to Sat D 6.30 to 10.30. **Closed:** Mon, Tue. **Meals:** alc (£4 to £8). **Service:** not inc. **Details:** Cards accepted. 34 seats. 12 seats outside. Wheelchair access. Music. Children allowed.

★ BEST CHEF ★ STEPHEN HARRIS ★

# The Sportsman

**Sophisticated cooking in a no-frills pub**
Faversham Road, Seasalter, Whitstable, CT5 4BP
Tel no: (01227) 273370
www.thesportsmanseasalter.co.uk
**Modern British | £30**
**Cooking score: 6**

In the somewhat bracing setting of the Seasalter coastal grazing marshes stands this simple pub with bare tables, paper napkins and basic cutlery, the simplicity of the setting giving no indication of the quality of the cooking to come. For here the brilliant, idiosyncratic Steve Harris cooks with an instinctive use of the best ingredients. From a winter menu might come a warm rock oyster with homemade chorizo, a little nibble of herring, apple jelly and cream, incredibly moreish pork scratchings and a few slices of own-cured ham. To follow, a trio of scallop dishes: with seaweed butter; with tomato powder and lardo (a delicacy made from pork fat); as a carpaccio topped with smoked brill roe and sorrel. Satisfaction, too, in the form of superb turbot, its flavour complemented by home-smoked pork belly and a sensational vin jaune sauce. On other occasions, visitors have enjoyed exemplary roast rack and shank of local lamb and an exquisite banana parfait with hazelnuts, caramel and chocolate sorbet. Attention to the best ingredients extends to bread ('the focaccia in particular'), butter (which is churned on the premises) and the wine – a fairly priced mix of France and New World bottles with the vast majority under £25.

**Chef/s:** Stephen Harris and Dan Flavel. **Open:** Tue to Sun L 12 to 2.30, Tue to Sat D 7 to 9. **Closed:** Mon, 25 and 26 Dec. **Meals:** alc (main courses £11 to £22). **Service:** not inc. **Details:** Cards accepted. 50 seats. Music. Children allowed. Car parking.

## Gastronomic hot spots

It's an illusive formula that turns a town or an area into a foodie hot spot: Ludlow and Rick Stein's Padstow have both been hailed as gastronomic phenomena, but there are other regions to look out for.

**Marlow** in Buckinghamshire is a strong contender for the Ludlow crown, a claim bolstered by proximity to the Bray stars.

**North Fife** sports a large number of reassuringly well-established restaurants; both **Ostlers Close** in Cupar and **The Cellar** at Anstruther are listed among the *Guide*'s longest-serving restaurants.

**East Kent** is experiencing a restaurant revival. The quality of food available in the rough triangle encompassing Faversham, Canterbury, Whitstable, Ramsgate and Dover has improved enormously, as has the number of places we can enjoy this glorious food in. Canterbury's **Goods Shed** farmers' market and restaurant is credited with kick-starting this revival. Once it was just **Read's** of Faversham, then came the **Sportsman** in Whitstable. Now, the likes of Toby Leigh (**Age and Sons**), Charles Lakin (**The Marquis at Alkham**) and David Flynn (**The Allotment**) have joined up-and-coming chefs at **The Fitzwalter Arms** and **The Three Mariners**. Whitstable, though, is the beating heart of the region, with its trio of **JoJo's**, **Wheelers Oyster Bar** and **Williams & Brown Tapas**.

## Wheelers Oyster Bar

Imaginative, on-song seafood
8 High Street, Whitstable, CT5 1BQ
Tel no: (01227) 273311
Seafood | £30
Cooking score: 4

Eating at Wheelers is very much a personalised experience. Not only is the place at capacity with just 16 diners, but the tiny 4-seater oyster bar (for seafood and fishy snacks) and the back parlour are heroically old-fashioned. Reporters reckon that Mark Stubbs has cranked up the cooking of late, and inspection found the kitchen very much on-song. While much effort goes into imaginative, modern fish dishes, they are not overworked: both a delicate mackerel tartare served alongside a shot glass of beetroot gazpacho, avocado purée and mustard cress salad, and a perfectly timed monkfish with a prawn and mussel laksa and buttered linguine revealed clean, clear flavours. A neat trio of rhubarb (sorbet, fool and tart) rounded off the meal with real zing. Presiding over it all, Delia Fitt greets her customers and remembers faces – her regulars arrive clutching wine, otherwise you are directed to the off-licence across the road.
**Chef/s:** Mark Stubbs. **Open:** Thur to Tue 1 to 7.30. **Closed:** Wed, 11 to 28 Jan. **Meals:** alc (main courses £17 to £21). **Service:** not inc. **Details:** Cards accepted. 16 seats. Air-con. Wheelchair access. Children allowed.

## Williams & Brown Tapas

A taste of Spain
48 Harbour Street, Whitstable, CT5 1AQ
Tel no: (01227) 273373
www.thetapas.co.uk
Spanish | £23
Cooking score: 2

**V**

Tables are closely packed at Christopher Williams' welcoming, simply decorated tapas bar. A wood floor and open-to-view kitchen tend to ratchet up the noise level – but shut your eyes and this could be Spain. Classics such as paella are given a modern workout when made with spinach, pine nuts and roast tomatoes, but the kitchen knows when to leave well alone when it comes to the likes of deep-fried fresh local sprats. Good raw materials are apparent in straightforward dishes, say, roast pork belly or Catalan honeyed free-range chicken. A short list of Spanish wines comes by the bottle (from £15.95) or glass (from £4.75).
**Chef/s:** Christopher Williams. **Open:** all week L 12 to 2 (2.30 Sat, 2.45 Sun), D 6 to 9 (9.45 Sat). **Closed:** 25 and 26 Dec. **Meals:** alc (main courses £9 to £13). **Service:** not inc. **Details:** Cards accepted. 32 seats. 6 seats outside. Air-con. No mobile phones. Music. Children allowed.

## READERS RECOMMEND

## The Pearson's Arms

Gastropub
The Horsebridge, Sea Wall, Whitstable, CT5 1BT
Tel no: (01227) 272005
**'Change for the better at this revamped seaside pub'**

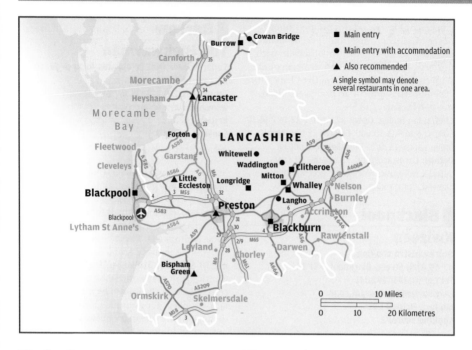

Map legend:
- ■ Main entry
- ● Main entry with accommodation
- ▲ Also recommended

A single symbol may denote several restaurants in one area.

## ■ Bispham Green

ALSO RECOMMENDED
### ▲ The Eagle & Child
Malt Kiln Lane, Bispham Green, L40 3SG
Tel no: (01257) 462297
www.ainscoughs.co.uk
**Gastropub**

Obscure North Country real ales, a bowling green and a farm shop are just some of the attractions at this enterprising country pub (circa 1820) a few miles from the M6. Food is also a big draw, and the kitchen adds a touch of exoticism to home-grown and local ingredients with good-value dishes ranging from crispy duck and pine nut salad (£6.50) to pan-fried pigeon breasts with porcini noodles and shallot essence (£12). Round off with apple and rhubarb crumble (£4.50). House wine is £12.60. Open all week.

## ■ Blackburn

NEW ENTRY
### The Clog and Billycock
**Lancashire food champion**
Billinge End Road, Pleasington, Blackburn, BB2 6QB
Tel no: (01254) 201163
www.theclogandbillycock.com
**Gastropub | £24**
**Cooking score: 3**
 £30

The newest gastro-horse in the Ribble Valley Inns stable works along comfortingly familiar lines. Take a seat somewhere in the spacious interior, probably near one of the trademark photos of local suppliers. Flap the huge menu like a wobble board, order at a pay point, and prepare for extraordinarily large portions. It's hard to go wrong, but über-local choices include a crumpet with fresh Lancashire curd cheese, cress and beetroot or a shared wooden platter of seafood with perky pickled accompaniments. Devilled Goosnargh

chicken or Fleetwood fish pie are among never-fail main courses and specials include plenty of seasonal game. An obsession with nursery puddings could lead to an encounter with tapioca, though the 'length of Lancashire' cheeseboard is difficult to pass by. Chilean house wines are £13.50.
**Chef/s:** Ian Rudge. **Open:** all week L 12 to 2 (8.30 Sun), D 6 to 9 (5.30 Sat). **Closed:** 25 Dec. **Meals:** alc (main courses £10 to £18). **Service:** not inc. **Details:** Cards accepted. 130 seats. 50 seats outside. No music. Wheelchair access. Children allowed. Car parking.

## Blackpool

### Kwizeen

**Quirky bistro cooking**
47-49 King Street, Blackpool, FY1 3EJ
Tel no: (01253) 290045
www.kwizeenrestaurant.co.uk
**Modern British | £25**
**Cooking score: 2**

A short hop from the Blackpool Tower, Kwizeen is set a little back from the Golden Mile. It is designed in perfect contemporary style, with curvy lines, a stripped-wood floor and simply dressed tables. Produce from the Lancashire countryside, as well as fish from the Fleetwood catch just up the coast, inform the stylish bistro cooking. Expect to start with something like mackerel niçoise with a poached egg and green beans, before following on with sea bass in curried lime butter, or tea-smoked wild mallard with Puy lentils and orange sauce. Finish, perhaps, with strawberry cheesecake and basil ice cream. House wines from Spain are a mere £10.
**Chef/s:** Marco Callé-Calatayud. **Open:** Mon to Fri L 11.45 to 1.45, Mon to Sat D 6 to 9 (10 Sat). **Closed:** Sun, first Sun after Valentines Day for 2 weeks, last week in Aug. **Meals:** alc (main courses £14 to £22). Set L £7.95 (2 courses) to £11. Set D £12.95 (2 courses) to £15.95. **Service:** not inc. **Details:** Cards accepted. 40 seats. No mobile phones. Music. Children allowed.

## Burrow

### The Highwayman

**Super-boozer that celebrates local produce**
Burrow, LA6 2RJ
Tel no: (01524) 273338
www.highwaymaninn.co.uk
**British | £23**
**Cooking score: 3**

'Is it a gastropub,' muses a reader, 'or just a pub that does really good food?' It's certainly no ordinary local, being one of a mini-chain of super-boozers under the Ribble Valley Inns umbrella. More atmospheric than its East Lancs siblings (the Three Fishes, the Clog and Billycock, see entries), one could pop in for a half of Thwaites Lancaster Bomber or Double Century, but many diners journey cross-county just for the food. The menu 'celebrates local produce', for example Flookburgh shrimps with blade mace butter, Herdwick mutton pudding and Lancashire curd tart, which the kitchen 'cooks well'. Ham-fisted presentation and unbalanced dishes are, however, sometimes evident. The wine list is definitely more gastropub than local, with representation from big names and regions starting at £13.50.
**Chef/s:** Michael Ward. **Open:** all week L 12 to 2 (12 to 8 Sun), D 6 to 9 (5.30 Sat). **Closed:** 25 Dec. **Meals:** alc (main courses £9 to £20). **Service:** not inc. **Details:** Cards accepted. 120 seats. 60 seats outside. Separate bar. No music. Wheelchair access. Children allowed. Car parking.

## ▊ Clitheroe

### Weezos

**North Country flavours and Afro vibes**
1-5 Parson Lane, Clitheroe, BB7 2JP
Tel no: (01200) 424478
www.weezos.co.uk
**Modern British | £27**
**Cooking score: 1**

Stosie Madi and Kathy Smith have brought a
cool African vibe to this listed toll house,
thanks to a chill-out backdrop of tribal masks
and ethnic music. It makes a vibrant setting for
inventive food inspired by a trusted network
of North Country suppliers: Bury black
pudding and spring onion fritters might open
the show, ahead of local partridge with pickled
pears or pan-roast fish of the day with chorizo
and spinach. Weezos also does a good line in
racy cocktails; otherwise there are interesting
wines from £13.95.
**Chef/s:** Stosie Madi. **Open:** Thur to Sat D only 7 to
12. **Closed:** Sun to Wed. **Meals:** alc (main courses
£15 to £19). **Service:** not inc. **Details:** Cards
accepted. 32 seats. 6 seats outside. Wheelchair
access. Music. Children allowed.

## ▊ Cowan Bridge

### Hipping Hall

**Assured cooking in a lovely setting**
Cowan Bridge, LA6 2JJ
Tel no: (01524) 271187
www.hippinghall.com
**Modern British | £50**
**Cooking score: 5**

 V

Chef Michael Wilson recently took over the
stoves at this peaceful, independently run
'restaurant-with-rooms' in the Lancashire
countryside. The setting – a seventeenth-
century house, but with a dining room dating
to the fifteenth – is lovely, with its attractive
gardens, neat lawns and shrubbery. In fine
weather a pre-dinner drink alfresco is a must.
Wilson's seasonally changing menus are
proudly rooted in classical cooking. The stars

are the well-made sauces and good local
ingredients. Roast poussin with albufera sauce
and poached sea bass with farfalle neri scallop
velouté make excellent choices, although
portioning could perhaps be more generous.
Some of Wilson's trendier combinations, for
example scallops with pea purée or pork belly
with langoustines and cauliflower purée,
won't strike the seasoned restaurant-goer as
particularly original. Desserts, meanwhile,
might be soothingly familiar choices of
Valrhona fondant and tonka bean ice cream,
or lemon chiboust and raspberries. Praise
comes for the wine list with its healthy
concentration of bottles in the £20 to £35
bracket, and wine by the glass from £4.50. A
word also for the youthful servers who know
the menu inside out and never miss a beat.
They can breathe out now – they're doing a
fine job.
**Chef/s:** Michael Wilson. **Open:** Fri to Sun L 12 to
1.30, all week D 7 to 9.30. **Closed:** 3 to 7 Jan.
**Meals:** Set L £29.50 (3 courses). Set D £49.50.
Gourmand D £60. **Service:** not inc. **Details:** Cards
accepted. 30 seats. Separate bar. No mobile
phones. Wheelchair access. Music. Car parking.

## ▊ Forton

### The Bay Horse Inn

**Head-turning Brit food**
Bay Horse Lane, Forton, LA2 0HR
Tel no: (01524) 791204
www.bayhorseinn.com
**Gastropub | £25**
**Cooking score: 3**

'What a pity Surrey cannot produce a
restaurant like this!' sighed one pair of
wanderers up north, offering high praise for
Craig Wilkinson's charming country pub. An
eighteenth-century watering hole in the
Trough of Bowland, with guest rooms over
the road in a converted grain store, it offers just
the ambience one hopes for, with its crazy
jumble of furniture and a big stone fireplace.
'Friendly and ultra-efficient' staff serve up
locally based food of head-turning quality,
from fine Lancashire-smoked salmon to lamb

shank with parsnip purée and pearl barley, or halibut with braised wild mushrooms. Not many will pass up the tempting desserts, such as crème brûlée with marinated figs. House wines are £12.95.

**Chef/s:** Craig Wilkinson. **Open:** Tue to Sun L 12 to 2 (3 Sun). Tue to Sat D 7 to 9.15. **Closed:** Mon, Tue after bank hols, 25 and 26 Dec. **Meals:** alc (main courses £12 to £22). Sun L £16.95 (2 courses) to £20.95. **Service:** not inc. **Details:** Cards accepted. 50 seats. 24 seats outside. Separate bar. Wheelchair access. Music. Children allowed. Car parking.

# Lancaster

## ALSO RECOMMENDED
## ▲ Quite Simply French

27A St Georges Quay, Lancaster, LA1 1RD
Tel no: (01524) 843199
www.quitesimplyfrench.co.uk
**French**

Sitting on the historic St Georges Quay, Lancaster's *rive gauche* if you will, this place aims to keep the tricolor flying with a menu of Gallic brasserie classics. Chicken and foie gras terrine with red onion and fennel chutney (£5.75) might be the curtain-raiser to a main course such as sea bass on tomato and coriander coulis (£15.95) or seared saddle of lamb sauced with red wine and rosemary (£16.95). Conclude with an Amaretto crème brûlée (£4.25). House French on an international list is £13.75. Open all week D, and Sun L.

### Please send us your feedback

To register your opinion about any restaurant listed in the Guide, or a new restaurant that you wish to bring to our attention, please visit the web address at the bottom of the page. Your feedback informs the content of the book and will be used to compile next year's reviews.

# Langho
## Northcote

**First-class food and ingredients**
Northcote Road, Langho, BB6 8BE
Tel no: (01254) 240555
www.northcote.com
**Modern British | £46**
**Cooking score: 6**

Rebranded from staid 'Northcote Manor', the snappily named Northcote is changing, but not so fast as to alienate longtime fans. The experience still begins over a drink in the awkward silence of the lounge, but the atmosphere picks up once the 'first-class, imaginative' food arrives and the staff chill out. If it's hard to get excited about a safe option of beef fillet with 'chipped potatoes' – whatever the provenance – the kitchen's championing of regional food and its 'constantly developing menu' definitely deserve effusive praise. Spot the trendy techniques, too: where else locally will you find 'chocolate brûlée, jelly, sorbet, malt and smoke' or oysters with citrus 'caviar'? Be warned – descriptions can fool, as was the case with 'melting ginger pudding' (a disappointingly dry sponge pud). More typical is Lancashire cheese soufflé with Morecambe Bay shrimps – 'a triumph of tastes' – or soft duck egg, morels and soldiers. Consistency is praised, even when the cooking is for large groups – 'it's impossible to tell if the executive chef is off-duty', enthuses one reader. Lunch is 'an absolute snip', with occasional discounts found online. A very special wine list offers idiosyncratic choices by the glass, several pages of half-bottles, 'spot-on' recommendations and unusual regional focuses (Portuguese whites). Bottles from £20.

**Chef/s:** Nigel Haworth and Lisa Allen. **Open:** all week L 12 to 1.30 (2 Sun), D 7 (6.30 Sat) to 9.30 (9 Sun). **Closed:** 25 Dec. **Meals:** alc (main courses £19 to £35). Set L £24.50. Set D £55 (5 courses). Sun L £30. Tasting menu £75 (8 courses). **Service:** not inc.

**Details:** Cards accepted. 60 seats. Separate bar. Wheelchair access. Music. Children allowed. Car parking.

## ▊ Little Eccleston

### ALSO RECOMMENDED
### ▲ The Cartford Inn
Cartford Lane, Little Eccleston, PR3 0YP
Tel no: (01995) 670166
www.thecartfordinn.co.uk
Gastropub

A 10-mile dash from the brassy bling of Blackpool brings you to this handome old refurbished pub in a quiet corner of the Fylde Peninsula. Outside is the River Wyre, inside, oak floors, huge roaring fires, contemporary artwork and a totally relaxed vibe. Local ingredients are put to good use in dishes including apple and Bury black pudding strudel with Lancashire cheese (£5.75) and oxtail, beef and local beer suet pudding (£11.50). House wine is £13.95. Closed Mon L and Sun D. Accommodation.

## ▊ Longridge

### Longridge Restaurant
The end of an era
104-106 Higher Road, Longridge, PR3 3SY
Tel no: (01772) 784969
www.heathcotes.co.uk
Modern British | £35
New chef
£5 OFF **V**

As the *Guide* went to press, we learnt that Chris and Kath Bell of the White Bull, Ribchester were to take over the running of Paul Heathcote's flagship restaurant. The place had been on the market, but this arrangement sees Paul Heathcote continuing as the owner. It is likely that the lively emphasis on local ingredients and regional dishes will remain as the Bells are no strangers to Longridge, having worked there in the past, and Chris's cooking is steeped in the modern gastropub classics, among them a proper Lancashire hotpot. The

wine list sprints through New and Old Worlds, starting at £14.95 (£3.85 a glass). Note: details below may change.
**Chef/s:** Chris Bell. **Open:** Tue to Fri L 12 to 2.30, Tue to Sat D 6 to 10 (11 Sat), Sun 12 to 9. **Closed:** Mon. **Meals:** alc (main courses £14 to £25). Set L £17.50 (2 courses) to £25. Sun L £25. Tasting menu £60 (9 courses). **Service:** not inc. **Details:** Cards accepted. 60 seats. Air-con. Separate bar. No mobile phones. Wheelchair access. Music. Children allowed. Car parking.

### Thyme
Great-value local pit-stop
1-3 Inglewhite Road, Longridge, PR3 3JR
Tel no: (01772) 786888
Modern European | £25
Cooking score: 2
 £5 OFF £30

A loyal Longridge servant for many years, Alex Coward aims to please all-comers in this pair of knocked-through terraced cottages. Light lunches provide easy-going, affordable nourishment for shoppers and business people who crowd into the pleasing, split-level dining room. By contrast, lively evening menus go walkabout in search of satisfaction: you might follow Greek spiced chicken 'sticks' or chicken liver and black pudding hotpot with the likes of grilled sea bass fillet, pesto-roasted vegetables and saffron sauce, or marinated duck breast and leg with oriental vegetables and crispy rice noodles. For afters, traditionalists drool over the prospect of 'mother's' marmalade-glazed Blackpool milk roll bread-and-butter pudding or Knickerbocker glory. House wine is £14.95.
**Chef/s:** Alex Coward. **Open:** Tue to Sun L 12 to 2 (11 to 4 Sun), Tue to Sat D 6 to 9.30. **Closed:** Mon. **Meals:** alc (main courses £13 to £19). Set L £8.95 (2 courses) to £10.95. Set D £11.95 (2 courses) to £13.95. Sun L £10.95 (2 courses) to £12.95. **Service:** not inc. **Details:** Cards accepted. 40 seats. Air-con. No mobile phones. Wheelchair access. Music. Children allowed.

## Mitton

### The Three Fishes

Celebrating Lancashire's larder
Mitton Road, Mitton, BB7 9PQ
Tel no: (01254) 826888
www.thethreefishes.com
British | £23
Cooking score: 3

The menu at Ribble Valley Inns' 'smart yet
unpretentious' and 'family-friendly' flagship is
a 'superb' collection of pub favourites and
'British delicacies that have been ignored' such
as mutton, trotters and game. Many go there,
however, simply for the competent, crowd-
pleasing classics like hotpot, fish and chips,
and desserts such as 'excellent' summer
pudding or burnt custard with rhubarb. The
changing roster of cask-conditioned beers,
wines (from £13.50) and soft drinks such as
sarsaparilla is impressive. The pub is praised for
'the warm welcome from every single member
of staff', which didn't, alas, extend to a fond
farewell at inspection. Reservations only for
weekday lunches and dinners.
**Chef/s:** Richard Upton. **Open:** all week L 12 to 2 (8
Sun), D 6 to 9 (5.30 Sat). **Meals:** alc (main courses
£9 to £20). **Service:** not inc. **Details:** Cards
accepted. 140 seats. 40 seats outside. Separate bar.
No music. Wheelchair access. Children allowed. Car
parking.

## Preston

### ALSO RECOMMENDED
### ▲ Bangla Fusion

Liverpool Old Road, Much Hoole, Preston,
PR4 5JQ
Tel no: (01772) 610800
www.banglafusion.co.uk
Indian

'Setting standards' for original Indian cuisine
in Lancashire, this enthusiastically endorsed
eatery is praised for its 'finer touches', opulent
surroundings and enterprising food. Baltis
and other curry house staples (from £8.95)
share the stage with 'creative' signature dishes

such as sizzling fusion duck with tortillas, or
spiced Rajshah scallops with tomato and garlic
sauce (£15.95). Sunday lunch is a family buffet
(from £9.95) and 'early doors' teatime menus
are a weekday bonus (Mon to Thur, 5 to 7).
House wine is £12.25. Closed Mon to Fri L.

### ▲ Grill Room at the Olive Press

23 Winckley Square, Preston, PR1 3JJ
Tel no: (01772) 252732
www.heathcotes.co.uk
Italian

A change of name and culinary allegiance for
the old Winckley Square Chop House,
bringing it in line with its Olive Press siblings.
'This isn't your run-of-the-mill Italian food',
enthuses a fan, who goes on to praise the
'friendly staff'. Carpaccio and seared tuna or
eggs al forna with truffle cream (£6.50),
spaghetti vongole, veal Milanese (£16.50) and
zabaglione (£6) are typical, alongside good-
value lunch deals and house Italian at £14.95.
Closed Sun and Mon. More reports please.

## Waddington

### Waddington Arms

Traditional food with capability and flair
West View, Clitheroe Road, Waddington, BB7 3HP
Tel no: (01200) 423262
www.waddingtonarms.co.uk
Gastropub | £19
Cooking score: 1

With the natural bounty of the Trough of
Bowland almost on the doorstep, and the
Bowland Brewery not much more than a mile
away, this is prime Lancashire gastronomic
territory. The tranquil Ribble Valley village is
home to this amenable pub, which serves
traditional British and French bistro dishes
with capability and flair. Duck and rabbit
terrine might kick things off, as a prelude to
steak, ale and mushroom pie, or seared tuna.
Finish with lemon tart. Wines start at £11.50,
with a generous selection in two glass sizes.

Chef/s: Jimmy Lovett. Open: all week L 12 to 2.30, D 6 to 9.30 (9 Sun). Closed: 25 Dec. Meals: alc (main courses £8 to £15). Set L and D £9.95 (2 courses) to £12.95. Service: not inc. Details: Cards accepted. 60 seats. 60 seats outside. No music. No mobile phones. Wheelchair access. Children allowed. Car parking.

## ■ Whalley

**NEW ENTRY**

### Food by Breda Murphy

Savoury delights and magnificent puds
Abbots Court, 41 Station Road, Whalley, BB7 9RH
Tel no: (01254) 823446
www.foodbybredamurphy.com
Modern British | £22
Cooking score: 2

**V**

The exterior of Ballymaloe-trained Breda Murphy's shop/deli/restaurant is inauspicious – a dull 1960s suburban brick house set back off the road beside a railway bridge. But step inside to tasteful music, 'posh kitchenalia' to buy, and a deli counter bursting with sweet and savoury delights. In the airy restaurant, carefully sourced ingredients make for 'simple, well-executed' dishes along the lines of perfectly cooked chicken livers with pancetta and red grapefruit. Follow, perhaps, with roast hake with fennel potato cake and mussel cream, or homemade lasagne with salad and cucumber pickle. Desserts are magnificent, especially a warm suet bread-and-butter pudding with honey glaze and vanilla anglaise. A short wine list opens at £13.95.
Chef/s: Gareth Bevan. Open: Tue to Sat L 10 to 6, Fri and Sat D 7 to 9.30 (themed nights, twice monthly). Closed: Sun, Mon, 25 Dec to 6 Jan. Meals: alc (main courses £7 to £13). Set D £42.50 (5 courses with live music). Afternoon tea £14. Service: not inc. Details: Cards accepted. 50 seats. 20 seats outside. No mobile phones. Wheelchair access. Music. Children allowed. Car parking.

## ■ Whitewell

### The Inn at Whitewell

An inn for all seasons
Whitewell, BB7 3AT
Tel no: (01200) 448222
www.innatwhitewell.com
Modern British | £28
Cooking score: 3

Deep in the Forest of Bowland, this greatly extended fourteenth-century manor has sedate charm in spades, from its handsome stonework and antiques to pristine landscaped gardens overlooking the River Hodder. These days it's something of an inn for all seasons, dishing out hospitality and also doing duty as a vintners and unofficial art gallery. Lunchtime visitors congregate in the splendid bars, while the more formal restaurant comes into its own for dinner. Either way, the kitchen has an eye for top-notch North Country produce, serving up grilled Bury black pudding with mustard mash, putting Mrs Kirkham's Lancashire into cheese and onion pies and partnering Goosnargh chicken with braised lentil and shallots. Seafood is from farther afield, whether it's Norfolk kippers or chargrilled baby squid with chorizo, while puds are of the wholesome, traditional kind. The lengthy wine list (from £13) treats the world as its cellar.
Chef/s: Jamie Cadman. Open: all week L 12 to 2, D 7.30 to 9.30. Meals: alc (main courses £15 to £25). Service: not inc. Details: Cards accepted. 70 seats. 30 seats outside. Separate bar. No music. Wheelchair access. Children allowed. Car parking.

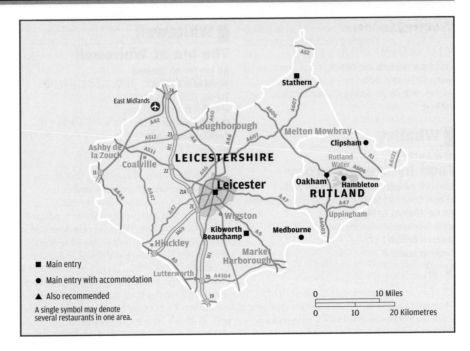

## Clipsham

### The Olive Branch

**Welcoming village pub**
Main Street, Clipsham, LE15 7SH
Tel no: **(01780) 410355**
www.theolivebranchpub.com
Gastropub | £28
Cooking score: 3

The Olive Branch appears rustic and unassuming – an impression reinforced by its beams, exposed stone walls, log fires and bare tables. It has the air of a true country local, albeit one with menus running from wild mushroom risotto to turbot with crab ravioli and crab bisque. The kitchen concentrates on excellent raw materials, most locally sourced, and details are not overlooked: praise is heaped on bread, local cheeses and homemade ice creams and sorbets. Pub staples such as Lincolnshire sausages with mustard mash and onion gravy are done very well, and classic puddings include egg custard or treacle tart.

The modern wine list is just right for the job, unfussy, imaginative and great value. Prices start at £14.
**Chef/s:** Sean Hope. **Open:** all week L 12 to 2 (5 Sat, 3 Sun), D 7 to 9.30 (9 Sun). **Closed:** 25 and 26 Dec, 1 Jan. **Meals:** alc (main courses £14 to £25). Set L £16.50 (2 courses) to £19.50. Set D £20 (2 courses) to £25. Sun L £24.50. **Service:** not inc.
**Details:** Cards accepted. 48 seats. 24 seats outside. Separate bar. Wheelchair access. Music. Children allowed. Car parking.

## Symbols

🛏 Accommodation is available

£30 Three courses for less than £30

**V** More than three vegetarian main courses

£5 OFF £5-off voucher scheme

🍷 Notable wine list

## Hambleton

### Hambleton Hall
**Cooking that hits the heights**
Hambleton, LE15 8TH
Tel no: (01572) 756991
www.hambletonhall.com
**Modern British | £70**
**Cooking score: 7**

Hambleton achieves the often elusive trick of being an elegant country house hotel that nonetheless retains the human touch, a tribute to the efforts of Tim and Stefa Hart over the three decades they have been running the place. 'From arrival to departure, they treat you as an individual,' attests one reporter, adding 'nothing is too much trouble.' It's a majestic Victorian building peeping over trees towards Rutland Water, which makes a fine backdrop to the business of eating. In surroundings that evoke the better class of interiors magazines, Aaron Patterson's cooking hits the heights. Menu descriptions sound refreshingly simple, and display a keen eye to the seasons. Game is a strong suit, as in loin of fallow deer, served enterprisingly with roast pineapple, gin and tonic jelly and cocoa sauce, but more classical ways of doing things are not scorned. Lamb might well come with aubergine caviar and mint sauce. To begin, consider a cannelloni roll containing both squid and chorizo, served with piquant peppers, or the witty Waldorf spin that mixes walnuts, grapes, apple and celery as accompaniments to lightly curried crab salad. Flavours and seasonings remain crystal-clear throughout, all the way to desserts such as hazelnut and chocolate fondant tart, served with Valrhona chocolate sorbet and an orange reduction sauce. A wine list of all the talents has been assembled, on which Germany gets a decent shake of the stick for once. Italy, Spain and Australia also look good. 'Wines of the Moment' start at £16.50.

**Chef/s:** Aaron Patterson. **Open:** all week L 12 to 1.30, D 7 to 9.30. **Meals:** alc (main courses £32 to £40). Set L £20 (2 courses) to £25. Set D £37 to £46. Sun L £41.50. Tasting menu £60. **Service:** 12.5%

(optional). **Details:** Cards accepted. 60 seats. Separate bar. No music. No mobile phones. Wheelchair access. Children allowed. Car parking.

## Kibworth Beauchamp

### Firenze
**Relaxed Italian with simple, satisfying food**
9 Station Street, Kibworth Beauchamp, LE8 0LN
Tel no: (0116) 2796260
www.firenze.co.uk
**Italian | £30**
**Cooking score: 3**

Lino and Sarah Poli have been running this enterprising Italian restaurant for a decade now. A light colour scheme makes the room feel pleasant and relaxed, while Lino's cooking aims to satisfy rather than push any boundaries – and a high level of satisfaction is certainly achieved. Warm salad of mackerel wrapped in pancetta with saffron vinaigrette has been a successful starter, as have pasta dishes such as sea bass ravioli with spinach and orange butter sauce, or buckwheat pasta with cabbage, potato and fontina cheese. Main courses of veal kidneys with spinach, pancetta and garlic sauce emphasise the simple, precise cooking with the several flavours counterpointing each other well. Hard-to-resist desserts might include a well-made hot pear tart with liquorice ice cream. The polished, all-Italian wine list casts its net wide and is a showcase for some of the country's most respected regional producers. For best value, home in on the 'Firenze selection' – a dozen attractive tipples from £13.95 (£3.95 a glass).

**Chef/s:** Lino Poli and Stuart Batey. **Open:** Mon to Sat L 12 to 3, D 7 to 11. **Closed:** Sun, 4 days Christmas, bank hols. **Meals:** alc (main courses £14 to £30). Set L £13.50 (2 courses). Set D £17.50 (2 courses) to £27.50 (4 courses). Tasting menu from £40. **Service:** not inc. **Details:** Cards accepted. 60 seats. Wheelchair access. Music. Children allowed.

## ▮ Leicester

**NEW ENTRY**

# Entropy

42 Hinckley Road, Leicester, LE3 0RB
Tel no: (0116) 2259650
www.entropylife.com
**Modern British | £25**
**Cooking score: 4**

Regeneration may have a little way to go in the neighbourhood, but Tom and Cassandra Cockerill's bar and restaurant is smart enough. The interior – two shops knocked into one – looks both rustic and modern with lots of pale wood, a colour scheme of chocolate and neutrals and views into the kitchen. A timely formula of all-day opening, flexible menus and a laid-back ambience delivers a daily changing repertoire that displays commendable seasonal focus. The food is nearly always interesting, prices pretty fair, and extras like homemade sourdough bread show quality from the off. Deep-fried Gloucester Old Spot cheeks with sauce gribiche, and moules marinière have impressed, as have salt-and-pepper squid, and rare hanger steak with green peppercorn sauce. In its way, the breakfast menu (served all day) is as much 'out of this world' as desserts like hot chocolate fondant with pistachio, rose geranium and a lychee and melon sorbet. Service is 'second to none', wines by the glass start at £3.75.
**Chef/s:** Tom Cockerill. **Open:** all week 12 to 10 (11 to 10 Fri, 10 to 10 Sat, 10 to 7 Sun). **Closed:** 25 and 26 Dec, 1 Jan. **Meals:** alc (main courses £9 to £16). **Service:** not inc. **Details:** Cards accepted. 40 seats. 40 seats outside. Air-con. Music. Children allowed.

## ▮ Medbourne

# Horse & Trumpet

Gastro-gilded menus and daring ideas
12 Old Green, Medbourne, LE16 8DX
Tel no: (01858) 565000
www.horseandtrumpet.com
**Modern British | £36**
**Cooking score: 5**

The Horse & Trumpet started life as a village inn – although it was probably a pretty grand hostelry judging by its pristine thatched roof, three-storey sandstone exterior and copious original features. Fast-forward three centuries and the place is now a high-ranking country restaurant-with-rooms that has benefited from sensitive and sympathetic improvement, not to mention considerable talent in the kitchen. Gary Magnani's menus are gilded with the trappings of gastro-fashion and he is prepared to tackle some pretty daring ideas along the way. A salad of Cornish crab is modernised with fennel biscuit, avocado cream and lemon verbena, scallops are tinged with cumin caramel, and beetroot adds a vivid edge to wild sea bass with lobster ravioli. Elsewhere, there's a sense of seasonal cohesion about breast of partridge with game sausage, dumplings, ceps and hazelnuts, although almond salsa is a surprising addition to rack of lamb with braised breast and rosemary gnocchi. There's no let-up when it comes to desserts, either: lemon curd with barley ice cream, basil meringue and raspberry syrup is one of the kitchen's more intricate flights of fancy. Like the food, the 80-bin wine list shows serious intent with a broad span and fair prices from £17.95 (£3.60 a glass).
**Chef/s:** Gary Magnani. **Open:** Tue to Sun L 12 to 1.45 (2 Sun), Tue to Sat D 7 to 9 (9.30 Sat). **Closed:** Mon, 2 weeks Jan, 26 Dec. **Meals:** Set L £16 (2 courses) to £20. Set D £20 (2 courses) to £27.50. Sun L £25. **Service:** not inc. **Details:** Cards accepted. 48 seats. 20 seats outside. No mobile phones. Wheelchair access. Music. Children allowed. Car parking.

## ▌Oakham

### Lord Nelson's House Hotel, Nick's Restaurant

**Well-considered modern food**
11 Market Place, Oakham, LE15 6DT
Tel no: (01572) 723199
www.nicksrestaurant.co.uk
**Modern European | £30**
Cooking score: 3

£5 OFF ➡ V

The owners of this timber-framed restaurant-with-rooms are friendly, straightforward and committed, service is capably handled, and new chef David Lem's food is generally well-considered. It nevertheless piles on the ingredients in earnestly modern fashion, producing, for example, a dish of crab and crayfish ravioli with tomato fondue, aubergine caviar and sauce vierge, and mains of roasted venison with a potato and beetroot hash, fig pithiviers, confit of Savoy cabbage, savoury fig and chocolate purée and red wine jus. Enterprising desserts have included warm dark chocolate cake with chestnut cappuccino and chocolate sauce. Around 30 roving wines start at £15.95 with an Australian Sauvignon and a South African Pinotage.
**Chef/s:** David Lem. **Open:** Tue to Sun L 12 to 3, Tue to Sat D 6 to 10. **Closed:** Mon, 25 and 26 Dec. **Meals:** alc (main courses £10 to £23). Set L and D £16 (2 courses) to £21. Sun L £15.95. **Service:** not inc. **Details:** Cards accepted. 40 seats. Separate bar. No mobile phones. Wheelchair access. Music. Children allowed. Car parking.

## ▌Stathern

### Red Lion Inn

**Upbeat pub food**
2 Red Lion Street, Stathern, LE14 4HS
Tel no: (01949) 860868
www.theredlioninn.co.uk
**Gastropub | £24**
Cooking score: 2

£5 OFF £30

This whitewashed inn dating from the mid-seventeenth century is sibling of the Olive Branch, Clipsham (see entry) and is to be found in the heart of the Vale of Belvoir. The atmosphere is as convivial as country inns should be, with local ingredients in the kitchen and a cooking style that brings the traditional pub repertoire up to date. Pressed Eastwell pork terrine with green bean and hazelnut salad might start you off, before sea bream with chorizo Parmentier and spinach comes into view. Prime Lincolnshire sausages from a local butcher are served with mustard mash and onion gravy, and there are homemade ice creams, sorbets and carrot cake to finish. Wines start from £12.75.
**Chef/s:** Edward Leslie. **Open:** all week L 12 to 2 (3 Sun), Mon to Sat D 6 to 9 (8.30 Mon). **Meals:** alc (main courses £9 to £18). Set L £12 (2 courses) to £16. Set D £15 (2 courses) to £20. Sun L £18. **Service:** not inc. **Details:** Cards accepted. 60 seats. 60 seats outside. Separate bar. Wheelchair access. Music. Children allowed. Car parking.

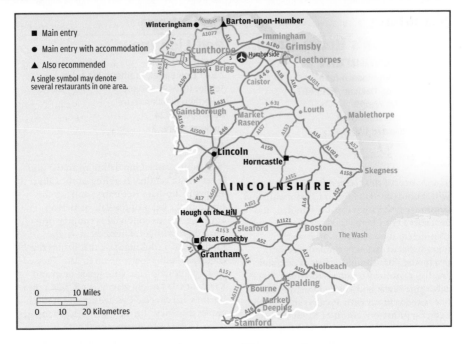

- ■ Main entry
- ● Main entry with accommodation
- ▲ Also recommended

A single symbol may denote several restaurants in one area.

## ■ Barton-upon-Humber

### ALSO RECOMMENDED
### ▲ Elio's

11 Market Place, Barton-upon-Humber, DN18 5DA
Tel no: (01652) 635147
**Italian**

Opened in 1983, Elio Grossi's engaging trattoria-with-rooms is an ever-popular fixture of the Humberside scene, noted for its conservatory/courtyard and the kitchen's fondness for fish. The day's specials could run from Scottish scallops with crispy bacon and leek sauce (£8.95) and Genovese-style red bream with olives, sun-dried tomatoes, pesto and pine kernels to osso buco in gremolata sauce (£15.95) or calf's liver veneziana. Pizzas, pasta, steaks and creamy desserts (£5.75) complete the package. Italian regional wines from £12.95 a litre. Open Mon to Sat D only.

## ■ Grantham

### NEW ENTRY
### Chequers Inn

**Popular seasonal favourite**
Main Street, Woolsthorpe by Belvoir, Grantham, NG32 1LU
Tel no: (01476) 870701
www.chequersinn.net
**Modern British | £27**
**Cooking score: 1**

£5 OFF   £30

The Chequers Inn is set among the gentle slopes of the Vale of Belvoir, and visitors might pass long summer evenings in the shaded gardens by the cricket pitch. When the seasons turn, the exposed brickwork of the adjoining bakehouse makes for a snug spot to enjoy dinner. On inspection, sluggish service was compensated by a starter of seared scallops, followed by a gutsy main of lamb served with Anna potatoes and spring vegetables. A cursory set of desserts might produce an apple crumble. House wines £14.

Chef/s: Mark Nesbit. **Open:** all week L 12 to 2.30 (4 Sun), D 6 to 9.30 (8.30 Sun). **Meals:** alc (main courses £10 to £18). Set L £11.50 (2 courses) to £15. Set D £16.50. Sun L £11.95 (2 courses). **Service:** not inc. **Details:** Cards accepted. 100 seats. 60 seats outside. No mobile phones. Wheelchair access. Music. Children allowed. Car parking.

## ▮ Great Gonerby

## Harry's Place

**A local treasure**
17 High Street, Great Gonerby, NG31 8JS
Tel no: (01476) 561780
**Modern French | £56**
**Cooking score: 7**
£5
OFF

Hidden behind large yew trees on the high street of a Lincolnshire backwater, this listed former farmhouse and wheelwright's is a fantastic resource for the local community. With just three tables, Harry and Caroline Hallam's set-up is domestic in scale and ambience (family photos and antiques), but this is backed up by professionalism where it counts. Harry's formula has served his customers well for 22 years – excellent raw materials showcased on a brief, regularly changing hand-written menu with just two choices per course – and he confidently keeps combinations fairly simple, timing accurate, and interweaves subtle flavours with stronger ones. A refreshing lack of undue fuss characterises dishes such as smoked Scottish salmon with orange caviar, vodka crème fraîche and a relish of mango, avocado, ginger, lime and coriander, or a main course of Lincolnshire salt marsh teal served with blackberries and a sauce of red wine, Madeira, sage, thyme, rosemary and mushrooms. Similarly, a well-reported fillet of wild halibut is perfectly timed and served with black beluga lentils and a sauce of red wine, coriander, chive and basil. Desserts such as prune and Armagnac ice cream served with passion fruit, or caramel mousse brûlée with strawberries and raspberries round things off gently. Caroline orchestrates things front-of-

house and the wine list extends to one hand-written side of A4, opening with Riojas at £20 (white) and £26 (red).
Chef/s: Harry Hallam. **Open:** Tue to Sat L 12.30 to 2, D 7 to 8.30. **Closed:** Sun, Mon, 1 week from 25 Dec, bank hols. **Meals:** alc (main courses £35). **Service:** not inc. **Details:** Cards accepted. 10 seats. No music. No mobile phones. Wheelchair access. Children allowed. Car parking.

## ▮ Horncastle

## Magpies

**A personally run Wolds favourite**
71-75 East Street, Horncastle, LN9 6AA
Tel no: (01507) 527004
www.dineatthemagpies.co.uk
**Modern British | £38**
**Cooking score: 5**
🍾★

Magpies is a quietly confident, personally run restaurant set in a row of black and white cottages. Inside, Caroline Gilbert is in charge of the mellow dining room, providing a welcome blend of discreet sophistication and relaxed charm. In the kitchen Andrew Gilbert likes to keep things simple, using pinpoint accuracy of timing, careful balance and pretty much faultless composition to make an impact. And make an impact he does. Expect a bedrock of modern British ideas with additions from France, Italy and beyond in starters such as saddle of rabbit stuffed with apple and sage, wrapped in Serrano ham and served on artichoke purée. For main course, loin of Lincolnshire lamb might arrive with Lancashire hotpot, while a fine piece of roast turbot may be voguishly paired with savoury Savoy cabbage, lobster mashed potato, broad beans and vanilla dressing. Desserts bring on vibrant assemblies such as a technically perfect hot pineapple tarte Tatin with coconut ice cream and candied chilli. Immense effort and care have gone into the wine list, which picks fine names from France and beyond and has a fair spread of prices. Some 17 house recommendations begin with Corney & Barrow French at £14.75.

**Chef/s:** Andrew Gilbert. **Open:** Wed to Fri and Sun L 12 to 2.30, Wed to Sun D 7 to 9. **Closed:** Mon, Tue, 27 to 30 Dec, bank hols. **Meals:** Set L £21 (2 courses) to £25. Set D £38. **Service:** not inc. **Details:** Cards accepted. 34 seats. 6 seats outside. Air-con. Separate bar. No mobile phones. Wheelchair access. Music. Children allowed.

## Hough on the Hill

### ALSO RECOMMENDED
### ▲ The Brownlow Arms

Grantham Road, Hough on the Hill, NG32 2AZ
Tel no: (01400) 250234
www.thebrownlowarms.com
**Gastropub**

This country inn dates from the seventeenth century and makes a big impression with its intimate, country house atmosphere. Dinner is the main event and the menu has a modern European flavour, opening with butter bean and bacon soup with white truffle oil (£4.95) before roast ribeye of lamb with gratin dauphinoise (£18.95) and finishing with caramel mousse, apple terrine and almond ice cream (£5.95). House wine £14.95. Open Sun L, Tue to Sat D. Accommodation.

## Lincoln

### NEW ENTRY
### The Old Bakery

26-28 Burton Road, Lincoln, LN1 3LB
Tel no: (01522) 576057
www.theold-bakery.co.uk
**Modern European | £35**
**Cooking score: 2**

£5 OFF 🍽 V

For some, this restaurant-with-rooms in Lincoln's Cathedral quarter is a 'very well run, decent operation' with a comfortable dining room and, as one couple found 'alfresco dining under glass' an added attraction. Menus offer lively, modern cooking based on well-sourced ingredients. There is a comforting familiarity about a lunch of fish and chips with tartare sauce or Lincolnshire sausages with English mustard mash potato and onion gravy, but it is

also worth exploring the evening à la carte: English boar salami with baby mozzarella and chorizo salad, and spring rack of lamb with its mini shepherd's pie and pink peppercorn sauce have been well received. Wines, from £13.50, are listed by style.

**Chef/s:** Ivano de Serio. **Open:** Tue to Sun L 12 to 3, D 7 to 9. **Closed:** 26 Dec, 1 Jan. **Meals:** alc (main courses £14 to £21). Set L £14 (2 courses) to £20. Set D £25 (2 courses) to £30. Sun L £16.50. **Service:** not inc. **Details:** Cards accepted. 65 seats. Air-con. Wheelchair access. Music. Children allowed.

### ALSO RECOMMENDED
### ▲ Wig & Mitre

32 Steep Hill, Lincoln, LN2 1LU
Tel no: (01522) 535190
www.wigandmitre.com
**Modern British**

'Food in perpetual motion' is the Hope family's description of the victuals served at their all-purpose eatery, housed in one of Lincoln's landmark ancient buildings. Drop by for breakfast, pick from the user-friendly daytime menu (served 9 to 6) or simply nip in for a drink. Otherwise, explore the seasonal carte and specials board for jazzed-up modern British dishes – perhaps pork cutlet with curly kale and roast celeriac (£12.95) or seared salmon with green Thai curry, followed by Russet apple and pear strudel (£4.95). Wines from £13.45. Open all week.

## Stamford

### READERS RECOMMEND
### Jim's Yard

**Modern French**
3 Ironmonger Street, Stamford, PE9 1PL
Tel no: (01780) 756080
www.jimsyard.biz
**'Superb food at reasonable prices'**

## ▌Winteringham

### Winteringham Fields

**Old-fashioned comfort and careful cooking**
Winteringham, DN15 9ND
Tel no: (01724) 733096
www.winteringhamfields.com
**Modern European | £52**
**Cooking score: 5**

🍷 ⊨ V

Winteringham Fields is an oddly sited stone-built restaurant-with-rooms with a well-packed feel from all the Victoriana – the panelling, well-padded chairs and sofas, cast iron ranges, and florid art certainly give it a definite personality. There are two dining rooms; the larger (and more modern) has a strident décor that divides opinion, but on the whole there's a feel of good, old-fashioned comfort about the place, one where handbags get their own stools and service is plentiful and attentive. Colin McGurran's cooking is careful and exact. Strongest successes have been registered with rare venison loin with wild mushrooms and a 'coco sauce', and pavé of Cornish halibut with a mussel and saffron fricassee and confit potatoes. Less glittering are complaints of under-seasoning letting down a pairing of crispy belly pork and king scallop with pak choi and cauliflower purée, and two courses from a seven-course surprise menu that were 'insipid and poor'. Elsewhere bread is good, the cheeseboard 'outstanding', and pre-dessert passion fruit soufflé has been praised in more than one report. Happily, the wine list keeps up the standards, with some decent offerings by the glass, bottles from £25, plus choices for those with deeper pockets.
**Chef/s:** Colin McGurran. **Open:** Tue to Sat L 12 to 3, D 7 to 10. **Closed:** Sun, Mon, 2 weeks Dec/Jan, 3 weeks Aug. **Meals:** Set L £35 (2 courses) to £39.95. Set D £65 (2 courses) to £75. Tasting menu £79. **Service:** not inc. **Details:** Cards accepted. 60 seats. Air-con. Separate bar. No music. No mobile phones. Wheelchair access. Car parking.

**Harry Hallam** Harry's Place

**Who or what inspired you to become a chef?**
As long as I can remember, food seems to have played a large (maybe obsessive!) part in my life. Early school day diaries have daily entries about food, e.g. 'today I put marmalade on my fried bread - it was yummy!'.

**If you hadn't become a chef, what would you have been?**
An architect, because I love drawing, or a surgeon as my biology teacher was always praising my knife work in dissection. (Would I have been able to pass the exams though?).

**What is the best meal you have ever eaten?**
Caroline's Kidneys Turbigo - still pink when I was two hours late home.

**What is your favourite restaurant and why?**
Le Gavroche, because of the impeccable service.

**What do you do to relax when out of the kitchen?**
Go to the north Norfolk coast to walk, or horse racing (Caroline studies the form closely!).

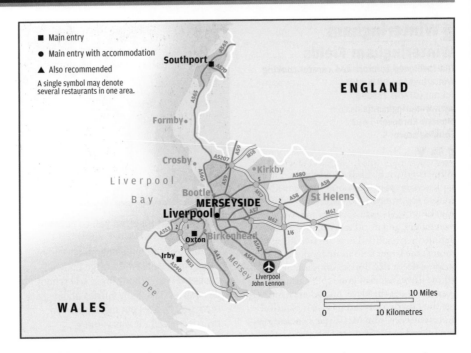

- ■ Main entry
- ● Main entry with accommodation
- ▲ Also recommended

A single symbol may denote several restaurants in one area.

ENGLAND

Southport

Formby

Crosby

Kirkby

Liverpool
Bay

Bootle
MERSEYSIDE
Liverpool

St Helens

Birkenhead

Oxton

Irby

Mersey

Liverpool
John Lennon

Dee

WALES

0                    10 Miles
0              10 Kilometres

## Irby

★ BEST NEW ENTRY 2010 ★

**NEW ENTRY**

## Da Piero
**Food that fills you with joy**
5 Mill Hill Road, Irby, CH61 4UB
Tel no: (0151) 6487373
www.dapiero.co.uk
Italian | £24
Cooking score: 5

£5 OFF   £30

Readers leave Irby's little Italian restaurant 'feeling happy with the world'. They attribute their joy to Sicilian chef Piero Di Bella's instinctive cooking and 'obvious love' for ingredients, which transcends a plain white room and out-of-the-way village location. As befits the area, portions are generous and prices reasonable, and the odd wait is attributable to hand-hewn food and a kitchen staff of one. The dishes that arrive by dumb-waiter from the kitchen above ooze quality, starting, perhaps, with tuna tartare made a shade paler with a carefully seasoned marinade and served with rocket, tomatoes and a jug of good balsamic. Pasta dishes are restrained, resisting Anglicisation and heavy sauces; spring might bring simple lemon linguine or spaghetti alla vongole, flecked with parsley and chilli and crowned with just-set clams. Secondi could be an unfussy plate of charred, bursting, homemade spicy sausage – pork through and through – with flavour-boosted lentils, or excellent Denbigh lamb cutlets with Wirral asparagus and fine creamed celeriac. Desserts are unashamed crowd-pleasers, done very well: homemade Amaretto ice cream is intense and creamy, chocolate semifreddo a stunner, even served with bizarrely out-of-place blobs of squirty cream. While Piero labours upstairs, wife Dawn is in charge front-of-house, dressing salads with the house olive oil (from the slopes of Mount Etna) and telling stories that unselfconsciously testify to the kitchen's high standards. An all-Italian wine list, featuring plenty of organic and unusual choices, starts at £15.75.

Chef/s: Piero Di Bella. **Open:** Tue to Sat D only 6 to 11 (12 Sat). **Closed:** Sun, Mon, 25 and 26 Dec, 1 and 2 Jan, 2 weeks Aug. **Meals:** alc (main courses £8 to £22). **Service:** not inc. **Details:** Cards accepted. 22 seats. Wheelchair access. Music. Children allowed.

## ▌Liverpool

### Blake's

Yeah, yeah, yeah...
Hard Day's Night Hotel, Central Buildings, 41 North John Street, Liverpool, L2 6RR
Tel no: (0151) 2432121
www.harddaysnighthotel.com
Modern British | £33
Cooking score: 4

 **V**

The Hard Day's Night Hotel exerts one hell of a pull for Beatles fans visiting the city. The theming isn't as tacky or overpowering as the name might lead you to expect, and in Blake's (after Sir Peter Blake, the artist responsible for the iconic image for *Sgt Pepper's Lonely Hearts Club Band*), the black-and-white portraits of the 60 historical figures that feature on the album cover are quite restrained. The menu keeps it simple too, with some eight starters ranging from scallops, cauliflower purée and curry oil to warm chicken sausage with a casserole of white bean and cep sauce. Mains bring pork fillet Wellington teamed with bacon and sage faggots, truffle mash, roasted roots and belly pork crackling, and sea bass with smoked haddock and clam and potato broth. A trio of blackcurrant – steamed pudding, parfait and crème brûlée – to finish should tempt the sweet-toothed. House wine is £14.95.
Chef/s: Andy Scott. **Open:** all week L 12 to 2.30, Mon to Sat D 6 to 10. **Meals:** alc (main courses £14 to £30). Set L and D £14.95 (2 courses) to £17.95. Sun L £16.95 (2 courses) to £19.95. **Service:** 10% (optional). **Details:** Cards accepted. 72 seats. Air-con. Separate bar. Wheelchair access. Music. Children allowed.

## London Carriage Works

Quintessential 'New Liverpool' experience
Hope Street Hotel, 40 Hope Street, Liverpool, L1 9DA
Tel no: (0151) 7052222
www.tlcw.co.uk
Modern British | £40
Cooking score: 3

£5 OFF **V**

There's a pleasing juxtaposition of town and country at the restaurant which is the lynchpin of Liverpool's smartest street, and also part of an expanding boutique hotel. The dining room, with its sculptural shards of glass and solid pillars, is resolutely urban, but the menu is littered with produce from the region's finest suppliers. Readers characterise the dishes as 'food you want to get stuck into'. Translation from page to plate can please or disappoint; on inspection, a starter salad of local goats' cheese croûtes was lively and robust, but a pasty rarebit topping did nothing for a fresh-tasting chunk of smoked haddock. Readers report some bang-on cooking, some near misses, and cheerful, unobtrusive service; clearly, at its best, this quintessential 'New Liverpool' experience can still deliver. A concise, restrained wine list starts at £14.95 (£3.90 a glass).
Chef/s: Paul Askew. **Open:** all week L 12 to 5, D 5 to 10. **Meals:** alc (main courses £15 to £28). Set L and D £18.95 (2 courses) to £23.95. Sun L £28 (3 courses). Tasting menu £60. **Service:** not inc. **Details:** Cards accepted. 100 seats. Air-con. Separate bar. Wheelchair access. Music. Children allowed.

## NEW ENTRY
## Panoramic

**Make a meal of the views**
34th Floor, West Tower, Brook Street, Liverpool,
L3 9PJ
Tel no: (0151) 2365534
www.panoramicliverpool.com
**Modern European | £40**
**Cooking score: 2**

Impressive even in the murk, the 'superb' views are the thing at this surprisingly intimate, business-friendly 34th-floor newcomer. Below, the Liver birds are but sparrows and the city scurries noiselessly. In the curvy, rust-and-biscuit room, where the lightbox tables glow in alien fashion from within, attempts at polished service succeed more often than they fail. Panoramic's ambition isn't always matched in the execution, but dishes done with a sure hand might include a plate of pretty, jewel-like vegetable carpaccio, crisp-skinned mackerel fillet with squat barrels of poached pear, or a mango dessert plate with a nod to coconut. A slimline wine list starts at £16 (£3.75 a glass). **Chef/s:** Chris Marshall. **Open:** all week L 12 to 2.30, D 6 to 10. **Closed:** bank hols. **Meals:** Set L £19.50. Set D £32 (2 courses) to £42. Sun L £25. **Service:** 10% (optional). **Details:** Cards accepted. 48 seats. Air-con. Separate bar. No mobile phones. Wheelchair access. Music. Children allowed.

## The Side Door

**Good-value ticket for culture vultures**
29a Hope Street, Liverpool, L1 9BQ
Tel no: (0151) 7077888
www.thesidedoor.co.uk
**Modern European | £25**
**Cooking score: 2**

£5 OFF  £30

Just around the corner from the Philharmonic Hall and Liverpool's theatreland hot spots, this unpretentious two-floored bistro is a handy ticket for culture vultures and foodies alike. Rustic bare floors and deep red walls set the tone for a menu that does some eclectic conjuring tricks with North Country

ingredients. Expect to find confit duck with creamed lentils alongside chilli-fried squid with king prawn and wild mushroom risotto or whole sea bass and caponata in competition with roast Goosnargh duck breast and sweet sherry shallots. Light lunches are brilliant value, and puddings play it straight, with the likes of Seville orange tart. Wines from £13. **Chef/s:** Sean Millar. **Open:** Mon to Sat L 12 to 2.30, D 5 to 10. **Closed:** Sun, 25 Dec, bank hols. **Meals:** alc (main courses £11 to £16). Set D £15.95 to £27.95. **Service:** not inc. **Details:** Cards accepted. 50 seats. Air-con. Wheelchair access. Music. Children allowed.

## 60 Hope Street

**A confident approach to local produce**
60 Hope Street, Liverpool, L1 9BZ
Tel no: (0151) 7076060
www.60hopestreet.com
**Modern British | £35**
**Cooking score: 3**

♿ V

With a decade of service now under its belt, 60 Hope Street's easy confidence makes for a relaxing meal whether you're below decks in the bar/bistro, or above in the restaurant. Readers praise the elegance of the generously proportioned dining rooms – this was a Georgian town house – and the kitchen's preference for local produce. However, inspection revealed inconsistencies. Crisp cauliflower fritters struggled under thick, pallid batter, and pan-fried salmon with Wirral asparagus, otherwise spot-on, suffered the attentions of a strangely sweet, off-kilter hollandaise. A redeeming chocolate and raspberry mousse tart looked splodgy but tasted spectacular. The cracking wine list packs a lot of interest and serious drinking opportunities into a few pages. Spread is global, although France leads the way. There's plenty for all palates and pockets from £13.95. **Chef/s:** Sarah Kershaw. **Open:** Mon to Fri L 12 to 2.30, Mon to Sat D 5 to 10.30. **Closed:** Sun, bank hols. **Meals:** alc (main courses £13 to £29). Set L £15.95 (2 courses) to £18.95. **Service:** not inc. **Details:** Cards accepted. 90 seats. 12 seats outside. Air-con. Separate bar. Music. Children allowed.

## Our inspectors' bugbears

**Exceedingly flash websites** that conceal useful information such as location with a barrage of flash animation and 'funky' tunes.

**Websites that fail to include pertinent information** like their opening times and phone numbers.

**Closely-packed tables in serried ranks**: why do so many modern restaurants have lines of tables for two with about nine inches of space between them?

**The waiter's warmth cooling suddenly when you ask to try the local tap water.**

**Serving that tap water tepid.**

**Set menus that bear no resemblance to the fireworks of the à la carte** – a good place makes the less expensive ingredients taste fabulous too.

And, of course, **menus that turn out to be much less enticing than on the website.**

**Menus riddled with supplements** applied to anything you'd actually want to eat.

**The extra mark-up on cheeses.**

**Inattentive service** once you arrive at the finishing stage. When you're ready, the bill should be dealt with swiftly and efficiently.

## Spire

**Beguiling contemporary food**
1 Church Road, Liverpool, L15 9EA
Tel no: (0151) 7345040
www.spirerestaurant.co.uk
Modern European | £25
Cooking score: 4

£5 £30
OFF

The restaurant is a cab-ride from the city centre in the Wavertree district, but well worth the trip. In a relaxed dining room of exposed brickwork, abstract art and café-style tables, you will find a beguiling version of contemporary European cooking. Start with an assemblage of fried halloumi, pomegranate, pea shoots and garlic cream, or a more Francophile foie gras and chicken liver parfait with elderflower jelly and brioche. Then go on to, perhaps, braised shoulder and fried chump of lamb with fennel purée, asparagus and green beans. Fish dishes are robustly handled – for example turbot comes with a vegetable ragoût, smoked bacon and shallots. The chocolatey desserts will win friends, but there might also be vanilla and raspberry pannacotta with Black Muscat jelly and shortbread. A thoroughly modern wine list deals in a good international assortment, rising from Chilean varietals at £14.95 to posh Burgundies and Californian stunners.
**Chef/s:** Matt Locke. **Open:** Tue to Fri L 12 to 2.30, Mon to Sat D 6 to 9 (9.30 Fri and Sat). **Closed:** Sun, first 2 weeks Jan. **Meals:** alc (main courses £13 to £17). Set L £9.95 (2 courses) to £12.95. Set D £12.95 (2 courses) to £14.95. **Service:** 10% (optional). **Details:** Cards accepted. 70 seats. Air-con. No mobile phones. Wheelchair access. Music. Children allowed.

# Oxton

★ WINE LIST OF THE YEAR ★

## Fraiche

**Flavour-filled, mind-expanding menus**
11 Rose Mount, Oxton, CH43 5SG
Tel no: (0151) 6522914
www.restaurantfraiche.com
**Modern French | £40**
**Cooking score: 7**

'None too shabby' report readers of Merseyside's most serious restaurant, with a little understatement. Chef-patron Marc Wilkinson is, notoriously, a one-man band, cooking alone for his 20-cover restaurant in a leafy conservation village not far from deepest Liverpool. He's also responsible for commissioning the caramel-coloured glass artworks that set a calm tone in the small room, and training a front-of-house team that has gained confidence and professionalism apace. Food, too, moves on; a spring inspection found less reliance on powders and piles, and impressive technical ability applied even-handedly in the pursuit of flavour rather than showing off. Set menus come in three guises, ascending in price and complexity from the three-course Elements through the six-course Signature to the surprise Bespoke option, which showcases the most daring of Wilkinson's dishes. That's not to say Signature doesn't expand the mind – who knew that tiny, crunchy passion fruit seeds provide just the right fruity acidity to offset sweet Menai mussels and rich cauliflower velouté? The menu might continue with soft, slow-cooked pork belly with intense raisin purée and an architecturally curved take on crackling, and a perfect piece of lemon sole with bright, citrus-soused quinoa. Earthy parsley root, and just a sprinkling of parsley sherbet might work impressively with a loin of Cumbrian lamb, and several services of different house-made breads are on hand to gather either the last lick of a fine, light sauce or the final smear of salty French seaweed butter. To finish, choose either from the well-kept – and firmly Gallic – cheese trolley, or the day's dessert, perhaps an artful rhubarb 'crumble' with a pleasingly miniature ball of coconut ice cream. The wine list plunders the world's vineyards for alluring flavours and intriguing styles, but you won't need a bulging wallet to appreciate its many gems. Half-bottles are a good way in, and there are accessible house selections from £19.
**Chef/s:** Marc Wilkinson. **Open:** Fri and Sat L 12 to 1.30, Wed to Sun D 7 to 9 (6 to 8 Sun). **Closed:** Mon, Tue, 25 Dec, first 2 weeks Jan. **Meals:** Set L £20 (2 courses) to £25. Set D £40. Bespoke menu £55.
**Service:** not inc. **Details:** Cards accepted. 20 seats. 8 seats outside. Separate bar. No mobile phones. Wheelchair access. Music.

# Southport

**NEW ENTRY**

## Bistrot Vérité

**Bustling village bistro**
7 Liverpool Road, Birkdale, Southport, PR8 4AR
Tel no: (01704) 564199
**Modern European | £20**
**Cooking score: 3**

Having departed Southport's Warehouse Brasserie to set up on his own, chef/proprietor Marc Vérité has pitched his new bistro just right for its villagey Birkdale location. A pale, pretty room edged with tongue-and-groove bustles with activity in the daytime, when a bowl of frothy soupe de poisson topped with chives and a generous rouille croûte might be just the ticket for lunch. By night, main courses chalked on the blackboard include crispy pork belly with caramelised peaches or a bowl of spaghetti with tiger prawn and a proper tomato and basil sauce. Follow, perhaps, with a classic French pud like crème brûlée. Service, led by Marc's wife Michaela, is generally sunny and speedy, and a brief wine list starts with selections at £12.95 (£3 a glass). House tipples are available by the carafe.
**Chef/s:** Marc Vérité. **Open:** Tue to Sat L 12 to 1.30, D 5.30 to 9.30. **Closed:** Sun, Mon, 25 and 26 Dec, 1 Jan. **Meals:** alc (main courses £9 to £15).
**Service:** not inc. **Details:** Cards accepted. 44 seats. 16 seats outside. Air-con. Music. Children allowed.

# Michael's

**Gently inventive cooking**
47 Liverpool Road, Birkdale, Southport, PR8 4AG
Tel no: (01704) 550886
www.michaelsbirkdale.co.uk
**Modern European | £25**
**Cooking score: 2**

Michael Wichmann has garnered himself a loyal following in well-heeled Birkdale village, with a repertoire of gently inventive bistro cooking served by knowledgeable staff. Hearty butternut squash and sweet potato soup, Loch Fyne smoked salmon wrapped around fennel and beetroot, and main courses such as buttery Goosnargh chicken breast with sugar snaps and tagliatelle, or sea bass fillets with creamed leeks make the running. Finish with the signature crème brûlée, perhaps served with strawberry and rhubarb compote. Higher lighting would help with reading the menus, and the December service was notably warmer than the room itself. A short wine list suffices, with bottles from £13.
**Chef/s:** Michael Wichmann. **Open:** Tue to Sat D 6 to 8.45 (9.30 Fri and Sat). **Closed:** Sun, Mon. **Meals:** alc (main courses £10 to £21). Set D Tue to Fri 6 to 7.30 (7 Fri) £13.95 (2 courses and wine) to £16.95. **Service:** not inc. **Details:** Cards accepted. 34 seats. Wheelchair access. Music. Children allowed.

# Warehouse Brasserie

**World food in a lively setting**
30 West Street, Southport, PR8 1QN
Tel no: (01704) 544662
www.warehousebrasserie.co.uk
**Global | £30**
**Cooking score: 2**

The Warehouse, Southport town centre's main draw, is an expansive, split-level space that answers accurately to the 'brasserie' description. It is run with the kind of bustling, but friendly, efficiency on which the genre stands or falls. A menu of world favourites usually features spring rolls of one sort or another (duck perhaps, with plum sauce dip), well-wrought pasta dishes, curries, and a

flavour-packed chicken breast on creamed Brussels sprouts with bacon, roast parsnip batons and a port reduction. Desserts such as banana and toffee crème brûlée will send you away happy. A keenly priced, serviceable wine list accompanies, with glasses from £3.95.
**Chef/s:** Darren Smith. **Open:** Mon to Sat L 12 to 2, D 5.30 to 10. **Closed:** Sun, 25 and 26 Dec, 1 Jan. **Meals:** alc (main courses £11 to £25). Set L £13.95 (2 courses) to £16.95. Set D £14.95 (2 courses) to £17.95. **Service:** not inc. **Details:** Cards accepted. 128 seats. Air-con. Separate bar. Wheelchair access. Music. Children allowed.

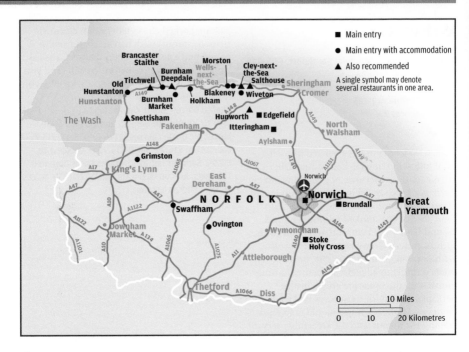

## ▌ Blakeney
### The White Horse Hotel
**Modern menus and careful cooking**
4 High Street, Blakeney, NR25 7AL
Tel no: (01263) 740574
www.blakeneywhitehorse.co.uk
**Modern British | £25**
**Cooking score: 1**

Up the steep hill from Blakeney's quay, this all-purpose inn looks smart after a refurbishment of the ground floor areas. The bar has been made more comfortable, while a new dining room is only slightly more refined. The kitchen continues to deal in straightforward modern dishes, offering among starters braised veal shank cannelloni, then carefully cooked cod with Jerusalem artichokes, Armand clams, pancetta and aïoli for mains. Desserts take in steamed fig sponge with star anise ice cream. House wine £11.95.

**Chef/s:** Duncan Philip. **Open:** all week 12 to 2.15, D 6 to 9. **Closed:** 25 Dec. **Meals:** alc (main courses £10 to £22). **Service:** not inc. **Details:** Cards accepted. 110 seats. 32 seats outside. Separate bar. No music. No mobile phones. Children allowed. Car parking.

## ALSO RECOMMENDED
### ▲ The Moorings
High Street, Blakeney, NR25 7NA
Tel no: (01263) 740054
www.blakeney-moorings.co.uk
**Modern British**

Visitors and locals flock to this cheerful café near Blakeney's quay, drawn by straightforward food and relaxed service. The kitchen is driven by an enthusiasm for Norfolk's produce, with soups, salads, sandwiches (local crab £4.25) and homemade cakes making up a flexible all-day menu. Lunch and dinner (check times in winter) bring smoked fish platters (£7.25) and loin of local venison (£16.50). House wine £14.50. Open all week.

## ▮ Brancaster Staithe
# The White Horse
Coastal pub with an incredible view
Brancaster Staithe, PE31 8BY
Tel no: (01485) 210262
www.whitehorsebrancaster.co.uk
Gastropub | £25
Cooking score: 3

🍽 V £30

The White Horse plays host to tourists, walkers and locals in equal measure and looks every inch the modern pub, from the cheering main bar to the light-filled conservatory dining room. And with the terrace making the most of views across vast salt marshes and a summer barbecue on the front patio, there's plenty of opportunity for outdoor eating. Fish is a strong suit: well reported local oysters (in tempura with wasabi mash, lemon syrup and tofu broth), excellent local mussels, as well as meaty medallions of monkfish with good aubergine caviar and red wine. Praise, too, for chicken with braised cabbage and bacon, and for a minute steak and red onion marmalade ciabatta from the excellent all-day bar menu. House wine is £13.
**Chef/s:** Rene Llupar. **Open:** all week L 12 to 2, D 6.30 to 9. **Meals:** alc (main courses £11 to £19). Bar menu available. **Service:** not inc. **Details:** Cards accepted. 90 seats. 100 seats outside. Separate bar. No mobile phones. Wheelchair access. Children allowed. Car parking.

READERS RECOMMEND
# The Jolly Sailors
Gastropub
Brancaster Staithe, PE31 8BJ
Tel no: (01485) 210314
www.jollysailorsbrancaster.co.uk
'Perfect for pizza and a pint – some of the best value along the north Norfolk coast'

## ▮ Brundall
# The Lavender House
Accomplished country cooking
39 The Street, Brundall, NR13 5AA
Tel no: (01603) 712215
www.thelavenderhouse.co.uk
Modern British | £39
Cooking score: 2

🍷

A hive of activity is afoot in this little Norfolk village, where Richard Hughes runs a cookery school as well as an accomplished restaurant in a thatched white cottage that dates from around 1540. You would expect local produce to feature strongly, and you would not be disappointed. Binham Blue, a cows'-milk cheese from north Norfolk, is fashioned into a full-flavoured starter with beetroot and orange, Brancaster mussels turn up in a main course teamed with turbot, lettuce and peas, and pheasant from Strumpshaw Fen comes with hazelnut cannelloni, pumpkin and caramelised apple. There's also a fine cheese trolley, as well as delights such as rhubarb ripple cheesecake with pink Champagne sorbet. A pedigree wine list is arranged by style, and keeps prices on a reassuringly tight rein, opening at £15.95.
**Chef/s:** Richard Hughes. **Open:** Sun L 12 to 2.30, Tue to Sat D 6 to 11. **Closed:** Mon. **Meals:** Set D £40 (6 courses). Tasting menu £58. Sun L £25. **Service:** not inc. **Details:** Cards accepted. 55 seats. Separate bar. Wheelchair access. Music. Children allowed. Car parking.

## ▮ Burnham Deepdale
ALSO RECOMMENDED
# ▲ Deepdale Café
Main Road, Burnham Deepdale, PE31 8DD
Tel no: (01485) 211055
www.deepdalecafe.co.uk
Café

The location on the north Norfolk coast makes this daytime venue popular with ramblers and bird-watchers alike. If you're up with the lark, there's a Big Breakfast for £6.75.

Otherwise, the food ranges from smoked haddock topped with a poached egg (£6.95) to a salad of homemade hummus with toasted pitta, glazed figs, olives and dips (£7.95) to a wide selection of sandwiches, with afternoon tea temptations in the shape of chocolate and Guinness cake (£1.75). Bring your own if you want to drink. Open all week.

## ▌Burnham Market

### The Hoste Arms

Quality catering for everyone
The Green, Burnham Market, PE31 8HD
Tel no: (01328) 738777
www.hostearms.co.uk
**Modern British | £35**
**Cooking score: 2**

🍷 ⇆ V

This is a former coaching inn overlooking Burnham Market's green, with a history extending back some 300 years or more. That might be said of several places in the *Guide*, but what distinguishes the Hoste is the singular quality of the operation, catering as it does for locals who have dropped in for a pint in the rustic bar and well-heeled weekenders intent on good food and wine. Successful dishes based largely on local ingredients have included an Oriental-style honey and soy-glazed pork belly with Vietnamese coleslaw, and sea bream with saffron and brown shrimp dressing. Great pains have clearly been taken over the wine list, which ranges from a wide selection by the glass (from £3.60 for Australian house) to first-growth clarets.
**Chef/s:** Aaron Smith. **Open:** all week L 12 to 2, D 6 to 9. **Meals:** alc (main courses £10 to £18). **Service:** not inc. **Details:** Cards accepted. 140 seats. 100 seats outside. Air-con. Separate bar. No music. Wheelchair access. Children allowed. Car parking.

**Tina Pemberton** The Café at Brovey Lair

### What made you want to become a chef?

I've travelled the world and been fascinated by local and ethnic produce. Since I was a student I have always enjoyed giving dinner parties. Friends used to flatter me by hardly ever asking me back and constantly encouraged me to run my own restaurant. In the end, against all the odds, I gave in.

### Which chefs do you admire?

Peter Gordon for his bold approach to fusion cooking and Donna Hay for the simplicity of her quick preparations, lots of flavour and a hint of spice. Correct food combining is as important as cooking. It's no good being creative just for effect. A lot of my early inspiration came from Wolfgang Puck, one of fusion's pioneers in California.

### What is your top culinary tip?

If you're cooking fish take it off the heat before it's cooked through. It must never be allowed to overcook. I have returned more fish dishes to the kitchen than I've eaten first time around. Fast, fresh and full of flavour is my mantra. Allow lots of time to prep so you can enjoy the company of your guests.

# Cley-next-the-Sea

## ALSO RECOMMENDED
## ▲ Cley Windmill
Cley-next-the-Sea, NR25 7RP
Tel no: (01263) 740209
www.cleywindmill.co.uk
**British**

Standing proud above the north Norfolk salt marshes, Cley Windmill is a photogenic heritage hot spot and an oddball hideaway – if you fancy bed and board in a tower. It also offers intimate evening meals to guests and visitors alike. The sum of £25 buys you a daily changing three-course dinner – perhaps pigeon salad with baby beetroot and seared pancetta, fillet of salmon on a herbed potato cake, and homemade meringue with poached berries and cream. House wine is £12.75. Open all week D only.

# Diss

## READERS RECOMMEND
## Weavers Wine Bar & Eating House
**British**
Market Hill, Diss, IP22 4JZ
Tel no: (01379) 642411
www.weavers-diss.com
**'Very dependable, sound bistro food, same chef/proprietor for more than 20 years'**

# Edgefield

## The Pigs
**Gutsy food in a proper pub**
Norwich Road, Edgefield, NR24 2RL
Tel no: (01263) 587634
www.thepigs.org.uk
**Gastropub | £20**
**Cooking score: 1**

**V**

This whitewashed country pub is a thoroughly characterful enterprise, where locally reared meats, North Sea fish, and game from local shoots are among the bill of fare,

and kids get their own menu. 'Iffits' are Norfolk's answer to tapas, including rarebit toasts and potted pork, while more substantial dishes encompass the ever-popular omelette Arnold Bennett, rosemary-roasted chicken breast stuffed with sausagemeat, or a six-ounce mutton burger with cucumber and mint chutney and pickled red cabbage, in a spelt bun. Wines are arranged by style, from £14.75.
**Chef/s:** Tim Abbott. **Open:** Tue to Sun L 12 to 2.30 (3 Sun), Tue to Sat D 6 to 9. **Closed:** Mon (except bank hols). **Meals:** alc (main courses £10 to £15). **Service:** not inc. **Details:** Cards accepted. 80 seats. 40 seats outside. Separate bar. Wheelchair access. Music. Children allowed. Car parking.

# Great Yarmouth

## Seafood Restaurant
**Welcoming, reliable and consistent**
85 North Quay, Great Yarmouth, NR30 1JF
Tel no: (01493) 856009
www.theseafood.co.uk
**Seafood | £35**
**Cooking score: 2**
£5
OFF

Miriam and Christopher Kikis have run their welcoming seafood restaurant for some 30 years, suggesting a rare level of reliability and consistency. They deal in 'superb fish, both execution and flavours'. Monkfish in a curry sauce or spicy seafood soup lead on to main courses like perfectly timed Dover sole with a herb butter and grilled skate with black butter, the last prompting one reporter to comment that 'good fish cooked in the classic style is hard to find'. In addition, there's lobster every which way and steaks for those who must. House wine from £12.75.
**Chef/s:** Christopher Kikis. **Open:** Mon to Fri L 12 to 1.45, Mon to Sat D 6.30 to 10.30. **Closed:** Sun, 2 weeks Christmas, 2 weeks May, bank hols. **Meals:** alc (main courses £11 to £22). Set L £15.95 (2 courses) to £21.95. Set D £27 (2 courses) to £35. **Service:** not inc. **Details:** Cards accepted. 42 seats. Air-con. Separate bar. Wheelchair access. Music. Car parking.

## Grimston

### Congham Hall, The Orangery

Not just a pretty face...
Lynn Road, Grimston, PE32 1AH
Tel no: (01485) 600250
www.conghamhallhotel.co.uk
**Modern British | £48**
**Cooking score: 3**

A handsome Georgian manor house not far
from Sandringham, Congham Hall boasts
grounds that are not just pretty to look at (the
Orangery restaurant has delicious parkland
views through tall windows), but which also
earn their keep. No fewer than 700 varieties of
herbs are grown in the kitchen garden. Jamie
Murch's kitchen is as much a hive of activity as
the garden, delivering a style of modernised
country cooking perfectly in keeping with the
surroundings. Start with seared scallops,
accompanied by fig chutney, parsnip purée
and truffle oil, or perhaps local roe deer served
carpaccio fashion, with Parmesan and
creamed horseradish. Main courses keep
things traditional, offering red mullet with
roasted fennel, or lamb chump with wild
mushrooms, salsify and red wine. Desserts end
things on a high with the likes of dark
chocolate and rum brûlée with coconut sorbet
and sugared pistachios. A lot of effort has gone
into developing the style-led wine list. The
bidding opens with a dozen carefully chosen
house recommendations from £20 (£5 a
glass), although value increases as you move
higher up the financial scale.
**Chef/s:** Jamie Murch. **Open:** all week L 12 to 2, D 7
to 9. **Meals:** Set L £16.25 (2 courses) to £20.75. Set D
£41 (2 courses) to £48. Sun L £23. **Service:** not inc.
**Details:** Cards accepted. 40 seats. 24 seats outside.
Separate bar. No music. No mobile phones.
Children allowed. Car parking.

## Holkham

### Victoria at Holkham

Idiosyncratic colonial hotel
Park Road, Holkham, NR23 1RG
Tel no: (01328) 711008
www.victoriaatholkham.co.uk
**Modern British | £30**
**Cooking score: 1**

Handsome Rajasthani furniture and Indian
artefacts suit the easy scale of the rooms at this
impressive Victorian building on the
Holkham Estate. As a postmodern country
house hotel it works: no pretentions, staff are
relaxed and half the clientele are in jeans. The
cooking style is broad-ranging, maybe lunch
of fish and chips or wild mushroom and
Parmesan pasta, with sea bass and braised
chicory, carrots, sultanas and orange sauce the
centrepiece at dinner. House wine is £15.
**Chef/s:** Roger Hickham. **Open:** all week L 12 to 2.30,
D 7 to 9. **Meals:** alc (main courses £12 to £18). Set L
£15.50 (2 courses) to £18.50. **Service:** not inc.
**Details:** Cards accepted. 70 seats. 100 seats
outside. Wheelchair access. Music. Children
allowed. Car parking.

## Holt

READERS RECOMMEND

### Wiveton Farm Café

Café
Wiveton Hall, Holt, NR25 7TE
Tel no: (01263) 740515
www.wivetonhall.co.uk/cafe.htm
'Colourful café that uses the farm's ingredients
– a real find'

# Hunworth

## ALSO RECOMMENDED
## ▲ The Hunny Bell
The Green, Hunworth, NR24 2AA
Tel no: (01263) 712300
www.thehunnybell.co.uk
Gastropub

Part of Henry Watt's Norfolk-based Animal Inns group (see entries for Wildebeest Arms and Mad Moose Arms), the eighteenth-century Hunny Bell looks over Hunworth's pretty green in the lovely Glaven Valley. Spruced-up in a smart, contemporary style, it's worth seeking out for Norfolk ales and daily menus that combine pub classics with more innovative dishes. Potted shrimps (£5.95), shepherd's pie topped with celeriac mash (£10.95), braised pork belly with chickpeas, tomato and chorizo stew (£13.95) and baked banana and chocolate cheesecake show the style. House wine £12.95. Open all week.

# Itteringham

## NEW ENTRY
## The Walpole Arms
First-class local food
The Common, Itteringham, NR11 7AR
Tel no: (01263) 587258
www.thewalpolearms.co.uk
Gastropub | £25
Cooking score: 1
£5 OFF  £30 

First-class fresh, local produce is the star turn at this extended brick-and-timber pub close to the River Bure on the edge of the Blickling Estate. Chicken, rabbit, chorizo and prawn paella, Morston mussels steamed in cider, onions and thyme, and sea bass served with saffron mash, baked tomato and gazpacho salsa give a Mediterranean feel to the daily changing menu. The low-beamed bar offers an open fire and local ales, while the larger, lighter restaurant opens out onto a terrace. House wine is £13.25.

Chef/s: Jamie Guy. Open: all week L 12 to 3 (5 Sun), Mon to Sat D 7 to 9. Closed: 25 Dec. Meals: alc (main courses £11 to £19). Service: not inc. Details: Cards accepted. 60 seats. 40 seats outside. Separate bar. Wheelchair access. Music. Children allowed. Car parking.

# Morston

## Morston Hall
A class act by the coast
The Street, Morston, NR25 7AA
Tel no: (01263) 741041
www.morstonhall.com
Modern British | £55
Cooking score: 5
£5 OFF  

'A perfect gem of North Norfolk!' exclaimed one reporter after sampling the pleasures of the Blackistons' secluded brick-and-flint mansion opposite Morston Quay. It may put on a grand face, with its high walls, Jacobean exterior and trim gardens, but the mood is as intimate and personable as can be and everyone has a good word to say about the 'terrific' service from keen young staff. After drinks in the conservatory, dinner revolves around a daily four-course menu (no choice) brimming with local flavours. At its most acutely seasonal, the kitchen might thrill with a risotto of local summer vegetables and beetroot foam, before Morston crab salad with Stiffkey samphire (picked a few miles away). Roast fillet of beef or lightly curried saddle of lamb are also true to the region – the latter served with coriander mash, celeriac and white wine jus. For dessert, blueberry soufflé has been singled out, although the finale might involve passion fruit tart with nectarine sorbet or artisan British cheeses. The impeccably chosen global wine list is organised by grape variety, and there is particularly fine drinking to be had from the French regions (note the Trimbach Alsace Rieslings) and the Antipodes. Prices start at £18 (£4 a glass).
Chef/s: Galton Blackiston, Richard Bainbridge and Samantha Wegg. Open: Sun L 12.30 for 1 (1 sitting), all week D 7.30 for 8 (1 sitting). Closed: 25 and 26

Dec, Jan. **Meals:** Set D £55 (4 courses). Sun L £34.
**Service:** not inc. **Details:** Cards accepted. 50 seats.
No music. No mobile phones. Wheelchair access.
Children allowed. Car parking.

# Norwich

## 1Up at the Mad Moose
Pub/brasserie on the up
2 Warwick Street, Norwich, NR2 3LD
Tel no: (01603) 627687
www.themadmoose.co.uk
Modern British | £25
Cooking score: 2

Out of the same stable as the Wildebeest Arms
(see entry), the Mad Moose inhabits a trendy
quarter of Norwich and treads a similar path
to its sibling. Pride of place goes to the sleek,
strikingly decorated 1Up restaurant on the first
floor of the Edwardian building, where
modish brasserie food is the deal. Expect
seared smoked eel with warm pigeon breast,
quince and lemon aïoli, ahead of confit pork
belly with horseradish gnocchi and butternut
squash, with desserts such as pineapple tarte
Tatin and star anise ice cream to finish.
Meanwhile, real ales and eclectic pub grub
nourish the crowds in the heavily populated
bar. House wine is £14.
**Chef/s:** Eden Derreck. **Open:** Sun L 12 to 3, Mon to
Sat D 7 to 9.30. **Closed:** 25 and 26 Dec. **Meals:** alc
(main courses £11 to £17). Set D £14 (2 courses) to
£18. Sun L £14 (2 courses) to £18. **Service:** not inc.
**Details:** Cards accepted. 48 seats. Separate bar.
Music. Children allowed.

## Tatlers
Assured eatery with well-judged food
21 Tombland, Norwich, NR3 1RF
Tel no: (01603) 766670
www.tatlers.com
Modern European | £20
Cooking score: 3

At ease in its substantial town house on one of
Norwich's oldest streets, Tatlers exudes an
assured informality. The lounge bar sports
leather armchairs, while two adjacent dining
rooms (which can get 'uncomfortably hot' in
summer) feature chunky wooden furniture
and modern art. Accommodating staff
offering tap water got an inspection meal off to
a flyer. Greater emphasis is now given to
British food and local ingredients, and a set
meal could be as simple as Norfolk asparagus
followed by seafood pie. The carte is more
elaborate, and a well-judged starter of smoked
haddock, crème fraîche, spinach and
Lincolnshire Poacher gratin might precede
perfectly slow-roasted belly pork with
broccoli and butter beans (slightly
undercooked), and an exemplary chocolate
brownie. Presentation is top notch, and the
house red (£15) full bodied.
**Chef/s:** Sean Creasey. **Open:** all week L 12 to 2.30,
Mon to Sat D 6 to 9.30. **Closed:** 25 and 26 Dec.
**Meals:** alc (main courses £10 to £18). Set L and D
£16 (2 courses) to £20. **Service:** not inc.
**Details:** Cards accepted. 70 seats. Separate bar.
Music. Children allowed.

## ALSO RECOMMENDED
### ▲ Mackintosh's Canteen
Unit 410, Chapelfield Plain, Norwich, NR2 1SZ
Tel no: (01603) 305280
www.mackintoshscanteen.co.uk
Modern British

Spread over two brightly airy storeys, with
views over old Norwich from the upper floor,
the Canteen offers a laid-back, unbuttoned
approach to all-day dining, together with a
canny version of crowd-pleasing brasserie
cooking. Well-conceived dishes take in

chargrilled chicken satay with guacamole and mango chutney (£5.95), salmon and spring onion fishcake and a richly sustaining take on shepherd's pie (£8.50). Finish with banana and toffee cheesecake and mascarpone (£5.25). Breakfasts, served every day, are another popular draw. Wines start at £13.95. Open all week.

## ▌Old Hunstanton

### The Neptune

**Chill-out vibes and ambitious food**
85 Old Hunstanton Road, Old Hunstanton, PE36 6HZ
Tel no: (01485) 532122
www.theneptune.co.uk
**Modern British | £38**
**Cooking score: 5**

£5 OFF 🛏

Calming vibes and a touch of romance lend a special feel to Kevin and Jacki Mangeolles' chill-out restaurant-with-rooms in a revamped seventeenth-century inn. Mellow tones, muted colours, candles and original fireplaces put everyone at their ease, and Kevin's food aims high. Given the setting, it is pretty elaborate stuff: loin of English veal is matched with cauliflower purée, deep-fried calf's tongue (a delicious 'first' for one visitor) with wild mushroom sauce, while red mullet could be paired up with broccoli purée, crab and green bean salad and pickled coconut. The kitchen is on good terms with local fishermen, and shows off their catch to telling effect, whether it's Thornham oysters or Brancaster lobster (packed into ravioli and served with pea purée). There's no denying that dishes are subtle and picture-perfect on the plate, although an inspector missed the 'wow factor' here and there. Dinner also comes with lots of top-end trappings – perhaps a mini-fish finger to start and a refreshing Pimms jelly with sweetened cucumber and apple cream as pre-dessert. To finish, a combo of milk chocolate mousse with ras-el-hanout caramel and chocolate sorbet hit the button with its gorgeous textures and 'fireworks in the mouth' – courtesy of popping candy. Jacki

oversees the suitably relaxed, chatty service and is the brains behind the sharp wine list. Eight house selections start at £15.95 (£3.60 a glass).
**Chef/s:** Kevin Mangeolles. **Open:** Sun L 12 to 2, Tue to Sun D 7 to 9. **Closed:** Mon, 26 Dec, 2 weeks Nov, 2 weeks Jan. **Meals:** alc (main courses £19 to £21). Sun L £18.50 (2 courses) to £23.50. **Service:** not inc. **Details:** Cards accepted. 24 seats. Separate bar. No mobile phones. Wheelchair access. Music. Car parking.

## ▌Ovington

### ★ BEST FISH RESTAURANT ★

### The Café at Brovey Lair

**Rave seafood in voguish surrounds**
Carbrooke Road, Ovington, IP25 6SD
Tel no: (01953) 882706
www.broveylair.com
**Pan-Asian and seafood | £48**
**Cooking score: 6**

£5 OFF 🛏 V

From the outside this looks like a private house, and inside, too, it seems like one, albeit very elegant in a *Vogue* shoot kind of way, with the brightly painted swimming pool and terrace giving a Mediterranean touch outside. The Pembertons offer 'a totally unique experience' that begins with a telephone discussion of likes and dislikes – the four-course menu is no choice and mostly fish – and ends (if you stay the night in one of two suites) with an unusual Cal-Mex breakfast. In between is dinner in the kitchen-cum-dining room with dishes prepared in front of you on the teppan grill. Tina Pemberton's cooking gives pan-Asian food a good name. She handles multiple flavours with assurance, turning out stir-fried sesame-coated chilli king prawns on a bean shoot salad with mint and coriander ahead of Portabello and oyster mushroom soup with miso and Japanese sea vegetables. For mains, Indian-spiced loin of wild halibut is baked with tamarind and coconut and comes with French beans stir-fried in pomegranate molasses, roasted red peppers, aubergine and basmati rice with pine nuts and cardamom. Bitter chocolate mocha truffle torte has impressed for dessert. Mike Pemberton handles service with panache. House wine is £16.95.

**Chef/s:** Tina Pemberton. **Open:** Mon to Sat L by arrangement, all week D 7.30 (1 sitting). **Closed:** 25 Dec. **Meals:** Set L and D £47.50 (4 courses). **Service:** 10%. **Details:** Cards accepted. 24 seats. 20 seats outside. Air-con. Separate bar. Wheelchair access. Music. Car parking.

## Salthouse

### ALSO RECOMMENDED
### ▲ Cookies Crab Shop

The Green, Salthouse, NR25 7AJ
Tel no: (01263) 740352
www.cookies.shopkeepers.co.uk
**Seafood**

The McKnespieys have been catching crabs and smoking fish on the north Norfolk coast for generations, and run their tiny set-up from an archetypal flint cottage overlooking the marshes. Eat in the shop, sit in the garden shed or relax under a parasol with one of their 'Royal' seafood salads (loaded with anything from lobster to eel), a bowl of kipper and tomato soup or a filled jacket potato. Prices from £5 to £13.50. Drink tea, Norfolk apple juice or BYO wine (no corkage). No cards. Open all week.

## Snettisham

### ALSO RECOMMENDED
### ▲ The Rose and Crown

Old Church Road, Snettisham, PE31 7LX
Tel no: (01485) 541382
www.roseandcrownsnettisham.co.uk
**Gastropub**

Crammed with period atmosphere, this fourteenth-century whitewashed pub is adorned with climbing roses and full of twisty passageways and beams within. As well as traditional favourites such as moules marinière, and beef bourguignon (£12.50), the kitchen also likes to try out new ideas, such as Thai-style red snapper in an oriental broth

with udon noodles and a tempura-battered tiger prawn (£15.75). Crème brûlée tart with banana ice cream and candied ginger (£5.20) is one of the more inventive desserts. House wines from £12.95. Open all week.

## Stoke Holy Cross
# The Wildebeest Arms

**Fashionable pub/restaurant**
82-86 Norwich Road, Stoke Holy Cross, NR14 8QJ
Tel no: (01508) 492497
www.thewildebeest.co.uk
**Modern European | £29**
**Cooking score: 2**

🍷 V £30

The Wildebeest (a member of a small group aptly called Animal Inns) is a white-faced creature that doubles as a local watering-hole and accomplished restaurant. The dining room is pleasingly informal, with bare tables and African masks, and the cooking ploughs a modern European furrow. Expect something like carpaccio of Norfolk venison with apple jelly, Parmesan and balsamic vinaigrette to start, followed by chargrilled beef fillet with celeriac purée, confit beetroot, Alsace bacon, pine nuts, shiitakes and Madeira. Lemon tart comes with rhubarb in two guises – poached and sorbet. A carefully annotated wine list reveals real passion in that department, with a raft of house selections at the standard price of £14.95 (£3.95 a glass) and good global coverage.

**Chef/s:** Dan Smith. **Open:** all week L 12 to 2 (12.30 to 2.30 Sun), D 7 to 9. **Closed:** 25 and 26 Dec. **Meals:** alc (main courses £13 to £25). Set L £13.95 (2 courses) to £16.95. Set D £16.50 (2 courses) to £19.95. **Service:** not inc. **Details:** Cards accepted. 90 seats. 20 seats outside. Wheelchair access. Music. Children allowed. Car parking.

## Swaffham
### Strattons

**Eco-friendly Palladian town house**
4 Ash Close, Swaffham, PE37 7NH
Tel no: (01760) 723845
www.strattonshotel.com
**Modern British | £40**
**Cooking score: 3**

🛏 V

The Scotts' pristine Palladian villa is not only an arty boutique hotel, but also flies the green flag with pride. Eco-friendly principles define just about everything, from the design and heating to the locally sourced, organic food. Meals are served in a quirkily decorated 'semi-basement' dubbed The Rustic. Dinner menus (fixed-price on Saturdays) are peppered with Norfolk flavours. Vanessa Scott offers dishes such as mackerel with roasted plums on toasted focaccia bread, and slow-roast leg of lamb with saffron, but reports suggest the kitchen performs unevenly: one couple were impressed by excellent bread and a complimentary cheeseboard taster, but not by a 'rather ordinary' dish consisting of leek mash, a 'small piece of cod' and mushroom gravy. Organic tipples (from £14) loom large on the wine list.
**Chef/s:** Vanessa Scott. **Open:** all week L 12 to 2, D 7 to 9 (8 Sun). **Closed:** 23 to 26 Dec. **Meals:** Set L £30 (2 courses) to £35. Set D £40. **Service:** not inc. **Details:** Cards accepted. 25 seats. 8 seats outside. No mobile phones. Music. Children allowed. Car parking.

## Titchwell
### ALSO RECOMMENDED
### ▲ Titchwell Manor

Titchwell, PE31 8BB
Tel no: (01485) 210221
www.titchwellmanor.com
**Modern European**

Remodelled with a sense of style, this large Victorian redbrick house on the coast road oozes rustic sophistication. Eat in any one of a series of rooms sporting open fires, clattering bare boards and leather sofas, or more formally in the garden conservatory. The kitchen works to a concise modern repertoire offering flexible menus. Mussels (£9) or fishcakes for lunch, an all-day tapas menu (from £3), and rump and 24-hour shin of Dexter beef (£19) as the centrepiece at dinner. House wine £14.50. Accommodation. Open all week.

## Wiveton
### Wiveton Bell

**Gastropub with clever seasonal menus**
Blakeney Road, Wiveton, NR25 7TL
Tel no: (01263) 740101
www.wivetonbell.co.uk
**Modern British | £25**
**Cooking score: 1**

🛏 V £30

Chef Nick Anderson made his name in King's Lynn, but recently decamped to this gastropub overlooking Wiveton's green and church. As a result, the cooking has moved up a gear and it's wise to book a table either in the spruced-up bar with its polished wooden floor, log fire and local art, or the conservatory dining room. Inventive seasonal menus tempt visitors to make the short drive inland for big bowls of Morston mussels, Briston pork belly with apple and cider jus, Cley smokehouse haddock, and sticky toffee pudding. House wine is £12.50.
**Chef/s:** Nick Anderson. **Open:** all week L 12 to 2.15 (3 Sun), D 6 to 9. **Closed:** 25 Dec. **Meals:** alc (main courses £9 to £18). Sun L £10.95. **Service:** not inc. **Details:** Cards accepted. 60 seats. 30 seats outside. Separate bar. No music. Children allowed. Car parking.

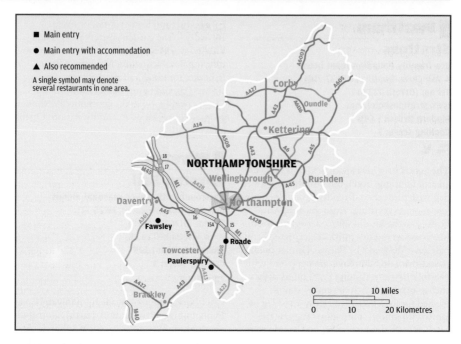

## Fawsley

**NEW ENTRY**
## Equilibrium at Fawsley Hall
**Historic building, cutting-edge food**
Fawsley Hall, Fawsley, NN11 3BA
Tel no: (01327) 892000
www.fawsleyhall.com
**Modern British | £59**
**Cooking score: 5**

£5 OFF

Fawsley Hall once played host to Good Queen
Bess and has seen centuries of gracious living
during its long life. Set in 200 acres of lush
parkland, it now houses a thoroughly modern
operation offering all the conference,
wedding, health and beauty facilities you
could wish for. The original Tudor kitchen
(complete with a grand inglenook) has been
transformed into Equilibrium – an
atmospheric setting for Nigel Godwin's
'highly complex and innovative' twenty-first
century cooking. Dinner revolves around a
ten-course tasting menu (with some choice

along the way). Elaborate strokes and high-
fashion gestures abound: just consider
Godwin's signature dish – an intricately
worked, tripartite creation involving a
ballottine of pigeon breast with foie gras,
celeriac rémoulade, hazelnuts and pickled
pear, alongside a plate of pigeon parfait with
brioche, plus a separate bowl of savoury
pigeon 'tea' containing confit leg wrapped in
gold leaf. Drama also extends to an appetiser
of smoked eel croquettes unveiled at the table
beneath and upturned martini glass filled with
smoke. Occasionally these deliberately
intricate devices miss a beat – a dessert of
artichoke crème brûlée, toasted oats and olive
oil gel came with a truffle ice cream so intense
it overpowered everything else. The wine list
mixes starry names with everyday bottles
from £19.

**Chef/s:** Nigel Godwin. **Open:** Tue to Sat D 7 to 9.30.
**Closed:** Sun, Mon, 24 to 26 Dec, 31 Dec. **Meals:** Set
D £59 (7 courses). **Service:** 12.5% (optional).
**Details:** Cards accepted. 26 seats. Separate bar. No
mobile phones. Wheelchair access. Music. Car
parking.

## ▌Paulerspury
### The Vine House
Beguiling home-from-home
100 High Street, Paulerspury, NN12 7NA
Tel no: (01327) 811267
www.vinehousehotel.com
Modern British | £30
Cooking score: 3

The 300-year-old limestone house (which was once two) is a thoroughly charming restaurant-with-rooms set in an equally alluring village not far from Towcester. Inside, the feel is homely but elegant, with bookshelves in the dining room and pleasant views on to the garden. A covered single table outside looks perfect for a summer-evening proposal. Marcus Springett cooks a three-course menu, using fresh, seasonal ingredients, starting perhaps with dry-cured bacon and mushroom risotto with smoked olive oil, and motoring on with red mullet in saffron and Indian spices, or Goosnargh duck with treacle-braised red cabbage and chocolate. Locally picked Victoria plums and blackcurrants go into a mousse, served with vanilla shortbread, to finish. Decent French stuff leads the vinous charge, with prices from £15.95.
**Chef/s:** Marcus Springett. **Open:** Tue to Sat L 12 to 2, Mon to Sat D 6 to 10 (9.30 Mon). **Closed:** Sun. **Meals:** Set L and D £26.95 (2 courses) to £29.95. **Service:** 12.5%. **Details:** Cards accepted. 33 seats. Separate bar. No music. Wheelchair access. Children allowed. Car parking.

## ▌Roade
### Roade House
Well-tuned modern food
16 High Street, Roade, NN7 2NW
Tel no: (01604) 863372
www.roadehousehotel.co.uk
Modern British | £31
Cooking score: 4

A few minutes' cruise off the M1, and you're in Roade, an unruffled village not far from Althorp and the motor-racing at Silverstone. This high-street hotel was once a village local called the White Hart. Bought by the Kewleys in 1983, it has become a winner with locals. 'This is my favourite restaurant', declares one regular. 'The welcome is warm and friendly and not stuffy at all, the surroundings are lovely and the food is wonderful.' The smartly appointed dining room, done in relaxing pale shades, is the scene for Chris's assured, unpretentious modern cooking, which might take in a main course of pot-roast pork belly with Irish black pudding and caramelised apple. Start with smoked haddock and salmon ravioli in prawn bisque, and end with something like ginger parkin, served with pineapple, spicy syrup and crème fraîche. The wine list is arranged by style, with prices from £15 for Languedoc house recommendations.
**Chef/s:** Chris Kewley. **Open:** Mon to Fri L 12 to 1.45, Sun 12 to 2, Mon to Sat D 7 to 9.30. **Closed:** bank hol Mon, between Christmas and New Year. **Meals:** Set L £20 (2 courses) to £23. Set D £26 (2 courses) to £31. **Service:** not inc. **Details:** Cards accepted. 45 seats. Air-con. Separate bar. No music. Wheelchair access. Children allowed. Car parking.

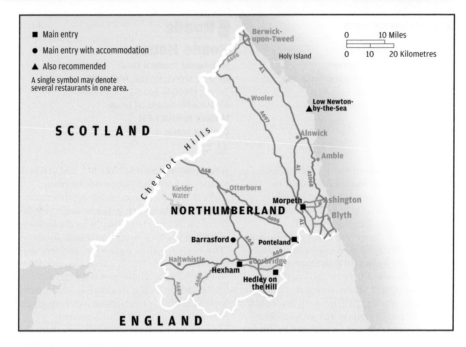

■ Main entry
● Main entry with accommodation
▲ Also recommended

A single symbol may denote
several restaurants in one area.

0    10 Miles
0    10    20 Kilometres

Berwick-upon-Tweed
Holy Island
Low Newton-by-the-Sea ▲
Wooler
SCOTLAND
Cheviot Hills
Alnwick
Amble
A68
Kielder Water
Otterburn
NORTHUMBERLAND
Morpeth
Ashington
Blyth
Barrasford ●
Ponteland
Haltwhistle
Corbridge
Hexham ■
Hedley on the Hill
ENGLAND

## Barrasford

### The Barrasford Arms
Barrasford, NE48 4AA
Tel no: (01434) 681237
www.barrasfordarms.co.uk
Gastropub | £25
Cooking score: 2

The bar may be traditional and its atmosphere lively, but by contrast the dining room is calmly decorated and complements chef/patron Tony Binks' robust cooking, with its generous portions, clear flavours and sound-quality ingredients. Farmhouse classics are prepared with care and presented with modern style, and there is a palpable level of achievement in a meal that opens with Northumbrian ham terrine with homemade piccalilli, goes on to local rack of lamb, and finishes with soft pistachio meringue. The short wine list is reasonably priced and offers nine by the glass (from £2.95) and house vino from £12.50.

Chef/s: Tony Binks and Simon Walsh. Open: Tue to Sun L 12 to 2 (3 Sun), Mon to Sat D 6.30 to 9. Closed: bank hol Mon. Meals: alc (main courses £9 to £16). Set L £11.50 (2 courses) to £14.50. Sun L £12.50 (2 courses) to £15. Service: not inc. Details: Cards accepted. 60 seats. 20 seats outside. Separate bar. Wheelchair access. Music. Children allowed. Car parking.

## Hedley on the Hill

### The Feathers Inn
Hedley on the Hill, NE43 7SW
Tel no: (01661) 843607
www.thefeathers.net
Gastropub | £21
Cooking score: 2

There's a genuine family feel to this former drovers' inn, and it is the beating heart of the rural community too. Daily changing menus support local produce and the kitchen bristles with honest endeavour. Chef Rhian Cradock's cook book collection is shared with guests and sets the scene for such delights as homemade black pudding of 'savoury richness' or grilled North Sea lobster with chunky chips, while homemade yoghurt with gooseberries and oats makes a splendid finale. Over 20 wines come by the glass with house bottles from £12.50, or try one of several north-east ales.

**Chef/s:** Rhian Cradock. **Open:** Tue to Sun L 12 to 2 (2.30 Sun), Tue to Sat D 6 to 8.30. **Closed:** 2 weeks Jan. **Meals:** alc (main courses £8 to £17). **Service:** not inc. **Details:** Cards accepted. 40 seats. 20 seats outside. No music. Children allowed. Car parking.

## ▮ Hexham

## Bouchon Bistrot

**French flair at reasonable prices**
4-6 Gilesgate, Hexham, NE46 3NJ
Tel no: (01434) 609943
www.bouchonbistrot.co.uk
**French | £23**
**Cooking score: 4**

£5 OFF   £30

Gregory Bureau's restaurant occupies three floors of a stark, stone-clad Grade II-listed building. While not blazing a revolutionary trail, the menu offers classic regional French dishes at reasonable prices and shows genuine flair along the way. Salade paysanne with boudin noir and smoked duck magret makes a promising start, or there could be oxtail terrine with sauce ravigote. Simple main courses might include roasted farmhouse chicken breast with wild mushrooms and gratin dauphinoise, and seared mullet with roasted fennel, tomato and ratte potatoes and dill sauce. Desserts end things on a high with a dark chocolate terrine with nut milk sauce. The international wine list won't break the bank either; there are a dozen choices by the glass with house French £12.75 a bottle.

**Chef/s:** Nicolas Duhill. **Open:** Tue to Sat L 12 to 2, D 6 to 9.30. **Closed:** Sun, Mon, 10 days Feb, bank hols. **Meals:** alc (main courses £12 to £17). Set L £9.95 (2 courses) to £12.95. Set D (6 to 7) £12.95 (2 courses)

to £14.95. **Service:** not inc. **Details:** Cards accepted. 130 seats. Air-con. Wheelchair access. Music. Children allowed. Car parking.

## READERS RECOMMEND

## Dipton Mill Inn

**Gastropub**
Dipton Mill Road, Hexham, NE46 1YA
Tel no: (01434) 606577
www.diptonmill.co.uk
**'Unpretentious, good quality and good value'**

## ▮ Low Newton-by-the-Sea

## ALSO RECOMMENDED
## ▲ The Ship Inn

Newton Square, Low Newton-by-the-Sea, NE66 3EL
Tel no: (01665) 576262
www.shipinnnewton.co.uk
**Gastropub**

Tucked into a little square a few yards from the beach, this whitewashed inn was once a fisherman's cottage. It's still got all its rustic Georgian character, and a good part of its modern charm is accounted for by the food, ordered at the bar from daily changing menus. Start with grilled goats' cheese with tomato and basil (£4.25), and proceed to lamb cutlets from a local butcher, served with mint sauce and cabbage (£11.50). Chocolate espresso cake is a must-have dessert (£4.50). House wine is £13.25. Open all week. Cash only.

### Symbols

🛏 Accommodation is available

£30 Three courses for less than £30

**V** More than three vegetarian main courses

£5 OFF £5-off voucher scheme

🍾 Notable wine list

## | Morpeth

NEW ENTRY
### Black Door Bar & Dining Rooms
Nicely ambitious food
59 Bridge Street, Morpeth, NE61 1PQ
Tel no: (01670) 516200
www.blackdoorbaranddiningrooms.co.uk
Modern British | £23
Cooking score: 2

£5 OFF **V**

A boon for any neighbourhood – and especially for this Northumberland market town – the Black Door is part of a small group with a good reputation. It's spread over three characterful floors, hung with prints of local castles in gilded frames. Service is pleasant, if casual, and the food displays a little welcome ambition in dishes like a starter of herb-rolled ballottine of poached salmon with a cool, oniony crème fraîche. Veggies get a good deal, with main courses such as a wedge of Parmesan polenta, crisp outside and creamy within, topped with a tomato sauce, wild mushrooms and a poached egg. An international wine list starts at £14 (£3.50 a glass).
**Chef/s:** Steve Burkitt. **Open:** all week L 12 to 3 (5 Sun), Mon to Sat D 5 to 11. **Closed:** 26 Dec, 1 Jan. **Meals:** alc (main courses £10 to £18). Set L £10 (2 courses) to £12.95. Set D £12.95 (2 courses) to £14.95. Sun L £14.95. **Service:** not inc. **Details:** Cards accepted. 90 seats. Air-con. Separate bar. Wheelchair access. Music. Children allowed.

## | Ponteland

### Café Lowrey
Brasserie favourites with panache
33-35 The Broadway, Darras Hall, Ponteland, NE20 9PW
Tel no: (01661) 820357
www.cafelowrey.co.uk
Modern British | £25
Cooking score: 4

£30

Ian Lowrey's bright, modern eatery is just a little way over the border into Northumberland. Properly dressed, well-spaced tables add class to the essentially informal approach, and the food is all about brasserie favourites presented with an unexpected level of panache. Grilled black pudding with mash, crispy onions and mustard cream is a loin-girding, cold-weather starter. Those of lighter tastes might open with a soufflé of Cheddar and spinach. Then it's on to fish, either simply grilled and served with mushy peas and chips, or in the shape of sea bass with crayfish and basil cream sauce. Meaty crowd-pleasers include the likes of sirloin steak or duck leg confit. Less familiar preparations might prove even more tempting, as in the venison loin that comes with goats' cheese mash, red cabbage and griottine cherries. Chocolate tart or crème brûlée round things off in style. Wines are an inspired international jumble, with prices from £13.50.
**Chef/s:** Ian Lowrey. **Open:** Sat and Sun L 12 to 2, Tue to Sat D 5.30 to 10. **Closed:** bank hols. **Meals:** alc (main courses £11 to £23). Set D £13.50 (2 courses) to £15.50. Sun L £13.95. **Service:** not inc. **Details:** Cards accepted. 70 seats. Air-con. Wheelchair access. Music. Children allowed. Car parking.

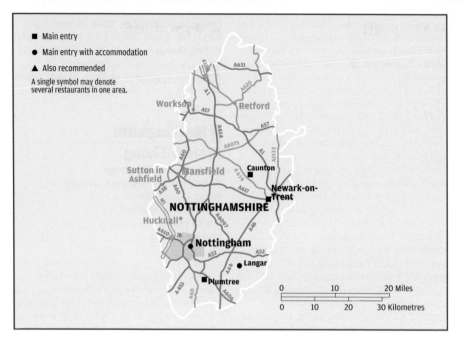

- ■ Main entry
- ● Main entry with accommodation
- ▲ Also recommended

A single symbol may denote
several restaurants in one area.

## Caunton

### Caunton Beck

**Handsome pub in quiet, leafy location**
Main Street, Caunton, NG23 6AB
Tel no: (01636) 636793
www.wigandmitre.com
Gastropub | £23
Cooking score: 2

Informality is the order of the day at this
meticulously restored sixteenth-century
cottage-cum-pub/restaurant. The low-
beamed bar area has a laid-back feel and leads
to an equally comfortable, accommodating
dining room. Food is available all day and the
flexible menu opens with breakfast (at 8am)
and goes on to 'very satisfying' twice-baked
Caunton Beck soufflé with Portobello
mushroom and Roquefort. Main courses such
as rack of Derbyshire lamb with a Burgundian
red wine and shallot sauce demonstrate the
kitchen's ability to source good quality
produce. Finish with griottine cherry
cheesecake. Good service, and a wine list
where prices are fair and interest high. House
vins de Pays are £13.45.
**Chef/s:** Valerie Hope and Andy Pickstock. **Open:** all
week 8am to midnight. **Closed:** 25 Dec. **Meals:** alc
(main courses £13 to £19). Set L and D £11 (2
courses) to £13.95. **Service:** not inc. **Details:** Cards
accepted. 90 seats. 30 seats outside. Separate bar.
No music. Wheelchair access. Children allowed. Car
parking.

## Langar

### Langar Hall

**Popular restaurant with on-target cooking**
Langar, NG13 9HG
Tel no: (01949) 860559
www.langarhall.com
Modern British | £30
Cooking score: 4

Langar Hall, a handsome early-Victorian
house with fine gardens and a cosy suite of
public rooms, runs trippingly along under the

watchful eyes of Imogen Skirving – who has been here 'forever'. Very little seems to change: there is still a good-value, two-course lunch, with a slightly pricier dinner option, as well as a seasonal carte with a repertoire that takes in plain and elaborate, classic and modern ideas. These range from twice-baked cheese soufflé, and roast cutlet and chargrilled leg of Langar lamb with root vegetables, to seared scallops with caramelised cauliflower and curry sauce, and roast duck breast and confit leg with Sauternes sauce. The cooking is generally on target and the mood is pleasant and unfussy, though the popularity of the restaurant has resulted in reports of service glitches this year. The wine list has a little bit of everything, to give range. House selections are £15.95.
**Chef/s:** Gary Booth and Toby Garratt. **Open:** all week L 12 to 2, D 7 to 10 (6.30 to 8.30 Sun). **Meals:** alc (main courses £13 to £23). Set L £12.50 (2 courses) to £17.50. Set D £20 (2 courses) to £25. Sun L £27. **Service:** 10% (optional). **Details:** Cards accepted. 60 seats. 15 seats outside. Separate bar. No music. No mobile phones. Wheelchair access. Children allowed. Car parking.

## ▋Newark-on-Trent

### Café Bleu
**Jazzy joint where Med meets Midlands**
14 Castle Gate, Newark-on-Trent, NG24 1BG
Tel no: (01636) 610141
www.cafebleu.co.uk
**Modern European | £28**
**Cooking score: 1**

Gallic *joie de vivre*, regular jazz nights and vibrant abstract artwork characterise the 15-year-old Café Bleu, which stands by the banks of the Trent, next to the ruins of Newark Castle (where King John famously met his end). A starter of roast wood pigeon with wild mushroom and chorizo broth might be followed by pan-fried turbot with spinach gnocchi, pea shoots and saffron butter. A side of steamed broccoli and Nottinghamshire Stilton is a welcome cameo appearance from the Midlands. House wines are £13.

**Chef/s:** Mark Cheseldine. **Open:** all week L 12 to 2.30 (2 Sat, 3 Sun), Mon to Sat D 7 to 9.30 (6.30 to 10 Sat). **Closed:** 25 and 26 Dec, 1 Jan. **Meals:** alc (main courses £11 to £18). **Service:** not inc. **Details:** Cards accepted. 80 seats. 50 seats outside. Wheelchair access. Music. Children allowed.

## ▋Nottingham

### French Living
**A patriotic foodie package**
27 King Street, Nottingham, NG1 2AY
Tel no: (0115) 9585885
www.frenchliving.co.uk
**French | £17**
**Cooking score: 1**

Stéphane and Louise Luiggi's self-styled 'capsule of Frenchness' is a generous celebration of all things Gallic. Out front is a deli/café dealing in all sorts of provisions, while the cellar is given over to a rustic, red-bricked bistro-style restaurant. The kitchen responds to its surroundings by dishing out bowls of bouillabaisse and cassoulet, as well as dipping into the bourgeois world of mouclade Rochelaise, medallions of pork with chopped gherkins and – of course – crème brûlée. French cheeses and wines (from £9.50) complete the patriotic package.
**Chef/s:** Jeremy Tourne. **Open:** Tue to Sat L 12 to 2 (2.30 Sat), D 6 to 10. **Closed:** Sun, Mon, 24 Dec to 2 Jan. **Meals:** alc (main courses £11 to £18). Set L £8.50 (2 courses) to £10.50. Set D £12.50 to £21.50 (3 courses). **Service:** 10% (optional). **Details:** Cards accepted. 43 seats. Air-con. Music. Children allowed.

## Hart's

**Food to knock your socks off**
1 Standard Court, Park Row, Nottingham,
NG1 6GN
Tel no: (0115) 9110666
www.hartsnottingham.co.uk
**Modern British | £35**
**Cooking score: 5**

Located in a delightfully understated listed
nineteenth-century building – formerly the
General Hospital – Tim Hart's Nottingham
venture (see also Hambleton Hall,
Hambleton, Leicestershire and Rutland) has
been catering for a down-to-earth, modern-
day city crowd for 13 years. 'Comfortable and
light', is how one visitor described the
ambience, and the service, too, has come in for
commendation: 'the joy of eating here is that
the service ensures you can relax and enjoy
yourself'. Gareth Ward's dishes deliver
imaginative pairings of good raw materials,
and offer seasonal focus and generous
portions. A starter of cannelloni of crab with
avocado, cucumber, coconut and passion fruit
'knocked the socks off' one reporter for
'astoundingly fresh flavours', while a main
course of poached and roast wild rabbit,
served with a slick of carrot and mango purée,
a dice of smoked bacon and crushed peas also
came 'bursting with flavour'. Hits at dessert
include banana parfait with peanuts, sesame
and toffee, and good sticky toffee pudding
with cream-cheese ice cream. Wines are set out
in style and the list offers good-value drinking
rather than impressing with unaffordable
bottles. House wine is £16.
**Chef/s:** Gareth Ward. **Open:** all week L 12 to 2, D 6
to 10 (9 Sun). **Closed:** 26 Dec, 1 Jan. **Meals:** alc
(main courses £14 to £22). Set L £13.95 (2 courses)
to £16.95. Set D £25. Pre-theatre £18 (2 courses).
Sun L £22. **Service:** 12% (optional). **Details:** Cards
accepted. 80 seats. 12 seats outside. Separate bar.
No mobile phones. Wheelchair access. Children
allowed.

## Larwood & Voce

**Cricketing foodie pub that's a winner**
Fox Road, West Bridgford, Nottingham, NG2 6AJ
Tel no: (0115) 9819960
www.larwoodandvoce.co.uk
**Gastropub | £24**
**Cooking score: 3**

V £30

The rejuvenated old boozer backs on to Trent
Bridge cricket ground – and, as you were
wondering, is named after the two English
cricketers who bowled out the Australians to
win the 1932-33 Ashes series. The interior ticks
all the gastropub style boxes: wood floors and
tables, leather sofas, bold wallpaper. In the
kitchen, ingredients are well chosen and
menus are in tune with the seasons, mixing
solid English fare with a smattering of
Mediterranean influences – say, warm black
pudding with crispy poached egg and fruity
brown sauce, ahead of cod with rösti potato,
green beans and chorizo. Local cheeses are an
alternative to buttermilk and yoghurt
pudding with poached Yorkshire rhubarb.
Breakfast is served at weekends. Wines are
divided by style and open at £13.50.
**Chef/s:** Christopher Reeve. **Open:** all week 12 to 10
(10 to 10 Sat, 10 to 6 Sun). **Closed:** 25 Dec.
**Meals:** alc (main courses £7 to £20). Set L £6.95 (2
courses) to £8.95. **Service:** not inc. **Details:** Cards
accepted. 95 seats. 32 seats outside. Separate bar.
Wheelchair access. Music. Children allowed. Car
parking.

**NEW ENTRY**
## Restaurant 1877

**Cutting-edge food in a Victorian building**
128 Derby Road, Canning Circus, Nottingham,
NG1 5FB
Tel no: (0115) 9588008
www.restaurant1877.com
**Modern British | £25**
**Cooking score: 2**

£30

Restaurant 1877 is housed in a handsome
building constructed in that year. It boasts an
atmosphere of measured calm, and a chef and

co-owner who has done the rounds of Nottingham's better restaurants. Mark Osborne's up-to-the-minute menu features foraged wild garlic, smoky essences and a name-check for his butcher, but his dishes are, at heart, unthreatening. Start with scallops with herb gnocchi, mango and chilli, perhaps, followed by beef with both nettle purée and salsa verde; the meat is good, though the flavours of English country verges and Italian sunshine might not be a natural pairing. Attention to detail shows in decent wine matches from a list that starts at £16 (£4.50 by the glass). Service is warm and capable.

**Chef/s:** Mark Osborne. **Open:** Tue to Sat L 12 to 2, D 6 to 10. **Closed:** Sun, Mon. **Meals:** alc (main courses £14 to £19). Set L £12.95 (2 courses) to £16.50. Set D £16.50 (2 courses) to £22.50. **Service:** 10% (optional). **Details:** Cards accepted. 68 seats. Air-con. Separate bar. No mobile phones. Wheelchair access. Music. Children allowed.

## Restaurant Sat Bains

**Cutting-edge cooking with passion**
Old Lenton Lane, Nottingham, NG7 2SA
Tel no: (0115) 9866566
www.restaurantsatbains.net
**Modern European | £60**
**Cooking score: 7**

It's an understated setting for one of the UK's top kitchens – a cluster of converted former nineteenth-century barns on a rural stretch just off the city's ring road (you'll need the SatNav). The interior is formal but not overdone, and tables in the stone-floored dining room and conservatory are discreetly well-spaced. Three tasting menus are offered, for which the praise flows forth: 'This is cutting edge . . . one dish, celeriac, chicken liver, truffle, was in the top three dishes of my life.' The pairing of unusual flavours and textures is clearly a passion, and while dishes can be complex, requiring a range of high skill levels to prepare, what is promised is delivered. One inspector was mightily impressed by the flavours in a delicate cube of smoked salmon with miso, tiny pickled florets

of cauliflower and nettle soup, and also by a lemon sole, well-timed, complete with an *Alice in Wonderland*-style 'drink me' bottle of peanut milk and accompanied by new season's asparagus. But the stand-outs of that meal were a Kilner jar layered with duck parfait and butternut squash purée and topped with mandarin sorbet – a wonderful play on sweetness and temperature – and a 'brilliantly conceived' dessert of rhubarb served with wild herb granita and almond granola. Bread is always well reported. At inspection, it was offered with a superb Lincolnshire Poacher butter, which made Brie de Meaux an odd choice to serve on toast with spring truffle – the only misstep in the seven courses tried. The tone of the service, headed by Amanda Bains, is generally one of courteous professionalism. Wines are organised by style, and contribute energetically to the cost of it all. No problem if you want to splurge out, but the decent affordable wines that most of us are after are sewn thinly, with bottles starting at £26.

**Chef/s:** Sat Bains. **Open:** Tue to Sat D 7 to 9. **Closed:** Sun, Mon, 2 weeks winter, 1 week spring, 2 weeks summer. **Meals:** Tasting menu £55 (5 courses), £69 (7 courses), £85 (10 courses). **Service:** 12.5%. **Details:** Cards accepted. 36 seats. Air-con. Separate bar. Wheelchair access. Music. Children allowed. Car parking.

## World Service

**Crowd-pleasing hotspot**
Newdigate House, Castle Gate, Nottingham, NG1 6AF
Tel no: (0115) 8475587
www.worldservicerestaurant.com
**Modern British | £40**
**Cooking score: 4**

It's a popular venue, hidden behind a high wall and fronted by an oriental garden and large terrace. Inside, the bar/restaurant is all dark wood, restrained colours and oriental artefacts, with an informal style and a repertoire of dishes that have evolved over the years. Menus are peppered with ideas that attempt to please all palates: not only a trio of salmon (smoked, grilled and home-cured),

ballottine of foie gras, and a well-timed lemon sole with warm new potato salad, spring vegetable and parsley velouté, but also monkfish and nori tempura with citrus and soy dressing, and cod cheeks teamed with crispy slow-roasted pork belly and oven-dried fig. A dull dessert of pistachio and carrot cake with blackcurrant parfait and Turkish delight has let the side down, but breads are fine and service is on-the-ball. The light lunch menu is good value and house wine is £14.
**Chef/s:** Chris Elson. **Open:** all week L 12 to 2 (2.30 Sun), 7 to 10 (9 Sun). **Closed:** 25 and 26 Dec, 1 Jan. **Meals:** alc (main courses £14 to £20). Set L £13 (2 courses) to £17.50. Sun L from £13.50. **Service:** 10% (optional). **Details:** Cards accepted. 80 seats. 30 seats outside. Air-con. Separate bar. Wheelchair access. Music.

## ALSO RECOMMENDED

### ▲ Delilah
15 Middle Pavement, Nottingham, NG1 7DX
Tel no: (0115) 9484461
www.delilahfinefoods.co.uk
**Café**

Although primarily a delicatessen – with an ample stock of cheeses, meats and wines – Delilah also serves tapas-style dishes, good sandwiches, salads, frittatas and fondues from a nine-stool counter at the back of the store. Weary shoppers might drop by for bruschetta with Moroccan tapenade, melted goats' cheese and wilted spinach (£5), griddled chorizo and halloumi kebabs, or various cheese and meat platters (£10) intended for sharing. Wines by the glass start at £4.50. Open all week.

### ▲ Iberico World Tapas
Shire Hall, High Pavement, Nottingham, NG1 1HN
Tel no: (0115) 9410410
www.ibericotapas.com
**Spanish/Tapas**

The vaulted basement beneath Nottingham's old Courthouse poses (almost convincingly) as a Moorish cellar, and provides a suitably arabesque ambience for this venture from the team behind nearby World Service (see entry).

A menu evenly divided between 'Spanish' and 'World' tapas sees customers torn between Iberian stalwarts such as patatas bravas (£3.50), squid with lime (£5), an ample stock of cheeses and charcuterie, and popular global dishes including butternut and pine nut risotto (£5) or black cod in spicy miso (£8). House wine is £15. Closed Sun and Mon.

## ▌Plumtree
### Perkins
*Ex-station's menus are just the ticket*
Station House, Station Road, Plumtree, NG12 5NA
Tel no: (0115) 9373695
www.perkinsrestaurant.co.uk
**Modern European | £29**
Cooking score: 2
 £30

'An exceptional country haven', is a reader's verdict of this Nottinghamshire bastion, run by the Perkins family since 1982. The railway station-turned-restaurant aims for a mix of traditional and modern cooking, which may explain why cream of celery and Stilton soup and home-smoked haddock mornay share the menu with crab cakes with Indian spiced coleslaw and own-smoked duck breast with confit leg and ginger pak choi, potato fondant and black cherry jus. It has hit just the right spot with many reporters this year. Set-price meals are very fair value. The wine list is well spread with house vins de pays d'Oc at £14.50.
**Chef/s:** Sarah Newham. **Open:** all week L 12 to 2 (3.30 Sun), Mon to Sat D 6.30 to 9.45. **Meals:** alc (main courses £14 to £18). Set L £11.95 (2 courses) to £15.95. Set D £19.95 (2 courses) to £24.50. Sun L £14.95 (2 courses) to £18.50. **Service:** not inc. **Details:** Cards accepted. 76 seats. 20 seats outside. Separate bar. Wheelchair access. Music. Children allowed. Car parking.

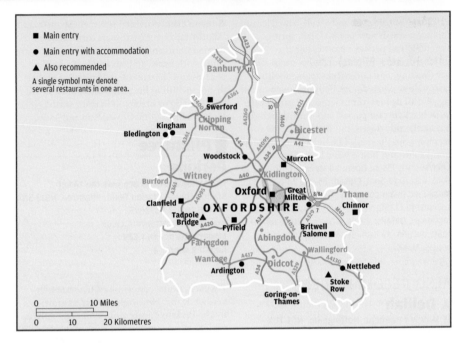

- ■ Main entry
- ● Main entry with accommodation
- ▲ Also recommended

A single symbol may denote several restaurants in one area.

0     10 Miles

0   10    20 Kilometres

## ■ Ardington

### The Boar's Head

**Pretty timber-framed all-rounder**
Church Street, Ardington, OX12 8QA
Tel no: (01235) 833254
www.boarsheadardington.co.uk
Modern British | £28
Cooking score: 3

 £30

Happily straddling the roles of pub and restaurant-with-rooms, this pretty timber-framed building is something of an all-rounder and the menus reflect this, ranging from bar snacks to a seven-course tasting menu. Choices from the carte might include scallops with black pudding and roasted foie gras, poached fillet of roe deer with sweet-and-sour celery and port sauce, British farmhouse cheeses with fruit cake or a pastry puff of apricots in rum with vanilla ice cream. One visitor noted that 'even the bread is baked on the premises', but there have also been reports of poor service. The interesting wine list comes down on the side of 'restaurant', but you can expect decent real ales in the bar. Wines start at £14.50.

**Chef/s:** Bruce Buchan. **Open:** all week L 12 to 2.15, D 7 to 9.30. **Closed:** 25 and 26 Dec, 1 Jan. **Meals:** alc (main courses £17 to £24). Set L £15 (2 courses) to £18.50. Sun L £23.50. Tasting menu £39.50.
**Service:** not inc. **Details:** Cards accepted. 40 seats. 30 seats outside. Separate bar. Wheelchair access. Music. Children allowed. Car parking.

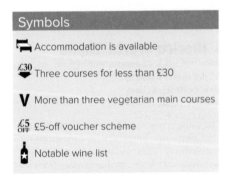

## Symbols

🛏 Accommodation is available

£30 Three courses for less than £30

**V** More than three vegetarian main courses

£5 OFF £5-off voucher scheme

🍷 Notable wine list

## Bledington

NEW ENTRY
### The Kings Head Inn
**Sensitive cooking in an idyllic spot**
The Green, Bledington, OX7 6XQ
Tel no: (01608) 658365
www.thekingsheadinn.net
Modern British | £25
Cooking score: 2

Honey-hued Cotswold buildings line
Bledington's lovely green, among them this
sixteenth-century former cider house. Inside,
a rare balance is struck between food and
drink. The bar remains the village boozer,
with benches, flagstone floors, local ales and
local drinkers, while two dining rooms – one
smart, the other pubby – cater for an
appreciative clientele. Food relies on prime,
often local, ingredients with Aberdeen Angus
beef (chargrilled rump and fillet or 'a juicy
sirloin') coming from the owner's uncle's herd.
Seafood such as tender mussels in a curry sauce
hails from Cornwall and rhubarb crème brûlée
makes a good finish. Wines from £13.95.
**Chef/s:** Charlie Loader. **Open:** all week L 12 to 2
(2.30 Sat and Sun), D 7 to 9 (9.30 Fri and Sat).
**Closed:** 25 and 26 Dec. **Meals:** alc (main courses
£10 to £19). **Service:** not inc. **Details:** Cards
accepted. 70 seats. 45 seats outside. Wheelchair
access. Music. Children allowed. Car parking.

## Britwell Salome

★ BEST UP-AND-COMING CHEF ★

NEW ENTRY
### The Goose
**Goose with the golden egg**
Britwell Salome, OX49 5LG
Tel no: (01491) 612304
www.gooserestaurant.com
Modern French | £75
Cooking score: 5

The Goose keeps its golden egg well hidden:
the modest brick and flint exterior of this
former pub scarcely hints at the delights

within. Inside, a comfy new lounge bar has an
adjacent space for eating, and there's a slightly
larger dining room behind, plus tables
outside. Furnishings are classy yet subdued,
with walls of bare brick or pastel shades. Staff
are young and well-drilled. Ryan Simpson has
created a menu in the modern British mould,
with French flourishes and well-sourced
(often local) ingredients. Readers have praised
'consistently excellent' cooking that's 'just the
right side of adventurous': à la carte first
courses include an innovative dish of crab
paired with grapefruit, as well as scallops with
veal sweetbreads. A superb-value set lunch
began with an amuse-bouche of vichyssoise
topped with smoked salmon and
(unnecessary) truffle oil. Next, warm duck
rillettes came in an intense reduction,
tempered by a perfectly poached duck egg, pea
foam, pea shoots and peas – a rich, memorable
dish. Main course of gorgeously succulent
salmon with crushed potatoes, green beans
and sauce vierge was followed by decadent,
dark chocolate tart with tonka bean ice cream.
The adequate wine list starts at £14.50.
**Chef/s:** Ryan Simpson. **Open:** Wed to Sun L 12 to 3
(8 Sun), Wed to Sat D 7 to 9 (6.30 to 9.30 Fri and
Sat). **Closed:** Mon, Tue, 26 to 14 Jan (except 31 Dec),
last week Aug, first week Sept. **Meals:** alc (main
courses £14 to £22). Set L £14.95 (2 courses) to
£17.95. **Service:** not inc. **Details:** Cards accepted. 40
seats. 20 seats outside. Air-con. Wheelchair access.
Music. Children allowed. Car parking.

## Chinnor
### The Sir Charles Napier
**Irresistible and original old charmer**
Sprigg's Alley, Chinnor, OX39 4BX
Tel no: (01494) 483011
www.sircharlesnapier.co.uk
Modern European | £34
Cooking score: 4

'If ever there was a place that regenerated the
spirit, it's the Napier – a deliciously
irresistible, quirky piece of gloryland high up
in the Chilterns', enthused one fan about this
consistent *Guide* veteran. Its lovable

eccentricity, animal sculptures and surreal *objets d'art* continue to charm the pants off everyone, and – as ever – owner Julie Griffiths remains the life and soul of the party. The food is potently seasonal, carefully rendered and convincing, with game a noticeably strong suit – perhaps thick slices of pitch-perfect venison with red onion tarte Tatin or 'deeply autumnal' breast of mallard with confit leg, beetroot purée and quince. Fish also shines, witness a memorable 'miniature' of caramelised scallops with teardrops of carrot purée, sultana and hazelnut dressing. Desserts are a treat, whether it's a jokey combo of banana crème brûlée with chocolate doughnuts and toffee popcorn or refreshing mango parfait with Kaffir lime and grapefruit sorbet. The wine list also comes up trumps: it's a deeply considered, creative global selection with France, Australia and California leading the way and house recommendations from £15.95.
**Chef/s:** Sam Hughes. **Open:** Tue to Sun L 11.30 to 2.30 (3.30 Sun), Tue to Sat D 6 to 9.30 (10 Sat). **Closed:** Mon, 25 to 27 Dec. **Meals:** alc (main courses £17 to £27). Set L Tue to Fri £15.50 (2 courses). Set D Tue to Fri £16.50 (2 courses). **Service:** 12.5% (optional). **Details:** Cards accepted. 70 seats. 70 seats outside. Air-con. Separate bar. Wheelchair access. Music. Children allowed. Car parking.

## Clanfield

NEW ENTRY
### Clanfield Tavern
**Hearty pub classics**
Bampton Road, Clanfield, OX18 2RG
Tel no: (01367) 810223
www.clanfieldtavern.com
Gastropub | £21
Cooking score: 2

£5 OFF £30

Sustainability, locally sourced and seasonal are the buzz words at Tom Gee's seventeenth-century Cotswold stone pub in picture-perfect Clanfield. Menus reflect the seasons, with hearty pub classics like Old Spot sausages with mash and onion gravy or a more robust slow-cooked blade of beef in red wine all

prepared from top-notch produce sourced from local farms and small suppliers. The lamb is reared next door and vegetables and herbs come from the kitchen garden out back. Eat at scrubbed tables in the rambling beamed and stone-walled bar or in the contemporary wood-floored conservatory dining room. House wine £11.50.
**Chef/s:** Nick Seckington. **Open:** Tue to Sun L 12 to 3 (3.30 Sun), Mon to Sat D 6.30 to 9 (5.30 to 8 Mon, 9.30 Fri and Sat). **Closed:** 25 Dec. **Meals:** alc (main courses £8 to 17). Set L £10 (2 courses) to £15. Set D £15 (2 courses) to £20. Sun L £14.95 (2 courses) to £17.95. **Service:** not inc. **Details:** Cards accepted. 85 seats. 20 seats outside. Wheelchair access. Music. Children allowed. Car parking.

## East Hendred

READERS RECOMMEND
### Eyston Arms
**Gastropub**
High Street, East Hendred, OX12 8JY
Tel no: (01235) 833320
www.eystons.co.uk
'Superior pub food in a truly lovely village'

## Fyfield
### The White Hart
**Age-old pub with modern, seasonal menus**
Main Road, Fyfield, OX13 5LW
Tel no: (01865) 390585
www.whitehart-fyfield.com
Modern British | £29
Cooking score: 2

Steeped in the history of the Reformation, the White Hart was a former chantry house, sold on to St John's College, Oxford, after the dissolution – and it still contains a secret escape-tunnel for priests. You can choose between the beamed interior or an outside table within sniffing distance of the aromatic herb garden to try the modern gastropub cooking. Antipasti and meze boards for sharing are one possibility, or else pursue a conventional three-course route, from seared peppered tuna with lime aïoli through mature beef fillet with steak and kidney pudding, salsify and foie gras sauce, to passion fruit tart with white chocolate sorbet. Wines, arranged by style, start at £15.50.

**Chef/s:** Mark Chandler. **Open:** Tue to Sun L 12 to 2.30 (3.30 Sun), Tue to Sat D 7 to 9.30. **Closed:** Mon. **Meals:** alc (main courses £13 to £19). Set L £15 (2 courses) to £18. Sun L £17 (2 courses) to £20. **Service:** not inc. **Details:** Cards accepted. 60 seats. 40 seats outside. Separate bar. No mobile phones. Music. Children allowed. Car parking.

## ▌Goring-on-Thames

### Leatherne Bottel

**Delightful waterside dining**
The Bridleway, Goring-on-Thames, RG8 0HS
Tel no: (01491) 872667
www.leathernebottel.co.uk
**Modern European | £40**
**Cooking score: 3**

**£5**
OFF

The setting is one to lift the spirits, the converted cottages on the banks of the Thames nothing less than beautiful and the riverside terrace an idyllic spot for summer lunches. Inside, there is an old–fashioned feel but Julia Abbey (née Storey) delivers dishes that are more contemporary than the setting suggests, showing adventurous flourishes within a modern European framework. Starters range from a mosaic of pigeon, ham hock and foie gras with apple and grape chutney to steak tartare with pickled radish and horseradish ice cream. Main courses bring venison with celeriac fondant, braised red cabbage with golden raisins and star anise, or cod with fennel confit, sweet cherry tomatoes, pak choi, shellfish and saffron sauce. Passion fruit tart makes a great dessert, and house wine is £20.

**Chef/s:** Julia Abbey. **Open:** all week L 12 to 2.30 (3 Sun), Mon to Sat D 7 to 9 (9.30 Fri and Sat). **Meals:** alc (main courses £18 to £25). Set L £19.50 (2 courses) to £24.50. Sun L £29.50. Tasting menu £58. **Service:** 10%. **Details:** Cards accepted. 45 seats. 50 seats outside. Separate bar. No music. No mobile phones. Wheelchair access. Children allowed. Car parking.

Wine service bugbears

Most restaurants rely on drinks for the bulk of their profit margin, but the multiplication factor – often up to 350% in London's West End – continues to depress restaurant-goers. If a bottle of ordinary Chablis is around £35, or a glass of house Champagne £12, you are certainly paying too much.

Over-enthusiastic topping up – when most diners are happy to do it for themselves – is a cause of profound irritation. But the practice, in more formal restaurants, of removing the bottle from the table altogether is also irksome. This can lead to the opposite of the topping-up problem, with dry glasses awaiting the attention of one of the preoccupied members of staff.

Drinking by the glass is widely popular, but the playing field on glass sizes is not level. Most now count a standard glass as 175ml and a large one as 250ml (a third of a bottle), but an uncomfortable number of restaurants still use the parsimonious 125ml as standard – sparkling wines are widely served in 125ml measures, for no particular reason. Dessert-wine measures may be tiny (as little as 70ml) but at least this recognises the higher alcohol content.

And which will be the first restaurant not to add the service-charge percentage to wine, when all it involves is opening a bottle?

## Great Milton
### Le Manoir aux Quat' Saisons
**Unashamed luxury and pure delight**
Church Road, Great Milton, OX44 7PD
Tel no: (01844) 278881
www.manoir.com
**Modern French | £95**
**Cooking score: 8**

🍷 ⊟ V

A pilgrimage to Raymond Blanc's manor house is on just about everyone's wish list – a chance to indulge in some of the pleasures and luxuries of the good life on a grand scale, if only for a few hours. For many visitors it's the sheer Englishness of the place that enthrals – whether you are playing croquet on the lawn or taking a tour of the organically inclined kitchen gardens. Everything about this world-class destination reflects its owner's personal vision of 'sustainable harmony', although the restaurant is very much Le Manoir's gently pulsating heart. Blanc may be a high-profile charmer, but he's also an intelligent and dutiful perfectionist in the kitchen. To appreciate the food to the full, come when the gardens are in bloom and eat in the conservatory, with its tent-like ceiling and summery glow. Take your pick from the carte, the menu du jour or one of the whole-table options culminating in the 10-course 'menu découverte'. The tag 'modern French' hardly does justice to the creative breadth of the cuisine on display here. Blanc is master of lightness, balance and intensity, with consummate technique and the talent to make food look exquisitely pretty on the plate. It's no surprise that he draws inspiration from faraway lands, and his accumulated wisdom shows in everything from a ceviche of tuna and scallop with shaved fennel salad, Oscietra caviar and lime dressing to roast Gressingham duck breast with braised chicory, confit of yuzu fruit, jasmine tea and raisin sauce. Disarmingly simple lunch dishes also have the power to seduce, whether it's a glorious springtime risotto of English asparagus, garden greens and Parmesan, or pan-fried Loch Duart salmon with sorrel, cucumber and a perfectly restrained wasabi beurre blanc. Superb home-baked breads remain a star turn, while desserts are wonders of eye-popping artistry that 'look like gifts': tiramisu flavours with cocoa sauce and coffee bean ice cream is a real dazzler. It hardly needs repeating that the welcome is effusively Gallic and service runs effortlessly on castors ('you would not know they were there', noted one happy soul). France naturally dominates the majestic wine list, which drools over the classics in meticulous detail, but also shows off treasures from elsewhere. In keeping with the Manoir's increasingly green credentials, organic and biodynamically produced bottles are given a decent airing too. Prices start at £26.50, with a useful selection from around £6 a glass.
**Chef/s:** Raymond Blanc and Gary Jones. **Open:** all week L 12 to 2.30, D 7 to 10. **Meals:** Set L £49. Set menus L and D £95 to £116. **Service:** not inc. **Details:** Cards accepted. 90 seats. Air-con. Separate bar. No music. No mobile phones. Wheelchair access. Children allowed. Car parking.

## Headington
**READERS RECOMMEND**
### The Black Boy
**Gastropub**
91 Old High Street, Headington, OX3 9HT
Tel no: (01865) 741137
www.theblackboy.uk.com
**'Reasonably priced, simple English food with quality'**

## Kingham
### Kingham Plough
**A country pub of some class**
Kingham, OX7 6YD
Tel no: (01608) 658327
www.thekinghamplough.co.uk
**Gastropub | £35**
**Cooking score: 4**

Traditional features abound in this old village pub opposite the green, but for all its slate and wood floors, exposed stone and impressive

beams there is nothing cobwebby about the operation. It provides an informal yet upmarket stage for Emily Watkins' modern British cooking. She makes the most of local produce such as Hereford beef (served with horseradish butter, triple-cooked chips and garden salad) or Daylesford chicken suprême (which arrives with a confit of the leg, chicken hearts and wild garlic and potato dumplings). Cornish octopus benefits from a well-matched accompaniment of wild garlic and tomato terrine, desserts stay dependably in the comfort zone of Cox's apple fritters with cider ice cream and rhubarb baked Alaska. While results on the plate have pleased most reporters, the same cannot be said for the service, which has been described as 'slow and unresponsive'. House wine from £14.50.
**Chef/s:** Emily Watkins. **Open:** all week L 12 to 1.45 (Sun 2.30), D 7 to 8.45 (Sun 6.15 to 7.45). **Closed:** 25 Dec. **Meals:** alc (main courses £12 to £22). **Service:** not inc. **Details:** Cards accepted. 70 seats. 20 seats outside. Separate bar. Wheelchair access. Music. Children allowed. Car parking.

## ▮ Murcott

★ BEST USE OF LOCAL PRODUCE ★

### The Nut Tree Inn
**Delightful pub with flavour-packed food**
Main Street, Murcott, OX5 2RE
Tel no: (01865) 331253
www.nuttreeinn.co.uk
**Modern British | £33**
**Cooking score: 5**

£5
OFF

'We enjoyed being pestered by Indian runner ducks', reported one enthusiastic diner, who appreciated the relaxed approach in this delightfully rustic Oxfordshire pub. While the birds were happily absent from the menu options, excellent pork and Dexter beef from the Nut Tree's own herds and spring lamb from local smallholdings featured prominently on the carte. Provenance is 'free-range, wild and organic wherever possible'. Michael North's cooking is exact and assured, coaxing the most flavour possible from these

top-quality ingredients. Roast best end of lamb was timed to a delicate pink, allowing the deep flavour to sing out – for one reporter it was among the best lamb ever tasted. Ballottine of Landes foie gras, its richness cut by poached rhubarb, and gently home-smoked Orkney salmon were starters which garnered praise. Large portions were also appreciated, while a bitter chocolate tart and hot lime and coconut soufflé were evidence of strong pastry skills. A properly made Welsh rarebit, followed by ham, egg and triple-cooked chips has featured on the good-value set lunch menu. Imogen North oversees the smooth, efficient service, whether in the low-beamed main restaurant, conservatory, bar or garden. House wines, including 'an amazing house red' are £15.95, with 11 selections by the glass. Mark-ups are notably reasonable.
**Chef/s:** Michael North. **Open:** all week L 12 to 2.30 (3 Sun), D 7 to 9 (6.30 to 8 Sun). **Closed:** Sun D in winter. **Meals:** alc (main courses £15 to £24). Set L and D £15 (2 courses) to £18. **Service:** not inc (except 10% for parties over 6). **Details:** Cards accepted. 60 seats. 60 seats outside. Music. Children allowed. Car parking.

## ▮ Nettlebed

### The White Hart
**Good value and piles of style**
28-30 High Street, Nettlebed, RG9 5DD
Tel no: (01491) 641245
www.whitehartnettlebed.com
**Gastropub | £25**
**New chef**

There may be no shortage of converted sixteenth-century inns around the country, but this one piles on the style, catering ambidextrously to locals as much as well-heeled out-of-towners on weekend breaks. There were changes in the kitchen as the *Guide* went to press, but it is likely that the appealing menu of good-value pub and bistro classics that takes in smoked mackerel rillette with horseradish, fish and chips and confit of duck with red cabbage, potato gratin and apple sauce, will continue. House wine is £13.95.

**Open:** all week L 12 to 2.30 (3 Sun), Mon to Sat D 6 to 9.30. **Meals:** alc (main courses £10 to £20). Set L £13.50 (2 courses) to £17.50. Sun L £14.95 (2 courses) to £17.95. **Service:** not inc. **Details:** Cards accepted. 80 seats. 40 seats outside. Separate bar. Wheelchair access. Music. Children allowed. Car parking.

# ■ Oxford

**NEW ENTRY**

## The Anchor Inn
**The best pub food in Oxford**
2 Hayfield Road, Oxford, OX2 6TT
Tel no: (01865) 510282
www.theanchoroxford.co.uk
Gastropub | £22
Cooking score: 2

£5 OFF  £30

Seek out this unassuming 1930s Art Deco building in the leafy suburb of Hayfield, best reached by strolling the Thames and canal paths from the city (parking awkward), and you will find the best pub food in Oxford. Bars are kitted out in period style, with high ceilings, stone fireplaces and huge gilt mirrors – a pleasing backdrop for Jamie King's modern British cooking. Using local and organic produce and sustainable fish from day boats, seasonal menus take in devilled lambs' kidneys and creamed spinach on toast, rack of lamb with lentils, chorizo and red wine sauce, and treacle tart with ginger ice cream. House wine is £13.55.
**Chef/s:** Jamie King. **Open:** all week L 12 to 2.30 (3 Sun), D 6 to 9.30 (7 to 9 Sun). **Closed:** 25 Dec. **Meals:** alc (main courses £10 to £17). Mon to Fri 1 course and drink £7.50. **Service:** not inc. **Details:** Cards accepted. 80 seats. 30 seats outside. Separate bar. Wheelchair access. Music. Children allowed. Car parking.

## Branca
**Crowd-pleasing livewire Italian**
111 Walton Street, Oxford, OX2 6AJ
Tel no: (01865) 556111
www.branca-restaurants.com
Italian | £25
Cooking score: 1

V

Everyone seems to have a great time at this exceedingly popular Italian brasserie. It gets packed with crowds drawn by the flexible all-day menu, but cheery staff cope admirably. There's something to suit all tastes, whether it's the 'delicious choice of antipasti', salads such as king prawn Caesar, risottos, pasta and pizza or more restaurant-style dishes along the lines of organic salmon and smoked haddock fishcakes and 'excellent duck and chips'. Lemon tart has been recommended for dessert. A concise Italian wine list opens at £13.75.
**Chef/s:** Michael McQuire. **Open:** all week 12 to 11. **Closed:** 24 and 25 Dec. **Meals:** alc (main courses £9 to £17). Set L and D £10.45 (2 courses). Sun L £10.95. **Service:** not inc. **Details:** Cards accepted. 100 seats. Air-con. Separate bar. Wheelchair access. Music. Children allowed.

## Cherwell Boathouse
**A riverside institution**
50 Bardwell Road, Oxford, OX2 6ST
Tel no: (01865) 552746
www.cherwellboathouse.co.uk
Modern British | £25
Cooking score: 1

£5 OFF

The river Cherwell is just a stone's throw from the glassed-in dining room, and punts for hire are drawn up outside – locations don't come more quintessentially English than this. The Verdin family's restaurant is an Oxford institution, noted for its thoughtful, impressive wine list and a short menu offering the likes of pheasant roulade with fruit chutney, grilled halibut with cheese and chive mash, and spotted dick with orange jelly and orange foam. House French is £12.75 and there's an excellent by-the-glass selection.

**Chef/s:** Carson Hill. **Open:** all week L 12 to 2 (2.30 Sat and Sun), D 6 to 9.30. **Closed:** 25 to 30 Dec. **Meals:** alc (main courses £13 to £18). Set L Mon to Fri £12.50 (2 courses) to £23. Set D £19.50 (2 courses) to £25. **Service:** 10% (optional). **Details:** Cards accepted. 65 seats. 40 seats outside. Separate bar. No music. Wheelchair access. Children allowed. Car parking.

## Gee's

**Well-run upmarket bistro**
61 Banbury Road, Oxford, OX2 6PE
Tel no: (01865) 553540
www.gees-restaurant.co.uk
**Modern British | £25**
**Cooking score: 2**

**V**

North Oxford's bourgeoisie adores Gee's. The dining room, a large Victorian conservatory, rang with urbane chatter on a sunny Saturday. Sunday jazz evenings are a long-standing attraction. This is a well-run establishment where smart staff serve upmarket bistro food. Lapses have been reported, though slips were few at a set lunch that began with lamb's kidneys in mustard sauce (on soggy toast) followed by expertly grilled mackerel on crunchy braised fennel. From the carte, fish soup, of rare intensity, was followed by locally sourced beef stew (with sublime gravy but glutinous mash). Puddings – luscious treacle tart with milk ice cream, perhaps – are alluring. The global wine list starts at £14.95, £11.50 a pichet.

**Chef/s:** Ben Aslin. **Open:** all week L 12 to 2.30 (3.30 Sun), D 6 to 10 (10.30 Fri and Sat). **Closed:** 25 Dec. **Meals:** alc (main courses £12 to £20). Set L £12.95 (2 courses) to £15.95. Set D £35. Sun L £19.95 (2 courses) to £22.95. Sun D jazz menu £15.50 (2 courses) to £19.50. **Service:** not inc. **Details:** Cards accepted. 85 seats. 40 seats outside. Air-con. Separate bar. Wheelchair access. Music. Children allowed.

**NEW ENTRY**
## Jamie's Italian

**Bustling branded café/bar**
24-26 George Street, Oxford, OX1 2AE
Tel no: (01865) 838383
www.jamiesitalian.com
**Italian | £20**
**Cooking score: 1**

**V**

Branding is prominent at Jamie Oliver's Italian brasserie chain: the merchandise displays, the chirpy-chappy menu, the eager young staff. The bustling Oxford original is a riot of rustic-industrial chic, while the basement dining rooms are darkly urban, with views of the uptempo kitchen. Food runs from 'ultimate' breakfasts to charcuterie, classic pasta pairings (including a well-constructed tagliatelle genovese), and mains of chargrills, salads and specials such as marinated sardines served cold. Organic house wine £10.95.

**Chef/s:** Will Lumb. **Open:** all week 12 to 11 (9am Fri, 10am Sat, 10am to 10.30pm Sun). **Closed:** 25 and 26 Dec. **Meals:** alc (main courses £9 to £17). **Service:** 10% (optional). **Details:** Cards accepted. 150 seats. Air-con. Separate bar. Wheelchair access. Music. Children allowed.

## ALSO RECOMMENDED

### ▲ Al-Shami

25 Walton Crescent, Oxford, OX1 2JG
Tel no: (01865) 310066
www.al-shami.co.uk
**Lebanese**

A popular local favourite that 'co-exists very happily' with the Oxford synagogue opposite, Al-Shami is noted for its bright surrounds, 'wonderful family atmosphere' and vibrant Lebanese food. Hot and cold meze (£1.80 to £4) are the undisputed stars of the show: try the kibbeh nayeh (ground raw lamb with bulgur wheat) and kellage halloum (grilled halloumi in bread). Mains are mostly high-protein chargrills and kebabs (from £6.20), plus baked fish and vegetarian options (say, rice and lentils with fried onions). Lebanese wines from £12. Open all week.

## ▲ Edamamé

15 Holywell Street, Oxford, OX1 3SA
Tel no: (01865) 246916
www.edamame.co.uk
**Japanese**

Tucked away in a pretty back street between New and Wadham Colleges, Edamamé is a friendly, enticing Japanese eatery with a loyal band of regulars. The informal menus invite the sampling of a selection of little dishes for sharing – pay £6 for stir-fried squid marinated in soy and ginger or breaded pork cutlet with fruity dipping sauce. Go on Thursday evenings for the sushi menu. Saké is £3 for a small flask, £5 for large. Open Wed to Sun L, Thur to Sat D.

## ▌Stoke Row

### ALSO RECOMMENDED
### ▲ The Crooked Billet

Newlands Lane, Stoke Row, RG9 5PU
Tel no: (01491) 681048
www.thecrookedbillet.co.uk
**British**

'A delight!' exclaimed one reader about this famously idiosyncratic Oxfordshire gem. Out in the middle of nowhere, it maintains a high profile – thanks to numerous film and TV appearances – and crowds come from all over to revel in its classy bohemian atmosphere, fine food and offbeat music events. Local flavours and eclectic ideas fill the handwritten menu, which embraces everything from aubergine polenta cakes with spinach dumpling (£7) to quince Bakewell tart (£5), via venison steak with haggis, roast figs and juniper sauce (£20). Global wines from £16.75. Open all week.

> ### Readers recommend
>
> A 'readers recommend' review is a genuine quote from a report sent in by one of our readers. We intend to follow up these suggestions throughout the year to come.

## ▌Swerford

## The Masons Arms

**Historic pub full of ideas**
Banbury Road, Swerford, OX7 4AP
Tel no: (01608) 683212
www.masons-arms.com
**Gastropub | £25**
**Cooking score: 2**
£5 OFF  £30

Bare floorboards, plain wood tables and soft colours set the tone for Bill Leadbeater's 300-year-old pub overlooking the Swere Valley. His wide-ranging contemporary ideas are incorporated into a menu that shows good materials and a dedication to offering value for money across the board. The lunchtime menu satisfies a range of appetites, from Caesar salad to home-baked ham, egg and chips. At dinner, sea trout comes with potato salad and beetroot relish, mains include slow-cooked 'crackled' shoulder of Old Spot pork or a well-reported lamb tagine. There are good British farmhouse cheeses, and wines start at £13.50.
**Chef/s:** Bill Leadbeater. **Open:** all week L 12 to 2 (2.30 Sun), Mon to Sat D 7 to 9. **Closed:** 25 and 26 Dec. **Meals:** alc (main courses £8 to £19). Set L £14.95 (2 courses) to £16.95. **Service:** not inc. **Details:** Cards accepted. 75 seats. 30 seats outside. Separate bar. Wheelchair access. Music. Children allowed. Car parking.

## ▌Tadpole Bridge

### ALSO RECOMMENDED
### ▲ The Trout at Tadpole Bridge

Tadpole Bridge, SN7 8RF
Tel no: (01367) 870382
www.troutinn.co.uk
**Gastropub**

Readers have praised the 'beautiful location', and indeed this dining pub has a setting straight out of *Wind in the Willows*. The menu embraces pub and restaurant fare – down-to-earth specials such as steamed beef and ale pudding (£12.95) rub shoulders with a classy salad of smoked eel and Noilly Prat jelly (£7.95) or local pork fillet with caramelised apple and black pudding (£14.95). The extensive, good-value wine list includes plenty from France, starting at £13.50. The 'superb staff' have made an impression on reporters too. Open all week.

## Woodstock

### The Feathers

**Higgledy-piggledy old charmer**
Market Street, Woodstock, OX20 1SX
Tel no: (01993) 812291
www.feathers.co.uk
**Modern British | £46**
**New chef**

🍴 V

Four seventeenth-century houses make up this attractive hotel near the entrance to Blenheim Palace. The place has a charming higgledy-piggledy feel – there's a series of little rooms with flagstone floors and deep sofas where you can enjoy drinks and bar meals. The dining room, too, runs through several rooms – linked by yellow wallpaper and background classical music – but here there's a more formal ambience. The departure of Russell Bateman – to Colette's at Chandler's Cross, Hertfordshire (see entry) – is bound to ring some changes. New man Marc Hardiman's menu includes scallops with crubeens, broccoli and lemon pith purée, and loin of lamb with white pudding and sweetbreads, Roscoff onion and broad beans with eucalyptus essence. Desserts run to passion fruit soufflé with its own sorbet. House wines from £17.
**Chef/s:** Marc Hardiman. **Open:** all week L 12 to 2.30, Mon to Sat D 7 to 9.30. **Meals:** Set L £19 (2 courses) to £24.50. Set D £46. Sun L £29. **Service:** 10% (optional). **Details:** Cards accepted. 40 seats. 40 seats outside. Separate bar. Wheelchair access. Music. Children allowed.

## Chris Bradley Mr Underhill's

**Who or what inspired you to become a chef?**
When we opened in 1981 we could not afford to employ a chef.

**What do you like cooking when you are 'off duty'?**
Anything Italian. When growing up in Glasgow in the sixties I lived with an Italian family for a short while who ran an outstanding deli.

**What is your favourite restaurant and why?**
I love going to restaurants; at my age it's impossible to single out just one.

**What do you do to relax when out of the kitchen?**
I'm allowed out of the kitchen?

**What is your top culinary tip?**
Use the very best ingredients and don't make it complicated just for the sake of it.

**What is the best part of your job?**
That moment when a member of staff clicks and realises that cooking will never be just a job for them.

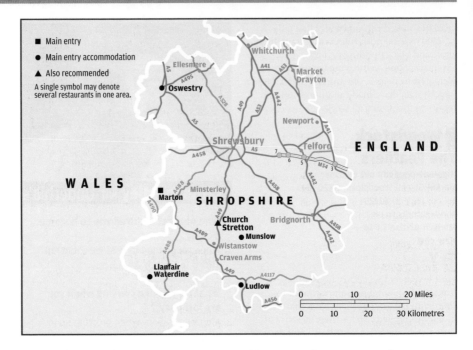

## ■ Church Stretton

### ALSO RECOMMENDED
### ▲ Berry's Coffee House

17 High Street, Church Stretton, SY6 6BU
Tel no: (01694) 724452
www.berryscoffeehouse.co.uk
Café

Berry's Coffee House is a hospitable 'little British café' housed in a Queen Anne town house with 'a great cosy atmosphere'. The focus is on locally sourced produce, with the daytime menu delivering a familiar repertoire – say, Welsh rarebit (made with local ale) and salads such as locally smoked salmon with dill sauce (£7.50). Homemade cakes are 'divine'. On Friday and Saturday evenings, shared plates of Shropshire charcuterie (£9) and local cheeses are backed up by blackboard specials. Staff are 'always lovely and helpful'. Wines from £11. Open all week.

## ■ Llanfair Waterdine

### The Waterdine

Seasonal cooking delivers the goods
Llanfair Waterdine, LD7 1TU
Tel no: (01547) 528214
www.waterdine.com
**Modern British | £33**
**Cooking score: 4**

£5 OFF 🛏

On the Shropshire/Wales border, the sixteenth-century drovers' inn still has some country pub trappings, although the focus is now on its intimate dining rooms. Ken Adams can clearly deliver the goods. His timing is assured, and the kitchen scores heavily with the quality of its raw materials, some of them home-grown: spiced black pudding on crushed apples with Hereford cider sauce is a spot-on modern starter, while flavourful leg of organic Welsh mountain lamb is roasted in Lebanese spices and served with a fine vegetable and anchellini (pasta) ragoût. Elsewhere, local game such as Mortimer

Forest deer might appear with pheasant, braised beetroot, celeriac and a good red wine sauce, while fresh Cornish hake is teamed with crab risotto. Desserts can astonish: try black rice pudding with pineapple and coconut cream or mulberry mousse with elderflower cream. The concise but impeccably chosen wine list opens at £17.50.

**Chef/s:** Ken Adams. **Open:** Thur to Sun L 12 to 1.30, Tue to Sat D 7 to 8.30. **Closed:** Mon (except bank hols), 1 week Jun, 1 week Sept. **Meals:** Set L £26.50 (2 courses) to £32.50. Set D £32.50. Sun L £22.50. **Service:** not inc. **Details:** Cards accepted. 24 seats. Separate bar. No music. No mobile phones. Wheelchair access. Children allowed. Car parking.

## ▌Ludlow
### La Bécasse
**Fine dining to knock your socks off**
17 Corve Street, Ludlow, SY8 1DA
Tel no: (01584) 872325
www.labecasse.co.uk
**Modern French | £55**
**Cooking score: 6**

£5
OFF

Alan Murchison's second restaurant (its sibling is L'Ortolan in Berkshire, see entry) provides proof that the words 'fine dining' need not imply 'uptight and stuffy'. A warm welcome sets the tone for service that is classy but low on pomp. Set snug to the street, the building is typical of picture-postcard Ludlow: quaint, but not stuck in the past (boldly striped carpets offset the gravitas of fine old wood panelling). The food, too, straddles convention and invention, with choices such as pan-fried halibut fillet with cauliflower, morteau sausage, honeycomb and curried lime emulsion. Will Holland's modern French cooking is characterised by great prettiness and flair; a lunchtime opener of glazed peanuts, guacamole dip and curried popcorn was the only occasion when 'unpretentious' teetered on 'unremarkable', but a cold carrot and orange soup delivered a trumpet blast of flavour. A coolly savoury jellied pig's head terrine was balanced by crispy squid, sauce gribiche and caper berries, while strawberry

and tarragon jus lifted a main course of chargrilled chicken ballottine with young leeks and wild garlic. Finally, bittersweet black pepper caramel was the master touch in a dessert of strawberry sorbet, fresh strawberries and a lemon crêpe. A substantial, wide-ranging wine list kicks off at £19.

**Chef/s:** Will Holland. **Open:** Wed to Sun L 12 to 2, Tue to Sat D 7 to 9 (9.30 Sat). **Closed:** Mon, Christmas and New Year. **Meals:** Set L £22 (2 courses) to £26. Set D £49 (2 courses) to £55. Tasting menu £60. Surprise menu £85. **Service:** 10% (optional). **Details:** Cards accepted. 40 seats. Separate bar. No mobile phones. Music. Children allowed. Car parking.

### Mr Underhill's
**Seductive cocktail of hospitality and food**
Dinham Weir, Ludlow, SY8 1EH
Tel no: (01584) 874431
www.mr-underhills.co.uk
**Modern European | £35**
**Cooking score: 7**

🍷 🍽

Chris and Judy Bradley's restaurant-with-rooms holds a special place in the affection of *Guide* readers and – more than 28 years down the line – visitors are still seduced by its very special 'cocktail of intimacy, wonderful hospitality and superb food'. The Bradleys also tell us that 'petits fours once taken home by our early-days guests are now being taken home by their children's children' – which says a great deal about their enduring longevity. This is a hands-on set-up *par excellence* and a tribute to dedication, caring stewardship and sheer hard work. It helps that the setting – an idyllic verdant hideaway beside the tumbling waters of Dinham Weir – never fails to cast its balmy spell, although the Bradleys' personal touch really shows in the good-humoured dining room. Evening meals are tailored to suit each table and guests are provided with their own named menu as a guide. What follows is a cavalcade of consummately crafted and perfectly delivered dishes – 'lots of little courses, lots of fantastic flavours'. Dinner is a long haul, but it never overwhelms, and service runs at just the right pace for maximum satisfaction. Proceedings always begin with a palate sharpener (say a trio of smoked salmon) before a seasonal soup (spicy tomato with sweet butternut squash foam in early summer). The seasonal drift might continue with a dish of Bridgnorth asparagus, soft egg sauce and herb crumb, followed by fish (pavé of halibut on crunchy greens with lemongrass and ginger broth). Centrepieces also take their cue from the regions and the calendar – perhaps roast rack and shoulder of Mill Farm lamb with garden sorrel, mint and pea purée. After that, it's time for dessert – say gariguette strawberry sponge with black pepper ice cream – and an array of cheeses (often 'very local to Ludlow') with tracklements. New this year is a four-course supper menu for those those don't want to partake of the full experience, but are happy to indulge in sharing platters and lighter offerings. As for wine, the Bradleys have tackled the thorny issue of escalating prices head-on, and their new list is a stunner, with an extended line-up of house selections, plus Italian and French bottles at the lower end of the scale. The bidding starts at £16.50 (£4.90 a glass).

**Chef/s:** Chris Bradley. **Open:** Wed to Sun D only 7.15 to 8.30. **Closed:** Mon, Tue, 1 week June. **Meals:** Set D £34.50 (4 courses) to £50 (7 courses). **Service:** not inc. **Details:** Cards accepted. 30 seats. 30 seats outside. No music. No mobile phones. Children allowed. Car parking.

## Symbols

 Accommodation is available

 Three courses for less than £30

**V** More than three vegetarian main courses

 £5-off voucher scheme

 Notable wine list

## ALSO RECOMMENDED

### ▲ The Clive
Bromfield, Ludlow, SY8 2JR
Tel no: (01584) 856565
www.theclive.co.uk
**Modern British**

Just north of Ludlow on the A49, this eighteenth century farmhouse is now a contemporary restaurant-with-rooms (with an adjoining bar and courtyard). Local produce drives the menu and dishes work best when kept simple. Lunch on terrine of pork and local game or home-cooked Shropshire ham with poached eggs (£9.95) or dine on saddle of venison with dauphinoise potatoes, braised red cabbage and Cassis sauce (£18.95). Local cheeses (from £5.95) are an alternative to sticky toffee pudding. House wine is £13.30. Open all week.

## Marton

### The Sun Inn
**Good, homely cooking**
Marton, SY21 8JP
Tel no: (01938) 561211
www.suninn.org.uk
**Modern British | £27**
**Cooking score: 1**

A stone-built country inn on the Shrewsbury to Montgomery road, this place has been the Sun Inn for 300 years. Run nowadays by the Gartell family, it is properly informal, with foursquare wooden tables beneath a low, beamed ceiling. Good homely cooking takes in salmon brandade with red pepper glaze, slow-roasted belly pork in honey and cider, served with Savoy cabbage and bacon, or a stew of John Dory, bream, scallops and prawns in saffron broth, followed by baked blueberry cheesecake. Wines start at £12.

**Chef/s:** Peter and Dominic Gartell. **Open:** Wed to Sun L 12 to 2 (2.30 Sun), Tue to Sat D 7 to 11. **Meals:** alc (main courses £12 to £17). Sun L £16.95 (3 courses). **Service:** not inc. **Details:** Cards accepted. 30 seats. 30 seats outside. Separate bar. No mobile phones. Wheelchair access. Music. Children allowed. Car parking.

## ▌Munslow

### The Crown Country Inn

**Doing justice to local ingredients**
Corvedale Road, Munslow, SY7 9ET
Tel no: (01584) 841205
www.crowncountryinn.co.uk
**Modern British | £25**
**Cooking score: 3**

Set below the rolling hills of Wenlock Edge, this listed Tudor inn was once a renowned 'Hundred House' where local justice was meted out to wrongdoers. These days it has a happier disposition, although there are still reminders of the past in the carved oak beams, flagstones and mighty inglenooks. Food is served in the bar and the first-floor Corvedale restaurant (once the courtroom), and the kitchen procures local ingredients for menus with a strong international bent. Crostini of black pudding and tomato fondue might appear alongside new season's Bridgnorth asparagus, while mains could embrace home-smoked chicken breast with red onion confit and wild mushrooms or crisp roast pork belly with chilli cornmeal fritter and white bean cassoulet. Artisan British cheeses are given full rein, and desserts always include a traditional hot pud. House wine is £13.95.
**Chef/s:** Richard Arnold. **Open:** Tue to Sun L 12 to 2, Tue to Sat D 6.30 to 9. **Closed:** Mon, 25 and 26 Dec, 1 and 2 Jan. **Meals:** alc (main courses £12 to £17). Set L and D £13 (2 courses) to £17.95. Sun L £18.95. **Service:** not inc. **Details:** Cards accepted. 60 seats. 24 seats outside. Separate bar. No mobile phones. Wheelchair access. Music. Children allowed. Car parking.

## ▌Oswestry

### Sebastians

**Homely French restaurant**
45 Willow Street, Oswestry, SY11 1AQ
Tel no: (01691) 655444
www.sebastians-hotel.co.uk
**French | £38**
**Cooking score: 3**

The Fishers have run their successful restaurant-with-rooms (housed in a sixteenth-century inn) for some 20 years. A comfortable lounge with log fire is a good place to start in winter months, before progressing to the peach-hued, beamed dining room with its old-fashioned chairs and smart linen. The monthly changing dinner menu – written in French for some reason, with English subtitles – takes you through four courses of traditional haute cuisine, with a sorbet before the main. Start with poached scallops on leeks topped with smoked salmon in white wine cream sauce, while a red wine sauce may be the medium for beef fillet on squash purée with crispy kale. Desserts are as English as 'crumble au rhubarbe', with matching mousse and a whisky-laced compote. A French-led wine list opens at £16.95.
**Chef/s:** Richard Jones and Mark Fisher. **Open:** Tue to Sat D 6.30 to 9.30. **Closed:** Sun, Mon, 25 and 26 Dec, 1 Jan, bank hol Mon. **Meals:** Set D £19.95 to £37.50. **Service:** not inc. **Details:** Cards accepted. 35 seats. 25 seats outside. Separate bar. No mobile phones. Wheelchair access. Music. Children allowed. Car parking.

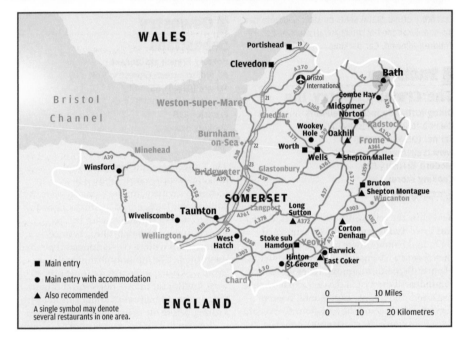

**WALES**

Portishead ■ 19
Clevedon ■
Bristol International ▲
A370
Bath ■
Combe Hay ▲
Midsomer Norton ▲
Radstock
Wookey Hole ■
Oakhill ▲
Frome
Worth ■
Wells ■
Shepton Mallet ▲
Bristol Channel
Weston-super-Mare
Cheddar
Burnham-on-Sea ●
Minehead
Glastonbury
Winsford ●
Bridgwater
Bruton ■
Shepton Montague ▲
Wincanton
SOMERSET
Wiveliscombe ●
Taunton ●
Langport
Long Sutton ▲
Corton Denham ▲
Wellington ●
West Hatch ■
Stoke sub Hamdon ▲
Yeovil
Barwick ▲
East Coker ▲
Hinton St George ■
Chard

**ENGLAND**

■ Main entry
● Main entry with accommodation
▲ Also recommended
A single symbol may denote several restaurants in one area.

| 0 | | 10 Miles |
|---|---|---|
| 0 | 10 | 20 Kilometres |

## ■ Barwick

### Little Barwick House

**Meticulously polished restaurant-with-rooms**
Barwick, BA22 9TD
Tel no: (01935) 423902
www.littlebarwickhouse.co.uk
**Modern British | £38**
**Cooking score: 6**

Tim and Emma Ford's eighteenth-century dower house continues to enchant visitors with its disarmingly serene outlook and ever-so-English sense of decorum. Set in three acres of distracting gardens and grounds (complete with an ancient cedar tree on the lawn) it glides along as a meticulously polished restaurant-with-rooms. Much depends on the output of Tim Ford's kitchen and his fruitful connections with the local food network: dependable supplies mean he can change his menu each day and keep everyone interested. Game always get a good outing in season, perhaps pink-roasted pigeon with braised lentils and spiced plums or saddle of wild rabbit with wild mushroom risotto and Calvados sauce. For those who fancy fish, the West Country ports provide red mullet (grilled and served with sun-blush tomatoes and basil dressing), sea bass (with white wine and chive sauce) and more besides. Unwavering consistency and highly skilled execution are also the hallmarks of finely crafted desserts such as exotic mango mousse and coconut pannacotta with marinated pineapple and passion fruit sorbet. Otherwise there are West Country farmhouse cheeses with quince paste for a savoury finale. The glorious global wine list is a prestigious, impeccably groomed selection that is aimed at connoisseurs and everyday quaffers alike. Top-end Aussies and Californians challenge the aristocratic French classics, and there are half-bottles in abundance. Six house recommendations start at £17.95.

**Chef/s:** Tim Ford. **Open:** Wed to Sun L 12 to 2, Tue to Sat D 7 to 9. **Closed:** Mon, 3 weeks from 25 Dec. **Meals:** Set L £20.95 (2 courses) to £24.95. Set D £32.95 (2 courses) to £37.95. Sun L £27.95.

**Service:** not inc. **Details:** Cards accepted. 40 seats. Air-con. Separate bar. No music. No mobile phones. Children allowed. Car parking.

# ▊ Bath

## Bath Priory

**Straight-down-the-line modern French classics**
Weston Road, Bath, BA1 2XT
Tel no: (01225) 331922
www.thebathpriory.co.uk
**Modern French | £65**
**Cooking score: 4**

🍷 🛏 V

The arrival of James Sheridan, cooking under executive chef Michael Caines, heralds a new, back-to-basics approach at this handsome manor house. Previous incumbent Chris Horridge's funky, hedgerow-inspired cuisine is gone, replaced by straight-down-the-line modern French classics. Thus you might find scallops with veal sweetbreads, pea purée and a morel velouté, or a terrine of confit rabbit and foie gras with poached cherries. Refined and accomplished, Sheridan's cooking boasts clean, contemporary flavours that are genuinely in tune with the seasons: an artfully arranged Provençal salad at a May lunch was a fitting introduction to the new season's vegetables, while a rhubarb and vanilla soufflé made a perfectly balanced conclusion. Occasional timidity means supporting flavours can get a little lost, for example the barely-there roast peach and five-spice that accompanied roast duck. High prices are tempered by the Priory's trademark generosity, evident in a bountiful supply of beautifully crafted nibbles and petits fours, and well-informed staff who are genuinely eager to please. Unusual producers find favour on the wine list, which offers a decent selection of half-bottles and a choice of 15 house selections from £26 (£6 a glass).
**Chef/s:** Michael Caines and James Sheridan. **Open:** all week L 12 to 2.30, D 7 to 9.30. **Meals:** Set L £26 (2 courses) to £32. Set D £54 (2 courses) to £65. Sun L £39. **Service:** not inc. **Details:** Cards accepted. 80 seats. No music. No mobile phones. Wheelchair access. Children allowed. Car parking.

NEW ENTRY
## Casanis

**Gallic bonhomie in abundance**
4 Saville Row, Bath, BA1 2QP
Tel no: (01225) 780055
www.casanis.co.uk
**French | £27**
**Cooking score: 1**

£5 OFF  £30 ▼

Adjacent to the city's Assembly Rooms, this relaxed bistro occupies a beautiful Georgian building in a lane with a distinctly Parisian look. Step inside and the cheery 'bonjour' from staff accentuates the Gallic flavour in an elegant dining room crammed with antiques from Provence. The candlelit tables are covered with white paper cloths, plus a solitary sprig of lavender for effect. The food is authentic French: a well-made snail and garlic ravioli with leek and chicken velouté could be followed by a daube of beef provençale and rosemary mash. Dessert could be a delicately flavoured lavender crème brûlée. House wine from £12.95.
**Chef/s:** Laurent Couvreur. **Open:** Tue to Sat L 12 to 2.30, D 6 to 10.30. **Closed:** Sun, Mon, 25 and 26 Dec, 1 week Jan, 1 week Aug. **Meals:** alc (main courses £12 to £18). Set L £11.50 (2 courses) to £15. Set D £16 (2 courses) to £20. **Service:** not inc. **Details:** Cards accepted. 52 seats. 12 seats outside. Wheelchair access. Music. Children allowed.

## Dukes Hotel, Cavendish Restaurant

**Elegant Georgian splendour**
Great Pulteney Street, Bath, BA2 4DN
Tel no: (01225) 787963
www.dukesbath.co.uk
**Modern British | £40**
**Cooking score: 3**

This splendid Palladian-style town house stands on one of Bath's showpiece streets. Among its inner jewels is a secluded walled patio garden overlooked by the neatly appointed Cavendish restaurant. Here Fran Snell takes sourcing seriously: Mendip venison loin accompanied by vegetable pavé, braised red cabbage and pear purée or roast fillet and slow-braised belly of pork teamed with butternut squash and apple and black pudding croquette typify the marriage of local ingredients with carefully controlled flavourings. Basics like slow-braised ox cheek and breast of free-range chicken are on the good-value lunch menu, alongside desserts such as apple, pear and sultana crumble. Main menu desserts bring more original combinations like Black Forest trifle with pistachio cream and cherry sorbet. House wine is £17.

**Chef/s:** Fran Snell. **Open:** Tue to Sun L 12 to 2.30, all week D 6.30 to 10. **Meals:** alc (main courses £18 to £24). Set L £12.95 (2 courses) to £15.95. Sun L £14.95. **Service:** 10% (optional). **Details:** Cards accepted. 40 seats. 40 seats outside. Separate bar. Music. Children allowed.

**NEW ENTRY**

# The Hop Pole

**Traditional pub, modern European food**
7 Albion Buildings, Upper Bristol Road, Bath, BA1 3AR
Tel no: (01225) 446327
www.bathales.com
**Gastropub | £23**
**Cooking score: 3**

Set on a busy main road close to the city centre, this may not be the most idyllic pub, but it is well worth a detour. A honey-stone building with a traditional pub feel, the former skittle alley is now a restaurant and the large garden is ideal for alfresco dining. The modern European food is seasonal, locally sourced and the cooking is confident with well-defined flavours, as in a starter of pan-fried duck livers, hot poached duck egg and buttered toast, followed by crispy belly of pork with Savoy cabbage, borlotti beans and mustard sauce. Simple desserts such as rhubarb and custard complete the picture. If you can resist the excellent ales, house wine is £11.

**Chef/s:** Chris Woodage and Mark Stevens. **Open:** Tue to Sun L 12 to 2 (3 Sun), Tue to Sat D 6.30 to 9. **Closed:** Mon. **Meals:** alc (main courses £8 to £16). **Service:** not inc. **Details:** Cards accepted. 50 seats. 60 seats outside. Music. Children allowed.

# King William

**Big on comfort food**
36 Thomas Street, Bath, BA1 5NN
Tel no: (01225) 428096
www.kingwilliampub.com
**Gastropub | £29**
**Cooking score: 2**

Shabby chic, with scrubbed pine tables and chalkboards listing everything from the name of the butcher to the wine of the month, this is a 'casual and unpretentious' local pub with good cooking. Straightforward British comfort food, using lovingly sourced seasonal ingredients, delivers brawn, watercress and Cornish potato salad, and shoulder and belly of pork, 'slow cooked to perfection' served with spinach in a creamy cider sauce. Desserts keep things simple with set vanilla cream and rhubarb syrup. Eat in the bar or over candlelight in the more formal upstairs dining room. House wine from £12. It's best to phone first before heading over for lunch – opening times may vary.

**Chef/s:** Adie Ware. **Open:** Tue to Sun L 12 to 3, all week D 6 to 10. **Closed:** 25 and 26 Dec. **Meals:** alc (main courses £11 to £20). Set D £24 (2 courses) to £29. Sun L £20 (2 courses) to £25. **Service:** 10% (optional). **Details:** Cards accepted. 40 seats. Separate bar. Music. Children allowed.

## Please send us your feedback

To register your opinion about any restaurant listed in the Guide, or a new restaurant that you wish to bring to our attention, please visit the web address at the bottom of the page. Your feedback informs the content of the book and will be used to compile next year's reviews.

The Good Food Guide 2010

## NEW ENTRY
# The Marlborough Tavern
**Ticks all the right gastropub boxes**
35 Marlborough Buildings, Bath, BA1 2LY
Tel no: (01225) 423731
www.marlborough-tavern.com
**Gastropub | £25**
**Cooking score: 3**
£5 OFF  £30

The Marlborough Tavern has been transformed from a run-down boozer into a sophisticated food pub. It's located just a few paces from Bath's famed Royal Crescent and comprises an airy, high-ceilinged room with a central bar – ticking all the right gastropub boxes with its sage tongue-and-groove, standard lamps and village hall furniture. While drinkers are as welcome as foodies, the food itself is simple, seasonal and locally sourced, with producers and provenance listed on a daily changing menu that might include whole lemon sole with anchovy and parsley butter, purple sprouting broccoli and mash or slow-roast belly of Wiltshire woodland Saddleback pork with chorizo, bacon and bean casserole and seasonal greens. An international wine list starts at £12.90.
**Chef/s:** Richard Knighting. **Open:** all week L 12.30 to 2.30 (4 Sun), Mon to Sat D 6 to 9.30. **Closed:** 25 Dec. **Meals:** alc (main courses £11 to £17). **Service:** not inc. **Details:** Cards accepted. 70 seats. 80 seats outside. Wheelchair access. Music. Children allowed.

## NEW ENTRY
# Minibar
**Great things come in small packages**
1 John Street, Bath, BA1 2JL
Tel no: (01225) 333323
www.bathminibar.com
**Spanish | £20**
**Cooking score: 2**
 £30

The clue is in the name: this is a tiny upstairs room, dominated by the bar on one side and a picture window overlooking Bath on the other. Perch on a stool at the stainless-steel counter that runs round the room and choose from the short menu of exquisitely put-together 'modern tapas' – perhaps a gorgeously rich dish of goats' cheese and aubergine with truffle honey, an impeccably sourced Spanish charcuterie plate, or a spanking-fresh crab 'martini', followed by a bitter-sweet chocolate and coffee pot de crème. The wine list, too, is small but perfectly formed. House wine £15.50.
**Chef/s:** Alex Grant. **Open:** Mon to Sat L 12 to 2.30, Tue to Sat D 5 to 10. **Closed:** Sun, 25 and 26 Dec, 2 weeks Jan. **Meals:** alc (tapas from £4 to £6). **Service:** not inc. **Details:** Cards accepted. 22 seats. Air-con. Music. Children allowed.

# The Queensberry Hotel, Olive Tree Restaurant
**Sumptuous dining and informed service**
4-7 Russel Street, Bath, BA1 2QF
Tel no: (01225) 447928
www.thequeensberry.co.uk
**Modern British | £38**
**Cooking score: 3**
£5 OFF

Four Georgian town houses knocked into one make up the lavish, chic Queensberry Hotel. There was an extensive refurbishment in 2008, and it is no surprise to find that the basement restaurant is now as sumptuous as the rest of the hotel. Low lighting, attentive, informed service and stylish table flowers set the mood. Nick Brodie's modern British menu uses seasonal ingredients to good effect, with starters such as Wye Valley asparagus and quails' eggs. Main courses might include Cornish brill unusually paired with chicken wings and a roast chicken sauce. Just the ticket, too, is a distinguished dessert of almond financier, glazed pear and pear sorbet. An extensive wine list is grouped by flavour for easy food matching; prices start at £15.
**Chef/s:** Nick Brodie. **Open:** Tue to Sun L 12 to 2 (12.30 Sun), all week D 7 to 10. **Meals:** alc (main courses £17 to £23). **Service:** not inc. **Details:** Cards accepted. 60 seats. Air-con. Separate bar. Music. Children allowed.

## The Royal Crescent Hotel, The Dower House

**Highly refined modern urban cooking**
16 Royal Crescent, Bath, BA1 2LS
Tel no: (01225) 823333
www.royalcrescent.co.uk
**Modern British | £60**
**Cooking score: 4**

The Dower House is tucked away behind the Royal Crescent Hotel in a secluded garden, and it goes in for a highly refined style of modern urban cooking (or 'ultra-modern and bitty' according to one reader). This translates as carpaccio of pork belly teamed with a Scottish langoustine, pickled kohlrabi, maple dressing and horseradish and caviar cream, or an autumnal main course that involved a version of bouillabaisse with rouille, black truffles and Parmesan croûtons served from a pumpkin at the table. Some have bemoaned the appearance throughout of those foams that Britain now seems heartily sick of, but as you head towards a dessert as diverting as a chocolate fondant parcel with passion fruit mousse and crème de cacao sorbet, you might just overlook the tendency. Service has been seen by some as 'slow and inefficient'. A brilliantly imaginative, quality-conscious, if expensive, wine list sees prices start at £26.
**Chef/s:** Gordon Jones. **Open:** all week L 12.30 to 2, D 7 to 9.30. **Meals:** Set L £18 (2 courses) to £25. Set D £50 (2 courses) to £60. Sun L £35. **Service:** not inc. **Details:** Cards accepted. 70 seats. 30 seats outside. Air-con. Separate bar. No mobile phones. Wheelchair access. Music. Children allowed.

## The White Hart

**Vintage pub on the up**
Widcombe Hill, Widcombe, Bath, BA2 6AA
Tel no: (01225) 338053
www.whitehartbath.co.uk
**Gastropub | £25**
**Cooking score: 3**

Reckoned to be one of Bath's oldest watering holes, the White Hart is renowned as a venue for drinking – especially when Bath are playing rugby at home – and it also provides hostel-style accommodation for travellers on a shoestring. These days, however, it is forging a reputation for assertive cooking, and observers say it now offers some of the 'most consistent' food in the city. Rupert Pitt keeps prices on a tight rein, but there's no shortage of confidence or quality on the plate. To start, you might fancy a terrine of pork and black pudding with apple and date chutney or smoked haddock risotto cake, while big-hearted mains could stretch from grilled free-range chicken breast with chorizo cassoulet to sea bream fillets with Jerusalem artichoke mash and sauce vierge. House wines start at £13.90 (£3.50 a glass).
**Chef/s:** Rupert Pitt, Jason Horn, Rachel Milsom and Luke Gibson. **Open:** all week L 12 to 2, Mon to Sat D 6 to 10. **Closed:** 25 and 26 Dec, 31 Dec, 1 Jan, bank hols. **Meals:** alc (main courses £11 to £15). **Service:** not inc. **Details:** Cards accepted. 52 seats. 40 seats outside. Separate bar. Music. Children allowed.

## ALSO RECOMMENDED

### ▲ The Garrick's Head

7-8 St Johns Place, Bath, BA1 1ET
Tel no: (01225) 318368
www.garricksheadpub.com
**Gastropub**

When on form, the Digneys' city-centre pub next to Bath's Theatre Royal delivers bold, no-frills classic British cooking built around a commitment to seasonality and local produce. The style is typified by pressed ham hock terrine with piccalilli (£6) or chargrilled mallard breast with confit leg and roast root vegetables (£14). But recent reports suggest that standards can be hit-or-miss. House wine is £12.50. Closed Sun D.

## ▲ Yak Yeti Yak

12 Pierrepont Street, Bath, BA1 1LA
Tel no: (01225) 442299
www.yakyetiyak.co.uk
**Nepalese**

The name should be in line for a comedy award, but the food is serious at this atmospheric Nepalese eatery. In a trippy basement setting of artefacts, prints and rugs, visitors can enjoy authentic food ranging from steamed momo dumplings (£4.80) to kukharako thukpa noodle soup (every Sherpa's 'staff of life'). Elsewhere, distinctive curries and vibrant vegetables embrace the likes of stir-fried pork bhutuwa (£7.10) and aloo tama (bamboo shoots, potatoes and black-eyed beans). One-plate lunches and early suppers (from £5.50) also hit the button. Drink Gurkha beer or house wine (£12.90). Open all week.

## ■ Bruton

**NEW ENTRY**
## At the Chapel

**Keen prices and an unusual setting**
High Street, Bruton, BA10 0AE
Tel no: (01749) 814070
www.atthechapel.co.uk
**Modern British | £20**
**Cooking score: 2**

In this sensitively converted chapel, nothing distracts from the splendour of the setting – white walls, dark wood floor, tall, curved windows and a single spectacular chandelier. The informal menu is equally well thought-out, with keenly priced crowd-pleasers such as burgers, terrines, salads and risottos. Attention to detail falters sometimes, but successes include a comforting chicken pie and perfectly seared calf's liver with a pile of buttery champ. The jewel in the crown is the wood-fired

oven, which turns out expertly crafted breads, pastries and pizzas for the restaurant and shop, plus peerless chocolate brownies and cakes. Wine from £13 a bottle.
**Chef/s:** Stephen Wesley. **Open:** all week 9 to 3 (11 to 3 Sun), Mon to Sat D 6 to 9.30. **Meals:** alc (main courses £9 to £18). **Service:** not inc. **Details:** Cards accepted. 65 seats. Separate bar. No music. Wheelchair access. Children allowed.

## ■ Clevedon
## Murrays

**An oasis of goodies for foodies**
87-93 Hill Road, Clevedon, BS21 7PN
Tel no: (01275) 341555
www.murraysofclevedon.co.uk
**Italian | £26**
**Cooking score: 4**

Murrays, an upmarket grocery-cum-neighbourhood deli and restaurant, is an oasis of good taste. Ogling the stock is a joy for anyone interested in food, be it goodies from Milan market or prime Somerset produce. The plain wood chairs and tables in the next-door-but-one restaurant look both rustic and modern, and Murrays' well-endowed larder drives the kitchen, giving it a strong Italian accent. Daily menus show commendable seasonal focus, so start, perhaps, with home-cured bresaola (a Somerset beef topside) with lemon and Fattoria Mose olive oil, or pappardelle with wild hare ragù. Follow with poached shoulder of local rose veal in a cream sauce with capers, cannellini beans, Savoy cabbage and mashed potatoes, or poached salt cod with butter beans, chilli mayonnaise and mixed leaves. Finish with generous desserts – maybe a caramelised passion fruit and Amalfi lemon tart with mascarpone. The appealing Italian wine list opens at £14.50.
**Chef/s:** Alex and Reuben Murray. **Open:** Tue to Sat L 12 to 2 (10 Sat), D 6 to 9.30. **Closed:** Sun, Mon, 24 Dec to 2 Jan. **Meals:** alc (main courses £10 to £21). Set L and D £15 (2 courses) to £20. **Service:** not inc. **Details:** Cards accepted. 72 seats. Air-con. Separate bar. No mobile phones. Wheelchair access. Music. Children allowed.

## Combe Hay

### The Wheatsheaf

**Sophisticated destination dining venue**
Combe Hay, BA2 7EG
Tel no: (01225) 833504
www.wheatsheafcombehay.com
**Modern British | £35**
**Cooking score: 5**

£5 OFF 🛏

Located in idyllic countryside just 15 minutes from Bath, this striking sixteenth-century former farmhouse oozes sophistication. Overlooking a lush valley complete with manor house and church, the exterior is clad in soft minty heritage shades. Inside, the pub has been stripped back to its original stone walls, flagstone floors and beams, with chic furnishings and Lloyd Loom chairs. Tables in the stunning, three-tiered garden are highly prized, and the owners have added a vegetable plot, hens and ducks in an attempt to make the kitchen more sustainable. Although it is still possible for walkers to pop in for a sandwich and pint of Butcombe bitter, this is very much a food destination, and chef Lee Evans's cooking has been tipped for stardom. There are some interesting flavour combinations in Cornish crab lasagne, mango, lemongrass and ginger foam or a main course of breast and confit of Wiltshire duck with Hispi cabbage and rhubarb tart, but reporters think the kitchen is trying too hard with ingredients 'quenelled and diced and turned to within an inch of their lives'. The 150-strong wine list is entirely European and majors on Bordeaux. House wine is £15.95 and there are 13 by the glass.
**Chef/s:** Lee Evans. **Open:** Tue to Sun L 12 to 2.30, Tue to Sat D 6.30 to 9 (9.30 Fri and Sat). **Closed:** Mon (except bank hols), first 2 weeks Jan. **Meals:** alc (main courses £15 to £24). Set L £14.95 (2 courses) to £18.95. Sun L £19.50 (2 courses) to £24.50. **Service:** 10% (optional). **Details:** Cards accepted. 50 seats. 30 seats outside. Music. Children allowed. Car parking.

## Corton Denham

### ALSO RECOMMENDED
### ▲ Queen's Arms

Corton Denham, DT9 4LR
Tel no: (01963) 220317
www.thequeensarms.com
**Modern British**

Right on the Somerset/Dorset border, this graciously gentrified hamstone inn still gives off a warming country vibe with its blazing fire and deep sofas. Enjoy a homemade pie and a pint in the bar, or opt for the terracotta-walled dining room, where menus highlight local ingredients including home-reared pork. Rabbit rillettes with spicy tomato chutney (£5.95) might by followed by rack of lamb with devilled kidneys and roasted mango (£16), with 'gooey' chocolate pudding (£5.90) to finish. Fascinating world beers and impressive wines by the glass (from £2.95). Open all week.

## East Coker

### ALSO RECOMMENDED
### ▲ Helyar Arms

Moor Lane, East Coker, BA22 9JR
Tel no: (01935) 862332
www.helyar-arms.co.uk
**Gastropub**

In the heart of a handsome feudal village, the fifteenth-century Helyar Arms is a cracking local, drawing a loyal drinking crowd. The food is good, too – worth the detour off the A37/A30 for Mathieu Eke's seasonally inspired menu that puts modern touches to traditional dishes. Bag a table by the fire in the homely, carpeted bar and tuck into pheasant, venison and rabbit terrine (£6.25), followed by shin of beef and Guinness stew with thyme dumplings (£13), and iced raspberry parfait (£6). House wine £13.50. Open all week. Accommodation.

## Hinton St George

### The Lord Poulett Arms

Vivid flavours in a revitalised pub
High Street, Hinton St George, TA17 8SE
Tel no: (01460) 73149
www.lordpoulettarms.com
Gastropub | £24
Cooking score: 3

Steve Hill and Michelle Paynton have breathed new life into this lovely hamstone pub in one of Somerset's most enchanting villages. Visitors now lap up its gentrified, rural chic interior, as well as partaking of outdoor pleasures in the fragrant herb garden, wildflower meadow and lavender-edged boules 'piste'. The menu covers a lot of ground and the kitchen generates vivid flavours in dishes such as beetroot and satsuma salad with goats' cheese and sour cherry vinaigrette or cumin and apple-glazed pork belly with spinach and polenta-crusted potatoes. There are also a few whiffs of the orient about, say, citrus-cured salmon with pomegranate, grapefruit and pickled ginger or Malaysian fish stew with rice noodles. Desserts pack an exotic punch with the likes of orange and cardamom crème brûlée accompanied by spiced shortbread. House wines start at £12.
Chef/s: Gary Coughlan. Open: all week L 12 to 2, D 7 to 9. Closed: 25 and 26 Dec, 1 Jan. Meals: alc (main courses £11 to £24). Sun L £16 (2 courses) to £19. Service: not inc. Details: Cards accepted. 70 seats. 40 seats outside. Separate bar. No music. Wheelchair access. Children allowed. Car parking.

## Long Sutton

### ALSO RECOMMENDED
### ▲ The Devonshire Arms

Long Sutton, TA10 9LP
Tel no: (01458) 241271
www.thedevonshirearms.com
Gastropub

The grandly porticoed former hunting lodge dominates the green in this sleepy village. The interior is more modern than you would expect, but is a 'nice place to relax and unwind'. Lunch in the bar is a mix of posh sandwiches, venison burger (£9.20) or bangers and mash, while dinner in the restaurant brings accomplished crab crème brûlée (£5.95) and duck breast and confit leg with creamy mash (£14.20). House wine £12.75. Open all week. Accommodation.

## Midsomer Norton

### The Moody Goose at the Old Priory

Ambitious food in a medieval priory
Church Square, Midsomer Norton, BA3 2HX
Tel no: (01761) 416784
www.theoldpriory.co.uk
Modern European | £40
Cooking score: 4

A converted twelfth-century priory in the prosperous backwaters of rural Somerset is the setting for Stephen Shore's affectionately nurtured set-up. The kitchen delivers 'slow food as it should be, with no fancy space dust or eclectic experiments', according to one reporter – but there's no shortage of enterprise or ambition, either. Local venison is paired with shiitake mushrooms and quince jelly, wild sea bass appears atop chorizo and cep risotto, and there's also room for Barbary duck breast with Puy lentils, orange and tarragon. Fine-tuned classic partnerships also show up strongly, as in a duo of fillet of beef and braised oxtail with girolles and Madeira sauce. Desserts might feature rhubarb and apple 'three ways' (a seasonal tribute to the Priory's walled garden), or you might prefer to finish with steamed date pudding and caramel sauce. The well-considered global wine list begins with a page of house selections from £17 (£4.50 a glass).
Chef/s: Stephen Shore. Open: Mon to Sat L 12 to 1.30, D 7 to 9.30. Closed: Sun, 25 and 26 Dec. Meals: alc (main courses £21 to £24). Set L £22.50 (2 courses) to £28.50. Set D £30. Service: not inc. Details: Cards accepted. 32 seats. Wheelchair access. Music. Children allowed. Car parking.

## Oakhill

ALSO RECOMMENDED
### ▲ The Oakhill Inn
Fosse Road, Oakhill, BA3 5HU
Tel no: (01749) 840442
www.theoakhillinn.com
**Gastropub**

A Somerset country inn with all the features
one hopes for − roaring fires in winter, tables
in the garden in summer, and lots of comfy
sofas − the Oakhill is run with warmth and
flair. A gastropub menu offers the likes of crab
cake with salad and mayonnaise (£5) to start,
and then fisherman's pie or slow-cooked pork
with goose-fat potatoes, roast roots and
brandied apple sauce (£13.50). Sticky toffee
pudding with toffee sauce (£5) is a favourite
dessert. Wines from £12. Closed Sun D.

## Portishead

**NEW ENTRY**
### The Lockhouse
**Estuary views and satisfying menus**
Lockside, Portishead, BS20 7AF
Tel no: (01275) 397272
www.thelockhouseportishead.co.uk
**Modern European | £25**
**Cooking score: 2**

Everybody approves of the principle behind
this Port Marine bar and restaurant that
occupies the site once filled by a tiny lock-
keeper's cottage − now extended to take in a
modern glass dining room and terrace.
Estuary views and busy vibes provide the
atmosphere, while the cheap all-day menu
(moules, chicken Caesar salad, beef burger),
bargains in the wine list (from £12.95) and the
ambitious evening carte supply satisfaction.
The performance on dishes as different as
scallops with cauliflower purée, fried golden
raisins and Muscatel vinaigrette, halibut
'lasagne' with gremolata, glazed baby carrots
and Madeira jus, and poached pear and ginger
tarte Tatin is satisfactory. Get directions when
booking.

**Chef/s:** Richard Gynn. **Open:** all week L 12 to 3 (6
Sun), D 6 to 10. **Meals:** alc (main courses £11 to
£19). Set L £13.95 (2 courses). Sun L £13.95.
**Service:** not inc. **Details:** Cards accepted. 60 seats.
32 seats outside. Air-con. Separate bar. Wheelchair
access. Music. Children allowed. Car parking.

## Shepton Mallet

ALSO RECOMMENDED
### ▲ Blostin's
29-33 Waterloo Road, Shepton Mallet, BA4 5HH
Tel no: (01749) 343648
www.blostins.co.uk
**Anglo-French**

Still rolling along after all these years, Nick
and Lynne Reed's homely restaurant remains a
model of local reliability. This is a small-scale,
almost domestic set-up with a cosy feel and
generous Anglo-French food − just the ticket
for a staunchly loyal crowd. Fixed-price
dinner menus (£18.95 for 3 courses) could
open with fish soup, before breast of duck
with roasted apples and cider or salmon with
creamy leeks and lemon butter. To finish,
perhaps white chocolate pannacotta. House
wine is £13.50. Open Tue to Sat D only.

## Shepton Montague

ALSO RECOMMENDED
### ▲ Montague Inn
Shepton Montague, BA9 8JW
Tel no: (01749) 813213
**Gastropub**

Affectionately known as the Monty, this
remote 200-year-old country boozer is famed
for its outdoor terrace and stupendous views
out towards Alfred's Tower. Food is of the
free-range, home-cooked variety, with West
Country ingredients showing up strongly on
the menu. Try duck liver parfait with pear and
vanilla relish (£5.50) before grilled chicken
breast with garlic mash and thyme sauce
(£14.50) or slow-baked pork with sage and
apple jus. Finish with tarte Tatin (£5.50) and a
glass of Burrow Hill Somerset Pomona.
House wine is £13.50. Closed Sun D.

## ▌ Stoke sub Hamdon

### The Priory House Restaurant

Personally run country charmer
High Street, Stoke sub Hamdon, TA14 6PP
Tel no: (01935) 822826
www.theprioryhouserestaurant.co.uk
**Modern British | £35**
**Cooking score: 5**

£5
OFF

The hamstone building on the high street was
built as a guest house for the village priory in
1789, and maintains its tradition of hospitality
as Peter and Sonia Brooks' relaxing country
restaurant. Just half a dozen tables ensure that
things remain manageable, and the
atmosphere of entering somebody's home is a
mighty appealing one. Peter's cooking is at the
gentler end of the modern British spectrum,
with combinations that make sense. Seared
scallops from Lyme Bay are teamed with
avocado, roasted red pepper, smoked bacon
and a lime dressing, while twin
accompaniments of beetroot chutney and
Sauternes jelly offset a classic foie gras terrine.
An occasional foray into Asian ways might
bring monkfish korma with Kashmiri apple
relish, rice pilaff and mini-poppadoms, or
there could be pink-roasted breast of Devon
duckling with braised red cabbage and apricot
sauce. Fruits cascade forth from a dessert
listing that might embrace summer berries set
in a Merlot jelly, or hot passion fruit soufflé
with a matching sorbet and crème anglaise.
Fine West Country cheeses await the less
sweet-toothed. A good slate of wines by the
glass from £4.50 heads up a list that offers
something from around the world for
everyone, with bottles starting at £14.
**Chef/s:** Peter Brooks. **Open:** Sat L 12.30 to 2, Tue to
Sat D 7 to 9. **Closed:** Sun, Mon, bank hols, 2 weeks
May, 2 weeks Nov. **Meals:** alc (main courses £19 to
£22). Set L £17 (2 courses) to £24. **Service:** not inc.
**Details:** Cards accepted. 20 seats. No mobile
phones. Wheelchair access. Music. Children
allowed.

## ▌ Taunton

### The Castle Hotel

A Somerset favourite
Castle Green, Taunton, TA1 1NF
Tel no: (01823) 272671
www.the-castle-hotel.com
**Modern British | £35**
**Cooking score: 4**

It still comes as a surprise to first-timers that
the Castle (it really was one) is plumb in the
centre of Taunton, behind a rather anonymous
high street. It is a vision from another era, an
impression confirmed by the faintly dated
interior, all spring greens and blossom pinks
in the dining room, with its crisply dressed
tables, giant candle lantern and 'even gianter
chandelier'. The cooking still tacks to the
country house style of a generation ago.
Dishes presented in trios are favoured, a crab
threesome for starters, including good
shredded white meat and tomato, as well as
glistening brown crab bavarois. Lamb in
spring offers another treble, with a denatured
shepherd's pie getting the vote. However,
performance can be patchy, dishes have been
let down by inaccurate timing or seasoning,
and the incidentals have been below par on
some occasions. There's little wrong with the
cheeseboard however – fine cheeses show a
wholly justified bias to the cream of the West
Country. A monster wine list is the principal
glory of the place, with France leading the
charge and shorter but reliable selections from
elsewhere. Wines by the glass start at £5. The
restaurant may be closed on Sunday and
Monday, so it's best to phone and book ahead.
**Chef/s:** Richard Guest. **Open:** all week L 12.30 to 2,
Mon to Sat D 7 to 10. **Meals:** alc (main courses £14
to £26). Set L and D £15 (2 courses) to £20 (except
Fri and Sat D). Sun L £30. **Service:** 12.5% (optional).
**Details:** Cards accepted. 70 seats. 30 seats outside.
Separate bar. No music. No mobile phones.
Wheelchair access. Children allowed. Car parking.

## The Willow Tree

**Hugely accomplished cooking and charm**
3 Tower Lane, Taunton, TA1 4AR
Tel no: (01823) 352835
**Modern British | £30**
Cooking score: 6

A listed seventeenth-century building, the
Willow Tree was once the Taunton moathouse
and enjoys a tranquil waterside setting. Darren
Sherlock and his partner Rita Rambellas left
the bustle of London behind and opened here
in 2002. They have created an enterprise of
great self-assurance and charm, and one that
enthusiastically celebrates the best the West
Country has to offer, from Newlyn fish to
locally reared meats, free-range ducks and
chickens, and, of course, the many fine
regional cheeses. It all happens in a
comfortable, smartly attired room with some
well-chosen pictures. The place opens five
evenings a week, plus the first Sunday of the
month for lunch, and Sherlock's sensitive,
hugely accomplished cooking has won many
converts. Poached salmon trout is fashioned
into a ballottine and served with a dressing of
smoked salmon, caviar and crème fraîche, or
there could be leek and white bean velouté
with truffle oil, to start. Main courses give
those quality meats and fish star billing,
whether in seared loin of venison with
creamed cauliflower and horseradish, roasted
button onions and roots, or sea bass with
crayfish and ginger risotto and coriander-
laced carrot purée. Desserts keep an eye on
seasonality with a spring menu that offers
poached rhubarb and custard tartlet and
lemon-curd ice cream. Chocoholics will make
a beeline for a hot fondant served with a plain
milk ice cream. Wines are a compact,
internationally jumbled selection, starting at
£16.95 (or £4.75 a glass) for a quartet of good
Australian and Argentinian varietals.
**Chef/s:** Darren Sherlock. **Open:** Tue to Sat D only
6.30 to 9.30. Open for L on first Sun of month.
**Closed:** Mon, Jan and Aug. **Meals:** Set D Tue and
Wed £22.50, Thur to Sat £29.50. **Service:** not inc.
**Details:** Cards accepted. 25 seats. 10 seats outside.
Separate bar. No mobile phones. Music. Children
allowed.

## ▌Wells

## Goodfellows

**For he's a jolly good fellow**
5 Sadler Street, Wells, BA5 2RR
Tel no: (01749) 673866
www.goodfellowswells.co.uk
**Modern European | £35**
Cooking score: 5
£5 OFF

Those in the know push through the inviting
French patisserie and café and head to the
restaurant at the back, where tables are
arranged around a central open-plan kitchen.
It's contemporary in style, with lots of stainless
steel, slate and marble (with extra seating up a
spiral staircase lit by a glass atrium). Here
Adam Fellows makes an impact by focusing
on 'lovely fresh fish'. An interesting
juxtaposition of ingredients – scallops with
pork rillettes, salmon with black pudding and
apple and honey-roast bacon – may raise
eyebrows but the results have 'really worked'
on the plate. In fact, there is an easy assurance
to much of the cooking, plus 'quite a light
touch' that's even seen in the odd meat dish like
roast breast of Gressingham duck with lentils
and celeriac and crispy vine leaf. Pan-fried
fillet of mackerel with soused vegetable,
saffron and spices is a good way to start, and
heroically local cheeses served with the
restaurant's excellent organic spelt and walnut
bread are a fine finale. 'Skilled but friendly and
unstuffy' describes the service, and the short
wine list is thoughtfully put together and
sensibly priced – house wine is £13.50.
**Chef/s:** Adam Fellows. **Open:** Tue to Sat L 12 to 2,
Wed to Sat D 6.30 to 9.30. **Closed:** Sun, Mon, 25 and
26 Dec, bank hol Mon. **Meals:** alc (main courses £10
to £23). Set L £16.50 (2 courses) to £19.30. Set D
£35. Tasting £55. **Service:** not inc. **Details:** Cards
accepted. 35 seats. Air-con. No mobile phones.
Wheelchair access. Music. Children allowed.

# The Old Spot

**Welcoming neighbourhood favourite**
12 Sadler Street, Wells, BA5 2SE
Tel no: (01749) 689099
Modern British | £28
Cooking score: 4

In a Georgian building with an elegant bay-windowed frontage, Ian and Clare Bates have established a thoroughly welcoming neighbourhood restaurant. It's quite a neighbourhood too, as you'll see from tables at the back, which have fabulous views over the green to the west front of Wells Cathedral. People return enthusiastically for favourite dishes, but the menus manage to be fresh, too. Start with grilled squid confidently seasoned with chilli, garlic and parsley, and go on with braised lamb shoulder with goats' cheese polenta and peperonata. An alternative route might be a majestically risen cep soufflé with Jerusalem artichoke and rocket salad, followed by roast pollack with fennel provençale, gremolata and olive oil mash. Reporters speak highly of the attention to detail and the quality of ingredients. Few will be able to resist desserts such as pannacotta with blood oranges in caramel. A concise and imaginatively chosen wine list has some helpful food suggestions, and a good list of bin-ends that don't stray above double figures. Prices open at £13.95.

**Chef/s:** Ian Bates. **Open:** Wed to Sun L 12.30 to 2.30, Tue to Sat D 7 to 10.30. **Closed:** Mon, 1 week Christmas. **Meals:** Set L £12.50 (2 courses) to £15. Set D £22.50 (2 courses) to £27.50. Sun L £15.50 (2 courses) to £18.50. **Service:** not inc. **Details:** Cards accepted. 50 seats. No music. No mobile phones. Wheelchair access. Children allowed.

## Great escapes

Our pick of out-of-the-way restaurants reward perseverance with peace. Just don't trust the satnav.

A sign halfway up the narrow lane from Chagford village to **Gidleigh Park** urges visitors to take heart; Michael Caines' food awaits.

In the crook of the River Hodder, **The Inn at Whitewell** offers shooting, fishing and fabulous walking from the front door.

The refurbished **Ardeonaig Hotel** is in a classic lochside setting, a surprising place to find chef/proprietor Pete Gottgens' extensive South African cellar.

An hour north-west from the Skye bridge, **The Three Chimneys** offers modern food in timeless island surroundings.

Thanks to chef James Sommerin's appearance on *Great British Menu*, more customers than ever are heading up the narrow track to **The Crown at Whitebrook**, in the serene Wye Valley.

In 67 acres dotted with sculpture, **The Samling** isn't far above busy Windermere, but it feels a world away.

Up, up and away from nearby Taunton, the comfy **Farmer's Inn** looks over the Somerset Levels from an idyllic hilltop spot.

## West Hatch

### The Farmer's Inn
Local produce and global dishes
West Hatch, TA3 5RS
Tel no: (01823) 480480
www.farmersinnwesthatch.co.uk
Gastropub | £25
Cooking score: 2

Hidden in the Somerset countryside, though within easy reach of Taunton, is this white-fronted, sixteenth-century inn with rooms. Inside, a series of interconnecting spaces feature a timber-framed bar, stripped wood tables and piles of logs ready to go on the fire should the weather be disobliging. Local produce is the name of the game, and it appears in some appealing global dishes. Rump of lamb with vegetable tagine and pistachio and coriander couscous is one possible main course, while horseradish-crusted trout fillets with tabbouleh make a thought-provoking starter. White chocolate and orange tart with Dorset clotted cream might bring you home again at meal's end. Local ales and ciders are not to be missed. A short wine list starts at £12.
Chef/s: Adam Boutwell. Open: all week L 12 to 2 (2.30 Sat and Sun), D 7 to 9 (9.30 Fri and Sat). Closed: 25 to 27 Dec. Meals: alc (main courses £10 to £17). Set L £12 (2 courses) to £15. Sun L £9.50. Service: not inc. Details: Cards accepted. 65 seats. 25 seats outside. Separate bar. Wheelchair access. Music. Children allowed. Car parking.

## Weston-Super-Mare

### The Cove
British
Birnbeck Road, Weston-Super-Mare, BS23 2BX
Tel no: (01934) 418217
www.the-cove.co.uk
'Delightful atmosphere, delicious food, lovely surroundings, great wine'

## Winsford

NEW ENTRY
### The Royal Oak
Eminently civilised village local
Halse Lane, Winsford, TA24 7JE
Tel no: (01643) 851455
www.royaloakexmoor.co.uk
Gastropub | £22
Cooking score: 1

Ed Hoskins and Kirsty Holden fly the seasonal and local flag in their eminently civilised thatched village inn. As much as possible is sourced from within 25 miles, and the kitchen makes good use of these ingredients for dishes like Exe Valley smoked trout with wild sorrel and lemon mayonnaise, Winsford lamb cutlets with braised lamb suet pudding, and a plate of West Country cheeses with sweet garlic and seed pickle. House wine from £11.95.
Chef/s: Richard Cowling. Open: all week L 12 to 3, D 6 to 9.30. Meals: alc (main courses £8 to £15). Service: not inc. Details: Cards accepted. 60 seats. 16 seats outside. Separate bar. No music. No mobile phones. Wheelchair access. Car parking.

## Wiveliscombe

NEW ENTRY
### The Barn at 10 The Square
Gem that's a real find
10 The Square, Wiveliscombe, TA4 2JT
Tel no: (01984) 629128
www.10thesquare.co.uk
Italian | £17
Cooking score: 4

'River Café in the heart of Somerset', is how one reader described the Barn, which is an extension of Sally Edwards' splendid period home. The fact that this place only opens in the evening for pre-booked groups of eight or more means that a little forward-planning is required, and lunches may be the better option for those travelling from afar. The café is set within a walled garden complete with a fish pond, which makes for wonderful alfresco dining in the summer. Sally cooks by herself in the small galley kitchen through which you have to pass to get to the bright, lofty dining area upstairs. Created with as much local, seasonal produce as she can find – some of it grown especially for her – the food is Italian-inspired: mushroom and mozzarella lasagne with rocket salad; chicken, pancetta, wine, cannellini beans and griddled polenta; baked pear with honey, Marsala, bay and crème fraîche. House wine from £13.50.

**Chef/s:** Sally Edwards. **Open:** Tues to Sun L 9.30 to 3 (11 Sun), D by arrangement for 8+. **Closed:** Mon. **Meals:** alc (main courses £7 to £9). **Service:** not inc. **Details:** Cards accepted. 20 seats. 30 seats outside. No mobile phones. Wheelchair access. Music. Children allowed.

## ▌Wookey Hole
### Wookey Hole Inn
**Quirky village pub**
High Street, Wookey Hole, BA5 1BP
Tel no: (01749) 676677
www.wookeyholeinn.com
**Gastropub | £28**
**Cooking score: 1**

'Love, peace and great food and wine' are promised at this idiosyncratic country inn opposite the famous caves, where a laid-back ambience forms a backdrop for some vivacious gastropub food. Smoked chicken and merguez sausage with a poached egg and salad might raise the curtain for mains such as sesame-crusted salmon with sweet chilli gnocchi and vegetable stir-fry. More chilli turns up in the chocolate tart, served with ginger ice cream. Wines start at £13.80 (£3.50 a glass).

**Chef/s:** Michael Davey. **Open:** all week L 12 to 2.30 (3.30 Sun), Mon to Sat D 7 to 9.30. **Closed:** 25 and 26 Dec. **Meals:** alc (main courses £14 to £24). **Service:** not inc. **Details:** Cards accepted. 70 seats. 100 seats outside. Separate bar. Wheelchair access. Music. Children allowed. Car parking.

## ▌Worth
**NEW ENTRY**
### The Pheasant Inn
**Real Italian food, made in Somerset**
Wells Road, Worth, BA5 1LQ
Tel no: (01749) 672355
www.the-pheasant-inn.com
**Italian | £25**
**Cooking score: 2**
**V** £30

With its skittles, cider and flagstones, The Pheasant looks like a conventional Somerset pub, but step inside the kitchen and the language changes to Italian – with authentic regional Italian food cooked from local produce. Service is warm and knowledgeable, with owner Roberto Perini running the restaurant as soon as he has finished making the fresh pasta. A starter of ravioli filled with ricotta and salmon served with a cheese and black truffle sauce and white truffle oil might be followed by pan-stewed Italian sausage with polenta, mushrooms and tomato sauce. A bottle of house wine is £13.

**Chef/s:** Mark Rushton. **Open:** all week L 12 to 4, D 7 to 9.30. **Meals:** alc (main courses £11 to £17). **Service:** not inc. **Details:** Cards accepted. 48 seats. 60 seats outside. Separate bar. Wheelchair access. Music. Children allowed. Car parking.

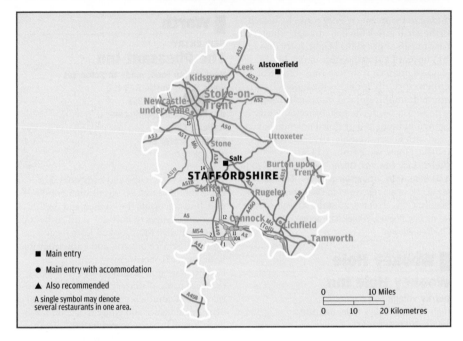

- ■ Main entry
- ● Main entry with accommodation
- ▲ Also recommended

A single symbol may denote several restaurants in one area.

## ■ Alstonefield

### The George

**Idyllic village pub**
Alstonefield, DE6 2FX
Tel no: (01335) 310205
www.thegeorgeatalstonefield.com
Gastropub | £24
Cooking score: 2

 V £30

Judging by the many reports from readers, the George simply oozes unpretentious country atmosphere. The simple décor runs to bare floorboards and plain wooden tables, but is still more defiantly pub than gastro, with the appealing menu offering homely dishes that don't stray too far from the pub classics repertoire. Haddock in a light crisp beer batter and Barnsley chop on a bed of bubble and squeak have found favour, as have starters of vegetable soup and roast tomato, garlic and goats' cheese risotto. Commitment to local produce extends to a farm shop, and house wine is £12.

**Chef/s:** Chris Rooney. **Open:** all week L 12 to 2.30, D 7 to 9 (8 Sun). **Closed:** 25 Dec. **Meals:** alc (main courses £9 to £17). **Service:** not inc. **Details:** Cards accepted. 40 seats. 20 seats outside. Separate bar. Wheelchair access. Children allowed. Car parking.

## ■ Beamhurst

### READERS RECOMMEND

### Restaurant Gilmore

**Modern British**
Strine's Farm, Beamhurst, ST14 5DZ
Tel no: (01889) 507100
www.restaurantgilmore.com
**'House speciality of Staffordshire blade of beef is excellent'**

## ▌Burton upon Trent

READERS RECOMMEND

### 99 Station Street

Modern British
99 Station Street, Burton upon Trent, DE14 1BT
Tel no: (01283) 516859
www.99stationstreet.com
'Good food, good atmosphere'

## ▌Salt

### The Holly Bush Inn

Fuss-free pub grub and fine ales
Salt, ST18 0BX
Tel no: (01889) 508234
www.hollybushinn.co.uk
Gastropub | £17
Cooking score: 2

 £5 OFF  £30

Born sometime in the twelfth century, this trimly thatched inn lays claim to being the 'second oldest licensed pub in the country', and it certainly looks the part with its carved beams, plank ceiling and knick-knacks. Real ale drinkers get full satisfaction from a splendid line-up of brews, and the food is a fuss-free assortment of honest pub grub with some neat local touches (braised lamb with apples and Packington free-range pork chops with a honey-mustard glaze) slipped in between the steaks and battered cod. 'Order the food at the bar and grab a table – quick' as no bookings are taken and the place fills up rapidly. House wine is £10.95.
Chef/s: Paul Hillman. Open: all week 12 to 9.30 (9 Sun). Closed: 25 and 26 Dec. Meals: alc (main courses £5 to £16). Service: not inc. Details: Cards accepted. 64 seats. 80 seats outside. No music. Wheelchair access. Children allowed. Car parking.

A walk, a pub and some grub

Raise a glass, feed the inner man (or woman) and cap it all with some leg-stretching across the great outdoors.

**The Gurnard's Head, Treen** Use this dramatically situated Cornish inn as a base camp for forays along the coastal path.

**The Drunken Duck Inn, Ambleside** Explore Tarn Hows and the low fells before heading back for a pint from the on-site Barngates Brewery.

**The Bell at Skenfrith, Skenfrith** Dreamy rustic Wales personified, complete with a river, castle and the wooded hills of the Monmow Valley. Simple seasonal food and an encyclopaedic wine list add charm.

**The Peat Spade Inn, Longstock** The Test Valley and the pleasures of the Test Way add to the allure of this bare-boarded pub-with-rooms in a thatched village.

**The Inn at Whitewell, Whitewell** If you want to see where much of your meal came from, head out for a trek through the neighbouring Trough of Bowland.

**The White Horse, Brancaster Staithe** A boon for fish fans, holidaymakers and lovers of north Norfolk's ozone-fuelled salt marshes. Ponder the views and enjoy some refreshment before heading out into the wide blue yonder.

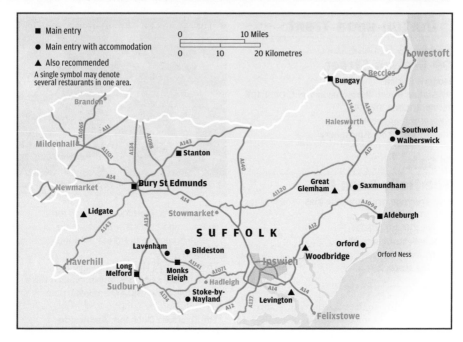

- ■ Main entry
- ● Main entry with accommodation
- ▲ Also recommended

A single symbol may denote several restaurants in one area.

0 _____ 10 Miles
0 ___ 10 ___ 20 Kilometres

# Aldeburgh

## The Lighthouse

**Dependable seaside favourite**
77 High Street, Aldeburgh, IP15 5AU
Tel no: (01728) 453377
www.lighthouserestaurant.co.uk
Modern British | £25
Cooking score: 2

£5 OFF    £30

An animated local institution, this happy-go-lucky venue has been lighting up the Aldeburgh scene for some 15 years. It gives off a cheery seaside vibe and serves the community admirably, feeding the Festival faithful, keeping the cinema crowds satisfied and looking after the residents come winter. The food is just the ticket, too, with keen prices, cosmopolitan ideas and plenty of seafood from the Aldeburgh boats. Whether you fancy fish and chips or duck confit with red cabbage, the kitchen can oblige, and it also rings the changes with Caribbean jerk chicken, sea bass on white wine risotto, and desserts such as chocolate nemesis. House wine is £12.95 (£3.25 a glass).
**Chef/s:** Guy Welsh and Sara Fox. **Open:** all week L 12 to 2 (2.30 Sat and Sun), D 6.30 to 10. **Meals:** alc (main courses £9 to £18). **Service:** not inc. **Details:** Cards accepted. 100 seats. 15 seats outside. Air-con. No music. No mobile phones. Wheelchair access. Children allowed.

## ALSO RECOMMENDED

### ▲ 152 Aldeburgh

152 High Street, Aldeburgh, IP15 5AX
Tel no: (01728) 454594
Modern European

A stone's throw from the beach and tucked back from Aldeburgh's busy High Street, this small bistro is perfectly in tune with its seaside town location. Expect a bright and contemporary feel inside, with plain tables, stripped wooden floors, simple modern artwork on plain walls and menus supplemented by chalkboard specials that feature locally landed fish. Mixed reports this year, but potted shrimps (£7.95) and pan-fried skate wing served with pancetta and caper butter (£13.95) have been praised. Finish with warm Bakewell tart with crème anglaise (£5.25). House wine £13.95. Reports please.

## ▲ Regatta

171 High Street, Aldeburgh, IP15 5AN
Tel no: (01728) 452011
www.regattaaldeburgh.com
Modern British

The sea is just a stroll away, so it's no surprise that local fish is a big player in this long-running, bright and breezy venue. Lobsters, sea bass, mackerel and more are listed on boards, and Regatta's own smokehouse also makes a contribution. Otherwise, dip into the regular menu, which features anything from baked goats' cheese in rosemary and shallot filo pastry (£11) to crisp pork belly with Thai spices (£12). Finish off with, say, caramel fudge and Malteser ice cream (£4). Wines from £12.95. Open all week.

## Bildeston

### The Bildeston Crown

Slick mix of ancient and modern
High Street, Bildeston, IP7 7EB
Tel no: (01449) 740510
www.thebildestoncrown.com
Modern British | £38
Cooking score: 4

This fifteenth-century, timber-framed former coaching inn re-opened after a sumptuous makeover five years ago, but visitors still feel the slick mixture of ancient and modern trappings 'can't make up their minds if they are city stylish or pastiche country'. Chris Lee is the driving force behind the menu and delivers contemporary classic food such as cumin-roasted scallops with chive pannacotta and cauliflower velouté. Presentation ensures that dishes look the part, but while materials are generally good, they sometimes have to

struggle to prove it: the mis-timing of fish has again been a complaint this year and the complex combinations in pork 'head to toe' left one reporter yearning for a vegetable. Crown classics such as fish and chips have been better reported, while desserts take in a perfectly executed chocolate fondant. Service is not sharp enough to match the ambition of the cooking. House wine is £20.

**Chef/s:** Chris Lee. **Open:** all week L 12 to 3, D 7 to 10. **Meals:** alc (main courses £12 to £20). Set L and D £15 (2 courses) to £18. Sun L £25. **Service:** not inc. **Details:** Cards accepted. 80 seats. 40 seats outside. Separate bar. No music. Wheelchair access. Children allowed. Car parking.

## Bungay

### Earsham Street Café

Food that's appealing on every level
13 Earsham Street, Bungay, NR35 1AE
Tel no: (01986) 893103
Modern British | £25
Cooking score: 2

The blue-fronted café is as unpretentious as they come, serving snacks and light dishes during the day, as well as a fuller lunch menu. Regulars will give thanks for the revival of evening openings on the last weekend of the month (book early!). The food is appealing on every level, from a starter like hot-smoked sprats with tomato bruschetta to mains such as fish pie topped with cheesy mash, or calf's liver and bacon with bubble and squeak and onion gravy. Dishes of the day are always worth a gander, bringing on perhaps braised oxtail with fine beans and mustard mash, before a comfort-food pudding like apple and cinnamon crumble with custard. Wines offer a broad selection by the glass (from £3.20), as befits a predominantly lunchtime venue.

**Chef/s:** Christopher Rice. **Open:** all week L 12 to 3.30 (2.30 Sun), last Fri and Sat of month D 7 to 9. **Closed:** Christmas, bank hols. **Meals:** alc (main courses £10 to £17). **Service:** not inc. **Details:** Cards accepted. 45 seats. 30 seats outside. Wheelchair access. Music. Children allowed.

## Bury St Edmunds

**★ READERS' RESTAURANT OF THE YEAR ★**
**EAST ENGLAND**

### Maison Bleue
Consistent French seafood restaurant
30-31 Churchgate Street, Bury St Edmunds,
IP33 1RG
Tel no: (01284) 760623
www.maisonbleue.co.uk
**Seafood | £25**
**Cooking score: 4**

 £30

The longstanding Maison Bleue is quite as customer-friendly now as it was when Regis Crépy (see the Great House, Lavenham) took it over in 1998. A comfortably appointed restaurant with white-clad tables and modern artworks, it is appreciated by locals as a highly reliable French restaurant, with the good-value lunch menu drawing special praise. Pascal Canevet keeps things light and modern, his menu embracing all things piscine. Fruits de mer are 'best in summer', skate wing meunière (with caperberry, lemon and croûtons) is a tried and true combination, but new juxtapositions are also employed – as when halibut fillet is served with honey, Tahitian vanilla and lime dressing. Meat dishes are more than token, and desserts include an 'unusual and delicious' slow-cooked Braeburn apple with brioche. Service is 'always excellent', and the wine list is well chosen with plenty of good drinking under £25 and house wines from £13.20.
**Chef/s:** Pascal Canevet. **Open:** Tue to Sat, L 12 to 2.30, D 7 to 9.30 (10 Fri and Sat). **Closed:** Sun, Mon, Jan, 2 weeks Aug. **Meals:** alc (main courses £14 to £24). Set L £13.95 (2 courses) to £16.95. Set D £25.95. **Service:** not inc. **Details:** Cards accepted. 65 seats. No mobile phones. Wheelchair access. Music. Children allowed.

## Great Glemham

### ALSO RECOMMENDED
### ▲ The Crown Inn
Great Glemham, IP17 2DA
Tel no: (01728) 663693
**Gastropub**

In a quiet village just a mile or so from the A12, the red-brick Crown, which dates from the seventeenth century, is a pleasant place in which to enjoy good food. Log fires, scrubbed tables and fresh flowers fill the homely bars, and menus bristle with great produce from local suppliers in and around the Alde Valley. Hearty dishes such as proper steak and kidney pudding (£9), beef and Guinness sausages with creamy mash and onion gravy, and warm chocolate tart with pistachio ice cream are typical. Wine from £12.99 a bottle. Closed Mon.

## Lavenham
### The Great House
Peerless reputation for French food
Market Place, Lavenham, CO10 9QZ
Tel no: (01787) 247431
www.greathouse.co.uk
**Modern French | £30**
**Cooking score: 4**

The Great House is a Lavenham institution with 25 years under its belt. It has carved out a formidable local reputation, thanks to the continuing efforts of Regis and Martine Crépy who, over the years, have imbued the place with an air of civilised charm. Refurbished in 2008, this timber-framed restaurant-with-rooms, 'seems to have taken a major step upwards with its facelift'. What is on offer is refined modern French cooking along the lines of carpaccio of native lobster with a white asparagus salad or a main course of wild sea bass marinated with olive oil, dill, and fennel seeds and served with a spaghetti of courgettes. Elsewhere, there's been praise for an assured duck foie gras ballottine with sultanas and roasted pistachios, Suffolk venison fillet with red wine and mustard sauce and red beetroot, and French lime cheesecake with red fruit marmalade. The value-for-money wine list opens at £12.95.

**Chef/s:** Regis Crépy. **Open:** Wed to Sun L 12 to 2.30, Tue to Sat D 7 to 9 (9.30 Fri and Sat). **Closed:** Mon, Jan, 2 weeks Jul/Aug. **Meals:** alc (main courses £15 to £24). Set L £16.95 (2 courses) to £18.95. Set D £28.95. **Service:** not inc. **Details:** Cards accepted. 50 seats. 24 seats outside. No mobile phones. Wheelchair access. Music. Children allowed.

# Levington

## ALSO RECOMMENDED
### ▲ The Ship Inn
Church Lane, Levington, IP10 OLQ
Tel no: (01473) 659573
**Gastropub**

This fourteenth-century pub is quite a looker, what with its thatched roof and pretty setting beside the River Orwell and the parish church. Inside, the low-ceilinged bar oozes atmosphere and drips with nautical paraphernalia, but the main eating action takes place in the rear dining room, overlooking the garden. Chef/landlord Mark Johnson delivers simple dishes along the lines of smoked bacon, vegetable and tomato soup (£4.75), steak and Suffolk ale pie (£9.75), and lemon and lime mousse (£5.60). House wine from £14.50. Open all week.

# Lidgate

## ALSO RECOMMENDED
### ▲ The Star Inn
The Street, Lidgate, CB8 9PP
Tel no: (01638) 500275
**Mediterranean**

A dyed-in-the-wool, pink-painted English inn formed of two cottages dating back to Elizabethan times, and with gardens front and back, the Star unexpectedly houses a Spanish restaurant. Expect clams in their shells with baby artichokes (£8.95) to start, and then lambs' kidneys in sherry with onions and bacon (£16.95) or textbook paella valenciana

with chicken, sausage, squid, mussels, langoustines and prawns in saffron rice (£17.95) to follow. Spanish wines feature strongly on the list, from £13. Closed Mon.

# Long Melford

## Scutchers
**Village restaurant with lots of choice**
Westgate Street, Long Melford, CO10 9DP
Tel no: (01787) 310200
www.scutchers.com
**Modern British | £30**
**Cooking score: 2**
£5 OFF

It's hard to miss the tall illuminated sign outside the fifteenth-century house that is home to the Barretts' modern bistro-style operation. A wide-ranging menu is based on tried-and-true culinary principles, taking in tempura-battered tiger prawns with spicy dipping sauce, calf's liver with bacon, mash and proper gravy, slow-roasted duck with orange sauce, or a rather luxurious fish ragoût that combines halibut, Dover sole and langoustines in a creamy, vermouth-based liquor. There's even caviar. Finish with apple and blackberry nutty crumble. A varietally organised wine list opens at £16.

**Chef/s:** Nick Barrett and Guy Alabaster. **Open:** Tue to Sat L 12 to 2, D 7 to 9.30. **Closed:** Sun, Mon. **Meals:** alc (main courses £12 to £24). Set L and D £18 (2 courses) to £24. **Service:** not inc. **Details:** Cards accepted. 60 seats. 15 seats outside. Air-con. Wheelchair access. Music. Children allowed. Car parking.

## Please send us your feedback

To register your opinion about any restaurant listed in the Guide, or a new restaurant that you wish to bring to our attention, please visit the web address at the bottom of the page. Your feedback informs the content of the book and will be used to compile next year's reviews.

## Monks Eleigh

### The Swan Inn

Imaginative cooking fits the bill
The Street, Monks Eleigh, IP7 7AU
Tel no: (01449) 741391
www.monkseleigh.com
**Gastropub | £24**
**Cooking score: 3**

£30

'A very pleasant local restaurant that sources carefully', just about sums up Carol and Nigel Ramsbottom's charming thatched village pub. Inside is unexpectedly contemporary, open-plan with modern polished wood floors and light, modern furniture. The sensible, regularly changing blackboard menu, underpinned by a classical theme, fits the bill perfectly. Local produce from a network of well-chosen suppliers is used to good effect: one winter visitor enjoyed a good-value set lunch of chickpea, pasta and vegetable soup followed by duck leg, with a rich chocolate truffle slice to finish. At other meals there have been home-cured gravlax, braised lamb 'osso buco' and chargrilled ribeye steak with hand-cut chips. Local cheeses have been praised, as has pannacotta with limoncello. House wine is £12.50.

**Chef/s:** Nigel Ramsbottom. **Open:** Tue to Sun L 12 to 2, D 7 to 9 (Sun D summer only). **Closed:** Mon, 25 and 26 Dec. **Meals:** alc (main courses £9 to £16). Set L and D £13.50 (2 courses) to £17.50. **Service:** not inc. **Details:** Cards accepted. 40 seats. 16 seats outside. Separate bar. No music. Children allowed. Car parking.

## Orford

### The Trinity, Crown and Castle

Welcoming mix of old and new
Orford, IP12 2LJ
Tel no: (01394) 450205
www.crownandcastle.co.uk
**Modern British | £35**
**Cooking score: 4**

≒ V

It might look like a Victorian hotel, but the Trinity's inner self harks back to the sixteenth century, albeit as a light, bright contemporary space with beamed ceilings, bare boards and polished tables in adjoining dining rooms. Menus, too, follow modern lines. Home-smoked trout combines with beetroot and new potato salad and horseradish cream, and pork belly lardons come with spiced pear, watercress salad and medlar jelly. More traditionally, Aberdeen Angus sirloin has been well-timed, enriched with Café de Paris glaze and served with good hand-cut chips, while pub-style lunches offer moules marinière, eggs Benedict and Suffolk steak and ale shortcrust pie. Warm loganberry jam and frangipane tart is a properly indulgent dessert. With plenty by the glass, the chatty, style-organised wine list suits the welcoming, unpretentious setting created by TV presenter Ruth Watson (Channel 4's *Country House Rescue*) and her husband David. Italian house white and Chilean red are £14.50.

**Chef/s:** David Williams. **Open:** all week L 12.15 to 2.15, D 6.45 to 9.15. **Closed:** 4 to 7 Jan. **Meals:** alc (main courses £14 to £20). Set L £20 (2 courses) to £25. Set D £25 (2 courses) to £35. Sun L £17.95 (2 courses) to £23.95. **Service:** not inc. **Details:** Cards accepted. 50 seats. Separate bar. No music. No mobile phones. Wheelchair access. Children allowed. Car parking.

## ALSO RECOMMENDED

### ▲ Butley Orford Oysterage
Market Hill, Orford, IP12 2LH
Tel no: (01394) 450277
www.butleyorfordoysterage.co.uk
**Seafood**

The Pinney family's vintage seafood café still stakes its reputation on the output of the owners' oyster beds and smokehouse, backed by supplies of fresh fish hauled from the inshore waters. Locals, holidaymakers and the Aldeburgh Festival crowd pack the place for plates of Butley bivalves (from £6.80), smoked Wester Ross salmon, cured sardines and more besides. Smoked chicken and ham salads appease the fish-phobes, and homely puds or Spanish ice creams (from £3.60) please everyone. House wine is £14.50. Open all week in season, but limited winter hours.

## ▮ Saxmundham

### The Bell Hotel
**Homely but inventive cooking**
31 High Street, Saxmundham, IP17 1AF
Tel no: (01728) 602331
www.bellhotel-saxmundham.co.uk
**Anglo/French | £25**
**Cooking score: 2**

The former coaching inn was once a pit-stop for George II on his journeys from the London court to his beloved Lowestoft. With the Aldeburgh Festival, Snape Maltings, a brace of RSPB reserves and the ravishing Suffolk coast all near to hand, the Bell hardly lacks for attractions, but Andrew Blackburn's cooking surely seals the deal. It's both homely and inventive, matching pollack with chorizo and butter beans in a starter, or serving roast venison loin with a sauce of bitter chocolate. A populist touch with desserts includes serving rice pudding with macerated prunes, or lacing the crème brûlée with whisky. House wines start from as little as £10.95.

**Chef/s:** Andrew Blackburn. **Open:** Tue to Sat L 12 to 2, D 6.30 to 9. **Closed:** Sun, Mon, 1 Jan, spring and autumn half-term. **Meals:** alc (main courses £14 to £17). Set L £12.50 (2 courses) to £15.75. Set D £19.50 (3 courses). **Service:** not inc. **Details:** Cards accepted. 26 seats. 15 seats outside. Separate bar. No mobile phones. Children allowed.

## ▮ Southwold

### Crown Hotel
**London by the seaside**
90 High Street, Southwold, IP18 6DP
Tel no: (01502) 722275
**Modern British | £30**
**Cooking score: 2**

Darling of the 'Sunday supplement set' and Southwold's floating out-of-town population, the Crown is about as metropolitan as you can get on the east Suffolk coast. The main action takes place in the throbbing Parlour – where it's 'first come, first served' and everyone is out to bag the best tables in the house. The kitchen deploys local ingredients (especially seafood) for dishes that sit comfortably with crowds weaned on big-city flavours. Expect mezze sharing plates, crusted chicken with feta fritters, roast Lowestoft cod with caper mash and sauce vierge, and puds such as coconut pannacotta with lemongrass sorbet. This is Adnams' flagship, and a showcase for one of the sexiest wine lists in the UK. Quirky gems and class acts abound, with 20 offered by the glass. Bottles start at £15.

**Chef/s:** Robert Mace. **Open:** all week L 12 to 2, D 6 to 9.30 (9 Sun). **Meals:** alc (main courses £13 to £20). **Service:** not inc. **Details:** Cards accepted. 70 seats. 32 seats outside. Separate bar. No music. No mobile phones. Wheelchair access. Children allowed. Car parking.

## Sutherland House

**Lots of style and low food miles**
56 High Street, Southwold, IP18 6DN
Tel no: (01502) 724544
www.sutherlandhouse.co.uk
Modern British | £30
Cooking score: 2

Food and rooms are bang-up-to-date at Peter and Anna Banks's fifteenth-century building in this upmarket seaside town. Beams, grand fireplaces and some fine plaster-work combine effortlessly with contemporary art, rich colours and modern lighting to create a relaxed ambience. Fresh, local and seasonal are buzz words, and the kitchen is truly passionate about food miles – the menu states the distance the main ingredients have travelled: 15 miles for a tapas-style starter of haddock chowder with quail's egg, one mile for braised beef with curly kale and horseradish foam, while grilled lemon sole accompanied by candied lemon, gnocchi and basil has 22 miles on the clock. Finish with a classic crème brûlée. House wine is £15.50.
**Chef/s:** Dan Jones. **Open:** all week L 12 to 3, D 7 to 9.30 (9 Sun). **Closed:** 25 Dec, Mon and Tue off season (Jan to May except bank hols). **Meals:** alc (main courses £11 to £21). Set L £9 to £24. **Service:** not inc. **Details:** Cards accepted. 50 seats. 30 seats outside. Wheelchair access. Music. Children allowed.

## Stanton

### The Leaping Hare

**Simplicity shines in a vineyard restaurant**
Wyken Vineyards, Stanton, IP31 2DW
Tel no: (01359) 250287
www.wykenvineyards.co.uk
Modern British | £27
Cooking score: 2

'Explore the Suffolk Wine Trail, then time your visit to Wyken Vineyard to coincide with lunch in the striking 400-year-old Suffolk barn' advises one visitor. A lofty, raftered ceiling, wood-burning stoves and wooden floors give a civilised charm to the split restaurant and informal café. Both offer modern daily menus that focus on quality home-grown or very local produce. Simplicity characterises the cooking, allowing clear flavours to shine through, as seen in a creamy leek and butternut squash risotto, Stowlangtoft lamb cutlets with ratatouille, and Wyken rhubarb custard tart with stem ginger ice cream. There's a Saturday morning farmers' market and the compact wine list includes Wyken Vineyards bottles from £14.
**Chef/s:** Jon Ellis. **Open:** all week L 12 to 2.30, Fri and Sat D 7 to 9. **Closed:** 25 Dec to 3 Jan. **Meals:** alc (main courses £13 to £18). Set L £18.95 (2 courses) to £22.95. Sun L £18.95. **Service:** not inc. **Details:** Cards accepted. 55 seats. 25 seats outside. Separate bar. No music. Wheelchair access. Children allowed. Car parking.

## Stoke-by-Nayland

**NEW ENTRY**

### The Crown

**Traditional dishes with a modern twist**
Park Street, Stoke-by-Nayland, CO6 4SE
Tel no: (01206) 262001
www.crowninn.net
Modern British | £25
Cooking score: 2

Spruced-up with a fresh, contemporary feel inside and clutch of stylish rooms behind, the Crown is a classy, modern-day inn set in a pretty village within easy reach of Lavenham and Constable Country. Low-beamed rooms, cosily lamp-lit and warmed by log fires, and ales from Suffolk brewers are complemented by a seasonal menu that draws on local produce and combines traditional dishes with modern ideas. Potted kippers with homemade piccalilli, braised wild rabbit or Blythburgh smoked pork chop with mustard sauce, and lemon and lavender crème brûlée are typical choices. The outstanding wine list opens with a Languedoc Grenache at £13.50 – don't miss the wine shop.

**Chef/s:** Mark Blake. **Open:** all week L 12 to 2.30, D 6 to 9.30 (10 Fri and Sat, 9 Sun). **Closed:** 25 and 26 Dec. **Meals:** alc (main courses £10 to £19). **Service:** not inc. **Details:** Cards accepted. 130 seats. 100 seats outside. Separate bar. No music. Wheelchair access. Children allowed. Car parking.

# Walberswick
## The Anchor

**A seaside breath of fresh air**
Main Street, Walberswick, IP18 6UA
Tel no: (01502) 722112
www.anchoratwalberswick.com
**Modern British | £25**
Cooking score: 2

Having been innkeepers in southwest London over a number of years, Mark and Sophie Dorber decided in 2004 to avail themselves of a breath of sea air. The result was the successful remaking of this Suffolk coastal pub, a mere 400 yards from the beach. Guest-rooms, a trio of bars and a restaurant menu cooked by Sophie are all part of the deal. Salt cod brandade with baked egg, local game terrine with plum chutney, and mains such as mutton hotpot with cabbage help reinforce the comforting domestic atmosphere, while the Provençal-style fish soup with rouille has been praised to the skies. Finish with meringue and brown bread ice cream. Wines start at £12.75, and beers, which have their own list, are treated just as seriously.
**Chef/s:** Sophie Dorber. **Open:** all week L 12 to 3, D 6 to 9. **Closed:** 25 Dec. **Meals:** alc (main courses £12 to £19). **Service:** not inc. **Details:** Cards accepted. 100 seats. 120 seats outside. Separate bar. No music. Wheelchair access. Children allowed. Car parking.

# Woodbridge

ALSO RECOMMENDED
## ▲ The Riverside

Quayside, Woodbridge, IP12 1BH
Tel no: (01394) 382587
www.theriverside.co.uk
**Modern British**

Sitting next to the River Deben is the gastro-arts complex of the Riverside, where a combined film and dinner deal (£30) should sort an evening out very comprehensively. Otherwise, look to the carte for rollmops in sour cream and chives (£6), with maybe sage-and lemon-crusted rump of Ketley Farm lamb (£17) or Loch Duart salmon with spring onion mash and garlic and chilli butter (£16) to follow. A range of inspired desserts (£6) includes caramelised pineapple with lemongrass granita. Wines from £14. Closed Sun D.

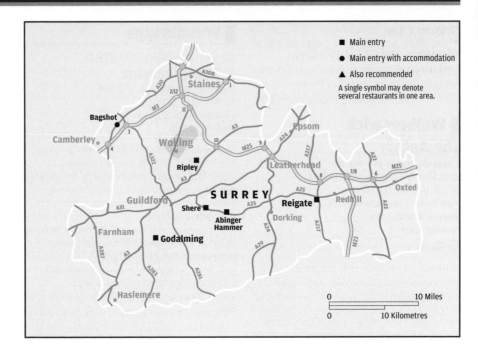

Map legend:
- ■ Main entry
- ● Main entry with accommodation
- ▲ Also recommended

A single symbol may denote several restaurants in one area.

## ▌Abinger Hammer

## Drakes on the Pond

**High-class village restaurant**
Dorking Road, Abinger Hammer, RH5 6SA
Tel no: (01306) 731174
www.drakesonthepond.com
**Modern British | £44**
**Cooking score: 5**

We somehow managed to position Drakes on the M25 last year. It is of course the A25 Guildford to Dorking road, a far pleasanter prospect. Certainly, the place itself, perched by the Pond (actually a large fishing lake), is a world away from all such hurly-burly, and the low-ceilinged dining room, with its deep blue carpet and pale primrose walls, looks like a welcome retreat. John Morris continues to set a high standard, producing food that follows the seasons, but with a fondness for mixing Anglo-French technique and oriental seasoning to good effect. A tian of crab and coconut comes with tempura-battered soft-shell crab and mango salsa, while scallops might be teamed with confit duck and orange in a sauce of tarragon and star anise. Main courses gently raise the game even higher, building layers of flavour in dishes such as loin and slow-cooked leg of rabbit, with a rabbit and potato hash, buttered spinach, puréed carrot and cardamom and a classical grain mustard sauce. The enveloping rich hues of toffee, chocolate and treacle are much in evidence among desserts, but there might also be lemon posset with ginger shortbread and lemon meringue ice cream. Lunch is a notable bargain given the quality. The French-led wine list starts at £18 (£4.75 a glass).
**Chef/s:** John Morris. **Open:** Tue to Fri L 12 to 1.30, Tue to Sat D 7 to 9.30. **Closed:** Sun, Mon, 25 and 26 Dec, 31 Dec and 1 Jan, 2 weeks late Aug. **Meals:** alc (main courses £24 to £28). Set L £19.50 (2 courses) to £23.50. **Service:** not inc. **Details:** Cards accepted. 30 seats. Air-con. No mobile phones. Wheelchair access. Car parking.

## ▌Bagshot

# Michael Wignall at the Latymer

**Original cooking from a serious chef**
Pennyhill Park Hotel, London Road, Bagshot, GU19 5EU
Tel no: (01276) 471774
www.pennyhillpark.co.uk
**Modern European | £58**
**Cooking score: 7**

⊟ V

The eating options at this pristine hotel surrounded by beautiful grounds take in a brasserie and the fine-dining Michael Wignall at the Latymer. The latter is a classy, almost club-like room with oak beams, panelling and mullioned windows. In contrast, the cooking is bright and modern. An opening salvo of tuna wrapped in aubergine, infused with lime and coriander created just the right effect. Originality and complexity are obsessions here, so it's no surprise that the tuna is accompanied by balsamic tapioca and fennel pannacotta, or that cannelloni-shaped Landais duck liver is wrapped with Jabugo ham and placed on top of a delicate film of camomile jelly, and accessorised with figs and camomile espuma. Squid is given star treatment; its ink used in a flaky crisp, and its body and tentacle served with king oyster mushrooms and finished off with a velvety smoked salmon velouté. This is a chef who takes his craft seriously – and there is no denying the effort and care of Michael Wignall and his team. Quail is poached, then glazed with Comté cheese and served with braised calf's tongue, wild asparagus, and confit onion purée – a perfect balance of flavours and textures. Aged prune parfait with a date cake, semi-dried figs and passion fruit sabayon further showed off the ability to mix flavours without over-indulgence. One reporter felt the restaurant needs to re-think its policy of not opening for lunch at weekends, and demanding credit card details for a weekday lunch when the restaurant was quiet. However, the service guarantees that you leave with a glow of contentment. The wine list is well-collated (and expensive), with even-handed selection of other countries beyond France. Prices start from £25. Two dozen by the glass (from £8.50) compensate for the lack of half-bottles.
**Chef/s:** Michael Wignall. **Open:** Tue to Fri L 12 to 2, Tue to Sat D 7 to 9.30 (10 Fri and Sat). **Closed:** Sun, Mon, 1 to 14 Jan. **Meals:** Set L £32 (3 courses). Tasting menu L £58. Set D £58 (3 courses). Tasting menu D £78. **Service:** not inc. **Details:** Cards accepted. 50 seats. Air-con. Separate bar. No music. No mobile phones. Wheelchair access. Car parking.

## ▌Cranleigh

**READERS RECOMMEND**

# Take it to the Table

**International**
127 High Street, Cranleigh, GU6 8AU
Tel no: (01483) 274036
'An upmarket deli combined with an excellent restaurant'

## ▌Forest Green

**READERS RECOMMEND**

# The Parrot Inn

**Gastropub**
Forest Green, RH5 5RZ
Tel no: (01306) 621339
www.theparrot.co.uk
'Open wood fires, friendly staff... and the menu is interesting and varied'

## ▌Godalming

# La Luna

**Living la dolce vita**
10-14 Wharf Street, Godalming, GU7 1NN
Tel no: (01483) 414155
www.lalunarestaurant.co.uk
**Italian | £28**
**Cooking score: 4**

£5 OFF 🍴 V £30

The brown tones of the dining room may strike a sober note, but the welcome at Godalming's reference-point Italian is effusively warm. Valentino Gentile cooks in the modern idiom, sourcing conscientiously (Nocellara olives and cold-pressed olive oil from Sicily, Freedom Food Scottish salmon, Orkney lamb) and allowing the main ingredients to speak for themselves. The menu is traditionally constructed, however, with antipasti such as carpaccio or smoked salmon followed by *primi piatti* pasta and risotto options (including ravioli of scamorza in minestrone sauce), and then the *secondi* main business. That salmon might appear simply dressed in orange and dill mayonnaise, or there could be lamb rump with rosemary jus and potato gratin. Steaks are seared to pink and served with a sauté of seasonal mushrooms. You know you'll want a tiramisu or pannacotta to finish – and you won't be disappointed – or consider lemon tart with blueberry coulis and orange zest mascarpone. A flag-waving wine list of Italian gems is on hand to add the icing to the cake. Pick your region from the map at the front, and explore with confidence. Prices open at £13.

**Chef/s:** Valentino Gentile. **Open:** Tue to Sat L 12 to 4, D 7 to 10. **Closed:** Sun, Mon. **Meals:** alc (main courses £9 to £18). **Service:** not inc. **Details:** Cards accepted. 50 seats. Air-con. No mobile phones. Wheelchair access. Music. Children allowed.

## ▌Reigate

## Tony Tobin @ The Dining Room

**Easy-paced neighbourhood eatery**
59a High Street, Reigate, RH2 9AE
Tel no: (01737) 226650
www.tonytobinrestaurants.co.uk
**Modern European | £37**
**Cooking score: 2**

Tony Tobin is no slouch when it comes to self-promotion – hence the personalised moniker of his bustling first-floor eatery. Soft lights and sweet music set the mood in the relaxed, mirrored dining room, and the food aims to satisfy all requirements. Various regularly changing menus follow the contemporary European route, offering the likes of marinated salmon with deep-fried oysters and

Champagne velouté ahead of breast of guinea fowl with confit leg, vanilla mash and lime jus. For dessert, how about gooseberry mousse with elderflower jelly? House wine is £15.95.
**Chef/s:** Tony Tobin and Jason Drew. **Open:** Mon to Fri and Sun L 12 to 2.30, Mon to Sat D 7 to 9.30 (10 Fri and Sat). **Closed:** 23 Dec to 3 Jan, bank hols. **Meals:** alc (main courses £18 to £28). Set L £12.50 (2 courses) to £18.50. Set D £18.50. Tasting menu £42. **Service:** 12.5%. **Details:** Cards accepted. 80 seats. Air-con. Separate bar. Music. Children allowed.

## The Westerly

**Charming, good-value bistro**
2-4 London Road, Reigate, RH2 9AN
Tel no: (01737) 222733
www.thewesterly.co.uk
**Modern British | £29**
**Cooking score: 4**

£5 OFF    £30

A snappy, modern interior of polished wood and simple furnishings sets the tone here for a refreshingly unpretentious slice of high street dining. Chef and co-proprietor Jon Coomb has won plenty of followers with his 'well-presented, beautifully cooked' bistro food. Kick off with terrine of chicken livers and bacon with cornichons and toast, then raise the comfort rating with excellent crisp belly of pork with morcilla and potato hotpot and Granny Smith purée. The St Clements cream is a good choice for dessert, but other options could include poached rhubarb and strawberries with Catalan cream. This is charming, unfussy cooking with service to match. The 'very good-value' set lunch comes highly recommended, and there are 'glasses of wine to suit all budgets'. The wine list hops between Europe and the New World, with wines neatly divided by style. Bottles start at £13.95.
**Chef/s:** Jon Coomb. **Open:** Wed to Fri L 12.30 to 3, Tue to Sat D 7 to 10. **Closed:** Sun, Mon, 25 Dec to 1 Jan. **Meals:** alc (main courses £16 to £19). Set L £17.50 (two courses) to £19.50. **Service:** not inc. **Details:** Cards accepted. 45 seats. Air-con. No music. Children allowed.

# Ripley

## Drake's Restaurant
**Experimental cooking and fascinating flavours**
The Clock House, High Street, Ripley, GU23 6AQ
Tel no: (01483) 224777
www.drakesrestaurant.co.uk
**Modern British | £46**
**Cooking score: 6**
£5
OFF **V**

The converted Georgian house, with a renovated clock on the front and a well-maintained walled garden, is the fulfilment of an ambition for Steve Drake. He pursues an invigorating, experimental approach to cooking, trying out unusual techniques and combinations in a style that wins converts. Presentation is generally immaculate, and the build-up of flavours in a dish can be fascinating. Pannacotta (a celery and almond version) might appear among the starters, along with roasted veal sweetbread and a mushroom biscuit, while a composition of venison for main course offers dual-cooked saddle (poached, then roasted), together with a burger of the meat and some cocoa gnocchi for good measure. Fish cookery is equally bold, perhaps adding celeriac fondant, onion purée and liquorice sauce to red mullet. At dessert stage, you won't be surprised to see vegetables and spices cropping up in the form of carrot and cumin cake with cumin syrup and orange ice cream. It's all served in a sympathetic, non-reverential atmosphere, a philosophy that extends to the sponsoring of the local junior-school pantomime. A fine wine list does the classic French regions in depth, before tearing off around the world. Prices are on the tough side, with even small glasses starting at £5.50.
**Chef/s:** Steve Drake. **Open:** Tue to Fri L 12 to 1.30, Tue to Sat D 7 to 9.30. **Closed:** Sun, Mon, 2 weeks Jan, 2 weeks Aug. **Meals:** Set L £21 (2 courses) to £26. Set D £38.50 (2 courses) to £46. Tasting menu £60. **Service:** not inc. **Details:** Cards accepted. 42 seats. No music. No mobile phones. Children allowed.

# Shere

## Kinghams
**Endearingly cosy village restaurant**
Gomshall Lane, Shere, GU5 9HE
Tel no: (01483) 202168
www.kinghams-restaurant.co.uk
**Modern British | £35**
**Cooking score: 3**
£5
OFF

Chef/proprietor Paul Baker has been driving this amenable village restaurant since 1993 and continues to deliver a convincing package for the denizens of rural Surrey and beyond. The building flaunts its endearingly cosy seventeenth-century charms, although the food keeps its feet planted in the present with the help of a daily fish specials board and some cleverly honed modern ideas. Seared scallops might be invigorated with a mango, pine nut and red pepper salsa, roasted venison appears in company with parsnip mousse, ginger shortbread and peppermint jus, while a dish of loin of lamb rolled with black pudding served on a root vegetable casserole adds a gutsy note to proceedings. To finish, hot steamed lemon pudding gets a lift from lemon mascarpone and raspberry compote. House wines are £15.95 (£4.50 a glass).
**Chef/s:** Paul Baker. **Open:** Tue to Sun L 12 to 3, Tue to Sat D 7 to 10. **Closed:** 25 Dec to 6 Jan. **Meals:** alc (main courses £11 to £23). Set L and D £16.50 (2 courses) to £22.45. Sun L £20.95. **Service:** not inc. **Details:** Cards accepted. 45 seats. 20 seats outside. No mobile phones. Music. Children allowed. Car parking.

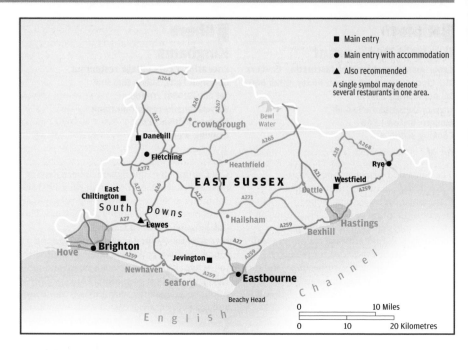

## ▌Brighton
### Bill's Produce Store

**Foodie market vibes**
The Depot, 100 North Road, Brighton, BN1 1YE
Tel no: (01273) 692894
www.billsproducestore.co.uk
**Modern British | £20**
**Cooking score: 3**

V

A high-profile offshoot of the original
Produce Store in Lewes, ex-greengrocer Bill
Collison's Brighton crowd-puller occupies a
converted bus depot that now serves as an
artisan local food market, wine shop, deli and
populist all-day eatery. From breakfast
onwards, the place deals in everything from
buttermilk pancakes and now-legendary fish
finger sandwiches to everything-included
lunch plates and daily specials (say, sardine,
caper and roasted pepper pizza). Come
evening, the kitchen puts on its gladrags for
hearty brasserie dishes such as Thai-spiced
pumpkin and coconut curry, beef and ale

casserole, chicken, mango and buckwheat
noodle salad or smoked haddock with leek
and mustard mash. After that, perhaps some
British cheeses or Bill's trademark aggafredo
(vanilla ice cream with espresso coffee). A
dozen gluggable wines start at £13.65 (£3.40
a glass); otherwise, there are juices, smoothies,
crushes and milkshakes aplenty.
**Chef/s:** Andy Pellegrino and Christy Robson. **Open:**
all week 8 to 5 (10 to 4 Sun), Mon to Sat D 5 to 10.
**Closed:** 25 and 26 Dec, 1 Jan. **Meals:** alc (main
courses £8 to £15). **Service:** not inc. **Details:** Cards
accepted. 96 seats. Air-con. Wheelchair access.
Music. Children allowed.

### Please send us your feedback

To register your opinion about any
restaurant listed in the Guide, or a new
restaurant that you wish to bring to our
attention, please visit the web address at
the bottom of the page. Your feedback
informs the content of the book and will be
used to compile next year's reviews.

## Due South

**Beach pebbles scrunch while you lunch**
139 Kings Road Arches, Brighton, BN1 2FN
Tel no: (01273) 821218
www.duesouth.co.uk
**Modern British | £33**
**Cooking score: 2**

 **V**

Located right on the beach, in the old
Victorian arches, Due South is within earshot
of plashing waves and the scrunch of pebbles.
The pan-European cooking, which is based
on local ingredients, delivers herb-crusted
Sussex goats' cheese with beetroot brioche, or
seared Brighton scallops with black pudding,
followed by roast Castle Farm beef ribeye,
smoked potato fondant and rosemary and
roast garlic jus. Vegetarian dishes show
imagination, as in parsnip and smoked
shiitake risotto, and meals end with rhubarb
crème brûlée or local cheeses. Wine prices
open at £14, and include a good selection of
organic and biodynamic gear.
**Chef/s:** Michael Bremner. **Open:** all week L 12 to
3.30, D 6 to 9.45. **Closed:** 25 and 26 Dec. **Meals:** alc
(main courses £9 to £28). **Service:** 12.5% (optional).
**Details:** Cards accepted. 55 seats. 40 seats outside.
Air-con. Wheelchair access. Music.

## The Foragers

**Refreshingly quirky and likeable local**
3 Stirling Place, Brighton, BN3 3YU
Tel no: (01273) 733134
www.theforagerspub.co.uk
**Gastropub | £26**
**Cooking score: 2**

This laid-back pub in a quiet back street in
Hove is refreshing and likeable – low-key
with a robustly seasonal and quirky attitude to
food. The daily changing menus are peppered
with seasonal ingredients – say, Tuscan-style
deep-fried local squid or twice-baked soufflé
(with local cowslip cheese, crushed blue
potatoes, roast red onion, wilted wild greens
and garlic cream) – which suggest
considerable dedication to sourcing. Slow-

cooked lamb stew comes with herb dumplings
and creamy mash, while wonderful comfort
desserts could feature sticky toffee cheesecake
or apple and cinnamon steamed pudding.
House wine is £11.65.
**Chef/s:** Georgina Clarke and Rebecca Misich. **Open:**
all week L 12 to 3 (4 Sat and Sun ), Mon to Sat D
6.30 to 10. **Closed:** 25 Dec. **Meals:** alc (main courses
£11 to £20). Set L £12.40 (2 courses) to £22. Set D
£19.50 (2 courses) to £25.50. **Service:** not inc.
**Details:** Cards accepted. 100 seats. 100 seats
outside. Wheelchair access. Music. Children
allowed.

## The Ginger Pig

**Gastropub cooking that's a cut above**
3 Hove Street, Brighton, BN3 2TR
Tel no: (01273) 736123
www.gingermanrestaurants.com
**Modern European | £22**
**Cooking score: 4**

Dreamed up by Brighton restaurateur Ben
McKellar (see following entry for
Gingerman), the Ginger Pig remains a pub
that attracts the locals, but it has also become a
destination restaurant for people who care
about food. It has a bright, warm, modern
feel, is run with well-honed professionalism,
and offers appealing, crowd-pleasing
contemporary menus bolstered by daily
blackboard specials. The kitchen shows sound
talent and avoids complication by
concentrating attention on the main
ingredients. Delicate flavours in a five-spiced
roast quail complemented by apple rémoulade
and a Madeira reduction, fresh local mackerel
teamed with potato, tarragon and olive salad
and a good romesco sauce, and proper hand-
cut chips accompanying chargrilled ribeye
steak epitomise careful buying and an unfussy
approach. Desserts range from spotted dick
and rum anglaise to chestnut and frangipane
tart with chocolate ice cream. The well-spread
wine list provides sound drinking from £14.
**Chef/s:** Ben McKellar and Joss Holland-Forrester.
**Open:** all week L 12 to 2 (12.30 to 4 Sat and Sun), D
6.30 to 10. **Meals:** alc (main courses £9 to £18). Set

L £10 (2 courses). **Service:** not inc. **Details:** Cards accepted. 55 seats. 35 seats outside. Separate bar. Wheelchair access. Music. Children allowed.

## Gingerman

**Cool hotspot that makes you happy**
21A Norfolk Square, Brighton, BN1 2PD
Tel no: (01273) 326688
www.gingermanrestaurants.com
**Modern European | £25**
**Cooking score: 3**

Ben McKellar's original Brighton restaurant, in a side-street off the seafront, has sailed on into its second decade with barely a blip. It's a cosy place done in muted tones, often jam-packed but run with appreciable front-of-house cool. 'Everything about this restaurant makes you feel happy', declares a reader who knows what's good for her. The assured modern European cooking might encompass a busy starter of wood pigeon with potato cakes, poached rhubarb, watercress and walnuts, followed perhaps by chargrilled rump of veal in a spiced tomato reduction, with Hispi cabbage, shallots and capers. Fish is always reliably well-timed, and desserts maintain the standard with limoncello pannacotta, served with hazelnut biscotti and candied lemon. The wine list opens at £15. **Chef/s:** Simon Neville-Jones and Ben McKellar. **Open:** Tue to Sun L 12.30 to 2, D 7 to 10. **Closed:** Mon, 1 week Christmas. **Meals:** Set L £10 (2 courses) to £15. Set D £25 (2 courses) to £30. Sun L £18 or £22. **Service:** not inc. **Details:** Cards accepted. 32 seats. Air-con. Music. Children allowed.

### Symbols

 Accommodation is available

 Three courses for less than £30

**V** More than three vegetarian main courses

£5 OFF £5-off voucher scheme

Notable wine list

## La Marinade

**Eclectic neighbourhood restaurant**
77 St Georges Road, Brighton, BN2 1EF
Tel no: (01273) 600992
www.lamarinaderestaurant.co.uk
**Modern European | £25**
**Cooking score: 1**

It's always showtime at Nick Lang's cosy neighbourhood gaff in Brighton's hip quarter. He's been dishing up the goods in this Regency terraced house since 2002 and still dips his hands into the global melting pot for racy ideas and ingredients. Much comes from the Med and Spain, whether it's charcuterie with pickled chillies and caperberries, chicken breast stuffed with Majorcan sobrasada sausage, or wild sea bass paired with Ortiz anchovies, capers and black olives. Rounding things off are desserts such as banana and sesame flambé. Wines from £12.95 also bang the eclectic drum. **Chef/s:** Nick Lang. **Open:** Thur to Sat L 12 to 3, Tue to Sat D 6 to 11. **Closed:** Sun, Mon. **Meals:** alc (main courses £13 to £16). Set L and D £11 (2 courses) to £15. **Service:** 12.5% on set menus. **Details:** Cards accepted. 40 seats. Air-con. Wheelchair access. Music. Children allowed.

## Real Eating Company

**All-day dining at its best**
86-87 Western Road, Brighton, BN3 1JB
Tel no: (01273) 221444
www.real-eating.co.uk
**Modern British | £20**
**Cooking score: 2**

**V**

The Real Eating Company is becoming something of a brand these days, with another deli/restaurant in Lewes (see entry) and cafés serving coffee, sandwiches and cakes in Horsham and Bournemouth. A passion to promote the very best in seasonal produce lies behind the whole operation, with a simple, compact brasserie-style menu delivering all-day dining at its very best. Potted crab, macaroni cheese or Sussex rump steak and chips are bolstered by daily specials such as aubergine Parmigiana or venison and pork faggots. A popular breakfast menu delivers eggs on toast, kippers or pancakes with maple syrup. House wine £14.

**Chef/s:** Alistair Warwick. **Open:** all week 8 to 6, Tue to Sat D 6.30 to 11. **Closed:** 25 and 26 Dec. **Meals:** alc (main courses £8 to £16). **Service:** 10% (optional). **Details:** Cards accepted. 42 seats. 16 seats outside. Air-con. Wheelchair access. Music. Children allowed.

## The Restaurant at Drakes

Sophisticated high-end cooking
43-44 Marine Parade, Brighton, BN2 1PE
Tel no: (01273) 696934
www.drakesofbrighton.com
Modern European | £43
Cooking score: 6

The restaurant at this stylish modern hotel on the eastern side of the Brighton seafront is no longer under the aegis of the Gingerman (see entries), but chef Andrew MacKenzie remains at the stoves, and the standard established over the last few years has been largely maintained. Olive-green banquettes and low lighting create an atmospheric evening ambience. The culinary approach is high-end, the menus casually multilingual (if erratically spelt), and much of what turns up impresses for both conception and sheer, burnished technique. A gently rich main course of pan-roasted halibut on jet-black squid-ink risotto comes topped with a homemade pasta frisbee of lobster, while Oxford beef ribeye is topped with a juice-drenched bundle of braised cheek in a deep, authoritative red wine sauce. A starter of red mullet terrine was less impressive – fridgey and under-seasoned, though it was partially saved by blobs of excellent tapenade. When pre-dessert and petits fours are both unremittingly chococentric, there seems little point in ordering a chocolate dessert – but the nougatine wafers sandwiching white chocolate mousse with malt custard and anglaise sauces was the real deal. Chilean house wines are £16 a bottle, £4 a glass.

**Chef/s:** Andrew MacKenzie. **Open:** all week L 12.30 to 2 (2.30 Sun), D 7 to 10. **Meals:** alc (main courses £15 to £25). Set L £15 (2 courses) to £20. Sun L £25. **Service:** 12.5% (optional). **Details:** Cards accepted. 45 seats. Air-con. Separate bar. No mobile phones. Music.

## Terre à Terre

Funky veggie favourite
71 East Street, Brighton, BN1 1HQ
Tel no: (01273) 729051
www.terreaterre.co.uk
Vegetarian | £28
Cooking score: 3

At Brighton's favourite vegetarian restaurant the room is big and bustly, with staff eager to please (and explain the menus). There is perhaps a suggestion that dishes are a little less complex and ambitious these days, but the cooking can still impress. A potato and onion latke flavoured with apple and Cheddar, accompanied by horseradish cream and a salad containing both shades of beetroot makes a satisfying dish, or there are Japanese assemblages that combine soba noodles dressed in mirin and miso, with smoked tofu, beanshoots, pomegranate seeds and wasabi cashews. Sides of bang-bang seasoned Smokey Scrunch chips or smoked tomato and rocket salad will help to fill any gaps. Desserts are as fortifying as the rest. Wines come in all sizes – glasses, half-bottles, half-litre carafes and bottles, the last from £17.25.

**Chef/s:** Dino Pavledis. **Open:** Tue to Sun 12 to 10.30 (11 Sat, 10 Sun). **Closed:** Mon, 25 and 26 Dec, 1 Jan. **Meals:** alc (main courses £11 to £15). **Service:** not inc. **Details:** Cards accepted. 80 seats. 14 seats outside. Air-con. Wheelchair access. Music. Children allowed.

## ALSO RECOMMENDED

### ▲ Hotel du Vin & Bistro

2-6 Ship Street, Brighton, BN1 1AD
Tel no: (01273) 718588
www.hotelduvin.com
**European**

The Brighton branch of the wine-centred hotel chain is just off the seafront in a century-old neo-Gothic building. As well as the two-storeyed bar area, a brasserie offers the group's trademark pan-European cooking, ranging from gravlax with fennel ceviche (£5.95) to confit duck leg in Madeira with dauphinoise (£14.95). Finish with poire Belle Hélène (£6.75). The extensive wine list that is the crowning glory of the place opens at £15 and has a world of choice to ponder. Flights of three small glasses of different wines, from £14.50, are an enterprising idea. Open all week.

## READERS RECOMMEND

### In Vino Veritas

**Modern European**
103 North Rd, Brighton, BN1 1YW
Tel no: (01273) 622522
www.in-vino-veritas.co.uk
'Small intimate restaurant with excellent wine list, now coming into its own'

## ▌Danehill

### The Coach & Horses

Upbeat downland pub
School Lane, Danehill, RH17 7JF
Tel no: (01825) 740369
www.coachandhorses.danehill.biz
**Gastropub | £25**
Cooking score: 2

Ian and Catherine Philpotts have created an upbeat rural pub brimming with charm and character. Overlooking the South Downs, it has stayed true to its roots with roaring fires and real ales in the interlinked bars, while a converted stable makes a suitably rustic dining room. Local sourcing is the foundation of the menus: game liver parfait with redcurrant and rosemary jam, and potted smoked haddock with sauce gribiche, perhaps, followed by confit leg of local rabbit or baked fillets of gurnard with smoked bacon and *fines herbes* risotto. The tidy wine list promises sound drinking from £12.75.
**Chef/s:** Lee Cobb. **Open:** all week L 12 to 2 (2.30 Sat, 3 Sun), Mon to Sat D 7 to 9 (9.30 Fri and Sat). **Meals:** alc (main courses £11 to £19). **Service:** not inc. **Details:** Cards accepted. 60 seats. 70 seats outside. Separate bar. Wheelchair access. Music. Children allowed. Car parking.

## ▌East Chiltington

### The Jolly Sportsman

Real pub with vibrant cooking
Chapel Lane, East Chiltington, BN7 3BA
Tel no: (01273) 890400
www.thejollysportsman.com
**Gastropub | £28**
Cooking score: 3

'A pub that still retains its pubby atmosphere', noted one reporter, who then went on to praise the food, the service and the wine list. It neatly sums up Bruce Wass's weather-boarded country hostelry. The interior is a mix of old and new (rough stone walls, warm colours and contemporary artworks), matched by vibrant, thoroughly modern cooking with an unerring feel for local produce. Poached mackerel is served with a Thai fish broth and could precede a trio of veal – loin, kidney and tongue – served with mustard mash and red wine vegetables. Warm walnut tart with bread pudding ice cream might head up desserts. Game casserole could appear on the good-value set lunch and house wine is £14.75.
**Chef/s:** Alistair Doyle and Bruce Wass. **Open:** Tue to Sun L 12 to 2.30 (4 Sun), Tue to Sat D 6 to 11. **Closed:** Mon, 25 and 26 Dec. **Meals:** alc (main courses £10 to £30). Set L £13.50 (2 courses) to £16.75. Sun L £18.50 (2 courses). **Service:** not inc. **Details:** Cards accepted. 80 seats. 40 seats outside. Air-con. Separate bar. No music. Wheelchair access. Children allowed. Car parking.

## Eastbourne

### The Mirabelle at the Grand Hotel

**Creative cooking amid old-school splendour**
Jevington Gardens, Eastbourne, BN21 4EQ
Tel no: (01323) 412345
www.themirabelle.co.uk
**Modern European | £37**
**Cooking score: 5**

£5 OFF 🍷 🛏 V

The redoubtable 'White Palace' – a Victorian 'wedding cake' edifice of epic proportions – is a *grande dame* among English seafront hotels. The BBC Palm Court Orchestra used to broadcast here, and there's still a whiff of the past about the vast first-floor Mirabelle restaurant, which looks for all the world like a ballroom with tables. Against a pale-pink backdrop of ruched drapes, legions of waiters wheel trolleys and lift domes in the old manner. Service is 'kindness itself' and the pianist has been 'much appreciated'. Given the old-school trappings, it's a surprise to find aspirational modern food on show, but Gerald Röser has honed a personal style based on lightness, seasonality and understated luxury. Pickled mirabelles provide some tart contrast to ballottine of foie gras, and the addition of snail porridge and fennel shavings to a dish of pork fillet suggests the kitchen has its finger on the pulse. Elsewhere, classic gestures assuage more conservative tastes – pike soufflé with smoked salmon and dill sauce, or fillet of Buccleuch beef with wild mushroom gratin and Madeira jus, say. Finally, spiced plum compote with star anise pannacotta and damson ice cream brings it all together for a big finish. The wine list is suitably grand in its range and depth, with a majestic selection representing the great, the good and the exceeding rare from France, backed up by stellar pickings from the New World. Prices start at £22 (£4.65 a glass).
**Chef/s:** Gerald Röser. **Open:** Tue to Sat L 12.30 to 2, D 7 to 10. **Closed:** Sun, Mon, 2 to 16 January. **Meals:** Set L £18 (2 courses) to £21.50. Set D £37 (3 courses). **Service:** inc. **Details:** Cards accepted. 50 seats. Air-con. Separate bar. No mobile phones. Wheelchair access. Music. Children allowed. Car parking.

## Fletching

### The Griffin Inn

**Cosy country inn with excellent menus**
Fletching, TN22 3SS
Tel no: (01825) 722890
www.thegriffininn.co.uk
**Modern European | £30**
**Cooking score: 3**

£5 OFF 🍷 🛏

The Pullan family runs the sort of pub that everyone would like to have as their local: a characterful village inn dating from the sixteenth century with an interior that feels 'homely and well-worn in the best sense', with plenty of dark brickwork and old beams. An early summer visit found Mediterranean fish soup and roast skate on the excellent chalkboard bar menu. There were also enjoyable Rye Bay scallops with spiced lentil dhal and wild rocket, and rump of Fletching lamb with Puy lentil salad, grilled courgette and anchovy dressing. A refreshing lemon balm pannacotta with mango salsa was a good finale. The view from the back garden out across the Ouse Valley is 'very special', something outdoor summer Sunday jazz and spit-roasts fully exploit. House wines from £13.50.
**Chef/s:** Andrew Billings, Peter White, Onik Minassian. **Open:** all week L 12 to 2.30 (3 Sat and Sun), Mon to Sat D 7 to 9.30. **Closed:** 25 Dec. **Meals:** alc (main courses £12 to £24). Sun L £30. **Service:** 10% (optional). **Details:** Cards accepted. 60 seats. 35 seats outside. Separate bar. No music. No mobile phones. Wheelchair access. Children allowed. Car parking.

# Jevington

## The Hungry Monk

Alluring, impressive institution
Jevington, BN26 5QF
Tel no: (01323) 482178
www.hungrymonk.co.uk
European | £34
Cooking score: 2
£5 OFF

It's been delighting visitors for more than four decades, and this impressively ancient flint building (once a retreat for famished pilgrims) has lost none of its allure over the years. Inside, cosy beamed lounges, blazing fires and comfy sofas put guests in just the right frame of mind for food with a generous spirit. Come for dinner and you might be treated to stuffed duck ballotine or twice-baked spinach and Gruyère soufflé ahead of Sussex veal with wild mushroom risotto or sea bass en papillote with a crushed potato cake. Banoffi pie was famously born here in 1972, and it heads a line-up of desserts that might also include apple and frangipane tart. House wine is £16.50.
**Chef/s:** Gary Fisher. **Open:** Sun to Fri L 12 to 2.30, all week D 6.45 to 9.30. **Closed:** 24 to 26 Dec. **Meals:** Set L £17.50 (2 courses) to £20.50. Set D £27.45 (2 courses) to £33.95. Sun L £29.95. **Service:** 12.5% (optional). **Details:** Cards accepted. 38 seats. Air-con. Wheelchair access. Music. Children allowed. Car parking.

# Lewes

## ALSO RECOMMENDED
## ▲ Real Eating Company

18 Cliffe High Street, Lewes, BN7 2AJ
Tel no: (01273) 402650
www.real-eating.co.uk
Modern British

The merits of this all-day restaurant/deli in the heart of Lewes are its unpretentious atmosphere and sound modern British cooking. Simplicity of presentation appears to be the maxim behind dishes such as venison bresaola with orange, rocket and Parmesan (£7) and crisp belly pork with mash and Agen prunes (£13). Breakfast produces sandwiches of Sussex bacon or sausage, while sticky toffee pudding is a good sweet (£6). Well-priced wines from £14. Open all week. See entry for Brighton, too.

# Rye

## The George in Rye

Local ingredients with a Mediterranean spin
98 High Street, Rye, TN31 7JT
Tel no: (01797) 222114
www.thegeorgeinrye.com
Modern European | £29
Cooking score: 1

A couple with family links to the duo behind London's Moro (see entry) have transformed this once-dilapidated Tudor hostelry into a bushy-tailed boutique hotel. Chef Rodrigo Grossman also did time at Moro, and his cooking has Mediterranean leanings – although ingredients are true to the locality. Whole sea bream is paired with rice pilaff, spinach and romesco sauce, while meat could be as down-home as Gloucester Old Spot pork belly with swede gratin. For dessert, the kitchen finds pleasure in simple things – perhaps chocolate, almond and Armagnac cake. House wine is £15.50.
**Chef/s:** Rodrigo Grossman. **Open:** all week L 12 to 3 (3.30 Fri to Sun), D 6.30 to 9.30 (10.30 Fri to Sun). **Meals:** alc (main courses £13 to £16). Set L £11.95 (2 courses) to £14.95. **Service:** not inc. **Details:** Cards accepted. 88 seats. 36 seats outside. Separate bar. No mobile phones. Music. Children allowed.

## Readers recommend

A 'readers recommend' review is a genuine quote from a report sent in by one of our readers. We intend to follow up these suggestions throughout the year to come.

## Landgate Bistro

**Dedicated local food supporter**
5-6 Landgate, Rye, TN31 7LH
Tel no: (01797) 222829
www.landgatebistro.co.uk
**Modern British | £26**
**Cooking score: 3**

A faithful servant of heritage honeypot Rye for years, the Landgate stands proud by one of the town's ancient gateways. Current owners have nailed their colours to the mast and are continuing the bistro's 'excellent traditions' when it comes to sourcing local ingredients. The supply lines are strong in these parts, and the kitchen takes full advantage with a seasonally charged menu that digs its heels into the British soil. Twelve-hour braised pork belly with apple and swede purée or wild duck breast with port reduction and Pink Fir Apple potatoes define the earthy style, with Rye Bay fish adding extra possibilities in the shape of, say, poached fillet of cod with chorizo and lentils. Details such as freshly baked sourdough bread and dressed Appledore salad leaves also impress, while desserts could range from lemon tart to prune and Armagnac crème brûlée. House French is £12.20.
**Chef/s:** Martin Peacock. **Open:** Sat and Sun L 12 to 3, Wed to Sat D 7 to 9 (9.15 Sat). **Closed:** Mon, Tue, Christmas and New Year bank hols. **Meals:** alc (main courses £10 to £17). Set D £14.90 (2 courses) to £17.90. Sun L £11.50 (2 courses) to £14.50.
**Service:** not inc. **Details:** Cards accepted. 32 seats. Separate bar. No mobile phones. Music. Children allowed.

**Giles Thompson** The Earl of March

### Who or what inspired you to become a chef?

Aged seven or so when riding 'shotgun' on the family butcher's delivery van in full butcher's dress. To be greeted by chefs and matron-like cooks who would make a huge fuss and spoil me rotten with pies and puds.

### What is your top culinary tip?

To poach an egg. First blanch it in boiling water for 10 seconds and cool quickly. Then poach the egg in the normal way to form the perfect shape every time.

### What is the best meal you have ever eaten?

Ducasse at Le Louis XV, Hotel De Paris, Monte Carlo. The vegetable nage with black truffle was a triumph.

### What do you like cooking when you are 'off duty'?

Sunday Roast. Pop it all in the oven - veg and all. Come back from the pub an hour or so later, open a bottle of wine - bliss!

### What do you do to relax when out of the kitchen?

Golf. Eating out with my two lovely daughters and seeing them develop into little foodies.

## Webbe's at the Fish Café

Enterprising seafood venture
17 Tower Street, Rye, TN31 7AT
Tel no: (01797) 222226
www.thefishcafe.com
**Seafood | £24**
**Cooking score: 4**

The warehouse-style building dates from 1907 and has converted easily into a light, contemporary ground-floor café. As the name suggests, the focus is on fish. There is no doubting the quality or the freshness of supplies, and the cooking is thankfully not over-ambitious: potted brown shrimps come with toasted soda bread, deep-fried sprats with cayenne, parsely and lemon, with shellfish platters or beer-battered cod and chips making a typical lunch (or steak for those who must). But another facet of the menu shows in the roast fillet of wild sea bass with brown shrimp and leek risotto with shellfish sauce and tiger prawn fritters or twice-cooked belly pork with Rye Bay scallops offered at dinner. Dessert choices seem half-hearted by comparison, many involving sorbets, ice creams, iced nougat and the like. House wine is £14.50. The evening-only dining room upstairs operates weekends in winter, Tue to Sat in summer.
**Chef/s:** Matthew Drinkwater. **Open:** all week L 12 to 2.30, D 6 to 9. **Meals:** alc (main courses £11 to £18). **Service:** not inc. **Details:** Cards accepted. 52 seats. Air-con. Wheelchair access. Music. Children allowed.

## ▋St Leonards on Sea

### St Clements

Modern British
3 Mercatoria, St Leonards on Sea, TN38 0EB
Tel no: (01424) 200355
www.stclementsrestaurant.co.uk
**'Excellent food just off the seafront'**

## ▋Westfield

### The Wild Mushroom

Immensely pleasing country restaurant
Woodgate House, Westfield Lane, Westfield, TN35 4SB
Tel no: (01424) 751137
www.wildmushroom.co.uk
**Modern British | £26**
**Cooking score: 2**

Locals and incomers receive the warmest of welcomes at Paul and Rebecca Webbe's beguiling Victorian farmhouse in a Sussex backwater. Theirs is an immensely pleasing country restaurant – small, cosy, impeccably run and firmly in touch when it comes to the food on the plate. Forget sepia-tinted flavours, this is the world of seared scallops in curry oil and Gressingham duck breast with five-spice sauce and caramelised plums. The region also plays its part (rack of South Downs lamb is paired with ratatouille) and desserts mix past and present for, say, pear and choc chip crumble with Poire William ice cream. House wine is £14.50.
**Chef/s:** Paul Webbe. **Open:** Tue to Fri and Sun L 12 to 2 (2.30 Sun), Tue to Sat D 7 to 10. **Closed:** Mon, 25 and 26 Dec, first 2 weeks Jan. **Meals:** alc (main courses £12 to £19). Set L £15.95 (2 courses) to £18.95. Sun L £22. **Service:** not inc. **Details:** Cards accepted. 44 seats. Separate bar. Wheelchair access. Music. Children allowed. Car parking.

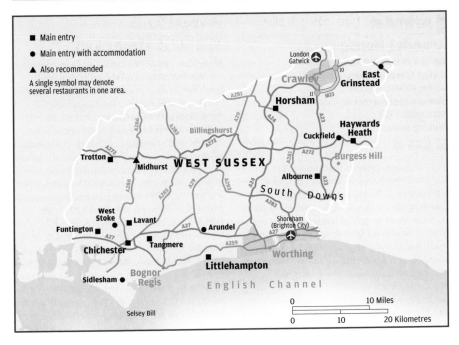

## ■ Albourne

### The Ginger Fox

Convivial country pub star
Henfield Road, Albourne, BN6 9EA
Tel no: (01273) 857888
www.gingermanrestaurants.com
**Modern British | £25**
**Cooking score: 4**

£30

Ben McKellar's country venture (see also
Gingerman, and the Ginger Pig, Brighton) is a
fully grown pub success story. Whether you
are taking advantage of the garden and
admiring the thatched roof topped with a fox
stalking a pheasant, or sitting inside amid
open fires, wood and stone floors, colourful
armchairs and leather banquettes, all is busy,
convivial and unreservedly good-natured.
Visitors have been delighted with the 'seasonal
food, the robust flavours, the game selection,
the well-cooked fish'. While the kitchen works
in tandem with regional producers,
inspiration comes from near and far:
homespun English diehards (braised oxtail
with parsnip mash) sit happily beside classic
European ideas (crispy plaice, squid and
chickpea salad ahead of local cod fillet with
white bean, wild mushroom and Toulouse
sausage). Desserts like 'an incredibly light'
steamed maple and walnut pudding or brioche
bread-and-butter pudding close proceedings.
House wine £13.50.
**Chef/s:** David Keates and Ben McKellar. **Open:** all
week L 12 to 2 (4 Sat, 12.30 to 4 Sun), all week D 6
to 10 (6.30 Sat and Sun). **Meals:** alc (main courses
£9 to £18). Set L £10 (2 courses). **Service:** not inc.
**Details:** Cards accepted. 50 seats. 90 seats outside.
Separate bar. Wheelchair access. Music. Children
allowed. Car parking.

## Arundel

### Arundel House

**Spot-on restaurant-with-rooms**
11 High Street, Arundel, BN18 9AD
Tel no: (01903) 882136
www.arundelhouseonline.co.uk
Gastropub | £26
Cooking score: 2

£5 OFF 🍴 🛏 🌐30

Visitors happily testify that this smart restaurant-with-rooms close to Arundel Castle 'hits all the right spots'. A reporter found breakfast excellent, but the main focus is on the short carte that has some Mediterranean undertones, ranging from a lively starter of layered spicy crab and aubergine on a rich tomato sauce, through salmon and smoked haddock lasagne, buttered spinach and dill crème fraîche, to confit pork belly with bubble and squeak rösti and lemon-braised Gem lettuce. Prices start at £18 on a wine list with a French backbone, fleshed out by bottles from elsewhere.
**Chef/s:** Luke Hackman. **Open:** Mon to Sat L 12 to 2, D 7 to 9.30. **Closed:** Sun, 23 to 27 Dec. **Meals:** Set L £14 (2 courses) to £18. Set D £24 (2 courses) to £28. **Service:** not inc. **Details:** Cards accepted. 32 seats. Music. Children allowed.

## Chichester

### Field & Fork

**Culinary magic that quietly shouts quality**
9 North Pallant, Chichester, PO19 1TJ
Tel no: (01243) 770827
www.fieldandfork.co.uk
Modern British | £26
Cooking score: 5

£5 OFF 🌐30

Field & Fork has branched out, opening in a smart minimalist space with added courtyard dining in Pallant House Gallery – found down the city's Georgian lanes. 'Every component, be it food provenance, service, style or good, old-fashioned hospitality, quietly shouts quality', noted one reporter. Sam Mahoney works his culinary magic with prime seasonal produce, delivering a lunch menu of spicy beef soup with sweet potato ahead of seafood and herb fishcakes with fennel, or a more robust South Downs lamb with butter bean cassoulet and smoked pancetta. In the evening two or three-course options (with wine choices) could take in dandelion and duck salad with duck liver terrine, or griddled smoked eel with fennel ceviche and horseradish dressing. A steamed fillet of hake with clams and miso with local sea kale and crayfish impressed at inspection, as did a cappuccino crème brûlée with warm soft brownie. The wines are reasonably priced and well chosen. Field & Fork's 22-seater Baffins Court Bistro is to be found off Chichester's East Street, tel no: (01243) 784888.
**Chef/s:** Sam Mahoney. **Open:** Tue to Sun L 10 to 5 (11 to 4 Sun), Wed to Sat D 6 to 10.30. **Closed:** Mon, 24 to 26 Dec. **Meals:** alc (main courses £9 to £15). Set D £21.95 (2 courses) to £25.95. **Service:** not inc. **Details:** Cards accepted. 40 seats. 40 seats outside. Air-con. Wheelchair access. Music. Children allowed. Car parking.

## Cuckfield

### Ockenden Manor

**Lordly country manor oozing history**
Ockenden Lane, Cuckfield, RH17 5LD
Tel no: (01444) 416111
www.hshotels.co.uk
Modern French | £50
Cooking score: 6

£5 OFF 🛏

Looking every inch the lordly English retreat, Ockenden Manor sits squarely in nine acres of lush, manicured grounds complete with a walled garden. The exterior bristles with chimneys, while an air of sedate formality imbues the main dining room; here, gilt-framed portraits, ornate hand-painted ceilings and stained glass windows create a mood of aristocratic gentility. Stephen Crane has been heading up the kitchen for more than a decade, and has honed a highly polished culinary style that fits the surroundings like a kid glove. His feel for intricacy and contrast shows in, say, grilled scallops with purple sprouting broccoli, crispy cuttlefish and crab velouté, while seasonal touches add an extra dimension to braised oxtail with boudin blanc or saddle of Balcombe venison – the latter paired with January King cabbage, wild mushrooms and Jerusalem artichokes. There is also skill and artistry in desserts such as liquorice crème brûlée with dark chocolate emulsion and orange sorbet. Ockenden does offer a full vegetarian menu, although one reader's experience was less than sympathetic – a mistaken pre-starter of pâté de foie gras and pieces of salmon in the soup suggest the kitchen doesn't really care for veggies! The serious wine list spends a lot of time in Bordeaux, before exploring other vinous territories. Ten house selections pegged at £20.50 offer the best value.

**Chef/s:** Stephen Crane. **Open:** all week L 12 to 2, D 6.30 to 9. **Meals:** Set L £14.95 (2 courses) to £20.90. Set D £49.50 (3 courses). Sun L £32.50. **Service:** not inc. **Details:** Cards accepted. 45 seats. 20 seats outside. Separate bar. No music. No mobile phones. Wheelchair access. Music. Children allowed. Car parking.

## ■ East Grinstead

### Gravetye Manor

**Country house grandeur with a light touch**
Vowels Lane, East Grinstead, RH19 4LJ
Tel no: (01342) 810567
www.gravetyemanor.co.uk
**Modern British | £52**
**Cooking score: 4**

🍾 🛏

The Elizabethan stone manor house is surrounded by wonderful gardens, designed by the Victorian horticulturist William Robinson. Inside, the décor revolves around oak panelling and open fires, with the formality of the traditional dining room matched by service that is somewhat stiff. On the food front, Mark Raffan's cooking is based on admirable principles, especially in sourcing materials from local specialists. The ambitious cooking makes liberal use of luxury ingredients, which is reflected in the price. But

there is a tendency to over-elaborate dishes that might stand on their own without embroidery. Note a roast breast of pheasant with a mousse of leg meat served with Savoy cabbage, horseradish butter and rich pheasant jus that failed to deliver consistent impact for one reporter. At dessert stage an ethereally light prune and Armagnac soufflé has impressed. The wine list is strong in Burgundy and Bordeaux, but there are good selections from elsewhere, notably Italy, Spain, South Africa and New Zealand and a commendable range of halves. Prices start at £19.

**Chef/s:** Mark Raffan. **Open:** all week L 12.30 to 2, D 7.30 to 9.30. **Meals:** alc (main courses £15 to £29). Set L £20 (2 courses) to £25. Set D £37.
**Service:** 12.5%. **Details:** Cards accepted. 50 seats. Separate bar. No music. No mobile phones. Wheelchair access. Children allowed. Car parking.

## ■ Funtington

### Hallidays

**Convivial village venue with local food**
Watery Lane, Funtington, PO18 9LF
Tel no: (01243) 575331
www.hallidays.info
**Modern British | £32**
**Cooking score: 2**

£5 OFF

Fashioned from a trio of thatched cottages dating back in part to late-medieval times, Hallidays is an intimate village venue at the foot of the Downs. The Stephensons run the place with conviviality and an eye for the best Sussex produce. Mussels cooked in scrumpy might be one way to start, or there might be game terrine with spiced oranges, followed by South Downs lamb with girolles, leeks and truffle oil. Hare features often, and there's usually roast rib of beef with Yorkshire pudding and horseradish cream for Sunday lunch. Crème brûlée with passion fruit sorbet and shortbread is an appealing way to end. Wines start at £14.25.

**Chef/s:** Andy Stephenson. **Open:** Wed to Fri and Sun L 12 to 3. Wed to Sat D 7 to 9.30. **Closed:** Mon, Tue, 2 weeks Aug, 1 week Mar. **Meals:** alc (main courses £13 to £18). Set L £17.50 (2 courses) to £22. Set D

£29 (2 courses) to £25. Sun L £22. **Service:** not inc.
**Details:** Cards accepted. 26 seats. Separate bar.
Wheelchair access. Music. Children allowed. Car
parking.

## Haywards Heath

### Jeremy's Restaurant at Borde Hill

**Big, bold flavours in a delightful setting**
Balcombe Road, Haywards Heath, RH16 1XP
Tel no: (01444) 441102
www.jeremysrestaurant.com
**Modern European | £35**
**Cooking score: 4**

£5
OFF

An enchanting location amid the verdant
delights of Borde Hill Gardens is a major asset
at Jeremy Ashpool's 'lovely, relaxed' restaurant.
You can indulge in a little vicarious pottering
while gazing from the windows of the sunnily
appointed dining room, which overlooks an
impeccably turned-out Victorian walled
garden. Jeremy Ashpool is known for his big,
bold flavours and colourful renditions of
modern European food – and his food is as
vivacious as Borde Hill's horticultural displays
themselves. Grilled mackerel is paired with a
ragoût of smoked haddock and celeriac
rémoulade, saddle of Balcombe Estate venison
gets seasonal embellishment in the form of
chestnut and truffle risotto, and there's
Southdown lamb too – perhaps a duo of
roasted loin and braised shank with butternut
squash purée. For dessert, new season's
rhubarb might be given a serious workout;
otherwise Scotch pancakes with cherry sauce
and buttermilk ice cream could win the day.
Monthly recommendations top the concise,
well-spread wine list; bottles start at £16.
**Chef/s:** Jeremy Ashpool and Richard Cook. **Open:**
Tue to Sun L 12.30 to 2.30, Tue to Sat D 7.30 to 10.
**Closed:** Mon, first two weeks Jan. **Meals:** alc (main
courses £15 to £22). Set L and D £17.50 (2 courses)
to £22.50. Sun L £26. **Service:** not inc.
**Details:** Cards accepted. 55 seats. 30 seats outside.
Separate bar. No mobile phones. Wheelchair
access. Music. Children allowed. Car parking.

## Horsham

NEW ENTRY
### Restaurant Tristan

**Tip-top lunches and dramatic dinners**
3 Stans Way, East Street, Horsham, RH12 1HU
Tel no: (01403) 255688
www.restauranttristan.co.uk
**Modern European | £36**
**Cooking score: 5**

£5
OFF

Tristan Mason's restaurant – his first as chef/
patron in a highly promising career – is
tucked away off a pedestrianised section of
East Street in the old part of Horsham. It's a
first-floor venue above a shop in a sixteenth-
century building. The pitched roof and beams
create a singular ambience, and smart table
settings set the tone. Mason's food displays a
high degree of technical skill, with tip-top
materials and the confidence to leave well
alone when required. A May lunch produced a
brace of mackerel fillets, sharply dressed with
savoury apple purée and lime and lemongrass
foam, followed by pink-cooked bavette steak,
with sticky red onion chutney, puréed
watercress and dabs of classic sauce albufera.
At dinner, things get decidedly dramatic, with
fish and meat combinations favoured –
perhaps turbot with daube of beef, salsify and
pickled wild mushrooms – and dishes that
show a keen understanding of people's natural
hankering for big, earthy flavours. Try milk-
fed lamb with tapenade potato purée, a black
pudding beignet and spring greens. Wizard
ways with chocolate produce a fondant worth
travelling for, served with *fleur de sel* ice cream
and crumbled hazelnuts, as well as superb
trufffles with coffee. The wine list isn't the
most exciting document, but it has some good
drinking. Bottles from £15.
**Chef/s:** Tristan Mason. **Open:** Tue to Sat L 12 to 2.30,
D 6.30 to 9.30. **Closed:** Sun, Mon, 25 Dec to 8 Jan,
last 2 weeks July. **Meals:** Set L £15 (2 courses) to
£20. Set D £28 (2 courses) to £36. **Service:** 12.5%
(optional). **Details:** Cards accepted. 36 seats.
Separate bar. No mobile phones. Wheelchair
access. Music. Children allowed.

## ▌Lavant

### The Earl of March

**Inspirational views and cracking food**
Lavant, PO18 OBQ
Tel no: (01243) 533993
www.theearlofmarch.co.uk
**Gastropub | £23**
**Cooking score: 4**
£5 OFF £30 ♥

Records show that William Blake penned *Jerusalem* while gazing across the vistas of the South Downs from this centuries-old coaching inn. That was in 1803, but the views out to Goodwood and beyond are still breathtaking. Of late, the pub has a new talking point – namely the cracking food emanating from Giles Thompson's kitchen. Years as executive chef at the Ritz have put him in good fettle, although his cooking is now tilted towards the well-heeled country set. Sussex game is a strong suit, but local flavours loom large across the seasonally attuned menu, whether it's grilled Southdown lamb cutlets with devilled kidneys and straw potatoes or sea bream from the coast with wilted spinach, tomato and caper salsa. For afters, consider winter fruit crumble or triple chocolate brownie. Otherwise, nestle into the bar with a pint and a lunchtime bite – perhaps hot roast pork on Sussex 'rough' bread or sausages and mash. House wine list is £15.50 (£3.75 a glass).
**Chef/s:** Giles Thompson and Mattie Thumshirn.
**Open:** all week L 12 to 2.30 (4 Sun), Mon to Sat D 5.30 to 9.30. **Meals:** alc (main courses £11 to £20). **Service:** not inc. **Details:** Cards accepted. 60 seats. 40 seats outside. Separate bar. Wheelchair access. Music. Children allowed. Car parking.

## ▌Littlehampton

### East Beach Café

**Stunning building with buzzy menus**
Sea Road, Littlehampton, BN17 5GB
Tel no: (01903) 731903
www.eastbeachcafe.co.uk
**Modern European | £24**
**Cooking score: 3**
£5 OFF **V** £30 ♥

Thomas Hetherwick's eyecatching design has won plaudits and many awards. Sitting on the beach it looks like a gigantic accumulation of driftwood, with full-length windows and an interior concept that's like eating beneath a towering iceberg. David Whiteside cooks an all-week lunch menu (with breakfasts too at weekends), and references many of today's buzz words. Salt-and-pepper chilli squid, ham hock and Puy lentil salad dressed in honey and mustard, saffron-scented fish chowder, braised shoulder of lamb with mash – it's all here. Kids will love the place, and they'll appreciate having their own menu, while puddings such as East Beach ice cream sundae will bring out the inner kid in all of us. An admirably concise wine selection just about covers most bases. Prices open at £12.95 (£3.95 a glass).
**Chef/s:** David Whiteside. **Open:** all week L 12 to 3 (3.30 Sun), all week D (Jun to Aug) 6.30 to 8.30, Thur to Sat D (Sept to Jun) 6.30 to 8. **Closed:** 23 to 26 Dec. **Meals:** alc (main courses £9 to £17). **Service:** not inc. **Details:** Cards accepted. 65 seats. 80 seats outside. Wheelchair access. Music. Children allowed. Car parking.

## ▌ Midhurst

ALSO RECOMMENDED
### ▲ The Duke of Cumberland Arms

Henley, Midhurst, GU27 3HQ
Tel no: (01428) 652280
**Gastropub**

This fifteenth-century, brick-and-stone cottage can be covered with wisteria and roses and found down a 'tricky to locate' tiny wooded lane off the A286. It's worth the trek for the garden alone. In the bar, low beams, a quarry-tiled floor, scrubbed pine tables, gas lamps and an open fire set the scene. Beer comes straight from the cask, but the food is bang-up-to-date: scallops with pea purée and bacon velouté (£8.50), Goodwood organic ribeye steak with pepper sauce (£16.95), and lemon tart with passion fruit granita. House wine is £10. Closed Sun D and Mon D.

## ▌ Sidlesham
### The Crab & Lobster

Hotspot lives up to its name
Mill Lane, Sidlesham, PO20 7NB
Tel no: (01243) 641233
www.crab-lobster.co.uk
**Gastropub | £35**
**Cooking score: 3**

Sam Bakose's hospitable style has attracted a loyal – and new – crowd since he took over a tired pub and transformed it into a chic hotspot. Located down a small Sussex lane hard by Pagham Harbour, all the gastropub prerequisites are here: fireplaces, flagstone floors, on-the-ball staff and a modern British menu punctuated with local produce. West Sussex beef and lamb, skate and sea bass from day boats, lobster and crab feature prominently – the last added to a risotto with Scottish scallops, or included in a fish pie with lobster, prawns and creamy leeks under a gratinated crust. At inspection, a fish soup with rouille passed with flying colours, as did

beer-battered fish and chips. Sixty-plus global wines are offered, but count on above-average pricing. Bottles start at £15.50.
**Chef/s:** Gavin Rees and Sam Bakose. **Open:** all week L 12 to 2.30, D 6 to 9.30. **Closed:** 25 Dec. **Meals:** alc (main courses £14 to £22). **Service:** not inc. **Details:** Cards accepted. 54 seats. 40 seats outside. No mobile phones. Wheelchair access. Music. Children allowed. Car parking.

## ▌ Tangmere
### Cassons

Good food at Goodwood
Arundel Road, Tangmere, PO18 0DU
Tel no: (01243) 773294
www.cassonsrestaurant.co.uk
**Modern British | £35**
**Cooking score: 2**
£5
OFF

Conveniently situated alongside the A27, this cream-and-blue restaurant is within easy reach of Goodwood. Originally two farm workers' cottages, it was refurbished in 2003 by a husband and wife team. They created a pretty, rustic dining room and comfortable bar area to go with the low beamed ceilings and king-sized inglenook. Vivian Casson shows her passion for cooking with confit of duck with honey and cider jus, seared salmon with beurre blanc or a beautifully presented crème brûlée and spun sugar basket. The set-price lunch is excellent value for food of this quality, portions are generous and service is friendly and efficient. There is an extensive wine list starting at £17 (£5 a glass).
**Chef/s:** Vivian Casson. **Open:** Wed to Sun L 12 to 2, Tue to Sat D 7 to 10. **Closed:** Mon, 25 and 26 Dec, 1 Jan. **Meals:** alc (main courses £19 to £27). Set L £17 (2 courses) to £21. Set D £27 (2 courses) to £35. Sun L £17.50 (2 courses) to £21.50. **Service:** not inc. **Details:** Cards accepted. 36 seats. 16 seats outside. Separate bar. No mobile phones. Wheelchair access. Music. Children allowed. Car parking.

## ▌Trotton

### The Keepers Arms

**Country pub with charm and views**
Terwick Lane, Trotton, GU31 5ER
Tel no: (01730) 813724
www.keepersarms.co.uk
**Gastropub | £27**
**Cooking score: 3**
£5 £30
OFF ▼

This upmarket inn certainly has alfresco
appeal, with its terrace and sylvan views.
Inside it's equally inviting, though an opened-
up space of easy-on-the-eye modernity gives
a more gastro than pub feel. But the place
hasn't forgotten its roots and the beamed bar
offers a choice of real ales and a blackboard
menu of bar staples. Clean-lined country
styling defines the large restaurant area –
pastel tones, lightwood floors and high-back,
cherry-coloured dining chairs. The kitchen,
too, keeps things simple – and seasonal. A very
fresh fillet of line-caught Solent sea bass with
a saffron and crayfish risotto, or roasted
Gressingham duck teamed with dauphinoise,
cabbage and bacon are typical of the style. A
short, fashionable wine list opens at £13.50.
**Chef/s:** Matt Appleton. **Open:** all week L 12 to 2
(2.30 Sun), D 7 to 9.30 (9 Sun). **Closed:** 25 and 26
Dec. **Meals:** alc (main courses £13 to £20).
**Service:** not inc. **Details:** Cards accepted. 50 seats.
20 seats outside. Separate bar. No mobile phones.
Wheelchair access. Music. Children allowed. Car
parking.

## ▌West Stoke

### West Stoke House

**Effortlessly civilised restaurant-with-rooms**
Downs Road, West Stoke, PO18 9BN
Tel no: (01243) 575226
www.weststokehouse.co.uk
**Modern British | £45**
**Cooking score: 6**

♦ ⇌

Built in 1760 and once part of Goodwood
Estate, West Stoke now makes the grade as an
effortlessly civilised restaurant-with-rooms –

a huge white house set in five acres of
landscaped grounds overlooking the Downs.
The place has improved by leaps and bounds
since Darren Brown donned his whites, and
his increasingly confident, intricately crafted
food is one reason for its high-profile success.
Menus are short, but ideas come thick and fast
in the kitchen. A starter of quail Kiev with
boudin, twice-cooked quail's egg, braised Puy
lentils, baby beetroot and red chard is a
typically complex starter, full of visual
contrasts, lightness and vivid textures.
Elsewhere, fillet of turbot is married with
cauliflower 'textures' and coriander shoots, sea
bass absorbs some Mediterranean warmth
thanks to deep-fried risotto, baby fennel,
confit lemon and aubergine caviar, and
venison is imbued with dark-hued autumnal
flavours – oxtail ravioli, wild mushrooms,
Savoy cabbage and butternut squash purée. To
finish, there are generally three desserts:
perhaps a cleverly contrived assiette of rhubarb
involving a soufflé, jelly, cheesecake and foam
or – on a different tack – milk chocolate
crunch with white chocolate ice cream and
walnut nougatine. France and other major
producing countries share out the spoils on the
auspicious wine list, which is noted for its
ungreedy prices, knowledgeable selections
and top-drawer producers. House
recommendations start at £16 (£4.50 a glass).
**Chef/s:** Darren Brown. **Open:** Wed to Sun L 12 to 2,
D 7 to 9. **Closed:** Mon, Tue, 25 and 26 Dec, first
week Jan. **Meals:** Set L £19.50 (2 courses) to £24.
Set D £35 (2 courses) to £45. Sun L £32.50.
**Service:** not inc. **Details:** Cards accepted. 50 seats.
Wheelchair access. Music. Children allowed. Car
parking.

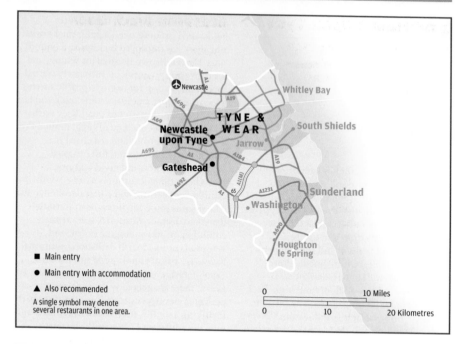

Legend:
- ■ Main entry
- ● Main entry with accommodation
- ▲ Also recommended

A single symbol may denote several restaurants in one area.

0    10 Miles
0    10    20 Kilometres

## ▌Gateshead

### Eslington Villa

**Victorian retreat, modern food**
8 Station Road, Low Fell, Gateshead, NE9 6DR
Tel no: (0191) 4876017
www.eslingtonvilla.co.uk
**Modern British | £25**
**Cooking score: 3**

The villa is an imposing Victorian mansion built around 1880 for a prominent local businessman, who clearly wanted a rural refuge away from the revolutionary industrial heat of the north east. There are two acres of leafy landscaped grounds and the place is blessed with eminently pleasing views. Those who come to eat as well as retreat can expect a menu of international standbys enlivened with a few creative flourishes: smoked haddock fishcakes and slow-cooked lamb shank with parsley mash are joined by Mediterranean bedfellows (wild mushroom risotto) and visitors from faraway lands

(marinated prawns with crispy won tons, tandoori-spiced monkfish). To finish, consider praline crêpe with orange salad or vanilla cheesecake with roasted plums. House wines from £13.50 kick off the 60-bin list.
**Chef/s:** Andrew Moore. **Open:** Mon to Fri and Sun L 12 to 2 (3 Sun), Mon to Sat D 7 to 10. **Closed:** 25 and 26 Dec, bank hols. **Meals:** Set L £17 (2 courses) to £19. Set D £19 (2 courses) to £23. Sun L £18. **Service:** not inc. **Details:** Cards accepted. 80 seats. 12 seats outside. Separate bar. Wheelchair access. Music. Children allowed. Car parking.

## Newcastle upon Tyne

### Blackfriars Restaurant

**Atmospheric dining and good ingredients**
Friars Street, Newcastle upon Tyne, NE1 4XN
Tel no: (0191) 2615945
www.blackfriarsrestaurant.co.uk
**Modern British | £25**
**Cooking score: 3**

Blackfriars confidently claims to be 'the oldest dining room in the UK'. The former Dominican refectory dates from 1239, and dining out rarely gets more atmospheric than here. There's something for every mood – a terrace menu, express lunch, evening menu and even banquets and pre-prepared picnics – while a passion for locally sourced ingredients is evident from placemats that are a map of local food and drink producers. Expect North Sea fishcake served with carrot, fennel and orange salad, sausage and mash or bavette of Northumbrian beef with pressed ox tongue, salsify and roasted shallot, and a dark chocolate cake with Lindisfarne mead marmalade ice cream for dessert. Service is 'very good'. House wine is £14.

**Chef/s:** Troy Terrington. **Open:** all week L 12 to 2.30 (4 Sun), Mon to Sat D 6 to 10. **Closed:** 25 and 26 Dec, bank hols. **Meals:** alc (main courses £9 to £19), Set L £12 (2 courses ) to £15. Set D £15 (2 courses) to £20. **Service:** 10% (optional). **Details:** Cards accepted. 70 seats. 50 seats outside. Air-con. Separate bar. Wheelchair access. Music. Children allowed.

### Brasserie Black Door

**Crunch-friendly favourites with a spin**
Biscuit Factory, Stoddart Street, Newcastle upon Tyne, NE2 1AN
Tel no: (0191) 2605411
www.blackdoorgroup.co.uk
**Modern British | £27**
**Cooking score: 4**

**V**

Following the demise of the fine-dining Black Door restaurant on Clayton Street, executive chef David Kennedy and many of the original team have pitched camp at their young blood brasserie in the trendy Biscuit Factory. Given that this is Europe's largest independent art emporium and gallery, it's no surprise that the interior is stuffed with contemporary prints, ceramics, sculptures and other exhibits. The menu's crunch-friendly prices are also an eye-opener, and the kitchen applies an eclectic spin to seasonal brasserie dishes ranging from seared chicken livers with pease pudding, walnuts and sherry vinegar dressing to chocolate and star anise truffle cake with blood orange sorbet. In between, it's a spirited show, taking in brill, chorizo and cockle risotto with pork scratchings, and lasagne of slow-cooked rabbit as well as steamed mutton pudding. Wines are an equally affordable bunch, from £14 (£3.50 a glass). The BD group also owns the Black Door Bar & Dining Rooms in Morpeth (see entry) and Café Black Door at Magnesia Bank, North Shields.

**Chef/s:** David Kennedy. **Open:** all week L 12 to 2 (4 Sun), Mon to Sat D 7 to 10. **Closed:** 25 and 26 Dec, 1 Jan. **Meals:** alc (main courses £10 to £18). Set L £10 (2 courses) to £12.95. Set D Mon to Thur £20 (2 courses) to £22.95 (inc wine). Sun L £9.95. **Service:** 10% (optional). **Details:** Cards accepted. 70 seats. Air-con. Separate bar. Wheelchair access. Music. Children allowed. Car parking.

## Restaurants with delis

**Ultracomida, Aberystwyth & Narberth**
Specialist produce from France, Spain and
Wales is given pride of place. A tempting
selection of tapas is also available.

**Valvona & Crolla Caffè Bar, Edinburgh**
Valvona & Crolla proclaims itself as
Scotland's oldest delicatessen (1934).
Lunch at the Caffè will uncover a repertoire
of Italian regional cooking.

**Bill's Produce Store, Brighton**
This colourful food market sells fruit,
flowers and herbs and also accommodates
a café. Drop in for milkshakes, smoothies
and the all-day breakfast menu.

**Delilah, Nottingham**
Browsing the cheeses and meats on sale
at this deli might make customers peckish.
Fortunately, a small counter at the back
of the store serves fondues, frittatas and
quality salads.

**Ottolenghi, Islington**
Piled high with Mediterranean and Middle
Eastern dishes, it's easy to see how this
bustling Islington eatery draws in the crowds.
Popular with brunching locals.

**Murrays, Clevedon, Somerset**
The stock of Italian artisan foods inspires
visitors to pop in to the restaurant
next-door-but-one, where Somerset
produce is met by Italian method.

## Café 21

**Smart Quayside favourite**
Trinity Gardens, Quayside, Newcastle upon Tyne,
NE1 2HH
Tel no: (0191) 2220755
www.cafetwentyone.co.uk
**Modern British | £33**
**Cooking score: 3**

Named after its original address at 21 Queen
Street, Terry Laybourne's city restaurant, now
on the Quayside, has played an integral part in
Newcastle's dynamic eating-out scene.
Curved leather banquettes, crisp napery and
quality glassware set the tone for Chris
Dobson's modern British brasserie food. A
breakfasty starter is all the rage these days –
here it's a warm salad of Craster kippers with
ratte potatoes and a poached egg. Mains try
out some interesting variations, such as
curried monkfish 'osso buco' with basmati rice,
or caramelised duck with five-spice in ginger
sauce, but there are old favourites too –
including three-week hung Northumbrian
beef steaks. Soft pistachio meringue with
plums and blackberries is a good way to finish.
An expertly-chosen wine list starts at £15.40
(£4 a glass) for Duboeuf house
recommendations.
**Chef/s:** Chris Dobson. **Open:** all week L 12 to 2.30 (4
Sun), D 5.30 to 10 (6 to 10 Sun). **Closed:** 25 and 26
Dec, 1 Jan. **Meals:** alc (main courses £15 to £29). Set
L and D £15 (2 courses) to £18. Sun L £16.
**Service:** 10% (optional). **Details:** Cards accepted.
129 seats. Air-con. Separate bar. Wheelchair access.
Music. Children allowed.

## Fisherman's Lodge

**Secret hideaway**
Jesmond Dene, Jesmond, Newcastle upon Tyne,
NE7 7BQ
Tel no: (0191) 2813281
www.fishermanslodge.co.uk
**Modern British | £40**
**New chef**

The Lodge feels like a secret hideaway, reached
via a single-track road with woodland on one
hand and the Ouse on the other. Built in 1850,

it was once the home of the man who brought electrification to Newcastle, and is only a five-minute drive from the city. A strong inventive streak has always characterised the cooking here, persisting through changes of the kitchen guard. But as we went to press, we heard that Fisherman's Lodge had been sold. We understand that the current staff will stay on, but a head chef has yet to be appointed. Reports please.

**Open:** Tue to Sat L 12 to 2, D 7 to 10. **Closed:** Sun, Mon, 25 and 26 Dec. **Meals:** alc (main courses £16 to £29). Set L £15.50 (2 courses) to £18.50. **Service:** not inc. **Details:** Cards accepted. 60 seats. 20 seats outside. Air-con. Separate bar. Wheelchair access. Music. Car parking.

## Jesmond Dene House
**Grandeur and contemporary style**
Jesmond Dene Road, Newcastle upon Tyne, NE2 2EY
Tel no: (0191) 2123000
www.jesmonddenehouse.co.uk
**Modern European | £47**
**Cooking score: 5**

🛏 **V**

Jesmond Dene House is as solidly established as the leafy river park from which it takes its name, and readers love the characterful mansion setting in a comfortable, contemporary boutique hotel. In summer, the conservatory feels fresh and lively; the main dining room is plusher and darker, perfect for winter nights. Pierre Rigothier uses Kielder venison and Northumbrian beef in dishes which taste as satisying as they look. At inspection, too much salt was the only thing that threatened to take the shine off otherwise impeccable starters of spring vegetable salad dressed with bagna cauda and delicate leaves from the herb garden, and silky foie gras terrine with punchy mango chutney and cocoa nibs. Less seasoning would also have improved slow-cooked pork with morels, and accurately steamed turbot with a Mediterranean tomato flourish. Desserts have the wow factor: for example an apple and hazlenut frangipane tart, or a chocolate sphere

which melted when hot, rich chocolate sauce was poured on it to reveal praline ice cream. The cheese trolley also represents serious temptation. A substantial selection of wines is available by the carafe, and great pains have been taken to offer interest for every pocket. Bottles start at £15 (£4 by the glass). Service is immaculate.

**Chef/s:** Pierre Rigothier. **Open:** all week L 12 to 2 (12.30 to 3 Sat, 12.30 to 3.15 Sun), D 7 to 9.30 (6 to 10 Sat and 7 to 9.30 Sun). **Meals:** alc (main courses £13 to £37). Set L £21 (2 courses) to £24. Set D £25. Sun L £25. **Service:** 10% (optional). **Details:** Cards accepted. 70 seats. 28 seats outside. Separate bar. Wheelchair access. Music. Children allowed. Car parking.

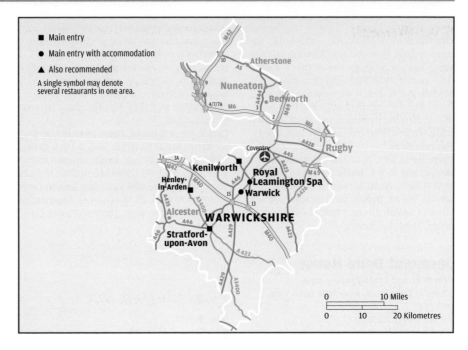

## Henley-in-Arden

**NEW ENTRY**

### The Bluebell

**Stylish pub with food that sings**
93 High Street, Henley-in-Arden, B95 5AT
Tel no: (01564) 793049
www.bluebellhenley.co.uk
**Gastropub | £25**
**Cooking score: 4**

 **V** 

The décor at this timber-framed 500-year-old high street pub is a stylish mix of ancient features with swanky modern design, flamboyant furniture, soft lighting and candles. The name of the game is to combine good-quality ingredients with uncomplicated modern cooking to produce a menu with broad appeal. Battered haddock with chips may be a pub cliché, but at inspection it was of cracking quality and accompanied by a pea purée and sauce gribiche that made the dish sing. Tender, tasty new season's herb-crusted lamb with spring onion crushed potatoes and mustard gravy was another hit. The meal was topped and tailed by good homemade bread and an impressive spiced Northern Irish cake with homemade lemon curd, and enhanced by service full of infectious enthusiasm. The consensus is that Duncan and Leigh Taylor 'run a superb establishment with true professionalism making customers feel welcome and cosseted'. House wine is £14.
**Chef/s:** Rob Round. **Open:** Tue to Sun L 12 to 2.30 (3.30 Sun), Tue to Sat D 6 to 9.30. **Closed:** Mon. **Meals:** alc (main courses £10 to £25). **Service:** not inc. **Details:** Cards accepted. 50 seats. 50 seats outside. Separate bar. Wheelchair access. Music. Children allowed. Car parking.

### Average price

The average price listed in main-entry reviews denotes the price of a three-course meal, without wine.

## Kenilworth

NEW ENTRY
### The Almanack
**Buzzing all-dayer**
Abbey End North, Kenilworth, CV8 1QJ
Tel no: (01926) 353637
www.thealmanack-kenilworth.co.uk
Gastropub | £23
Cooking score: 1

V

This latest opening from Peach Pubs is a stylish property in the heart of town. It's more bar/restaurant than full-blown gastropub and there's a distinct retro feel, with the lounge curving around a vast island bar to smart dining areas and an open-to-view kitchen. The place buzzes all day (from 8am) offering everything from bacon sandwiches and cappuccino to deli-boards, roasts of the day, chargrilled 28-day aged steaks and updated pub classics like sausages with spring onion mash and mustard jus. House wine from £14. **Chef/s:** Corin Earland. **Open:** all week L 12 to 2.30 (4 Sun), D 6 to 10 (9 Sun). **Closed:** 25 Dec. **Meals:** alc (main courses £10 to £16). Set L £10.50 (2 courses). **Service:** not inc. **Details:** Cards accepted. 120 seats. 50 seats outside. Air-con. Wheelchair access. Music. Children allowed.

### Restaurant Bosquet
**Ever-popular Gallic charmer**
97A Warwick Road, Kenilworth, CV8 1HP
Tel no: (01926) 852463
www.restaurantbosquet.co.uk
French | £32
Cooking score: 4

Since setting out their stall in 1981, Bernard and Jane Lignier have gained a reputation as an endearing double act – thanks to their infectious Gallic charm and the mood of chatty domesticity that permeates their affable little restaurant. The rich, bold flavours of Bernard's native south-west France define much of his food, which is why he is generous with the foie gras and cooks his chips in goose fat. Devotees of this overtly earthy style revel in the delights of herb-crusted saddle of lamb with butter-bean stew, breast of pheasant stuffed with apricots on a port and chestnut sauce, and saddle of venison with truffle oil, chocolate and Cassis sauce. Fish dishes vary with the market, and the roll call of desserts might range from blueberry and almond tart to raspberries and strawberries with a Muscat sabayon. Jurançon, Madiran, Cahors and other names from the south-west dominate the patriotically French wine list. Prices start at £15.50. **Chef/s:** Bernard Lignier. **Open:** Tue to Fri L 12 to 1.15, Tue to Sat D 7 to 9.15. **Closed:** Sun, Mon, 1 week Christmas, 2 weeks Aug. **Meals:** alc (main courses £20 to £22). Set L and D £31.50. **Service:** not inc. **Details:** Cards accepted. 26 seats. No music. No mobile phones. Wheelchair access. Children allowed.

## Leamington Spa

NEW ENTRY
### Mallory Court
**Stunning dishes pack a flavour punch**
Harbury Lane, Leamington Spa, CV33 9QB
Tel no: (01926) 330214
www.mallory.co.uk
Modern British | £50
Cooking score: 5

V

Mallory Court's ancient appearance is deceptive. The country house hotel was actually built just before the First World War and styled after Lutyens, with lovely pitched roofs and mullioned windows. Inside, the dining room is just the right side of elegant: oak panelling, soft lighting and views across 10 acres of manicured grounds. Simon Haigh is a master at turning great ingredients into stunning dishes, whether it's local lamb or superb fish (a strong suit), or luxuries like foie gras and lobster. Although there may be drizzles and swirls aplenty, dishes pack a genuine flavour-filled punch for all their delicacy and balance. To start, hand-dived scallops may be teamed with pancetta and cauliflower, while mains of, perhaps, meltingly braised oxtail with lardons or pan-roast loin of venison with butternut squash show that meat cookery is of the highest order too. Desserts are glorious. Fruit is imaginatively treated, whether a pineapple parfait with rice pudding cannelloni or a baked lemon cream with spiced figs. The hotel has been added to sympathetically, and now offers the option of a more informal brasserie. Wines are a swanky bunch, but expect to invest more than £30 for a decent bottle from the weighty list.

**Chef/s:** Simon Haigh. **Open:** Sun to Fri L 12 to 1.45, all week D 6.30 to 9. **Meals:** Set L £23.50 (2 courses) to £27.50. Set D £39.50. Sun L £35. **Service:** not inc. **Details:** Cards accepted. 35 seats. 20 seats outside. Separate bar. Wheelchair access. Music. Children allowed. Car parking.

# ▌Stratford-upon-Avon

## Malbec

**Good-value food worth seeking out**
6 Union Street, Stratford-upon-Avon, CV37 6QT
Tel no: (01789) 269106
www.malbecrestaurant.co.uk
**Modern European | £26**
**Cooking score: 2**

Centrally located and offering good-value food that's prepared from quality ingredients, Simon Malin's restaurant is worth seeking out. Reporters recommend booking a table in the pretty panelled and flagstoned ground-floor dining room (as 'you would not want to be downstairs unless in a big party') and heap praise on the 'exceptional value' of a Friday 'steak night', and the set lunch. A spring carte delivered pea and mint soup with goats' cheese and black pepper gnocchi followed by fillet of pollack with wilted lettuce, peas and asparagus with caper mayonnaise. Bread could be improved, but service is 'attentive and efficient' and wines reasonably priced from £14.95.

**Chef/s:** Simon Malin. **Open:** Wed to Sat L 12 to 1.45, Tue to Sat D 7 to 9.30. **Closed:** Sun, Mon, 1 week Oct. **Meals:** alc (main courses £14 to £18). Set L £10 (2 courses) to £15. **Service:** not inc. **Details:** Cards accepted. 36 seats. No mobile phones. Music. Children allowed.

# ▌Warwick

## Rose and Crown

**Busy, convivial all-day pub**
30 Market Place, Warwick, CV34 4SH
Tel no: (01926) 411117
www.roseandcrownwarwick.co.uk
**Gastropub | £23**
**Cooking score: 1**

Perched at a corner of Warwick's Market Place, this is as good a 'townie' pub as you will find. Whether taking advantage of outside tables, sitting in the lively main bar or eating in the dining room at the rear, all is busy, convivial and unreservedly good-natured. There's something to eat at almost any time of the day, with the brasserie menu offering good renditions of smoked fish chowder, pork schnitzel or steak with béarnaise. Short list of global wines from £13.50.

**Chef/s:** Gavin Allcock. **Open:** all week B 8.30 to 11, L 12 to 2.30, D 6.30 to 10. **Closed:** 25 Dec. **Meals:** alc (main courses £10 to £17). Sun L £11.50 to £12.50. **Service:** 10% (optional). **Details:** Cards accepted. 45 seats. 30 seats outside. Air-con. Separate bar. Wheelchair access. Music. Children allowed.

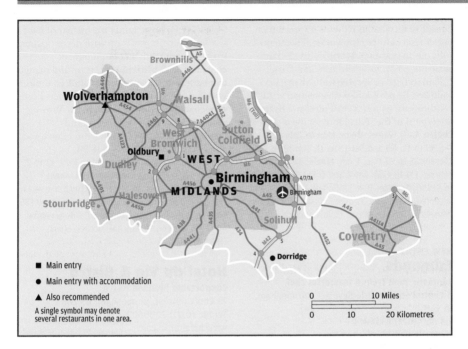

- ■ Main entry
- ● Main entry with accommodation
- ▲ Also recommended

A single symbol may denote
several restaurants in one area.

| 0 | | 10 Miles |
| 0 | 10 | 20 Kilometres |

## ▌ Birmingham

### Bank

**Rock-solid second-city brasserie**
4 Brindleyplace, Birmingham, B1 2JB
Tel no: (0121) 6334466
www.bankrestaurants.com
**Modern British | £28**
**Cooking score: 2**

The sibling of Bank Westminster (see entry,
London), this Brummie stalwart makes the
most of the of its futuristic Brindleyplace
setting with a windowed frontage. A wall of
wine racks at the back will tempt the
discerning drinker, if the view of the brigade
at work in the open-to-view kitchen doesn't
distract the eye. The brasserie menus deal in
the likes of chilli squid with Thai noodle salad,
and cottage pie with pickled red cabbage. A
persistent Asian influence means crispy duck
and green curries are usually in evidence too.

Finish with New York-style cheesecake and
blueberry compote. A good two-page jumble
of wines accompanies, opening at £14.95.
**Chef/s:** Stephen Woods. **Open:** all week L 12 to 4
(11.30 Sat and Sun), D 4.30 to 10.45 (11 Sat, 9.45
Sun). **Meals:** alc (main courses £10 to £22). Set L
and D £12.50 (2 courses) to £15. **Service:** 12.5%
(optional). **Details:** Cards accepted. 250 seats. 100
seats outside. Air-con. Separate bar. Wheelchair
access. Music. Children allowed.

### cielo

**Straightforward, comforting cooking**
6 Oozells Square, Brindleyplace, Birmingham,
B1 2JB
Tel no: (0121) 6326882
www.cielobirmingham.com
**Italian | £35**
**Cooking score: 1**

Andy Waters remains as executive chef at this
smart Oozells Square Italian – a handy
arrangement as his own restaurant (see
Edmunds) is close by. What you get is
straightforward and comforting Italian

cuisine that treats ingredients respectfully, rather than culinary fireworks,. The menu rolls out in traditional format, divided into antipasti, pasta, meat and fish, and dolce. Calamari fritti or spaghetti alla matriciana, followed by pork loin with creamed wild mushrooms, pancetta and cider, and tiramisu are typical of the style. House wine is £14.95.
**Chef/s:** Andy Waters. **Open:** Mon to Thur L 12 to 3, D 5.30 to 11, Fri and Sat 12 to 11, Sun 12 to 10. **Closed:** 25 to 27 Dec, 1 Jan. **Meals:** alc (main courses £11 to £25). Set L and D £12.95 (2 courses) to £15.95. **Service:** 10% (optional). **Details:** Cards accepted. 104 seats. 32 seats outside. Air-con. Wheelchair access. Music. Children allowed.

**NEW ENTRY**
## Edmunds
**Fantastic food from a masterful chef**
6 Central Square, Brindleyplace, Birmingham, B1 2JB
**Tel no: (0121) 6334944**
www.edmundsbirmingham.com
**Modern European | £41**
**Cooking score: 6**
£5 OFF **V**

Chic, urban Edmunds in busy Brindleyplace is a world away from Andy Waters' original restaurant, a rustic little affair in rural Henley-in-Arden. The food, too, has undergone a renaissance, growing from 'quality home cooking', as he described it, to determinedly fine dining. Smartly subdued lighting, modern artworks, low-back cream chairs – it's formal right down to the razor-sharp creases in the tablecloths and the gleam on the glassware. It would all be an empty gesture without fantastic food, of course, and the kitchen doesn't disappoint. Waters, a classically trained chef, has not let his days in Lyon and Switzerland box him into a culinary corner. The menu is Francophile to be sure, but plenty of contemporary touches save it from time-warp territory. Go for luxury – scallop ravioli with creamed Avruga caviar sauce, perhaps – or try something ever so slightly humbler, but still seriously upmarket, such as neck of lamb confit and loin cutlet. It's all masterfully done,

from a chef who certainly has no fear of hard work. Standards don't slip with dessert either, from a wonderfully unctuous pavé of chocolate with pistachio ice cream and mango to a light, bright lemon and raisin iced mousse with lemon curd sauce. Beverley Waters heads service with disarming friendliness. Wines accommodate differing pockets and incorporate a range of styles from France and elsewhere. House wine is £18.50.
**Chef/s:** Andy Waters. **Open:** Mon to Fri L 12 to 2, Mon to Sat D 7 to 10. **Closed:** Sun, 4 weeks throughout the year. **Meals:** Set L £19 (2 courses) to £21. Set D £35 (2 courses) to £41. Tasting menu £55. **Service:** 10% (optional). **Details:** Cards accepted. 40 seats. Air-con. Wheelchair access. Music. Children allowed.

## Hotel du Vin & Bistro
**Comfortable branded bistro**
25 Church Street, Birmingham, B3 2NR
**Tel no: (0121) 2000600**
www.hotelduvin.com
**European | £35**
**Cooking score: 2**
🍷 🛏 **V**

Turn right on entry to Birmingham's former Eye Hospital and find not a French bistro but the kind of unashamed tribute – all nicotine-coloured walls, wine bottles and hop garlands – that's a genre in its own right. At Hotel du Vin, it's done with enough conviction to boost the restaurant beyond dreary hotel status. In accordance with house style, food is appealingly direct and hearty, though not exclusively French. Start, perhaps, with charcuterie with Italian garnishes, followed by a nicely-aged steak with a pat of horseradish butter, or calf's liver with shallot mash and a mildly devilled sauce. Service is inconsistent, though well-meaning. True to its name, Hotel du Vin puts wine high on the agenda. The list is a global firecracker, with peerless drinking opportunities across the range. A fine crop of house recommendations start the ball rolling from £14.75 (£3.90 a glass).

**Chef/s:** Nick Turner. **Open:** all week L 12 to 2, D 6 to 10. **Meals:** alc (main courses £12 to £20). Set L £15 (2 courses). Sun L £20. **Service:** 10% (optional). **Details:** Cards accepted. 100 seats. Air-con. Separate bar. No music. Wheelchair access. Music. Children allowed. Car parking.

**NEW ENTRY**
## Jyoti's Vegetarian
**Fresh, zingy treats and great value**
1045 Stratford Road, Hall Green, Birmingham, B28 8AS
Tel no: (0121) 7785501
www.jyotis.co.uk
**Indian vegetarian | £20**
**Cooking score: 1**

V

Indian vegetarian eateries are thin on the ground, but this one is going great guns. Behind a sweet centre packed with multi-coloured goodies is a brightly lit café, with one wall bearing a photo of Jamie Oliver (he rates their curries as 'wicked' apparently). Masses of choice includes fresh, zingy treats like pani puri and chana betata, while vegetable kofta come in the same star anise fragrant sauce as an unctuous aubergine curry. Desserts are traditional and very sweet. Great value and friendly staff. Bring your own wine.
**Chef/s:** Mr and Mrs Joshi. **Open:** all week 12.30 to 10. **Meals:** alc (main courses £5 to £13). Set L and D £24 (3 courses). **Service:** not inc. **Details:** Cards accepted. 36 seats. Air-con. Wheelchair access. Music. Children allowed.

## Metro Bar & Grill
**Cool big-city customer**
73 Cornwall Street, Birmingham, B3 2DF
Tel no: (0121) 2001911
www.metrobarandgrill.co.uk
**Modern European | £25**
**Cooking score: 2**

V

This contemporary urban restaurant wears its classy credentials with good grace. It's smart but not flashy, full of big-city bustle and customers are likely to receive a warm welcome in the bar before sitting down to white-clothed tables. The menu features many modern favourites (classics, even) as well as a few more experimental ideas, their common denominator being a feeling for comfort – from salt-and-pepper squid or smoked haddock fishcake, to chicken breast with chestnut stuffing and bread sauce or a Metro burger with Monterey Jack cheese and tomato relish. House wine is £14.50.
**Chef/s:** Chris Kelly and Darren Husted. **Open:** Mon to Fri L 12 to 2.30, Mon to Sat D 6 to 10. **Closed:** Sun, 25 Dec to 2 Jan, bank hols. **Meals:** alc (main courses £10 to £21). Set D £14.50 (2 courses) to £17.50. **Details:** Cards accepted. 80 seats. Air-con. Separate bar. Music. Children allowed.

## Opus
**Bullish Brummie championing British produce**
54 Cornwall Street, Birmingham, B3 2DE
Tel no: (0121) 2002323
www.opusrestaurant.co.uk
**Modern British | £30**
**Cooking score: 2**

£5 OFF

Opus looks thoroughly urban, but it has been just as careful as many a country village eatery in sourcing from pedigree suppliers – from Carlingford oysters to free-range meats. A chef's table in the kitchen allows up to eight diners a backstage view of proceedings through five inventive courses. There's plenty going on out front too, in the form of quail with pumpkin risotto and bacon, Dover sole on the bone with lemon thyme butter, or slow-braised collar of pork with creamed potatoes and winter veg. Desserts ramp up the indulgence factor with Valrhona chocolate tart and salted peanut ice cream. An inspired international wine list starts at £14.50.
**Chef/s:** David Colcombe. **Open:** Mon to Fri L 12 to 2.15, Mon to Sat D 6 to 9.30 (7 to 10 Sat). **Closed:** Sun, bank hols, 25 Dec to 1 Jan. **Meals:** alc (main courses £13 to £35). Set L and D £15.50 (2 courses) to £18.50. **Service:** 10% (optional). **Details:** Cards accepted. 85 seats. Air-con. Separate bar. No music. Wheelchair access. Children allowed.

## Purnell's

**Good humour, serious skill**
55 Cornwall Street, Birmingham, B3 2DH
Tel no: (0121) 2129799
www.purnellsrestaurant.com
**Modern British | £40**
**Cooking score: 6**

£5
OFF

Occupying a red-brick corner plot in
Birmingham's business district and decorated
with views of urban landmarks, Purnell's is
very much a city restaurant. Since setting up
here in 2007, Glynn Purnell has kindled a
reputation for humour and inventiveness,
underpinned by real skill. The seven-course
'Purnell's Tour' takes in the greatest hits from
the à la carte, sparked in many cases by
childhood memories. To start, a cube of
wobbly, smooth cheese custard, speared with
pineapple jelly, is inspired homage to the naff
party snack, and exhibits the sweetness
towards which many of the dishes tend. Meat
and fish are handled deftly, as seen in coconut-
poached brill with spiced lentils and toffee and
cumin carrots, or beef rump with a delicate
dusting of liquorice powder and orange-
scented pearl barley ristotto. Desserts, such a
masterfully puffy warm chocolate mousse
with mango sorbet and crunchy crystallised
rose petals, or the just-enough serving of
crème brûlée in an eggshell, are another high
point. Over coffee and peanut butter chocolate
lollies, diners feel connected to the kitchen,
with the brigade's ribald laughter leaking
happily through the service door. Less
welcome on inspection was patchy service
which seriously threatened to undermine the
experience, though readers have also enjoyed
'wonderful' front-of-house attentions. A
restrained wine list has a slight French skew
and bottles from £19.95 (glass £5.50).
**Chef/s:** Glynn Purnell. **Open:** Tue to Fri L 12 to 1.30,
Tue to Sat D 7 to 9.30. **Closed:** Sun, Mon, 1 week
Easter, 2 weeks end Jul/Aug, 1 week Christmas.
**Meals:** Set L £17 (2 courses) to £20. Set D £33.95 (2
courses) to £39.95. Tasting menu £65.
**Service:** 12.5% (optional). **Details:** Cards accepted.
45 seats. Separate bar. Wheelchair access. Music.

## Simpsons

**Civilised city high-flier**
20 Highfield Road, Edgbaston, Birmingham,
B15 3DU
Tel no: (0121) 4543434
www.simpsonsrestaurant.co.uk
**Modern French | £40**
**Cooking score: 6**

In a city not short of culinary fireworks,
Simpsons' reputation is assured. The solid
suburban setting of this restaurant-with-
rooms could make you expect something
staid. It's true that moments of wild abandon
are rare, but Luke Tipping's cooking embraces
Thai, Indian and southern Mediterranean
flavours without abandoning French
technique and sensibilities. Thus, while
readers report 'one of the best' cheeseboards, a
meal might just as easily finish with
shockingly light orange mousse or Thai
mango crumble. The conservatory dining
rooms have a pale, tasteful charm. Colour
comes from looking either onto the pretty
terrace or into the kitchen, through windows
sensibly sized to give both diners and chefs
some privacy. Start, perhaps, with Scottish
lobster and exotic accompaniments: creamy
coconut rice, pineapple, battered shallot rings
and a curry foam. On inspection, a burnt
garnish of coconut shavings marked a fleeting
low point. To follow, Cornish lamb might
become a summery semi-salad, partnered
with artickokes, radishes, feta and lovage,
while duck gets the Thai treatment with a
spring roll, pak choi and star anise. A varied
clientele reflects the appeal of good-value set
menus at lunch and dinner. The French-
dominated wine list has plenty of big bottles
and starts at £22 (£7 by the glass). Doubling
that will open things up considerably.
**Chef/s:** Luke Tipping. **Open:** all week L 12 to 2 (2.30
Sat and Sun), Mon to Sat D 7 to 9 (9.30 Fri and Sat).
**Closed:** bank hols. **Meals:** alc (main courses £20 to
£27). Set L £30. Set D £32.50. Tasting menu £70.
**Service:** 12.5% (optional). **Details:** Cards accepted.
70 seats. 30 seats outside. Air-con. No music.
Wheelchair access. Children allowed. Car parking.

**NEW ENTRY**

## Turners

**Some of the best value in Birmingham**
69 High Street, Harborne, Birmingham, B17 9NS
Tel no: (0121) 4264440
www.turnersofharborne.com
Modern British | £35
Cooking score: 6

£5
OFF

Mirrors lining the top half of one wall bring light and width to this rather corridor-like restaurant, but there's no danger of forgetting where you are – the names of the chef and co-owner are emblazoned across the top. The décor is sensibly simple, almost stark, with a quarry-tiled floor and midnight blue panelling. It's bold, though, like the food. Richard Turner had already made a name for himself locally, in particular when cooking at the late Paris in the Mailbox. Now in his own place, he can give his creativity full rein. The result is well-pitched, remarkably priced food. Lunches and the fixed-price dinners on their 'auberge' nights early in the week must be among the best value in Birmingham. Excellent homemade bread is the precursor to, perhaps, chicken liver and foie gras parfait with Madeira jelly ('the best thing I've ever eaten in a restaurant') or loin of monkfish wrapped in Parma ham and served with bejewelled couscous. To finish, a vanilla pannacotta has also impressed. Vegetarians may get a rather intriguing variation on egg and chips – a deep-fried hen's egg with two potato croquettes and potato foam, all fragrant with truffle oil and accompanied by spinach and salsify. Service is attentive, if a little impersonal. House wine is £19.50.
**Chef/s:** Richard Turner. **Open:** Tue to Fri L 12 to 2.30, Tue to Sat D 6.30 to 9.30. **Closed:** Sun, Mon, 23 Dec to 2 Jan, 23 Aug to 8 Sept. **Meals:** Set L £17.50 (2 courses) to £21.50. Set D £32.50 (2 courses) to £39.50. Tasting menu £55. **Service:** not inc. **Details:** Cards accepted. 30 seats. Air-con. No mobile phones. Wheelchair access. Music. Children allowed. Car parking.

## Chez Jules

**French**
5A Ethel Street, Birmingham, B2 4BG
Tel no: (0121) 6334664
www.chezjules.co.uk
'Great food with no fuss'

## ▍Dorridge

### The Forest

**Revamped railway hotel**
25 Station Approach, Dorridge, B93 8JA
Tel no: (01564) 772120
www.forest-hotel.com
Modern European | £23
Cooking score: 2

 £30

Commuters alighting at Dorridge BR station probably wouldn't guess that the nearby Forest was originally a suburban railway hotel, but step past the original Victorian façade and it's clear that the place has been fast-tracked into the present with a chic bar, conference facilities and an upbeat brasserie-style restaurant. The kitchen follows suit, and the food 'does more than enough to excite the palate', according one reporter. A risotto of red wine, radicchio and bone marrow sets the tone, before grilled sea bream with baked fennel, mussels and saffron or something casual such as chargrilled piri-piri chicken. For afters, consider vanilla pannacotta with garibaldi biscuits. House wine is £13.95.
**Chef/s:** Dean Grubb. **Open:** all week L 12 to 2.30 (3 Sun), Mon to Sat D 6.30 to 10. **Closed:** 25 Dec. **Meals:** alc (main courses £8 to £25). Set L and D Mon to Fri £13 (2 courses) to £15.50. Sun L £14.50 (2 courses) to £17.50. **Service:** 10% (optional). **Details:** Cards accepted. 70 seats. 60 seats outside. Air-con. Separate bar. Wheelchair access. Music. Children allowed. Car parking.

## ▮ Oldbury

NEW ENTRY

### Saffron

Bold colours and expert spicing
909 Wolverhampton Road, Oldbury, B69 4RR
Tel no: (0121) 5521752
www.saffron-online.co.uk
Indian | £20
Cooking score: 2
£5 OFF **V** £30

Saffron doesn't hold back on colour. A red and black scheme dominates, from the stylish chairs to the striking angular wall which separates the bar from the dining room. Spicing is expert and can be whisperingly delicate, particularly in a fine saffron-dusted sea bass. The til tinka version of king prawns is crunchy with red sesame and spiced with mace and cardamom, while more upmarket dishes such as lobster peri-peri appear among generous offerings of old favourites and regional specialities. A laminated dessert menu may cause a slight sinking of the heart, but fear not, the puddings are good and mostly homemade, carrot halva being particularly fine. House wine weighs in at £10 a bottle.

**Chef/s:** Gregory Gomes. **Open:** all week L 12 to 2.30, D 5.30 to 11.30. **Meals:** alc (main courses £6 to £19) Set L £4.95 (2 courses). Sun L £6.95. **Service:** not inc. **Details:** Cards accepted. 96 seats. Air-con. Separate bar. Wheelchair access. Music. Children allowed. Car parking.

## ▮ Solihull

READERS RECOMMEND

### Da Santino

Italian
12 Dorridge Square, Solihull, B93 8HN
Tel no: (01564) 772547
'Retro Italian restaurant serving delicious and highly authentic food'

## ▮ Wolverhampton

ALSO RECOMMENDED

### ▲ Bilash

2 Cheapside, Wolverhampton, WV1 1TU
Tel no: (01902) 427762
www.thebilash.co.uk
Indian

Set in Wolverhampton's financial quarter, opposite St Peter's church, Bilash is an Indian restaurant that is a cut above the norm. Elegant décor and a service approach that is consistently praised in reader reports make for a successful formula, and the cooking is highly rated too. Tangri kebabs of chicken, marinated and cooked in the tandoor (£5.90), are interesting for their Thai-style spicing. More familiar territory is explored with lamb tikka hasina (£12.90), and the show-stopping Goan tiger prawn masala (£22.90). Wines from £17.90. Closed Sun.

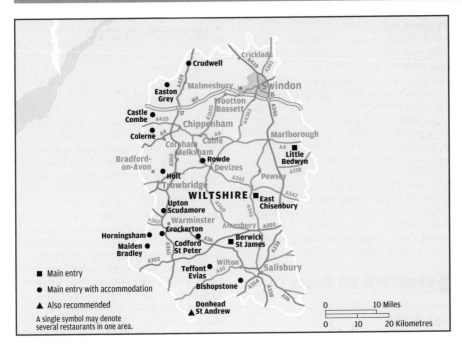

- ■ Main entry
- ● Main entry with accommodation
- ▲ Also recommended

A single symbol may denote several restaurants in one area.

0        10 Miles

0      10      20 Kilometres

## ■ Berwick St James

**NEW ENTRY**

### The Boot Inn

Cracking pub food
High Street, Berwick St James, SP3 4TN
Tel no: (01722) 790243
www.bootatberwick.co.uk
Gastropub | £22
Cooking score: 1

£5 OFF    £30

Handy for Stonehenge, this brick-and-flint Wadworth pub is at the heart of a sleepy village deep in the Wiltshire Downs. It serves some cracking pub food. The changing chalkboard in the homely, carpeted bar lists traditional British dishes prepared as much as possible from local and seasonal produce. Lunch brings thick-cut sandwiches, or there could be seared chicken livers and wild mushrooms on toast, hearty beef and ale pie, and rhubarb fool with ginger shortbread. The pretty garden is a summer bonus. Wines from £12.50.

**Chef/s:** Giles Dickinson. **Open:** Tue to Sun L 12 to 3, Tue to Sat D 6.30 to 9 (9.30 Fri and Sat). **Closed:** Mon. **Meals:** alc (main courses £10 to £16). **Service:** not inc. **Details:** Cards accepted. 45 seats. 30 seats outside. Wheelchair access. Music. Children allowed. Car parking.

## ■ Bishopstone

**NEW ENTRY**

### Helen Browning at the Royal Oak

Country pub with organic cred
Cues Lane, Bishopstone, SN6 8PP
Tel no: (01793) 790481
www.royaloakbishopstone.co.uk
Gastropub | £25
Cooking score: 3

£5 OFF    £30

Here's a proper country pub, off a narrow country road, down an even narrower one, full of books, chalkboard menus and things for the kids to do. Helen Browning's organic

Eastbrook Farm provides pork, beef, eggs and much of the fruit and veg. Lunch is a simple affair – an organic burger with beetroot julienne and triple-cooked chips or a big fat fishcake of grey mullet, perhaps, with a dessert of properly runny Seville orange posset. In the evenings, the menu stretches its legs a little into a three-course format that might progress from pancakes with air-dried ham and turnip purée, through ribeye steak with mash and salad, to silky-smooth chocolate tart. Service is all charm and chat, and a short wine list does its job succinctly, from £4 a glass.

**Chef/s:** Liz Franklin. **Open:** all week L 12 to 2.30 (4 Sat and Sun), D 6.30 to 9.30 (8.30 Sun). **Meals:** alc (main courses £9 to £20). **Service:** not inc. **Details:** Cards accepted. 40 seats. 20 seats outside. Music. Children allowed. Car parking.

## ▌Bradford on Avon

READERS RECOMMEND
### Fat Fowl
**Modern European**
Silver Street, Bradford on Avon, BA15 2JX
Tel no: (01225) 863111
www.fatfowl.com
'All-day café/restaurant with a varied menu, much of it is locally sourced'

## ▌Castle Combe

NEW ENTRY
### The Manor House Hotel, Bybrook Restaurant
**Modern country-house cuisine**
Castle Combe, SN14 7HR
Tel no: (01249) 782206
www.manorhouse.co.uk
**Modern British | £52**
**Cooking score: 5**
£5 OFF ▭ V

At the heart of the medieval village of Castle Combe, the Manor House has stood in one form or another since the fourteenth century. It is surrounded by as many acres of woodland and park as there are days in the year, and its championship golf course is a powerful draw

for the swingers. The cooking in the chandeliered Bybrook Restaurant exercises its own attractive powers in the hands of Richard Davies, who offers a highly refined style of country house cuisine in the modern British mould. An appetiser cup of foamy soup, and a shot-glass of foamy pre-dessert, are therefore de rigueur, but in between lie some more substantial dishes. Sautéed Skye scallops appear on butternut squash purée with slivers of chorizo and diced poached pear to create a well-conceived assemblage of flavours. Micuit salmon with goose foie gras, apple and celeriac has become a signature starter. Mains might go down the familiar route of wrapping monkfish in Parma ham, or partnering slow-cooked cannon of lamb with honey-glazed swede and a soubise of caramelised onion. Warm, sticky almond and banana financier sponge with creamy rum and raisin ice cream is a nice way to finish. The wine list majors in big names and mature vintages, with glass prices from £7.

**Chef/s:** Richard Davies. **Open:** Sun to Fri L 12.30 to 2, all week D 7 to 9.30 (10 Sat). **Meals:** Set L £17 (2 courses) to £21. Set D £30 (2 courses) to £52. Sun L £27.50. **Service:** not inc. **Details:** Cards accepted. 55 seats. 15 seats outside. Separate bar. No mobile phones. Wheelchair access. Music. Children allowed. Car parking.

## ▌Codford St Peter

### The George Hotel
**Friendly inn with classy cooking**
High Street, Codford St Peter, BA12 0NG
Tel no: (01985) 850270
**Modern British | £25**
**Cooking score: 4**
£5 OFF ▭ £30

Just off the A36 in a Wiltshire village, the George is handy if you've just braved the tourist hordes at Stonehenge. Sitting opposite the Woolstore theatre, it features a large walled garden and cosy, low-ceilinged interiors. The friendly ambience is such that you might stop in just for a pint or a glass of wine, but then you'd miss Boyd McIntosh's rather classy British pub cooking. Start with a smoked salmon salad with capers, or perhaps a serving of chicken livers with black pudding and crispy bacon, and go on to Cumberland sausages with mustard mash and onion gravy, or garlic-roasted mackerel with pickled ginger and tomato salad. Other fish specials are chalked up on the board. Vegetarians might opt for sweet pepper, courgette and leek risotto with Parmesan and basil oil. Desserts include treats like dark chocolate marquise with cherry ice cream, homemade meringue nests with fresh fruit and cream, and apple and peach crumble. The less sweet-toothed might be tempted by a platter of French and English cheeses. A short wine list starts at £13.95 (£3.50 a glass).

**Chef/s:** Boyd McIntosh and Joel Deverill. **Open:** Wed to Mon L 12 to 2, Mon and Wed to Sat D 6.30 to 9. **Closed:** Tue. **Meals:** alc (main courses £9 to £20). Set L and D £9.95 (2 courses). **Service:** not inc. **Details:** Cards accepted. 55 seats. 60 seats outside. Music. Children allowed. Car parking.

## ■ Colerne
### Lucknam Park
**Fascinating food in sumptuous surroundings**
Colerne, SN14 8AZ
Tel no: (01225) 742777
www.lucknampark.co.uk
**Modern European | £65**
**Cooking score: 6**

£5 OFF 🛏 V

The Lucknam Park experience begins as you process along the stately, tree-lined driveway that leads up to this palatial Palladian mansion. Set in 500 acres of manicured parkland, it is a model of aristocratic gentility – although the hotel has been puffed up with all manner of latter-day accoutrements, from the obligatory luxury spa to an equestrian centre. Housed in the original ballroom (resplendent with a fabulous hand-painted ceiling, crystal chandeliers and gold silk drapes), the Park Restaurant makes a suitably sumptuous backdrop for Hywel Jones' cooking. Diners can look forward to confident, innovative food that challenges the notion of soft-centred country house cooking by bringing on board

carrot escabèche, salted grapes, sweetbread dumplings and other modish extras. Elsewhere, monkfish is given some Middle Eastern lustre with roast couscous, Fowey mussels and cauliflower tagine, while loin of Brecon venison benefits from butternut squash risotto fritters, apple and sloe gin sauce. Among the starters, confit of citrus-cured salmon is paired with beetroot 'four ways' and a 'compression' of Roundway Hill pork is matched with roast langoustines and ravigote dressing. Desserts are endlessly fascinating conceits: a cube of Valrhona chocolate with mascarpone sorbet, or a nouveau/classic amalgam of exotic fruit ravioli alongside rum and raisin financier. The upper-crust, international wine list brings serious names to the table, with prices from £22.

**Chef/s:** Hywel Jones. **Open:** Mon to Sat D 7 to 10, Sun L 12 to 2. **Meals:** Sun L £35. Set D £65 to £75. **Service:** not inc. **Details:** Cards accepted. 50 seats. No music. No mobile phones. Wheelchair access. Children allowed. Car parking.

## ■ Crockerton
### The Bath Arms
**Proper pub, proper food**
Clay Street, Crockerton, BA12 8AJ
Tel no: (01985) 212262
www.batharmscrockerton.co.uk
**Gastropub | £22**
**Cooking score: 3**

🛏

This seventeenth-century coaching inn close to Longleat has all the relaxed and friendly unpretentiousness that one hopes for in a pub. The cooking, more modern than you would expect from the traditional surroundings, has a commitment to seasonal produce, such as game terrine or a well-flavoured plate of pheasant with parsnip mash and tongue cassoulet on a winter menu. Reporters have enjoyed black bream 'cooked to perfection with a delicate sauce', while other main courses might include sticky beef with braised red cabbage or bar classics like mixed grill and shepherd's pie. Chocolate brownie with the pub's own very good coffee ice cream is a popular dessert. Value for money is extremely good, not least in the short, lively list of wines from £14.50.

**Chef/s:** Dean Carr. **Open:** all week L 12 to 2, D 6.30 to 9. **Meals:** alc (main courses £7 to £15). **Service:** not inc. **Details:** Cards accepted. 80 seats. 100 seats outside. Wheelchair access. Music. Children allowed. Car parking.

## ▌Crudwell

### The Rectory Hotel

**Serenity, local menus and decadent desserts**
Crudwell, SN16 9EP
Tel no: (01666) 577194
www.therectoryhotel.com
**Modern European | £30**
**Cooking score: 3**

The three-storeyed Georgian manor house enjoys a particularly tranquil setting, with a modern dining room panelled in light wood overlooking the walled garden and its sunken Victorian baptismal pool (the place was once a rectory, remember). Peter Fairclough cooks a locally based menu of brasserie-style dishes, with confit duck leg on a salad of chorizo and hazelnuts to begin, perhaps followed by sea bass with king prawn linguine, or calf's liver with pancetta risotto. Immaculately presented desserts such as dark chocolate tart with lavender ice cream, or orange and vanilla crème brûlée with Pimm's granita and orange salad, end things on a high. The wine list covers a lot of territory succinctly, with prices starting from £13.95 (£3.75 a glass).

**Chef/s:** Peter Fairclough. **Open:** all week D only 7 to 9 (9.30 Sat). **Meals:** alc (main courses £15 to £18). **Service:** not inc. **Details:** Cards accepted. 20 seats. 20 seats outside. Separate bar. Wheelchair access. Music. Children allowed. Car parking.

## ALSO RECOMMENDED

### ▲ The Potting Shed

Crudwell, SN16 9EW
Tel no: (01666) 577833
www.thepottingshedpub.com
**Gastropub**

With rambling rooms, beams and open fires, this wonderful village pub has period feel by the pint (as well as real ale in the bar), served up with quirky design touches and expansive gardens. But it's not just the décor that's a clever blend of old and new. Familiar reworked British classics include braised oxtail terrine (£5.50), chicken, leek and tarragon pie, and poached smoked haddock with parsley mash (£12.50), with produce locally sourced or own-grown. Wines from £13.95. Closed Sun D. An offshoot of the Rectory Hotel (see entry).

## ▌Donhead St Andrew

## ALSO RECOMMENDED

### ▲ The Forester

Lower Street, Donhead St Andrew, SP7 9EE
Tel no: (01747) 828038
**Modern British**

Cornish seafood is one of the stars at this landlocked sixteenth-century hostelry on the Wiltshire/Dorset border. In a gentrified, *Country Living* setting, fish-loving visitors can sample the likes of Fowey mussels, pan-fried razor clams or full-blooded bouillabaisse (£15.50). Others might prefer to kick off with oxtail ravioli, pickled red cabbage and horseradish cream (£6.50) before a chargrilled burger, English rose veal T-bone or seared calf's liver with leek and sage mash. After that, perhaps apple crumble and custard (£4.50). House wine is £13.50. Closed Sun D.

## East Chisenbury

**NEW ENTRY**
### Red Lion

East Chisenbury, SN9 6AQ
Tel no: (01980) 671124
www.redlionfreehouse.com
**Modern British | £25**
**Cooking score: 5**

£30

The best of England's country pubs often need seeking out, amid the high hedges and twisty lanes of leafy B-roads. In summer, it is an idyllic run to the Red Lion, and one pair of diners who braved the snowstorms of February still thought it was well worth the effort. The colossally talented Guy Manning arrived here via London's Chez Bruce (see entry), New York and Martin Berasategui in San Sebastian. The pub has been sensitively renovated, with brick pillars and a huge old fireplace left in situ. The menus feature the pick of local produce, with virtually everything made in-house. Middle White pork is a show-stopper, turning up at a Sunday lunch in the form of the roasted loin, still baby-pink, with magic wands of crackling, crunchy 'roasties', and a section of baked onion. Start, perhaps, with a creamy dish of tender cockles cooked with potato and celery, finish with banoffi pie in a glass. Presentations are restaurant standard, but the topping-up of bread (and even that moreish crackling) show that the pub ethos has not been forsaken. Stone, Vine and Sun supply the inspired, single-page wine list. Glasses are from £3.50.
**Chef/s:** Guy Manning and Brittany Manning. **Open:** Wed to Sun L 12.30 to 2.30 (3.30 Sun), Tue to Sun D 6.30 to 9.30 (8.30 Sun). **Closed:** Mon, 10 days Jan. **Meals:** alc (main courses £10 to £16). **Service:** 10% (optional). **Details:** Cards accepted. 40 seats. 20 seats outside. Separate bar. Wheelchair access. Music. Children allowed. Car parking.

## Easton Grey

## Whatley Manor

Devastatingly good-looking cooking
Easton Grey, SN16 0RB
Tel no: (01666) 822888
www.whatleymanor.com
**Modern French | £68**
**Cooking score: 7**

£5 OFF 🍷 🛏

Two courtyards of honey-stone buildings form the heart of this expansive manor-house hotel. Everything inside is grand but homely: the rambling lounges, the light hallways, even the sofas — which is where you begin the evening with canapés such as foie gras velouté with balsamic jelly, or tender beetroot topped with crème fraîche. Wood panelling and rug-strewn floors sit comfortably with modern furnishings, and leaded windows look out over romantic gardens. The dining room, simply decorated with abstract art, is more modest than the sprawling lounges might suggest. Service is impeccable; staff appear (and disappear) right on cue, and a similar crisp precision shapes the cooking. You could start with an amuse of tomato essence (unassuming in its tall, clear glass, it tastes ripe, intense and greenhouse-fresh) alongside deep-fried goats' cheese with olive tapenade. The same mature and rounded cheese formed the heart of a punchy ravioli starter, teamed with apple sorbet, almond purée and cubes of celery and pink pepper gel on blood-red slivers of beetroot. This is devastatingly good-looking food with impeccably balanced flavours; a main course of John Dory fillets and langoustine tails with crisp summer vegetables and white prawn foam proved the point. Quick-fire pre-desserts of blackcurrant and clove foam followed by Earl Grey pannacotta with lemon jelly thyme foam were an odd couple, one loud, the other retiring, but a strawberry and kalamansi soufflé stole the show, flanked by strawberries every which way, from whole to sorbet. Classic petits fours along the lines of madeleines, pâté de fruits and homemade chocolates are best savoured back in the lounge. The wine list is a

formidable slate, but its worldwide scope isn't intimidating and prices are kind enough to allow for top-class drinking at every level. There is excellent stuff from £17.50 a bottle, and plenty of desirable options by the glass.
**Chef/s:** Martin Burge. **Open:** Wed to Sun only D 7 to 10. **Closed:** Mon and Tue. **Meals:** Set D £68, Tasting menu £85. **Service:** 10%. **Details:** Cards accepted. 40 seats. Separate bar. Car parking.

## ▌Holt
## The Tollgate Inn
**As English as afternoon tea**
Ham Green, Holt, BA14 6PX
Tel no: (01225) 782326
www.tollgateholt.co.uk
Modern British | £25
Cooking score: 3
£5 OFF 🛏 £30

Bedecked with flowers and warmed by a wood-burning stove, this stone-built inn is as English as afternoon tea. It was previously a weaving shed, then a Baptist chapel, and later an ordinary locals' bar – and now it has become a popular dining destination, thanks to owners Alison Ward-Baptiste and Alexander Venables. Bolstered by an impressive list of local ingredients, Alexander's menus deliver a welcome blend of British and French influences: perhaps bouillabaisse of Cornish fish with aïoli and rouille, followed by traditional beef Wellington with minted peas. Finish with local cheeses or panettone bread-and-butter pudding with butterscotch sauce and caramel ice cream. Other choices include good value set-price menus, and 'light bite' lunch options. A substantial global wine list opens at £13.10.
**Chef/s:** Alexander Venables. **Open:** Tue to Sun L 12 to 2, Tue to Sat D 7 to 9. **Closed:** Mon, 25 Dec, 1 Jan. **Meals:** alc (main courses £14 to £19). Set L £12.50 (2 courses) to £14.95. Set D £16.75 (2 courses) to £18.75. Sun L £12.50. **Service:** not inc. **Details:** Cards accepted. 60 seats. 40 seats outside. Separate bar. No mobile phones. Wheelchair access. Music. Car parking.

## ▌Horningsham
## The Bath Arms
**Idiosyncratic inn with highly satisfying food**
Longleat Estate, Horningsham, BA12 7LY
Tel no: (01985) 844308
www.batharms.co.uk
Gastropub | £30
Cooking score: 2
🚃 V

The seventeenth-century, ivy-clad coaching inn stands at the gates of Longleat House and is decorated in idiosyncratic style. It's a fitting setting for cooking that doesn't aim to thrill with outlandish ideas, but still achieves highly satisfying results thanks to skilful techniques and well-sourced ingredients. Thus lunch, served in the bar, dining room and (weather permitting) front and back terraces, might feature rare beef sandwiches, pork chop or faggots, while dinner in the restaurant brings game terrine ahead of seared calf's liver with braised shin and garlic mash. Double chocolate brownie is a popular dessert. Wines from £13.50.
**Chef/s:** Frank Bailey. **Open:** all week L 12 to 2.30, D 7 to 9 (9.30 Fri and Sat). **Meals:** alc L (main courses £5 to £17). Set L £13.50 (2 courses) to £17.50. Set D £24.50 (2 courses) to £29.50. Sun L £12.50. **Service:** not inc. **Details:** Cards accepted. 44 seats. 44 seats outside. Separate bar. Wheelchair access. Music. Children allowed. Car parking.

## ▌Little Bedwyn
## The Harrow at Little Bedwyn
**Fine dining with wines to match**
Little Bedwyn, SN8 3JP
Tel no: (01672) 870871
www.theharrowatlittlebedwyn.co.uk
Modern British | £40
Cooking score: 6
🍾

A modest red brick exterior, complete with pub sign, belies the elegant interior of this restaurant of interconnected rooms, with garden terrace for al fresco dining. Roger and Sue Jones' proud mission statement – 'We believe in real farming, free-range and real food' – is supplemented by a list of their local and regional suppliers. Top-quality ingredients are treated sensitively, showing real skill and intelligence. Readers praise the cooking for its 'lightness of touch' and 'original teaming of flavours and textures'. Witness crisp English asparagus topping a pea risotto of exquisite creamy sweetness and an equally impressive well-timed sea bass fillet with enoki mushrooms and red wine jus. Exciting meat dishes include a platter of Welsh lamb, comprising best end chop, fillet, cottage pie and lamb's fries, or braised ox cheek paired with oxtail and foie gras ravioli. Desserts such as raspberry soufflé and summer pudding are well executed. Service matches the excellence of the food and drink. Every dish on the carte and tasting menus has suggested wine pairings – fittingly so, given the depth and quality of the wine list. The set-lunch menu (£30) includes two glasses of wine. House selections start at £21 on a wine list that is an extensive and alluring collection of modern and classic bottles. There are 12 by the glass. Our questionnaire was not returned, so some of the information below may have changed.

**Chef/s:** Roger Jones. **Open:** Wed to Sun L 12 to 2, Wed to Sat D 7 to 9. **Closed:** Mon, Tue, 2 weeks Christmas, 2 weeks Aug. **Meals:** alc (main courses £24). Set L £30. Set D £40 to £120. **Service:** not inc. **Details:** Cards accepted. 32 seats. 28 seats outside. Wheelchair access. Music.

## Maiden Bradley

**NEW ENTRY**
### The Somerset Arms
**A real find**
Church Street, Maiden Bradley, BA12 7HW
Tel no: (01985) 844207
www.thesomersetarms.co.uk
**Gastropub | £22**
**Cooking score: 2**

£5 OFF 🍽 £30

Lisa Richards and Rachel Seed breathed new life into this plain brick pub in 2008 and have not looked back since. It's set in a classic estate village midway between Longleat and

Stourhead, and the quirky interior has been revamped with style – heritage paints, stone and wood floors, blazing fires, fat candles on scrubbed tables – and it is 'popular with everyone from gamekeepers to gentry'. Robust dishes from short, Mediterranean-inspired menus include pan Catalan with monkfish, chorizo and butter bean stew, with chilli chocolate pot and orange shortbread to finish. A real find. House wine £12. More reports please.

**Chef/s:** Rachel Seed. **Open:** Tue to Sun L 12 to 3 (3.30 Sun), Tue to Sat D 6 to 9.30. **Closed:** Mon. **Meals:** alc (main courses £8 to £18). **Details:** Cards accepted. 36 seats. 16 seats outside. Separate bar. Music. Children allowed. Car parking.

## Rowde

### The George & Dragon
**Charming pub with sumptuous seafood**
High Street, Rowde, SN10 2PN
Tel no: (01380) 723053
www.thegeorgeanddragonrowde.co.uk
**Modern British | £25**
**Cooking score: 4**

£5 OFF 🍽 V £30

It's unusual to find beautifully cooked fresh seafood in the heart of the Wiltshire countryside, but that's what the George & Dragon does really well. The charming former meeting house and inn dates back to the fourteenth century. Exposed beams, wood floors and open fires give the restaurant and bar a cosy, welcoming atmosphere. Skilful cooking shows a light, modern touch, using uncomplicated flavours in predominantly fish-based dishes. Check the blackboard for specials such as whole crab, lobster and seasonal treats from Cornwall. Begin with seared scallops with hollandaise, or a fishy hors d'oeuvre. Typical mains are monkfish with prosciutto, wild mushrooms and grainy mustard sauce, otherwise try a Wiltshire pork chop with herb stuffing and red cabbage. Desserts stick mainly with homely favourites like chocolate and orange bread-and-butter pud or crème brûlée. Wines start at £14.50 a bottle, with 10 by the glass from £4.

Chef/s: Christopher Day. Open: all week L 12 to 3 (4 Sun), Tue to Sat D 7 to 10 (6.30 to 10.30 Sat).
Meals: alc (main courses £10 to £25). Set L £14.50 (2 courses) to £17.50. Service: not inc.
Details: Cards accepted. 35 seats. 40 seats outside. Separate bar. No mobile phones. Wheelchair access. Music. Children allowed. Car parking.

# ▌Teffont Evias
## Howard's House
**Hospitality in a hidden valley**
Teffont Evias, SP3 5RJ
Tel no: (01722) 716392
www.howardshousehotel.co.uk
Modern British | £45
Cooking score: 3

'You are always treated so well here', says one reader of this peaceful country hotel and restaurant. A seventeenth-century dower house in a lush, hidden valley, it's an impossibly pretty location with immaculate gardens and a smartly traditional interior. The menu is nicely in tune with the surrounding landscape. Caramelised belly of Wiltshire pork with braised lentils and apple and Calvados sauce might pave the way for breast of local guinea fowl with bubble and squeak potato cake and Madeira jus. For pudding try a 'superb' mandarin soufflé with mandarin sorbet. The substantial wine list covers the major French regions but also brings in a good sprinkling of New World names. Prices start at £15.75 a bottle.
Chef/s: Nick Wentworth. Open: all week L 12.30 to 1.45, D 7 to 9. Closed: 1 week Christmas. Meals: Set L £22.50 (2 courses) to £27. Set D £23.50 (2 courses) to £27.95. Sun L £22.50. Service: not inc.
Details: Cards accepted. 26 seats. 20 seats outside. Wheelchair access. Music. Children allowed. Car parking.

# ▌Upton Scudamore
## The Angel Inn
**An updated inn of substance**
Upton Scudamore, BA12 0AG
Tel no: (01985) 213225
www.theangelinn.co.uk
Modern British | £30
Cooking score: 3

At the heart of a little village on the edge of Salisbury Plain, the Angel is an updated country inn of substance, complete with a south-facing walled garden, a high-ceilinged bar and a civilised dining room. Complimentary home-baked bread and a blackboard of specials (including fish from Brixham) add an extra dimension to meals here, and the kitchen isn't short on ideas. A 'cushion' of smoked salmon receives a cockle and parsley oil dressing, roast pollack fillet appears atop wilted greens with a mussel, lemongrass and coconut broth, while seared pigeon breast and spring vegetable casserole is finished with crème de Cassis. Homemade ice creams and sorbets are alternatives to desserts such as egg custard tart or peanut parfait on a honeycomb base with chocolate mousse. House wines start at £13.75.
Chef/s: Nick Cooper. Open: all week L 12 to 2, D 6.30 to 9.30. Closed: 25 and 26 Dec, 1 Jan.
Meals: alc (main courses £9 to £20). Set L £10.95 (2 courses) to £14.95. Service: not inc. Details: Cards accepted. 60 seats. 40 seats outside. Separate bar. Wheelchair access. Music. Children allowed. Car parking.

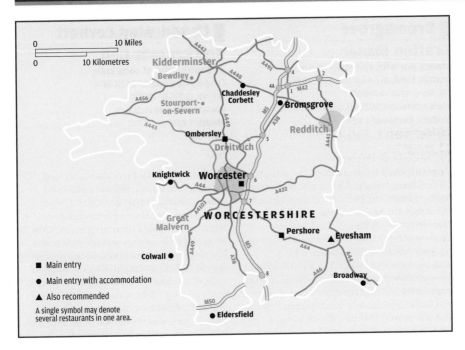

- ■ Main entry
- ● Main entry with accommodation
- ▲ Also recommended

A single symbol may denote several restaurants in one area.

## ▮ Broadway

### Russell's

**Boutique brasserie with panache**
20 High Street, Broadway, WR12 7DT
Tel no: (01386) 853555
www.russellsofbroadway.co.uk
**Modern British | £35**
**Cooking score: 4**

£5 OFF 🛏 V

Renowned furniture designer Gordon Russell once had his headquarters in this Cotswold stone building in touristy Broadway. The bright, relaxing dining room is a joy, and there are outdoor tables on a front patio and in the courtyard for summer eating. Matt Laughton cooks a broad-minded, contemporary brasserie-style menu that coasts from starters like grilled sardines with chorizo, orange and coriander to mains such as Cornish whiting with cherry tomatoes, polenta and romesco dressing or rump steak with truffle oil mash, artichoke and wild mushrooms in balsamic syrup. There are pastas and antipasti in both starter and main-course sizes, as well as slates of tapas, and meals end with such indulgences as chocolate mousse with caramelised orange and ginger ice cream. The concise wine list offers an even spread of both hemispheres, with a dozen house selections at the uniform price of £18 (£4.50 a glass).
**Chef/s:** Matt Laughton. **Open:** all week L 12 to 2.30, Mon to Sat D 6 to 9.30. **Meals:** alc (main courses £12 to £28). Set L £12 (2 courses) to £15. Set D £15 (2 courses) to £22.95. Sun L £22.95. **Service:** not inc. **Details:** Cards accepted. 55 seats. 30 seats outside. Air-con. No mobile phones. Wheelchair access. Music. Children allowed. Car parking.

## Bromsgrove

### Grafton Manor

**Stately pile with spiced-up menus**
Grafton Lane, Bromsgrove, B61 7HA
Tel no: (01527) 579007
www.graftonmanorhotel.co.uk
Modern European | £29
Cooking score: 3

Commissioned by the Earls of Shrewsbury in 1567, this rambling red-brick pile is now the Morris family seat and a destination venue for Birmingham's business community. It's also a favoured stop-off for travellers en route to Worcestershire's rural backwaters and fans of idiosyncratic food. The kitchen takes a European view of things, but it overlays its western endeavours with a mildly affectionate exploration of Indian cuisine. Bombay prawns and chicken bhuna add some spice to a menu that works its way through vodka-cured salmon with pear, apple and beetroot salad, wild mushroom fricassee and braised belly pork with carrot purée and caramelised apples. The Subcontinent resurfaces with desserts such as Hyderabadi apricots with mango and coriander sorbet – or you might prefer to keep faith with Lord of Grafton's whisky steamed pudding. Wines are affordably priced from £11.65.
**Chef/s:** Tim Waldren and Adam Harrison. **Open:** Sun to Fri L 12 to 2.30, Mon to Sat D 7 to 9. **Closed:** first week Jan. **Meals:** Set L £22.50. Set D £28.95 to £33.75 (4 courses). **Service:** not inc. **Details:** Cards accepted. 60 seats. Separate bar. No music. No mobile phones. Wheelchair access. Children allowed. Car parking.

## Chaddesley Corbett

### Brockencote Hall

**A country hotel of some class**
Chaddesley Corbett, DY10 4PY
Tel no: (01562) 777876
www.brockencotehall.com
French | £38
New chef

The interior of this lovingly maintained Victorian mansion reflects the owners' individual taste: easy pastels, floral drapes, comfortable upholstered seating and fine white table linen in the dining room. With 25 years and more in the business, Alison and Joseph Petitjean have perfected the personable approach that has delighted a generation of visitors, evident in everything from the good housekeeping to the welcoming staff. Chef Didier Philipot moved on just as the *Guide* went to press and we learned of his successor, John Sherry, too late for us to send an inspector, but it is likely that the typical country house combination of luxury (foie gras and truffles, for example) and hard labour will continue. The wine list offers house wines from £16 a bottle.
**Chef/s:** John Sherry. **Open:** all week L 12 to 1.30, D 7 to 9.30. **Meals:** alc (main courses £18 to £28). Set L £15 (2 courses) to £19. Set D £26.30 (2 courses) to £34.30. Sun L £27.50. **Service:** not inc.
**Details:** Cards accepted. 75 seats. Separate bar. No mobile phones. Wheelchair access. Music. Children allowed. Car parking.

## Colwall

### Colwall Park Hotel

**Appealing mock-Tudor retreat**
Walwyn Road, Colwall, WR13 6QG
Tel no: (01684) 540000
www.colwall.co.uk
**Modern British | £35**
**Cooking score: 3**

£5 OFF

This substantial mock-Tudor hotel stands in the shadow of composer Edward Elgar's beloved Malvern Hills. Inside, the impressive oak-panelled Seasons Restaurant provides a suitably elegant backdrop for meals with a contemporary British tone and a fondness for regional produce – everything from Longdon Marsh lamb to a Three Counties cheeseboard. The kitchen serves roast loin of venison with a juniper-scented jus, pairs roast tenderloin of pork with braised belly, cider fondant and Calvados jus, and pleases fish-lovers with seared halibut, buttered spinach and warm tartare juices. If you fancy a sweet finish, try pineapple and black pepper tarte tarte Tatin or pistachio crème brûlée. French bottles (from £15.95) claim pole position on the wine list. **Chef/s:** James Garth. **Open:** all week L 12 to 2.30, D 7 to 9. **Meals:** alc (main courses £19 to £22). Set L £17 (2 courses) to £20. **Service:** not inc. **Details:** Cards accepted. 40 seats. Air-con. Separate bar. No mobile phones. Wheelchair access. Music. Children allowed. Car parking.

## Eldersfield

### The Butchers Arms

**Village pub with down-to-earth cooking**
Lime Street, Eldersfield, GL19 4NX
Tel no: (01452) 840381
www.thebutchersarms.net
**Gastropub | £29**
**Cooking score: 4**

£30

'Step back in time as you enter this traditional country pub' notes a reporter of James and Elizabeth Winter's two-room hostelry that dates from the sixteenth century. It's as you might expect: simple décor with a wood burner, low ceilings and real ales served straight from the cask in the tiny bar; the dining room is even smaller and tables highly prized. A glance at the menu shows a kitchen heroically striving for local and seasonal output – Bath chaps (pig's cheek) come with black pudding and Bramley apples – but it is the sensibly modernist approach that strikes most forcibly. This is down-to-earth cooking taking in 'tender and succulent' Gressingham duck, accompanied by lentils, cabbage and rhubarb compote, or wild Cotswold roe deer with bashed neeps and golden beetroot. Then, perhaps, an 'equally successful' treacle tart with white chocolate ice cream for dessert. A short, Eurocentric wine list opens at £15.95. **Chef/s:** James Winter. **Open:** Tue to Sun L 12 to 2.30, Tue to Sun D 7 to 8.45. **Closed:** Mon, 25 and 26 Dec, 10 days early Jan. **Meals:** alc (main courses £14 to £19). **Service:** not inc. **Details:** Cards accepted. 24 seats. Children allowed. Car parking.

## Evesham

### ALSO RECOMMENDED
### ▲ The Evesham Hotel

Cooper's Lane, Evesham, WR11 1DA
Tel no: (01386) 765566
www.eveshamhotel.com
**Modern British**

Originally a Tudor farmhouse, renovated in the Georgian era, this white-fronted hotel has been run by the Jenkinsons since the 1970s. An atmosphere of good-humoured hospitality prevails, and the menus aim to offer a wide range of choice. Alluring options might be scallops in Dijon mustard and green olive sauce (£8.75), roast lamb rump with honey-roast apple and parsnip and rosemary jus (£16.50) and a good spread of vegetarian dishes. Finish with strawberry cheesecake served with strawberry and basil compote (£5.20). Wines from £17. Open all week.

## ▌Hadley Heath

### The Hadley Bowling Green Inn

Gastropub
Hadley Heath, WR9 0AR
Tel no: (01905) 620294
www.hadleybowlinggreen.com
'Everything was fresh, delicious and perfectly cooked; service friendly'

## ▌Knightwick

### The Talbot

Teme Valley cuisine
Knightwick, WR6 5PH
Tel no: (01886) 821235
www.the-talbot.co.uk
British | £32
Cooking score: 1

The Clift family have clocked up 25 years at their fifteenth-century coaching inn overlooking the River Teme. It's very much a pub with a restaurant, rather than the other way around, matched by a well-executed cooking style that is rustic rather than refined. An industrious kitchen makes the best of local and seasonal supplies – rabbit casserole, cold raised pork and game pies, pot-roasted shoulder of mutton – and produces its own bread and preserves; even beer is brewed on the premises. House wine is £12.25.
**Chef/s:** Kate Parffrey. **Open:** all week L 12 to 2, D 6.30 to 9 (7 Sun). **Meals:** alc (main courses £10 to £22). Set D £27. Sun L £27. **Details:** Cards accepted. 30 seats. 30 seats outside. No music. No mobile phones. Wheelchair access. Children allowed. Car parking.

## Also recommended

Also recommended entries are not scored but we think they are worth a visit.

## ▌Ombersley

### Venture In

Past meets present
Ombersley, WR9 0EW
Tel no: (01905) 620552
Anglo-French | £36
Cooking score: 3

The name is an open invitation to cross the threshold of Ombersley's oldest building. Dating from 1430, this quaint half-timbered edifice is a trademark heritage assortment of weathered beams, thick stone walls and a giant inglenook. It even has its own ghost. The place may reek of history, but the kitchen bypasses memory lane in favour of food peppered with re-inventions and sharp accents: confit pig's cheek and bacon with sweet onion marmalade might precede breast and leg of pheasant with a game faggot, braised barley and sweet pickled red cabbage. A separate fish menu features the likes of monkfish wrapped in bacon with mushroom risotto and red wine sauce, while desserts have included prune and Armagnac tart with coffee ice cream. Around 70 well-spread wines kick off with house selections at £15.
**Chef/s:** Toby Fletcher. **Open:** Tue to Sun L 12 to 2, Tue to Sat D 7 to 9.30. **Closed:** Mon, bank hols, 1 week Christmas, 2 weeks Feb, 2 weeks Aug. **Meals:** Set L £22 (2 courses) to £26. Set D £36. Sun L £26. **Service:** not inc. **Details:** Cards accepted. 32 seats. Air-con. Wheelchair access. Music. Car parking.

## ▌Pershore

### Belle House

Fine materials and careful cooking
Bridge Street, Pershore, WR10 1AJ
Tel no: (01386) 555055
www.belle-house.co.uk
Anglo-French | £28
Cooking score: 3

The conversion of this red-brick Georgian town house is both dramatic and sympathetic – its ornate ceiling and wood panelling have been left intact for succeeding generations. Calm, precise service sets the tone, and both fine materials and careful presentation distinguish Steve Waites' cooking. An enthusiastic reporter mentions carrot and coriander soup, perfectly poached sea bass in saffron broth, and steamed salmon with aubergine caviar, confit cherry tomatoes and a beurre blanc as standout summer lunch dishes. Dinner might bring a main course of lamb, braised and roasted, and served with a portion of the sweetbreads adorned with sweet potato purée and ricotta. Finish with strawberry crème brûlée with a poppyseed tuile. A well-constructed list of quality wines encompasses a good spread of house selections, from £14.95 (£3.50 a glass).

**Chef/s:** Steve Waites and Sue Ellis. **Open:** Tue to Sat L 12 to 2, D 7 to 9.30. **Closed:** Sun, Mon, 1 to 14 Jan, 1 week Aug. **Meals:** Set L £14 (2 courses) to £21. Set D £22.50 (2 courses) to £28. **Service:** not inc. **Details:** Cards accepted. 80 seats. Air-con. Separate bar. Wheelchair access. Music. Children allowed.

# ▌Worcester

## Brown's
**Riverside restaurant that's big on style**
24 Quay Street, South Quay, Worcester, WR1 2JJ
Tel no: (01905) 26263
www.brownsrestaurant.co.uk
**Modern European | £30**
**Cooking score: 3**

The modish interior of this contemporary grain mill conversion on the banks of the River Severn (not visible from the restaurant) suggests upmarket fineries from the kitchen. But the menu is rooted reliably in seasonal British produce, delivered in a modern style that brings new life to old flavours. Expect starter choices like oxtail consommé with beetroot and mustard relish, and mains of confit pork belly with scallops, black pudding and creamed mustard celeriac, or dry-aged Herefordshire beef fillet teamed with a braised blade 'cottage pie' and smoked mushroom jus. Desserts, too, are given an original spin: try rhubarb and custard omelette Rothschild.

Readers declare the 'Express Lunch' to be good value for money. Service is attentive, and house wine weighs in at £18.

**Chef/s:** Iain Courage. **Open:** all week L 12 to 2.30 (3 Sun), Mon to Sat D 5 to 9.30. **Closed:** 25 and 26 Dec, 1 Jan. **Meals:** alc (main courses £14 to £39). Set L £9.95 (2 courses) to £12.95. Set D £20. Sun L £19.95. **Service:** not inc. **Details:** Cards accepted. 70 seats. 10 seats outside. Separate bar. Wheelchair access. Music. Children allowed.

## The Glasshouse
**Easy-going cosmopolitan all-rounder**
Danesbury House, 55 Sidbury, Worcester, WR1 2HU
Tel no: (01905) 611120
www.theglasshouse.co.uk
**Modern British | £28**
**Cooking score: 3**

Cool vibes and flexible, all-round appeal are big selling points at this cosmopolitan, three-floor brasserie – although food is never far from the limelight. Co-founder Shaun Hill is now turning heads at the Walnut Tree, Llanddewi Skirrid (see entry, Wales) but his spirit lives on in the Glasshouse kitchen. Chef Tom Duffill delivers the kind of must-eat, big-hearted dishes made famous by his mentor: there's no mistaking grilled ox tongue with duck hash, salsa verde and soft-boiled egg or roast loin of pork with spiced lentils and chorizo, while iced nougatine parfait with roasted plums should finish things off admirably. 'The chance to eat and drink for less than £20' at lunchtime is a pull for readers; you can also sample everything on the sharp global wine list by the glass or carafe. Bottles start at £15.

**Chef/s:** Tom Duffill. **Open:** Mon to Sat L 12 to 2.30, D 5 to 10. **Closed:** Sun. **Meals:** alc (main courses £13 to £20). Set L £10 (2 courses) to £15. Set D £16.95 (2 courses) to £21.95. **Service:** not inc. **Details:** Cards accepted. 100 seats. 20 seats outside. Air-con. Separate bar. Wheelchair access. Music. Children allowed.

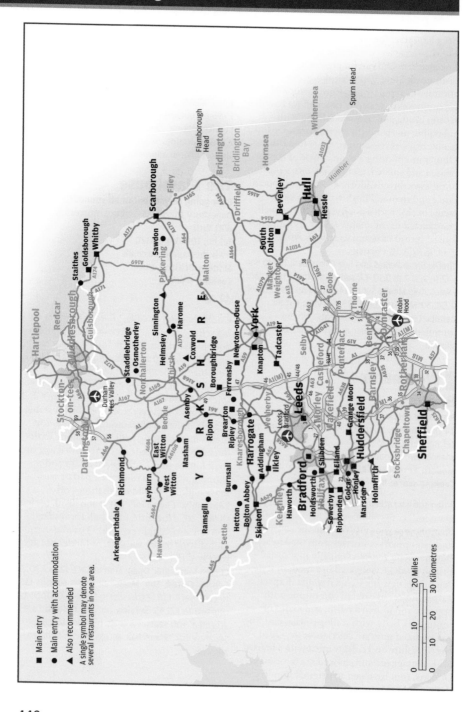

## ▌Addingham

### The Fleece Inn

**Down-home Yorkshire champion**
154 Main Street, Addingham, LS29 0LY
Tel no: (01943) 830491
**Modern British | £23**
**Cooking score: 3**

A North Country crowd-puller and still resolutely a down-home village boozer, the Fleece seems to have the lot, from gnarled beams in the drinkers' bar to a full-to-bursting summertime courtyard. It's just the spot for food that speaks broad Yorkshire, and t' menu does the business: roast beef sandwiches with dripping are great with a pint, and punters are also well-fed with trencherman helpings of pigeon and prune terrine with blackberry jam, Whitby fish pie and slabs of roast belly pork with red cabbage. Elsewhere, the kitchen forsakes its local roots and takes a tour for coq au vin, wok-fried king prawns, and scallops wrapped in bacon with chorizo and tomato risotto. Affordably priced wines start at £12.95 (£3.65 a glass). The same team also owns the Wellington Inn at Darley, near Harrogate, HG3 2QQ; tel no: (01423) 780362.

**Chef/s:** Andrew Cressy. **Open:** Mon to Sat L 12 to 2.15, D 6 to 9.15, Sun 12 to 8. **Meals:** alc (main courses £9 to £19). **Service:** not inc. **Details:** Cards accepted. 100 seats. 100 seats outside. Air-con. Separate bar. No music. Wheelchair access. Children allowed. Car parking.

## ▌Arkengarthdale

### ALSO RECOMMENDED
### ▲ Charles Bathurst Inn

Langthwaite, Arkengarthdale, DL11 6EN
Tel no: (01748) 884567
www.cbinn.co.uk
**Gastropub**

The CB has enjoyed a startling rebirth from an unloved boozer to a fully switched-on country inn. Game terrine, rump of lamb (£14.95), pork belly and sticky toffee pudding

hit the right notes after a wintry walk in Arkengarthdale, but things can get erratic: overseasoned rabbit consommé for example, and forgetting to torch the whisky and oat crème brûlée (£5.25). Fewer components and fewer dishes could sort out the glitches in an otherwise warm and welcoming refuge. House wine £12.95. Open all week. Accommodation.

## ▌Asenby

### The Crab & Lobster

**Eccentric pub for fish fans**
Dishforth Road, Asenby, YO7 3QL
Tel no: (01845) 577286
www.crabandlobster.co.uk
**Seafood | £35**
**Cooking score: 3**

It may look like just another Yorkshire country inn (apart from the old advertising signs plastered on the walls and crustacean effigies on the thatched roof), but step inside and you'll find a riot of eccentric memorabilia at every turn. As you might expect from the name, seafood is the main culinary business of the day, whether you are eating in the bar, restaurant or airy pavilion. Make a start with a mussel stir-fry spiked with chilli, ginger and coriander, move on to a chunk of cod with pot-roast belly pork, duck-fat roasties and five-spice sauce, and round off with something comforting such as baked apple with cinnamon cheesecake. For lunch, try a club sandwich – packed with fish, of course. House wines start at £21 (£3 a glass). Luxury accommodation is available at the nearby Crab Manor Hotel.

**Chef/s:** Stephen Dean. **Open:** all week L 12 to 2, D 7 to 9 (6.30 to 9.30 Sat). **Meals:** alc (main courses £16 to £44). Set L £14 (2 courses) to £17. **Service:** not inc. **Details:** Cards accepted. 90 seats. 50 seats outside. Separate bar. Wheelchair access. Music. Children allowed. Car parking.

## Beverley

NEW ENTRY
### Whites Restaurant
Careful, creative cooking
12a North Bar Without, Beverley, HU17 7AB
Tel no: (01482) 866121
www.whitesrestaurant.co.uk
Modern British | £32
Cooking score: 2

Beverley is Hull's smarter sister, which pretty much describes John Robinson's restaurant by the old town walls. Wood floors, dark, modern furniture and white napery make for a slightly stark lunchtime vibe, but imagine candles flickering in the evening, and you've got a sophisticated venue. Lunch is good value for such careful, creative cooking – think starters like smoked salmon mousse with pea and mint salsa, or chunky pork terrine. Mille-feuille of Fourme d'Ambert with leeks and roasted red onions is a pretty plate, local lamb shoulder with mash and shallots is satisfyingly dense and earthy, and two perfect cheeses arrive with homemade oat biscuits and celery pickle as a finale. Wine starts at £16, with a glass for £4.50.
Chef/s: John Robinson. Open: Tue to Sat L 10 to 3, D 6.30 to 11. Closed: Sun , Mon, 2 weeks Christmas. Meals: alc (£18 to £20). Set L £13.50 (2 courses) to £15.95. Set D £16 (2 courses) to £20. Service: not inc. Details: Cards accepted. 30 seats. No mobile phones. Wheelchair access. Music. Children allowed.

## Bolton Abbey

### The Devonshire Arms, Burlington Restaurant
A maestro works his magic
Bolton Abbey, BD23 6AJ
Tel no: (01756) 710441
www.thedevonshirearms.co.uk
Modern British | £58
Cooking score: 5

🍷 🍽 V

Steve Smith was only weeks into his job as head chef when the Guide went to press last year. In the intervening period he's worked his magic on the Burlington restaurant, and moved into top gear with a choice of three expertly wrought menus: à la carte, a six-course Tasting Menu and a Menu Prestige. Elsewhere, the timeless qualities of this country house hotel endure: the lovely backdrop of Lower Wharfedale, the plush elegance of the lounges. All is set for haute cuisine, made clear by Smith's description of his oeuvre. The menu is written in Terse, that contemporary language of the ambitious kitchen. Each dish is noted by its headline protein – beef, for example – then comes the rarified embellishment (and his punctuation): 'smoked sirloin – braised shin and tongue Parsley purée and risotto – Trompette – Bourguignonne jus'. There is a clearly personal style in the food, too, with obvious favouring of certain ingredients and techniques. Suffice it to say that Smith's technique involves smoking, marinating, pressing, reducing and slow-cooking, resulting in highly technical dishes, delicately portioned and intensely flavoured. Desserts astonish and delight – parsnip was the theme of a plate containing brioche pain perdu, parsnip ice cream and candied bacon with cumin caramel and tea jelly. And it comes as a pleasant surprise to open a wine list of this weight and quality and find drinkable bottles under £25 – a sign of an intelligent pricing policy that is to be applauded.

Chef/s: Steve Smith. **Open:** Sun L 12 to 2, Tue to Sun D 7 to 10. **Closed:** Mon. **Meals:** Set D £58. Sun L £35. Tasting menu £65. Prestige menu £70. **Service:** 12.5% (optional). **Details:** Cards accepted. 70 seats. Separate bar. No mobile phones. Wheelchair access. Children allowed. Car parking.

**NEW ENTRY**

## The Devonshire Brasserie
Daring dining in the Dales
Bolton Abbey, BD23 6EX
Tel no: (01756) 710710
www.thedevonshirearms.co.uk
**Modern British | £23**
**Cooking score: 2**

🍴 V £30

Even after a decade or so, there's still an electric shock on entering the Devonshire Brasserie. When, in this most sedate and conservative of Yorkshire locations, the Duchess of Devonshire daringly chucked out the chintz and the faux fishing tackle and revamped the interior with a vibrant green, pink and purple colour scheme, it made everyone re-think eating out in the Dales. Splash out on lobster, prawn and crab cocktail followed by duck breast with prunes, or settle for modern English brasserie staples from steaks to superior sausage and mash, and finish with trusty lemon tart. Beautiful Wharfedale views reassure you that some things never change. Wine from £13.95 a bottle.
**Chef/s:** Christopher Woodward. **Open:** all week L 12 to 2.30 (4 Sun), D 6 to 9.30. **Meals:** alc (main courses £11 to £24). **Service:** 12.5% (optional). **Details:** Cards accepted. 72 seats. 40 seats outside. Air-con. Wheelchair access. Music. Children allowed. Car parking.

## ▌Boroughbridge

## The Dining Room
Convincing food from a local favourite
20 St James Square, Boroughbridge, YO51 9AR
Tel no: (01423) 326426
www.thediningroomonline.co.uk
**Modern British | £30**
**Cooking score: 4**

£5 OFF

Part of a terrace on Boroughbridge's main square, this green-painted Queen Anne house is just the kind of personable restaurant that attracts a bevy of loyal followers. The Astleys are local favourites who continue to garner praise for their enthusiastic approach – especially when it comes to seeking out seasonal ingredients. Take a drink in the upstairs lounge before moving down to the eponymous dining room with its long drapes and elegant knick-knacks. Chris Astley's cooking avoids risk-taking in favour of well-tried mainstream ideas: dishes such as smoked haddock and saffron risotto, sea bass with vermouth sauce or duck confit with wild mushroom sauce and local black pudding are not going to take the world by storm, but they are convincing and capably executed. Kick off with, perhaps, baked goats' cheese and vine tomato tart, and conclude with new season's Yorkshire rhubarb and liquorice ice cream. Wines from France and the New World are at the heart of the lively list, which starts at £16.95.
**Chef/s:** Chris Astley. **Open:** Sun L 12 to 2. Tue to Sat D 7 to 9.15. **Closed:** Mon, bank hols, 26 Dec, 1 Jan. **Meals:** alc (main courses £14 to £23). Set D £23.95 (2 courses) to £27.95. Sun L £19.50 (2 courses) to £25. **Service:** not inc. **Details:** Cards accepted. 32 seats. 22 seats outside. Separate bar. Music. Children allowed.

## ALSO RECOMMENDED

### ▲ The Crown Inn

Roecliffe, Boroughbridge, YO51 9LY
Tel no: (01423) 322300
www.crowninnroecliffe.com
**Gastropub**

Handy for the A1, this old coaching inn sits on the green in a picture-perfect village. Refurbishment has smartened things up, making the most of oak beams, stone floors and big fires, and the food measures up too. Top quality local ingredients are put to good use in starters such as wild mushroom risotto laced with Wensleydale cheese and crisp leeks (£5.50), and mains of Lincoln Red daube of beef with caramelised onions and organic mushrooms (£10.95). House wine starts at 13.95.

## █ Bradford

### Mumtaz

**Kashmiri blockbuster**
386-400 Great Horton Road, Bradford, BD7 3HS
Tel no: (01274) 571861
www.mumtaz.co.uk
**Indian | £16**
**Cooking score: 2**

 **V**

The Mumtaz group is now a major brand with global pulling-power, whose customers include the Bollywood elite. The enormous glass-fronted premises house a chic bar and restaurant that wouldn't look out of place on a film set, and it serves an extensive menu of Kashmiri-influenced food. A good way to start is with the spice-marinated lamb boti – skewers of tender meat. The wealth of choice to follow extends from tiger prawn dopiaza to chicken karahi with okra, and some excellent vegetarian specialities. Carrot halva and ras malai are among the sweet options. The freshly-squeezed juices will distract you from the fact that this is an alcohol-free zone.

**Chef/s:** Mumtaz Khan. **Open:** all week 11am to midnight (1 Fri and Sat). **Meals:** alc (main courses £6 to £16). **Service:** not inc. **Details:** Cards accepted. 275 seats. Air-con. Wheelchair access. Music. Children allowed. Car parking.

### Prashad

**Showcasing vibrant vegetarian dishes**
86 Horton Grange Road, Bradford, BD7 2DW
Tel no: (01274) 575893
www.prashad.co.uk
**Indian Vegetarian | £15**
**Cooking score: 2**

Mohan and Kaushy Patel have been showcasing Indian vegetarian food since opening their deli in 1986; the restaurant followed in 2004. Gujarati and Punjabi cooking form the bedrock of the menu. Dazzling pethis (deep-fried, spiced coconut in a fluffy potato casing) make an outstanding appetiser, or you might go for roadside snacks like pani puri (filled with potato and chickpeas and served with a spicy herb juice). Vegetables might involve richly spiced aubergine and peas cooked in a balti and dahl enlivened with courgettes. Thirst-quenchers include lassi and fruit juices. Unlicensed.

**Chef/s:** Kaushy Patel and Minal Patel. **Open:** Tue to Fri L 11 to 3, D 6 to 10.30, Sat and Sun 11 to 10.30. **Closed:** Mon, 25 and 26 Dec, 1 and 2 Jan. **Meals:** alc (main courses £6 to £11). **Service:** not inc. **Details:** Cards accepted. 30 seats. Wheelchair access. Music. Children allowed. Car parking.

## READERS RECOMMEND

### Zouk Tea Bar and Grill

**Indian**
1312 Leeds Road, Bradford, BD3 8LF
Tel no: (01274) 258025
www.zoukteabar.co.uk
**'The best Pakistani restaurant! Great atmosphere, wonderful staff'**

## ■ Brearton

NEW ENTRY

### The Malt Shovel
Dedicated to first-class food
Main Street, Brearton, HG3 3BX
Tel no: (01423) 862929
www.themaltshovelbrearton.co.uk
European | £24
Cooking score: 3

V

Back in the 1970s Jürg Bleiker ran a *Guide* favourite, the Old Deanery at Ripon (see entry). A fish-smoking business followed and now, with enviable energy, he has returned to the stove with son D'Arcy and daughter-in-law Anna, front-of-house. It's an atmospheric pub, with a candlit bar, elegant panelled red room, conservatory, and a menu that references Bleiker's Swiss roots in veal osso buco, wiener schnitzel and rösti potato. If smoked haddock with whisky, cream and Gruyère has a retro ring, it is indeed a throwback to Bleiker's Deanery repertoire. Chilli squid with chorizo and a simply fried whole red bream hit a more contemporary note while a lemon posset makes a refreshing finish to a confident, well-tuned meal. An original wine list (from £15.95) lifts it all sharply above off-the-peg gastropubbery. **Chef/s:** Jürg Bleiker. **Open:** Wed to Sun L 12 to 2 (3 Sun), Wed to Sat D 6 to 9. **Closed:** Mon, Tue. **Meals:** alc (main courses £10 to £24). **Service:** not inc. **Details:** Cards accepted. 55 seats. 15 seats outside. Separate bar. No music. No mobile phones. Wheelchair access. Children allowed. Car parking.

## ■ Burnsall

### Devonshire Fell
Modern brasserie in stunning Dales location
Burnsall, BD23 6BT
Tel no: (01756) 729000
www.devonshirehotels.co.uk
Modern European | £29
Cooking score: 4

£5  £30
OFF

The sturdy stone Fell had become the weaker link in the Devonshire trio of Wharfedale eateries, but with new chef Dan Birk it's taken a sharp upward turn. He comes with an impressive CV and brings technique, timing and elegant presentation that applies as well to the bar menu of sausage and mash and steak and ale pie as to the à la carte. Choose starters of sea bass fillet and miniature ratatouille or tender slices of wood pigeon breast on Bury black pudding with a silky celeriac purée. Follow with Dales lamb, sea bream or an outstanding dish of tender venison on sautéed Savoy cabbage, caramelised root vegetables and a deep grand-veneur sauce, sweetened with redcurrant and a hint of bitter chocolate. Desserts of parfaits, brûlées, tarts and pannacottas all stay on the money. Factor in fabulous Wharfedale views, smart bedrooms and this is once again a cherishable Dales asset. House wine is £16. **Chef/s:** Daniel Birk. **Open:** all week L 12 to 3, D 6.30 to 9.30 (10 Fri and Sat, 9 Sun). **Meals:** alc (main courses £16 to £18). Set L and D £23 (2 courses) to £29. Sun L £11.95. **Service:** 12.5% (optional). **Details:** Cards accepted. 40 seats. Separate bar. Wheelchair access. Music. Children allowed. Car parking.

# Coxwold

ALSO RECOMMENDED
## ▲ The Abbey Inn
Byland Abbey, Coxwold, YO61 4BD
Tel no: (01347) 868204
www.bylandabbeyinn.co.uk
Gastropub

Seasonal, regional produce is at the heart of the business at this atmospheric English Heritage-owned inn opposite the ruins of Byland Abbey. A light bite of warm Wensleydale cheese and caramelised onion tarlet (£6.50) or roast rack of shearling lamb with a little pan of mutton and turnip stew (£14.50) typify choices in the rustic dining rooms. Desserts could feature organic Byland Blue pannacotta with Pontefract liquorice ice cream (£4.50), and wines, arranged by style, open at £14.50. Closed Sun D, Mon and Tue.

# East Witton
## The Blue Lion
Assured Yorkshire cooking
East Witton, DL8 4SN
Tel no: (01969) 624273
www.thebluelion.co.uk
Modern British | £28
Cooking score: 4

Sitting at a junction next to a traffic island of green, in this peaceful little village near Leyburn, is an eighteenth-century former coaching inn built of grey stone. With comfortable guest rooms and a few outdoor tables, it's run with appreciable hospitality. The scene for John Dalby's assured Yorkshire cooking is a rather smart dining room, with well-hung pictures and a paisley carpet. The choice is extensive, but dishes never get tiresomely complicated, and the quality of ingredients always beams forth. Try a homemade pork pie with pickled onions and piccalilli to start, or perhaps more exotic deep-fried soft-shell crab seasoned Chinese-style with chilli and ginger, and served with a fennel salad. Then consider a main course such as slow-braised, masala-spiced mutton with cumin-scented sweet potato. Fish might be a fillet of black bream accompanied by well-made lemon thyme risotto, and then there's a menu of dessert temptations, which may feature something light like lemon posset with raspberries and lemon-curd shortbread, in among the chocolate, toffee and caramel. A well-chosen dozen wines by the glass, half-litre or bottle thriftily opens a list that finds some splendid examples in all the regions it covers. Prices start at £14.95 a bottle for house Languedoc.
Chef/s: John Dalby. Open: all week L 12 to 2.15, D 7 to 9.15. Closed: 25 Dec. Meals: alc (main courses £11 to £27). Service: not inc. Details: Cards accepted. 70 seats. 30 seats outside. Separate bar. No music. Wheelchair access. Children allowed. Car parking.

# Elland
## La Cachette
Great-value bistro
31 Huddersfield Road, Elland, HX5 9AW
Tel no: (01422) 378833
www.lacachette-elland.com
Modern European | £24
Cooking score: 3
£5 OFF | V £30

The name may suggest some kind of secret hideaway, but this happy-go-lucky venue has been around long enough for the word to be out on the street. Inside, it's bistro through and through, with continental touches, candlelit corners and party booths for big bashes adding to the congenial vibe. Light lunches please the locals, but the kitchen ups its game for an evening menu that mixes standards with more contemporary ideas. Fishcakes, beef bourguignon and roast pheasant with steamed game pudding share the honours with, say, sea bass fillet, braised fennel and truffled olive oil potatoes or rump of lamb with spiced couscous and balsamic jus. Bringing up the rear is a cast list of desserts that might include blackcurrant and Cassis mousse with liquorice syrup. Prices are too attractive to ignore, and the great value extends to the seriously considered wine list, which gives equal billing to Europe and the New World. Ten house selections start at £13.70 (£2.80 a glass). **Chef/s:** Jonathan Nichols. **Open:** Mon to Sat L 12 to 2.30, D 6 to 9.30 (10 Fri and Sat). **Closed:** Sun, 2 weeks after 25 Dec, bank hols (exc Christmas). **Meals:** alc (main courses £9 to £23). Set L £11.95 (2 courses). Set D £19.95. **Service:** not inc. **Details:** Cards accepted. 90 seats. Air-con. Separate bar. No mobile phones. Wheelchair access. Music. Children allowed.

## Ferrensby
### The General Tarleton
**A beacon with full-blooded food**
Boroughbridge Road, Ferrensby, HG5 OPZ
Tel no: (01423) 340284
www.generaltarleton.co.uk
**Modern British | £26**
**Cooking score: 4**

A beacon out on the country roads just off the A1, the General Tarleton has evolved along similar lines to its cousin, the trendsetting Angel at Hetton (see entry), and there's still some resonance in its flexible pub/restaurant style and full-blooded cooking. Billed as 'food with Yorkshire roots', the menu touts 'traceability and seasonality', with much talk of ingredients gleaned from within 30 miles of the GT's kitchen. Seafood 'moneybags' and crispy squid with belly pork continue to garner plaudits, likewise pressed, slow-cooked shoulder of Dales lamb (perhaps served with confit garlic, broad bean and thyme jus). Other hot contenders might include homemade black pudding with crispy bacon and a poached egg, hotch-potch of Yorkshire pork with mock goose pie, and chargrilled haunch of Holme Farm venison in red wine sauce. The sweet menu also comes up trumps with the likes of iced nougatine parfait or treacle tart with Dales clotted cream. There's plenty of invigorating drinking on the well-annotated wine list, with wallet-friendly bottles from £15.

**Chef/s:** John Topham. **Open:** all week L 12 to 2, D 6 to 9.15. **Meals:** alc (main courses £10 to £19). Set L £10 (2 courses) to £14. Set D £15 (2 courses) to £18. Sun L £22.95. **Service:** not inc. **Details:** Cards accepted. 120 seats. 80 seats outside. No music. Wheelchair access. Children allowed. Car parking.

## Golcar
### The Weavers Shed
**From garden to kitchen**
86-88 Knowl Road, Golcar, HD7 4AN
Tel no: (01484) 654284
www.weaversshed.co.uk
**Modern British | £45**
**Cooking score: 5**

The Jacksons' idiosyncratic restaurant-with-rooms, housed in an eighteenth-century woollen mill, has been impressing Yorkshire folk – and those from further afield – since 1993. Locally sourced and home-grown ingredients are the name of the game, the latter coming from a kitchen garden in a nearby village, and including such items as cardoons and black cabbage. Stephen Jackson has always kept a conscientious weather eye on metropolitan culinary trends, and you will find dishes such as scallops with hummus and chorizo, or gnocchi with squash, chard, pine nuts, raisins and Curthwaite (a Cumbrian goats' cheese) on the menu. That said, there is a definite undertow of traditional British culinary ways too, evident in main courses such as Goosnargh chicken with buttered leeks, wild garlic mash and bread sauce. To finish, the benchmark Kirkham's Lancashire, served with Eccles cake, shows a broad-minded readiness to embrace the old regional foe, while Yorkshire's very own rhubarb might appear poached alongside a frozen trifle of the same. A stunning wine list, complete with maps and painstaking notes, is offered, with house wines at a uniform price of £15.50 (£4 a glass), and noteworthy selections from southern France and California, among many other fine things.

**Chef/s:** Stephen Jackson. **Open:** Tue to Fri L 12 to 2, Tue to Sat D 7 to 9. **Closed:** Sun, Mon, 2 weeks Christmas. **Meals:** alc (main courses £17 to £28). Set L £14.95 (2 courses) to £17.95. **Service:** not inc. **Details:** Cards accepted. 24 seats. Separate bar. No mobile phones. Music. Children allowed. Car parking.

## ◼ Goldsborough

### The Fox & Hounds

**Hideaway with vibrant, spot-on food**
Goldsborough, YO21 3RX
Tel no: (01947) 893372
www.foxandhoundsgoldsborough.co.uk
**Modern European | £28**
**Cooking score: 5**

Last year was something of an *annus horribilis* for the Fox and Hounds – an electrical fire closed them for six months. But they're back after a low-key makeover, and on sparkling form. Jason Davies's understated and exemplary cooking skills are as sharp as ever, but a revised menu, plus an upgrading of the wine list, extra tables and bags of local sourcing have subtly strengthened this hideaway pub on the Yorkshire coast. Every dish, from a soothing sage and butternut squash risotto, and a salad of langoustines, fennel and chilli to some inventive bruschettas (crab and chilli or shin beef and garlic) was spot-on in composition and delivery. Whitby-landed fish always features strongly here, and halibut with porcini-infused potatoes or skate wing with crushed potatoes were both finished with vibrant herby salsas. Slow-roast belly pork with crackling is a well-honed favourite, served with cannellini beans, curly kale and a mustard dressing. The expanded dessert menu has featured a perfect plum and almond tart or a very chocolatey truffle cake. As with Sue Davies's ebullient front-of-house style, the whole operation is a happy marriage of homeliness and excellence. House wine is £14.
**Chef/s:** Jason Davies. **Open:** Wed to Sun L 12 to 1, Wed to Sat D 6.30 to 8. **Closed:** Mon, Tue, bank hols, Christmas, New Year. **Meals:** alc (main courses £11

to £18). **Service:** not inc. **Details:** Cards accepted. 28 seats. 8 seats outside. No mobile phones. Wheelchair access. Music. Children allowed. Car parking.

## ◼ Grange Moor

### The Kaye Arms

**Food you can rely on**
29 Wakefield Road, Grange Moor, WF4 4BG
Tel no: (01924) 848385
www.thekayearms.com
**Modern British | £25**
**Cooking score: 3**

**V**

Inside this solid roadside pub it's a 1980s timewarp of swirly patterned carpets, Anaglypta wallpaper and ersatz panelling with a soundtrack to match. But service is smiley and warm, and there's an air of relaxed unpretentiousness all around. The 'famous' twice-baked cheese soufflé is 'a wonder' – feather-light with the right amount of saltiness – while plump, gamey pigeon breast sitting on a savoury rhubarb pie in a puddle of red wine jus has been pronounced 'one of the most perfect dishes I've had all year'. It's the kind of 'well-cooked and presented food you can rely on in these uncertain times'. The global wine list has bottles starting at £15.95, with glasses from £3.25. Farmyard animal pens are beside the car park.
**Chef/s:** Simon Dyson. **Open:** Mon to Fri L 12 to 2.30, D 5.30 to 9.30, Sat and Sun 12 to 9.30. **Closed:** 25 Dec. **Meals:** alc (main courses £11 to £25). Early bird D £19.95. Sun L £19.95. **Service:** not inc. **Details:** Cards accepted. 85 seats. 40 seats outside. Air-con. Separate bar. No mobile phones. Wheelchair access. Music. Children allowed. Car parking.

## Harome

### The Star Inn

**Unwavering quality all the way**
High Street, Harome, YO62 5JE
Tel no: (01439) 770397
www.thestaratharome.co.uk
Modern British | £40
Cooking score: 6

The energy of Andrew and Jacquie Pern is extraordinary. They have responded to the clamour of business at the Star by fitting out a new 40-seat dining room, and there is also a new fish and cocktail bar. They still run the deli and butcher in nearby Helmsley, and have also bought the Pheasant Hotel there. The Star is equipped with a new kitchen, and the kitchen garden goes from strength to productive strength. Is there anything they don't do? The Star alone – an inn since the fourteenth century – would be reason enough to celebrate, as was verified by one couple who risked a 250-mile round trip for lunch on the *Guide*'s say-so and came away in raptures. Andrew Pern is blessed with a supreme confidence that comes from having the culinary equivalent of perfect pitch, demonstrated in dishes such as the starter of soused halibut with blue potato salad and horseradish vodka – an indisputable success that kick-starts the tastebuds. The commitment to regionality is unimpeachable – you might proceed to loin of local lamb adorned with local goats' cheese and served with local asparagus in a lavender vinaigrette. However that doesn't rule out continental ways of doing things, as in sea bass with garlic-roast snails, shaved summer truffle and bourguignon-style sauce. Quality is unwavering all the way through to pleasantly startling desserts like chocolate and stout pudding with black treacle ice cream. Nor does the wine list let the side down, with its fairly priced miscellany of great pedigree growers, and wide choice by the glass from £4.50.

**Chef/s:** Andrew Pern. **Open:** Tue to Sun L 11.30 to 2 (12 to 6 Sun), Mon to Sat D 6 to 9.30. **Closed:** 25 and 26 Dec. **Meals:** alc (main courses £14 to £23). **Service:** not inc. **Details:** Cards accepted. 100 seats. 50 seats outside. Separate bar. No mobile phones. Wheelchair access. Music. Children allowed. Car parking.

## Harrogate

### Hotel du Vin & Bistro

**Stout, spa town brasserie**
Prospect Place, Harrogate, HG1 1LB
Tel no: (01423) 856800
www.hotelduvin.com
Modern European | £35
Cooking score: 2

Knowing a restaurant is part of a chain is rarely a big draw for regular readers of the *Guide* and the loss of star chef Tom Van Zeller has meant not everyone leaves happy. But this prominent spa town brasserie is clearly a stout enough institution to carry on as if nothing has happened. At best, dishes are perfectly judged and the French-influenced menu offers some unusual treats like crispy frogs' legs with pea purée, but it's the excellent range of locally sourced meat that really warrants attention. Hotel du Vin's reputation for fine wines at affordable prices is fully justified, and the huge, easy-to-navigate list casts its net wide for quality drinking. France naturally looms large, but there are rich pickings from interesting sources around the globe. Prices start at £14.75

**Chef/s:** Murray Wilson. **Open:** all week L 12 to 3 (12.30 to 1 Sun), D 7 to 9.45. **Meals:** alc (main courses £13 to £20). Set L £10.95 (1 courses + glass of wine + coffee). Sun L £12.95 (1 course) to £18.50 (2 courses) to £23.50 (3 courses). **Service:** 10% (optional). **Details:** Cards accepted. 75 seats. 30 seats outside. Separate bar. No music. No mobile phones. Wheelchair access. Children allowed.

## Orchid Restaurant

**Exciting Asian flavours**
Studley Hotel, 28 Swan Road, Harrogate, HG1 2SE
Tel no: (01423) 560425
www.orchidrestaurant.co.uk
**Pan-Asian | £25**
**Cooking score: 2**

The basement of the Studley Hotel is an unlikely setting for a pan-Asian restaurant, but Orchid puts on a real show with its lacquered tables, clay pots and bamboo steamers. The menu is a cook's tour across the Far East, with stop-offs for Szechuan bang-bang chicken, Japanese usuyaki beef and Korean steamed dumplings with black vinegar dip. For something more substantial, look to Thailand for red duck curry or Malaysia for wok-fried seafood with sambal sauce and pungent shrimp paste. Sushi and sashimi are added to the mix on Tuesday evenings, and the wine list is tailor-made for the food – note the gems from the Trimbach Estate, Alsace. Prices start at £15.50.
**Chef/s:** Kenneth Poon. **Open:** Mon to Fri and Sun L 12 to 2, all week D 6 to 10. **Closed:** 25 and 26 Dec. **Meals:** alc (main courses £9 to £20). Set L £9.95 (2 courses) to £12.95. Set D £21.95. Sun L £15. **Service:** 10% (optional). **Details:** Cards accepted. 95 seats. Air-con. Separate bar. Wheelchair access. Music. Children allowed. Car parking.

## Oxford Street Brasserie

**Buzzy, talked-about all-rounder**
34a Oxford Street, Harrogate, HG1 1PP
Tel no: (01423) 505300
www.oxfordstreetbrasserie.com
**Modern European | £30**
**Cooking score: 4**

 **V**

Just two minutes' walk from Harrogate International Centre and the town's theatre, David Robson's all-rounder has earned a local reputation for its cosmopolitan buzz and approachable modern food – despite its rather inauspicious location above a shop. Robust Euro-inspired dishes such as morteau sausage with lentils and Savoy cabbage, slow-cooked pork belly with spiced apple and crackling, or butter-roast cod with pak choi and curried mussels display a strong brasserie backbone. Desserts offer just the right degree of temptation – hot chocolate soufflé with raspberry smoothie or vanilla pannacotta with salted caramel, for example. Also check out the daily list of far-from-predictable vegetarian specials on the board. Factor in a child-friendly attitude, bargain-priced set menus and plentiful chef-watching opportunities in the open kitchen, and it's easy to see why the Oxford Street Brasserie is getting noticed. Three-dozen global wines also play their part, with decent drinking from £12.95 (£3.40 a glass).
**Chef/s:** David Robson. **Open:** Tue to Sat L 12 to 2.30, D 5.30 to 9.30. **Closed:** Sun, Mon, 25 and 26 Dec, 1 Jan. **Meals:** alc (main courses £13 to £16). Set L and early D £10 (2 courses) to £12.50. **Service:** 10% (optional). **Details:** Cards accepted. 38 seats. Air-con. No mobile phones. Music. Children allowed.

## Sasso

**Low-key hideaway with stand-out pasta**
8-10 Princes Square, Harrogate, HG1 1LX
Tel no: (01423) 508838
www.sassorestaurant.co.uk
**Italian | £28**
**Cooking score: 5**

Hidden away in an uncluttered basement on Princes Square, Stefano Lancellotti's 'enoteca' is a low-key affair that fits somewhere between a candles-in-Chianti bottles trattoria and a modish new-wave Italian hangout. Polished tables and a smattering of artwork provide the understated backdrop to food that is a confident mix of rustic and big-city flavours, with lots of influences from across Italy. Seasonal specials offer a telling snapshot of the kitchen's approach to fish: scallops are served in a carbonara sauce with Parmesan, crispy pancetta and salted dry ricotta, while fresh tuna is grilled in a sesame crust with capers, pine nuts and Sicilian-style sultanas in a Marsala, honey and olive oil emulsion.

Homemade pasta also stands out – perhaps pigeon tortelloni on a celery sauce with sweet tomato confit. Lancellotti doffs his cap to France for saddle of rabbit, which is stuffed with artichokes and fontina cheese, then cooked in a brew of beer, honey and wholegrain mustard. Desserts are embedded in the creamy Italian tradition of tiramisu and luscious semifreddo with caramelised walnuts. The wine list is a serious slate with strength in depth when it comes to the Italian regions. House selections from Friulli start at £13.95, rising to potent, wallet-emptying 2000 Venetian Amarone at £480.

**Chef/s:** Stefano Lancellotti. **Open:** all week L 12 to 3 (4 Sun), Mon to Sat D 6 to 12. **Closed:** bank hols, 25 and 26 Dec, 1 Jan. **Meals:** alc (main courses £10 to £22). Set L £8.95 (2 courses). Sun L £15.95 (2 courses) to £18.95. **Service:** not inc. **Details:** Cards accepted. 100 seats. 20 seats outside. No music. Music. Children allowed.

# Haworth

## Weavers

**A Brontë bonus**
15 West Lane, Haworth, BD22 8DU
Tel no: (01535) 643822
www.weaverssmallhotel.co.uk
**Modern British | £25**
**Cooking score: 3**

Haworth's tourist footfall is formidable – hardly surprising, given that it's the home of the Brontë Parsonage. Pilgrims would do well to book ahead for nearby Weavers too. It's a sympathetically run, professional small hotel, housed in what was once a group of cotton weavers' cottages. A jumble of furniture and warm lighting make a welcome backdrop to the Rushworths' imaginative approach, which cannily mixes English tradition (belly pork, ham hock and black pudding with piccalilli, sausages and mash with onion gravy) with the odd dash of cosmopolitan modishness, as in seared scallops with pea purée and pancetta. Local game and poultry are among the star ingredients, and you're bound to want to

finish with something like chocolate crumb pudding with honeycomb ice cream. Glasses of wine start at £3.55, bottles from £14.75. **Chef/s:** Jane and Colin Rushworth and Adam Vendetouli. **Open:** Wed to Fri L 11.30 to 2.30, Tue to Sat D 6.30 to 9.30. **Closed:** Sun, Mon, 10 days after 25 Dec. **Meals:** alc (main courses £12 to £23). Set L and D £15.50 (2 courses) to £17.50. **Service:** not inc. **Details:** Cards accepted. 65 seats. Air-con. Separate bar. No mobile phones. Music. Children allowed.

# Helmsley

## Feversham Arms Hotel

**Gentrified mix of modern and traditional**
High Street, Helmsley, YO62 5AG
Tel no: (01439) 770766
www.fevershamarmshotel.com
**Modern European | £75**
**Cooking score: 4**

At this nineteenth-century coaching inn turned proper country-house hotel (with ubiquitous spa), Simon Rhatigan has fostered a decidedly gentrified and old-fashioned English air. Within the main dining room an air of light formality reigns. Simon Kelly delivers a menu that straddles both traditional and contemporary – a modern take on ham, egg and chips as a starter and slow-cooked pork belly with braised red cabbage for lunch, contrasting with seared foie gras, apple fondant and apple jelly, and East Coast cod, lobster linguine and Champagne velouté for dinner. Among desserts, blueberry mousse with pistachio ice cream and lime jelly appealed to one diner, or try red wine-poached figs with pain perdu and yoghurt sorbet. Most reporters are happy, but some mention poor timing and service errors. Prices start at £20 on the international wine list. **Chef/s:** Simon Kelly. **Open:** all week L 12 to 2, D 7 to 9.30. **Meals:** alc (main courses £18 to £24). Set D £33. **Service:** not inc. **Details:** Cards accepted. 70 seats. 30 seats outside. Separate bar. No mobile phones. Wheelchair access. Music. Children allowed. Car parking.

# Hessle

## Artisan

**No gimmicks, just first-class food**
22 The Weir, Hessle, HU13 0RU
Tel no: (01482) 644906
www.artisanrestaurant.com
Modern European | £39
Cooking score: 5

High praise has been flowing in for this tiny 16-cover restaurant in the shadow of the Humber Bridge near Hull. 'Fantastic flavours and textures', enthuses one reporter, 'extremely friendly and welcoming', notes another. Even the exceptionally short menu – two starters, two mains, two puddings and cheese – fails to draw complaints. There are no pretentions or gimmicks, just first-class food and anyone feeling short-changed can actually eat through the whole menu – though in smaller portions – with the 'Taste of Everything' option. What Richard Johns has always been good at is the kind of cooking that allows the inherent quality of ingredients to shine. The freshest fish appears in main courses such as sea bass on herb risotto; the meat alternative might be a definitive slow-cooked local pork with crackling. This meal also saw first courses of scallops and bacon with cauliflower purée, and rose veal with foie gras velouté, both delivered with pinpoint accuracy. There is much praise, too, for Lyndsey Johns' tirelessly warm service front-of-house. This a classic example of the very best of small enterprise. Wines from £20.50 a bottle.

**Chef/s:** Richard Johns. **Open:** Tue to Sat D only from 7, (L by arrangement). **Closed:** Sun, Mon, 1 week Christmas, 1 week Easter. **Meals:** Set D £32 (2 courses) to £39. Tasting menu £50 (6 courses). **Service:** not inc. **Details:** Cards accepted. 16 seats. Air-con. No mobile phones. Wheelchair access. Music. Children allowed. Car parking.

# Hetton

## The Angel Inn

**Culinary delights in Dales 'restro-pub'**
Hetton, BD23 6LT
Tel no: (01756) 730263
www.angelhetton.co.uk
Modern British | £29
Cooking score: 3

£5 OFF 🍴 V £30

'We'll certainly do *that* again', declared one flushed pair, who had let a dollop of winter cheer into their lives by spending a February evening by the fire at the Angel. 'Warm and professional service' is universally commended, and the hordes of loyal returnees explain why this place has been a consistent *Guide* entry over so many years. They come back to the creeper-covered, oak-beamed, log-fired inn for the polished cooking, which runs a gamut from old favourites like the still-popular signature moneybag of seafood served with lobster sauce, to bang-up-to-date dishes such as seared wild halibut with butternut purée and mussels in a caviar butter sauce. Mutton from Bolton Abbey is good to see, presented here as the roasted loin and braised flank, with crushed courgettes and basil mash. Sticky toffee pudding has its devoted adherents, or you might ring the changes with a poached tamarillo. The Bar Brasserie serves nibbles and sandwiches, as well as many dishes from the main carte. A fantastic wine list opens with some food-matching suggestions, before lighting out into classical French, modern Italian and southern-hemisphere directions. Prices start at £17 (£3.10 a glass).

**Chef/s:** Mark Taft. **Open:** Sun L 12 to 2, Mon to Sat D 6 to 9.30. Bar brasserie open all week L and D. **Closed:** 1 week Jan. **Meals:** alc (main courses £12 to £22). Set D £15.95 (2 courses) to £36.50. Sun L £25. **Service:** not inc. **Details:** Cards accepted. 40 seats. 30 seats outside. Air-con. Separate bar. No music. Wheelchair access. Children allowed. Car parking.

## ◼ Holdsworth

### Holdsworth House
**Sophisticated dining in Jacobean splendour**
Holdsworth Road, Holdsworth, HX2 9TG
Tel no: (01422) 240024
www.holdsworthhouse.co.uk
Modern British | £30
Cooking score: 3

£5 OFF 🍽 V

Set 'rather incongruously in the burbs of Halifax', this splendid Jacobean country house has plenty to offer: leaded windows, creaky floors, huge studded doors, a gleaming dark oak staircase, tapestries, candlelit tables and mature gardens. There's nothing ancient about the cooking, though. Yorkshire asparagus spears with crispy poached hen's egg and pink grapefruit hollandaise followed by rump of spring lamb teamed with lamb faggot, Anna potato, baby carrots and fèves nail the local produce promise, while cannon of beef with sauté kidney, onion jam roly-poly, watercress and spinach purée with artichokes is a good-humoured modern take on an old classic. With rhubarb délice and ginger ice cream for pudding, you may need to pace yourself. A sophisticated wine list opens at £14.95.
**Chef/s:** Lee Canning. **Open:** all week L 12 to 2, D 6 to 9.30 (9 Sun). **Meals:** alc (main courses £15 to £20). Set L and D £15.95 (2 courses) to £19.95. Sun L £15.95. **Service:** not inc. **Details:** Cards accepted. 40 seats. Separate bar. Wheelchair access. Music. Children allowed. Car parking.

## ◼ Holmfirth

### ALSO RECOMMENDED
### ▲ The Butchers Arms
38 Towngate, Hepworth, Holmfirth, HD9 1TE
Tel no: (01484) 682361
www.thebutchersarmshepworth.co.uk
Gastropub

You are deep in *Last of the Summer Wine* territory here – but there's no whiff of quaintness about this freshly refurbished Grade II-listed pub, despite the stone floors, beams and roaring fires. Pressed ham hock terrine (£6.95) is a cracking start, or go for a bowl of properly satisfying, creamy parsnip soup. Follow with pot-roast pheasant with braised red cabbage (£15.95), or braised slab of beef with balsamic onions and Parmesan mash (£16.95). House wine £12.50. Closed Sun D.

## ◼ Honley

### Mustard and Punch
**Industrious local favourite**
6 Westgate, Honley, HD9 6AA
Tel no: (01484) 662066
www.mustardandpunch.co.uk
Modern British | £22
Cooking score: 3

£5 OFF £30

A sophisticated but unpretentious restaurant in the centre of Honley, Mustard and Punch's reputation is built on sterling British produce. Grilled black pudding on herb crushed potatoes with Granny Smith jus, and Yorkshire rump steak with sautéed potatoes, onion rings and peppercorn sauce typify the style, while French/European accents are seen in dishes such as seared scallops with boudin noir and cauliflower purée followed by pan-fried calf's liver with beetroot risotto. For dessert, maybe chilled rice pudding with Agen prune and sultana caramel. Everything from breads to ice cream is homemade, and the three-course dinner represents great value for money. Wines are priced from £13.95 a bottle.
**Chef/s:** Richard Dunn and Wayne Roddis. **Open:** Mon to Sat D only 6 to 9.30. **Closed:** Sun, bank hols, 28 Dec to 4 Jan. **Meals:** Set D £19.95 (2 courses) to £21.50. **Service:** not inc. **Details:** Cards accepted. 55 seats. Air-con. Wheelchair access. Music. Children allowed. Car parking.

### Average price

The average price listed in main-entry reviews denotes the price of a three-course meal, without wine.

## Huddersfield

### Bradley's Restaurant

Cheery bastion of good value
84 Fitzwilliam Street, Huddersfield, HD1 5BB
Tel no: (01484) 516773
www.bradleysrestaurant.co.uk
**Modern British | £26**
Cooking score: 2

£5 OFF  **V**  £30

Andrew Bradley's restaurant has been feeding the citizens of Huddersfield and beyond since 1993, and continues to deliver the goods. The split-level dining room is a cheery bastion of good value: business lunches and 'early bird' deals (with wine included) keep the crowds coming back – although the regular menu is also on target. Expect lively, unpretentious cooking with some Mediterranean accents: seared scallops come with new potatoes, salsa verde and pancetta, roast rump of lamb is accompanied by minted pea tortellini and ratatouille, and red mullet fillets are served with pumpkin and spinach risotto. Close with, say, strawberry Bakewell tart. House wine is £13.95. A sister restaurant is at 46–50 Highgate, Heaton, Bradford BD9 4BE, tel no: (01274) 499890.
**Chef/s:** Eric Paxman and Daniel Kidd. **Open:** Mon to Fri L 12 to 2, Mon to Sat D 6 to 10 (5.30 Fri and Sat). **Closed:** Sun, bank hols. **Meals:** alc (main courses £10 to £19). Set L £6.95 (2 courses) to £9.50. Set D £12.95 (2 courses) to £16.95. **Service:** not inc. **Details:** Cards accepted. 120 seats. Air-con. Separate bar. No mobile phones. Wheelchair access. Music. Children allowed. Car parking.

### Dining Rooms @ Strawberry Fair

Shoppers' salvation
14-18 Westgate, Huddersfield, HD1 1NN
Tel no: (01484) 513103
www.strawberry-fair.com
**Modern European | £21**
Cooking score: 1

**V**  £30

An independently owned department store in a restored Victorian shopping emporium is a good place to pick up some quality cookware or glass, as well as to refresh yourself in the daytime dining room. Handsomely turned out in minimal fashion with black chairs and white walls, it makes a soothing space for modern bistro cooking. The choice runs from quiches and risottos of the day, through mains such as grilled bream with sorrel hollandaise or chicken and asparagus pie, to rhubarb sponge with custard. A handful of wines starts at £11.
**Chef/s:** Rachel Miller. **Open:** Mon to Sat L 11.30 to 3. Breakfast (from 9.30) and afternoon tea available. **Closed:** Sun, 25 and 26 Dec, bank hols. **Meals:** alc (main courses £7 to £10). Set L £13.50 (2 courses). **Service:** not inc. **Details:** Cards accepted. 46 seats. Air-con. Wheelchair access. Music. Children allowed.

## Hull

### Boars Nest

Classic cooking in an old butcher's
22-24 Princes Avenue, Hull, HU5 3QA
Tel no: (01482) 445577
www.theboarsnesthull.com
**Modern British | £28**
Cooking score: 2

£30

You may not have known that boars built nests, but this one is roosting in a converted Edwardian butcher's shop, where the old railing and green and white tiles still form part of the décor. Classic British cooking is the name of the game, meaning that you might begin with fried chicken livers with pickled mushrooms, and go on to a whole stuffed gilthead bream. Some of the classics are of the more modern bent, as when lamb shoulder is crusted in walnuts and Stilton and served with garlic potato purée, while tandoori monkfish with coriander rice noodles represents another strain of British culinary orientation altogether. To finish sticky toffee pudding comes with treacle ripple ice cream and caramelised quince. Wines start at £17.

**Chef/s:** Simon Rogers. **Open:** all week L 12 to 2 (3 Sun), D 6.30 to 10 (9 Sun). **Closed:** 26 Dec, 1 Jan. **Meals:** alc (main courses £10 to £22). Set L £8 (2 courses) to £10. Set D £20 (3 courses inc wine). Set Sun L £10 (3 courses). **Service:** 10% (optional). **Details:** Cards accepted. 62 seats. 16 seats outside. Separate bar. Wheelchair access. Music. Children allowed.

## ◼ Ilkley

### The Box Tree

**Overflowing gastronomic jewel box**
35-37 Church Street, Ilkley, LS29 9DR
Tel no: (01943) 608484
www.theboxtree.co.uk
**Anglo-French | £60**
**Cooking score: 6**

🍾

Coq au vin and sherry trifle were highlights back in 1965 when Malcolm Reid, Colin Long and the Box Tree first came to the attention of the *Guide*. The restaurant became the most talked about outside London, but later fell to near bankruptcy – until Simon Gueller put it back on the culinary map. Despite some judicious de-cluttering, the Box Tree remains the same overflowing jewel box it ever was, but thankfully service is no longer so starched. Prices are high, but rewards exceptional: from a starter of roast quail on a risotto of white truffle oil, and mains of thyme-crusted turbot on a grain mustard sauce, combinations are well thought out, flavours bold and servings generous, with short shrift for blobs and dots. 'Classic techniques with a modern twist' is how Gueller describes his style, typified by his superb ballottine of salmon, wrapped in herbs, served here with nothing fancier than a little

crème fraîche and a few sprigs of curly endive. Desserts are less exciting, but the overall finding is unquestionably that of a superior restaurant well and truly on song. Pedigree French classics are the main contenders on the auspicious wine list, although fine bottles from other quarters are also worth the investment. Prices start at £21.

**Chef/s:** Simon Gueller. **Open:** Fri to Sun L 12 to 2, Tue to Sat D 7 to 9.30. **Closed:** Mon, 27 to 30 Dec, first week of Jan. **Meals:** alc (mains £27 to £30). Set L £20 (2 courses) to £28. Set D £30 (3 courses). Sun L £30. **Service:** not inc. **Details:** Cards accepted. 56 seats. Air-con. Separate bar. Wheelchair access. Music. Children allowed.

### Farsyde

**Great-value town brasserie**
1-3 New Brook Street, Ilkley, LS29 8DQ
Tel no: (01943) 602030
www.thefarsyde.co.uk
**Modern British | £25**
**Cooking score: 3**

V

When Gavin Beedham, one-time head chef at the Devonshire Arms at Bolton Abbey, set up in 1995, he brought bold bistro flavours and top chef expertise to a town with little middle ground between wine bars and the upmarket Box Tree (see entry). Since then he's moved to bigger premises, decorated in the same warm hues of orange and yellow, and broken up the space with intimate booths. Red pepper and butternut squash soup and poached salmon on celeriac purée with a parsley salsa showed reliable form. The vegetables – dauphinoise potatoes, ratatouille and roast roots – were a cut above the usual 'bouquetière', while desserts hit the spot with sticky toffee pudding and chocolate tart. Accomplished rather than original, is ther verdict. Wines start at £10.75.

**Chef/s:** Gavin Beedham. **Open:** Tue to Sat L 11.30 to 2, D 6 to 10. **Closed:** Sun, Mon, 25 and 26 Dec, 1 and 2 Jan. **Meals:** alc (main courses £13 to £16). Set L £14.95 (3 courses). Set D £14.50 (2 courses). **Service:** not inc. **Details:** Cards accepted. 82 seats. Air-con. Separate bar. Wheelchair access. Music. Children allowed.

**NEW ENTRY**
## Ilkley Moor Vaults
**Thoughtful, wholesome food**
Stockeld Road, Ilkley, LS29 9HD
Tel no: (01943) 607012
www.ilkleymoorvaults.co.uk
British | £20
Cooking score: 2
£5 OFF £30

Don't be put off by the slightly shabby exterior of this rambling pub in genteel Ilkley. Inside 'is more homely than home': flagged floors, open fires, scrubbed pine tables and standard lamps with chintzy shades. Joe McDermott is putting thoughtfully sourced ingredients to good use in wholesome dishes such as homemade smoked sausage with pickled peppers and mustard, homity pie and roast vegetables, or subtle smoked haddock with mustard sauce, spinach and crushed Jersey Royals. Finish with spiced bread pudding with cream, or rhubarb and apple crumble with custard. The wine list takes in Europe and the New World. House selections start at £3.30 a glass.
**Chef/s:** Joe McDermott and Sabi Janak. **Open:** all week L 12 to 2.30 (3 Sun), Mon to Sat D 6 to 9 (9.30 Fri and Sat). **Meals:** alc (main courses £9 to £17). **Service:** not inc. **Details:** Cards accepted. 60 seats. 30 seats outside. Separate bar. No music. Wheelchair access. Children allowed. Car parking.

## Knapton

**NEW ENTRY**
### The Red Lion
**Head-turningly good pub grub**
Main Street, Knapton, YO26 6QG
Tel no: (01904) 793957
Gastropub | £18
Cooking score: 3
£30

A typical pub menu of fish and chips, shepherd's pie, steak and chips and a handful of familiar specials doesn't normally turn the head of the *Guide*. But when these dishes are so sensibly and enjoyably done that they could be

a model for every such menu, it's well worth noticing. This is Roux-trained Annie Prescott's first solo venture – after four years at Melton's in York (see entry) – and she's matched expertise and village pub simplicity to excellent effect. The standards are upholstered by a touch of seasonal flair – local spring asparagus was on sale next to the handpumps on the bar. At £3.95, crème brûlée is an object lesson in price and execution, as are well-chosen house wines at £11.95.
**Chef/s:** Annie Prescott. **Open:** Tue to Sun L 12 to 3 (4 Sun), all week D 7 to 11 (6 to 12 Wed to Sat). **Closed:** 25 Dec. **Meals:** alc (main courses £7 to £17). **Service:** not inc. **Details:** Cards accepted. 62 seats. 12 seats outside. Wheelchair access. Music. Children allowed. Car parking.

## Leeds

### Anthony's at Flannels
**Anthony Flinn does urban cool**
68-78 Vicar Lane, Leeds, LS1 7JH
Tel no: (0113) 2428732
www.anthonysatflannels.co.uk
Modern European | £18
Cooking score: 4
£30

You would expect the chic, minimalist Flannels designer clothing store to have a suitably trendy restaurant and, on the light, loft-style top floor, Anthony's at Flannels fits the bill. It's part of the expanding culinary empire of Leeds' favourite son, Anthony Flinn, and the air of restrained extravagance – lent by crisp white linen, heavy cutlery and formal service – raises expectations of something special on the food front. On the whole, the food delivers, but don't expect the scientific gastronomy of mothership Anthony's Restaurant in Boar Lane (see entry). Eggs Benedict for brunch, posh sandwiches, salads of, say, cured hams and cheese or steaks with all the trimmings, are just as popular as a set lunch that offers scallops with broad beans, apple, pea shoots and crisp jamón ahead of lamb neck with wild garlic, carrots, celeriac and pearl onions. House wines from £13.95.

**Chef/s:** Ryan McAlister. **Open:** Tue to Sun 10 to 4.30 (11 Sun). **Closed:** Mon, 25 and 26 Dec, Easter Sun. **Meals:** alc (main courses £8 to £22). Set L £14.50 (2 courses) to £18. **Service:** 10% (optional). **Details:** Cards accepted. 55 seats. Air-con. Separate bar. Wheelchair access. Music. Children allowed.

## Anthony's Restaurant
**Avant-garde excellence**
19 Boar Lane, Leeds, LS1 6EA
Tel no: (0113) 2455922
www.anthonysrestaurant.co.uk
**Modern European | £42**
**Cooking score: 7**

When Anthony Flinn and family launched this iconic venue, they aimed high. Why not establish a destination restaurant in a basement on one of the city's less chi-chi streets? Why not bring the ever-curious approach of elBulli, where Flinn famously staged, to Yorkshire? Why not offer a beer list, temptingly annotated, alongside the house Champagne? As readers suggest of a visit here, life is too short not to. Certain elements of the experience remain resolutely understated. The dining room is neutral and low on fripperies, and the bread is a perfect white sliced farmhouse loaf in miniature. Prices, too, lack pretension: a three-course set lunch is remarkable value at £23.95. On the plate, there's a delicious push-and-pull between Flinn's classical ability and his roguish tendencies. Start with a relatively simple ham hock consommé, the aniseed-inflected liquid poured over crispy, tender strands of meat at the table, or a more evolved plate of smoked beef carpaccio with thick smoked feta and three – just three – super-charged pieces of peanut. Between the meat and a scattering of micro-leaves, little teardrops of pomelo wake everything up. A main course might be John Dory with butter-poached oysters and a citrus-spiked avocado cream, taking turns with jamón bellota and an oyster 'leaf', which has the briny taste of said shellfish. Dessert could be a delicate ginger and sesame parfait with clear rhubarb consommé, or a comforting banana cake topped with caramel and surrounded at the table with warm mozzarella velouté, which tastes for all the world like rich, slightly rummy bedtime milk. The short but strong wine list is divided by style, with prices from £14.50 (£4.20 a glass), and the offer of 50ml glasses of dessert tipples from £2 should wow fans of 'stickies'.

**Chef/s:** Anthony James Flinn. **Open:** Tue to Sat L 12 to 2, D 7 to 9.30. **Closed:** Sun, Mon, Christmas to New Year. **Meals:** Set L £19.95 (2 courses) to £23.95. Set D £34 (2 courses) to £42. Tasting menu £60. **Service:** not inc. **Details:** Cards accepted. 40 seats. Air-con. Separate bar. No mobile phones. Wheelchair access. Music. Children allowed.

## Brasserie Forty 4
**Dependable, on-the-money food**
44 The Calls, Leeds, LS2 7EW
Tel no: (0113) 2343232
www.brasserie44.com
**Modern European | £30**
**Cooking score: 3**
🍾

Part of the Calls complex down by the waterside, this dependable city-centre brasserie has weathered the shake-ups following the closure of Pool Court and emerged in good shape. The mood is laid-back and cosmopolitan, a feeling enhanced by the swanky curved bar, vibrant canvases and showpiece arched window looking out on to the river. Smart, on-the-money food is the style, and it shows across the range, from pigeon breast with chorizo mash and red wine sauce to the house dessert – chocolate fondue served with marshmallows and fresh fruit. In between, teriyaki ostrich with deep-fried lotus root alongside traditional roast pheasant might raise a few eyebrows, but there's also a daily fish menu that keeps it simple with the likes of John Dory with crushed new potatoes and pesto. The wine list is a city slicker, from its Dom Perignon Champagnes to Kiwi stars and cutting-edge Cousiño-Macul Chileans. Prices start at £15.50, and 17 are offered by the glass.

**Chef/s:** Roy Dickinson. **Open:** all week L 12 to 2 (1 to 3 Sat, 1 to 5 Sun), all week D 6 to 10 (6 to 10.30 Sat, 5 to 8 Sun). **Closed:** bank hols, 25 and 26 Dec. **Meals:** alc (main courses £12 to £17). Early bird Set D £21.50 (3 courses). Sun L £14.25 (2 courses) to £17.50. **Service:** 10% optional. **Details:** Cards accepted. 120 seats. 18 seats outside. Air-con. Separate bar. Wheelchair access. Music.

## Fourth Floor
**All this and shopping too...**
Harvey Nichols, 107-111 Briggate, Leeds, LS1 6AZ
Tel no: (0113) 2048000
www.harveynichols.com
**Modern British | £25**
**Cooking score: 4**

'There is much to enjoy here', enthused one reporter, citing the atmosphere, service and, of course, the food; as at other branches of the Harvey Nichols chain, it is the ensemble that wins fans. This Leeds outpost strikes a contemporary pose with its open kitchen, long bar and rooftop views over the city. The food 'is consistently good', with sound sourcing lending substance to the operation. The kitchen sends out broadly based dishes ranging from Thai-style mussels with coconut broth to carpaccio of venison with broad bean and pea shoot salad with sloe gin syrup. Local roots are celebrated – via Lishman's ribeye with parsnip purée, confit garlic and sage jus – while a balanced dish of poached sea trout comes with spring greens, broad beans and brown crab given 'a little oomph' with some harissa. The wine list is high-class, generally fairly priced and with some good drinking under £25. House wine is £17.50.
**Chef/s:** Richard Walton-Allen. **Open:** all week L 12 to 3 (4 Sat and Sun), Tue to Sat D 5.30 to 10 (from 7 Sat). **Closed:** 25 Dec, 1 Jan, Easter Sun. **Meals:** alc (main courses £11 to £19). Set L £15.50 (2 course) to £18.50. Set D £18.50 (2 courses) to £21. Sun L £15. **Service:** 10% (optional). **Details:** Cards accepted. 80 seats. 20 seats outside. Air-con. Separate bar. No mobile phones. Wheelchair access. Music. Children allowed.

## No. 3 York Place
**Spot-on dishes at affordable prices**
3 York Place, Leeds, LS1 2DR
Tel no: (0113) 2459922
www.no3yorkplace.co.uk
**Modern British | £25**
**Cooking score: 4**

After many years of high-end dining, this gem of the Leeds business district risked everything by stripping away its finery. What some thought could be a move downmarket turned out to be just a piece of judicious pruning. Several years on it has proved to be a canny decision: no more heavy linen to add to the costs, more affordable prices, and a more manageable wine list. After a slightly shaky handover last year, when Martel Smith passed the baton to his pupil Simon Silver, recent reports attest to 'spot-on' cooking, and this French-influenced brasserie is back on form with some marvellous dishes like a 'wonderful' lobster risotto, sea bass with buttered noodles and sauce vierge, and a beef fillet in a wild mushroom sauce. The shortened wine list is still impressive and prices start at £14.
**Chef/s:** Simon Silver. **Open:** Mon to Fri L 12 to 1.30, Mon to Sat D 6.30 to 9.30 (10 Sat). **Closed:** Sun, 25 Dec to 7 Jan, bank hols. **Meals:** alc (main courses £13 to £19). Set L and D £14 (2 courses) to £18. **Service:** 10% (optional). **Details:** Cards accepted. 52 seats. Air-con. Separate bar. Wheelchair access. Music. Children allowed.

## The Olive Tree
**Greece is the word**
Oaklands, 55 Rodley Lane, Leeds, LS13 1NG
Tel no: (0113) 2569283
www.olivetreegreekrestaurant.co.uk
**Greek | £22**
**Cooking score: 1**

For more than 20 years, people have flocked to the Olive Tree to enjoy classic Greek food in the incongruous setting of an English-style country home. Maybe it's the fond holiday

memories brought back by a menu packed with typical Hellenic cooking: generous meze, spicy keftedes, taramasalata or some lovely pastries. Not everything is up to scratch, sadly, but the loyal following seems undeterred. The list offers a rare chance to enjoy some Greek wines, among others, and it starts at £13.45. There are two more branches in Headingly and Chapel Allerton.
**Chef/s:** Andreas Jacouvu and George Psarias. **Open:** all week L 12 to 2, D 6 to 10. **Closed:** 25 and 26 Dec, 1 Jan. **Meals:** alc (main courses £11 to £20). Set D £10.95 (2 courses) to £13.95. Sun L £9.95. **Service:** 10% (optional). **Details:** Cards accepted. 150 seats. Separate bar. Wheelchair access. Music. Children allowed.

**NEW ENTRY**
# Piazza by Anthony
**Treasure in Leeds**
The Corn Exchange, Call Lane, Leeds, LS1 7BR
Tel no: (0113) 2470995
www.anthonysrestaurant.co.uk
**Modern European | £20**
**Cooking score: 3**
V

The mighty Victorian Corn Exchange is Leeds' most treasured building – and Anthony Flinn its most treasured chef. Under the impressive domed roof of the Exchange, Piazza by Anthony combines retail – a bakery, patisserie, chocolatier and cheese shop – with a bar, private dining rooms and a café for spuds and soup. The Flinnmeister can be seen in the bakery, up to the elbows in dough but with one eye on the brasserie which occupies the circular central space. Broad grey stripes and oversized hurricane lamps surround those eating from a well-constructed, all-day menu of easy but refined dishes. To start, ham hock terrine, edged with pistachios and a 'hazelnut crunch' is piggy indeed, and roast halibut is spanking fresh with clams and a full-on shellfish cream sauce. House wine is £13.95, there's plenty of interest under £20.

**Chef/s:** Alex Knott. **Open:** all week 10 to 10. **Closed:** 25 and 26 Dec, 1 Jan. **Meals:** alc (main courses £8 to £32). **Service:** 10% (optional). **Details:** Cards accepted. 118 seats. Separate bar. Wheelchair access. Music. Children allowed.

# Salvo's
**Family-run Italian landmark**
115 Otley Road, Headingley, Leeds, LS6 3PX
Tel no: (0113) 2755017
www.salvos.co.uk
**Italian | £24**
**Cooking score: 2**
V

While nearby restaurants are half-empty, people will wait hours for a table at this Leeds institution. After 30 years, Salvo's is more popular than ever. Cash-strapped students drop in for affordable but extremely good pizza, while others splash out on fancier fare such as slow-braised beef in red wine with truffled potato cake. A decent wine list starts at £13.95. Those in the know opt for Salumeria, John and Gip Dammone's deli a few doors away at 109 Otley Road, which becomes a wonderfully intimate restaurant by night. Their set menus, themed by region, are genuine feasts.
**Chef/s:** Gip Dammone and Giuseppe Schirripa. **Open:** all week L 12 to 2 (12.30 to 9 Sun), D 6 to 10.30 (5.30 to 11 Fri and Sat). **Closed:** 25 and 26 Dec, 1 Jan. **Meals:** alc (main courses £9 to £18). Set L £8.95 (2 courses) to £11.45. Set D £12.50 (2 courses) to £14.95. Sun L £12.95 (2 courses) to £15.95. **Service:** not inc. **Details:** Cards accepted. 70 seats. 20 seats outside. Air-con. Separate bar. No mobile phones. Wheelchair access. Music. Children allowed.

## Also recommended
Also recommended entries are not scored but we think they are worth a visit.

## ALSO RECOMMENDED

### ▲ Hansa's

72-74 North Street, Leeds, LS2 7PN
Tel no: (0113) 2444408
www.hansasrestaurant.com
**Indian Vegetarian**

Owner Mrs Hansa Dabhi heads an all-woman kitchen team in this Leeds evergreen, which has been delivering subtly hued Gujarati vegetarian food since 1986. The menu encompasses a full range authentic specialities, from 'sharuaat' starters including steamed patra (stuffed colcassia leaves), chilli paneer and patudi gram flour rolls to masala dosa with sambar and coconut chutney and bhagat muthiya (chickpea koftas with potatoes, £7.25). Textbook kulfi and shrikand round things off. Thalis from £10.95. House wine is £13.95. Open Sun L and Mon to Sat D.

### ▲ Sukhothai

8 Regent Street, Chapel Allerton, Leeds, LS7 4PE
Tel no: (0113) 2370141
www.thaifood4u.co.uk
**Thai**

Traditional artwork, carvings and a waterfall are among the visual delights at this Thai restaurant, which is named after the old capital. Graceful service included an unforgettable birthday serenade for one reader, and the fairly priced menus extend expansively across the range, from fishcakes with peanut chilli sauce (£3.95) to 'Weeping Tiger' beef sirloin served on a sizzling platter and choo chee sea bass in coconut and lime-leaf curry (£10.50). Finish with banana crêpe filled with sweet sticky rice and topped with honey (£3.50). Wines from £11.95. Closed Mon L.

## ▌Leyburn

# The Sandpiper Inn

**Cosy local with hearty dishes**
Market Place, Leyburn, DL8 5AT
Tel no: (01969) 622206
www.sandpiperinn.co.uk
**Modern British | £28**
**Cooking score: 3**

It all looks reassuringly Yorkshire cosy when the candles cast their shadows under the low beams, and hearty dishes from the blackboard menu are delivered to the dark green dining room. Smoked salmon and crab salad with mango salsa, pigeon and butternut squash risotto, Dales lamb with dauphinoise potatoes and ratatouille are all effective, and with a genuine nod to local suppliers, though 'we'd like it if Jonathan Harrison broadened his repertoire'. Other familiar dishes are competently presented. A lemongrass and raspberry parfait with meringue and cream may be the most fancy of the desserts, but a reporter judged the 'just chewy' grains of the rice pudding and caramelised oranges as 'fantastic'. That same reporter found the service amateurish, others have found it friendly and attentive. House wines from £13.95 a bottle.

**Chef/s:** Jonathan Harrison. **Open:** Tue to Sun L 12 to 2.30 (2 Sun), D 6.30 to 9 (7 to 9 Sun). **Closed:** Mon, some Tue in low season, 25 and 26 Dec. **Meals:** alc (main courses £11 to £18). **Service:** not inc. **Details:** Cards accepted. 40 seats. 20 seats outside. Separate bar. No mobile phones. Music. Children allowed.

## ▌Marsden

### The Olive Branch

**Classic food and treasure-trove wine**
Manchester Road, Marsden, HD7 6LU
Tel no: (01484) 844487
www.olivebranch.uk.com
**Modern British | £30**
**Cooking score: 4**

£5 OFF 🍷 🍴

An elegant village restaurant-with-rooms has been fashioned from what was a no-frills country pub. There's still a pleasing element of rusticity, with bare wood tables and a decked area for outdoor eating. Paul Kewley's food lifts things into a whole other realm, with a vast menu that deals in classic modern British dishes, as well as some old favourites. Baked Whitby crab gratinated with Parmesan is a nice bistro-ish way to start, but there are also oysters in season, and the more refined likes of foie gras terrine with Riesling jelly and panettone. Mains bring on braised lamb shank with saffron risotto or properly aged beef from Hartshead Moor. Desserts go French with crème brûlée and lemon tart. Some food and wine matching tips open the extravagantly broad list, which is a treasure-trove of fine producers and many mature vintages at extremely fair prices – an object lesson to others. Prices open at £14.95.
**Chef/s:** Paul Kewley. **Open:** Sun L 1 to 8.30, all week D 6.30 to 9.30 (8.30 Sun). **Closed:** 26 Dec, 2 weeks Jan. **Meals:** alc (main courses £16 to £24). Set L £13.95 (2 courses) to £18.95. **Service:** not inc. **Details:** Cards accepted. 68 seats. 12 seats outside. Separate bar. No mobile phones. Wheelchair access. Music. Children allowed. Car parking.

## ▌Masham

### Samuel's at Swinton Park

**Fine dining in a stunning country manor**
Masham, HG4 4JH
Tel no: (01765) 680900
www.swintonpark.com
**Modern British | £42**
**Cooking score: 5**

£5 OFF 🍴

Castellated and grand, Swinton Park does English country house splendour with knobs on. Yet under the forbidding weight of portraits, silk brocades and gilded ceilings, Simon Crannage's menu is artfully restrained. An amuse-bouche of silky white onion velouté, topped with a heady truffle foam set the tone for a high-scoring meal. Chicken and foie gras terrine, garnished with dots of flageolet bean purée and truffle dressing looked potentially prissy, but the richness of the foie gras surged through. Another starter of goats' cheese on walnut 'crunch' had lots going on – cheese, walnuts, red pepper jelly, puréed aubergine, baby leaves – but balanced out into a satisfying whole. Mains were equally accomplished. A very slow-cooked blade of beef dutifully fell apart on the fork and was soothingly matched with wild mushrooms, baby onions and a soft celeriac purée. Salmon fillet came with the sharp, fresh citrusy flavours of pickled cucumber, saffron potatoes and melted prawn and lime butter. A generous cheese course had half a dozen Yorkshire and French specimens, crackers, grapes, membrillo, lemon jelly, figs and chutney. Only thin coffee and an over-chilled and too-dense lemon mousse failed to deliver, with service and the wine list amply fit for purpose. The beefy wine list starts at £17.99.
**Chef/s:** Simon Crannage. **Open:** Wed to Sun L 12.30 to 2, all week D 7 to 9.30. **Meals:** Set L £19 (2 courses) to £24. Set D £42 (3 courses). Sun L £26.50. Tasting menu £62. **Service:** not inc. **Details:** Cards accepted. 60 seats. 20 seats outside. Separate bar. No mobile phones. Wheelchair access. Music. Children allowed. Car parking.

## Vennell's

**Top cooking, top value**
7 Silver Street, Masham, HG4 4DX
Tel no: (01765) 689000
www.vennellsrestaurant.co.uk
**Modern British | £27**
**Cooking score: 5**

The slightly suburban feel of this family operation just off Masham's handsome market square belies its seriously accomplished cooking. Jon Vennell's dinner menu restrains itself to four choices per course but the pay-off is in quality. Among starters including flawless Stilton soufflé and a prettily presented beef carpaccio with shavings of Parmesan and truffle oil, only scallop ravioli fell short of the high benchmark for flavour. Slow-cooked belly pork and crackling served on mustard mash and gorgeously collapsing roast shallots is touted as Vennell's signature dish (supported by readers calling it 'exquisite' and 'full of flavour') while a Calvados and sweetcorn sauce adds an inspired sweet touch. More bold notes are struck by a buttery parsley and garlic risotto, topped with a generous slab of sea trout. Desserts are confident: a delicate chocolate and Grand Marnier bavarois with a pistachio biscuit; seasonal stalks of Yorkshire rhubarb and a dainty rhubarb and almond tart with vanilla ice cream and a super-sticky, cut-above-the-norm sticky toffee pudding. Prices are remarkably keen for a chef at the top of his game. House wine from £13.25.
**Chef/s:** Jon Vennell. **Open:** Sun L 12 to 4, Tue to Sun D 7.15 to 12. **Closed:** Mon, 1 to 14 Jan. **Meals:** Set D £21 (2 courses) to £27.50. Sun L £17.50. **Service:** not inc. **Details:** Cards accepted. 30 seats. Separate bar. No mobile phones. Music. Children allowed.

## █ Newton-on-Ouse

## Dawnay Arms

**Clever spin on Yorkshire grub**
Newton-on-Ouse, YO30 2BR
Tel no: (01347) 848345
www.thedawnayatnewton.co.uk
**Gastropub | £25**
**Cooking score: 4**

Martel Smith quit smart high-end cooking in Leeds for this riverside country pub – it's been a wise move. He hasn't changed the feel of the place – it still has its flagged floor, beams and chunky wooden tables, and local drinkers are still catered for – but the contemporary dining room indicates wider horizons. The style of food suits the pub well: down-to-earth, parsimonious in the best sense (using humble materials to good effect), unfussy and exploring local supplies – as homemade black pudding with crispy pork belly and a first-class apple and vanilla chutney or Whitby crab cakes reveal. The skill level is high, notably in a fine honey-roast breast of duck served with a casserole of game sausage and white beans, and in baked fillet of cod with Yorkshire rarebit crust and Savoy cabbage. Impressive desserts include baked egg custard tart with Yorkshire rhubarb compote. House wine is £13.95.
**Chef/s:** Martel Smith. **Open:** all week L 12 to 2.30 (6 Sun), D 6 to 9.30. **Meals:** alc (main courses £10 to £20). Set D £11.95 (2 courses) to £14.95. Set D £12.95 (2 courses) to £15.95. Sun L £14.95 (2 courses) to £17.95. **Service:** not inc. **Details:** Cards accepted. 80 seats. 80 seats outside. Separate bar. Wheelchair access. Music. Children allowed. Car parking.

# Osmotherley

## Golden Lion

No-frills food with a retro flavour
6 West End, Osmotherley, DL6 3AA
Tel no: (01609) 883526
www.goldenlionosmotherley.co.uk
Modern European | £23
Cooking score: 3

A tourist-friendly location on the fringes of the North York Moors National Park explains why a motley mix of energetic outdoor types, farmers and holidaymakers regularly descend on this eighteenth-century sandstone inn-with-rooms overlooking the village square. The Golden Lion thrives on traditional country hospitality and generous Yorkshire virtues, with honest, no-frills food high on the agenda. Regular menus have a decidedly retro flavour – think king prawns in garlic butter, avocado and crispy bacon salad, salmon fishcakes with spinach and sorrel sauce or suet-crusted steak and kidney pudding with mash and garlic cabbage. Daily blackboard specials throw in a few more intriguing modern ideas, while desserts revert to type with, perhaps, raspberry ripple cheesecake, Middle Eastern orange cake with marmalade cream or warm apple, prune and walnut cake. House wine is £14.95.
**Chef/s:** Chris and Judy Wright and Sam Hind. **Open:** Wed to Sun L 12 to 2.30, all week D 6 to 9. **Closed:** 25 Dec. **Meals:** alc (main courses £8 to £19). **Service:** not inc. **Details:** Cards accepted. 90 seats. 20 seats outside. Music. Children allowed.

## Please send us your feedback

To register your opinion about any restaurant listed in the Guide, or a new restaurant that you wish to bring to our attention, please visit the web address at the bottom of the page. Your feedback informs the content of the book and will be used to compile next year's reviews.

# Ramsgill

★ READERS' RESTAURANT OF THE YEAR ★
NORTH EAST

## The Yorke Arms

Class and wizardry at an adorable retreat
Ramsgill, HG3 5RL
Tel no: (01423) 755243
www.yorke-arms.co.uk
Modern British | £50
Cooking score: 6

Drive up to the outer reaches of Nidderdale, past Gouthwaite Reservoir, and you'll come face to face with Frances and Bill Atkins' adorable restaurant-with-rooms. Once a coaching inn and shooting lodge, it has been transformed into an eminently civilised, courteously run rural retreat full of atmosphere and antique furnishings. 'Frances Atkins' reputation precedes her', observed one visitor, and much depends on her confident, sophisticated approach to North Country supplies. Nidderdale lamb is a major attraction, local mutton and veal turn up from time to time (the latter served luxuriously with chicken sausage and foie gras ravioli) and bumper supplies of seasonal game are put to particularly good use – witness saddle and slow-cooked leg of hare with butternut squash, roasted onion skins and rosemary gnocchi. Elsewhere, fish from the coast is given incisive treatment, with creative ideas such as roast wild sea bass with chervil root, watercress, shrimp, chicken and tomato reduction. Desserts are a showcase for top-end technical wizardry: consider caramel bavarois with mango, green apple and brittle pastry. If you fancy a taster rather than the full works, nip into the bar for black pudding cooked in brioche with poached egg, or maybe gratin of scallops with spinach or a toasted steak sandwich. There are wows aplenty on the distinguished and well-balanced wine list: strong showings from Burgundy, Bordeaux and the Rhône are matched by some fine Italians and Aussie heroes. House selections start at £16.

# RAMSGILL

**Chef/s:** Frances Atkins. **Open:** all week L 12 to 2, D 7 to 9 (8 Sun, residents only). **Meals:** alc (main courses £19 to £35). Set L £30 (3 courses). Tasting menu £75. Sun L £29 to £35. **Service:** not inc. **Details:** Cards accepted. 50 seats. 20 seats outside. Separate bar. No mobile phones. Music. Children allowed. Car parking.

## Richmond

NEW ENTRY
### The Punch Bowl Inn
Simple, hearty gastropub grub
Low Row, Richmond, DL11 6PF
Tel no: (01748) 886233
www.pbinn.co.uk
Gastropub | £23
Cooking score: 1

Despite mutterings that the twinkly spotlights and pine tables are more wine bar than Dales pub, the Cody family are to be congratulated for breathing new life into an historic inn that had been closed for three years before they took over. The modern/rustic menu, written up on a mirror above the stove, is the same gastropub formula used at their Charles Bathurst Inn (see entry). Cooking is simple, hearty and effective: thick cheese and broccoli soup, a generous plateful of pork tenderloin stuffed with apricots, and crème brûlée sparked up by honey and whisky. House wine is £14.50.
**Chef/s:** Andrew Short. **Open:** all week L 12 to 2, D 6.30 to 9. **Closed:** 25 Dec. **Meals:** alc (main courses £9 to £20). **Service:** not inc. **Details:** Cards accepted. 60 seats. Air-con. No mobile phones. Music. Children allowed. Car parking.

### Please send us your feedback

To register your opinion about any restaurant listed in the Guide, or a new restaurant that you wish to bring to our attention, please visit the web address at the bottom of the page. Your feedback informs the content of the book and will be used to compile next year's reviews.

## Ripley
### The Boar's Head Hotel
Antiquity and modern cooking
Main Street, Ripley, HG3 3AY
Tel no: (01423) 771888
www.boarsheadripley.co.uk
Modern British | £35
Cooking score: 1

This sturdy stone hotel sits squarely at the centre of the estate village of Ripley, and Lady Ingilby, the chatelaine of Ripley Castle, takes an active part in menu planning. Dine among sparkling silver beneath gilded ancestral portraits, or more casually in the bistro. Recent reports have found the cooking more competent than inspired, delivering prawn and lovage mousse with smoked mackerel and horseradish cream, and loin of spring lamb with tomatoes and chickpeas at lunch, and more ambitious salmon with scallops and marinated beetroot or a monkfish and braised oxtail combo for dinner. House wine is £14.50.
**Chef/s:** Oliver Stewart. **Open:** all week L 12 to 2.30, D 6 to 9. **Meals:** alc (main courses £12 to £19). Set L and D £18 (2 courses) to £21.50. **Service:** not inc. **Details:** Cards accepted. 80 seats. 100 seats outside. Separate bar. Wheelchair access. Music. Children allowed. Car parking.

## Ripon
### The Old Deanery
Inventive food in an amazing building
Minster Road, Ripon, HG4 1QS
Tel no: (01765) 600003
www.theolddeanery.co.uk
Modern British | £32
Cooking score: 2

Close to Ripon cathedral, this 'amazing building' sports a harmonious combination of traditional elements (candlelight in the restaurant, a log fire in the bar) and understated contemporary styling. The 'consistently good' food fits in nicely, being classic but never tired or dated. Braised leg of duck with Puy lentils and red wine leads the way, followed by fillet of sea bass with smoked haddock mash and vermouth beurre blanc. Desserts, too, riff on familiar themes: try rhubarb fool, crumble and granita or apricot tarte Tatin. There's a lawned garden for alfresco dining. Wines start at £14.60.

**Chef/s:** Barrie Higginbotham. **Open:** all week L 12 to 3, Mon to Sat D 7 to 9. **Closed:** 25 Dec, 1 Jan. **Meals:** Set L £12.50 (2 courses) to £15.50. Set D £26.50 (2 courses) to £31.50. Sun L £18.95. **Service:** not inc. **Details:** Cards accepted. 66 seats. 45 seats outside. Separate bar. Wheelchair access. Music. Children allowed. Car parking.

## READERS RECOMMEND

### Lockwoods
**Modern British**
83 North Street, Ripon, HG4 1DP
Tel no: (01765) 607555
www.lockwoodsrestaurant.co.uk
'Small and very friendly. Early bird menu is fantastic value for money'

## ▌Ripponden

### El Gato Negro Tapas
**Spain reigns in the Pennines**
1 Oldham Road, Ripponden, HX6 4DN
Tel no: (01422) 823070
www.elgatonegrotapas.com
**Spanish | £29**
**Cooking score: 5**
£5 OFF  V  £30

Black cats seem to be lucky in any language, and this 'gato negro' has certainly worked its magic for the folk of West Yorkshire. Chef Simon Shaw decided to swap the bright lights of Harvey Nichols' Fifth Floor in Knightsbridge (see entry) for some down-home rusticity when he took over this defunct boozer in the scenic Pennine village of Ripponden and started surprising the locals with authentic Spanish tapas. Thankfully the interior rejects castanet clichés in favour of sophisticated good looks, laid-back vibes and DIY menus (just tick the boxes to order). The

owners have pitched this place to perfection, and regularly nip off to Spain in search of ingredients – top-drawer charcuterie (including acorn-fed jamón Ibérico and chorizo Leon), regional cheeses, Catalan bread, honey and other artisan provisions. Order several items from a list that might include roast pork belly with morcilla, apple and pea purée, grilled squid with chilli, lemon and garlic, and classic patatas bravas with aïoli. Little details also mean a lot – anchovy fillets on crostini, sourdough bread for dipping, dishes of punchy Syrian lentils – and you can feel comfortably at home with desserts such as crème brûlée 'to die for'. The wine list backpacks its way across Spain and also jets off to the Spanish 'New World'. Reasonably priced drinking starts at £13.95 (£3.50 a glass).

**Chef/s:** Simon Shaw. **Open:** Sat L 12 to 2, Sun L 12.30 to 5, Wed to Sat D 6 to 9.30 (10 Sat). **Closed:** Mon, Tue, 25 Dec to 6 Jan, 2 weeks Aug. **Meals:** alc (tapas £3 to £14). Set D £30 for 2 (inc wine). **Service:** not inc. **Details:** Cards accepted. 35 seats. Wheelchair access. Music. Children allowed.

## ▌Sawdon

**NEW ENTRY**
### The Anvil Inn
**Top-class food worth finding**
Main Street, Sawdon, YO13 9DY
Tel no: (01723) 859896
www.theanvilinnsawdon.co.uk
**Gastropub | £23**
**Cooking score: 2**
🛏 £30

This comfortably renovated village pub serves up top-class, impeccably sourced food. Scan the daily changing menu at ease in a battered leather chair in the blacksmith's former workshop – the stone fireplace and chimney intact – but the nostalgia ends there. Mark Wilson's skill is evident in dishes such as twice-baked soufflé of roast garlic and red onion with Fountains Gold cheese, or daube of beef slow-braised in red wine with shallot marmalade and mash. Lemon curd baked Alaska with raspberry coulis is a subtle, quivering plateful. House wine is £14.95. Walkers, cyclists, lunching ladies and locals mill about, enjoying the relaxed vibe and unforced bonhomie that exists here. Worth making the effort to find.

**Chef/s:** Mark Wilson. **Open:** Tue to Sun L 12 to 2 (3 Sun), Tue to Sat D 6.30 to 9. **Closed:** Mon, 25 and 26 Dec, 1 Jan, bank hols. **Meals:** alc (main courses £10 to £18). **Service:** not inc. **Details:** Cards accepted. 30 seats. 12 seats outside. Music. Children allowed. Car parking.

## Scarborough

## Lanterna
**Cheery Italian old-stager**
33 Queen Street, Scarborough, YO11 1HQ
Tel no: (01723) 363616
www.lanterna-ristorante.co.uk
Italian | £35
Cooking score: 3

**V**

With its central location and cheery atmosphere, this Scarborough stalwart attracts locals and visitors with the quality and worth of its food. Produce imported from Italy sits side by side with fine Yorkshire raw materials, and often results in dishes such as Yorkshire pudding filled with insalata di carne cruda (raw marinated chopped fillet of veal) and sanguinaccio – black pudding served with polenta and caramelised onions. Elsewhere, classic Piemontese preparations are the order of the day, with dishes mobilising plenty of flavours – from homemade pasta via risotto with porcini mushrooms and filleto alla piemontese (fillet steak with butter and garlic) to rich, creamy desserts. Between October and January, the prized white truffle of Piedmont stars on its own menu. The Italian wine list opens at £13.

**Chef/s:** Giorgio Alessio. **Open:** Mon to Sat D only 7 to 9.30 (10 Sat). **Closed:** Sun, 24 and 25 Dec, 2 weeks end Oct, 2 weeks Feb. **Meals:** alc (main courses £14 to £45). **Service:** not inc. **Details:** Cards accepted. 30 seats. Air-con. Wheelchair access. Music. Children allowed.

READERS RECOMMEND

## The Green Room Restaurant
**Modern British**
138 Victoria Road, Scarborough, YO11 1SL
Tel no: (01723) 501801
www.thegreenroomrestaurant.com
'Lovely modern food made with very good ingredients'

## Sheffield

## Artisan
**Sheffield all-rounder**
32-34 Sandygate Road, Crosspool, Sheffield, S10 5RY
Tel no: (0114) 2666096
www.relaxeatanddrink.com
**Modern British | £27**
Cooking score: 3

£5 OFF **V** £30

Crosspool is a leafy, slightly down-at-heel suburb of Sheffield, so Artisan, with its gentleman's club look of dark red walls, dark wood floors and furniture is quite a surprise. The service is cheerful, the atmosphere friendly and a range of menus include tapas and steak. A plate of olives, beetroot hummus and interesting bread kick-starts a meal that could go on to a crab tian with pea purée and lobster oil – the crab nicely dressed with a hint of cumin, although a fishcake was less successful at inspection. Old-school desserts such as crème brûlée are enjoyable. Upstairs is the Canteen (formerly Catch), which is much lighter in every way – floors, furniture, price, mood. The wine list starts at £16.

**Chef/s:** Simon Wild and Anton Corso. **Open:** all week L 12 to 2 (3 Sat and Sun), D 6 to 10. **Meals:** alc (main courses £12 to £28). Set L £18 (2 courses) to £22. Set D £20 (2 courses) to £27. Sun L £16.50. 2 courses for £12 in Canteen. **Service:** not inc. **Details:** Cards accepted. 90 seats. Air-con. Separate bar. Wheelchair access. Music. Children allowed.

## The Cricket Inn

**Reborn boozer with cosmopolitan vibes**
Penny Lane, Totley, Sheffield, S17 3AZ
Tel no: (0114) 2365256
www.relaxeatanddrink.com
Gastropub | £21
Cooking score: 2

£5 OFF **V** £30

Sheffield's favourite restaurateur Richard Smith (of Artisan fame, see entry) is one of the brains behind this resurgent pub in a well-to-do suburb of the city. The fact that it's next to the local cricket pitch gives the place a certain rustic afterglow, while the fashionable interior adds some agreeable cosmopolitan vibes. Regular menus, blackboard specials and cut-price deals cover a lot of ground, with Derbyshire steaks, sharing platters and British cheeses alongside homemade Scotch eggs with black pudding, crab cakes and glazed lamb shank with pesto mash. There are fish finger butties as well, plus a slate of puds including pineapple syllabub. House wine is £14 and 'the beer's great, too'.
**Chef/s:** Jack Baker. **Open:** Mon to Fri L 12 to 2.30, D 5 to 9, Sat 12 to 9.30, Sun 12 to 8. **Closed:** 25 Dec. **Meals:** alc (main courses £9 to £28). Set L and D £12. Ladies L £10. Sun L £16. **Service:** not inc. **Details:** Cards accepted. 70 seats. 85 seats outside. Wheelchair access. Music. Children allowed. Car parking.

## Greenhead House

**Friendly stalwart with flair**
84 Burncross Road, Chapeltown, Sheffield, S35 1SF
Tel no: (0114) 2469004
www.greenheadhouse.com
Modern European | £40
Cooking score: 2

'Like being invited into the home of a special friend,' observed a fan of Neil and Anne Allen's 25-year-old stalwart of the Sheffield scene. Set in a cottagey suburban house with a lovely walled garden, it continues to please a loyal band of followers and – despite limited opening hours – there's no lack of enthusiasm

or flair in the kitchen. Dinner menus change each month, allowing for new ideas to come on stream – perhaps traditional pansotti pasta filled with ricotta and mortadella served with pistachio sauce, or casseroled hare topped with chestnut and sage crumble. Sweets have included a 'very potent' Drambuie crème brûlée. House wine is £16.90.
**Chef/s:** Neil Allen. **Open:** Fri L 12 to 1, Wed to Sat D 7 to 8.30. **Closed:** Sun to Tue, Christmas to New Year, 2 weeks Easter, 2 weeks Aug. **Meals:** Set D £39.95 to £44.25 (4 courses). **Service:** not inc. **Details:** Cards accepted. 30 seats. 10 seats outside. Separate bar. No music. Wheelchair access. Children allowed. Car parking.

**NEW ENTRY**
## Moran's Restaurant

**Thrilling food in a surprising spot**
289 Abbeydale Road South, Dore, Sheffield, S17 3LB
Tel no: (0114) 2350101
www.moranssheffield.co.uk
Modern European | £27
Cooking score: 4

£5 OFF £30

It's easy to miss Moran's, and when you do find it you will dither at the door. It's not much more than a Portakabin set between a garden centre and a firm of insolvency practitioners. But persevere. Smiley staff set a standard that doesn't falter – much like the food. Soy-marinated monkfish scampi with red pepper salsa and lime mayonnaise comes with a crisp, light batter that shatters on impact, the fish sweet, the salsa a thrilling accompaniment. Mussels in Goan ginger and coconut curry is 'a sublime notion, pulled off confidently'. Roast guinea fowl (teamed with haggis, neeps and tatties, roast baby onions and whisky sauce) hits all the right subtle notes, while roast breast of Gressingham duck with a duck and apricot sausage, sweet potato mash and port and orange sauce is a delicate, elegant twist on a standard classic. Vanilla crème brûlée, espresso granita and hazelnut sablé biscuit completes the picture. House wines from £13.95.

**Chef/s:** Bryan Moran. **Open:** Wed to Sun L 12 to 2.30 (3 Sun), Tue to Sat D 7 to 9.30. **Closed:** Mon, 1 to 14 Jan. **Meals:** alc (main courses £13 to £20). Sun L £15.95 (2 courses) to £18.95. **Service:** not inc. **Details:** Cards accepted. 56 seats. 12 seats outside. Air-con. Separate bar. No mobile phones. Wheelchair access. Music. Children allowed. Car parking.

# ▌Shibden
## Shibden Mill Inn
**Handsome, whatever the season**
Shibden Mill Fold, Shibden, HX3 7UL
Tel no: (01422) 365840
www.shibdenmillinn.com
**Modern British | £24**
**Cooking score: 3**

Deep in the cleft of a lush wooded valley, this handsome, sprawling whitewashed inn welcomes with its rambling series of rooms and outdoor space. It has the seasons covered: in winter there are low lights, dark walls and roaring fires; in summer, the attractive garden makes the most of the spectacular location. The comprehensive menu is supplemented by daily specials, and might start with open ravioli of wild mushroom with watercress sauce or poached rabbit with black pudding. Olive-crusted trout could follow, served with seafood minestrone, or there could be flaked ham hock and two fried eggs with homemade tomato relish and chips. Egg custard tart with rhubarb compote and cinnamon ice cream is 'a heavenly plate'. Staff are 'always friendly', the thorough wine list opens at £13.95 (£3.95 a glass).
**Chef/s:** James Cooper. **Open:** all week L 12 to 2 (7.30 Sun), Mon to Sat D 6 to 9.30. **Meals:** alc (main courses £10 to £18). **Service:** not inc. **Details:** Cards accepted. 120 seats. 60 seats outside. Wheelchair access. Music. Children allowed. Car parking.

# ▌Sinnington
## ALSO RECOMMENDED
## ▲ The Fox and Hounds
Main Street, Sinnington, YO62 6SQ
Tel no: (01751) 431577
www.thefoxandhoundsinn.co.uk
**Modern British**

The stone-built inn on the edge of the North York Moors has a pleasingly unreconstructed feel, with a comfortable lounge bar and homely dining room. It's been accommodating weary travellers, in one way or another, since the eighteenth century. These days, modern bistro classics make up the menus, with scallops, black pudding, watercress and orange (£7.95) to start, perhaps followed by slow-cooked shoulder of lamb with dauphinoise and baby vegetables (£14.25). Eight house wines are all £13.50. Open all week.

# ▌Skipton
## Le Caveau
**Atmospheric subterranean dining**
86 High Street, Skipton, BD23 1JJ
Tel no: (01756) 794274
www.lecaveau.co.uk
**Anglo-French | £28**
**Cooking score: 2**

Secreted beneath the pavements of Skipton's main drag (voted 'Great British Street 2009'), this likeable neighbourhood restaurant occupies a sixteenth-century 'caveau' that now bubbles with atmosphere and Yorkshire hospitality. Its barrel-vaulted ceiling, mighty beams and rugged stone walls make a pleasing backdrop for Richard Barker's brand of unshowy Anglo-French cooking. Starters of pressed guinea fowl and pheasant terrine with Sauternes grape chutney could give way to chargrilled Dales ribeye steak with celeriac purée and Madeira jus or slow-baked lamb shank in red wine, garlic and rosemary. To finish, perhaps lemon tart with lime marmalade ice cream. House wine £12.95.

Chef/s: Richard Barker. **Open:** Tue to Fri L 12 to 2, Tue to Sat D 7 to 9.30 (5.30 to 9.45 Sat). **Closed:** Sun, Mon, 1 week Jan, 1 week June, 2 weeks Sept. **Meals:** alc (main courses £12 to £22). Set L £9.50 (2 courses) to £12. Set D £12 (3 courses). **Service:** not inc. **Details:** Cards accepted. 26 seats. Separate bar. No mobile phones. Music. Children allowed.

## ▌ South Dalton
### The Pipe & Glass Inn
**Good service, good value, a lovely atmosphere**
West End, South Dalton, HU17 7PN
Tel no: (01430) 810246
www.pipeandglass.co.uk
Gastropub | £25
Cooking score: 4

**V**

The countryside around the estate village of Dalton is green and appealing. The Pipe & Glass is no ordinary village inn – it's more a combination of pub and serious contemporary restaurant. James Mackenzie's menus are well considered and built around good, often local, ingredients. His cooking focuses on care and skill, rather than convoluted complexity, as demonstrated by crispy wild rabbit rissoles served with cockles, capers and sorrel. The same goes for main courses of Barnsley lamb chop teamed with devilled kidneys and served with nettle and mint sauce, rosemary boulangère potatoes and spiced pickled red cabbage; or for venison suet pudding with chanterelle mushrooms, butter-braised celery and carrots with crispy smoked bacon. For dessert, 'irreproachable' ginger burnt cream with poached rhubarb compote has been recommended. 'Good service, good value and a lovely atmosphere' sum it all up. House Chilean is £13.95.
Chef/s: James Mackenzie. **Open:** Tue to Sun L 12 to 2 (4 Sun), Tue to Sat D 6.30 to 9.30. **Closed:** Mon, 25 Dec, 1 week Jan. **Meals:** alc (main courses £9 to £20). **Service:** not inc. **Details:** Cards accepted. 80 seats. 60 seats outside. Air-con. Separate bar. No mobile phones. Wheelchair access. Music. Children allowed. Car parking.

## ▌ Sowerby
### The Travellers Rest
**A country inn with contemporary flair**
Steep Lane, Sowerby, HX6 1PE
Tel no: (01422) 832124
www.travellersrestsowerby.co.uk
Modern British | £26
New chef

 £5 OFF £30

Much like the interior, the cooking at this sturdy hilltop inn successfully marries traditional pub classics with more contemporary sensibilities. From starters along the lines of warm salad of wood pigeon with bacon to enormous plates of roast beef ('excellent and very local') topped with equally enormous Yorkshire puddings, reporters have found much to be happy about. But Rob Turner arrived just as the *Guide* went to press, too late for us to receive any reports on his progress. A short but very well-chosen wine list starts at £11.95.
Chef/s: Rob Turner. **Open:** Sat and Sun L 12 to 2.30 (7 Sun), Wed to Sat D 5 to 9 (9.30 Fri, 5.30 to 10 Sat). **Closed:** Mon, Tue. **Meals:** alc (main courses £9 to £19). Sun L £17.95. **Service:** not inc.
**Details:** Cards accepted. 60 seats. 30 seats outside. Wheelchair access. Music. Children allowed. Car parking.

## ▌ Staddlebridge
### McCoys at the Tontine
**Singular restaurant-with-rooms**
Staddlebridge, DL6 3JB
Tel no: (01609) 882671
www.mccoystontine.co.uk
Modern British | £40
Cooking score: 4

Built in the first decade of the nineteenth century by private subscription, the Tontine Inn was designed to mop up business on the Thirsk to Yarm turnpike. The coming of the railways put rather a dent in its throughput, but the modern era has seen the place reborn as a singular restaurant-with-rooms. The style is

French bistro-meets-modern British, with starters taking in king scallops with pancetta-wrapped rabbit loin in shallot and caper dressing. Effective main courses might be chicken breast with truffled leek cannelloni, wild mushrooms and vermouth. Desserts include a homely blackberry, lemon and ginger sponge with custard. The wine list sources some imaginative choices from Australia and New Zealand, as well as doing justice to the classic regions of France. Trawling through will reveal plenty of choice under £20. House wines are from £18.50.
**Chef/s:** Stuart Hawkins. **Open:** all week L 12 to 2, D 6.30 to 9 (9.45 Fri and Sat, 8.30 Sun). **Closed:** 25 and 26 Dec, 1 and 2 Jan. **Meals:** alc (main courses £18 to £25). Set L £14.95 (2 courses) to £16.95. Sun L £21.95. **Service:** not inc. **Details:** Cards accepted. 84 seats. Music. Children allowed. Car parking.

## Staithes
### Endeavour
**Passionate about fish cookery**
1 High Street, Staithes, TS13 5BH
Tel no: (01947) 840825
www.endeavour-restaurant.co.uk
Seafood | £31
Cooking score: 4

The Endeavour appears simple and unassuming – an impression reinforced by steep, narrow staircases, old wood panelling and cosy dining room. Charlotte Willoughby and Brian Kay's passion is fish cookery, and their well-considered, unflashy dishes have pulled in the punters since 2001. The haul from local boats is the starting point, with fish curing done on the premises, so that a mousse of home-salted cod and soused mackerel fillet or a plate of home-smoked pollack might open proceedings. Main courses bring fillet of Scarborough turbot with apple wafers and an apple and Calvados sauce, or a cassoulet of local seafood – turbot, ling, gurnard, scallop and squid – with smoked bacon and cannellini beans. The standard menu also pleases carnivores, with confit of rabbit legs on spiced apricot couscous. Wind up with rich

lemon mousse and lemon curd ice cream. House wine is £13. Note that the restaurant now opens for lunch and dinner on Friday and Saturday only. Booking is essential.
**Chef/s:** Charlotte Willoughby and Brian Kay. **Open:** Fri and Sat L 12.30 to 2, D 7 to 9. **Closed:** Sun to Thur. **Meals:** Set L £19 (2 courses) to £21. Set D £26 (2 courses) to £32. **Service:** not inc. **Details:** Cards accepted. 16 seats. No mobile phones. Music. Children allowed. Car parking.

## Tadcaster
### Singers
**Modern menus with lots of choice**
16 Westgate, Tadcaster, LS24 9AB
Tel no: (01937) 835121
www.singersrestaurant.co.uk
Modern European | £26
Cooking score: 2

An old stone house in historic Tadcaster, Singers is named for the musical theming in the dining room, where pictures of the great and the good of the past adorn the walls, and the tables are dedicated to noted vocalists. A modern brasserie approach characterises the cooking, and choice is appealingly wide. Start perhaps with salmon, sole and crab roulade with spinach and pear salad, and go on to venison steak with beetroot and mascarpone risotto and a Burgundy jus. Nobody will go home bereft when the pudding menu includes thick-crusted apple pie with 'lots of proper custard'. A short, serviceable wine list opens at £13.95.
**Chef/s:** Adam Hewitt and John Appleyard. **Open:** Tue to Sat D only 6 to 9.30. **Closed:** Sun, Mon, 24 Dec to 1 Jan. **Meals:** alc (main courses £17 to £18). Set D £16.95 to £25.95. **Service:** not inc.
**Details:** Cards accepted. 38 seats. Air-con. Separate bar. Wheelchair access. Music. Children allowed.

## ▌West Witton

# The Wensleydale Heifer

**Contemporary seafood in rural surroundings**
Main Street, West Witton, DL8 4LS
Tel no: (01969) 622322
www.wensleydaleheifer.co.uk
**Seafood | £30**
**Cooking score: 3**

🛏 **V**

'They don't get any better than this', writes one dedicated fish and chip eater of 60 years' experience. Not that this whitewashed pub restricts itself to superior fish and chips – this is really a full-blown and fairly pricey seafood restaurant. With 70 covers served in a warren of smartly decorated rooms and a raft of different menus, it's eager to please, and for the most part does – if somewhat impersonally. Herb-crusted cod with mussels, mash, spinach and a fennel cream sauce was competent, well presented and generous. Ditto tuna loin with marinated fennel, green beans and tiger prawns, but busy plates and over-complicated dishes can detract from the essential quality of the ingredients. 'No-one had time to say hello or goodbye' on a Saturday night, but lunchtime service is 'smooth and professional'. House wine is £16.50.
**Chef/s:** David Moss. **Open:** all week 12 to 2.30, 6 to 9.30. **Meals:** alc (main courses £14 to £22). Set L and D £14.50 (2 courses) to £16.95. Sun L £15.50 (2 courses) to £18.95. **Service:** 10% (optional).
**Details:** Cards accepted. 70 seats. 50 seats outside. Separate bar. Wheelchair access. Music. Children allowed. Car parking.

## ▌Whitby

# Green's

**Bags of ambition**
13 Bridge Street, Whitby, YO22 4BG
Tel no: (01947) 600284
www.greensofwhitby.com
**Modern British | £30**
**Cooking score: 4**

Rob and Emma Green's restaurant 'certainly aims to please', according to one fan who loved its 'brilliant new décor' and ambitious food. The place now operates on two levels, with an unfussy bistro menu downstairs (think moules frites, duck breast salad and mixed grills) and increasingly sophisticated stuff in the first-floor restaurant. Green's is located close to Whitby's swing bridge and the quay, so it's no surprise that fresh seafood is a strength – the local trawlers and their skippers even get a name-check on the menu. The kitchen can turn its hand to anything from Thai seafood ragoût to turbot fillets with a little shellfish thermidor, cauliflower purée and fennel salad, while meaty endorsements have included a trio of local estate venison (including a steamed suet pudding) and chargrilled Yorkshire beef with a mini cottage pie. After that, desserts such as chocolate tart with white chocolate and Cointreau ice cream add a little sweetness to proceedings. 'Reasonably priced' wines start at £13.95.
**Chef/s:** Rob Green. **Open:** Mon to Fri L 12 to 2, D 6.30 to 9.30 (10 Fri), Sat 12 to 10, Sun 12 to 9.30. **Closed:** 25 and 26 Dec, 1 Jan. **Meals:** alc (main courses £13 to £24). Set D £33.50 (2 courses) to £39.95. Sun L £10.95. **Service:** not inc.
**Details:** Cards accepted. 50 seats. Air-con. No mobile phones. Wheelchair access. Music. Children allowed.

## Magpie Café

**Doyen of seaside cafés**
14 Pier Road, Whitby, YO21 3PU
Tel no: (01947) 602058
www.magpiecafe.co.uk
Seafood | £20
Cooking score: 2

£5 OFF

In a handsome, white-fronted Georgian building overlooking the harbour, the Magpie is an unpretentious, family-friendly restaurant that offers a menu of impeccably fresh fish and seafood from the Whitby boats. A bowl of kipper soup will be a boon on a cold day, but culinary influences from further afield bring on sesame, ginger and honey king prawns with rice, and sea bass with pancetta and tomato sauce. Even a simple plate of haddock and chips is a joy. Look out for Lindisfarne oysters in season, and save room for one of the numerous desserts. Five house wines come at £12.95, or £3.25 a glass.

**Chef/s:** Ian Robson and Paul Gildroy. **Open:** all week 11.30 to 9. **Closed:** 24 to 26 Dec, 1 Jan, 2 weeks Jan. **Meals:** alc (main courses £7 to £21). **Service:** not inc. **Details:** Cards accepted. 130 seats. Air-con. Wheelchair access. Music. Children allowed.

# York

## J. Baker's Bistro Moderne

**Affordable fine dining and fun**
7 Fossgate, York, YO1 9TA
Tel no: (01904) 622688
www.jbakers.co.uk
Modern British | £28
Cooking score: 5

£5 OFF

A high roller right in York's gastro-epicentre, Jeff Baker's self-styled 'bistro moderne' is pitched squarely as a populist venue for our times. Rather than desperately seeking accolades, it aims to deliver good food for all at prices that won't crash the system. The ground-floor restaurant lives and breathes laid-back cosmopolitan style, with subdued colours, a few pictures and flower arrangements providing the backdrop, while upstairs is a seductive chocolate room dedicated to toothsome delights. At lunchtime, a flexible grazing menu rules: order and eat at your own pace from a snappy assortment of little dishes including snail and chestnut 'ragoo' or black pudding pasties with hazelnut pease pudding. Evening meals raise the bar with forthright, fancy-free offerings such as crunchy lamb belly with smoked eel, eggplant and pimento or slow-cooked pork cheeks with Thai ketchup, seared squid and buttered noodles. Jeff Baker may be serious about food, but he has a sense of fun and isn't averse to playing a few mischievous tricks on the taste buds. A starter dubbed 'pot of tea and bacon buttie' involves pheasant, pancetta and prunes, roast Yorkshire mallard is served with 'leftover Xmas pudding' and desserts include the deliciously tongue-in-cheek peanut butter and jelly sandwich with sarsaparilla. House wines from £13.95 head the praiseworthy, price-conscious list.

**Chef/s:** Jeff Baker. **Open:** Tue to Sat L 12 to 2.30, D 6 to 10. **Closed:** Sun, Mon, first week Jan. **Meals:** Set menu £24 (2 courses) to £38 (7 courses). **Service:** 10% (optional). **Details:** Cards accepted. 56 seats. Separate bar. Wheelchair access. Music. Children allowed.

**NEW ENTRY**

## Le Langhe

**Top-quality ingredients simply prepared**
The Old Coach House, Peasholme Green, York, YO1 7PW
Tel no: (01904) 622584
www.lelanghe.co.uk
Italian | £25
Cooking score: 3

For years, only locals found their way to this Italian deli with a tiny café at the back, but in 2008 the owners moved to bigger, brighter premises beside the city walls bringing their enticing deli/café to a wider clientele. The menu is deceptively simple, based around imported cheeses and meats: prosciutto, bresaola or maybe culatello served on a board

with good bread and maybe some artichokes and olives. Specials might include pasta with aubergine and tomato, while a recent four-course tasting menu featured Italian hams, an exquisite homemade pasta with pumpkin and goats' cheese, tender pigeon breast on a sauce of juniper and blackcurrant with tiny fried potatoes, and, to finish, fig and pistachio tart, served with an impressive selection of Italian wines. Quaffing starts at £14 a bottle.
**Chef/s:** Ottavio Bocca. **Open:** Mon to Sat L 10 to 5.30. **Closed:** Sun, 25 and 26 Dec, Easter, bank hols. **Meals:** alc (main courses £10 to £15). **Details:** Cards accepted. 30 seats. 20 seats outside. Wheelchair access. Children allowed.

## Melton's

**Much-loved York bolt-hole**
7 Scarcroft Road, York, YO23 1ND
Tel no: (01904) 634341
www.meltonsrestaurant.co.uk
Modern European | £30
Cooking score: 5

£5 OFF 🍷

The long-standing Melton's is quite as customer-friendly now as it was when it opened in 1990. A small, agreeably intimate restaurant with a deep blue frontage, it is appreciated by locals as a highly reliable neighbourhood address, with the 'early bird' menu (and it's a generous definition of the 'early' concept) drawing special praise. 'We eat like lords while spending a more modest amount of money', a reader vouchsafes. Firmly supporting local 'food heroes', Michael Hjort's menus change monthly, and might encompass the likes of mussel risotto with saffron air, beef shin with black olives and gremolata, and pannacotta with rhubarb and vodka. Fish is sensitively handled, as in a main course of brill with caramelised red onions and beurre blanc, served with Pink Fir Apple potatoes and seasonal greens. Choice for vegetarians might include main dishes such as cannellini bean and sprouting broccoli fritters with smoked paprika relish, or tomato-dressed polenta with Portabello mushrooms and pak choi. Wine suggestions to go with the latest menu dishes are only one of the commendable aspects of an extensive list that zips niftily about the globe in search of value. House wines are £15, or £3.75 for a small glass.
**Chef/s:** Michael Hjort and Greg Birch. **Open:** Tue to Sat L 12 to 2, D 5.30 to 9.45. **Closed:** Sun, Mon, 2 weeks Christmas, 1 week Aug. **Meals:** alc (main courses £14 to £18). Set L £22.50. **Service:** not inc. **Details:** Cards accepted. 42 seats. Air-con. Music.

## Melton's Too

**Boisterous bistro for all-comers**
25 Walmgate, York, YO1 9TX
Tel no: (01904) 629222
www.meltonstoo.co.uk
Modern European | £20
Cooking score: 2

V

The laid-back younger brother of Melton's (see entry), 'Mtoo' occupies a seventeenth-century building on three levels – embracing a ground-floor snug/bar, bistro and a loft for events and gigs. It's a boisterous, open-minded place that caters admirably for all-comers: 'even "picky" teenagers like eating here', noted one reporter. Food runs through the day, from breakfast trays, tapas and filled Yorkshire puddings to lively modern dishes built from regional ingredients. Carpaccio of Ledston Estate venison could be followed by bouillabaisse, penne with meatballs or slow-roast rare-breed pork with cider and apples. For afters, perhaps Yorkshire rhubarb crumble with custard. Drinks range from real ales and fruity cordials to affordable wines (from £12).
**Chef/s:** Michael Hjort. **Open:** all week 10.30 to 10.30. **Closed:** 25 and 26 Dec, 1 Jan. **Meals:** alc (main courses £9 to £12). Express L £6.90. Set L and early D £12.50 (2 courses) to £17. **Service:** not inc. **Details:** Cards accepted. 130 seats. Air-con. Wheelchair access. Music. Children allowed.

## Middlethorpe Hall

A vision of Palladian splendour
Bishopthorpe Road, York, YO23 2GB
Tel no: (01904) 641241
www.middlethorpe.com
**Modern British | £43**
Cooking score: 3

Middlethorpe Hall conjures up visions of aristocratic stature and Palladian splendour. The stately, three-storey William and Mary mansion (now owned by the National Trust) seems to have it all, from acres of parkland complete with a ha-ha to opulent interiors awash with vintage portraits, panelling and antiques. Grandeur extends to the impeccably groomed dining room, where visitors can look forward to food that pitches Yorkshire flavours against modern European themes. Honey-glazed pork cheeks with apple purée rub shoulders with duck confit and chorizo terrine with braised lentils, while slow-cooked local beef fillet with cottage pie and Savoy cabbage sits alongside baked lemon sole, crab mousse, artichokes and chive butter sauce. For dessert, expect, say, hot apple and blackberry soufflé or tiramisu. France rules on the upper-crust wine list, with prices from £16.50.
**Chef/s:** Nicholas Evans. **Open:** all week L 12.30 to 1.45, D 7 to 9.45. **Meals:** alc (main courses £19 to £28). Set L £17 (2 courses) to £23. Sun L £26. **Service:** inc. **Details:** Cards accepted. 60 seats. 32 seats outside. Separate bar. No music. Wheelchair access. Children allowed. Car parking.

NEW ENTRY
## Ye Olde Punchbowl Inn

TV pub that's a handy asset
Marton cum Grafton, York, YO51 9QY
Tel no: (01423) 322519
www.yeoldepunchbowl.co.uk
**Gastropub | £28**
Cooking score: 2

Cynics may look suspiciously on this village pub, the subject of a television series in which Richard Fox and Neil Morrissey joshed their way past grumpy locals to create their own micro-brewery and pub refurb in the space of a few weeks. Yet this well-heeled village has gained a handy asset. The interior has been pleasantly updated with wood floors, rustic brick, and a muted palette, the 'home-grown' ale is good, the menu simple, satisfying and not over-ambitious. Sweet potato and garlic risotto, a generous salmon fishcake served with a chive beurre blanc and a slow-roast shoulder of lamb with wild mushrooms and mint potato mash are typical. Crème brûlée and sticky toffee pudding head a list of familiar favourites. House wine from £12.95.
**Chef/s:** John Malia. **Open:** all week L 12 to 2.30 (5.30 Sun), Mon to Sat D 5.30 to 9 (6 to 9.30 Fri and Sat). **Meals:** alc (main courses £12 to £20). **Service:** not inc. **Details:** Cards accepted. 80 seats. 20 seats outside. Wheelchair access. Music. Children allowed. Car parking.

# SCOTLAND

Borders, Dumfries & Galloway,
Lothians (inc. Edinburgh),
Strathclyde (inc. Glasgow), Central, Fife,
Tayside, Grampian, Highlands & Islands

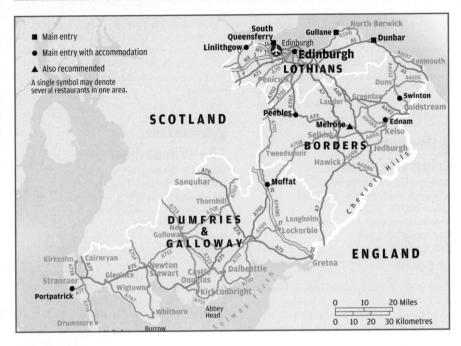

- ■ Main entry
- ● Main entry with accommodation
- ▲ Also recommended

A single symbol may denote several restaurants in one area.

## Ednam

### Edenwater House

**Magical place with recipe for success**
Ednam, TD5 7QL
Tel no: (01573) 224070
www.edenwaterhouse.co.uk
**Modern European | £35**
Cooking score: 4

This fine old stone manse by the church is a pretty magical place, but has become so by dint of hard labour. With views all round, a husband and wife team, a fine wine cellar and good cooking for dinner that comes with no choices on the menu, it receives lots of reader endorsements. Many dishes have pleased: crab and crayfish risotto, followed by wild halibut with glazed fennel, warm potato salad with dill and lemon spinach or a satisfying venison steak with rösti with parsnip purée, red cabbage and jus flavoured with bitter chocolate. It is a fair recipe for success, with Jacqui Kelly's food reckoned to be satisfying and substantial

without being weighty. Jeff Kelly informs us of plans to create a wine-tasting room where diners may sample wines before choosing, and to expand an already interesting and unusual list. House wine from £15.

**Chef/s:** Jacqui Kelly. **Open:** Mon to Sat D only 8 (1 sitting). Non-residents Thur to Sat only. **Closed:** last 2 weeks Dec, first 2 weeks Jan. **Meals:** Set D £35. **Service:** not inc. **Details:** Cards accepted. 16 seats. No music. No mobile phones. Car parking.

## Melrose

### ALSO RECOMMENDED
### ▲ Burt's Hotel

Market Square, Melrose, TD6 9PL
Tel no: (01896) 822285
www.burtshotel.co.uk
**Modern British**

This whitewashed building on the market square dates from 1722 and is still laden with period character. In the green dining room, a refined style of country house cooking is offered, with fixed-price dinner menus of two courses (£28.50) or three (£33.75). Expect grilled red mullet with melon and feta couscous in port syrup, followed by saddle of lamb with garlic butter fondants, creamed Savoy cabbage and redcurrant and rosemary jus, then warm treacle tart with whisky and ginger ice cream and crème anglaise. House wines are £14.95. Open all week.

## ■ Peebles

### Cringletie House

**Bold style in a baronial pile**
Edinburgh Road, Peebles, EH45 8PL
Tel no: (01721) 725750
www.cringletie.com
**Modern British | £43**
Cooking score: 4

£5 off ▮ ⊟ V

Built in 'laird of the manor' style around 1861, this imposing baronial pile is surrounded by 28 acres of grounds complete with a listed dovecote and one of Scotland's oldest working walled gardens. Meals are served in the elegant first-floor Sutherland Room, where the fine views, carved oak fireplace and hand-painted trompe l'oeil ceiling may distract your attention from the food on the plate. But not for long. A challenging starter of crispy pork belly with roasted scallops, balsamic onions and marinated squid is typical of the kitchen's bold style. Main courses sustain the momentum with – perhaps – duck breast on butternut squash and pancetta risotto or vanilla-poached salmon with a horseradish crust, beetroot and wilted pak choi. As for desserts, consider 'chocolate and cherry heaven' or 'apple mayhem' (tarte Tatin with apple sorbet and Cringletie-style apple pie). The knowledgeably assembled, ever-changing wine list is a fascinating read, coloured by the owners' travels to vineyards across the globe. Current star turns include Pinot Grigio Seghesio from Sonoma County, USA and quaffable Santa Cecilia Nero d'Avola from Planeta in Sicily. Prices start at £19.90 (£4.90 a glass).

**Chef/s:** Craig Gibb. **Open:** Sun L 12 to 2, all week D 7 to 9. **Meals:** Set D £42.50. Tasting menu £65. Sun L £22.50. **Service:** not inc. **Details:** Cards accepted. 40 seats. Separate bar. No mobile phones. Wheelchair access. Music. Children allowed. Car parking.

## ■ Swinton

### The Wheatsheaf

**Reputable Borders inn**
Main Street, Swinton, TD11 3JJ
Tel no: (01890) 860257
www.wheatsheaf-swinton.co.uk
**Modern British | £30**
**New chef**

£5 off ⊟

The Wheatsheaf combines the assets of an inn with the attributes of an upmarket country hotel, and the emphasis is firmly on food. A new head chef was appointed too late for any feedback, so reports please. Local ingredients, Scottish meat and fish direct from the boat at Eyemouth show up on the dinner menu, which might open with breast of wood pigeon and black pudding on celeriac with orange and redcurrant sauce, followed by roast rack of Borders lamb with a basil and mustard crust, or grilled fillet of halibut with a walnut, parsley and lemon crust. For dessert, there might be white chocolate cheesecake with a strawberry sorbet. House wine is £12.55. **Chef/s:** Scott MacIntyre. **Open:** all week L 12 to 2, D 6 to 9. **Closed:** 25 and 26 Dec, 1 Jan. **Meals:** alc (main courses £15 to £20). **Service:** not inc. **Details:** Cards accepted. 45 seats. Separate bar. Wheelchair access. Music. Children allowed. Car parking.

# Moffat

## Well View

Enduring family set-up
Ballplay Road, Moffat, DG10 9JU
Tel no: (01683) 220184
www.wellview.co.uk
Modern European | £38
Cooking score: 4

The Schuckardts set up shop in Moffat in 1984, and named their congenial little guest house after the sulphurous well that was once the focal point of this Victorian spa town. More than 25 years down the line, they are still keeping it in the family and treating visitors to a dose of relaxed, domestic hospitality – plus the prospect of carefully crafted food with classical inclinations. The formula of ingredients-led, four-course dinners with no choice until dessert isn't about to change, and meals always begin with a little canapé taster to kick-start the appetite. After that, you might be offered carrot and apricot soup with warm bread before – say – roast duck breast with stir-fried vegetables and red wine jus. For dessert, the choice might extend to chocolate chip steamed pudding with crème anglaise or Ecclefechan butter tart with two sauces. Well View is no longer licensed, but guests are offered complimentary glasses of wine (white or red) with their meal.

**Chef/s:** Janet and Lina Schuckardt. **Open:** Sun L 1, all week D 7.30 (1 sitting). **Meals:** Set D £38 (4 courses). Sun L £22. **Service:** not inc. **Details:** Cards accepted. 10 seats. No mobile phones. Music. Children allowed. Car parking.

## Symbols

 Accommodation is available

 Three courses for less than £30

**V** More than three vegetarian main courses

 £5-off voucher scheme

 Notable wine list

# Portpatrick

## Knockinaam Lodge

Glorious isolation, splendid food
Portpatrick, DG9 9AD
Tel no: (01776) 810471
www.knockinaamlodge.com
Modern European | £50
Cooking score: 5

You can almost imagine the high drama of some swashbuckling romantic novel being played out amid the wooded glens and rugged cliffs that form a backdrop to this isolated Victorian hunting lodge. Built in 1869, it is now surrounded by 30 acres of lavish gardens, with lawns running down to a private sandy beach overlooking the Irish Sea. Long-serving chef Tony Pierce is a key figure, and visitors can enjoy the fruits of his fine-tuned culinary labours in the sedate dining room. French influences point up his sharply defined, seasonal menus, although the kitchen is loyal to Scotland when it comes to sourcing top-drawer ingredients. Meals follow the well-tried country house format – four courses, with cheese or a dessert to finish. A February dinner might progress from grilled fillet of Luce Bay sea bass with chive hollandaise to a bowl of cauliflower, onion and truffle soup. After that, perhaps roast cannon of Galloway lamb partnered by a potato and thyme rösti, confit shallot and grilled black pudding. Hot passion fruit soufflé could bring proceedings to a close, before coffee and petits fours in the comfy lounge. 'Welcome to the wonderful world of wine!' proclaims the list – and wondrous it is, too. Owner David Ibbotson is an enthusiast whose cherry-picked selection spans the globe, from rare French gems to exciting Aussie discoveries. Half-bottles abound and house recommendations start at £20.

**Chef/s:** Tony Pierce. **Open:** all week L 12 to 2, D 7 to 9. **Meals:** Set L £37.50 (4 courses). Set D £50 (5 courses). Sun L £27.50. **Service:** not inc. **Details:** Cards accepted. 26 seats. Separate bar. No mobile phones. Wheelchair access. Music. Car parking.

## ▌Dunbar

### Creel Restaurant

Good-value creative cooking
25 Lamer Street, The Old Harbour, Dunbar,
EH42 1HJ
Tel no: (01368) 863279
www.creelrestaurant.co.uk
**Modern British | £26**
Cooking score: 3

Logan Thorburn runs an industrious kitchen at his unassuming wood-panelled bistro near the harbour, supporting local suppliers and with much made on the premises. There is the option of set-price lunches and a good-value evening carte, and a pleasing sense of creativity runs through both. Steamed local langoustines with homemade mayonnaise is familiar enough, but more novel is braised chorizo with red pepper and Merlot, toasted corn bread and aïoli. Main courses might include breast of chicken with a cassoulet of fresh vegetables, Toulouse sausage and cannellini beans, or grilled fillet of grey mullet with bacon, boiled egg and baby potato salad with spicy tomato and sour cream dressing. Wines on the modest, good-value list start at £15.95.
**Chef/s:** Logan Thorburn. **Open:** Thur to Sun L 12 to 2, Thur to Sat D 6.45 to 9. **Closed:** Mon to Wed, 25 Dec. **Meals:** alc D (main courses £11 to £17). Set L £12.50 (2 courses) to £16.50. Sun L £15.50 (2 courses) to £21.50. **Service:** not inc. **Details:** Cards accepted. 36 seats. No mobile phones. Wheelchair access. Music. Children allowed.

## ▌Edinburgh

### Abstract

Sassy décor and food to match
33-35 Castle Terrace, Edinburgh, EH1 2EL
Tel no: (0131) 2291222
www.abstractrestaurant.com
**Modern French | £37**
Cooking score: 4

Abstract paints a highly contemporary picture with a sassy, urbane look of faux snakeskin tables and chairs, signature artwork, striking wallpaper, gold ceiling and contemporary lighting. The food lives up to the setting, its fine-tuned kitchen, now headed by Geoff Malmedy who previously ran the kitchen at Abstract, Inverness (see entry), delivering some colourful, innovative modern French cooking. Quality seasonal ingredients from the Scottish larder provide the inspiration, witness a great-value lunch main course of red gurnard in a langoustine bouillon, served with crunchy vegetables. Starters deliver the same pizzazz, perhaps an assiette of asparagus (chilled soup, tempura, mousse and carpaccio), while the carte cranks up the ante with the likes of slow-cooked Borders beef teamed with oyster croustilliant, horseradish macaroni and tarragon jelly. The international wine list is suitably French-led and dominated by some starry names, with house selections starting at £18. The adjoining Piano Bar is as sleekly attired as the attentive, professional service.
**Chef/s:** Geoff Malmedy. **Open:** Tue to Sat L 12 to 2, D 6 to 10. **Closed:** Sun, Mon. **Meals:** alc (£16 to £25). Set L £12.95 (2 courses) to £16.95. Tasting menu £55. **Service:** 12.5% (optional). **Details:** Cards accepted. 60 seats. Air-con. Separate bar. Wheelchair access. Music. Children allowed.

## Atrium

**One of Edinburgh's elder statesmen**
10 Cambridge Street, Edinburgh, EH1 2ED
Tel no: (0131) 2288882
www.atriumrestaurant.co.uk
**Modern European | £40**
**Cooking score: 4**

Tucked behind the Castle, in the heart of Edinburgh's theatreland, the Atrium is now one of the elder statesmen of the culinary renaissance that took place in the Scottish capital in the 1990s. Blond wood, masses of natural daylight and discreet lighting in the evening give the interiors a bright and relaxing feel. Neil Forbes still produces virtually everything in-house, using a wealth of produce from farms in the area, together with regional cheeses. The cooking style is obviously contemporary, but strikes some traditional chords too: halibut from Fraserburgh with lobster ravioli, squid and sea kale, or Peelham Farm lamb with crushed roots, boulangère potatoes and a mushroom jus. Scallops from Gigha might get the juices flowing, perhaps furnished with sweet potato purée. For those who love rich desserts, a steamed pudding with marmalade, syrup and lemon curd will answer the call. An enterprising, carefully annotated wine list is cosmopolitan in its spread, with prices from £18.50.

**Chef/s:** Neil Forbes. **Open:** Mon to Fri L 12 to 2, Mon to Sat D 6 to 10. **Closed:** Sun, 25 and 26 Dec, 1 and 2 Jan. **Meals:** alc (main courses £19 to £24). Set L £14 (2 courses) to £18. Set D £27 (3 courses). Tasting menu £55. **Service:** not inc. **Details:** Cards accepted. 80 seats. Air-con. No music. Wheelchair access. Children allowed.

## The Balmoral, Number One

**Star restaurant in a majestic hotel**
1 Princes Street, Edinburgh, EH2 2EQ
Tel no: (0131) 5562414
www.restaurantnumberone.com
**Modern European | £58**
**Cooking score: 6**

If you arrive in Edinburgh at Waverley station, or just make a beeline for Princes Street, you'll find the Balmoral looming magnificently before you. The majestic clock tower sets the tone, the interiors have all the marbled and corniced splendour you can handle, and in Number One, with its comfortable opulence, the place has a star restaurant. Nor does the cooking simply stick to the tried and tested – it displays a nicely inventive impulse that maintains interest all the way through. Crab appears in two guises, as a mille-feuille of the white meat and a pannacotta of the brown, spiked with wasabi mayonnaise. Mains bring on good Scottish meats, such as venison and Borders beef, the latter presented with oxtail ravioli, squash purée and braised leeks, and choice seafood, such as a pairing of John Dory and langoustine in shellfish sauce, with a supporting cast of morels, asparagus and peas. Desserts keep up the pace with poached rhubarb, pistachio financier and honey parfait, or one of the hot soufflés (an Earl Grey version was a hit for one reader). Wines by the glass (from £8) and half-bottles head up a list that does France in comprehensive detail, including superb Burgundies from Olivier Leflaive, before lighting out elsewhere. Prices look tough, but undeniable quality prevails.

**Chef/s:** Craig Sandle. **Open:** all week D only 6.30 to 10. **Closed:** first 2 weeks Jan. **Meals:** Set D £57.50. Tasting menu £62.50. **Service:** 12.5% (optional). **Details:** Cards accepted. 50 seats. Air-con. Separate bar. No mobile phones. Wheelchair access. Music. Children allowed.

## Best value in Scotland

**Creel Restaurant, Dunbar** A sense of creativity runs through both set-price lunches and a good-value evening carte.

**David Bann, Edinburgh** A vegetarian restaurant with a keenly priced menu.

**The Dogs, Edinburgh** No-frills bistro where prices are a steal.

**The Colonsay, Scalasaig, Isle of Colonsay** Good food and good value just 100 metres from the ferry.

**Fins, Fairlie** The guarantee of excellent, seasonal fish and good lunch and dinner deals.

**La Vallée Blanche, Glasgow** Noted for keenly priced lunch and pre-theatre offers.

**The Doll's House, St Andrews** A straightforward, flexible cooking style at affordable prices.

**The Apron Stage, Stanley** Tiny 18-seater restaurant noted for its simple food and sensible prices.

**Crannog, Fort William** The two-course lunch is the deal to go for.

**Rocpool, Inverness** Lunch and early evening set meals are worth exploring.

## The Bonham

Oodles of über-cool Caledonian chic
35 Drumsheugh Gardens, Edinburgh, EH3 7RN
Tel no: (0131) 2747444
www.thebonham.com
**Modern European | £35**
Cooking score: 4

Fashioned from a Victorian town house, the Bonham is Caledonian chic personified and sets out its stall as a self-avowed, über-cool boutique hotel with a serious modern restaurant attached. Contemporary artwork and gigantic mirrors catch the eye in the fashionable dining room, where Brittany-born Michel Bouyer's food continues to impress. He fuses ideas from his home patch with modern European influences and a love of seasonal Scottish produce – witness roast breast of Hugh Grierson organic chicken with a ballottine of the leg, Stornoway black pudding, green pea risotto and salsify jus. Elsewhere, a mousse of East Lothian wild garlic is embellished with roasted snails and shallot cream, while butter-cooked halibut keeps company with herring egg caviar, buckwheat pancake and leek barigoule. To close the show, try the witty 'after dinner duo' (cappuccino mousse with Earl Grey ice cream and lemon confit) or the Bonham 'savoury sweet' (French-baked scone, vanilla pannacotta and mini cheese soufflé). Fifty wines start at £16.50.
**Chef/s:** Michel Bouyer. **Open:** all week L 12 to 2.30 (12.30 Sun), D 6.30 to 10. **Meals:** alc (main courses £15 to £50). Set L and D £13.50 (2 courses) to £16. **Service:** not inc. **Details:** Cards accepted. 48 seats. Wheelchair access. Music. Children allowed. Car parking.

# Café St Honoré

**Romantic Parisian charm**
34 NW Thistle Street Lane, Edinburgh, EH2 1EA
Tel no: (0131) 2262211
www.cafesthonore.com
**French | £30**
**Cooking score: 3**

A slice of *fin de siècle* France hidden away down a quirky little lane in New Town, Café St Honoré is 'doing well' and the new team has settled easily into its stride. The place still drips romantic Parisian charm with its soft jazz, candlelight and mirrors, although the food has evolved of late. These days, the kitchen also supports Scottish producers, buys organic where possible and takes on board influences from the Mediterranean. Ballottine of chicken with lyonnaise potatoes and Borders beef bourguignon now share the limelight with pearl barley, butternut squash and goats' cheese risotto or wild sea bass with squid ink linguine, herb oil and mussel cream. After that, don't be surprised to see Yorkshire rhubarb and almond trifle alongside tarte Tatin. The global wine list starts with French house selections from £16 (£4.75 a glass).
**Chef/s:** Ben Radford. **Open:** all week L 12 to 2.15, D 5.30 to 10 (6 Sat and Sun). **Closed:** 24 to 26 Dec, 31 Dec to 2 Jan. **Meals:** alc (main courses £14 to £24). Set L and D £15 (2 courses) to £19.50. **Service:** 10% (optional). **Details:** Cards accepted. 40 seats. Air-con. Wheelchair access. Music. Children allowed.

# Centotre

**Buzzing all-day Italian caffè**
103 George Street, Edinburgh, EH2 3ES
Tel no: (0131) 2251550
www.centotre.com
**Italian | £28**
**Cooking score: 2**

£5 OFF  V  £30

Readers have certainly warmed to Victor and Carina Contini's 'trendy but truly Italian' caffè/bar/deli in a converted banking hall: they love its infectious fun atmosphere, clued-up service, reasonable prices and 'steadily reliable' food. All the classics are here, from fresh pasta

(aubergine-stuffed ravioli with Sicilian sugo), inventively topped pizzas and salads of every description, to artisan Lombardy cheeses and luscious homemade gelati. The menu also promises robust platefuls of chargrilled piccante sausages with cabbage, potato and pancetta stew, corn-fed chicken with garlic, rosemary and white wine, and bowls of steamed Shetland mussels and clams spiked with chilli. The food is matched by a 'fantastic' selection of pedigree regional Italian wines from £14.95.
**Chef/s:** Carina Contini. **Open:** Mon to Sat 7.30am to 10pm (11pm Fri and Sat). Sun 11 to 8. **Meals:** alc (main courses £7 to £22). Set L £13.95 (2 courses and glass of wine). Sun L £14.95. **Service:** not inc. **Details:** Cards accepted. 146 seats. 40 seats outside. Air-con. Separate bar. Wheelchair access. Music. Children allowed.

# David Bann

**Vibrant veggie food and good puds**
56-58 St Mary's Street, Edinburgh, EH1 1SX
Tel no: (0131) 5565888
www.davidbann.co.uk
**Vegetarian | £21**
**Cooking score: 2**

 V £30

Just off the Royal Mile, in Edinburgh's old town, David Bann's vegetarian restaurant offers sexily lit surroundings – and a menu that will prove exotically diverting to both veggies and meat eaters. Dishes are described in detail: roasted squash, pine nut and basil ravioli with homemade organic curd cheese and herb oil might preface udon noodles with pak choi, shiitake mushrooms and home-smoked tofu, in a sauce of red pepper, ginger, garlic, lime, chilli, soy, mirin and coriander. And topped with mooli. Oh, and cucumber. It all represents a vibrant, healthily inventive approach to flesh-free cooking. To finish, expect conventionally luscious desserts like dark chocolate soufflé with vanilla ice cream and white chocolate sauce. A thoughtfully chosen wine list with good notes opens with Argentinian Viognier and Cabernet Sauvignon at £12.50.

**Chef/s:** David Bann. **Open:** all week L 11 to 5, D 5 to 10 (10.30 Sat and Sun). **Closed:** 25 and 26 Dec, 1 and 2 Jan. **Meals:** alc (main courses £10 to £13). **Service:** not inc. **Details:** Cards accepted. 80 seats. Air-con. Separate bar. No music. Wheelchair access. Children allowed.

★ BEST VALUE RESTAURANT ★

**NEW ENTRY**

# The Dogs

**Buzzy bistro for credit crunch times**
110 Hanover Street, Edinburgh, EH2 1DR
Tel no: (0131) 2201208
www.thedogsonline.co.uk
**Modern British | £17**
**Cooking score: 4**

**V**

The dogs of the name greet you downstairs, and there is a huge painting of a Golden Labrador behind the bar in one of the two upstairs dining rooms. Otherwise, this is a no-frills bistro with a clutter of dark tables and unmatched chairs. Menus are deceptively simple, prices a steal, and the atmosphere informal and relaxed. This is a vibrant place, buzzing with happy customers, and the food makes a great impact. Zingy soups are full of complex flavours and are accompanied by artisan bread. A seemingly unsophisticated wild mushroom risotto was found to be first-rate at inspection, while a main course of talapia (similar to red snapper) was 'pan-fried to perfection', pork belly was tender with a crispy skin, and tasty chicken breast was served with homemade skirlie and clapshot. This was followed by a 'heavenly' honey and lemon posset with homemade ginger biscuit. Wines start at £11.95.
**Chef/s:** James Scott and Jamie Ross. **Open:** all week L 12 to 4.30, D 5 to 10. **Closed:** 25 Dec, 1 Jan. **Meals:** alc (main courses £8 to £25). **Service:** not inc. **Details:** Cards accepted. 57 seats. No music. Children allowed.

# Forth Floor

**Open-plan foodie paradise**
Harvey Nichols, 30-34 St Andrews Square, Edinburgh, EH2 2AD
Tel no: (0131) 5248350
www.harveynichols.co.uk
**Modern European | £35**
**Cooking score: 3**

All branches of Harvey Nichols name their restaurant after the floor it occupies. This being Edinburgh, they called it the Forth Floor and the 'gorgeous views' take in most of the city. It's a flexible set-up, with a bar, all-day brasserie dealing in classics such as Caesar salad and Toulouse sausage with potato salad, and a more formal restaurant open for lunch and dinner. The latter is 'comfortable and relaxed', serving food that appeals for its honesty and simplicity – starters include Cullen skink and grilled red mullet with aubergine caviar and braised baby fennel. Variety is ensured at main course stage with roasts of lamb chump or venison loin alongside baked North Sea turbot with salt cod fritters. True to Harvey Nicks' reputation, the Forth Floor wine list is a star turn. In-form and in-vogue producers are given full rein (no tired old has-beens here) and there's a fabulous choice from around the globe. Prices can hit the roof, although the smart money is on the own-label house selections (from £17.50) and swanky choice by the glass.
**Chef/s:** Stuart Muir. **Open:** all week L 12 to 3 (3.30 Sat and Sun), Tue to Sat D 6 to 10. **Closed:** 25 Dec, 1 Jan. **Meals:** alc (main courses £17 to £26). Set L £28.50 (2 courses) to £34.50. Set D £32.50 (2 courses) to £39. **Service:** 10% (optional). **Details:** Cards accepted. 60 seats. 10 seats outside. Air-con. Separate bar. Wheelchair access. Music. Children allowed. Car parking.

# La Garrigue

**The flavour of Languedoc**
31 Jeffrey Street, Edinburgh, EH1 1DH
Tel no: (0131) 5573032
www.lagarrigue.co.uk
French | £28
Cooking score: 3
£5 OFF  £30

Jean-Michel Gauffre presents his native Languedoc dishes in an informal setting best described as reinvented rustic: attractive, tactile tables and chairs are by the late sculptor and furniture maker Tim Stead. No attempt is made to shock with outrageous ingredients: fish soup or smoked ham shank terrine with a spicy lentil dressing might be followed by slow-cooked pork belly with braised chicory and pumpkin mash or a rich casserole of shin of beef in red wine. The cooking suits the tone of the place, robust and rustic, and certainly draws a loyal following. Desserts are straightforward and well crafted (lavender crème brûlée, chocolate parfait), the set lunch menu good value and the compact wine list focuses on the Languedoc, with prices from £14.50.
**Chef/s:** Jean-Michel Gauffre. **Open:** Mon to Sat L 12 to 2.30, D 6.30 to 9.30. **Closed:** Sun, 1 week Jan. **Meals:** Set L £13.50 (2 courses) to £15.50. Set D £24.50 (2 courses) to £28. **Service:** 10% (optional). **Details:** Cards accepted. 45 seats. Air-con. Wheelchair access. Children allowed. Car parking.

# Haldanes at The Albany

**Edinburgh favourite comes home**
39A Albany Street, Edinburgh, EH1 3QY
Tel no: (0131) 5568407
www.haldanesrestaurant.com
Modern British | £28
Cooking score: 3
£5 OFF  £30

Haldanes looks comfortable and relaxed after moving back to its original home in the light basement of the Albany Hotel. It's a surprisingly modern affair, intimate yet unstuffy and genuinely friendly. A cosy lounge bar offers leather sofas and tub chairs to match the high-back versions in the dining area, where beige and brown tones provide the backdrop for Jack Vettriano prints. Prime Scottish ingredients are the culinary springboard for fixed-priced menus that mix classics such as Cullen skink with more modern ideas like baked fillet of halibut in a clam, mussel and crayfish broth, or roast loin of pork accompanied by a pork and foie gras sausage roll, spring cabbage and pomme purée. Classic French vintages and gluggable regional selections loom large on the thoughtfully assembled wine list. Enticing labels are much in evidence, with South Africa and California also making valuable contributions. House selections start at £16.
**Chef/s:** George Kelso. **Open:** Tue to Fri L 12 to 1.45, all week D 5 to 9. **Closed:** 24 and 25 Dec, 2 and 3 Jan. **Meals:** Set L £10 (2 courses) to £15. Set D £22.75 (2 courses) to £27.75. **Service:** not inc. **Details:** Cards accepted. 50 seats. Separate bar. No music. No mobile phones. Children allowed.

# Kalpna

**Indian vegetarian champion**
2-3 St Patrick Square, Edinburgh, EH8 9EZ
Tel no: (0131) 6679890
www.kalpnarestaurant.com
Indian Vegetarian | £19
Cooking score: 2
£5 OFF  V  £30

Now into its third decade, Ajay Bhartdwaj's revitalised restaurant remains one of the true champions of Indian vegetarian cooking and a 'recurring favourite' with readers. The menu offers a highly distinctive cocktail of dishes drawn from Gujarat, South India and Rajasthan, so expect a creative mix of the familiar and the esoteric. Pakoras, dhosas and bhindi masala share the billing with specialities such as saam savera (spinach leaves wrapped around homemade paneer, saffron, ginger and vegetables) and signature dam aloo kashmiri (stuffed potato 'barrels' with two contrasting sauces). Lunch is a buffet and thalis are excellent value. Drink mango lassi, beer or the house wine (£11.75).

**Chef/s:** Ajay Bhartdwaj. **Open:** Mon to Sat L 12 to 2, all week D 5.30 to 10.30 (6 to 10 Sun). **Closed:** 25 and 26 Dec, 1 Jan. **Meals:** alc (main courses £6 to £11). Set L £7 (2 courses) to £8. Set D £13.50. **Service:** 10% (optional). **Details:** Cards accepted. 50 seats. Air-con. Music. Children allowed.

## The Kitchin

**Waterfront star**
78 Commercial Quay, Leith, Edinburgh, EH6 6LX
Tel no: (0131) 5551755
www.thekitchin.com
**Modern European | £55**
**Cooking score: 6**

Amid the hive of activity that is the Leith development, it's not easy for individual restaurants to stand out – yet that is what Kitchin's has managed since opening in 2006. Housed in what was once a whisky distillery, it faces the maritime piazza and chic waterfront dwellings, and has a sexy atmosphere of subdued lighting. The food is modern Scottish, ingredients-led from best regional supply lines. But a French accent is noticeable in the willingness to use the kinds of raw materials others shy away from: crispy pig's ear turns up in a salad to accompany an array of roasted Anstruther langoustines, with boned and rolled pig's head to boot. The game season produced superbly cooked woodcock for one reporter, innards and all. Those looking for a less challenging way through the menu might opt for pressed leek terrine with hazelnut and Jerusalem artichoke dressing to begin, followed by seared Eymouth sea bass, served with potato purée in a white wine sauce given point with grain mustard and clams. Sea buckthorn berries are an item you may not have expected to find on the dessert menu, but there they are in a sorbet with spiced chocolate gâteau. The cooking is done justice by an artfully composed wine list, French-weighted but with much else besides. Wines by the glass, from £8, are brilliant.
**Chef/s:** Tom Kitchin. **Open:** Tue to Sat 12.30 to 1.45 (2 Fri and Sat), D 6.45 to 10 (10.30 Fri and Sat). **Closed:** Sun, Mon, 21 Dec to 13 Jan, 1 week July.

**Meals:** alc (main courses £24 to £34). Set L £24.50 (3 courses). Set D £45.50 (2 courses) to £54.50. Tasting menu £60. **Service:** not inc. **Details:** Cards accepted. 50 seats. Air-con. Separate bar. No mobile phones. Wheelchair access. Music. Children allowed. Car parking.

## Plumed Horse

**Small restaurant wins big praise**
50-54 Henderson Street, Edinburgh, EH6 6DE
Tel no: (0131) 5545556
www.plumedhorse.co.uk
**Modern European | £32**
**Cooking score: 5**

A small-scale restaurant with big ideas, Tony Borthwick's Plumed Horse is perhaps 'not in the best location in Leith' but it is certainly on song according to this year's crop of reports. Visitors have praised the 'well-prepared and well-presented food, with fresh local ingredients', the 'friendly and attentive' staff, the fact that tables are 'not too close together', and that the chef circulates 'for comments'. The menu formats are simple: fixed-price for lunch and dinner. High-quality, native ingredients are at the core of a culinary philosophy that draws inspiration from far and wide to come up with starters of ravioli of smoked salmon with capers, sweetcorn purée, smoked salmon and passion fruit oil, and main courses of sautéed loin of lamb with slow-poached shoulder and spinach mousse crepinette, spring root vegetables, pearl barley with lamb jus. And to finish there might be hot banana soufflé with toffee ice cream. Nine wines by the glass – carefully chosen to suit the food – open the wine list (from £5). There's a good half-bottle selection, and the rest is a varied assortment with plenty of easy-drinking bottles at reasonable prices. House wine is £18.
**Chef/s:** Tony Borthwick. **Open:** Tue to Sat L 12 to 1.30, D 7 to 9. **Closed:** Sun, Mon, 25 and 26 Dec, 2 weeks July. **Meals:** Set L £23. Set D £30 and £43. **Service:** not inc. **Details:** Cards accepted. 36 seats. Air-con. No mobile phones. Wheelchair access. Music.

## Restaurant Martin Wishart

**The jewel in the crown**
54 The Shore, Leith, Edinburgh, EH6 6RA
Tel no: (0131) 5533557
www.martin-wishart.co.uk
**Modern French | £60**
**Cooking score: 8**

🍷 V

'Sometimes when you eagerly anticipate a meal in a restaurant many people have recommended, the actual experience disappoints. Not in this case: the food we ate at lunch was truly outstanding.' Verdicts like this are what successful restauraureuring is all about – raising the bar and still clearing it. That couple's lunch included a 'terrific' lobster ravioli with pig's trotter, followed by great John Dory, and will live as long in their memories as some of the almost equally spectacular Edinburgh theatre they saw. The Leith development area is a thriving hub of great eating, and isn't too far from the city centre. The undoubted jewel in the crown is Martin Wishart's place. First-timers may be surprised by the understated décor of pale coffee, light wood and mirrored pillars, which does nothing to announce the culinary fireworks. Dishes that don't sound especially promising in the description turn out to be triumphs of culinary judgment – a reporter who risked starting with the ceviche of halibut cured in mango and passion fruit declared: 'I could have eaten it again and again.' Nor are we confined only to the prime cuts and no-brainers. A veal dish brings together kidney, tongue and sweetbreads with cabbage in an armagnac jus, accompanied by the signature potato mousseline enriched with pungently delicious Epoisses (unpasteurised cows' cheese). Confit cod in olive oil is earthily partnered with sautéed snails, Jerusalem artichoke and a jus given depth with Périgord truffle. Desserts aim for lightness rather than a cholesterol *coup de grâce*, but ideas are still good, as in assiette of rhubarb and yoghurt with ginger beer sorbet and a lemongrass sauce. A wine list to beat the band is excellent in France, and only marginally less impressive outside Europe. Hearteningly, it's easier to get change from £30 than you might anticipate. Only a little more, and a wealth of opulent choice open up. There's also a good spread by the glass, from £5.50.
**Chef/s:** Martin Wishart. **Open:** Tue to Sat L 12 to 2.30, D 6.30 to 9.30. **Closed:** Mon, 25 and 26 Dec, 2 weeks Jan. **Meals:** Set L £24.50 (3 courses). Tasting menu £60 to £65. **Service:** not inc. **Details:** Cards accepted. 48 seats. No mobile phones. Wheelchair access. Music. Children allowed.

## Rhubarb at Prestonfield

**Decadent dining at a romantic hotel**
Prestonfield House, Priestfield Road, Edinburgh, EH16 5UT
Tel no: (0131) 2251333
www.prestonfield.com
**Modern European | £50**
**Cooking score: 4**

🛏 V

A no-expense-spared makeover has transformed historic Prestonfield House (once home to the city's Lord Provost) into one of Edinburgh's most romantic hotel destinations, and it comes complete with a suitably dramatic restaurant. Rhubarb occupies two opulently restored Regency rooms resplendent with dusky, exotic colour schemes, exquisite drapes and extravagant floral displays – plus parkland views from its windows. The kitchen makes its own luxurious contribution, delivering food that mixes contemporary eclecticism with some old-world classics. Hand-dived scallops with Ibérico de Bellota, quince and macadamia nuts puts down a challenging marker, ahead of braised haunch and roast loin of Glen Almond roe deer with pistachio, smoked garlic and sweet potato – although you could play safe with lemon sole meunière or lamb cutlets Reform with mint hollandaise. Intricate desserts naturally find room for rhubarb in various clever forms; otherwise you might finish with gingerbread-and-butter pudding, orange curd, cardamom ice cream and white chocolate flake. House wine at £21 opens an encyclopaedic list.

Chef/s: John McMahon. Open: all week L 12 to 2 (3 Sat and Sun), D 6 to 10 (11 Fri and Sat). Meals: alc (main courses £12 to £33). Set L £16.95 (2 courses) to £30. Set D £25 (2 courses) to £30. Service: not inc. Details: Cards accepted. 90 seats. 20 seats outside. Separate bar. Wheelchair access. Music. Children allowed. Car parking.

## Valvona & Crolla Caffè Bar

**Edinburgh's foodie Godfather**
19 Elm Row, Edinburgh, EH7 4AA
Tel no: (0131) 5566066
www.valvonacrolla.com
Italian | £20
Cooking score: 3

£5 OFF  V  £30

A visit to the Contini family's seminal delicatessen is 'an education in itself' according to one fan, but there's much more to this remarkable enterprise than food shopping. Born in 1934, it has progressed 'from market stall to dotcom' and is now famed for its vintage décor, exceptional wines and robust Italian cooking. Call in at any time for stuzzichini nibbles, 'sandwiches' made from hand-crafted panetella bread or a plate of antipasti; otherwise make a meal of it with lunch. Pizzas and salads support a daily line-up that might include pennette with smoked salmon in a parsley sauce spiked with vodka, followed by grilled wild boar chops with baby new potatoes and grilled treviso. For afters, specially imported Milanese ice creams are a must; otherwise try pistachio polenta cake. V&C's dazzling array of Italian regional wines is second to none in Scotland, and you can pick any bottle from their full line-up at retail price (plus £6 corkage). House wines start at £12.45. The Continis also run the VinCaffè in Multrees Walk shopping complex, tel no: (0131) 557 0088.

Chef/s: Pina Trano. Open: Mon to Sat 8.30am to 6 (8am to 6.30 Fri and Sat), Sun 10.30 to 4. Closed: 25 and 26 Dec, 1 and 2 Jan. Meals: alc (main courses £10 to £15). Service: not inc. Details: Cards accepted. 86 seats. Air-con. Separate bar. No mobile phones. Wheelchair access. Music. Children allowed.

## The Vintners Rooms

**Leith's living history**
The Vaults, 87 Giles Street, Leith, Edinburgh, EH6 6BZ
Tel no: (0131) 5546767
www.thevintnersrooms.com
French | £35
Cooking score: 4

A stunning monument to Leith's historic wine trade and a romantic destination *par excellence*, the Vintners Rooms is perfectly placed above the old cellars on Giles Street. The main restaurant is seductively secreted in the original auction room – a historically charged space full of chandeliers, candles and cherubs, hand-worked stucco and mighty stone fireplaces. By contrast, the kitchen's heart is in France, although it peps up its endeavours with some warm Mediterranean tones. A 'trilogie' of foie gras or seafood en croûte with wild rocket and Parmesan could give way to rack of lamb with aubergine caviar or Dover sole meunière with olive oil crushed potatoes, while desserts run to crêpes Suzette or chocolate fondant with pistachio ice cream. The stylishly updated bistro area (complete with a swanky zinc bar and oriental rugs) is now open throughout the day for drinks and light dishes. Needless to say, the wine list is a treasure trove – with not a cobweb in sight. Lovers of vintage French and patrician Italian drinking are in for a treat, but exciting modern labels also make their presence felt. House selections are £18.50 (£4.50 a glass).

Chef/s: Patrice Ginestrière. Open: Tue to Sat L 12 to 2, D 7 to 10. Closed: Sun, Mon, 26 Dec to 7 Jan. Meals: alc (main courses £15 to £30). Service: not inc. Details: Cards accepted. 64 seats. Separate bar. Wheelchair access. Music. Children allowed. Car parking.

### Average price

The average price listed in main-entry reviews denotes the price of a three-course meal, without wine.

# Witchery by the Castle

**Hubble bubble...**
Castlehill, Royal Mile, Edinburgh, EH1 2NF
Tel no: (0131) 2255613
www.thewitchery.com
**Modern British | £42**
Cooking score: 2

There's more than a suggestion of Gothic theatricality about this atmospheric sixteenth-century building on Edinburgh's Royal Mile. Dramatic tapestries, flowing drapes and flickering candles set the tone in the lavish restaurant – or you can eat in the Secret Garden room. Recent reports have cited a few lapses in the kitchen – especially with the handling of vegetables – but the cooking is generally sound. Smoked Loch Etive eel with Argyll heritage potato salad and horseradish cream has been applauded, likewise brioche bread-and-butter pudding with caramelised apple and puff-candy ice cream. In between, expect the likes of corn-fed duck breast and confit leg with foie gras bonbon, buttered black cabbage and quince jelly. The immense 1,000-bin wine list is an extraordinarily diverse collection with very 'tolerable' mark ups. Prices start at £17.50.

**Chef/s:** Douglas Roberts. **Open:** all week L 12 to 4, D 5.30 to 11.30. **Closed:** 25 and 26 Dec. **Meals:** alc (main courses £15 to £34). Set L and D £12.95 (2 courses) to £30. **Service:** not inc. **Details:** Cards accepted. 100 seats. Air-con. No mobile phones. Music.

## ALSO RECOMMENDED

### ▲ Fishers Bistro

1 Shore, Leith, Edinburgh, EH6 6QW
Tel no: (0131) 5545666
**Seafood**

Sited on the harbour-front in thriving Leith, the white-fronted Fishers has evolved from being a seafood speciality restaurant to offering locally reared meat and game too. With a sister establishment in the city, it has a solid fanbase for dishes such as tempura skate wing with preserved lemon tartare (£5.50),

and main courses like sea trout on wilted spinach with a soft-boiled egg, roasted red peppers and hollandaise (£14.95) or duck leg confit with chilli-roasted sweet potatoes and tamarind sauce. Desserts include the likes of black cherry frangipane or chocolate and brandy truffle cake, both with cream or ice cream (£4.30). Wines on an extensive list start at £12.95. Open all week.

## ▌Gullane

# La Potinière

**Consistently outstanding**
34 Main Street, Gullane, EH31 2AA
Tel no: (01620) 843214
www.la-potiniere.co.uk
**Modern British | £40**
Cooking score: 6

La Potinière has been a fixture of the *Guide* for a good many years, but when Mary Runciman and Keith Marley took over this singular-looking grey-stone house in 2002 they raised the bar even higher with their innovative cooking. Readers continue to be impressed with every detail of the set-up, from the 'friendly, informative and timely service' to the 'excellent' wine and food. As a kitchen double act, Mary and Keith succeed in blending fabulous Scottish produce with refined technique to deliver precise, uncluttered dishes in the contemporary idiom. Expect a 'burst of intense flavours' from specialities such as Parmesan- and parsley-crusted halibut with smoked mussel, chive and tomato risotto and a Noilly Prat sauce. Simplicity is the key to their refreshing short menus, which might run from starters of fennel mousse with orange and fennel salad via loin and haunch of roe deer with damson gin sauce to warm chocolate pudding with raspberry compote. Wines start at £16.

**Chef/s:** Mary Runciman and Keith Marley. **Open:** Wed to Sun L 12.30 to 1.30, D 7 to 8.30. **Closed:** Mon, Tue, Christmas, 3 weeks Jan. **Meals:** Set L £18.50 (2 courses) to £22.50. Set D £40. **Service:** not inc. **Details:** Cards accepted. 30 seats. No music. No mobile phones. Wheelchair access. Children allowed. Car parking.

## ▌Linlithgow

### Champany Inn

Aberdeen Angus reigns
Champany Corner, Linlithgow, EH49 7LU
Tel no: (01506) 834532
www.champany.com
British | £55
Cooking score: 3

Steak is king at the Champany Inn, and prime Aberdeen Angus has reigned here for more than 25 years. The Davidsons have turned what was a collection of sixteenth-century farm buildings clustered around a horse-driven flour mill into a destination for aficionados of well-hung, chargrilled slabs of class-A animal protein. However, if a butchered-to-order, three-week T-bone, porterhouse or ribeye isn't your bag, perhaps thick-cut double lamb chops, lobster or organic cod and chips will do the trick. The main event is preceded by specialities from Champany's own 'smokepot' and a few Scottish-hued starters (Brechin black pudding with rösti or West Coast scallops with truffled celeriac purée). Quality is second to none across the board, but it involves serious financial outlay; if something more wallet-friendly is required, head for the adjoining Chop & Ale House. The food keeps regal company with a breathtaking, 600-bin wine list that runs from rarefied French classics and Spanish treasures to an unrivalled cornucopia of South African gems personally selected by Clive Davidson and his sommelier. Own-label Cape selections start at £18.50.
**Chef/s:** Clive Davidson. **Open:** Mon to Fri L 12 to 2, Mon to Sat D 6.30 to 10. **Closed:** Sun, 25 and 26 Dec, 1 and 2 Jan. **Meals:** alc (main courses £28 to £42). Set L £19.50 (2 courses). Set D £39. **Service:** 10%. **Details:** Cards accepted. 50 seats. 25 seats outside. Separate bar. No music. No mobile phones. Wheelchair access. Car parking.

## ▌South Queensferry

NEW ENTRY
### The Boat House

Splendid location on the River Forth
22 High Street, South Queensferry, EH30 9PP
Tel no: (0131) 3315429
www.theboathouse-sq.co.uk
Seafood | £30
Cooking score: 3

It's easy to miss this place on the cobbled street of South Queensferry. But go past the ground-floor deli and descend into the bowels of the building and you will find the two sparkling white rooms that constitute the restaurant, complete with magnificent views. The main emphasis is on fish, sourced from all over Scotland and beyond, but there's fillet steak Café de Paris, too. Simple treatment of the seafood shows off its freshness, whether queen scallops in garlic butter or wild Scottish halibut with herb hollandaise. Finish off with a sticky toffee pudding. Wines from £13.95.
**Chef/s:** Paul Steward. **Open:** Sat and Sun L 12 to 2.30, all week D 5.30 to 10. **Meals:** alc (main courses £16 to £23). **Service:** not inc. **Details:** Cards accepted. 45 seats. Children allowed.

## ALSO RECOMMENDED

### ▲ Dakota Forth Bridge

Ferrymuir Retail Park, South Queensferry, EH30 9QZ
Tel no: (0870) 4234293
www.dakotahotels.co.uk
Seafood

This black glass-plated monolith is located on the outskirts of Edinburgh. The minimalist Grill majors in carefully sourced seafood ranging from crispy monkfish cheeks with tartare sauce (£7.50) and crab linguine (£12.50) to sharing platters of roasted shellfish in wild garlic butter. Chargrilled steaks, lamb curry and spring vegetable risotto assuage other palates, while desserts might run to pavlova with rhubarb jelly and custard (£6.50). House wine is £15.95. Open all week.

# Annbank

## Enterkine Country House

**Relaxed intimacy and cosseted dining**
Annbank, KA6 5AL
Tel no: (01292) 520580
www.enterkine.com
**Modern European | £45**
**Cooking score: 4**

From the moment you meander along the avenue of mature trees leading up to Enterkine House, you can tell that this pristine 1930s residence is run with the relaxed intimacy of a family home rather than a formal country hotel. The cosseted mood shines through in the dining room, which has the bonus of appetising views over the River Ayr. The kitchen uses carefully sourced Scottish ingredients, and the menu could feature anything from hand-dived Kintyre Bay scallops to Blackface lamb from Castle Douglas. Terrine of veal cheeks with Buccleuch oxtail and shallot jam makes a rich, unctuous opener, while mains might feature breast of red-legged partridge partnered by a seasonal contingent of Savoy cabbage purée, celeriac, organic parsnips and girolles. Desserts also show plenty of complexity – witness a combo of caramelised fig and honey parfait with toffee sauce, nougatine wafer, bee pollen and Agen prunes. The global wine list opens with house recommendations at £21.50.

**Chef/s:** Paul Moffat. **Open:** all week, L 12.30 to 2, D 7 to 9. **Meals:** Set L £16.50 (2 courses) to £18.50. Set D midweek £30, Set D weekend £45. Sun L £25. **Service:** not inc. **Details:** Cards accepted. 40 seats. No mobile phones. Music. Children allowed. Car parking.

### Readers recommend

A 'readers recommend' review is a genuine quote from a report sent in by one of our readers. We intend to follow up these suggestions throughout the year to come.

## Ballantrae
### Glenapp Castle
**Confident cooking in baronial splendour**
Ballantrae, KA26 0NZ
Tel no: (01465) 831212
www.glenappcastle.com
**Modern British | £55**
**Cooking score: 6**

£5 OFF 🛏

Glenapp Castle is a fine example of Scottish baronial splendour – all turrets and castellated walls – with glorious views across the Ayrshire coast to Ailsa Craig, Arran and the Mull of Kintyre. Within, well-appointed public rooms have a comfortable country house feel, and staff create a welcoming atmosphere that's anything but uptight. In the kitchen a clear sense of purpose is evident. Adam Stokes' daily changing six-course dinners run along a clear format, with choice only at main course and dessert stage. He combines local produce and a few luxuries with contemporary ideas. These prime ingredients are then handled with due confidence and care, with dishes such as smoked ham hock tortellini with pea purée and an Arran mustard sauce, and beef fillet with a truffle and foie gras cromesquis, braised onions and a red wine sauce showing creative use of traditional ingredients. The cooking of fish has been praised, and the consensus of readers is that 'the soufflés are a perfect dessert'. Hot chocolate fondant with Galliano and banana ice cream and bee pollen is an interesting idea. The wine list covers most bases (from £25) and there is a good selection by the glass.
**Chef/s:** Adam Stokes. **Open:** all week L 12.30 to 2.30, D 7 to 10. **Closed:** Christmas, 2 Jan to mid Mar. **Meals:** Set L £35. Set D £55 (6 courses). **Service:** not inc. **Details:** Cards accepted. 34 seats. No music. No mobile phones. Wheelchair access. Car parking.

**Also recommended**

Also recommended entries are not scored but we think they are worth a visit.

## Carradale
### Dunvalanree
**Home-from-home with local flavours**
Port Righ, Carradale, PA28 6SE
Tel no: (01583) 431226
www.dunvalanree.com
**Modern British | £26**
**Cooking score: 2**

£5 OFF 🛏 £30

The 'long and winding road' that leads to the door of Dunvalanree House is actually the B842, and it brings visitors to the Milsteads' home-from-home on the honeypot Mull of Kintyre. Alan plays host while Alyson cooks with honest intent and an eye for local produce. There's nothing flash about her food, but natural flavours are allowed to work their magic in dishes such as seared Kilbrannan scallops with coriander and lime, rack of Ifferdale lamb or fillet of Kintyre venison on celeriac mash with red wine sauce. Desserts could include crème brûlée with raspberries, or the more satisfyingly calorific hot chocolate cake, soused in a chocolate and Drambuie sauce. The wine list was about to change as we went to press, but expect sound drinking from around £14.
**Chef/s:** Alyson Milstead. **Open:** all week D only 7.30 (1 sitting). **Closed:** Christmas. **Meals:** Set D £22 (2 courses) to £26. **Service:** not inc. **Details:** Cards accepted. 20 seats. No mobile phones. Wheelchair access. Music. Children allowed. Car parking.

## Crinan
### Crinan Hotel, Westward
**Unbeatable location**
Crinan, PA31 8SR
Tel no: (01546) 830261
www.crinanhotel.com
**Modern European | £25**
**Cooking score: 3**

🛏 £30

The white-painted, family-run hotel perches on the coast opposite the Isle of Jura and has been part of this small fishing hamlet for more than two centuries. Nick and Francis Ryan are rightly proud of their materials, especially seafood: Loch Crinan jumbo prawns landed just a couple of hours earlier, locally caught lemon sole, and venison from Jura. There have been changes in the kitchen this year, with long-standing sous chef Gregor Barra stepping up to the plate, and recent reports have been mixed. Dinner continues to be a set-price, four-course affair with organic chicken liver parfait with Cumberland sauce a typical start, and sabayon of fresh berries a light finish. A well-chosen wine list opens at £15.50.

**Chef/s:** Gregor Bara. **Open:** all week L 12 to 2.30, D 6 to 8.30. **Closed:** 23 to 28 Dec. **Meals:** alc (main courses £10 to £24). Set D £45 (4 courses). **Service:** not inc. **Details:** Cards accepted. 50 seats. 20 seats outside. Separate bar. No music. Wheelchair access. Children allowed. Car parking.

## ▌Dalry
## Braidwoods
**Precision, deep flavours, flawless food**
Drumastle Mill Cottage, Dalry, KA24 4LN
Tel no: (01294) 833544
www.braidwoods.co.uk
**Modern British | £38**
**Cooking score: 6**

The atmosphere of homeliness is in evidence as soon as you roll up outside Keith and Nicola Braidwood's north Ayrshire restaurant. It occupies a pair of 200-year-old, low-roofed, whitewashed millers' cottages. Inside, the place has been smartly – but not intimidatingly – designed, with modern chairs and good tableware. Fixed-price menus are the drill, with two or three courses at lunch, and three or four at dinner. Start with whole boneless roasted quail stuffed with black pudding on spiced red cabbage compote or scallops from Wester Ross, divertingly accompanied by tomato and coriander dahl. The intermediate course at dinner might offer a choice of Parmesan tart or saffron-laced Arbroath smokie soup, before the evening proceeds with best end of local lamb with baby spinach or grilled turbot with green olive

tapenade on langoustine and leek risotto. The cooking throughout achieves a high order of precision, coaxing maximum depth of flavour from flawless raw materials, and it's all rounded off with the likes of caramelised rice pudding adorned with warm Agen prunes in Armagnac. House wines and a seasonally changing selection of specials head up a list that locates fine growers from all over western Europe and the southern hemisphere. Prices start at £19.95 (£4.50 a glass).

**Chef/s:** Keith Braidwood. **Open:** Wed to Sun L 12 to 1.30, Tue to Sat D 7 to 9. **Closed:** Mon, first 3 weeks Jan, first 2 weeks Sept. **Meals:** Set L £21 (2 courses) to £25. Set D £38. Sun L £27.50. **Service:** not inc. **Details:** Cards accepted. 24 seats. No music. No mobile phones. Wheelchair access. Children allowed. Car parking.

## ▌Fairlie
## Fins
**Simple, spanking-fresh fish**
Fencefoot Farm, Fairlie, KA29 0EG
Tel no: (01475) 568989
www.fencebay.co.uk
**Seafood | £27**
**Cooking score: 2**

£5 OFF  £30 ▼

The guarantee of excellent, seasonal fish, much of it from Jill and Bernard Thains' own boat, is a huge draw. Fresh raw materials – there is fillet steak for those who must – are treated in a straightforward manner. Three Cumbrae oysters served on ice or smoked salmon from their own smokehouse, followed by a generous lemon sole baked with a herb crust and served with citrus lemon butter, have proved that simple can be best. Both lunch and dinner menus are bolstered by blackboard specials, with straightforward desserts and a short, affordable wine list that complements the food well. Prices start at £14.50.

**Chef/s:** Jane Burns. **Open:** Tue to Sun L 12 to 2.30, Tue to Sat D 7 to 9. **Closed:** Mon, 25 and 26 Dec, 1 and 2 Jan. **Meals:** alc (main courses £11 to £26). Set L £12 (2 courses) to £17. Set D £15 (2 courses) to

£20. **Service:** not inc. **Details:** Cards accepted. 30 seats. 20 seats outside. No mobile phones. Wheelchair access. Music. Car parking.

## █ Glasgow

### An Lochan
**Livewire city eatery**
340 Crow Road, Glasgow, G11 7HT
Tel no: (0141) 3386606
www.anlochan.co.uk
**Seafood | £20**
**Cooking score: 1**
£5 OFF  £30 🍷

Following the success of their venture in Tighnabruaich (see entry), the McKies decided to spread the word among Glasgow's city crowd. Sourcing is all-important in this lively eatery, with much gleaned from the family's home base in Argyll. Seafood platters are a big hit, alongside anything from scallops wrapped in pancetta with black pudding mash to parsley-crusted lythe fillet with carrot purée. Meat fans might choose pheasant with pearl barley and chocolate risotto, while hazelnut parfait could close the show. House wine is £13.95. A third outlet is now open at Glendevon, Tormaukin, Perthshire, tel no: (01259) 781252.
**Chef/s:** Claire McKie. **Open:** Tue to Sun L 12 to 3, Tue to Sat D 6 to 9. **Closed:** Mon, 25 and 26 Dec, 1 and 2 Jan. **Meals:** alc (main courses £12 to £27). Set L £10.95 (2 courses) to £13.95. Set D £12.95 (2 courses) to £15.95. **Service:** not inc. **Details:** Cards accepted. 40 seats. 12 seats outside. No mobile phones. Wheelchair access. Music. Children allowed.

### Brian Maule at Chardon d'Or
**Gallic sensibility and Scottish produce**
176 West Regent Street, Glasgow, G2 4RL
Tel no: (0141) 2483801
www.brianmaule.com
**French | £40**
**Cooking score: 4**

The porticoed entrance to the elegant Victorian town house in the heart of Glasgow sets the tone. Starched napery and gleaming glassware also look the part, and there is an enveloping atmosphere of relaxation to the whole operation. At least for the diner, that is. French-trained Brian Maule is hard at work behind the scenes on a cuisine comprised of Gallic sensibility allied to quality Scottish produce. Isle of Skye scallops are teamed with aubergine caviar and chorizo as a curtain-raiser. Mains might showcase best beef sirloin with a serving of the braised cheek, simply garnished with creamy mash and red wine sauce. At dessert, classics such as crème brûlée share the billing with cinnamon parfait accompanied by spiced plums. The wine list offers a good balance of western European and southern hemisphere bottles, with plenty of pedigree growers and mature vintages. House wines start at £21.15.
**Chef/s:** Brian Maule. **Open:** Mon to Fri L 12 to 2, Mon to Sat D 6 to 10 (10.30 Sat). **Closed:** Sun, bank hols, 25 and 26 Dec, first 2 weeks Jan, 2 weeks Jul/Aug. **Meals:** alc (main courses £21 to £27). Set L and D £16.50 (2 courses) to £19.50. Tasting menu £55 (6 courses). **Service:** 10% (optional). **Details:** Cards accepted. 140 seats. Air-con. Separate bar. Music. Children allowed.

## Gamba

**Zesty modern seafood**
225a West George Street, Glasgow, G2 2ND
Tel no: (0141) 5720899
www.gamba.co.uk
**Seafood | £35**
**Cooking score: 3**

£5
OFF

Still going strong after 12 years, Alan Tompkins and Derek Marshall's basement restaurant is a lively space with a strong Mediterranean feel and informal atmosphere. The menu is almost exclusively seafood-based, with a couple of token meat offerings and little choice for vegetarians. It takes a zestful contemporary approach, coming up with a modern take on prawn cocktail (crayfish with Charentais melon, chilli jam and lemon), and delivering sashimi of tuna with wasabi, soy and pickled ginger. It also finds room for more straightforward things such as lemon sole simply grilled in browned lemon butter, or roast monkfish with stewed red cabbage, redcurrant and rosemary, as well as chocolate and orange custard for dessert. House wine is £16.
**Chef/s:** Derek Marshall. **Open:** Mon to Sat L 12 to 2.30, D 5 to 10.30. **Closed:** Sun, 25 and 26 Dec, 1 and 2 Jan. **Meals:** alc (main courses £13 to £28). Set L and pre-theatre £15.95 (2 courses) to £18.95.
**Service:** not inc. **Details:** Cards accepted. 66 seats. Air-con. Separate bar. No mobile phones. Music.

## Michael Caines at ABode Glasgow

**Trademark intricate food**
129 Bath Street, Glasgow, G2 2SZ
Tel no: (0141) 5726011
www.michaelcaines.com
**Modern European | £38**
**Cooking score: 5**

£5
OFF

Part of the ABode group of boutique hotels set up by Michael Caines and Andrew Brownsword (the AB of the title), this venture occupies what was the legendary Arthouse – a dazzling Edwardian building that was once home to prime minister Sir Edward Campbell-Bannerman. It's a complete package that includes a casual grill and late-night bar, although pride of place goes to the chic ground-floor restaurant. Day-to-day cooking is in the hands of Craig Dunn, but it's not difficult to spot Michael Caines' signature and thumbprint on the menu. A starter such as confit salmon with spinach and herb tortellini, herb purée and lavender cream sets the ambitious tone, before intricate mains of, say, cumin-poached pheasant with Puy lentils, leg confit, choucroute and baby onions. Fish also shows up impressively elsewhere – poached wild sea bass accompanied by scallop and truffle mousse, artichoke barigoule and carrot and coriander purée is suitably complex. As for dessert, there is much to delight in the shape of flambéed pear Tatin with clotted ice cream and ginger pear juice or coconut mousse with mango and pineapple compote and mango sorbet. A temperature-controlled wine 'cave' ensures the 100-bin wine list is kept in tip-top condition. Expect fine drinking across the range, with accommodating prices from £19.25 (£4.60 a glass).
**Chef/s:** Craig Dunn. **Open:** Tue to Sat L 12 to 2.30, D 6 to 10. **Closed:** Sun, Mon, first 2 weeks Jan, 2 weeks Jul. **Meals:** alc (main courses £20 to £23). Set L £12.95 (3 courses). Set D £19.95 (3 courses). Tasting menu £55 (7 courses). **Service:** 12% (optional). **Details:** Cards accepted. 44 seats. Air-con. No mobile phones. Wheelchair access. Music. Children allowed. Car parking.

## Stravaigin

**Consistently creative cooking**
28 Gibson Street, Glasgow, G12 8NX
Tel no: (0141) 3342665
www.stravaigin.com
**Global | £30**
**Cooking score: 2**

£5
OFF

A regular who praises the utter consistency of this Glasgow stalwart sums up the cooking as 'creative, flavourful and unique'. Against a backdrop of rough-cast stone walls and beamed ceilings, a setting of contemporary, light-touch elegance has been created. The menus make resourceful use of Scotland's larder – Shetland crab is teamed with a chilli-spiked sweet potato cake and minted tomato salsa as one way to begin, while the mains run from Thai-style seafood broth with rice noodles and sambal to tamari-glazed duck breast with sesame-roast yam and kimchi. To finish, a classic pannacotta or a fine international cheese selection. The carefully annotated wine list has glass prices from £3.65.

**Chef/s:** Daniel Blencowe. **Open:** Fri to Sun L 12 to 3.30 (2.30 Fri), all week D 5 to 11. **Closed:** 25 and 26 Dec, 1 Jan. **Meals:** alc (main courses £13 to £22). Set pre-theatre D £12.95 (2 courses) to £15.95. **Service:** not inc. **Details:** Cards accepted. 76 seats. Air-con. Separate bar. No mobile phones. Music. Children allowed.

---

**★ READERS' RESTAURANT OF THE YEAR ★**
**SCOTLAND**

# Ubiquitous Chip

**Still in fine fettle**
12 Ashton Lane, Glasgow, G12 8SJ
Tel no: (0141) 3345007
www.ubiquitouschip.co.uk
**British | £40**
**Cooking score: 4**

The Chip sails on, a Glasgow institution since 1971, still evolving and still in fine fettle. Down a cobbled lane in the heart of the West End, the place boasts four separate dining areas, including the covetable cobblestoned courtyard with mezzanine. Scotland's proud larder is the mainstay of Ian Brown's menus, which essay a broad sweep from peat-smoked Finnan haddie and lentil tart with rhubarb sauce as a robust opener, to mains such as Argyll venison, Perthshire pigeon and Orkney salmon. Lamb three ways was good in parts for one visitor, the flavour of the cheaper cuts – leg stuffed with mussels and some minced lamb in a bridie pie – impressing more than the loin. Desserts such as marmalade steamed pudding with whisky custard will

help to fill any holes. The magisterial wine list has always been one of the principal joys, with its global reach, superb growers and considerate price range. House wines start at £16.95, or £4.25 a glass.

**Chef/s:** Ian Brown. **Open:** all week L 12 to 2.30 (12.30 to 3 Sun), D 5 to 11 (6.30 Sun). **Closed:** 25 Dec, 1 Jan. **Meals:** Set L £23.85 (2 courses) to £29.85. Set D £34.85 (2 courses) to £39.85. **Service:** not inc. **Details:** Cards accepted. 190 seats. Air-con. Separate bar. No music. Wheelchair access. Children allowed.

# La Vallée Blanche

**Idiosyncratic bistro**
360 Byres Road, Glasgow, G12 8AY
Tel no: (0141) 3343333
www.lavalleeblanche.com
**French | £25**
**Cooking score: 3**

One of Glasgow's more divertingly styled restaurants, La Vallée Blanche is named in reference to its French ski resort ambience – no matter that it actually sits above a record store on Byres Road. Some decent modern bistro cooking is offered, in the form of starters such as tea-smoked salmon with vegetables à la grecque, quails' eggs and beetroot, and mains that might team Peterhead halibut with piquillo peppers, grilled courgettes, roasted tomatoes and olive oil or braised ox cheek with provençal pomme purée. It all seems to win people over in its idiosyncratic way, not least with desserts like hot banana soufflé served with gingerbread ice cream. A tiny, single-page listing of French wines makes choosing pretty straightforward. Prices start at £18.50, or £3.95 a glass.

**Chef/s:** Neil Clark. **Open:** Tue to Sun L 12 to 3 (4 Sat and Sun), D 5.30 to 10 (10.30 Sat and Sun). **Closed:** Mon, 25 and 26 Dec, 1 Jan. **Meals:** alc (main courses £11 to £23). Set L £9.95 (2 courses) to £12.95. Set pre-theatre D £12.50 (2 courses) to £14.95. Sun L £9.95 (2 courses) to £12.95. **Service:** not inc. **Details:** Cards accepted. 76 seats. Air-con. Music. Children allowed.

## READERS RECOMMEND

### The Left Bank

**Modern British**
33-35 Gibson Street, Glasgow, G12 8NU
Tel no: (0141) 3395969
www.theleftbank.co.uk
'Great all-day cafe, love the weekend brunch'

## Isle of Colonsay

### The Colonsay

Get away from it all...
Scalasaigh, Isle of Colonsay, PA61 7YP
Tel no: (01951) 200316
www.thecolonsay.com
**Modern British | £25**
**Cooking score: 2**

The remote island of Colonsay is 'a magical place', a real get-away-from-it-all idyll, so it's a surprise to find a boutique-style hotel just 100 metres from the ferry. The reworking of this eighteenth-century inn, with the bar serving as the island's hub, has been a huge success. The kitchen calls on island produce and their own garden-grown goodies as well as fish from local boats, and menus are kept within reasonable limits. Simple Colonsay crab with brown crab dressing makes a good start, then go on to cod with sorrel hollandaise and silver beet or a fricassee of chicken legs with lyonniase potatoes. House wine is £12.
**Chef/s:** James Gaskell. **Open:** all week L 12 to 2, D 6 to 9. **Closed:** Nov and Feb. **Meals:** alc (main courses £8 to £20). Set L £11.50 (2 courses) to £15.50. Set D £12.95 (2 courses) to £15. **Service:** not inc.
**Details:** Cards accepted. 60 seats. 30 seats outside. Separate bar. Wheelchair access. Children allowed. Car parking.

**Tom Kitchin** The Kitchin

**Who or what inspired you to become a chef?**
I'm not sure how it all began really, but growing up in the Scottish countryside and seeing first-hand the fantastic fare Scotland boasts was a big inspiration. My first job in the industry was in a local country pub and I still remember my excitement at the kitchen buzz – I think that was when I knew I really wanted to be a chef.

**Which chefs do you admire?**
My old chef Pierre Koffmann, who used to have La Tante Claire in London. He's retired now but he had three Michelin stars for 20 years. He trained Marco Pierre White and Gordon Ramsay and I trained with him too. Working for Pierre was tough, but it taught me so much and now he's a great friend and mentor.

**What is the best part of your job?**
I love sourcing the produce used for the restaurant: getting the first game and the first asparagus of the season ensures that I get the freshest, most seasonal produce for the restaurant. My suppliers are my most valued source of knowledge and have become an integral part of my team.

## Isle of Eriska
### Isle of Eriska Hotel
**Stunning island location**
Ledaig, Isle of Eriska, PA37 1SD
Tel no: (01631) 720371
www.eriska-hotel.co.uk
**British | £40**
**Cooking score: 4**
£5 OFF 🚗

Beppo and Chay Buchanan-Smith's hotel is in the Scottish Baronial style, standing on a 300-acre private island with its own vehicle-access bridge. Extravagant refurbishments have transformed the rather staid restaurant into a stylish, contemporary setting that 'now matches the excellent local food'. Robert MacPherson has been chef here since 1987, and his menus reflect a thorough knowledge of the surrounding area and its producers. Readers love the 'depth of flavours and elegance on the plate' of dishes such as Argyll lamb's neck ravioli with woodland mushroom and pumpkin risotto, roasted chervil root and garlic velouté, perhaps followed by saddle of West Highland venison with honey-braised red cabbage and skirlie gâteau, candied quince and rowan jelly jus. You could finish with mille-feuille of blood orange with liquorice-iced parfait. The hotel now has an impressive open cellar, displaying an international selection of wines priced from £13.
**Chef/s:** Robert MacPherson. **Open:** all week D only 8 to 9. **Closed:** 3 to 27 Jan. **Meals:** Set D £40. **Service:** not inc. **Details:** Cards accepted. 50 seats. Air-con. Separate bar. No music. No mobile phones. Wheelchair access. Children allowed. Car parking.

## Isle of Mull
**READERS RECOMMEND**
### Café Fish
**Seafood**
The Pier, Main Street, Torbermory, Isle of Mull, PA75 6NU
Tel no: (01688) 301253
www.thecafefish.com
'All fresh, and tastes amazing... honest, good food served with flair'

### Mediterranea
**Italian**
Aros, Salen, Isle of Mull, PA72 6JG
Tel no: (01680) 300200
'Excellent cooking by an Italian in Scotland'

## Maidens
**READERS RECOMMEND**
### Wildings
**Modern British**
Harbour Road, Maidens, KA26 9NR
Tel no: (01655) 331401
'Excellent food at a very reasonable cost'

## Oban
### Ee-Usk
**Straightforward seafood**
North Pier, Oban, PA34 5QD
Tel no: (01631) 565666
www.eeusk.com
**Seafood | £30**
**Cooking score: 1**

This harbourside restaurant fulfils its function as a contemporary eating house with a bright, eclectic feel and a flexible menu that plays seafood as its trump card. Mussels, langoustines, scallops and prawns are all locally caught; also expect Thai fish cakes and seafood pasta, even haddock and chips. There have been mixed reports this year citing a lack of attention to detail and offhand service especially in the busy summer months, but others love the 'magnificent views' and 'fabulous seafood'. House wine is £13.50.

**Chef/s:** Jane Scott. **Open:** all week L 12 to 3, D 6 to 9.30. **Closed:** 25 Dec, 26 Dec, 1 Jan. **Meals:** alc (main courses £12 to £20). **Service:** not inc. **Details:** Cards accepted. 106 seats. 20 seats outside. Air-con. No mobile phones. Wheelchair access. Music. Children allowed. Car parking.

## ALSO RECOMMENDED

### ▲ Waterfront
1 The Railway Pier, Oban, PA34 4LW
Tel no: (01631) 563110
www.waterfrontoban.co.uk
**Seafood**

Housed in what was once a seamen's mission, this west coast restaurant offers a seafood-based menu showcasing the best of the Argyll haul. Local mussels are served in tomato, garlic and chilli (£6.95), and might be followed by pesto-grilled salmon with crab spring rolls and basmati rice (£9.95), or grilled haddock with leek mash and Cheddar glaze (£9.95), but there's Highland venison and braised beef too. Finish with chocolate marquise and winter fruit compote (£4.50). Wines from £15.50. Open all week.

## ▌Tighnabruaich

### An Lochan
**Local food favourite with stunning views**
Tighnabruaich, PA21 2BE
Tel no: (01700) 811239
www.anlochan.co.uk
**Modern British | £35**
**Cooking score: 3**
£5 OFF 🛏

The McKies have put all their energy into running this re-branded Victorian hotel by the Kyles of Bute and, following an extreme boutique makeover, it's now a destination for fans of locally sourced food. The Shinty Snug features pub/bistro staples, but the sharp, in-vogue restaurant menu aims much higher. Here you might find butter-poached langoustines paired with beetroot terrine, truffled goats' cheese and red wine emulsion, ahead of 'sous vide' loin of venison (courtesy

of local stalker 'Winston Churchill') with braised red cabbage, blackcurrant jelly, roast parsnip and potato infusion. On-trend intricacy is also the theme of desserts such as carrot and orange fondant with beetroot tartare and lavender ice cream. The whole package is enhanced by 'effortless service' and – of course – stunning views. The list features 60 well-chosen wines from £13.95. An Lochan also operates in Glasgow (see entry) and Tormaukin, Perthshire.

**Chef/s:** Paul Scott. **Open:** all week L 12.30 to 2.30, D 6.30 to 9. **Closed:** 2 weeks Christmas. **Meals:** alc (main courses £11 to £24). **Service:** not inc. **Details:** Cards accepted. 40 seats. Separate bar. No mobile phones. Wheelchair access. Music. Children allowed. Car parking.

## ▌Troon

### MacCallums Oyster Bar
**Famed for its Scottish fish**
The Harbour, Troon, KA10 6DH
Tel no: (01292) 319339
**Seafood | £25**
**Cooking score: 2**

The converted hydraulic pump house by the harbour, filled with America's Cup memorabilia, is a highly attractive prospect. Part of a seafood business, Scotland's renowned fish naturally puts in an appearance, not only oysters and lobsters, but crispy ginger and chilli squid with oriental dip, grilled langoustines with garlic butter and sea bass with creamed mash and ratatouille. Alternatives might be the well-reported Cullen skink or smoked haddock and Arbroath smokie thermidor gratin, while chorizo, olive and spicy bean casserole makes a fitting accompaniment to crisp-skinned grilled bream. Fish-friendly whites dominate the wine list, which opens at £18.95.

**Chef/s:** Phillip Burgess. **Open:** Tue to Sun L 12 to 2.30, Tue to Sat D 6.30 to 9.30. **Closed:** Mon, Christmas to New Year. **Meals:** alc (main courses £9 to £28). **Service:** not inc. **Details:** Cards accepted. 43 seats. Wheelchair access. Music. Children allowed. Car parking.

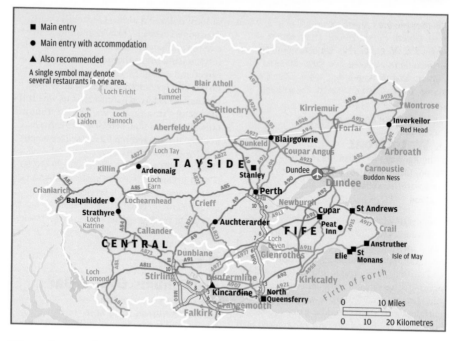

Legend:
- ■ Main entry
- ● Main entry with accommodation
- ▲ Also recommended

A single symbol may denote several restaurants in one area.

## Ardeonaig

### Ardeonaig Hotel

**Daring flourishes in an enchanting setting**
South Road, Loch Tay, Ardeonaig, FK21 8SU
Tel no: (01567) 820400
www.ardeonaighotel.co.uk
**Modern British | £27**
**Cooking score: 4**

Pete Gottgens is a fourth-generation hotelier, born in South Africa, who endeavours to bring a ray of Cape sunshine to the shores of Loch Tay. There are not many places where a commitment to local produce is pursued with such conviction – a flock of 150 Blackface sheep and a few head of Highland cattle are among the assets. A couple who are loyal fans note that cooking is continually developing – including some daring flourishes – but always within reason. The starter of smoked Scrabster haddock with a lightly fried quail egg, buttered leeks and grain mustard sauce is a classic winner, but so are main courses such as

hare sirloin with a pasty of the leg meat and seasonal baby roots. Venison gets good notices too, usually in the form of the fillet cooked a la plancha, and served with herbed polenta, wild lochside mushrooms and Madeira jus. South African chocolate mielie pudding is the house dessert special. If your knowledge of Cape wine production is a little rusty, here's the chance to brush up. A guide to the different regions prefaces a diverse, thrilling selection of fine growers. Prices are on the high side – they start at £19.50 – but the quality is excellent.
**Chef/s:** Pete Gottgens. **Open:** all week L 12 to 5, D 7 to 10. **Meals:** alc (main courses £13 to £30). Set L £14.50 (2 courses) to £19.50. Set D £26.50 (3 courses). Tasting menu £49 (7 courses).
**Service:** not inc. **Details:** Cards accepted. 40 seats. 40 seats outside. Separate bar. No mobile phones. Wheelchair access. Music. Car parking.

### Average price

The average price listed in main-entry reviews denotes the price of a three-course meal, without wine.

## ▌Auchterarder

### Andrew Fairlie at Gleneagles

**Sleek, luxurious French cuisine**
Auchterarder, PH3 1NF
Tel no: (01764) 694267
www.andrewfairlie.com
**Modern French | £75**
**Cooking score: 7**

First there is the hotel – a spectacular French-style château set deep in 850 acres of grounds landscaped by Capability Brown. It's not only a big, bold international tourist destination but also the world's most famous golfing resort. Andrew Fairlie's self-named restaurant operates as an autonomous business within the confines of the place, and there's a strong sense of personal identity about the set-up – from the letters 'AF' entwined on a lectern at the entrance to a portrait of the man himself on the black walls of the dining room. It's a discreet, cosseted space, full of luxurious intent and wholeheartedly dedicated to the arcane business of fine dining. Whether you choose the carte or one of the whole-table options (dégustation and menu du marché), you can expect overtly ambitious food based around top-drawer ingredients from Scottish sources and Rungis Market in Paris. The accent is resoundingly French, and Andrew Fairlie is master of refined contemporary flavours, working wonders with foie gras, Anjou squab pigeon, line-caught turbot and other aristocrats of the table. Home-smoked lobster – cured over old whisky barrels then served with warm lime and herb butter – is a signature dish, and many specialities involve high-flown juxtapositions of different bits from the same animal: Peelham Farm grass-fed veal loin is matched with shin and sweetbreads, while lamb cutlet is paired with slow-cooked neck and herb stuffing. Otherwise, two people might fancy sharing a whole roast poulet noir served disarmingly with creamed potatoes. Desserts are fashioned with technical mastery and a feel for contrast and texture – perhaps caramelised pine nut mousse with iced orange parfait or carpaccio

of strawberries set alongside lemon and fig cake and olive oil sorbet. Finally, you can wallow in the ripe pleasures of cheeses from Fromagerie Boursault. The wine list sets out to impress, although you'll need much more than pocket money to explore and appreciate its range. Prices start at £25, but jet rapidly into the stratosphere.
**Chef/s:** Andrew Fairlie and Stephen McLaughlin. **Open:** Mon to Sat D only 6.30 to 10. **Closed:** Sun, 24 and 25 Dec, 3 weeks Jan. **Meals:** Set D £75 to £95 (6 courses). **Service:** not inc. **Details:** Cards accepted. 52 seats. Air-con. No mobile phones. Wheelchair access. Music. Car parking.

## ▌Balquhidder

### Monachyle Mhor

**Creative food to bowl you over**
Balquhidder, FK19 8PQ
Tel no: (01877) 384622
www.mhor.net
**Modern British | £46**
**Cooking score: 5**

In the heart of the Trossachs National Park, this boutique hotel (once a farmhouse) sets itself apart from the surrounding greenery with a façade of delicate cherry-blossom pink. Safe houses were painted pink during the Jacobite rebellion, and the legendary Rob Roy was born in the area. The Lewis family has been in possession here since 1983, with Tom at the stoves since the mid-nineties – and reporters continue to be bowled over. 'As well as the high level of creativity and the matching of complementary or contrasting tastes, the very important pacing of courses and knowledgeable service are also exceptional', enthused one reporter. The four-course dinner menu might start out with a pairing of seared red mullet and peppered squid, accompanied by white asparagus, Parma ham and hollandaise, followed by a soup (perhaps cauliflower with shaved Parmesan and truffle oil). Main course offers a choice of three, including maybe Gressingham duck breast with red cabbage in Madeira sauce and potato purée spiked with lime and vanilla. Dessert could be cherry clafoutis in brandy-laced cherry soup with vanilla ice cream. Vegetarians have a separate menu to choose from. The wine list is a dream selection, usefully arranged by grape variety, packed with quality growers and knowledgeably served. Pinot Noirs are especially good. Glass prices start at £4.

**Chef/s:** Tom Lewis. **Open:** all week L 12 to 1.45, D 7 to 8.45. **Meals:** alc L (main courses £16 to £19). Set D £46. Sun L £32. **Service:** not inc. **Details:** Cards accepted. 42 seats. 30 seats outside. Separate bar. No mobile phones. Wheelchair access. Music. Children allowed. Car parking.

## Muthill

READERS RECOMMEND
### Barley Bree
French
6 Willoughby Street, Muthill, PH5 2AB
Tel no: (01764) 681451
www.barleybree.com
'Pleasingly balanced food from a French chef'

## Strathyre
### Creagan House
Dreamy views and leisurely dining
Strathyre, FK18 8ND
Tel no: (01877) 384638
www.creaganhouse.co.uk
French | £30
Cooking score: 4

£5
OFF

If dreamy locations are your thing, this extended seventeeth-century farmhouse might be just what you're looking for. It stands in a sheltered valley at the head of Loch Lubnaig, with forests, crags and valleys all around. Guests assemble at 7.30 for dinner at 8 in the stately baronial hall – but if that smacks of staid country house conservatism, think again. Gordon Gunn's cooking is a surprising fusion of Scottish and French influences, with 'understated subtlety' counting for more than big gestures. A starter of truffled langoustine mousseline with hand-dived Orkney scallops

and a Chartreuse-scented sauce shows his style and dedication to native produce. Proceedings might continue with poached halibut embellished with an oyster beignet and Avruga caviar velouté, or venison with baked fig, gin and juniper sauce. You can also pay a little extra for Aberdeen Angus beef fillet 'served in your favourite way', before meals conclude with homemade desserts and Scottish cheeses. The well-spread wine list opens with eight house recommendations from £12.80 (£8.95 a carafe).

**Chef/s:** Gordon Gunn. **Open:** Fri to Tue D only 7.30 (1 sitting). **Closed:** Wed, Thur, 24 to 26 Dec, 21 Jan to 5 Mar, 4 to 19 Nov. **Meals:** Set D £29.50.
**Service:** not inc. **Details:** Cards accepted. 14 seats. Separate bar. No music. No mobile phones. Wheelchair access. Car parking.

## Anstruther
# The Cellar
**Virtuous seafood and stunning wine**
24 East Green, Anstruther, KY10 3AA
Tel no: (01333) 310378
www.cellaranstruther.co.uk
**Seafood | £38**
**Cooking score: 6**
£5 OFF

Nothing about Peter and Susan Jukes' remarkable dining room seems to be affected by the passing of time. Once a cooperage and herring smokery, it still extols the simple virtues of seafood and wine in a comfortingly familiar setting of tiled floors and rough stone walls. A vintage grandfather clock marks the hours as guests enjoy Peter Jukes' enthusiastic adventures into the world of seafood cookery. Menus change daily depending on the catch, the market and the weather – so freshness is never in doubt. Ideas have been fine-tuned over the years and some dishes are hardy piscine perennials, while others spring surprises on the Cellar's loyal following of tourists and golfing emigrés from St Andrews. The house fish soup – a crayfish bisque glazed with cream and Gruyère – tops the bill; otherwise you might begin with a simple omelette packed with smoked haddock. If there's halibut in the day's haul, it might be grilled and served with greens, pine nuts, smoky bacon and a pot of hollandaise. Cod could be smeared with a pesto crust and dished up with pak choi, mash and balsamic dressing. Those with a penchant for meat could be offered grilled medallions of beef with wild mushrooms, 'stovies' and grain mustard sauce, before meals come to a close with cheese and desserts – perhaps a layered terrine of chocolate mousse with orange liqueur custard. Peter Jukes has also lavished care and affection on his stunning, highly personal wine list. Runs of fragrant Alsace varietals, Chablis and New Zealand Sauvignons suit the food admirably and prices (from £17.50) are fair.
**Chef/s:** Peter Jukes. **Open:** Fri and Sat L from 1, Mon to Sat D 6.30 to 9.30. **Closed:** Sun, 24 to 26 Dec, 1 Jan. **Meals:** Set L £15 (2 courses) to £23.50.

Set D £34.95 (2 courses) to £39.95. **Service:** not inc. **Details:** Cards accepted. 38 seats. Separate bar. No music. No mobile phones. Wheelchair access. Children allowed.

## Cupar
# Ostlers Close
**Astounding quality at a hidden gem**
25 Bonnygate, Cupar, KY15 4BU
Tel no: (01334) 655 574
www.ostlersclose.co.uk
**Modern British | £36**
**Cooking score: 5**
£5 OFF

An air of carefully nurtured domesticity hangs over the Grahams' modest restaurant tucked down a 'close' (alley) off Cupar's main street. But for all its homeliness this is a slick operation: service from Amanda Graham is beyond reproach and husband Jimmy's cooking delivers understated dishes of often astounding quality. Much care goes into the sourcing of ingredients and over nigh-on three decades a well-established network of local and regional suppliers has been built up. 'The starters were excellent,' noted one reporter, 'but the mains, including a stupendous slow-cooked trio of pork were so flavoursome we had to be restrained from asking for "seconds".' Others have endorsed the seafood: 'turbot with roasted vegetables, langoustines, scallops and a bouillabaise sauce – was outstanding', while game could be breast of wood pigeon with celeriac purée on a date and Puy lentil sauce, or roe venison with wild mushrooms, roast root vegetables and a red wine sauce. Puddings are also 'first-rate', with praise for a steamed Seville orange marmalade sponge with cream custard and orange ice cream. The wine list shows careful selection at fair prices; bottles from £17.
**Chef/s:** James Graham. **Open:** Sat L 12 to 1.30, Tue to Sat D 7 to 9.30. **Closed:** Sun, Mon, 25 and 26 Dec, 1 and 2 Jan, 2 weeks Apr and Oct. **Meals:** alc (main courses £18 to £22). Set D (Tue to Fri, Nov to Apr) £26. **Service:** not inc. **Details:** Cards accepted. 26 seats. No music. No mobile phones. Wheelchair access.

## Elie

### Sangster's
**Well-crafted cooking**
51 High Street, Elie, KY9 1BZ
Tel no: (01333) 331001
www.sangsters.co.uk
**Modern British | £36**
**Cooking score: 5**

Elie is a pretty Fife village, where the jewel in the high street crown is Bruce Sangster's engaging, comfortably domestic restaurant – a fireplace and simple furnishings make you feel you're in someone's home. The local-is-best philosophy reigns, and it finds its highest point in the orchard fruits and herbs that come from the restaurant's own kitchen garden. The four-course dinner menu might begin with a roast Ross-shire scallop in a sauce of brown lentils, cumin and coriander, or with the favourite twice-baked soufflé of Tobermory Cheddar ('so light, I expected it to float off the plate', enthuses a reader). After an intermediate course, which may be a confit duck leg in parsley dressing, main courses are about fine Scottish produce treated imaginatively and sensitively. Venison loin might come with a portion of hotpot, red cabbage compote and a port and red wine sauce, or there could be well-timed sea bream in a classical, but appreciably light, vermouth sauce. The finale brings pear crumble parfait with vanilla and butterscotch sauces, or Scottish cheeses with truffle honey. A well-annotated wine list contains much to delight from both Old World and New, at unobjectionable prices. A range of house offerings starts at £18.50.
**Chef/s:** Bruce Sangster. **Open:** Wed to Fri and Sun L 12.30 to 1.30, Tue to Sat D 7 to 8.30. **Closed:** Mon, 25 and 26 Dec, first 3 weeks Jan, 2 weeks early Nov. **Meals:** Set L £18 (2 courses) to £21. Set D £30 (2 courses) to £36. Sun L £25. **Service:** not inc. **Details:** Cards accepted. 28 seats. No mobile phones. Wheelchair access.

## Kincardine

**ALSO RECOMMENDED**
### ▲ The Unicorn
15 Excise Street, Kincardine, FK10 4LN
Tel no: (01259) 739129
www.theunicorn.co.uk
**Gastropub**

A coal fire warms the bar area and there are worn, comfy leather sofas, but otherwise this seventeenth-century coaching inn tucked away off the main road to Glasgow has a clean, contemporary look. Smooth, rich and well-made chicken liver parfait (£5.75), and nicely pink Buccleuch lamb rump (£16.95) are what to expect in the brasserie, alongside straightforward wines from £4.50 a glass. Service has been described as friendly and welcoming. Open all week.

## North Queensferry

### The Wee Restaurant
**A gem under the Forth bridge**
17 Main Street, North Queensferry, KY11 1JG
Tel no: (01383) 616263
www.theweerestaurant.co.uk
**Modern European | £26**
**Cooking score: 3**

Not quite as wee as some, managing to seat fully two dozen covers at capacity, but there is no getting away from the feeling of cosiness and intimacy. The Woods do a lot to make the place a destination in the area, with wine-tasting evenings and even a room for private parties now. Craig's cooking exerts its own magnetic attraction, in a version of modern Scottish food with European influences. Shetland mussels are cooked with bacon, pine nuts, Parmesan and basil, while mains bring on garlic-roasted cod with spiced aubergine risotto, baby artichokes and salsa verde, or a reinvention of the southern French speciality cassoulet, with Toulouse sausage and Puy lentils accompanying roast breast of mallard. Finish with plum clafoutis and vanilla ice cream. Wines start at £14.75.

Chef/s: Craig Wood. **Open:** Tue to Sat L 12 to 2.30, D 6 to 9. **Closed:** Sun, Mon. **Meals:** alc (main courses £17 to £19). Set L £14.75 (2 courses) to £18.50. **Service:** not inc. **Details:** Cards accepted. 36 seats. No mobile phones. Music. Children allowed.

## Peat Inn
### The Peat Inn
Blue-chip food lover's paradise
Peat Inn, KY15 5LH
Tel no: (01334) 840206
www.thepeatinn.co.uk
**Modern British | £50**
Cooking score: 6

The Smeddles continue to raise the bar at this long-standing, iconic restaurant. Since taking over in 2006, they have unfailingly treated customers with engaging politeness, made them feel at home, and fed them good food and wine. 'A food lover's paradise', enthused one satisfied reader. The quality shines out from Geoffrey Smeddle's restrained but inventive cooking. Every menu teems with authentic seasonal and regional produce. A spring dinner might gather asparagus, Anstruther lobster, St George's mushrooms and wild leeks; in autumn it rustles with pomegranates, walnuts, quince and chestnuts. The food straddles both traditional and contemporary and skill levels are high, notably in a pairing of langoustines and crisp pork belly with marinated cauliflower and shallot dressing, or in a main course of roast breast and confit leg of wild mallard, served with creamed Savoy cabbage, bacon, potato purée and pearl onions. Carrot, orange and ginger soup with just a trace of cardamom, and field-reared veal, served with parsnips, carrots, quince and chestnuts and a juniper-flavoured sauce, have also found favour, as has the 'very good value' lunchtime table d'hôte. Among desserts, hot pineapple and coconut soufflé with spiced lemongrass ice cream appealed to one diner. An assured wine list completes this blue-chip operation with prices from £21.

Chef/s: Geoffrey Smeddle. **Open:** Tue to Sat L 12.30 to 2, D 7 to 9. **Closed:** Sun, Mon, 25 and 26 Dec, 1 to 15 Jan. **Meals:** alc (main courses £16 to £23). Set L £16. Set D £32. Tasting menu £50. **Service:** not inc. **Details:** Cards accepted. 45 seats. Separate bar. No music. No mobile phones. Wheelchair access. Children allowed. Car parking.

## St Andrews
### The Seafood Restaurant
Dramatic dining
The Scores, Bruce Embankment, St Andrews, KY16 9AB
Tel no: (01334) 479475
www.theseafoodrestaurant.com
**Seafood | £45**
Cooking score: 4

The glass-fronted restaurant perched above the West Sands beach in St Andrews is like an Edward Hopper painting when it's all lit up in the evening – minus the air of melancholy. It's a dream location, and fitting for the fresh wares the place specialises in. Pittenweem crab dressed in lemon and coriander is a good curtain-raiser, served with sweetcorn purée and tomato fondue. The main course ratio is traditionally four fish to one meat – perhaps breast of Gressingham duck with sweet potato and Parma ham pressé, salsify, and foie gras sauce. The fish treatments are often quite meaty, though, as in grilled halibut with dauphinoise, and a chowder of mussels, leeks and pancetta. Dessert could be custard tart with rhubarb (poached and sorbet) and honeycomb. A quality wine list is stronger in Europe than the New World, with prices from £22 and a good choice of half-bottles.

Chef/s: Scott Swift. **Open:** all week L 12 to 2.30 (3 Sun), D 6.30 to 10. **Closed:** 25 and 26 Dec, 1 Jan. **Meals:** Set L £22 (2 courses) to £26. Set D £40 (2 courses) to £45. **Service:** not inc. **Details:** Cards accepted. 60 seats. 20 seats outside. Air-con. No music. No mobile phones. Wheelchair access. Children allowed.

## ALSO RECOMMENDED

### ▲ The Doll's House

3 Church Square, St Andrews, KY16 9NN
Tel no: (01334) 477422
www.houserestaurants.com
**Modern European**

In the centre of St Andrews in a traffic-free square, the Doll's House is a versatile all-rounder with a diverse clientele. There's an informal atmosphere as well as a straightforward cooking style that blends modern and traditional ideas. Starters of locally smoked salmon with spiced crab and chilli oil (£6.45) and mains of pork chop with apple purée and mixed shoots (£12.95) are typical of the style. Good value extends to the wine list, which opens at £13.95. Open all week.

### ▲ Vine Leaf

131 South Street, St Andrews, KY16 9UN
Tel no: (01334) 477497
www.vineleafstandrews.co.uk
**Modern British**

Personally run restaurant tucked down a winding pend (lane) in the heart of St Andrews. The flexible menu (priced at £23.50/£25.95 for 2/3 courses) casts its net wide for ample, generous dishes to suit all appetites. Fresh crab, ginger and lemon tart, slow-cooked lamb with rösti potatoes and pistou vegetables, a trio of game (wild venison steak, duck and pigeon breast) with port and redcurrant sauce and sticky toffee pudding show the style. Credible wines from £15.90. Open Tue to Sat D only.

## ▊ St Monans

### The Seafood Restaurant

A classy catch

16 West End, St Monans, KY10 2BX
Tel no: (01333) 730327
www.theseafoodrestaurant.com
**Seafood | £37**
**Cooking score: 5**

The picturesque string of fishing villages on the East Fife coast begs a classy fish eatery and has landed it in the clean-cut, whitewashed Seafood Restaurant which overlooks the harbour at St Monans. The Firth of Forth all but laps up to the doorstep, and there's a sunny terrace for pre-dinner drinks. Inside there's a gloriously light-filled dining room simply done out with tongue-and-groove panelling, dove grey floorboards, fresh, white linen tablecloths and panoramic views out to the Isle of May. The menu is as cool and confident as the décor: half-a-dozen dishes at each course that might begin with Kilbrandon oysters and Bloody Mary sauce or home-cured gravlax with orange beurre blanc. Follow it with smoked haddock and poached egg or halibut with crushed potatoes and a cep velouté of real depth and flavour. Match it with a glass of Pouilly Fumé and finish with a miniature marmalade pudding and marmalade ice cream. The well-spread, fish-friendly wine list has plenty of decent drinking for around £20, and a fair showing by the glass too.
**Chef/s:** Craig Millar and Roy Brown. **Open:** all week L 12.30 to 2.30 (3 Sun), D 6.30 to 9.30 (8.30 Sun). **Closed:** Mon and Tue from Sept to May, 25 and 26 Dec, 1 Jan. **Meals:** Set L £20 (2 courses) to £25. Set D £32 (2 courses) to £37. **Service:** not inc. **Details:** Cards accepted. 40 seats. 36 seats outside. Separate bar. No music. No mobile phones. Wheelchair access. Children allowed. Car parking.

# ■ Blairgowrie

## Kinloch House Hotel

Magnificence and rich, creative food
Blairgowrie, PH10 6SG
Tel no: (01250) 884237
www.kinlochhouse.com
**Modern British | £48**
Cooking score: 5

🍷 🛏

Set in 25 acres of lush countryside, with a grand oak-panelled entrance hall and first-floor picture gallery, this is a house of some magnificence, but it is run with a personal approach that makes visitors feel at home. The cooking occupies the centre ground of country house opulence, offering fixed-price menus at lunch and dinner. A tian of crab with avocado, tomato and gazpacho is appealing in its straightforward richness, while accompaniments deepen the impact of dishes – thus roast loin of lamb comes with sautéed sweetbreads, dauphinoise potatoes, confit garlic and a rosemary sauce. Desserts display the same degree of creativity in pineapple mousse with passion fruit jelly and coconut sorbet. Simpler things are done well too: at lunch there could be a plate of Inverawe smoked salmon with homemade brown bread, and slow-cooked feather blade steak with horseradish potato purée, roast vegetables and a red wine sauce. Kinloch House takes wine seriously, picking fine names from France and beyond. The list opens with wines by the glass (from £6.50), while 24 house selections (from £23.50) give a good overview of the quality here.
**Chef/s:** Andrew May. **Open:** all week, L 12 to 2, D 7 to 8.30. **Closed:** 14 to 28 Dec. **Meals:** Set L £18.50 (2 courses) to £23.50. Set D £48. **Service:** not inc. **Details:** Cards accepted. 40 seats. Separate bar. No music. No mobile phones. Wheelchair access. Children allowed. Car parking.

# ■ Inverkeilor

## Gordon's

Food-focused family enterprise
Main Street, Inverkeilor, DD11 5RN
Tel no: (01241) 830364
www.gordonsrestaurant.co.uk
**Modern British | £44**
Cooking score: 5

'A fantastic family-run restaurant,' just about sums up the enthusiastic popular support for this splendid enterprise operating out of a Victorian residence in a little village not far from beautiful Lunan Bay. The intimate, beamed interior comes complete with stained glass windows set into sandstone walls and rugs strewn over its wood floors; an open fire burns in the grate, and Maria Watson runs front-of-house with cheery good humour. Gordon and son Garry hold sway at the stoves, and the kitchen certainly knows how to let the cooking stand up on its own. 'It's all about the food', observed one contented soul. Recent meals have delivered some very impressive modern dishes indeed, including pitch-perfect wood pigeon on cep and chive risotto with Pinot Noir jus, and wild sea bass atop a potato galette with sweetcorn and mussel fricassee. Incidentals and extras are equally tantalising – perhaps an 'exceptional' mid-course of cauliflower and Maris Piper velouté perked up with truffle oil, or a deliciously surprising pre-dessert of lemon mousse and raspberry sorbet. Desserts themselves cover everything from stylish comfort food (Baileys croissant-and-butter pudding) to more modish pear soufflé with marzipan ice cream, tonka bean anglaise and pear tuile. The well-spread 50-bin wine list is helpfully organised by grape variety, with prices starting at £16.
**Chef/s:** Gordon and Garry Watson. **Open:** Wed to Fri and Sun L 12 to 1.45, Tue to Sun D 7 to 8.30. **Closed:** Mon, second and third week in Jan. **Meals:** Set D £27 (3 courses) to £44 (4 courses). **Service:** not inc. **Details:** Cards accepted. 24 seats. No music. No mobile phones. Wheelchair access. Children allowed. Car parking.

# Perth

## The Anglers Inn

Skilful cooking in a smart pub
Main Road, Guildtown, Perth, PH2 6BS
Tel no: (01821) 640329
www.theanglersinn.co.uk
**Modern British | £25**
Cooking score: 3

Jeremy and Shona Wares moved from 63 Tay
Street (see entry), their in-town restaurant, to
this main street pub six miles from Perth in
May 2007. Clean and simple has been their
rule for renovation: an open-plan room with
the bar tucked discreetly in one corner, white
linen-clad, well-spaced tables, and modern
pictures create a contemporary feel. Jeremy's
cooking is direct and skilful, using local
produce in a traditional way. An inspection
lunch saw a pork, bacon and apricot terrine
teamed with onion chutney and a main course
of seasonal St George's mushroom with lovage
puff pastry, both an exercise in flavours and
textures. Elsewhere, rump of lamb with
chargrilled Provençal vegetables, couscous
and rosemary vinaigrette has found favour.
There's a small, well-chosen wine list with
options by the glass from £3.50
**Chef/s:** Jeremy Wares and Cat Listen. **Open:** all
week L 12 to 2, D 6 to 9 (8 Sun). **Meals:** alc (main
courses £12 to £25). Set L £12.95 (2 courses) to
£14.95. Set D £14.95 (2 courses) to £17.95. Sun L
£16.95. **Service:** not inc. **Details:** Cards accepted.
60 seats. 25 seats outside. Separate bar. No music.
Wheelchair access. Children allowed. Car parking.

## Deans @ Let's Eat

Elaborate food in classic surrounds
77-79 Kinnoull Street, Perth, PH1 5EZ
Tel no: (01738) 643377
www.letseatperth.co.uk
**Modern British | £26**
Cooking score: 4

Located on a busy street corner not far from
the city centre, Deans is a smart restaurant
with a slightly formal, old-fashioned feel and
a lounging sofa area for before and after the
meal. Willie Deans' assured cooking shows
classical French influences with dishes that are
quite elaborate ('lots of different components
to a dish') but always 'beautifully presented'.
Start perhaps with chargrilled tuna with
wasabi mayonnaise, crispy onions, potato and
lemon salad with a red pepper dressing.
Follow with pink medallion of prime Scottish
beef fillet served on a slow-cooked casserole,
with a timbale of white and black pudding
with truffled celeriac purée. For one reporter
'it is the desserts that make the restaurant so
special'. These might include hot raspberry
soufflé, red berry ice cream with vanilla and
raspberry sauce. Margo Deans and her front-
of-house team ensure that the atmosphere is
'unstuffy'. Wines start at £14.50.
**Chef/s:** William Deans. **Open:** Tue to Sat L 12 to 2,
Tue to Sat D 6 to 9.30 (6.30 Fri and Sat). **Closed:**
Sun, Mon, 2 weeks Jan, 1 week Jul, 1 week Oct.
**Meals:** alc (main courses £12 to 15). Set L £13.95 (2
courses) to £16.95. Set D £20 (2 courses) to £25.
**Service:** not inc. **Details:** Cards accepted. 60 seats.
No mobile phones. Wheelchair access. Music.
Children allowed.

## 63 Tay Street

**Local ingredients treated with respect**
63 Tay Street, Perth, PH2 8NN
Tel no: (01738) 441451
www.63taystreet.co.uk
**Modern British | £31**
Cooking score: 2

£5
OFF

Judging by the enthusiastic feedback this year, this informal restaurant across a busy road from the River Tay attracts a strong local following. Graeme Pallister knows where to source the best local produce and how to treat it with respect. Wild garlic soup with lemon oil is a light and appealing starter. Main courses might be a pork loin chop with mushrooms and Gruyère and apple sauce, or pan-fried Sea trout with fresh pasta, mouclade of mussels and brown shrimp. Finish with iced nougatine parfait with poached pineapple and caramel sauce. The wide-ranging wine list is reasonably priced. Bottles start at £14.50.
**Chef/s:** Graeme Pallister. **Open:** Tue to Sat L 12 to 2, D 6.30 to 9. **Closed:** Sun, Mon, 26 Dec to 15 Jan, 1 week July. **Meals:** alc (main courses £11 to £18). Set L £19.50 (3 courses). Set D £31.25 (3 courses). **Service:** 10% for parties over 8. **Details:** Cards accepted. 36 seats. No mobile phones. Music. Children allowed.

# ▊ Stanley

**NEW ENTRY**

## The Apron Stage

**Small is beautiful**
5 King Street, Stanley, PH1 4ND
Tel no: (01738) 828888
www.theapronstage.co.uk
**Modern British | £25**
Cooking score: 3

£30
▼

Shona Drysdale and Jane Nicoll used to be part of the team that put Let's Eat in Perth on the map and in this new venture, an evocative and unusual 18-seater restaurant, their passion for food is vividly celebrated. A mix of trompe l'oeil mirrors, pale colours and painted furniture gives a masterful illusion of space, while a simple counter separates diners from a miniscule kitchen. Given such limitations, the short blackboard menu makes sense. It offers, perhaps, a light potato pancake topped with goats' cheese, rocket and two thin slices of Parmesan ('perfect in its flavour, freshness and simplicity'), then a just-pink trio of lamb cutlets with lyonnaise potatoes. The 20 or so wines are a knowledgeable selection, with bottles from £13.75 (£3.50 a glass).
**Chef/s:** Shona Drysdale. **Open:** Fri L 12 to 2, Wed to Sat D 6.30 to 9.30. **Closed:** Sun, Mon, Tue. **Meals:** alc (main courses £13 to £18). Set L £13 (2 courses) to £15.75. **Service:** not inc. **Details:** Cards accepted. 18 seats. No mobile phones. Wheelchair access. Music. Children allowed.

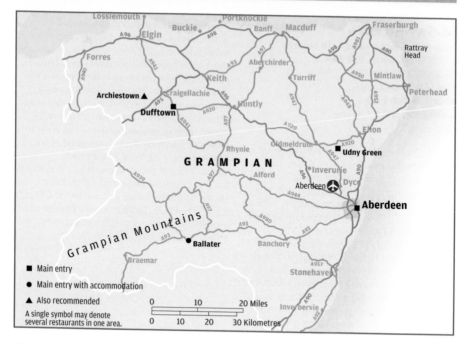

- ■ Main entry
- ● Main entry with accommodation
- ▲ Also recommended

A single symbol may denote several restaurants in one area.

0   10   20 Miles

0   10   20   30 Kilometres

## ▌Aberdeen

### Silver Darling

**Fish-loving harbourside heavyweight**
Pocra Quay, North Pier, Aberdeen, AB11 5DQ
Tel no: (01224) 576229
www.silverdarlingrestaurant.co.uk
**Seafood | £38**
**Cooking score: 6**

It's apt that this high-ranking fixture of the Aberdeen restaurant scene should take its title from the old Scottish nickname for herrings. Seafood is king here, and the culinary business of the day is conducted in a conservatory-style dining room on the first floor of the granite city's old Customs House. Inviting views of the harbour and the boats add an extra fillip to proceedings, as customers enjoy some of the most invigorating fish cookery in the area. Didier Dejean's French roots help to anchor the kitchen, although his food is shot through with vivid eclectic influences that add an exciting extra dimension to proceedings. A scattering of Parma ham 'dust' is applied to seared scallops, while rock turbot is poached in Beaujolais then served daringly with black and white pudding. Elsewhere, a starter of sea bass and sea trout sashimi with white asparagus, mint dressing and sokura cress tips its hat to oriental fusion, while steamed wild sea bass on red pesto couscous with fennel, basil and black olive coulis acknowledges a debt to the Med. To conclude, it's showtime with an 'array of little pots of crème brûlée' or poached peach in grenadine syrup with crème fraîche and almond mousse. The respectable wine list puts its weight behind fish-friendly, Old World whites. Prices start at £21.
**Chef/s:** Didier Dejean. **Open:** Mon to Fri L 12 to 1.30, Mon to Sat D 6.30 to 9.30. **Closed:** Sun, 2 weeks Christmas and New Year. **Meals:** alc (main courses £19 to £22). Set L £15.50 (2 courses) to £19.50. **Service:** not inc. **Details:** Cards accepted. 45 seats. No mobile phones. Wheelchair access. Music. Children allowed.

## Archiestown

ALSO RECOMMENDED
▲ **Archiestown Hotel**
The Square, Archiestown, AB38 7QL
Tel no: (01340) 810218
www.archiestownhotel.co.uk
**Modern British**

Plumb in the midst of the Highland whisky trail, Archiestown's village square is the location for this stone-built Georgian manor-house hotel. Modern Scottish cooking uses good local produce in dishes such as venison and chicken liver pâté with spiced plum and apple chutney (£7.50), cod on citrus mash with prawn and lemon butter (£18.50) or lamb rump on balsamic potatoes and onions. Finish with cranachan cheesecake and raspberry compote (£5.50). Wines start at £17.50. Open all week.

## Ballater

### Darroch Learg
**Bastion of Scottish family hospitality**
Braemar Road, Ballater, AB35 5UX
Tel no: (013397) 55443
www.darrochlearg.co.uk
**Modern British | £45**
Cooking score: 6

Built in the 1880s, this splendidly situated hotel has been run by the Franks family for over 40 years. David Mutter has run the kitchen for the past 15 years, delivering the kind of touch that leaves readers gasping for superlatives: 'We had simply the most fabulous cooking. Everything from start to finish showed great care, and the ingredients are first-rate.' Wood pigeon, lamb, Angus beef and smoked haddock are the pick of the Highland larder. The latter might appear in a raviolo to begin, served with a velouté of the fish, while pigeon is also wrapped up, this time in pastry, and served with spiced pear chutney. Main courses use strong supporting flavours to set off their principal components, so that halibut is accompanied by Puy lentils, a crab

croquette and shellfish sauce, while Gressingham duck breast comes with a black pudding pithiviers, shallot jam and olives. The six-course tasting menu gives a grand tour of the style, concluding, perhaps, with pannacotta, served with cherries in mulled wine and homemade shortbread. A serious, authoritative wine list accompanies. 'Brief Encounters' is an interesting selection of temporary listings, there's a good choice in halves, and wines by the glass start at £6.50.
**Chef/s:** David Mutter. **Open:** Sun L 12.30 to 2, all week D 7 to 9. **Closed:** Christmas, last 3 weeks Jan. **Meals:** Set D £46 (3 courses). Tasting menu £56. Sun L £25. **Service:** not inc. **Details:** Cards accepted. 48 seats. Wheelchair access. Music. Children allowed. Car parking.

### The Green Inn
**Classic techniques and local ingredients**
9 Victoria Road, Ballater, AB35 5QQ
Tel no: (013397) 55701
www.green-inn.com
**Modern British | £39**
Cooking score: 4

Rather more grand inside than the word 'inn' suggests, this smart but homely restaurant-with-rooms sits in the heart of the village overlooking the church green. Run by the O'Halloran family, with son Chris in the kitchen, its public rooms are full of personal touches and provide ample opportunity for lounging. At the core of the menu are classic techniques and close-at-hand ingredients, often enlivened with flavours from further afield. Typical of the style are ravioli of Loch Fyne langoustine and organic salmon with a lemongrass and chervil velouté, followed by roast Gressingham duck with pak choi, glazed apple and celeriac purée, honey and cracked pepper sauce. Desserts continue in a similar vein, for instance baby pear and ginger tarte Tatin with candied ginger ice cream. The interesting wine list favours France and offers plenty around the £20 mark.

**Chef/s:** Chris O'Halloran. **Open:** Tue to Sat D only 7 to 9. **Closed:** Sun, Mon, 2 weeks Jan, 3 weeks Nov. **Meals:** Set D £32.50 (2 courses) to £38.50. **Service:** not inc. **Details:** Cards accepted. 28 seats. Separate bar. No mobile phones. Wheelchair access. Music. Children allowed.

## Dufftown
### La Faisanderie

**French cooking with fine local ingredients**
2 Balvenie Street, Dufftown, AB55 4AD
Tel no: (01340) 821273
French | £28
Cooking score: 3

The Pheasantry – as the name translates – is a fond Frenchman's *hommage* to all things Scottish, plumb in the heart of Speyside whisky country. Chef/patron Eric Obry sources all produce locally. He even shoots his own venison, and many of the clientele are game-stalkers and fisherfolk too. In cosy, comfortable surroundings, the food uses French technique to the best effect: langoustine and mushroom ravioli in shellfish bisque, haggis-stuffed pheasant with onion compote and a sauce of honey, whisky and cream, or the daily changing fish specials. Finish with citrus and star anise brûlée with lavender sablé biscuit, or a gander at the Franco-Scottish cheeseboard. An exclusively French list opens with a quartet of Languedoc house wines at £11.90. It is advisable to check opening times.
**Chef/s:** Eric Obry. **Open:** Sat and Sun L 12 to 1.30, Thur to Mon D 6 to 8.30 (7 to 9 Fri and Sat). **Closed:** Tue, Wed, 2 weeks Nov, 2 weeks Feb. **Meals:** alc (main courses £16 to £19). Set L £14.50 (2 courses) to £17.95. Set D £28 (3 courses). **Service:** not inc. **Details:** Cards accepted. 28 seats. Wheelchair access. Music. Children allowed.

## Udny Green
### Eat on the Green

**Scottish favourites with a modern spin**
Udny Green, AB41 7RS
Tel no: (01651) 842337
www.eatonthegreen.co.uk
Modern European | £42
Cooking score: 2

The dining area has been extended into what was the old post office at this former inn overlooking the village green, yet the place still feels homely. Traditional Scottish modes are given a modern spin in dishes that display great clarity of flavour. Start with something like an array of seafood hors d'oeuvres with lemon and lime crème fraîche, before going on to chargrilled Angus sirloin with roasted shallots, pink peppercorn cream and chips, or steamed halibut teamed with scallops and langoustines in a Cognac-spiked shellfish bisque. Fine British cheeses are the alternative to desserts like caramelised lemon tart with raspberry sorbet. The wine list is full of dependable names at prices that shouldn't disturb, opening at £14.
**Chef/s:** Craig Wilson. **Open:** Wed to Fri and Sun L 12 to 2, Wed to Sun D 6.30 to 8.30 (9 Fri and Sat). **Closed:** Mon and Tue. **Meals:** alc (main courses £19 to £24). Set L £18.95 (2 courses) to £21.95. Set Sat D £42. Sun L £19.95 (2 courses) to £24.95. **Service:** not inc. **Details:** Cards accepted. 70 seats. Wheelchair access. Music. Children allowed. Car parking.

### Please send us your feedback

To register your opinion about any restaurant listed in the Guide, or a new restaurant that you wish to bring to our attention, please visit the web address at the bottom of the page. Your feedback informs the content of the book and will be used to compile next year's reviews.

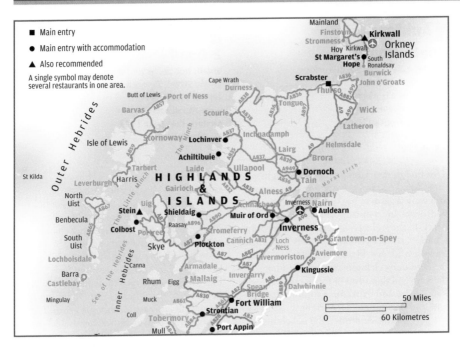

- ■ Main entry
- ● Main entry with accommodation
- ▲ Also recommended

A single symbol may denote several restaurants in one area.

## Achiltibuie

### Summer Isles Hotel

Traditional dining and splendid sunsets
Achiltibuie, IV26 2YG
Tel no: (01854) 622282
www.summerisleshotel.co.uk
**Modern European | £54**
Cooking score: 4

Despite a change of ownership in 2008, the magnetic attractions of this remote Highland getaway are intact. Chris Firth-Bernard remains in the kitchen, sending out a full-blooded five-course dinner with all the trimmings every night at 8 o'clock sharp, ideally as the sun sets in the picture window behind the lovely, lonely Summer Isles. The performance begins with a round or two of canapés in the lounge – an oyster, perhaps, or a warm cheese straw – before a no-choice dinner in the candlelit dining room. Expect local seafood: scallops, mussels steamed with saffron, monkfish filo parcels or Achiltibuie

lobster in a butter sauce. Desserts come by the trolley-load. Indulge in one – or all – of: raspberry soufflé, chocolate log, tarts and pavlovas, berries and cream. The cheese trolley is equally groaning with British and French cheeses, celery, grapes, figs and chutney. Dinner here pays scant heed to fads and fashion, sticking to reliable, much-loved dishes in the Summer Isles tradition. A 400-bin wine list does full justice to the food. Prices start around £20.
**Chef/s:** Christopher Firth-Bernard. **Open:** all week L 12.30 to 2, D 8 (1 sitting). **Closed:** Nov to Easter. **Meals:** Set L £25. Set D £54 (5 courses). **Service:** not inc. **Details:** Cards accepted. 28 seats. Separate bar. No music. No mobile phones. Wheelchair access. Children allowed. Car parking.

### Average price

The average price listed in main-entry reviews denotes the price of a three-course meal, without wine.

## Auldearn

### Boath House

**Astute, quietly confident cooking**
Auldearn, IV12 5TE
Tel no: (01667) 454896
www.boath-house.com
**Modern European | £65**
Cooking score: 5

This fine Regency house has all the right ingredients: 20 acres of streams, lake, woods and walled garden, bags of charm, fine bedrooms and a distinguished kitchen at its heart. In the warmly decorated dining room, Charles Lockley's cooking exudes and inspires quiet confidence. Fixed-price lunches, with dinner a daily changing six-course affair, deliver food that's 'full of freshness and flavour', backed by accurate timings, balance and fine attention to detail right through to the petits fours. At dinner, the no-choice menu offers an intriguing array of dishes, from white bean and truffle soup, via rabbit with lentils, pear and hazelnut to 'impeccably fresh' scallops with leek, dill and egg cream. There's some fine and original cooking in main courses, too, with proper appreciation of the importance of flavour: the combination of wheat grain, bacon and parsley root went perfectly with venison. After that you might encounter fine British cheeses and puddings like spiced custard with pineapple and pistachio cake. The wine list concentrates on France but all countries turn out a slate of well-reviewed bottles at fair prices (from £19).
**Chef/s:** Charles Lockley. **Open:** all week L 12.30 to 2, D 7 to 9. **Meals:** Set L £21 (2 courses) to £28.50. Set D £65 (6 courses). **Service:** not inc. **Details:** Cards accepted. 28 seats. No music. No mobile phones. Wheelchair access. Children allowed. Car parking.

## Dornoch

### 2 Quail

**Small, but perfectly formed**
Castle Street, Dornoch, IV25 3SN
Tel no: (01862) 811811
www.2quail.com
**Modern European | £38**
Cooking score: 4

The sandstone building on Dornoch's main street houses a restaurant-with-rooms for which the word 'intimate' might have been coined. Just a dozen places are offered at dinner, which makes a refreshing change if you're in town for a spot of golfing and don't want the whole corporate package. Eating in the tartan-carpeted dining room feels as much like being invited into someone's house as can be – except that Michael Carr's cooking is several cuts above the domestic norm. The short, three-course dinner menus deal in the likes of salmon in an oriental stir-fry, to begin, with maybe beef fillet and foie gras in truffled sherry sauce to follow. It is all prepared in a positive, confident style often marked by finely judged richness. That's certainly the case in a dessert such as dark chocolate marquise with black cherries. The short wine list is a serviceable international collection starting at £16.50 for house French.
**Chef/s:** Michael Carr. **Open:** Tue to Sat D only 7 to 9. **Closed:** Sun, Mon, 2 weeks Christmas, 2 weeks Feb/Mar. **Meals:** Set D £38. **Service:** not inc. **Details:** Cards accepted. 12 seats. No mobile phones. Music. Children allowed.

## ■ Fort William

## Crannog

**Packed with good fishy things**
Town Pier, Fort William, PH33 6DB
Tel no: (01397) 705589
www.crannog.net
**Seafood | £21**
Cooking score: 2

Perched on the lochside, Crannog is an unmistakable landmark, with its bright white front and red roof. West Highland seafood presented with the minimum of intervention is the cheering philosophy, with the likes of Cullen skink and a version of moules marinière to start, followed by the house bouillabaisse, based on tomato and fennel, packed with good fishy things, and topped with an aïoli croûton. Otherwise, look to the all-important blackboard for the fish specials of the day. There's meat if you want it, in the form of ribeye steak with celeriac mash, plus maple and date pudding for afters. Wines start at £14.50.
**Chef/s:** Robbie MacDonald and Stewart MacLachlan. **Open:** all week L 12 to 2, D 6.30 to 9.30. **Closed:** 25 Dec, 1 Jan. **Meals:** alc (main courses £11 to £20). Set L £9.95 (2 courses). **Service:** not inc. **Details:** Cards accepted. 60 seats. Separate bar. Wheelchair access. Music. Children allowed. Car parking.

## Inverlochy Castle

**Modern cooking at a magnificent pile**
Torlundy, Fort William, PH33 6SN
Tel no: (01397) 702177
www.inverlochycastlehotel.co.uk
**Modern European | £64**
Cooking score: 6

Subtlety and understatement can't have figured in the vocabulary of the first Lord Abinger when he created this magnificent Victorian pile. Set in the foothills of Ben Nevis close to its thirteenth-century namesake, the castle is an imposing beast, amply adorned with chandeliers and antiques. The views are spectacular, not least because the hotel overlooks its own lake. Against such a stoutly traditional backdrop, Philip Carnegie's modern cooking is something of a surprise, but follows comfortably on the heels of his predecessor, Matthew Gray. Dinner is a formal affair, overseen by 'pleasant, attentive' staff. Local produce underpins a starter of Loch Linnhe prawns with veal sweetbreads, pearl barley and truffle, while others, such as foie gras and green peppercorn ballottine with rhubarb jelly and Poilâne bread, rely on top-class ingredients from further afield. Main courses reflect the same dedication to sourcing the best ingredients, with choices ranging from roasted leg of rabbit with white beans and butternut squash to poached halibut with crab-stuffed potatoes and roast shimeji mushrooms. This is dining with a sense of occasion, so expect statement desserts such as hot passion fruit soufflé with a chocolate beignet, or perhaps lemon rice pudding with griottine cherry compote and granita. Alternatively, there are cheeses with oatcakes and homemade walnut bread. The lengthy wine list covers France in detail, then strikes out to countries as diverse as Germany, Chile and the USA. Bottles are priced from £34.
**Chef/s:** Philip Carnegie. **Open:** all week L 12.30 to 1.30, D 6 to 10. **Meals:** Set L £28.50 (2 courses) to £35. Set D £64. Sun L £35. **Service:** not inc. **Details:** Cards accepted. 30 seats. 6 seats outside. No music. No mobile phones. Wheelchair access. Music. Children allowed. Car parking.

## READERS RECOMMEND

## Lochleven Seafood Cafe

**Seafood**
Onich, Fort William, PH33 6SA
Tel no: (01855) 821048
www.lochlevenseafoodcafe.co.uk
'**A stunning, off-the-beaten-track setting serving excellent fresh seafood**'

## Grantown on Spey

READERS RECOMMEND
### The Glass House
**Modern British**
Grant Road, Grantown on Spey, PH26 3LD
Tel no: (01479) 872980
www.theglasshouse-grantown.co.uk
'Food is uniformly excellent, being well cooked and presented'

## Inverness

### Abstract at Glenmoriston Town House
**Minimalist chic, aspirational cuisine**
20 Ness Bank, Inverness, IV2 4SF
Tel no: (01463) 223777
www.abstractrestaurant.com
**Modern European | £43**
**New chef**

Sitting pretty beside the banks of the River Tay, Glenmoriston Town House is not only one of Scotland's top luxury hotels, it's also home to Abstract – a fashion-conscious restaurant with a good line in minimalist chic. Occupying part of the ground floor, its sleek style is matched by cooking with aspirations, intricacy and voguish gastro trademarks. Chef Geoff Malmedy has departed, to take over the kitchen at the Edinburgh branch of Abstract (see entry). We were notified about the arrival of his replacement, William Hay, too late to respond with an inspection. New menus are unavailable as we go to press, but previously, complex embellishments, meat/fish combos and jokey contrasts defined the contemporary French-inspired repertoire. Reports please. The wine list puts its faith in luxurious drinking from the French regions and beyond. Prices start at £18.
**Chef/s:** William Hay. **Open:** Tue to Sat D only 6 to 10. **Closed:** Sun, Mon, one week Jan. **Meals:** alc (main courses £15 to £28). Tasting menu £50. **Service:** not inc. **Details:** Cards accepted. 45 seats. No music. No mobile phones. Wheelchair access. Children allowed. Car parking.

### Rocpool
**Effervescent brasserie in an elegant hotel**
1 Ness Walk, Inverness, IV3 5NE
Tel no: (01463) 717274
www.rocpoolrestaurant.com
**Modern European | £27**
**Cooking score: 2**

In an elegant hotel on the banks of the Ness, Rocpool is a thriving brasserie operation offering modern European cooking based on good Highland produce. Dishes can be complex, as in a starter that combines grilled Emperor prawns and crisp squid with chorizo, pak choi, chilli jam and crème fraîche, or a main course of Parmesan and herb-crusted chicken escalope with roasted pumpkin, avocado, feta and lemon. Those looking to eat more simply might try the Classics menu, and choose Cullen skink, followed by fillet steak with new potatoes, green beans and salsa rosso. Finish with sticky toffee pudding and vanilla ice cream. A decent selection of wines by the glass starts at £3.75.
**Chef/s:** Steven Devlin. **Open:** Mon to Sat L 12 to 2.30, all week D 5.45 to 10 (9.30 Sun). **Closed:** 25 and 26 Dec, 1 and 2 Jan. **Meals:** alc (main courses £9 to £20). Set L £10.95 (2 courses). Set D £12.95 (2 courses, 5.45 to 6.45). **Service:** not inc. **Details:** Cards accepted. 55 seats. Air-con. Wheelchair access. Music. Children allowed.

## Isle of Islay

READERS RECOMMEND
### An Taigh Osda
**Modern British**
Bruichladdich, Isle of Islay, PA49 7UN
Tel no: (01496) 850587
www.antaighosda.co.uk
'Excellent menu, all memorable, would definitely come here again'

## Isle of Skye
# The Three Chimneys
**Enchanting cooking in a magical place**
Colbost, Isle of Skye, IV55 8ZT
Tel no: (01470) 511258
www.threechimneys.co.uk
**Modern British | £55**
**Cooking score: 5**

🍷 🚗

It's a sublime setting on the shores of Loch Dunvegan, the isolation total and thrilling: a century-old stone croft dwelling with rooms in a separate building, and views to the Outer Hebrides. In this magical environment, Michael Smith's cooking conjures up more enchantment. Drawing resourcefully on regional fare, he brings off a balancing act of old and new Scottish traditions. Dishes may sound quite complex in the billing, but they achieve well-judged culinary logic on the plate, and the quality of materials is sensational. A duo of hot-smoked salmon and smoked haddock with quail's egg mimosa starts things confidently, while a meatier pairing teams up wild rabbit and hare with tattie (potato) scones, Ayrshire bacon and Agen prunes. Main courses maintain the pace with the likes of citrus-steamed turbot, sea bass and squid in a razor clam and sorrel velouté, or loin of lamb with haggis, clapshot and spring greens. Frosted blaeberries garnish a dark chocolate and amaretti délice with crème fraîche. It all comes with a serious wine list. Starting with glasses from £4.50, it soon lights out all over the vinous globe, with thickets of excellent producers, helpful notes and reasonable choice below £25.
**Chef/s:** Michael Smith. **Open:** Mon to Sat L 12.30 to 2, all week D 6.30 to 9.30. **Closed:** Sun L Nov to Mar, 7 to 28 Jan. **Meals:** Set L £25 (2 courses) to £32. Set D £55. Tasting menu £77. **Service:** not inc. **Details:** Cards accepted. 36 seats. Separate bar. No music. No mobile phones. Wheelchair access. Car parking.

## ALSO RECOMMENDED
## ▲ Loch Bay
1-2 Macleod Terrace, Stein, Isle of Skye, IV55 8GA
Tel no: (01470) 592235
www.lochbay-seafood-restaurant.co.uk
**Seafood**

A miniscule cottage slap-bang on the jetty, Loch Bay naturally goes for spanking fresh seafood in a big way. Local divers bring scallops, and there's organic salmon from Orkney; otherwise the boats land anything from lobsters and king prawns to sea bream, hake and halibut. Expect grilled razor clams with parsley butter (£6.50) or Cullen skink ahead of John Dory or monkfish with olive oil and citrus juices (£16). Homely sweets might include apple and apricot crumble (£5.20). House wines from £14.25. Open Tue to Sat, Easter to end Oct.

## READERS RECOMMEND
## Ullinish Country Lodge
**Modern British**
Struan, Isle of Skye, IV56 8FD
Tel no: (01470) 572214
www.theisleofskye.co.uk
'Stunning location, historic connections, good food'

## Kilberry
## READERS RECOMMEND
# Kilberry Inn
**Modern British**
Kilberry, PA29 6YD
Tel no: (01880) 770223
www.kilberryinn.com
'One of Scotland's best-kept secrets'

# Kingussie

## The Cross
Natural-born enchantment
Ardbroilach Road, Kingussie, PH21 1LB
Tel no: (01540) 661166
www.thecross.co.uk
**Modern British | £50**
Cooking score: 5

A little piece of Arcadia in the Scottish Highlands, David and Katie Young's converted tweed mill by the bubbling Gynack Burn is pure, natural-born enchantment, whether you are whiling away the hours on the idyllic riverside terrace or ensconced in the rustic stone-walled dining room. The kitchen's commitment to ingredients is mightily impressive, right down to the different varieties of potato deployed in various dishes (Yukon Gold purée with fillet of Scrabster turbot, wild mushrooms and samphire, or Sharpe's Express alongside fillet of dry-aged Greenfield Farm beef, say). Dinner is a short fixed-price menu with a couple of simple supplements – a well-tried formula that continues to cast its spell. A tian of Kyle of Lochalsh langoustines, vine tomato and avocado is a bright way to start, before – say – roast loin of Perthshire venison with juniper jus, soured cabbage, spinach cream and parsnip boulangère. Desserts are perfectly conceived and impeccably balanced confections – perhaps spiced pear cake with salted butterscotch sauce and organic yoghurt ice cream. The organic theme is picked up by the wine list – a sheer delight that sees France and Spain out front, closely followed by exciting New World challengers. In keeping with the prevailing mood, wines are deliberately served 'without too much fuss' or ceremonial posturing. Prices start at £20.
**Chef/s:** David Young and Becca Henderson. **Open:** Tue to Sat D only 7 to 9. **Closed:** Sun, Mon, mid-Dec to early Feb (except Hogmanay). **Meals:** Set D £50 (4 courses). **Service:** not inc. **Details:** Cards accepted. 20 seats. Separate bar. No music. No mobile phones. Wheelchair access. Children allowed. Car parking.

# Kirkwall
## ALSO RECOMMENDED
### ▲ Dil Se
7 Bridge Street, Kirkwall, KW15 1HR
Tel no: (01856) 875242
www.dilserestaurant.co.uk
Indian

The modern, glass-fronted Bangladeshi-run restaurant behind the harbour is the most northerly outpost of Indian cooking in the UK. Head chef Motin Uddin delivers a menu that takes in most of the usual suspects – tandoori king prawns (£16.95), chicken tikka (£11.95) – but the cooking is consistently good, served with nice puffy naans and vegetable dishes such as saag bhaji (spiced spinach with garlic). Orkney ice cream served with gulab jamun is a fitting finish. House wine is £11.95. Open all week 4 to 11.

# Lochinver
## Albannach
Stellar chill-out with impeccable cooking
Baddidarroch, Lochinver, IV27 4LP
Tel no: (01571) 844407
www.thealbannach.co.uk
**Modern British | £50**
Cooking score: 6

Remoteness is a virtue at Colin Craig and Lesley Crosfield's tall white house on the shores of Loch Inver. For 20 years they have been providing solace and sustenance for scores of walkers, climbers and those who simply want to indulge in a little well-deserved R&R. Their dedication to local sourcing is admirable, although current constraints mean that they sometimes have to look further afield for supplies. Whatever the provenance, the results are generally impeccable. A typically glowing report details 'one of the best meals ever eaten' – crab tartlets with avocado, aubergine terrine and 'astonishingly tender' roe deer with truffle-infused butternut squash purée being the high points. On another night, the unhurried five-

course menu might track its way through seared wood pigeon breast with juniper cabbage and wild mushroom raviolo ahead of a tian of Mediterranean vegetables and goats' cheese, before alighting on wild Stornoway salmon with samphire, broad beans, coriander and lime sauce. Then it's off again for cheeses (Cuddy's Cave and Wigmore, say) and – finally – a typically unshowy dessert such as chocolate and walnut délice. Colin Craig was undertaking some serious work on his glorious wine list as our deadline approached, but it's safe to assume that stellar bottles from France will remain the most precious commodities. Prices currently start at £16.
**Chef/s:** Colin Craig and Lesley Crosfield. **Open:** all week D only 7.30 for 8 (1 sitting only). **Closed:** 4 Jan to 10 Mar, Mon to Wed in Nov, Dec and Mar (except Christmas 2 weeks). **Meals:** Set D £50 (5 courses). **Service:** not inc. **Details:** Cards accepted. 20 seats. No music. No mobile phones. Car parking.

## ▌Muir of Ord

### The Dower House
Cosseted domesticity in a stone lodge
Highfield, Muir of Ord, IV6 7XN
Tel no: (01463) 870090
www.thedowerhouse.co.uk
**Modern British | £38**
Cooking score: 2

More of a private residence than a hotel, Robyn and Mena Aitchison's early-Victorian stone lodge (originally a thatched farmhouse) is still a picture of cosseted domesticity. Guests are treated to evening meals in the country-house dinner party tradition – a touch of polite formality here, some homely bonhomie there. The menu doesn't allow for choice, so you might be offered lobster on tagliatelle with its own vinaigrette followed by local beef fillet with wild mushrooms or – on another night – roast quail on bulgur wheat before seared scallops with rosemary and anchovy dressing. To finish, expect caramelised strawberry crêpes, apricot tart or something similar. House wine is £18.

**Chef/s:** Robyn Aitchison. **Open:** all week D only 7.30 (1 sitting). **Closed:** Nov, Christmas. **Meals:** Set D £38. **Service:** not inc. **Details:** Cards accepted. 16 seats. Separate bar. No music. No mobile phones. Wheelchair access. Car parking.

## ▌Newtonmore
READERS RECOMMEND
### Blasta
Modern British
Main Street, Newtonmore, PH20 1DA
Tel no: (01540) 673231
www.blasta-restaurant.co.uk
'Excellent locally sourced ingredients, spot-on service, good atmosphere'

## ▌Plockton
### Plockton Inn
Simply succulent, naked seafood
Innes Street, Plockton, IV52 8TW
Tel no: (01599) 544222
www.plocktoninn.co.uk
**Seafood | £20**
Cooking score: 2

🛏 V 💧

They call Plockton 'the jewel in the Highlands' crown' and in shimmering spring sunshine who would argue? The hotel sits sweetly in the middle of a long row of whitewashed fishermen's cottages overlooking the loch, with both palm trees and camellias in the pocket-sized garden by the shore. The daily changing menu is inevitably fish-centric. The prawns travel yards from the jetty to the kitchen and arrive on your plate sweet, succulent and unadorned. Smoked salmon comes from the Sleepy Hollow Smokehouse at Aultbea, while poached haddock, pan-fried herring and simply flash-fried scallops flesh out the seafood litany. Decent, reasonably priced wines and local beer complete the picture. Wines from £13.50 a bottle.
**Chef/s:** Mary Gollan and Susan Trowbridge. **Open:** all week L 12 to 2.15, D 6 to 9. **Closed:** 25 and 26 Dec. **Meals:** alc (main courses £8 to £22).

Service: not inc. **Details:** Cards accepted. 50 seats. 20 seats outside. Separate bar. Music. Children allowed. Car parking.

## ▌Port Appin

### Airds Hotel

**Smart, intimate hotel with local food**
Port Appin, PA38 4DF
Tel no: (01631) 730236
www.airds-hotel.com
**Modern British | £50**
Cooking score: 5

Reached down a narrow, winding track off the main Oban to Fort William road, this smart, intimate hotel offers serene views across Loch Linnhe. In the kitchen Paul Burns takes native produce as his starting point – hand-dived local scallops with Stornaway black pudding and grape chutney, and local turbot and salmon wrapped in pastry with mushroom and served with a beurre blanc. Meat options have included prime Scotch beef fillet with foie gras, fondant potato and red wine sauce. At their best, flavours and textures work effectively and a couple who stayed for two nights reported a 'very competent and professional kitchen'. Dinner is a short, four-course, set-price affair, incorporating a mid-meal soup and culminating in desserts such as vanilla mousse with poached berries and a raspberry coulis. Quality is undisputed on a wide-reaching wine list that offers good drinking for under £25. House white and red are £21.95.
**Chef/s:** Paul Burns. **Open:** all week L 12 to 2, D 7.30 to 9.30. **Closed:** 2 days each week Nov to Jan. **Meals:** Set L £21.95 (2 courses) to £24.95. Set D £49.50 (4 courses). **Service:** not inc. **Details:** Cards accepted. 32 seats. No music. No mobile phones. Wheelchair access. Car parking.

## ▌St Margaret's Hope

### The Creel

**A delight, with rapturous views**
Front Road, St Margaret's Hope, KW17 2SL
Tel no: (01856) 831311
www.thecreel.co.uk
**Seafood | £35**
Cooking score: 7

Well worth the 13-mile drive from Kirkwall, this Orkney restaurant-with-rooms in a white-painted house on the seafront is a delight. With rapturous views over the open sea, it's hardly surprising that fish and shellfish are the strong suits – as in starters of grilled mackerel fillets in toasted oatmeal with rhubarb chutney, or scallops baked in their shells with parsley butter. It's the type of cooking that obstinately refuses to make a show of itself, and succeeds because of its simplicity and superb ingredients. Majestic main courses such as roasted hake with langoustines and spinach, or halibut with roasted peppers and parsnip purée remind you why you love seafood cookery. Meat-eaters might be regaled with two cuts of mutton – pot-roast leg and braised shank – in a sauce of barley and Pinot Noir. The chef's special plate is the smart way to finish: a line-up of chocolate mousse, meringues, crème caramel, a brandy snap and butterscotch sauce, or go for the selection of fine British cheeses with oatcakes. The short, stylistically grouped wine collection keeps the emphasis on value. There will be something there to suit whatever you're eating; from £14. Alan and Joyce Craigie have been running this place since 1985, so news that they have put the place on the market can only be received with regret. Ring to check they are still open for business.
**Chef/s:** Alan Craigie. **Open:** Wed to Sun D only 7 to 8.30. **Closed:** Mon, Tue, Oct to Easter. **Meals:** Set D £32 (2 courses) to £38. **Service:** not inc. **Details:** Cards accepted. 34 seats. No music. No mobile phones. Wheelchair access. Children allowed. Car parking.

## St Ola

### The Foveran

Modern British
Kirkwall, St Ola, KW15 1SF
Tel no: (01856) 872389
www.foveranhotel.co.uk
'Seafood to die for – it's so fresh and plump'

## Scrabster

### The Captain's Galley

Sustainable seafood by the harbour
The Harbour, Scrabster, KW14 7UJ
Tel no: (01847) 894999
www.captainsgalley.co.uk
Seafood | £40
Cooking score: 3

A sympathetically restored, nineteenth-century salmon station and ice house by Scrabster harbour is the evocative setting for the Cowies' seafood restaurant. Jim is on a mission to select the pick of the catch from the boats. Only sustainable species from 'non-pressure' local stocks make the grade; even so, there can be up to 10 different varieties on offer each night. Sea bass is given a honey and soy glaze, loin of cod is dusted with curry spices and a duo of split langoustines and roast gurnard is jazzed up with red pepper sauce vierge and crispy chorizo. The kitchen clearly takes a lively global view of things when it comes to flavour, although some reporters found the whole experience 'lukewarm' in every sense of the word. Round off proceedings with the 'infamous' hot chocolate pudding or ginger crème brûlée with orange and Armagnac-soaked prunes. Wines start at £14.75.
Chef/s: Jim Cowie. Open: Tue to Sat L 12.30 to 2.30, D 7 to 9. Closed: Sun, Mon, 25 and 26 Dec, 1 and 2 Jan. Meals: Set L £18 (2 courses) to £23. Set D £32 (2 courses) to £39.75. Service: not inc. Details: Cards accepted. 25 seats. Separate bar. Wheelchair access. Music. Children allowed. Car parking.

## Shieldaig

### Tigh an Eilean Hotel

Homespun hospitality
Shieldaig, IV54 8XN
Tel no: (01520) 755251
www.stevecarter.com/hotel/rest.htm
Modern British | £44
Cooking score: 3

£5 OFF ⌂

The name Tigh an Eilean ('house by the island') offers visitors the prospect of pure Highland enchantment amid some of Scotland's most dramatic scenery. Chris and Cathryn Field are purveyors of homespun hospitality and champions of local produce – especially seafood. The pick of the catch is delivered from jetty to kitchen, and it's deployed for lively dishes ranging from crab gratin with pink grapefruit to halibut fillet on linguine with asparagus velouté. Meat fans also have plenty to cheer about, with the likes of Provençal herb-crusted Blackface lamb on offer. To finish, Spain vies with Scotland when it comes to cheese and desserts (tarta de Santiago, say). House wine is £16.50. The Fields recently opened their all-day Shieldaig Bar & Coastal Kitchen next to the hotel, serving seafood and wood-fired pizzas with great views to boot.
Chef/s: Chris Field. Open: all week D only 7 to 8.30. Closed: Nov to Mar. Meals: Set D £44. Service: not inc. Details: Cards accepted. 24 seats. Separate bar. No music. No mobile phones. Children allowed. Car parking.

## Stonehaven

### The Tolbooth

Seafood
Old Pier, Stonehaven Harbour, Stonehaven, AB39 2JU
Tel no: (01569) 762287
www.tolbooth-restaurant.co.uk
'Freshly caught seafood'

## ▌Strontian

# Kilcamb Lodge

Tranquil, comfortable country house
Strontian, PH36 4HY
Tel no: (01967) 402257
www.kilcamblodge.co.uk
**Modern European | £48**
**Cooking score: 5**

🍷 🍽

At David and Sally Fox's extended eighteenth-century stone house on the shores of Loch Sunart, tranquillity and space are part of the pull. It's a comfortable, 'non-pretentious' country house, and while another new chef has taken over, reports continue to praise the cooking and the 'second-to-none' service. Dinner is a daily changing four-course affair offering a pair of choices at starter and main course stage. Tammo Siemers' cooking keeps to established principles, with nothing to jar the nerves. Fresh fish and seafood is always offered, perhaps in the form of seared scallops with cauliflower tempura and walnut dressing or red mullet with confit fennel and orange dressing. Meats are well selected too: game in the shape of a starter of seared pigeon breast with poached figs and juniper jus, or a main course roast fillet of beef teamed with braised oxtail and served with pickled onions and carrots. A good wine list is arranged by grape variety. France dominates, but choice is wide-ranging, with prices starting at £19.75 for an Argentinian Torrontes and £23.75 for a South African Shiraz.

**Chef/s:** Tammo Siemers. **Open:** all week L 12 to 1.30, D 7.30 to 9.30. **Meals:** Set L £14.75 (2 courses) to £17.50. Set D £35 (2 courses) to £48 (4 courses). Sun L £14.50. **Service:** not inc. **Details:** Cards accepted. 26 seats. Separate bar. No mobile phones. Wheelchair access. Music. Car parking.

## Adam Stokes  Glenapp Castle

**Who or what inspired you to become a chef?**
I was always cooking and experimenting when young.

**If you were to have one abiding principle in the kitchen, what would it be?**
Accurate cooking and consistency is the key!

**What is the best meal you have ever eaten?**
Had a special meal at Restaurant Neichel in Barcelona.

**Which chefs do you admire?**
John Campbell, Gordon Ramsay, not only for cooking but for business too.

**What do you do to relax when out of the kitchen?**
Spending time with my wife and driving the roads of Scotland.

**What do you like cooking when you are 'off duty'?**
Traditional method curries.

**What is the best part of your job?**
Working with the finest ingredients. Seeing the development of young chefs.

# WALES

Glamorgan, Gwent, Mid-Wales, North-East Wales, North-West Wales, West Wales

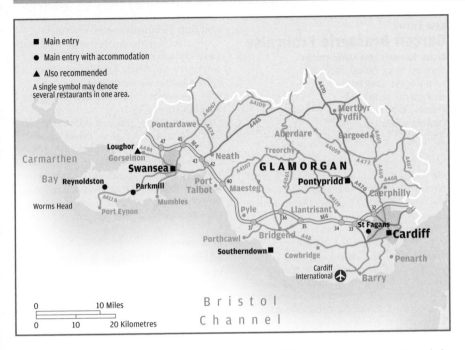

- ■ Main entry
- ● Main entry with accommodation
- ▲ Also recommended

A single symbol may denote several restaurants in one area.

## Bridgend

### READERS RECOMMEND
## Bokhara Brasserie
**Indian**
Court Colman Manor, Bridgend, CF31 4NG
Tel no: (01656) 720212
www.court-colman-manor.com
**'It came as a shock to find a very good tandoori in a Welsh country house'**

## Cardiff

## Le Gallois
**Sophistication, flamboyance and charm**
6-10 Romilly Crescent, Cardiff, CF11 9NR
Tel no: (029) 2034 1264
www.legallois.co.uk
**Modern European | £30**
**Cooking score: 4**

Sophistication is the keynote here, but Le Gallois also strikes a relaxing chord. Charming French staff, loungeable chairs in the bar and a spacious dining room make it easy to while away longer than you intended. The food is a modish, often imaginative take on classic themes. An inspection lunch included a pastel-pretty starter of salmon quenelles with perfectly seasoned crab bisque, while sweet, fall-apart-tender confit duck found the ideal foil in the slight acidity of a sun-dried tomato and leek risotto. A dessert of carrot cake, while down-to-earth wholesome, did not sit comfortably with the generally more flamboyant cooking style, which in the evening might produce wood pigeon faggot with black pudding, game jus, carrot froth, mushy peas and a poached quail's egg, or pork belly with a chou farci of pork livers and Agen prunes with cider gastrique. The wines – mostly French and with good regional coverage – start at £14.50.

**Chef/s:** Grady Atkins. **Open:** Tue to Sun L 12 to 3, Tue to Sat D 6.30 to 10. **Closed:** Mon, 25 Dec to 5 Jan. **Meals:** alc (main courses £14 to £21). Set L £15.95 (2 courses) to £18.95. **Service:** 10% (optional). **Details:** Cards accepted. 60 seats. Air-con. Separate bar. Wheelchair access. Music. Children allowed. Car parking.

## NEW ENTRY
# Garçon Brasserie Française

**Bistro flavours and Gallic charm**
Mermaid Quay, Cardiff, CF10 5BZ
Tel no: (029) 2049 0990
www.garcon-resto.co.uk
French | £27
Cooking score: 1

Styled for maximum Gallic charm, Garçon is the younger sibling of longstanding Cardiff favourite Le Gallois (see entry). The food here is classic bistro fare: think moules marinière, cassoulet and tarte Tatin. Fresh, good-quality ingredients make it worth a visit, but an inspection meal revealed elements of unpredictability: a crisp pastry parcel of melting goats' cheese came with tomato chutney but minus the promised tapenade, while beautifully fresh sea bass arrived with an unadvertised mushroom and cream sauce. Wines start at £14.95.
**Chef/s:** Gareth Farr. **Open:** all week 12 to 10 (11 Sat and Sun, 9 Mon). **Closed:** 25 and 26 Dec, 1 Jan. **Meals:** alc (main courses £10 to £25). Set L and D £12.95 (2 courses) to £15.95. **Service:** not inc. **Details:** Cards accepted. 100 seats. 30 seats outside. Air-con. Wheelchair access. Music. Children allowed.

# Gilby's

**Comfort food and ambitious flourishes**
Old Port Road, Culverhouse Cross, Cardiff, CF5 6DN
Tel no: (02920) 670800
www.gilbysrestaurant.co.uk
Modern European | £30
Cooking score: 2

£5
OFF

Housed in a converted eighteenth-century barn conversion on the outskirts of Cardiff, Gilby's is a restaurant that lives something of a double life. On the one hand, a repertoire of emphatically Welsh comfort food draws the crowds from the city, with a Wye valley smoked salmon and chive mousse proving a popular starter. On the other hand, executive

chef Kurt Fleming is not afraid to apply continental technique to Welsh produce, with a pan-fried fillet of bass and crispy confit chicken on a sauté of broccoli and thyme spätzle among the more ambitious mains on offer. A generous wine list sees house wines weighing in at £15.
**Chef/s:** Kurt Fleming. **Open:** all week L 12 to 2.30 (3 Sun), Mon to Sat D 5.45 to 10. **Closed:** 26 and 27 Dec, 1 Jan. **Meals:** alc (main courses £10 to £28). Set L £14.95 (2 courses) to £19.95. Set D early eve £19.95. Sun L £19.95. **Service:** not inc. **Details:** Cards accepted. 100 seats. 50 seats outside. Separate bar. No mobile phones. Wheelchair access. Music. Children allowed. Car parking.

## NEW ENTRY
# Mimosa Kitchen & Bar

**Fashionable newcomer by the bay**
Mermaid Quay, Cardiff, CF10 5BZ
Tel no: (029) 2049 1900
www.mimosakitchen.co.uk
Modern European | £22
Cooking score: 2

V

Mimosa proudly announces itself as Cardiff's 'first gastro bar', and slate floors and steel surfaces give a stark, contemporary feel. Surprising, then, that much of the menu is so fiercely patriotic: on inspection a starter of traditional Welsh lamb cawl (soup), served with Gorwydd Caerphilly cheese proved impressive. A main course of crispy wild sea bass served with new potatoes and fennel was further evidence of a kitchen playing to its strengths, but be warned; the nightclub-esque atmosphere might not be to everyone's taste. A modest wine list is overshadowed by a very reasonable cocktail menu, starting at £5.75.
**Chef/s:** Alun Roberts. **Open:** all week 10 to 10 (9.30 Sun). **Closed:** 25 and 26 Dec. **Meals:** alc (main courses £8 to £17). Sun L £12.95 (2 courses) to £14.95. **Service:** not inc. **Details:** Cards accepted. 67 seats. 40 seats outside. Air-con. Separate bar. Wheelchair access. Music. Children allowed.

## NEW ENTRY
# Mint & Mustard

**Neighbourhood Indian with big ideas**
134 Whitchurch Road, Cardiff, CF14 3LZ
Tel no: (029) 2062 0333
www.mintandmustard.com
**Indian | £22**
**Cooking score: 2**

£5 OFF  **V**  £30

Mint & Mustard is set in an unassuming suburb of Cardiff and passers-by might struggle to distinguish it from the innumerable Indian restaurants that line the streets. But once inside it's clear why M&M's quirky brand of superior subcontinental cooking pulls in so many punters: a starter of Bombay chaat served with chutney and gram flour vermicelli is evidence of considerable chutzpah in an ambitious kitchen. Meanwhile, a main of chicken Chettinad is symptomatic of a menu dominated by South Indian – particularly Keralan – dishes. A respectable wine list opens at £12 a bottle.
**Chef/s:** Anand George. **Open:** Sun to Fri L 12 to 2.30, all week D 6 to 11 (10.30 Sun). **Meals:** alc (main courses £5 to £12). Set D £27. **Service:** not inc. **Details:** Cards accepted. 60 seats. Air-con. Separate bar. Music. Children allowed.

# Patagonia

**South America meets South Wales**
11 Kings Road, Cardiff, CF11 9BZ
Tel no: (029) 2019 0265
www.patagonia-restaurant.co.uk
**Modern European | £35**
**Cooking score: 3**

£5 OFF

Welsh-Argentinian cooking might seem an unlikely marriage, but Joaquin and Leticia Humaran's neighbourhood restaurant continues to turn heads by applying some Hispanic swagger to Celtic fare. By day a humble coffee house – with a sideline in pastas and risottos – as evening approaches the lights are dimmed, and the two-tier dining area effortlessly transforms into a small but stylish showcase for the couple's innovative cooking.

A near pitch-perfect starter of rabbit and medjool date terrine wrapped in Parma ham, perhaps, followed by an equally accomplished main of Gressingham duck breast served with parsnip and celeriac purée and an Earl Grey jus. Unsurprisingly, the cursory wine list shows a South American bias, with house wine opening the bidding at £13 a bottle.
**Chef/s:** Joaquin Humaran. **Open:** Tue to Sat D 6.30 to 10. **Closed:** Sun, Mon, 25 Dec to 15 Jan.
**Meals:** Set D £24.90 (2 courses) to £28.90.
**Service:** not inc. **Details:** Cards accepted. 42 seats. Air-con. Wheelchair access. Music. Children allowed. Car parking.

# Woods Brasserie

**Crowd-pleasing food with a view**
The Pilotage Building, Stuart Street, Cardiff, CF10 5BW
Tel no: (029) 2049 2400
www.woods-brasserie.com
**Modern European | £25**
**Cooking score: 2**

**V**  £30

Now entering its tenth year in the stately Pilotage Building at Cardiff Bay, Woods' formula for modern brasserie food in stylish surroundings has changed little over the last decade. A superior spot for people-watching, the restaurant is especially atmospheric when the rain from the bay beats against the glass walls of the dining room. On inspection, a starter of roasted scallops with a slightly disappointing parsnip and vanilla purée was redeemed by a main of Welsh lamb with Hispi cabbage, served with a baby shepherd's pie. Elsewhere on the menu, a perennially popular grill option offers a selection of steaks. House wines open at £17.
**Chef/s:** Wesley Hammond. **Open:** all week L 12 to 2 (3 Sun), D 5.30 to 10. **Closed:** Sun D Sept to June.
**Meals:** alc (main courses £11 to £22). Set L £13.50 (2 courses) to £16.50. Sun L £14.95 (2 courses) to £17.95. **Service:** not inc. **Details:** Cards accepted. 90 seats. 50 seats outside. Air-con. Separate bar. Wheelchair access. Music. Children allowed.

## Loughor

### ALSO RECOMMENDED
### ▲ Hurrens Inn on the Estuary

13 Station Road, Loughor, SA4 6TR
Tel no: (01792) 899092
www.hurrens.co.uk
**Modern European**

A stylish little restaurant with views of North Gower and the Loughor estuary, Hurrens serves up modern, internationally inspired food made with fresh, largely Welsh ingredients. Typical dishes include pan-fried pigeon salad with Perl Las cheese (£5.95), chargrilled wild boar with a mustard crust, red cabbage, apple and thyme jus (£16.50) and apple and blackberry crumble (£5). Wines from £14.95. Open Tue to Sun L and Tue to Sat D.

## Mumbles

### READERS RECOMMEND
### Labaire's

**British**
93 Newton Road, Mumbles, SA3 4BN
Tel no: (01792) 366006
'Food is local, fresh and lovingly prepared'

## Parkmill

NEW ENTRY
### Maes-Yr-Haf

**Serious dining in a valley**
Parkmill, SA3 2EH
Tel no: (01792) 371000
www.maes-yr-haf.com
**Modern British | £30**
Cooking score: 3

£5 OFF 🚗

An excellent boutique hotel with a 'wonderful atmosphere', Maes-Yr-Haf has plugged a gap in Gower's dining scene by offering serious cooking in a stylish modern setting. The food is sometimes inventive, but draws on classic/traditional themes. Tender confit duck leg

rillettes with translucent beetroot carpaccio and hazelnut dressing has impressed, as has breast of guinea fowl (again, beautifully tender) served on a clear-flavoured tarragon risotto with buttered greens and mushroom fricassee. There are some inexplicable frills (creamed potato supporting a lattice-cut crisp on a plate of cod and chips) but the cooking is accurate and flavours are on the money – as in a balanced dessert of Welsh cakes with strawberries, cream and balsamic ice cream. Wines start at £13.95 a bottle.
**Chef/s:** Christos Georgakis. **Open:** Tue to Sun L 12 to 2.30 (4 Sun), Tue to Sat D 7 to 9.30. Open Mon Apr to Aug. **Closed:** 25 and 26 Dec, 2 weeks Jan. **Meals:** alc (main courses £14 to £25). Set L £13.95 (2 courses) to £16.95. Sun L £17.95. **Service:** not inc. **Details:** Cards accepted. 44 seats. 40 seats outside. Separate bar. Wheelchair access. Music. Car parking.

## Pontypridd

### The Bunch of Grapes

**Buzzing gastropub with snappy food**
Ynysangharad Road, Pontypridd, CF37 4DA
Tel no: (01443) 402934
www.bunchofgrapes.org.uk
**Gastropub | £25**
Cooking score: 1

£5 OFF  £30

Originally frequented by passing canal boat tradesmen, the Bunch of Grapes now lures diners with 'great locally-sourced food, great ales and a relaxed informal atmosphere buzzing with life'. The stylish but traditional interior includes a conservatory adorned with a living vine. Expect snappy gastropub food: choices range from salmon, prawn and cockle pie with hand-cut chips and green herb salad to posh burgers (homemade relishes are available to take away). Wines start at £12.95.
**Chef/s:** Sebastien Vanoni. **Open:** all week L 12 to 3 (3.30 Sun), Mon to Sat D 6 to 9.30. **Meals:** alc (main courses £13 to £17). **Service:** not inc. **Details:** Cards accepted. 62 seats. 24 seats outside. Separate bar. Wheelchair access. Music. Children allowed. Car parking.

## ▮ Reynoldston

### Fairyhill

Local food and a gorgeous setting
Reynoldston, SA3 1BS
Tel no: (01792) 390139
www.fairyhill.net
**Modern British | £45**
Cooking score: 4

In the heart of Gower, this 'secluded and charming' country house is a world away from the daily grind. It stands amid 24 acres of parkland, threaded with countless walks. The interior is homely and traditional, with a large lounge and plentiful sofas for pre- or post-dinner drinks. 'Knowledgeable and unobtrusive' staff add to the sense of luxury. The food is simple, fresh and local. For the lowest food miles you could try air-dried Welsh Black beef with citrus dressing, capers and Parmesan, followed by mélange of local seafood with vegetable fettuccine and laverbread velouté. Round it off with treacle and walnut tart with clotted cream. Lunches are 'particularly good value' and the wine list takes in everything from classics to lively new finds from around the world. Bottles are priced from £15.50, with a good selection under £25.
**Chef/s:** James Hamilton. **Open:** all week L 12 to 2, D 7 to 9. **Closed:** 25 and 26 Dec, first 3 weeks Jan. **Meals:** alc (main courses £15 to £25). Set L £15.95 (2 courses) to £19.95. Set D £35 (2 courses) to £45. Sun L £24.50. **Service:** not inc. **Details:** Cards accepted. 60 seats. 20 seats outside. Separate bar. Wheelchair access. Music. Car parking.

## ▮ St Fagans

### The Old Post Office

Delivering first-class food
Greenwood Lane, St Fagans, CF5 6EL
Tel no: (02920) 565400
www.theoldpostofficerestaurant.co.uk
**Modern European | £28**
Cooking score: 3

Four miles from Cardiff, this former post office and police station continues to serve its sleepy village as an unpretentious but nonetheless accomplished restaurant. A short walk to the entrance at the back reveals a conservatory extension decked out in a contemporary but cosy style. Much of the menu remains faithful to the region's maritime heritage. A starter of soused mackerel and potato salad might be followed by skate wing with anchovies and black butter, or perhaps fresh crab risotto. Slow-roasted belly pork with mash and roast fennel is another tempting main. House wines are £12.
**Chef/s:** Simon Kealy. **Open:** Tue to Sun L 12 to 3, Tue to Sat D 7 to 9.30. **Closed:** Mon, 25 to 27 Dec, 2 weeks Jan, 2 weeks August. **Meals:** alc (main courses £12 to £18). Set L £11.95 (2 courses) to £14.95. Set D £15 (2 courses) to £20. **Service:** not inc. **Details:** Cards accepted. 38 seats. 30 seats outside. Air-con. Separate bar. Wheelchair access. Music. Children allowed. Car parking.

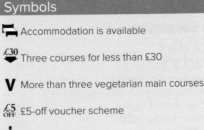

### Symbols

🛏 Accommodation is available

£30 Three courses for less than £30

V More than three vegetarian main courses

£5 OFF £5-off voucher scheme

🍾 Notable wine list

## ▌Southerndown

### La Plie

Fine dining and a warm welcome
52 Beach Road, Southerndown, CF32 0RP
Tel no: (01656) 880127
www.laplierestaurant.co.uk
Modern French | £36
Cooking score: 2

£5
OFF

A red-brick building standing on a windswept corner looking out across rolling fields may seem an unlikely location for fine dining. Once inside, however, the warm welcome from friendly, professional staff hints at what's to come. Soft lighting bounces off the cream walls in the small, high-ceilinged room. Chairs are comfortable and tables are covered in immaculate linen. Chef/owner Leon Matt Powell has a background in classically based establishments and this shows in a starter of grilled red mullet with pan-fried squid, squid ink gnocchi and sauce nero, and a main course of braised shoulder of rose veal en crépinette with buttered sea kale and roasted golden beetroot. House wine £15.
**Chef/s:** Leon Matt Powell. **Open:** Wed to Sun L 12.30 to 2, Thur to Sat D 7.30 to 10. **Closed:** Mon, Tue, first week Jan, bank hols (open 25 Dec). **Meals:** Set L £16 (2 courses) to £20. Set D £29 (2 courses) to £36. **Service:** not inc. **Details:** Cards accepted. 26 seats. 4 seats outside. No mobile phones. Wheelchair access. Music. Children allowed. Car parking.

## ▌Swansea

### Darcy's

Snug seafront eatery with sweeping views
698 Mumbles Road, Swansea, SA3 4EH
Tel no: (01792) 361616
Modern British | £25
Cooking score: 1

£30

Close to the tip of the Mumbles headland, Darcy's commands sweeping views of Swansea Bay from its spot on the seafront.

Inside the narrow dining room, light blue walls give a nautical feel, while crisp linen and exposed brickwork balance snugness with sophistication. The short menu shows an inclination towards seafood: a starter of asparagus with poached egg and hollandaise sauce might be followed by catch of the day – say, crispy sea bass, served with boulangère potatoes. House wines start at £12 a bottle.
**Chef/s:** Bryony Jones. **Open:** Wed to Sun L 12.15 to 2 (2.30 Fri to Sun), Tue to Sat D 6.15 to 9 (9.30 Fri and Sat). **Closed:** Mon. **Meals:** alc (main courses £11 to £26). Set L £14 (2 courses) to £17. **Service:** not inc. **Details:** Cards accepted. 40 seats. Air-con. No mobile phones. Wheelchair access. Music. Children allowed.

### Didier & Stephanie

Classic, classy French cooking
56 St Helen's Road, Swansea, SA1 4BE
Tel no: (01792) 655603
French | £30
Cooking score: 4

Nearing its tenth birthday, Didier Suvé and Stephanie Danvel's little island of French sophistication keeps things classic, classy and precise. The interior is a feast of buttery yellows and bare wood. In the kitchen, Didier works with Welsh ingredients (bar a few imported French specialities) to produce food that manages the rare trick of being both familiar and thrilling. Visitors repeatedly praise the consistency of what's on offer here. From one dish to the next, Didier keeps all the balls in the air, deftly handling tastes, textures and timing. Typical of the unfussy style are a croustillant of French black pudding with mustard dressing, followed by pan-fried wild sea bass with saffron sauce. Dessert might be tarte Tatin served with crème fraîche. The Francophile wine list kicks off at £12.90.
**Chef/s:** Didier Suvé. **Open:** Tue to Sat L 12 to 2, D 7 to 9. **Closed:** Sun, Mon, 2 weeks Christmas. **Meals:** alc (main courses £14 to £18). Set L £13.90 (2 courses) to £16.50. **Service:** not inc. **Details:** Cards accepted. 25 seats. Air-con. Music. Children allowed.

## Hanson at the Chelsea Restaurant

**A flair for seafood**
17 St Mary Street, Swansea, SA1 3LH
Tel no: (01792) 464068
www.hansonatthechelsearestaurant.co.uk
Modern British | £28
Cooking score: 3

 £30

Tucked down a pedestrianised side street, this smart little restaurant remains Swansea's best bet for fish and seafood. Andrew Hanson's cooking is big on colour, flavour and freshness, thanks – in part – to the proximity of Swansea marina. Pan-fried scallops with a glaze of ginger-scented hollandaise, warm asparagus and crispy cockle salad followed by local Dover sole with fresh lemon and parsley butter are typical maritime offerings, while plentiful fish-free options could include a deep-fried croquette of goats' cheese with red onion marmalade, followed by slow-cooked navarin of lamb with gratin dauphinois. Leave room for desserts such as hot apple crêpes or lemon tart. Wines from £11.95.
**Chef/s:** Andrew Hanson. **Open:** Mon to Sat L 12 to 2, all week D 7 to 10. **Closed:** 25 and 26 Dec, bank hols. **Meals:** alc (main courses £10 to £22). Set L £11.95 (2 courses) to £16.50. Set D £20 (2 courses) to £25. **Service:** not inc. **Details:** Cards accepted. 34 seats. No mobile phones. Wheelchair access. Music. Children allowed.

## Slice

**Confident, pint-sized contender**
75 Eversley Road, Swansea, SA2 9DE
Tel no: (01792) 290929
www.sliceswansea.co.uk
Modern British | £30
Cooking score: 3

Customers sit upstairs in the pint-sized dining room of this wedge-shaped building, while Phil Leach is hard at work in the glass-fronted kitchen down below. The relatively short menu allows him to produce food of consistently high quality, with no corner-cutting. This is refined but uncomplicated food, based around the best ingredients the region can offer. Trendy British themes such as pork belly with caramelised apples, creamed potato and cider sauce are beautifully handled, while stunningly fresh fish is key to starters such as grilled mackerel fillet with warm potato salad and horseradish dressing. Desserts range from the traditional sticky toffee pudding to classics such as chocolate marquise with white chocolate sorbet. Wines start at £12.95.
**Chef/s:** Philip Leach. **Open:** Thur to Sun L 12 to 2, D 6.30 to 9. **Closed:** Mon to Wed, 25 Dec to 22 Jan. **Meals:** Set L £15 (2 courses) to £20. Set D £30. **Service:** not inc. **Details:** Cards accepted. 18 seats. No music. No mobile phones.

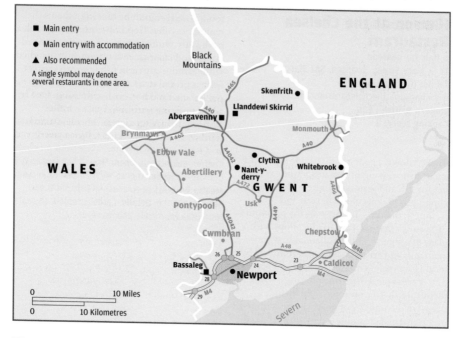

■ Main entry
● Main entry with accommodation
▲ Also recommended
A single symbol may denote
several restaurants in one area.

## Abergavenny

### The Hardwick

**Intelligent food in a welcoming setting**
Old Raglan Road, Abergavenny, NP7 9AA
Tel no: (01873) 854220
www.thehardwick.co.uk
**Modern British | £30**
**Cooking score: 4**

Stephen Terry's welcoming roadside
gastropub has plenty of admirers, including
one who ranks the triple-cooked chips as
'better than Heston's'. The interior – 'warm
and cosy, with a roaring log fire' – is a mix of
bare wood and reclaimed furniture. The menu
is built on stunning ingredients such as Black
Mountain Smokery hot- and cold-smoked
salmon with salted cucumber and crème
fraîche, followed by braised shoulder and roast
loin of local, organic lamb with fried polenta,
roast winter vegetables and salsa verde.
Desserts continue along traditional lines, with
an upmarket take on bread-and-butter
pudding or rhubarb-and-custard crumble.

While the friendly, attentive staff please most
visitors, 'erratic service' has been noted when
this popular pub is packed. The cosmopolitan
wine list is divided by style, making it easy to
tell oaked from unoaked, full-bodied from
light. Bottles start at £14.50.
**Chef/s:** Stephen Terry. **Open:** Tue to Sun L 12 to 3,
Tue to Sat D 6.30 to 10. **Closed:** Mon, 25 and 26
Dec. **Meals:** alc (main courses £12 to £20). Set L
£17.95 (2 courses) to £21. Sun L £18.95 (2 courses) to
£22.50. **Service:** not inc. **Details:** Cards accepted.
70 seats. 20 seats outside. Separate bar. No mobile
phones. Wheelchair access. Music. Children
allowed. Car parking.

### READERS RECOMMEND

### The Angel Hotel

**Modern British**
15 Cross Street, Abergavenny, NP7 5EN
Tel no: (01873) 857121
www.angelhotelabergavenny.com
**'Astounded by the high quality of the menu'**

The Good Food Guide 2010

## Bassaleg

### Junction 28

**Internationally inspired food**
Station Approach, Bassaleg, NP10 8LD
Tel no: (01633) 891891
www.junction28.com
**Modern European | £20**
Cooking score: 2

This tranquil, leafy spot was originally the site of the old Bassaleg railway station. Part of the restaurant is decked out in the style of an old railway carriage, which is – trust us – considerably less tacky than it sounds. The menus offer 'beautifully served food with lots of flavour and lots of choice': starters range from lamb kofta to a baked suet pudding packed with winter game. Classic French cooking dominates the main courses, with occasional international diversions, as in a duo of monkfish with tempura prawns, pea purée and tartare sauce. Finish with lemon posset. Wine starts at £13.50.
**Chef/s:** Jean Jacques Payel. **Open:** all week L 12 to 2 (4 Sun), Mon to Sat D 5.30 to 9.30. **Closed:** 26 Dec, 1 Jan, last week Jul, first week Aug. **Meals:** alc (main courses £11 to £19). Set L £11.95 (2 courses) to £13.95. Set D £16.95 (3 courses). Sun L £12.95 (2 courses) to £14.95. **Service:** not inc. **Details:** Cards accepted. 160 seats. Air-con. Separate bar. Wheelchair access. Music. Children allowed. Car parking.

## Clytha

### The Clytha Arms

**Traditional pub with classy food**
Clytha, NP7 9BW
Tel no: (01873) 840206
www.clytha-arms.com
**Modern British | £29**
Cooking score: 3

A converted dower house beside the old Abergavenny to Raglan road, this traditional-looking pub has a delightful fire-warmed bar where locals chat and six real ales are always on tap. But it also has a trick up its sleeve – namely the classy food that appears in the place of ordinary pub grub. You'll need to order from the restaurant menu to fully experience this; kick off with goats' cheese dumplings with wild mushrooms before a main course of grilled quail with spring risotto, followed by plum pudding with rum butter. Other options include tapas (fried cheese-stuffed chillies or Penclawdd cockles with laverbread) and bar meals such as steak, beer and pickled walnut pie. Plenty of thought has gone into the ambitious wine list, which touts classics and new trendies with equal gusto. Prices (from £13.95) are fair, and there's a well-considered selection by the half-bottle and glass.
**Chef/s:** Andrew Canning. **Open:** Tue to Sun L 12 to 3, Tue to Sat D 6 to 12. **Closed:** Mon, 25 Dec. **Meals:** Set L and D £19.95 (2 courses) to £23. Sun L £17 (2 courses) to £20. Tapas and Bar menu available. **Service:** not inc. **Details:** Cards accepted. 60 seats. Air-con. Separate bar. No music. Children allowed. Car parking.

## Llanddewi Skirrid

### The Walnut Tree

**Flourishing in Shaun Hill's hands**
Llanddewi Skirrid, NP7 8AW
Tel no: (01873) 852797
www.thewalnuttreeinn.com
**Modern British | £32**
Cooking score: 5

Shaun Hill has now settled in as chef and joint owner of this resurgent restaurant, which had closed down before he stepped into the breach. 'The makeover of the Walnut Tree has been entirely successful', pronounces one reader, clearly noting that love and attention have been lavished on every aspect of this sturdy, whitewashed building beneath Skirrid mountain. Hill is very much hands-on at the stove, but while he cooked solo in his previous venture (the Merchant House in Ludlow), he now shares the task with a brigade of chefs. The straight-talking cooking references Hill's Merchant House days, pulling together top-notch ingredients and classic techniques with deceptive insouciance. From calves' brains with brown butter to cassoulet of goose, lamb and sausage, there are plenty of fortifying choices. However, for a lighter touch, look to griddled squid with chilli, mint and borlotti beans followed by Roquefort tart with roasted chicory and walnut salad. Desserts range from sticky toffee pudding with clotted cream to blood orange and raspberry mousse. The wine list fulfils its promise to prioritise quality, interest and artisan growers – and the result is an engaging and surprisingly reasonably priced list of 80-plus bins, with bottles starting at £16.

**Chef/s:** Shaun Hill and Roger Brook. **Open:** Tue to Sat L 12 to 3, D 7 to 10. **Closed:** Sun, Mon, one week Christmas. **Meals:** alc (main courses £9 to £20). Set L £15 (2 courses) to £20. **Service:** not inc. **Details:** Cards accepted. 60 seats. 20 seats outside. Air-con. Separate bar. No music. Wheelchair access. Children allowed. Car parking.

## Nant-y-derry
### The Foxhunter
Proper, honest food
Nant-y-derry, NP7 9DN
Tel no: (01873) 881101
www.thefoxhunter.com
**Modern British | £30**
Cooking score: 4

The old stationmaster's house is light, calm and stylishly understated, its 'well-deserved reputation' built on 'proper honest food, no foams or other pretentious nonsense'. Understandable when chef and co-proprietor Matt Tebbutt is influenced by time spent with mentors such as Marco Pierre White, and by the wealth of excellent ingredients available locally. Dishes range from posh peasant food (pigeon soup with braised lentils and winter vegetables or seafood bourride with rouille and garlic bruschetta) to modern riffs on classic themes – lamb gigot with creamed cocoa beans, purple broccoli, rosemary and anchovy butter or roast wild boar with dauphinoise potato, red cabbage and apple and

star anise purée. The latter approach extends to desserts such as clementine and ginger steamed pudding with orange sauce and crème fraîche. The lengthy wine list has something for all palates and pockets, and its neatly balanced global portfolio ranges from French regional certainties to upbeat Aussie contenders. Prices start at £14.95.

**Chef/s:** Matt Tebbutt. **Open:** Tue to Sun L 12 to 2.30, Tue to Sat D 7 to 9.30. **Closed:** Mon, 25 and 26 Dec, 1 Jan. **Meals:** alc (main courses £13 to £21). Set L £18.95 (2 courses) to £23.95. Sun L £20.95 (2 courses) to £25.95. **Service:** not inc. **Details:** Cards accepted. 50 seats. 12 seats outside. Separate bar. Wheelchair access. Music. Children allowed. Car parking.

## Newport
### The Chandlery
Top-drawer local ingredients
77-78 Lower Dock Street, Newport, NP20 1EH
Tel no: (01633) 256622
www.thechandleryrestaurant.com
**Modern British | £27**
Cooking score: 4

£30

There are no prizes for guessing that this double-fronted, Grade II-listed building was once a ship's chandlery, but since 2002 it has served the denizens of Newport and beyond as a stylish restaurant spread over two floors. Contemporary design blends sympathetically with original period features in the lounge and rambling dining areas, where the mood is congenial. Top-drawer native ingredients form the cornerstones of the kitchen's efforts, whatever the occasion. Light lunches of antipasti, Welsh rarebit or free-range bangers and mash could give way to more ambitious grills and a host of carefully honed specialities ranging from Andrew Morgan's venison with celeriac purée, roast beetroot and Black Mountain jus to baked cod with Penclawdd cockles, spring onion and cheese mash. Start with smoked Pant Mawr cheese and chicken boudin with Puy lentils, and end with local honey and hazelnut parfait with mango sauce, or vanilla pannacotta with rhubarb compote.

Around four dozen well-considered wines kick off with house selections from £13.95 (£3.50 a glass). **Chef/s:** Simon Newcombe. **Open:** Tue to Fri and Sun L 12 to 2, Tue to Sat D 7 to 10. **Closed:** Mon. **Meals:** alc (main courses £12 to £18). Set L £11.95 (2 courses) to £14.50. **Service:** not inc. **Details:** Cards accepted. 80 seats. Air-con. Separate bar. Music. Children allowed. Car parking.

## The Crown
**Classic strokes and bold invention**
The Celtic Manor Resort, Coldra Woods, Newport, NP18 1HQ
Tel no: (01633) 413000
www.celtic-manor.com
**Modern European | £48**
**Cooking score: 5**

Destination tourism, leisure and corporate hospitality on a grand scale are the hallmarks of the sprawling Celtic Manor Resort. Crowning it all is the new flagship restaurant – a contemporary design triumph that sends out all the right signals with its walnut floors, chandeliers cascading from elliptical coffered ceilings and a bespoke glass screen by the chef's table. The whole set-up is a tie-in with the Crown at Whitebrook (see entry), and executive chef James Sommerin oversees both venues – although Tim McDougall is responsible for the day-to-day running of the kitchen. Native produce is treated with due respect for a repertoire that mixes bold invention with a solid grounding in the classics. A starter of semi-cured Welsh beef with preserved truffle, quails' eggs and smoked Berkswell cheese sets the tone, ahead of roast veal loin with twice-cooked sweetbreads, asparagus and warm tomato and olive vinaigrette. When it comes to fish, the kitchen looks to the orient for thrills – serving wasabi cream and white radish salad with mi-cuit of sea trout, adding smoked eel tempura to a dish of halibut with beetroot essence, and partnering braised skate wing with clam curry. Desserts also deliver top-end surprises in the shape of, say, poached tamarillo with vanilla cheesecake and citrus lace 'bisquit'. The wine list is a fascinating, exhaustive tour of some of the world's most auspicious vineyards. Don't miss the special wine flights or the sommelier's selection, served in Riedel tasting glasses. Prices start at £23 (£5.25 a glass). **Chef/s:** Tim McDougall. **Open:** Tue to Sat L 12 to 2, D 7 to 10. **Closed:** Sun, Mon, 1 to 14 Jan. **Meals:** Set L £14.95 (2 courses) to £19.95. Midweek set D £19.95 (2 courses) to £28. Set D £47.50. Tasting menu £65 (6 courses). **Service:** not inc. **Details:** Cards accepted. 45 seats. Separate bar. No mobile phones. Wheelchair access. Music. Car parking.

## Skenfrith
## The Bell at Skenfrith
**Beautiful pub in a breathtaking setting**
Skenfrith, NP7 8UH
Tel no: (01600) 750235
www.skenfrith.co.uk
**Gastropub | £30**
**Cooking score: 4**

£5 OFF

What a setting: a river, castle and wooded hills mean that before you even sit down to eat, this pristine gastropub feels like Wales on a plate. Inside, expect real fires, cosy corners and a superbly stocked bar. The dining area opens onto a pretty patio and garden; there's also a burgeoning kitchen garden. The food remains simple and seasonal, but new chef Andrew Birch has raised the bar, with deft seasoning and flavour combinations. An inspection lunch opened with chicken terrine and a dainty mustard-spiked salad of celeriac and endive, after which a crisp-skinned piece of pork belly with mash, apple-infused sauce and vibrant peas and broad beans showed just how good 'local' can be. Iced lemon parfait with strawberry soup made a bright and balanced ending. William Hutchings has created a walk-in wine cellar and his encyclopaedic list now has a 'map' to aid navigation, so trawl your way through the pages of clarets, Champagnes and more. House selections start at £14. **Chef/s:** Andrew Birch. **Open:** all week L 12 to 2.30, D 7 to 9.30 (9 Sun). **Closed:** Tue Nov to Mar, end Jan to early Feb. **Meals:** alc (main courses £15 to £19.

Set L £15 (2 courses) to £19). Sun L £19 (2 courses) to £23. **Service:** not inc. **Details:** Cards accepted. 60 seats. 30 seats outside. No music. No mobile phones. Wheelchair access. Children allowed. Car parking.

## Whitebrook

### The Crown at Whitebrook

**Top-drawer restaurant-with-rooms**
Whitebrook, NP25 4TX
Tel no: (01600) 860254
www.crownatwhitebrook.co.uk
**Modern European | £45**
**Cooking score: 7**

♦ ⇌

'Everything about this sophisticated little restaurant-with-rooms is immaculately presented and carefully executed', noted one satisfied reporter. A smooth team of 'efficient, knowledgeable and friendly staff' gets a visit off on the right foot, beginning with drinks in the expansive lounge area (where there are plenty of sofas, books and magazines), then on to the smart dining area, decked out in calming coffees and creams. Framed by excellent canapés and petits fours, a six-course lunchtime tasting menu was superb value for money. Cauliflower pannacotta with apple velouté and a 'delightfully alien-looking' cauliflower crisp preceded braised ham hock, which came as a breadcrumb-encased patty teamed with tender langoustine, celery and mustard. Plump tortellini of sweet butternut squash, lemony goats' cheese and hazelnut showed James Sommerin's ability to create balanced, deeply satisfying meat-free dishes. However a show-stopping pairing of medium-rare beef sirloin with fall-apart braised brisket, artichoke and lentils was enough to banish any thoughts of vegetarianism. The use of fresh herbs is excellent, and nowhere is this more apparent than in the bright, piercing flavours of a dessert of blood orange jelly with honeycomb, vanilla ice cream and tarragon. Beside such a dazzling array, only the breads (which would be perfectly satisfactory lower down the scale) seemed pedestrian and overly doughy. Dine in the evening, and a weightier selection of dishes might open with smoked eel, confit pig's trotter, sweetcorn and chilli followed by oven-roasted loin of venison with chestnut, celeriac, espresso and dark chocolate, and ending with maple-glazed fig with iced cinnamon and honey for dessert. An impeccably tutored sommelier is on hand to offer guidance when it comes to the increasingly impressive wine list, which is helpfully organised by grape varietals. Gilt-edged selections abound and there is plenty to catch the eye from £19.50 a bottle.

**Chef/s:** James Sommerin. **Open:** all week L 12 to 2, Mon to Sat D 7 to 9 (9.30 Fri and Sat). **Closed:** 2 weeks Christmas. **Meals:** Set L £25 (2 courses) to £28. Set D £45. Sun L £28. Tasting menu £70 (8 courses). **Service:** not inc. **Details:** Cards accepted. 30 seats. No mobile phones. Wheelchair access. Music. Car parking.

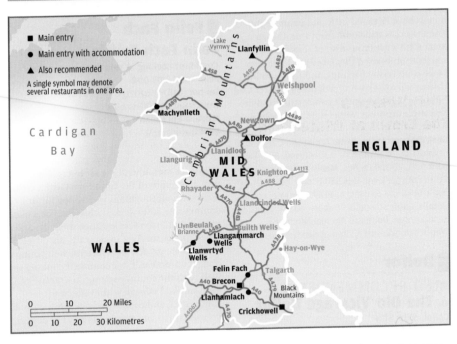

## Brecon

### Tipple'n'Tiffin

**Informal canalside snacking and dining**
Theatr Brycheiniog, Canal Wharf, Brecon,
LD3 7EW
Tel no: (01874) 611866
**Modern British | £20**
Cooking score: 1

This canalside restaurant has 'attentive, informal' service and a flexible menu of dishes to be enjoyed tapas-style or in a more conventional three-course format. Typical of the unpretentious, global style are game sausages on root mash with caramelised shallot and claret gravy, local goats' cheese and caramelised onion tartlets, and chicken tikka skewers on mixed pepper couscous. Finish with homemade puddings such as chocolate fondant or treacle tart. A short, international wine list includes plenty by the glass. Bottles from £11.50.

**Chef/s:** Louise Gudsell. **Open:** Mon to Sat L 12 to 2.30, D 6 to 9. **Closed:** Sun, 2 weeks Christmas. **Meals:** alc (main courses £8 to £10). Set L £15 (2 courses) to £20. Set D £20 (2 courses) to £25. **Service:** not inc. **Details:** Cards accepted. 40 seats. 40 seats outside. Wheelchair access. Music. Children allowed. Car parking.

## Crickhowell

### Nantyffin Cider Mill Inn

**Generous dishes in old apple store**
Brecon Road, Crickhowell, NP8 1SG
Tel no: (01873) 810775
www.cidermill.co.uk
**Modern British | £25**
Cooking score: 2

Described as 'country inn and dining room', this pink-painted inn has a cosy bar with a welcoming fire. The dining room is in the spacious apple store. After a change of ownership in 2007, Marius Petre from Romania was promoted to head chef, but menus have changed little and many of the raw materials still come from a nearby farm. Start with a generous dish of seared pigeon suprême on braised Puy lentils in a red wine sauce with crispy parsnips, and follow with a traditional roast such as rack of Gloucester Old Spot pork. Finish with a comforting rhubarb and apple crumble. Wines start at £13.95 a bottle.

**Chef/s:** Marius Petre. **Open:** Tue to Sun L 12 to 2.30 (3 Sun), Tue to Sat D 6 to 9.30. **Closed:** Mon exc bank hols, 25 and 26 Dec. **Meals:** alc (main courses £11 to £18). Set L and D £12.50 (2 courses) to £16.50. Sun L £14.95 (2 courses) to £17.95. **Service:** not inc. **Details:** Cards accepted. 90 seats. 40 seats outside. Separate bar. No music. No mobile phones. Wheelchair access. Children allowed. Car parking.

# ▌Dolfor

## ALSO RECOMMENDED
## ▲ The Old Vicarage Dolfor
Dolfor, SY16 4BN
Tel no: (01686) 629051
www.theoldvicaragedolfor.co.uk
**Modern British**

Tim and Helen Withers' guesthouse and restaurant is all country charm and elegance inside, though the kitchen garden with its happy hens is more reminiscent of *The Good Life*. The mostly organic menu (£25 for three courses) offers an impressive hike through the best produce the surrounding landscape can offer, from a starter of Mochdre ham, red onion and blue cheese tart to a main course of local venison with braised red cabbage. For dessert, perhaps sticky toffee pudding. Wines start at £14. Open all week D only.

# ▌Felin Fach

## Felin Fach Griffin
**Confident cooking in relaxing surroundings**
Felin Fach, LD3 0UB
Tel no: (01874) 620111
www.felinfachgriffin.co.uk
**Modern European | £35**
**Cooking score: 3**

While it's undoubtedly more restaurant than pub, the genius of the Felin Fach Griffin is that it contains all the things you'd hope for in a country inn, just tweaked a bit to create a sense of occasion – so there are huge sofas, a piano, woodsmoke, an Aga, stone walls, an immaculate garden and efficient, welcoming staff. Ricardo Van Ede's confident cooking sits well with the country setting: try tartare of local smoked salmon with watercress pannacotta, and then Herdwick lamb with young carrots and shepherd's pie. For dessert, maybe creamed rice pudding with passion fruit caramel and sorbet. The drinks list includes some good bottled beers and an impressive, international selection of wines, many of them organic. House recommendations start at £15.50.

**Chef/s:** Ricardo Van Ede. **Open:** all week L 12.30 to 2.30 (12 to 2.30 Sun), D 6.30 to 9.30. **Closed:** 24 and 25 Dec, 4 days Jan. **Meals:** alc (main courses £15 to £19). Set L £15.90 (2 courses) to £18.90. Set D £21.50 (2 courses) to £27.50. Sun L £18.90. **Service:** not inc. **Details:** Cards accepted. 60 seats. 25 seats outside. Separate bar. No mobile phones. Wheelchair access. Music. Children allowed. Car parking.

# Llanfyllin

## ALSO RECOMMENDED
## ▲ Seeds

5 Penybryn Cottages, High Street, Llanfyllin,
SY22 5AP
Tel no: (01691) 648604
**Modern British**

Puzzles, books, paintings and masks from around the world make this an atmospheric little refuge. Slate floors and a wood-burning stove add to the cosy charm. The menu offers three courses for £25.25, and generally sings from the traditional/classic song sheet, with a few Mediterranean flourishes. Sun-dried tomato and spring onion risotto followed by roast rack of Welsh lamb with Dijon and herb crust are typical of the style. Lemon posset or Eton mess bring proceedings to a very British close. Wines start at £13.75. Open Thur to Sun L, Tue to Sat D.

# Llangammarch Wells

## Lake Country House

Food that's been to finishing school
Llangammarch Wells, LD4 4BS
Tel no: (01591) 620202
www.lakecountryhouse.co.uk
**Modern British | £39**
Cooking score: 2

£5 OFF 🍽

One reader was charmed by the 'slightly shabby elegance' of this grand country house, whose dining room is all swags, chintz and chandeliers. The cooking takes raw local ingredients and sends them to finishing school: pressing of confit of Welsh lamb, globe artichokes and thyme with sweet pickled fennel might be followed by braised shin of Welsh beef with potato purée, wild mushrooms, spiced red onion jam and Madeira reduction. For dessert, maybe iced apple and parsnip parfait with cumin caramel syrup and green apple sorbet. An impressive wine list kicks off at £21.50 a bottle.

**Chef/s:** Sean Cullingford. **Open:** all week L 12.30 to 2, D 7.15 to 9.15. **Meals:** Set L £15 (2 courses) to £18. Set D £38.50 (4 courses). **Service:** not inc. **Details:** Cards accepted. 40 seats. Separate bar. No music. No mobile phones. Wheelchair access. Children allowed. Car parking.

# Llanhamlach

**NEW ENTRY**
## Peterstone Court

A true Brecon beacon
Llanhamlach, LD3 7YB
Tel no: (01874) 665387
www.peterstone-court.com
**Modern British | £30**
Cooking score: 4

£5 OFF 🍷 🍽

This handsome Georgian manor is set in the Brecon Beacons National Park, with excellent views of some of the highest peaks of South Wales. The present owners have been here for five years and used to own the Nantyffin Cider Mill Inn (which they sold in 2007). The nearby family farm provides seasonal raw materials such as meat (including Middle White rare breed pigs), vegetables, herbs and fruit. The kitchen's mantra is 'we believe in slow food' – and confit of Welsh lamb proved they practise what they preach; its rich flavour showed signs of long marination and slow roasting. Equally impressive at a test meal was a risotto of wild mushrooms and truffles, a well-made ballotine of Glaisfer chicken served with braised cabbage and boulangère potatoes in a light thyme jus, and rhubarb parfait rolled in crumble and topped with Chantilly cream. The 60-bin wine list is notable for its range, quality and refreshingly painless mark ups. 'Pouring wines' open the bidding at £12.95.
**Chef/s:** Robert Taylor and Sean Gerrard. **Open:** all week L 12 to 2.30 (3 Sun), D 7 to 9.30. **Meals:** alc (main courses £9 to £23). Set L £11.50 (2 courses) to £13.50. **Service:** not inc. **Details:** Cards accepted. 50 seats. 40 seats outside. Separate bar. No mobile phones. Wheelchair access. Music. Children allowed. Car parking.

## Llanwrtyd Wells

### Carlton Riverside

**Imaginative food and charming service**

Irfon Crescent, Llanwrtyd Wells, LD5 4ST

Tel no: (01591) 610248

www.carltonriverside.com

**Modern British | £38**

**Cooking score: 6**

£5 OFF

'Considering the dreary location, this place is just wonderful', writes one reader. Not everyone would see a Victorian spa town set in dramatic Welsh countryside as dreary, but you'd be hard pressed to dispute the glowing endorsement of Carlton House. An attractive stone building beside the River Irfon, it houses Mary Ann and Alan Gilchrist's smart restaurant-with-rooms and atmospheric cellar bar/bistro. Mary Ann and Alan are 'lovely people' who always charm their guests – he an attentive host, she in the kitchen. Mary Ann's 'imagination and ingenuity' are showcased on the special no-choice menu offered to short break guests. Typical dishes include crab and brown shrimp ravioli, suprême of Gressingham duck with punchnep (turnips cooked Welsh-style), buttered cabbage, braised chicory and a citrus and honey sauce, and chocolate fondant with Merlyn liqueur ice cream. Her regular menu might offer air-dried ham with beetroot roulade, slow-roasted belly pork with red cabbage, apple and crackling, and rosewater terrine with raspberry coulis. Alan's impressive international wine list includes plenty of half-bottles. Bottles start at £14.50.

**Chef/s:** Mary Ann Gilchrist. **Open:** Mon to Sat D 7 to 8.30. **Closed:** Sun, 14 to 30 Dec. **Meals:** alc (main courses £15 to £25). Set D £17.50 (2 courses) to £22.50. **Service:** not inc. **Details:** Cards accepted. 20 seats. No music. No mobile phones. Wheelchair access. Children allowed.

**Best value in Wales**

**Mimosa Kitchen & Bar, Cardiff**
Cardiff's 'first gastro bar' has a fiercely patriotic, well-priced menu.

**Mint & Mustard, Cardiff**
Quirky but superior Indian cooking at reasonable prices.

**Hanson at the Chelsea, Swansea**
Swansea's best bet for fish and seafood.

**Junction 28, Bassaleg** Classic French/international cooking with good lunch and dinner deals.

**Tipple'n'Tiffin, Brecon**
A flexible menu of tapas-style or more conventional three-courses.

**The Wynnstay, Machynlleth** Welcoming staff and a menu built around local supplies.

**56 High Street, Mold** The two-course lunch and dinner are a steal.

**Tir a Môr, Criccieth** Bargain menu offered on Tuesday to Thursday evenings.

**Ultracomida, Aberystwyth**
A choice of tapas and a keenly priced, daily three-course menu.

**Angel Vaults, Carmarthen** Great set three-course lunch and dinner menus.

## Lasswade Country House

**Country hotel with lovely views**
Station Road, Llanwrtyd Wells, LD5 4RW
Tel no: (01591) 610515
www.lasswadehotel.co.uk
**Modern British | £32**
Cooking score: 2

Over the last nine years Roger and Emma Stevens' Edwardian country hotel has grown in confidence, thanks in part to reliable local supply lines and high-quality seasonal raw materials. Open for dinner only, the kitchen reveals its full mettle with a short-choice, three-course menu. For one very satisfied couple the cooking overtook the stunning views as 'the star of the show', delivering tea-smoked salmon, Welsh Black steak with mushrooms, and a filo pastry basket filled with fruits in elderflower wine to finish. A short wine list starts at £12.50 with most under £20.
**Chef/s:** Roger Stevens. **Open:** all week D 7.30 to 9. **Closed:** 25 Dec. **Meals:** Set D £32. **Service:** not inc. **Details:** Cards accepted. 20 seats. No music. No mobile phones. Wheelchair access. Car parking.

## ▮ Machynlleth
## The Wynnstay

**Bursting with character**
Maengwyn Street, Machynlleth, SY20 8AE
Tel no: (01654) 702941
www.wynnstay-hotel.com
**Modern British | £25**
Cooking score: 2

This 'quirky' coaching inn with welcoming staff simply bursts with character and personal touches. Modern and traditional features rub along nicely together, both in terms of the colourful décor and the menu. Chef and co-proprietor Gareth Johns 'clearly has a little black book of local suppliers' but his inspiration is wide-ranging. You could start with Welsh goose ravioli in spinach and tomato sauce, followed by breast of Montgomery duck with liquorice and orange. Desserts run from chocolate tart to 'Welsh' summer pudding. The chattily annotated wine list has a personal feel, and opens at a friendly £13.95.
**Chef/s:** Gareth Johns. **Open:** all week L 12 to 2, D 6.30 to 9. **Meals:** alc (main courses £12 to £16). Sun L £12.95 (2 courses) to £14.95. **Service:** not inc. **Details:** Cards accepted. 80 seats. 40 seats outside. Separate bar. No music. Wheelchair access. Children allowed. Car parking.

## ▮ Pontdolgoch

**READERS RECOMMEND**
## The Talkhouse

**Modern British**
Pontdolgoch, SY17 5JE
Tel no: (01686) 688919
www.talkhouse.co.uk
**'Good food in a former country pub'**

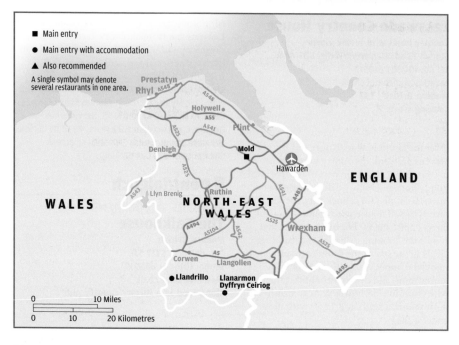

■ Main entry
● Main entry with accommodation
▲ Also recommended

A single symbol may denote several restaurants in one area.

Prestatyn
Rhyl
Holywell
Flint
Denbigh
Mold
Hawarden
**ENGLAND**
Llyn Brenig
Ruthin
**WALES**
**NORTH-EAST WALES**
Wrexham
Corwen
Llangollen
● Llandrillo
Llanarmon Dyffryn Ceiriog

0        10 Miles
0     10     20 Kilometres

## Llanarmon Dyffryn Ceiriog

### The West Arms Hotel

**Rustic inn with cutting-edge food**
Llanarmon Dyffryn Ceiriog, LL20 7LD
Tel no: (01691) 600665
www.thewestarms.co.uk
**Modern European | £33**
Cooking score: 3

🛏 V

'Great food and friendly waiters', enthuses one fan of this rustic delight, set in a remote spot at the foot of the Berwyn mountains. A former drovers' inn, it delivers all the wonky floors, bare beams and inglenooks you could wish for, yet the food has a contemporary edge. Seared scallops with chive mash and cream, leek and bacon sauce opens proceedings on a sophisticated note, and mains toe the line with the likes of roasted partridge breast with bacon, chestnut, Savoy cabbage and natural juices. Round it off with chilled Grand

Marnier soufflé with orange and pineapple salad. The wine list loiters in France then strikes out to places as diverse as Australia, Chile and the Lebanon. Bottles start at £14.95. **Chef/s:** Grant Williams. **Open:** all week L 12 to 2, D 7 to 9. **Meals:** Set D £27.95 (2 courses) to £32.90. **Service:** 10% (optional). **Details:** Cards accepted. 70 seats. 42 seats outside. Separate bar. Wheelchair access. Music. Children allowed. Car parking.

## Symbols

🛏 Accommodation is available

💷30 Three courses for less than £30

**V** More than three vegetarian main courses

£5 OFF £5-off voucher scheme

🍾 Notable wine list

## Llandrillo

### Tyddyn Llan
**Fine dining without pretensions**
Llandrillo, LL21 0ST
Tel no: (01490) 440264
www.tyddynllan.co.uk
**Modern British | £45**
Cooking score: 7

£5 OFF 🍷 🛏

One reader sums the cooking up very well: 'local fresh food prepared in a perfectly simple but elegant way'. Bryan Webb is an expert cook who doesn't try to impress with flourishes of culinary wizardry and presentation. He and his wife Susan run this small Georgian mansion with a certain ease that is appreciated by visitors. The interior is both homely and tasteful: comfortable lounges with open fires, a tiny bar that opens on to a small dining room with tongue-and-groove walls that, in turn, leads to a larger, classically designed extension. The kitchen focuses mainly on raw materials from local suppliers with some ingredients from further afield – salmon from Loch Duart, smoked salmon from Loch Fyne and cheese from Neal's Yard Dairy – while the cooking is a well-travelled, open-minded take on modern British. At a spring lunch, the Middle Eastern imam bayaldi was an unusual starter – a combination of aubergine, tomatoes and golden raisins, topped with a dollop of yoghurt. For main course, duck confit was accompanied by Savoy cabbage in 'a lovely cider and apple sauce', and roast wild bass was teamed with laverbread butter sauce. A star among desserts was a light pannacotta with blood oranges and grappa. The wine list includes five pages of bottles under £25, and there is a 'top wine bargains' section created for 'these recessionist times'. Prices start at £18.
**Chef/s:** Bryan Webb. **Open:** Fri and Sat L 12.30 to 2, Sun L 12.45 to 2.30, all week D 7 to 9.30. **Closed:** last 2 weeks Jan. **Meals:** Set L £21.50 (2 courses) to £28. Set D £38 (2 courses) to £45. Sun L £28.

**Service:** not inc. **Details:** Cards accepted. 40 seats. 8 seats outside. Separate bar. No music. No mobile phones. Wheelchair access. Children allowed. Car parking.

## Mold

### 56 High Street
**Charmer with a fish focus**
56 High Street, Mold, CH7 1BD
Tel no: (01352) 759225
www.56highst.com
**Seafood | £25**
Cooking score: 3

£5 OFF £30 🍷

This 'great little find' stands opposite the beautiful fourteenth-century church on Mold's High Street. 'Wonderful service from start to finish' is one of its charms; another is the 'beautifully cooked and presented' food. The focus is on fish and seafood, but meat and vegetarian options are always on the menu. Kick off with appetisers such as shell-on prawns, before launching into a starter of, say, mussels from the Menai Strait cooked marinière-style or in a Thai broth. Fresh fish mains might include red mullet fillets with haricot bean and potato cassoulet, grilled smoked chorizo and red pepper dressing. Beef fillet topped with black pudding, Stilton and bacon could be among the meat alternatives. Finish with lemon tart and raspberries. Wines start at £11.95.
**Chef/s:** Karl Mitchell, Kirsten Robb and Martin Fawcett. **Open:** Tue to Sat L 12 to 3, D 6.30 to 9.30 (6 to 10.30 Fri and Sat). **Closed:** Sun and Mon. **Meals:** alc (main courses £12 to £19). Set L £8.95 (2 courses). Set D £13 (2 courses). **Service:** not inc. **Details:** Cards accepted. 50 seats. Air-con. No mobile phones. Wheelchair access. Music. Children allowed. Car parking.

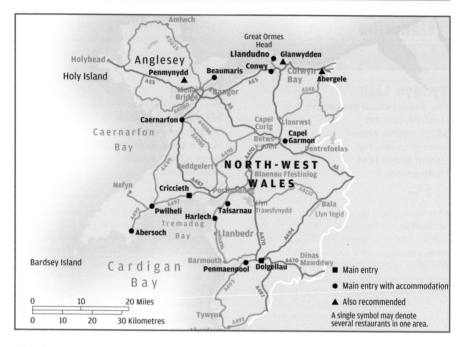

Map legend:
- ■ Main entry
- ● Main entry with accommodation
- ▲ Also recommended

A single symbol may denote several restaurants in one area.

0   10   20 Miles
0   10   20   30 Kilometres

## ■ Abergele

### ALSO RECOMMENDED
### ▲ The Kinmel Arms

St George, Abergele, LL22 9BP
Tel no: (01745) 832207
www.thekinmelarms.co.uk
**Modern British**

An eighteenth-century coaching inn with a contemporary interior, the Kinmel Arms offers 'consistently good food' served by 'friendly, knowledgeable staff'. Try Menai mussels steamed with lemongrass, chilli, garlic and coconut milk (£5.95) ahead of slow-braised shoulder of Welsh lamb with leeks, fondant potato, kidney and liver ragoût, port and rosemary jus (£17.55), then squeeze in a dessert of pecan and pear pie with a bourbon and milk chocolate ice cream (£5.55). Wines start at £13.95. Closed Sun and Mon.

## ■ Abersoch

### Porth Tocyn Hotel

Far-reaching menus and views
Bwlch Tocyn, Abersoch, LL53 7BU
Tel no: (01758) 713303
www.porth-tocyn-hotel.co.uk
**Modern European | £39**
**Cooking score: 4**

After more than 28 years in the hands of the Fletcher-Brewer family, this small country-house hotel has that particular kind of loved, well-tended atmosphere that comes with time and devotion. Inside, a series of interconnecting rooms is decked out with homely furnishings, while the grounds comprise immaculate gardens and farmland with sea views. In the kitchen, John Bell and Louise Fletcher-Brewer cook up a confident combination of classic/traditional and modern/international themes, to be enjoyed in the dining room along with more of those spectacular views. Typical of the scope is a starter of hot chorizo with butter bean and Parma ham salad, followed by roast pork fillet stuffed with garlic and thyme mousse with a red wine and sage reduction. Finish with glazed vanilla rice pudding and shortbread. The lengthy wine list offers everything from classics to newer, international finds, all of them grouped by style. Bottles start at £14.95. **Chef/s:** John Bell and Louise Fletcher-Brewer. **Open:** all week L 12 to 2, D 5.15 to 9 (9.30 in high season). **Closed:** early Nov to 2 weeks before Easter. **Meals:** Set D £32.50 (2 courses) to £39. Set Sun L £23. **Service:** not inc. **Details:** Cards accepted. 50 seats. 30 seats outside. Separate bar. No music. No mobile phones. Wheelchair access. Car parking.

## Bangor

READERS RECOMMEND
### Blue Sky Café
Eclectic
236 High Street, Bangor, LL57 1PA
Tel no: (01248) 355444
www.blueskybangor.co.uk
'Well-hidden café with an exciting selection of cakes'

## Beaumaris
### Ye Olde Bulls Head Inn
Anglesey aristocrat
Castle Street, Beaumaris, LL58 8AP
Tel no: (01248) 810329
www.bullsheadinn.co.uk
Modern British | £39
Cooking score: 5

This Bull of impeccable pedigree dates from 1472. It has undergone numerous transformations but retains its aristocratic aura, having lodged the likes of Dr Johnson, Charles Dickens and Princess Victoria. The Loft is a destination restaurant in the eaves of the building. It combines the traditional and the modern, with its beams and rafters and its twenty-first century stylish décor. Hefin Roberts is now in charge of the kitchen, and

pulls out all the stops on his 'imaginative, well-executed' menu – from appetisers and excellent breads, via the complimentary demi-tasse of soup and the pre-dessert, right through to the petits fours. At inspection, a starter of lightly seared Anglesey king scallops had a subtle sweetness, and was stylishly presented with braised lentils and spiced onion fritters. Chwaen Goch Farm black beef fillet came with braised oxtail, thyme and garlic creamed potatoes, roasted vegetables and peppercorn sauce, while sole paupiette was accompanied by crab tortellini, confit lemon, kohlrabi and fennel. Finish, perhaps, with a pineapple upside-down cake with pineapple carpaccio and pink peppercorn syrup. Smartly chosen wines from the classic French regions form the backbone of the venerable wine list, although there's ample choice from elsewhere for those who fancy something more zesty. House selections weigh in at £18.50. The downstairs conservatory brasserie (with a separate kitchen) serves more informal food. **Chef/s:** Hefin Roberts. **Open:** Mon to Sat D only 7 to 9.30 (6.30 Fri and Sat). **Closed:** Sun, 25 and 26 Dec, 1 Jan. **Meals:** Set D £32 (2 courses) to £38.50. **Service:** not inc. **Details:** Cards accepted. 45 seats. Separate bar. No music. No mobile phones. Car parking.

## Blaenau Ffestiniog

READERS RECOMMEND
### Bistro Moelwyn
Modern British
10 High Street, Blaenau Ffestiniog, LL41 3DB
Tel no: (01766) 832358
www.bistromoelwyn.co.uk
'Good food in an informal setting'

## Borth y Gest

READERS RECOMMEND
### Moorings Bistro
Modern British
4 Ivy Terrace, Borth y Gest, LL49 9TS
Tel no: (01766) 513500
www.mooringsbistroborthygest.com
'A friendly bistro overlooking the bay'

## Caernarfon
### Rhiwafallen

**Stylish restaurant-with-rooms**
Llandwrog, Caernarfon, LL54 5SW
Tel no: (01286) 830172
www.rhiwafallen.co.uk
**Modern British | £35**
Cooking score: 2

Readers enjoy the 'welcoming' atmosphere and 'varied choice of food' in this stylish former farmhouse set in two acres of grounds. Renovated using natural materials such as wood and slate, it retains its traditional charm, albeit with a contemporary edge. The menu skips with flair and imagination through excellent Welsh ingredients, from a Pant-Ys-Gawn goats' cheese and coconut fritter with peppered pineapple and toasted brioche to a main course of twice-cooked belly of Anglesey pork with celeriac purée, red cabbage, roast pears and star anise jus. Finish with tarte Tatin and rum-and-raisin ice cream. House wine is £14.95.
**Chef/s:** Rob John. **Open:** Sun L 12.30 to 2, Tue to Sat D 7 to 9. **Closed:** Mon, 25 and 26 Dec, 1 and 2 Jan. **Meals:** Set D £35. Sun L £19.50. **Service:** not inc. **Details:** Cards accepted. 20 seats. Air-con. Separate bar. No mobile phones. Wheelchair access. Music. Car parking.

## Capel Garmon
### Tan-y-Foel Country House

**A very personal country house**
Nr Betws-y-Coed, Capel Garmon, LL26 0RE
Tel no: (01690) 710507
www.tyfhotel.co.uk
**Modern British | £45**
Cooking score: 6

The traditional Welsh stone exterior of this country house belies the fresh, light modernity of its interior. Original features such as exposed stonework shine out all the more in this chintz-free zone. The setting is spectacular. Expect sweeping views of the

Conwy Valley and Snowdonia National Park, and a restaurant decorated in the same understated, modern style as the rest of the building. Chef/proprietor Janet Pitman's short, daily changing menus give carefully sourced, often local or home-grown ingredients the modern British treatment: typical of the style are a starter of carpaccio of beef with shredded celeriac and walnuts and Stilton mustard dressing followed by pan-seared breast of Gressingham duck with smoked paprika and chorizo risotto and basil fennel cream sauce. You could finish with Welsh cheeses or a warm chocolate mousse. This is assured and consistent cooking, all of it Janet's own work (as she's on her own in the kitchen, vegetarians and other special dietary requirements are not generally catered for). An interesting and well-balanced wine list offers over 100 bins, including plenty of classics and some lively New World finds. Bottles start at £25. Bookings by prior arrangement only.
**Chef/s:** Janet Pitman. **Open:** all week D 7.30. **Closed:** 21 to 27 Dec, 31 Dec to 4 Jan. Limited availability in Jan. **Meals:** Set D £42 (3 courses). **Service:** not inc. **Details:** Cards accepted. 10 seats. No music. No mobile phones. Car parking.

## Conwy
### Castle Hotel, Dawson's Restaurant

**Traditional but not stuffy**
High Street, Conwy, LL32 8DB
Tel no: (01492) 582800
www.castlewales.co.uk
**Modern British | £24**
Cooking score: 2

Busy wallpaper and a buzzy atmosphere enliven this former coaching inn at the heart of town. Refurbished with a modern slant but retaining the magnificent paintings of Victorian artist and illustrator John Dawson-Watson (who spent his last days in Conwy), the setting has a sense of occasion without feeling stuffy. The menu fits in nicely, offering traditionally inspired dishes such as smoked haddock and potato soup followed by lamb hotpot with bacon and tarragon dumplings and pickled red cabbage. A separate list of pubby 'favourites' includes fish and chips and chicken korma. Wines from £13.95.

**Chef/s:** Graham Tinsley. **Open:** all week 12 to 9.30. **Meals:** alc (main courses £11 to £18). Set L £16 (2 courses) to £24. Set D £16 (2 courses) to £24. Sun L £17 to £19. **Service:** 10% (optional). **Details:** Cards accepted. 70 seats. 8 seats outside. Separate bar. Wheelchair access. Music. Children allowed. Car parking.

## Criccieth

### Tir a Môr

**Thriving bistro with honest, generous dishes**
1-3 Mona Terrace, Criccieth, LL52 0HG
Tel no: (01766) 523084
www.tiramor.com
**European | £25**
**Cooking score: 2**

£30

Minimalist in style but big on charm, this welcoming little bistro is thriving in the hands of chef/proprietor Laurent Hebert and his Welsh-speaking wife. The restaurant's name translates as 'land and sea' and the menu delivers a nice balance of both. Expect honest, generous dishes with a French/Mediterranean slant – perhaps fresh mussels in a white wine and cream sauce followed by Welsh lamb noisettes with tomato fondue and rosemary-scented jus, and chocolate parfait for dessert. From Tuesday to Thursday a bargain set-price menu offers three courses and a glass of wine for £18.50. Wines start at £13.95.

**Chef/s:** Laurent Hebert. **Open:** Tue to Sat D 6 to 9.30. **Closed:** Sun, Mon, 26 Dec to 1 Feb. **Meals:** alc (main courses £13 to £20). Set D £18.50 (3 courses). **Service:** not inc. **Details:** Cards accepted. 36 seats. Wheelchair access. Music. Children allowed.

## Dolgellau

### Dylanwad Da

**Friendly coffee shop and restaurant**
2 Ffôs-y-Felin, Dolgellau, LL40 1BS
Tel no: (01341) 422870
www.dylanwad.co.uk
**Modern British | £25**
**Cooking score: 2**

 £5 OFF    £30

This welcoming, stone-fronted restaurant and coffee shop has a growing reputation for daytime tapas, while the evening menu remains focused on the simple, confident cooking that has kept it on the map for over 20 years. Typical of the style are spicy lamb meatballs followed by steak au poivre or Pommery chicken. For dessert, perhaps lemon and lime tart. Dylanwad Da means 'good influence' and is a play on the name of proprietor Dylan Rowlands. As well as being chef, Rowlands personally imports a good selection of European wines to bolster his lengthy wine list. Bottles are priced from £13.50.

**Chef/s:** Dylan Rowlands. **Open:** Thur to Sat L 10 to 3, D 7 to 9. **Closed:** Sun to Wed, Feb. **Meals:** alc (main courses £13 to £18). Set L and D £16 (2 courses) to £21. **Service:** not inc. **Details:** Cards accepted. 28 seats. Separate bar. No mobile phones. Wheelchair access. Music. Children allowed.

### READERS RECOMMEND

### Bwyty Mawddach

**Modern British**
Maesygarnedd, Llanelltyd, Dolgellau, LL40 2TA
Tel no: (01341) 424020
www.mawddach.com
**'Brasserie food in smart surroundings'**

## Glanwydden

**ALSO RECOMMENDED**
### ▲ The Queen's Head
Glanwydden, LL31 9JP
Tel no: (01492) 546570
www.queensheadglanwydden.co.uk
**Gastropub**

A former wheelwright's cottage in the heart of the village, the 'always reliable' Queen's Head is a smart gastropub serving down-to-earth food. You could try crispy duck leg with onion marmalade (£6.25) ahead of a hearty main course of sautéed lamb's liver and bacon with mash and onion gravy (£10.50). Fish options such as 'big fat, juicy' Anglesey scallops glazed with Gruyère are 'always a good bet'. Wines start at £16.50 a litre. Open all week.

## Harlech
### Castle Cottage
**Sophisticated take on traditional favours**
Y Llech, Harlech, LL46 2YL
Tel no: (01766) 780479
www.castlecottageharlech.co.uk
**Modern British | £34**
**Cooking score: 2**

Two venerable houses have been brought gently into the twenty-first century to make this stylish restaurant-with-rooms. The menu follows suit, delivering a sophisticated take on traditional flavours, as in a starter of black pudding, egg, bacon and croûton salad. Other dishes, such as sea bass on salt cod creamed potatoes with basil and white wine cream sauce, have a European tone. Finish with homely treats such as lemon posset or sticky sponge pudding. A decent wine list starts at £15.
**Chef/s:** Glyn Roberts. **Open:** all week D 7 to 9.30. **Closed:** 3 weeks Nov. **Meals:** Set D £34 (3 courses). **Service:** not inc. **Details:** Cards accepted. 40 seats. Separate bar. No mobile phones. Wheelchair access. Music. Children allowed. Car parking.

## Llanberis

**READERS RECOMMEND**
### The Peak
**Modern British**
86 High Street, Llanberis, LL55 4SU
Tel no: (01286) 872777
www.peakrestaurant.co.uk
**'Sophisticated food in a simple setting'**

## Llandudno
### Bodysgallen Hall
**Food with a sense of occasion**
Llandudno, LL30 1RS
Tel no: (01492) 584466
www.bodysgallen.com
**Modern British | £43**
**Cooking score: 5**

The National Trust now owns Bodysgallen Hall, but its management and staff remain unchanged. A beautifully restored seventeenth-century house, it stands in over 200 acres of grounds with views to Conwy Castle, Snowdonia and the sea. In the kitchen, head chef Gareth Jones continues to produce light, fresh, seasonal food with a sense of occasion. Dinner could begin with lightly smoked quail breast with cider and green apple jelly, pickled mushrooms and soft-boiled egg, followed by herb-poached fillet of Welsh beef with sticky ox cheek and celery salt mash. Desserts continue in the same elegant vein with the likes of pear tarte Tatin with vanilla-glazed blackberries and Kir Royale sorbet. If you hanker after something a little less formal, try the new 1620 Brasserie in the former coach house. Despite admirable efforts to create a contemporary, relaxed vibe, the atmosphere here can seem 'sedate'. However, it's helped along by 'cheerful, efficient service' and by an amiable menu that runs from lunchtime salads and paninis to sturdy mains such as fish pie or braised lamb shank with mustard mash and rosemary sauce. A snappy, worldwide wine list opens at £14.50 and includes plenty by the glass. Back in the main restaurant, the choice is extensive and impressive, with prices from £18.

**Chef/s:** Gareth Jones. **Open:** Tue to Sun L 12.30 to 1.45, D 7 to 9.30. **Closed:** Mon. **Meals:** alc (main courses £17 to £26). Set L £19 (2 courses) to £23. Set D £30 (2 courses) to £43. Sun L £27. **Service:** inc. **Details:** Cards accepted. 50 seats. Air-con. Separate bar. No music. No mobile phones. Wheelchair access. Children allowed. Car parking.

## St Tudno Hotel, Terrace Restaurant

**Polished old-school elegance by the sea**
Promenade, Llandudno, LL30 2LP
Tel no: (01492) 874411
www.st-tudno.co.uk
**Modern British | £32**
Cooking score: 4
£5 OFF 🍷 🛏

In essence this is an old school seaside hotel: elegant, traditional and family-run for 35 years. Set opposite Llandudno's promenade, it has impressive sea views, but the Terrace Restaurant has 'views' of Italy, thanks to the enormous murals of Lake Como that run its entire length. The food here is as polished and classically inspired as the hotel's décor and makes good use of Welsh ingredients. A crème brûlée of Gorau Glas cheese with crab apple jelly and beetroot glaze might be followed by duet of Welsh spring lamb with rosemary boulangère and roast garlic jus. Given the location, you can expect decent seafood offerings, such as pan-roasted fillet of local sea bass with Conwy mussels and Madeira jus. Desserts walk the classic/modern line with the likes of tonka bean brûlée with vanilla salt, passion fruit parfait and plum financier. The weighty, well-travelled wine list is a delight, and starts at £15.50 a bottle.

**Chef/s:** Ian Watson. **Open:** all week L 12.30 to 2, D 7 to 9.30 (9 Sun). **Meals:** alc (main courses £17 to £23). Set L £18 (2 courses) to £22. Sun L £19.95. **Service:** not inc. **Details:** Cards accepted. 65 seats. Air-con. Separate bar. No mobile phones. Music. Car parking.

## ■ Penmaenpool

## Penmaenuchaf Hall

**Oak-panelled opulence and fine food**
Penmaenpool, LL40 1YB
Tel no: (01341) 422129
www.penhall.co.uk
**Modern British | £40**
Cooking score: 3
£5 OFF 🍷 🛏

No less a figure than the Victorian poet Gerard Manley Hopkins thought this region a retreat for the battered senses, and said so in verse. Sheltering in the foothills of Cader Idris, in the Snowdonia National Park, Penmaenuchaf is a country house of oak-panelled opulence, where the slate-floored dining room enjoys wonderful views over the gardens. A productive blend of traditional and modern styles distinguishes the cooking, taking you perhaps from a serving of duck three ways (smoked, confit and parfait) with celeriac rémoulade, via an intermediate course such as pea cappuccino, to straightforward but well-executed main courses such as grilled halibut in ginger sauce or best end of lamb with ratatouille and rosemary jus. Dessert may be lavender crème brûlée with Champagne sorbet. Wines of the Month, a Collector's Choice listing and a roll call of 11 house selections at the uniform price of £17.50 (hurrah!) are the hallmarks of an imaginative and commendable approach to wine.

**Chef/s:** Justin Pilkington. **Open:** all week L 12 to 2, D 7 to 9.30. **Meals:** alc (main courses £22 to £26). Set L £15.95 (2 courses) to £17.95. Set D £40. Sun L £17.95. **Service:** not inc. **Details:** Cards accepted. 40 seats. Separate bar. Wheelchair access. Music. Car parking.

### Average price

The average price listed in main-entry reviews denotes the price of a three-course meal, without wine.

## ■ Penmynydd

### ALSO RECOMMENDED
### ▲ Neuadd Lwyd Country House

Penmynydd, LL61 5BX
Tel no: (01248) 715005
www.neuaddlwyd.co.uk
**Modern British**

Originally a rectory, this Victorian country house has spectacular views towards Snowdonia. The elegant dining room makes full use of these, and in summer the French doors are flung open for alfresco dining. The four-course, no-choice menu (£39) majors in Welsh ingredients: perhaps local oak-smoked chicken with a tian of avocado and tomato concassé with pesto dressing followed by pan-seared fillet of Menai sea bass with vegetables cooked with Carmarthen ham and a herb butter sauce. Wine from £12.95. Open Thur to Sat D only (by arrangement).

## ■ Pwllheli
### Plas Bodegroes

**Expertly cooked and beautifully presented food**
Nefyn Road, Pwllheli, LL53 5TH
Tel no: (01758) 612363
www.bodegroes.co.uk
**Modern British | £43**
**Cooking score: 6**

🍶 🍽

A Georgian manor house set in secluded gardens on the rugged Llyn Peninsula, Plas Bodegroes has a 'relaxing atmosphere, beautiful surroundings and amazing artwork everywhere'. Its long-standing reputation for classy dining is built on excellent ingredients from the surrounding area, including fresh lobsters, crab and, of course, Welsh lamb and beef. The garden provides a significant portion of the herbs and vegetables. Chef and co-proprietor Chris Chown is now joined in the kitchen by Aled Williams, and their 'expertly cooked and beautifully presented' food combines classic and traditional Welsh

elements. One diner deemed a mousseline of scallops, crab and laverbread with crab sauce 'possibly the best starter I have ever eaten'. Mains such as grilled halibut topped with Welsh rarebit make it easy to stick with seafood, but roast loin of mountain lamb with braised shoulder gâteau, pea purée and rosemary may prove a tempting diversion. Bara brith-and-butter pudding with Penderyn whisky ice cream brings things to a patriotic close. The wine list covers France in loving detail, but also roams the world, rooting out plenty of lesser-known gems. There are plenty of half-bottles; whole ones start at £16.

**Chef/s:** Christopher Chown and Aled Williams.
**Open:** Sun L 12.30 to 2, Tue to Sat D 7 to 9.30.
**Closed:** Mon, Dec to early Mar. **Meals:** Set D £42.50 (4 courses). Sun L £18.50. **Service:** not inc.
**Details:** Cards accepted. 40 seats. Separate bar. No mobile phones. Wheelchair access. Music. Children allowed. Car parking.

### ALSO RECOMMENDED
### ▲ Y Daflod at Tafarn Y Fic

Llithfaen, Pwllheli, LL53 6PA
Tel no: (01758) 750473
www.tafarnyfic.com
**Modern British**

At this simple bistro on the first floor of a community-owned village pub, self-taught Hefina Pritchard offers genuine and substantial dishes, and her farmer husband, Tomos, is an amiable front-of-house host. Start, perhaps, with roast red pepper filled with tomato and garlic and served with tapenade (£4.75), followed by pork stuffed with basil, hazelnuts and apricots, served with balsamic sauce (£14). Finish with white chocolate cheesecake with ginger and rhubarb (£4.75). Wines start at £10.50. Open Thur to Sat D only.

**Also recommended**
Also recommended entries are not scored but we think they are worth a visit.

## Talsarnau
### Maes-y-Neuadd
**Romantic medieval manor**
Talsarnau, LL47 6YA
Tel no: (01766) 780200
www.neuadd.com
**Modern British | £35**
Cooking score: 4

£5 OFF

The epithet 'mansion in the meadow' is a suitably romantic tag for this gracious fourteenth century granite manor set amid lush grounds overlooking Cardigan Bay. Maes-y-Neuadd's green-fingered horticulturists get a name-check on the menu for their sterling work in the revitalised walled garden – and the organic fruits of their labours filter through to the kitchen, along with supplies from local producers. Lunch is a light affair, but the bar is raised for fixed-price dinners that might open with steamed salmon and pan-fried silver bream with pea purée, crispy kale and lemon butter. The main course might be roasted halibut with mushroom risotto and laverbread saffron sauce, before the 'grand finale' ushers in Welsh cheeses, a pair of puddings and homemade ice creams. Despite a few recent grumbles from readers, 'standards are being maintained' here and the pedigree of the wine cellar is never in doubt. The list trots all the way from Wales to the Antipodes in search of top-notch tipples, although an attractive collection of bottles around £17 is the pick of the crop for crunch-conscious drinkers.

**Chef/s:** Peter Jackson and John Owen Jones. **Open:** all week L 12 to 1.45, D 7 to 8.45. **Meals:** alc (main courses £9 to £15). Set L £14.50 (2 courses) to £19. Set D £30 (2 courses) to £35. Sun L £17.95. **Service:** not inc. **Details:** Cards accepted. 65 seats. 18 seats outside. Separate bar. No music. No mobile phones. Wheelchair access. Children allowed. Car parking.

**Bryan Webb** Tyddyn Llan

**Who or what inspired you to become a chef?**
My mum baked a lot and, with the choice of going down the mines, I chose to move away and become a chef; I was very lucky.

**If you hadn't become a chef, what would you have been?**
I would have loved to have been a radio DJ.

**What is the best meal you have ever eaten?**
The one that sticks in my memory has to be the first time I ate at Chez Panisse, for my 40th birthday. It was so amazingly fresh and tasty.

**Which chefs do you admire?**
Shaun Hill: I love his food and he is such a nice person. Sally Clarke for her fresh approach to ingredients. Michael Caines for his ABode Hotel restaurants. Richard Corrigan for being Richard.

**If you were to have one abiding principle in the kitchen, what would it be?**
If it's not right, do not serve it.

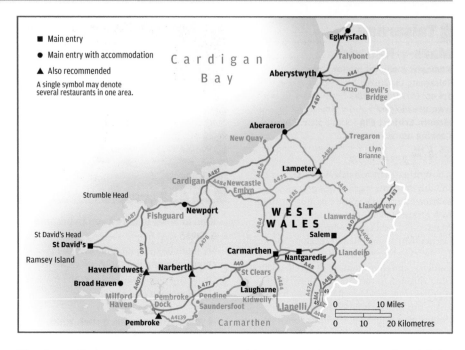

■ Main entry
● Main entry with accommodation
▲ Also recommended

A single symbol may denote
several restaurants in one area.

Cardigan Bay

Eglwysfach
Talybont
Aberystwyth
A44
A4120 Devil's Bridge
Aberaeron
New Quay
Tregaron
Llyn Brianne
Lampeter
Cardigan Newcastle Emlyn
Strumble Head
Fishguard Newport
St David's Head
St David's
Ramsey Island
Haverfordwest Narberth
Broad Haven
Milford Haven Pembroke Dock Pendine Saundersfoot
Pembroke
Laugharne Kidwelly Llanelli
St Clears
Carmarthen Nantgaredig
Salem
WEST WALES Llanwrda Llandeilo
Llandovery

0        10 Miles
0    10    20 Kilometres

## Aberaeron

### Harbourmaster

**Chic flagship with harbour views**
Pen Cei, Aberaeron, SA46 OBT
Tel no: (01545) 570755
www.harbour-master.com
**Modern British | £30**
**Cooking score: 3**

£5 OFF

A chic boutique hotel right at the harbour's edge, the Harbourmaster remains the flagship for a new breed of Welsh restaurants-with-rooms. The dining room occupies the former harbourmaster's building, while the buzzing bar and lounge are in a converted warehouse next door. The past year has brought mixed experiences for readers, especially with the bar food, but a recent inspection meal in the restaurant suggests a return to form following the appointment of a new head chef. Small scallops were helped along by accurately seasoned Puy lentils, crispy bacon and intense cauliflower purée, and a big, tender piece of sirloin came medium as requested, with light, crisp skinny fries and a burgeoning organic salad. For dessert, a refreshing, light-as-air rhubarb trifle. Wines from £13. Reports please.

**Chef/s:** Simon Williams. **Open:** all week L 12 to 2.30, D 6 to 9. **Closed:** 25 Dec. **Meals:** alc (main courses £15 to £22). Set L £12.50 (2 courses) to £15. Sun L £18.50. **Service:** not inc. **Details:** Cards accepted. 55 seats. 15 seats outside. Separate bar. Wheelchair access. Music. Car parking.

## Aberystwyth

### ALSO RECOMMENDED
### ▲ The Treehouse
14 Baker Street, Aberystwyth, SY23 2BJ
Tel no: (01970) 615791
www.treehousewales.co.uk
**Café**

Located on the first and second floors of an excellent organic food shop, this bistro-cum-coffee house makes use of produce sold downstairs. Thus everything is organic, there are lots of vegetarian and vegan dishes, and cheek-by-jowl tables create an informal atmosphere. The cooking is genuine and wholesome: split pea and mint soup with excellent homemade bread roll (£3.50/£4.25), Mediterranean lamb casserole with vegetables (£8.60) and a lemon tart (£2.50). Organic wines are £8.95 a bottle. Open all day Mon to Sat, closed D.

## ▲ Ultracomida

**31 Pier Street, Aberystwyth, SY23 2LN**
**Tel no: (01970) 630686**
**www.ultracomida.co.uk**
**Modern European**

In the heart of Aberystwyth close to the seafront and the pier, this delicatessen and café offers a cornucopia of specialist produce from Wales, Spain and France. Tapas such as fishcakes with aïoli or Manchego cheese fritters cost £3 to £4 each, while the daily menu (£9.50 for two courses, £13 for three) might offer smoked mackerel pâté and toast followed by sweet potato and chickpea hotpot, with orange crema catalana for dessert. Wines from £10.50 a bottle. Filled barras and bocatas are also available to take away. Open Mon to Sat L and Fri D. There is a branch in Narbeth (see entry).

## ■ Broad Haven
## The Druidstone

**Bohemian rhapsody**
**Broad Haven, SA62 3NE**
**Tel no: (01437) 781221**
**www.druidstone.co.uk**
**Eclectic | £30**
**Cooking score: 2**

In contrast with the modern-rustic styling that has become *de rigueur* for restaurants of a certain type, this rambling country house has a gorgeously authentic, rough-round-the-edges bohemian air. A family affair that has evolved through decades of ownership, it occupies one of the most heart-stoppingly beautiful locations in the UK. The sea sparkles

below you; watch it from the terraces, or walk down to the secluded bay. Back in the warm, the simple, hearty food ranges from wok-fried chicken with cashew nuts and oyster sauce to pork fillet with bacon, Puy lentils and cider. Finish with banoffi pie. Wines start at £11.80.
**Chef/s:** Angus Bell, Andrew Bennett and Matt Ash. **Open:** all week L 12.30 to 2.30, D 7 to 9.30. **Meals:** alc (main courses £14 to £19). **Service:** not inc. **Details:** Cards accepted. 36 seats. 50 seats outside. Separate bar. No music. Wheelchair access. Children allowed. Car parking.

## ■ Carmarthen

**NEW ENTRY**
## Angel Vaults

**Smart town-centre dining**
**10 Nott Square, Carmarthen, SA31 1PQ**
**Tel no: (01267) 238305**
**www.theangelvaultsrestaurant.co.uk**
**Modern British | £25**
**Cooking score: 1**

'Definitely worth checking out', this relative newcomer in the heart of Carmarthen has slick styling, charming staff and views of Nott Square. The menu is classically based and makes good use of trendy/traditional ingredients such as beetroot, belly pork or mackerel. On a lunch visit a fat, nicely crisped salmon fishcake impressed. In the evening tarte Tatin of sweet red onion and Carmarthenshire goats' cheese, 28-day aged sirloin with mushroom duxelles, and raspberry crème brûlée are typical choices. Wines from £11.95. More reports please.
**Chef/s:** Andrew Thomas. **Open:** Tue to Sun L 12 to 2.30, Tue to Sat D 6.30 to 9.30. **Closed:** Mon. **Meals:** alc (main courses £14 to £20). Set L £11.95 (2 courses) to £15.95. Set D £24.50. Sun L £17.50. **Service:** not inc. **Details:** Cards accepted. 75 seats. 12 seats outside. Air-con. Separate bar. Wheelchair access. Music. Children allowed.

## Stephen Terry  The Hardwick

**Who or what inspired you to become a chef?**

Mr Paul Ward. My first college lecturer who inspired me to go to London and bore an uncanny resemblance to Anton Mosimann!

**What is the best meal you have ever eaten?**

My main course of slow roast pork belly with apple at a dinner at Y Polyn restaurant celebrating Camarthenshire produce and producers.

**Which chefs do you admire?**

Ruth Rogers, Rose Gray, Theo Randall, Alistair Little, Galvin brothers, Rowley Leigh, Anthony Demetri, Tim Hughes, Mark Hix, Simon Hopkinson, Andrew Pearn.

**What is your top culinary tip?**

Less is more.

**What did it mean to be awarded 'Best Use of Local Produce' in The Good Food Guide 2009?**

Extremely happy for all the local producers that supply us. They may not have been named individually, but they know who they are and it is as much their award as it is The Hardwick's.

## ▌Eglwysfach

### Ynyshir Hall

**Smart dining with frills and thrills**
Eglwysfach, SY20 8TA
Tel no: (01654) 781209
www.ynyshir-hall.co.uk
**Modern British | £65**
**Cooking score: 5**
£5 OFF 🍷 🛏

A 'charming, modest country house' that once belonged to Queen Victoria, Ynyshir Hall sits in a wooded valley surrounded by a glorious 14-acre garden. Beautiful at any time of year, the grounds are resplendent in April and May with rhododendrons and azaleas. Next door is a 1000-acre RSPB reserve, originally part of the estate. Owned by Von Essen Hotels since 2006, Ynyshir is still run by owners-turned-shareholders Joan and Rob Reen. Rob (an artist) is responsible for the pictures on the walls and the jewel-like colour schemes, which reflect the blaze of colour outside. Equally artful is chef Shane Hughes' exact and adventurous cooking. Described as 'sensational' and 'stimulating', this is dining with frills (cheese straws and a beetroot mousse among canapés in the bar) and thrills – notably one reader's 'spectacular' vanilla soufflé into which passion fruit sauce was poured at the table. In between come refined, beautifully balanced dishes with deceptively simple descriptions: perhaps crab lasagne with tomato fondue, followed by Welsh lamb with thyme and garlic potato, aubergine and tomato. The lengthy, international wine list kicks off at a reasonable £16 a bottle. Ask the 'excellent sommelier' to recommend some of the 25 wines by the glass.

**Chef/s:** Shane Hughes. **Open:** all week L 12.30 to 1.45, D 7 to 8.45. **Meals:** Set L £25 (2 courses) to £32. Set D £65 (5 courses). Sun L £32. Tasting menu £80. **Service:** not inc. **Details:** Cards accepted. 30 seats. Separate bar. No mobile phones. Wheelchair access. Music. Children allowed. Car parking.

# Haverfordwest

## ALSO RECOMMENDED
## ▲ The George's
24 Market Street, Haverfordwest, SA61 1NH
Tel no: (01437) 766683
www.thegeorges.uk.com
**Eclectic**

This grotto-like restaurant does a roaring trade in simple homemade food. Much of the 'intriguing décor' is for sale, and you'll find everything from clothes to crystals in the shop at the rear. The menu makes good use of local ingredients, including produce from the restaurant's own Victorian garden on the outskirts of Haverfordwest. You could start with the chef's country pâté (£5.50) followed by seafood chowder (£14.50). Popular desserts include the George's 'famous' sticky toffee pudding (£5.50). Wines from £11. Open Tue to Sat L, Fri and Sat D.

# Lampeter

## ALSO RECOMMENDED
## ▲ Ty Mawr Mansion
Cilcennin, Lampeter, SA48 8DB
Tel no: (01570) 470033
www.tymawrmansion.co.uk
**Modern British**

A gaggle of Hollywood starlets stayed at Ty Mawr while filming nearby, and they doubtless enjoyed not only the majestic Aeron Valley, but also the mansion itself, which is a haven of Georgian splendour on a domestic scale. The bilingual menus take in seared Anglesey scallops with linguine and saffron cream (£9.95), roast breast and braised leg of local pheasant with celeriac purée and shallot and chestnut sauce (£19.95), and bitter chocolate tart with orange and praline anglaise and crème fraîche (£8.95). A wine list of decent international spread starts at £13.50 for a pair of French blends. Open Mon to Sat D.

# Laugharne

## The Cors
**Quirky and very romantic**
Newbridge Road, Laugharne, SA33 4SH
Tel no: (01994) 427219
www.the-cors.co.uk
**Modern British | £26**
**Cooking score: 3**
£5 OFF | £30

Idiosyncratic and very romantic, this restaurant-with-rooms occupies a Victorian villa lost in an otherworldly bog garden ('cors' is Welsh for bog). Garden and menu are the work of chef/proprietor Nick Priestland, and both smack of someone doing exactly what he wants and doing it well. His simple, precise cooking is a showcase for local ingredients: dressed crab salad with country-style toast or bruschetta with local goats' cheese and roasted peppers make fresh springtime starters, while roasted fillet of organic Welsh Black beef with green peppercorns and red wine jus is a full-blooded main course. For vegetarians, there's fennel and Parmesan au gratin with a chilli ginger sauce and potatoes. A list of 20-plus worldwide wines starts at £13.
**Chef/s:** Nick Priestland. **Open:** Sun L 12 to 3, Thur to Sat D 7 to 12. **Closed:** Mon to Wed, last week Nov. **Meals:** alc (main courses £15 to £22). **Service:** not inc. **Details:** Cards accepted. 24 seats. 12 seats outside. Separate bar. No mobile phones. Wheelchair access. Music. Car parking.

## ALSO RECOMMENDED
## ▲ Stable Door
Market Lane, Laugharne, SA33 4SB
Tel no: (01994) 427777
www.laugharne-restaurant.co.uk
**Spanish**

Originally a seventeenth-century stable block in the grounds of Laugharne Castle, this place was also once a watering-hole frequented by Dylan Thomas. A menu of traditional tapas dishes (from £2.75) sits alongside daily specials such as leek and potato soup (£5), sirloin steak with garlic butter and gratin potatoes (£15.95) and chocolate and orange truffle torte (£4.50). Vegetarians might opt for spinach and ricotta cannelloni on tomato and red pepper sauce. Wines start from £12.50 (£3.25 a glass). Open Fri to Sun L, Thur to Sat D.

## Llanboidy

READERS RECOMMEND
### Jabajak
**Modern British**
Banc y llain, Llanboidy, SA34 0ED
Tel no: (01994) 448786
www.jabajak.co.uk
**'Food was clearly fresh and just tasted superb... awesome wine list'**

## Nantgaredig
### Y Polyn
**Hearty eating in a country haven**
Nantgaredig, SA32 7LH
Tel no: (01267) 290000
www.ypolynrestaurant.co.uk
**Modern British | £29**
**Cooking score: 3**

Balancing trends with tradition, Y Polyn stands firm as a haven of stylish rusticity deep in the Carmarthenshire countryside. A stream edges alongside the former tollhouse, and trees rise protectively behind it. For fine days, there is a sheltered terrace and small garden. Inside, a wood-burning stove, large sofas and scrubbed farmhouse tables set the tone for a hearty, homely style of eating. Excellent local ingredients, including some home-reared meats, are served with confident simplicity: perhaps Carmarthen ham with celeriac rémoulade, followed by fish pie. In addition to the regular menu, the new 'credit crunch lunch' offers the likes of French onion soup or roast pollock with pease pudding, at £12.50 for three courses. Desserts continue in a comforting vein, with, for instance, sherry trifle or treacle tart. The wine list opens at £13.50.

**Chef/s:** Susan Manson and Maryann Wright. **Open:** Tue to Sun L 12 to 2, Tue to Sat D 7 to 9. **Closed:** Mon. **Meals:** alc (main courses £9 to 11). Set L £10 (2 courses) to £12.50. Set D £28.50. **Service:** not inc. **Details:** Cards accepted. 46 seats. 15 seats outside. Separate bar. Wheelchair access. Music. Children allowed. Car parking.

## Narberth

ALSO RECOMMENDED
### ▲ Ultracomida
Narberth, SA67 7AR
Tel no: (01834) 861491
www.ultracomida.com
**Modern European**

A stylish deli full of wonderful smells. Like its counterpart in Aberystwyth (see entry), it specialises in Spanish, Welsh and French produce, some of which is used in its small restaurant. Here you can dip into tapas such as chorizo cooked in red wine (£4) or hummus and toast, or try slow-cooked, organic lamb casserole from the lunchtime set menu (£11 for two courses; £13 with dessert). Wines start at £10.50. Open Mon to Sat 12 to 4.30 and Fri D.

## Newport
### Cnapan
**Home-from-home with big flavours**
East Street, Newport, SA42 0SY
Tel no: (01239) 820575
www.cnapan.co.uk
**Modern British | £29**
**Cooking score: 2**

The Coopers have been in residence at this amicable Pembrokeshire home-from-home since 1984, so it's not surprising that Cnapan is treasured for its family atmosphere and irrepressible hospitality. Whether you are staying over or simply passing through, you can expect unshowy food that's big on natural flavour and far-flung influences. Dinner can spring a few surprises, so be prepared for scallops on asparagus and fennel purée with caper dressing followed by a heartier dish of honey-roast duck breast with clementine, five-spice and port sauce. For pudding, how about rhubarb and orange crème brûlée or mango sorbet with Cointreau and mango drizzle? House wines start at £12.50.

**Chef/s:** Judith Cooper. **Open:** Wed to Mon D 6.30 to 9. **Closed:** Tue, Dec 25, Jan to mid March. **Meals:** Set D £23 (2 courses) to £29. **Details:** Cards accepted. 36 seats. Separate bar. No mobile phones. Wheelchair access. Music. Children allowed. Car parking.

**NEW ENTRY**

## Llys Meddyg

**Pembrokeshire food champion**
East Street, Newport, SA42 0SY
Tel no: (01239) 820008
www.llysmeddyg.com
**Modern European | £35**
Cooking score: 4

Llys Meddyg was originally a coaching inn, then a doctor's residence before Ed and Louise Sykes transformed the building into a stylish restaurant-with-rooms. There is an arty ground-floor restaurant and a rustic but cosy cellar bar with a flagstone floor and wood-burning stove. Chef Scott Davis is a champion of local Pembrokeshire produce from land and sea. His seemingly simple cooking belies a sound technique – witness a dinner in spring that opened with Newport crab cake consisting of nothing but dark and white meat (no potatoes) crowned with papaya in a mustard sauce, followed by meltingly tender shoulder of lamb topped with a cardamom crust and served with cockles. Baked New York cheesecake with blood orange sorbet and tarragon syrup made a perfect finish. On the short, fairly priced list, house wine is £14.50.

**Chef/s:** Scott Davis. **Open:** Tue to Sun L 12 to 2 (3 Sun), Tue to Sat D 7 to 9. **Meals:** alc (main courses £18 to £23). Set L £15.50 (2 courses) to £18.50. Sun L £18.95. **Service:** not inc. **Details:** Cards accepted. 40 seats. 50 seats outside. Separate bar. No mobile phones. Music. Children allowed. Car parking.

## ▓ Pembroke

### ALSO RECOMMENDED
### ▲ Old Kings Arms

Main Street, Pembroke, SA71 4JS
Tel no: (01646) 683611
www.oldkingsarmshotel.co.uk
**Modern British**

It calls itself a 'fifteenth-century kitchen restaurant', and this homely room does indeed have a time-warp domestic charm, from its bare beams hung with copper pots and pans to the log fire that blazes on colder days. Expect simple, generous dishes such as confit leg of duckling on juniper cabbage (£7.15), seared Welsh lamb fillet on wilted greens with a port and redcurrant sauce (£16.95) and lemon posset (£4.20). Wines start at £10.25 a bottle. Open all week.

## ▓ St David's

## Cwtch

**Beautiful ingredients and no flummery**
22 High Street, St David's, SA62 6SD
Tel no: (01437) 720491
www.cwtchrestaurant.co.uk
**Modern British | £28**
Cooking score: 3

'Cwtch' is Welsh for a hug, or the snug of a pub, and as one diner observed: 'it lived up to its name in terms of atmosphere. Very snug, cosy and welcoming.' A stylishly informal restaurant on St David's main street, Cwtch's interior has a stripped-back simplicity that lets the lovely old building do the talking. A similar restraint is seen in the cooking, which never obscures beautiful ingredients with flummery. This is an ideal place to sample the region's best produce, from local charcuterie with celeriac rémoulade and beef dripping toast to St Brides Bay halibut with Penclawdd cockle fishcake and sauce vierge. Finish with bara brith pudding with Pembrokeshire cream or a plate of glorious Welsh cheeses with quince jelly. The nicely annotated international wine list includes a good selection by the glass. Bottles start at £13. **Chef/s:** Matthew Cox. **Open:** Tue to Sun D 6 to 11. **Closed:** Mon, 7 to 24 Jan. **Meals:** Set D £23 (2 courses) to £28. **Service:** not inc. **Details:** Cards accepted. 55 seats. Wheelchair access. Music. Children allowed.

## Morgan's

**Sleek and modern all round**
20 Nun Street, St David's, SA62 6NT
Tel no: (01437) 720508
www.morgans-restaurant.co.uk
**Modern British | £30**
**Cooking score: 2**

Originally a nineteenth-century school house, Morgan's is just 100 metres from beautiful St David's Cathedral – but you won't see it because this cathedral is, unusually, set in a hidden valley. Considering the historic surroundings, the restaurant's interior is surprisingly sleek and modern, and the food follows suit, offering an imaginative take on an impressive array of local ingredients. Try twice-baked Caerfai cheese soufflé followed by fillet of Pembrokeshire beef with bacon and shallot rösti potato, braised spinach, shallot purée and a crisp onion ring, then finish with a homemade chocolate brownie with chocolate sauce and ginger ice cream. Wines from £13.
**Chef/s:** Tara Pitman. **Open:** Wed to Mon D 6.30 to 10. **Closed:** Tue. **Meals:** alc (main courses £13 to £20). **Service:** not inc. **Details:** Cards accepted. 36 seats. Separate bar. No music. No mobile phones. Wheelchair access. Children allowed.

## ALSO RECOMMENDED

### ▲ Refectory at St David's

St David's Cathedral, St David's, SA62 6RH
Tel no: (01437) 721760
**Modern British**

There's been a change of hands, but the simple, healthy menu at this informal eatery is still worth applauding. Set deep in the Cathedral complex, its first floor has lovely views of the grounds. Try smoked salmon and horseradish quiche with rosemary roasted potatoes and salad (£6.45), pizza and salad or leek, potato and Perl Las cheese soup (£3.10). A selection of organic wines starts at £11. Open all week; closed evenings except in high summer.

## ▌ Salem

## Angel

**Culinary fireworks in a quiet village**
Salem, SA19 7LY
Tel no: (01558) 823394
www.angelsalem.co.uk
**Modern British | £25**
**Cooking score: 4**

£5 OFF  £30

The quiet village of Salem may seem an unlikely place for culinary fireworks, but Rod Peterson's cooking keeps this sleepy part of Carmarthenshire firmly on the map for food-lovers. The Angel still functions as a pub – albeit a smart one – but the main draw is undoubtedly the restaurant. Wood floors, antique furniture and well-spaced tables create a sense of occasion, and the food delivers on this promise. The style is modern British, with a grounding in the classics and an eye for Welsh traditions, as in a main course of delice of salmon with a Welsh rarebit glaze, buttered leeks and poached egg. Local ingredients feature strongly: you could start with Swansea Bay mussels marinière, followed by Welsh beef steak pudding with mushroom jus and béarnaise sauce. Dessert might be lemon crème brûlée or white chocolate and raspberry trifle. A respectable selection of international wines starts at £13.95.
**Chef/s:** Rod Peterson. **Open:** Wed to Sun L 12 to 3.30, Tue to Sat D 6 to 11. **Closed:** Mon. **Meals:** alc (main courses £10 to £18). **Service:** not inc. **Details:** Cards accepted. 80 seats. 16 seats outside. Separate bar. No mobile phones. Wheelchair access. Music. Children allowed. Car parking.

# CHANNEL
# ISLANDS

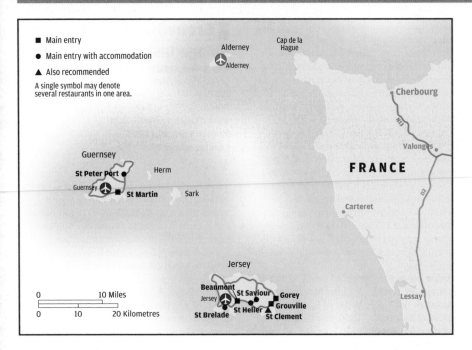

## ▌ Beaumont, Jersey

### Bistro Soleil

**Simple, with local specials**
La Route de la Haule, Beaumont, Jersey, JE3 7BA
Tel no: (01534) 720249
**Modern British | £26**
**Cooking score: 1**

A panoramic view of St Aubin's Bay makes an appropriate backdrop to this simple bistro, as locally caught fish and seafood are a feature of the specials board. The main menu takes in reliable favourites such as 'very good' scallops with crisp belly pork and braised faggot with creamed mash and apple compote, but recent reports have been mixed, indicating that food and service are 'really not up to it'. House wine is £14.75. Reports please.
**Chef/s:** Ian Jones. **Open:** Tue to Sun L 12 to 2 (2.30 Sun), Tue to Sat D 6.45 to 9.30. **Closed:** 25 and 26 Dec, bank hols. **Meals:** alc (main courses £11 to £23). Set L £10 (2 courses) to £12.50. Set D £15. Sun L £15. **Service:** not inc. **Details:** Cards accepted.

55 seats. 40 seats outside. Separate bar. Wheelchair access. Music. Children allowed. Car parking.

## ▌ Gorey, Jersey

### Suma's

**Polish and pleasure aplenty**
Gorey Hill, St Martin, Gorey, Jersey, JE3 6ET
Tel no: (01534) 853291
www.sumasrestaurant.com
**Modern European | £32**
**Cooking score: 5**

£5 OFF **V**

Shored by a good local reputation and the fact that it is Longueville Manor's baby sister (see entry), Suma's additional pull is its fantastic location and terrace views over Gorey's stone-walled fishing harbour and historic castle. Daniel Ward's cooking establishes a refined but unpretentious tone – no violent shocks, just a high degree of polish and pleasure. Plump, fresh and perfectly timed local scallops, for example, served with nothing more than dressed salad leaves (though they can be teamed equally successfully with cauliflower purée, apple jelly, crisp pancetta and soft lentils) or a main of wild sea bass alongside crushed Charlotte potatoes, sauce vierge and picked white crab meat. Equal billing is given to meat, perhaps a smoked chicken and ham hock terrine with homemade piccalilli and toasted country bread, or a duo of venison with braised cabbage, cranberries, roast beetroot and redcurrant sauce. Desserts deliver crowd-pleasing profiteroles filled with Jersey cream and a hot Valrhona chocolate fondant with a whisky ice cream, soft Spanish turron and chocolate sauce. The well-assembled wine list offers a reasonably priced global choice of around 70 bins. Chilean house selections start at £9.75.

**Chef/s:** Daniel Ward. **Open:** all week L 12 to 2.30, D 6.15 to 9.30. **Closed:** Christmas to mid Jan. **Meals:** alc (main courses £13 to £19). Set menu £16.50 (2 courses) to £18.50. Sun L £22.50. **Service:** 10%. **Details:** Cards accepted. 40 seats. 16 seats outside. Air-con. Separate bar. Wheelchair access. Music. Children allowed.

## ALSO RECOMMENDED
### ▲ Castle Green
La Route de la Cote, Gorey, Jersey, JE3 6DR
Tel no: (01534) 840218
www.jerseypottery.com
**Gastropub**

Breathtaking views of Mont Orgueil Castle and Grouville Bay are a bonus at this pubby venue within the Jersey Pottery complex. Castle Green is an ideal spot for a family re-fuel, although the main menu pulls no punches when it comes to flavours or ideas. Jersey produce looms large, whether it's hand-dived scallops with butternut squash risotto (£9.50/£16) or pork and black butter sausages with parsnip purée, Savoy cabbage and red wine jus (£11.95). Wines from £13.50. Closed Sun D and all Mon.

## ▮ Grouville, Jersey
### Village Bistro
**Impressive results and a quaint setting**
Gorey Village Main Road, Grouville, Jersey, JE3 9EP
Tel no: (01534) 853429
www.villagebistrojersey.com
**Modern European | £28**
**Cooking score: 3**

V

The Copps' attractive bistro in a peaceful Jersey village is housed in a former church, and makes the most of the Channel Island sun in summer with tables in a courtyard garden. Sarah Copp has established a good local network of supplies and the results are plain for all to see in cooking that brings an impressive degree of finish to essentially simple dishes. A warm tartlet of smoked haddock and leek, topped with a quail egg and served with curried crème fraîche, offers a full-flavoured starter, and might be the prelude to roast rack of lamb with salsify, carrots and dauphinoise in a garlic and thyme jus. It's all served in an atmosphere of civility and cheer. A quartet of French and Argentinian house wines comes at £13 a bottle.

**Chef/s:** Sarah Copp. **Open:** Tue to Sun L 12 to 2.30 (4 Sun), Tue to Sat D 7 to 10.30. **Closed:** Mon. **Meals:** alc (main courses £14 to £19). Set L £13.50 (2 courses) to £15.75. Set D £18.50. Sun L £18.50. **Service:** not inc. **Details:** Cards accepted. 36 seats. 24 seats outside. No mobile phones. Wheelchair access. Music. Children allowed.

## ▌St Brelade, Jersey

### The Atlantic Hotel, Ocean Restaurant
**Confident food and awesome views**
Le Mont de la Pulente, St Brelade, Jersey, JE3 8HE
Tel no: (01534) 744101
www.theatlantichotel.com
**Modern British | £50**
**Cooking score: 4**

🍷 ⇆ V

With its stunning sub-tropical gardens, a championship golf course next door and some of the most jaw-dropping sea views in Jersey, it's no wonder this dapper hotel is a must-visit holiday destination. The classy Ocean Restaurant – all maritime blues, whites and beiges – takes full advantage of the setting, and Mark Jordan's polished cooking makes a point of plundering Jersey's seasonal larder for ingredients. Proceedings might begin with a miniature tasting of local crab or hand-dived scallops paired with honey-baked pork belly and creamed cabbage. Moving on, you might see roast rump of spring lamb, squab pigeon with foie gras and golden raisin jus or seared fillet of line-caught sea bass with crushed Jersey Royals, tortellini and fish 'bubbles'. To finish, vanilla ice cream with strawberry marshmallow, mint jelly and chocolate leaves should put you in holiday mood. Sommelier Sergio dos Santos knows his way around the prestigious wine list, which cruises through France at its leisure and also picks up fascinating stuff from elsewhere (including a bottle or two from Jersey itself). Half-bottles are numerous and house selections start at £18 (£5 a glass).
**Chef/s:** Mark Jordan. **Open:** all week L 12.30 to 2.30, D 7 to 10. **Closed:** Jan. **Meals:** Set L £20 (2 courses) to £25. Set D £50. Sun L £30. **Service:** not inc. **Details:** Cards accepted. 65 seats. Separate bar. No mobile phones. Wheelchair access. Music. Children allowed. Car parking.

## ALSO RECOMMENDED
### ▲ Wayside Café
Le Mont Sohier, St Brelade, Jersey, JE3 8EA
Tel no: (01534) 743915
**Café**

Situated on the beach, overlooking the bay, the restaurant enjoys gorgeous views of the tides and surrounding coastline. Those in the know go on fine days and grab an outside table. The day's specials are chalked up on a board, and there are breakfasts, all-day snacks and sandwiches, as well as Thai duck salad (£5), followed by red mullet with saffron mash and Provençal dressing (£13), and treats like passion fruit and raspberry meringue roulade (£4.95). Wines from £11.95. Open all week.

## ▌St Clement, Jersey

## ALSO RECOMMENDED
### ▲ Green Island Restaurant
Green Island, St Clement, Jersey, JE2 6LS
Tel no: (01534) 857787
**Modern European**

The beachside restaurant is perched (quite securely) at the top of the slipway at Green Island, with panoramic sea views and an outdoor terrace for fine-weather dining. A Mediterranean influence informs dishes such as prawn and scallop saffron risotto with mascarpone (£8.80), herb-crusted brill with crab linguine, and roast rack of lamb with potato and celeriac rösti and root vegetable cassoulet (£18.50). Indulgent desserts might take in warm chocolate brownie with red berry compote, chocolate sauce and blackcurrant sorbet (£6.25). Wines from £14.50. Closed Sun D and all Mon.

## Shaun Rankin  Bohemia

**Who or what inspired you to become a chef?**
My mother.

**If you hadn't become a chef, what would you have been?**
Marine biologist.

**What is the best meal you have ever eaten?**
Roast lobster, chips and béarnaise sauce.

**What is your favourite restaurant and why?**
Les Maisons de Bricourt, Cancale.

**If you were to have one abiding principle in the kitchen, what would it be?**
Don't be late.

**What do you do to relax when out of the kitchen?**
Fishing.

**What is the best part of your job?**
Working with passionate people.

**What's coming up next for you?**
Watch this space!

## St Helier, Jersey

### Bohemia

Cooking up a storm
Green Street, St Helier, Jersey, JE2 4UH
Tel no: (01534) 880588
www.bohemiajersey.com
**Modern European | £50**
**Cooking score: 7**

Sophisticated boutique opulence is the name of the game at the trendsetting, ultra-hip Club Hotel & Spa in St Helier's fashionably moneyed financial quarter, just a short walk from the beach. Try to ignore the noisy hubbub and scrum of bodies in the throbbing bar if you are heading for the style-conscious wood and leather-panelled Bohemia restaurant, where cool affluence prevails and chef Shaun Rankin is cooking up a storm. As you might expect, freshly landed Jersey seafood gets a good outing and it's subjected to fiercely contemporary treatment: grilled red mullet and roast scallops find themselves in company with cauliflower purée, blood orange, white chocolate and Fourme d'Ambert cheese, while roast turbot is accompanied by Puy lentils, Savoy cabbage, Périgord truffle and a beignet of celeriac purée and pig's trotter. Elsewhere, intricately contrived ideas are spread across the carte, from a terrine of foie gras with caramelised pineapple chop, passion fruit jam, mango sorbet and ginger crumbs, via roast Anjou pigeon with Roquefort risotto, pickled walnuts and Asian pear to Amaretto parfait with salted caramel, barley ice cream and lemon curd. The kitchen is also prepared to inject some up-to-the-minute pizazz into classic partnerships: a 'three-hour' local duck egg is served cunningly with Jerusalem artichoke velouté and confit of chicken wings, while roast loin of Yorkshire venison appears in a new guise, with smoked chocolate tortellini and a smattering of world-larder exotica (Medjool dates, ginger and scented quinoa). Given the voguish tone of the menu (and the equally voguish surrounds), it's no surprise to find meals interspersed with all manner of amuse-bouches, extras, mid-courses and shot glasses. Multi-course tasting menus are served at the six-person chef's table, and the serious-minded, 140-bin wine list looks to neighbouring France for most of its inspiration. Bottle prices start at £16.50, with around 20 Verre de Vin selections from £4.50 a glass.

**Chef/s:** Shaun Rankin. **Open:** Mon to Sat L 12 to 2.30, D 6.30 to 10. **Closed:** Sun, 25 to 27 Dec. **Meals:** Set L £18.50 (2 courses) to £21.50. Set D £42.50 (2 courses) to £49.50. Tasting menu £75. **Service:** 10% (optional). **Details:** Cards accepted. 66 seats. Air-con. Separate bar. Wheelchair access. Music. Children allowed. Car parking.

## ▌St Martin, Guernsey
## The Auberge
**Modish island brasserie**
Jerbourg Road, St Martin, Guernsey, GY4 6BH
Tel no: (01481) 238485
www.theauberge.gg
**Modern European | £27**
**Cooking score: 5**

**V**

A fantastic location high on the cliffs within easy reach of St Peter Port adds to the allure of this well-established brasserie-style restaurant. The dining room has been given a modish minimalist look, with big picture windows offering panoramic views across Le Pied du Mur Bay to Guernsey's island neighbours. Locally sourced produce – especially daily consignments of seafood from the boats – is at the heart of dishes that are vigorously creative. A starter of marinated red mullet escabèche is embellished with pink grapefruit, pickled cucumber and avocado cream, while crispy capers and wasabi cream add a flourish to beef carpaccio. Unexpected componets also find their way into main courses – witness tagliatelle nero and fennel ceviche with skate or mushroom tartare and curried king prawns alongside fillet of brill. Classic steaks (served with various sauces and chunky chips) are just the ticket for meat fans, while cleverly crafted desserts might run to banana tempura with banana parfait and cinnamon foam, or peach tarte fine with

lemon and lime crème fraîche and peach sorbet. Around 40 wisely chosen global wines start at £17.50 (£6.25 a glass).

**Chef/s:** Daniel Green. **Open:** all week L 12 to 2, Mon to Sat D 7 to 9. **Closed:** 25 and 26 Dec, 1 Jan. **Meals:** alc (main courses £13 to £19). Set L £14.95 (2 courses). Set D £18.95. Sun L £22.95. **Service:** 10% (optional). **Details:** Cards accepted. 50 seats. 20 seats outside. Wheelchair access. Music. Children allowed. Car parking.

## READERS RECOMMEND

## La Barbarie
**Seafood**
Saints Bay, St Martin, Guernsey, GY4 6ES
Tel no: (01481) 235217
www.labarbariehotel.com
'**Excellent local seafood and fish**'

## ▌St Peter Port, Guernsey
## La Frégate
**Chic dining with fabulous views**
Les Cotils, St Peter Port, Guernsey, GY1 1UT
Tel no: (01481) 724624
www.lafregatehotel.com
**Modern European | £30**
**Cooking score: 4**

Perched high above St Peter Port, this tastefully upgraded eighteenth-century manor gazes down on the harbour and the dramatic 800-year-old Castle Cornet, offering visitors 'some of the best views anywhere'. Cool, airy modernism is the theme in the restaurant, with its bare boards, abstract artworks and startling floral arrangements – although the food follows a more mainstream path. Local seafood and Guernsey produce are deployed for Euro-accented dishes ranging from roast sea bass with seared scallops, fennel cream and vanilla froth to luxury-laden medallions of beef with truffle gnocchi and foie gras sauce. Chateaubriand and crêpes Suzette hark back to the days of trolleys and flambés, but the kitchen also rings the changes by offering crispy duck pancakes with teriyaki dressing and chicken breast with pea risotto and a Sauternes reduction. Desserts include iced raspberry and lychee parfait with a 'minestrone' of red fruits and poached peaches. House wine is £14.95.

**Chef/s:** Neil Maginnis. **Open:** all week L 12 to 2, D 7 to 9.30. **Meals:** alc (main courses £14 to £19). Set L £16.50 (2 courses) to £19. Set D £25 (2 courses) to £30. Sun L £18.95. **Service:** not inc. **Details:** Cards accepted. 80 seats. 40 seats outside. Air-con. Separate bar. No music. Children allowed. Car parking.

## ALSO RECOMMENDED
### ▲ Da Nello
46 Pollet Street, St Peter Port, Guernsey, GY1 1WF
Tel no: (01481) 721552
**Italian**

Nello Ciotti brings a taste of sunny Italy to Guernsey with his long-running restaurant in a granite-walled, eighteenth-century cottage – complete with a covered piazza. 'Amazing seafood' from the Guernsey boats is a big draw: expect anything from signature lobster linguine to grilled scallops with balsamic syrup and crispy bacon. Otherwise, start with aubergine Parmigiana (£5.90) and move on to medallions of beef with Barolo sauce (£15.95). House wine £14.50. Open all week.

### ▲ Le Nautique
Quay Steps, St Peter Port, Guernsey, GY1 2LE
Tel no: (01481) 721714
www.lenautiquerestaurant.co.uk
**French**

Gunter Botzenhardt's restaurant caters admirably for visitors who make the seasonal trek to this harbour town. Sustenance comes in the shape of globetrotting fish dishes including Thai crab cakes with mango and banana salsa (£7.50), and sea bass with ginger, chilli, pineapple and fresh coriander (£15.50). Meat dishes (confit roast duckling, caramelised apples and Calvados sauce) are worth exploring. House wine £16.50. Closed Sun.

## ▮ St Saviour, Jersey
### Longueville Manor
**Beacon of country house elegance**
St Saviour, Jersey, JE2 7WF
Tel no: (01534) 725501
www.longuevillemanor.com
**Modern British | £55**
**Cooking score: 5**
🍷 🍴

*Guide* regular Longueville has been in the Lewis family for half a century, and remains a beacon of grand country-house elegance and solicitude. It was built in the fourteenth century and is surrounded by 15 acres of woodland and grounds – including a Victorian kitchen garden – and is run with sympathetic warmth and professionalism. Chef Andrew Baird has clocked up a fair few years here (his third decade is upon us), and the results are there for all to see, in cooking that takes its cue from the seasons and its influences from modern French modes. Poached sea bass is teamed with crab gratin in one main course, while meatier options might be loin and shoulder of lamb with flageolets and baby vegetables, or marrow-crusted Angus fillet with braised cheek and béarnaise. Top and tail with inventive dishes such as grilled scallops, belly pork, trompettes, honey and five-spice, and pineapple wrap with riz au lait, pannacotta and kiwi. The Taste of Jersey menu is worth the punt, incorporating perhaps crab, halibut and pork from the vicinity, with Longueville's own honey in the form of a soufflé. The monster wine list is a delight – it doesn't just concentrate lazily on France, but has fine, authoritative selections from Italy, New Zealand and South America too. An excellent glass selection starts at £4.75.

**Chef/s:** Andrew Baird. **Open:** all week L 12 to 2, D 7 to 10. **Meals:** Set L £17 (2 courses) to £20.50. Set D £47.50 (2 courses) to £55. Sun L £30. **Service:** service included. **Details:** Cards accepted. 60 seats. 35 seats outside. Separate bar. No music. No mobile phones. Wheelchair access. Children allowed. Car parking.

# NORTHERN IRELAND

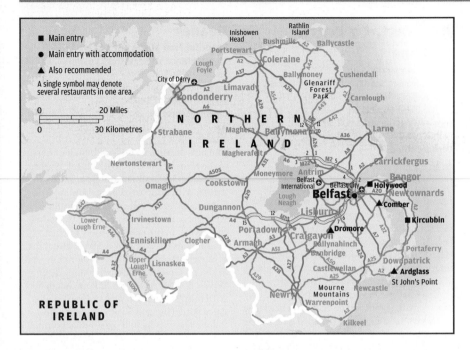

## Ardglass, Co Down

### ALSO RECOMMENDED
### ▲ Curran's Bar & Seafood Steakhouse

83 Strangford Road, Chapeltown, Ardglass, Co Down, BT30 7SP
Tel no: (028) 4484 1332
www.curransbar.net
**Seafood**

Spanking fresh fish is Curran's strong suit. Its seafood platter (£35 for two sharing) is a star of the menu: langoustines, prawns, crab cakes, mussels, smoked mackerel, clams, crab claws – perfect with homemade wheaten bread and a glass of chilled white wine. It's billed as a starter, so pace yourself if you want to go on to chargrilled salmon or steak with peppercorn cream. Old-fashioned desserts include apple crumble (£4). House wine from £12. Open all week.

## Ballyrobert, Co Antrim

### READERS RECOMMEND
### Oregano
**Modern British**
29 Ballyrobert Road, Ballyrobert, Co Antrim, BT39 9RY
Tel no: (028) 9084 0099
www.oreganorestaurant.com
'A modern menu that combines flair and imagination'

## Bangor, Co Down

### READERS RECOMMEND
### Esplanade Bar
**Modern British**
12 Ballyholme Esplanade, Bangor, Co Down, BT20 5LZ
Tel no: (028) 9127 0954
'Food and service excellent, with a beautiful view over Ballyholme Bay'

## ▌Belfast, Co Antrim

### Cayenne
**Sexy fusion sizzler**
7 Ascot House, Shaftesbury Square, Belfast, Co Antrim, BT2 7DB
Tel no: (028) 9033 1532
www.cayenne-restaurant.co.uk
Global | £30
Cooking score: 4

🍷 V

Much of Paul and Jeanne Rankin's Belfast restaurant empire has been decimated by the downturn, but this globally inclined sizzler is still running on high octane. It woos a fashion-conscious young city crowd with its electric mix of multi-media events, arty interiors and voguish global flavours. A glance at Cayenne's gastro-passport reveals trips to the Far East and beyond, with a sexy repertoire that runs all the way from black cod miso with radish salad and pickled ginger slaw to Italian lemon cheesecake with candied pine nut and milk sorbet. In between, expect a riot of fusion in the shape of red-braised pork with seared scallops, celeriac and sesame-fried onions, blackened monkfish with roast aubergine and Indian rösti or daube of beef with garlic mash and shiitake mushrooms. After dinner, enjoy the sensory blast of a Hot Causeway (Bushmills whiskey, Drambuie, honey, cloves and lemon topped with hot water). Wines are broadly categorised by grape, and the list is as invigorating as the food, with a canny choice of trendy top-end names at fine-tuned prices. Prices start at £16.95 (£3.95 a glass).
**Chef/s:** Paul Rankin. **Open:** Thur and Fri L 12 to 2.15, all week D 6 to 11 (5 Sun). **Closed:** 25 Dec, 1 Jan, 12 July. **Meals:** alc (main courses £14 to £23). Set L £12 (2 courses) to £15.50. Set D £20. **Service:** not inc. **Details:** Cards accepted. 150 seats. Air-con. Separate bar. Wheelchair access. Music. Children allowed.

### Deanes
**Beautiful food at the city's heart**
36-40 Howard Street, Belfast, Co Antrim, BT1 6PF
Tel no: (028) 9033 1134
www.michaeldeane.co.uk
**Modern British | £40**
Cooking score: 5

V

The hub of Michael Deane's Belfast empire is in the heart of the city: a delightful, bright, contemporary dining room fronting two streets, with floor-to-ceiling windows, fashionably grey walls, black chairs and white table linen. At the bottom end of the room, chefs work in the open-to-view kitchen, sending out beautifully presented dishes such as butternut squash soup with pumpkin seeds or the ever-popular smoked salmon from Walter Ewing. Aged loin of Fermanagh beef with buttered green beans, scallion potato, sauce bordelaise and bone marrow could follow. Desserts include an unusual pomme genoise – poached apples, apple sorbet and liquorice ice cream. It's worth noting, too, that fixed-price lunches are excellent value for the quality of the produce and the highly skilled cooking. The wine list leans towards France with a list of fine vintages, but there's more than a nod towards the rest of Europe and the New World. House wine is £22.
**Chef/s:** Derek Creagh. **Open:** Tue to Sat L 12 to 3, D 6 to 10. **Closed:** Mon, Sun, 25 and 26 Dec, 1 Jan, bank hols, 12 and 13 July. **Meals:** alc (main courses £17 to £26). Set L £17.50 (2 courses) to £21.50. Tasting menu £55 (5 courses) to £75 (10 courses). **Service:** 10% (optional). **Details:** Cards accepted. 80 seats. Air-con. Separate bar. Wheelchair access. Music. Children allowed.

**NEW ENTRY**
## Deanes at Queens
**Buzzing brasserie**
1 College Gardens, Belfast, Co Antrim, BT9 6BQ
Tel no: (028) 9038 2111
www.michaeldeane.co.uk
**Modern British | £27**
**Cooking score: 3**

Deanes at Queens – part of the Michael Deane gastro-circus – can be found on College Gardens, a stone's throw from the University, and there's a great buzz due to its friendly service and please-all menu of popular brasserie classics. The bright, airy dining space is long, with a polished wood floor, plain tables and a bar running practically the entire length, behind which on-show chefs prepare the likes of salt-and-chilli squid with wasabi aïoli, and belly pork with fresh linguine, shaved fennel, lemon and parsley. The set lunch menu, in particular, is good value. It offers say, tomato and roast red pepper soup with basil pesto, beer-battered fish and chips, and double chocolate steamed pudding. House wine from £14.95.
**Chef/s:** Chris Fearon. **Open:** Mon to Sat L 12 to 3, D 5.30 to 9 (10 Wed to Sat). **Closed:** Sun, 1 Jan, Easter Mon and Tue, 11 and 12 July, 25 and 26 Dec. **Meals:** alc (main courses £11 to £18). Set L £15 (2 courses) to £17.50. Set D £22.50 (2 courses) to £27.50. **Service:** 10% (optional). **Details:** Cards accepted. 150 seats. 20 seats outside. Air-con. Wheelchair access. Music. Children allowed.

## James Street South
**Assured big-city food**
21 James Street South, Belfast, Co Antrim, BT2 7GA
Tel no: (028) 9043 4310
www.jamesstreetsouth.co.uk
**Modern European | £35**
**Cooking score: 5**

Tucked just behind City Hall, this popular restaurant has a bright, spacious dining room. Light floods in through the high, arched windows and there's contemporary artwork on the white walls. Here Niall McKenna gets to show off his considerable talents with a sophisticated modern European menu. The cooking blends classical and contemporary ideas and the set lunch, in particular, seems good value. For unhurried diners, an interesting à la carte might feature starters of honeyed pork belly with asparagus and hollandaise, or carpaccio of venison with honey, red pepper, shaved asparagus and olive oil dressing. To follow, there might be rump of spring lamb with caramelised shallot, aubergine and pea, or saddle of rabbit with confit root vegetables, black trompette mushrooms and shallot jus. Desserts include apple crumble with lavender anglaise and whiskey jelly. An appropriately modern wine list offers a good choice at mostly fair prices. House wine is £18.
**Chef/s:** Niall McKenna. **Open:** Mon to Sat L 1 to 2.45, all week D 5.45 to 10.45 (5.30 to 9 Sun). **Closed:** 25 and 26 Dec, 1 Jan, Easter Sun and Mon, 12 July. **Meals:** alc (main courses £15 to £20). Set L £14.50 (2 courses) to £16.50. Set D (pre theatre Mon to Thur) £16.50 (2 courses) to £19.50. Set D £16.50 (2 courses) to £18.50. **Service:** not inc. **Details:** Cards accepted. 65 seats. Air-con. Separate bar. Wheelchair access. Music. Children allowed.

**NEW ENTRY**
## Menu by Kevin Thornton
**Old favourites with a creative twist**
Fitzwilliam Hotel Belfast, 1-3 Great Victoria Street, Belfast, Co Antrim, BT2 7BQ
Tel no: (028) 9044 2130
www.fitzwilliamhotelbelfast.com
**Modern European | £35**
**Cooking score: 5**

Three elegant rooms make up the dining space in this cosmopolitan restaurant in the Fitzwilliam Hotel. Polished wood floors, regal high-backed red chairs, subdued lighting and intimate booths along the walls set a tone that suggests a serious approach to food. However, the atmosphere is pleasingly unceremonious. Kevin Thornton's cooking is solidly grounded in classic techniques, but, rather than restricting his style, this acts as a springboard for his creative flair. For example, old favourites are given a very modern twist: bacon and cabbage have long been a staple of the Irish diet, here they combine in a very successful terrine with shallot vinaigrette and leek purée. Mains focus on local ingredients: grilled fillet of Fermanagh Angus beef partnered with béarnaise sauce and pont neuf potatoes, Kettyle's free-range chicken with tagliatelle, lemongrass and lime sauce. Equally straightforward are desserts of bourbon vanilla crème brûlée with Bushmills whiskey snap or chocolate fondant with passion fruit sorbet. The global wine list starts at £19.

**Chef/s:** Kevin Thornton and Patrick Leonard. **Open:** Mon to Fri L 12.30 to 2.30, all week D 5.30 to 10 (11 Fri and Sat). **Meals:** alc (main courses £13 to £23). **Details:** Cards accepted. 130 seats. Air-con. Separate bar. No mobile phones. Wheelchair access. Music. Children allowed.

---

**★ READERS' RESTAURANT OF THE YEAR ★
NORTHERN IRELAND**

## Mourne Seafood Bar
**Fish fresh from the Lough**
34-36 Bank Street, Belfast, Co Antrim, BT1 1HL
Tel no: (028) 9024 8544
www.mourneseafood.com
**Seafood | £25**
**Cooking score: 3**

Although right in Belfast city centre, there's more than a hint of 'rustic' about Mourne Seafood Bar. The entrance is through their fish shop (where the pick of the catch from Carlingford Lough is sold from Wednesday to Saturday) and the dining room is long and slightly narrow, with a banquette along the red-brick wall. As well as the regular menu, there's a good daily list of blackboard specials. Chowder is a favourite, as is smoked mackerel, while mains may include whole fish on the bone or a hearty casserole of salmon, mussels, clams and hake in a herbed tomato broth with potatoes, red onions and fresh tomatoes. Buttermilk pannacotta with berries is just one of a good dessert selection. Wines from £14.

**Chef/s:** Andy Rea. **Open:** all week L 12 to 5 (4 Fri and Sat, 1 to 6 Sun), Tue to Sat D 5 to 9.30 (10.30 Thur, Fri and Sat). **Closed:** 25 and 26 Dec, 1 Jan, 17 Mar. **Meals:** alc (main courses £8 to £18). **Service:** not inc. **Details:** Cards accepted. 70 seats. 8 seats outside. Air-con. Wheelchair access. Music. Children allowed.

## Nick's Warehouse
**Fine ingredients and good-value lunches**
35-39 Hill Street, Belfast, Co Antrim, BT1 2LB
Tel no: (028) 9043 9690
www.nickswarehouse.co.uk
**Modern British | £30**
**Cooking score: 3**

Nick and Kathy Price have been here since 1989, working to updated classic formulae and applying sound techniques (plus influences from further afield) to fine Irish produce. The good-value lunch menu might start with carrot and coriander soup and move on to beef and mushroom casserole. At dinner, expect monkfish medallions with spiced aubergine and basil dressing ahead of chargrilled dry-cured bacon with sautéed mushrooms, Savoy cabbage, roast potatoes and blue cheese sauce, or grilled cod with potato purée and an oxtail-filled beef tomato. House wine from £14.

**Chef/s:** Sean Craig. **Open:** Tue to Sat L 12 to 3, D 6 to 10. **Closed:** Sun, Mon, 25 and 26 Dec, 1 Jan, 13 to 14 March. **Meals:** alc (main courses £11 to £22). Set D £16.50 (2 courses) to £19.50 (Tue to Thur). **Service:** not inc. **Details:** Cards accepted. 135 seats. Air-con. Separate bar. Wheelchair access. Music.

---

| Symbols | |
|---|---|
| ⌐ | Accommodation is available |
| £30 | Three courses for less than £30 |
| V | More than three vegetarian main courses |
| £5 OFF | £5-off voucher scheme |
| 🍾 | Notable wine list |

**NEW ENTRY**
## No 27 Talbot Street
**High-quality modern food**
27 Talbot Street, Belfast, Co Antrim, BT1 2LD
Tel no: (028) 9031 2884
www.no27.co.uk
**Modern British | £30**
**Cooking score: 3**
£5
OFF

One of the Cathedral Quarter's newer restaurants, No 27 is busy, even on weekday evenings, with visitors drawn back by the high quality of the cooking. The room is long, with pale walls making an excellent backdrop for some striking paintings. Belfast seems to be intent on reviving the 'on-show' kitchen, and here at the back three chefs can be seen busily preparing the day's menu. Starters run to chargrilled squid with salsa and coriander salad or lobster niçoise. Main courses are divided equally between meat and fish, say hake with cherry tomatoes, sauté potatoes and balsamic dressing or calf's liver in red wine jus. Desserts include white chocolate and mango cheesecake or key lime pie with strawberries. Wines on the global list start at £16.
**Chef/s:** Alan Higginson. **Open:** Mon to Fri L 12 to 3, Tue to Sat D 6 to 10. **Closed:** Sun, 25 and 26 Dec, 1 Jan, Easter Mon. **Meals:** alc (main courses £14 to £23). **Service:** not inc. **Details:** Cards accepted. 70 seats. Air-con. Separate bar. Wheelchair access. Music.

## ALSO RECOMMENDED
### ▲ Coco
7-11 Linenhall Street, Belfast, Co Antrim, BT2 8AA
Tel no: (028) 9031 1150
www.cocobelfast.com
**Modern British**

Jason Moore is the new owner of this city-centre restaurant, which was formerly Paul Rankin's Roscoff Brasserie. He has made a few changes to style, décor and menu, and now serves brasserie-style food with a distinctly global flavour. A simple lunch could be an oriental crispy duck salad (£4.50), risotto or cod and chips. Dinner brings seared foie gras with mango and coriander salsa, and honey-roast belly pork with root vegetable and barley risotto (£14.50). A global selection of wines starts at £14.50. Closed Sat L and Sun D.

## READERS RECOMMEND
### The Ginger Tree
**Japanese**
23 Donegal Pass, Belfast, Co Antrim, BT7 1DQ
Tel no: (028) 9032 7151
'Delicious Japanese food'

### Me:nu
**Seafood/Steakhouse**
15-17 Donegal Pass, Shaftesbury Square, Belfast, Co Antrim, BT7 1DQ
Tel no: (028) 9024 4257
www.menubelfast.co.uk
'A real find, a seafood/steakhouse with excellent, sophisticated cooking'

# ▌Comber, Co Down

## ALSO RECOMMENDED
### ▲ The Old Schoolhouse Inn
100 Ballydrain Road, Comber, Co Down, BT23 6EA
Tel no: (028) 9754 1182
www.theoldschoolhouseinn.com
**French**

In 1983, Terry and Avril Brown rescued Ballydrain school and converted it into a restaurant. It still has the cast-iron radiators, wall clock, high windows, sepia pictures, globe and even some old uniforms, but the cooking is far removed from school dinners of old. Avril sources local ingredients and her two-course dinner (£19.95) offers a good range of local fish – seared halibut and hake – although the house speciality is Finnebrogue venison (£6 supplement). An excellent wine list is very reasonably priced, with house selections from £13.95. Open all week D only.

| Also recommended |
| --- |
| Also recommended entries are not scored but we think they are worth a visit. |

## Dromore, Co Down

### ALSO RECOMMENDED
### ▲ Boyles of Dromore
8-12 Castle Street, Dromore, Co Down, BT25 1AF
Tel no: (028) 9269 9141
www.boylesofdromore.com
**Modern French**

Found in a row of early nineteenth-century cottages opposite the castle ruins, Boyles' striking pink-and-green painted exterior extends a firm invitation to venture inside: the welcoming fire, cottagey atmosphere and Raymond Murray's cooking won't disappoint. Starters might include a terrine of chicken with onion marmalade (£5.65) followed by pale-smoked Portavogie haddock served with spinach and mash, topped with a delicately poached egg (£18.50), and the popular iced cappuccino parfait (£5.25) for dessert. Wines from £11.50. Open Fri to Sun L, Wed to Sun D.

## Holywood, Co Down
### Bay Tree Coffee House
**Real gem with loads of fans**
118 High Street, Holywood, Co Down, BT18 9HW
Tel no: (028) 9042 1419
www.baytreeholywood.com
**British | £20**
**Cooking score: 2**
£5 OFF  **V**  £30

The reputation of Sue Farmer's simple restaurant spreads far beyond its immediate locale and it continues to offer good value to a packed room. A light lunch might be red onion, goats' cheese and thyme tartlet with salad, but if you are after something more filling, look for creamy chicken and sweetcorn pie with a crunchy mash topping and follow with rich chocolate fudge cake. Dinner brings chicken liver pâté with redcurrant jelly, then haddock with parsley butter and mash. Sue's famed cinnamon scones catch the eye for dessert – so renowned you can buy them to take away. House wine is £13.50. A real gem.

**Chef/s:** Sue Farmer. **Open:** all week L 12 to 3, (10 to 2.45 Sun), Mon and Wed to Sat D 6 to 9.30. **Closed:** 25 to 27 Dec, 1 Jan, 12 and 13 July. **Meals:** alc (£6.50 to £17.50). **Service:** not inc. **Details:** Cards accepted. 60 seats. Wheelchair access. Music. Children allowed. Car parking.

## Kircubbin, Co Down
### Paul Arthurs
**On-the-money bistro cooking**
66 Main Street, Kircubbin, Co Down, BT22 2SP
Tel no: (028) 4273 8192
www.paularthurs.com
**Modern British | £25**
**Cooking score: 3**
**V**  £30

Having launched his bistro-style restaurant above a chippie in 2002, Paul Arthurs was in the throes of expanding the premises as this year's *Guide* went to press. A new ground-floor dining room-cum-carvery is promised, which will double PA's seating capacity. In the meantime, customers can enjoy the rustic surrounds of the upstairs room (think exposed brickwork, wood floors and bold artwork) while sampling on-the-money eclectic dishes. Bowls of mussels from nearby Strangford Lough are a mainstay, although starters also run to creamed crab risotto with lemongrass, chilli and coriander. To follow, consider confit of duck with foie gras, honey and ginger or corn-fed chicken fillet with macaroni, garlic and chorizo. Irish cheeses could round off the show, unless your fancy turns to something homely and sweet – perhaps bread-and-butter pudding. House wine is £14.50.
**Chef/s:** Paul Arthurs. **Open:** Sun L 12 to 2.30, Tue to Sat D 5 to 9.30. **Closed:** Mon, 25 and 26 Dec. **Meals:** alc (main courses £15 to £18). **Service:** not inc. **Details:** Cards accepted. 45 seats. 20 seats outside. Music. Children allowed.

# MAPS

# MAP 6

- ■ Main entry
- ● Main entry with accommodation
- ▲ Also recommended

A single symbol may denote
several restaurants in one area.

0        10 Miles

0    10      20 Kilometres

Note: Maps 1 to 5 can be found at the front
of the London section

## Isles of Scilly
Same scale as main map

Tresco ▲
Hugh Town ●   St Mary's
     ● Isles of Scilly
     (St Mary's)

Lundy

Bud

Padstow ●   Rock ●   ■ St Kew
St Merryn ■    Wadebridge

Newquay
Watergate Bay ■ ●
Newquay   A392   Bodmin   A38

Kelsey Head      CORNWAL

     Lostw

St Austell   Fow
     A390   Polp

A30   ● Truro
St Ives ■   Redruth
  Camborne   A39
Treen ●   Hayle      ● Portscatho
St Just   Penzance    ● St Mawes
Land's End ●     A394   ▲ Falmouth
Land's End   Sennen   ● Perranuthnoe   Helston   Falmouth Bay
   Mousehole Porthleven ● Mawgan
     Mount's
     Bay
    Lizard
    Lizard
    Point

Bristol
Channel

Weston-super-Mare

21 A38

Cheddar

Lynton

Minehead

Burnham-
on-Sea

22

A371

Ilfracombe

Winsford

A39

Bridgwater

23

Glastonbury

A39

Street

A361

A39

Braunton

**Barnstaple**

SOMERSET

Langport

Bideford

South
Molton

Knowstone

Wiveliscombe

▲ Bampton

Wellington

Taunton

A361

Long Sutton ▲

Stoke sub
Hamdon

Great
Torrington

A39

A388

A386

Rackenford

A361

West
Hatch

25

M5

A358

Hinton
St George

A303

Ilminster

Chard

A30

Crewkerne

Tiverton

27

Hatherleigh

A3072

Holsworthy

A3072

A377

Crediton

A3072

A396

28

Honiton ▲

Gittisham

A373

Axminster

A358

A3066

Bridport

shwater

Okehampton

DEVON

A30

Exeter ✈

Rockbeare

A30

Newton
Poppleford

A3052

Seaton

Lyme
Regis

West
Bay

Virginstow

29

30

Topsham

A376

Sidmouth

Lyme Bay

Lewdown

Chagford

A382

Exeter

31

Lydford

A386

nceston

Lifton

Dartmoor

Exmouth

Bovey
Tracey

A380

Dawlish
Teignmouth

Gulworthy

A390

Tavistock

Ashburton

A38

Newton
Abbot

Shaldon

skeard

A388

Buckfastleigh

A385

Torquay

Plymouth
City ✈

South
Brent ▲

Paignton

A4387

Saltash

A38

Ivybridge

Totnes

Brixham

East Looe

Plymouth

A379

Dartmouth

Millbrook

A361

A379

Strete

Kingsbridge ▲

Bigbury-on-Sea

Salcombe

Start
Point

## Channel
## Islands
Not to same scale

Alderney ✈

Alderney

St Peter Port ▲ ✈

Guernsey

Herm

Sark

St Martin

**Guernsey**

**Jersey**

Beaumont

St Saviour

Jersey ✈

Gorey

Grouville

St Brelade

St Helier ▲

St Clement

## MAP 7

- ■ Main entry
- ● Main entry with accommodation
- ▲ Also recommended

A single symbol may denote
several restaurants in one area.

```
0                    10 Miles
0        10        20 Kilometres
```

9

Tewkesbury
Bourton-on-the-
Eldersfield  Corse Lawn  9  Winchcombe
Stow-the-
Upper
Cheltenham  10  Slaughter
Gloucestershire  11
Ross-on-Wye  Gloucester  11A  Compton Abdale ▲
Cinderford  GLOUCESTERSHIRE
Monmouth  Arlingham  Northl
Whitebrook  13  Stroud  Coln St Aldwyns
South
Sapperton  Fairford
Chepstow  Dursley  Tetbury  Cirencester
Crudwell  Crickl
Bassaleg  26  25  23  Thornbury  Didmarton ▲
Pontypridd  24  Caldicot  21  Swindo
Caerphilly  28  Newport  22  20/15  Easton  Malmesbury  16
Llantrisant  29  17  16  Grey  17
32  18A  Bristol Filton  Wootton
St Fagans  Avonmouth  19  Castle Combe  Bassett
35  34  33  Portishead  19  1  Chippenham
Cardiff  Clevedon ■  18  A420
Cowbridge  Penarth  Colerne  A4
Corsham  WILTS
Cardiff  Barry  Bristol  Bath  Melksham  Rowde
International  Bristol  Bradford-  Pewse
International  on-Avon
Weston-  Combe Hay  Holt  Devizes
super-Mare  Midsomer  Trowbridge  East
Cheddar  Norton  Chisenbury
Burnham-  Radstock  Upton
on-Sea  22  Wookey  Scudamore
Minehead  Hole  Oakhill ▲  Frome  Warminster
Worth  Wells  Horningsham  Crockerton  Amesbury
23  Shepton  Maiden  Codford
Bridgwater  Glastonbury  Mallet  Bradley ▲  St Peter  Berwi
Street  Shepton  Bruton  Teffont Evias ■  St Jan
SOMERSET  Montague  Wilton
Langport  Long  Corton  Wincanton  Salisbur
Taunton  Sutton  Denham  Gillingham  Bishopstone
Wiveliscombe  Trent ▲  Shaftesbury  Donhead  Farnham
▲ Bampton  West  Stoke sub  St Andrew  Stuckt
Wellington  Hatch  Hamdon  Yeovil  Sturminster
27  Hinton  Sherborne  Newton
Ilminster  St George  Barwick  Ringwo
Chard  Crewkerne  East Coker  Blandford
Tiverton  Forum  Wimborne
28  Minster  Bournemouth
Honiton ▲  Axminster  DORSET  Poole
Exeter  Gittisham  Piddletrenthide  Bournemou
29  Rockbeare  Bridport  Poole
Newton  Lyme  Dorchester  Christchu
30  Poppleford  Regis  West Bay  Wareham  Bournemou
Topsham  Seaton  Poole
31  Sidmouth  Lyme Bay
Exmouth  Weymouth ▲  Swana
Dawlish  Fortuneswell  St Alban's
Teignmouth  Easton  Head
■ Shaldon  Bill of Portland

6

Swerford

oreton-
Marsh
Chipping
Norton
Kingham
dington
wer
dington

Woodstock

BUCKINGHAMSHIRE

Newton
Longville

Willian

Hitchin

Stevenage

Datchworth

Hunsdon

Leighton
Buzzard

Luton

London
Luton

Welwyn Garden
City

Hertford

Bicester

Murcott

Aylesbury

Long
Crendon

Dinton
Ford

Frithsden

Dunstable

OXFORDSHIRE

Witney

Kidlington

Thame

Berkhamsted

HERTFORDSHIRE

St Albans

Cheshunt

Oxford

Great
Milton

Chinnor

Chesham

Hemel
Hempstead

Watford

Enfield

Burford
Clanfield

Tadpole
Bridge

Fyfield

Britwell
Salome

Radnage

Great
Missenden

Amersham

Chandler's
Cross

Bushey

Abingdon

High
Wycombe

Nettlebed

Marlow

Harrow

GREATER

Wantage

Didcot

Ardington

Goring-on-Thames

Stoke
Row

Hurley

Cookham

Bray

Slough

Wembley

London

LONDON

Wallingford

East
Garston

BERKSHIRE

Chieveley

Frilsham

Reading

Maidenhead

Paley
Street

Windsor

Bracknell

London
Heathrow

Staines

Richmond

Bromley

rlborough

Marsh
Benham

Newbury

Shinfield

Wokingham

Bagshot

Woking

Epsom

Croydon

Hungerford

Little
Bedwyn

Highclere

Thatcham

Baughurst

Camberley

Fleet

Farnborough

Ripley

SURREY

Leatherhead

Old Burghclere

Basingstoke

Aldershot

Guildford

Redhill

Andover

Farnham

Shere

Abinger
Hammer

Dorking

Reigate

Popham
Services

Alton

HAMPSHIRE

Alresford

Liphook

Haslemere

Godalming

London
Gatwick

Crawley

East
Grinstead

Longstock
Stockbridge

Winchester

West Meon

Petersfield

Horsham

Danehill

Haywards Heath

Cuckfield

Romsey

Eastleigh

Droxford

Trotton

Midhurst

WEST SUSSEX

Billingshurst

Burgess Hill

East
Chiltington

Southampton

Shedfield

West
Stoke

Lavant

Albourne

Waterlooville

Havant

Funtington

Tangmere

Shoreham
(Brighton City)

Lewes

Southampton

Hythe

Fareham

Emsworth

Chichester

Arundel

Worthing

Brighton

nhurst

Brockenhurst

Beaulieu

Gosport

Southsea

Bognor
Regis

Littlehampton

ymington

Buckler's
Hard

Cowes

Portsmouth

Sidlesham

Barton on Sea
Yarmouth

Ryde

Seaview

Selsey Bill

Newport

ISLE OF WIGHT

Sandown

Shanklin

Isle of Wight

Ventnor

Clanfield

Marborough

Baughurst

Chiltern Hills

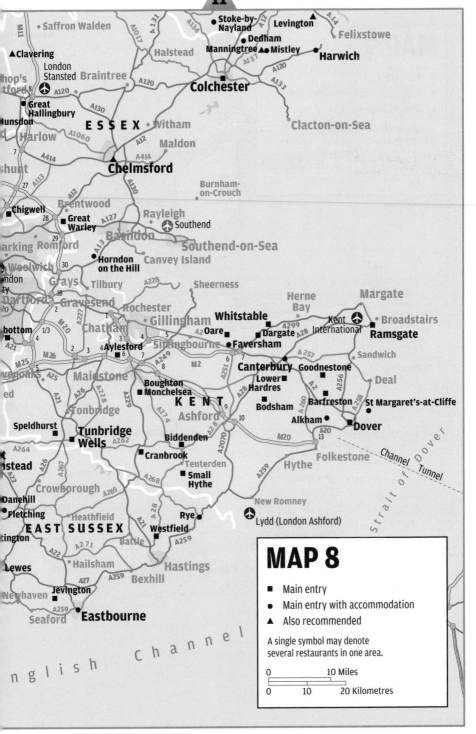

**MAP 8**

- ■ Main entry
- ● Main entry with accommodation
- ▲ Also recommended

A single symbol may denote
several restaurants in one area.

0          10 Miles

0     10     20 Kilometres

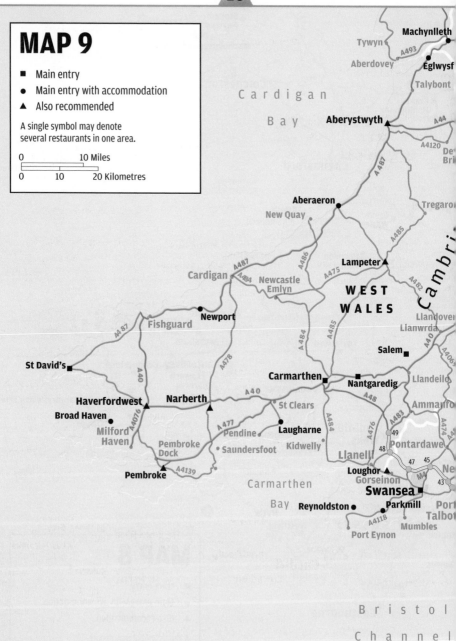

# MAP 9

- ■ Main entry
- ● Main entry with accommodation
- ▲ Also recommended

A single symbol may denote several restaurants in one area.

| 0 | | | 10 Miles |
| 0 | 10 | | 20 Kilometres |

Machynlleth
Tywyn
A493
Aberdovey
Eglwysf
Talybont
Cardigan
Bay
Aberystwyth
A44
A4120
De
Bri
A487
Aberaeron
New Quay
Tregaro
A485
Cambri
Lampeter ▲
WEST
A475
A482
WALES
Cardigan
A487
A484
Newcastle
Emlyn
Llandove
Lianwrda
Newport
A40
Fishguard
A487
A484
A485
Salem ■
A40
A4069
St David's ■
A40
Carmarthen ■
Nantgaredig ■
Llandeilo
A478
A48
Haverforwest
Narberth ▲
St Clears
Ammanfo
Broad Haven ●
A4076
A477
Pendine
Laugharne ●
A484
A476
A483
A474
Milford
Haven
Pembroke
Dock
Saundersfoot
Kidwelly
Llanelli
49
Pontardawe
48
47 45
Pembroke ▲
A4139
Carmarthen
Loughor ▲
Ne
Bay
Reynoldston ●
Gorseinon
Swansea ■
43
Parkmill
Por
Talbo
A4118
Mumbles
Port Eynon

B r i s t o l

C h a n n e l

Ilfracombe
Lynton
A361
A39

Lundy

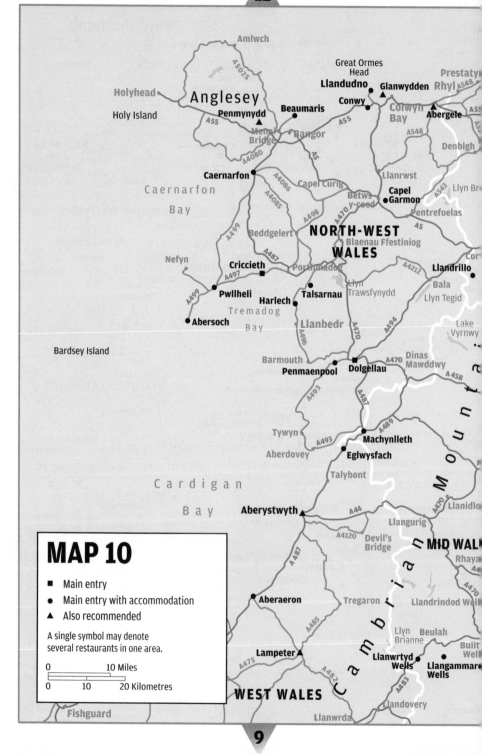

**MAP 10**

■ Main entry

● Main entry with accommodation

▲ Also recommended

A single symbol may denote several restaurants in one area.

| 0 | 10 Miles |
| 0 | 10 | 20 Kilometres |

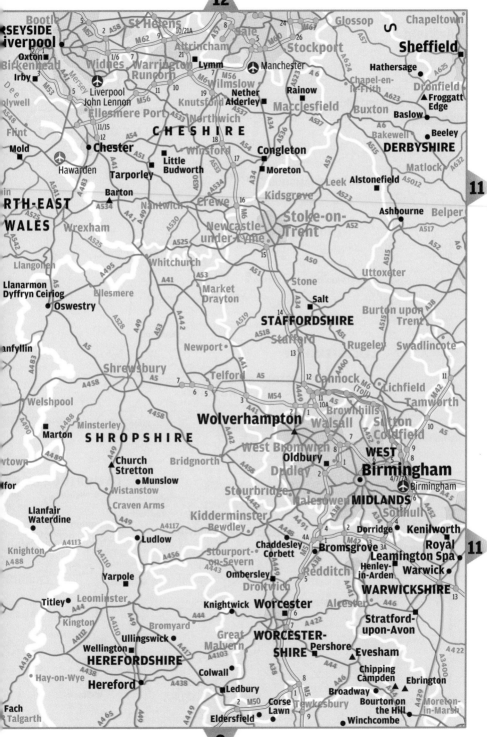

# MAP 11

- ■ Main entry
- ● Main entry with accommodation
- ▲ Also recommended

A single symbol may denote
several restaurants in one area.

0           10 Miles

0     10       20 Kilometres

blethorpe

Skegness

Wells-next-the-Sea

Brancaster Staithe
Titchwell
d Hunstanton
Hunstanton
e Wash

Cley-next-the-Sea
Burnham Deepdale
Morston
Salthouse
Sheringham
Holkham
Blakeney
Wiveton
Cromer

Burnham Market
Snettisham
Hunworth
Edgefield

Fakenham
Itteringham
Aylsham
North Walsham

Grimston
King's Lynn

East Dereham
Norwich
Norwich
Brundall
Great Yarmouth

Swaffham
Ovington
Wymondham
Stoke Holy Cross
Lowestoft

Downham Market
Attleborough
Beccles

Bungay

ttleport
Brandon
Thetford
Diss
Halesworth

Ely
Southwold
Walberswick

Mildenhall
Stanton

Fordham
Bury St Edmunds
Great Glemham
Saxmundham

rningsea
Newmarket
Lidgate
Stowmarket
Aldeburgh

Little Wilbraham
SUFFOLK
Orford

nxton
Haverhill
Lavenham
Bildeston
Woodbridge
Orford Ness

Long Melford
Monks Eleigh
Hadleigh
Ipswich

Saffron Walden
Stoke-by-Nayland
Levington
Felixstowe

vering
Sudbury
Dedham
Manningtree
Mistley
Harwich

Braintree
Halstead
Colchester
The Naze

N O R F O L K

**8**

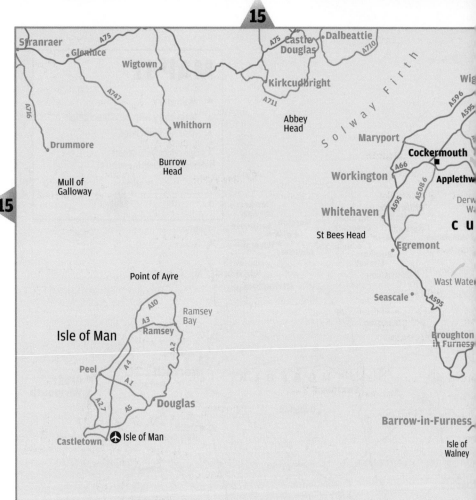

**15**

**15**

Stranraer

Glenluce

A75

Wigtown

A747

A716

Drummore

Whithorn

Burrow Head

Mull of Galloway

Castle Douglas

Dalbeattie

A710

Kirkcudbright

A711

Abbey Head

Solway Firth

Maryport

Wig

A596

A595

Cockermouth

Applethw

A66

Workington

A508 6

A595

Whitehaven

Derw W.

C U

St Bees Head

Egremont

Wast Wate

Point of Ayre

Ramsey Bay

Seascale

A595

Isle of Man

A10

A3

Ramsey

A2

Broughton in Furness

Peel

A4

A1

A27

A5

Douglas

Castletown

Isle of Man

Barrow-in-Furness

Isle of Walney

I  r  i  s  h       S  e  a

# MAP 12

- ■ Main entry
- ● Main entry with accommodation
- ▲ Also recommended

A single symbol may denote
several restaurants in one area.

0          10 Miles
0      10      20 Kilometres

**10**

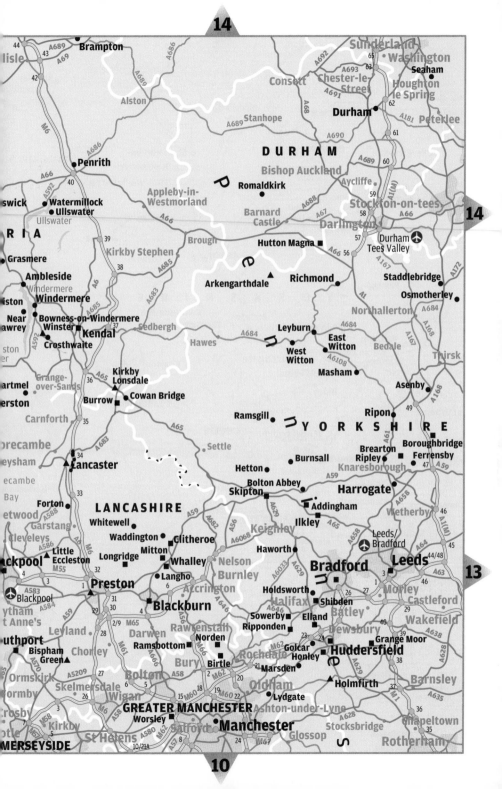

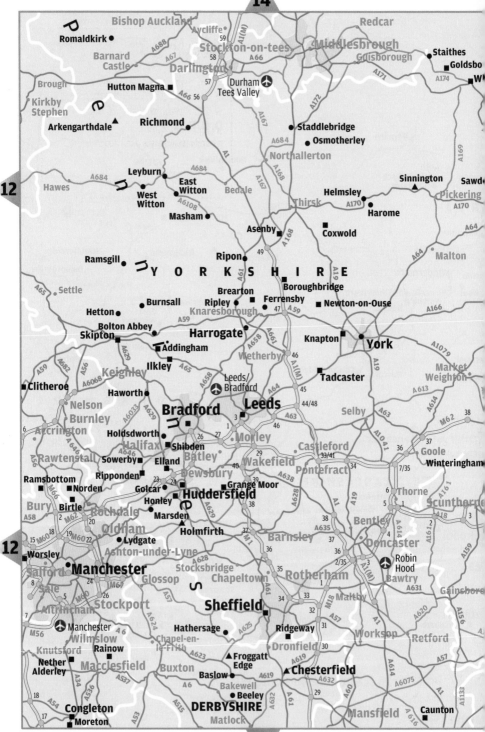

# MAP 13

- ■ Main entry
- ● Main entry with accommodation
- ▲ Also recommended

A single symbol may denote
several restaurants in one area.

| 0 | | 10 Miles |
|---|---|---|
| 0 | 10 | 20 Kilometres |

Scarborough

Filey

A165

Flamborough
Head

A614

Bridlington

Driffield A165

Bridlington
Bay

Hornsea

A1035

Beverley

ssle Hull

Withernsea

Barton-upon-
Humber

A1077

A1033

Humber

A15

Immingham
A180

Spurn Head

Humberside

Grimsby

Cleethorpes

A18

gg

A1173

A46

Caistor

A18

A16

A1031

A631

Market
Rasen

Louth

Mablethorpe

A157

A153

A16

A52

A158

A1028

coln

Horncastle

Partney

LINCOLNSHIRE

A155

A158

Skegness

11

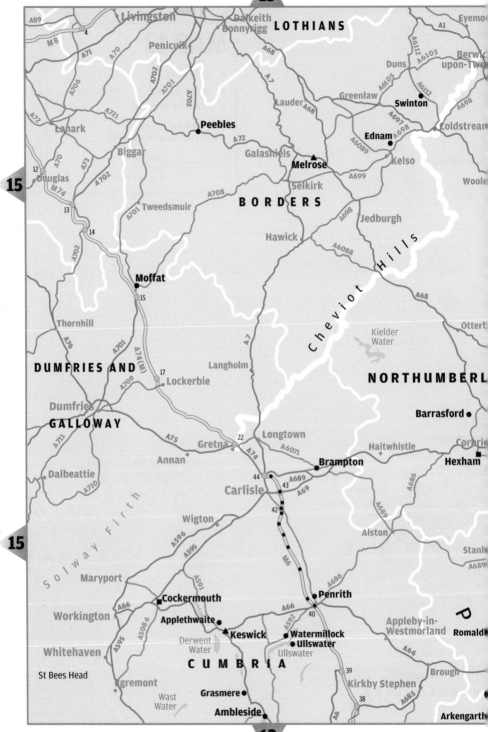

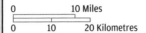

# MAP 14

- ■ Main entry
- ● Main entry with accommodation
- ▲ Also recommended

A single symbol may denote
several restaurants in one area.

0        10 Miles

0      10      20 Kilometres

Holy Island

▲ Low Newton-
by-the-Sea

Alnwick

Amble

A1

A1068

Morpeth

Ashington

Blyth

596

A1

Newcastle

nteland

Whitley Bay

Newcastle
upon Tyne

TYNE &
WEAR

South Shields

Jarrow

A695

dley on
he Hill

A692

Gateshead

A1231

Sunderland

65

Washington

A693

63

Seaham

bsett Chester-le-
Street

A691

Houghton le Spring

A68

62

Durham

A181

Peterlee

A690

61

Hartlepool

DURHAM

A689

60

Bishop
Auckland

Aycliffe

A1(M)

Redcar

A688

59

A67

Stockton-on-tees

58

Middlesbrough

arnard
stle

A66

Darlington

Guisborough

Staithes

A171

A174

Goldsborough

Whitby

Hutton
Magna

A66

56

57

Durham
Tees Valley

A172

Richmond

A167

Staddlebridge

A171

13

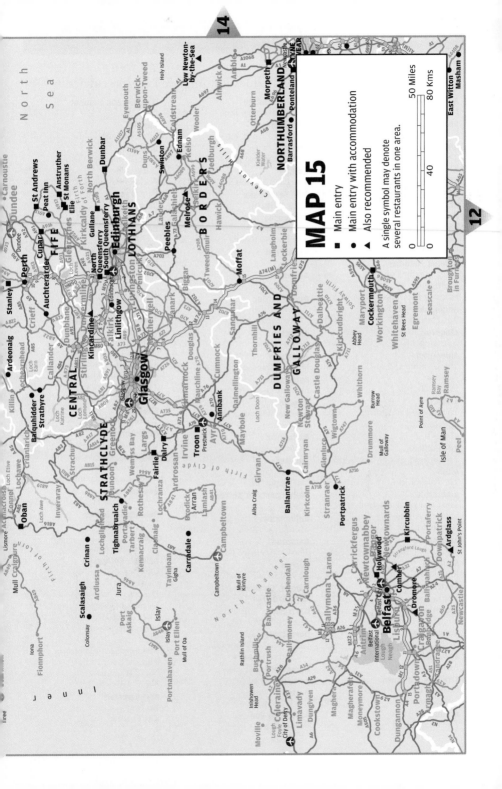

## Note: The INDEX BY TOWN does not include London entries.

The Good Food Guide 2010

The Good Food Guide 2010

# THANK YOUS

This book couldn't happen without a cast of thousands. Our thanks are due to the following contributors, amongst many others:

Mr A Ahmed
Mrs Joanne Abbott
Mrs Catherine Abel
Mrs Elizabeth Abernethy
Mr Anthony Abrahams
Miss Julia Acaster
Mrs Geri Ackroyd
Mrs Theresa Acutt
Mr Alasdair Adam
Mr Anthony Adams
Mr David Adams
Mr Francis Adams
Mrs Gale Adams
Mr Mark Adams
Mr Rob Adams
Mr Andy Adcock
Ms Helen Aesa
Mr Sayed Ahmed
Mrs Valerie Aikman
Mr John Aird
Mrs Charlotte Alder
Mrs Debbie Alexander
Miss Ambia Ali
Mr S Ali
Mr Douglas Allan
Mrs Gillian Allan
Mr John Allan
Miss Sophie Allan
Mr Alex Allcock
Mr Ian Allen
Mr Richard Allen
Mrs Susan Allen
Miss Maria Aller
Mr John Allington
Mrs Helen Almond
Mrs Norma Alsopp
Mrs Kathleen Alston
Miss Lubna Altajir
Mr Tom Alves
Mr David Ambrose
Mrs Lynn Anders
Ms Jenny Anderson
Mr Mark Anderson
Mrs Nitila Anderson
Mr Ronald Anderson
Mrs Flora Andrews
Mr James Andrews
Mr Igor Andronov
Mr Michael Angus
Mr Christopher Aniyi
Mr A Annessou
Mrs Margaret Appleby
Mrs Marie Appleby
Mrs Cynthia Archer
Ms Cheryl Armer-Clarkson
Mrs Jean Armstead
Mrs Debra Armstrong
Mr Jonathan Armstrong
Mrs Charlotte Ashby
Mr John Ashcroft
Mr Guy Ashton
Mr Nicolas Ashurst
Mrs Catherine Ashwell
Miss Nicola Ashworth
Mrs Candy Atcheson
Miss Andre Atherton
Ms Margaret Atherton
Mrs Cath Atkins
Mr Ian Atkins
Mr Paul Atkins
Mrs Caroline Atkinson
Mr Jeremy Austin
Mrs Judith Austin
Mr Tony Austin
Mr David Axford
Miss Emily Babb
Mr Steve Babbage
Mr Ian Bacon
Mrs Julie Badrick
Ms Susan Bahman
Mr Barry Bailey
Mrs Kate Bailey
Mr Tristan Bailey
Miss Louise Baines
Mr R Bairamian
Mr Jim Baird
Mr Alvin Baker

Mr David Baker
Mrs Jillian Baker
Mr Volker Balk
Miss Carrie Ball
Mr George Ball
Ms Tina Ball
Mr Colin Ballantyne
Miss Ana Ballon
Mr Richard Bamford
Mrs Ishi Bancil
Mr Craig Banks
Miss Sophie Bannerman
Mrs Gill Baque
Mrs Rebecca Barber
Mrs Roslyn Barber
Mrs Susanna Barber
Mr John Barker
Mrs Sally Barker
Mrs Susan Barker
Mr Arthur Barlow
Miss Claire Barlow
Mrs Margaret Barlow
Mrs Amanad Barnes
Ms Eleanor Barnes
Mr Steve Barnes
Mr Paul Barnett
Mr Stephen Barnett
Mr William Barnett
Ms Gabriele Baron
Mr Mark Baron
Mrs Penny Barr
Mrs Amanda Barrass
Mrs Rosie Barrett
Mr Iain Barrie
Mr Ashley Barron
Ms Anna Barry
Mr Ronan Barry
Ms Pam Barsby
Mrs Beth Bartels
Miss Alison Bartholomew
Mrs Fiona Bartholomew
Mrs Cherry Bartles-Smith
Mrs Amanda Bartlett
Mr Robin Bartlett
Mrs Michele Bartley
Mr Andrew Barton
Mr Will Barton
Mr Sohail Bashir
Mr Tim Batchelor
Mr Derek Bates
Mr Thomas Bates
Mr Peter Bathgate
Mr Sam Batstone
Mr Charles Batt
Ms Sue Batt
Miss Stephanie Bauyer
Mr William Bavin
Ms Ailee Baxter
Mr Duncan Baxter
Mrs Jackie Baxter
Mrs Lyn Baxter
Mr Susi Bazzinotti
Mr Paul Beaber
Mr Paul Beach OBE
Miss Christie Beavan
Mrs Julia Bebington
Revd Geoffrey Beck
Mrs Maureen Becker
Mrs Pamela Beech
Mr Nick Beeton
Mr Tony Beirne
Mr Peter Belfield
Mrs Suzanne Bell
Mrs Lucy Bellamore
Mr James Bellord
Mrs Teresa Belmar
Mrs Natasha Benbow
Mr John Bence
Mrs Emma Benjafield
Mr Antony Benjamin
Mr Redouane Bennani
Mr John Bennett
Mrs Maura Bennett
Mr Peter Bennett
Mr Ronald Bennett
Mr Eric Benoist
Mrs Suzanne Benson

Miss Amie Bentley
Mr Gerard Bentley
Mr Jon Bentley
Mrs Christine Benzie
Mr Martin Berridge
Ms Rebecca Berry
Mr Simon Berry
Mr W Best
Mr Daniel Bevan
Mrs Heather Bewers
Mrs Sharda Bhandari
Mr Savraj Bhangra
Mr Jonathan Bibbings
Mr Terry Bibbu
Mrs Hannah Bichard
Mr Charles Bickford
Mrs Susan Bickley
Mr Simon Bidgood
Mr Adrian Biggs
Mr Jamshed Bilimoria
Mr Stephen Bingham
Ms Leann Binns
Mr Charles Birch
Mr Ken Birch
Mr Chris Bird
Mr Joe Birtwell
Mr Brian Bishop
Mrs Jan Bishop
Mrs Rebecca Bishop
Mr Mark Bixter
Mrs Vivienne Blackburn
Ms Sheila Blackhurst
Mrs Jacqueline Blain
Mr T Blain
Mrs Alma Blair
Miss Maggie Blair
Mrs Debra Blakemanbarratt
Mr Dave Bland
Mrs Mary Bland
Mr Danny Blee
Miss Rosie Blewitt
Mr Edward Blincoe
Ms Alicia Blum-Ross
Mr Colin Blyth
Mr Geoffrey Blyth
Miss Susie Blyth
Mr Tony Blythe
Mr Marc Board
Mr Andy Boase
Mrs Anne Boggis
Mrs Maggie Bointon
Mrs Marion Bokkelkamp
Mrs Sandra Bolland
Mrs Julia Bolwell
Mr Peter Bolwell
Mrs Susan Bonci
Ms Cherry Bond
Miss Jacqueline Bond
Mr Neil Bonsall
Mr Richard Bonwick
Miss Jackie Boorman
Mr Ben Booth
Miss Emma Booth
Mr Neil Booth
Mr Peter Booth
Mrs Linda Bott
Mrs Fifi Boucher
Miss Graldine Bouchet
Mrs Amy Bouchier
Mrs Denise Bourdages
Mr Rej Bourdages
Mr Peter Bourne
Mr N Bowbanks
Mr Bryan Bowen
Miss Suzanne Bowen
Mr Mike Bowler
Mrs Sally Boycott
Mrs Meriel Boyd
Mr Thomas Boyes
Ms Gill Bracey
Mr Anthony Bradbury
Mr Colin Bradfield
Mrs Debbie Bradley
Mr Nigel Bradley
Mr Nicholas Braithwaite
Mr Roger Braithwaite
Mrs Helen Brasher

Mrs Joan Braune
Mrs Angela Bray
Mr Frederick Bray
Mrs Sally Bray
Mr Barrie Brears
Ms Margaret McBrein
Mrs Catherine Brennan
Mr Denis Brennan
Mrs Denise Bretton
Mr Karel Bretveld
Mrs Joan Brice
Miss N Brierley-Downs
Mr Andrew Briggs
Mrs Carol Briggs
Mr John Briggs
Ms Sacha Bright
Mr David Briscoe
Mr Simon Bristowe
Mr Clive Brittain
Ms Doris Broad
Mr David Brokenshire
Mrs Carole Brooke
Mr Richard Brooke
Mr Nigel Brooke-Smith
Mr Daniel Brooks-Dowsett
Mr John Broomfield
Mr Adrian Brown
Mr Alasdair Brown
Miss Anika Brown
Mr Antony Brown
Mrs Caroline Brown
Mrs Diana Brown
Mrs Dorothy Brown
Mr Douglas Brown
Miss Elizabeth Brown
Mrs Gemma Brown
Mr Gerry Brown
Mrs Jackum Brown
Mr James Brown
Mrs Janice Brown
Mrs Kris Brown
Ms Linda Brown
Mrs Louise Brown
Mr Martin Brown
Mrs Sharon Brown
Mr Sue Brown
Mrs Nansi Browne
Mrs Judy Browning
Mr Steven Brownley
Mr Kyle Bruce
Mrs Susan Bruce
Mr Richard Brundle
Mr Tony Brunskill
Mr John Bryant
Mr Beppo Buchanan-Smith
Miss Laura Buckenham
Mrs Elizabeth Buckingham
Mrs Tracey Buckley
Mrs Lucy Buick
Mr David Buisson
Miss Alex Buist
Mr David Bull
Mrs Hilary Bull
Mr Matthew Bull
Mrs Carol Bulloch
Mr Gary Bullock
Mr Chris Bulman
Mrs Susie Bulman
Mrs Rita Bulmer
Mr Harry Buls
Ms Helen Bunter
Mrs Pamela Burbidge
Mr Geoffrey Burcher
Miss Susie Burden
Mrs Jan Burgess
Mrs Susan Burgess
Mr Keith Burkin
Ms Lesley Burn
Ms Lisa Burnett
Mrs Angela Burniston
Mrs Cara Burns
Mr Gearoid Burns
Mr Neil Burns
Miss Rachel Burns
Mr Robert Burns
Miss Sonia Burns
Mr Michael Burnside

Mr Stanley Burnton
Mr Edmund Burrell
Mrs Jillian Burrell
Mrs Jill Burrington
Ms Liz Burton
Mrs Rosie Burton
Ms Julie Butcher
Miss Lucy Butcher
Miss Sandy Butcher
Mr Malcolm Butler
Mr Matthew Butt
Mr Craig Byford
Mr Adrian Caddick
Mrs Samantha Cadman
Mr Chris Cadogan
Mr Laurie Cairns
Mr Tim Caley
Mr Graham Callander
Mrs Cynthia Calton
Mr Tom Calver
Mr David Camden
Mr Dexter Cameron
Mrs Nancy Camp
Mr Ian Campbell
Miss M Campbell
Mr William Campbell
Mr B Campbell-Baldwin
Mrs K Campbell-Cave
Mrs Ann Campion
Mrs Betty Carey
Mr Martin Carey
Mr Scott Cargill
Miss Helen Carney
Ms Amanda Carnie
Ms Sue Caroline
Mr Peter Carr
Mr Steve Carratt
Mr Steve Carrick
Mr Edward Carroll
Mr Michael Carroll
Mrs Rebecca Carroll
Mrs June Carson-Leafe
Mrs Laura Carstairs
Mr Dave Carter
Mr Mark Carter
Miss Gemma Casey
Mr Robert Casey
Mr Roger Casey
Mr Robert Cassen
Miss Barbara Cates
Mr Alan Cator
Mrs Helen Cattell
Mr Michael Chadwick
Mrs Christine Chamberlain
Ms Carolyn Champion
Mr Cyril Chan
Mr John Chandler
Ms Barbara Chaplin
Mr Craig Chapman
Mr Miles Chapman
Mr Peter Chapman
Mrs Elspeth Charles
Ms Frances Chatten
Mrs Margaret Chaundy
Mr Paul Cheetham
Mrs Sylvia Cheetham
Mr Beppe Chelli
Mr Giuseppe Chelli
Ms G Cheng
Mr William Chesneau
Mr Daniel Chesterman
Mr Alan Chesters
Mr Karyn Chiesa
Mr Steve Childs
Mr Martin Chillcott
Mr Richard Chinn
Mrs Jessica Chivers
Mr Ron Choy
Mr John Christopher
Mr David Churchward
Ms Margaret Clancy
Miss Lauren Clark
Mr Graham Clark
Mr Jon Clark
Mr Mike Clark
Mrs Martha Clark
Miss Jennifer Clarke

Miss Rachel Clarke
Mr Colin Clarkson
Mr Ian Clarkson
Mrs Gillian Claugher
Mrs Jackie Clay
Mrs Lynne Clay
Mr David Claypole-Smith
Miss Kirsty Clegg
Mrs Barbara Clements
Ms Kim Clifford
Mrs Sarah Clothier
Mrs Kate Clover
Mr Keith Cobham
Mrs Gillian Cockburn
Mr John Cockell
Mrs Kim Cockitt
Ms Sally Cockle
Mr Andrew Coe
Mr Christopher Coggins
Miss Naomi Cohen
Mrs Rosalind Cohen
Mr Graham Cole
Mrs Juliet Cole
Prof Malcolm Cole
Mr Sam Cole
Mr Wayne Coleman
Mrs Christine Colgrave
Miss Emilie Colin
Mr Steve Collard
Mrs Mollie Collett
Mrs Ann Collier
Mr Keith Collier
Mr Mike Collier
Mr Jean Collin
Mr John Collings
Mr Antony Collins
Mr Alexis Colombo
Mr Raymond Comer
Miss Louise Compton
Mrs Siobhan Compton
Mr Bernie Conlon
Mr Brian Connelly
Mr Paul Conner
Mr Alfred Connolly
Mr Phillip Conquest
Mr Peter Constable
Mr Soli Contractor
Miss Sheila Conway
Mr Barry Cook
Mrs Brenda Cook
Mrs Emma Cook
Mrs Michelle Cook
Mrs Sonya Cook
Miss Verity Cook
Mr Stephen Cooling
Mr Stephen Coombes
Mr Chris Coombs
Miss Sian Coombs
Sir Adrian Cooper
Mrs Edra Cooper
Mr John Cooper
Mr Robert Cooper
Mrs Sara Coote
Miss Grace Copestake
Mrs J Copley
Miss Rose Copsey
Mr Steve Corcoran
Mr Charles Cordy-Simpson
Ms Catherine Cork
Mrs Mandy Cornick
Ms Jo Cornley
Mr John Cornwell
Mr Nicholas Cosin
Mr Hugh Coster
Mr Richard Cotterill
Ms Lis Coulthard
Mr Richard Coulthard
Mr Steve Coupe
Mr Trevor Coupe
Mrs Dorothy Cowan
Ms Lorna Cowan
Mr Stuart Cowie
Ms Laura Cowley
Mrs Angela Cox
Mrs Christine Cox
Mr David Cox
Mr Eden Cox
Mr David Coyle
Mr Edward Cracknell
Mrs Marion Cracknell
Miss Elizabeth Craggs
Mr Gary Craig
Mr Lee Craig

Mr Nigel Crane
Mr Kevin Cranston
Mr Philip Creed
Mr Mark Crichton
Mrs Patricia Criddle
Mrs Nicola Crilly
Miss Denise Crisell
Mrs Margaret Crisell
Mr Nigel Crocker
Miss Sue Crofts
Mrs Vicky Croiala
Mrs Jayne Crook
Mr Andrew Cross
Ms Julia Cross
Mr Richard Cross
Mrs Susan Cross
Mrs Pam Crossen
Mr G Crossley
Mrs Sandra Crouch
Mr Peter Crowcroft
Miss Carlene Crowe
Ms Rosalind Crowe
Mr Gareth Crump
Mr Roger Cull
Ms Jane Culling
Ms Margaret Cumberland
Mr Steve Curd
Mr Brendan Curley
Miss Colette Curnyn
Mrs Paula Curry
Mrs Susan Curtis
Mr William Curtis
Miss J Cutler
Mr Paul Cutts
Mrs Sheila Cutts
Ms Margaret Daintith
Miss Veena Dalal
Ms Liza Dale
Mrs S Dale
Mr Jeffrey Daly
Mrs Julie Dangoor
Mr Tim Daniel
Mrs Pearl Daniel
Mr Jack Daniels
Mr Mark Daniels
Mrs Elizabeth Daplyn
Mr Ian Daplyn
Mr Brian Darby
Mr Clifford Darlington
Mr Paul Darlow
Mrs Maxine Darrock
Mr Daniel Darwood
Mrs Rosemary Dash
Mr Ian Davenport
Mrs Ellie Davidson
Ms Layla Davidson
Mrs Lisa Davidson
Mr Alexander Davies
Mr Alun Davies
Mr Andy Davies
Mrs Cath Davies
Mrs Chris Davies
Mrs Deb Davies
Mr Duncan Davies
Mrs Elizabeth Davies
Miss Erica Davies
Mr Gareth Davies
Miss Helen Davies
Mr Huw Davies
Miss Lindsey Davies
Mr M Davies
Mr Mark Davies
Mrs Meryl Davies
Mrs Molly Davies
Mr Paul Davies
Mr Russell Davies
Ms Sharon Davies
Mr Duncan Davis
Mr Edward Davis
Ms Lynn Davis
Mr Neville Davis
Ms Alison Davison
Miss Coralie Davison
Mr Mark Davison
Miss Sarah Davison
Miss Pereen D'Avoine
Miss Claire Daw
Mr Antony Dawe
Miss Angela Dawson
Mr David Dawson
Mr Peter Dawson
Mr Peter Day
Mr Richard Day

Mrs Fiona Deal
Mr James Deal
Miss Hannah Dean
Mr David Deane
Mrs Charlotte Deasy
Mr Philip Deaville
Miss Samantha Deb
Mr Nicholas Dee
Mr Peter Deering
Mr Samuel De'Laney-Curtis
Mrs Kay Delves
Mr Michael Dempsey
Mrs Sandra Dennis
Mr Rodney Densem
Miss Helen Derrett
Mrs Caroline De Souza
Mr Christopher Detton
Mr James Deveraux
Mrs Miriam Dickens
Mr David Dickie
Miss Kishi Dickinson
Mrs M Dickinson
Mr David Dickson
Mr Ian Dickson
Mrs Maria Digby
Mr Chris Dillabough
Miss Jo Dillon
Mrs Hazel Dimambro
Mrs Gillian Dimsdale
Mr Ralph D'Inverno
Mrs Linda Dippy
Mr Frankie Dixon
Mr Michael Dixon
Mr Peter Dixon
Mr Roy Dixon
Ms Sieglinde Dlabal
Mr Robert Doak
Mr George Dobbie
Mrs Anna Dober
Mr Darren Docker
Mr Marcus Dodd
Mr Martin Dodd
Miss Caroline Dodds
Mr Byron Dolan
Mr I Donaldson
Miss Kate Donaldson
Mrs Pina Donaldson
Mr John Donlon
Mr Bob Donnelly
Mr Gary Donoghue
Mr John Doran
Mr Bill Dorman
Mr Paul Dormer
Mr Alberto Doro
Miss Jo Doswell
Miss Nicola Douglas
Mrs Michele Dowell
Mr Mark Downey
Mr James Downie
Mr Paul Downie
Mr Sean Dowson
Mr Charles Doxat
Mr John Driscoll
Mrs Linda Drummond
Mr Ron Du Bois
Mr Noel Dsouza
Mr Mark Duddridge
Mrs Isabel Duffett-Smith
Mr Charlie Duggan
Mrs Rachel Duggan
Mr Neville Duncan
Mr Peter Dunkley
Mrs Christine Dunn
Mr Thomas Dunn
Ms Lynn Dunning
Mr P Dunning
Mr Francis Durham
Mrs Hazel Durham
Mrs Linda Durrant
Mrs Wendy Durrant
Mr Benjamin Duve
Mr Dom Dwight
Mrs Alyson Dyer
Mr John Dyer
Miss Lizzie Dyer
Mr Ross Dykes
Ms Anne Eames
Ms Penny Earle
Mr Mike and Janet Earnshaw
Miss Diana East
Miss Beth Eccles
Mrs Cynthia Eddison
Mrs Linda Edge

Mrs Jackie Edgecombe
Mr Kev Edgington
Mr Nigel Edmonds
Mr Colin Edwards
Mr George Edwards
Mr Glyn Edwards
Mrs Jan Edwards
Mrs Jane Edwards
Mrs Janice Edwards
Mr John Edwards
Mrs Nicky Edwards
Mr Osian Edwards
Mr Philip Edwards
Miss S Edwards
Mrs Jocelyn Eglin
Mr John Elbert
Mr Gary Elflett
Mr Ronald Elis
Mr Lee Ellepen
Mr Richard Eller
Mrs Andrea Elles
Mr Adam Elliott
Mrs Angela Ellis
Miss Bethan Ellis
Mrs Jo Ellis
Mr Michael Ellis
Mr Simon Ellis
Mrs Sue Ellis
Mr David Ellse
Mr Christopher Elston
Mr Jonathon Elwood
Mr John Enell
Miss Sophie Eni
Mr Nick Errington
Mrs Melanie Eskenazi
Miss Jane Esplen
Miss Dionne Etan-Thorpe
Mr Andrew Evans
Mr Anthony Evans
Mr Colin Evans
Mr Gareth Evans
Mr Geoff Evans
Mr Gordon Evans
Mr John Evans
Miss Joscelyn Evans
Ms Maureen Evans
Mr Mick Evans
Mr Neville Evans
Mr Ramon Evans
Miss Sam Evans
Mrs Susan Evans
Mrs Christine Everitt
Mr John Exelby
Mrs Fiona Fairbairn
Mrs Maura Falla
Mrs Jacqueline Faller
Mr Tony Falloni
Mr Graham Fallows
Mrs Wedad Fanous
Mrs Liz Farler
Mrs Joan Farnworth
Mr Terry Farr
Miss Genaya Farrell
Ms Elizabeth Farrell
Mrs Fiona Farrow
Mrs Josie Fawcett
Mr Peter Fawcett
Mrs Ginny Fazackerley
Mr Anthony Feiler
Mr Mike Fenwick
Mr Alberto Feruglio
Mr Colin Field
Mrs Denise Field
Mr Michael Fieldhouse
Mr Neville Filar
Mrs Ranan Filippeli
Mr Malcolm Fincken
Mr Daniel Fineberg
Miss Jo Finley
Mr Andre Finn
Mrs Joan Firth
Mr Dene Fisher
Mr Leigh Fisher
Mr Brian Fitchett
Mrs Georgina Fitzgerald
Mr Patrick Fitzpatrick
Mr Terence Flanagan
Mr Kieran Flatt
Mr Garth Fletcher
Miss Grace Fletcher
Mr Ian Fletcher
Miss Jasmine Fletcher
Mr John Fletcher

Mrs Fiona Flint
Ms Sarah Flint
Ms Ann Flintham
Miss Kate Flintham
Mr Stewart Flisher
Mr Martin Flower
Miss Timi Fodor
Ms Annabel Fogden
Mr Miklos Font
Mrs Edwina Foote
Mr James Forbes
Ms Louise Ford
Mr Nigel Ford
Ms Patricia Ford
Mr Peter Ford
Miss Stephanie Ford
Mr Tom Ford
Mr Bennet Foreman
Miss Elauan Foreman
Mr Charles Forgan
Mrs Pam Forrest
Mrs Beatrice Forster
Mr James Forster
Mrs Anne-Marie Forsyth
Mrs Nichola Foss
Mrs Barbara Foster
Mrs Elaine Foster
Mr Ian Foster
Mrs Marie Foulds
Ms Natalie Foward
Mr Nick Fowler
Mr Cameron Fox
Mr Harry Fox
Mr Sean Fox
Mr Xavier Fradera
Miss Nicola France
Ms Christine France
Mrs Lisa Francis
Mr Victor Frank
Mrs Maureen Frankcom
Mr Gordon Franklin
Mr Alexander Fraser
Mr and Mrs C Fraser
Ms Catherine Fraser
Mrs Janet Fraser
Mrs May Fraser
Mr Stephen Fraser
Mr Brendan Frawley
Mrs Christine Freeman
Mr Paul Freeman
Mr Peter Freeman
Miss Sarah Freeman
Miss Celine Frimpong
Mrs Sue Fulford
Mrs Susan Furneaux
Mr Peter Furness
Mr Rich Furness
Miss Caroline Gaboardi
Mr Adam Gaca
Mrs Elizabeth Gadsby
Mrs Sandra Gailans
Mr Paul Galatis
Mr John Gale
Mr Selwyn Gale
Miss Tam Gambie
Ms Pernille Gammelmark
Mr Dave Gane
Ms Patty Gann
Mrs Carla Gardiner
Mr John Gardner
Mrs Sandra Gardner
Mrs Sharon Garner
Ms Sheelagh Garner
Ms Joanna Garrard
Mr John Garrat
Mrs Patricia Gartan
Mrs Jeanie Garven
Mrs Ghislaine Garvey
Mrs Meg Garvie
Mr John Gascoigne
Mr Ian Gaskin
Mrs Monica Gauntlett
Mrs Christine Gavan
Mrs P Gavey
Mr Devon Gayle
Mrs Amanda Gayton
Miss Sophie Gear
Mr Mark Geffryes
Mr George Gellatly
Mr Tony Georgakis
Mr David George
Mr Kenneth George
Miss Helen Georgescull

Mr Chris Georgiou
Mrs Christine Gerezdi
Mrs Anthea Gerrie
Mrs Kaye Gibbard
Mrs Annette Gibbons
Ms Alex Gibbons
Mrs Jane Gibson
Mr Gary Giddens
Mrs Denise Gifford
Mr Andrew Gilbrenny
Mrs Anne Giles
Mr Bernard Giles
Mr George Gill
Ms Neena Gill
Mrs Barbara Gillian
Mrs Catherine Gillie
Mr Ewan Gillies
Ms Erica Gillingham
Mr Roland Gilmore
Mr Graham Gingell
Mr Bryan Glastonbury
Mr John Glaze
Mr Keith Gleadall
Mr Alan Gleeson
Mrs Vickie Glew
Mrs Mary Goatman
Mrs Laurence Gobet
Mrs Bethan Godden
Mr Nick Godden
Mr David Godding
Mr Bryan Godfree
Ms Di Godfrey
Mrs Jane Godfrey
Ms M Godfrey
Ms C Godsmark
Mrs E Godsmark
Ms Mia Goldberg
Mr Michael Good
Ms Carrie Goodair
Miss Victoria Goodall
Mr George Goodbody
Mrs Jenni Goodman
Mr Ian Goodwin
Mrs Margaret Goodwin
Mr Ken Goody
Mrs Diana Gordon
Mr William Gordon
Ms Dawn Gordon
Mrs Diana Gordon
Mrs Jacqui Goring
Mr Darren Gorman
Mr Paul Gormley
Miss Cat Goryn
Mr Matthew Gould
Mrs Joanne Gowing
Mr Adrian Graham
Mrs Erica Graham
Mrs Gillian Graham
Mrs Christine Grandison
Mr David Grant
Mrs Hilary Grant
Mrs Jacki Grant
Mrs Susan Grant
Ms Floriana Grasso
Mr Gordon Gray
Mrs Helen Gray
Mrs Hollie Gray
Mr Quentin Gray
Mr Stuart Gray
Mr Adrian Greason-Walker
Mr Leigh Greaves
Mr Mark Greaves
Mr Alastair Green
Mrs Caroline Green
Mr James Green
Mr Jonathan Green
Mr Martin Green
Mr Michael Green
Ms Natasha Green
Mrs Reidunn Green
Mr Tony Green
Mrs R Greenhalgh
Miss Nichola Greenhalsh
Mr Alan Greenwood
Mr Brian Greenwood
Mrs Charlotte Greenwood
Mr Arthur Gregg
Mrs J Gregory-Newman
Mr Michael Grenfell
Mr Matthew Grey
Miss Meinir Lloyd Griffiths
Ms Jill Griffiths
Mr Tom Griffiths

Mr John Grime
Mr and Mrs Grimes
Mr David Grimes
Mr Michael Gross
Mr Arthur Grosset
Mr Nigel Groves
Miss Sarah De Gruchy
Mrs Agnes Grunwald-Spier
Mr David Gunnersen
Mr Ian Gunning
Mr Philip Gurney
Miss Joanna Gurr
Miss Therese Gustafson
Mrs Sara Guven
Mrs Colleen Guy
Miss Stacie Hack
Mr Chris Haddock
Mrs Linda Haddock
Miss Lucy Haddon
Miss Kate Haden
Mr Alan Hagan
Mr David Hague
Miss Alexandra Hales
Mr Andrew Halkett
Mrs Hilary Hall
Mr John Hall
Mr John Halliwell
Miss Laura Hallows
Ms Penny Hamer
Mr John Hamilton
Mrs Katie Hamilton
Mrs Christine Hammond
Mr Keith Hammond
Mr Peter Hampton
Mr D Hancock
Mr Robert Hancock
Mr Simon Handley
Mr Gordon Hands
Mr Graham Hanford
Ms Catherine Hankey
Mrs Meg Hankinson
Mr Ben Hanks
Mr Sir Jeremy Hanley
Mr Gerry Hanna
Mr Philip Hanna
Mrs Jacqueline Hanratty
Mr Ian Hanreck
Miss Louise Hanson
Mr Paul Hanson
Mr David Harbottle-Sear
Mr George Nicholas Harby
Mrs Meryl Hardacre
Ms Emma Hardaker-Jones
Mr James Harding
Ms Jamie Harding
Mr K Harding
Mr Paul Harding
Mrs Anne Hardy
Mrs Julie Hargraves
Ms Justine Harkness
Mr John Harltey
Mrs Ali Harper
Mrs Mary Harrington
Mr David Harris
Miss Eleanor Harris
Ms Julie Harris
Mrs Libby Harris
Mrs Lisa Harris
Mr P Harris
Mrs Sam Harris
Miss Sara Harris
Mr Steve Harris
Mrs Angela Harrison
Mr Barry Harrison
Mr James Harrison
Mrs June Harrison
Miss Lesley Harrison
Mr Tony Harrison
Mr John Hart
Mrs Rosemary Hartfall
Mrs Velia Hartland
Mr John Hartley
Mrs Pippa Hartley
Ms Jan Harvey
Mrs Rebecca Harwood
Mr John Haslam
Miss Rose Haslem
Mr Abdul Hassan
Mr Andrew Hastings
Mrs Pamela Hastings
Mrs Claire Hawkins
Mr Jeremy Hawkins
Mrs Lucy Hawkins

Mr Peter Hawksworth
Mr Ralph Haworth
Miss Kate Haydock
Mr John Hayes
Ms Sally Hayes
Ms Beverley Hayter
Mr Mel Hayward
Mrs Pam Hayward
Mrs Lynn Hazell
Ms Sue Head
Mrs Tracey Heath
Mr Frederic Heathcote
Mr Geoff Heathcote
Mrs Mary Heathcote
Miss Patricia Heatherington
Mrs Jude Heaton
Mr Don Heeley
Mr Yann Helle
Miss Ashlea Helliar
Mr Christopher Helliar
Mr Steve Helliwell
Mrs Jane Hemingway
Mrs Kathleen Henderson
Mr Ed Henson
Mr Martin Henson
Mr David Henwood
Miss Kate Hepherd
Mr Andy Herrity
Mr Clark Herron
Mr Robert Hersey
Mr Gad Heuman
Mr Andrew Hewitt
Mrs Angela Hewitt
Mr Graham Hewitt
Mr Howard Heywood
Mr David Hicks
Mr Michael Higgins
Mr Philip Higgins
Mr Liam Hill
Mrs Lynda Hill
Mr Mark Hill
Miss Nichola Hill
Mrs Pam Hill
Miss Sara Hill
Mr Tim Hills
Mrs Lisa Hills
Mrs C Hindmarch
Mr Eric Hinds
Mrs Deborah Hirons
Mr William Hirst
Mrs Lynn Hiskey
Mr John Hitcham
Mr Chris Hobbs
Miss Sarah Hobbs
Mrs Elizabeth Hobson
Mr Peter Hobson
Miss Margaret Hocking
Miss Margaret Hodge
Mr Tony Hodgkins
Ms Kate Hodson
Mr Perran Von Hoehen
Mrs Tracy Hoggarth
Mrs Lindsey Holdsworth
Mrs Isobel Holland
Mrs Margaret Holland
Miss Jennie Holland-Brown
Mr Stuart Hollings
Mr David Holloway
Mrs Joan Holloway
Mr Mark Holloway
Miss Cathryn Holmes
Mrs Joy Holmes
Mr Keith Holmes
Miss Kim Holmes
Mr Gareth Holt
Mr Harold Holt
Mrs Sarah Holyoake
Mr Peter Hood
Mrs Fiona Hooper
Mr Oliver Hopkins
Mr David Hornby
Mr John Hornby
Miss Vivien Hornidge
Ms Teresa Horscroft
Mr Jonathan Horsnell
Mr Alex Horton
Miss Luci Hortop
Ms Zoe Horwich
Mrs Teri Hottinger
Mr David Hough
Mrs Alicia Houghton
Mr Steven Hourston
Mrs Debbie Howard

Mr Malcolm Howard
Mr Steve Howard
Mrs Caroline Howe
Mrs Alyson Howell
Mrs Michelle Howell
Mrs Sue Howes
Miss Katherine Howgego
Mr Chris Howland-Harris
Mr James Howley
Ms Larissa Hoyte
Miss Martina Hruskova
Mr Don Hubbard
Mr Robert Hubbard
Mr Melvyn Hudd
Mrs Bethan Hughes
Mr David Hughes
Mr Jon Hughes
Ms Margaret Hughes
Mrs Pat Hughes
Mr Robert Hughes
Mr Robin Hughes
Mr Tim Hughes
Mr Steven Hughs
Mr Philip Huke
Mr Allan Hull
Mrs Margaret Hull
Mrs Roz Hull
Mrs Elizabeth Humber
Mrs Marian Humphreys
Mr Ralph Humphries
Mr Adam Hunt
Mr Geoff Hunt
Mr Jake Hunt
Mr Martin Hunt
Miss Natasha Hunter
Ms Karen Hunter
Mr Graham Huntington
Mrs Joanna Huntington
Mrs Debbie Huntley
Mr Rashidul Huque
Mr Sam Hurd
Mr Keith Hurdman
Mr Chris Hurrell
Mr Faisal Hussain
Mr Syed Hussain
Mrs Judith Hussey
Miss Naomi Hussey-Yeo
Mrs Helen Hutchings
Miss Jo Hutchins
Mr Peter Hutchins
Mr David Hutchison
Mrs Victoria Hutton
Mr Reg Huyton
Mr David Hyett
Mrs Sarah Ibbetson
Mr Julian Ideson
Mr James Igoe
Mr Russell Iles
Mrs Sue Illingworth
Ms Rachel Illsley
Mr John Impey
Mr Tom Inglis
Miss Katie Ingram
Mr Peter Ingram
Mr Jorge Inzulza
Mrs L Ironton
Ms Laura Irvine
Mr Stewart Irvine
Mr Mick Irving
Mr Ahmed Ismaail
Mrs Beryl Iverson
Mrs Jane Ives
Mrs Denise Izon
Mr Terry Izzard
Mrs Claire Jackson
Mr David Jackson
Mr John Jackson
Ms Lesley Jackson
Miss Natalie Jackson
Mr Peter Jackson
Mr Richard Jackson
Mrs Susan Jackson
Mr Lyndon Jacob
Mr David James
Mrs Hilary James
Mrs Iona James
Ms Julie James
Mrs Louise James
Mr Matt James
Mr Richard James
Mr Robert Jamieson
Mrs Hilary Janin

Mr Geoffrey Jarvis
Mr Peter Jarvis
Ms Tara-Melissa Jarvis
Ms Anmaria Jason
Mrs Rebecca Jawara
Mr Antony Jay
Mr Keith Jay
Mrs Caroline Jaycock
Mr Martin Jeeves
Mrs Tracey Jefferies
Mr David Jeffrey
Miss Lucie Jeffrey
Mrs Rosemary Jeffries
Mr Nicholas Jenkin
Mr Phillip Jenkins
Mr Steven Jenkins
Mr Ben Jenkinson
Miss Kat Jennings
Mr Roy Jennings
Mr Stuart Jennings
Miss Alison Jerome
Mr David Jervois
Mrs Theresa Jessey
Mr David Jessop
Mr Barry Jewitt
Mr Pat Jewitt
Mr Hyam Joffe
Mrs Tahera Joglu
Mrs Helen John
Mr Michael John
Mr Barry Johnson
Miss Beverley Johnson
Miss Kathryn Johnson
Mr Philip Johnson
Mr Richard Johnson
Mrs Charlotte Johnston
Mr Christine Johnston
Mr Steve Johnston
Mrs Jane Johnstone
Ms Kathryn Johnstone
Mrs Jill Jolliffe
Mr Antony Jones
Mrs Alison Jones
Mrs Barbara Jones
Mr Chris Jones
Mr Clive Jones
Mr David Jones
Miss Donna Jones
Mrs Edra Jones
Mrs Elizabeth Jones
Mr Gareth Jones
Mrs Helen Rees Jones
Mr Ian Jones
Mr John Jones
Mrs Lucy Jones
Mr Nathan Jones
Mr Nigel Jones
Mr Phil Jones
Mrs Rachel Jones
Ms Susan Jones
Mr Tom Jones
Mrs Vivienne Jones
Mr John Jordan
Miss Luise Juhr
Mr Charles Kail
Mr Yush Kalia
Mr Michael Kaltz
Miss H Kay
Mr Nick Kealey
Miss Claire Keane
Ms Sheelagh Keddie
Mr David Keeble
Miss Kate Keith
Mr Adam Kellett-Long
Mrs Heather Kellie
Mrs Felicity Kelsall
Mrs Kirsty Kemp
Ms Verity Kemp
Mr Nick Kennedy
Mrs Jennifer Kenrick
Mr David Kent
Mrs Elaine Kent
Mr John Kenward
Miss Caroline Kenyon
Mrs Eileen Kenyon
Ms Emily Kerrigan
Miss Janet Kershaw
Miss Sarika Keshri
Miss Imogen Ketchley
Mrs Ferdawsia Khan
Miss Mehreen Khan
Mr Raja Khan
Mrs Aisha Khan-Evans

Mr Hassan Khorsan
Mr Vimal Khosla
Mr John and Margaret Kilby
Mr Neil Kilpatrick
Mrs Deborah Kimmett
Miss Amanda King
Mr Gabriel King
Mr Jonathan King
Miss Samantha King
Mrs Sharon King
Miss Victoria Kingsley
Mr Colin Kirby
Mr Mark Kirkbride
Mrs Susan Kitchener
Mr Terry Kitching
Mrs Riki Kittel
Miss Ana Klien
Mr Gabriel Knapik
Mr John Kneward
Mr John Knight
Mr Karl Knight
Mr Keith Knight
Miss Kerry Knight
Miss C Knutsen
Mr Mike Kobylak
Ms Kerry Kohler
Mrs Robyn Kristad
Mrs Valerie Krol
Miss Dawn Kubicek
Mr Prem Kumar
Mr George Kyriacou
Mrs Monique Labuschagne
Miss Janet Laflin
Mrs Anne Laforce
Mr Ian Laidlaw-Dickson
Mr Amal Lalit
Mr Jim Lambourn
Mr Liam Lananiter
Mrs Jackie Lancaster
Mr Allan Landsburgh
Mr John Lane
Mr Phillip Lane
Mr Jack Lang
Mrs Anne Langan
Ms Marie Langan
Mrs Michael L'Angellier
Mrs Karen Langridge
Mr Robert Langston
Mr Richard Lankester
Mr Nicholas Lash
Mrs Gabrielle Le Lasseux
Mr E Latham
Mrs Karen Latter
Miss Toni Lavender
Mr Kerry Law
Mrs Samantha Laws
Mrs Angeline Lawson
Mr Martin Lawson
Mr David Leach
Mr Adrian Leary
Mrs Linda Leary
Mrs Rachelle Ledsam
Mr Richard Lee
Mrs Sharon Lee
Mr James Leek
Mr Peter Leged
Mr John Legg
Mr Trevor Legg
Mr Michael Leggatt
Mrs Ursula Lehner
Mr John Leighton
Ms Marika Leino
Miss Vicky Leith
Mr Gareth Leng
Mrs Ros Lennard
Miss Jessica Leschnikoff
Mrs Sue Levitt
Mr Richard Levy
Miss Justyna Lewandowska
Mr John Lewin
Mr C Lewis
Mrs Catherine Lewis
Mr Garth Lewis
Mr John Lewis
Mrs Karen Lewis
Mr Philip Lewis
Ms Carrie Leyva
Dr Simon Li
Mr Henry Liddell
Mrs Denise Liebermann
Mr R Light
Mr Clive Lindemann
Mrs Carole Lindey

Mrs Marion Lindsey-Noble
Mrs Ivana Linehan
Mr John Ling
Mrs Vicky Ling-Williams
Mr David Linnell
Mr Robert Lishman
Mr Ian Lister
Mr M Llewelyn
Mrs Annie Lloyd
Mrs Caroline Lloyd
Mr Colin Lloyd
Mr Gerald Lloyd
Mrs Kirstie Lloyd
Mr David Lock
Mrs Caroline Locker
Mrs Angela Lockyer
Mrs H Von Loggerenberg
Mr Barry Long
Mr Christopher Long
Mr David Long
Mr Mathew Long
Mr Michael Long
Mr A Longstaff
Mrs Vicky Lorych
Mr Marc Lough
Mrs Frances Loughridge
Mr John Paul Lowdon
Mr Dominic Lowe
Mr Mike Lowndes
Miss Susanna Lucas
Mr Adrie Van Der Luijt
Mrs Lucilla Lunn
Mr Rob Lutz
Mr Brian Lynch
Mrs Maureen Lyon
Mr Sarah Maberley
Mrs Audrey Macdonald
Ms Fiona Macdonald
Mr Paul Macdonald
Miss Satu Macdonald
Mrs Catrin Macdonnell
Mrs Jane Macgillivray
Mr Hugh Mackintosh CBE
Mr Tony Mackenzie
Mrs Marion Mackie
Mr Ian Maclennan
Mrs Therese Macleod
Mrs Janice Maclugash
Mr Ziya Mactaggart
Ms Janet Madden
Mrs Jessica Madge
Mrs X Madill
Miss Tara Magan
Mr Stephen Maher
Ms Eleanor Maidment
Mrs Beatrice Majoko
Mr Ivor Makinson
Mrs Janette Makinson
Mr John Malcolm
Mr Christopher Male
Mr Kevin Malia
Mr Ian Malone
Mrs Sylvia Malone
Mr Scott Malyon
Mr Ajith Manage
Ms Samay Mancliffe
Ms Mairead Manifold
Mr Paul Manley
Mr David Mann
Miss Katy Mann
Mr David Mannion
Mr Trevor Mansfield
Mr Jacques Marchal
Mr James Marchant
Mr Scott Mariani
Ms Lisa Marie
Mr David Marigold
Mrs Sarah Marjoram
Mr Laurence Marks
Mrs Charles Markus
Ms Carole Marling
Mr Ben Marlow
Mrs Brenda Marlow
Mr Aaron Marsden
Mrs Eileen Marsh
Mr Barry Marshall
Mr John Marshall
Mr Jonathan Marshall
Mrs K Marshall
Mrs Valerie Marshall
Mrs Claire Martin
Mrs Diana Martin
Mr Graham Martin

Mrs Isobel Martin
Mrs Jane Martin
Mr James Martin
Mr Paul Martin
Mr Steve Martin
Mrs Robin Martin-Jenkins
Miss Anna Mason
Mrs S Wilding Masson
Mr Tim Mather
Ms Kwee Matheson
Mr Roy Mathias
Mrs Beryl Matthews
Mr Chris Matthews
Mr Graham Matthews
Mrs Helen Matthews
Mrs Jillian Matthews
Miss Susan Matthews
Mr Jack Maunders
Mr Frederic Maurice
Ms Charlotte Maurissen
Mr James Mawhinney
Mrs Julie Maxwell
Mr Ian May
Mrs Margaret May
Mr Michael May
Mr Rod Mayall
Mr Damian Maye
Mr Colin Mayers
Mrs Maria Mayes
Mr S Le May-Grellan
Mrs Julie Maykels
Mr Gary Maynard
Miss Sandra Maynard
Mr Stuart McAdam
Ms Shenagh McAfee
Mr P McAleenan
Mr Andrew McAlpine
Mr Norman McAndrew
Mr Rob McArdle
Mr Jim McAvinchey
Mr Margaret McBrein
Mr Derek McBride
Mrs Joanne McBride
Ms Margaret McBrien
Mr Graham McCabe
Miss Carol McCallum
Mrs Sarah McCandlish
Mrs Sarah McCann
Miss Anna McCarthy
Mr Fred McCarthy
Mr James McCarthy
Miss Diane McCluskey
Mrs Karen McComiskie
Mr Steve McCoy
Mrs Fiona McCree
Mr Steven McCreesh
Mr Laurence McCurrich
Miss Ruth McDavid
Mrs Helen McDermott
Mrs Lee Nee McDermott
Mr Bruce McDonald
Miss Jane McDonald
Ms Kate McDowall
Mr Jamie McGarry
Mr Alex McGeorge
Mr Tommy McGee
Mr Mark McGill
Mr John McGinnell
Miss Becky McGovern
Mrs Linda McGowan
Mr Joe McGrane
Mr Ian McGregor
Miss Laura McGregor
Mrs Geraldine McGuckin
Mr Ed McHugh
Ms Jan McHugh
Mrs Sue McHugh
Mrs Kate McIlroy
Mr Neil McIntosh
Mr Alex McIntyre
Mr Malcolm McIntyre
Mrs Siobhan McKee
Ms Keira McKenna
Mrs Carol McMenamin
Ms Wendy McMillan
Mr Brian McMorrough
Mr Alastair McMurdo
Mr Ian McNicoll
Mr Andrew McPherson
Mr Neil McRae
Mrs S McTiernan
Mrs Alison McVicar
Mr Ellis Mead

Mr Daren Meadow
Mr Ian Meadows
Mr Nathan Meadows
Mr Anthony Meakin
Ms Jibby Medina
Mr John Medlock
Mr David Mee
Mr Johnson Meech
Miss Alexandra Megan
Mrs Sandra Megginson
Mr Ben Mein
Ms Maggie Mellon
Mr David Mellow
Ms Laure Meloy
Mrs Barbara Melville
Mr David Melzack
Miss Helena Memory
Ms Katherine Mendelsohn
Miss Sonia Mendoza
Mrs Nick Mercer
Mr Mark Mercereau
Ms Helena Merriman
Ms A Merton
Mr Peter Messenger
Ms Debbie Metcalfe
Mr Joerg Meyer
Mr Neil Meyrick
Miss Michelle Michael
Mrs J Michell
Miss Anna Middleton
Ms Jane Middleton
Miss Samantha Middleton
Mrs Dorothy Midson
Mrs Francesca Migliuolo
Mrs Cheryl Millar
Mrs Mary Millar
Mrs B Miller
Ms Paulette Miller
Mr Robert Miller
Mr Ian Millington
Mr John Millins
Mr Nicholas Millins
Mr Clive Mills
Mr Jerry Mills
Mr Justin Mills
Mrs Norah Mills
Mrs Margaret Milner
Ms Jenny Milnes
Mrs Rachel Milnes
Mr Richard Mineards
Mr Patrick Minns
Ms Caroline Minshull
Mr Ben Mitchell
Ms Grace Mitchell
Mrs Helen Mitchell
Mrs Janet Mitchell
Mr Spencer Mitchell
Mr John Modd
Ms Sarah Mohun
Mr Margaret Moloney
Mrs Judith Molyneux
Mrs Diane Monk
Mrs Michaela Monk
Miss Julie Monkman
Mrs Kathy Montanaro-Acott
Mr Alan Montgomery
Mrs Linda Montgomery
Miss Rachel Moodie
Mr Prakash Moolgavkar
Mr David Moore
Mrs Kathleen Moore
Mr Nicholas Moore
Mrs Pam Moore
Mrs Dawn Moran
Mrs Sarah Moreland
Mr Stephen Morey
Ms Brenda Morgan
Mr Jim Morgan
Mrs Lisa Morgan
Mr Mike Morgan
Miss Victoria Morgan
Mrs Wendy Morgan-Brown
Mr John Moring
Mr Dave Morley
Mr Anthony Morris
Mr David Morris
Mrs Hilary Morris
Mr Leon Morris
Miss Sally Morris
Ms Susan Morris
Mrs Susan Morrish
Mr Kingsley Morrison
Mr Andrew Morritt

Miss Jane Morton
Mr Alan Mosca
Mr Laurence Moseley
Ms Ritu Motashaw
Miss Cara Mottram
Mrs Victoria Mowat
Miss Katy Mowbray-Brown
Mr E Mozid
Dr M Muers
Mr Sidney Muller
Ms Lami Mulvey
Mrs Cathy Mumford
Mr Brian Munro
Mrs Gail Munro
Mr David Munson
Mrs Ronnie Murdin
Mr Jim Murphy
Mr Justin Murphy
Miss Charlotte Murray
Mr David Murray
Ms Joanne Murray
Miss Karen Murray
Mrs Linda Murray
Mrs Teresa Murrey
Mr Richard Mustill
Mr Colin Mutch
Mrs Jacquie Myers
Mrs Karen Myers
Mrs Linda Nash
Mr Anil Nataly
Mrs Bina Nataly
Ms Jayne Nation
Mr Barry Natton
Mrs Sarah Naybour
Mrs Becky Naylor
Mr Edward Naylor
Miss Lucy Neal
Miss Emma-Jayne Needle
Mrs Sian Neil
Mr Dominic O'Neill
Mrs Judith Neill
Mr Alex Nelson
Mr Edward Nelson
Mr Tim Neobard
Miss Julie Nerney
Mr Iain Nesbitt
Mrs Kathy Nettleship
Mrs Sally Newall
Mrs M Newkirk
Mrs Amanda Newman
Mr Daniel Newman
Mr John Newman
Mrs Zoe Newton
Ms Denise Ng
Ms Dorothy Ng
Mr Christopher Nicholas
Mr Eric Nicol
Mr Keith Nichols
Mrs Christine Nicolas
Mrs Gill Nightingale
Mrs Fiona Nixon
Mrs Natalie Nixon
Miss Jenny Nobes
Mrs Iris Nolan
Ms Vivien Norbid
Mr Robert Norgrove
Mr Chuck Norman
Mr John Norman
Mrs Dawn Norris
Mr Geraint Norris
Mr N North
Mr John Nottage
Mrs Gillian Nugent
Mrs Pamela Oakes
Ms Jan Brown OBE
Mrs Erla O'Byrne
Mr Duncan Ockendon
Mr Michael O'Connor
Mrs Sarah Odell
Mrs Katharine Odgers
Ms Caroline Ogden
Ms Catherine Ogden
Mr Lionel Ogden
Mrs Angela Ogilvie
Mrs Jane O'Gorman
Mrs Kerri O'Hare
Mrs Irene O'Keeffe
Mr Jonathan Oldknow
Mrs Susan Oliver
Mr Roberto Olmos
Mr David Oram
Mrs Chantel Ormerod
Mr Robert Orr

Mr Connal Orton
Mr Richard Osborne
Mrs Theresa Osen
Mr Jamie Osman
Miss Mags Ostrowka
Mrs Kirstine Oswald
Mr Gareth Owen
Mr John Owen
Mrs Joyce Owen
Mrs Freda Owens
Mr Graham Oxendale
Mrs Kiran Pachoo
Mrs Meriel Packman
Mr John Page
Mr Tim Paine
Miss R Paley
Miss Wendy Palframan
Miss Anne Palin
Mrs Evie Palmer
Mrs Lynfa-Sian Palmer
Miss Sandra Palys
Mr Dinesh Panch
Mr Thomas Pangbourne
Miss Madelein Papenfus
Mrs Louise Parbat
Mrs Carol Parietti
Mr Ray Parish
Mr Martin Parker
Mrs Ruth Parker
Ms Catherine Parkin
Mr John Parkin
Mrs Bren Parkins-Knight
Miss Angela Parks
Mrs Debra Parks
Mrs Nancy Parks
Mr Steve Parks
Miss Sandra Parodi
Mrs Alexandra Parr
Ms Susie Parr
Mrs Gill Parramore
Mr Dave Parrott
Mr Neil Parrott
Mrs Jan Parry
Mr Trevor Parsley
Mr Henry Partridge
Miss Daniela Passi
Miss Bridie Passmore
Mr Adam Patel
Mr Imran Patel
Miss Nishi Patel
Mr Otddle Patel
Mr S Patel
Ms Vina Patel
Mr John Paterson
Mr John Patis
Mr Alex Paton
Mr Kyle Pattinson
Ms Pauline Pattison
Mr Christian Patton
Mr Ross Pavey
Mr Michael Pawson
Mr David Payne
Miss Lucy Payne
Miss Clare Pearce
Mr Graham Pearce
Mrs Michelle Pearce
Mrs Penny Pearce
Mr Raymond Pearce
Mrs Susan Pearce
Mr Geoff Pears
Mrs Karen Pearson
Mr Matt Pearson
Mr Adrian Penge
Mr Jason Penge
Mrs Bev Pennal
Mr Thomas Peplinski
Miss Orianna Perez
Ms Jane Perfect
Mr Rob Perfitt
Mrs Sue Perrott
Miss Anne Perry
Mrs Charley Perry
Mrs Jennifer Perry
Mr John Perry
Mrs Julie Perry
Mr Christopher Peters
Mrs Megan Peters
Mr Lionel Petitcorps
Mr Brian Pettifer
Mr Tony Phillimore
Mrs Janet Phillips
Mr Keith Phillips
Mrs Liz Phillips

Mrs Lynne Phillips
Mr Mark Phillips
Mr Thomas Phillips
Mrs A Pickering
Mr David Piersenne
Mr Andy Pilcher
Mrs Sue Pilcher
Mrs Susi Pink
Ms Louise Pinkney
Mr Stuart Pinnell
Mrs Heather Pitch
Mrs Mary Pitts
Miss Lizzy Platt
Mr Michael Plummer
Mr Paul Pocock
Ms Kay Pollock
Mr Robert Pollock
Mrs Hazel Pomfret
Mr Richard Pook
Ms Fiona Porter
Mrs Valerie Posner
Mr John Potter
Miss Liz Potter
Mr Trevor Potter
Mr Brian Powdrill
Miss Sarah Powley
Mr Kenneth Pratt
Mr William Prentice
Mrs Claire Prettejohn
Mr Christopher Price
Ms Joanne Price
Mr John Price
Mr Stephen Price
Mrs Olesia Priest
Mr John Prince
Miss Lisa Prince
Mr Ben Prior
Mr Michael Prior
Mrs Elaine Prisk
Mr Matthew Prothero
Miss Annabel Prow
Miss Charlotte Prow
Mrs Mary Pryce
Mr Terence Pryce
Mr Robert Pullar
Mr Steve Pullen
Mrs Melanie Pullin
Mr Charles Pycraft
Mrs Gillian Pyke
Miss Lauren Pyke
Ms Alexandra Le Quaife
Ms Jeanne Quigley
Mrs Heather Quinlan
Mr J P Quinn
Mrs Linda Quinn
Miss Tamara Qutteineh
Mr Clive Rabson
Mr Alan Radcliffe
Mr Kim Radford
Miss Vivien Radford
Mr Matt Raines
Mr Susilan Rajalingam
Mrs Klim Ramos
Mr Alan Ramshaw
Mr Alan Randall
Miss Jennifer Randall
Mr Derek Ransom
Mr Peter Ranson
Mr Aklas Rashid
Mr Alastair Rattray
Miss E Raven
Mr Matt Ravenhill
Mr Nick Ravenscroft
Mrs Carol Rawnsley
Mr Bobby Rayit
Mr Philip Rayner
Mrs Aileen Rea
Mr Graham Read
Mrs Laurette Read
Ms Margaret Read
Mr Roger Read
Mrs Anna Redbourn
Mrs Angela Redfern
Mr Nick Redfern
Mr Neil Redford
Ms Sue Redpath
Mrs Carmen Reed
Mrs Pamela Reed
Mr Dudley Rees
Ms Tara Rees
Mr Richard Rees-Jones
Mr Malcolm Reeves
Mr Peter Reeves

Mrs Sue Reeve
Miss Alison Reid
Mr Ken Reid
Mrs Nicola Reid
Mr Stephen Renouf
Mrs Diana Renton
Mr Peter Renton
Mr Robert Renton
Miss Diana Resiga
Ms Saskia Restorick
Mr Angus Rex
Mrs Jane Reynolds
Mr Liam Reynolds
Mrs Siobhan Reynolds
Mr Craig Rhodes
Miss Jane Rhodes
Mr Matthew Rhodes
Mr Rizwan Dham Riaz
Mrs Ann Rich
Mrs Julie Richards
Mr Keith Richards
Mr Noel Richards
Mr Roy Richards
Mrs Rosemary Richards
Mr Steve Richards
Mr Christopher Richardson
Mr Glyn Richardson
Mr Grant Richardson
Mr Neil Richardson
Miss Helen Ridout
Mr Colin Riley
Mrs Linda Riley
Mr David Riordan
Mrs Brigid De Rivaz
Mrs Irene Rizza
Mrs Angela Roberts
Mr Glyn Roberts
Mrs Jane Roberts
Mrs Jennifer Roberts
Mrs Johanna Roberts
Miss Kate Roberts
Mr Lee Roberts
Mrs Margaret Roberts
Mrs Patricia Roberts
Mr Trevor Roberts
Miss Abi Robertson
Mr Ian Robertson
Miss Kate Robertson
Ms Sonia Robertson
Mrs Teresa Robertson
Mr Jason Robilliard
Mr William Robins
Mr Chris Robinson
Mrs Jayne Robinson
Miss Margaux Robinson
Mr Richard Robinson
Mr Stuart Robinson
Mr Tom Robinson
Mrs Vicky Robinson
Mr Christopher Robson
Mr E Robson
Miss Natalia Robson
Ms Isabelle Roche
Mr J Rochelle
Mr Craig Rodger
Ms Rachel Rodgers
Miss Maria Rodriguez
Ms Ruth Roebuck
Mrs Eileen Roerig
Mrs Sally Roff
Mr Norman Roger
Mr Frank Rogers
Mrs Julie Rogers
Mr Kevin Rogers
Mr Larkin Rogers
Mr Martin Rogers
Mrs Margaret Rogers
Mrs Maggie Rolls
Mr E Roney
Mr Bernard Roome
Mrs Margaret Roper
Mrs Gemma Ross
Mrs Hilary Ross
Mr Hugh Ross
Mr J Ross
Mr Stuart Ross
Mrs Jean Rosser
Mr Stephen Rosser
Dr Colin Roth
Mrs Ann Rougvie
Mr Richard Round
Mr Kay Rouse
Mr Johnathan Routledge

Mr Antony Rowe
Mr David Rowe
Mr John Rowe
Mr Michael Rowe
Mr Tudor Rowe
Miss Emma Rowlands
Mr Stuart Rowland
Mrs Jill Rowley
Ms Gemma Rowley
Mrs Rachel Rowley
Mrs Isabelle Rowse
Mrs Rosalyn Rowse
Mr Phil Royall
Mrs Pauline Rozendaal
Mr Bernard Rubin
Mrs Julie Ruck
Miss Frances Rudge
Mr Andrew Rupp
Mr Craig Russell
Mr David Russell
Miss Edwina Russell
Mrs Pauline Rutter
Mr Peter Rutter
Mr Mark Ryan
Mr William Rymer
Miss Nosheen Sadaf
Mr Merouane Saf
Mr Keith Sale
Mrs Maria Sale
Mrs Lyn Sales
Mr Geoff Salt
Mr Keith Salway
Mrs Jaqui Sampson
Mr Oliver Samuel
Mr Mike Samuels
Mrs Christine Sanders
Mr Richard Sanders
Ms Manjit Sandhu
Mr A Sandison
Mr Rodney Sandler
Mrs Charlotte Sands
Mr Ian Sanford
Mr Edward Sargent
Mr Kate Sargeson
Mrs Jennifer Sarony
Mr Adam Saunders
Mr Stuart Sauntson
Mr Philip Savage
Mr Robert Savage-Hanford
Mr Andrew Saveall
Mrs Valerie Sawtell
Mr Peter Sawyer
Ms Sandy Scaife
Mr Alan Scarrott
Miss Lucinda Schofield
Mr Ronald Schwarz
Mr Jeremy Scorey
Mr Ian Scott
Mr Paul Scott
Mr Lesley Scott-Miller
Ms Jane Scullion
Mr Mark Seaman
Mr William Seaman
Miss Claire Sebastian
Mrs Jane Seddon
Mrs Marie Sedgewick
Mr Christopher Seel
Mr David Sefton
Miss Dawn Sell
Mr Craig Selley
Mrs Nicola Selwood
Mr Brian Sequeira
Mr Ken Serle
Miss Vanessa Setterington
Mrs Anne Seymour
Ms Jane Seymour
Mr James Shackelton
Mr Andrew Shanahan
Mrs Elaine Sharp
Mr Chris Shaw
Mr David Shaw
Miss Freddie Shaw
Mr John Shaw
Mrs Helen Sheaff
Mr William Shearer
Mr Anthony Sheehan
Miss Tabassum Sheikh
Mrs Sally Sheinman
Mr Andrew Shepherd
Mrs Liz Shephard
Mr Charles Sherwin
Ms C Sherwood-Roberts
Mr Stan Sheward

Mrs Jill Shields
Mr David Shoesmith
Miss Linda Shone
Mrs Regina Shortland
Mrs Samantha-Jo Shoults
Mrs Alice Shrimpton
Mr George Shuttleworth
Mrs Marjorie Siddall
Mrs Linda Siggins
Mr P Silcox
Mr Mark Sills
Mr Stewart Sim
Miss Emma Simarro
Mrs Josephine Simeone
Mr Reginald Simeone
Mr Peter Simm
Mr Jonathan Simmons
Mr Andrew Simon
Mrs Catherine Simonini
Mrs Jane Simpson
Mr Jean Simpson
Mrs Barbara Sims
Miss Charlie Sims
Mr Michael Sims
Mr Adam Singer
Mr Bishen Singh
Mrs Anne Sked
Mrs Christine Skeen
Miss Amanda Skelton
Mrs Alison Skinner
Ms Amanda Skinner
Mr Anthony Skinner
Mr Darren Skinner
Mrs Heather Skinner
Mr David Slater
Miss Pippa Slater
Mr Eastwood Slator
Mrs Amanda Sleight
Mr David Sleight
Mrs Monica Slowikowska
Ms Judith Smallwood
Ms M Smallwood
Mrs Sarah Smallwood
Mrs Diana Smart
Mrs Christine Smeaton
Mr Tom Smeaton
Mr Joyce Smeets
Mr Andrew Smith
Mr David Smith
Mrs Dorothy Smith
Mr Duncan Smith
Mr Edwin Smith
Miss Felicity Smith
Miss Geida Smith
Mr James Smith
Mrs Jan Smith
Miss Jenny Smith
Mr John Smith
Mrs Karen Smith
Mr Kim Smith
Mr Mark Smith
Mr Matthew Smith
Mr Neil Smith
Miss Nicola Smith
Mrs R Smith
Miss Rebecca Smith
Mr Ron Smith
Mrs Sonia Smith
Mrs Susan Smith
Mr Stanley Smith
Mr Zac Smith
Mr Duncan Smyth
Mr and Mrs Smythe
Mrs Jo Snow
Mrs Linda Soar
Miss Umber Sohail
Mr Rajan Sokhi
Ms Anita Soley
Mr Miguel Somoza
Miss Yasmine Soopramanien
Mr Sebastian Sora
Mr Derek Southern
Mrs Gina Southey
Mrs Paula Southgate
Mrs Lesley Spankie
Mr Carlo Spano
Mrs Penny Speers
Mr Andrew Speight
Mr Barbara Spence
Mrs Catriona Spence
Mr Charles Spence
Mrs Beverley Spencer
Mrs Christine Spencer

Mr John Spenser
Mrs Linda Spencer
Mr Nigel Spencer
Mrs Diana Spiers
Mr Peter Spindley
Miss Claire Squance
Mrs Trudi Squirrell
Miss Helen Stallard
Ms Pam Stanier
Mrs Louise Stanley
Mrs Emma Stansfield
Mrs Annalisa Stanton
Mrs Fiona Stapley
Mrs Rebecca Stark
Mr Trevor Steedman
Ms Mel Steel
Mr Colin Steele
Mrs Jenny Stenhouse
Mrs Colleen Stenning
Mr Chris Stephens
Mr William Stephens
Mrs Diana Stern
Mrs Margarete Stetter
Mrs Christine Steuer
Mr Alan Stevens
Mr Andrew Stevens
Mr Owen Stevens
Mr S Stevens
Miss Alexandra Stevenson
Mr J Stevenson
Mr Andrew Stewart
Mr Ian Stewart
Mr James Stewart
Mr Keith Stewart
Mr Nick Stewart
Mr Allen Stidwell
Mrs F Stillwell
Mr Roger Stimson
Miss Laura Stirling
Mr Dave Stokes
Miss Kate Stokes
Mrs Erika Stone
Mr Martin Stone
Mr Michael Stone
Miss Nicola Storey
Mr Ron Storey
Mr John Stott
Mrs Mary Emma Strange
Mrs Mary Ann Strathdene
Mr John Straughan
Mrs Jennifer Streat
Mrs Sarah Street
Mr Dave Streeter
Mr Charles Strickland
Mr Trevor Strickley
Mrs Alexandria Stringer
Miss Victoria Stringer
Ms Carolyn Strong
Miss Claire Strong
Miss Claire Stuart
Mr Neil Stuart
Mr Michael Stubbs
Mr Peter Stubbs
Mr James Sturtridge
Mrs Bee Styche
Mrs Sylvia Suddons
Mr Varun Sudunagunta
Mrs Merryn Sudworth
Mr Stephane Suet
Mrs Christine Sullivan
Miss Ruzia Sultana
Miss Becky Surridge
Mr Martyn Sutcliffe
Mr Amanda Sutherland
Mrs Ann Sutherland
Mr Ian Sutherland
Mr Maurice Sutton
Mr Thomas Swallow
Mr John Swanton
Ms Kate Swift
Mr Michael Swift
Mr Ian Swingland
Mrs Sabrina Sykes
Ms Sarah Sykes
Mrs Sheila Symonds
Mr Adam Szafranek
Ms Diana Szalai
Mr Richard Tadman
Mr Douglas Talintyre
Mrs Angela Tansley
Mr Bryan Tansley
Mr Colm Tarpey
Mr Michael Tarry

Mrs Anne Tate
Mr Denis Tate
Mrs Valerie Tate
Miss Chloe Tattershall
Mrs Judy Tayler-Smith
Mrs Alison Taylor
Miss Andrea Taylor
Mrs Angela Taylor
Mr David Taylor
Mr Geoffrey Taylor
Mrs Janet Taylor
Mrs Jean Taylor
Mrs Julie Taylor
Mrs Katherine Taylor
Ms Marianne Taylor
Mr Mike Taylor
Mr Peter Taylor
Mr Philip Taylor
Mr Roger Taylor
Mr Steven Taylor
Mrs Susie Taylor
Mr Vince Taylor
Mr Rex Teater
Mrs Carolyn Temple
Mr Alan Templeton
Mrs Fionnuala Tennyson
Mr Frank Terdrey
Mr Stephen Theunissen
Mrs S Thiers-Ratcliffe
Miss Elinor Thomas
Mrs Jennifer Thomas
Dr John Thomas
Mrs Kaye Thomas
Mr M Thomas
Mr Richard Thomas
Mr Simon Thomas
Mr William Thomas
Mr Barrington Thompson
Mr J Thompson
Mr James Thompson
Mr Nick Thompson
Ms Nicola Thompson
Mr Roger Thompson
Mr Stuart Thompson
Mrs Tina Thompson
Mrs Amanda Thomson
Miss Lisa Thomson
Mr John Thornburn
Mrs Maureen Thorne
Mrs Stephanie Thorne
Mr David Thornton
Mrs Linda Thorpe
Mr Bob Thurlow
Mrs Eve Thynne
Mr Steve Tilsley
Mr Terry Timms
Mrs Vicki Tinkler
Miss Jenny Tinsley
Ms Audrey Tippetts
Miss Rachael Titley
Ms Jan Todd
Mr Jason Tolputt
Ms Lynnea Toltz
Mrs Caroline Tomes
Mr Michael Tomlinson
Mr Paul Tompson
Mr Paul Toomer
Mr David Topple
Miss Jo Towell
Mr Brian Towers
Mrs Denise Townsend
Mrs Diana Townsend
Mrs Linda Townsend
Mr Mike Trace
Mrs John Tranter
Ms Cate Travers
Mr Rodney Treadwell
Mr Stefan Trebacz
Ms Claire Tree
Mrs B Trehair
Mr Steven Trembath
Ms Sylvia Trench
Mrs Caroline Trevor
Mr Jack Trewhella
Mr Bob Trigg
Mr George Trollpe
Mrs Susan Trotman
Mr Christopher Trotter
Ms Pamela Trotter
Miss Kate Troup
Mr Dee Truong
Mr David Tubby
Mr Robert Tuck

Mrs Tudor-Williams
Mr Adam Tulk
Mr Chris Tunstall
Mr Brian Turner
Mr Geoff Turner
Mrs Hilary Turner
Mr Ian Turner
Mr John Turner
Mrs Louise Turner
Mrs Marie Turner
Mr Tom Turner
Mr Rick Turnock
Mrs Samantha Turpin
Mr David Turton
Ms Jill Turton
Mr Chris Twining
Mrs Debbie Twist
Mrs Angela Tyreman
Mr Shuja Ullah
Mr Ralph Ullmann
Mr Valerie Underdown
Miss Alison Underhill
Mrs Mary Unwin
Mr Peter Upton
Mr Kathleen Vallance
Mrs Kate Vann
Ms Claire Vassallo
Miss Sarah Vaughan
Mrs Fiona Veerman
Mrs Susan Velamail
Ms Patricia Venn
Mrs Jenny Venning
Miss Donna Vince
Mrs Lisa Vince
Mrs S Virdee
Mr Michael Vollentine
Miss Sophie Voller
Miss Van Der Voort
Mrs June Voy
Ms Bhavini Vyas
Ms Clara Wade
Ms Kate Wafer
Mr Nick Wagner
Ms Sheena Wagstaff
Mrs Carmel Waldron
Mr Jon Wale
Mr Ann Walker
Mrs Elizabeth Walker
Mrs Emma Walker
Mr John Walker
Ms Neil Walker
Mrs Penny Walker
Mr Peter Walker
Mr Thomas Walker
Mrs Catherine Wallace
Mrs Karen Wallace
Miss Amy Wallis
Mr Edgar Wallner
Mrs Louise Walmsley
Mr Adrian Walsh
Mr Andrew Walsh
Mr Brian Walsh
Mrs Clare Walsh
Mr John Walsh
Ms Toni Walsh
Mr Philip Walter
Mr Simon Walters
Mrs Joan Walton
Ms Yuet-Mai Wan
Mr and Mrs Ward
Mr Andy Ward
Mr Chris Ward
Mr David Ward
Mr Harry Ward
Mr David Wares
Mr Darren Warner
Mr Richard Warner
Mr Andrew Warwick
Miss Becky Warwick
Mr Stephen Washington
Miss Nicola Waterworth
Mr Chris Wathern
Mrs Angharad Watkin
Mr David Watkins
Mr David Watson
Mr Jeremy Watson
Mr Kenneth Wattam
Mr Anthony Watts
Mr Peter Watts
Mrs Kay Weatherly
Ms Mary Webb
Mrs Sharon Webb
Ms Marilyn Wedgwood

Mrs Andreanna Weedon
Mrs Brenda Weeks
Mrs Luisa Weinzierl
Mrs Maddie Weir
Mr Roger Weldhen
Mrs Sarah Wells
Mr Ian Welsby
Mr Thomas Welsh
Miss Helen Wentzel
Mr and Mrs J West
Dr Margaret West
Mr Paul West
Mrs Sally West
Ms Caroline Westgate
Mr Tim Westmacott
Mr Trevor Weston
Mr David Westrup
Miss Gayle Westwood
Mr Jack De Wet
Mr Kevin Whalley
Mrs Susan Wharton
Mr Brian Wheatley
Mr Grahame Wheelband
Mrs Diana Wheeler
Mrs Lynne Wheeler
Mr Simon Wheeler
Mr Paul Whelan
Ms Clare Whiston
Mrs Debra White
Mrs Dolores White
Mr Edmund White
Mrs Patricia White
Mr T White
Mr Paul Whitefoot
Mr Colin Whitehead
Mrs Tina Whitfield
Mr Peter Whittam
Mr Martin Whittet
Mr Roger Whitton
Mr Tony Whitty
Mr David Whitwam
Ms Jill Whyms
Mr Heide Wickes
Mr Bill Wiffen
Mrs Katherine Wigfield
Miss Lynn Wigglesworth
Mrs J Wilson
Mrs Rosemary Wild
Mr Anthony Wilde
Mr Ernest Wilde
Mr Janet Wilde
Mrs Joan Wilde
Mrs Helen Wildey
Mr Bill Wilkins
Mrs Catherine Wilkins
Mrs Dianne Wilkins
Mrs Judi Wilkins
Mr Barry and Elaine
   Wilkinson
Mr John Wilkinson
Mr Mark Wilkinson
Mr Richard Wilkinson
Mr Rob Wilkinson
Mrs Catherine Wilks
Mr Paul Willan
Mr Greg Willcox
Mr Roger William
Mr Adrian Williams
Mr Alan Williams
Mrs Alma Williams
Mrs Anthea Williams
Mr Gareth Williams
Mr Jason Williams
Mr Marcus Williams
Mr Max Williams
Miss Naomi Williams
Mr Paul Williams
Mr Peter Williams
Mr Shane Williams
Mr Stewart Williams
Mrs Susan Williams
Miss Zoe Williams
Mrs Gill Williamson
Mr Michael Williamson
Mr Anthony Wills
Mrs Andrea Wilmot
Mr Andy Wilmot
Mr Roger Wilmot
Mr Anthony Wilson
Mrs Beverley Wilson
Mr Craig Wilson
Mr Duncan Wilson
Mrs Elaine Wilson

Mrs Gillian Wilson
Mrs Gina Wilson
Mrs Sue Wilson
Mrs Margaret Wiltshire
Mr Norman Windsor
Mr Phillip Windsor
Mrs Linda Winnett
Mr Tony Winrow
Mrs Christine Winson
Mr Bob Winteringham
Mrs Lyn Winters
Mr William Wisedale
Miss Kasia Wojcik
Mr James Womack
Ms Aiysha Wona
Mr Andrew Wong
Ms Angelina Wong
Ms Jasmin Wong
Miss Ursula Wong
Miss Amy Wood
Mr David Wood
Mr Debbie Wood
Mrs Gill Wood
Mr James Wood
Ms Lucie Wood
Ms Lynn Wood
Mrs Patricia Wood
Mr Robert Wood
Miss Sarah Wood
Mr Stephen Wood
Mrs Sue Wood
Mr Tony Wood
Mr Paul Woodcock
Mrs Claire Woodhead
Mrs Gillian Woods
Mr David Woodward
Mrs Karen Woolley
Mrs Stephanie Woolley
Mrs Elizabeth Worley
Mr Peter Worth
Mr Matthew Worthington
Mrs Delyth Wotherspoon
Mrs A Wragg
Mr David Wright
Mr F Wright
Mr Paul Wright
Mr Ros Wright
Mrs Amanda Wyatt
Mr David Wyatt
Mr Norman Wyatt
Mr Russell Wyatt
Mr Richard Wyld
Mr Jianfeng Xing
Miss Keri Yardley
Mr Robert Yates
Mrs Trudy Yeardley
Mr John Yearley
Mr Adam Yeo
Miss Zeliha Yilmaz
Mr Alastair Young
Mrs Catherine Young
Mrs Colleen Young
Miss Helen Young
Miss Katrina Young
Mrs Kay Young
Mr Neil Young
Mr Philip Young
Mr Richard Young
Miss Seona Young
Miss Tanouchi Yuji
Mr Tanouchi Yuji
Mr Paul Zacharek
Mr Sherry Zameer
Mr David Zerdin
Mr Biao Zhong
Mrs Anne Zouroudi